Teaching Students with Learning Problems

Sixth Edition

Cecil D. Mercer
University of Florida

Ann R. Mercer
Gainesville, Florida

Merrill
Prentice Hall

Upper Saddle River, New Jersey
Columbus, Ohio

Library of Congress Cataloging-in-Publication Data

Mercer, Cecil D.
  Teaching students with learning problems / Cecil D. Mercer, Ann R.
Mercer. --6th ed.
    p. cm.
  Includes bibliographical references and indexes.
  ISBN 0-13-089296-3
  1. Learning disabled children--Education. 2. Learning disabled
children--Education--United States. I. Mercer, Ann R. II. Title.
LC4704 .M473   2001
371.9--dc21   00-036173
                                                        CIP

Vice President and Publisher: Jeffery W. Johnston
Executive Editor: Ann Castel Davis
Editorial Assistant: Pat Grogg
Production Editor: Sheryl Glicker Langner
Production Coordination: Terry Routley, Carlisle Communications, Ltd.
Design Coordinator: Diane C. Lorenzo
Photo Coordinator: Nancy Harre Ritz
Cover Designer: Rod Harris
Cover photo: Uniphoto
Production Manager: Laura Messerly
Director of Marketing: Kevin Flanagan
Marketing Manager: Amy June
Marketing Services Manager: Krista Groshong

This book was set in Helvetica and Stone Serif by Carlisle Communications, Ltd., and was printed and bound
by R. R. Donnelley & Sons Company. The cover was printed by Phoenix Color Corp.

Photo credits: Shirley Zeiberg/PH College, p. 1; Anthony Magnacca/Merrill, pp. 3, 145, 233, 235, 319, 401, 431,
469; Anne Vega/Merrill, pp. 25, 65, 97, 265; Linda Peterson/Merrill, p. 47; Julie Peters/Merrill, p. 121; Scott
Cunningham/Merrill, pp. 173, 185, 371, 449, 524, 531, 587; Todd Yarrington/Merrill, p. 217; Barbara
Schwartz/Merrill, pp. 287, 297, 364, 383, 441, 565; Laima Druskis/PH College, p. 571

Merrill
Prentice Hall

10 9 8 7 6 5
ISBN 0-13-089296-3

To the many students with learning problems who have touched and inspired their teachers with their hard work, courage, and smiles.

Why Do I Teach?

When asked why I teach,
I reply,
"Because of the splendid company I keep."

Within my classroom, I see the farmer, the builder, the nurse, and the mechanic.
They are young and strong and eager to learn and play.
Nearby sit the doctor, the laborer, the attorney, and the salesman.
All are unbiased and full of life each and every day.
The minister, the teacher, the actress, and the counselor are also with me.
It's truly amazing, all the wonderful people I see.

These are the ones who will shape the future
And heal the sick, farm the land, serve others, plan, and pray.
They will grow to become an influence in many diverse ways.
Although I may not see them in their prime,
I can say I knew them well at another time.
I knew them all as youngsters who were proud, or bold, or shy, or kind.
And each one I taught and counted as mine.

There's an easy answer to why I teach.
It's definitely because of the splendid company I keep.

C.D.M.
A.R.M.

ABOUT THE AUTHORS

Cecil D. Mercer is a distinguished professor of education at the University of Florida. He received his Ed.D. in special education from the University of Virginia in 1974. Cecil has written numerous articles and books on educating exceptional students. One of his major works is *Students with Learning Disabilities*, and he is coauthor of the *Strategic Math Series* and the *Great Leaps Reading Program*. Cecil remains involved in the educational programs of exceptional students through his participation in in-service and classroom activities in public and private schools, and he is a featured keynote and workshop speaker at many national conferences. Cecil is a member of the International Dyslexia Association Board of Directors and has served on the Learning Disabilities Association of America Professional Advisory Board. He has been awarded the College of Education Teacher of the Year award three times at the University of Florida.

Ann R. Mercer is an educational diagnostician in Gainesville, Florida, and a former special education teacher of students with emotional disabilities and students with learning problems at both the elementary and secondary levels. Ann is coauthor of *Self-Correcting Learning Materials for the Classroom* in addition to several articles and book chapters in the field of special education. Ann and Cecil have three sons, Kevin, Greg, and Ken, and a golden retriever named Buckley.

PREFACE

Most educators can recall key events that made lasting impressions on their minds or hearts. One such event occurred in 1968 during a PTA meeting at a small elementary school next to the Blue Ridge Mountains in Virginia. The officers of the PTA were concerned about the uninterested, unmotivated, and misbehaving students in their school, and they asked me to discuss the topic. More than 70 people—parents, teachers, and central office staff—entered the small cafeteria for the PTA meeting.

Within a few minutes I was introduced. I told the audience that I was delighted to be with them and wanted to begin by giving them a short test. The test consisted of a problem involving the transporting of a chicken, a fox, and a bag of chicken feed across a lake. However, the problem was designed so that it was impossible to answer correctly. I gave these instructions: "This is a short test that most people with average ability finish in one minute. When I say 'Begin,' please start. Ready?" Toward the end of the minute, many of the assemblage were mumbling, fidgeting, and attempting to look at others' papers. I called time and asked how many had solved the problem. Nobody raised a hand. With a puzzled expression I said, "You must be tired. I'll give you another minute. Slow learners usually can solve it in two minutes."

Although I had anticipated some frustration, the behavior of this group of adults during the next minute was somewhat surprising. Many cheated, some cursed, others broke my pencils, and still others crumpled up the test and tossed it aside. At the end of the minute I informed them that time was up. I asked several people how they felt. Responses included: "I feel like punching you in the mouth." "I want to leave and never come back." "I'd like to give you a piece of my mind." "What's the answer to this [expletive] thing?"

Within two minutes, this situation had prompted adults to cheat, swear, want to leave, destroy property, threaten physical violence, and talk rudely. I pointed out that what had happened to them was the same thing that often happens to students with learning problems. Tasks are assigned that are too difficult or practically impossible for them to do correctly. Moreover, failure to do these tasks generally is viewed as a reflection of one's ability. The point was clear: Both students and adults are inclined to act aggressively or avoid situations in which they are given inappropriate tasks.

With adults reacting so quickly and intensely to this type of failure, I was reminded of what happens to youngsters who customarily face failure within the schools. Ann and I enthusiastically share the conviction of many educators that students with learning problems have a right to educational programs tailored to their unique needs. To us, individualized programming involves *the student working on appropriate tasks or content over time under effective motivational conditions*. The primary purpose of this book is to prepare special education professors and teachers, resource room teachers, remedial education teachers, and general classroom teachers for the challenges of individualized programming for students with learning or behavioral problems.

Individualized programming requires an understanding of subject matter, assessment, effective teaching practices for each content area, instructional activities, independent work activities, and commercial programs and software. Moreover, the complex needs of students with learning problems and the abundance of interventions necessitate that special education teachers collaborate with general education teachers, other professionals, and parents. As teachers of elementary, secondary, and university students, we have had difficulty finding a text that covers all of these areas. Resource and classroom teachers as well as special education professors often refer to one text for instructional activities, another for teacher-made materials, another for scope and sequence skills lists, another for assessment, and yet another for descriptions of commercial materials and software. This book provides a comprehensive, practical *text* for special education and remedial education methods courses; a *resource* for special education and remedial education in-service programs; and a *handbook* for individual teachers.

New in This Edition

As a result of feedback from reviewers and users of the fifth edition, this sixth edition features some noteworthy changes, including the addition of the National Institutes of Health research on reading assessment and interventions in phonological awareness, phonics, comprehension strategies, and fluency. Moreover, reviewers indicate that the coverage of collaboration, inclusion, content enhancements, effective teaching practices, classroom management, phonological awareness, cultural diversity, affective development, functional curriculum, problem solving, explicit and implicit instruction, successful transition practices, and the use of adult volunteers or paraprofessionals in the classroom is timely and comprehensive. Also, descriptions of tests, materials, and software have been updated throughout this edition. We hope this edition will help other teacher educators and teachers to accomplish instructional goals more easily.

Acknowledgments

Many individuals deserve special attention for their contributions to this book. Appreciation and thanks go to the reviewers Jim Burns, College of St. Rose (New York), Rori R. Carson, Eastern Illinois University, Roberta Strosnider, Hood College (Maryland), and Cynthia Dieterich, Cleveland State University. We also express our gratitude to the many students who read the fifth edition and provided valuable suggestions for improving it. Thanks to Ann Davis, administrative editor, for her encouragement, support, patience, and belief that we would meet deadlines. Finally, we always will be indebted to students, parents, and teachers who have shared their successes and frustrations with us through the years.

Cecil D. Mercer
Ann R. Mercer

DISCOVER THE COMPANION WEBSITE ACCOMPANYING THIS BOOK

The Prentice Hall Companion Website: A Virtual Learning Environment

Technology is a constantly growing and changing aspect of our field that is creating a need for content and resources. To address this emerging need, Prentice Hall has developed an online learning environment for students and professors alike—Companion Websites—to support our textbooks.

In creating a Companion Website, our goal is to build on and enhance what the textbook already offers. For this reason, the content for each user-friendly website is organized by chapter and provides the professor and student with a variety of meaningful resources. Common features of a Companion Website include:

For the Professor—

Every Companion Website integrates **Syllabus Manager™**, an online syllabus creation and management utility.

- **Syllabus Manager™** provides you, the instructor, with an easy, step-by-step process to create and revise syllabi, with direct links into Companion Website and other online content without having to learn HTML.

- Students may logon to your syllabus during any study session. All they need to know is the web address for the Companion Website and the password you've assigned to your syllabus.

- After you have created a syllabus using **Syllabus Manager™**, students may enter the syllabus for their course section from any point in the Companion Website.

- Class dates are highlighted in white and assignment due dates appear in blue. Clicking on a date, the student is shown the list of activities for the assignment. The activities for each assignment are linked directly to actual content, saving time for students.

- Adding assignments consists of clicking on the desired due date, then filling in the details of the assignment—name of the assignment, instructions, and whether or not it is a one-time or repeating assignment.

- In addition, links to other activities can be created easily. If the activity is online, a URL can be entered in the space provided, and it will be linked automatically in the final syllabus.

- Your completed syllabus is hosted on our severs, allowing convenient updates from any computer on the Internet. Changes you make to your syllabus are immediately available to your students at their next logon.

For the Student—

- **Chapter Objectives**—outline key concepts from the text

- **Interactive Self-Quizzes**—complete with hints and automatic grading that provide immediate feedback for students

  After students submit their answers for the interactive self-quizzes, the Companion Website **Results Reporter** computes a percentage grade, provides a graphic representation of how many questions were answered correctly and incorrectly, and gives a question by question analysis of the quiz. Students are given the option to send their quiz to up to four email addresses (professor, teaching assistant, study partner, etc.).

- **Message Board**—serves as a virtual bulletin board to post—or respond to—questions or comments to/from a national audience

- **Net Searches**—offer links by key terms from each chapter to related Internet content

- **Web Destinations**—links to www sites that relate to chapter content

To take advantage of these and other resources, please visit the *Teaching Students with Learning Problems* Companion Website at

www.prenhall.com/mercer

CONTENTS

PART

I

Foundations
of Teaching

CHAPTER 1

Creating Responsive
Learning Environments

The following are some of the pleas that university students heard recently while assessing the reading skills of elementary students in general education classes. "Please teach me to read!" "Are you here to help me learn to read?" "Will you help my teacher to teach me to read?" Other youngsters refused to read or cried when they could not read the words. The university students maintained that the reading passages were too difficult until they were told that the passages were from the students' reading books and were controlled for readability. Thus, each youngster was asked to read passages at his or her respective grade level. Unfortunately, this scenario is widespread because students of all ages experience the frustration of low achievement and school failure. Moreover, these students are capable of achieving at a higher level.

Cegelka and Berdine (1995) report that 25 to 40 percent of all students are estimated to have significant academic problems. Numerous societal problems contribute to the poor school performance of youngsters. These problems include limited or no family support, poverty, increased student diversity, crime, high dropout rates, and substance abuse. Also, several school-related problems contribute to the poor achievement of students. Problems result from the practice of many educators to adopt curriculum materials that have never been field tested, adhere to one instructional approach for all students, and fail to lessen the gap between research and practice. Also, decreasing financial and community support weakens the ability of school personnel to meet the needs of all students.

This text focuses on teaching students who will experience extensive school failure if they do not receive instruction that is responsive to their needs. Educational methodology exists to help these individuals realize their learning potential and become independent and contributing members of society. The contents of this text are written within the context of four beliefs. First, all individuals are capable of learning. It is apparent that not all students are capable of learning the same thing, but most can master the basic curricula of schools. Second, the teaching talent to help all students learn according to their potential exists in most schools today. Third, the knowledge gap between what is known about effective teaching and what is routinely practiced in classrooms is enormous. Schools and educational programs can be structured to educate all students. Research findings must be acted on to help teachers and students. Fourth, all students need a safe, caring, and positive learning environment, and one of the best ways to care for students is to teach them in a manner that ensures success. Dr. Hiam Ginott (Milwaukee Public Schools, 1990, p. 30) reminds teachers of the need to create caring environments:

> I have come to a frightening conclusion that,
>
> I am the decisive element in the classroom.
>
> It is my personal approach that creates the climate.
>
> It is my daily mood that makes the weather.
>
> As a teacher I possess tremendous power to make a child's life miserable or joyous.
>
> I can be a tool of torture or an instrument of inspiration.
>
> I can humiliate or humor, hurt or heal.
>
> In all situations it is my response that decides whether a crisis will be escalated or de-escalated, and a child humanized or de-humanized.

The following section briefly describes many of the students who face academic achievement deficits if not provided with effective instruction in caring environments.

STUDENTS AT RISK FOR SCHOOL FAILURE

Efforts to respond to the needs of students who fail in school without special help have resulted in the creation of several programs that serve specific groups of students. Examples of such programs are special education, Title I, bilingual education, and migrant education. These programs are supported by federal legislation (the Individuals with Disabilities Education Act [IDEA]), and each program includes criteria for student eligibility. Special education serves students with disabilities who qualify in one of the following categories: specific learning disabilities, speech or language impairments, mental retardation, emotional disturbance, multiple disabilities, hearing impairments, orthopedic impairments, other health impairments, visual impairments, autism, deaf-blindness, and traumatic brain injury. In addition, students with attention deficit disorders and attention-deficit hyperactivity disorders may be eligible for special education services under IDEA (under the Other Health Impaired category or under other disability categories) or may be served in federally sponsored programs (Section 504 of the Rehabilitation Act of 1973). The learning problems for the majority of students identified for special education are categorized as mild. The learning and behavior difficulties of students with mild mental disabilities, learning disabilities, emotional disabilities, and attention deficit disorders are stressed in planning their respective educational programs; however, it also is important to recognize the secondary learning difficulties exhibited by students with physical or sensory disabilities. Students with physical or sensory disabilities frequently have significant problems learning academic content as well as social skills. Thus, many of these individuals need special instruction to address their learning difficulties.

Title I programs focus on serving students who are both low achieving and from low-income homes, and the programs are organized to be supplemental to services already available in the general education classroom. In their review of variables related to learning, Wang, Haertel, and Walberg (1993/1994) report that the home environment/parental support variable is highly related to student learning (i.e., it ranked fourth out of 28 variables). Some positive attributes of a home environment include high but realistic expectations about schoolwork, an authoritative rather than a permissive or authoritarian approach for discipline, a positive and supportive parent–child relationship, an educative atmosphere supportive of education, and daily routines and organization that facilitate doing homework (Ysseldyke, Christenson, & Kovaleski, 1994). Typically, low socioeconomic home environments have fewer of these positive attributes, and the teacher should consider this when instructing students with learning problems who are from such environments. Borich (1992) notes that teachers of low-socioeconomic students should be warm and encouraging, and let students know that help is available; present ma-

terial in small pieces, at a slow place, and with an opportunity for practice; stress factual knowledge; immediately help a student who needs help; and supplement the standard curriculum with specialized material to meet the needs of individual students.

Many students with learning problems have culturally and linguistically diverse backgrounds. It is important for teachers to value students' cultural differences and provide comfortable ways for these students to share their rich heritage with others. These activities help students respect variations among individuals and provide minority students with events that foster positive self-worth and motivation. Moreover, by becoming acquainted with the cultures of diverse learners, the teacher can adapt curriculum, instruction, and management strategies to accommodate their learning preferences and needs. Due to language differences between school and home and values that are often at odds with society's values, these students face obstacles that impede school success. Moreover, the high poverty rates within some subgroups (e.g., African American and Hispanic) adversely affect school success. From their review of the literature, Olson and Platt (2000) report that six values deserve consideration in helping culturally diverse students achieve school success. Table 1.1 presents these six areas in terms of the prominent values in American schools and the potentially conflicting values held by the respective subgroups. Knowledge of these values helps teachers adapt instruction for these students. In some cases the teacher can alter instruction to accommodate different values (e.g., use instructional games for some students and cooperative learning for others); in other situations the teacher can help the student embrace a value that is important to success (e.g., encourage the student to complete work on time through the use of advance organizers, planning, and goal setting).

Characteristics of Students at Risk for School Failure

It is apparent that disabilities, poverty, limited family support, cultural differences, language differences, ineffective teaching, and lack of educational funding contribute to the serious failures

TABLE 1.1

Prominent values in American schools and values of culturally diverse groups

Prominent Values in American Schools	Values of Culturally Diverse Groups
Competition—value winning in direct competition with others	*Cooperation*—value working together and being social (African American, Hispanic, and Native American)
Individual Autonomy—value adult or mature behaviors in youth	*Dependency on Authority or Family*—value youth being dependent on family or authority (African American, Hispanic, and Asian)
Time as Primary Emphasis—value being on time, completing work on time, and taking timed exams	*Time as Secondary Emphasis*—value time as important but secondary to relationships and performance (African American and Hispanic)
Focus on High Achievement—value high academic achievement	*Focus on Affective Development*—value development of personality and self-concept in conjunction with achieving (African American, Hispanic, and Native American)
Focus on Future—motivation connected to future needs	*Focus on Immediate*—motivation connected to today's needs (African American and Hispanic)
Focus on Informal Atmosphere—value informal casual classroom environment where students ask many questions	*Focus on Formal Atmosphere*—value respect for authority or adults, and value listening over speaking (Native American and Asian)

experienced by 15 to 25 percent of the school population. These youngsters all share the unfortunate experience of low academic achievement that results from problems in receiving instruction, connecting new knowledge with prior knowledge to create new learning that is organized and stored in a meaningful way, and/or recalling new information in such a way that it can be expressed or displayed at the appropriate time.

Although students at risk for school failure all experience academic failure without special instruction, their individual learning characteristics vary considerably. They are a heterogeneous group whose educational programs must be planned on the basis of individual characteristics and needs. In planning for students with learning problems, it helps to examine their learning characteristics. Information about some of the primary cognitive, affective, and behavioral characteristics of students with learning problems is presented in Table 1.2. Consideration of these characteristics helps teachers select, adapt, and implement techniques, strategies, and approaches that enable students with learning problems to succeed. Fortunately, numerous instructional procedures exist to help students with learning problems succeed. Frequently, one strategy works for many different students and has positive effects across cognitive, affective, and behavioral domains.

Legislation and court decisions direct that the special needs of students with learning problems must be met, as much as possible, in classes with peers without disabilities. The placement of students with disabilities in general education classes necessitates that general and special education teachers cooperate in planning and delivering instruction. Currently, general education teachers are providing more direct instruction to learners with disabilities than ever before and are working closely with special education teachers. To succeed in school, students with learning problems need a systematic instructional program that is planned according to their individual needs. To ensure that the plan is implemented throughout the day, it must be cooperatively planned by both general and special education teachers.

TABLE 1.2
Some characteristics of students with learning problems

Cognitive Characteristics

Cognitive and Metacognitive Deficits
From a knowledge base of 11,000 statistical findings across 28 categories, Wang et al. (1993/1994) examined the influence of each category on student learning. The metacognitive and cognitive processes of students ranked second and third on their influence on student learning. *Metacognition* refers to a learner's knowledge (awareness) of thinking processes or strategies (such as planning, evaluating effectiveness of ongoing activities, checking the outcomes of effort, and correcting difficulties) and the ability to regulate or monitor these processes or strategies to learn successfully. Knowledge about a student's metacognition appears to hold promise for designing instruction. Instructional practices (e.g., mnemonics and think alouds) designed to help students with cognitive and metacognitive difficulties are featured throughout the text.

Low Academic Achievement
Low academic achievement occurs in all areas (i.e., language, reading, math, spelling, written expression, and content subjects) and is a primary characteristic of students with learning problems. Language and reading problems are the most prominent. Because language skills and academic functioning are closely related, it sometimes is difficult to determine whether a student's major problem is language or reading.

Poor Memory
Many students with learning problems have difficulty remembering information presented visually or auditorially. Teachers frequently report that these students forget spelling words, math facts, vocabulary words, and directions. Some authorities maintain that these students do not spontaneously use techniques that facilitate memory (e.g., rehearsal or forming associations).

Attention Problems and Hyperactivity
To succeed in school, a student must recognize and maintain thought on relevant classroom tasks and must be able to shift attention to new tasks. Students with attention problems are unable to screen out extraneous stimuli and are attracted by irrelevant stimuli. Attention deficits and related behaviors received substantial coverage with the introduction of the term *attention deficit disorder (ADD)* in the 1982 *Diagnostic and Statistics Manual of Mental Disorders* (American Psychiatric Association, 1982). Moreover, increased awareness of attention deficits occurred with the revised publication of the manual in 1987 (American Psychiatric Association, 1987), in which the disorder term was changed to *attention-deficit hyperactivity disorder (ADHD).* The 1994 edition of the manual includes three subtypes of ADHD: predominantly hyperactive type, predominantly inattentive type, and combined type (American Psychiatric Association, 1994).

Perceptual Disorders
Perceptual problems (such as the inability to recognize, discriminate, and interpret sensation), especially visual and auditory disabilities, traditionally have received much attention from authorities on learning disabilities. In a review of the research, Garnett (1992) notes that spatial deficits are a factor in math learning for some students. According to C. R. Smith (1998, pp. 116–117), "Visual-perceptual processes appear to be important to reading and math achievement at young ages and, in very subtle ways, relate to some later spelling, writing, and conceptual difficulties. They do not seem to be a major contributor to the skills needed for progress in many higher level academic areas." An emphasis on perceptual factors is not prominent; however, some authorities continue to examine perceptual factors with a cautious but curious mindset.

Affective Characteristics

Poor Social Skills
Difficulties with social skills can be as debilitating as academic problems to students who have learning problems. Examples of social skills in which some students with learning problems lack competence include greeting someone, accepting criticism, receiving compliments, saying no, and giving positive feedback. The social skills deficits of some students are caused by their inability to understand social cues. Because of their inability to interact appropriately with teachers and peers, students with social skills deficits frequently have low social status among their peers.

(continued on next page)

TABLE 1.2
(continued)

> ### Poor Self-Concept
> Frustrated by their learning difficulties, many students with learning problems act disruptively and acquire negative feelings of self-worth (Bender & Wall, 1994). Rather than learning and developing attitudes about tasks they can do, youngsters with learning problems often learn what they can't do. This lack of positive self-regard often results in poor self-concept and self-esteem. Montgomery (1994) found that some students with learning disabilities have a low self-concept regarding academics but do not differ from their high-achieving peers and peers without disabilities on self-concepts related to other areas (e.g., affect, family, physical, and social).
>
> ### Poor Motivation
> Given the repeated academic failure that many students with learning problems experience, it is not surprising that they are less motivated to perform than their peers without disabilities. When early attempts to succeed in school meet with failure, it is common for students to believe that success is beyond their abilities and efforts. Consequently, many develop a learned helplessness and lose their intrinsic motivation to prove their competence. Thus, they become externally motivated because they believe that success is dependent upon external factors and beyond their control (C. R. Smith, 1998).
>
> ### Debilitating Mood States
> Little research on the mood states of students with learning problems exists; however, some research on students with learning disabilities offers noteworthy findings. This research indicates that students with learning disabilities have higher levels of anxiety, worry, oversensitivity, minor somatic complaints, loneliness, and depression than students without disabilities (Bender & Wall, 1994; Margalit & Shulman, 1986; Sabornie, 1994).
>
> ## Behavioral Characteristics
>
> ### Adaptive Behavior Deficits
> Students with learning problems frequently exhibit adaptive behavior deficits that interfere with academic achievement and social relationships. Adaptive behavior or *adaptivity* "is a proactive process through which individuals organize their lives in purposeful, flexible, and advantageous ways to meet the demands of multiple environments" (Weller, Watteyne, Herbert, & Crelly, 1994, p. 282). Adaptive behavior is a multidimensional variable and includes social coping, relationships, pragmatic language, and production (i.e., how one produces work).
>
> ### Disruptive Behavior
> Disruptive behavior may be the result of social skills deficits or frustration over lack of academic success. Disruptive behavior generally includes acts that interrupt or interfere with appropriate activities. Disruptive behavior inhibits the learning or work of others and requires the teacher or supervisor to stop productive events and deal with the disruption. The behavioral problems of numerous students with learning problems are well documented (Bender & Smith, 1990; McKinney & Feagans, 1984). Some students display disruptive aggressive behavior toward others (e.g., fighting and acting out). Their low tolerance for frustration often leads to outbursts that include name calling, sarcasm, or swearing. These behavioral problems frequently lead to disruptive events in inclusive classrooms and prompt educators to view the behavioral difficulties of students with learning problems as serious deterrents to their school success. One behavior that is very disruptive to the teaching–learning process is high absenteeism. Teachers must constantly make plans to help absent students catch up on their learning and work. Moreover, the academic progress of absent students is impeded.
>
> ### Withdrawal
> Bender and Smith (1990) report that some students with learning problems exhibit significantly more shy and withdrawn behavior than do their normally achieving peers. Social withdrawal may result from the students' previous failures at interaction or a feeling of incompetence because of academic failure. Some students may become so socially isolated that they are unable to interact in a positive manner with peers or adults. Because loneliness and social withdrawal frequently appear within the context of depression and suicide, it is essential to develop interventions and preventive strategies.

☀ INDIVIDUALIZED
EDUCATIONAL PROGRAMS

Meeting the needs of a diverse group of students is a formidable task for both general and special education teachers. Primary and elementary teachers are faced with helping youngsters acquire basic skills, develop independent learning strategies, and explore careers. While teaching more than 100 students daily, secondary teachers are faced with helping adolescents acquire specific vocational skills, learning strategies, and academic knowledge. These teachers must be able to alter the type and amount of instruction. Altering the *type* of instruction may involve putting reading passages on tape or teaching the student a strategy for writing a paragraph. Altering the *amount* of instruction entails providing more extensive teacher modeling of concepts, using elaborated feedback, or providing more independent practice.

Individualized instruction refers to instruction that enables the student to work on appropriate tasks or content over time under conditions that motivate. This individualized approach does not imply that each student must be taught one to one. It *does* mean, however, that students receive daily instruction tailored to their educational needs. It can occur within various instructional arrangements, including seatwork, small groups, peer teaching, and large groups. The teacher matches the learner, the task, and instructional interventions to ensure optimal student growth.

Some specific components of individualized instruction consist of instructional objectives based on assessment, variable entry points into the curriculum, variable pacing, active participation of the learner in decision making, a variety of instructional arrangements (e.g., large groups, small groups, and cooperative learning) as a function of the task and learning level, and criterion-referenced evaluation of the learner. An *individualized educational program (IEP)* outlines the plan (i.e., the outcomes, curriculum, teachers' responsibilities, schedule, and settings) that facilitates individualized instruction.

As mentioned previously, the Individuals with Disabilities Education Act is aimed at special education. IDEA reauthorizes Public Law (PL) 94-142 (adopted in 1975), and it incorporates the amendments to PL 94-142, including PL 99-457 (adopted in 1986), PL 101-476 (adopted in 1990), and PL 105-17 (adopted in 1997). Essentially, IDEA guarantees a free, appropriate public education for all individuals with disabilities through age 21. Although PL 94-142 primarily deals with educational programs, PL 99-457 and PL 101-476 include mandates and incentives to provide services for infants, toddlers, and their families. Moreover, the amendments provide guidelines for assisting adolescents to make transitions from secondary school to postschool settings. The law provides the following four basic educational rights for students with disabilities:

1. A thorough, nondiscriminatory assessment of the parameters of the specific disability, with no single measure being the only criterion for evaluation.
2. The right to a free, appropriate education tailored to the needs of each individual.
3. Placement in the "least restrictive environment," with maximum emphasis on enhancing participation in the general curriculum and placing the youngster with a disability in a program with youngsters without disabilities whenever possible.
4. The provision of supplementary aid and services to help ensure the success of the educational program.

An IEP must be designed and implemented for each student (age 3 through 21) with a disability. The legislative intent of the IEP is to serve three primary functions: management, communication, and accountability (California Department of Education, 1994). The management function exists because the IEP is a planning tool designed to ensure that eligible students receive appropriate services based on the individual needs of the student. The communication function exists because the IEP requires a multidisciplinary team to work together to develop a written plan that details appropriate services and learner outcomes. Accountability exists because student progress toward specified objectives must be monitored and periodically reviewed. According to Public Law 94-142, the IEP must state the student's current performance levels; annual and short-term instructional objectives; special services and the extent of general classroom participation; the projected date for initiation and anticipated duration of such services; and criteria, evaluation procedures, and schedules for determining progress. In addition, the 1997 amendments require that if a student with disabilities has behavioral problems, a proactive behavioral intervention plan, based on functional behavioral assessment, must be included in the student's IEP. Moreover, Public Law 99-457 provides an *individualized family service plan* (IFSP) for infants and toddlers (birth through age 2) with disabilities. The IFSP documents the early-intervention services required by these children and their families.

The IEP and the IFSP both require that the written plan be developed by a multidisciplinary team, which includes the parents, and be based on a multidisciplinary assessment of unique needs. At the IEP meeting, a multidisciplinary team determines at least one short-term objective for each annual goal. The goals are major statements, and parental permission must be given for one to be added or deleted, whereas short-term objectives are steps taken to obtain a stated goal and can be added at the teacher's discretion.

Figure 1.1 shows an IEP format that incorporates the essentials of a plan. Part B enables the teacher to outline the short-term objectives for the academic year. The organization of Part B can be modified (e.g., for each objective, list the date initiated, materials, evaluation, date achieved, and person responsible) so that the short-term objectives are not segmented according to grading periods. It is a good practice for the special education teacher to work with a student and his or her teachers for several sessions before the IEP conference. During this time, the special education teacher can determine realistic objectives and specific teaching techniques.

Participants in IEP Meetings

The law specifies who must participate in IEP meetings: (1) a representative of the schools, other than the child's teacher, who is qualified to provide or supervise special education, (2) the student's teachers (a special education teacher and a general education teacher), (3) one or both parents, (4) the student, when appropriate, and (5) others at the discretion of the parent or school personnel. For students with disabilities who are evaluated for the

first time, a member of the evaluation team or an individual knowledgeable about the evaluation procedures must attend the IEP meeting.

Schools must follow certain procedures regarding parental participation to ensure the presence of parents at the meeting. Specific steps include the following:

1. Notify parents early enough. The purpose, time, and location of the meeting and the persons who will be in attendance should be included in the notice.
2. Schedule the meeting at a mutually agreed upon time and place.
3. If neither parent can attend, use other methods to ensure parental participation, such as telephone calls or home visits.
4. If a meeting is held without a parent in attendance, document attempts to involve the parents (e.g., telephone calls, copies of correspondence, and records of home visits).
5. Provide a copy of the student's IEP to the parent upon request.

Finally, the law states that, when appropriate, the student is to participate in the planning of his or her IEP. Although the participation of the student in the meeting often would be minimal, it may be especially effective to include the secondary level student in the planning of a program.

Components of an IEP

Levels of Performance   On the IEP, level-of-performance data must be precise enough to aid the teacher in formulating initial objectives. Norm-referenced or criterion-referenced evaluation instruments are designed to provide such data. In a norm-referenced evaluation, a student's performance is compared with others' scores; in a criterion-referenced evaluation, a student's performance is described in terms of fixed criteria. Evaluating student progress with standardized achievement tests is common. However, this practice is not warranted because standardized tests do not directly assess the content included in a student's curriculum and, thus, student learning and teacher effectiveness are being evaluated according to content that the teacher has not taught. Criterion-referenced instruments and informal measures seem to be more suitable than tests that primarily yield comparative scores. These instru-

FIGURE 1.1
Individualized educational program

Part A: IEP

Identification Information

Name: Greg Creswell
School: Village Elementary School
Birthdate: 5-15-87   Grade: 6
Parent's Name: Keith Melissa Williams
Address: 1300 Johnson Street
Raleigh, N.C.
Phone: Home: none   Office: 932-8161

Continuum of Services

	Hours per week
General class	20 hrs
Resource teacher in general classroom	6 hrs
Resource room	4 hrs
Reading specialist	
Speech/language therapist	
Counselor	
Special class	
Transition class	
Others:	

Yearly Class Schedule

	Time	Subject	Teacher
1st semester	8:30 - 9:20	math	Rivera
	9:30 - 10:20	language arts	Barton (Resource)
	10:30 - 11:20	social studies	Barton
	11:30 - 12:20	science	Rivera
		lunch	
	1:10 - 2:00	art	Shaw
	2:10 - 3:00	P.E.	King
2nd semester	8:30 - 9:20	math	Rivera
	9:30 - 10:20	language arts	Barton (Resource)
	10:30 - 11:20	social studies	Barton
	11:30 - 12:20	science	Rivera
		lunch	
	1:10 - 2:00	art	Shaw
	2:10 - 3:00	P.E.	King

Testing Information

Test Name	Date Admin.	Interpretation
K-TEA	9-10-99	Spelling: standard score: 82 Math: standard score: 104 Reading: standard score: 79
informal test of phonics	9-13-99	knows 6 of 20 phonics rules
CBM probe	9-13-99	reads 3rd grade level reader at 84 correct wpm with 70% comprehension.
CBM probe	9-16-99	reads 4th grade level reader at 60 correct wpm with 40% comprehension.
social skills checklist	9-16-99	gets along well with others but has difficulty dealing with critical feedback.

Checklist

9-7-99	Referral by Ann Tharin
9-9-99	Parents informed of rights; permission obtained for evaluation
9-16-99	Evaluation compiled
9-17-99	Parents contacted
9-20-99	Total committee meets and subcommittee assigned
9-24-99	IEP developed by subcommittee
9-27-99	IEP approved by total committee

Committee Members

Ann Tharin
Referral Teacher: John Thomas
Other LEA representative: Melissa Williams
Parents
Teachers: Mary Rivera
Joan Barton
Alice King

Date IEP initially approved: 9-27-99

Health Information

Vision: good
Hearing: excellent
Physical: good
Other:

(continued on next page)

FIGURE 1.1
(continued)

Part B.1.: IEP (Complete for each subject area)

Student's Name: *Greg Croswell*   Subject Area: *Reading*

Level of Performance: *Can identify 6 of 20 phonics rules. Reads 3rd grade book—84 wpm; 70% comprehension.*   Teacher: *Joan Benton - Resource Teacher*
Reads 4th grade book—60 wpm; 40% comprehension.

Annual Goals:
1. *Given passages from middle of 4th grade reader, Greg will read 110 wpm correctly with 80% comprehension.*
2. *Greg will identify and use 20 phonics rules.*
3.

	First Grading Period Sept.—Oct.	Second Grading Period Oct.—Nov.	Third Grading Period Nov.—Dec.	Fourth Grading Period Jan.—Feb.	Fifth Grading Period Feb.—Apr.	Sixth Grading Period Apr.—June
Objectives	*Referred*	*1. Read initial level 3rd grade passages at 110 correct wpm with 70% comprehension.* *2. Recognize and use 8 phonics rules*	*1. Read middle level 3rd grade passages at 110 correct wpm with 80% comprehension.* *2. Recognize and use 11 phonics rules.*	*1. Read upper level (end of book) 3rd grade passages at 110 correct wpm with 80% comprehension.* *2. Recognize and comprehend 14 phonics rules.*	*1. Read initial level 4th grade passages at 110 correct wpm with 80% comprehension.* *2. Recognize and use 17 phonics rules*	*1. Read middle level 4th grade passages at 110 correct wpm with 80% comprehension.* *2. Recognize and use 20 phonics rules.*
Agent		*Resource Teacher-1 General Teacher-2*	*Resource Teacher-1 General Teacher-2*	*Resource Teacher-1 General teacher-2*	*Resource Teacher-1 General Teacher-2*	*Resource Teacher-1 General Teacher-2*
Evaluation		*1. CBM reading probe at 3rd grade level 2. Informal test of phonics rules applications*	*1. CBM reading probe at 3rd grade level 2. Informal test of phonics rules & applications*	*1. CBM reading probe at 3rd grade level 2. Informal test of phonics rules & applications*	*1. CBM Reading Probe at 4th grade level 2. Informal test of phonics rules and applications*	*1. CBM Reading probe at 4th grade level 2. Informal test of phonics rules and applications*

12

Source: Adapted from *Developing and Implementing Individualized Education Programs* (pp. 419–420), 3rd ed., by B. B. Strickland and A. P. Turnbull, 1990, Upper Saddle River, NJ: Merrill/Prentice Hall. Copyright 1990 by Prentice-Hall Publishing Company. Reprinted by permission.

ments typically include systematic skill sequences and provide information that directly leads to objectives (e.g., instruct student in sums to 9 facts). Currently, curriculum-based measurement is the best practice for evaluating student performance and progress on IEPs. Levels of performance may be assessed in the following areas: social adaptation, emotional maturity, prevocational–vocational skills, psychomotor skills, and academic achievement. Formal and informal assessment devices are discussed in Chapter 3, and specific tests are presented in each of the respective curriculum area chapters. In addition, scope and sequence skills lists are included in Appendix A.

Annual Goals   Annual goals must be tailored to individual needs—academic and otherwise—and must encompass the entire spectrum of short-term objectives in each specified area. They must be measurable and describe what the student should be able to do at the end of the school year. Although teachers are not held accountable if the IEP is implemented as written and the student does not achieve the projected growth, they are responsible for setting realistic expectations and providing systematic instruction toward these goals. Annual goals that are likely for a student with mild disabilities include the following:

- Student will read fourth-grade-level material fluently with comprehension.
- Student will learn the multiplication facts through the 9s.
- Student will work independently and complete assigned current tasks.

For the teacher who uses a scope and sequence skills list to identify instructional objectives and to monitor progress, the process of writing annual goals may be less time-consuming. By coding the scope and sequence skills list, the teacher simply can write the annual goals using the code. For example, a student's present level of performance may be reading skill No. 3.14, and the annual goal may be to reach reading skill No. 4.26. In this approach, the short-term objectives become the skills listed between 3.14 and 4.26. When using coding, the teacher must ensure that parents understand the organization of the instructional objectives.

Short-Term Objectives   Short-term objectives must be listed and described in specific,

measurable terms. These objectives help boost present levels of performance toward annual goals. As noted previously, this task is much simpler if criterion-referenced evaluation measures are used, because the mastery of specific skills is targeted readily on a continuum of listed competencies. Short-term objectives that are likely to be used with some students with mild disabilities are as follows:

- Student will recognize and say the sounds of the initial consonants *r* and *w* 100 percent of the time.
- Student will correctly write his or her name within 30 seconds.
- Student will read the next story in his or her reader at 150 correct words per minute with 90 percent comprehension.

Description of Services   A statement of the specific services and materials provided for the student includes who teaches the student, what content is included in the instructional program, and what materials are used. Also, because Public Law 94-142 requires that the student be educated in the least restrictive environment, the extent of the student's participation in the general education program must be established. For example, the plan may state that the student functions in the general classroom for all but one hour a day. The role of the general education teacher then is noted (e.g., the child will sit in the front of the general classroom and will use individualized spelling tapes developed jointly by the general education teacher and the special education teacher.)

Dates of Service   The plan outlines the projected dates for initiation and anticipated duration of services.

Evaluation   The use of objective criteria and frequent assessment are encouraged. However, the law requires only an annual evaluation to determine whether the annual goals are being achieved. Evaluation procedures are presented in Chapter 3 and in each of the respective curriculum area chapters.

Using the IEP

The IEP is a substantial improvement over past planning strategies used by many educators; however, it is not sufficient for delivering an individualized program. Bateman (1977) compared the components of diagnostic prescriptive teaching (an individualized programming approach) and the IEP. Both require assessment of the student's current level and specification of goals and objectives. However, only prescriptive teaching specifies the teaching tasks inherent in the objectives (such as antecedent events, student responses, consequent events, and daily evaluation for each task).

During the past 15 years, IEPs have undergone few changes. S. Smith (1990) maintains that in many situations IEPs are not useful documents. In a review of IEPs, Giangreco, Dennis, Edelman, and Cloninger (1994) found that IEPs "did not adequately communicate the individual needs of students, nor did they seem to serve as a useful resource to guide their general education experiences" (p. 295). Given the reform movements in education, it may be an opportune time to make some major changes in IEPs. In the following passage, Giangreco et al. (p. 295) comment on needed changes:

> We suggest that efforts be focused on improving the quality and usefulness of IEPs by, at least in part, reconceptualizing the minimum requirements and extending beyond those minimums. IEP goals, objectives, and supports should be internally and externally congruent and be designed to improve valued life outcomes. That is, . . . content of the IEP should be reflected in what is taught within general education class activities, and student outcomes should be truly meaningful.

Although the IEP is recognized as a major step toward the improvement of educational services for students with learning problems, the accompanying data management system can be quite burdensome to the teacher. Developing, writing, and monitoring the IEP require a great deal of teacher time, although a computer offers an excellent tool to help educators manage it. Jenkins (1987) compared computer-generated IEPs and handwritten IEPs and found that computer-generated IEPs were of higher quality and took significantly less time to write.

The following are some computer applications in IEP management:

- *Create new IEPs.* A computer can be used to develop an IEP (e.g., store and retrieve demographic data, test scores, annual goals, short-term objectives, and other data).

- *Monitor procedural safeguards.* A computer can be used to provide the steps in the IEP process (e.g., receipt of parental consent for assessment, notification of IEP meeting, and annual review date) and the respective status regarding each step. Hayden, Vance, and Irvin (1982) provide an example of a computerized procedural safeguard procedure that features 21 steps.

- *Update records.* A student's IEP can be displayed readily and modified easily on a computer. For example, progress on short-term objectives can be added. Moreover, the updated or existing record can be printed quickly for parents, teachers, or multidisciplinary team members.

- *Analyze and interpret test data.* Test results can be scored and analyzed on a computer. Programs are available that include scoring and analysis for the WISC-III, the K-ABC, and the *Woodcock-Johnson III Tests of Cognitive Abilities* and *Tests of Achievement.*

- *Monitor academic progress.* A list of curriculum skills can be programmed, and student progress can be monitored.

Computer applications to IEP management are obviously extensive. Some school districts have developed their own IEP management programs tailored to their specific needs.

EDUCATIONAL SERVICES AND RELATED PRACTICES

Selecting the appropriate school setting for serving students with learning problems is a complex and important task. This decision affects the quality of instruction provided and determines who does the teaching and who becomes the student's peer group. In essence, the placement decision significantly influences the student's attitude, achievement, and social development. In making the placement decision, educators are required by law to select the setting that represents the student's least restrictive environment.

Least Restrictive Environment and Mainstreaming

According to IDEA, the term *least restrictive environment (LRE)* means that, to the extent appropriate, students with disabilities should be educated with students without disabilities. The IEP committee collectively decides the student's least restrictive environment by determining the setting that best meets the student's social and educational needs. Selecting the student's "most enabling environment" is a more positive way of conceptualizing LRE. Historically, students with disabilities were pulled out of general classrooms and placed in self-contained classes. LRE is based on the premise that placing youngsters who have disabilities with youngsters who do not results in improved academic and social development for students with disabilities and reduces the stigma associated with being educated in segregated settings.

IDEA does not mention the term *mainstreaming;* however, the term is widely used. Mainstreaming springs from the least restrictive environment concept and is used extensively to refer to the practice of integrating students with disabilities socially and instructionally into general education as much as possible. Some authorities debate the similarities and differences of mainstreaming and LRE; however, when both are practiced responsibly, they are similar. When mainstreaming simply involves placing students who have disabilities with normally achieving students without regard for the optimal social and academic growth of the individual student, it is not being practiced responsibly.

The least restrictive principle stresses the need for using a continuum of services sensitive to diverse needs. Figure 1.2 presents a core of necessary alternatives to serve a heterogeneous population of students with disabilities. The three major categories of services are general class, special class, and special school. The alternatives are arranged in the figure from bottom to top in the order in which segregation, labeling, and severity of need of the recipients usually increase. In establishing objectives for a student with learning problems, it is important to adopt a tentative commitment to a program level and not consider placement in any program as permanent or terminal. Educators must provide these youngsters with programs that continuously respond to their unique needs. Whenever feasible, a student needs to move from the more restricted setting to the most integrated placement. In addition, placement within a particular program alternative needs to be considered when it appears a change would be beneficial. For example, a student may be moved from one general classroom to another because a specific teacher has certain qualities or uses an instructional program that is suited specifically to the student.

The appropriate use of the various service alternatives requires careful planning. General class-based services and related practices, which most frequently involve students with learning problems, are presented next.

The General Education Class

A high percentage of students who have the ability to learn the basic curriculum spend most of their time in general education classes. In this placement, the student spends most of the day with youngsters of the same age.

Keogh (1990) notes that the key to success for the student with disabilities placed in the general classroom is the general classroom teacher. Factors that deserve consideration include the teacher's attitude toward having a student with a disability in the classroom, the teacher's judgment of the student's capacity to make progress, the teacher's ability to deal with peer acceptance problems, and the teacher's skill in dealing with the emotional behavior and problems that may result from the student's inability to compete academically with other students. It is apparent that the general classroom teacher has an enormous responsibility, and it is important that these teachers receive preparation and useful support (e.g., teacher assistance teams or coaching). Moreover, a student with a learning difficulty should not be placed in a general classroom with a teacher who does not believe that the student will profit.

Special Materials and Consultation   Occasionally, a teacher can manage with the help of additional materials such as a supplementary reading series, learning strategy materials, computer-assisted instruction, content enhancement materials, or manipulative materials for math. To be successful, the teacher must have a reasonable student–teacher ratio (e.g., mid-20s-to-1 or lower), especially in the earlier grades (Mueller, Chase, & Walden, 1988). The teacher also may be provided with limited consultation, usually by a learning disabilities teacher. Consultation may consist of demonstrating the use of materials or equipment, performing an assessment, developing specific

FIGURE 1.2
Continuum of educational placements for students with disabilities

Source: From *Students with Learning Disabilities* (p. 191), 5th ed., by C. D. Mercer, 1997, Upper Saddle River, NJ: Merrill/Prentice Hall. Copyright 1997 by Prentice-Hall Publishing Company. Reprinted by permission.

learning strategies, or providing an in-service program. Collaborative consultation is a service that should be inherent in all general class-based service alternatives. (Consultation skills are discussed later in this chapter.)

Itinerant Services General class teachers sometimes have students in class whose difficulties are not severe enough to warrant resource room instruction or special class placement. In such cases, an itinerant teacher usually visits the schools periodically and focuses on teaching skills and special materials. These consultation services range from

daily to biweekly visits, with the classroom teacher still having the basic responsibility for the student. Obviously, the itinerant teacher must carefully schedule visits to avoid interrupting the activities of the general classroom teacher. Occasionally, itinerant services are bolstered by volunteers or teacher aides.

Resource Room Assistance Many students with learning problems spend the majority of the day in a general class and go to the resource room for a specified period of time (e.g., 45 to 60 minutes) each day. The resource room teacher, located in the school, works closely with numerous teachers to coordinate the instructional programs of the students. Because the resource room teacher provides daily services to about 20 to 30 students with disabilities and their respective teachers, the role demands a highly competent, personable individual.

Speece and Mandell (1980) surveyed 228 general educators about resource room services. The teachers indicated that resource room teachers should provide nine support services:

1. Attend parent conferences (74.2 percent)
2. Meet informally to discuss student progress (74.2 percent)
3. Provide remedial instruction in the resource room (67.0 percent)
4. Provide information on behavioral characteristics (54.5 percent)
5. Provide academic assessment data (53.9 percent)
6. Schedule meetings to evaluate student progress (52.7 percent)
7. Provide materials for classroom (52.1 percent)
8. Suggest materials for classroom (52.1 percent)
9. Provide written reports of students' activities and progress (51.5 percent).

Because many of these services require consultation from resource room teachers, Speece and Mandell, as well as Idol (1989), encourage more in-service and preservice programs that emphasize the development of consultation skills.

Most students with learning disabilities are served in one of three types of resource room models: categorical, cross-categorical, or noncategorical. Categorical programs serve only students with learning disabilities. Cross-categorical programs serve exceptional students from several categorical areas (i.e., educable mentally retarded, emotionally disabled, and learning disabled). Noncategorical programs meet the educational needs of students with mild learning problems, whether classified as disabled or not.

From a review of the research, C.R. Smith (1998) reports that some research supports the effectiveness of resource room services in increasing the attending behavior and academic achievement of the students served. Moreover, she notes that peer acceptance and self-concepts of students attending resource rooms do not appear to diminish. C. R. Smith, however, notes that

the resource room model has several disadvantages associated with pulling students out of their general classes, including the following:

- The student may miss valuable lessons in the general education class while attending the resource room.
- The student may miss some enjoyable activities (e.g., music, physical education, and art) in the general education class while attending the resource room.
- The student may feel stigmatized for leaving the general classroom to receive special help.
- The resource room and general classroom teacher may fail to coordinate instruction.

To deal with these disadvantages, push-in models as opposed to pullout models are being developed. In the push-in models, the resource room teacher provides instruction in the general education classroom. The resource room teacher's activities may include working with an individual student, team teaching with the general education teacher (by teaching the entire class independently or together), and teaching small groups of students in certain content areas. When the resource room teacher works with *all* students periodically, the stigma associated with having a teacher only for students who have learning problems is decreased. As previously mentioned, these integrated arrangements have yielded equivocal academic gains with less cost than resource room programs.

The Content Mastery Center Program at Corsicana High School in Corsicana, Texas, is an example of a resource room in which the general educator has primary responsibility for teaching specific content areas, while the special educator teaches specific strategies or skills to students who need additional instruction. The goal of the Content Mastery Center is to ensure that students with disabilities who are enrolled in general classes progress satisfactorily and receive passing grades. The Center is available to students during any class time when they are not receiving direct instruction from the general classroom teacher, and students decide when to use the Center. A Weekly Grade Check Form, filled out by general classroom teachers, reports the grades and performance of each mainstreamed student and alerts the Center's staff that a student may need to be urged to use the Center's services. The Center is staffed full time by a learning disabilities teacher and an aide, and it offers excellent curriculum resources. All of the school textbooks are available in the Center, with important information in each book highlighted. Textbooks and library books on tape, along with audiotape players, also are provided, as well as materials for classroom projects for students who need ideas, materials, and help designing a project. In addition to giving small-group instruction, helping with projects, and keeping in touch with parents on a regular basis, the Center's teachers provide one-to-one tutoring and individualized instruction according to individual student needs.

Reintegration of Students

To meet the requirements of educating students with learning problems in their least restrictive or most enabling environment, educators must constantly evaluate each student's needs and progress to determine whether a placement change is appropriate, especially if the student's needs appear to warrant a less restrictive service model. Thus, for students in more restrictive placements, educators frequently must examine the feasibility of reintegrating each student successfully into the general classroom. Critics maintain that too many students with disabilities are identified, labeled, and placed in special education settings without appropriate emphasis given to changing these students' programs or returning these students to the mainstream.

Sabornie (1985) stresses the need for educators to consider the social consequences of integrating students who have disabilities with students without disabilities. Sabornie concludes that educators must teach essential social skills to students with disabilities to ensure that students without disabilities will not be negative toward them. Salend and Lutz (1984) surveyed general and special educators in elementary schools to ascertain which social skills are considered critical to successful functioning in the mainstream setting. The 15 competencies identified are organized into three categories: interacting positively with others, obeying class rules, and displaying proper work habits. Although there are numerous similarities

among the competencies needed to succeed in elementary and secondary settings, Salend (1998) notes that the expectations for success in the higher grades are more stringent regarding classroom decorum and behavior. He also reports that junior high school educators tend to be more stringent than their senior high school counterparts.

Ellett (1993) surveyed secondary teachers to determine student skills and behaviors that they considered necessary for success in general classrooms. She developed the following rank ordering of student competencies (skills or behaviors) important to success in secondary classes:

1. Follows directions in class
2. Comes to class prepared with materials
3. Uses class time wisely
4. Makes up assignments and tests
5. Treats teachers and peers with courtesy
6. Completes and turns in homework on time
7. Works cooperatively in student groups
8. Completes tests with a passing grade
9. Appears interested in content
10. Takes notes in class
11. Scans a textbook for answers and information
12. Volunteers to answer questions in class
13. Writes neatly
14. Is able to give oral reports and speeches

It is apparent that academic and social skills criteria provide placement teams with critical information for determining whether the student is ready to be reintegrated into the mainstream setting.

Anderson-Inman (1986) suggests an excellent four-step transenvironmental programming model for planning and implementing a program to prepare students for success in mainstream settings. The four steps include environmental assessment, intervention and preparation, generalization, and evaluation of target environment. Environmental assessment entails the determination of the setting demands (e.g., skills and behaviors) of the targeted mainstream setting. Intervention and preparation involves teaching students the skills and behaviors needed to meet the setting demands. In generalization, students are encouraged to use the skills in the general classroom. Finally, evaluation involves determining how well the students acquire and use the skills in the mainstream environment.

Specific guidelines for reintegration include the following:

- Help students and parents adjust to modifications or a reduction of special education services.
- Include the respective teachers and solicit their observations of the student in relation to placement decisions.
- Use fading techniques when changing placements.
- Be sure the new classroom teacher can make the necessary minor adjustments (Chalfant, 1985; Ellett, 1993).
- Make certain the exiting criteria include the same variables used in identifying and placing the student (Chalfant, 1985).

Obviously, dismissal from a special education program originates from a reevaluation of the student's needs and progress. The IEP format offers the teacher an excellent opportunity to examine the possibility of reintegration. If observations indicate that a change is warranted, the teacher can initiate a meeting or reevaluate the existing IEP.

MOVEMENT FROM MAINSTREAMING TO INCLUSION

When Public Law 94-142 was passed in 1975, it mandated that students with disabilities be provided services in their least restrictive environment. Restriction was interpreted in terms of the amount of time students were educated in classes with their peers without disabilities. Thus, mainstreaming emphasized keeping students with mild disabilities in general education classes as much as possible. Mainstreaming was implemented in collaboration with the continuum of special education placement options listed previously in this chapter. Although some students with mild disabilities remained in part-time and full-time special classes, the most popular service delivery format was the resource room. Most students with mild disabilities attended the resource room for one or two periods a day and remained in general education classes for the remainder of the day. In the resource room, the students received special help as outlined in their IEPs. The dual system of general education placements supported with selected special education placements continued without serious challenges until 1986. Beginning in 1986,

the Regular Education Initiative (REI) promoted the position that students with disabilities be educated in general education classes without pullout special education services.

The Regular Education Initiative

Madeleine Will, Assistant Secretary for the Office of Special Education and Rehabilitative Services in the Reagan administration, and other educators (M. C. Reynolds, 1989; Stainback & Stainback, 1987; Wang, Reynolds, & Walberg, 1986) promoted a system of service delivery to special education students referred to as the Regular Education Initiative. The REI included major revisions in how services are provided to students with learning disabilities. It maintained that a dual system of general and special education is not necessary and that students with learning disabilities can be served more effectively within the general education setting. In essence, the REI recommended that the continuum of special education service alternatives be eliminated and that students with learning disabilities, as well as other special education students, be served totally within the general classroom.

The REI emerged because Will (1986) and several of her colleagues (Wang et al., 1986) maintained that negative consequences occur when special education students are separated from their peers without disabilities to receive instructional services. Specifically, Will offered the following statements as a rationale for the REI:

- Some students with learning or behavioral problems who need special services do not qualify for special education.
- Students are stigmatized when they are put in special education placements that separate them from their normally achieving classmates.
- Special education students usually are identified after they develop serious learning problems; therefore, the emphasis is on failure rather than prevention.
- The special education system, with its eligibility requirements and rigid rules, may not lead to cooperative school–parent relationships.

The REI stimulated much debate and discussion among special educators. It was agreed that general and special educators need to coordinate their services and educate special education students according to their least restrictive environment; however, there was much concern about completely changing the current continuum of services available through special education. During the latter part of the 1980s, the REI position became part of the inclusion movement.

The Inclusion Movement

During the early 1990s, the REI position gained substantial momentum within the context of inclusion. The inclusion movement, however, highlighted the social value of inclusive classes and the need to place individuals with severe disabilities in general education classes (Fuchs & Fuchs, 1994). Also, the inclusion movement stressed strong opposition to the continuum of placements. Likewise, opposition to educating students with and without disabilities in general education classes without the continuum of alternative placements increased. This section examines the relative positions on where students with disabilities should be educated.

The Inclusion Position   Sapon-Shevin notes that inclusion embraces the vision that all students be served in their neighborhood schools in the general classroom with individuals their own age (O'Neil, 1994/1995). These inclusive schools are restructured to be supportive, nurturing communities that meet the needs of all individuals within them, with substantial resources and support for students and teachers. Sapon-Shevin maintains that little evidence exists to support the education of students in segregated settings. She espouses that inclusive schools are based on the belief that the world is an inclusive community with people who vary not only in terms of disabilities but in race, class, gender, and religious background. To prepare students to live in an inclusive world, it is important for them to learn and grow within communities that are similar to the world they will live in as adults. Sapon-Shevin believes that educators should begin with the assumption that all students are included and their needs will be met in inclusive settings.

The Continuum of Alternative Placements Position   During the mid-1970s, the consensus of advocates for students with disabilities was that students with disabilities should be part of mainstream classes. This viewpoint was incorporated into Public Law 94-142 with the least restrictive environment mandate. This mandate was retained in the Individuals with Disabilities Education Act of 1990. However, Yell (1995) notes that results of litigation show that IDEA supports the continuum of placements rather than forcing the placement of students with disabilities in the general classroom. He states, "At times, the mainstream will be the appropriate placement; however, IDEA and case law interpreting the LRE mandate are clear that for some students with disabilities, the appropriate and least restrictive setting will not be the regular education classroom. . . . The most important placement factor must be the individual needs of the student" (p. 402).

The need for a continuum of alternative placements is based on the assumption that options ranging from full-time placement in general education classrooms to placement in special residential schools or hospitals are essential to meet the diverse needs of students with disabilities. Kauffman notes that educators must justify every placement decision, inclusive or otherwise (O'Neil, 1994/1995). He states, "Sure, we ought to meet special needs in a regular class when that's possible. But there isn't anything wrong with meeting special needs outside the regular class if that is required. In fact, the law and best practice say we must consider both possibilities" (O'Neil, 1994/ 1995, p. 7).

In essence, the continuum of alternative placements position assumes that students with disabilities need optional placements to learn in a manner commensurate with their potential. Prescriptive educations are needed to help them become independent and productive members of society. An inspection of the two positions reveals that both support the idea of educating students in general classes. The inclusion position adopts a general education class placement only, whereas the continuum of alternative placements position recommends the continuation of placement options.

Rationale for Inclusion

Statements of the rationale for inclusion include the following:

• Many inclusionists believe that placing students in integrated or inclusive settings is morally right. Stainback, Stainback, East, and Sapon-Shevin (1994) state that many educators think that grouping students homogeneously based on a common characteristic is inappropriate for moral reasons involving equality.

• Both identification and consequent labeling of students within special education categories harm students. Labels lower students' self-esteem and cause others to develop biased viewpoints (e.g., lower expectations) toward them. Inclusion decreases the need to label.

• The efficacy of placing students categorically identified in special education placements apart from the mainstream has not been established.

• According to Sapon-Shevin, placing students outside the mainstream lessens schoolwide efforts to develop responsible inclusive settings for serving students with disabilities (O'Neil, 1994/1995).

• Through collaboration among special educators, general educators, parents, and other service providers, the educational needs of all students can be met in general education classes.

• Placing students with and without disabilities together provides educators with opportunities to teach youngsters to understand and appreciate individual differences. Sapon-Shevin notes that these experiences help prepare students to function in inclusive societies (O'Neil, 1994/1995).

There is a great deal of conviction and passion surrounding the inclusion movement. Baker, Wang, and Walberg (1994/1995) state, "As schools are challenged to effectively serve an increasingly diverse student population, the concern is not *whether* to provide inclusive education, but *how to implement* inclusive education in ways that are both feasible and effective in ensuring schooling success for all children, especially those with special needs" (p. 34). Moreover, Sapon-Shevin believes that "inclusion is much bigger than special education, much bigger than individual classrooms; it's even much bigger than the school. Inclusion really calls for a fundamental restructuring of the school districts and the schools" (O'Neil, 1994/1995, p. 9).

Rationale for Continuum of Alternative Placements

Statements of the rationale for continuum of alternative placements include the following:

• The general class placement and the continuum of placements apart from the mainstream are necessary to meet the intense and diverse needs of students with disabilities.

• The history of special education documents the enormous efforts that parents, legislators, educators, and organizations have expended in securing these varied and intense service delivery alternatives. Inclusion threatens the loss of service options that advocates have spent years obtaining.

• The availability of the continuum of alternative placements has been mandated by law since 1975. The mandate reflects the wishes of many parents, educators, and legislators, and the loss of these service options violates the civil rights of students with disabilities (Kauffman & Hallahan, 1995).

• Research regarding the continuum of placements has serious methodological problems and was conducted so long ago that it has little relevance to current practices in special classes (Hallahan & Kauffman, 1994).

• General education teachers are not prepared to work with students who have disabilities. Keogh (1988) states, "It is disturbing that the national reports are unanimous in their conclusion that the present system does not provide quality education to regular students. Can we assume that in its present form it will be adequate to incorporate the educational needs of pupils with learning and achievement problems?" (p. 20).

• Many general educators do not support inclusion. Albert Shanker (1994/1995), president of the American Federation of Teachers, questions how teachers can meet the extraordinary demands of teaching in an inclusive classroom when they already are overburdened with overcrowded classes, persistent social problems, a diversity of learners, and a lack of training to teach students with various disabilities.

• There is no clear evidence that inclusion is appropriate for all students with disabilities, and evidence of its benefit for average and above-average students is lacking.

Research on the Inclusion and Continuum of Alternative Placements Issue

A solid research base has not been established regarding the efficacy of service alternatives to students with disabilities. Methodological problems, conflicting research results, and the changing demographics (e.g., increasing diversity) of America's schools make it difficult to interpret and apply earlier studies to today's schools. (For reviews of earlier research, see Carlberg and Kavale, [1980]; Fuchs and Fuchs [1994]; Gartner and Lipsky [1987]; Kauffman and Hallahan [1995]; M. C. Reynolds [1989]; Waxman, Wang, Anderson, and Walberg [1985]; and Wiederholt and Chamberlain [1989].) Because recent research appears to have more implications for serving students with mild disabilities, this section presents some of the major contemporary studies.

Efficacy of Inclusion: ALEM   The Adaptive Learning Environments Model (ALEM) was developed as a program to demonstrate the feasibility of inclusion. The ALEM is a large-scale, full-time mainstreaming program in which students who are nondisabled, disabled, and at risk are integrated in the general classroom. While its advocates (M.C. Reynolds, Wang, & Walberg, 1987; Wang & Zollers, 1990) report that ALEM is successful, other researchers are less positive. Fuchs and Fuchs (1988) and Bryan (1988) evaluated the statistical evidence available in the ALEM research and conclude that support is lacking to call ALEM successful. On the basis of the findings, they note that it is premature to endorse a merger of general and special education. Kauffman and Hallahan (1993) note that it is clear that ALEM has not been effective in meeting the needs of students with mild-to-moderate disabilities.

Efficacy of Inclusion: Four Research Projects   From 1989 to 1993, the Office of Special Education and Rehabilitative Services supported four research projects to study the education of students with mild disabilities within the general classroom. The four projects were led by the following researchers: Sharon Vaughn and Jeanne Schumm at the University of Miami; Keith Lenz, Jean Schumaker, and Don Deshler at the University of Kansas; Sue Gordon, Maureen Riley, and Catherine Morocco at the Education Development Center in Newton, Massachusetts; and Lynn Fuchs and Douglas Fuchs at Vanderbilt University. The research teams represented varying

philosophical positions, used different research methodologies, and involved hundreds of elementary and secondary teachers from numerous curriculum areas. Amazingly, from this kaleidoscope of differences emerged a common core of vital findings about some of the challenges that teachers face when they attempt to educate a class of academically diverse students. The Joint Committee on Teacher Planning for Students with Disabilities (1995) reports the following four common themes:

Theme 1

Teachers are sensitive to and concerned about at-risk students in their classes. The researchers found that teachers were greatly concerned about students in their classes who struggled to meet academic demands. These attitudes existed among elementary and secondary teachers. Unfortunately, many of the teachers were perplexed about what to do when some students failed to keep up with the rest of the class.

Theme 2

Specific instructional procedures and tools are workable and effective for most students in general education classrooms. Several planning strategies and instructional approaches were developed by the researchers for use in general education classrooms. The researchers found that when teachers were given sufficient instruction and opportunities to receive feedback regarding their applications, they were able to incorporate the strategies and approaches successfully into their instructional activities. Teachers were satisfied with the new procedures, and the majority of students, including high, middle, and low achievers, benefited. The following procedures highlight some of the features of the varied instructional approaches:

- Teachers viewed students from a holistic perspective and shared the results of their teaching and discussed ways to meet unique needs of diverse students.
- Teachers used self-questions to guide them in planning and structuring lesson content in ways that enable all students to learn.
- Teachers used classwide peer tutoring and curriculum-based measurement to afford more

opportunities for individually focused intensive instruction.

- Teachers selected the critical content and used graphic organizers to structure the content in learner-friendly ways.

Theme 3

Consideration must be given to the complex realities of the general classroom setting when planning a program to meet the needs of students with disabilities. Instructional procedures that were most readily adopted were those most easily incorporated into the flow of existing routines and perceived as benefiting all students in the classroom. Some of the realities facing general education teachers included pressure to cover a lot of content, raise the performance level of learners, teach large groups, prepare for multiple classes with little planning time during the school day, and work with other teachers and staff without much time for collaboration. Pressure escalates when parents and community leaders claim that instructional programming for inclusive classrooms risks compromising the quality of education for students without disabilities.

Theme 4

Some students with mild disabilities did not benefit from the adjustments made in the general education classroom. A few students across all projects did not benefit from the instructional procedures. The researchers offered the following as plausible explanations for the lack of achievement:

- The instructional procedures lacked the power to influence the performance of certain students.
- The classroom teacher lacked the training to individualize instruction for unique learners.
- Because of the pressure to cover the content in the curriculum, the classroom teacher did not have sufficient time for the students to achieve mastery.
- The demands of the class were so extensive that the teacher overlooked the difficulties of students with disabilities and assumed that learning had occurred.
- The students with disabilities were absent frequently.

The demands of the inclusive classroom were so extensive that teachers had neither the time nor the energy to ensure that all students mastered the skills or content. The numerous pressures combine to create a difficult setting within which teachers are able to meet the needs of students with disabilities who have unique, and often severe, learning deficits.

The researchers from the four projects overwhelmingly reached the following consensus: "In order for students with disabilities to be successfully included in the general education classroom, educators need to think in terms of '*supported* inclusion,' not simply 'inclusion'" (Joint Committee on Teacher Planning for Students with Disabilities, 1995, p. 5). The researchers provide the following set of instructional conditions to implement supported inclusion:

- Teachers must be philosophically committed to meeting the needs of all students in the general education classroom.
- Teachers must have time to plan and think about the needs of diverse learners.
- Teaching practices that meet the needs of all students must be incorporated into the instructional program.
- General education teachers must collaborate with special education teachers to assess, teach, and monitor student progress.
- Short-term, intensive instruction from a special education teacher needs to be available for some students with disabilities.
- Sustained instruction in basic skills or learning strategies that cannot be provided in general education classes must be available to some students with disabilities.

In essence, supported inclusion promotes the process of educating as many students as possible in the general education class. For those students who fail to make acceptable progress in the general class, however, short-term and long-term instruction in alternative settings is recommended.

Perspective on the Movement from Mainstreaming to Inclusion

Although inclusion has theoretical appeal and promising directions, existing realities remind professionals and parents that it is premature to eliminate the continuum of alternative placements. Educators have not yet widely implemented the rapidly accruing knowledge and technology about teaching in general or special education settings. The proverbial gap between research and practices is larger than ever. Singer (1988) states, "Proponents of the [REI] argue that the best solution is to abandon the current system, but in doing so, I fear that we would be throwing out the baby with the bathwater" (p. 419). No more structural changes are needed until the quality of instruction in all settings is improved.

There is evidence that students with disabilities, as well as other students with learning problems, are not making acceptable progress. It is apparent that business as usual is not acceptable in either the mainstream or in special education settings. Changes are needed and must be implemented according to a systematic plan that incorporates what is known about the change process in schools. Keogh (1990, p. 190) highlights the needed focus in this change process in the following passage:

> It is clear that major changes are needed in the delivery of services to problem learners, and that these services need to be the responsibility of regular as well as special educators. It is also clear that teachers are the central players in bringing about change in practice. It follows, then, that our greatest and most pressing challenge in the reform effort is to determine how to improve the quality of instruction at the classroom level.

Four years later, Keogh (1994, p. 68) provides additional insights into the change process:

> We are now in a time of enormous change, and the potential for progress is real. At the same time, there are many threats to progress, some from social/political and economic conditions, others from conflicts and dissensions within our profession. Real progress requires that we address both policy and research issues. As a start I paraphrase Broadbent [1973] and suggest that we are forced to think.

Citizens, educators, and parents all want schools in which every student receives an appropriate education in a safe and caring environment. All individuals also want a society whose diverse members value one another's rights and cultures. To accomplish these visions, educators must maintain the passion for ideals but retain the wisdom that comes from an awareness of the realities of educating a diverse population with limited funds. It is not a time for segregation through fanaticism and bitterness. Division fueled by antagonism weakens the educational profession and makes it vulnerable to funding cuts and movements not in the best interests of students or teachers. It is time to work together toward the shared goal of educating all students. Also, it is time to realize that many individuals feel strongly about both the inclusion ideas and the need for a continuum of alternative placements. Keogh (1994) challenges educators to stop and think. Thinking is enhanced through listening; thus, educators should listen and then think about what parents and peers are saying during these troubled times in special education. The following quotes deserve attention and thought:

- According to Kauffman (1994), "Hirschman (1986) observed that many who become impatient with the social welfare programs of government—of which general and special education are examples—offer radical reform or restructuring as the solution to problems that are correctable through patient, deliberate improvements within the current structure. The popular, structuralist approach to reform, however, typically leads to disappointment because only the structure changes; actual treatment, the hardest thing to change, is not modified as the structure changes" (p. 617).

- Sapon-Shevin states, "I have never, ever met a parent of a child with disabilities who did not hope that the child would someday have friends and connections with the broader community" (O'Neil, 1994/1995, p. 7).

- Morse (1994) notes, "Special education is declared a caring profession, yet little is said about the rehabilitative function of teacher caring as an essential special education ingredient, even in the discussion of the increasing number of children stultified by not being cared for. . . . Caring by consultation requires even more imaginative extension. Yet caring is what many special children most need" (p. 538).

- Brandt (1994/1995) concludes, "I endorse the testimony of numerous pioneering educators and satisfied parents that it works—under the

Success in learning is the key variable in any classroom setting.

right conditions. But I also concede that conditions are often far from right in many schools. Looking at the arguments for and against inclusion . . . I think of Tevye in the musical *Fiddler on the Roof* saying, 'He's right—but she's also right'" (p. 3).

• Wilmore (1994/1995), an educator and parent of a child with disabilities, states, "Every committee must think, What if this child were my child? Think about the child's tomorrows. Think about what we do now that will affect those tomorrows. We can't afford to make mistakes" (p. 62).

☀ PROGRAM FACTORS AND LEAST RESTRICTIVE ENVIRONMENT

In School A, placing a student with learning disabilities in an inclusive program may be the least restrictive environment, whereas in School B, part-time placement in a resource room would be the least restrictive environment for the same student. This scenario exists because the quality of services varies across districts, schools, teachers, and placements. School A has several general education teachers who are excellent at tailoring instruction to meet the needs of the student with learning disabilities. School B has a learning disabilities resource teacher who does an excellent job of teaching students to achieve academic

gains and use learning strategies to become more independent learners. Unfortunately, the general education teachers at School B are not sensitive to the instructional needs of students with learning disabilities. The variations in mainstream settings led Bender and his associates (Bender & Ukeje, 1989) to research why some mainstream teachers receive students with learning problems and tailor instruction appropriately, while other teachers respond negatively to mainstreaming. Bender, Vail, and Scott (1995) report that teachers with less positive attitudes toward mainstreaming use effective mainstream instructional strategies less frequently.

When the instructional and social needs of students with disabilities are met in inclusive settings, it is the most appropriate placement. The question of what constitutes an effective inclusive program is becoming increasingly important. Fortunately, several researchers are investigating the factors of effective mainstream environments. Ysseldyke and Christenson (1993) developed *The Instructional Environment System—II* to help educators evaluate learning environments. This scale was developed, in part, on empirically based teaching practices that facilitate positive student outcomes for learners with mild disabilities.

Several researchers (Wang & Baker, 1985/1986; Waxman et al., 1985) reviewed empirical studies of adaptive instruction used in inclusive settings. They identified the following instructional features as promoting successful mainstreaming:

- An instructional match is maintained for each student.
- Individualized pacing for achieving instructional goals is maintained.
- Student progress is monitored, and continuous feedback is provided.
- Students are involved in the planning and monitoring of their learning.
- A broad range of techniques and materials is used.
- Students help one another to learn.
- Students are taught self-management skills.
- Teachers engage in instructional teaming.

This section features program factors that promote the successful inclusion or successful academic achievement of students with mild disabilities. Topics include teachers teaching teachers, the special education or at-risk teacher, and teacher–parent collaboration.

Teachers Teaching Teachers

The Individuals with Disabilities Education Act has had a widespread effect on the identification, instructional, and placement practices in special education. For example, collaboration between general education teachers and special education teachers now is required. It is the responsibility of educators to employ the interactive framework established by Public Law 94-142 to ensure that all students are educated in the least restrictive environment. In addition to the need for general and special education teachers to collaborate to meet the diverse needs of students with disabilities, there are other compelling reasons for working together. Cook and Friend (1991) note that the information explosion necessitates a need for shared expertise. Also, the increasing trend toward site-based management implies that administrators, teachers, parents, and community members must be able to make responsible decisions concerning school quality. Various special education/general education "teaching teams" (Thousand & Villa, 1990) have emerged to meet the challenge of educating students with disabilities in the general classroom. Moreover, Robert Fulghum (1988) reminds us of the importance of helping one another: "And it is still true,

no matter how old you are—when you go out into the world, it is best to hold hands and stick together" (p. 6).

A teachers-helping-teachers approach focuses on meeting the needs of students with disabilities within the general class before considering formal special education services and more segregated placements. Much of the promise of these activities rests on the assumption that, in a supportive and trusting environment, teachers can support and teach one another to individualize instruction better. Consequently, as teachers become more competent, the general or mainstream setting improves and referrals to special education decrease.

Strategies for Increasing Consultation Time Specific strategies for increasing consultation time have been implemented successfully at the elementary, middle, and secondary school levels (West & Idol, 1990). These strategies include the following:

- Create times when large numbers of students can be brought together for grade-level or schoolwide activities under the supervision of a few teachers.
- Have the principal regularly teach one period a day.
- Cluster students working on similar assignments into larger groups under the supervision of a few teachers.
- Hire a permanent substitute who "floats" from classroom to classroom as needed.
- Designate a specific time each week for staff collaboration.
- Designate one day each month or one day per grading period as "Collaboration Day."
- Extend the school day for about 20 minutes twice weekly to provide collaboration periods for teachers.

West and Idol (1990) note that numerous different and creative strategies have been used to support collaborative consultation. Developing strategies to create time for consultation requires more than administrative and logistical support. The collegial problem-solving process must be valued by both teachers and administrators (Phillips & McCullough, 1990; West & Idol, 1990). Finally, some of the components that are needed to develop and maintain effective consultations include administrative support, teacher input into decision making, collaborative consultation training, support teams to work with peer collaboration teams, and the use of language that all participants understand (Olson & Platt, 2000).

Collaborative Consultation   Collaborative problem-solving aimed at preventing student learning and behavioral problems offers a viable alternative to the overused and costly refer–test–place paradigm. The results of a survey of members of the Council for Exceptional Children (1989) on professional development needs illustrate the need for more collaboration. The three top-ranked items from the survey indicate the need for more collaboration with general education teachers and other special program teachers, the coordination of special education with other programs and services, and an improved relationship between general and special education.

West and Idol (1990) point out the differences between consultative and collaborative relationships. In consultative relationships, one professional confers with another to seek guidance. In collaborative relationships, two or more professionals work together with parity and reciprocity to solve problems. When collaborative consultation initially was conceptualized as a special education service model, the following definition emerged (Idol, Paolucci-Whitcomb, & Nevin, 1986, p. 1):

> Collaborative consultation is an interactive process which enables people with diverse expertise to generate creative solutions to mutually defined problems. The outcome is enhanced, altered, and different from the original solutions that any team member would produce independently. The major outcome of collaborative consultation is to provide comprehensive and effective programs for students with special needs within the most appropriate context, thereby enabling them to achieve maximum constructive interaction with their nonhandicapped peers.

In essence, mutual empowerment is an important goal of educational collaboration.

The major goals of collaborative consultation are to prevent behavioral and learning problems, ameliorate learning and behavioral problems, and coordinate instructional programs (West, Idol, & Cannon, 1988). For collaborative consultation to be most effective, a formal set of problem-solving stages is recommended. The most commonly accepted stages (Idol et al., 1986; West et al., 1988) include the following:

Stage 1:   *Goal/entry.* Roles, objectives, responsibilities, and expectations of the consultant and consulter are negotiated.

Stage 2:   *Problem identification.* The problem is defined clearly and discussed until all members have a mutual understanding of the problem.

Stage 3:   *Intervention recommendations.* Interventions are generated and prioritized in the expected order of implementation. Written, measurable objectives are developed to detail specific interventions for each aspect of the problem, establish criteria to determine whether the problem has been solved, and spell out the roles of the student and respective team members and identify appropriate resources needed for delivering interventions.

Stage 4:   *Implementation recommendations.* Implementation is provided according to established objectives and activities. Timelines and respective personnel responsible for selected interventions are specified. In the collaborative model, the consultant typically assumes a modeling role that phases out as the consulter gains expertise and confidence with the intervention.

Stage 5:   *Evaluation.* The success of the intervention strategies is assessed. This assessment includes measures of the student, consultant, consulter, and system change.

Stage 6:   *Redesign.* The intervention is continued, modified, or discontinued based on the evaluation of the intervention strategies.

West and Idol (1990) report that team consensus is reached at each stage before going to the next step. Moreover, they note that adherence to the stages allows for a systematic and efficient approach to solving problems.

Collaborative consultation may occur as a simple problem-solving process in a variety of contexts. Educational reforms are being suggested and demanded to provide learners who have disabilities with appropriate educational programs in their least restrictive environments. Many educators are calling for general and special educators to work together more closely to serve students with learning and behavioral problems. Consequently, many team approaches are being developed in which collaborative consultation may occur. Some models being proposed include teacher assistance teams (Chalfant & Pysh, 1989), mainstream assistance teams (Fuchs, Fuchs, & Bahr, 1990), cooperative professional development (Glatthorn, 1990), coaching (Showers, 1985), peer collaboration (Pugach & Johnson, 1988), and cooperative teaching (Bauwens, Hourcade, & Friend, 1989).

Teacher Assistance Teams   Kirk and Chalfant (1984) discuss a teacher assistance team (TAT) model that has helped teachers reduce the number of inappropriate referrals and resolve many students' problems. Each team consists of three elected teachers, the teacher seeking help, and parents or others as needed. The referring teacher provides information concerning the student's strengths and weaknesses and attempted interventions. Typically, the team conducts a problem-solving meeting by delineating specific objectives with the teacher, brainstorming intervention alternatives, selecting or refining intervention(s), and planning follow-up activities. The teacher leaves the meeting with a copy of the interventions. A follow-up meeting is planned in two to six weeks to determine whether the suggestions are working.

The TAT model was evaluated in three states for two years. Of the 200 students served in the study, the teams helped the classroom teacher resolve the difficulties of 133 students, or 66.5 percent. Of the 116 students who were underachieving, the teams could meet the needs of 103 (88.7 percent) without referring them to special education. Moreover, schools with teacher assistance teams cut their diagnostic costs by about 50 percent (Kirk & Chalfant, 1984). In another study, Chalfant and Pysh (1989) examined the practices of 96 first-year teacher assistance teams in seven states. Results indicate that the TAT model generated interventions that improved student performance, increased the appropriateness of special educa-

tion referrals, created effective strategies for students without disabilities, and assisted mainstream teachers in serving students with disabilities in their classrooms. Moreover, teacher satisfaction about TAT involvement was positive (i.e., 88 percent positive statements versus 12 percent negative statements). Principal support, team attributes, and teacher support were identified as major factors contributing to TAT effectiveness. In addition, Graden, Casey, and Christenson (1985) report success with a prereferral system that uses teacher-to-teacher consultation and group problem-solving sessions.

Coaching   The team approach of coaching also is generating enthusiasm among educators (McREL Staff, 1984/1985; Showers, 1985). Peer coaching involves the formation of a small group of teachers for peer observation. Teachers observe one another's classrooms, get feedback about their teaching, experiment with improved techniques, and receive support (McREL Staff, 1984/1985). Three-person coaching teams engage in a three-phase process involving discussion and planning, observation, and feedback.

In the discussion and planning phase, the teachers focus on the improved technique or strategy they want to learn and outline the specific essential behaviors or actions for implementing the new technique. In the observation phase, Teacher 1 observes Teacher 2, who observes Teacher 3, who observes Teacher 1. A format to guide data collection (e.g., a checklist, log, or tape recorder) helps observation. In the feedback phase, the observer and the teacher meet to discuss the observations. To help maintain the professional nature of coaching, the teachers must never talk to a third person about observations or let a team member draw others into personal problems. Periodically, the coaching teams meet in a support group of 6 to 12 with other coaching teams to plan and offer support for one another. Showers (1985) reports that coaching builds a community of teachers who continuously engage in the study of improved teaching. The coaching process becomes a continuous cycle in which common necessary understandings emerge for improved teaching through collegial study of new knowledge and skills.

The effects of coaching are impressive. Showers (1985) reports that coaching provides the essential follow-up for training new skills and strategies. Also, coaching is more effective than lecture and demonstration in providing classroom applications (McREL Staff, 1984/1985). In a study in which coached and uncoached teachers received the same training (e.g., theory, demonstration, and practice), Showers (1990) found that 80 percent of the coached teachers transferred the newly learned skills to their classes, whereas only 10 percent of the uncoached group transferred the skills. Coaching appears to help educators develop a broader repertoire of skills for meeting the diverse needs of students in mainstream settings.

Peer Collaboration   One way of enhancing classroom teachers' abilities to design and adapt educational interventions for mainstreamed students is through peer collaboration (Pugach & Johnson, 1988). Peer collaboration is based on the assumption that when general education teachers work together using a systematic problem-solving strategy, they can develop appropriate instructional and behavioral interventions for all of their students.

Peer collaboration involves pairs of teachers who engage in a highly structured dialogue about a problem involving a single student, a group of students, or a whole class. The structured dialogue includes opportunities for self-questioning, summarizing, and predicting with regard to the specific problem concerning the teacher. Each teacher in the dyad has a specific role. The Initiator is the teacher who shares the problem and ultimately solves the problem. The Facilitator guides the partner through each step in the dialogue to arrive at a solution. Table 1.3 presents the four steps included in the peer-collaboration process.

According to Pugach and Johnson (1988), as this process is systematically repeated, the general format of the dialogue becomes an internal-

TABLE 1.3
Steps included in the peer-collaboration process

Problem Description and Clarifying Questions
In this step, the Initiator provides the partner with a short, written description of the problem. Next, the Facilitator reads the problem and asks the partner whether there are any clarifying questions to be asked. For example, the written problem might be "Robert fails to complete classroom and homework assignments." The Initiator might ask questions such as "When does the behavior occur?" or "Are there any occasions when he does complete his work?" The Facilitator also can guide the process by asking, "Are there questions you could ask yourself about his classroom and homework assignments?" The purpose of this type of probing is to lead the Initiator to a general area of the problem rather than suggest specific areas for examination. The goal is to enable the Initiator to "recognize a pattern of behavior and form a summary" (Pugach & Johnson, 1988, p. 76).

Summarizing
After the problem is clarified, the Initiator summarizes the problem. The summary includes the clarified behavior pattern of the student, the teacher's response to the behavior, and the relevant factors in the classroom environment under the teacher's control.

Interventions and Predictions
During this step, at least three possible interventions are proposed by the Initiator, and predictions are made regarding potential outcomes for each intervention. The role of the Facilitator is to help the partner arrive at an intervention that is practical and minimally disruptive to the teacher and the class.

Evaluation Plan
During the last step in the process, a reasonably simple plan is developed to document and evaluate the effectiveness of the intervention. For example, in Robert's case, the Initiator may realize that a check-off sheet for Robert to mark as he completes assignments may help him complete his work. The intervention also can include a special notebook in which Robert records all of his homework assignments. His performance on both tasks should be monitored daily for two weeks. Finally, the Initiator and the partner may agree to meet in two weeks to discuss whether to continue the intervention or begin the peer-collaboration process again.

ized problem-solving strategy. Peer collaboration can provide general classroom teachers with a strategy to accommodate students with disabilities in the mainstream classroom. In a synthesis of their research on peer collaboration, Pugach and Johnson (1990) report that classroom teachers exhibited the following behaviors as a result of training in the peer-collaboration process:

- The focus of problem identification shifted away from the student to factors directly under the teacher's control.
- The teachers generated potential interventions for all problems targeted in a peer-collaboration session.
- The teachers effectively resolved over 85 percent of the problems targeted through peer collaboration.
- The teachers felt significantly more confident in their ability to manage classroom problems.
- Positive attitudes increased toward their class as a whole.

Cooperative Teaching   West and Idol (1990) note that the term *cooperative teaching* has been used interchangeably with *team teaching.* Cooperative teaching appears to be a viable model for integrating students with disabilities into the mainstream setting. Bauwens and Hourcade (1991, p. 20) define cooperative teaching as

> an educational approach in which general and special educators work in a co-active and coordinated fashion to jointly teach heterogeneous groups of students in educationally integrated settings (i.e., general education classrooms). In cooperative teaching both general and special education teachers are simultaneously present in the general classroom, maintaining joint responsibilities for specified education instruction that is to occur within the setting.

Using their definition as a framework, Bauwens and Hourcade discuss three different configurations of cooperative teaching: team teaching, complementary instruction, and supportive learning activities.

In a *team-teaching* arrangement, two teachers share instructional responsibility for a common body of content-area knowledge. The general and special educator jointly plan and instruct the same academic content to all students. Negotiation is a critical feature of this process. The teachers negotiate how the content will be presented, the time frames for instruction, and specific responsibilities for each part of the unit or lesson. In *complementary instruction,* the general educator has primary responsibility for teaching specific content areas, while the special educator teaches specific strategies or skills (e.g., notetaking, summarizing, or identifying main ideas in reading) to students who need additional instruction. In contrast to the team-teaching arrangement, in which teachers share equal responsibility for the same content, the complementary instruction arrangement features separate but related responsibility for instruction. Finally, in the *supportive learning activities* arrangement, the general and special educator collaboratively determine the major content and instructional goals for any lesson. The teachers jointly identify activities to support and extend the lesson. Within the supportive learning activities arrangement, the general educator primarily is responsible for teaching the content; however, the special educator reinforces and enriches the content by implementing supportive learning activities. For example, the special educator may have expertise in computer applications to extend the mathematics unit on decimals and percents. Moreover, the special educator can enrich and support content areas through the use of interest centers.

Communication Skills for Collaboration
In addition to being familiar with various models for collaboration, teachers need to use effective communication skills to implement collaboration successfully. Parity, shared responsibility, accountability, and mutual goals cannot be mandated. These characteristics result from reciprocal relationships among volunteers who value collaboration and believe it can work to help students and themselves. Idol and West (1991) provide the following principles of successful collaborative consultation skills:

- Create an atmosphere of mutual trust and respect so that team members feel safe in sharing information.
- Provide nonevaluative feedback when others are speaking.

- Use jargon-free language when sharing ideas.
- Be aware that nonverbal body language can communicate positive or negative messages.
- Give and receive feedback willingly and effectively, without confrontation.

Adapting and modifying teacher–teacher and teacher–student interactions and teaching repertoires demands considerable risk-taking by teachers. General and special educators who share responsibility for modifying their instruction to meet the diverse needs of students with disabilities need to establish a trusting relationship to help support their efforts toward change. Training in the principles in Covey's (1989) *The Seven Habits of Highly Effective People* and Covey, Merrill, and Merrill's (1994) *First Things First* provides an excellent foundation to help individuals develop and maintain collaborative relationships that foster positive changes.

The Special Education or At-Risk Teacher

Although numerous variables (e.g., funding, support, and cooperation) affect the quality of instructional services provided to students with disabilities, the teacher remains the most important influence in program quality. To deliver direct services, the special education or at-risk teacher must demonstrate the most effective empirically based assessment and teaching practices discussed in the remaining chapters of this text. To deliver indirect services, the teacher needs effective consultation skills to work with teachers of mainstreamed students, school-based assistance teams, and parents. Because more students with disabilities are being educated in the mainstream environment, the trend is moving toward using consultative services to help students succeed in mainstream classrooms. Generally, the research on the outcomes of consultation appears promising for reducing referrals to special education and helping students achieve in mainstream classrooms (Heron & Kimball, 1988; Idol, 1988; Polsgrove & McNeil, 1989). Heron and Kimball report that "the data currently available justify consultation as an appropriate service for facilitating the education of all students in the least restrictive en-

vironment, and it is clear that the database regarding the efficacy of specific consultation practices continues to emerge" (p. 27).

Consultation   Collaborative consultation represents an increasingly popular process regarding how numerous experts view the dynamics of problem solving in consultation. Special education teachers as well as mainstream teachers need training to become efficient in collaborative consultation. West and Cannon (1988) worked with a 100-member interdisciplinary expert panel to generate consultation competencies needed by general education and special education teachers to meet the educational needs of students with disabilities in general classrooms. The panel identified 47 essential competencies in nine categories. The categories receiving the highest ratings were interactive communication; personal characteristics; equity issues, values, and beliefs; collaborative problem solving; and evaluation of consultation effectiveness. Staff development competencies were rated as important but not essential. Categories that received ratings indicating less importance to the consultation process were consultation theory and models, consultation research, and system change.

Idol (1988) recommends that a consulting teacher should have completed a supervised practicum experience in school consultation and should have knowledge of all types of exceptional learners, all special education service delivery models, the history of special education, and special education legislation and legal rights of exceptional persons. In addition, Idol notes that a consulting teacher should have demonstrable skills in using assessment techniques (e.g., curriculum-based assessment, criterion-referenced testing, classroom observation, and standardized tests); applying basic remediation techniques for academic skill deficits (e.g., study skills strategies); applying basic behavior management techniques for individuals as well as groups of students, applying accommodation techniques to special needs learners in mainstream settings (e.g., materials modification, principles of reinforcement, and computer-assisted instruction); transferring learned skills from supportive service programs to the classroom; measuring, monitoring, and evaluating academic and behavioral progress in students; and using effective communication and working collaboratively with other adults.

Viable knowledge regarding consultation is increasing, and it needs to be a part of a special education teacher's preservice and staff development training. Tindal, Shinn, and Rodden-Nord (1990) provide a model that includes consideration for realistic school-based variables that influence the consultation process. This model includes 11 variables that are organized within three dimensions—people, process, and procedural implementation.

People Variables

1. Consultant background and skills—history, experiences, knowledge, resources
2. Consulter background and skills—history, experiences, knowledge, resources, teacher tolerance
3. Client background and skills—history, experiences, knowledge, resources
4. Administrator background and skills—history, experiences, knowledge, resources

Process Variables

5. Problem-solving relationship between consultant and consulter—problem identification and problem remediation
6. Theoretical perspective of consultation—behavioral, organizational, mental health
7. Stage in consultation—problem identification, problem corroboration, program development, program operationalization, program evaluation
8. Activity structure—assessment, assessment/direct intervention, assessment/indirect intervention, indirect service to system

Procedural Implementation Variables

9. Type of data—judgments, observations, tests
10. Program intervention—context, materials, interactive techniques
11. Evaluation strategies—qualitative, quantitative (individual-referenced, criterion-referenced, norm-referenced)

Tindal et al. note that the model should be used to help teachers consider important variables as they implement consultation in applied educational settings.

Teacher–Parent Collaboration

Teachers should work closely with parents to promote learning in school and at home. In a survey of the 20 variables most highly rated by a 12-member team of experts as being important for learning in children, M. C. Reynolds, Wang, and Walberg (1992) list three variables that involve parents. These experts report that to promote learning, parents should show affection for their child, display interest in their child's schoolwork, and expect academic success.

Foremost, parents should provide the child with a home environment of warmth, acceptance, and understanding. The child needs and deserves a comfortable place to retreat from the pressures, demands, and frustrations of daily living. Kronick (1977, p. 327) captures the essence of this responsibility:

> Our most primary goal must be to ensure that the home is a relaxed and pleasant place, a source of strength to the child. It should not shield the child from the world but give courage to cope with it. This means that the child must feel like an accepted, valued member of the family, sharing plans, decisions, special occasions, and concerns. I strongly feel that the home must be the child's anchor and that other considerations are secondary. Therefore, if you have to discard home remediation to create this kind of atmosphere, then discard it.

When parents are involved and cooperative, the home becomes the supportive foundation that the child needs to face the changing demands of school. Teachers and parents should recognize their roles as complementary and supplementary and view their relationship as a partnership to foster the child's progress.

Establishing Cooperation Teachers and parents often harbor attitudes about each other that inhibit mutual cooperation. These attitudes sometimes manifest themselves through teacher blaming or parent blaming. Such dissonance benefits no one. Its sources should be identified and strategies should be pursued to promote a cooperative and working relationship.

Initial progress toward cooperation hinges on development of mutual respect. Barsch (1969) suggests that parents prefer a teacher who approaches them as individuals, treats them with dignity, and conveys a feeling of acceptance. A parent does not want to be treated as simply a parent of a child with disabilities. Barsch points out, "As teachers are able to convey a feeling of acceptance of the person, the parent is reciprocally more accepting of whatever counsel the teacher may offer" (p. 11).

Many obstacles can inhibit cooperative parent–teacher relationships. However, the common goal should enable both to transcend the obstacles and work together. The following selected activities may foster teacher–parent cooperation:

- Provide parents with training on how to tutor their child.
- Invite parents to volunteer in the classroom.
- Develop an informative and consistent communication system between the teacher and the parents regarding homework. Initiate communication regularly, communicate about a problem early enough to resolve it, follow through on what is said, and communicate clearly (Jayanthi, Nelson, Sawyer, Bursuck, & Epstein, 1995).
- Communicate frequently through home notes, phone messages, progress reports, parent–teacher conferences, parent nights, e-mail, and at-school events.
- Ask parents to help with academics by reading to their child, signing homework, asking about their child's school day, helping their child practice math facts or spelling words, and taking their child to the library (National Institute of Education, 1985).
- Invite parents to go on field trips or visit the classroom.
- Focus on listening to parents in an effort to gain understanding and show respect.
- Help parents become informed advocates for their child.
- Provide transportation and child care services for parents to attend school meetings or events.

The changing demography in the United States challenges educators to develop techniques for effectively engaging linguistically diverse parents. Wilson and Hughes (1994) report that one in seven people speaks a language other than English at home. Some major factors that influence these parents' involvement are length of residence in the United States, English proficiency, availability of support groups and bilingual staff, and prior experience. Moreover, teachers should learn about the family's customs, values, concerns, and expectations. Wilson and Hughes offer the following techniques for engaging these parents:

- Employ an interpreter for parent conferences.
- Print all signs, school communications, and notes in the language spoken by the family.
- Send parents a large amount of written and visual information over an extended time.
- Videotape some class activities and share them with the parents.

Parent–Teacher Conferences   Parent–teacher conferences create an environment in which parents feel they are working cooperatively with school personnel. Many school districts encourage the special education teacher to meet with the parents before the child begins receiving special education services. Duncan and Fitzgerald (1969) found that early meetings with parents served to prevent or reduce attendance problems, the number of dropouts, and discipline problems. Also, early meetings were associated with higher grades and good future communication.

The initial parent–teacher conference is extremely important. To prepare, the teacher should examine the child's records and review pertinent information such as present status (i.e., chronological age, grade, class, and previous teacher), physical appearance and history, educational status, personal traits, and home and family characteristics. The teacher should also identify objectives for the meeting and develop an appropriate agenda. The conference time should be convenient for all attending, and the meeting place should be arranged to promote communication.

Successful conferences typically consist of six parts: (1) establishing rapport, (2) obtaining pertinent information from the parents, (3) providing information, (4) collaborating with parents to reach a consensus on a plan, (5) summarizing the conference and planning follow-up activities, and (6) evaluating the conference (Salend, 1998; Stephens & Wolf, 1989). Starting with neutral topics and providing a comfortable seat help establish rapport. To obtain information, the teacher should state the purpose of the conference, ask open-ended questions, recognize parents' feelings by responding empathetically, and avoid irrelevancies (such as marital problems). To provide information, the teacher should start with positive statements about the child's behavior and provide samples of work when possible, avoid educational jargon, and share anticipated plans. To collaborate with parents, the information presented by both parties must be considered. Active listening and flexibility facilitate reaching a consensus on a plan. To summarize the conference, the teacher should briefly review the main points concerning the student's progress, restate the activities that will be implemented to deal with identified weaknesses and problems, and answer any questions. The teacher and parents should discuss and agree on follow-up strategies and schedule another meeting, if necessary. The conference should end on a positive note, and the teacher should thank the parents for their input and interest and offer to be available for any future questions concerning their child. Finally, evaluation consists of noting each person's satisfaction with the meeting. Sample questions include: Was a folder of the student's representative work prepared for the parents? Was the teacher able to explain the academic remediation strategy to the parents? Was the teacher able to provide an adequate report of social and emotional progress? and Was the teacher able to solicit and respond to questions raised by the parents?

Listening is the key to communication, and both parties must listen. A good listener gains much information that often can help solve problems. Parents like to talk to a teacher who listens sympathetically, calmly, and nonjudgmentally. Active listening involves increased levels of responding, body animation, and questioning. Eye contact is a basic component of good listening, whereas fatigue, strong feelings, too much talking, and environmental distractions deter active listening. Simpson (1996) notes that to facilitate the communication process, the effective listener must demonstrate skills in attention, acceptance, and empathy, as well as use specific listening strategies (e.g., door-opening statements, clarifying statements, restating content, reflecting affect, silence, and summarizing). He states that

"the professional who attempts to respond to parents prior to listening to them, or the educator who too hastily assumes the position of 'telling' parents what to do or 'answering' their questions when they simply desire the opportunity to talk, will rarely offer the most satisfactory conferencing relationship" (p. 120).

Parents are major stakeholders in their child's educational program and, because of the emotions involved, it is not uncommon for a teacher to encounter parental criticism or anger. Jones and Jones (1995) provide some helpful techniques for teachers to deal with parental criticism and confrontation:

- Maintain a calm and pleasant manner.
- Use active listening and avoid becoming defensive. Look genuinely interested during the process. These behaviors defuse emotions.
- Ask what the parent wishes to accomplish.
- Set a time limit if necessary and give consideration to scheduling another meeting.
- Ask the parent whether the student is aware of the problem of concern.
- Be honest and rely on specific data.
- Let the parent know specifically what will be done to deal with the problem.

Parents as Teachers   From generation to generation, parents transmit customs, unique family habits, and traditions. Society expects parents to teach values and social skills, but should parents teach academics? The literature is mixed on the general effectiveness of parental tutoring. Some experts claim it is effective, whereas others question it. Basically, it is an individual decision that can be made intelligently if selected guidelines are followed.

Each individual must decide about home tutoring. According to Kronick (1977), the basic consideration is whether tutoring can be accomplished without depriving any family member of the resources (e.g., time, money, and activities) that should be directed toward maintaining a well-balanced life. Essentially, home tutoring is feasible if the overall experience is pleasant for the child and the parent.

If the decision is made to engage in parental tutoring, attention must be directed toward doing a good job. Guidelines include the following:

- Give simple instructions and precisely convey the requirements of the task.
- Be flexible regarding the length of the session. Sometimes the child will not attend to the work for a concentrated period of time. In these instances, settle for 2 to 5 minutes of concentrated work instead of insisting on completed work at the risk of creating frustration and tension (Weiss & Weiss, 1976).
- Maintain a tutoring log of the child's performance or a written record of observations (e.g., types of errors, questions asked, and rate of responses) made during the tutoring. These observations can be shared with the teacher and may assist in making future plans. Keeping a record of the child's progress is often helpful.
- Do not extend formal tutoring indefinitely. Periodically halt the tutoring. Supplement or replace it by incorporating the remedial tasks in everyday chores and games (Kronick, 1977).
- Make an effort to select the best time for the session. Many parents report that immediately following the evening meal is a good time (Weiss & Weiss, 1976). Also, choose a place for the session that does not restrict the activities of the other family members and is not too distracting. Tutor at the same time and place to establish an expectation for the activity.
- Identify appropriate levels and make sure the child can complete the task. Tutoring sessions should be success oriented. Work should be challenging but not too difficult.
- Limit the length of the tutoring session to about 15 minutes for children up to grade six and up to 30 minutes for older students (Cummings & Maddux, 1985).
- Use creative techniques in reviewing and teaching new material, and practice activities in ways that reduce boredom (Cummings & Maddux, 1985).
- Let the child know when a mistake has been made but do so in a positive or neutral manner. Provide encouragement and praise the learner for trying.
- Give the child time to become familiar with the task materials. Provide the child with an overview or introduction before beginning formal instruction.
- Encourage the child to make judgments or choices on the basis of evidence rather than by guessing or appealing to authority. Give the child time to think about the problem.
- Make sure that the tutoring sessions are pleasant for both the parent and the child.

Perspective on Teacher–Parent Collaboration   With the trend toward more parental involvement in identification, placement, and educational programming, school personnel must prepare themselves to work more closely and effectively with parents. The teacher must be supportive, sensitive, and informative during crucial parental adjustment periods. Both parties must realize that the optimal growth of the child will emerge only from a pilgrimage of problem-solving ventures. Frustration and hard work surely will accompany the search for services; however, joy likely will accompany the solution. This process beckons the teacher and the parent to develop precise assessment techniques and gather information about resources, techniques, and materials.

INSTRUCTIONAL VARIABLES RELATED TO STUDENT LEARNING

Numerous factors related to student achievement are outside of the direct control of the teacher; however, the quality of instruction within the classroom remains a major factor in student learning. Teachers and teacher educators have a responsibility to examine the research and apply the findings as they develop teacher practices. The instructional variables that follow highlight the major findings of selected research in general and special education. When a teacher incorporates these practices into daily instruction, the likelihood of improving the achievement of students increases.

Focus on Time for Learning

In their review of teaching research, Stevens and Rosenshine (1981) report that successful teachers maintain a strong academic focus. Effective teachers instruct students to spend more time working directly on academic tasks in texts, workbooks, instructional materials, and peer-mediated instruction. They assign and hold students responsible for more homework and test students more frequently.

The importance of an academic focus also receives support from research on engaged time. *Engaged time* is the time a student actually spends performing an academic task (e.g., writing, reading, or computing). An extensive study of teaching activities that make a difference in student achievement was conducted as part of a six-year Beginning Teacher Evaluation Study funded by the National Institute of Education through the California Commission for Teaching Preparation and Licensing. Denham and Lieberman (1980) report that one of the major contributions of the study is its emphasis on academic learning time—that is, the time a student spends engaged in academic tasks of appropriate difficulty. As expected, the study found that academic learning time is related to student achievement. Specifically, Fisher et al. (1980) report that the time allocated to a content area is associated positively with learning in that area, and the engaged time that students spend successfully performing reading or mathematics tasks is associated positively with learning. Thus, a cornerstone of good teaching is establishing appropriate academic instructional objectives and designing intervention programs that maximize opportunities for the student to work successfully on tasks related to the objectives (Howell & Nolet, 2000). Unfortunately, several researchers (Larrivee, 1986; Ysseldyke & Algozzine, 1995) report that students' engaged time in many classrooms is relatively low.

Haynes and Jenkins (1986) examined the instruction that special education students receive in resource rooms. One of their findings revealed that the amount of reading instruction per day varied from class to class. One class received about 58 minutes a day, and another class received about 17 minutes a day. As expected, the students who spent more time in reading instruction learned more about reading. In an observation of 230 elementary students with mild disabilities, Rich and Ross (1989) found that noninstructional time (e.g., transitions, housekeeping, wait time, and free time) accounted for almost three hours of the school day. Moreover, researchers report that achievement and academic engagement time are greater during teacher-directed behavior than during independent work (Sindelar, Smith, Harriman, Hale, & Wilson, 1986).

The finding that academic learning time is related positively to more student learning is consistent in the research for both general education students and students with learning problems (A. Reynolds, 1992). To foster a positive and productive learning environment, students should spend as much time as possible engaged in meaningful academic tasks.

Gettinger (1991) found that students with learning disabilities required significantly more time to achieve mastery on a reading comprehension task than students without learning disabilities. In essence, students with learning problems need ample time for learning, high rates of success, and strategies on how to learn and retain relevant information. Greenwood (1991) used classwide peer tutoring with at-risk elementary students to increase time on academic tasks over a five-semester period. The peer tutoring group achieved academic gains that were superior to a control group of comparable students.

Researchers claim that achievement is improved in two ways: by increasing the student's learning time and by decreasing the time a student needs to learn. Instructional factors that increase engaged time or decrease time needed for learning a specific skill include relevant learning tasks, effective classroom management, clearly stated learning expectations, timely and specific feedback, teacher–student interaction, reinforcement for learning, and continuous monitoring to meet instructional objectives (Anderson, 1984; Rieth & Evertson, 1988). Table 1.4 presents some specific suggestions for increasing instructional time and engaged time.

Ensure High Rates of Student Success

The need for students to experience high levels of success has substantial research support. In this research, *success* refers to the rate at which the student understands and correctly completes exercises (Borich, 1992). Success is defined according to the difficulty level of the materials. In high success, the student understands the task and makes occasional careless errors. With moderate success, the student partially understands the material and makes numerous mistakes. In low success, the student does not comprehend the

TABLE 1.4

Suggestions for increasing engaged time

General Suggestions for Increasing Engaged Time

Schedule more instructional time.

Teach students to make transitions quickly.

Use effective teaching techniques (see Chapter 4).

Strive to motivate students.

Be organized and prepared.

Increase teacher instructional interactions with students.

Maintain a balance between teacher-led and seatwork time.

Suggestions for Increasing Engaged Time During Teacher-Led Instruction

Use signals to remind students to attend (see SLANT in Chapter 4).

Be enthusiastic.

Maintain a brisk pace.

Illustrate content with interesting metaphors or stories.

Ask questions frequently and involve all students.

Praise students for effort and being on task.

Highlight the importance of content and its relation to daily life.

Suggestions for Increasing Engaged Time During Independent Work

Use a variety of seatwork activities, instructional games, self-correcting materials, and computer-assisted instruction.

Teach students to work independently.

Use peer tutoring pairs and classwide peer tutoring.

Make independent work relevant and meaningful.

Use cooperative learning groups.

Praise students for doing seatwork.

Check independent work for progress.

Monitor independent work through scanning and moving around the classroom.

Give clear and concise directions.

Evaluate independent work.

Post student work in the classroom.

Give independent work at each student's instructional level.

---

material. Student engagement in academic work is related highly to rate of success (i.e., instruction that produces moderate-to-high success rates results in increased achievement). Apparently, during high success more content is covered at the learner's appropriate instructional level. The positive relationship between achievement and high success rate is documented, especially when the instruction is didactic or expository.

One of the primary findings of the Beginning Teacher Evaluation Study (Fisher et al., 1980) is that learning improves most when students have a high percentage of correct responses during teacher questioning and seatwork. Stevens and Rosenshine (1981) suggest that a reasonable success rate appears to be at least 80 percent during instruction and 90 percent at the end of a unit. Ideally, the task should maintain an appropriate level of challenge (i.e., require effort to succeed). Fisher et al. (1980, pp. 17–18) highlight this point:

Common sense suggests that too high a rate of high-success work might be boring and repetitive and could inhibit the development of persistence. Probably, some balance between high success and more challenging work is appropriate. Also, we found that older students and/or students who were generally skilled at school learning did not require as high a percentage of time at the high-success level. Apparently these students had learned problem solving—how

TABLE 1.5

Selected instructional features that promote student success

Area	Instructional Feature
Content	Is useful or relevant
	Is clearly specified
	Is instructionally organized for easy learning
Assessment	Enables appropriate placement
	Provides frequent feedback regarding programs
	Leads to the establishment of realistic but high goals
Learning experience	Allows ample time for learning
	Provides support to facilitate learning
	Has students actually experience high rates of progress
	Reinforces achievements and efforts
Self-Regulation	Permits students to work independently
	Permits students to self-monitor their progress in some lessons
	Allows students to participate in goal setting and the selection of some activities
Collaboration	Includes peer teaching
	Includes collaboration in group activities

Source: From *Students with Learning Disabilities* (p. 234), 5th ed., by C. D. Mercer, 1997, Upper Saddle River, NJ: Merrill/Prentice Hall. Copyright 1997 by Prentice-Hall Publishing Company. Reprinted by permission.

to take a task they did not completely understand and work it out. Such students are able to undertake the challenge of more difficult material, as long as they eventually experience success. . . . When students worked with materials or activities that yielded a low success rate, achievement was lower.

Borich (1992) claims that the research suggests that students need to spend about 60 to 70 percent of their time on tasks that allow almost complete understanding with occasional careless errors. Instruction that promotes high success not only contributes to improved achievement but also fosters increased levels of self-esteem and positive attitudes toward academic learning and school (Wyne & Stuck, 1982).

In a study of success rates, Rieth and Frick (1983) found that learners with mild disabilities experience 43 percent high task success, 45 percent medium task success, and 12 percent low task success. Fisher et al. (1978) found that normally achieving students experience 45 percent high task success, 52 percent medium task success, and 3 percent low task success. The relatively low rates of high task success for both groups and the higher rate of low task success for the learners with mild disabilities underscore the need for better instructional matches and the con-

tinuous monitoring of student progress (Rieth & Evertson, 1988). Lack of success can lead to anxiety, frustration, inappropriate behavior, and poor motivation. In contrast, success can improve motivation, attitudes, academic progress, and classroom behavior.

Although many variables contribute to student success, the degree to which an appropriate instructional match is accomplished for each student must be viewed as the cornerstone of teaching that promotes high rates of success. The teacher's ability to diagnose relevant student characteristics (e.g., skill level, prior knowledge, strategy use, interests, and motivation) and task factors (e.g., level of difficulty, time to achieve mastery, and relevance) influences the quality of the instructional match (Christenson, Ysseldyke, & Thurlow, 1989). In essence, the teacher must match the learning task to the student's aptitude (i.e., diagnostic teaching function) to develop an instructional program that ensures student success. As presented in Table 1.5, Wang (1987) highlights some of the features of learning environments that promote successful learning outcomes. Borich (1992) notes that moderate-to-high success rates not only help learners achieve mastery of lesson content but also provide a foundation for students to become independent learners and engage in higher order thinking. This development becomes more likely when explicit instruction is coupled with strategies or self-directed instruction.

Provide Positive and Supportive Learning Environments

It is well known that students learn more when the school and classroom environments are positive and supportive (Christenson et al., 1989). For example, Samuels (1986) reports that an academic focus with a humanistic orientation increases student achievement. The teacher is the key individual who influences the tone of a classroom. The teacher arranges physical (e.g., lighting, temperature, and seating) and academic variables (e.g., scheduling, method of lesson presentation, test dates, and homework) and establishes the affective nature (e.g., encouragement, competitiveness, and cooperation) of the classroom. Teacher expectations, encouragements, evaluations, attentiveness, and attitudes greatly influence students' perceptions of themselves as learners. Because many students with learning problems have negative perceptions of their academic abilities, general and special education teachers must create and maintain a supportive classroom setting for them. When the teacher is cheerful, supportive, and enthusiastic, students tend to feel more comfortable and model those actions and attitudes. This can result in a pleasant, productive learning environment for all learners. Teachers easily can notice when things go wrong in the classroom, but *effective* teachers comment on positive classroom happenings. Sprick (1985) notes that learning is greater and behavior is more appropriate in classrooms in which teachers attend more to positive events than to negative events. Specifically, he reports that teachers who maintain a 3:1 ratio of attention to positive over negative events are likely to have a well-managed classroom of high-achieving students. Goodlad (1984) found that teachers with positive styles used about 10 percent of their time handling behavior problems, whereas teachers with predominantly negative styles spent about 42 percent of their time managing students' inappropriate behavior. Sprick reports that, unfortunately, most classroom teachers attend to negative events

three times more often than they attend to positive events. R. M. Smith, Neisworth, and Greer (1978, p. 85) convey the importance of the positive approach:

> Liberal amounts of praise, support, and encouragement are found in every good classroom. By emphasizing children's good points, the teacher can build their confidence and desire to tackle more difficult activities. Failure to use such encouragement is a mistake teachers cannot afford to make. The development of a healthy social interaction in the classroom has never been accomplished through criticism and ridicule.

Several educators (Borich, 1992; Brigham, Scruggs, & Mastropieri, 1992) maintain that teacher enthusiasm is an important aspect of teacher effort, is positively correlated to student achievement, and helps establish a positive and supportive learning environment. Brigham et al. examined the effects of teacher enthusiasm on the learning and behavior of junior high school students with learning problems. Their results indicate that enthusiastic presentations yield higher academic achievement and lower levels of off-task behavior. They characterize enthusiastic presentations according to eight elements: (1) varied, uplifting, and rapid vocal delivery, (2) dancing, wide-open eyes, (3) frequent, demonstrative gestures, (4) dramatic and varied body movements, (5) varied, emotive facial expressions, (6) varied word usage, (7) ready animated acceptance of ideas and feelings, and (8) exuberant overall energy level. Conversely, they describe five elements of unenthusiastic teacher behavior: (1) standing or sitting in the same place, (2) speaking in a monotone or inexpressive voice, (3) making infrequent eye contact, (4) using few animated facial expressions, and (5) generally interacting less with students. Borich maintains that no one can sustain a heightened level of enthusiasm for a long time without becoming emotionally fatigued. He states that a proper level reflects a balance of gesturing, eye contact, vocal inflections, and movement, which signals to most students the teacher's vigor, involvement, and intent.

Brophy and Good (1986) and Alderman (1990) report that a positive learning environment and student learning are enhanced when teachers believe that *all* students can learn and that teachers can make a difference. Christenson et al. (1989) state that a positive learning environment is built upon the use of realistic expectations for student learning, the development of instructional plans that consider student characteristics and needs, the use of reinforcement for student productivity, the use of active monitoring of student progress, and the belief that all students will experience academic success. Alderman notes that in a positive classroom, errors are viewed as a natural and important part of the learning process rather than as an indication that the student lacks ability. Moreover, a positive approach is enhanced by the appropriate use of reinforcement for desirable academic, on-task, and social behaviors. The positive effect of reinforcement on academic achievement and work behaviors is well established (Blankenship & Lilly, 1981; Lovitt, 1995). The teacher may consider the following questions to examine his or her potential influence on creating a positive and supportive learning environment:

- Am I enthusiastic most of the time?
- What is my attitude toward students?
- What is my attitude toward peers?
- Do I support all students?
- Do I admit mistakes and remain comfortable?
- Do I change my opinion with new information?
- Am I happy?
- Is my job fulfilling?
- Do I take care of my physical and emotional health?
- Am I a good listener?
- Do I laugh and smile much?

Students' descriptions of good teachers (Lovitt, 1977) reflect the importance of being positive. The students in Lovitt's study noted that good teachers compliment students, let students come to them for assistance, help all students, use good manners, trust students, join in class humor, explain more than once, and ask students for help. The students were concerned with fair play, inclusion in the action, and getting work done in a quiet and orderly room. They wanted their teachers to be real people with senses of humor. When the teachers behaved more like this, the academic performance of the students improved: "As the teacher did more things that pleased the students, they did more to please the teacher" (Lovitt, 1977, p. 94).

Plan and Maintain a Motivational Environment

The initial step in preventing classroom behavioral problems is to keep students motivated and, thus, engaged in the learning process. *Motivation* is used to describe what focuses or energizes a student's attention, emotions, and activity. It explains why students choose certain activities over others (e.g., do homework or talk on the telephone). Motivators can be internal or external, and they represent things or events that influence choices. Internal motivators come from within the individual (e.g., the desire to read a sports magazine). External motivators come from within the environment (e.g., parental pressure to do homework). When both internal and external sources motivate in the same direction, the effect is powerful. To motivate effectively, the teacher should be aware of a student's internal motivators, such as interests, needs, and aspirations, and external motivators, such as peer influence or teacher approval. Borich (1992) maintains that the key to motivation is to bring internal and external motivators together to engage students in active learning. He encourages teachers to find out students' needs, interests, and aspirations and to use these to personalize learning and, thus, motivate students to learn.

Many students with learning problems lose their motivation for learning as a result of a history of frustration and school failure. When teaching students with limited motivation, the teacher should plan systematic procedures to increase motivation. Van Reusen and Bos (1994) examined the effects of motivation strategy instruction on the participation of secondary students with learning disabilities in planning their IEPs. This instruction required the students to examine their strengths and limitations and identify their needs and aspirations. The purpose of the motivation strategy instruction was to involve the learners in key aspects of the learning process and increase the students' commitment to learn. Compared with students with learning disabilities who did not receive the motivation strategy training, the treatment group identified more goals and communicated more effectively during their IEP conferences. These findings highlight the importance of involving students with learning disabilities in the planning of their educational program. Specifically, the motivation strategy instruction helped the teachers and students recognize needs, interests, and aspirations that were important for motivating these students.

Setting realistic instructional goals and determining specific mastery criteria are important to student motivation (Christenson et al., 1989). Clifford (1990) encourages teachers to establish learning goals that represent a moderate success probability. She notes that students often attribute success with easy tasks to task ease, and attribute success with extremely difficult tasks to luck. Clifford states, "It is only success at moderately difficult . . . tasks that we explain in terms of personal effort, well-chosen strategies, and ability; and these explanations give rise to feelings of pride, competence, satisfaction, persistence, and personal control" (p. 22). Similarly, Alderman (1990) notes that the linking of success to one's own efforts is critical for the development of motivation in students.

Once goals are established, student motivation is enhanced by monitoring progress toward these goals and delivering feedback on how to correct errors through learning strategies and study skills (Porter & Brophy, 1988; Wang, 1987). Table 1.6 features strategies for motivating students as suggested by Alderman (1990), Brigham et al. (1992), Brophy (1987), Christenson et al. (1989), Porter and Brophy (1988), and Salend (1998).

☀ REFERENCES

Alderman, M. K. (1990). Motivation for at-risk students. *Educational Leadership, 48*(1), 27–30.

American Psychiatric Association. (1982). *Diagnostic and statistical manual of mental disorders* (2nd ed.). Washington, DC: Author.

American Psychiatric Association. (1987). *Diagnostic and statistical manual of mental disorders* (3rd ed., revised). Washington, DC: Author.

American Psychiatric Association. (1994). *Diagnostic and statistical manual of mental disorders* (4th ed.). Washington, DC: Author.

Anderson, L. W. (1984). Instruction and time-on-task: A review. In L. W. Anderson (Ed.), *Time and school learning* (pp. 142–163). New York: St. Martin's Press.

Anderson-Inman, L. (1986). Bridging the gap: Student-centered strategies for promoting the transfer of learning. *Exceptional Children, 52,* 562–572.

Baker, E. T., Wang, M. C., & Walberg, H. J. (1994/1995). The effects of inclusion on learning. *Educational Leadership, 52*(4), 33–35.

Barsch, R. H. (1969). *The parent teacher partnership.* Arlington, VA: Council for Exceptional Children.

Bateman, B. D. (1977). Prescriptive teaching and individualized education programs. In R. Heinrich & S. C. Ashcroft (Eds.), *Instructional technology and the education of all handicapped children.* Columbus, OH: National Center on Media and Materials for the Handicapped.

Bauwens, J., & Hourcade, J. J. (1991). Making co-teaching a mainstreaming strategy. *Preventing School Failure, 35*(4), 19–24.

Bauwens, J., Hourcade, J. J., & Friend, M. (1989). Cooperative teaching: A model for general and special education integration. *Remedial and Special Education, 10*(2), 17–22.

Bender, W. N., & Smith, J. K. (1990). Classroom behavior of children and adolescents with learning disabilities: A meta-analysis. *Journal of Learning Disabilities, 23,* 298–305.

Bender, W. N., & Ukeje, I. C. (1989). Instructional strategies in mainstream classrooms: Prediction of the strategies teachers select. *Remedial and Special Education, 10*(2), 23–30.

Bender, W. N., Vail, C. O., & Scott, K. (1995). Teachers' attitudes toward increased mainstreaming: Implementing effective instruction for students with learning disabilities. *Journal of Learning Disabilities, 28,* 87–94, 120.

Bender, W. N., & Wall, M. E. (1994). Social-emotional development of students with learning disabilities. *Learning Disability Quarterly, 17,* 323–341.

Blankenship, C., & Lilly, M. S. (1981). *Mainstreaming students with learning and behavior problems: Techniques for the classroom teacher.* New York: Holt, Rinehart & Winston.

Borich, G. D. (1992). *Effective teaching methods* (2nd ed.). Upper Saddle River, NJ: Merrill/Prentice Hall.

Brandt, R. (1994/1995). Overview: What is best? *Educational Leadership, 52*(4), 3.

Brigham, F. J., Scruggs, T. E., & Mastropieri, M. A. (1992). Teaching enthusiasm in learning disabilities classrooms: Effects on learning and behavior. *Learning Disabilities Research & Practice, 7,* 68–73.

Broadbent, D. E. (1973). *In defense of empirical psychology.* London: Methuen.

TABLE 1.6
Strategies for motivating
students to learn

Plan for Motivation
Create a supportive and positive environment.
Program for success by maintaining a match between task and student
  capabilities.
Develop meaningful learning outcomes.
Relate content to students' interests and their daily lives.
Use metaphors, anecdotes, stories, and examples to embellish
  understanding.

Motivate Through Appropriate Expectations
Communicate positive expectations.
Communicate challenging expectations.
Teach goal setting and help students link efforts to outcomes.

Use Extrinsic Incentives for Students Who Require Them
Praise sincere effort.
Reward good or improved performances.
Point out pragmatic values of learning.
Structure appropriate competitive activities.
Provide students with many opportunities to respond.
Provide immediate feedback to student responses.
Periodically use a game format.

Recognize and Provide Intrinsic Motivation
Teach self-management.
Involve students in planning selected instructional activities.
Provide ample time for students to achieve mastery.
Give students choices in selecting activities or topics.
Allow students to complete products.
Use fantasy or simulation activities.
Challenge students with higher order thinking activities.
Use cooperative learning and peer tutoring.
Discuss rationales for learning specific skills and content.
Induce students to develop their own motivation.
Encourage students to move from extrinsic to intrinsic motivators.
Use activities that arouse curiosity.

Use Strategies to Promote Motivation
Teach basic social skills.
Model interest in learning.
Project intensity.
Be enthusiastic about content and learning.
Be enthusiastic when presenting and interacting.
Use advance organizers to establish attending and importance.
Use explicit modeling to teach understanding.
Use a variety of independent learning activities (e.g., self-correcting
  materials and computer-assisted instruction).
Model metacognition through "think alouds" while problem solving.
Minimize anxiety during learning activities.
Monitor progress and adjust instruction accordingly.
Vary grouping arrangements.
Use culturally relevant materials and examples.
Use students' names, experiences, hobbies, and interests in lessons.

Source: From *Students with Learning Disabilities* (p. 238), 5th ed., by C. D. Mercer,
1997, Upper Saddle River, NJ: Merrill/Prentice Hall. Copyright 1997 by Prentice-Hall
Publishing Company. Reprinted by permission.

Brophy, J. (1987). Synthesis of research on strategies for motivating students to learn. *Educational Leadership, 45*(2), 40–48.

Brophy, J., & Good, T. L. (1986). Teacher behavior and student achievement. In M. C. Wittrock (Ed.), *Handbook of research on teaching* (3rd ed., pp. 328–375). Upper Saddle River, NJ: Prentice Hall.

Bryan, J. (1988, April). *Perspectives on the regular education initiative.* Paper presented at the meeting of the Council for Exceptional Children, Washington, DC.

California Department of Education. (1994). *I can learn: A handbook for parents, teachers, and students.* Sacramento, CA: Author.

Carlberg, C., & Kavale, K. (1980). The efficacy of special versus regular class placement for exceptional children: A meta-analysis. *The Journal of Special Education, 14*, 295–309.

Cegelka, P. T., & Berdine, W. H. (1995). *Effective instruction for students with learning difficulties.* Boston: Allyn & Bacon.

Chalfant, J. C. (1985). Identifying learning disabled students: A summary of the National Task Force report. *Learning Disabilities Focus, 1*(1), 9–20.

Chalfant, J. C., & Pysh, M. V. (1989). Teacher assistance teams: Five descriptive studies of 96 teams. *Remedial and Special Education, 19*(6), 49–58.

Christenson, S. L., Ysseldyke, J. E., & Thurlow, M. L. (1989). Critical instructional factors for students with mild handicaps: An integrative review. *Remedial and Special Education, 10*(5), 21–31.

Clifford, M. M. (1990). Students need challenge, not easy success. *Educational Leadership, 48*(1), 22–26.

Cook, L., & Friend, M. (1991). Collaboration in special education: Coming of age in the 1990s. *Preventing School Failure, 35*(2), 24–27.

Council for Exceptional Children. (1989). Survey of CEC members' professional development needs. *Teaching Exceptional Children, 21*(3), 78–79.

Covey, S. R. (1989). *The seven habits of highly effective people.* New York: Simon & Schuster.

Covey, S. R., Merrill, A. R., & Merrill, R. R. (1994). *First things first.* New York: Simon & Schuster.

Cummings, R. E., & Maddux, C. D. (1985). *Parenting the learning disabled: A realistic approach.* Springfield, IL: Charles C Thomas.

Denham, C., & Lieberman, A. (Eds.). (1980). *Time to learn.* Washington, DC: National Institute of Education.

Duncan, L. W., & Fitzgerald, P. W. (1969). Increasing the parent-child communication through counselor-parent conferences. *Personnel and Guidance Journal, 47,* 514–517.

Ellett, L. (1993). Instructional practices in mainstreamed secondary classrooms. *Journal of Learning Disabilities, 26,* 57–64.

Fisher, C. W., Berliner, D. C., Filby, N. N., Marliave, R., Cahen, L. S., & Dishaw, M. M. (1980). Teaching behaviors, academic learning time, and student achievement: An overview. In C. Denham & A. Lieberman (Eds.), *Time to learn.* Washington, DC: National Institute of Education.

Fisher, C. W., Berliner, D. C., Filby, N. N., Marliave, R., Cahen, L. S., Dishaw, M. M., & Moore, J. E. (1978). *Teaching and learning in the elementary school: A summary of the Beginning Teacher Evaluation Study.* San Francisco: Far West Laboratory for Educational Research and Development.

Fuchs, D., & Fuchs, L. S. (1988). Evaluation of the adaptive learning environments model. *Exceptional Children, 55,* 115–127.

Fuchs, D., & Fuchs, L. S. (1994). Inclusive schools movement and the radicalization of special education reform. *Exceptional Children, 60,* 294–309.

Fuchs, D., Fuchs, L. S., & Bahr, M. W. (1990). Mainstream assistance teams: A scientific basis for the art of consultation. *Exceptional Children, 57,* 128–139.

Fulghum, R. (1988). *All I really need to know I learned in kindergarten.* New York: Ballantine Books.

Garnett, K. (1992). Developing fluency with basic number facts: Intervention for students with learning disabilities. *Learning Disabilities Research & Practice, 7,* 210–216.

Gartner, A., & Lipsky, D. K. (1987). Beyond special education: Toward a quality system for all students. *Harvard Educational Review, 57,* 367–395.

Gettinger, M. (1991). Learning time and retention differences between nondisabled students and students with learning disabilities. *Learning Disability Quarterly, 14,* 179–189.

Giangreco, M. F., Dennis, R. E., Edelman, S. W., & Cloninger, C. J. (1994). Dressing your IEPs for the general education climate: Analysis of IEP goals and objectives for students with multiple disabilities. *Remedial and Special Education, 15,* 288–296.

Glatthorn, A. A. (1990). Cooperative professional development: Facilitating the growth of the special education teacher and the classroom teacher. *Remedial and Special Education, 11*(3), 29–34, 50.

Goodlad, J. I. (1984). *A place called school.* New York: McGraw-Hill.

Graden, J. L., Casey, A., & Christenson, S. L. (1985). Implementing a prereferral intervention system. Part I. The model. *Exceptional Children, 51,* 377–384.

Greenwood, C. R. (1991). Longitudinal analysis of time, engagement, and achievement in at-risk versus non-risk students. *Exceptional Children, 57,* 521–534.

Hallahan, D. P., & Kauffman, J. M. (1994). Toward a culture of disability in the aftermath of Deno and Dunn. *The Journal of Special Education, 27,* 496–508.

Hayden, D., Vance, B., & Irvin, M. S. (1982). Establishing a special education management system—SEMS. *Journal of Learning Disabilities, 15,* 428–429.

Haynes, M. C., & Jenkins, J. R. (1986). Reading instruction in special education resource rooms. *American Educational Research Journal, 23,* 161–190.

Heron, T. E., & Kimball, W. H. (1988). Gaining perspective with the educational consultation research base: Ecological considerations and further recommendations. *Remedial and Special Education, 9*(6), 21–28, 47.

Hirschman, A. O. (1986). *Rival views of market society and other recent essays.* New York: Viking.

Howell, K. W., & Nolet, V. (2000). *Curriculum-based evaluation: Teaching and decision making* (3rd ed.). Belmont, CA: Wadsworth/Thomson Learning.

Idol, L. (1988). A rationale and guidelines for establishing special education consultation programs. *Remedial and Special Education, 9*(6), 48–58.

Idol, L. (1989). The resource/consulting teacher: An integrated model of service delivery. *Remedial and Special Education, 10*(6), 38–48.

Idol, L., Paolucci-Whitcomb, P., & Nevin, A. (1986). *Collaborative consultation.* Austin, TX: PRO-ED.

Idol, L., & West, J. F. (1991). Educational collaboration: A catalyst for effective schooling. *Intervention in School and Clinic, 27,* 70–78.

Jayanthi, M., Nelson, J. S., Sawyer, V., Bursuck, W. D., & Epstein, M. H. (1995). Homework-communication problems among parents, classroom teachers, and special education teachers: An exploratory study. *Remedial and Special Education, 16*(2), 102–116.

Jenkins, M. W. (1987). Effect of a computerized individual education program (IEP) writer on time savings and quality. *Journal of Special Education Technology, 8*(3), 55–66.

Joint Committee on Teacher Planning for Students with Disabilities. (1995). Planning for academic diversity in America's classrooms: Windows on reality, research, change, and practice. *Effective School Practices, 14*(2), 1–53.

Jones, V. F., & Jones, L. S. (1995). *Comprehensive classroom management: Creating positive learning environments for all students* (4th ed.). Boston: Allyn & Bacon.

Kauffman, J. M. (1994). Places of change: Special education's power and identity in an era of educational reform. *Journal of Learning Disabilities, 27,* 610–618.

Kauffman, J. M., & Hallahan, D. P. (1993). Toward a comprehensive delivery system for special education. In J. I. Goodlad & T. C. Lovitt (Eds.), *Integrating general and special education* (pp. 73–102). Upper Saddle River, NJ: Merrill/Prentice Hall.

Kauffman, J. M., & Hallahan, D. P. (Eds.). (1995). *The illusion of full inclusion: A comprehensive critique of a current special education bandwagon.* Austin, TX: PRO-ED.

Keogh, B. K. (1988). Improving services for problem learners. Rethinking and restructuring. *Journal of Learning Disabilities, 21,* 19–22.

Keogh, B. K. (1990). Narrowing the gap between policy and practice. *Exceptional Children, 57,* 186–190.

Keogh, B. K. (1994). What the special education research agenda should look like in the year 2000. *Learning Disabilities Research & Practice, 9,* 62–69.

Kirk, S. A., & Chalfant, J. C. (1984). *Academic and developmental learning disabilities.* Denver: Love.

Kronick, D. (1977). A parent's thoughts for parents and teachers. In N. G. Haring & B. Bateman, *Teaching the learning disabled child.* Upper Saddle River, NJ: Prentice Hall.

Larrivee, B. (1986). Effective teaching for mainstreamed students is effective teaching for all students. *Teacher Education and Special Education, 9,* 173–179.

Lovitt, T. C. (1977). *In spite of my resistance: I've learned from children.* Upper Saddle River, NJ: Merrill/Prentice Hall.

Lovitt, T. C. (1995). *Tactics for teaching* (2nd ed.). Upper Saddle River, NJ: Merrill/Prentice Hall.

Margalit, M., & Shulman, S. (1986). Autonomy perceptions and anxiety expressions of learning disabled adolescents. *Journal of Learning Disabilities, 19,* 291–293.

McKinney, J. D., & Feagans, L. (1984). Adaptive classroom behavior of learning disabled students. *Journal of Learning Disabilities, 16,* 360–367.

McREL Staff. (1984/1985, Winter). Coaching: A powerful strategy for improving staff development and inservice education. *Noteworthy,* pp. 40–46.

Milwaukee Public Schools. (1990). *One at a time, together! Best practices: Integrated programming and therapy.* Milwaukee, WI: Milwaukee Public Schools,

Department of Exceptional Education and Supportive Services.

Montgomery, M. S. (1994). Self-concept and children with learning disabilities: Observer-child concordance across six context-dependent domains. *Journal of Learning Disabilities, 27,* 254–262.

Morse, W. C. (1994). Comments from a biased viewpoint. *The Journal of Special Education, 27,* 531–542.

Mueller, D. J., Chase, C. I., & Walden, J. D. (1988). Effects of reduced class size in primary classes. *Educational Leadership, 45*(5), 48–50.

National Institute of Education. (1985, February). *Research in brief.* Washington, DC: Author.

Olson, J. L., & Platt, J. M. (2000). *Teaching children and adolescents with special needs* (3rd ed.). Upper Saddle River, NJ: Merrill/Prentice Hall.

O'Neil, J. (1994/1995). Can inclusion work? A conversation with Jim Kauffman and Mara Sapon-Shevin. *Educational Leadership, 52*(4), 7–11.

Phillips, V., & McCullough, L. (1990). Consultation-based programming: Instituting the collaborative ethic in schools. *Exceptional Children, 56,* 291–304.

Polsgrove, L., & McNeil, M. (1989). The consultation process: Research and practice. *Remedial and Special Education, 10*(1), 6–13, 20.

Porter, A. C., & Brophy, J. (1988). Synthesis of research on good teaching: Insights from the work of the Institute for Research on Teaching. *Educational Leadership, 45*(8), 74–85.

Pugach, M. C., & Johnson, L. J. (1988). Peer collaboration. *Teaching Exceptional Children, 20,* 75–77.

Pugach, M. C., & Johnson, L. J. (1990). Meeting diverse needs through professional peer collaboration. In W. Stainback & S. Stainback (Eds.), *Support networks for inclusive schooling: Interdependent integrated education* (pp. 123–137). Baltimore, MD: Paul H. Brookes.

Reynolds, A. (1992). What is competent beginning teaching? A review of the literature. *Review of Educational Research, 62,* 1–35.

Reynolds, M. C. (1989). An historical perspective: The delivery of special education to mildly disabled and at-risk students. *Remedial and Special Education, 10*(6), 7–11.

Reynolds, M. C., Wang, M. C., & Walberg, H. J. (1987). The necessary restructuring of special and regular education. *Exceptional Children, 53,* 391–398.

Reynolds, M. C., Wang, M. C., & Walberg, H. J. (1992). The knowledge bases for special and general education. *Remedial and Special Education, 13*(5), 6–10, 33.

Rich, H. L., & Ross, S. M. (1989). Student's time on learning tasks in special education. *Exceptional Children, 55,* 508–515.

Rieth, H., & Evertson, C. (1988). Variables related to the effective instruction of difficult-to-teach children. *Focus on Exceptional Children, 20*(5), 1–8.

Rieth, H. J., & Frick, T. (1983). *An analysis of the impact of instructional time with different service delivery systems on the achievement of mildly handicapped students* (Final Grant Research Report). Bloomington: Indiana University, Center for Innovation in Teaching the Handicapped.

Sabornie, D. J. (1985). Social mainstreaming of handicapped students: Facing an unpleasant reality. *Remedial and Special Education, 6*(2), 12–16.

Sabornie, D. J. (1994). Social-affective characteristics in early adolescents identified as learning disabled and nondisabled. *Learning Disability Quarterly, 17,* 268–279.

Salend, S. J. (1998). *Effective mainstreaming: Creating inclusive classrooms* (3rd ed.). Upper Saddle River, NJ: Merrill/Prentice Hall.

Salend, S. J., & Lutz, J. G. (1984). Mainstreaming or mainlining: A competency based approach to mainstreaming. *Journal of Learning Disabilities, 17,* 27–29.

Samuels, S. J. (1986). Why children fail to learn and what to do about it. *Exceptional Children, 53,* 7–16.

Shanker, A. (1994/1995). Full inclusion is neither free nor appropriate. *Educational Leadership, 52*(4), 18–21.

Showers, B. (1985). Teachers coaching teachers. *Educational Leadership, 42*(7), 43–48.

Showers, B. (1990). Aiming for superior classroom instruction for all children: A comprehensive staff development model. *Remedial and Special Education, 11*(3), 35–39.

Simpson, R. L. (1996). *Working with parents and families of exceptional children and youth* (3rd ed.). Austin, TX: PRO-ED.

Sindelar, P., Smith, M., Harriman, N., Hale, R., & Wilson, R. (1986). Teacher effectiveness in special education programs. *The Journal of Special Education, 20,* 195–207.

Singer, J. D. (1988). Should special education merge with regular education? *Educational Policy, 2,* 409–424.

Smith, C. R. (1998). *Learning disabilities: The interaction of learner, task, and setting* (4th ed.). Boston: Allyn & Bacon.

Smith, R. M., Neisworth, J. T., & Greer, J. G. (1978). *Evaluating educational environments.* Upper Saddle River, NJ: Merrill/Prentice Hall.

Smith, S. (1990). Individualized education programs (IEPs) in special education—From intent to acquiescence. *Exceptional Children, 57,* 6–14.

Speece, D. L., & Mandell, C. J. (1980). Resource room support services for regular teachers. *Learning Disability Quarterly, 3*(1), 49–53.

Sprick, R. S. (1985). *Discipline in the secondary classroom: A problem-by-problem survival guide.* West Nyack, NY: The Center for Applied Research in Education.

Stainback, S., & Stainback, W. (1987). Integration versus cooperation: A commentary on "Educating children with learning problems: A shared responsibility." *Exceptional Children, 54,* 66–68.

Stainback, S., Stainback, W., East, K., & Sapon-Shevin, M. (1994). A commentary on inclusion and the development of a positive self-identity by people with disabilities. *Exceptional Children, 60,* 486–490.

Stephens, T. M., & Wolf, J. S. (1989). *Effective skills in parent/teacher conferencing* (2nd ed.). Columbus, OH: School Study Council of Ohio, College of Education, The Ohio State University.

Stevens, R., & Rosenshine, B. (1981). Advances in research on teaching. *Exceptional Education Quarterly, 2*(1), 1–9.

Thousand, J. S., & Villa, R. A. (1990). Sharing expertise and responsibilities through teaching teams. In W. Stainback & S. Stainback (Eds.), *Support networks for inclusive schooling: Interdependent integrated education* (pp. 151–166). Baltimore, MD: Paul H. Brookes.

Tindal, G., Shinn, M. R., & Rodden-Nord, K. (1990). Contextually based school consultation: Influential variables. *Exceptional Children, 56,* 324–336.

Van Reusen, A. K., & Bos, C. S. (1994). Facilitating student participation in individualized education programs through motivation strategy instruction. *Exceptional Children, 60,* 466–475.

Wang, M. C. (1987). Toward achieving educational excellence for all students: Program design and instructional outcomes. *Remedial and Special Education, 8*(3), 25–34.

Wang, M. C., & Baker, E. T. (1985/1986). Mainstreaming programs: Design features and effects. *The Journal of Special Education, 19,* 503–521.

Wang, M. C., Haertel, G. D., & Walberg, H. J. (1993/1994). Synthesis of research: What helps students learn? *Educational Leadership, 51*(4), 74–79.

Wang, M. C., Reynolds, M. C., & Walberg, H. J. (1986). Rethinking special education. *Educational Leadership, 44*(1), 26–31.

Wang, M. C., & Zollers, N. J. (1990). Adaptive instruction: An alternative service delivery approach. *Remedial and Special Education, 11*(1), 7–21.

Waxman, H. C., Wang, M. C., Anderson, K. A., & Walberg, H. J. (1985). Adaptive education and student outcomes: A quantitative synthesis. *Journal of Educational Research, 78*(4), 228–236.

Weiss, H. G., & Weiss, M. S. (1976). *Home is a learning place: A parents' guide to learning disabilities.* Boston: Little, Brown.

Weller, C., Watteyne, L., Herbert, M., & Crelly, C. (1994). Adaptive behavior of adults and young adults with learning disabilities. *Learning Disability Quarterly, 17,* 282–295.

West, J. F., & Cannon, G. S. (1988). Essential collaborative consultation competencies for regular and special educators. *Journal of Learning Disabilities, 21,* 56–63, 28.

West, J. F., & Idol, L. (1990). Collaborative consultation in the education of mildly handicapped and at-risk students. *Remedial and Special Education, 11*(1), 22–31.

West, J. F., Idol, L., & Cannon, G. (1988). *Collaboration in the schools: Communicating, interacting, and problem solving.* Austin, TX: PRO-ED.

Wiederholt, J. L., & Chamberlain, S. P. (1989). A critical analysis of resource programs. *Remedial and Special Education, 10*(6), 15–27.

Will, M. C. (1986). Educating children with learning problems: A shared responsibility. *Exceptional Children, 52,* 411–415.

Wilmore, E. L. (1994/1995). When your child is special. *Educational Leadership, 52*(4), 60–62.

Wilson, C. L., & Hughes, M. (1994). Involving linguistically diverse parents. *LD Forum, 13*(3), 25–27.

Wyne, M., & Stuck, G. (1982). Time and learning: Implications for the classroom teacher. *The Elementary School Journal, 83,* 67–75.

Yell, M. L. (1995). Least restrictive environment, inclusion, and students with disabilities: A legal analysis. *The Journal of Special Education, 28,* 389–404.

Ysseldyke, J. E., & Algozzine, B. (1995). *Special education: A practical approach for teachers* (3rd ed.). Boston: Houghton Mifflin.

Ysseldyke, J. E., & Christenson, S. L. (1993). *The Instructional Environment System—II.* Longmont, CO: Sopris West.

Ysseldyke, J. E., Christenson, S., & Kovaleski, J. F. (1994). Identifying students' instructional needs in the context of classroom and home environments. *Teaching Exceptional Children, 26*(3), 37–41.

CHAPTER 2

Planning and Organizing Instruction

C hapter 1 focuses on creating responsive educational environments within the context of student needs and characteristics, teacher–teacher collaboration, and teacher–parent collaboration. Moreover, it promotes the adoption of a philosophy that embraces research concerning instructional variables that promote learning. Whereas Chapter 1 concerns macrofactors such as human resources and legal requirements, Chapter 2 focuses on micro-factors such as planning and organizing the many details that accompany teaching. Arranging the classroom, selecting instructional materials, developing homework guidelines, and scheduling are only a few of the details that teachers must plan and organize.

When instruction engages student attention and participation continuously without interruptions, digressions, and diversions, it usually is the result of extensive teacher planning. Given the importance of teacher planning, it is imperative that teachers receive recognition and support for planning activities. In a report on teacher planning, Lenz, Deshler, and Schumaker (1990) provide some helpful information about teacher planning:

- The time that teachers spend planning after school hours varies greatly. The average amount of planning time is 76 minutes.
- The average time teachers spend planning during the summer is 59 hours.
- Many teachers report that their most productive planning occurs in unstructured settings (e.g., driving a car, walking the dog, or taking a shower). Teachers generally agree that during-school planning involves "top structure" planning (i.e., scheduling, determining class structure, and responding to administrative tasks), whereas "deep structure" planning (i.e., how to clarify a difficult concept or develop a motivating activity) is accomplished away from school.
- Teachers report that the biggest obstacles to planning for an academically diverse class are insufficient time, lack of opportunity to develop or discover motivating and ability-appropriate materials and activities, and lack of knowledge concerning students' abilities and academic history.

This chapter presents planning and organizing instruction in the areas of physical arrangements, instructional arrangements (including choosing and using materials), scheduling, classroom equipment, and material organization system.

PHYSICAL ARRANGEMENTS

The decisions a teacher makes regarding the physical arrangements of a classroom have an important effect on the success of instructional activities and classroom management. Cegelka and Berdine (1995) note that physical arrangements influence the time students spend in active learning, the time students spend attending, and the amount of disruptive behavior. Thoughtfully designed classrooms enable teachers and students to access materials easily and move around the room without creating congestion. Also, in well-designed classrooms teachers easily can see the students and, in turn, students easily can see and hear teacher presentations. In planning physical arrangements it is helpful to consider the arrangement of students, materials, and special areas.

Arrangement of Students

When selecting an arrangement for students, it helps to begin by determining where the teacher will present whole-class instruction. The position of the chalkboard and overhead projector screen usually determines the best location for teacher presentations. The following considerations in arranging students are important:

- *Arrange students so that they easily can see and hear teacher presentations.* The students should readily see any content presented on the chalkboard or overhead projector screen and easily hear the teacher.
- *Arrange students so that the teacher has easy access to any student.* Easy access helps the teacher provide individual help, offer private feedback, and prevent crisis situations.
- *Arrange students so that the teacher easily sees the students.* This enables the teacher to monitor the students by frequently scanning the classroom. Scanning increases on-task behavior and is especially important during student-directed activities. Sprick (1991) reports that scanning is an important factor in teaching, and effective teachers typically scan the classroom about once every 15 seconds.

- ***Decide whether desks are to be arranged in clusters or rows.*** Options on arranging student desks include using isolated desk areas, clusters, rows, or combinations. Because placing desks in clusters tends to promote socialization and interactions among students, many educators (Emmer, Evertson, & Worsham, 2000) suggest placing student desks in rows, especially at the beginning of the school year. Moreover, students should neither sit with their backs to major instructional areas nor face distractions (e.g., windows, doorways, or other students).
- ***Place difficult-to-teach or off-task students in the middle of the room near the front.*** These students need more monitoring than other students; placing them close to the teacher helps the teacher monitor their attention and behavior.

Arrangement of Materials

The appropriate location of materials facilitates the flow of instructional activities and improves classroom management. In arranging materials, several considerations are important:

- ***Keep frequently used materials easily accessible.*** Although the specific materials frequently used by the teacher and the students depend on the academic area or subject being taught, basic items usually include paper, markers, rulers, scissors, chalk and erasers, transparencies and water-soluble pens, masking tape, glue, and a stapler. To help students maintain the materials that they supply, it is helpful to send a list home for parents, and the teacher should have an ample supply of items needed by students. Frequently used materials should be arranged on accessible bookshelves and in cabinets.
- ***Ensure that high-traffic areas are free of congestion.*** High-traffic areas are usually around group work places, the pencil sharpener, the trash can, the teacher's desk, certain bookshelves, computers, doorways, and student desks. These high-traffic areas should not be close to each other and should be easily accessible.

Arrangement of Special Areas and Centers

An important consideration in planning the arrangement of a classroom is to designate selected areas for specific activities (e.g., math area, language area, or study area). In many classrooms space is needed for small-group instruction, centers, and individual work. Several types of areas are presented next.

Academic Areas   It is sometimes necessary to divide instructional spaces in the academic areas. In the elementary grades, these areas typically include reading, math, language, handwriting, spelling, and subjects such as science, social studies, and health. Each area provides room for several students and a space for storing materials. In the intermediate and secondary grades, fewer academic areas are specified in a classroom; however, instructional areas may be set up for various branches of a particular subject. For example, an English teacher may have areas for literature, grammar, listening, and free reading.

Teacher Areas   The teacher needs areas for small-group and large-group instruction. In addition, the teacher needs some space for storing materials and personal articles. The teacher's space should provide a good vantage point for monitoring the ongoing activities in the room.

Individual Student Areas   Each student needs a place to store materials, to sit during whole-class or cooperative learning activities, and to work on independent seatwork. Typically, students are assigned a desk. It often is helpful to provide students who are highly distractible or having a difficult day with a quiet work area, such as carrels or desks located away from the flow of activity. However, it is important that such carrels be viewed as a positive place to learn, not as punishment.

Audiovisual Area   It is helpful to designate areas for using movie, filmstrip, or overhead projectors. Listening centers are also needed for using a tape recorder, record player, videocassette recorder, or computer. Many classrooms do not provide a separate audiovisual area. In these situations, some space may serve dual functions (e.g., a reading area/listening station).

General Considerations

In planning a classroom arrangement, the total effect should be pleasant and inviting. Teachers must take the resources and space available and arrange the class to suit their style and the content being taught. A sample general education classroom floor plan is presented in Figure 2.1, and a resource room plan is featured in Figure 2.2. Teachers may modify these to fit their needs. The sample arrangement of a general education classroom (Figure 2.1) provides a good vantage position for the teacher, easy access to students, a small-group instruction area, and a whole-class presentation format that allows the students to see the teacher at the chalkboard or material on the overhead projector screen.

FIGURE 2.1
Sample floor plan for a general education classroom

FIGURE 2.2

Sample floor plan for a large resource room

Source: From *The Resource Teacher: A Guide to Effective Practices* (p. 56), 2nd ed., by J. L. Wiederholt, D. D. Hammill, and V. L. Brown, 1983, Austin, TX: PRO-ED. Copyright 1983 by Allyn & Bacon. Reprinted by permission.

Class Size   The limited research that exists on the effects of special-education class size indicates that smaller student-teacher ratios result in more positive student outcomes than do larger ratios (Forness & Kavale, 1985). The research in general education is more extensive. Mueller, Chase, and Walden (1988) present results from Program Prime Time in Indiana concerning the effects of a reduced class size in primary grades. Specifically, they report that a reduced class size in primary grades results in a less hectic atmosphere, better teacher morale, more individualized instruction,

and improved student achievement, particularly by at-risk students and students with learning problems. In a synthesis of the research on the effects of class size, Robinson (1990) found that the most positive effects of small classes (22 or fewer students) occur in kindergarten through third grade and especially benefit the achievement of at-risk students; the positive effects of class size on student achievement decrease as grade levels increase; reducing class size has little effect on student achievement if teachers continue to use the same instructional methods in smaller classes that they used in larger classes; and reductions in class size have small positive effects on achievement when compared to many less costly learning interventions and strategies. The improved learning of at-risk students and students with learning problems in smaller classes is likely the result of the teachers having the opportunity to respond to the students' individual instructional needs.

☼ INSTRUCTIONAL ARRANGEMENTS

Six basic instructional arrangements that are available to teachers are presented in Figure 2.3. The large-group instruction, small-group instruction, and one student with teacher arrangements are teacher-directed and require continuous teacher participation. Adult helpers with students, students teaching students, and material with student require indirect teacher involvement and periodic teacher participation. Careful use of these six instructional arrangements is a key factor in individualizing instruction for a class of students with diverse needs. For example, when a teacher uses small-group instruction or the one student with teacher arrangement, the remaining students can be engaged meaningfully in learning activities through indirect teacher involvement (e.g., students teaching students or material with student). The skillful orchestration of these arrangements helps the teacher maintain student participation and attention.

Large-Group Instruction

The large class sizes that exist in many schools necessitate large-group instruction. When the content is appropriate for all students, large-group instruction can be an effective way of presenting new content or discussing pertinent information. Typically, the large-group format is appropriate for such activities as story telling, presenting show and tell, discussing interesting events, taking a field trip, brainstorming, playing a game, or viewing videotapes. If the teacher uses effective presentation strategies such as demonstration, modeling, and guided practice (presented in Chapter 4) and supplements them with cooperative learning, small-group instruction, follow-up direct instruction, or engaging seatwork activities, large-group instruction can be effective for teaching academics and social skills to students with diverse needs.

Advantages and Disadvantages of Large-Group Instruction   Large-group instruction is time-efficient and prepares students for the type of instruction that primarily is used in secondary schools, community colleges, and universities. Also, experiences in large groups may help students with disabilities make the transition from special to general education settings. Moreover, general education and special education teachers who co-teach may share the responsibilities of teaching the large group. The primary disadvantage of large-group instruction is that it does not allow for the teacher to deal easily with the diverse abilities and skill levels present in most classrooms. In large groups, questions may go unanswered, distracted students may remain off-task, and students who need more intensive instruction may fail to receive it. For high-ability students, large-group instruction frequently moves too slowly, whereas for low-ability students, it usually moves too quickly. In either situation, behavioral problems are likely to result because of boredom or frustration.

Guidelines for Large-Group Instruction   Large-group instruction is more likely to accommodate students with different learning needs and rates if the following guidelines and techniques are used:

- ***Keep instruction short.*** Suggested amounts of time for large-group instruction according to grade level include: kindergarten or first grade—5 to 15 minutes; second or third grade—5 to 20 minutes; fourth or fifth grade—5 to 25 minutes, sixth or seventh grade—5 to 30 minutes, and eighth through twelfth grade—5 to 40 minutes.
- ***Use questions to involve students in the lesson.*** Emmer et al. (2000) encourage teachers to make sure that each student has opportunities to participate frequently. Choral or group responses are good ways to involve all students simultaneously. Also, teachers should guard against calling on the same students too often. Positive participation is enhanced if the teacher asks high-ability students the most difficult questions and offers less demanding questions to low-ability students.

FIGURE 2.3
Instructional arrangements

Large group with teacher

Small group with teacher

One student with teacher

Adult helpers with students:
Paraprofessionals
Volunteers
Parents

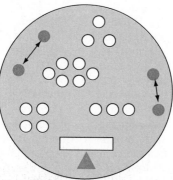

Students teaching students:
Peer tutoring
Classwide peer tutoring
Cooperative learning

Material with student:
Seatwork activities
Self-correcting materials
Instructional games
Technological tools
Homework

KEY:

▲ Teacher

● Student receiving
direct instruction
in specified arrangement

○ Student

△ Adult Helper

■ Material

• *Use lecture–pause routines.* The lecture–pause procedure involves the teacher lecturing for 6 to 12 minutes and then pausing for about 3 minutes to allow students divided into groups of three to follow the RAP procedure:

R–*Read* your notes or questions.

A–*Ask* other students about your notes (e.g., spellings, missing information, or questions about the content).

P–*Put* corrections or answers to questions in your notes.

• *Encourage active participation among lower performing students while maintaining the involvement of higher achieving students.* Heads Together (Kagan, 1989/1990) is a teacher-questioning strategy that combines elements of teacher-directed and peer-mediated instruction. Students are placed into four-member learning teams, each consisting of one high achiever, two average achievers, and one low achiever. The students number themselves 1 through 4 and sit together during teacher-directed lessons. When the teacher directs a question to the entire class, the teams "put their heads together" to determine the best answer. The teacher then asks, "How many Number __ (1s, 2s, 3s, or 4s) know the answer?" After one randomly selected student responds, the teacher asks whether other students with the selected number agree with or want to expand on the answer. Because students are given time to discuss possible answers before responding and it is not known which group member will be selected to respond, it is more likely that everyone, including low achievers, will know the correct responses.

• *Use visual aids to promote understanding of lecture material.* Diagrams are useful, especially in helping students understand relationships. Concept diagramming (presented in Chapter 13) and story mapping (presented in Chapter 8) are visual diagramming approaches that are used frequently.

• *Maintain a lively pace.* A lively pace helps maintain student attention. Because thinking time is always faster than speaking time, it is important to keep the lecture moving at an appropriate pace to hold interest.

• *Use frequent "change-ups."* Sprick (1981) notes that "change-ups" are anything the teacher does to vary the presentation. Selected change-up activities include varying voice levels, varying rate of talking, illustrating a point with a story, telling a joke, having students follow a sequence of directions (such as look at ceiling, floor, windows, and chalkboard), and allowing students to stand up to stretch.

• *Determine the rules for behavior during presentations.* Mnemonics such as SLANT (presented in Chapter 4) are excellent for reminding students of behavioral expectations during lectures.

• *Determine the rules for behavior during discussions.* Rules for discussions are imperative to prevent call-outs and put-downs. A good rule for discussions is "Raise your hand to request to ask a question or answer a question."

• *If students misbehave, praise students who follow the rules.* This reinforces students for appropriate behavior, communicates teacher expectations, and provides a model for misbehaving students.

• *Use flexible grouping.* With flexible grouping, the teacher instructs the large group by using direct instruction procedures, such as descriptions and demonstration, but individualizes guided instruction and independent practice. The small groupings for individualized instruction would differ from lesson to lesson because different students would need various levels of help as a function of the lesson content.

• *Use participation buddies to promote student involvement.* In this technique (Fister & Kemp, 1995), the teacher divides students into teams of two and asks the class a question. Each student is instructed to think of the answer and then share it with his or her buddy. The partners then can share their answers with the class.

• *Use response cards to promote participation.* Each student is given a card with *True* on one side and *False* on the other side. The teacher makes a statement and asks the students to decide whether it is true or false. After a few seconds, the teacher instructs the students to show their answers by placing their cards on their chests with *True* or *False* displayed. Then the teacher gives the correct answer, discusses it, and praises students for participating. This activity can be modified by presenting multiple-choice items on an overhead or handout and asking students to display (or signal) their card answers (i.e., *a, b, c,* or *d*) to specific questions.

• *Use Ask, Pause, and Call.* The teacher can *ask* a question, *pause* for several seconds to allow thinking time, and *call* on an individual or group for the response (Fister & Kemp, 1995).

• *Use signals to avoid surprise call-ons.* The teacher can prearrange a subtle cue (e.g., standing near the student's desk) that lets certain students know in advance that they will be called on next to answer a question or read a passage (Fister & Kemp, 1995).

Small-Group Instruction

The small-group arrangement typically consists of three to seven students and represents a major format for teaching academic skills. Although it can be a highly effective arrangement for all students, small-group instruction is especially recommended for students with learning problems. In establishing small groups for instruction, the teacher attempts to group students who have similar instructional needs in a specific academic area. Groups can be based on placement in a reader or on need for instruction in selected phonics rules, paragraph writing, or specific math facts. To accommodate different rates of learning, the composition of the groups should remain flexible. If a student makes rapid progress, it may be advisable to place the student in a different group for instruction.

In an examination of general education classroom practices, Slavin (1988) reports that little research exists concerning the merits of within-class instructional grouping for reading instruction; however, research on such grouping in mathematics is available and clearly supports grouping for instruction. Specific findings indicate that the effects are greater for low achievers than for average and high achievers. Other research on this approach also indicates positive benefits (Anderson, Evertson, & Brophy, 1979; Carnine, Silbert, & Kameenui, 1997). To improve its effectiveness, these researchers recommend placing the students in a semicircle facing the teacher. They note that distractible students tend to perform better when they are in the middle of the group and about two feet from the teacher.

Advantages of Small-Group Instruction
It is difficult to meet the learning needs of a heterogeneous group of students during large-group instruction, and small-group instruction provides an effective alternative. Moreover, small-group instruction is especially important for students who are learning basic skills in reading, writing, and math; thus, small-group instruction occurs more frequently during the elementary grades. Compared with large-group instruction, specific advantages of small-group instruction include the following:

• Students are able to participate more during the instruction.

• Teachers are able to provide more instruction, praise, and feedback.

• Students are able to progress at their own rates (i.e., both high achievers and low achievers are able to progress at rates commensurate with their abilities).

• Small-group instruction typically is less boring.

• Teachers using small-group instruction are able to monitor the progress of students better and make teaching modifications.

• Small-group instruction provides students with language differences with a more comfortable setting for participating and asking for clarification.

• The small-group arrangement is especially important for students with learning and behavioral problems because many of these students lack the skills to work and learn independently. They frequently have difficulty recognizing relationships, making associations, remembering information, using or activating an effective learning strategy, or discovering new knowledge. Thus, they need and prosper from the direction, structure, and intensity of the teacher-directed small-group setting (Cegelka & Berdine, 1995).

• A small-group follow-up can be helpful to students who do not learn sufficiently during large-group teacher presentations. The teacher can extend an invitation to a teacher-directed small-group follow-up session (e.g., "Please join me at the table if you need help with the seatwork assignment") so that certain students can meet while other class members work on the assignment independently or in cooperative groups (Cegelka & Berdine, 1995).

Disadvantages of Small-Group Instruction
Most of the disadvantages of small-group instruction involve teacher preparation time and

managing students doing their seatwork while others are participating in a small group. Compared with large-group instruction, specific disadvantages of small-group instruction include the following:

- Students are required to do more seatwork.
- Teachers must do more planning (e.g., a reading teacher must plan small-group lessons as well as seatwork activities for students when they are not in their small group).
- Teachers must organize more instructional variables (such as grouping students, managing transitions, and monitoring seatwork activities while teaching).
- Teachers must provide more instruction in the respective academic or content area.

Guidelines for Small-Group Instruction

Because the rewards in student learning and motivation can be substantial when small-group instruction is used, the teacher should approach small-group instruction positively. The advantages of small-group instruction can be attained and the disadvantages minimized if effective guidelines are followed:

- *Establish rules for small-group instruction.* In addition to reminding students that general classroom rules apply in small-group lessons, the teacher should have some specific rules for these lessons (e.g., "Always bring your materials—pencil, book, and workbook—to small-group lessons" and "Wait quietly for the teacher to begin the lesson"). Also, if the teacher previously has not developed the rules and behavioral expectations for making the transition of going to small-group instruction, this routine needs to be taught. Finally, it is important to remind students who are out of the group to follow the classroom rules regarding seatwork.

- *Make the groups as homogeneous as possible.* Grouping the students according to ability and skill helps the teacher tailor instruction for the students in the group. Because the lowest performers need more intense instruction (i.e., more elaboration, examples, praise, feedback, and practice), it helps to keep their group as small as possible. Sprick (1981) notes that three groups usually are needed in reading, whereas two groups often are sufficient in math.

- *Maintain flexible groupings.* To ensure that students progress at their own rates, it helps for the groupings to remain flexible. For example, a student who makes rapid progress may be placed in a different instructional group.

- *Locate the small group in an area that allows the teacher to scan the entire class.* When working with a small group, the teacher should be able to see the rest of the class. It also helps to select a location that minimizes distractions for the students. For example, students in the small group should sit where they do not see other students doing seatwork. Seatings away from high-traffic areas such as the pencil sharpener, waste basket, or audiovisual center also reduce potential distractions.

- *Place the students in a semicircle so that their shoulders align with the shoulders of the students beside them.* This alignment provides an equal opportunity for all students to participate in group activities. When a student's shoulders are six or more inches behind the others, he or she tends to feel outside of the group. Sprick (1981) suggests using two semicircle rows of students when there are nine or more students in the group. Students in the back row sit in chairs; those in the front row sit on the floor. For sitting on the floor not to be aversive, Sprick recommends making it a privilege (e.g., "Tonya, Greg, and Jason have done such a nice job of attending to the lesson today, they get to sit on the floor mats next time").

- *Use motivation activities during small-group work.* Motivation techniques include providing much positive praise during the initial small-group session, using descriptive praise, using group praise (e.g., occasionally conduct a group handshake), using some choral responding to involve everyone, and maintaining enthusiasm and a lively pace during the lesson.

One Student with Teacher

Intensive tutorial teaching frequently is used to help students with learning problems learn a new skill. In addition, one-to-one instruction is appropriate for students who are learning skills that are different from the rest of the class. One-to-one tutoring is a powerful instructional arrangement. In the one-to-one arrangement, the student has the opportunity to ask questions, explain reasoning or strategies, receive instructional feedback, correct errors, and prevent further learning problems with specific skills or content. Bloom (1984) states, "We were astonished at the consistency of the findings and at the great differences in student cognitive achievement, attitudes, and self-concept under tutoring as compared with group methods of instruction" (p. 4). One-to-one teaching can be used spontaneously to prevent or relieve frustration. When teachers observe students having difficulty during group instruction or seatwork, they can give them attention at the first opportunity.

Often, 3 to 5 minutes is just the amount of time needed to help a student understand a concept, receive corrective feedback, understand directions, and feel motivated to continue working. When one-to-one instruction is scheduled daily for students with learning problems, the students know they will have some time with the teacher to receive help. Elementary teachers and resource room teachers have fewer students or are with them for a longer time; thus, it is easier for them than for intermediate and secondary level teachers to offer one-to-one instruction. When teachers use one-to-one instruction, they must plan such activities as seatwork, peer tutoring, computer-assisted instruction, or cooperative learning activities for the rest of the class.

Adult Helpers with Students

The use of volunteers and paraprofessionals in classrooms has increased substantially during the last decade. With class sizes increasing and students with special needs becoming more prevalent, it is logical for educators to turn to paraprofessionals as a supportive instructional arrangement. Furthermore, paraprofessionals provide vital, cost-effective services to teachers and students. Traditionally, paraprofessionals have been used for clerical tasks, but their roles as instructors are increasing. They provide a powerful resource for increasing the engaged learning time of students with learning and behavioral problems. For recruiting volunteers and paraprofessionals, it is helpful to contact parent–teacher associations, service organizations, parents, church groups, and senior citizen groups. School personnel should interview potential paraprofessionals thoroughly to ensure that they un-

derstand the roles and responsibilities of the position and are suitable for the job.

Planning and Implementing Paraprofessional Programs   To plan and implement an effective paraprofessional program, the following factors should be considered:

- ***Roles of paraprofessionals.*** McKenzie and Houk (1986) provide an inventory of paraprofessional skills and teacher needs (see Figure 2.4). This inventory helps teachers outline their needs and helps paraprofessionals identify their skills. When both parties use the inventory, it is possible to determine whether a match exists between paraprofessional skills and teacher expectations. If significant gaps exist, it is important to explore the possibility of training the "willing" paraprofessional to acquire more skills or matching the paraprofessional with another teacher who has different needs. An examination of the numerous important tasks in the inventory indicates that the paraprofessional has an opportunity to make a difference in the classroom. Moreover, the teacher has an opportunity to specify the paraprofessional's duties in such areas as diagnostic support, instruction, behavior management, classroom organization, and clerical support.

- ***Training paraprofessionals.*** Paraprofessionals and volunteers need training to prepare them for their respective roles. The following activities should be included in their training: (1) tour the school and meet key school personnel, (2) explain the need for confidentiality and the rules that govern it, (3) review the dress code and appropriate standards of behavior, (4) review the communication system, (5) demonstrate how to operate equipment related to instruction and special needs of students, (6) discuss schedules, school events, emergency procedures, and absences, and (7) introduce training in instructional procedures regarding presentation techniques, guided practice, corrective feedback, encouragement, and independent practice activities. Skills in instructional procedures can be developed and refined through ongoing in-service, readings, videos, and collaboration with teachers and other paraprofessionals.

- ***Collaboration.*** After the teacher and paraprofessional clarify role expectations, it helps to outline the specific tasks of the paraprofessional,

FIGURE 2.4
Inventory of paraprofessional skills and teacher needs

Name _____ **Date** _____

Directions: Listed below are a number of tasks which a paraprofessional may perform. If you are a paraprofessional, mark with a "P" those activities/duties which you feel you could conduct. If you are a teacher, mark with a "T" those areas in which you intend to use a paraprofessional.

Instructional Support
1. _____ Reinforce concepts already presented by the teacher, by assisting students in reading, math, spelling, articulation, vocabulary development, signing, mobility, and/or self-care.
2. _____ Listen to students read.
3. _____ Read to students.
4. _____ Supervise independent or small-group work.
5. _____ Modify written materials; e.g., tape record stories, rewrite to lower level.
6. _____ Help students work on projects or assignments.
7. _____ Help students select library books.
8. _____ Assist physically disabled students; e.g., feeding, positioning.
9. _____ Help students explore careers and special interests.
10. _____ Practice vocabulary with non-English-speaking students.
_____ Other. Please describe.

Behavior Management Support
11. _____ Provide and/or supervise earned reinforcement.
12. _____ Supervise time out.
13. _____ Be a resource for students who are experiencing stress.
14. _____ Monitor progress on contracts.
15. _____ Enhance students' self-concept by providing positive feedback.
_____ Other. Please describe.

Diagnostic Support
16. _____ Correct and grade assigned activities.
17. _____ Observe and record academic behavior and progress; e.g., math facts learned, vocabulary growth, reading rate.
18. _____ Observe and record social behavior(s).
19. _____ Administer informal assessments; e.g., unit tests and criterion-referenced measures.
_____ Other. Please describe.

Classroom Organization
20. _____ Make instructional games.
21. _____ Develop and manage learning centers.
22. _____ Prepare displays.
23. _____ Locate instructional materials.
24. _____ Assist in daily planning.
25. _____ Make bulletin boards.
_____ Other. Please describe.

Clerical Support
26. _____ Type.
27. _____ Duplicate materials.
28. _____ Take attendance.
29. _____ Record grades.
30. _____ Other. Please describe.

Source: From "Paraprofessionals in Special Education" (p. 249) by R. G. McKenzie and C. S. Houk, 1986, *Teaching Exceptional Children, 18,* 246–252. Copyright 1986 by The Council for Exceptional Children. Reprinted by permission.

determine the skills needed to do the tasks, and provide training or demonstration of the procedures or strategies needed to do the tasks. Daily meetings are helpful to review the day, plan the next day, and make needed modifications in activities or duties. One of the most important aspects of these meetings is for the pair to maintain communication and a collaborative framework for evaluation, training, and problem solving. Also, the teacher should recognize the contributions of the paraprofessional.

• ***Working with culturally and linguistically diverse students.*** In some settings it is helpful to have paraprofessionals who speak languages other than English or who understand diverse cultures. These qualifications enable the paraprofessional to assist non-English-speaking students or students from diverse backgrounds. Miramontes (1991) developed a Multilingual/Multiethnic Instructional Services team to coordinate services to students from culturally and linguistically diverse backgrounds. In this model, paraprofessionals assist in developing and providing instructional programs, incorporate students' primary languages and cultures in their program, serve as positive ethnic and linguistic role models, and provide school–community liaison services.

Students Teaching Students: Peer Tutoring

The students-teaching-students instructional arrangement provides teachers with a viable resource of instructional support and offers students the opportunity for intensive practice on academic tasks tailored to individual needs. It features students working independently and thus frees the teacher to work with other students individually or in small-group sessions. In a mainstream classroom of heterogeneous learners, instructional arrangements that allow students to practice needed skills or learn subject content independently are critical to the academic success of students with learning problems. Although students teaching students occurs in a multitude of formats, most peer instructional arrangements feature either peer tutoring or cooperative learning.

Description of Peer Tutoring Tutorial instruction (e.g., parents teaching their children or older siblings instructing younger siblings) was probably the first pedagogy among primitive societies. As early as the first century A.D., Quintilian in his *Institutio Oratoria* discussed teaching settings in which older children tutored younger children. Today, a basic definition of peer tutoring is *an instructional arrangement in which the teacher pairs two students in a tutor–tutee relationship to promote learning of academic skills or subject content.* The teacher determines the academic task and provides the instructional materials. Although peer tutoring is used to foster social skills, positive relationships, and self-esteem for both students, the emphasis is usually on the learning progress of the tutee. To maintain effective peer tutoring, the teacher monitors behavior and praises both the tutor and the tutee for performing their respective duties.

Research on Peer Tutoring Several studies have focused on the effectiveness of peer tutoring. Levin, Glass, and Meister (1984) examined the effectiveness of peer tutoring in terms of reading and math outcomes and found that peer tutoring produced more than twice as much achievement as computer-assisted instruction, three times more than reducing the class size from 35 to 30 students, and almost four times more than lengthening the school day by one hour. Osguthorpe and Scruggs (1986) reviewed studies in which special education students served as tutors. They found that tutees who received instruction from special education students made academic gains in a variety of content areas. Moreover, many of the tutors benefited academically and socially from being the tutor. These findings encourage both general and special education teachers to set up many different tutor–tutee pairs to promote social integration as well as academic gains among students with and without learning problems.

Scruggs and Richter (1985) reviewed 24 studies in which students with learning disabilities were involved in tutoring interventions. They note that investigators favored the use of peer tutoring, and most studies support the continued use of tutoring with students with learning problems. Other studies have investigated the comparative effects of peer tutoring for students with and without learning problems. The educational implications from the peer-tutoring research is similar for students in general education and special education. Tutor and tutee benefits in academics (i.e., achievement gains across academic and content areas) are reported for students with and without learning problems, whereas the effect of peer tutoring on the enhancement of social skills and self-concept remains inconclusive for students both with and without learning problems (Cohen, Kulik, & Kulik, 1982; Osguthorpe & Scruggs, 1986). Moreover, the research indicates that peer-tutoring program variables are more important to student achievement than are student variables such as age, ability, grade, and training. Relevant program variables include structured settings, lower order target skills, teacher-developed achievement measures, and programs of shorter longitudinal duration. Also, math achievement appears to be greater than achievement in reading and other subject areas in peer-tutoring programs (Cohen et al., 1982). Because of the effect of program variables, it is not surprising that both students with and students without learning problems benefit from peer-tutoring programs of similar design and content.

Peer tutoring appears to hold much promise. It can improve academic skills, foster self-esteem, develop appropriate behaviors, and promote positive relationships and cooperation among peers. It benefits both tutor and tutee, and once the program is designed it requires less of the teacher's time than most instructional arrangements. Also, it is tailor-made to help students with learning problems achieve in mainstream settings.

Programming Guidelines for Peer Tutoring

The development and implementation of a successful peer-tutoring program require the consideration of numerous factors. The following twelve steps represent best practices from the research and literature regarding the factors involved in planning and implementing peer tutoring:

1. ***Determine goals of peer tutoring.*** Although peer tutoring is used primarily to help students with academic achievement, some educators report that it is effective for improving socialization skills, classroom behaviors, self-concept, and interpersonal relationships. Some appropriate goals include the following:
- Provide tutees with an opportunity to practice and learn targeted academic skills (e.g., spelling words, math facts, and word recognition) until mastery is achieved.

- Provide tutees with an opportunity to review and learn subject content (e.g., definitions of science terms and identification of countries on a map).
- Provide tutors and tutees with an opportunity to develop appropriate social skills (e.g., giving encouragement, giving corrective feedback, clarifying directions or subject matter, and providing cues and prompts).
- Provide tutors with an opportunity to review or practice recently learned skills or content.
- Enhance the self-concepts of tutors and tutees by making positive statements about their skills or abilities and by providing them with success experiences in both social and academic areas.

2. ***Target skills or content for the peer tutoring pairs.*** When the entire class is working on skills (e.g., spelling words) or content (e.g., presidents of the United States) presented in a recent lesson, the teacher may have each pair working with the same content. In other situations, peer tutoring provides students who need extra practice with the opportunity to receive it. Generally, the content or skills targeted should include material the teacher already has presented to the students. In selecting content and skills, it is helpful to consider the following research findings:
- Peer tutoring has resulted in academic gains for tutors and tutees within most academic areas.
- Gains in math have been greater than in other academic areas for tutors and tutees.
- Peer tutoring pairs seem to achieve best when working on lower level skills such as spelling words or math facts.
- Peer tutoring appears to work better on molar-level activities such as number of words written or read correctly than on singular skill activities such as decoding skills.
- The targeted skills and content should be similar to those used in the classroom.
- Student gains usually are more evident on curriculum-based measures than on standardized tests.

3. ***Select materials.*** In addition to paper and pencils, materials needed for a peer-tutoring program usually include the following:
- Directions for tutor and tutee.
- An academic task presented on flash cards, a worksheet, or pages in a textbook.
- An assessment sheet on which the tutor can record correct and incorrect responses.

- Scoring procedures if tutee performance is to be evaluated.

A sample tutor instruction sheet for flash cards is presented in Table 2.1, and a sample record sheet is provided in Figure 2.5.

4. ***Design procedures for tutor and tutee.*** The procedures instruct the tutor how to present the academic task, score the tutee responses, provide feedback for correct and incorrect responses, and record the total performance score of the tutee. The procedures instruct the tutee how to respond (e.g., written, timed, or verbal) to the academic task. Finally, the procedures detail the rewards for the tutor and tutee for the achievement of specified goals (e.g., tutee passes a weekly quiz on the tutoring content with 90 percent accuracy or achieves 80 percent accuracy during the session).

5. ***Assign tutor–tutee pairs.*** Several configurations of tutor–tutee assignments are used in peer tutoring. Across-class tutoring involves students from one class going to another class to tutor. Across-class tutors are usually older or high achievers. Pullout tutoring involves the tutee going to a specialized setting to work with a tutor from another class. These two arrangements require administrative support and scheduling among the classes involved. A third type of tutoring, intraclass tutoring, yields good results and requires less schoolwide planning. Intraclass tutoring involves students within the same class serving as tutors and tutees for each other. The tutoring interaction may be either one-way or reciprocal. In reciprocal tutoring the tutor and tutee exchange roles during the tutoring session so that each has an opportunity to serve as teacher and learner. Unless there are students who have chronic problems with each other, tutor-tutee assignments can be random. After a specified time (such as one week to one month), the tutor–tutee assignments are randomly changed (e.g., tutors or tutees select names of a partner from a container). Low achievers can act as tutors for high achievers when the tutoring materials include the correct answers for the tutor. This enables the tutor with learning problems to check the answer and provide feedback to tutees who are high achievers. This format enables a heterogeneous group of students to tutor each other and engage in reciprocal tutoring.

TABLE 2.1

Sample tutor instruction sheet for flash cards

Step 1:	At the beginning of the tutoring session, get the folder of tutor materials.
Step 2:	Sit directly opposite and facing the tutee.
Step 3:	Check to see that the tutor materials include record sheets, flash cards, blank cards, and pencils.
Step 4:	Ask whether the tutee is ready to begin.
Step 5:	Remove the record sheet, pencil, and flash cards from the folder.
Step 6:	Hold up the flash cards one at a time with the card facing the tutee.
Step 7:	Instruct the tutee to read aloud the number fact or word.
Step 8:	Count to 3 silently. If the tutee does not respond or responds incorrectly, say, "The answer is _____. Say it." After the tutee repeats the answer, place the card at the bottom of the stack.
Step 9:	If the tutee does not respond or responds incorrectly, mark a "–" next to the number fact or word in the first trial column of the record sheet.
Step 10:	If the tutee responds correctly, mark a "+" next to the number fact or word, and say, "Good job," "Great," or "Super." Place the card on the table.
Step 11:	After the tutee attempts all of the cards, present them again, and mark a "+" or "–" in the second trial column of the record sheet.
Step 12:	Present the cards a third time, and mark a "+" or "–" in the last trial column of the record sheet.
Step 13:	Look at the data sheet. If there are three "+"s for a number fact or a word, provide a blank card and a pencil and instruct the tutee to write the number fact or word. Have the tutee file this card in the tutee's mastery box.
Step 14:	Ask the tutee to move the marker on the Ladder of Success chart to the correct spot according to how many number facts or words the tutee has learned.
Step 15:	Place the materials back in the folder and return the folder to its place.

FIGURE 2.5

Sample tutor record sheet

Tutor Record Sheet

Tutor _____   Date _____

Tutee _____

Mark either a "+" or a "−" depending on the tutee's response (+ = correct; − = incorrect)

Math Fact or Word	Trial 1	Trial 2	Trial 3	Math Facts or Words Not Learned
1				
2				
3				
4				
5				
6				
7				
8				
9				
10				

How did you feel about today's session?

_____

Do not write below this line

Percent correct _____   Percent incorrect _____

Number learned _____   Number not learned _____

---

6. ***Train tutors.*** Tutor training procedures are included in most peer-tutoring programs. The duties of tutors typically include introducing new material, presenting items, correcting errors, prompting and praising correct answers, testing and recording progress, and assigning points for progress. Tutor training procedures consistently include a combination of the following: orientation to the rationale and goals of tutoring, a description of the materials and procedures, teacher demonstration of tutoring skills, tutor imitation and role playing of procedures with feedback, intermittent guidance when needed, and praise for following the procedures correctly. In essence, tutor training follows the direct instruction sequence (use an advance organizer, describe the behavioral expectations, demonstrate the behavioral expectations, and so on) used to teach behavioral expectations such as classroom rules. Sample guidelines for helping the tutor succeed include the following:

- Make the relationship with your partner positive because it is the most important part of any tutoring program.
- Greet your partner as you would a good friend. Be friendly and open. Make your partner feel at ease. Call your partner by name.

- Listen carefully to your partner. Be interested. Ask questions.
- Be patient. Be respectful. Build confidence by helping your partner succeed.
- Believe in your partner! You will both succeed and you will both be learning. Remember, everyone is different and everyone learns at an individual pace.

Figure 2.6 presents a sample tutor checklist for the teacher to use for training and feedback.

7. ***Train tutees.*** A primary task of the tutees is to try their best to do the tasks presented by the tutor. Specific duties include following directions, receiving feedback appropriately, and maintaining attention. Tutees typically are trained with the same direct instruction sequence used to teach tutors.

8. ***Teach social skills used in peer tutoring.*** For peer tutoring to occur in a positive and supportive environment, the teacher should teach social skills such as accepting a partner, giving and accepting corrective feedback, and praising a partner. Each of these skills is taught through the direct instruction sequence. Teacher demonstrations of nonexamples (such as rudeness or put-downs) and discussions of how those behaviors make people feel help teach the importance of good social skills, as do teacher demonstrations and role playing of how to greet a partner with a smile and a gesture (such as a high-five).

9. ***Review rules.*** The teacher reminds the students that the classroom rules apply during peer tutoring. Rules to emphasize during peer tutoring are "Make transitions quickly" and "Use whisper voices." Again, the behavioral expectations for these rules are taught using the direct instruction sequence.

10. ***Schedule the peer-tutoring sessions.*** Most researchers recommend about 20 minutes for one-way tutoring sessions and 30 minutes for reciprocal sessions. Positive achievement results primarily from two or more sessions weekly.

11. ***Conduct a tutoring session.*** In addition to planning the peer-tutoring program and adapting curriculum materials, teachers must supervise the sessions, evaluate progress, and make periodic revisions. Initially the teacher needs to supervise the peer-tutoring sessions closely and provide corrective and positive feedback. Once the students become proficient in their respective tutor–tutee roles, the teacher can scan the tutoring sessions while working with a small group or individual students. Some educators report good results when the teacher periodically meets with tutor–tutee pairs to discuss progress. Also, researchers have found that tutor and tutee performance contingencies positively affect maintenance of effective peer tutoring interactions as well as academic achievement (Greenwood, Carta, & Hall, 1988; Maheady, Harper, & Sacca, 1988). For managing misbehavior during peer-tutoring sessions, Sprick (1981) recommends the following:

- Ignore misbehavior unless it persists.
- If misbehavior is chronic, reassign the pair to other partners.

FIGURE 2.6

Sample tutor checklist

Tutor _____						
Date	Date	Date	Date	Date	Date	
____	____	____	____	____	____	Collects material
____	____	____	____	____	____	Goes to work space
____	____	____	____	____	____	Describes lesson to partner
____	____	____	____	____	____	Praises correct responses
____	____	____	____	____	____	Shows enthusiasm
____	____	____	____	____	____	Provides corrective feedback
____	____	____	____	____	____	Uses positive manner
____	____	____	____	____	____	Follows directions without assistance
____	____	____	____	____	____	Speaks in a quiet voice
____	____	____	____	____	____	Keeps records
____	____	____	____	____	____	Replaces material at end of session

- Do not get involved in minor disputes.
- Praise pairs for appropriate behavior.
- For persistent misbehavior, implement owing-time consequences.
- Develop a signal (e.g., tap a note on a toy xylophone) to remind the class to work quietly.

12. ***Evaluate the peer-tutoring program.***
The achievement of tutees can be evaluated by examining the daily progress sheets completed by tutors. Weekly quizzes on the skills or content covered in peer tutoring also help monitor progress. Social skills progress may be monitored through systematic observation of the tutoring pairs, and affective domains may be evaluated through interviews or questionnaires.

With appropriate planning, student training, and teacher support, peer tutoring can be a viable instructional alternative. To maintain the tutors' involvement, their efforts can be recognized by activities such as displaying their pictures on bulletin boards, allowing them to meet before school, offering awards, providing reinforcing events such as meetings with faculty or administrators, publishing articles about the program, and having the principal recognize tutors.

Students Teaching Students: Classwide Peer Tutoring

Peer-mediated instructional programs deserve consideration from general education and special education teachers. Classwide peer tutoring enables the teacher to engage all students in a classroom simultaneously in a variety of academic tasks. It involves restructuring the classroom so that pairs of students work together on academic activities.

Description of Classwide Peer Tutoring

ClassWide Peer Tutoring (Delquadri, Greenwood, Whorton, Carta, & Hall, 1986; Greenwood, Delquadri, & Carta, 1988) was developed at the Juniper Gardens Children's Project in Kansas City, KS, and is designed to help students with mild disabilities improve their basic skills. *ClassWide Peer Tutoring* is an integrated behavior management and direct instruction procedure based upon reciprocal peer tutoring and group-oriented reinforcement contingencies (e.g., cooperative learning). The method includes three features to increase

on-task behavior and amount of practice of academic skills: (1) peers are used to supervise responding and practice, (2) a game format is used that includes points and competing teams to motivate students and maintain interest, and (3) a weekly evaluation plan ensures gains in individual and class progress. The teacher trains students to be effective tutors by carefully explaining and demonstrating error-correction procedures and the point system to be followed in the tutoring sessions. Corrective feedback is given during supervised practice opportunities.

The *ClassWide Peer Tutoring* system features the following basic arrangement:

1. Daily tutoring slots of about 30 minutes are required. Each student tutors for 10 minutes and then receives 10 minutes of tutoring. An additional 10 minutes are spent counting points and posting results.

2. On Monday the tutor–tutee pairs for the week are selected. The pair sit next to or across from each other and begin a 10-minute tutoring session. For example, if the task is spelling, the tutor monitors the spelling and awards two points for each word written correctly. The tutee earns one point for correctly respelling a word after the tutor has detected an error and gives the correct spelling. The tutor marks points on a Tutoring Point Sheet. At the end of 10 minutes, the tutoring roles are reversed.

3. During the tutoring sessions, the teacher moves among the students and awards bonus points for correct tutoring behavior.

4. After the second 10-minute session, each student counts the number of points earned as both tutor and tutee. The class is divided into two teams by having students draw from a container that holds squares of two different colors. The point totals for each student are recorded in one of two team columns on a chart. The team earning the highest number of points is the winning team for the day or week. The composition of the two teams changes periodically.

5. On Friday the teacher conducts a more intensive assessment of each student's progress on the skills from that week.

Peabody Classwide Peer Tutoring (D. Fuchs, Mathes, & Fuchs, 1993), developed at George Pea-

Teacher modeling facilitates peer-mediated instruction.

body College of Vanderbilt University, is a research-based instructional alternative that extends the Juniper Gardens Children's Project model so that students engage in strategy-based reading practice. Three major reading activities are included: partner reading, paragraph shrinking, and prediction relay. In partner reading, students take turns reading aloud, correcting errors, and retelling what they read. In paragraph shrinking, students take turns reading the paragraph aloud, correcting errors, and stating the main idea of each paragraph in ten or fewer words. In prediction relay, students take turns predicting what happens next, reading the next passage aloud, correcting errors, verifying predictions, summarizing the text, and making more predictions. Peabody Classwide Peer Tutoring usually is conducted during three weekly 35-minute sessions. Instructional adaptations for classwide peer-mediated instruction include students working on different materials, students using different instructional techniques, and the teacher circulating to provide individual tutoring.

Research on Classwide Peer Tutoring   Maheady, Sacca, and Harper (1988) used *ClassWide Peer Tutoring* in secondary mainstream settings to improve the academic and social performance of students with learning disabilities. Moreover, Maheady, Harper, and Sacca (1988) note that numerous researchers report success with *Class-Wide Peer Tutoring* at the elementary school level. The *Classwide Peer Tutoring* program was developed over an eight-year period and has been field-tested extensively. Research data indicate that *ClassWide Peer Tutoring* improves students' engagement in academic tasks, increases academic achievement gains, and enhances cooperative peer relations (Greenwood et al., 1984; Maheady, Harper, & Mallette, 1991).

Peabody classwide peer-mediated instruction for reading and math was combined with curriculum-based measurement and field-tested in inclusive classrooms with outstanding results. Efficacy studies were conducted for two successive years in general education classrooms that included students with learning disabilities. The studies involved more than 150 teachers and 3,500 students. Each study yielded impressive statistically significant outcomes (Joint Committee on Teacher Planning for Students with Disabilities, 1995). Workshops and training materials are available that enable teachers to instruct their students to implement curriculum-based measurement and classwide peer-mediated instruction. (For information, contact Lynn Fuchs or Douglas Fuchs at Vanderbilt University, Box 328, Peabody, Nashville, TN 37203; 615/343-4782.)

Programming Guidelines for Classwide Peer Tutoring To develop and implement a successful classwide peer tutoring program, the following guidelines are presented:

• Provide social skills training to those students who need it to work together cooperatively. Useful skills include accepting a partner, encouraging and praising your partner, taking turns, using quiet voices, and stopping activity on signal. Demonstrating and reinforcing these skills greatly enhances the success of peer tutoring.

• For partner reading, pair a high-level reader with a low-level reader and use the following sequence: (1) the high-level reader reads aloud for 5 minutes, (2) the low-level reader reads aloud the same text for 5 minutes, and (3) the low-level reader sequences the major events of what has been read for 1 minute if in second or third grade, or for 2 minutes if in fourth, fifth, or sixth grade.

• For paragraph shrinking, pair a high-level reader with a low-level reader and use the following sequence: (1) for 5 minutes, the high-level reader continues reading new text in the story, stopping after each paragraph to summarize the paragraph and (2) for 5 minutes, the low-level reader continues with new text, summarizing each paragraph.

• For prediction relay, pair a high-level reader with a low-level reader and use the following sequence: (1) continuing with new text, the high-level reader reads aloud for 5 minutes, stopping after each page to check the previous prediction, summarize the page, and predict what will happen on the next page and (2) the low-level reader continues to read new text aloud for 5 minutes, stopping after each page to check the previous prediction, summarize the page, and make a prediction.

• For lower level skills such as spelling or math facts, use scoring similar to basketball. The student who announces the word or math fact responds to a correct answer by saying "Two points" and circles two points on a score sheet. For an incorrect response, the announcer says, "Sorry, Partner, the correct spelling (or math fact) is _____. Go for a foul shot." Then the partner practices writing the word (or math fact) correctly three times. To encourage the practice of foul shots (error correction), the teacher periodically gives bonus points for players writing the word or math fact correctly three times.

• Assign each pair of students to one of two class teams and pool together the weekly points of the pairs of students to get a weekly team score. When team total scores are announced, it is important to celebrate each team's score and minimize competition. Moreover, the weekly spelling or math test scores for each team can be compiled and recorded. Each team can be encouraged to beat last week's score or set new records.

• Use classwide peer tutoring two or three times a week.

• Avoid long-term pairing of students who do not get along with each other. Teams may be changed weekly or biweekly.

Students Teaching Students: Cooperative Learning

Cooperative learning represents another instructional arrangement in which peers work independently. Because of its success with diverse groups of students (Mainzer, Mainzer, Slavin, & Lowry, 1993) and the independent nature of their work, it represents a viable approach for promoting successful mainstreaming. During the last decade, cooperative learning has enjoyed increasing popularity and enthusiastic support from general educators and special educators.

Description of Cooperative Learning There are many forms of cooperative learning, but they all involve students working in teams or small groups to help one another learn (Slavin, 1991). Because cooperative learning provides students with an opportunity to practice skills or learn content presented by the teacher, it supplements teacher instruction. Cooperative learning emphasizes team goals, and team success is achieved only if each individual learns. A basic definition of cooperative learning is *an instructional arrangement in which small groups or teams of students work together to achieve team success in a manner that promotes the students' responsibility for their own learning as well as the learning of others.*

Student Team Learning (STL) techniques represent the most extensive practices used in cooperative learning. STL methods emphasize that team goals can be achieved only if each member achieves selected academic objectives. Slavin (1991) notes that the concepts of team reward, individual accountability, and equal opportunities for success are central to all STL methods. Team rewards are earned when a team achieves at or above a predetermined criterion level. Because all teams that achieve criterion are successful (rewarded), teams are not in competition for an all-or-nothing reward. Individual accountability is featured because team success depends on the individual learning of all team members. Team success is evaluated by the composite performances (e.g., scores) of team members on a quiz of material assigned to the group. This relationship of individual performance to team performance fosters activities that involve team members helping one another learn the targeted academic content. Equal opportunities for success are provided because each team member helps the team by improving on past performance. This challenges low, average, and high achievers to do their best because their respective performances all are valued by the team.

Student Teams-Achievement Divisions (STAD) (Slavin, 1978, 1986) and Teams-Games-Tournament (TGT) (DeVries & Slavin, 1978; Slavin, 1986) are two cooperative learning methods that are adaptable across subject areas and grade levels. In STAD, a heterogeneous group of four students are assigned to a team. After the teacher presents a lesson, the team works together to ensure that all students have mastered the lesson. Then the students take individual quizzes without peer help. The students' quiz scores are compared with their past averages, and points are awarded if their performances meet or exceed their earlier efforts. The points are totaled to yield a team score, and teams that meet criteria are rewarded (e.g., they receive certificates). This cycle of activity usually takes three to five class periods. STAD works best with academic material that has single correct answers (e.g., math computations and map skills). TGT uses the same teacher presentation, group assignment, and teamwork format as STAD. The quizzes, however, are replaced with weekly tournaments. In these tournaments students compete with players from other teams to earn points to add to their respective team scores. Students compete at three-member tournament tables with others who have similar skill levels on the target skills. The winners at the tournament tables each earn the same number of points for his or her team. All students have an equal opportunity for success because low achievers competing with other low achievers can earn as many points as high achievers competing with high achievers. As with STAD, TGT takes three to five classes and is most appropriate with content featuring single answers.

In addition to STAD and TGT, two comprehensive curricula exist for specific content and grades. Team Assisted Individualization (TAI) (Slavin, Madden, & Stevens, 1990) is designed for mathematics in third through sixth grade. Cooperative Integrated Reading and Composition (CIRC) (Slavin, Stevens, & Madden, 1988) is designed for reading in third through fifth grade.

Research on Cooperative Learning   Most research on cooperative learning focuses on the STL techniques developed at Johns Hopkins University. In a synthesis of research on cooperative learning, Slavin (1991) reports the following:

- The most successful approaches for improving academic achievement include group goals and individual accountability. In these settings, groups are rewarded based on the performances of the respective team members.
- In studies featuring group goals and individual accountability, the achievement effects of experimental/control comparisons consistently favor cooperative learning. Specifically, in 37 of 44 studies of at least four weeks' duration, the significantly positive effects favor cooperative learning, whereas none favor traditional methods.
- The positive achievement effects of cooperative learning appear consistent across grades (two through twelve), subject areas, and school settings (rural, urban, and suburban).
- Effects are equally positive for high, average, and low achievers.
- The positive effects of cooperative learning are reported consistently in affective areas (e.g., self-esteem, intergroup relations, attitudes toward school, and ability to work cooperatively).

Slavin et al. (1990) report excellent results in math achievement and affective measures with Team Assisted Individualization for students with academic disabilities in mainstream settings. Likewise, Cooperative Integrated Reading and Composition groups for reading and writing yield excellent outcomes for students without disabilities as well as students with academic disabilities in mainstream settings (Slavin et al., 1988). Slavin (1989/1990) states, "Cooperative learning seems to be an extraordinary success. It has an excellent research base, many viable and successful forms, and hundreds of thousands of enthusiastic adherents" (p. 3).

Programming Guidelines for Cooperative Learning Team goals and rewards, individual accountability, and equal opportunities appear to be the essential components of a cooperative learning program. Guidelines adapted from those presented in peer tutoring are appropriate for planning and implementing cooperative learning:

* Determine goals of cooperative learning.
* Target selected skills or contingent lessons for the teams.
* Select materials, including the quizzes or tournament questions.
* Design procedures for team members to help one another.
* Assign students of varying achievement levels to the same teams.
* Train teams to help one another.
* Teach social skills for teamwork.
* Review classroom rules and teach new rules.
* Schedule the cooperative learning sessions for three to five days a week.
* Conduct a cooperative learning session.
* Evaluate the cooperative learning program.

The January 1990 issue of *Exceptional Leadership* focuses on cooperative learning and includes numerous resources for its effective use.

Material with Student: Seatwork Activities

Learning Considerations From a learning perspective, the material-with-student or independent seatwork arrangement provides the student with opportunities to practice skills that the teacher has presented. Practice helps the student move through the learning sequence that begins with acquisition and progresses to the higher levels of proficiency, maintenance, and generalization. For many students with learning problems, the mastery of skills and content requires extensive practice.

From a review of the research on practice, Dempster (1991) reports several findings that have implications for classrooms:

* Given equivalent practice time, two or more opportunities with the same material are more effective than a single opportunity.
* Spaced practice promotes better learning than massed practice.
* Relative to massed practice, the effectiveness of spaced practice increases as the frequency of the practice activity increases.
* Cumulative questions or tasks promote effective learning.
* Frequent, spaced practice seems to produce a more elaborate understanding of the topic than massed practice.

Direct classroom implications of Dempster's (1991) findings include the following suggestions for planning effective practice:

* Incorporate spaced reviews or practice (including questions from previous and current lessons) into a variety of activities (such as discussions, seatwork, peer tutoring, and homework).
* Organize lessons so that a brief time is used to review the main points of the previous day's lesson. Include review tasks or questions on seatwork activities.
* Once or twice a month, conduct a comprehensive practice session featuring discussions and seatwork.

Teacher Considerations From a teacher's perspective, a material-with-student arrangement not only provides students with opportunities to improve achievement but also allows the teacher some freedom to work with small groups or individual students. Although planning seatwork activities and teaching students to work independently is time-consuming, it is worth the effort. Well-designed material-with-student activities can make the school year pleasant and productive. Some guidelines for planning and implementing an effective independent seatwork program follow:

* ***Ensure that the independent work assignments are tailored to the student's instructional level.*** Preceding independent practice with demonstration or guided practice is a good way to

ensure that the assignment is instructionally appropriate.

• *Use a variety of independent seatwork activities.* Varying the activities provides the teacher with alternatives and tends to increase student motivation and time on-task. Suitable activities include self-correcting materials, instructional games, computer-assisted instruction, and tape recorder-assisted instruction. These activities are presented in this chapter and in the curriculum area chapters throughout the text.

• *Consider work folders for daily assignments.* A work folder is a flexible system of communication between the teacher and the individual student. Work folders can be used to communicate the day's assignments. They provide a place for keeping charts and completed work and for giving feedback. After students have used the work folders for a while, they can enter the room, pick up their folders, and begin work without teacher intervention. A check-off sheet can be placed in the folders to help students determine which tasks are completed and which need to be studied.

• *Prepare some cushion activities to accommodate students finishing their work at different times.* Activities include starting another assignment, writing on the computer, working in a learning center, listening to a tape, assisting another student, or reading a book or magazine.

• *Modify the format of worksheets to improve learner friendliness.* Because some students become anxious when given a full worksheet of problems to complete, it helps to divide worksheets into fewer problems. This enables students to complete as much work (e.g., two short worksheets) without feeling overwhelmed. Also, a full worksheet can be divided into sections and students are encouraged to work on one section at a time.

• *Design procedures that enable students to ask questions while doing independent seatwork.* Procedures that prevent constant interruptions from students while the teacher is working with a small group include (1) assigning student helpers to answer questions, (2) developing a signal (e.g., a desk sign that signifies that the student has a question) that allows the student to continue working until help arrives, and (3) designating an area of the room where one student at a time can go when he or she has a question.

• *Ensure that students understand the instructions for their seatwork activities before starting small-group instruction.* This is especially important when new assignments or a new format (e.g., self-correcting material or computer) are used.

• *Use the direct instruction teaching sequence to teach the behavioral expectations for independent seatwork.*

Material with Student: Self-Correcting Materials

Students spend much classroom time working with instructional materials on their own; thus, the materials used should not lead to frustration, failure, and the practicing of errors. To some degree, a material serves as a teacher. The more teacher functions it can serve, the more useful it is. Inexpensive materials can provide instructions, present a stimulus or task, and provide feedback about correctness of student responses.

Self-correcting materials give the student immediate feedback without the teacher being present. Self-correcting materials are especially useful with students with learning problems who have a history of academic failure. It is important to reduce their failure experiences, particularly public failures. When the student makes a mistake with a self-correcting material, it is a private event—no one else knows. Only the student sees the error, and the error can be corrected immediately. Furthermore, if immediate feedback is not provided, mistakes will be practiced until the teacher corrects the student at a later time. With self-correcting materials, the student is corrected immediately and practices only the correct response.

Self-correcting materials help students maintain attention to academic tasks. The student can approach each response with a game-playing attitude: "I bet I get this one right!" When self-correcting materials are used, some cheating should be expected at first. Although many students initially enjoy beating the system, eventually it becomes more fun to select an answer and see whether it is correct. If cheating persists, a checkup test or posttest on the featured content can be administered. The student soon realizes that cheating on the material will not help on the checkup test.

There are many ways to make self-correcting materials, including the use of answer keys, matching cards, puzzles, pocket calculators, and computers. The materials should be simple so that a demonstration enables students to use them. The best use of these materials is to provide practice or drill on areas that the teacher already has introduced.

Students should not be required to use the same self-correcting material for a long time. The teacher should vary the content periodically, exchange materials with another teacher, give students a choice of which material they wish to use, have students make their own content for the self-correcting device, or put away selected materials for a while. By changing self-correcting materials from time to time, the teacher can maintain student interest and involvement.

The remainder of this section provides examples of feedback devices that can be used to make self-correcting materials. Some of the self-correcting materials are presented with construction guidelines, while others are simple to make. The same device or material often can be used with different content. Throughout this book, self-correcting materials are presented in the different curriculum areas.

Flap A flap can be made of any flexible material such as cloth, vinyl wallpaper, construction paper, or thin cardboard. When using this device, the student can bend the flap up or to the side to reveal the answer to the question or problem. Figure 2.7 illustrates an Answer Box with a flap to provide feedback.

Instructional objective: See math fact or problem—say answer; see math fact or problem—write answer; see contraction words—write contraction; see percentage problem—write answer.

Feedback response: A flap is placed over the mouth. When the flap is raised, the answer is revealed. Vinyl wallpaper is flexible and serves as a good flap.

Materials: A cardboard box (e.g., cigar or school supply box); 3″ × 5″ index cards; contact paper or lamination; a small wooden block, about 3″ × 3 1/2″.

Construction: Cut out three squares in the lid of the box so that they form two eyes and a mouth. Cut a section out of the right side of the box so that the index cards can be fed into the box from the side. Paint the box inside and out. Laminate a picture of a face on the box and place the eyes and the mouth over the squares. Place a flexible flap over the mouth. Prepare index cards with problems and answers so that the problem appears in the "eyes" and so that the flap over the mouth can be lifted to reveal the answer. For math problems, use a grease (overhead projector) pencil to write the math operation (+, −, ×, ÷) in the space between the "eyes."

Directions: The student inserts a stack of selected cards into the Answer Box. Then the student responds (orally or by writing) to the problem presented in the two windows. The student lifts the flap over the mouth to reveal the answer and check the response.

Modifications: The card formats can be varied to present a variety of math problems and reading tasks. Possible card formats include the following:

Initial consonants   Division

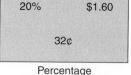

Percentage

Windows Small windows can be cut in materials to provide feedback. The correct answer can be in the window or, when two or more windows are used, the items in the windows can match to show a correct response. Figure 2.8 illustrates the use of windows.

Instructional objective: Any objective in which a matched pair can be devised (problems on one wheel and the correct answers on another wheel) can be selected. See math problem—select answer; see picture—select word; see picture—select initial sound.

Feedback device: Windows provide feedback. When a correct match is obtained in the front windows, the objects, symbols, or numbers match in the back windows. Thus, to check an answer the student looks at the back windows.

FIGURE 2.7
Answer Box

Outside view

Flap

Block of wood

Stack of cards

Inside view

Materials: Poster board, brass fasteners; small pictures or symbols.

Construction: Cut two horizontal pieces of poster board with matching dimensions. Cut two windows on the same horizontal line in each piece so that the windows line up with each other when the pieces are placed together (back to back). Decorate and laminate each piece and make the center holes for the fasteners. Cut circles with dimensions that enable the outer 1″ ridge to pass through the windows when the center of the wheel is lined up with the poster board hole. Write, draw, or paste problems on one wheel and put answers on a corresponding wheel. Write, draw, or glue symbols, objects, or numbers on the back of each wheel set.

Directions: The student selects a wheel set that presents an appropriate task. The student places the wheels between the two rectangular pieces, lines up the holes, and inserts the brass fasteners. The stu-

dent then rotates the task wheel until a problem is presented in the window. Next, the student rotates the other wheel and selects one of the answers that passes through the window. Once an answer is selected, the student flips over the material and checks to see whether the answer is correct. A correct answer yields matching objects in the two windows on the back.

Modifications: The teacher can make numerous wheel sets and code them according to skill area. Wheels that are to be used together (a wheel set) should have matching codes. The tasks that can be placed on the wheels are almost limitless. The size of the material can be varied to accommodate different-size windows.

Stylus   Feedback can be provided by using a stylus with certain types of stimulus cards. The Poke Box in Figure 2.9 illustrates the use of a stylus.

FIGURE 2.8
Spinning Wheels

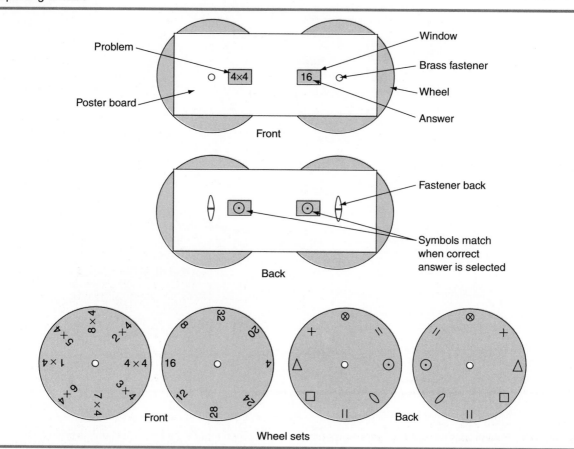

Wheel sets

Instructional objective: Any instructional target that features a multiple-choice answer format can be used with the Poke Box. See math problem—choose or write answer; see sentence—choose missing word; see paragraph—choose title.

Feedback response: The student inserts a stylus in one of the holes below the answers and pulls the card to see whether it comes out of the box. If the correct hole is selected, the card is removed easily from the box because the area below the correct answer is cut and offers no resistance to the stylus.

Materials: A cardboard or wooden box big enough to hold 3″ × 5″ or 5″ × 8″ index cards; a large rubber band; a thin stick or poker; index cards.

Construction: Cut the front end of the box so that most of the index card is visible, but leave a horizontal strip at the bottom of the box about 1″ high. Using a hole punch or drill, make three evenly spaced holes across the front of the box about 1/2″ from the bottom. At each end of the front of the box, drill or punch a hole that extends beyond the dimensions of the index cards. Insert a broken rubber band from the inside of the box on both sides, and tie the ends in knots on the outside of the box. (The rubber band holds the cards and pushes them to the front of the box.) Paint the box inside and out. Make holes in the index cards so that they line up with the holes in the box. Cut out one answer slot on each card. Attach the stylus to the box. Prepare index cards with problems or questions on top and possible answers beneath.

FIGURE 2.9
Poke Box

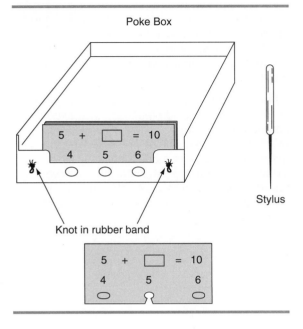

Poke Box

Stylus

Knot in rubber band

Line up the answers with the appropriate holes. To prevent a student from tearing the card by pulling too hard on an incorrect choice, strengthen the holes with gummed reinforcers.

Directions: The student says, writes, or chooses the answer to the problem card. Then the student pokes the stylus in the hole representing the answer. If the choice is correct, the problem card can be pulled up and out of the box and the next problem card is presented.

Modifications: The size of the box can vary so that large cards can be used. Some Poke Boxes feature 8″ × 11½″ cardboard cards. The large space provides room for short stories and multiple-choice comprehension questions. The teacher can put the problem or story on a separate worksheet and put the answer selections on the cards.

Matching Cards   Sets of cards are prepared with the problem or question on one card and the answer on another card. The back of the set of cards contains a match of some sort or a picture completion. After selecting an answer to a problem, the student turns over the cards. If the appropriate answer is chosen, the objects, numbers, colors, or pictures on the back will either match or fit together to complete a picture.

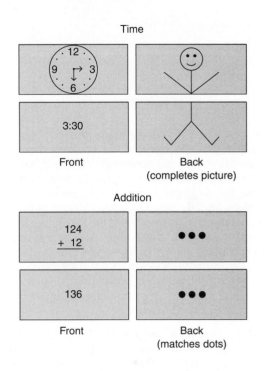

Time

Front

Back
(completes picture)

Addition

124
+ 12

●●●

136

●●●

Front

Back
(matches dots)

Answer on Back   A problem is presented on one side of a stimulus card, and the answer is placed on the other side.

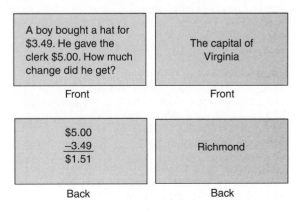

A boy bought a hat for $3.49. He gave the clerk $5.00. How much change did he get?

Front

The capital of Virginia

Front

$5.00
−3.49
$1.51

Back

Richmond

Back

Tab A tab is pulled from a pocket in the learning material to reveal an answer or answers.

Pocket Pockets can be made easily by stapling envelopes to the back of the learning material. Pockets usually hold some type of answer key. In addition, pockets can be coded to provide feedback. For example, library card pockets can be used for sorting stimulus cards. A code is on the back of the stimulus card and the library pocket. If a card is placed in the correct pocket, the codes match. Many instructional targets can be taught with this format. For example, if the stimulus cards show words from the categories of noun, pronoun, verb, and adjective, there would be a pocket corresponding to each category.

Holes Problems are written on one side of a card or sheet, and a hole is punched beside or underneath each item. The answer to each problem is written on the back of the card next to or under the hole. The student sees the problem, writes or says the answer, puts a pipe cleaner or pencil in the hole, and turns over the card to check the response. This format can be used for teaching opposites, plurals, synonyms, word problems, and so on. Manila folders can be used to make this material.

Clips Clips such as clothespins or paper clips can be used to provide feedback. For example, a cardboard pizza wheel can be divided into segments with a task stimulus presented in each segment. Responses are made by clipping clothespins to the edge of the segments. To check answers, the board is turned over to see whether the code on the pizza board matches the code on the clothespin.

Front

Back

Strips in a Folder Strips are cut in one side of a manila folder, which is then laminated. Worksheets containing problems and answers are inserted into the folder so that only the problem is presented. The student uses a grease pencil or a felt-tip pen to write the responses under each problem. Then the worksheet is pulled upward, and the answers appear in the strip.

Worksheet

68	57	27
−19	−28	−19
49	29	8

66	37	82
−47	−17	−45
19	20	37

Folder with
strips cut out

Top of
worksheet

Folder with
strips closed

Worksheet pulled
up to reveal answers

Material with Student: Instructional Games

Once students with learning problems understand the concept involved in a new skill or strategy, they need practice to achieve mastery or automaticity. Instructional games help students maintain interest during practice. Familiar game procedures such as checkers, cards, dice, spinners, and start-to-finish boards are useful. Game content can be individualized for students by putting questions on cards and requiring players to answer a question on a card selected from his or her personalized stack (e.g., multiplication facts for

one player and word meanings for another player). If the question is answered correctly, the student gets to take a turn (e.g., roll dice or spin a spinner) in the game. To maintain a high level of academically engaged time, students should maintain a good pace during games. A fast pace is facilitated by limiting the number of players to two or three for games in which students take turns or by setting a limit on response time.

Lavoie (1993) notes that some students with learning problems do not like games because they are concerned that they do not possess the knowledge or skills needed to win in a game format. He points out that games are only motivating when students think that they have a good chance of winning. Students are more likely to think they can win if the game features content or skills at the students' independent practice level. Also, cooperative game formats should be used until the students have the maturity to handle competitive games.

The games should be individualized for student needs. If a game has many uses, it saves the gamemaker's time and helps the student learn new skills in a familiar format. Games can be made self-correcting, or an answer key can be provided. This allows students to play the game without direct teacher supervision. Chance factors (e.g., lose a turn, take an extra turn, and skip two spaces) boost interest, and familiar formats (such as a game board) allow students to play independently.

Manila folders are good game boards because they are sturdy and conveniently sized, have tabs for easy reference, and are easy to store in a file cabinet. Rules are readily available if written on the back of each folder. Lamination makes the game board more durable and attractive. The teacher can purchase kits with blank laminated boards that have established routes for markers to travel, unmarked spinners, and blank playing cards. Several publishers market these materials. Finally, the teacher may wish to make a rough draft of a game and test it before making the finished product.

Two teacher-made instructional games are presented next (Figures 2.10 and 2.11). In addition, games involving cards, dominoes, chips, dice, and so on are presented in the curriculum area chapters.

FIGURE 2.10

Simple game-board format

Simple Board Game

Instructional objective: Any instructional task that can be presented on a card and performed in a few seconds is suitable.

Feedback device: Answer key and peer correction provide feedback.

Materials: Poster board (or a manila folder); index cards; golf tees; dice; tasks for the cards.

Construction: Draw a segmented road, race track, rocket path, football field, mountain path, or any other start-to-finish sequence on poster board. Decorate the board to accent the game theme (e.g., racing cards, football, joggers, or mountain climbers). Make a stack of task cards with an accompanying answer key. For example, if the task card says $4 \times 4 =$ ___, the answer key would read $4 \times 4 = \underline{16}$.

Directions: A player rolls the dice, picks up a task card, and says an answer. If no player challenges this answer, the player moves the marker the number on the dice. If the answer is challenged, it is looked up on the answer key. If it is correct, the player gets another turn. If it is incorrect, the marker is not moved and the challenger takes a turn.

Modifications: Omit the challenge factor, or mark spaces so that when a player lands on them a chance card (e.g., *Move back three spaces* or *Take an extra turn*) is picked up.

Mystery Detective

Instructional objective: Reading comprehension. See sentence clue card—select the meaning of underlined portion in terms of how, what, when, who, why, or where.

Feedback device: Tabs with numbers that match those on the clue cards are used to provide feedback. For example, a number on a *What* card will be on the tab labeled *What*. Thus, a correct response results in a number match between the card and the tab.

Materials: Poster board for game board, tabs, and clue cards; dice; pictures or drawings for decoration; objects to move from start to jail.

Construction: Cut a slot in the poster board and tape an additional piece of cardboard to the poster board to form a pocket with the slot at the top. Cut six tabs of a length that exposes the name of the tab but not the numbers when inserted fully in the pocket. On the game side of the board draw a "start-to-jail" winding, segmented road. Make a stack of sentence clue cards. Underline a portion of each sentence that corresponds to one of the how, what, when, who, why, or where questions. Place a number in the right top corner of each clue card. Do not repeat the numbers. Make six tabs, one for each of the questions. On each tab list the numbers that match the clue cards. Laminate the material to increase its durability.

FIGURE 2.11
Mystery Detective Game

Directions: A player rolls the dice and picks up a clue card. The player determines whether it is a how, what, when, who, why, or where clue and selects one of the tabs. If the number on the sentence clue card is on the tab chosen, the player's marker is moved the number of spaces indicated on the dice. If the number on the sentence clue card is not on the tab, the player's marker is not moved. The next player does the same thing, and the first player whose marker is put in jail wins.

Modifications: Use this game format to practice syllabication by labeling each tab with a number to indicate the number of syllables on corresponding word cards. Instead of using the pocket on the game board, put each tab in an envelope or in a separately constructed pocket. To make the game more exciting, mark "Trouble" or "Good News" on certain squares. When a marker lands on a marked square, the player picks up a card and does the activity on the card (e.g., *Go ahead three spaces*).

Material with Student: Technological Tools

Peck and Dorricott (1994) claim that technological tools can improve students' abilities, change the way they work and think, and provide a new access to the world. As the Information Age rapidly continues to emerge, educators need to examine the instructional possibilities of the new technologies for educating students with learning problems in the 21st century. Hancock and Betts (1994) discuss the use of technology for instruction according to research-verified applications, emerging applications, and future applications. These applications of technology are featured in Table 2.2.

The computer can be used as a tool for classroom management as well as classroom instruction. With computer-managed instruction, teachers can more efficiently develop individualized educational programs and keep records. Computers can store sequences of instructional objectives and student performance information, track student progress, and generate proper forms and required recordkeeping data (L. S. Fuchs, Fuchs, & Hamlett, 1989).

Computer-assisted instruction, or CAI, refers to software that is designed to provide instruction. The computer offers some unique advantages in instructing students with learning problems. Attributes of CAI that appear useful in helping students

achieve include the following (Fitzgerald, Fick, & Milich, 1986; Lindsey, 1987; Peck & Dorricott, 1994):

- Instruction is individualized by branching students to items appropriate for them.
- Tasks are analyzed and presented in meaningful sequences.
- Progress is at the student's own rate.
- Reinforcement of individual student responses is immediate.
- Existing software enables the student to increase the rate of correct responses.
- Animation, sound effects, and game-playing situations make drill and practice multisensory and motivating.
- Programs that simulate real-life experiences allow the student to make decisions and see the consequences.
- Strategies related to problem solving can be adapted for the computer through such programs as adventure games and software that teaches how to program.
- The computer can be programmed to use the student's name when giving lessons. A computer is nonjudgmental and allows the student to make mistakes in a nonthreatening environment.
- Students need to learn how to use technology to succeed in the Information Age.

Educational software can differ in method or mode of delivery as well as in quality. Ellis and Sabornie (1986) discuss six modes of delivery:

1. *Drill and practice.* Computer-assisted drill and practice supplements other forms of instruction. It is designed to integrate and consolidate previously learned material.

2. *Tutorial.* The role of teacher is assumed by the computer, and material is presented in a programmed learning format. The student moves from one step to the next by answering questions and can be branched to remedial or review segments as well as to more advanced levels of the program.

3. *Educational games.* Games are designed to develop general problem-solving methods and strategies while maintaining interest and motivation.

4. *Simulations.* Simulations attempt to model the underlying characteristics of a real phenomenon so that its properties can be studied. They

TABLE 2.2
Profile of technology for instruction

Applications with Research Verification

Calculators
In addition to arithmetic, algebraic, and trigonometric functions, modern calculators feature plotting and graphing capabilities. These functions enable the student to view computation results in graphic form.

Computer-Assisted Instruction (CAI)/Integrated Learning Systems (ILS)
Select drill and practice programs have yielded small but positive effects on learning. In some schools, CAI that features ILS (including individualized academic tutorials) has produced impressive gains with urban students who are underachieving.

Distance Education
With distance education, learners in remote locations gather at a site that has cable or satellite receivers, phone lines, and video cameras. This equipment allows one- or two-way audio and video contact with a course provider. Hughes Corporation's Galaxy is a distance education program that beams daily lessons to schools through satellite hookup.

Laser Videodiscs
Laser videodisc programs enable the learner to interact with print and still or moving images. These programs do not require a computer. Disc players with remote controls and bar-code readers that select and present images are available for a few hundred dollars.

Microcomputer-Based Labs (MBLs)
These labs use microcomputers and probes to sense temperature, pH levels, and light intensity. Computer labs represent a means for providing hands-on science experiences.

Presentation Software
Overhead projectors and other audiovisual technologies effectively support lectures and demonstrations. A computer combined with a large-screen monitor or LCD display panel is a powerful medium for presenting visual material. Adding multimedia capability permits enhancements such as sound, graphics, and video images.

Telecommunications
The dissemination of large quantities of information to many people simultaneously is available through telecommunications networks. Students can use telecommunications services for assessing publications, training materials, and collected data.

Applications with Emerging Support

Computerized Adaptive Testing (CAT)
With CAT, the test questions vary according to the test taker's responses. An incorrect answer is followed by an easier question, whereas a correct response generates a more difficult question. Initial studies report that CAT provides more accurate results regarding a person's knowledge level in less time than traditional test formats.

Interactive Multimedia
This computer technology links information from multiple sources and enables the user to interact with program content. Most interactive multimedia programs contain text, line drawings, maps, graphs, animated graphics, voice narration, music, and video clips featuring full motion and color.

Multi-User Dimensions (MUDs)
Using MUDs, individuals with a computer and modem communicate through telecommunications services to play out roles in an imaginary context. MUDs are able to transport the user to any place in any time. MUDs provide opportunities for individuals to pursue collaborative and creative activities that extend beyond typical writing or drama exercises.

Text-to-Speech
Computers can translate text to speech. This function is a popular enhancement for early grades and non-English-speaking populations.

TABLE 2.2
(continued)

> *Voicemail*
> Digital voicemail systems are commonplace and offer an excellent medium for delivering information to students. Each student can be assigned a private mailbox with a personal information number (PIN), and parents, teachers, and other students can access the individual's mailbox from any touchtone phone.
>
> *Word Processing*
> Word processing programs are used widely in schools to help students develop writing skills. These programs have been particularly effective with students who are low achievers.
>
> ### Future Applications
>
> *Broadband Networks*
> Through these networks, two-way, delay-free transmissions are delivered to the home through cable or satellite.
>
> *Groupware*
> Groupware allows users in a network to jointly author, share, and disseminate electronic documents, or to join in group decision-making ventures.
>
> *Knowbots*
> *Knowbots,* which stands for *knowledge robots,* are automated systems for collecting, screening, and organizing data.
>
> *Pen-Based Computing*
> Data are entered through pen-based applications that use touch-screen icons and handwriting recognition, instead of through a keyboard.
>
> *Speech-to-Text*
> These voice-aware applications enable users to vocally control computer functions.
>
> *Virtual Reality*
> Users wear special goggles connected to a data input device that engulfs the user in a three-dimensional environment emulating the real world.
>
> *Wireless Connectivity*
> Wireless technology, like the cellular phone, enables teachers and students to share information regardless of their location.

Source: From *Students with Learning Disabilities* (pp. 250–251), 5th ed., by C. D. Mercer, 1997, Upper Saddle River, NJ: Merrill/Prentice Hall. Copyright 1997 by Prentice-Hall Publishing Company. Reprinted by permission.

can incorporate many game features but are intended to model some reality.

5. ***Problem solving.*** The computer can be used to solve real-world problems. For example, students may write computer programs to test possible solutions to a variety of problems.

6. ***Word processing.*** A word processor is a tool for writing instruction. Ease of correcting errors, availability of spelling and grammar checkers, elimination of the need to rewrite after revisions are made, and use of a printer that produces neat copies help teach writing to students with learning problems.

CAI is promising, but limited information exists concerning how computers can best be applied in the classroom. However, it is apparent that the use of appropriate software can motivate students with learning problems through individualized instruction and needed academic practice (Majsterek & Wilson, 1993).

Wiens (1986) suggests three specific criteria for evaluating software to use in teaching students with learning problems. First, software should use the computer's capacity to present the materials better than traditional methods. Voice synthesis, interaction, animation, and response monitoring are features of successful CAI. Moreover, Shuell and Schueckler (1988) note that to transcend traditional methods, CAI programs must use the student's knowledge base, provide guided and independent practice, give corrective feedback, present materials in steps that facilitate learning, provide clear lesson overviews and goals, conduct periodic performance evaluations, and finish with a summary and review of the lesson's main points. Wiens's second criterion for good software is that the teacher must be able to modify or adapt the program to develop appropriate instructional matches for individual learners. The third criterion is that the CAI program should include a way to collect student response data so that teachers can monitor student progress. Actually, the teacher should expect software to report graphic representations of progress on easily generated printouts.

In addition to the many general uses of the computer for students with learning problems, specific applications are also suited to these students. Grimes (1981) notes that for students who have difficulty maintaining on-task attention, computer programs can promote attention with color cueing, animation, underlining, and varying print sizes. For students who respond impulsively, the computer can provide cues or hints to inhibit impulsive responding. For those who take a lot of time to respond (reflective responders), computer programs can be tailored to allow extra response time.

Majsterek and Wilson (1993) reviewed several CAI studies that focused on teaching basic skills to students with learning problems. They conclude that CAI with well-designed software based on sound educational principles and tailored to the learning needs of students with learning problems can produce equivalent or slightly less than equivalent learning with less teacher time than traditional instruction. Other reports of CAI (Ellis & Sabornie, 1986; Hasselbring, Goin, & Bransford, 1988; Woodward & Carnine, 1988) conclude that student achievement usually is greater when CAI supplements rather than replaces teacher-directed instruction. Keefe and Candler (1989) report mixed results on the effectiveness of using word processors with students who have learning problems. However, several individual studies report good results when CAI is used to teach students with learning disabilities (e.g., spelling—L. S. Fuchs et al., 1989; world geography—Horton, Lovitt, Givens, & Nelson, 1989; reading—Torgesen, Waters, Cohen, & Torgesen, 1988; health—Woodward, Carnine, & Gersten, 1988).

Future successful technology-assisted instruction depends on a closer working relationship between educators and software manufacturers. Various software programs for language, reading, spelling, written expression, math, learning strategies and study skills, and transition education are presented in their respective chapters. Appendix B lists addresses of producers and distributors of educational software.

Material with Student: Homework

Homework continues to be a widely practiced activity in schools. Many consider it an important component for improving the quality of American education (Heller, Spooner, Anderson, & Mims, 1988). Olympia, Sheridan, and Jenson (1994) define *homework* as academic work assigned by teachers that extends the practice of academic skills into other environments. Cooper (1989) notes that homework implies completion during non-school hours, but in actuality most students have options to do the work during study hall, library time, or subsequent classes. An important aspect of homework includes programming for academic skill generalization through working in numerous environments. Heller et al. outline the components of homework as it relates to special education. They report that a homework activity must be teacher-directed, include only previously taught skills, be an extension of schoolwork, be evaluated, be based on instructional objectives appropriate to the student, and occur outside school hours.

High rates of achievement are related to the amount of time students are actively engaged in academic tasks. Homework represents a viable method to help students with learning problems engage in academic tasks and improve achievement. The positive relationship of homework to achievement has been well documented for students with learning problems (Jenson, Sheridan, Olympia, & Andrews, 1994). Minimally competent students can compensate for lower ability through increased home study. Specifically, it helps them move through the acquisition, proficiency, maintenance, and generalization stages of learning (Mims, Harper, Armstrong, & Savage, 1991) and provides an opportunity for the teacher to control the temporal aspects of practice (i.e., spaced vs. massed practice) that are most effective for learning (Dempster, 1991).

In a synthesis of research on homework in general education, Cooper (1989) reports that homework positively affects achievement but that the effect varies considerably across grade levels. In essence, he notes that the effects of homework are substantial for secondary students and minimal for elementary students. For middle school students, the effects are good but are only about half as beneficial as for secondary students. Cooper also reports that the optimal amount of homework varies across grade levels.

Although there is a limited amount of research on homework practices, Patton (1994) highlights 35 recommended practices from the available research and literature. He discusses practices in the areas of management, assignments, student competencies, and parental involvement. Patton notes that 14 of the recommended practices have empirical validation, 25 have literature-based support, and 5 have field-based support. It is apparent that research is limited, but a validation base for effective practices is emerging.

In a survey of homework practices of 88 teachers of students with learning disabilities, Salend and Schliff (1989) found that most teachers (80 percent) use homework regularly but fail to use quality practices consistently. They report that 85 percent of the teachers experience problems in getting students to complete their homework. Salend and Schliff note that students' low motivation may be related to the failure of the learning disabilities teachers to give feedback on homework (43 percent do not discuss or review homework), incorporate homework into grading policies (42 percent do not regularly grade homework), or involve parents in the homework process (only 41 percent solicit feedback from parents). From the limited research on the effects of homework on students with learning disabilities, it appears that quality practices are related to positive student achievement.

Guidelines from the literature (Al-Rubaiy, 1985; Armstrong & McPherson, 1991; Frith, 1991; Mims et al., 1991) and research (Cooper, 1989; Patton, 1994; Rosenberg, 1989) are available to promote best practices in homework:

• *Assign a reasonable amount of homework.* From his synthesis of the homework research, Cooper (1989) recommends the following amount of homework: First through third grade—one to three 15-minute assignments per week; fourth through sixth grade—two to four 15- to 45-minute assignments per week; seventh through ninth grade—up to five 45- to 75-minute assignments a week; tenth through twelfth grade—up to five 75- to 120-minute assignments a week. The purpose of homework at the elementary level is to help students develop good study habits, practice newly acquired skills, and realize that learning can take place in nonschool environments. For students in seventh to twelfth grade, homework becomes essential to academic achievement and school success. To regulate the amount of time students spend on homework, the teacher should check with students or parents periodically about how much time homework is taking. For example, it is not uncommon for students with learning disabilities to spend twice as much time doing an assignment as students without disabilities (Jenson et al., 1994). Accommodations for students with learning problems include the following: (1) separate large assignments into smaller chunks, (2) provide more time to complete the assignment, (3) offer incentives for completing homework to students who are distractible, off-task, or impulsive, and (4) organize student groups that can work together. For example, O'Melia and Rosenberg (1994) report good progress on homework completion through cooperative homework teams. Moreover, teachers who work in teams need to plan together on assigning homework. Because students take classes from different teachers in the upper grades, the teachers should work cooperatively to develop appropriate amounts of homework.

• *Make homework an integral part of the learning process.* Nicholls, McKenzie, and Shufro (1994) compared perspectives of students with and without learning problems on the relevance of homework. Most students with learning problems viewed homework as an imposition and remotely related to life skills, whereas most students without learning problems viewed homework as important and related to life skills. When the teacher discusses the rationale for homework and informs students of the specific objectives (such as mastery of skills) of each assignment, students are able to appreciate homework's value. Rosenberg

(1989) reports that when teachers discuss, review, explain, and evaluate homework assignments with students who have learning problems, homework becomes an effective learning activity. Al-Rubaiy (1985) notes that a feeling of ownership of the assignment is promoted when students recognize the value of homework. Homework should not be busy work or used as punishment.

• *Plan homework assignments at the student's instructional level.* Teachers must ensure that assignments represent an appropriate match between the student's ability or skill level and the difficulty level of the assignment. This instructional match usually is maintained when the teacher assigns homework to practice or review material that the student has been taught.

• *Make sure the student understands the assignment.* Understanding the purpose and instructions for the assignment is critical (Jenson et al., 1994). When the assignment is similar to classwork, clarity is facilitated. When the assignment is new or different, the teacher should demonstrate the task and provide some guided practice on a portion of the assignment. Understanding also is facilitated when directions are clear and simple and when students are asked to explain the task.

• *Evaluate homework.* Teachers should evaluate all homework assignments and maintain a cumulative record of the results. Assigning a grade encourages students to complete assignments and develop a sense of responsibility. Moreover, for students who do not test well, homework provides an opportunity to improve their grades and display their skills and knowledge (Mims et al., 1991).

• *Reinforce the completion of homework.* Teachers should indicate that homework is important to help students learn and develop responsibility. Students should be encouraged when they complete their homework. Encouragement may be private (verbal praise, note sent home, sticker, or high grade) or public (bulletin board display of work or display of names with homework stars). Also, the entire class or teams of students may be encouraged when each member has completed the assignment or improved in the number of assignments completed.

• *Involve parents in homework.* In a study of parents of students with learning disabilities, Kay,

Fitzgerald, Paradee, and Mellencamp (1994) examined parental perspectives on homework. They found that parents felt inadequate to help with homework. They desired more information on how to help their children with homework and wanted a two-way communication system that would help them become partners on their child's instructional team. Initially, the teacher should send a letter to parents regarding homework policies and practices. Because letters do not always represent a functional medium of communication to homes, it may be necessary for the teacher to discuss homework in parent conferences, at PTA meetings, during parent nights at school, or on the telephone. Information for parents should include the purpose of homework, the expected frequency of homework, the approximate amount of time assignments should take, homework evaluation procedures, effects of homework on grades, and suggestions for parents on how to help with homework. Tips regarding parental involvement include the following:

• Schedule a specific time and place for homework.
• Supervise the homework session by periodically checking with the student to determine progress, rather than overseeing every task.
• Provide an environment conducive to learning. The area needs to be well lighted and free of distractions.
• Provide the student with appropriate materials.
• Sign and date completed homework assignments.
• Encourage and praise the student for doing homework.
• Share with the teacher any concerns involving the amount of work or the difficulty level of the assignments.

• *Facilitate homework through effective support systems.* Frith (1991) suggests using peer tutoring for checking and assessing homework and for giving corrective feedback, using computer-assisted instruction for students who have access to computers, encouraging parents to support the value of homework with their actions and words, and developing monitoring systems (such as graphs or checklists) for homework.

In his concluding remarks concerning homework, Frith (1991, p. 49) states:

For maximum usefulness, homework assignments need to be made in the context of a strong support system that includes assistance from teachers and peers as well as parents. A strong support system will increase positive impressions that students have toward homework, especially when it might appear that these assignments are imposing on their free time. Regardless of perspective, homework is certainly important, and it should be viewed as an integral component of the instructional program—not only in regular education but in special education as well.

☀ SCHEDULING

Schedules are vital for accomplishing instructional goals in an organized manner. They indicate which activities will occur and when they will occur. Most students with learning problems need the organization and routine typical of systematic scheduling. Furthermore, scheduling greatly affects the pace of instruction. It ensures that enough classroom time is spent in high-priority curriculum areas and that enjoyable activities are interspersed with less appealing activities.

A well-planned daily schedule greatly aids the teacher in providing effective instruction and collaboration; however, developing an appropriate schedule is hard work. A teacher needs knowledge and skills in individualized programming (Chapter 1), assessment for teaching (Chapter 3), instructional approaches and techniques (Chapter 4), curriculum materials (Chapter 4), and classroom management (Chapters 4 and 5). Scheduling techniques presented in this section include general scheduling techniques, scheduling at the elementary level, scheduling at the secondary level, and scheduling in the resource room.

General Scheduling Techniques

The following suggestions and techniques apply to improving scheduling practices in various program settings (resource room and general classroom) and at all grade levels:

- **Schedule for maximum instructional time.** To allocate academic time, Schloss and Sedlak (1986) suggest that teachers plan time to practice new skills within a demonstration-practice-feedback-mastery paradigm, build planning time into the schedule and adhere to it, consider time needed for transitions and setups, and pace the instruction quickly during sessions allocated to academics.

- **Proceed from short work assignments to longer ones.** At first, some students may be unable to work on a seatwork assignment for a long period (such as 30 to 45 minutes). The teacher can break the task into short lessons that the student can manage independently. When task complexity, rather than time, is a problem for the student, it may be helpful to break the task into steps. Eventually, time and task complexity can be increased as the student develops academic and self-management skills.

- **Alternate highly preferred with less preferred tasks.** In scheduling, it often helps if a less preferred activity is followed by a highly preferred activity. For example, if reading is preferred over math, math is scheduled first and followed by reading. If none of the academic subjects is preferred, it may be necessary to use nonacademic activities (such as art, recess, music, and physical education) as preferred activities.

- **Provide a daily schedule for each student.** A daily schedule provides needed structure to students with learning problems. It also presents them with expectations and a sequence of events in advance. Developing a daily schedule is easier if students understand that events will occur at the same time each day. This is accomplished by giving students a schedule form, perhaps on a ditto or chalkboard, that specifies the time of events for the day. On assignments that are progressive (such as assignments in a text or workbook, or long-term writing, art, or science projects), students may record the starting point for the next day on the schedule. When scheduling changes are needed, the teacher explains the new events or assignments.

- **Schedule assignments that can be completed in a school day.** Students need the opportunity to begin each day with a "clean slate." They then do not have to worry about yesterday's incomplete or incorrect work. To make sure students are able to complete their work, the teacher should be certain assignments are at the student's instructional level, make initial assignments short and increase them gradually, provide leeway time for completing work, reinforce on-task behavior, provide answer keys and self-correcting materials, and make some assignments continuous (weekly), with daily aims and a completion date specified.

• ***Provide time cues.*** The schedule designates the time allotted for each assignment. Many students with learning problems have difficulty managing their time and need reminders or cues. Several techniques may be used as time reminders. For example, the teacher can cut sections that are the same size as the face of the classroom clock out of circular pieces of cardboard. When these circular pieces are placed on the clock face, they display blocks of time on the clock (e.g., a circle with $1/4$ section cut out displays a 15-minute block of time). The student receives time cues by observing the proportion of time exposed on the clock and the location of the minute hand in that exposed section. Secondly, the teacher can set a kitchen timer for the amount of time allotted to an activity. The timer may occasionally be used with an individual student on a given activity. The sound of the timer ticking and the movement of the dial remind the student to continue working.

• ***Schedule activities in a complementary manner.*** In an individualized program, teachers must organize student activities and plan time to provide individual assistance. Because some subjects require more teacher assistance than others, it often helps if the entire class is not working on the same subject at the same time. Math, spelling, and handwriting usually require less teacher assistance than reading. Thus, a teacher may be able to provide more individual assistance if part of the class is scheduled to work on math while others are working on reading.

• ***Plan a variety of activities.*** Sometimes academic instruction is more effective if one activity is not too long and if a variety of activities are planned. Many teachers organize a 45-minute instructional period into three 15-minute segments. A sample math lesson may include the following activities: direct teacher instruction, listening station (for taped instruction), or self-correcting material activity. In this plan, students may be divided into three groups and rotated through the activities. The option of working in an interest center may be added for students who complete their work early.

• ***Consider alternative schedules.*** To reduce instructional fragmentation, discipline problems, and student failure, some schools have redesigned the traditional school schedule to include block scheduling (Canady & Rettig, 1995). For example, parallel-block scheduling with a 100-minute time block is used at the elementary level, and a four-block schedule with 90-minute time blocks is used at the middle school level. Another middle school method is to reorganize the 180-day school calendar to a 75-75-30 plan in which courses end after two 75-day terms; during the final six weeks, students are enrolled in specialized courses that provide enriching activities or additional learning time to master grade-level objectives. At the secondary level, block scheduling can include a 4×4 semester plan (i.e., four 90-minute blocks for 90 days) or a Day 1/Day 2 schedule so that students have fewer classes daily and fewer class changes. These scheduling approaches attempt to address students' differing needs for learning time and improve the quality of time that students spend at school.

Scheduling at the Elementary Level

General class and special class elementary teachers often teach the same students for a large portion of the school day. Moreover, in cooperative or team-teaching situations in mainstream classrooms, the general education teacher and the special education teacher need to plan the schedule together. This requires scheduling a variety of activities: opening exercises, reading, math, recess, art, and so on. The following four steps can be used to schedule entire school days:

1. ***Analyze the day's events.*** The first step in developing a daily schedule is to analyze the daily events and determine how much time the teacher is responsible for planning. This time is affected by nonacademic school activities and supportive instructional services. After the teacher has determined the amount of time students are at lunch, resource room instruction, physical education, art, and so on, the teacher knows how much time must be scheduled. In a 6-hour school day, the classroom teacher probably needs to schedule $4^{1}/_{2}$ to 5 hours. Planning $4^{1}/_{2}$ to 5 hours of daily instruction for 180 days a year is a sizable project.

2. ***Plan opening exercises.*** Opening exercises usually require 15 to 20 minutes; they develop rapport and prepare students for the day's activities. The teacher can use this time to observe the attitudes, moods, and physical appearance of the students. Common activities for opening exercises include collecting lunch money; taking attendance; saluting the flag; recognizing special days

(such as birthdays and holidays); discussing the schedule of activities for the day; and discussing current events, weather, or the date. For the young student who cannot read, pictures can be used to designate activities.

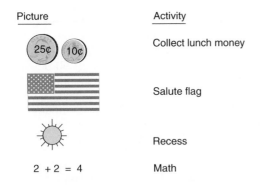

Picture	Activity
25¢ 10¢	Collect lunch money
	Salute flag
	Recess
2 + 2 = 4	Math

3. ***Schedule academic instruction.*** Although many students are more alert and easier to motivate in the morning than in the afternoon, Dunn, Beaudry, and Klavas (1989) report that most students with learning problems are more alert in the afternoon. Therefore, it helps to plan some intensive learning activities in the afternoon. Also, because students function at different academic levels, students should be divided into small groups for academic instruction.

4. ***Plan closing exercises.*** Closing exercises usually require 10 to 15 minutes; they are designed to tie together the school day in a pleasant, orderly manner. Some closing activities include cleaning up, returning materials, determining what to take home, reviewing the day's activities, and discussing the next day's major events. The teacher should strive to finish the day in a positive manner with each student.

The sample schedule presented in Table 2.3 stresses systematic and small-group academic work in reading and math in the morning and group-oriented activities in the afternoon. The schedule also provides time to complete unfinished work. This extra time permits slower students to finish their work and other students to work ahead or select interesting activities. The teacher may use this time to provide individual attention or conduct assessments. These flexible time periods reduce pressure and enable the teacher to individualize in-

struction. Often it is easier to assign math or spelling seatwork than reading seatwork; thus, the teacher may wish to give math or spelling seatwork to students when they are not receiving small-group reading instruction.

Scheduling at the Secondary Level

A typical secondary school schedule includes a homeroom period, five or six class periods, and a lunch period. Class periods are about 50 minutes, and the teacher usually has one period for planning. Because a fixed schedule of periods exists at the secondary level, it may seem that teachers do not need to do much daily scheduling. However, because lessons must fit into 50-minute segments, planning is essential to ensure efficient use of instructional time.

In scheduling, an opening exercise may be limited to an explanation of the activities for the period, and a closing exercise may simply consist of allowing time to put away materials. Some secondary classes are structured so that students enter the room, get their work folders, and begin working. The teacher moves from group to group, or individual to individual, offering assistance and reinforcement. In this arrangement, opening activities are omitted, but time is scheduled for returning folders.

In planning for a period, it may be a good idea to divide students into groups and schedule appropriate activities for each group. With this format a teacher may rotate through the groups. Some content is taught adequately to the whole group; however, when this arrangement is used, the teacher must ensure that all students understand the lecture material (e.g., by taking questions from students). The teacher should expect students with learning problems to need additional help during seatwork. This help may be provided by a classmate, special material, an aide, or the teacher.

The following general scheduling considerations may be used with adolescents with learning problems:

• If there is flexibility in scheduling electives, students can select courses in which they have a good opportunity to succeed. Scheduling that results in a heavy load or an unsympathetic teacher can cause serious difficulties for a learner with problems.

TABLE 2.3
Sample schedule

Time	Activity		
8:30	Opening exercises		
8:50	Setting up and beginning work		
9:00	Reading period (small groups)		
	Group A	*Group B*	*Group C*
9:00	Group with teacher	Listening center	Paper-pencil task
9:15	Listening center	Paper-pencil task	Instructional game
9:30	Paper-pencil task	Instructional game	Group with teacher
9:45	Instructional game	Group with teacher	Listening center
10:00	Recess		
10:20	Math period (small groups)		
	Group 1	*Group 2*	*Group 3*
10:20	Paper-pencil task	Cooperative learning group	Group with teacher
10:35	Cooperative learning group	Group with teacher	Criterion test, timing, or math game
10:50	Group with teacher	Criterion test, timing, or math game	Paper-pencil task
11:05	Criterion test, timing, or math game	Paper-pencil task	Cooperative learning group
11:20	Prescribed and selected activities including: choosing a free activity, going to the library, using an interest center, working on unfinished tasks, performing timings, taking a test, or playing an instructional or recreational game. The teacher may use this time to work with students who have been absent or out of the room, provide feedback, and give individual attention.		
11:45	Story time, handwriting, or content area (science, social studies)		
12:00	Lunch		
12:30	Spelling, language arts (involving classwide peer tutoring on Tuesdays and Thursdays)		
1:00	Physical education, music, art, or motor development		
1:30	Recess		
1:45	Content area (science, social studies, geography, career education, or citizenship)		
2:05	Prescribed and selected activities		
2:20	Closing activities		
2:30	Dismissal		

• A course load must reflect student needs. There should be a balance between demanding and less-demanding courses. Course substitution also may be used. If the school offers less-demanding courses that satisfy required credits, the student with learning problems can avoid courses in which he or she is likely to be unsuccessful.

• Expanded course offerings are used in some settings to accommodate the student with learning problems. In these situations the special education staff teaches some content areas in a different setting.

Scheduling in the Resource Room

The resource room teacher is faced with a tedious and time-consuming scheduling task, primarily because students participate in more than one instructional setting with two or more teachers.

The following issues complicate resource room scheduling:

- The student's academic, emotional, and social needs must be considered when determining the best time to schedule resource room instruction. If the student leaves the general class for the resource room during an academic lesson, will needed academic instruction be missed? If the student leaves during a nonacademic activity (such as art, physical education, or music), will the student resent missing a desirable activity?
- Classroom teachers usually have preferred times for sending students to the resource room.
- Students who come to the resource room at a specified time may have different instructional needs. For example, one student may need help with a specific math skill, whereas another student may need to work on reading comprehension.
- In some situations it is helpful if the resource room teacher teaches in the general class setting.
- Because students are participating in parallel and complementary instructional programs, with different teachers working on the same instructional objectives, the resource room teacher must schedule time for conferring with classroom teachers.

Despite numerous scheduling difficulties, the resource program remains an important instructional model for serving students with learning problems. The following techniques and suggestions are helpful in resource room scheduling:

- Students may come to the resource room at different times, depending on the day. For example, they may come at a certain time three days a week and at another time two days of the week. With this schedule the students do not consistently miss a given subject or activity in the general class.
- A resource teacher may choose to provide instruction in the various academic areas at fixed times during the day. With this type of schedule, reading, math, handwriting, and spelling are taught at a specified time, and students may come to the sessions they need. Thus, a student may come to the resource room for a half-hour of instruction one or more times daily to receive help in problem areas.
- To maximize the efficient use of time, the resource room teacher must encourage and reinforce being on time and making a quick transition from task to task.
- To decrease the likelihood that students will disrupt the general classroom when they return from the resource room, the resource teacher may give students an assignment to work on until the general classroom teacher can involve them in the ongoing activities. Also, the teacher may assign a student the responsibility of helping the returning student to begin work.

CLASSROOM EQUIPMENT

Instructional equipment can be used to meet the specific needs of students with learning problems. For example, audiovisual equipment can be used to instruct students with specific modality preferences, and manipulative devices often help to hold the attention of a distractible learner. Use of a tape recorder, overhead projector, and small-item materials is presented in this section. The use of computers and computer software is discussed in the section on technological tools.

Tape Recorder

Cassette recorders have several advantages. They are simple to operate, the recorder and tapes are small and easy to store, and tapes are relatively inexpensive. Headphones enable individual students to operate a recorder without distracting classmates. Instructional applications of a tape recorder include the following:

- A tape can be made of reading material (e.g., literature, stories, and magazines). The student can read along with the tape to practice reading. Thus, the tape can provide feedback, increase speed, and help the student identify and practice difficult words.
- In a language activity, the student can use a tape recorder to make a tape of a story. Later, the student can write the story from the tape with a peer, aide, or teacher.
- Oral directions can be put on tape to accompany seatwork activities. The student who has difficulty with oral directions can play the tape until the directions are understood.
- Spelling tapes are useful for practice and taking tests. One commonly used format gives the spelling word; the word used in a sentence; and a

pause, a beep, and the word spelled correctly. The pause can be eliminated by having the student stop the tape recorder to write the word and then start it to check the spelling.

- Stories, facts, or a report of an event can be recorded. News programs, commercials, telephone messages, weather reports, and teacher-made content can be used. The student listens and then responds to comprehension questions. For example, a weather report is taped and the student is required to answer the following questions: High temperature? Low temperature? Any rain? Forecast for tomorrow? What season is it?

- One-minute samples of instrumental music can be taped for students to use in conducting timings. The tapes usually begin with the word "start" and end with the word "stop." The teacher may prefer to use only the words and omit the music. In place of a kitchen timer, tapes of different time spans can be used to mark the end of any timed activity.

- Correction tapes can be used to provide feedback to students who have completed math seatwork.

- Music can be recorded on tapes for students to listen to when they have completed an assignment. Also, pleasant background music can be played while students are engaged in activities such as cleaning up, settling down after recess, free-choice, seatwork, or art.

- At the secondary level, class lectures and discussions can be taped. These tapes can be used to help students review or understand the material.

Overhead Projector

An overhead projector is readily available to classroom teachers and is used to display an image on a screen from a transparency. Transparencies can be teacher-made or purchased. They allow the user to write on, color in, and point at specific details while discussing them. Overhead projectors can be used to project images on light-color surfaces without darkening the room. Because an overhead projector greatly accents the visual image, it aids students who are easily distracted by extraneous visual stimuli. The teacher can block out all stimuli that do not relate to the item being studied or completed.

Guidelines for effective use of transparencies on an overhead projector include the following:

- Prepare transparencies ahead of time.
- Type or write in clear, bold lines on plain paper. Use a pencil or marker containing a carbon base, or put the original through a copy machine. Then make the transparency quickly by putting the original through a Thermofax copier or transparency maker.
- Make letters at least $1/4''$ high. Orator or bulletin type from a primary typewriter projects adequately.
- Simplify and be concise. Use a maximum of six or seven lines of copy and six or seven words per line.
- Use simple graphic drawings. Have diagrams ready ahead of time rather than using teaching time to put complicated illustrations on a transparency.
- Emphasize key points by capitalizing, underlining, circling, and boxing.
- Use color for clarity, emphasis, and variety. The acetate background itself can be a color instead of clear. Also, colored pieces of acetate can be attached in key spots, or color markers can be used on the acetate.
- Turn the projector off and on to shift students' attention.
- Use the revelation technique (covering the visual with a sheet of paper and revealing items one at a time) to avoid distractions and keep the class interested. Students who are taking notes may appreciate being shown the complete visual first as an overview before the masks are applied.
- Use the techniques of overlays and masking (revelation) to break down a whole into its component parts.
- Locate the screen so that everyone in the room can see it clearly. Position it as high as possible, and tilt it forward to project an appropriate image.
- When writing while talking, check the screen periodically to be sure the students are seeing what is being discussed. Write clearly.
- Keep extra markers or pencils on hand.
- Make color lifts of artwork on magazine paper.
- Use transparencies in place of a chalkboard to focus attention, thereby saving time and space because the lesson can be used again. Also,

class control and eye contact can be maintained better than at a chalkboard.

Uses of an overhead projector include the following:

• Class schedules and homework assignments can be put on an overhead to save chalkboard space for student and teacher use throughout the day. To check on the schedule or finish copying a homework assignment, the student can turn on an overhead projector and complete the task.

• An overhead projector can be used for administering many kinds of tests: computation facts, word problems, cloze spelling tests, fill-in-the-blank items, and multiple-choice items.

• An overhead projector can be used to display the category being discussed. Words, phrases, sentences, poems, drawings, and pictures are useful stimuli in facilitating relevant interactions.

• An overhead projector is useful for playing reading comprehension and spelling games. The teacher gradually exposes the letters of a word, the definition of a word, a sentence, or a paragraph. The students attempt to respond correctly with the fewest cues possible. With the letters of a word, students attempt to finish spelling the word; with the definition, they identify the word that matches the definition. In the sentence task, students try to complete the sentence correctly. The paragraph task involves providing a title for the paragraph. It often helps to divide students into teams and allow each group to give a response as another cue is presented.

• A spinner can be made on a transparency, placed on an overhead, and used for a variety of instructional activities and games. The teacher or student spins it, and it points to letters, numbers, words, or math facts. The spinner can be used to determine the number of points a specific task item is worth, select a math problem (by pointing to it), select one word at a time until the student can make a sentence, or select a letter for the student to sound out or add to previous letters to spell a word. These games are suitable for the student–teacher pair, two or more students, or a large group divided into teams.

• The overhead projector can be used to develop experience stories with small groups of students. In this activity, the group contributes to the story while the teacher writes it on the transparency.

• Students can use the overhead projector to display stories developed in language experience activities. The stories can be read to the class or copied by selected students. In addition, the class can help the student title the story.

• It often is easier for the teacher to lecture while using an overhead projector than while using a chalkboard. It is easier to point to or uncover material on an overhead than to write on a chalkboard. With an overhead, the teacher does not need to write and talk simultaneously or have students wait while the teacher writes.

• Many students enjoy writing on a transparency and seeing it presented on a screen. This activity is especially useful in practicing handwriting.

• An overhead projector can be used to project figures, pictures, letters, or numbers on a black chalkboard. The student can trace over the projected images to practice handwriting or develop fine motor skills, or this activity can be used as reinforcement.

Small-Item Materials

Inexpensive materials that are useful in a classroom include the following:

• *Miniature chalkboard.* One side of a piece of three-ply cardboard, about 15″ × 18″, can be painted with several coats of chalkboard paint (available at school supply and paint stores). Also, the smooth side of a Masonite board can be painted and the rough side can be used as a flannelboard. These boards can be made for students to use at their desks.

• *Flannelboard.* A heavy piece of cardboard can be covered with flannel. Also, the rough side of a piece of Masonite can be used for a flannelboard. Figures for the board can be made from foam-backed material or felt. Flannelboards are available commercially in various sizes, and some have easel backs. Uses include presenting vocabulary or spelling words, listing important rules, displaying parts of an outline, displaying graphs and fractions, presenting pictures representing difficult concepts, and displaying map outlines.

- *Game materials.* Materials commonly used with game boards can be collected and stored in an accessible location. Golf tees, Playskool characters, and items from old games are good markers; dice and spinners are good number indicators. Manila folders are excellent for drawing start-to-finish game-board formats and are easy to store.
- *Construction materials.* Various materials should be collected, such as pictures (e.g., of specific sounds, story starters, and so on), school supply or cigar boxes, oatmeal boxes, egg cartons, shoe boxes, water-base marking pens, plastic term-paper holders, tobacco or coffee cans, tongue depressors, library card holders, poster board, oaktag paper, wooden cubes, pizza discs, envelopes, and clothespins. These and other materials are useful for constructing instructional materials. The instructional games and self-correcting materials presented in this chapter and the instructional activities featured throughout the curriculum area chapters require many of these items.
- *Typewriter.* A manual typewriter can stimulate learning and be fun to use (e.g., in practicing spelling and typing stories). Also, a typewriter is helpful for students with handwriting difficulties.
- *Durable coverings.* Materials used frequently can be covered with a transparent adhesive material or with plastic spray. The student can mark on the material and wipe off the markings with a damp cloth. Also, a consumable workbook can be protected for repeated use. The teacher can trim two pieces of acetate to the size of the workbook, lay the acetate on the inside of each cover, and tape it to the cover along the outer edge. To do the work on a page, the student simply flips the acetate over the page and uses a crayon or grease pencil. This can be erased, leaving the workbook blank so that it can be used by another student. Another method is to cut cardboard into 8″ × 11″ pieces and tape acetate to it, either along the left side only or along both the sides and the bottom, forming a pocket to hold worksheets.
- *Magnetic board.* A magnetic board can be used for students to respond on, to present tasks, or to display work. Work or tasks are displayed easily by taping a paper clip to the back of the stimulus card or worksheet. The paper clip clings to the magnetic board and holds up the material.
- *Tracing screen.* A wire screen with a cardboard edge makes an excellent tracing screen. When paper is placed over the screen and written on with a crayon, the letters become raised and can be used for tracing.
- *Mirror.* A door-mounted or full-length mirror is excellent for teaching grooming and self-concept activities. The mirror provides direct feedback to a student about appearance.

MATERIAL ORGANIZATION SYSTEM

To plan and deliver individualized instruction in a systematic and continuous manner, a great deal of organization is needed. For the beginning teacher, the development of a system is a large undertaking; however, without it much frustration and anxiety can result. For example, without a system of filing instructional materials that accounts for storage and retrieval, the beginning teacher can spend hours trying to locate needed materials. Thus, one of the initial jobs for a teacher is to develop a filing and storage system and refine it with use.

Before the first day of teaching, the teacher begins to make bulletin boards, dittos, instructional games, worksheets, interest centers, overheads, and special project activities. A filing system helps the teacher organize and add to these materials. In addition, the system can be refined as the teacher develops priorities.

Table 2.4 presents a general filing system. The categories would change depending on the subjects being taught. As it develops, the system would become more specific. For example, numerous subcategories would be listed under phonics as materials and activities are collected and developed (e.g., individual consonant sounds, blends, vowel sounds, and digraphs). In the academic areas, a highly specific filing system can be developed from scope and sequence skills lists, commercial programs, or curriculum guides. By making the system open-ended, the teacher can add categories as needed. New ideas or materials collected from teachers, books, in-service meetings, university classes, or commercial programs can be filed into the system readily and used when needed.

TABLE 2.4
Sample categorical outline for
a filing system

I. Academic Areas
   R. Reading
      R-1   Phonological awareness materials and activities
      R-2   Readiness materials and activities
      R-3   Phonics materials and activities
      R-4   Comprehension materials and activities
      R-5   Whole-word materials and activities
      R-6   Whole language materials and activities
      R-7   Literature-based materials and activities

   M. Math
      M-1   Readiness materials and activities
      M-2   Quantity materials and activities
      M-3   Place value materials and activities
      M-4   Addition materials and activities
      M-5   Subtraction materials and activities
      M-6   Multiplication materials and activities
      M-7   Division materials and activities
      M-8   Fractions materials and activities
      M-9   Percentages materials and activities
      M-10 Word problems materials and activities
      M-11 Money materials and activities
      M-12 Algebra materials and activities

Other academic areas (language, spelling, social studies) would be developed
according to subareas and specific skills.

II. Management and Motivation Areas
      B.B.   Bulletin boards
      I.C.   Interest centers
      L.C.   Learning centers
      C.R.   Classroom rules
      S.   Scheduling materials (e.g., forms)
      E.C.   Evaluation center materials (e.g., charts, forms, stopwatches,
            and logs)
      G.   Games
      A.V.   Audiovisual materials
      S.C.   Self-correcting materials
      R.M.   Reinforcement materials
      C.A.   Classroom arrangement materials
      C.S   Computer software and CD ROMs
      C.M.   Computer manuals

☀ REFERENCES

Al-Rubaiy, K. (1985, Summer). . . . And now for your homework assignment. *The Directive Teacher*, 3–5.

Anderson, L. M., Evertson, C. M., & Brophy, J. E. (1979). An experimental study of effective teaching in first grade reading groups. *Elementary School Journal, 79,* 193–223.

Armstrong, S. W., & McPherson, A. (1991). Homework as a critical component in social skills instruction. *Teaching Exceptional Children, 24*(1), 45–47.

Bloom, B. (1984). The search for methods of group instruction as effective as one-to-one tutoring. *Educational Leadership, 41*(8), 4–18.

Canady, R. L., & Rettig, M. D. (1995). The power of innovative scheduling. *Educational Leadership, 53*(3), 4–10.

Carnine, D., Silbert, J., & Kameenui, E. J. (1997). *Direct instruction reading* (3rd ed.). Upper Saddle River, NJ: Merrill/Prentice Hall.

Cegelka, P. T., & Berdine, W. H. (1995). *Effective instruction for students with learning difficulties.* Boston: Allyn & Bacon.

Cohen, P. A., Kulik, J. A., & Kulik, C. C. (1982). Educational outcomes of tutoring: A meta-analysis of findings. *American Educational Research Journal, 19*(2), 237–248.

Cooper, H. (1989). Synthesis of research on homework. *Educational Leadership, 47*(3), 85–91.

Delquadri, J., Greenwood, C. R., Whorton, D., Carta, J. J., & Hall, R. V. (1986). Classwide peer tutoring. *Exceptional Children, 52,* 535–542.

Dempster, F. N. (1991). Synthesis of research on reviews and tests. *Educational Leadership, 48*(7), 71–76.

DeVries, D. L., & Slavin, R. E. (1978). Teams-games-tournament (TGT): Review of ten classroom experiments. *Journal of Research and Development in Education, 12,* 28–38.

Dunn, R., Beaudry, J. S., & Klavas, A. (1989). Survey of research on learning styles. *Educational Leadership, 46*(6), 50–58.

Ellis, E. S., & Sabornie, E. J. (1986). Effective instruction with microcomputers: Promises, practices, and preliminary findings. *Focus on Exceptional Children, 19*(4), 1–16.

Emmer, E. T., Evertson, C. M., & Worsham, M. E. (2000). *Classroom management for secondary teachers* (5th ed.). Boston: Allyn & Bacon.

Fister, S. L., & Kemp, K. A. (1995). *TGIF: But what will I do on Monday?* Longmont, CO: Sopris West.

Fitzgerald, G., Fick, L., & Milich, R. (1986). Computer-assisted instruction for students with attentional difficulties. *Journal of Learning Disabilities, 19,* 376–379.

Forness, S. R., & Kavale, K. A. (1985). Effects of class size on attention, communication, and disruption of mildly mentally retarded children. *American Educational Research Journal, 22*(3), 403–412.

Frith, G. (1991). Facilitating homework through effective support systems. *Teaching Exceptional Children, 24*(1), 48–49.

Fuchs, D., Mathes, P. G., & Fuchs, L. S. (1993). *Peabody classwide peer tutoring reading methods.* Unpublished teacher's manual. (Available from Douglas Fuchs, Box 328, George Peabody College, Vanderbilt University, Nashville, TN 37203.)

Fuchs, L. S., Fuchs, D., & Hamlett, C. L. (1989). Effects of alternative goal structures within curriculum-based measurement. *Exceptional Children, 55,* 429–438.

Greenwood, C. R., Carta, J. J., & Hall, R. V. (1988). The use of peer tutoring strategies in classroom management and educational instruction. *School Psychology Review, 17*(2), 258–275.

Greenwood, C. R., Delquadri, J. C., & Carta, J. J. (1988). *ClassWide Peer Tutoring: Programs for spelling, math, and reading.* Delray Beach, FL: Educational Achievement Systems.

Greenwood, C. R., Dinwiddie, G., Terry, B., Wade, L., Stanley, S. O., Thibadeau, S., & Delquadri, J. C. (1984). Teacher- versus peer-mediated instructions: An eco-behavioral analysis of achievement outcomes. *Journal of Applied Behavior Analysis, 17,* 521–538.

Grimes, L. (1981). Computers are for kids: Designing software programs. *Teaching Exceptional Children, 14,* 48–53.

Hancock, V., & Betts, F. (1994). From the lagging to the leading edge. *Educational Leadership, 51*(7), 24–29.

Hasselbring, T. S., Goin, L. I., & Bransford, J. D. (1988). Developing math automaticity in learning handicapped children: The role of computerized drill and practice. *Focus on Exceptional Children, 20*(6), 1–7.

Heller, H. W., Spooner, F., Anderson, D., & Mims, A. (1988). Homework: A review of special education classroom practices in the Southeast. *Teacher Education and Special Education, 11,* 43–51.

Horton, S. V., Lovitt, T. C., Givens, A., & Nelson, R. (1989). Teaching social studies to high school students with academic handicaps in a mainstreamed setting: Effects of a computerized study guide. *Journal of Learning Disabilities, 22,* 102–107.

Jenson, W. R., Sheridan, S. M., Olympia, D. E., & Andrews, D. (1994). Homework and students with learning disabilities and behavior disorders: A practical, parent-based approach. *Journal of Learning Disabilities, 27,* 538–548.

Joint Committee on Teacher Planning for Students with Disabilities. (1995). Planning for academic diversity in America's classrooms: Windows on reality, research, change, and practice. *Effective School Practices, 14*(2), 1–53.

Kagan, S. (1989/1990). The structural approach to cooperative learning. *Educational Leadership, 47*(4), 12–15.

Kay, P. J., Fitzgerald, M., Paradee, C., & Mellencamp, A. (1994). Making homework work at home: The parent's perspective. *Journal of Learning Disabilities, 27,* 550–561.

Keefe, C. H., & Candler, A. C. (1989). LD students and word processors: Questions and answers. *Learning Disabilities Focus, 4,* 78–83.

Lavoie, R. D. (1993, March). *Batteries are not included: Motivating the reluctant learner.* Paper presented at the Learning Disabilities Association International Conference, Washington, DC.

Lenz, B. K., Deshler, D. D., & Schumaker, J. B. (1990). *The development and validation of planning routines to enhance the delivery of content to students with handicaps in general education settings* (Progress report). Lawrence: University of Kansas Center for Research on Learning.

Levin, H., Glass, G., & Meister, C. (1984). *Cost-effectiveness of four educational interventions.* Stanford, CA: Institute for Research on Educational Finance and Governance, Stanford University.

Lindsey, J. D. (1987). *Computers and exceptional individuals.* Upper Saddle River, NJ: Merrill/Prentice Hall.

Maheady, L., Harper, G. F., & Mallette, B. (1991). Peer-mediated instruction: A review of potential applications for special education. *Reading, Writing, and Learning Disabilities International, 7,* 75–103.

Maheady, L., Harper, G. F., & Sacca, M. K. (1988). Peer-mediated instruction: A promising approach to meeting the diverse needs of LD adolescents. *Learning Disability Quarterly, 11,* 108–113.

Maheady, L., Sacca, M. K., & Harper, G. F. (1988). Classwide peer tutoring with mildly handicapped high school students. *Exceptional Children, 55,* 52–59.

Mainzer, R. W., Jr., Mainzer, K. L., Slavin, R. E., & Lowry, E. (1993). What special education teachers should know about cooperative learning. *Teacher Education and Special Education, 16,* 42–50.

Majsterek, D., & Wilson, R. (1993). Computer-assisted instruction (CAI): An update on applications for students with learning disabilities. *LD Forum, 19*(1), 19–21.

McKenzie, R. G., & Houk, C. S. (1986). The paraprofessional in special education. *Teaching Exceptional Children, 18,* 246–252.

Mims, A., Harper, C., Armstrong, S. W., & Savage, S. (1991). Effective instruction in homework for students with disabilities. *Teaching Exceptional Children, 24*(1), 42–44.

Miramontes, O. B. (1991). Organizing for effective paraprofessional services in special education: A multilingual/multiethnic instructional service team model. *Remedial and Special Education, 12*(1), 29–36.

Mueller, D. J., Chase, C. I., & Walden, J. D. (1988). Effects of reduced class size in primary classes. *Educational Leadership, 45*(5), 48–50.

Nicholls, J. G., McKenzie, M., & Shufro, J. (1994). Schoolwork, homework, life's work: The experience of students with and without learning disabilities. *Journal of Learning Disabilities, 27,* 562–569.

Olympia, D. E., Sheridan, S. M., & Jenson, W. R. (1994). Homework: A natural means of home-school collaboration. *School Psychology Quarterly, 9,* 60–80.

O'Melia, M. C., & Rosenberg, M. S. (1994). Effects of cooperative homework teams on the acquisition of mathematics skills by secondary students with mild disabilities. *Exceptional Children, 60,* 538–548.

Osguthorpe, R. T., & Scruggs, T. E. (1986). Special education students as tutors: A review and analysis. *Remedial and Special Education, 7*(4), 15–26.

Patton, J. R. (1994). Practical recommendations for using homework with students with learning disabilities. *Journal of Learning Disabilities, 27,* 570–578.

Peck, K. L., & Dorricott, D. (1994). Why use technology? *Educational Leadership, 51*(7), 11–14.

Robinson, G. E. (1990). Synthesis of research on class size. *Educational Leadership, 47*(7), 80–90.

Rosenberg, M. S. (1989). The effects of daily homework assignments on the acquisition of basic skills by students with learning disabilities. *Journal of Learning Disabilities, 22,* 314–323.

Salend, S. J., & Schliff, J. (1989). An examination of the homework practices of teachers of students with learning disabilities. *Journal of Learning Disabilities, 22,* 621–623.

Schloss, P. J., & Sedlak, R. A. (1986). *Instructional methods for students with learning and behavior problems.* Boston: Allyn & Bacon.

Scruggs, T. E., & Richter, L. (1985). Tutoring learning disabled students: A critical review. *Learning Disability Quarterly, 8,* 286–298.

Shuell, T. J., & Schueckler, L. M. (1988, April). *Toward evaluating software according to principles of learn-*

ing and teaching. Paper presented at the meeting of the American Educational Research Association, New Orleans.

Slavin, R. E. (1978). Student teams and achievement divisions. *Journal of Research and Development in Education, 12,* 39–49.

Slavin, R. E. (1986). *Using student team learning* (3rd ed.). Baltimore, MD: Center for Research on Elementary and Middle Schools, Johns Hopkins University.

Slavin, R. E. (1988). Synthesis of research on grouping in elementary and secondary schools. *Educational Leadership, 46*(1), 67–77.

Slavin, R. E. (1989/1990). Research on cooperative learning: Consensus and controversy. *Educational Leadership, 47*(4), 52–54.

Slavin, R. E. (1991). Synthesis of research on cooperative learning. *Educational Leadership, 48*(5), 71–82.

Slavin, R. E., Madden, N. A., & Stevens, R. J. (1990). Cooperative learning models for the 3 R's. *Educational Leadership, 47*(4), 22–28.

Slavin, R. E., Stevens, R. J., & Madden, N. A. (1988). Accommodating student diversity in reading and writing instruction: A cooperative learning approach. *Remedial and Special Education, 9*(1), 60–66.

Sprick, R. S. (1981). *The solution book: A guide to classroom discipline.* Blacklick, OH: SRA.

Sprick, R. S. (1991). *Discipline and responsibility: A team approach.* Eugene, OR: Teaching Strategies.

Torgesen, J. K., Waters, M. D., Cohen, A. L., & Torgesen, J. L. (1988). Improving sight-word recognition skills in LD children: An evaluation of three computer program variations. *Learning Disability Quarterly, 11,* 125–132.

Wiens, W. (1986). Computer assisted learning in the learning assistance centre. *B.C. Journal of Special Education, 10,* 17–28.

Woodward, J., & Carnine, D. (1988). Antecedent knowledge and intelligent computer-assisted instruction. *Journal of Learning Disabilities, 21,* 131–139.

Woodward, J., Carnine, D., & Gersten, R. (1988). Teaching problem solving through a computer simulation. *American Educational Research Journal, 25*(1), 72–86.

CHAPTER 3

Assessing Students for Instruction

Ysseldyke and Algozzine (1995, p. 198) aptly state the basic goal of assessment practices:

The ultimate goal of assessment is to identify problems with instruction and to lead to instructional modifications. A good share of present-day assessment activities consist of little more than meddling. . . . We must use assessment data to improve instruction. . . . The only way to determine the effectiveness of instruction is to collect data.

To aid instructional programming, assessment should provide information in two areas. First, information is needed to help the teacher select *what* to teach the individual student. Second, information is needed to help the teacher determine *how* to teach the student. When the teacher determines how the student learns best, he or she can arrange variables such as physical setup of the class, social interaction patterns, and reinforcement strategies to make the instructional program most effective.

Information for determining what and how to teach an individual is gathered by both formal and informal evaluation procedures. Formal evaluation consists of administering published norm-based standardized tests; informal evaluation typically involves nonstandardized assessment devices and procedures. Formal testing is used primarily to document and identify the particular problem and appropriate label (e.g., learning disability) of a student. Informal testing is used primarily to plan instruction and evaluate student progress continuously. Many educators prefer informal over formal assessment, and in recent years its popularity has grown (McLoughlin & Lewis, 1994). For example, the curriculum-based measurement section in this chapter presents an informal assessment approach that is receiving extensive attention. Each of the curriculum area chapters in this book discusses formal and informal assessment procedures.

☀ INDIVIDUALIZED PROGRAMMING: A CONTINUOUS PROCESS OF ASSESSMENT AND TEACHING

Individualized programming refers to an instructional program that enables the student to work on appropriate tasks or content over time under conditions that motivate. As noted in Chapter 1, individualized instruction can occur within various instructional arrangements, including seatwork, small groups, peer teaching, and large groups. The teacher matches the learner, the task, and instructional interventions to ensure optimal student growth. The process of individualized programming can be subdivided in numerous ways; the four steps presented in Table 3.1 cover the essential components.

Step I: Assess to Identify Target Skill or Content

The purpose of Step I is to determine *what* to teach the student. Successful instruction begins with the selection of an appropriate learning task. A teacher's thorough understanding of the instructional task or content is germane to effective teaching. To identify the target skill, the teacher first conducts an assessment. The tests for the assessment may be based on a variety of sources such as a scope and sequence skills list (see Appendix A) and may include criterion-referenced tests or teacher-made tests. The teacher analyzes the student's test performances to discover which specific skills have been mastered, and then he or she selects instructional objectives. These target skills should be described as precisely as possible. For example, an instructional objective in geography might be as follows: Given an unlabeled map of the world, the student will label the seven continents with 100 percent accuracy within 2 minutes. Once the initial instructional objectives are selected, subsequent objectives are derived from day-to-day assessment procedures.

Assessment for what to teach is required at all grade and age levels. The model presented in Figure 3.1 provides guidelines for assessment of what to teach.

Determine Scope and Sequence of Skills or Content to Be Taught Teachers frequently are responsible for determining short- and long-range instructional objectives in numerous curriculum areas (such as reading, math, science, and vocational education). To do this effectively, the teacher must understand the scope and sequence of skills or content in the curriculum areas. For example, a sixth-grade teacher may have students whose math skills span several grade levels; some students

TABLE 3.1
Four steps of individualized programming

Procedure	Example
Step I: Assess to identify target skill or content	Subtract two-digit number from three-digit number with double regrouping.
Step II: Determine factors likely to facilitate learning	Student is easily discouraged, especially when given a lot of work. Student continuously wants feedback on performance. Student has some difficulty with oral directions.
Step III: Plan instruction	Provide oral directions slowly and have student repeat them. Give practice seatwork that features a few items. Provide immediate feedback verbally when teaching and through self-correcting materials during seatwork.
Step IV: Begin daily data-managed instruction through three phases:	
Presentation Procedures	
Use an advance organizer	Use an advance organizer to connect the skill to prior learning, identify the skill, provide a rationale for the skill, and introduce the materials.
Describe and model	Break down the target skill into component parts and model or demonstrate the skill or subskill to the student while carefully explaining each step.
Practice Procedures	
Conduct guided practice	Have the student practice the selected task (skill or subskill) with guidance (such as instruction, cues, and prompts) from the teacher. Provide corrective feedback and reinforcement.
Conduct controlled practice to mastery	Have the student practice the selected task (skill or subskill) in controlled materials to a specified criterion. Provide corrective feedback and reinforcement.
Conduct independent practice	Have the student practice the total task to a mastery criterion. Provide corrective feedback and reinforcement.
Generalization and Independent Learning Procedures	
Use generalization training	To foster generalization, have the student practice the task presented in various materials (such as probes and general curriculum workbooks) and settings (such as resource room, general class, and home) to a specified criterion. Provide corrective feedback and reinforcement.
Use independent learning training	For independent active learning, have the student practice a task-specific learning strategy (such as self-questioning for comprehension). Encourage the student to use metacognitive strategies to self-regulate learning (e.g., use mnemonic devices to remember test-taking strategies).

need help with regrouping in two-digit subtraction problems, whereas others are working with decimals and percentages. A knowledge of scope and sequence skills gives the teacher a clear understanding of the skills a student has and has not mastered.

Task analysis can help teachers adopt, adapt, or make teaching materials. It is essential for determining the sequence of skills to be included in a material or program. Task analysis consists of dividing a learning project into parts to identify the

FIGURE 3.1

Assessment model for determining what to teach

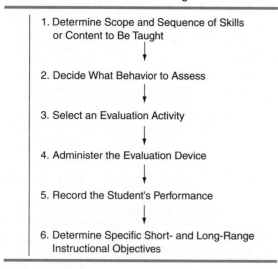

1. Determine Scope and Sequence of Skills or Content to Be Taught

2. Decide What Behavior to Assess

3. Select an Evaluation Activity

4. Administer the Evaluation Device

5. Record the Student's Performance

6. Determine Specific Short- and Long-Range Instructional Objectives

skills needed. The notion that learning is cumulative—that skills build upon one another—is basic in task analysis.

Task analysis uses precise instructional objectives because they allow the teacher to sequence instruction. A well-formulated objective for a task includes a condition (parameters of task), a criterion, and a terminal behavior. *Enabling behaviors* are the prerequisite skills for performing the specified behavior. Enabling behaviors are determined by working backward from the terminal behavior. This process builds a hierarchy of skills. Tasks can be examined according to difficulty level, temporal order, or developmental sequence (McLoughlin & Lewis, 1994). *Difficulty level* stresses teaching easy material prior to teaching more difficult material. The following example illustrates a difficulty level task analysis with the terminal behavior of reading a simple sentence:

Terminal behavior: Read a simple sentence.

Prerequisite skills:

1. Performs left-to-right eye movement.
2. Associates sounds of letters with symbols.
3. Blends sounds into words.
4. Reads words.

Temporal level refers to a sequence of tasks that have a logical temporal order. For example, teach-

ing the concept of place value should precede instruction in computation problems that require regrouping. A more apparent temporal task analysis consists of putting on a sock before putting on a shoe. A *developmental sequence* involves a gradual progression through subskills that build on one another. Learning math in the order of counting, addition, subtraction, multiplication, and division is an example of a developmental sequence.

Frank (1973) outlines four steps in task analysis: (1) clearly state the terminal behavior, (2) identify the subskills of the terminal behavior and sequence them from simple to complex, (3) informally assess to see which subskills the student already can perform, and (4) start teaching in sequential order, beginning with the easiest subskill that the student has not learned.

Commercial programs and criterion-referenced tests are good sources of scope and sequence skills lists. To be useful, a scope and sequence skills list should organize the sequence into component areas and present the major skills or content in each area. This type of list helps the teacher to grasp the total content or sequence and to see it in a hierarchical or logical nature. For each skill listed in a sequence, the teacher can develop a device or procedure for assessing it. For example:

Skill: Given the two base words on contractions, the student writes contractions.

Sample assessment item:

Write a contraction for:

1. can not   _____
2. you are   _____
3. they are   _____
4. we will   _____
5. I am   _____
6. he is   _____
7. do not   _____

Criterion 7/7

Scope and sequence skills lists that are useful in designing assessment programs are included in Appendix A. Lists are provided for reading, spelling, handwriting, written expression, and math. Although scope and sequence skills lists have content validity and logic, their content and ordering have not been confirmed through research.

Therefore, teachers should use their own judgment in selecting and adapting them.

Decide What Behavior to Assess   Deciding what behavior to assess begins at a global level and becomes specific. At the global level the area of assessment (such as spelling or reading) is selected, usually based on referral information, teacher observation, or results from standardized testing. Assessment at the global level involves sampling the student's behavior within a wide span of skills in the area. For reading, skills in word attack, word recognition, word comprehension, and passage comprehension may be sampled. Resources for constructing tests that assess across a span of skills include graded curriculum materials, scope and sequence skills lists, and standardized tests. Problem areas are identified, which helps the teacher select specific skill areas for further assessment. For example, the student may demonstrate a problem with word recognition in reading. Word recognition then becomes an area for specific skill testing. The specific skill assessment provides information that leads directly to determining instructional objectives (e.g., student needs to work on short vowel sounds). In summary, determining what behavior to assess follows four stages: (1) select global area, (2) conduct assessment across a wide span of skills, (3) note problem areas, and (4) conduct specific skill assessment.

Select an Evaluation Activity   The teacher has many choices in selecting evaluation activities: commercial tests, curriculum tests, portfolios, criterion-referenced skill inventories and checklists, and teacher-made instruments (e.g., a curriculum-based measurement device or an informal reading inventory). As the decision is being made, several factors are considered, including purpose, cost, time, and relevance of the activity or test for classroom instruction.

The teacher must consider whether the activity is for surveying a span of skills or for assessing a specific skill. If skill-span assessment is needed, the activity is usually noncontinuous (e.g., twice a year), whereas with specific skill assessment it is continuous (perhaps daily or weekly).

Specific skill assessment is used during the initial evaluation to determine instructional objectives. It also is used in daily instruction to evaluate a student's progress in specific skills. Because of its frequent use, the teacher must select activities that are easy to use and not time-consuming. Additional information on frequent assessment is provided in this chapter in the section on monitoring student performance.

Administer the Evaluation Device   The teacher usually administers the evaluation device for the initial assessment. As noted previously, the initial assessment involves evaluating both a wide span of skills and specific skills. Because this procedure involves much decision making (e.g., identifying problem areas, noting error patterns, and selecting specific skills for assessment), it usually is done by the teacher or a diagnostician. After the initial assessment is completed and instructional objectives are determined, procedures for monitoring progress are established. These procedures are usually easy to administer, score, and interpret. The teacher may assign this evaluation to the student, a teacher aide, a classroom volunteer, or a classmate. Many students enjoy monitoring their own progress.

It is important for the evaluator to establish rapport and to note the student's attitude. Because the teacher is trying to determine whether a student has mastered a skill, the evaluation can be administered flexibly. For example, if a student does not appear to be trying, the teacher may wish to stop the activity, talk with the student, and then start the activity from the beginning. During self-evaluation activities, the teacher must periodically check on the student to ensure that he or she is making serious efforts and following the correct procedures. When standardized tests are used primarily to obtain a quantitative score, the administration and scoring procedures are followed closely.

Record the Student's Performance   The teacher needs to record two types of student performance: performance on daily work and mastery of skills. Daily progress usually is recorded by means of teacher-made activities (such as spelling tests, learning charts, and performance on worksheets). Overall skill mastery usually is recorded on individual progress charts. Scope and sequence lists provide a good format for recording skill mastery. In addition, some commercial materials provide individual progress sheets for recording student performance. A detailed discussion of recordkeeping procedures is presented later in this chapter.

Determine Specific Short- and Long-Range Instructional Objectives After administering the assessment, the teacher must analyze the data and create instructional objectives. Good objectives specify the target behavior in observable terms, delineate the conditions under which the behavior occurs, and describe the criterion for successful performance. Short-term objectives should contribute directly to the mastery of long-term objectives. For example, the following short- and long-term objectives are related:

> *Long-term objective:* Given the graphemes of 44 phonemes, the student will say the correct phoneme with 90 percent accuracy.

> *Short-term objective:* Given the graphemes for consonant blends, the student will say the phoneme with 90 percent accuracy.

When the instructional objectives are established, the first step in individualized programming is achieved.

Step II: Determine Factors Likely to Facilitate Learning

This step focuses on determining *how* to teach the individual student. Knowing how to teach the student greatly increases the efficiency of instruction. For example, Tony's teacher may notice that Tony completes his seatwork much faster when responses do not require him to write small-sized letters or numbers. The teacher then can give Tony worksheets that provide large writing spaces, and his performance on seatwork tasks should improve. This type of information is obtained through sources and direct observation (e.g., interviewing the parents, chatting with the teacher, reading cumulative files, and using behavioral checklists); that is, it is obtained without administering standardized tests. A detailed discussion of assessment for determining how to teach is presented later in this chapter.

Step III: Plan Instruction

This step is guided by the tenet of data-based instruction; that is, any humane teaching procedure that produces appropriate progress toward instructional objectives is good teaching. This orientation reduces the time spent planning elaborate teaching methods because it stresses that good teaching is a function of student progress. Thus, a teacher uses fundamental teaching principles (discussed in Chapter 4) and monitors student progress to determine whether instructional changes are needed. However, the efficiency of instruction improves if the teacher is sensitive to learner behaviors that cue her or him on how to instruct the student. Thus, this step entails the development of a teaching plan that combines the *what to teach* information gathered in Step I with the *how to teach* information gathered in Step II. Chapters 2 and 4 present detailed discussions of instructional planning.

Step IV: Begin Daily Data-Managed Instruction

Teachers of students with learning problems encounter variable performances from many of their students. Teachers must know, however, whether a student is making adequate progress toward specified instructional objectives so that they can modify instructional procedures. Evaluation must be frequent and provide information for making instructional decisions. If a student masters a task, the teacher initiates a new task and repeats the teach–test–teach cycle. If a student does not master the task, four options are available for the teacher: repeating the same instructions, modifying the instructional procedures, introducing a new teaching strategy, or changing to an easier task. Again, when the teacher selects one of the options, the teach–test–teach cycle is repeated.

Typically, learning a new skill requires three progressive stages: acquisition, maintenance, and generalization. However, in their analysis of research on generalization, Deshler, Schumaker, and Lenz (1984) found that specific instructional tactics promote generalization. Therefore, they report that generalization may be conceptualized better as a framework for the entire instructional sequence than as a stage that the learner passes through after acquisition. The instructional sequence of presentation, guided practice, independent practice, generalization, and independent active learning includes the tactics that foster generalization. Chapter 4 features these instructional procedures, and Chapter 13 presents a detailed example of a similar teaching sequence that has been used successfully to teach low-achieving adolescents.

Although many teachers share common orientations, no two teachers teach exactly alike. They select from numerous theories, strategies, and techniques to create individual styles. In creating an individualized programming approach, the teacher strives to achieve optimum growth in each student. To accomplish this, instruction must be planned according to student progress—instructional decisions must be based on student performance data. Evidence exists that teachers' perceptions of student progress without learner data frequently are incorrect (Miramontes, Cheng, & Trueba, 1984; Utley, Zigmond, & Strain, 1987). It is not sufficient for a teacher to "feel" that an approach is effective. Evaluation results need to document the effectiveness of specific interventions. This book presents various ways of monitoring student progress. This chapter features procedures used in data-based instruction, which includes curriculum-based measurement and precision teaching. These procedures are among the most precise and effective techniques currently being applied in the classroom.

STAGES OF LEARNING

Numerous authorities present stages of student learning that are fundamental to designing and implementing effective instruction (Alberto & Troutman, 1999; Idol, 1993; D. D. Smith, 1981). Nelson and Polsgrove (1984) report that a database is emerging for the practice of matching teaching procedures to the student's stage of learning for a specific skill. Thus, teaching practices for each stage in the learning sequence are being recommended and evaluated.

Many educators believe that the entry-level learning stage is a critical factor in planning teaching activities. D. D. Smith (1981) presents the commonly recognized stages of learning. As featured in Figure 3.2, the stages include initial and advanced acquisition, proficiency, maintenance, generalization, and adaption. This section briefly describes the stages of learning and suggested teaching strategies for each.

FIGURE 3.2
Stages of learning

Source: Adapted from *Teaching the Learning Disabled* (p. 68), by D. D. Smith, 1981, Upper Saddle River, NJ: Prentice Hall. Copyright 1981 by Prentice-Hall Publishing Company. Reprinted by permission.

Acquisition Stage

During the acquisition stage, the learner performance ranges from 0 percent accuracy (i.e., no knowledge of how to perform the task) to a 90 to 100 percent range of accuracy. During this stage the instructional goal focuses on helping the student perform the skill accurately.

D. D. Smith (1981) recommends some major strategies for teaching a student at the acquisition stage. During initial acquisition, priming tactics are suggested, including rationales for learning a specific skill, physical guidance, shaping, demonstration, modeling, match-to-sample tasks, and cueing and prompting. Also, programming tactics are used during initial acquisition and feature backward and forward chaining and errorless learning. For the advanced acquisition stage, refinement tactics are used and feature feedback, specific directions, error correction, reward for accuracy, and criterion evaluation.

Proficiency Stage

In the proficiency stage, the learner attempts to learn the skill at an almost automatic level. The aim is for the student to perform the task both accurately and quickly. The tactics differ from those used at the acquisition stage. Tactics at this level focus on increasing performance speed.

Learning at the proficiency stage is enhanced by the use of goal setting, teacher expectations, rationales for increasing rate, positive reinforcement, and progress monitoring. Moreover, self-management is suggested for social skills development.

Maintenance Stage

After high levels of learning have occurred at the proficiency stage, the student enters the maintenance stage. The goal of instruction here is to maintain the high level of performance. Idol (1993) notes that students at this stage are expected to retain both accuracy and fluency with the skill once direct instruction or reinforcement has been withdrawn. Students with learning problems frequently encounter much difficulty at this stage because it requires retention (memory) of the skill. Tactics at this stage concentrate on maintaining high levels of learning.

Learning during the maintenance stage involves periodic practice; however, for the student with learning problems, practice is not always suffi-

cient and other tactics are necessary. Maintenance and retention are also fostered by overlearning, mnemonic techniques, intermittent schedules of reinforcement, social reinforcement, and intrinsic reinforcement (self-management).

Generalization Stage

During the generalization stage, the learner performs the skill in different times and situations. This means that the student demonstrates proficiency in the skill in different settings (e.g., at home, in the classroom, and at work) and with different people (e.g., the learning disabilities teacher, general classroom teacher, parent, and boss). Generalization is an area of great difficulty for many students with learning problems and, unfortunately, remains an area of limited research (D. D. Smith & Luckasson, 1992). Investigators have discovered that generalization does not automatically occur with students who have learning problems—it must be systematically taught. Alberto and Troutman (1999) refer to the learning stages within the context of a response hierarchy. They maintain that the functional use of the learned response increases as the student's learning progresses from acquisition to maintenance. Thus, acquisition, proficiency, and maintenance appear to be prerequisites of generalization. (Chapter 4 discusses generalization.)

Adaption Stage

In the adaption stage, the learner applies a previously learned skill in a new area of application without direct instruction or guidance. Simply, this skill may be referred to as problem solving. To illustrate, problem solving occurs when a student who has mastered multiplication facts "discovers" that division is the reverse of multiplication and proceeds to answer division facts accurately and independently. D. D. Smith (1981) maintains that students with learning problems are rarely taught adaption-level skills, despite their importance.

Commentary on Learning Stages

Unfortunately, research documenting successful approaches for developing generalization and problem-solving skills is limited. Most studies document effectiveness only for short-term effects; however, some research in skill generalization appears promising. For example, Idol (1993) reports on eight projects in which generalization occurred through the use of behavioral tactics. Other investigators (Lloyd, Saltzman, & Kauffman, 1981; Schumaker, Deshler, Alley, & Warner, 1983) are using behavioral tactics in teaching rule or strategy learning, with positive results regarding generalization.

Combinations of the behavioral approach with other approaches (e.g., cognitive) are being used to teach higher order skills (Berliner, 1989; Deshler & Lenz, 1989; Graham & Harris, 1994). (Chapters 4 and 13 present techniques for teaching students to be independent learners and problem solvers.)

☀ MONITORING STUDENT PERFORMANCE FOR DETERMINING WHAT TO TEACH

During instruction, the teacher decides whether the task difficulty level is appropriate; that is, the student should perform the task without prolonged failure or frustration. Earned success is a key concept in monitoring task difficulty. The student must view the task as demanding enough to realize some sense of accomplishment when it is completed.

Data-based instruction focuses on the direct and continuous measurement of student progress toward specific instructional objectives. It is a widely used teaching approach that features the interactive nature of assessment and instruction, and it illustrates the dynamic and ongoing process involved in determining and monitoring what to teach. Data-based instruction has roots in applied behavior analysis, precision teaching, direct instruction, and criterion-referenced instruction. Many educators (Alberto & Troutman, 1999; Howell & Nolet, 2000; Kerr & Nelson, 1998) concur that it holds much promise for both current and future teaching practices.

Research in curriculum-based assessment (CBA) has provided a renewed impetus for data-based instruction. *CBA* refers to any approach that uses direct observation and recording of a student's performance in the school curriculum as a basis for obtaining information to make instructional decisions (Deno, 1987). Within this model, *curriculum-based measurement (CBM)* refers to the use of specific procedures whereby a student's academic skills are assessed from repeated rate samples using stimulus materials taken from the student's curriculum. The primary uses of CBM are to establish district or classroom performance standards, identify students who need special instruction, and monitor individual student progress toward long-range goals.

Using Curriculum-Based Measurement to Establish Performance Standards

When CBM is used to establish performance standards, measures are developed from the school curriculum and administered to all the students in a target group (e.g., all fourth graders in a school or district). The results provide data to determine standards of performance. Using CBM to establish standards involves four components: (1) material selection, (2) test administration, (3) performance display and interpretation, and (4) decision-making framework (Tindal & Marston, 1990).

Material Selection   Selecting appropriate material from the school curriculum begins the assessment process. Appropriate material is at the level the teacher expects the student to master by the end of the school year and may include the following:

- Reading—200 word passages from a fourth-grade-level basal book without poetry, exercises, or excessive dialogue.
- Spelling—all words from a fourth-grade spelling curriculum proportionally divided into alternate test forms.
- Math—alternate forms of 36 randomly selected computation problems that proportionally represent the fourth-grade math curriculum.

The object is to select several samples of the school curriculum in a respective academic area and administer them to all students. A comparison of all students on the same measure provides a norm-referenced database for making instructional decisions.

Test Administration   Administration procedures include using standardized formats and scoring performance in terms of rate correct per minute. A sample reading administration format includes the following steps:

1. Randomly select a passage from the goal-level material.

2. Place it in front of and facing the student.
3. Keep a copy for the examiner.
4. Provide directions.
5. Have the student read orally for 1 minute.
6. Score the student's performance in terms of number of words read correctly, and note errors for instructional purposes.

It is helpful to administer two or three passages and record the average score.

Performance Display and Interpretation

When all students in the grade or class are tested and the average score for each student is computed, the teacher can develop a plot of the entire group. Guidelines for developing a box plot are presented in Table 3.2, and Figure 3.3 presents sample box plots of 31 fifth-grade students. The top and bottom Ts represent the 90th and 10th percentiles. The box includes the middle 50 percent of the population, with the bottom line representing the 25th percentile, the top line representing the 75th percentile, and the middle line representing the 50th percentile.

The circles outside of the 10th and 90th percentiles are individuals with extreme values. The data from this sample reveal that some students read very poorly and probably need to receive specialized services (e.g., Title I or special education), whereas other students are extremely fluent in the material. The two passages were selected according to grade-level readability, but the average for Passage A, 152 words read correctly, is significantly higher than the average for Passage B, 137 words read correctly. Thus, an important consideration in

FIGURE 3.3
Box plots of oral reading fluency for a fifth-grade class

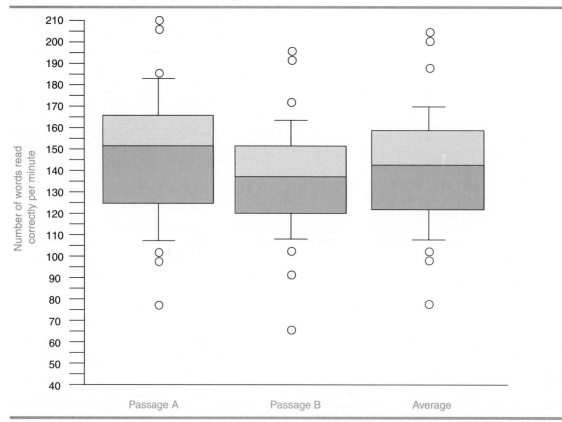

TABLE 3.2
Guidelines for developing a box plot

Step 1: Rank the scores from highest to lowest.

Step 2: Determine the percentage value of a single score. Compute each score's value by dividing 1 by the total number of scores. For example, in a ranking of 31 scores, each score equals approximately 3.2% (1/31 = .032).

Step 3: Determine the points in the ranking for 90%, 75%, 25%, and 10%. Because each score in a ranking of 31 student scores is worth 3.2%, the top three scores account for the highest 10%. A line drawn immediately under the third score represents the 90% level. Using the same procedure, a line drawn under the eighth score (3.2 × 8 = 25.6%) represents the 75% level.

	Example:	181	
		180	
		178	90% level
		164	
		161	
		159	
		153	
		150	75% level
		149	

(149 through 62—lowest of 31 scores)

Step 4: Find the median score (50th percentile). The median is the middle score. It represents the score at which 50% of the scores are below it and 50% of the scores are above it. It takes three steps to find the median: (1) rank-order the scores, (2) count the total number of scores, and (3) divide the total number of scores so that one score is in the middle. For an odd number of scores, the score in the middle in the median. For an even number of scores, the median is interpolated by computing the average of the two middle scores.

Step 5: Use the 90%, 75%, 25%, and 10% levels as well as the average to draw the box plot on a graph. Plot individual scores above 90% and below 10%. For example:

Step 6: Interpret the box plot for grouping students, planning instruction, establishing long-range goals, setting standards (such as establishing mastery criteria), or identifying students who need special help.

using this system is to sample multiple passages to minimize differing levels of difficulty that exist from passage to passage.

Decision-Making Framework   These data enable teachers to identify low performers who need special instruction, divide students into instructional groups, plan instructional programs, and establish long-range goals. Hall and Tindal (1989) used this type of assessment to create three reading groups (low group—below 16th percentile, middle group—between 16th and 84th percentile, and high group—above 84th percentile).

For teachers who work with low-performing and special education students, however, the real power of this assessment system is its applicability in establishing a formative evaluation system. By administering successively lower or higher level materials from other grade levels and comparing performance to the normative levels for those grades, it is possible to establish both current functioning and appropriate goal-level functioning. Rather than placing students into an instructional material according to the percentage correct, as is done with informal reading inventories, a placement validated through research can be made by placing the student in the level in which he or she is most comparable to others. For example, if a fifth-grade student performs most closely to students who are using a third-grade reading material, placement in this material is justified; furthermore, judgments of appropriate goals can be established (e.g., successful performance in fourth-grade material by the end of the school year).

Individually Referenced Data Systems

Since Lindsley (1964, 1971) introduced precision teaching about 25 years ago, many educators have recognized the value of data-based instruction. Other systems that use the methodology of applied behavior analysis to develop data-based instructional procedures include Exceptional Teaching (White & Haring, 1980), Data-Based Program Modification (Deno & Mirkin, 1977), and Individually Referenced CBA (Tindal & Marston, 1990). The salient features of all of these systems are direct measurement, repeated measurement, graphing data, long-range goal performance monitoring, short-range goal performance monitoring, and data analysis and instructional decisions.

Direct Measurement   One of the most important features of data-based instruction (individually referenced CBM) is its emphasis on direct, continuous, and precise measurement of behavior. Direct measurement entails focusing on relevant classroom behaviors (e.g., oral reading rate or math computation rate).

Repeated Measurement   Repeated measurement requires that a behavior be counted and recorded over a period of time. Howell, Kaplan, and O'Connell (1979) note that performance is a single measure of behavior on one occasion, whereas learning is a change in performance over time. When more than one performance is recorded, the teacher can tell whether the student is staying the same, getting better, or regressing. As more data are gathered, a teacher's perception of learning becomes more accurate. Such continuous data help the teacher make daily instructional decisions.

Kerr and Nelson (1998) provide some practical guidelines for adjusting the frequency of monitoring:

- Use session-by-session (one or more daily) recording when student progress is rapid through a small-step sequence.
- Use daily recording when student behavior fluctuates and daily program adjustments are needed.
- Use daily recording when the daily progress of the student is needed for intervention modifications.
- Use biweekly or weekly probes when student progress is slow.
- Use biweekly or weekly probes when general monitoring of behavior is needed and frequent program adjustments are not needed.
- Use biweekly, weekly, or monthly probes when evaluating maintenance of generalization of previously mastered skills.

Although daily measurement provides the best data for making teaching decisions, research indicates that twice-weekly monitoring of academic performance is as effective as daily monitoring for promoting academic achievement (Fuchs, 1986).

In addition to the most common practice of recording permanent products, a variety of observational recording techniques is available. Recording techniques are presented in Table 3.3 and include event recording, interval recording, time sampling,

TABLE 3.3
Observational recording techniques

Technique	Data Collection Method	Example	Illustration	Summary Data
Event Recording Focus: Frequency of behavior Aim: Increase or decrease frequency of behavior Advantages: Provides exact count of behavior occurrences Ease of data collection (e.g., tallies on card) Suitable to recording academic responses (e.g., tallies of reading errors)	Record each observed occurrence of behavior.	Count the number of times a student completed assignments for five school days.	Assignments Day Due Completed 1 5 // 2 4 // 3 5 /// 4 6 /// 5 7 ///// 27 16	Total number (frequency): 16 Number of assignments completed out of total assignments: 16/27
Interval Recording Focus: Frequency of behavior Aim: Increase or decrease frequency of behavior Advantages: Can observe several behaviors or students simultaneously Good for very high frequency behaviors	Divide a specified observation period into equal intervals that are typically 30 seconds or less. Within each interval, record whether the behavior occurred (+) or did not occur (–) at any time during the interval.	Record whether or not a student was "attending" to the seatwork materials at some time during the interval.	1 minute 1 minute + – + + + – + + + – + + – – + +	Percentage of time in which the student exhibited the behavior $$\frac{\text{Number of intervals attending}}{\text{Total number of intervals}} = 5/8 = 62.5\%$$
Time Sampling Focus: Frequency of behavior Aim: Increase or decrease frequency of behavior Advantages: Can observe several behaviors or students simultaneously Can record behavior without continuously observing	Divide specified observation period into equal intervals of several minutes or more duration. Observe at the end of each interval and record whether the behavior occurred (+) or did not occur (–).	Record whether a student was or was not "on task" at the end of every 5 minutes during a 40 minute period.	40 minutes + – + + – – + +	Percentage of time the student exhibited the behavior: $$\frac{\text{Number of intervals on task}}{\text{Total number of intervals}} = 4/8 = 50\%$$
Duration Recording Focus: Duration of behavior Aim: Increase or decrease duration of behavior Advantages: Provides the amount or percentage of time the student engages in behavior	Record the amount of time the student is engaged in the activity during the observation period. Turn a stopwatch on when the activity starts, and turn it off when the activity is over. Repeat this process throughout the observation period.	Record the amount of engaged time the student spent on the math assignment.	Observation time: 10:00–10:30 Start Stop Duration (minutes) 10:04 10:08 4 10:11 10:16 5 10:21 10:23 2 10:26 10:30 4 15	Percentage of time the student engaged in the activity: $$\frac{\text{Number of minutes engaged}}{\text{Total number of minutes}} = 15/30 = 50\%$$

(continued on the next page)

TABLE 3.3
(continued)

Technique	Data Collection Method	Example	Illustration	Summary Data
Latency Recording Focus: Duration of latency behavior Aim: Increase or decrease latency duration Advantages: Easily collected Provides data on how long it takes student to begin appropriate activity Provides data on how long student can delay response (e.g., going to bathroom)	Record the time it takes for a student to begin an activity once the antecedent stimulus (signal) has been provided. Turn a stopwatch on after the signal to begin an activity has been provided, and turn it off when the student begins the activity.	Record the amount of time it took a student to get his or her reading book and join the reading group after being instructed to do so.	Signal Begin Latency (minutes) 11:02 11:05 3 11:03 11:06 3 11:01 11:02 1 11:04 11:07 3 10:59 11:01 2 12	Daily average of time lapse between being told to begin and actually beginning: $\dfrac{\text{Latency time}}{\text{Number of days}} = 12 \div 5 = 2.4$ minutes
Anecdotal Recording Focus: Complete description of student's behaviors Aim: Determine which behaviors are important for designing intervention and determine tactics to enhance intervention Advantages: Provides data that facilitate the development of instructional objectives and interventions	Record all behaviors of the student during a specified time period.	Record behaviors displayed during science laboratory period.	Time: 1:05 Antecedent: Teacher passes out lab materials and explains experiment. Behavior: Sally stares out the window. She talks to students around her. Consequence: Teacher talks to Sally about the experiment.	Narrative report.
Permanent Product Recording Focus: Student outcomes that result in a permanent product (e.g., written work or tape)—most common recording procedure used by teachers (e.g., math papers, book reports, and projects) Aim: Monitor student progress and provide feedback on correct and incorrect responses Advantages: Easy to collect Teacher does not have to observe student directly Provides data on student progress Extremely versatile (e.g., useful in all content areas) Sample of behavior is a durable product May be recorded at teacher's convenience	Collect assignments and provide feedback regarding correct and incorrect responses.	Collect spelling papers and return with percentage correct on top of paper. 60% correct Spelling Test 1. ~~~~~~ 2. ~~~~~~ 3. ~~~~~~	Number correct (frequency) Percentage correct: $\dfrac{\text{Number correct}}{\text{Total number}} \times 100$ Rate correct/incorrect per minute

duration recording, latency recording, anecdotal recording, and permanent product recording. The observation techniques are especially useful in assessing classroom behavior that is related to academic success. (For more detailed descriptions of recording techniques, see Alberto and Troutman [1999], Howell and Nolet [2000], or Kerr and Nelson [1998].)

Graphing Data   For data to be useful, the information must be displayed in an easy-to-read format. This involves creating a visual display so that raw data can be analyzed. In data-based instruction, graphing is the most common method of presenting data. Kerr and Nelson (1998) report that graphs serve three important purposes: (1) they summarize data in a manner that leads to daily decision making, (2) they communicate intervention effects, and (3) they provide feedback and reinforcement to the learner and teacher.

Data must be converted into a form that allows for consistent graphing. Basically, this involves reporting three types of data: number correct, percentage (the number of correct responses divided by the total number of responses and then multiplied by 100), or rate (the number correct divided by the time).

The basic format for graphing is a *line graph* that includes two axes. The horizontal axis is the abscissa, or *x*-axis. The vertical axis is the ordinate, or *y*-axis. As shown in Figure 3.4, the *x*-axis is used to record the time factor (i.e., the observation period). The *y*-axis is used to record performance on the target behavior. An example of a line graph on equal-interval graph paper is presented in Figure 3.5.

A *bar graph* uses vertical bars to display data (i.e., vertical bars represent levels of performance). A bar graph is easy to interpret and provides the teacher and student with a clear

FIGURE 3.4
Sample *x*- and *y*-axes

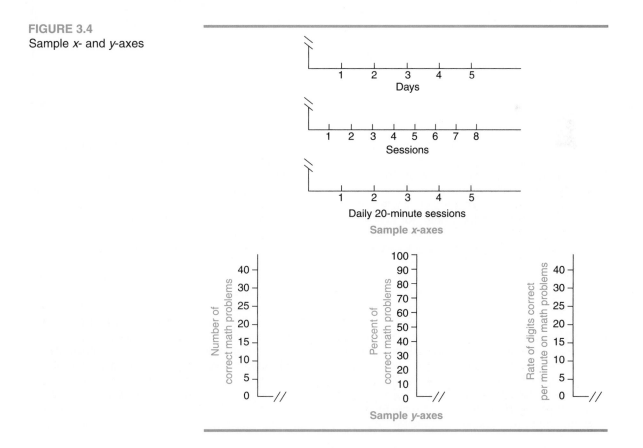

FIGURE 3.5
Sample line graph

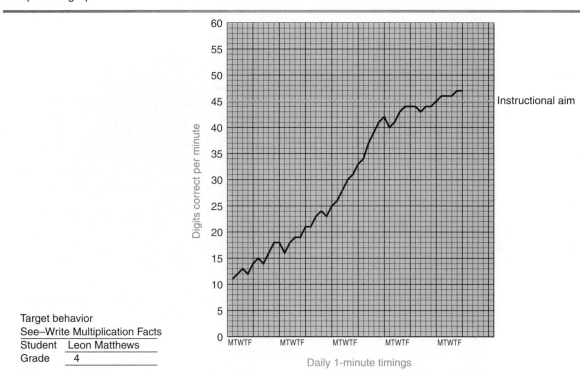

Target behavior
See–Write Multiplication Facts
Student   Leon Matthews
Grade   4

picture of performance. Figure 3.6 shows some sample bar graphs.

Another type of graph, the *ratio graph,* is particularly suited to charting rate data. Data for ratio graphing are converted into rate per minute and are charted on a semilogarithmic grid. Number of correct and incorrect responses on an instructional target (such as see word—say word) for a specified time period (frequently 1 minute) provides the data for the graph. Such graphs are a major tool of applied behavior analysis or, more specifically, precision teaching.

Long-Range Goal Performance Monitoring
Individually referenced CBM procedures typically use *performance monitoring charts.* These charts display progress toward a long-range instructional goal. Measurement usually occurs twice weekly from a random sample of a pool of items that measure the same skill. The items represent the goal

level the student wants to attain by the end of the semester or year. Figure 3.7 presents a CBM long-range goal performance monitoring chart. The student's baseline includes the first three data points. The needed rate of improvement is displayed by the broken goal line. It begins at the baseline median at the end of two weeks and proceeds to the goal proficiency criterion on the twentieth week. The ten scores after the first vertical intervention line represent the student's progress under Intervention A. The trend line superimposed over these scores is an estimate of the student's rate of improvement. When the trend line is compared with the goal line, it is apparent that the student's progress is too slow and an instructional modification is needed. The second vertical line represents a new intervention. Because the data points after Intervention B display an improved rate of progress consistent with reaching the goal on time, the teacher maintains Intervention B. If

FIGURE 3.6
Sample bar graphs

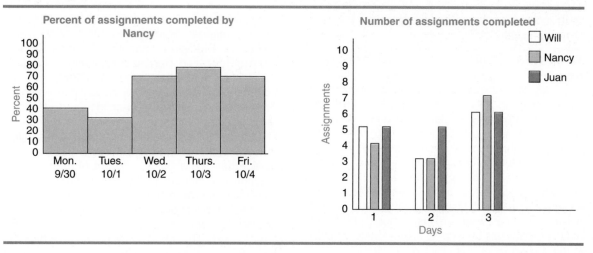

FIGURE 3.7
Long-range goal performance monitoring chart

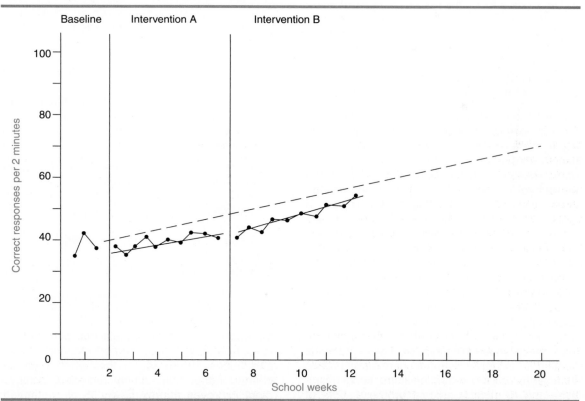

Source: From *Students with Learning Disabilities* (p. 286), 5th ed., by C. D. Mercer, 1997, Upper Saddle River, NJ: Merrill/Prentice Hall. Copyright 1997 by Prentice-Hall Publishing Company. Reprinted by permission.

113

the trend line is steeper than the goal line, the goal proficiency criterion is increased.

Short-Range Goal Performance Monitoring Another type of chart, a *mastery monitoring chart,* is used to monitor progress on successive short-term goals. When the student masters a short-term goal, a new goal is established, and monitoring continues through a series of short-term goals. The pool of measurement items changes each time the student masters a goal. Although mastery monitoring requires additional teacher work, it has several advantages: the charting system reflects traditional curriculum skill hierarchies, a close tie exists between instruction and measurement, and information is available on what to teach. Mastery monitoring is used widely in precision teaching.

Specifically, in precision teaching, the teacher performs the following steps:

1. Selects a target behavior
2. Develops a task sheet or probe for evaluation of student progress in daily timings
3. Graphs the data two to five times a week and sets instructional aims that correspond to a standard of fluency
4. Designs the instructional program
5. Analyzes data and makes instructional decisions

Target behaviors usually are determined by administering probe sheets. These sheets include academic tasks and are used to sample the student's behavior. Typically, the student works on the probe sheet for 1 minute, and the teacher records the rate of correct and incorrect responses and notes any error patterns. Figure 3.8 displays a probe sheet of a task for assessing addition facts with sums to 9. The instructional objective usually is not established until the student has performed the task on the probe sheet several times. This provides a more reliable index of the student's performance than one test. The original assessment probe may be used, or a new probe sheet can be designed to stress specific facts (e.g., addition involving zero).

Several materials are available for implementing a precision teaching system. These materials contain an extensive list of academic skill probes that can be used to determine instructional objectives and to monitor student progress. One of these materials is *A Resource Manual for the Development and Evaluation of Special Programs for Exceptional Students* (Volume V-D: Techniques of Precision Teaching), Florida Department of Education, Bureau of Education for Exceptional Students, Tallahassee, FL 32399.

Precision teachers record student performances and graph the results. The chart in Figure 3.9 shows math progress across several skills, and changes in performance are displayed proportionally. In this procedure, the relative rate of learning is more apparent than the absolute amount of learning. For example, if a student's rate of writing multiplication facts increases from 10 per minute to 20 per minute in a week, the rate of change ($\times$2) is as great as that of a student who goes from 20 to 40 in the same time period. The chart also provides space for recording raw data. This helps in checking the chart and enables the student to note progress by examining the slope of the raw data.

Teachers who prefer a simple graph can use an equal-interval chart, as illustrated in Figure 3.5. This kind of chart can be drawn on square-ruled graph paper. The teacher records the frequency of the behavior along the vertical axis and the number of sessions or timings on the horizontal axis. An example of an equal-interval chart on unlined paper is presented in Figure 3.10. Two advantages of equal-interval charts are that they are easy to understand and easy to obtain.

The value of using graphs is recognized for several reasons:

- Graphs provide a visual description of data and reduce large amounts of data.
- Graphs simplify the presentation of results and facilitate communication of program results and student learning.
- Graphs reflect important characteristics of performance.
- Graphs facilitate the use of data to plan and modify instruction.
- Graphs provide informational and often motivational feedback.

Moreover, research suggests that achievement is associated with graphed performances. Fuchs and Fuchs (1986) report that when data are charted rather than simply recorded, achievement improves approximately .5 of a standard deviation unit.

FIGURE 3.8
Probe sheet used to present addition facts—sums to 9

Name _____ Correct _____ Error _____

Date _____ Comments _____

6 + 2	5 + 3	4 + 4	9 + 0	8 + 1	2 + 7	5 + 0
8 + 0	4 + 3	1 + 1	3 + 2	5 + 2	3 + 6	5 + 4
7 + 1	4 + 2	3 + 3	8 + 1	7 + 0	2 + 5	4 + 0
1 + 0	3 + 1	2 + 2	6 + 1	5 + 4	1 + 6	0 + 0
3 + 4	2 + 4	2 + 1	3 + 1	3 + 0	4 + 5	5 + 1
6 + 3	7 + 2	1 + 2	1 + 3	1 + 4	1 + 5	1 + 8

Data Analysis and Instructional Decisions
Instructional aims or goals provide the student and teacher with a framework to analyze data and evaluate student progress. When instructional aims are expressed in terms of percent correct, it generally is accepted that 80 percent correct responses represent mastery. The instructional aim also may be expressed in terms of rate. Rate is equal to the number of movements divided by the number of minutes observed. In precision teaching, the instructional aim usually is defined in terms of rate of correct and incorrect responses per minute. In CBM, it usually is defined according to rate of correct responses per minute only. Rate

is a sensitive ratio measure that readily reflects the effects of instructional interventions.

Ideally, the aim should represent a mastery level of the skill. Data concerning rates that reflect mastery (i.e., proficiency) in academic tasks have long been lacking. Although disagreement still exists concerning proficiency-level rates, enough data (Howell & Nolet, 2000; Mercer, Mercer, & Evans, 1982) are available to suggest proficiency-level trends on selected academic tasks.

Certain learner characteristics, such as age, grade level, and achievement level, influence the establishment of appropriate aims. Because research has not conclusively determined specific

FIGURE 3.9
Proportional chart showing math progress across several skills

FIGURE 3.10
Equal-interval chart

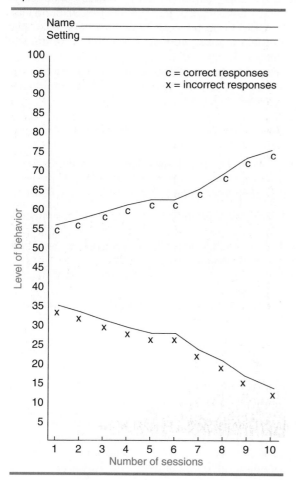

aims for academic tasks, teachers must use their own judgment in setting aims with individual students. One way of facilitating aim selection is to collect rate data from students who are achieving satisfactorily and use their performances as aims (see the section on using CBM to establish performance standards), or the teacher can perform the task and use a proportion of this performance as an aim. Another way to determine goal level is to obtain two of three or three of three scores on similar grade-level passages within the 55-to-75 words per minute correct range and locate the median of these three baseline scores. If the student is being measured at or above third-grade

reader level, multiply the number of weeks in the instructional period by 2 and add this to the baseline median score. For example:

(Weeks × 2) + Baseline median = Goal
(30 × 2) + 60
60 + 60 = 120 words per minute

If the student is being measured below the third-grade reader level, multiply the number of weeks in the instructional period by 1.5 and add this to the baseline median score. For example:

(Weeks × 1.5) + Baseline median = Goal
(30 × 1.5) + 60
45 + 60 = 105 words per minute

In addition to using performance standards (provided in the curriculum area chapters), peer assessment, or student baseline to establish instructional aims, the teacher may use the adult/child proportional formula (Koorland, Keel, & Ueberhorst, 1990):

$$\frac{\text{Student aim (to be computed)}}{\text{Student tool skill rate}} = \frac{\text{Adult task performance rate}}{\text{Adult tool skill rate}}$$

For example:

Student tool skill rate =
see/write 70 correct digits per minute

Adult task performance rate =
see/write 80 correct math facts digits per minute

Adult tool skill rate =
see/write 130 correct digits per minute

$$\frac{x}{70} = \frac{80}{130}$$

$x = (70 \times 80) \div 130$; $x = 5{,}600 \div 130$; $x = 43.07$
Student aim = 43 correct math facts digits per minute

Charted data enable the teacher to determine whether the student is making acceptable progress. Data analysis is enhanced when it is charted to display both baseline data (i.e., present levels of performance) and intervention data (i.e., data gathered during intervention). Each time an intervention change is made, a vertical line is drawn on the chart to indicate the change. The purpose of charting data is to help the teacher make accurate decisions about teaching strategies (e.g., when to continue or change a procedure). Significant learning patterns often emerge that enable the teacher to find possible reasons for success or failure and make decisions based on data. The most desirable pattern is clear-cut: an increase in the rate of appropriate or correct responses and a decrease in the rate of inappropriate or incorrect responses.

Students with learning problems often are identified because they have difficulty keeping up with instruction. These students fall further and further behind. Analyzing a student's learning pattern can help identify learning problems so that the teacher can make appropriate decisions about instruction.

Changes in student performance over time can be assessed with several specific measures (see Figure 3.11):

- *Level of performance*—refers to immediate changes in level of performance that occur when an intervention is introduced.
- *Slope*—refers to the rate of change in a trend line that reflects the values of the data points.
- *Variability*—refers to the inconsistency of performance.
- *Overlap*—refers to data values that are common across different interventions.

An additional measure, quantification of weekly rate, involves determining the weekly rate and comparing with the performance aim rate. For example, if the weekly rate of improvement is 2.5 words read correctly per minute and the aim is 2.0, then the student is making good progress. The procedure to quantify the weekly rate of improvement is to (1) find the value on the vertical axis of the median of the last three data points, (2) find the value on the vertical axis of the median of the first three data points, and (3) subtract the end value from the beginning value and divide the difference by the number of weeks of instruction.

Research supports the use of rules for making decisions when analyzing the data. Fuchs and Fuchs (1986) found that formative evaluation involving data-utilization rules is associated with an average increase in student achievement of .5 standard deviation over formative evaluation without such rules. An example of a rule is the three-day rule, in which the teacher makes an instruc-

tional modification if the student's progress is unsatisfactory (i.e., below aim) for three consecutive days. Fuchs, Fuchs, and Hamlett (1989) found that for CBM to be most effective, teachers must use the data to evaluate instruction and make modifications. Tindal and Marston (1990) provide a detailed discussion of data-analysis techniques and decision rules for goal-oriented and treatment-oriented decision making.

Basic Guidelines for Monitoring Student Performance

Howell et al. (1979) offer numerous guidelines for implementing data-based instruction. They note that such instruction is most successful when:

- The teacher initially counts only priority behaviors.
- The teacher identifies strategies to facilitate timing and recording behaviors.
- The teacher evaluates the recorded data frequently.
- The teacher uses probes or curriculum-referenced testing.
- The system remains a tool for teaching rather than a "cause" and is only used as long as it helps the student.

Howell et al. also list the following strategies to facilitate timing and recording behaviors:

- The teacher can take group timings, especially on written activities. Some teachers, for example, time 1-minute handwriting samples, 1-minute math fact sheets, and 1-minute spelling activities.
- Students can record time stopped and started. This can be done easily with a rubber stamp of a clock on the students' worksheets.
- A kitchen timer or prerecorded tape can be used to time sessions.
- Students can work together and time and record data for one another. This works well with flash-card drills.
- Students can read into a tape recorder. Teachers later can record correct and error rates for either samples of behavior or the total session.
- Mechanical counters can be used. Single- and dual-tally counters as well as beads and golf score counters are available.

FIGURE 3.11
Four measures of change in student performance over time

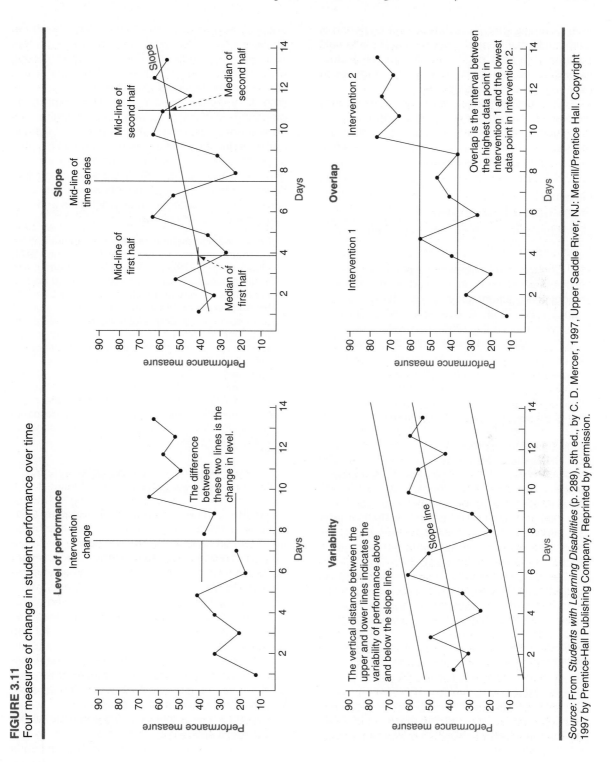

Source: From *Students with Learning Disabilities* (p. 289), 5th ed., by C. D. Mercer, 1997, Upper Saddle River, NJ: Merrill/Prentice Hall. Copyright 1997 by Prentice-Hall Publishing Company. Reprinted by permission.

- Counting should be done for a fixed period of time each day. Counting for different intervals confuses the data pattern because such factors as endurance, boredom, and latency of response may enter into the data analysis.
- One-minute timings can be used because they are easy to chart and no rate plotter is necessary.
- Aides, peers, student teachers, and volunteers can be trained to help develop materials and to count and record behaviors.

Commentary on Data-Based Instruction

Highlights of research on data-based approaches include the following:

- Considerable evidence supports the positive association between data-based monitoring and student achievement gains (Fuchs, 1986; Fuchs & Fuchs, 1986; Rieth & Evertson, 1988; Tindal & Marston, 1990; White, 1986). In a meta-analysis of formative evaluations, Fuchs and Fuchs found that data-based programs that monitored student progress and evaluated instruction systematically produced .7 standard deviation higher achievement than nonmonitored instruction. This represents a gain of 26 percentage points. Moreover, White reports outstanding gains for students involved in precision teaching programs.
- CBM measures have good reliability and validity (Fuchs, 1986; Fuchs, Fuchs, & Maxwell, 1988; Howell & Nolet, 2000; Tindal & Marston, 1990).
- Self-selected goals yield better performance than assigned goals (Fuchs, Bahr, & Rieth, 1989).
- When teachers establish moderately to highly ambitious goals, students achieve better (Fuchs, Fuchs, & Deno, 1985).
- CBM combined with classwide peer tutoring has proven to be an effective practice for classes of diverse learners (Joint Committee on Teacher Planning for Students with Disabilities, 1995).

In a national survey of 136 learning disabilities teachers, Wesson, King, and Deno (1984) found that the majority (53.6 percent) of the 110 teachers who knew of direct and frequent measurement used it; however, those who did not use it believed it was too time-consuming. The position that data-based instruction is time-consuming is prominent among users and nonusers of direct

and frequent measurement; however, Wesson et al. report that direct and frequent measurement does not need to be so. Fuchs, Wesson, Tindal, Mirkin, and Deno (1981) report the results of a study in which teachers were trained to reduce the time they spend in direct measurement (e.g., preparing, directing, scoring, and graphing) by 80 percent. According to Wesson et al., "Trained and experienced teachers require only two minutes to prepare for, administer, score, and graph student performance" (p. 48). They also report that direct and frequent measurement is no more time-consuming than other evaluation activities,and they sum up the issue as follows (p. 48):

> Since related research reveals that frequent measurement involves achievement (Bohannon, 1975; Mirkin et al., 1979), the proposition that direct and frequent measurement is a waste of critical instructional time is without a factual basis. . . . Given its benefits, direct and frequent measurement must be used on a more widespread basis in special education. One implication of the present study is that teachers may need more training and experience in procedures for conducting direct and frequent measurement. . . . Furthermore, experience should improve measurement efficiency. Once these two frequently cited obstacles are minimized, direct and frequent measurement may enjoy more widespread use and may serve to improve the performance of many more students.

ASSESSMENT FOR DETERMINING HOW TO TEACH

Once the teacher determines the student's instructional needs by assessing what to teach, the important process of determining how to teach begins. This process focuses on environmental variables influencing the student's achievement. Learning deficits often are attributed to problems within the student, and thus the student is viewed as responsible for the learning problems. Many educators now recognize that environmental factors (such as inadequate teaching) may trigger and sustain low achievement and inappropriate behaviors. Thus, in planning instruction for the student with learning problems, both student and environmental factors must be considered.

Unfortunately, teacher training and material development inadequately emphasize how to teach. The efficiency of the instructional process depends

Individualized assessment leads to appropriate instruction across academic areas.

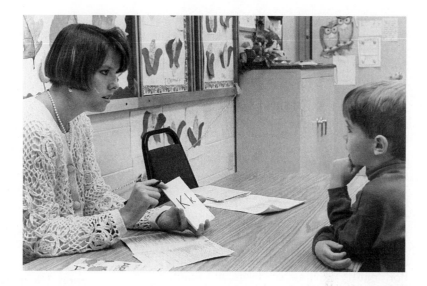

on how well a teacher or diagnostician determines and manipulates factors that best facilitate a student's learning. For example, Ms. Allen, a classroom teacher, observed that because Ronnie constantly asks classmates whether his responses are correct, he is not using his time wisely during spelling seatwork. To improve the situation, Ms. Allen made a spelling tape with the week's word list spelled correctly on it, which Ronnie uses to study the words. If Ronnie subsequently learns an average of one word more a day without increasing the time spent on spellng, the instructional program has become more efficient. Ronnie will learn many more spelling words during the school year without increasing the amount of time he spends on spelling seatwork. This ability to analyze how a student learns best influences the selection of materials, methods, and procedures used in the intervention program. It is perhaps the foremost skill that distinguishes the professionally trained teacher from other supportive instructional personnel.

Formats for Determining How to Teach

Systematic Observation   Systematic observation of the student is one of the teacher's most valuable ways of obtaining information about a student's optimal learning conditions. In systematic observation, it often is important to record

more than a specific behavior. Information for determining how to teach often comes from observing antecedent and consequent events as well: (1) what precedes behavior (teacher asked Johnny to read in a large group), (2) behavior (Johnny cried), and (3) what follows behavior (teacher coaxed Johnny). Systematic observation is simple to use and can be done in a variety of settings. Guidelines for successful observation include the following:

- Select the behavior to be observed. Make sure the target behavior is identifiable to the extent that it is measurable.
- Select a method of recording the behavior and record its frequency.
- Describe the conditions under which the observations are made. These include time, place, activity, antecedent event, and consequent event.

Observation is more effective when the observer has a specific reason or question formulated to guide the observation. Furthermore, observational data collected over time can strengthen the teacher's confidence in the data. Technology for measuring systematic observation focuses on two key factors: (1) selecting the target behavior and (2) recording the frequency of the behavior. Table 3.3, which was presented in the section on individually referenced data systems, presents observational recording techniques.

Formal Assessment Only a few formal tests focus on assessing factors relating to how to teach, and they have not proven to aid instructional programming. Factors that can be manipulated to improve learning are not assessed readily by formal testing. Most formal tests are administered only once, and repeated observations are needed to analyze the effects of various factors on behavior.

Criterion Tests Criterion tests primarily assess what to teach. However, because they can be used to evaluate the effects of instruction, they also are useful in determining *how* to teach. For example, a teacher may divide a list of spelling words into two lists to determine whether a multisensory spelling activity or a flash-card drill is more effective. By administering a criterion test on each set of words, the teacher can compare the student's performances and make a decision about the effectiveness of the two treatments.

Rating Scales A rating scale is a series of statements or questions that require some judgment about the degree or frequency of the behavior or characteristics described in each statement. Sample formats of rating scales include the following:

Numerical Scale

Select the number that best describes the individual.

_____ Frequency of adult supervision required

1. Always
2. Often
3. Occasionally
4. Rarely
5. Almost never

Graphic Scale

Select a place on the line that best describes the individual.

Frequency of adult supervision required:

Always	Often	Occasionally	Rarely	Almost never

Some formal rating scales that may be useful in assessing students with social, emotional, and behavioral problems are presented in Chapter 5. Occasionally, teachers make or use rating scales for parents to complete. These are helpful to use with parents who do not have the time to observe and record their child's behavior systematically. A teacher also may wish to give a rating scale to students to obtain information about areas such as the student's reinforcement preferences, interests, and attitudes about school.

Interviews Information obtained from interviews with parents, teachers, and students can be used to determine how to teach. Through interviews, the teacher can obtain information about specific techniques to use with the student. Also, information can be obtained about the student's interests, favorite activities, problem areas, and attitudes, as well as how the student is perceived at home.

Charting Charting holds much promise for determining how to teach. In charting, a student's daily performance on a probe sheet is recorded on a graph. The graph provides a measure of the student's progress over time. The teacher analyzes the graph pattern and makes instructional decisions regarding which antecedent and consequent events to maintain or change. The teacher can manipulate an antecedent event (such as seating arrangement) or consequent event (e.g., award points for work) and analyze the chart to see whether performance improves, declines, or remains the same. Charts mainly have been used to determine what to teach, but some educators now use probe assessment and charts to evaluate learning style. Charting itself is reinforcing to some students and may help to improve student performance.

Alternative Assessment Dissatisfaction with group-administered standardized tests of achievement and the content of traditional test items are two factors that have provided impetus to the alternative assessment movement. The terms (e.g., *authentic assessment, direct assessment, outcome-based assessment, portfolio assessment,* and *performance assessment*) used to describe the movement reflect some of the concerns with the artificial nature of traditional tests. Worthen (1993) notes that these approaches are called "alternative assessment" for two reasons: "First, all are viewed as *alternatives* to traditional multiple-choice, standardized achievement tests; second, all refer to *direct* examination of student *performance* on significant tasks that are relevant to life outside of school" (p. 445).

Alternative assessment represents some changes in what is assessed and how assessment takes place. First, authentic tasks are emphasized and tasks that represent meaningful subskills are minimized. For example, writing a letter is a worthwhile real-life task, whereas completing a worksheet on punctuation is not stressed. Second, student performance is assessed directly across numerous formats, including writing, oral discourse, portfolios, or demonstrations. Third, higher order thinking is stressed by requiring students to explain, demonstrate, or document their thinking processes. This often is demonstrated through portfolio assessment, which is the most widely used alternative assessment.

Portfolios have the potential to reveal much about their creators and can give teachers insights into their students' growth. According to Paulson, Paulson, and Meyer (1991), "A portfolio is a purposeful collection of student work that exhibits the student's efforts, progress, and achievements in one or more areas. The collection must include student participation in selecting contents, the criteria for selection, the criteria for judging merit, and evidence of student self-reflection" (p. 60). Portfolios are being applied to academic areas for several purposes: to demonstrate student effort, to document student achievement, to enhance assessment information from other sources, and to document the quality of educational programs. In portfolio assessment, the student collects and reflects on examples of her or his own work in a specific area. For example, in addition to results from classroom tests, written responses to literature, checklists, and tapes, a reading portfolio should include samples of student work, the student's observational notes, self-evaluations, and progress notes contributed by both the teacher and the student (Valencia, 1990).

From a review of the portfolio literature, Salvia and Ysseldyke (1998) maintain that portfolio assessment consists of six elements:

1. Valued outcomes are targeted for assessment.
2. Authentic tasks (real work) are used for assessment.
3. Selected tasks involve cooperative endeavors among students and between the teacher and the student.

4. Multiple dimensions (e.g., content, strategies, methods of inquiry, and work processes) are used to evaluate learning.
5. The completion of products includes reflection and self-evaluation.
6. Assessment and instruction are integrated.

Portfolios also should be created for a specific purpose. Without direction, a portfolio can become a collection of papers or products. The Vermont Portfolio Project developed guidelines for writing portfolios. Abruscato (1993, p. 475) notes that the writing portfolio includes the following six work samples of writing completed during the school year, as well as the student's response to a formal or standard writing assessment given to all students within a grade level:

1. A table of contents
2. A "best piece"
3. A letter
4. A poem, short story, play, or personal narrative
5. A personal response to a cultural, media, or sports exhibit or event, or to a book, current issue, math problem, or scientific phenomenon
6. One prose piece from any curriculum area other than English or language arts (for fourth-graders) and three prose pieces from any curriculum area other than English or language arts (for eighth-graders)
7. The piece produced in response to the uniform writing assessment, as well as related outlines, drafts, etc.

The student is a participant in the assessment process and learns to set goals and evaluate learning in progress. Thus, portfolio assessment offers the opportunity to observe student performance in a context where the student solves problems and makes judgments about his or her own performance. The teacher can use the information about the behaviors and attitudes of readers and writers of differing abilities to tailor instruction. Portfolios also can be used during parent–teacher conferences. At the end of the year, several works can be selected from the portfolio that exemplify what has changed for the student in that time, and these works can become a final portfolio to serve as a continuing document of progress from year to year.

Salvia and Ysseldyke (1998) caution educators to approach portfolio assessment carefully. They note that many valid concerns, which need to be addressed before this method can become a best practice, surround the use of portfolio assessment. Specifically, they summarize their findings in the following passage (p. 294):

> Despite an initial surge of interest in the use of portfolios, several concerns and limitations have not been systematically addressed: selecting the criteria for including work in a student's portfolio, determining the nature of student participation in content selection, ensuring sufficient content generated by a student to reach valid decisions, and finding a way to make portfolio assessment more reliable, with consistency of scoring and breadth of sampling of student performances. In addition, there are concerns about biased scoring, instructional utility, and efficiency. Portfolio assessment will remain difficult and expensive for schools, and educators who wish to pursue this alternative should give serious attention to how portfolios are assembled and evaluated. Objectivity, less complexity, and comparability are the keys to better practice.

ASSESSMENT AREAS FOR DETERMINING HOW TO TEACH

The first step in determining how to teach is to identify the major areas of assessment. Figure 3.12 presents the major areas that are basic in assessment for determining how to teach: expectation factors, stimulus events, response factors, and subsequent events. The primary function of this section is to alert the teacher to these areas. A general awareness of relevant instructional factors can be useful in teaching all students. For example, if a teacher is sensitive to expectancy and response

FIGURE 3.12
Important factors in assessing how to teach

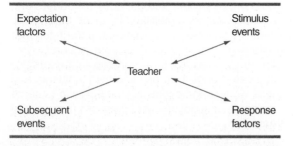

factors and stimulus and subsequent events in daily observations, subtle changes can lead to improved student learning. Once the assessment areas are determined, the important factors need to be identified under each.

Expectation Factors

Expectation refers to an individual's orientation to the learning situation. Two types of generalized expectations are recognized. The first involves the expectation of a particular type of consequence (such as social approval, achievement, tangible reward, failure, or punishment), which governs whether a person perceives a situation as being similar to past situations. The second generalizes from other situations involving a similar problem-solving activity, but differing in consequence. Thus, problem-solving activities encountered in a variety of situations may generalize to another situation, no matter the consequence. Motivation often is equated with expectation, because expectation may serve as an incentive (or deterrent) for approaching, continuing, or avoiding the learning task. A student who receives verbal praise for writing spelling words may expect that if the words are written, some desirable event will follow. Conversely, if a student receives a low grade or criticism for writing spelling words, expectation can serve as a deterrent, and the student avoids the learning task. Thus, expectation of success or failure can influence the student's motivation toward the learning task.

Numerous expectations significantly influence learning outcomes and student behavior. Four expectation areas are discussed: learner expectations, teacher expectations, peer expectations, and parental expectations.

Learner Expectations Using a checklist-rating scale, the teacher can answer three important questions:

1. Does the student frequently exhibit negative expectation reactions?
2. To whom or to what are the negative reactions directed?
3. What are the stated reasons for the negative reactions?

By answering these questions, the teacher obtains information that is helpful in planning instruction. For example, if the student is embarrassed to read orally around others and thus dislikes reading, the teacher may allow the student to record reading assignments on a tape recorder or to read in a one-to-one situation with the teacher or a friend. Minor instructional adjustments often can result in increased student motivation, more efficient learning, and better student expectations.

Self-report activities are excellent ways to obtain information about a student's negative and positive expectations. Sentence completion is a popular self-report activity. For example:

1. I learn best when _____.
2. I am really happy when _____.
3. When I work hard, my teacher _____.
4. My least favorite thing at school is _____.
5. When I do not try, my teacher _____.

Rating scales are another type of self-report that is used frequently. For example:

(a) I learn math quickly.	1 2 3 4 5	I do not seem to understand math.
(b) Classmates really like me.	1 2 3 4 5	Classmates do not like me much.
(c) I have a lot of friends.	1 2 3 4 5	I do not have many friends.

Teacher Expectations   Teachers develop perceptions of a student that, in turn, create certain expectations of the student. When the teacher expects and accepts less from the student than the student is capable of giving, the expectations may impede both learning progress and social development. Rosenthal and Jacobson's (1966) work generated much interest in this phenomenon, which is frequently referred to as the *self-fulfilling prophecy.* Brophy and Good (1974) report that "the idea that teacher expectations can function as self-fulfilling prophecies appears to be an established fact rather than a mere hypothesis" (p. 77).

Characteristics such as race, special education label, sex, appearance, and achievement level of older siblings have been shown to influence teacher expectations (Algozzine & Mercer, 1980). A teacher who expects inappropriate behavior or poor academic progress likely may get it. Fortunately, the reverse of this phenomenon holds much promise. R. M. Smith, Neisworth, and Greer (1978, p. 84) affirm the importance of the teacher's influence:

The teacher's attitude toward children and education determines to a very real degree how children perceive school, themselves, and each other—and how much progress they actually make. Teachers can make learning pleasant or punishing; they can create motivation or fear; they can produce excited anticipation or dread. A teacher's personal style and approach, more than anything else, create the climate and mood which will characterize the classroom.

Because teacher expectations influence students' success, an assessment of how to teach must include an examination of teacher expectations. Factors that deserve consideration in analyzing teacher expectations include the following:

- The teacher assigns work that is too difficult or too easy.
- The teacher expects the student to misbehave.
- The teacher is quick to tell the student about an incorrect response.
- The teacher makes negative predictions about the student's future (e.g., "He'll drop out of school").
- The teacher has difficulty listening to the student.

Peer Expectations   Through daily interactions with classmates, students learn to view themselves as leaders, followers, fringers, or isolates. Acceptance by peers helps students gain confidence and self-assurance which, in turn, foster better performance on academic tasks; peer rejection can produce anxiety and self-doubt. Peer influence is a function of numerous factors, including age, home stability, and socioeconomic level. Because elementary-age and younger students tend to value home and adult praise more than adolescents, there is less peer influence with them than with adolescents. Above all, the teacher must avoid contributing to one student's negative perception of another student. The teacher must recognize student leaders and understand classroom alliances in order to promote a healthy social climate. The teacher also must be aware of peer values, especially those relating to academic achievement and social behavior. Once the social climate is ascertained, the teacher can use peer tutoring, modeling, role playing, seat assignments, and the control of peer attention to promote peer expectations that foster the growth of individual students.

Questionnaires on class norms and personal values as well as observations of student behavior provide useful information about peer values and class social patterns. Debilitating factors of importance in analyzing peer expectations include the following:

- The student is an isolate.
- Many peers criticize the student.
- A certain group likes or dislikes the student.
- Peers view the student as a low achiever.
- The student displays no apparent quality that peers value.

Parental Expectations   Parental expectations can influence a student's academic and social growth. If a parent highly values and reinforces academic work, the student is likely to receive encouragement and praise from parents for doing homework and performing well in school. Parental support is often a key factor in maintaining a student's motivation and achievement. Positive parental expectations can help in the student's development; however, parental expectations that are negative, too high, or too low can harm the student's academic and social development. The student who must constantly face living up to parents' unrealistic expectations may begin to hate school and eventually may rebel against both the school and the parents. Also, the student may start getting into trouble to receive parental attention. If parents do not value academic achievement, the student does not receive much encouragement or praise from parents for doing schoolwork. In home situations in which fighting or goofing off in school is valued, the student receives encouragement for behavior that is directly opposed by the school.

The teacher must be sensitive to both helpful and harmful parental expectations. Helpful expectations should be encouraged, and harmful ones should be approached in a problem-solving manner. The common goal of optimal growth for the student frequently enables the teacher and parents to overcome obstacles and work cooperatively. Factors that deserve attention in assessing parental expectations include the following:

- Parents tell the student not to worry about getting good grades.
- Parents do not encourage the student to complete homework.
- Parents allow the student to stay home from school when the student is not sick.

- Parents select a vocational goal for the student that is not compatible with the student's interest or ability.
- Parents frequently insist that the student be placed in a higher reading or math group.
- Parents talk about how the student will never achieve.
- Parents do not encourage self-expression from the student.

Stimulus Events

Stimulus (or antecedent) events include an array of materials, instructional methods, and classroom settings that set the stage for the student to respond. Because the teacher controls or determines many of the stimulus events in the classroom, they must be examined to understand how students learn best. The teacher can observe the student, directly ask the student, or use questionnaires to gather information about individual preferences. Stimulus events can be sorted into the categories of physical setting; instructional arrangements, techniques, and materials; and learning style preferences. Figure 3.13 presents a rating scale of stimulus events that affect learning.

Physical Setting   Section I of Figure 3.13 presents variables of interest in analyzing the environmental conditions that affect a student's performance, both positively and negatively. Physical properties (e.g., noise, temperature, lighting, and spatial factors) can be manipulated to suit the student's learning preferences.

In a survey of research on learning styles, Dunn, Beaudry, and Klavas (1989) found that from 10 to 40 percent of students, dependent upon age, gender, and achievement, exhibit learning preferences regarding quiet vs. sound, bright or soft lighting, warm or cool temperatures, and formal vs. informal setting designs. When choices are available, the student or the teacher can choose a setting suitable to the activity and individual preferences. For example, students who prefer bright lighting and cool temperatures may perform well next to the classroom windows and away from the heat ducts.

Instructional Arrangements, Techniques, and Materials   This area covers a wide range of stimulus events that dramatically affect learning. For example, regarding instructional arrangements,

FIGURE 3.13
Rating scale of stimulus events that affect learning

Key
3 — always happens   *2* — frequently happens
1 — sometimes happens   *0* — never happens

Key
3 — always happens   *2* — frequently happens
1 — sometimes happens   *0* — never happens

I. Physical Properties
  A. Noise
    1. The student likes to work in a
       quiet area.   3 2 1 0
    2. The student frequently asks the
       teacher to repeat directions.   3 2 1 0
  B. Temperature
    1. The student prefers warmer areas
       of the room.   3 2 1 0
    2. The student has allergies that
       are sensitive to air quality (such as
       when the furnace is first turned on).   3 2 1 0
  C. Lighting
    1. The student prefers well-lighted
       areas of the room (e.g., near a
       window).   3 2 1 0
    2. The student has difficulty seeing
       the chalkboard.   3 2 1 0
  D. General Physical Factors
    1. The student is distracted near
       windows, pencil sharpener,
       or sink.   3 2 1 0
    2. The student likes to work in close
       proximity to the teacher.   3 2 1 0
    3. The student is distracted by
       messy or cluttered areas.   3 2 1 0

II. Instructional Arrangements
    1. The student works well in a small
       group.   3 2 1 0
    2. The student works well in a one-
       to-one situation with the teacher.   3 2 1 0
    3. The student works well in peer-
       mediated situations.   3 2 1 0
    4. The student works well alone
       with seatwork.   3 2 1 0
    5. The student works well in
       cooperative learning groups.   3 2 1 0
    6. The student works well with a
       teacher aide or volunteer.   3 2 1 0

III. Instructional Techniques
    1. The student needs much
       demonstration of expected
       behavior.   3 2 1 0

    2. The student likes input regarding
       instruction.   3 2 1 0
    3. The student needs simple
       instructions.   3 2 1 0
    4. The student readily models the
       behavior of peers.   3 2 1 0
    5. The student readily models the
       behavior of the teacher.   3 2 1 0
    6. The student needs prompts and
       cues to maintain behaviors.   3 2 1 0
    7. The student likes working with
       equipment (e.g., tape recorder,
       computer, and overhead
       projector).   3 2 1 0
    8. The student has low frustration
       tolerance.   3 2 1 0
    9. The student reponds well when
       the teacher asks questions.   3 2 1 0
   10. The student needs a lot of time
       to complete work.   3 2 1 0
   11. The student works best in the
       morning (or afternoon).   3 2 1 0
   12. The student works slowly and
       inaccurately.   3 2 1 0
   13. The student does not perform
       well under timed conditions.   3 2 1 0
   14. The student enjoys working
       against a timer.   3 2 1 0
   15. The student enjoys charting
       correct and incorrect responses.   3 2 1 0
   16. In approaching a new task, the
       student becomes easily
       frustrated.   3 2 1 0
   17. In approaching a new task, the
       student tries to distract the
       teacher.   3 2 1 0
   18. In approaching a new task, the
       student refuses to attempt it.   3 2 1 0
   19. The student responds well to
       different academic materials
       or activities (specify _____).   3 2 1 0

(continued on next page)

FIGURE 3.13
(continued)

Key
3 — always happens   2 — frequently happens
1 — sometimes happens   0 — never happens

IV. Materials
    1. The student likes or needs self-correcting materials. 3 2 1 0
    2. The student likes or needs instructional games using game boards. 3 2 1 0
    3. The student likes or needs instructional games using cards. 3 2 1 0
    4. The student needs worksheets with only a few items. 3 2 1 0
    5. The student needs lots of writing space on worksheets. 3 2 1 0
    6. The student needs visual cues on seatwork (e.g., arrows, green dots to note starting place, and lines to show place for responses). 3 2 1 0
    7. The student enjoys chalkboard activities. 3 2 1 0
    8. The student responds well to manipulative materials (e.g., puppets in language, cubes and abacus in math, and calculator in math or spelling). 3 2 1 0
    9. The student enjoys doing work with flash cards. 3 2 1 0
   10. The student enjoys making materials (e.g., flash cards, game boards, and card decks). 3 2 1 0
   11. The student enjoys working with computers. 3 2 1 0

V. Learning Style Preferences
  A. Visual Preference Indicators
    1. The student enjoys reading a book. 3 2 1 0
    2. The student enjoys seeing a filmstrip. 3 2 1 0
    3. The student enjoys looking at pictures. 3 2 1 0
    4. The student enjoys watching a movie. 3 2 1 0
    5. The student enjoys playing a concentration game. 3 2 1 0
    6. The student remembers material from an overhead. 3 2 1 0

Key
3 — always happens   2 — frequently happens
1 — sometimes happens   0 — never happens

    7. The student remembers what is seen in a film. 3 2 1 0
  B. Auditory Preference Indicators
    1. The student enjoys hearing a record. 3 2 1 0
    2. The student enjoys hearing a tape. 3 2 1 0
    3. The student enjoys hearing a story. 3 2 1 0
    4. The student follows auditory directions. 3 2 1 0
    5. The student remembers what the teacher says. 3 2 1 0
    6. The student likes talking to people. 3 2 1 0
    7. The student listens to people well. 3 2 1 0
  C. Tactile Preference Indicators
    1. The student likes to draw. 3 2 1 0
    2. The student likes to manipulate objects. 3 2 1 0
    3. The student likes to trace things. 3 2 1 0
    4. The student likes to work with clay or finger paints. 3 2 1 0
  D. Kinesthetic Preference Indicators
    1. The student remembers material from motor activities. 3 2 1 0
    2. The student remembers what he or she writes. 3 2 1 0
    3. The student likes to play motor games. 3 2 1 0
    4. The student likes to do experiments. 3 2 1 0
    5. The student likes to operate a tape recorder, keyboard, calculator, or other machines. 3 2 1 0

VI. Summary of Stimulus Events
_____
_____
_____
_____

Dunn et al. (1989) found that many students in third through eighth grade learn better in well-organized small groups than either alone or with the teacher. Students in eighth grade and above tended to learn better when they worked alone. Moreover, Dunn et al. report that in all classes examined there were students who preferred to learn by themselves, others who wished to work with peers, and others who liked working with the teacher. It is likely that these instructional arrangement preferences can be determined or managed by providing students with choices and then monitoring their progress in the different arrangements. Studies of underachievers, dropouts, at-risk students, and vocational education students reveal that as a group they are not morning people (Griggs & Dunn, 1988; Tappenden, 1983). For these groups, achievement improved when learning occurred during late morning, afternoon, or during the evening. Overall, Dunn et al. report that most students are not "early birds" and prefer learning in the late morning or afternoon.

Sections II, III, and IV of Figure 3.13 include factors related to instructional arrangements, techniques, and materials. Once the teacher identifies preferred instructional factors, the task of determining what to do is usually straightforward. The teacher can provide special places for students to go for isolation, rest and quiet, letting off steam, rewarding themselves, private instruction, talking with the teacher, and working alone or in a group. If a student learns well alone in the afternoon, the teacher can schedule those arrangements for the student. If a student is frustrated easily during seatwork or always wants feedback, the teacher can give the student self-correcting activities. If a student lacks interest, the teacher can remind the student of the importance of the skill or use instructional games. If a student writes slowly and needs a lot of mobility (physical activity), the teacher can provide larger spaces on worksheets to write answers or allow the student to work on a chalkboard.

Learning Style Preferences Determining learning styles has received much attention, and assessing modality (form of sensation) preferences has been a key concern. Diagnosticians and teachers usually administer various tests (such as *Learning Style Inventory* or *Detroit Tests of Learning Aptitudes—4*) to determine a student's learning style preferences and make instructional recommendations. If the student performs better in the visual modality, for example, instruction that stresses visually oriented materials and techniques is recommended. This strategy has been practiced in special education for years and now appears to be gaining momentum in general education. Although the learning style approach has widespread use and intuitive appeal, it remains highly controversial. It has not been supported in the educational psychology research (Miller, 1981), in the special education research (Kavale & Forness, 1987, 1990), or in the reading research (Snider, 1992). Other researchers (Brunner & Majewski, 1990; Dunn et al., 1989) claim the learning style approach has substantial support. (For detailed coverage regarding the learning style controversy, see the following journal issues: E*ducational Leadership,* October 1990; *Exceptional Children,* January 1990; and *Remedial and Special Education,* January/February 1992.)

It appears that educators should not rely heavily on tests to determine learning style strengths and weaknesses. Using informal measures, the teacher may discover both a student's learning style preference and the conditions under which the preference exists—that is, it may depend upon the particular task. Classroom tasks can be used to assess modality strengths and weaknesses. For example, three learning channel combinations can be assessed: see—write (see multiplication fact—write answer), hear—write (hear word—write word), and see—say (see word—say word). The practice of examining modality preferences by using classroom tasks can help determine how a student learns.

Section V of Figure 3.13 presents some factors that may point to a student's modality preferences. If a modality strength or weakness is suspected, classroom observations can validate or refute the suspicion. However, if a student has a visual learning problem, for example, an auditory strength does not necessarily exist.

Response Factors

Tasks usually require students to make a motor or verbal response, or both. Selecting the type of response (such as pointing, making gestures, or writing) for an instructional activity can be crucial in the activity's design. Some students function better if the response requires extensive motor involvement (e.g., write numerals, connect dots, push button, operate tape recorder, color items, or arrange items on a feltboard); others function better with simple verbal responses (such as "yes" and "no"). Repsonse time also deserves attention. If a student writes numerals slowly or talks rapidly without thinking, these tendencies need to be considered in planning instruction. A long delay between the presentation of a task and a response may relate to several factors (e.g., task is too difficult, lack of attention to or low interest in the task, or the student is seeking teacher attention). A short delay with correct responses may indicate that the student has mastered the task, whereas a short delay with incorrect responses may suggest that the student is responding without thinking, not trying, racing others, or seeking attention.

The logical organization of the response also should be noted. Some responses require concept ordering (e.g., following steps in solving a problem or discussing concepts from smallest to largest), whereas others require language ordering (e.g., the organization of several thoughts with supportive statements). Many students with learning problems need assistance in organizing responses. Some responses do not appear to be related to the question or involve interpreting the question based on different cultural experiences. Asking the student to explain a unique response often provides the teacher with insights about student experiences, interests, or concerns.

Finally, it may help to note the student's reaction when the correct answer is not known. Some students become frustrated quickly and react with anger or apathy, whereas others make derogatory comments about themselves or stop trying. Also, the student may not be following instructions. Thus, it is helpful to listen to students' questions and comments. Important factors in analyzing response preferences include the following:

- The student likes simple one-word responses.
- The student likes brief discussions.
- The student likes extensive dialogue.
- The student exhibits speech problems.
- The student likes to verbalize responses while touching the item.
- The student likes to write and say responses.
- The student likes to sing and clap.
- The student likes to respond by pointing.

- The student copies work from a near position.
- The student copies work from a far position.
- The student uses a pencil holder.
- The student writes slowly.
- The student writes quickly and neatly.
- The student writes too big for the space allowed.
- The student has physical abnormalities that interfere with writing or speaking.

Subsequent Events

Consequences greatly influence behavior and can be used to motivate students and manage their behavior. Social praise, special activities and privileges, evaluation marks, positive physical expression, awards, tokens, and tangible objects are some positive consequences frequently used to reinforce, and thus influence, student behavior. The teacher has many ways to determine what reinforces a student. The teacher simply can ask the student or note free-time preferences for activities or objects. Some teachers use a reinforcement menu, featuring a variety of consequences from which the student chooses a favorite item or activity.

To use consequent events most effectively, the teacher must consider timing, amount, and ratio of reinforcement. Some students need immediate reinforcement to maintain a behavior; others can tolerate a delay in reinforcement without decreasing the occurrence of the behavior. Also, some students require a great deal of reinforcement only for certain changes. For example, when the teacher is attempting to establish a new behavior, much reinforcement may be needed. As the learning proceeds, reinforcement may be reduced.

Analysis of the Student Learning Profile

Expectation factors, stimulus events, response factors, and subsequent events must be weighed in relation to one another in planning instruction. It is necessary to consider all four factors together to form instructional strategies that best facilitate learning. After each factor has been assessed and viewed as a whole, a profile may be written. The profile can display numerous patterns and supply a simple list of do's and don'ts for designing an individual program. Table 3.4 presents a student learning profile and treatment plan.

TABLE 3.4
Student learning profile and treatment plan

Assessment Area and Findings	Treatment
Learner Expectations	
Thinks teacher dislikes him	Ask for a favor once a day, or ask the student a personal interest question each day (e.g., "Did you like that football game?").
Senses defeat in reading	Pair reinforcement with effort in reading.
Teacher Expectations	
Assigns work that is too difficult in reading	Provide realistic successes in reading.
Tends to pick on student	Use sensitive responses to incorrect responses.
Peer Expectations	
Is with peers who do not value reading	Seat student near peers who value reading.
Is liked and respected by peers	Use peer teaching, with student being tutor or tutee.
Parental Expectations	
Is pushed by parents to work hard	Tell parents not to tutor unless it is a pleasant experience.
Has concerned and cooperative parents	Encourage parents to praise effort as well as correct product.
Physical Properties	
Is allergic to dust	Seat student away from chalk trays.
Prefers cooler areas of room	Allow student to work away from furnace ducts.
Prefers well-lighted areas	Seat student near a window.
Likes to work near other students	Assign work at a table with students who work hard.
Arrangements	
Dislikes one-to-one instruction	Make one-to-one instruction pleasant.
Enjoys small-group activities	Use small-group instruction.
Instructional Techniques	
Gets bored with same task	Practice academic skills through the use of a tape recorder, instructional games, self-correcting materials, and computer software.
Has low frustration tolerance in reading	Allow student to practice reading on tape recorder before reading orally to the teacher.
Works slowly	Let student work against a timer.
Needs prompts and cues to maintain behavior	Use contingency contracts with a variety of activities.
Instructional Materials	
Dislikes reading worksheets	Use language experience approach in reading.
Likes games	Use instructional games.
Likes worksheets with only a few items	Use worksheets that are partially completed.
Dislikes cluttered worksheets or materials	Use Language Master or tape recorder.
Learning Style Preferences	
Responds well in all modalities	Present tasks in various modalities.
Response Factors	
Writes slowly and sloppily	Encourage use of a plastic pencil holder.
Prefers short verbal responses coupled with simple motor responses	Use point-and-say responses.
Writes too big for space allowed	Give a lot of room for writing on worksheets or use chalkboard for writing.
Subsequent Events	
Does not respond to one-word praise but enjoys smiles and handshakes	Follow good effort with a smile, touch, and encouraging phrase.
Requests immediate feedback	Use answer keys, peer feedback, and self-correcting materials.
Likes high letter grades	Write big letter grades on good work.
Has difficulty with feedback on incorrect items	Use a variety of sensitive responses for incorrect work.

Analysis of the student learning profile is useful primarily for guiding teacher observations in the different assessment areas. An instructional plan based on an assessment for determining how to teach should be viewed as an estimate. When the right variables are manipulated appropriately, the plan is effective; however, when the assessment is incorrect, the plan should be adjusted. All treatment plans should be monitored closely to ensure their efficacy and the student's progress. Thus, assessment for determining how to teach is similar to assessment for determining what to teach in that both are ongoing processes.

Perspective on Assessing for How to Teach

Efforts should be made to provide a systematic assessment of learning environments. *The Instructional Environment System—II* (TIES—II) (Ysseldyke & Christenson, 1993) provides educators with an assessment device for evaluating and obtaining information about an individual student's instructional environment. The learning environment is examined across 12 instructional-environment components (e.g., motivational factors, relevant practice, and informed feedback), and 5 home-support-for-learning components (e.g., discipline orientation and parental participation) that are considered to be related to instructional outcomes for students. TIES—II can be used to describe the extent to which a student's academic or behavioral problems relate to factors in the instructional environment, as well as to identify starting points in designing appropriate instructional interventions for individual students. This type of assessment provides educators with a systematic procedure for examining factors that facilitate planning how to teach.

Mercer and Corbett (1991) provide a viable example of how an educator used observations to assess expectation, response, and reinforcement factors that related to how to teach an individual student. An educational diagnostician was asked to test a 13-year-old student, Stephanie, who was being seen in a hospital-based pediatric clinic. When he arrived to test her, he discovered that her folder had been misplaced. So, he proceeded to test her without the benefit of background information. In the beginning of the testing session,

Stephanie worked intensely; however, as testing continued, she lowered her head and mumbled incorrect answers. When the examiner asked whether she was okay, she did not respond. Through continued efforts to talk with Stephanie, he realized that she stopped trying when the test items became difficult. He explained that the tests covered material through the twelfth grade and that she was expected to miss some items. He asked her to try to do her best, and he mentioned that they would take a refreshment break periodically throughout the testing. Stephanie liked the idea of taking breaks and promised to do her best. When Stephanie's test responses were scored, she achieved average or above average scores in reading, math, and spelling.

Several days later, the examiner was asked to present the test results at a staffing conference. Much to the examiner's dismay, the pediatrician, the psychologist, and the language clinician reported that Stephanie performed at a very low level. In fact, they agreed that she was "trainable mentally retarded" with a full-scale IQ of 37. Furthermore, they noted that she had been in a special class for students with mental disabilities for about eight years. When the educational diagnostician presented Stephanie's scores, he reported average or above-average scores for a 13-year-old individual. The team was puzzled with the results, but discussions revealed that Stephanie had lowered her head and mumbled incorrect responses throughout the testing sessions with all of the team members except the educator. It was agreed that the student's scores in the educational testing were the most valid, and the team recommended that she be placed in a general education class with some temporary support services. Stephanie made appropriate progress in the general education setting.

In this example, observations (such as the student lowers her head and mumbles incorrect responses) led the examiner to hypothesize that Stephanie stopped trying when item difficulty increased. Through discussion with her, the examiner determined that his hypothesis appeared accurate. Student–examiner interactions led to the student agreeing to do her best on all items. The data documented that Stephanie's academic achievements were average or above average. Due to the examiner's ability to obtain and apply qualitative and quantitative information, Stephanie's performance and life improved dramatically. Thus, through interaction with the participant, the examiner was able to make adaptations during assessment that led to significant changes in the student's educational life.

GRADING

The practice of grading students is a fundamental component of the educational system. Grades serve several important functions, including providing feedback to students regarding their learning; providing feedback to parents regarding their child's learning progress; guiding decisions concerning promotion, graduation, and academic awards; determining eligibility for extracurricular activities; helping determine college admission; and providing feedback to employers.

Despite its major role in assessing and providing feedback to students, parents, and institutions (colleges and employers), limited agreement exists concerning the most appropriate grading practices. The discussions about grading become more uncertain when students with learning problems are considered, particularly when those students are included in general education classes. Questions about the equity of using different standards to evaluate students within the same classroom arise. Specifically, educators and parents question whether it is fair to award the same grade and course credit to students who do not meet the class performance standards as are given to students who do meet the standards. On the other hand, proponents of individualized grading claim that to do otherwise burdens students who are already at a disadvantage for competing fairly with their peers. They believe students with special needs deserve the opportunity to earn motivating grades when they give substantial effort to learn. Also, Wood (1998) reminds educators that numerous students with disabilities do not require grading adaptations if appropriate modifications (such as content enhancements, explicit teaching techniques, and sensitive testing conditions) are available in the learning environment. In spite of the importance of grades in our educational system and the numerous problems encountered by teachers, the issue of grading has received relatively little attention by teacher educators.

Grading can be viewed from three primary viewpoints: criterion-referenced, self-referenced, and norm-referenced (Terwilliger, 1977). Criterion-referenced grading stresses the learning of specified objectives to a mastery criterion. Self-referenced grading is based on the student's progress as compared with some perception of the student's ability. Effort is an important factor in the self-referenced viewpoint. Norm-referenced grading assesses the student's strengths and weaknesses in relation to the performance of others. This view assumes some level of competence in the comparison group.

Grades have been defined as symbols (letters or numbers) that relate to a student's quality of achievement or performance rather than to the amount of work expended. Grades represent a value judgment about the quality of a student's achievement relative to a course of objectives during a specified time period (Terwilliger, 1977). Generally, grades are used to compare performances among students or to reflect achievement in terms of an established standard. Although many grading systems exist, the most commonly used systems involve letters (A, B, C, D, and F) or numbers (1, 2, 3, 4, and 5). These letter or number grades reflect levels of performance ranging from outstanding to failing. Percentage ranges typically are used to determine criteria for an assigned letter grade (e.g., 90 to 100 percent = A).

Types of Alternative Grading

Many students with disabilities or learning problems cannot succeed in general education classes without the use of alternative grading criteria. Although general education teachers commonly assign grades to all of their students, they should collaborate with special education teachers regarding the grades of students with disabilities. Also, the type of grading system and the grading responsibilities of all involved teachers should be determined before the school year begins.

Results of a national survey of classroom grading practices of general education teachers indicate that teachers find certain grading adaptations (such as pass/fail grades, portfolios, multiple grades, and grading for effort) to be helpful for students both with and without disabilities (Bursuck et al., 1996). The following types of grading alternatives have been used to accommodate the special needs of students in inclusion classes (DeBoer, 1994; Salend, 1998; Wood, 1998):

- *Individualized educational program grading approach.* This approach determines grades on the basis of a student's progress on goals and objectives specified on the student's individualized educational program (IEP). Because IEP learning objectives are based on the student's needs and include criterion-performance levels, evaluation based on them appears logical.
- *Pass/fail systems.* The pass/fail system establishes criteria for passing or failing. The achievement of minimum course competencies earns a *P* grade, while failure to achieve minimum course competencies results in an *F* grade.
- *Mastery level/criterion systems.* Content or skills are divided into subcomponents. Mastery is achieved when a student reaches a criterion level on a specified subcomponent. Mastery level systems usually follow a sequence that includes a pretest, instruction activities, and a posttest. The sequence is repeated as the student masters subsequent skills or content.
- *Point systems.* In these systems, points are assigned to various activities. The point totals that the student earns correspond to specific grades (e.g., A, B, C, and D), and a minimum number of points are needed to earn a passing grade. Figure 3.14 provides an example of a point system.
- *Contract grading.* Contracting for grades has been used successfully in special education for years and is easily applied in general education classes. The teacher and student sign a contract that specifies the work to be completed, how the grade is determined, and the timeline for completion. Chapter 5 includes a sample contract.
- *Multiple grading.* With multiple grading the teacher grades the student in several areas, typically including ability, effort, and achievement. The ability grade is based on the student's expected or predicted progress. The effort grade is based on the time and energy the student devotes to learning. The achievement grade reflects the student's mastery of the material to a specified criterion. With multiple grading, it is common for the student to receive ability, effort, and achievement grades in each content area (Salend, 1998). The grading system displayed in Figure 3.14 in-

cludes multiple grading because grades are assigned for tests, quizzes, projects, homework, and participation.

- *Shared grading.* When two or more teachers work together to teach a student, they collaborate to assign a grade. The grade is based on each teacher's observations of progress according to established guidelines for assessing performance. Shared grading typically occurs when two or more teachers (e.g., special education, Title I, or general education teachers) instruct the same student in a specified content area.
- *Student self-comparison.* The teachers and students meet to determine appropriate instructional goals within the curriculum. Progress on these goals is monitored by the students and the teachers, and a grade is assigned according to the amount of progress. In some self-comparison systems the students evaluate themselves and determine their own grades.
- *Level grading.* Grading is individualized by using a subscript to note the level of difficulty on which the students' grades are based. For example, a grade of B indicates that the student is doing B-range work, and a 1, 2, or 3 is combined with the letter grade to indicate difficulty level. For example, B_1 means B work on above-grade-level material; B_2 means B work on grade-level material, and B_3 means B work on below-grade-level material (DeBoer, 1994).
- *Descriptive grading.* Teachers write descriptive comments regarding each student's performance, attitude, effort, and learning preferences. Examples (such as a portfolio of student work) are included to illustrate achievement and effort.

Guidelines for Developing an Effective Grading System

From a review of the research on grading, Rojewski, Pollard, and Meers (1990) report that grading issues are highlighted but reports of successful practices are limited. Although the research is limited regarding proven grading practices, selected educators (Dempster, 1991; Rojewski et al., 1990; Sprick, 1985) provide some viable directions for developing grading systems for students with learning problems:

- *Determine grades on the basis of course objectives.* A major percentage of a final grade

FIGURE 3.14
A grading system with points
and multiple evaluations

Student Grade Sheet

Student _____

Subject area _____

Tests:
  1. Score _____ /100 points
  2. Score _____ /100 points
  3. Score _____ /100 points
  4. Score _____ /100 points   Total _____ /400 points

Quizzes:
  1. Score _____ /20 points
  2. Score _____ /20 points
  3. Score _____ /20 points
  4. Score _____ /20 points   Total _____ /80 points

Project or Paper:
  1. Score _____ /120 points   Total _____ /120 points

Homework:
  1. Score _____ /10 points
  2. Score _____ /10 points
  3. Score _____ /10 points
  4. Score _____ /10 points
  5. Score _____ /10 points
  6. Score _____ /10 points
  7. Score _____ /10 points
  8. Score _____ /10 points
  9. Score _____ /10 points
  10. Score _____ /10 points   Total _____ /100 points

Weekly participation:
Week 1 _____ /20 points
Week 2 _____ /20 points
Week 3 _____ /20 points
Week 4 _____ /20 points
Week 5 _____ /20 points
Week 6 _____ /20 points   Total _____ /120 points
                                          Final Score _____ /820 points

should be based on the student's mastery of course objectives (Rojewski et al., 1990; Sprick, 1985). For example, a failing grade indicates that the student did not master the course objectives. Students who achieve mastery receive an average grade (e.g., C), and students who exceed the objectives receive higher grades (e.g., B or A). Grading on mastery of clearly defined course objectives provides each student with an opportunity to pass the course. When students can pass a course on the basis of mastered course objectives, they realize that they can suc-ceed regardless of the performance of other students. Their grade is not determined on the basis of their performance relative to other students, as is practiced when normal curve grading is used. Thus, students with learning problems are not competing with higher performing students for grades. In mainstream classes it helps if the teacher plans lessons or units with three progressive levels of information: (1) information that all students should learn, (2) information that most students should learn, and (3) information that some students should learn (Joint

Committee on Teacher Planning for Students with Disabilities, 1995). Chapter 4 discusses this type of pyramid planning.

• *Use multiple evaluation methods.* Final grades should be based on a variety of activities, including tests, quizzes, projects or papers, homework, and class participation. For students who have difficulty taking tests, these multiple evaluations provide an opportunity to demonstrate their skills or knowledge. The grading system presented in Figure 3.14 includes multiple evaluations. Sprick (1985) provides extensive criteria for evaluating class participation (i.e., managing a system that deals with tardiness, disruptions, absences, and late work).

• *Teach students to understand the grading system.* The procedure of assigning points to activities and basing grades on a point total helps students with learning problems understand the grading system. Sprick (1985) notes that many students who are low achievers do not understand grading systems and seldom know what their current grades are throughout the school year. He points out the importance of teaching students to understand their grades and of having students maintain a weekly record of their grades in each class or subject area.

• *Monitor the performance of students frequently and give feedback.* It is important for students to participate in frequent evaluation activities and receive feedback on their performances. Dempster (1991) notes that frequent testing yields higher levels of achievement than infrequent testing. Also, he reports that tests on material recently presented promotes learning. Emmer, Evertson, and Worsham (2000) report that regular feedback provides students with needed information and reduces the time they practice errors if responses are incorrect. The curriculum-based measurement procedures described previously in this chapter provide an excellent system for frequently monitoring student performances.

• *Remember that an effective grading system is a motivational tool.* Sprick (1985, p. 35) stresses that the grading system is a motivational tool that the teacher controls:

> An effective grading system is more than an evaluation tool; it is also an instructional tool and a motivational tool. If designed and implemented well, a grading system can encourage students to try their best each day. An increase in daily motivation increases the chance that students will keep up with the work and learn how to demonstrate mastery of course objectives.

• *Determine whether district-wide grading procedures exist.* District-wide procedures are especially important when teachers are designing an alternative to traditional grading and marking methods for students with disabilities. District-wide procedures typically include guidelines for decisions about failing students and report card formats for communicating to parents and students. If district-wide procedures do not exist, efforts should be made to develop them. Consistency in grading is facilitated if district-wide procedures are available (Anderson & Wendel, 1988).

• *Use alternative grading systems for students with learning problems.* The teacher can select from the list of alternative grading systems to accommodate the needs of students with learning problems. These alternative systems should be planned with consideration for the student's ability, effort, achievement, and learning goals.

TESTING MODIFICATIONS

Teachers routinely assess their students' performance through the use of teacher-made tests. Success on most of these tests requires that the students have well-developed attention and memory skills (Salend, 1998). Thus, teacher-made tests may be an obstacle for students whose ability to take these tests successfully is limited because of their disabilities. To minimize the problems that students with learning difficulties may experience, several test adaptations are offered. Table 3.5 includes 25 test modifications that have been used to help students with learning problems succeed in the mainstream. Gajria, Salend, and Hemrick (1994) examined the extent to which 64 general education teachers used these test modifications. Their findings resulted in a rank ordering of test modifications used by general education teachers for mainstream students. The list in Table 3.5 includes modifications used by 50 percent or more of the teachers. Their results also indicate that the following seven modifications were used by less than half of the teachers:

TABLE 3.5
Test modifications for students with learning problems

Test Modifications	Percentage of Use by Teachers
1. Provide ample space for students to respond to items on test protocol.	96.9%
2. Space items so as not to interfere with one another.	95.3%
3. Prepare tests that are typewritten rather than handwritten.	90.6%
4. Allocate more time to complete the test.	90.6%
5. Place a blank beside each item on matching test questions rather than have students draw lines.	90.6%
6. Monitor students' performance during the test.	82.8%
7. Limit the number of choices to a maximum of four on multiple-choice test questions.	81.3%
8. Present items in a predictable hierarchical sequence.	79.7%
9. Give shorter, more frequent tests rather than fewer, more comprehensive tests.	79.7%
10. Read directions and test items to students.	79.7%
11. Use cues to enhance understanding of the major elements and directions.	76.6%
12. Require only brief response or outline form on essay test questions.	74.4%
13. Define unfamiliar or abstract words.	71.9%
14. Limit the number of matching items to ten.	71.9%
15. Provide a pool of responses for fill-in-the-blank test questions.	70.3%
16. Change the setting in which the student takes the test.	62.5%
17. Allow students to choose the number of questions they must answer.	62.5%
18. Avoid using *never, not, sometimes,* or *always* in true–false test questions.	60.9%
19. Adjust the reading level of the test to meet the students' needs.	59.4%
20. Decrease the number of test items.	57.8%
21. Place answers vertically under multiple-choice test questions.	57.8%
22. Place an equal number of choices in both columns on matching test questions.	57.8%
23. Avoid ambiguous choices such as *all of the above* or *none of the above* on multiple-choice test questions.	54.7%
24. Employ subsections that divide open-ended essay test questions.	54.7%
25. Allow students to dictate their responses.	50.0%

1. Give a sample test in advance.
2. Allow use of technological equipment in the presentation of test items.
3. Allow use of technological equipment for student responses.
4. Use alternative scoring procedures.
5. Provide a model of a correct response for each set of test directions.
6. Place lengthier items in the left-hand column on matching test questions.
7. Provide an answer check sheet that lists the components expected on essay test questions.

From an inspection of the results, Gajria et al. conclude that teachers are most likely to make testing modifications that they perceive maintain academic integrity, are effective, and require minimum individualization in terms of planning, extra time demands, and resources. In essence, the teachers used test modifications that they believed applied to all students.

Another area that has received much attention is the use of testing accommodations, modifications, and adaptations for students with disabilities when they are administered standardized tests such as state-sponsored minimum competency tests, achievement tests, the *Scholastic Aptitude Test,* and the *Graduate Record Exam.* Thurlow, Ysseldyke, and Silverstein (1995) divide some of the common accommodations, modifications, and adaptations into the following four areas:

1. *Presentation format*—Braille editions of test, use of magnifying equipment, large-print edition of test, oral reading of directions, signing of directions, and interpretation of directions

2. *Setting of test*—alone in a test carrel, with small groups, at home, and in special education class
3. *Response format*—mark response in test book, use template for responding, point to response, give response orally, give response in sign language, use typewriter for responding, use computer for responding, and receive assistance and interpretation with responses
4. *Timing of test*—extended time, more breaks during testing, and extending testing sessions over several days

Thurlow et al. note that a fundamental issue involves applying test modifications that remove or limit irrelevant sources of difficulty without altering the measurement of the construct being assessed. Limited research exists regarding test modifications; however, Beattie, Grise, and Algozzine (1983) found several modifications that enhanced the performance of third grade students with learning disabilities on the *Florida State Student Assessment Test*. These modifications include ordering items in terms of difficulty, allowing complete sentences to be on one line rather than splitting them into two lines to maintain margins, and using arrows and stop signs to guide students through test sections.

For students whose disabilities interfere with their ability to demonstrate their knowledge or skills, testing modifications are essential for them to succeed in mainstream classes or mainstream society. Responsible testing practices are needed to enable capable individuals with disabilities to earn good grades, gain acceptance to colleges and universities, and enter the job market.

☀ RECORDKEEPING

Recordkeeping for instructional purposes refers to the process of collecting and organizing data on student progress. Keeping a record of student progress enables the teacher to make timely instructional decisions. Also, recordkeeping is necessary to plan and implement individualized educational programs and to report student progress to parents.

Because students receive instruction in a wide range of skills that vary greatly in complexity, the task of recording student progress is not simple. Data collection can become quite cumbersome and awkward; thus, teachers may view it as a neg-

ative part of the instructional process. However, recordkeeping provides the teacher with essential information and therefore is a positive component of the instructional program. When recordkeeping is developed and managed correctly, many benefits are realized:

• Students often enjoy participating in recording their progress.
• Teachers can gain satisfaction from having documented student progress.
• Teachers can target learning difficulties and make timely interventions.
• Teachers can share the progress of students with parents, principals, and other school personnel.
• The data can be used to help make program and placement decisions.

A recordkeeping system must serve two primary functions. First, a composite or master form is needed to record the progress of students on major objectives across all curriculum areas. For the elementary teacher, this form includes several curriculum areas; for a secondary teacher, it may include only one area. Progress recorded on the composite form serves as a basis for evaluating students and reporting information to others. Second, a system is needed to record and evaluate the progress of students on daily or weekly instructional objectives. Suggestions and activities for recording student progress are featured in the curriculum area chapters throughout the text.

Composite Recordkeeping

The first step in developing a composite recordkeeping system is to organize instructional objectives. These objectives must be specific, measurable, and organized in steps small enough to reveal short-term progress (days to weeks). Instructional objectives that are in a sequence must be listed in a hierarchical manner. Nonsequential objectives (e.g., social skills objectives such as taking turns in a game or raising a hand to talk) should be clustered in a meaningful way. The sequential objectives on the composite form should be in larger steps than the daily instructional objectives.

The composite record of student progress provides the teacher with information for grouping the students for instruction. Students who are working on the same or similar objectives in a specific subject area may be organized into a small group for instruction. Once the initial instructional groups are established, the daily recording of student progress enables the teacher to change grouping patterns throughout the year. The student thus can move to and from groups on the basis of progress. The composite record also helps the teacher with the difficult problem of grading students.

Some commercial materials organize the objectives and provide the teacher with recordkeeping forms. Curriculum guides developed by school curriculum committees often outline the instructional objectives by subject area across grade levels. In addition, scope and sequence skills lists (such as those provided in Appendix A) provide a framework for organizing objectives.

A composite recordkeeping form should be kept simple. Also, because it is used for a long period by numerous people, it helps to use sturdy material. The sample form presented in Table 3.6 is organized by subject area for simplicity; for sturdiness, it may be constructed on a manila folder. When a folder is used, materials (such as criterion test results) may be placed in it for recording.

Daily Recordkeeping

To establish a daily recordkeeping system, short-term instructional objectives must be identified and arranged in a sequential order whenever pos-

sible. Criteria for mastery of the objectives must be established. Students should learn to evaluate and record their daily performances as much as possible.

A student progress book frequently is used. This is suitable especially for the secondary teacher who teaches the same subject to many students. Table 3.7 presents a progress book of daily or short-term objectives in social studies. Also, Table 3.8 presents a format for recording performances on spelling words in which the number of correct and incorrect responses is recorded.

For some instructional objectives that relate to social skills, observations may be recorded on tally sheets. For example, the teacher may wish to reduce out-of-seat behavior during math seatwork. Also, a tally sheet may be used to record academic responses. The teacher can make a tally each time the student capitalizes the first word in a sentence or responds correctly to a specific question.

The recordkeeping formats presented in this section provide the teacher with a variety of options for establishing a daily recording system. No matter which format is selected, the following steps must be followed in planning a data-recording system:

Step 1: Write a measurable short-term objective.

Step 2: Determine the measurement dimension to be used (e.g., accuracy, rate correct and incorrect, or frequency).

TABLE 3.6
Class progress record in reading

Students' Names	Instructional Objective: Pages in Textbook											
	1–5	6-11	12-20	21-26	27-31	32-40	41-43	44-47	48-51	52-58	59-64	65-68
1. Archer, B.	9/3	9/10	9/19	9/26	9/30	10/6	10/11	10/19	10/24	10/31		
2. Dillard, W.	9/3	9/16	9/30	10/11	10/24	10/31						
3. Gruggs, G.	9/7	9/18	10/4	10/23								
4. Hiller, D.	9/8	9/20	10/7	10/20	10/27							
5. Hunt, T.	9/7	9/19	10/4	10/22								
25. West, R.	9/4	9/15	9/19	9/30	10/6	10/12	10/27					

Note: Each objective is based on pages completed in a commercial material (e.g., workbook or reader).

TABLE 3.7

Progress book of short-term objectives in social studies

Students' Names	Social Studies Objectives							
Boyer, R.	79 9/20	80 9/21	81 9/22	82 9/24	87 9/25	88	89	90
Chestnut, W.	91 9/14	92 9/17	93 9/18	101 9/19	102 9/20	103 9/22	104	105
Martin, A.	49 9/20	52 9/22	53 9/24	54 9/25	55	80	81	82
Parker, D.	79 9/8	80 9/10	81 9/11	82 9/12	87 9/13	88 9/14	89 9/19	90
Rice, S.	91 9/17	92 9/19	93 9/20	101 9/22	102	103	104	105

Note: Because social studies objectives may not always be sequential, the numbers may not always be consecutive.

TABLE 3.8

Format for recording performances on spelling words

	Name: Bobby Richards		
Date	Spelling List Number	Correct Responses	Error Responses
10/2	1	14	6
10/3	1	16	4
10/4	1	17	3
10/5	1	20	0
10/6	2	15	5
10/9	2	16	4
10/10	2	19	1
10/11	3	11	9
10/12	3	16	4
10/13	3	17	3
10/16	3	19	1
10/17	4	17	3
10/18	4	20	0

Step 3: Decide how often to assess the behavior (e.g., daily 1-minute sample, 10-minute criterion test, weekly unit test, or all out-of-seat behavior during math seatwork).

Step 4: Establish a consistent schedule for measuring the behavior.

Step 5: Select a recording format.

REFERENCES

Abruscato, J. (1993). Early results and tentative implications from the Vermont Portfolio Project. *Phi Delta Kappan, 74,* 474–477.

Alberto, P. A., & Troutman, A. C. (1999). *Applied behavior analysis for teachers* (5th ed.). Upper Saddle River, NJ: Merrill/Prentice Hall.

Algozzine, B., & Mercer, C. D. (1980). Labels and expectancies for handicapped children and youth. In L. Mann & D. A. Sabatino (Eds.), *The fourth review of special education* (pp. 287–313). New York: Grune & Stratton.

Anderson, K. E., & Wendel, F. C. (1988). Pain relief: Make consistency the cornerstone of your policy on grading. *The American School Board Journal, 175*(10), 36–37.

Beattie, S., Grise, P., & Algozzine, B. (1983). Effects of test modifications on the minimum competency performance of learning disabled students. *Learning Disability Quarterly, 6,* 75–77.

Berliner, D. C. (1989). The place of process-product research in developing the agenda for research on teacher thinking. In J. Lowyck & C. Clark (Eds.), *Teacher thinking and professional action* (pp. 3–21). Belgium: Leuven University Press.

Bohannon, R. (1975). *Direct and daily measurement procedures in the identification and treatment of reading behaviors of children in special education.*

Unpublished doctoral dissertation, University of Washington, Seattle.

Brophy, J. E., & Good, T. L. (1974). *Teacher-student relationships.* New York: Holt, Rinehart & Winston.

Brunner, C. E., & Majewski, W. S. (1990). Mildly handicapped students can succeed with learning styles. *Educational Leadership, 48*(2), 21–23.

Bursuck, W., Polloway, E. A., Plante, L., Epstein, M. H., Jayanthi, M., & McConeghy, J. (1996). Report card grading and adaptations: A national survey of classroom practices. *Exceptional Children, 62,* 301–318.

DeBoer, A. (1994). *Grading alternatives.* Presentation conducted at Project TIDE Training, Myrtle Beach, SC.

Dempster, F. N. (1991). Synthesis of research on reviews and tests. *Educational Leadership, 48*(7), 71–76.

Deno, S. L. (1987). Curriculum-based measurement. *Teaching Exceptional Children, 20*(1), 41–42.

Deno, S. L., & Mirkin, P. K. (1977). *Data-based program modification.* Reston, VA: Council for Exceptional Children.

Deshler, D. D., & Lenz, B. K. (1989). The strategies instructional approach. *International Journal of Disability, Development, and Education, 36*(3), 203–224.

Deshler, D. D., Schumaker, J. B., & Lenz, B. K. (1984). Academic and cognitive interventions for LD adolescents: Part I. *Journal of Learning Disabilities, 17,* 108–117.

Dunn, R., Beaudry, J. S., & Klavas, A. (1989). Survey of research on learning styles. *Educational Leadership, 46*(6), 50–58.

Emmer, E. T., Evertson, C. M., & Worsham, M. E. (2000). *Classroom management for secondary teachers* (5th ed.). Boston: Allyn & Bacon.

Frank, A. R. (1973). Breaking down learning tasks: A sequence approach. *Teaching Exceptional Children, 6,* 16–29.

Fuchs, L. S. (1986). Monitoring progress among mildly handicapped pupils: Review of current practice and research. *Remedial and Special Education, 7*(5), 5–12.

Fuchs, L. S., Bahr, C. M., & Rieth, H. J. (1989). Effects of goal structures and performance contingencies on the math performance of adolescents with learning disabilities. *Journal of Learning Disabilities, 22,* 554–560.

Fuchs, L. S., & Fuchs, D. (1986). Effects of systematic formative evaluation: A meta-analysis. *Exceptional Children, 53,* 199–208.

Fuchs, L. S., Fuchs, D., & Deno, S. L. (1985). The importance of goal ambitiousness and goal mastery to student achievement. *Exceptional Children, 52,* 63–71.

Fuchs, L. S., Fuchs, D., & Hamlett, C. L. (1989). Effects of instrumental use of curriculum-based measurement to enhance instructional programs. *Remedial and Special Education, 10*(2), 43–52.

Fuchs, L. S., Fuchs, D., & Maxwell, L. (1988). The validity of informal reading comprehension measures. *Remedial and Special Education, 9*(2), 20–28.

Fuchs, L. S., Wesson, C., Tindal, G., Mirkin, P., & Deno, S. (1981). *Teacher efficiency in continuous evaluation of IEP goals* (Research Report No. 53). Minneapolis: University of Minnesota Institute for Research in Learning Disabilities.

Gajria, M., Salend, S. J., & Hemrick, M. A. (1994). Teacher acceptability of testing modifications for mainstreamed students. *Learning Disabilities Research & Practice, 9,* 236–243.

Graham, S., & Harris, K. R. (1994). Implications of constructivism for teaching writing to students with special needs. *The Journal of Special Education, 28,* 275–289.

Griggs, S. A., & Dunn, R. (1988). High school dropouts: Do they learn differently from those who remain in school? *The Principal, 35*(1), 1–8.

Hall, T., & Tindal, G. (1989). Using curriculum-based measures to group students in reading. In G. Tindal, K. Essick, C. Skeen, N. George, & M. George (Eds.), *The Oregon Conference '89: Monograph.* Eugene: University of Oregon College of Education.

Howell, K. W., Kaplan, J. S., & O'Connell, C. Y. (1979). *Evaluating exceptional children: A task analysis approach.* Upper Saddle River, NJ: Merrill/Prentice Hall.

Howell, K. W., & Nolet, V. (2000). *Curriculum-based evaluation: Teaching and decision making* (3rd ed.). Belmont, CA: Wadsworth/Thomson Learning.

Idol, L. (1993). *Special educator's consultation handbook* (2nd ed.). Austin, TX: PRO-ED.

Joint Committee on Teacher Planning for Students with Disabilities. (1995). Planning for academic diversity in America's classrooms: Windows on reality, research, change, and practice. *Effective School Practices, 14*(2), 1–53.

Kavale, K. A., & Forness, S. R. (1987). Substance over style: Assessing the efficacy of modality testing and teaching. *Exceptional Children, 54,* 228–239.

Kavale, K. A., & Forness, S. R. (1990). Substance over style: A rejoinder to Dunn's animadversions. *Exceptional Children, 56,* 357–361.

Kerr, M. M., & Nelson, C. M. (1998). *Strategies for managing behavior problems in the classroom* (3rd ed.). Upper Saddle River, NJ: Merrill/Prentice Hall.

Koorland, M. A., Keel, M. C., & Ueberhorst, P. (1990). Setting aims for precision learning. *Teaching Exceptional Children, 22*(3), 64–68.

Lindsley, O. (1964). Direct measurement and prosthesis of retarded behavior. *Journal of Education, 147,* 62.

Lindsley, O. R. (1971). Precision teaching in perspective: An interview with Ogden R. Lindsley. *Teaching Exceptional Children, 3*(3), 114–119.

Lloyd, J., Saltzman, N. J., & Kauffman, J. M. (1981). Predictable generalization in academic learning as a result of preskills and strategy training. *Learning Disability Quarterly, 4,* 203–216.

McLoughlin, J. A., & Lewis, R. B. (1994). *Assessing special students* (4th ed.). Upper Saddle River, NJ: Merrill/Prentice Hall.

Mercer, C. D., & Corbett, N. L. (1991). Enhancing assessment for students at risk for school failure. *Contemporary Education, 62,* 259–265.

Mercer, C. D., Mercer, A. R., & Evans, S. (1982). The use of frequency in establishing instructional aims. *Journal of Precision Teaching, 3*(3), 57–63.

Miller, A. (1981). Conceptual matching models and interactional research in education. *Review of Educational Research, 51,* 33–84.

Miramontes, O., Cheng, L., & Trueba, H. T. (1984). Teacher perceptions and observed outcomes: An ethnographic study of classroom interactions. *Learning Disability Quarterly, 7,* 349–357.

Mirkin, P., Deno, S., Tindal, G., & Kuehnle, K. (1979). *Formative evaluation: Continued development of data utilization systems* (Research Report No. 23). Minneapolis: University of Minnesota Institute for Research in Learning Disabilities.

Nelson, C. M., & Polsgrove, L. (1984). Behavior analysis in special education: White rabbit or white elephant? *Remedial and Special Education, 5*(4), 6–17.

Paulson, F. L., Paulson, P. R., & Meyer, C. A. (1991). What makes a portfolio a portfolio? *Educational Leadership, 48*(5), 60–63.

Rieth, H., & Evertson, C. (1988). Variables related to the effective instruction of difficult-to-teach children. *Focus on Exceptional Children, 20*(5), 1–8.

Rojewski, J. W., Pollard, R. R., & Meers, G. D. (1990). Grading mainstreamed special needs students: Determining practices and attitudes of secondary vocational educators using a qualitative approach. *Re-*

medial and Special Education, 12(1), 7–15, 28.

Rosenthal, R., & Jacobson, L. (1966). Teachers' expectancies: Determinants of pupils' IQ gains. *Psychological Reports, 19*(1), 115–118.

Salend, S. J. (1998). *Effective mainstreaming: Creating inclusive classrooms* (3rd ed.). Upper Saddle River, NJ: Merrill/Prentice Hall.

Salvia, J., & Ysseldyke, J. E. (1998). *Assessment* (7th ed.). Boston: Houghton Mifflin.

Schumaker, J. B., Deshler, D. D., Alley, G. R., & Warner, M. M. (1983). Toward the development of an intervention model for learning disabled adolescents: The University of Kansas Institute. *Exceptional Education Quarterly, 4,* 45–74.

Smith, D. D. (1981). *Teaching the learning disabled.* Upper Saddle River, NJ: Prentice Hall.

Smith, D. D., & Luckasson, R. (1992). *Introduction to special education: Teaching in an age of challenge.* Boston: Allyn & Bacon.

Smith, R. M., Neisworth, J. T., & Greer, J. G. (1978). *Evaluating educational environments.* Upper Saddle River, NJ: Merrill/Prentice Hall.

Snider, V. E. (1992). Learning styles and learning to read: A critique. *Remedial and Special Education, 13,* 6–18.

Sprick, R. S. (1985). *Discipline in the secondary classroom: A problem-by-problem survival guide.* West Nyack, NY: The Center for Applied Research in Education.

Tappenden, V. J. (1983). Analysis of the learning styles of vocational education and nonvocational education students in eleventh and twelfth grades from rural, urban, and suburban locations in Ohio. *Dissertation Abstracts International, 44,* 1326a.

Terwilliger, J. S. (1977). Assigning grades—Philosophical issues and practical recommendations. *Journal of Research and Development in Education, 10,* 21–39.

Thurlow, M. L., Ysseldyke, J. E., & Silverstein, B. (1995). Testing accommodations for students with disabilities. *Remedial and Special Education, 16*(5), 260–270.

Tindal, G. A., & Marston, D. B. (1990). *Classroom-based assessment: Evaluating instructional outcomes.* Upper Saddle River, NJ: Merrill/Prentice Hall.

Utley, B. L., Zigmond, N., & Strain, P. S. (1987). How various forms of data affect teacher analysis of student performance. *Exceptional Children, 53,* 411–422.

Valencia, S. (1990). A portfolio approach to classroom reading assessment: The whys, whats, and hows. *The Reading Teacher, 43,* 338–340.

Wesson, C. L., King, R. P., & Deno, S. L. (1984). Direct and frequent measurement of student performance: If it's good for us, why don't we do it? *Learning Disability Quarterly, 7,* 45–48.

White, O. R. (1986). Precision teaching—Precision learning. *Exceptional Children, 52,* 522–534.

White, O. R., & Haring, N. G. (1980). *Exceptional teaching* (2nd ed.). Upper Saddle River, NJ: Merrill/Prentice Hall.

Wood, J. W. (1998). *Adapting instruction to accommodate students in inclusive settings* (3rd ed.). Upper Saddle River, NJ: Merrill/Prentice Hall.

Worthen, B. R. (1993). Critical issues that will determine the future of alternative assessment. *Phi Delta Kappan, 74,* 444–454.

Ysseldyke, J. E., & Algozzine, B. (1995). *Special education: A practical approach for teachers* (3rd ed.). Boston: Houghton Mifflin.

Ysseldyke, J. E., & Christenson, S. L. (1993). *The Instructional Environment System— II.* Longmont, CO: Sopris West.

CHAPTER 4

Teaching Students and Managing Instruction

The first chapter of this text, "Creating Responsive Learning Environments," stresses the need to understand the characteristics and needs of learners, maximize the use of human resources (e.g., teachers, parents, and students), identify and plan for students with mild disabilities according to federal legislation, and recognize some factors that promote school success for learners with mild disabilities. The second chapter, "Planning and Organizing Instruction," considers physical arrangement of the classroom, instructional arrangements (e.g., large-group instruction, students teaching students, and material with student), and logistical factors such as scheduling, homework practices, and use of classroom equipment. The third chapter, "Assessing Students for Instruction," discusses the importance of assessment within the context of instruction and learning. Monitoring student performance, alternative grading, and test modifications are featured topics. These three chapters set the stage for the focus of this chapter—interactive teaching and factors that directly influence it.

Interactive teaching begins when the teacher and the students are engaged with one another to promote student learning. The intensity of interactive teaching is apparent when one realizes that the typical elementary teacher participates in 1,000 daily interactions (Jackson, 1968) and makes about 5,000 daily decisions (Goldberg, 1990). Interactive teaching is the hub of the instructional process and demands careful planning and skillful orchestration and implementation.

☀ A CONTINUUM OF INSTRUCTIONAL CHOICES

Classes that include students with mild disabilities typically also include average achievers, high achievers, low achievers, and culturally diverse learners. These students bring a kaleidoscope of prior knowledge, personal needs, and cultural experiences to the classroom. This diversity necessitates that teachers use instructional procedures that make it possible for all students to learn. Too often, however, educators become narrowly focused on a single perspective of teaching and learning. For example, a teacher who is a social constructivist may dismiss highly behavioral approaches. Likewise, a teacher who is a behaviorist may refuse to try constructivistic approaches. In either case, instructional choices are reduced and learners are denied the instructional options they need.

Mather and Roberts (1994) underscore the need to recognize individual differences and to select an instructional method or a combination of methods that helps a student achieve. Although a single instructional method is seldom effective for all students in a classroom, some educators cling to a particular method, insisting that all students will succeed if it is implemented correctly. Mather and Roberts note that the notion of teaching "harder" using a previously unsuccessful method is similar to "shouting English to a non-English speaker" (p. 55). Neither is likely to create enhanced results. Dixon and Carnine (1994) implore educators to stop emphasizing educational ideologies and, instead, to concentrate on the value of specific instructional practices. "Dogma . . . taints our perceptions in ways that serve no useful purpose for learners" (p. 357).

This section focuses on two instructional approaches that have been characterized as mutually exclusive: explicit teaching and implicit teaching. These two broad, yet distinct, approaches encompass most commonly used teaching practices (Mercer, Lane, Jordan, Allsopp, & Eisele, 1996). From a pragmatic perspective, they appear compatible, and both are needed to address the needs of students in a diverse classroom.

Explicit teaching is instruction in which the teacher serves as the provider of knowledge. Explicit teaching is based on the belief that when learning is complex and difficult for learners, the teacher must provide extensive support to students and transmit knowledge that facilitates learning. Skills and concepts are presented in a clear and direct fashion that promotes student mastery. In explicit instruction, the teacher provides an explanation or model of a skill or concept, guides students through application of the skill or concept in a variety of situations, and provides many opportunities for independent application that will ensure mastery and generalization. Explicit instruction emphasizes student mastery, and its principles are compatible with behavioral theory, direct instruction, task analysis, product-oriented effective teaching research, and exogenous constructivism.

TABLE 4.1

Explicit-to-implicit continuum of instructional choices

Explicit Instruction	Interactive Instruction	Implicit Instruction
Much direct teacher assistance	Balance between direct and nondirect teacher assistance	Nondirect teacher assistance
Teacher regulation of learning	Shared regulation of learning	Student regulation of learning
Directed discovery	Guided discovery	Self-discovery
Direct instruction	Strategic instruction	Self-regulated instruction
Task analysis	Balance between part-to-whole and whole-to-part	Unit approach
Behavioral	Cognitive/metacognitive	Holistic
Exogenous constructivism	Dialectical constructivism	Endogenous constructivism

Implicit teaching is an instructional ideology that assumes that students are naturally active learners who construct new personalized knowledge through linking prior knowledge and new knowledge. An authentic context augments the development of this knowledge as students make connections between classroom activities and real-world problem solving (Cobb, Yackel, & Wood, 1992; Englert, Tarrant, & Mariage, 1992). Thus, in implicit instruction, the teacher facilitates student learning and creates situations in which students can discover new knowledge and construct their own meanings. Skills and concepts are learned through exposure in meaningful contexts. In implicit instruction, the teacher guides students only as much as is necessary for them to build their own understandings. Scaffolding, or teacher support through questioning and explaining, is provided only as needed. A community of learners is developed in which students collaborate to discover alternative ways to solve problems and construct new knowledge. Implicit instruction emphasizes the thinking processes involved in learning; it is compatible with holistic theory and social constructivism.

Between the explicit and implicit extremes is *dialectical* or *interactive teaching,* which is based on the belief that knowledge is a collaborative enterprise and that instruction should include both explicit and implicit methods. In these collaborative interactions, the teacher provides instruction (e.g., offering metacognitive explanations, modeling cognitive processes, asking leading questions, and providing encouragement) as necessary to guide student discovery. A key feature of this supportive instruction is that the dialogue between the teacher and the students provides the learners with the support and guidance they need to achieve a goal efficiently.

Table 4.1 provides a continuum of explicit-to-implicit instructional choices with descriptive components. The continuum includes Moshman's (1982) three levels of constructivism: exogenous, dialectical, and endogenous. These three levels parallel explicit, interactive, and implicit instruction.

Explicit and implicit approaches are viewed by many educators as incompatible and dichotomous. Heshusius (1989, 1991) and Poplin (1988) criticize the explicit approaches employed by many special educators as being too reductionistic and mechanistic. They believe that an implicit approach to teaching is better suited to the construction of knowledge by learners. In contrast, Engelmann (1988) and Liberman and Liberman (1990) insist that learners need explicit instruction to master many basic concepts and develop problem-solving and higher order thinking. They view implicit teaching as ineffective and inefficient for many learners.

The student population's increasing diversity compels educators to view student learning needs along a continuum. Student factors and content factors influence the appropriateness of instructional options along the continuum. Most educators favor explicit teaching when students with moderate-to-mild disabilities are the target population. This position is understandable when the characteristics of these learners are considered.

Students with histories of problems in automaticity, metacognitive strategies, memory, attention, generalization, proactive learning, and motivation cannot plausibly engage in efficient self-discovery learning (i.e., implicit teaching).

Howell and Nolet (2000) provide guidelines regarding student factors when selecting an instructional approach. Howell and Nolet suggest using a more implicit approach when the student has an adaptive or flexible motivational system, has significant prior knowledge of the task or concept, and encounters consistent success with the content. They recommend a more explicit approach when the student has a rigid motivational pattern, lacks significant prior knowledge, or encounters repeated failure on the task.

In addition to student characteristics, the nature of the content of instruction guides educators in their selection of instructional approaches. Howell and Nolet (2000) provide guidelines regarding curriculum or content factors when selecting an instructional approach. They recommend a more implicit approach when the task is simple, well-defined, conceptual in nature, and able to be completed by a general problem-solving strategy. On the other hand, an explicit approach is more appropriate when the task is complex, is poorly defined, has missing information, or requires a task-specific strategy. Explicit instruction is warranted if the content is critical to subsequent learning or requires a high level of proficiency. If time is limited or if a priority on mastery exists, an explicit approach works best. Finally, a hazardous task requires explicit instruction. For example, a person learning to operate heavy equipment needs specific information regarding correct procedures and possible hazards, rather than self-discovering such information.

Setting Demands of an Implicit Learning Environment

An implicit learning environment places substantial demands on the learner. The following list highlights some of the most pertinent demands and their relationship to some of the learning characteristics of students with learning problems (Mercer, Jordan, & Miller, 1996):

• Learners must have sufficient prior knowledge to construct new and appropriate meaning from understanding connections between prior learning and new information. Many students with learning problems exhibit severe learning discrepancies in academics. Thus, many of these students have inadequate amounts of prior knowledge.

• Learners must attend to teacher presentations, teacher–student interactions, and student–student interactions regarding academics. Many students with learning problems have difficulty sustaining attention to relevant visual or auditory stimuli.

• Learners must use cognitive and metacognitive processing to acquire, remember, and construct new knowledge in a manner that is authentic to their lives. Students with learning problems typically exhibit cognitive and metacognitive deficits that hinder information processing (Torgesen, 1990). Specifically, some of these students are described as having difficulty in assessing their abilities to solve problems, identifying and selecting appropriate strategies, organizing information to be learned, monitoring problem-solving processes, evaluating problems for accuracy, and generalizing strategies to appropriate situations.

• Students must be active participants in their own learning. Many students with learning problems have histories of academic failure that contribute to the development of learned helplessness in academics. It is postulated that such learned helplessness results from students repeatedly trying to read words or solve problems when they have little or no understanding of content or concepts. This lack of understanding fosters the student's dependency on the teacher and thus promotes the belief that external help is needed to read words or solve problems correctly. Repetition of this event promotes and strengthens learned helplessness.

• Students must engage in group discussions to work in cooperative learning arrangements. These collaborative and cooperative events help establish a community of learners and require oral language skills (e.g., presenting organized information, making persuasive arguments, and participating in debates) and appropriate social skills (e.g., listening, taking turns, and respecting others' opinions). The use of language is extensive, and the language demands of cooperative group activities increase in each grade level. Also, social skills deficits among individuals with learning problems are high.

- To become self-regulated learners, students must recognize their own learning characteristics, develop their own metacognitive strategies, and maintain a proactive attitude about learning. Many students with learning problems have been described as *passive learners,* which refers to students who are cognitively passive because they typically do not participate actively or self-regulate their own learning. Also, many of these students are characterized as having motivational deficits due to their passivity.

Examination of the setting demands and prevalent characteristics of students with learning problems demonstrates that many such students lack the attributes, skills, and knowledge needed to succeed in an implicit setting. These and other students at risk for school failure require much teacher support and direction to begin moving toward becoming self-regulated lifelong learners. The teaching practices on the explicit end of the continuum of instructional choices (such as directed modeling, teaching to mastery, scaffolding, think alouds, and the use of mnemonics) can serve as a springboard to help students become more proactive and successful learners. The range of teaching practices along this continuum provides a framework for educating a diversity of learners. Explicit teaching or teacher-directed learning is needed immediately to help the more immature learners, whereas implicit teaching helps mature learners (e.g., those with rich prior knowledge, proactivity, and social acumen) continue their growth.

Research Base for a Continuum of Instructional Choices

Research conducted across curriculum areas indicates that students of diverse abilities respond differently to instruction. The findings of this research provide a foundation for an instructional continuum.

Language   Warren and Yoder (1994) contend that instructional choices in the field of language and communication are needed and that, during some developmental stages, certain choices are clearly better than others. For example, direct, explicit instruction was compared with milieu teaching (an approach that combines student-directed activities with teacher prompts) and was found to be more effective for instruction in advanced linguistic skills (Yoder, Kaiser, & Alpert, 1991). In contrast, explicit instruction was not as effective as milieu teaching for early vocabulary instruction.

Reading   Stanovich (1994) asserts that the selection of an appropriate approach to reading instruction depends upon the learner and the skill. With skills close to perceptual input systems (i.e., specific information such as phonological relationships and vocabulary), the need for explicit instruction is great. On the other hand, as the type of skill moves away from perceptual input systems (i.e., less specific information such as inferential comprehension), implicit instructional approaches become more powerful.

According to Stanovich (1994), explicit instruction and teacher-directed strategy training are more effective for teaching word recognition skills, especially for at-risk children, children with learning disabilities, and children with special needs. Numerous researchers have demonstrated that explicit instruction helps students at risk for learning problems acquire reading and spelling skills (Bradley & Bryant, 1985; Chall, 1989; Engelmann, 1988; Evans & Carr, 1985; Iverson & Tunmer, 1993). Moreover, programs for such students have improved reading skills using explicit instruction (Slavin et al., 1994).

Writing   Graham and Harris (1994) note that by the end of the primary grades, average-achieving students often have reached a level of fluency in the mechanics of writing that provides freedom in getting thoughts on paper (i.e., planning and content generation). Students with special needs do not reach this level of fluency as early as other students (Graham, 1990). The incidental methods of whole language and process approaches may be insufficient for students at risk for learning failure. Graham and Harris explain that students with special needs require more than frequent, meaningful, authentic writing to achieve good writing skills. They propose research on writing approaches that integrate explicit instruction with more authentic writing activities. Such approaches have shown promising results, but additional research is needed.

Math   The findings of mathematics research indicate that students can benefit from instruction that includes both explicit and implicit methods (Mercer, Jordan, & Miller, 1994). The literature supports explicit methods such as description of procedures, modeling of skills (during which the teacher uses "think alouds" or describes the thinking process as problems are solved), use of cues and prompts, direct questioning of students to ensure understanding, and practice to mastery. Implicit methods such as linking information to prior knowledge, reflection on learning, interactive discourse about concepts, and discovery methods also are recommended.

Science   Scruggs and Mastropieri (1994) point out the lack of attention in research to implicit science instruction for students with special needs. They describe their continuing research in special education classrooms that use an inquiry (implicit) approach to science. Scruggs and Mastropieri conclude that students with mild disabilities can construct scientific knowledge but that they need much support to succeed. Teachers must provide highly structured coaching and behavioral management techniques.

Perspective on a Continuum of Instructional Choices

Struggles to advance a single instructional paradigm occur almost exclusively at the university level and, fortunately, the ideological extremes are seldom found in actual classrooms. Educational researchers must remember the needs of individual students and individual teachers. Restricting the range of instructional choices in the name of paradigmatic purity serves no useful purpose. Educational research should support the implementation of instructional practices that are most appropriate to meet individual educational needs. Accepting a broader view of instructional practice is a good place to start. The following personal story provides an interesting perspective on the need to consider a range of viewpoints in constructing a responsive learning environment.

Several years ago, Ann and I took a snow skiing lesson in Utah. Our ski instructor was wonderful. His experiences included teaching skiing to many individuals with physical disabilities. When the lessons began, I was fearful, anxious, and excited. The skiing equipment, the slopes, the ice, the ski lifts, and gravity were all intimidating. During the process of the lessons, I had the following experiences:

1. During the first 10 minutes of instruction, I went backward down the little knoll we were on and could not get up. Ann laughed, and the ski instructor smiled.

2. When approaching the ski lift, I tried to hurry and fell down on the path under the lift. The operator stopped the ski lift and instructed a person to help me get up. Ann laughed from her vantage point on the ski lift above me, and the ski instructor smiled.

3. Upon exiting the ski lift, I saw Ann and the ski instructor sprawled on the ground. I was unaware that skiing was required to exit the lift; however, I made an incredible move to avoid hitting my wife and the instructor. Unfortunately, I did not see the person on the top of the slope about to launch down the mountain. I joined this person with force, and we proceeded to tumble down the slope. Ann looked concerned, and the ski instructor enjoyed a hearty laugh.

The instructor worked with Ann and me for several hours. He explicitly taught us how to fall, get up with skis on, turn, traverse a slope, and snow plow to slow down. He described, modeled, and gave corrective feedback and encouragement. Slowly, I gained confidence, but I continued to work hard at skiing. Finally, the instructor said, "If I could stop you from thinking so much about all the techniques, I could help you discover the ease and joy of skiing." Then he told me to stop looking at my skis and to look at the mountain across the valley and ski down the mountain. He told me that I was ready and could do it. I tried it, and I skied the mountain without looking down. What an exhilarating experience! The techniques that the instructor had taught seemed to develop naturally. He was indeed a gifted teacher.

When reflecting about the ski instructor's teaching, I realized that he had used a continuum of explicit and implicit instruction. Initially, he taught me the basics explicitly and gave me confidence. As I learned, he became more implicit. In the end, he challenged me to discover skiing at a more advanced level.

Just as I was challenged by skiing the mountain, students of all ability levels are challenged by academic concepts that often are difficult to understand and attain. However, the use of both explicit and implicit instructional components has the potential to help a diversity of learners acquire and use academic skills and content. Educators should teach students how to fall, get up, self-correct, and discover the mountains of fun that learning can provide. They should teach them how to use the equipment (e.g., computers, rulers, calculators, objects, and books), explore concepts, correct errors, slow down and think, collaborate, and discover the joys of learning.

The curriculum area chapters of this text provide a wealth of activities, strategies, and techniques that can be used within the context of the explicit-to-implicit instructional continuum. Because most students with learning problems need much teacher assistance, explicit and interactive instruction are emphasized. For example, the Direct Instruction Model developed at the University of Oregon and the Strategic Intervention Model developed at the University of Kansas Center for Research on Learning are included as effective instructional practices that respectively represent explicit and interactive instruction.

☀ SYSTEMATIC TEACHING STEPS

Teaching styles are developed individually, but they should not be based on whims, biases, or personal opinions. Teachers and teacher educators have a responsibility to examine the research and apply the findings as they develop teacher practices. Greenwood, Arreaga-Mayer, and Carta (1994) found that students in classrooms in which teachers used research-based interactive teaching practices had higher academic engagement times and achievement scores than students in classrooms in which teachers used other methods. To ensure appropriate academic progress, teachers must use well-designed lessons with students with learning problems. Archer et al. (1989) present a lesson design for students with disabilities that is based on effective teaching research. The components of their design plus components from the research are discussed and organized in terms of (1) opening the lesson, (2) conducting an interactive presentation, (3) closing the lesson, and (4) using continuous teaching components. The information included in the tables in this section was compiled from the following sources: Anderson, Brubaker,

Alleman-Brooks, and Duffy (1985); Anderson, Evertson, and Emmer (1980); Anderson, Raphael, Englert, and Stevens (1991); Bickel and Bickel (1986); Brophy and Good (1986); Christenson, Ysseldyke, and Thurlow (1989); Deno and Fuchs (1987); Ellis, Deshler, Lenz, Schumaker, and Clark (1991); Englert et al. (1992); Fisher et al. (1980); Gage and Needels (1989); Lenz, Bulgren, and Hudson (1990); Mercer (1997); Olson and Platt (2000); Rieth and Evertson (1988); Rosenshine and Stevens (1986); and Scruggs, Mastropieri, Sullivan, and Hesser (1993). When a teacher incorporates these practices into daily instruction, the likelihood of improving the achievement of students increases.

Opening the Lesson

The first task in opening a lesson is to gain the students' attention. This usually is accomplished through verbal cueing such as "Let's get started," "Eyes on me," or "Time to start." Verbal statements frequently are more effective if they are followed by teacher "wait time" to permit follow through and eye contact with students. Lavoie (1993) recommends the use of a focusing activity to help capture students' attention. This activity, which is especially useful for beginning the day's first lesson, can involve asking a high-interest question related to current events. For example, when the teacher asks, "Does anyone know what surprising event happened at the beach yesterday?" the students quickly may become engaged in a discussion about whales beaching themselves. After a brief discussion on whales, the teacher can shift students' attention to the lesson. Nonverbal cues are another technique for gaining students' attention (e.g., the teacher stands in a specific area and visually scans the class, or the teacher points to a poster that says *Look at the teacher and listen*). Throughout the day the teacher must redirect students' attention from one activity to another. In doing this, the teacher should announce the transition clearly and ensure that students know her or his expectations. Specific expectations are taught readily by teaching students a mnemonic that cues expected behaviors (e.g., the SLANT mnemonic, which is presented later in this chapter).

Once the students are attending, the teacher helps them connect the lesson to prior knowledge (e.g., the previous lesson or related experience).

TABLE 4.2

Competencies for opening a lesson

Gain students' attention by using verbal or nonverbal cues, or introduce a high-interest focusing topic.
State expectations for each transition, and consider using a mnemonic device (e.g., SLANT) to teach expectations.
Connect the lesson to prior learning or knowledge.
Review and reteach if prior knowledge is insufficient.
Identify the lesson's target skill, strategy, or content.
Provide a rationale for learning the skill, strategy, or content.
Discuss the relevance of the skill, strategy, or content until an authentic context is realized. Authenticity may be achieved within the context of school activities, community events, or future demands.
Have students identify what they know and set goals indicating what they expect to learn.

This procedure usually includes such statements as "Last time, we learned to solve multiplication problems by using objects" or "Yesterday we practiced finding words within words." Also, it helps to ask questions that allow students to demonstrate their skill or knowledge level. For example, the teacher can ask, "In a multiplication problem such as *27 × 4*, what does the *4* represent?" or "What words can you find in the word *together*?"

Next, the teacher introduces the target skill, strategy, or knowledge for the lesson and provides a rationale for learning it. Included in this step is a focus on setting goals (e.g., "Today we are going to learn to solve multiplication problems by drawing. Drawing the problems will help you understand multiplication better and enable you to solve them without using objects"). Such statements introduce the skill and the goal as well as provide a rationale for learning. Hasselbring (1994) suggests the use of anchoring activities to help connect the lesson content to real-world situations. Anchoring activities involve having the class discuss the relevancy of the skill, strategy, or content within an authentic context. Mercer, Jordan, and Miller (1996) note that authenticity may be accomplished by discussing the skill, strategy, or content within the context of school activities (e.g., passing tests), community events (e.g., computing the best price of an item), or future demands (e.g., getting a job or graduating from secondary school). Finally, it helps for the students to identify their objectives by evaluating their current learning status and predicting learning outcomes. Having students identify what they know, what they will learn, and how they know whether they have learned provides a

nice context for guiding their learning process. Table 4.2 lists a summary of competencies for opening a lesson.

Conducting an Interactive Presentation

The interactive presentation is the heart of the instructional process and actively involves the teacher presenting and interacting with the students. To do this, the teacher uses explicit modeling and guided practice to teach new material. These procedures are essential in helping most students with learning problems to succeed in school.

Explicit Modeling The purpose of explicit modeling is to "paint pictures" for learners in such a way that understanding is ensured. The teacher instructs the students to watch, listen, and think while the teacher models. Through teacher "think alouds," learners observe metacognitive processes used in learning skills, content, or strategies. Two excellent procedures are used in modeling: (1) the teacher asks a question and provides the answer; the students hear and observe the teacher think aloud while modeling the strategy, and (2) the teacher asks a question, and the students help provide the answer; the teacher and the students perform the strategy together, and the teacher continues to provide modeling. The opportunity to observe and experience these thought processes helps learners activate their own thinking processes. Thus, explicit modeling becomes essential for immature learners (e.g., those who have limited prior knowledge or are passive learners) to acquire and use essential

TABLE 4.3
Competencies for explicit
modeling

Provide step-by-step demonstrations of covert and overt procedures
involved in learning new information or applying strategies.
Use think alouds to model covert processes involved in learning strategies
or problem solving (e.g., the teacher asks a question aloud and answers it
aloud while describing covert and overt processes).
Provide examples and nonexamples to show distinctive and nondistinctive
concept features.
Maintain a lively pace while modeling, but allow enough time for students to
understand the content or strategy.
Model with enthusiasm.
Model task-specific learning strategies (i.e., perform the task) and self-
instructions (e.g., self-monitoring or problem solving) to help students
achieve.
Prompt student involvement with questions and check understanding during
modeling.
Correct student responses and help students expand responses.
Note organization, relationships, and clues in the new material that elicit
learning strategies.

knowledge. For example, Montague (1992) used explicit modeling of cognitive and metacognitive strategies to teach students with learning disabilities to solve word problems successfully. The specific cognitive strategies modeled included the following: (1) *read* for understanding, (2) *paraphrase* in your own words, (3) *visualize* a picture or diagram, (4) *develop* a plan to solve the problem, (5) *estimate* the answer, (6) *compute,* and (7) *check* to make sure everything is right. Table 4.3 lists a summary of competencies for explicit modeling. Teacher modeling is a key to academic success for many students. Just do it!

Guided Practice   After explicit modeling and before independent practice, the teacher directs the active participation of students in guided practice. Guided practice primarily consists of the teacher prompting students and checking their work. Prompts enable the teacher to help students perform the task so that initial practice will be successful. Prompts consist of asking leading questions, repeating and rephrasing lesson content, pointing to a specific word or number, providing examples and nonexamples, giving feedback, doing tasks partially, doing a task with students, and providing manual guidance. After students perform the task with prompts, the teacher checks to see whether they can work successfully without prompts. The teacher constantly monitors student

progress and gives corrective feedback until students are ready to work independently. If students have difficulty, the teacher may repeat the model, prompt, and check procedures in quick succession.

The teacher should use a continuum of assistance to determine how much support students need and what kind of prompts and cues are necessary. For example, some students may need little assistance after appropriate modeling and, thus, minimal monitoring and feedback to complete the task. Other students may need to be reminded to complete certain steps in the task, or they may need more explanation about some aspect of the task. The teacher provides more or less explicit instruction during guided practice, based upon individual student needs. As students demonstrate accuracy in the skill, the teacher decreases the amount of assistance. Table 4.4 presents a summary of competencies for conducting guided practice.

Closing the Lesson

In closing a lesson, the teacher summarizes the lesson's skills or concepts and connects them to future learning. The typical components of a closing are (1) a review of the lesson content, (2) a preview of the next lesson, and (3) the introduction and assignment of independent practice (Archer, Gleason, & Isaacson, 1995).

TABLE 4.4
Competencies for conducting
guided practice

Provide clear directions and expectations for tasks used during guided
practice.
Use prompts to ensure student success. For example:
  Ask leading questions (e.g., "Did you check your work?").
  Point and cue (e.g., point to a word or number, and cue students to think
  aloud).
  Give examples and nonexamples.
  Model the task.
  Repeat the directions or rephrase lesson content.
  Provide wait time.
  Instruct students to check their work.
  Do the task with students.
Use prescriptive prompts to guide successful learning.
Reduce assistance when students are successful, and increase assistance
  when students have difficulty.
Check student work continuously to ensure success.
Provide instruction based on student errors (e.g., repeat the model, prompt,
  and check sequence for students who are having difficulties).
Summarize students' accomplishments, and encourage them to enter
  independent practice.

Review   During review, the critical information presented in the lesson is summarized. Also, the teacher checks student understanding with a final practice or by questioning students. For example, the teacher might ask students to solve a math problem by drawing it, and then monitor their work to check for understanding. The teacher can also determine student understanding through questions (e.g., "What is the first step in drawing a math problem?").

Preview   The preview consists of introducing the next lesson. It provides students with a meaningful temporal context for their learning (e.g., what they are learning and doing, and what they will learn and do). Also, expectations concerning how they can apply their accumulating knowledge are discussed.

Independent Practice   The teacher acknowledges how much students have learned in the lesson and informs them that they are now ready for independent work. Independent work is designed to assist students to master the lesson's skill, strategy, or content. Thus, practice activities should relate to the lesson's objectives. The recommended success level during independent practice is 90 to 100 percent (Christenson et al., 1989). Students can complete independent prac-

tice in class and as homework, and they can work individually or in small groups. Table 4.5 presents competencies for conducting independent practice. An interactive presentation culminates with independent practice and involves three phrases: I do it (teacher modeling), we do it (guided practice), and you do it (independent practice). When a student experiences difficulty, any of these three phases may be used to ensure success.

Using Continuous Teaching Components

Although interactive teaching follows a linear sequence of teacher activities (e.g., advance organizer to independent practice), teachers constantly are engaged in a multiplicity of thoughts and behaviors during interactive presentations. For example, while conducting guided practice, a teacher may be making mental notes on how to improve the lesson, assessing student progress, adapting directions to help individual students, providing feedback, and enhancing the lesson's authenticity to promote generalization. This section features some of the teaching components that occur throughout the interactive teaching presentation. The skillful use of these components increases the likelihood of academic success of students who have learning problems.

TABLE 4.5
Competencies for conducting independent practice

Review the task and describe the assignment and the criteria (e.g., neatness, accuracy, and promptness) used to evaluate it.

Explain the rationale of the assignment and its importance.

Check to ensure that students understand the assignment through questioning and reviewing homework and previous assignments.

Demonstrate strategies and procedures for completing independent practice activities.

Maintain records of students' performance and provide results of evaluations to students.

Provide for error-correction activities during seatwork.

Praise or reinforce students for independent work effort and assignment completion.

Circulate among students to monitor progress and assist students.

Frequently scan the classroom to see whether students are working.

Ensure that students experience high rates of success during seatwork.

Hold students accountable for independent work.

Have students complete missed assignments and correct errors.

Ensure that independent work relates to academic goals.

Provide peer tutoring and cooperative-learning grouping arrangements for students mature enough to interact appropriately.

Provide a variety of independent practice activities (e.g., instructional games, self-correcting materials, computer-assisted instruction, tape recorder-assisted instruction, and quality homework practices).

Instruct students to generalize and apply knowledge across settings and situations.

Monitoring Progress and Providing Feedback Monitoring progress involves the teacher frequently checking on students' behavior and academic work and adapting instruction to ensure that an appropriate instructional match is being maintained. Good and Brophy (1986) note that active and frequent monitoring is the key to student learning. Active monitoring includes checking to see whether students understand the task requirements and the procedures needed to complete the task correctly. To check understanding, the teacher asks each student to demonstrate how to complete the task. When the student performs the task, the teacher is able to note errors and help the student make corrections. Because these procedures enable the teacher to catch errors before extensive practice, high success rates are maintained (Christenson et al., 1989). Moreover, Rieth and Evertson (1988) report that active teacher monitoring (e.g., moving rapidly around the classroom, checking work, and interacting substantively with students) increases the on-task academic responses of students with learning problems. In a review of pro-grams for at-risk students, Slavin and Madden (1989) report that the most effective programs involve frequent assessment of student progress so that programs can be modified according to individual needs. In essence, the most effective teachers maintain a productive flow of activity through continuous scanning and monitoring (Christenson et al., 1989). (Chapter 3 describes numerous techniques for monitoring student progress.)

A significant finding of the Beginning Teacher Evaluation Study (Fisher et al., 1980) is that academic feedback is positively associated with student learning. Feedback serves two important functions: (1) it helps students distinguish between correct and incorrect responses and (2) it informs students of their progress. Rieth and Evertson (1988) note that all major reviews of effective teaching cite feedback as among the most essential teacher behaviors for promoting positive learning outcomes. In a study of mainstream teachers, Larrivee (1986) found that teachers who gave frequent positive feedback, persistent feedback to students who respond incorrectly, and supportive responses to high and low achievers significantly enhanced the academic performance of mainstreamed students. Moreover, in a synthesis of research on good teaching, Porter and Brophy (1988) report that good teachers monitor students' understanding through regular appropriate feedback. Wang (1987) reports that feedback strongly promotes mastery of content and skills for further learning, ability to study and learn independently, ability to plan and monitor learning activities, motivation for continued learning, and confidence in one's ability as a learner.

In a review of academic monitoring procedures, Fuchs (1986) reports that when students' academic programs were monitored systematically and developed formatively over time, the students achieved an average of .7 standard deviation unit higher (i.e., equivalent to 26 percentage points) than did students whose programs were not monitored systematically. Baechle and Lian (1990) found that direct feedback significantly improved the performance of students with learning problems in interpreting metaphors. Moreover, Collins, Carnine, and Gersten (1987) note that basic and elaborative feedback significantly improved student performance on reasoning-skill tasks. In a comparison of basic and elaborative feedback, they found that elaborative feedback produced the greatest skill acquisition. Kline, Schumaker, and Deshler (1991) report excellent results with elaborated feedback in the teaching of academic-specific learning strategies to adolescents with learning problems. In a math strategies program, Mercer and Miller (1992) report that the following elaborated feedback sequence is effective in teaching students with learning problems to acquire, retain, and apply basic math facts:

1. Grade the student's work.
2. Praise the student for the correct responses.
3. Chart the results on a graph and discuss the progress toward the mastery criteria.
4. Note the incorrect responses.
5. Point out error patterns and demonstrate correction procedures, if needed.
6. Instruct the student to correct errors using rules and information taught in the lesson.
7. Praise the student for error corrections.

Interestingly, when kindergartners are questioned about their abilities (e.g., "Who can draw?" "Who can sing?" "Who can dance?"), most will respond enthusiastically with "I can!" However, when college students are asked the same questions, many do not respond affirmatively, or they give responses that are timid and tempered with qualifiers (e.g., "I can draw a tree"). It is unfortunate that, after years of schooling, college students fail to exhibit the confidence and enthusiasm that kindergartners display. A plausible reason for their timidness is that they have a history of being punished for incorrect responses, which has resulted in a loss of confidence and a fear of risk taking.

Teacher reactions to incorrect responses influence student achievement and self-esteem. Rather than seeking help from other students, the student who responds incorrectly should participate in correcting the answer. The teacher can prompt a correct response (e.g., pause, repeat the question, rephrase the question, or provide a clue) or give the answer and ask the student to answer the question again. Thus, the student always finishes with a correct response, and the teacher praises the student for listening. The teacher should view errors as teaching opportunities, and the learner should view errors as learning opportunities. Perhaps these orientations will produce more confident adult learners.

Although the literature is replete with studies that document the importance of feedback, studies analyzing the behavior of general education and special education teachers report low frequencies of feedback to special education students (Rieth & Evertson, 1988). Table 4.6 presents competencies for monitoring progress and providing feedback. Curriculum-based measurement (discussed in Chapter 3) provides teachers with a viable method of monitoring student progress and providing systematic feedback.

Promoting Generalization   As the emphasis on teaching students to be independent learners and active problem solvers increases, generalization is becoming an instructional focus of effective teaching. *Generalization* refers to the occurrence of relevant behavior in different, non-training situations (i.e., across subjects, settings, people, behaviors, or time) without the scheduling of the same events that were present in the training conditions (Stokes & Baer, 1977). For example, generalization to new situations occurs

TABLE 4.6
Competencies for monitoring progress and providing feedback

Competencies for Monitoring Progress
Monitor progress continuously to maintain an instructional match between the instructional task and the student's ability, skill, and existing knowledge.
Monitor to check understanding of task demands by asking the student to perform a sample task.
Monitor to ensure high rates of success.
Use a systematic recordkeeping system to monitor progress.
Use the results of monitoring to initiate interventions to improve student learning.
Check homework, grade and comment on homework, and return homework quickly.

Competencies for Giving Feedback
Give frequent positive feedback for student successes.
Provide informative feedback (e.g., note error patterns and highlight positive features) to students when making written or verbal corrections.
Involve students in setting instructional goals and discuss performance in terms of goals.
View errors as teaching opportunities and reteach (e.g., provide modeling or guided practice) on the basis of student performance.
Correct careless errors immediately.
Require students to correct errors and remember what to do when they encounter similar problems.
Praise students for error correction.
Use student performance data to make instructional decisions (e.g., repeat lesson, move to next lesson, or change lesson).
Acknowledge correct responses quickly and continue with the lesson or ask another question.
Repeat the part of the response that is correct when a student hesitates but answers correctly, and explain why the response is correct.
Reteach when a student answers incorrectly due to lack of knowledge.

when a student demonstrates proficiency in math facts and continues to respond quickly and accurately when these facts are embedded in calculation problems.

Ellis, Lenz, and Sabornie (1987) report that various types of generalization are stressed throughout the instructional process. Specifically, they identify four levels:

1. *Antecedent generalization* involves changing negative student attitudes that may eventually affect generalization behaviors.
2. *Concurrent generalization* involves learning the skill well enough to be able to generalize it.
3. *Subsequent generalization* involves applying the skill to various situations, contexts, and settings.
4. *Independent generalization* involves the student using self-instruction (e.g., cognitive behavior modification) to mediate generalization.

These levels reflect the student's progress during learning. Ellis et al. report that two types of generalization can occur at each level:

1. In *stimulus generalization,* the learned skill is used in conditions that are different than those encountered in training. This leads to the transfer of skills to different settings.
2. In *response generalization,* the newly learned skill is combined with previously learned skills to produce a different, nontrained skill. Essentially, the skill is adapted for use with different stimuli. For example, a student learns the concept of place value and uses it to regroup in addition problems.

The Learning Strategies Curriculum developed at the University of Kansas Center for Research on Learning is one of the few curriculums that systematically incorporates generalization training within the teaching sequence. (Chapter 13 presents the teaching sequence used in the learning strategies curriculum.)

Attributional retraining is a technique that has been used successfully to teach students with learning problems to generalize (Borkowski, Weyhing, & Carr, 1988). Students with learning problems tend to attribute academic success to ease of task or luck and attribute failure to low ability (Ellis, 1986). These misconceptions highlight the need for attributional retraining. Once students learn that successes are the result of their own efforts, they are more likely to feel in control of their learning and develop more independent learning behaviors. (Chapter 5 presents attributional retraining.)

Independent generalization is the product of highly developed metacognitive processes involving self-evaluation, self-monitoring, self-recording, self-goal setting, and self-reinforcement (Ellis et al., 1987). These metacognitive skills reflect a thinking process that is acquired through self-instructional training (Borkowski, Estrada, Milstead, & Hale, 1989). During the acquisition of a skill, the concept of "thinking for yourself" is incorporated into the instructional program. Preparing students with learning problems to use metacognition requires them to develop a system of self-questioning. For example, students can ask themselves the following questions as they begin and proceed through an academic task:

1. Why am I learning this?
2. What am I supposed to learn?
3. What do I already know about it?
4. What ideas are important?
5. How is the information organized?
6. How am I going to learn it?
7. How am I going to remember it?
8. Where am I going to use it?
9. When am I going to use it?
10. How do I apply it?

When students use these self-questions, they actively participate in their learning tasks. They are developing generalization skills by considering how, when, and where they will apply the knowledge they are gaining.

Pressley and Harris (1990) note that teachers must help students realize that generalization of a strategy leads to improved performance. Furthermore, teachers must help students know when and where a learned strategy can be used profitably. Table 4.7 presents competencies for promoting generalization.

Fostering Independence

The practice of teaching students to become independent learners has emerged as a viable component in effective teaching research (Porter & Brophy, 1988; Pressley & Harris, 1990; Wang, 1987). Wang notes that self-responsibility for one's own learning and behavior is enhanced when academic tasks are perceived as important to functioning in society, ample time is allowed for mastery, and effective study skills are used. Moreover, she reports that student involvement in instructional activities and decisions (e.g., goal setting, selection of practice activities, self-monitoring of progress, and lesson completion through independent study) fosters independent learning. Knapp, Turnbull, and Shields (1990) discuss the balance between teacher-directed and learner-directed instruction to foster independent learning: "The key is to strike the right balance between teacher direction and student responsibility, so that students understand what they are doing (and why) and that, over time, their capacity for self-regulated learning increases" (p. 6).

Eaton and Hansen (1978, p. 215) assert the importance of self-management skills:

> Students who can successfully manage their own social and academic behaviors learn critical life skills. They learn to accept responsibility for their own actions and for their own learning. Students who can manage their own learning experience the thrill of knowing they can succeed at some very difficult tasks. They can replace their image of failure with one of self-confidence. In actuality, self-management is the *real* goal of schooling. It teaches a person "how" to learn.

Students with learning problems typically have difficulty with self-regulation (Rooney & Hallahan, 1985). Consequently, many lack self-control strategies that are fundamental to achieving success at school and home. Self-regulation is an essential component of the independent behavior needed to succeed as a student and as an adult. When students work independently, the teacher can perform essential teaching activities more freely. In essence, it allows students to do independent practice.

TABLE 4.7
Competencies for promoting generalization

Have students discuss the rationale for using content or strategy.
Have students identify settings for using content or strategy.
Identify cues in settings that remind students to use content or strategy.
Enlist assistance of other teachers to encourage generalization of content or strategy.
Identify metacognitive processes needed to remember and apply content or strategy.
Set goals to use content or strategy in different contexts.
Teach content or strategy to mastery.
Relate content or strategy use to students' personal lives.
Use a variety of activities in teaching content or strategy (e.g., different teachers, peer instruction, and various practice activities).
Teach content or strategy that is likely to be reinforced or useful in students' natural environments.
Enlist parental help to encourage use of content or strategy at home.
Use a variety of formats (e.g., objects, pictures, media, and computer-assisted instruction) to teach content or strategy.
Encourage students to use content or strategy in their daily lives.
Point out to students that successes are related to their own efforts.
Encourage students to engage in self-management through self-recording, self-evaluation, and self-reinforcement activities.
Provide students with problem-solving instruction through metacognitive strategies (e.g., use of mnemonics that key strategy use).
Teach students to set goals and monitor progress toward their goals.

Numerous approaches exist for teaching self-regulation. Three useful techniques for teaching self-regulation are self-recording, self-evaluation, and self-reinforcement. The steps for teaching each of these three techniques are (1) provide the rationale, (2) demonstrate and model, and (3) practice with feedback (Hughes, Ruhl, & Peterson, 1988). Each technique can be used alone or in combination with related techniques.

Self-recording involves counting and recording one's own behavior, on the assumption that such actions will influence one's behavior. For example, the daily recording of one's weight is likely to influence one's intake of calories or fat grams. Event and interval recording are appropriate for most self-recording situations. The steps for teaching self-recording include the following:

1. ***Provide the rationale.*** This step involves selecting a behavior that needs changing (e.g., the need to complete more seatwork) and discussing how self-recording can be used to change it.

2. ***Demonstrate and model.*** In this step a recording form and a method of observation are selected. The teacher demonstrates self-recording

by using the observation method and recording the results on the form. Next, the student performs self-recording and receives feedback until understanding is certain.

3. ***Practice with feedback.*** In this step the student practices self-recording with prompts and corrective feedback. As the student becomes proficient in self-recording, the teacher reduces prompts, praise, and feedback.

Self-evaluation is the component of self-regulation that teaches the student to judge how well he or she is doing. The following steps for teaching self-evaluation are used:

1. ***Provide the rationale.*** The importance of evaluating one's work is discussed. The notion that evaluation enables the student to determine whether his or her performance is satisfactory is stressed. Also, the point is made that it helps the student to know whether more effort is needed.

2. ***Demonstrate and model.*** In this step a self-evaluation form is selected. It usually requires the student to mark digits (0, 1, 2) that correspond to a grading scale of poor progress (0), some

progress (1), and good progress (2). The teacher demonstrates using the form and has the student model the behavior to ensure that he or she understands the process.

3. ***Practice with feedback.*** The student practices self-evaluation with teacher feedback until proficiency is achieved.

Self-reinforcement is a technique for self-regulation that involves the student reviewing his or her progress to determine whether reinforcement has been earned. The steps for teaching self-reinforcement include the following:

1. ***Provide the rationale.*** This step focuses on teaching the importance of earning reinforcement by helping the student identify appropriate reinforcers. The rationale establishes standards of performance for the earning of reinforcements, and it specifies when and how the student is to be rewarded.

2. ***Demonstrate and model.*** The teacher uses mock data, recording sheets, and a reinforcement menu to demonstrate self-reinforcement. The teacher tells the student when reinforcement criteria are met and selects the reward. The student performs the same behavior with teacher feedback until understanding is apparent.

3. ***Practice with feedback.*** The student practices self-reinforcement by using self-recording and self-evaluation. Students are encouraged to give praise subvocally when selecting the reinforcer (e.g., "I worked hard and now I get a reward"). The teacher provides corrective and positive feedback until the student becomes proficient by self-reinforcement.

Hughes et al. (1988) used a combination of self-recording, self-evaluation, and self-reinforcement to help learners with mild disabilities improve their independent work behavior during seatwork. They note that some generalization to other times occurred among their students.

Individualized instruction is easier to organize and carry out if students are involved in managing their own programs. Students may participate in the following activities involving self-management:

- Select activities from a list designed to help them achieve objectives.
- Manage their own work schedules using check-off sheets.

- Use audiovisual equipment independently.
- Select instructional materials and return them to the proper place.
- Tutor one another when feasible.
- Ask for adult help when necessary.
- Self-correct work.
- Administer timings on probes for targeted behaviors.
- Model appropriate learning and social behavior for one another.
- Develop techniques for modifying their own behavior.
- Find solutions to social conflicts without teacher intervention.

The major approach for teaching students to become independent learners is strategy instruction. According to Deshler and Lenz (1989, p. 205),

> A strategy is an individual's approach to a task. It includes how a student thinks and acts when planning, executing, and evaluating one's performance on a task and its outcomes. . . . In other words, a strategy is seen as a "tool" that can be used by learners to facilitate their analysis of the demands of a given problem, to help them make decisions regarding the best way(s) to address the problem, and to guide their completion of the task, including a careful monitoring of the effectiveness of the process along the way.

Pressley and Harris (1990) state that strategies are procedures for accomplishing academic tasks. Examples of strategies include clustering information to memorize it, using self-questioning to enhance reading comprehension, and using a first-letter mnemonic strategy to remember information (e.g., using *Daddy, Mother, Brother,* and *Sister* to remember the *divide, multiply, bring down,* and *subtract* steps in division).

Techniques and procedures of effective strategy instruction begin with matching student abilities and needs to the strategy selected for instruction. Once the match is determined, the teacher points out the benefits of the strategy and discusses (with student input) how and when to use it. The heart of effective strategy instruction is teacher modeling. During the modeling, the teacher thinks aloud as the strategy is applied to meaningful academic tasks. The student then is given ample opportunity to practice the strategy on tasks that gradually increase in difficulty level. The teacher remains supportive as control of strategy use is

TABLE 4.8
Competencies for fostering independence

Stress the importance of instructional content (i.e., skills, content, or strategies) and its relevance to daily functioning.
Allow ample time to reach mastery.
Encourage generalization.
Teach effective study skills.
Involve students in goal setting and point out how their errors relate to goal achievement.
Help students connect their degree of effort to positive and negative consequences.
Encourage students to be proactive about learning (e.g., set goals).
Provide students with strategies that foster independent learning (e.g., using mnemonics, clustering information to memorize it, and using self-questioning to ensure comprehension).
Model metacognitive or regulatory self-statements to help students self-instruct, self-monitor, and self-evaluate.
Model being a learner.

transferred gradually to the student. Finally, the student is encouraged to transfer strategy use across settings (e.g., special education setting, general class setting, and homework) and content subjects (such as using a reading strategy in social studies and science). During the transfer phase, the student needs to realize and acknowledge the benefits of using a strategy. The learning strategies developed at the University of Kansas Center for Research on Learning have been used successfully throughout the nation with adolescents who have learning problems. Table 4.8 presents competencies for fostering independence.

Using Questions

Asking questions during presentations and follow-up discussions is a key part of the teaching process. The purpose of teacher questioning is multifaceted and frequently can determine how well students with learning problems succeed. Questions are used to involve the student, promote learning, monitor student progress and adjust instruction, and manage the flow of the lesson. Questions can be used to help involve the student by gaining her or his attention and stimulating interest and curiosity. Moreover, they can lead the student to reflect on prior learning and self-evaluate progress. Thus, questions often are useful in beginning a lesson or discussion. Questions also can be used to promote learning. For example, review questions help students remember prior knowledge and link it to new information. Recall ques-

tions help students rehearse basic information and promote memory of important details. Questions reinforce specific concepts and prompt students to recall and apply the information.

Sequential questions can lead students to discover connections; divergent questions can promote higher order thinking. Questions enable the teacher to monitor student progress because student responses readily indicate whether students are acquiring and understanding the lesson content. Student responses also help the teacher diagnose students who need additional help on instructional modifications. Finally, questions enable the teacher to adjust the flow of the lesson. If student responses indicate that the lesson is easy, the pace can be increased; when student responses indicate that the lesson is difficult, the pace can be decreased.

Both convergent and divergent questions can be used in the instructional process. Convergent questions limit the answer to a single response or to a small number of responses and usually relate to content the learner previously has read or heard (e.g., What is the tallest mountain in North America?). Convergent questions are direct or closed questions and begin with verbs such as *define, describe, identify, summarize, paraphrase,* or *rephrase.* Convergent questions elicit responses relating to the acquisition of facts, rules, and action sequences. About 80 percent of all classroom questions are convergent (Borich, 1992). These lower level cognitive questions encourage student participation and promote factual knowledge.

Divergent questions are open-ended questions with several correct responses (e.g., What role do you think sports play in building self-discipline?). These questions require higher level cognitive responses than convergent questions and begin with verbs such as *relate, distinguish, differentiate, formulate, compose, produce, justify,* or *decide.* Divergent questions call for responses that relate to the acquisition of concepts, patterns, or abstractions, and they elicit a variety of appropriate responses. About 20 percent of all classroom questions are divergent (Borich, 1992). Students with learning problems have more difficulty with divergent questions than convergent questions. To prepare students with learning problems to answer divergent questions, they need to be given a foundation of concepts and knowledge through explicit instruction. Table 4.9 provides competencies for

using questions when instructing students with learning problems.

☀ CLASSROOM MANAGEMENT

Managing student behavior and teaching are simultaneous and ongoing activities. When teachers plan instruction according to their students' abilities and effectively use the systematic teaching steps to deliver instruction, most management problems disappear. Management primarily involves getting students to work on tasks independently or in small groups, or to attend to teacher-directed lessons or discussion. If students perceive a task as worthwhile and one that they can do successfully, getting them to attend or engage in it is fairly easy. On the other hand, if the task is perceived as too difficult or irrelevant, it is almost impossible

TABLE 4.9
Competencies for using questions

Use review questions to ensure that students know prior content.
Use questions with specific and concrete examples that are familiar.
Use step-by-step questions that gradually become more complex.
Use questions that rephrase or review the answers to previous questions.
Provide students with wait time (i.e., 3 to 5 seconds) after asking a question.
Provide one or two probable answers in a question to guide students in the appropriate direction.
Use questions and answers in a game format (e.g., the class gets a point when a student responds correctly, and the teacher gets a point when the teacher provides the correct response).
Use questions to individualize instruction (e.g., ask more convergent questions than divergent questions to low achievers).
Use questions to increase lesson clarity (e.g., "What are you going to do when you have read the story?").
Use questions to check for understanding.
Use rapidly paced questions in basic skill instruction in which short, factual answers can encourage learning and students are responding quickly.
To maintain group attention, call on a student after, rather than before, a question.
Promote higher order thinking through questions with more than one correct answer.
Promote higher order thinking through questions that encourage application (i.e., questions with *apply* and *use*), analysis (i.e., questions with *relate* and *distinguish*), synthesis (i.e., questions with *formulate* and *create*), and evaluation (i.e., questions with *justify* and *appraise*).
Use convergent questions that elicit correct answers about 75 percent of the time.
Respond to incorrect answers in a sensitive and helpful manner.
Use divergent questions that encourage students to respond with substantive answers (including incorrect, incomplete, and "I don't know" answers) about 25 percent of the time.
Instruct students to construct questions.
Attend to who is answering questions correctly during discussions.
Call on nonvolunteers and ask students to elaborate on other students' answers.
Wait or pause for about 3 seconds after asking a question and calling on a student to enable the student to offer a substantive response (e.g., give a correct or incorrect answer, ask for clarification, or say "I don't know").

to get students to work on it for more than a few minutes. Thus, successful management begins with good teaching.

Classroom Tone

The teacher has the power to invite or not invite each student to learn. The teacher's attitudes, attentiveness, enthusiasm, support, and expectations strongly influence how students feel about themselves as learners. Thus, the teacher creates the affective tone of the classroom and sets the stage for learning. Teacher behavior significantly influences student behavior. To maximize the positive aspects of teacher influence, the teacher must be a good role model. The following questions help the teacher assess his or her potential to influence students in a positive way:

- Do I strive to maintain good physical health?
- Do I strive to maintain good emotional health?
- Do I treat students with respect?
- Do I enjoy teaching?
- Do I behave confidently (e.g., in walking and talking)?
- Do I have a positive attitude toward students and peers?
- Do I accept the challenge of educating all learners?
- Do I change my position when a compelling reason exists to do so?
- Am I happy?
- Am I effective at helping students learn?
- Do I listen to students and peers well?
- Do I have a sense of humor?

Classroom Rules

Because it is not possible for the teacher to conduct quality instruction or for students to work productively without guidelines for behavior and procedures, all effectively managed classrooms have rules and procedures. Rules and procedures help students function in the complex social and emotional environment of the classroom. Classroom rules are essential for establishing the expected behaviors of students and the teacher. Rules help structure the learning environment and provide students with guidelines to follow, and they offer the teacher a framework for reinforcing behaviors.

Rule Guidelines   Numerous educators (Emmer, Evertson, & Worsham, 2000; Sprick, 1981) offer guidelines for planning and establishing rules for classrooms:

- ***Select the minimum number of rules.*** It is difficult to remember and enforce a large number of rules. Usually, four to six rules are sufficient for operating a classroom efficiently. Suggested rules for primary students include the following:
- Always try your best.
- Raise your hand to say something.
- Get along with your classmates.
- Work quietly during seatwork.
- Listen when the teacher or someone else is talking.

Sample rules for older students include the following:
- Bring essential materials to class.
- Be in your seat and ready to work when the bell rings.
- Respect and be polite to others.
- Be quiet and stay seated when someone is talking.
- Respect the property of other people.
- Obey all school rules.

- ***State the rules positively.*** Negatively stated or "don't" rules imply that the teacher expects students to misbehave. Moreover, a positively stated rule automatically excludes many misbehaviors and includes many desired behaviors. For example, the rule "Respect and be polite to others" excludes numerous misbehaviors (such as teasing, name calling, butting in line, and hitting classmates) and includes many appropriate behaviors (e.g., sharing materials, saying "thank you," saying "please," and talking quietly). Positively stated rules provide nonthreatening, assertive expectations without making the teacher appear to be a dictator.
- ***Determine consistent consequences for rule fulfillment or infraction*** (e.g., students who obey rules earn free time and students who break rules lose recess time). The consequences for obeying and breaking rules should be understood by all students. Rules without consequences have little effect on behavior; thus, consistent teacher follow-through is critical. Also, rules and their consequences should be applied in an equitable manner; bending the rules for specific students or situations should be avoided.

- *Tailor rules to individual classroom goals and to individual teaching styles* (e.g., wanting students to work independently and allowing a certain level of noise during seatwork).
- *Include school rules within class rules.* This reminds students that school rules apply in the classroom.

The presentation of rules should be done as soon as possible after the teacher is responsible for a new group of students. Rule presentations usually begin with a group discussion concerning the need for rules. This discussion helps students understand the need for the rules, have a sense of ownership of the rules, and assume responsibility for their own behavior. Student involvement often is promoted by the teacher soliciting reasons for having rules and why particular rules are important. Typical student responses may include that rules protect individual and group rights, prevent violence, and permit normal activities to take place. After this general discussion, the rules are presented one at a time. The following steps are helpful in presenting specific rules:

1. *Present each rule and discuss why it is important.* The teacher may solicit discussions from the students regarding the usefulness and importance of each rule.
2. *Clarify each rule and the expected behaviors associated with it.* The teacher should give and recognize examples and nonexamples of behaviors associated with each rule. The teacher may model behaviors associated with the rule and ask students to demonstrate appropriate rule-based behaviors.
3. *Once a rule has been presented and discussed, immediately begin to reinforce students for appropriate rule-based behaviors* (e.g., "I liked the way you raised your hand when you wanted to say something").
4. *Discuss the consequences for breaking the rules.* For example, initial failure to obey rules may result in the teacher ignoring the student until the rules are followed. Continued misbehavior may result in loss of recess time.

Teaching Behavioral Expectations for Rules and Classroom Routines

Generally it takes the teacher from one to two weeks to communicate the behavioral expectations for rules and classroom routines. During these beginning weeks, the teacher should teach students what is expected in performing classroom routines such as checking attendance, arriving late to class, leaving the room as a group or individually, bringing materials to class, using the pencil sharpener, participating in group discussions, completing seatwork, making transitions (e.g., changing from one content area to another, moving from small groups to individual work, and getting ready for lunch), performing peer tutoring, using classroom equipment, turning in seatwork and homework, and responding to classroom interruptions. These routines occur frequently, and appropriate behaviors should be established as quickly as possible. Teachers and classrooms are unique, and each teacher must clarify behavioral expectations for numerous situations: What is expected during seatwork? Is talking allowed? What is expected during whole-class discussions? What do students do to get teacher help? What are the procedures for making transitions from one activity to another (such as from lunch to academic work)? These activities occur many times during a school day, and explicitly teaching students what is expected saves the teacher many hours of corrective feedback during the school year.

For teaching the appropriate behavior regarding classroom rules and routines, it is helpful to use the following direct instruction teaching format:

1. *Use an advance organizer.* In this step the teacher links the lesson to previous discussions about rules and reminds students of the need for rules and routines. The teacher notes that rules and routines maintain both students' rights and a productive environment. Next, the teacher introduces a specific behavioral expectation (e.g., "Raise your hand if you have something to say") or a class of behavioral expectations associated with a routine (e.g., making the transition from reading to math activities). Finally, the teacher and the students briefly discuss the rationale for the lesson's behavioral expectations.
2. *Describe the behavioral expectations.* In this step the teacher explicitly describes the specific behaviors required to perform the target activity appropriately. For example, in presenting how to make the transition from seatwork to small-group reading, the teacher describes the steps (e.g., get reading materials out of your desk, stand up and quietly push your chair under your desk, walk to your reading group without disturbing your classmates, quietly pull out your chair at the reading table, be

seated, and patiently wait for the teacher to begin reading). Some teachers help students remember the behaviors by using mnemonics. In teaching behavioral expectations for teacher lectures, the SLANT mnemonic is useful:

S—*Sit* up straight.

L—*Lean* forward in your desk.

A—*Act* interested.

N—*Nod* occasionally to signal understanding.

T—*Track* the teacher with your eyes.

3. ***Demonstrate the behavioral expectations.*** In this step the teacher models the behaviors. For example, in teaching the routine of making a transition from seatwork to small-group reading, the teacher performs each behavioral activity while talking aloud about it. A good technique for demonstrating the behavior is for the teacher to ask a question and then answer it: "What's the first thing I need to do to get ready for reading group? Let's see, I need to get my reading materials together." Then the teacher gets each material while talking about it: "I need my reading book, a pencil, and some paper."

4. ***Conduct guided practice with feedback.*** In this step the teacher instructs the students to model a target behavior (e.g., raising hand or using quiet voices) or a class of behaviors within a routine (such as going to a reading group). When the students exhibit the behaviors, the teacher provides positive and corrective feedback.

5. ***Conduct independent practice with feedback.*** In this step the students perform the behavior(s) per instructions without models, cues, or prompts, and the teacher provides positive praise for correct procedures and gentle verbal corrections for incorrect behaviors. It is helpful to tell students how the activity or routine should proceed prior to the event. At the conclusion of a routine or activity, the teacher tells students how well they performed: "You did a great job of making transitions to reading groups today. I'm so proud of you."

6. ***Maintain behavioral expectations.*** Once the formal lesson on a specific behavior or class of behaviors (routine) is conducted, the teacher continues to teach the behavioral expectations during daily events. For example, during the first two weeks, the teacher uses descriptive praise for correct behavior (e.g., "You did a great job raising your hand for help and waiting quietly for me to come to you") and gentle verbal reprimands for correction. These reprimands simply involve restating the rule: "Please

remember to raise your hand if you want my help or attention" or "Please remember to bring your reading book and pencil to reading group." Descriptive praise and gentle verbal reprimands help clarify the behavioral expectations and indicate a teacher's commitment to them (Sprick, 1981). Once the behavioral expectations are understood and most students are behaving appropriately (e.g., in two to three weeks), the teacher gradually reduces the amount of reinforcement for correct behaviors and implements consequences for students who consistently do not behave appropriately.

Engaging Students

Students with learning problems often have difficulty attending or maintaining on-task behavior. Techniques exist to help these youngsters engage in schoolwork. Fister and Kemp (1995) provide several activities to promote engagement. The You–Me Game involves putting a You–Me chart on the chalkboard. Each time students use predetermined steps for attending (e.g., SLANT), a tally is recorded for the students on the *You* side. When students fail to use the attending strategy, the teacher quickly marks a point under the *Me* side and says "I got you!" Another technique Fister and Kemp provide is Participation Budding, which promotes student participation. Students choose or are assigned partners, and the teacher poses a question to the class. Each student thinks about the answer and then turns to his or her assigned buddy to share the answer. The partners then share the answers with the rest of the class.

The section on maintaining a motivational environment in Chapter 1 provides some excellent techniques for the teacher to use to help students with learning problems attend and engage. Also, Table 4.10 provides a list of competencies for managing instruction and students' behavior in the classroom. These competencies are organized into three areas: communicating expectations, engaging interactions, and instructing for engagement.

ACCOMMODATING STUDENTS WITH LEARNING PROBLEMS IN GENERAL EDUCATION CLASSROOMS

Teaching students with learning problems in inclusive settings is challenging (see the section on inclusion in Chapter 1). Both general education

TABLE 4.10
Competencies for managing instruction and behavior

Communicating Expectations
Establish a positive, expectant, and orderly classroom environment.
Maintain a positive classroom environment through enthusiasm, encouragement, and a positive disposition.
Establish rules that involve respect for others.
Clearly state what behaviors are expected and what behaviors are not tolerated.
Introduce and discuss rules, procedures, and consequences for following rules and breaking rules.
Post rules, discuss rules, and provide rationale for rules.
Establish classroom routines and procedures to promote flow of activities.
Hold students accountable for work and keep records of progress.
Communicate expectations and provide structure for learning (e.g., instructional groupings, prescriptive seat-
    work, accessible materials, and support for working).

Engaging Interactions
Use task-specific and descriptive praise.
Use a hierarchy of reinforcers to adapt to level of student maturity (e.g., food, objects, tokens, points, praise,
    activity, or sense of mastery).
Maintain a 3:1 ratio of teacher attention to positive classroom events vs. negative classroom events.
Provide positive reinforcement for appropriate behavior or effort, successful task completion, and the learning of
    new or difficult material.
Gradually shift reinforcement from appropriate behavior to learning accomplishments.
Provide students with verbal reminders to follow rules.
Use nonverbal signals when feasible to direct students in a manner that does not disrupt the class.
Deliver specific praise contingently.
Engage in frequent positive and supportive interactions.
Reinforce student accomplishments.
Frequently scan the classroom.
Arrange the classroom to facilitate smooth transitions and ease of student monitoring.

Instructing for Engagement
Ensure that students have the ability or skills to acquire the targeted content or perform the strategy or
    procedure being taught.
Correct student behavior in a way that helps students understand the appropriate behavior for the situation.
Instruct students to understand and follow rules through demonstrating, modeling, giving examples and
    nonexamples, reinforcing students for following rules, correcting students for not following rules, and
    applying consequences for students who break rules.
Foster self-management in students through self-monitoring, self-recording, and self-evaluating.
Provide explicit instruction in classroom routines.
Provide more teacher-led instruction than independent work.
Use metaphors, anecdotes, and concrete examples to help students connect new content with their existing
    knowledge.
Circulate throughout the classroom to check the accuracy of work and progress of students.
Engage students in talk about their own thinking.
Ask students to interact with one another and collaborate on problem-solving tasks.

and special education teachers seek accommodations that foster the learning and management of a class of heterogeneous learners. Several researchers (Fagen, Graves, Healy, & Tessier-Switlick, 1986; Schumm & Vaughn, 1995) note the importance of identifying accommodations that are reasonable to ask of teachers in inclusive settings. This section features accommodations that appear reasonable. They are organized according to accommodations involving materials, interactive instruction, and student performance.

Accommodations Involving Materials

Students spend a large portion of the school day interacting with materials. Most instructional materials give teachers few activities or directions for teaching a large class of students who learn at different rates and in various ways. This section provides material accommodations that enhance the learning of diverse students. Frequently, paraprofessionals, volunteers, and students can help develop and implement various accommodations. Material accommodations include the following:

- **Use a tape recorder.** Many problems with materials are related to reading disabilities. The tape recorder often is an excellent aid in overcoming this problem. Directions, stories, and specific lessons can be recorded on tape. The student can replay the tape to clarify understanding of directions or concepts. Also, to improve reading skills, the student can read the printed words silently as they are presented on tape.

- **Clarify or simplify written directions.** Some directions are written in paragraph form and contain many units of information. These can be overwhelming to some students. The teacher can help by underlining or highlighting the significant parts of the directions. Rewriting the directions is often helpful. For example:

  Original directions: This exercise will show how well you can locate conjunctions. Read each sentence. Look for the conjunctions. When you locate a conjunction, find it in the list of conjunctions under each sentence. Then circle the number of your answer in the answer column.

  Directions rewritten and simplified: Read each sentence and circle all conjunctions.

- **Present small amount of work.** The teacher can tear pages from workbooks and materials to present small assignments to students who are anxious about the amount of work to be done. This technique prevents students from examining an entire workbook, text, or material and becoming discouraged by the amount of work. Also, the teacher can reduce the amount of work when it appears redundant. For example, the teacher can request the student to complete only odd-numbered problems or items with stars by them, or can provide responses to several items and ask the student to complete the rest. Finally, the teacher can divide a worksheet into sections and instruct the student to do a specific section. A worksheet is divided easily by drawing lines across it and writing *go* and *stop* within each section.

- **Block out extraneous stimuli.** If a student is easily distracted by visual stimuli on a full worksheet or page, a blank sheet of paper can be used to cover sections of the page not being worked on at that time. Also, line markers can be used to aid reading, and windows can be used to display individual math problems.

- **Highlight essential information.** If an adolescent can read a regular textbook but has difficulty finding the essential information, the teacher can mark this information with a highlight pen.

- **Locate place in consumable material.** In consumable materials in which students progress sequentially (such as workbooks), the student can make a diagonal cut across the lower right-hand corner of the pages as they are completed. With all the completed pages cut, the student and teacher can readily locate the next page that needs to be corrected or completed.

- **Provide additional practice activities.** Some materials do not provide enough practice activities for students with learning problems to acquire mastery on selected skills. Teachers then must supplement the material with practice activities. Recommended practice exercises include instructional games, peer teaching activities, self-correcting materials, computer software programs, and additional worksheets.

- **Provide a glossary in content areas.** At the secondary level, the specific language of the content areas requires careful reading. Students often benefit from a glossary of content-related terms.

- **Develop reading guides.** A reading guide provides the student with a road map of what is written and features periodic questions to help him or her focus on relevant content. It helps the reader understand the main ideas and sort out the numerous details related to the main ideas. A reading guide can be developed paragraph-by-paragraph, page-by-page, or section-by-section.

Accommodations Involving Interactive Instruction

The task of gaining students' attention and engaging them for a period of time requires many teaching and managing skills. Teaching and interactions should provide successful learning experiences for each student. Some accommodations to enhance successful interactive instructional activities are provided:

• *Use explicit teaching procedures.* Many commercial materials do not cue teachers to use explicit teaching procedures; thus, the teacher often must adapt a material to include these procedures. Simmons, Fuchs, and Fuchs (1991) provide an instructional template to help teachers include explicit teaching steps within their lessons (i.e., present an advance organizer, demonstrate the skill, provide guided practice, offer corrective feedback, set up independent practice, monitor practice, and review). This template reminds teachers of steps to use before, during, and after instruction:

Before Instruction

• Note time allocated for instruction (total instructional time and estimated time for teacher-directed instruction).
• Determine lesson objective (The student will be able to. . . .).
• List preskills to review ("Before we begin, let's review. . . .").

During Instruction

• Frame lesson ("Today we're going to learn. . . ."; "This is important because. . . .").
• Present target skill ("Listen and watch as I show you. . . .").
• Guide practice ("Let's try this one together").
• Correct errors and provide feedback (correct response—"That's right"; hesitant response—"Good" and repeat rule or procedure; and incorrect or no response—use prompts on process errors and model correct response on factual errors).
• Prepare for independent practice ("Let's do the first one together").

After Instruction

• Monitor independent practice (circulate throughout the room and provide feedback to students through brief interactions).
• Review new skills (review skills at the end of the lesson and systematically throughout the instructional year).

• *Repeat directions.* Students who have difficulty following directions are often helped by asking them to repeat the directions in their own words. The student can repeat the directions to a peer when the teacher is unavailable. Lewis and Doorlag (1999) offer the following suggestions for helping students understand directions:
• If directions contain several steps, break down the directions into subsets.
• Simplify directions by presenting only one portion at a time and by writing each portion on the chalkboard as well as stating it orally.
• When using written directions, be sure that students are able to read and understand the words as well as comprehend the meaning of the sentences.

• *Maintain daily routines.* Many students with learning problems need the structure of daily routines to know and do what is expected.

• *Provide a copy of lecture notes.* The teacher can give a copy of lecture notes to students who have difficulty taking notes during presentations.

• *Provide students with a graphic organizer.* An outline, chart, or blank web can be given to students to fill in during presentations. This helps students listen for key information and see the relationships among concepts and related information.

• *Use step-by-step instruction.* New or difficult information can be presented in small sequential steps. This helps learners with limited prior knowledge who need explicit or part-to-whole instruction.

• *Combine verbal and visual information.* Verbal information can be provided with visual displays (e.g., on an overhead or handout).

• *Write key points or words on the chalkboard.* Prior to a presentation, the teacher can write new vocabulary words and key points on the chalkboard or an overhead.

• *Use balanced presentations and activities.* An effort should be made to balance oral presentations with visual information and participatory activities (Farlow, 1996). Also, there should be a balance between large-group, small-group, and individual activities.

• *Use mnemonic instruction.* Mnemonic devices can be used to help students remember key information or steps in a learning strategy.

- *Emphasize daily review.* Daily reviews of previous learning or lessons can help students connect new information with prior knowledge.

Accommodations Involving Student Performance

Students vary significantly in their ability to respond in different modes. For example, students vary in their ability to give oral presentations; participate in discussions; write letters and numbers; write paragraphs; draw objects; spell; work in noisy or cluttered settings; and read, write, or speak at a fast pace. Moreover, students vary in their ability to process information presented in visual or auditory formats. The following accommodations involving mode of reception and expression can be used to enhance students' performance:

- *Change response mode.* For students who have difficulty with fine motor responses (such as handwriting), the response mode can be changed to underlining, selecting from multiple choices, sorting, or marking. Students with fine motor problems can be given extra space for writing answers on worksheets or can be allowed to respond on individual chalkboards.
- *Provide an outline of the lecture.* An outline enables some students to follow the lesson successfully and make appropriate notes. Moreover, an outline helps students to see the organization of the material and ask timely questions.
- *Encourage use of graphic organizers.* A graphic organizer, as illustrated in Figure 4.1, involves organizing material into a visual format. To develop a graphic organizer, the student can use the following steps: (1) list the topic on the first line, (2) collect and divide information into major headings, (3) list all information relating to major headings on index cards, (4) organize information into major areas, (5) place information under appropriate subheadings, and (6) place information into the organizer format.
- *Place students close to the teacher.* Students with attention problems can be seated close to the teacher, chalkboard, or work area and away from distracting sounds, materials, or objects.
- *Encourage use of assignment books or calendars.* Students can use calendars to record assignment due dates, list school-related activities, record test dates, and schedule timelines for schoolwork. Students should set aside a special section in an assignment book or calendar for recording homework assignments.
- *Reduce copying activities.* Copying activities can be minimized by including the information or activity on handouts or worksheets.

FIGURE 4.1
A graphic organizer

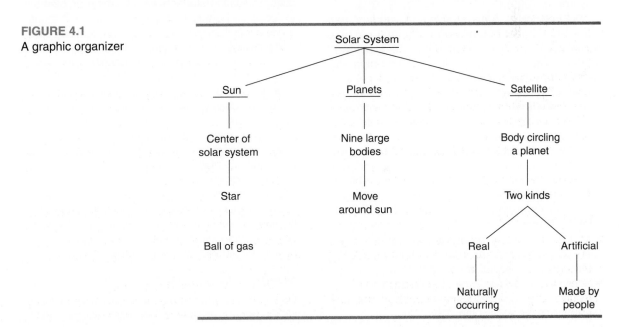

● *Have students turn lined paper vertically for math.* Lined paper can be turned vertically to help students keep numbers in appropriate columns while computing math problems (Fagen et al., 1986).

● *Use cues to denote important items.* Asterisks or bullets can denote questions or activities that count heavily in evaluation. This helps students spend time appropriately during tests or assignments.

● *Design hierarchical worksheets.* The teacher can design worksheets with problems arranged from easiest to hardest. Early success helps students begin to work.

● *Allow use of instructional aids.* Students can be provided with letter and number strips to help them write correctly. Number lines, counters, and calculators help students compute once they understand the mathematical operations.

● *Display work samples.* Samples of completed assignments can be displayed to help students realize expectations and plan accordingly.

● *Use peer-mediated learning.* The teacher can pair peers of different ability levels to review their notes, study for a test, read aloud to each other, write stories, or conduct laboratory experiments. Also, a partner can read math problems for students with reading problems to solve (Cegelka & Berdine, 1995).

● *Encourage note sharing.* A student can use carbon paper or a notebook computer to take notes and then share them with absentees and students with learning problems. This helps students who have difficulty taking notes to concentrate on the presentation.

● *Use flexible work times.* Students who work slowly can be given additional time to complete written assignments.

● *Provide additional practice.* Students require different amounts of practice to master skills or content. Many students with learning problems need additional practice to learn at a fluency level.

● *Use assignment substitutions or adjustments.* Students can be allowed to complete projects instead of oral reports or vice versa. Also, tests can be given in an oral or written format. For example, if a student has a writing problem, the teacher can allow her or him to outline information and give an oral presentation instead of writing a paper (Cegelka & Berdine, 1995).

The accommodations listed in this section provide a framework for helping students with learning problems achieve in general education classrooms. Throughout this book, activities, techniques, and strategies are presented that embellish these accommodations. The planning and teaching chapters (Chapters 1 through 3) and the curriculum area chapters (Chapters 6 through 14) provide more detailed accommodations.

☀ SELECTING CURRICULUM

Curriculum primarily involves what is taught in the school and consists of learning outcomes that society considers essential for success. A curriculum is established before students enter the school, and it represents what society values as important for becoming a productive citizen and successful individual. If the curriculum accurately represents what is important, it should not be altered, because students deserve an opportunity to acquire this valued knowledge and skills. To accommodate some students with learning problems, it is necessary to prioritize the content to ensure that the most important content is mastered. This position is highlighted in the belief that "less is more." Specifically, it refers to covering highly valued content extensively so that students achieve understanding and mastery. Another way of accommodating students with learning problems is to focus on how to teach the curriculum. Although some curriculum materials simply present objectives and activities, most materials influence how to teach through their organization, sequencing, and activities. Other materials provide extensive directions in how to teach (e.g., teacher scripts). Students with learning problems learn better when instruction follows research-supported interactive teaching activities (e.g., explicit modeling, corrective feedback, and monitoring of progress), which were presented earlier in this chapter. Because only 3 percent of published curriculum materials are field tested and validated before marketing (Sprick, 1987), educators need to select curriculum materials carefully. This section presents some factors to consider when selecting curriculum materials or designing a curriculum for students with learning problems.

Material Selection Factors

Given the large number of commercial materials, selection often is difficult. Educators who are making decisions on curriculum material selection should consider effective curriculum material design practices.

Curriculum Materials Should Promote Best Instructional Practices   The extensive research findings regarding teaching practices (Englert et al., 1992) should be incorporated in curriculum materials. For example, procedures should be included that help the teacher provide good advance organizers, clarify objectives, model concepts explicitly, provide meaningful examples, teach generalization, give helpful feedback, tie the content to something important, and accommodate learner diversity. Teachers deserve to have materials that remind or guide them to use best practices. Teachers are constantly required to adapt, modify, or restructure curriculum materials to include best teaching practices. For many students with learning problems, these teacher procedures represent the difference between success or failure.

Curriculum Materials Should Foster Learner Understanding   Many students have experienced the arduous task of memorizing information (e.g., dates, facts, and math formulas) that becomes isolated cognitively (i.e., it does not connect with anything meaningful or relevant). Baker, Simmons, and Kameenui (1994) note that content needs to be presented in relation to "big ideas." These big ideas are concepts or strategies that facilitate efficient learning across a range of examples. The big ideas serve as anchors through which "small ideas" can be connected and understood. Baker et al. suggest that big ideas are especially useful in teaching content areas. For example, they suggest the big idea of using the problem–solution–effect sequence to teach history. This sequence provides a generalizable strategy for understanding historical events and their interrelatedness. When faced with a *problem,* people throughout history have used moving, inventing, dominating, accommodating, or tolerating to *solve* problems. Attempts to solve problems produce *effects* that often produce another problem; thus, the cycle continues. This cyclical approach helps learners understand history because meaning is clearer and historical events are associated more readily to current events.

Prater (1993) discusses the importance of teaching concepts effectively to students with learning disabilities. She reports that such students have difficulty learning concepts through observation and experience, and thus need explicit concept instruction to succeed in school and life. Prater presents the following sequence of steps that are well-grounded in theory and empirical evidence for teaching students to understand concepts:

1. Define the instructional objectives.
2. Analyze the task used for demonstrating knowledge of the concept.
3. Define the concept and label it.
4. Select the number and sequence of examples and nonexamples.
5. Elaborate the defining attributes.
6. Provide immediate feedback.

Materials that feature these steps are noteworthy. Moreover, metaphors, multiple examples, demonstrations, think alouds, and tying content to something relevant also facilitate understanding.

Curriculum Materials Should Guide the Assessment of Relevant Prior Knowledge   The assessment of prior knowledge needed to learn something new should be featured in curriculum materials. This assessment can guide the review of prerequisite knowledge or the teaching of important prerequisite content. Also, continuously monitoring student progress helps the teacher know when she or he must reteach, review, or introduce new material. The curriculum area chapters in this text present assessment formats and procedures that help assess prior knowledge and learning progress.

Curriculum Materials Should Guide Mastery Learning   Most students with learning problems do not succeed with the spiral curriculum approach of exposing specific content to students, and then moving on to a new topic without regard for how well the students learned the original material. This "spray and pray" approach usually results in frustration and minimal learning. Curriculum materials that include goal setting and mastery criteria and feature explicit presentations of new content followed by meaningful and varied practice activities help teachers determine whether individual students are achieving mastery. (Mastery learning is discussed in Chapter 3 and in the curriculum area chapters.)

Curriculum Materials Should Promote Generalization   Although teaching for generalization is presented in the section of this chapter on using continuous teaching components, the influence of curriculum materials on generalization should be examined. Features such as multiple examples, big ideas, meaningfulness, mastery learning, and application activities that specifically require the learner to connect the new knowledge to daily living foster generalizations.

Recently, much has been written about making content more meaningful through authentic learning and integrated instruction. *Authentic learning* is meaningful to the student and is based on the assumption that learners connect prior knowledge with new knowledge to construct meaning (Newmann & Wehlage, 1993). Also, authentic learning assumes that the learner uses a systematic or disciplined strategy to construct meaning that results in discourse, products, or performances that have value beyond success in school. Baker et al. (1994) note that curriculum materials featuring conspicuous strategies (i.e., general steps that students follow when solving a problem) aid students with learning problems, especially when the strategies are explicit, concise, and generalizable. Newmann and Wehlage present five standards that are basic to authentic learning: (1) higher order thinking is required, (2) depth of knowledge is obtained (mastery), (3) learning is connected to the world beyond the classroom, (4) substantive conversation occurs, and (5) social support for student achievement is provided. *Integrated* or *unit instruction* promotes generalization by teaching a concept across subject areas. For example, to teach likenesses and differences among people, students can measure heights and weights of people in math, read stories about individuals with disabilities in reading, and examine the likenesses and differences of people's hair with a microscope in science. A curriculum structure that promotes authentic learning standards or teaches concepts across subject areas enhances generalization.

Curriculum Materials Should Provide Guidelines for Learner Diversity Curriculum materials offering viable suggestions for students who learn at different rates help a teacher meet the needs of diverse learners. Materials that include best teaching practices greatly reduce student frustrations and minimize learning diversity. Materials that provide for mediated scaffolding help teachers re-

spond to a wide range of learners. *Mediated scaffolding* refers to personalized guidance, instruction, assistance, and support that a teacher, peer, task, or material provides a learner. It is temporary guided instruction that gradually is removed as the learner acquires skills. Mediated scaffolding may be included in materials through sample teaching scripts, additional examples, metaphors or anecdotes, and meaningful practice activities. Finally, materials that offer suggestions for cooperative learning, computer-assisted instruction, peer-mediated instruction, instructional games, and grouping arrangements help teachers plan and respond to diverse learners. In essence, the curriculum material should be designed to reach all students and challenge advanced achievers to higher order thinking. It appears more prudent to teach low and average achievers well and challenge high achievers than to frustrate low achievers while focusing primarily on high achievers.

Guidelines for Designing a Curriculum

From his research and review of curriculum and practice activities, Carnine (1989) provides guidelines for designing a curriculum that is most likely to increase accuracy and decrease instructional time to mastery:

- ***Introduce information cumulatively.*** This procedure avoids memory overload by introducing new pieces of information one at a time. Each new piece of information is presented after the previous piece has been learned. For example, a student can learn one continent at a time until all seven are learned.
- ***Build retention.*** To increase memory and decrease the likelihood of errors, a review of difficult material should occur within a couple of days of initial learning. Moreover, students need practice in discriminating a newly learned concept from similar concepts. Supervised practice is important in the initial stages of discrimination practice. Solving problems involving the multiplication and division of fractions is an example of discrimination practice.
- ***Separate confusing elements and terminology.*** When similar symbols are to be taught

A well-planned lesson leads to student engagement and learning.

(such as 6 and 9, + and ×, or b and d), the teacher should introduce one of the symbols at a time. Once a symbol or term is learned, the similar one can be introduced.

- **Make learning more meaningful by stressing relationships.** First, the teacher should stress the relationship of components to the whole. For example, the teacher can instruct students to use their knowledge of sound-symbol correspondence to decode words, or the teacher can point out how a comprehension strategy can be applied to books across subject areas. Second, the teacher should stress the application of known information to unknown information. For example, the teacher can point out that the multiplication of 5s involves counting by 5s or that the commutative property of addition (i.e., $a + b = c$, $b + a = c$) applies to multiplication.

- **Reduce processing demands.** Processing demands are decreased by teaching a strategy or algorithm first and then teaching the information in increasingly difficult stages. For example, teaching letter-sound correspondences first reduces the processing requirements for decoding words, and teaching addition (i.e., easiest information) before multiplication decreases the processing demands of learning multiplication.

- **Require faster responses.** Requiring faster responses helps students develop automatic responses.

PLANNING UNITS AND LESSONS

A lesson that maintains students' attention and participation and proceeds smoothly without interruptions, digressions, and diversions has usually been carefully planned: Effective teaching and classroom management do not "just happen." In planning for academically diverse classes, teachers focus on developing interesting activities that motivate and encourage student involvement. Many teachers report that their most productive planning occurs in unstructured settings (e.g., driving a car, walking the dog, or taking a shower). Teachers generally agree that during-school planning involves "top structure" planning (i.e., scheduling, determining class structure, developing units, and responding to administrative tasks), whereas "deep structure" planning (e.g., how to clarify a difficult concept within a lesson or develop a motivating activity) is accomplished away from school.

The planning of units and lessons is germane to effective instruction. Units and lessons provide the framework for structuring teaching to accomplish short- and long-range learning outcomes. Lenz, Bulgren, Schumaker, Deshler, and Boudah (1994) define a unit of instruction as *a chunk of content that is distinguishable from a previous chunk of content through a closure or transition activity* (e.g., a test or project).

FIGURE 4.2
Unit planning format

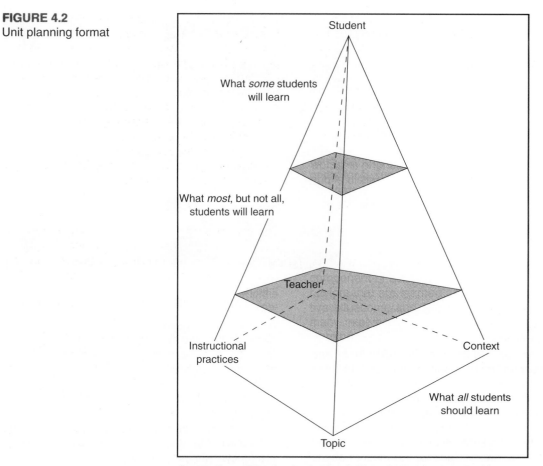

Source: From "Planning for Academic Diversity in America's Classrooms: Windows on Reality, Research, Change, and Practice" (p. 10), by Joint Committee on Teacher Planning for Students with Disabilities, 1995, *Effective School Practices, 14*(2), 1–53. Copyright 1995 by the Association for Direct Instruction. Reprinted by permission.

Schumm, Vaughn, and Leavell (1994) provide a format for planning units for teachers to use in planning instruction for diverse classes. As noted in Figure 4.2, the format includes a structure that enables the teacher to differentiate outcomes according to students' learning characteristics. This graphic organizer enhances the teacher's proficiency in planning units to promote learning for all students. As illustrated in Figure 4.2, Level 1 represents the basic concepts, content, or skills that the teacher wants all learners to master. The information at this level is critical for understanding the content of the unit and is usually more general

than information in Levels 2 and 3. The functional teacher question at this level is "What do I want *all* students to learn?" Level 2 represents a higher level of information than Level 1. It focuses on information that the teacher considers next in importance for understanding or applying the content or skills. The functional teacher question at this level is "What do I want *most* students to learn?" Level 3 represents supplemental information that is more complex or detailed. The functional teacher question at this level is "What information may *some* students learn?" A student's mastery of information at the different levels is not determined by abilities. Because a student's prior knowledge and interests vary across topics, a student's learning will vary across topics. Access to information at all levels should be available to all students.

The following questions pertaining to the topic, the teacher, and the students provide guidelines for helping the teacher use the level format to plan units (Joint Committee on Teaching Planning for Students with Disabilities, 1995):

- What prior knowledge do the students and do I have of this topic?
- How interesting is the topic to individual students and to me?
- How many new concepts are introduced, and how complex are they?
- How can I relate this material to previous instruction?
- Have I taught this material before?
- What resources are available to me for this unit?
- Will students' communication skills make comprehension of a particular concept difficult?
- Will students with reading difficulties be able to function independently while learning about the concept from the text?
- Will students with behavioral or attention problems be able to concentrate on this material?
- Will my students have the vocabulary they need to understand this concept?
- What experiences have my students had that will relate to this concept?
- Is there some way to relate this concept to the cultural and linguistic backgrounds of my students?

Planning Routines for Units

The level format for planning units can be combined readily with unit planning routines to develop a unit responsive to the needs of diverse learners. Lenz et al. (1994) discuss unit planning routines that help teachers become explicit with students about learning outcomes, the relationship of chunks of information, and activities that will facilitate learning. They note that these unit planning routines help students with learning problems understand and retain information. The routines involve thinking about the content of a unit, the outcomes of the unit, and the development of a graphic device to display the organization and relationship of the

unit content. The unit organizer in Figure 4.3 features the use of a unit planning routine for teaching multiplication facts. The suggested order for planning a unit, as illustrated in Figure 4.3, is to title the current unit, provide the title of the last unit, determine the next unit, indicate the global picture, draw the unit map, list the unit outcomes, and determine the unit schedule. Lenz et al. offer an excellent routine for planning units of content in inclusive classrooms at the secondary level. (Chapter 13 provides additional information on teaching content to adolescents.)

Lesson Planning Format

The planning format for lessons is similar to the unit planning format. It helps the teacher explicitly determine what will be taught and how it will be taught. This planning adds essential details to the teaching of the lessons within a unit. The lesson planning format features teacher planning to determine what all students will learn, what most students will learn, and what some students will learn (Schumm et al., 1994). These levels are identical to those featured in Figure 4.2 in the unit planning format. Schumm et al. provide the following sequence to guide the development of the lesson planning format:

1. Identify content according to the three levels (i.e., what all will learn, what most will learn, and what some will learn).
2. Use the following questions to guide the "context" of instruction:
   - Are there scheduled interruptions (e.g., holidays or special events) that may alter instructional time?
   - How will the class size affect instruction of the lesson?
   - Do the students work well individually, in small groups, or in pairs? Which students need to be grouped together?
   - What resources exist to teach this lesson?
   - What methods will be used for motivation?
   - What instructional strategies and adaptations can be implemented to promote learning for all students?
   - What learning strategies are needed to help students master these concepts?
   - What independent work and homework assignments are appropriate for this lesson?

FIGURE 4.3
A unit organizer

The Unit Organizer
Global Picture

Acquiring, maintaining, and applying basic computation skills

Last unit	Current unit	Next unit
Multisensory subtraction	Multisensory multiplication	Multisensory Division

Unit schedule

8/19	Concrete Lessons pp. 18–34
8/23	Representational Lessons pp. 35–53
8/28	Abstract & Review Lessons pp. 54–69
9/4	Acquisition Test
9/6	Fluency & Problem-Solving Lessons pp. 70–89
9/11	Monitor Fluency & Word Problem Solving Until Mastery pp. 90–94

Unit map

Multiplication facts

Concrete experiences

Representational experiences

Abstract experiences

Problem solving & abstract experiences

Unit Outcomes

Students are able to demonstrate understanding of multiplication facts through objects.

Students are able to demonstrate understanding of multiplication facts through drawings.

Students are able to compute multiplication facts at a fluent rate.

Students are able to solve multiplication facts word problems with and without extraneous information.

Students are able to apply and generalize multiplication facts by creating word problems from daily experiences.

- How will student learning be monitored? How will student learning be assessed at the end of the lesson and at the end of the unit?
3. Develop an agenda for the lesson.
4. List needed materials.
5. Determine seatwork and homework assignments.
6. Determine what method will be used to evaluate student learning.

The lesson plan design that includes the systematic teaching steps in Table 4.11 could be adapted readily to include the three levels of content in the lesson planning format. The differentiated learning outcomes (Levels 1, 2, and 3) can be incorporated in the lesson by adapting instruction during the modeling, guided practice, independent practice, feedback, and generalization steps. Advanced students (i.e., students working on content at Level 3) could develop a booklet of multiplication problems encountered in their daily lives or could solve more complex problems by applying the strategies they have learned. Students with learning difficulties in multiplication

TABLE 4.11
Math lesson design for teaching diverse learners

Step 1:   Introduce the lesson
Use a focusing activity to gain student attention.
Connect the lesson to previous learning or lesson.
Identify the target skill, strategy, or content.
Provide a rationale for learning the skill, strategy, or content.
Discuss the relevancy of the skill, strategy, or content until an authentic context is realized. Authenticity may be achieved within the context of school activities, community events, or future demands.

Step 2:   Describe and model the skill or strategy
The teacher requests the students to attend while the teacher demonstrates the skill or strategy. To help students understand the demonstration, the following two procedures are used:
Procedure 1: The teacher asks a question and then answers the question. The students hear and observe the teacher think aloud while modeling metacognitive strategies.
Procedure 2: The teacher asks a question and the students help provide the answer. The students participate by answering the question and solving the problem. The teacher and the students perform the strategy together, and the teacher continues to provide modeling.

Step 3:   Use scaffolding to guide practice and interactive discourse
Procedure 1: The teacher guides students through problem-solving strategies without demonstration unless it is required. Guidance is provided as needed and the following supportive techniques are used:
  • The teacher asks specific leading questions and models if necessary (e.g., "What is the first step in solving a problem?").
  • The teacher provides prompts regarding declarative knowledge (e.g., "Use a variable [letter] to represent the unknown in the word problem").
  • The teacher provides cues regarding procedural knowledge (e.g., "Remember to isolate the variable in solving the equation").
Procedure 2: The teacher instructs students to do the task and reflect on the process and product. The teacher provides support on an as-needed basis and uses fewer prompts and cues. The students are encouraged to become more independent.

Step 4:   Conduct independent practice to mastery
Students are encouraged to reflect (i.e., estimate, predict, check, and create) and work without teacher assistance. Activities include group projects to explore multiple ways to solve problems (e.g., using objects, pictures, drawings, and algorithms) or the creation of authentic contexts for solving problems (e.g., conducting a survey and using math to present and describe the results). A variety of practice arrangements are used, including cooperative learning, peer tutoring, instructional games, self-correcting materials, and computer-assisted instruction.

Step 5:   Provide feedback
Procedure 1: Focus on successes. Discuss student performance or product in terms of a predetermined learning goal. Tie student efforts and thinking processes to success.
Procedure 2: Focus on error correction. View errors as opportunities for the teacher to teach and for the students to learn. Ask students to note errors and correct. If needed, guide their correction through questions, metaphors, and modeling. Also, have students work together to correct errors.

Step 6:   Teach generalization and transfer
Reflect on applications of new knowledge across settings and situations.
Encourage students to create meaningful math word problems related to new knowledge.
Have students work on more difficult problems. For example, if they have learned multiplication facts 0 to 81, have them attempt problems such as 12×6 using the strategies they have learned. With word problems, challenge students to solve those involving more than one operation. Have students collaborate to solve the challenging problems.

(i.e., students working on content at Level 1) could receive extra modeling or guided practice, more independent practice activities with computers, or more time to achieve mastery.

☀ POSTINSTRUCTIONAL ACTIVITIES

Information regarding the relationship between competent teachers and involvement in postinstructional tasks is limited. However, it is assumed that the following postinstructional activities improve teaching effectiveness: reflecting on one's actions and students' responses; staying current on subject matter and educational issues by reading journals, texts, or professional organization literature; taking advanced education courses; and interacting with colleagues to coordinate teaching plans (Reynolds, 1992). It also is recognized that postinstructional activities combine with planning activities.

Teacher Reflection and Collaboration

One of the primary activities of postinstruction involves the process of reflecting about teaching. Brandt (1991, p. 3) highlights the importance of reflecting in the following passage:

> Everyone needs opportunities for self-renewal, but those responsible for developing other human beings need them most of all. Thinking deeply about what we are doing leads us to ask better questions, break out of fruitless routines, make unexpected connections, and experiment with fresh ideas.

Reynolds (1992) reports that competent teachers reflect on their teaching to find out what teaching behaviors are successful and unsuccessful with students. This process helps teachers refine their teaching practices. Reynolds notes that reflection occurs during as well as after interactions with students. During interactions, teachers gather information from student comments, actions, and written work to determine levels of student understanding. These multiple forms of assessments provide information that enables teachers to reflect on what practices are effective or ineffective and to improve their teaching. Reynolds notes that as teachers gain experience and become more competent, their reflections change from concerns

about classroom management, the quality of their explanations, how they respond to questions, and student participation to concerns about student understanding and instructional events that seem especially noteworthy. With experience, teachers seem to develop a system for organizing, understanding, and using the enormous amount of information gained from experience. Because of the learning differences of students, the focus on student understanding is important in guiding teachers to make adjustments that enable all students to succeed.

One of the primary techniques for fostering teacher reflections is journal writing. Smyth (1989) suggests the following questions to guide reflections that are applicable to teacher journal writing:

- What do I do? (Elicits description of practice.)
- What does this mean? (Elicits principles of instruction.)
- How did I come to be this way? (Elicits awareness beyond the classroom and situates practices in a broader cultural milieu.)
- How might I do things differently? (Elicits action.)

Although reflection is often a private or individual event, it is facilitated through collaborative activities. Working together with colleagues often helps teachers gain personal insights and create synergistic solutions. (Collaboration is featured in Chapter 1.) The following collaborative questions can foster reflection:

- Will curriculum-based assessment allow teachers to assess the progress of students in a manner that provides insight into effective instructional activities and learner differences?
- How can teachers more effectively involve parents in school activities?
- How can teachers effectively combine elements of whole language instruction with phonological awareness instruction to improve reading instruction?

An additional collaborative/reflective activity involves establishing an educators' forum to focus on school problems.

Mohlman, Sparks-Langer, and Colton (1991) report that educators can foster professional growth through performing microteaching followed by writing in reflection journals, conducting self-analysis of video- and audiotapes, conducting action research projects, and collaborating about student learning and teaching. They note that case studies of teaching and learning events that highlight specific context, practices, content, and ethical and moral dilemmas help teachers develop a valuable repertoire of ideas, skills, and attitudes. Finally, Mohlman et al. indicate that teachers need time to understand, interpret, and personalize information from research, theories, and experts.

PERSPECTIVE ON INSTRUCTIONAL COMPONENTS

When teachers examine the many instructional components that are recommended for good teaching, it is understandable if they feel a little overwhelmed. The instructional components related to positive student outcomes represent a formidable list to incorporate into daily teaching practices. Fortunately, the growing knowledge base about effective teaching can enlighten educators about best teaching practices; however, a unifying theory or framework to organize the knowledge base and guide the application of best teaching practices is missing. The examination of teaching in terms of planning, interactive teaching, and postinstructional activities helps organize the many components of teaching into a manageable framework for improving the practice of teaching. If one considers that many of the supported instructional practices are interrelated, the task of effective teaching becomes more reasonable. For example, the competency involving monitoring student progress is inherent in several planning activities (e.g., provide time for learning, ensure success, and strive to motivate), interactive teaching activities (e.g., monitor progress and give feedback), and postinstructional activities (e.g., reflect on student learning and activities that are effective or ineffective).

When examining all the aspects of good teaching, it is nice to remember that students can bring much joy to teaching. As Lovitt (1977) points out, "Youngsters are, by definition, fresh. . . . They see life differently. . . . They often develop their own approaches and language systems for dealing with and talking about their lives. . . . Children entertain

teachers; they keep them sane, pure in spirit, and incorruptible" (p. 201). It helps if the teacher appreciates students and expects to enjoy their freshness, humor, questions, and ideas.

Perhaps the most important source of knowledge about good teaching is the students. In a paper on "The Good Teacher" presented at a conference titled "Education from Cradle to Doctorate," Clark (1989) notes that students' thoughts and stories about good teachers almost invariably concern four fundamental human needs: (1) to be known, (2) to be encouraged, (3) to be respected, and (4) to be led. Moreover, he discusses the voices of students concerning good teaching (pp. 18–19):

> In the language of children, their good teachers nurture them by treating them as intelligent people who can become even more intelligent, by taking the time to learn who we are and what we love, treating us fairly by treating us differently, by explaining why he teaches and acts as he does, by telling stories of her own life outside school and listening to ours, by letting me have a bad day when I can't help it. The good teacher is both funny and serious. We can laugh together, and this makes me feel happy and close. She puts thought into surprising us in ways that we will never forget. He draws pictures that show how ideas are connected; we don't feel lost or afraid that we will be sent away or humiliated. The good teacher loves what he is teaching, but does not show off or put distance between us and him. The good teacher sets things up so that children can learn how to learn from one another. She knows how to be a friend while still a responsible adult. . . . The good teacher puts people first, say the children. The good teacher acts from love and caring, and is loved and cared for in return.

REFERENCES

Anderson, L. M., Brubaker, N. L., Alleman-Brooks, J., & Duffy, G. G. (1985). A qualitative study of seatwork in first-grade classrooms. *Elementary School Journal, 88,* 123–140.

Anderson, L. M., Evertson, C. M., & Emmer, E. T. (1980). Dimensions in classroom management derived from recent research. *Journal of Curriculum Studies, 12,* 343–346.

Anderson, L. M., Raphael, T. E., Englert, C. S., & Stevens, D. D. (1991). *Teaching writing with a new instructional model: Variations in teachers' beliefs, instructional practice, and their students' performance.* Paper presented at the annual meeting of the American Educational Research Association, Chicago, IL.

Archer, A. L., Gleason, M. M., & Isaacson, S. (1995). Effective instructional delivery. In P. T. Cegelka & W. H. Berdine, *Effective instruction for students with learning difficulties* (pp. 161–194). Boston: Allyn & Bacon.

Archer, A., Isaacson, S., Adams, A., Ellis, E., Morehead, J. K., & Schiller, E. P. (1989). *Academy for effective instruction: Working with mildly handicapped students.* Reston, VA: Council for Exceptional Children.

Baechle, C. L., & Lian, M. J. (1990). The effects of direct feedback and practice on metaphor performances in children with learning disabilities. *Journal of Learning Disabilities, 23,* 451–455.

Baker, S. K., Simmons, D. C., & Kameenui, E. J. (1994). Making information more memorable for students with learning disabilities through the design of instructional tools. *LD Forum, 19*(3), 14–18.

Bickel, W. W., & Bickel, D. D. (1986). Effective schools, classrooms, and instruction: Implications for special education. *Exceptional Children, 52,* 489–500.

Borich, G. D. (1992). *Effective teaching methods* (2nd ed.). Upper Saddle River, NJ: Merrill/Prentice Hall.

Borkowski, J. G., Estrada, M. T., Milstead, M., & Hale, C. A. (1989). General problem-solving skills: Relations between metacognition and strategic processing. *Learning Disability Quarterly, 12,* 57–70.

Borkowski, J. G., Weyhing, R. S., & Carr, M. (1988). Effects of attributional retraining on strategy-based reading comprehension in learning-disabled students. *Journal of Educational Psychology, 80*(1), 46–53.

Bradley, L., & Bryant, P. E. (1985). *Rhyme and reason in reading and spelling.* Ann Arbor: University of Michigan Press.

Brandt, R. (1991). Overview: Time for reflection. *Educational Leadership, 48*(6), 3.

Brophy, J., & Good, T. L. (1986). Teacher behavior and student achievement. In M. C. Wittrock (Ed.), *Handbook of research on teaching* (3rd ed., pp. 328–375). Upper Saddle River, NJ: Prentice Hall.

Carnine, D. (1989). Teaching complex content to learning disabled students: The role of technology. *Exceptional Children, 55,* 524–533.

Cegelka, P. T., & Berdine, W. H. (1995). *Effective instruction for students with learning difficulties.* Boston: Allyn & Bacon.

Chall, J. S. (1989). Learning to read: The great debate 20 years later. *Phi Delta Kappan, 70,* 521–538.

Christenson, S. L., Ysseldyke, J. E., & Thurlow, M. L. (1989). Critical instructional factors for students with mild handicaps: An integrative review. *Remedial and Special Education, 10*(5), 21–31.

Clark, C. M. (1989, October). *The good teacher.* Paper presented at the Norwegian Research Council for Science and the Humanities Conference: "Education from Cradle to Doctorate," Trondheim, Norway.

Cobb, P., Yackel, E., & Wood, T. (1992). A constructivist alternative to the representational view of mind in mathematics education. *Journal of Research in Mathematics Education, 23,* 2–33.

Collins, M., Carnine, D., & Gersten, R. (1987). Elaborated corrective feedback and the acquisition of reading skills: A study of computer-assisted instruction. *Exceptional Children, 54,* 254–262.

Deno, S. L., & Fuchs, L. S. (1987). Developing curriculum-based measurement systems for data-based special education problem solving. *Focus on Exceptional Children, 19*(8), 1–16.

Deshler, D. D., & Lenz, B. K. (1989). The strategies instructional approach. *International Journal of Disability, Development and Education, 36,* 203–224.

Dixon, R., & Carnine, D. (1994). Ideologies, practices, and their implications for special education. *The Journal of Special Education, 28,* 356–367.

Eaton, M. D., & Hansen, C. L. (1978). Classroom organization and management. In N. G. Haring, T. C. Lovitt, M. D. Eaton, & C. L. Hansen, *The fourth R: Research in the classroom* (pp. 191–217). Upper Saddle River, NJ: Merrill/Prentice Hall.

Ellis, E. S. (1986). The role of motivation and pedagogy on the generalization of cognitive strategy training. *Journal of Learning Disabilities, 19,* 66–70.

Ellis, E. S., Deshler, D. D., Lenz, B. K., Schumaker, J. B., & Clark, F. L. (1991). An instructional model for teaching learning strategies. *Focus on Exceptional Children, 23*(6), 1–24.

Ellis, E. S., Lenz, B. K., & Sabornie, E. J. (1987). Generalization and adaptation of learning strategies to natural environments: Part I: Critical agents. *Remedial and Special Education, 8*(1), 6–20.

Emmer, E. T., Evertson, C. M., & Worsham, M. E. (2000). *Classroom management for secondary teachers* (5th ed.). Boston: Allyn & Bacon.

Engelmann, S. (1988). The Direct Instruction Follow Through model: Design and outcomes. *Education and Treatment of Children, 11,* 303–317.

Englert, C. S., Tarrant, K. L., & Mariage, T. V. (1992). Defining and redefining instructional practice in special education: Perspectives on good teaching. *Teacher Education and Special Education, 15,* 62–86.

Evans, M. A., & Carr, T. H. (1985). Cognitive abilities, conditions of learning, and the early development of reading skill. *Reading Research Quarterly, 20,* 327–350.

Fagen, S., Graves, D., Healy, S., & Tessier-Switlick, D. (1986). Reasonable mainstreaming accommodations for the classroom teacher. *The Pointer, 31*(1), 4–7.

Farlow, L. (1996). A quartet of success stories: How to make inclusion work. *Educational Leadership, 53*(5), 51–55.

Fisher, C. W., Berliner, D. C., Filby, N. N., Marliave, R., Cahen, L. S., & Dishaw, M. M. (1980). Teaching behaviors, academic learning time, and student achievement: An overview. In C. Denham & A. Lieberman (Eds.), *Time to learn.* Washington, DC: National Institute of Education.

Fister, S. L., & Kemp, K. A. (1995). *TGIF: But what will I do on Monday?* Longmont, CO: Sopris West.

Fuchs, L. S. (1986). Monitoring progress of mildly handicapped pupils: Review of current practice and research. *Remedial and Special Education, 7*(5), 5–12.

Gage, N. L., & Needels, M. C. (1989). Effects of systematic formative evaluation on student achievement. *Exceptional Children, 53,* 199–208.

Goldberg, M. F. (1990). Portrait of Madeline Hunter. *Educational Leadership, 47*(5), 41–43.

Good, T. L., & Brophy, J. E. (1986). School effects. In M. C. Wittrock (Ed.), *Handbook of research on teaching* (3rd ed., pp. 570–602). Upper Saddle River, NJ: Prentice Hall.

Graham, S. (1990). The role of production factors in learning disabled students' compositions. *Journal of Educational Psychology, 82,* 781–791.

Graham, S., & Harris, K. R. (1994). Implications of constructivism for teaching writing to students with special needs. *The Journal of Special Education, 28,* 275–289.

Greenwood, C. R., Arreaga-Mayer, C., & Carta, J. J. (1994). Identification and translation of effective teacher-developed instructional procedures for general practice. *Remedial and Special Education, 15,* 140–151.

Hasselbring, T. S. (1994). *TECH TALK: A multimedia teleconference* [video]. Orlando, FL: Orange County Public Schools.

Heshusius, L. (1989). The Newtonian-mechanistic paradigm, special education, and contours of alternatives: An overview. *Journal of Learning Disabilities, 22,* 403–415.

Heshusius, L. (1991). Curriculum-based assessment and direct instruction: Critical reflections on fundamental assumptions. *Exceptional Children, 57,* 315–329.

Howell, K. W., & Nolet, V. (2000). *Curriculum-based evaluation: Teaching and decision-making* (3rd ed.). Belmont, CA: Wadsworth/Thomson Learning.

Hughes, C. A., Ruhl, K. L., & Peterson, S. K. (1988). Teaching self-management skills. *Teaching Exceptional Children, 20*(2), 70–72.

Iverson, S., & Tunmer, W. E. (1993). Phonological processing skills and the Reading Recovery Program. *Journal of Educational Psychology, 85,* 112– 126.

Jackson, P. W. (1968). *Life in the classrooms.* New York: Holt, Rinehart & Winston.

Joint Committee on Teacher Planning for Students with Disabilities. (1995). Planning for academic diversity in America's classrooms: Windows on reality, research, change, and practice. *Effective School Practices, 14*(2), 1–53.

Kline, F. M., Schumaker, J. B., & Deshler, D. D. (1991). Development and validation of feedback routines for instructing students with learning disabilities. *Learning Disability Quarterly, 14,* 191–207.

Knapp, M. S., Turnbull, B. J., & Shields, P. M. (1990). New directions for educating the children of poverty. *Educational Leadership, 48*(1), 4–8.

Larrivee, B. (1986). Effective teaching for mainstreamed students is effective teaching for all students. *Teacher Education and Special Education, 9*(4), 173–179.

Lavoie, R. D. (1993, March). *Batteries are not included: Motivating the reluctant learner.* Paper presented at the Learning Disabilities Association International Conference, Washington, DC.

Lenz, B. K., Bulgren, J., & Hudson, P. (1990). Content enhancement: A model for promoting the acquisition of content by individuals with learning disabilities. In T. E. Scruggs & B. Y. L. Wong (Eds.), *Intervention research in learning disabilities* (pp. 122–165). New York: Springer-Verlag.

Lenz, B. K., Bulgren, J. A., Schumaker, J. B., Deshler, D. D., & Boudah, D. (1994). *The unit organizer routine* (Instructor's manual). Lawrence, KS: Edge Enterprises.

Lewis, R. B., & Doorlag, D. H. (1999). *Teaching special students in general education classrooms* (5th ed.). Upper Saddle River, NJ: Merrill/Prentice Hall.

Liberman, I. Y., & Liberman, A. M. (1990). Whole language vs. code-emphasis: Underlying assumptions and their implications for reading instruction. *Annals of Dyslexia, 40,* 51–77.

Lovitt, T. C. (1977). *In spite of my resistance: I've learned from children.* Upper Saddle River, NJ: Merrill/Prentice Hall.

Mather, N., & Roberts, R. (1994). Learning disabilities: A field in danger of extinction? *Learning Disabilities Research & Practice, 9,* 49–58.

Mercer, C. D. (1997). *Students with learning disabilities* (5th ed.). Upper Saddle River, NJ: Merrill/Prentice Hall.

Mercer, C. D., Jordan, L., & Miller, S. P. (1994). Implications of constructivism for teaching math to students with moderate to mild disabilities. *The Journal of Special Education, 38,* 290–306.

Mercer, C. D., Jordan, L., & Miller, S. P. (1996). Constructivistic math instruction for diverse learners. *Learning Disabilities Research & Practice, 11,* 147–156.

Mercer, C. D., Lane, H. B., Jordan, L., Allsopp, D. H., & Eisele, M. R. (1996). Empowering teachers and students with instructional choices in inclusive settings. *Remedial and Special Education, 17,* 226–236.

Mercer, C. D., & Miller, S. P. (1992) *Strategic math series: Multiplication facts 0 to 81.* Lawrence, KS: Edge Enterprises.

Mohlman, G., Sparks-Langer, S., & Colton, A. B. (1991). Synthesis of research on teachers' reflective thinking. *Educational Leadership, 48*(6), 37–44.

Montague, M. (1992). The effects of cognitive and metacognitive strategy instruction on the mathematical problem solving of middle school students with learning disabilities. *Journal of Learning Disabilities, 25,* 230–248.

Moshman, D. (1982). Exogenous, endogenous, and dialectical constructivism. *Developmental Review, 2,* 371–384.

Newmann, F. M., & Wehlage, G. G. (1993). Five standards of authentic instruction. *Educational Leadership, 50*(7), 8–12.

Olson, J. L., & Platt, J. M. (2000). *Teaching children and adolescents with special needs* (3rd ed.). Upper Saddle River, NJ: Merrill/Prentice Hall.

Poplin, M. S. (1988). The reductionist fallacy in learning disabilities: Replicating the past by reducing the present. *Journal of Learning Disabilities, 21,* 389–400.

Porter, A. C., & Brophy, J. (1988). Synthesis of research on good teaching: Insights from the work of the Institute for Research on Teaching. *Educational Leadership, 45*(8), 74–85.

Prater, M. A. (1993). Teaching concepts: Procedures for the design and delivery of instruction. *Remedial and Special Education, 14*(5), 51–62.

Pressley, M., & Harris, K. R. (1990). What we really know about strategy instruction. *Educational Leadership, 48*(1), 31–34.

Reynolds, A. (1992). What is competent beginning teaching? A review of the literature. *Review of Educational Research, 62,* 1–35.

Rieth, H., & Evertson, C. (1988). Variables related to the effective instruction of difficult-to-teach children. *Focus on Exceptional Children, 20*(5), 1–8.

Rooney, K. J., & Hallahan, D. P. (1985). Future directions for cognitive behavior modification research: The quest for cognitive change. *Remedial and Special Education, 6*(2), 46–51.

Rosenshine, B., & Stevens, R. (1986). Teaching functions. In M. C. Wittrock (Ed.), *Handbook of research on teaching* (3rd ed., pp. 376–391). Upper Saddle River, NJ: Prentice Hall.

Schumm, J. S., & Vaughn, S. (1995). Meaningful professional development in accommodating students with disabilities: Lessons learned. *Remedial and Special Education, 16,* 344–353.

Schumm, J. S., Vaughn, S., & Leavell, A. (1994). Planning pyramid: A framework for planning for diverse student needs during content area instruction. *The Reading Teacher, 47*(8), 608–615.

Scruggs, T. E., & Mastropieri, M. A. (1994). The construction of scientific knowledge by students with mild disabilities. *The Journal of Special Education, 28,* 307–321.

Scruggs, T. E., Mastropieri, M. A., Sullivan, G. S., & Hesser, L. S. (1993). Improving reasoning and recall: The differential effects of elaborative interrogation and mnemonic elaboration. *Learning Disability Quarterly, 16,* 233–240.

Simmons, D. C., Fuchs, D., & Fuchs, L. S. (1991). Instructional and curricular requisites of mainstreamed students with learning disabilities. *Journal of Learning Disabilities, 24,* 354–360.

Slavin, R. E., & Madden, N. A. (1989). What works for students at risk: A research synthesis. *Educational Leadership, 46*(5), 4–13.

Slavin, R. E., Madden, N. A., Dolan, L. J., Wasik, B. A., Ross, S. M., & Smith, L. J. (1994). "Whenever and wherever we choose": The replication of "Success for All." *Phi Delta Kappan, 75,* 639–647.

Smyth, J. (1989). Developing and sustaining critical reflection in teacher education. *Journal of Teacher Education, 40*(2), 2–9.

Sprick, R. S. (1981). *The solution book: A guide to classroom discipline.* Blacklick, OH: SRA.

Sprick, R. S. (1987). *Solutions to elementary discipline problems* [audiocassette tapes]. Eugene, OR: Teaching Strategies.

Stanovich, K. E. (1994). Constructivism in reading education. *The Journal of Special Education, 28,* 259–274.

Stokes, T. F., & Baer, D. M. (1977). An implicit technology of generalization. *Journal of Applied Behavior Analysis, 10,* 349–367.

Torgesen, J. (1990). Studies of children with learning disabilities who perform poorly on memory span tasks. In J. K. Torgesen (Ed.), *Cognitive and behavioral characteristics of children with learning disabilities* (pp. 41–58). Austin, TX: PRO-ED.

Wang, M. C. (1987). Toward achieving educational excellence for all students: Program design and instructional outcomes. *Remedial and Special Education, 8*(3), 25–34.

Warren, S. T., & Yoder, P. J. (1994). Communication and language intervention: Why a constructivist approach is insufficient. *The Journal of Special Education, 28,* 248–258.

Yoder, P. J., Kaiser, A., & Alpert, C. (1991). An exploratory study of the interaction between language teaching methods and child characteristics. *Journal of Speech and Hearing Research, 34,* 155–167.

CHAPTER **5**

Promoting Social, Emotional, and Behavioral Development

Students with learning problems often have difficulty with social skills and emotional development and with maintaining appropriate behavior. Problems in social skills result in difficulty interacting with others, whereas emotional difficulties generally involve problems within oneself (e.g., low self-concept). Students with behavioral problems often disrupt others or undermine their own learning progress. Problems in these areas frequently overlap; for example, a student with a poor self-concept regarding academics may withdraw from social interactions during academic activities and engage in off-task behavior (e.g., daydreaming) throughout the school day. Although it is not always apparent whether social, emotional, or behavioral problems contribute to a student's academic difficulties, they usually interfere with learning and thus limit academic success. On the other hand, learning difficulties can contribute to social, emotional, and behavioral problems by causing the student to face excessive academic failure and frustration.

Experts maintain that it is not sufficient to treat academic deficits in isolation and that educational plans must consider the social, emotional, and behavioral characteristics and needs of students with learning problems (Bender, 1994). Through appropriate instruction the teacher can help students improve their social, emotional, and behavioral development. Table 5.1 includes profiles of students and related interventions for selected social, emotional, and behavioral characteristics.

☀ ASSESSMENT OF SOCIAL, EMOTIONAL, AND BEHAVIORAL DEVELOPMENT

Assessment of social, emotional, and behavioral development involves various types of measurement and evaluation procedures. In addition to student behavior in the classroom, a thorough assessment of social, emotional, and behavioral factors considers student self-concept and attitudes as well as behavior outside the classroom. To provide a broad and natural picture of the student, an ecological assessment includes an evaluation of the student's behavior and status in various environments in which he or she functions. Currently, no single test can yield a comprehensive, reliable, valid, and useful assessment of social skills or emotional and

behavioral problems. Thus, several instruments and procedures are required to assess social, emotional, and behavioral development. Helpful information may be obtained from teachers, parents, students, and peers as well as from records of social, developmental, and educational history.

During assessment of social, emotional, and behavioral development, the type of behavior and its frequency, intensity, and duration should be considered. When assessment consists of a combination of various methods, contexts, and sources of data, the social, emotional, and behavioral problems of students can be identified and can lead to appropriate educational interventions. This section presents several techniques and measures available to assess social, emotional, and behavioral development. Included are commercial observer-rater instruments, commercial measures of adaptive behavior, self-report instruments, sociometric techniques, and naturalistic observations.

Commercial Observer-Rater Instruments

With these instruments an observer (e.g., teacher, guidance counselor, social worker, school psychologist, or family member) completes either a checklist or a rating scale. Checklists generally are used to record the presence or absence of specific characteristics or behaviors. Rating scales are designed to indicate the frequency of a particular behavior or the degree to which certain characteristics are present. Teacher ratings frequently are used to assess behavioral problems in classrooms. These ratings usually are conducted with published checklists, scales, or questionnaires. These formats are most useful for general screening and initial identification of student behavioral problems, as well as for measuring student progress over time. Table 5.2 provides nine instruments to use in assessing social, emotional, and behavioral development.

Traditionally, teacher ratings of social skills have received less attention than emotional and behavioral problems, but this is changing. Gresham and Elliott (1990) authored an instrument that involves teacher ratings of social skills (see Table 5.2). The teacher version of the *Social Skills Rating System* (Gresham & Elliott, 1990) features items that represent a broad range of behaviors (e.g., positive behaviors such as sharing, giving

TABLE 5.1
Profiles of students and related interventions for selected social, emotional, and behavioral characteristics

Social Skills Deficits
Nobody seems to like Barry. He often is called rude or inconsiderate. For example, he may continue to relate the details of a neighborhood rumor even though the face of one of his classmates is red with embarrassment, or he thoughtlessly may interrupt a serious conversation between two adults. He cannot tell when his listeners have lost interest. To help Barry identify critical social and nonverbal cues, his teacher involves him in role playing and games such as charades. A social skills curriculum also is used.

Poor Self-Concept
Melanie, a secondary school student, has faced repeated failure and frustration throughout her school years. She has few friends and seldom initiates social interactions or takes part in school activities. When given an academic task, Melanie frequently responds, "That's too hard for me. I can't do it." Melanie's English teacher, who has taken an individual interest in her, has minimized her anxiety about failure through the use of support and success techniques. The teacher is helping Melanie attribute her failures to insufficient effort and praises her for effort regardless of the accuracy of her responses. She also uses Melanie as a peer tutor to enhance her feelings of self-worth.

Dependency
As a young child, Brad was very dependent on his mother. She gave him excessive attention and assistance. Now, he frequently turns to his teacher with requests such as "Help me" or "Show me how." Brad's teacher is trying to provide him with appropriate academic tasks and success experiences and is reinforcing him for effort. Brad also works independently with self-correcting materials and computer software programs that provide him with immediate feedback without the teacher being present.

Loneliness
Tessa usually works, plays, and eats alone. She sits quietly at her desk, staring into space, rather than working or participating in discussions. She seldom willingly joins group activities or even initiates a conversation. She does not share and frequently makes negative comments that reduce the likelihood of further interaction (e.g., "You sure are dumb. Don't you know how to do anything right?"). Tessa's teacher is providing her with much support and praise and gradually is encouraging various interpersonal relationships. Peer teaching and instructional games in which Tessa is paired with a competent, accepting student are providing Tessa with appropriate peer contact. The teacher systematically reinforces any group participation or positive social interaction.

Disruptive Behavior
Larry is often out of his seat or yelling across the room. He starts fights over minor incidents, such as tripping or butting in line. Larry's teacher is using social skills training and behavior modification techniques to reduce his disruptive behavior. She reinforces and praises him for appropriate behavior and ignores him as much as possible when he is being disruptive. When she must reprimand him, she does so quietly so that others cannot hear.

Hyperactivity
Richard's mother describes her son as having been in a state of perpetual motion since he was very young. It seems impossible for him to sit still for even a few minutes. At mealtime, he quickly stuffs his food in his mouth and is then once again on the go. In the classroom Richard also is easily excitable and constantly in motion. For example, he frequently is out of his seat, shuffling papers, moving his feet or legs, or tapping his pencil on his desk. Richard's activity level causes him to have frequent accidents (e.g., while riding his bicycle), and he sometimes unintentionally hurts a classmate when playing too rough on the playground. Richard takes Ritalin every morning under his doctor's prescription, and his classroom teacher structures Richard's daily work schedule according to his attention span, reinforces him when he is less active, and frequently allows him to perform tasks that permit him to move about the room.

Distractibility
According to her teacher, Amy is highly distractible and has a short attention span. She can work on an assignment for a short time, but she is diverted quickly by any noise or motion in the room. She stares out the window or daydreams, and her assignments go uncompleted. Her teacher uses a carrel to isolate Amy from potentially distracting auditory and visual stimuli. She also encourages Amy to use verbal mediation (i.e., quietly talking to herself about what she is doing) while performing a task and gives her praise for on-task behavior.

(continued on next page)

TABLE 5.1
(continued)

> *Impulsivity*
> Jane's impulsivity is evident in class. She is usually the first person to complete and hand in a worksheet, always without checking the accuracy of her responses. Jane's grades in math especially have been affected by her tendency to respond impulsively, even though she usually can correct a wrong response when given the opportunity. She talks out of turn, and without thinking says things that may hurt someone's feelings. Jane's teacher is encouraging her to pause before acting or speaking. In math, her teacher has Jane estimate the answers and check her work. Also, through contingency contracts, Jane is reinforced according to an accuracy criterion (percent correct) for each task.

Source: From *Students with Learning Disabilities* (p. 625), 5th ed., by C. D. Mercer, 1997, Upper Saddle River, NJ: Merrill/Prentice Hall. Copyright 1997 by Prentice-Hall Publishing Company. Reprinted by permission.

compliments, and following rules, as well as problem behaviors such as aggression, hyperactivity, and social withdrawal). Another dimension of the *Social Skills Rating System* involves the teacher specifying whether each behavior is critical, important, or unimportant for the classroom system. These ratings indicate which behaviors are priority for social skills intervention. Maag (1989) indicates that teacher ratings are valuable for identifying students and problematic behaviors that can be assessed further through naturalistic observations.

Parental ratings also have been used extensively to rate children's atypical behaviors and adaptive behavior. Five of the behavior rating instruments included in Table 5.2 are suitable for parental use. Parental ratings of social skills have received limited attention, but the *Social Skills Rating System* (Gresham & Elliott, 1990) includes a version for parents to rate their children's social skills on cooperation, assertion, self-control, and responsibility. An important feature of the instrument is the inclusion of a frequency dimension and an importance dimension for each social skill rated.

Commercial Measures of Adaptive Behavior

Adaptive behavior refers to the way an individual adjusts to the demands and changes in the physical and social environment. The interview technique frequently is used to obtain information from parents about the student's current nonacademic functioning, whereas teachers typically respond on written questionnaires concerning the student's social and emotional behavior. Adaptive behavior

assessment scales generally include items for measuring personal self-sufficiency, independence in the community, and personal and social responsibility. Three measures of adaptive behavior are presented in Table 5.3.

Self-Report Instruments

Self-report techniques allow students to report on their own specific behaviors. Self-report procedures obtain information directly from the students; thus, the information is totally subjective. Its validity depends on the willingness of students to report the information and on their ability to understand and perform the task. Some commercial self-report instruments have built-in lie scales to screen for defensiveness and unrealistic levels of social desirability. Commercial self-report instruments are presented, as are the Q-sort technique and various informal techniques.

Commercial Self-Report Instruments Self-report measures are the primary means for assessing students' self-concepts and for identifying areas that cause students anxiety or concern. Students respond directly to test items concerning themselves. Table 5.4 includes seven commercial self-report instruments for assessing self-concept. Self-report instruments have several weaknesses because of the potential for bias, the desire to give responses that please, social desirability, and reading-level difficulties (Gresham & Elliott, 1989). Consequently, self-report measures of students' social skills are not used as widely as sociometrics, teacher ratings, and other measures. However, the self-report version of the *Social Skills*

TABLE 5.2

Observer-rater instruments

Instrument	Age/Grade	Respondent
Behavior Assessment System for Children (Reynolds & Kamphaus, 1992)	2½–18 years	Teacher, parent, student

The system provides teacher, parent, and self-reports, as well as a structured developmental history and observed classroom behavior of the student. The teacher rating scale includes items (such as "Bullies others" and "Adjusts well to new teachers") related to adaptive and problem behaviors in school settings, whereas the parent rating scale pertains to behaviors exhibited in community and home settings. The self-report measure of personality includes short true–false statements concerning personal thoughts and feelings. The teacher and parent scales use a 4-point rating scale of frequency, and all three scales yield composite scores of problem behaviors. Additional student information is obtained on the development history survey of social, psychological, developmental, educational, and medical areas, and during a 15-minute classroom observation maladaptive and adaptive behaviors are coded and recorded. Two computerized formats for easy scoring are available.

Instrument	Age/Grade	Respondent
Behavior Evaluation Scale—2 (McCarney & Leigh, 1990)	Kindergarten– 12th grade	Teacher

The scale yields behavioral information about students according to five subscales: learning problems, interpersonal difficulties, inappropriate behavior, unhappiness/depression, and physical symptoms/fears. The 76 items are stated in observable and measurable terms, and raw scores are weighted according to severity and frequency of observed behaviors.

Instrument	Age/Grade	Respondent
Behavior Rating Profile—2 (Brown & Hammill, 1990)	1st–12th grade	Teacher, parent, student, peers

Six independent measures of behavior are included: teacher rating scale, student rating scale (school), parent rating scale, student rating scale (home), sociogram, and student rating scale (peer). The three student rating scales are embedded in a 60-item true–false format, and the parent and teacher rating scales each contain 30 items that the respondents classify on a 4-point scale. The sociogram provides information about the student's sociometric status within the classroom. The results of the profile can be used to identify students whose behavior is perceived to be deviant and to identify specific settings in which behavioral problems are prominent. Also, the profile can be useful in identifying persons whose perceptions of a student's behaviors are different from those of other respondents.

Instrument	Age/Grade	Respondent
Comprehensive Behavior Rating Scale for Children (Neeper, Lahey, & Frick, 1990)	6–14 years	Teacher

The teacher uses a 5-point scale to indicate how descriptive of the student each of 70 statements is. Nine scales are included: inattention-disorganization, reading problems, cognitive deficits, oppositional-conduct disorder, motor hyperactivity, anxiety, sluggish tempo, daydreaming, and social competence. Thus, the scale focuses on cognitive as well as emotional and behavioral dimensions.

Instrument	Age/Grade	Respondent
Devereux Behavior Rating Scale— School Form (Naglieri, LeBuffe, & Pfeiffer, 1993)	5–18 years	Teacher, parent

The scale is especially effective as a screening device to identify the existence of behaviors that fall within the normal range and behaviors that indicate a severe emotional disturbance. Two 40-item versions, one for children age 5 through 12 years and one for adolescents age 13 through 18 years, feature separate sets of appropriate items. The four subtests focus on interpersonal problems, inappropriate behaviors/feelings, depression, and physical symptoms/fear. Administration time is about 5 minutes, and item-level scores help identify specific problem behaviors.

(continued on next page)

TABLE 5.2
(continued)

Instrument	Age/Grade	Respondent
Revised Behavior Problem Checklist (Quay & Peterson, 1987)	Kindergarten– 8th grade	Teacher, parent, anyone familiar with the student

A rating system is used that distinguishes among behaviors not observed, observed but mild, and observed and severe. Problem behaviors are classified according to six domains: conduct disorder, socialized aggression, attention problems or immaturity, anxiety or withdrawal, psychotic behavior, and motor excess.

Social-Emotional Dimension Scale (Hutton & Roberts, 1986)	5½–18½ years	Teacher

The 32-item norm-referenced rating scale can be used to assess students who are at risk for conduct disorders, behavioral problems, or emotional disturbance. Student performance is assessed in six areas: physical/fear reaction, depressive reaction, avoidance of peer interaction, avoidance of teacher interaction, aggressive interaction, and inappropriate behavior.

Social Skills Rating System (Gresham & Elliott, 1990)	3–18 years	Teacher, parent, student

There are three rating forms (teacher, parent, and student) that evaluate a broad range of behaviors. The social skills scale (on all three forms) evaluates positive social behaviors (such as cooperation, assertion, responsibility, empathy, and self-control). The problem behavior scale (on the teacher and parent forms) measures behaviors that can interfere with the production of social skills (such as aggression, anxiety, and hyperactivity). The academic competence scale (on the teacher form) is an index of academic functioning. Items on each scale are rated according to perceived frequency and importance. SSRS *ASSIST* software provides computerized scoring and reporting as well as behavioral objectives and suggestions for planning intervention.

Walker Problem Behavior Identification Checklist (Walker, 1983)	Preschool–6th grade	Teacher

The checklist takes about 15 minutes to administer and consists of 50 statements describing behaviors that may interfere or compete with successful academic performance. The items are designed to measure five behavioral factors: acting out, withdrawal, distractibility, disturbed peer relations, and immaturity.

Rating System (Gresham & Elliott, 1990) represents an attempt to develop a reliable and valid self-report measure of social skills. It includes one version for third through sixth grade and another one for seventh through twelfth grade. The scales yield scores in the areas of cooperation, assertion, self-control, and empathy.

Q-Sort Technique   The Q-sort technique is a procedure for investigating self-concept that can be used to identify areas for behavior modification. The technique focuses on determining the degree of discrepancy between an evaluation of

the "real" self and the "ideal" self. The procedure offers a way to select specific social, emotional, and behavioral problems for intervention.

The student is given a set of cards containing statements that must be sorted onto a pyramid formboard. A sample list of 25 statements suitable for elementary school students is presented in Table 5.5, and Figure 5.1 shows the behavior formboard. The formboard contains nine categories that form a continuum from *most like me* to *most unlike me*. The student is given the same number of descriptor cards as there are squares in the pyramid. In sorting the items, the student must

TABLE 5.3
Measures of adaptive behavior

Instrument	Age/Grade	Respondent
AAMR Adaptive Behavior Scale—School (Lambert, Nihira, & Leland, 1993)	3–18 years	Teacher, parent, anyone familiar with the student

The school edition covers social and daily living skills and behaviors. Part I evaluates personal independence in daily living (e.g., independent functioning, self-direction, and responsibility). Part II measures social maladaptive behaviors (e.g., conformity, trustworthiness, and self-abusive behavior). The scale domains are grouped into five factors: personal self-sufficiency, community self-sufficiency, personal-social responsibility, personal adjustment, and social adjustment. The responder must circle the highest level of functioning demonstrated by the student, answer "yes" or "no" to a series of statements, or rate the statements in each item as occurring never, occasionally, or frequently. The scale yields standard scores and percentiles for each domain, and a software scoring and report system is available.

Instrument	Age/Grade	Respondent
Scales of Independent Behavior— Revised (Bruininks, Woodcock, Weatherman, & Hill, 1996)	Infant–adult	Teacher, parent, student, anyone familiar with the student

The instrument provides a noncognitive measure of adjustment in social, behavioral, and adaptive areas. It assesses functional independence and adaptive behavior in motor skills, social interaction and communication skills, personal living skills, and community living skills. Also, an optional problem behavior scale focuses on general externalized, internalized, and asocial maladaptive behaviors. Because the instrument is linked conceptually and statistically to the *Woodcock-Johnson Psycho-Educational Battery—Revised*, adaptive behavior can be measured based on cognitive ability. Administration time is 45 to 60 minutes for the full-scale form and 15 to 20 minutes for the short form or early development form. A computer scoring and reporting program is available.

Instrument	Age/Grade	Respondent
Vineland Adaptive Behavior Scale (Sparrow, Balla, & Cicchetti, 1984)	Birth–18 years (survey and expanded forms); 3–12 years (classroom edition)	Teacher, parent, anyone familiar with the student

Three versions are available: (1) interview edition, survey form—aids in screening or classification decisions, (2) interview edition, expanded form—provides specific prescriptive information that can be used for educational programming, and (3) classroom edition—allows for direct observation of adaptive behavior of students and uses a checklist format. The scale assesses adaptive behavior in four areas: communication, daily living skills, socialization, and motor skills. The survey and expanded forms also measure maladaptive behavior. Standard scores and percentiles are available for each area and subarea as well as total adaptive behavior, and *Vineland ASSIST* software provides helpful score conversion.

arrange the cards so that each square is used and none is left blank or used twice. First, the student is asked to complete a *real sort* by sorting the items onto the formboard to best reflect her or his own beliefs about her or his classroom behavior. After the responses of the real sort are recorded, the student is asked to complete an *ideal sort* in which the same items are arranged on the formboard to indicate how she or he would *like* to be in

daily classroom activities. During sorting, the student may rearrange the cards as many times as needed. The teacher compares the student's responses on the real sort with the responses on the ideal sort and notes items that differ greatly (i.e., by four or more points). These items can become target behaviors for intervention.

The behavioral Q-sort also can be administered to parents or teachers. Thus, comparisons

TABLE 5.4
Self-report instruments

Instrument	Age/Grade
Coopersmith Self-Esteem Inventories (Coopersmith, 1981)	8–15 years

The self-report questionnaires consist of short statements (e.g., "I'm a failure" and "I can usually take care of myself") to be answered "like me" or "unlike me." The inventories are designed to measure attitudes toward the self in social, academic, and personal contexts. The school form contains 58 items that produce a total score, a lie score, and attitude scores toward social self/peers, home/parents, and school/academics.

| *Culture-Free Self-Esteem Inventories—2* (Battle, 1992) | 5 years and older |

The inventories contain a 60-item form (or a 30-item brief form) that measures students' self-esteem in five areas: general, peers, school, parents, and lie (defensiveness) scales. The 40-item adult form includes four areas: general, social, personal, and lie scales. Yes–no responses can be either written or spoken. The test screens for possible intervention and yields percentiles for total and subtest scores.

| *Multidimensional Self-Concept Scale* (Bracken, 1992) | 5th–12th grade |

The instrument includes six 25-item scales in the following areas: social, competence, affect, academic, family, and physical. Each area can be assessed independently. The test yields standard scores and can be administered in about 20 minutes. The manual provides specific recommendations for improving self-concept.

| *Piers-Harris Children's Self-Concept Scale* (Piers & Harris, 1984) | 8–18 years |

The scale covers many areas of self-concept, including physical appearance, popularity, anxiety, and happiness-satisfaction. The student responds with "yes" or "no" to 80 declarative statements (e.g., "I am good looking" and "My classmates make fun of me"). The items are written on a third-grade reading level, and both positive and negative statements are included. Suggested administration time is 15 to 20 minutes.

| *Self-Esteem Index* (Brown & Alexander, 1991) | 7–18 years |

This norm-referenced measure indicates how individuals perceive and value themselves. The index includes four scales: academic competence, family acceptance, peer popularity, and personal security (physical appearance and personal attributes). The student classifies each item on a scale ranging from *always true* to *always false*. In addition to a global self-esteem score, the four scales yield standard scores and percentile ranks.

| *Student Self-Concept Scale* (Gresham, Elliott, & Evans-Fernandez, 1992) | 3rd–12th grade |

The scale includes 72 items that relate to the perceived confidence and importance of specific behaviors influencing the development of a student's self-concept. The student rates items on three dimensions (self-confidence, importance, and outcome confidence) to measure self-concept in three areas: academic (e.g., reading skills and listening to teacher), social (e.g., playing with others and sharing), and self-image (e.g., general self-concept and global self-perception). The scale can be individually or group-administered in about 20 to 30 minutes.

| *Tennessee Self-Concept Scale: Second Edition* (Fitts & Warren, 1996) | 7 years and older |

The scale is designed to measure self-concept and provides scores in 15 areas, including identity, behavior, satisfaction, physical self, moral self, personal self, family self, social self, and academic/work self. Each descriptive statement (e.g., "I have a healthy body" and "I have a lot of self control") is answered on a 5-point scale from *completely false* to *completely true*. The child form, written at a second-grade reading level, can be used with 7- through 14-year-old students, and the adult form, written at a third-grade reading level, is designed for individuals 13 years of age and older. Each form requires about 10 to 20 minutes to complete.

TABLE 5.5

Elementary-level school items on the behavioral Q-sort

1. Gets work done on time
2. Pokes or hits classmates
3. Gets out of seat without permission
4. Scores high in spelling
5. Plays with objects while working
6. Scores high in reading
7. Disturbs neighbors by making noise
8. Is quiet during class time
9. Tips chair often
10. Follows directions
11. Smiles frequently
12. Often taps foot, fingers, or pencil
13. Pays attention to work
14. Works slowly
15. Throws objects in class
16. Reads well orally
17. Talks to classmates often
18. Scores high in English
19. Talks out without permission
20. Rocks in chair
21. Scores high in arithmetic
22. Asks teacher questions
23. Uses free time to read or study
24. Works until the job is finished
25. Walks around room during study time

Source: Adapted from *Communicating with Parents of Exceptional Children: Improving Parent–Teacher Relationships* (p. 46) by R. L. Kroth, 1975, Denver, CO: Love. Copyright 1975 by Love Publishing Company. Reprinted by permission.

can be made between others' perceptions of the student's school behavior (both real and ideal) and the student's own perceptions. The teacher's rating of the student's behavior can be compared with the student's own rating. When the comparisons on a specific behavior (such as "Pays attention to work") are very different, that behavior can be selected for examination and intervention.

Informal Self-Report Techniques Informal self-report techniques provide a general idea of a student's problems. Each student who participates should be assured that the information provided is confidential and that only honest answers help the teacher. Wallace, Larsen, and Elksnin (1992) note that teacher-developed measures of self-concept

are generally as reliable and valid as those of widely used research instruments. Four frequently used informal self-report techniques are checklists, questionnaires, interviews, and autobiographies.

In a teacher-made checklist, students are asked to indicate which behaviors or descriptions they believe apply (such as "Has a lot of friends," "Finishes classwork," and "Gets mad quickly"). Checklists are easy to administer and can give the teacher some insights concerning how the students view themselves. For example, students are presented with a list of adjectives and are instructed to check all words they consider to be descriptive of themselves. Sample items include the following:

_____	absent-minded	_____	noisy
_____	athletic	_____	friendly
_____	lonely	_____	cooperative
_____	intelligent	_____	quiet
_____	popular	_____	happy

Several kinds of questionnaires are designed to obtain information about a student's personal, social, and emotional behaviors. The yes–no or true–false format is useful and easy to administer:

1. Are you usually very friendly?   Yes   No
2. Do you get mad often?   Yes   No
3. I usually like to be by myself.   True   False

Questionnaires using open-ended questions or sentence completion require students to complete the statements. Thus, students express themselves in their own words. Such a format requires more time and ability on the part of the students, but it often yields more meaningful information than the yes–no or true–false format. Sample items from a sentence completion questionnaire include the following:

1. I work best when _____.
2. I get angry when _____.
3. When I feel lonely I _____.

Specific information also can be obtained from students through interviews. They provide an opportunity for students to express opinions and feelings about themselves and others. Interview techniques even can be extended into daily conversations, providing a flexible and ongoing source of information. In an interview, the teacher should relate the discussion questions to the stu-

FIGURE 5.1
Behavior formboard

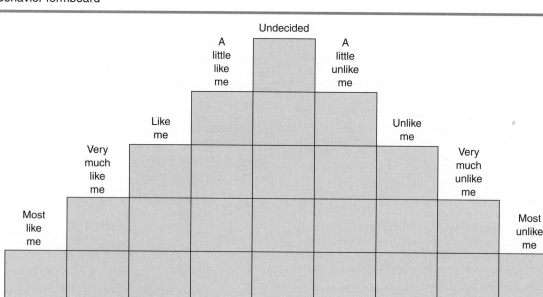

Source: From *Communicating with Parents of Exceptional Children: Improving Parent–Teacher Relationships* (p. 44) by R. L. Kroth, 1975, Denver, CO: Love. Copyright 1975 by Love Publishing Company. Reprinted by permission.

dent's particular area of difficulty. The interview is most effective when conducted in private and rapport reflecting an honest interest in the student is established. Interview questions should be kept to a minimum and should be broad instead of specific to require the student to develop a topic or express an opinion. If the teacher receives proper consent, the interview can be recorded so that it is available for later study. If recording is not possible, note taking during the interview should be minimal but immediate.

In autobiographies, students give written accounts of their lives or reveal their feelings about themselves and others. Personal experiences, ambitions, or interests can be described. Students who have difficulty in expressive writing can record oral presentations. The type of autobiography depends upon the student's age and maturity. Students can be asked to respond to specific questions or be given a topic, such as "Things That Upset Me." Autobiographical material then can be analyzed for present or potential problem areas.

Sociometric Techniques

Sociometric techniques are commonly used to assess social skills and related problems (Maag, 1989). Sociometric methodology typically is grouped into three categories: peer nominations, peer ratings, and peer assessment. A sociogram provides a visual record of the group's social structure.

Peer Nominations   This procedure involves asking students to nominate peers according to *nonbehavioral* criteria (such as preferred work partners, best friends, or preferred play partners). These criteria are viewed as nonbehavioral because they refer to activities (e.g., play) or attributes (e.g., best friend) rather than specific behaviors (e.g., asks for the opinion of others). Thus, nominations assess attitudes and preferences for engaging in selected activities with peers. Peer nominations can be fixed choice (i.e., the student nominates a limited number of peers) or unlimited choice (i.e., the student nominates as many peers as desired). It helps if a printed list of the names of all class members is provided, and responses should be kept secret. Nominations can be weighted (i.e., the order of nominations is considered with weights assigned in a rank-order manner) or unweighted (McConnell & Odom, 1986). Peer nominations also can be keyed to negative criteria (e.g., least preferred play partner). Research suggests that positive and negative nominations are not at opposite ends of the same continuum but measure two distinct dimensions of sociometric status (Gresham & Reschly, 1988; McConnell & Odom, 1986).

Coie, Dodge, and Coppotelli (1982) and Dodge (1983) have generated empirical support for the peer nomination approach. Coie et al. provide a classification system for peer nominations that identifies five sociometric status groups: popular, neglected, rejected, controversial, and average. These groups are then evaluated in terms of *liked most* and *liked least*. These techniques provide a detailed description of the social status of a student in a peer group and identify behavior correlates for each sociometric group. For example, rejected students exhibit high rates of aggressive and disruptive behaviors and low rates of cooperative, peer-reinforcing behaviors, whereas neglected students display high rates of shy, withdrawn, and fearful behaviors and low rates of positive social interactions (Dodge, 1983).

Peer Ratings   In a peer rating, *all* students in a classroom rate one another on a Likert-type scale according to *nonbehavioral* criteria. These criteria are similar to peer nominations in that areas such as *play with* and *work with* preferences are used. A student's score on a peer rating is the average rating received from peers. Gresham and Elliott (1989) note that these ratings tend to indicate a student's overall acceptance level within the peer group. Peer ratings feature several advantages over peer nominations. First, every student in the class is rated rather than only a few students. Second, a student's rating scores are more reliable because they are based on a larger number of raters. Third, peer ratings typically do not involve the use of negative criteria, thereby reducing ethical objections to sociometric assessments. Disadvantages of peer ratings include stereotypical ratings (i.e., giving many peers the same rating) and central tendency errors (i.e., rating

peers in the middle of the scale) (McConnell & Odom, 1986).

Peer Assessment   In peer assessment, students are asked to nominate or rate peers on several *behavioral* characteristics. Students hear or read behavioral descriptions and then nominate or rate individuals according to the descriptions. One of the more popular peer assessment techniques is the *Guess Who?* technique (Kaufman, Agard, & Semmel, 1985). Students nominate peers who fit behavioral descriptions involving such dimensions as disruptive behavior, smartness, dullness, and quiet/good behavior.

Sociogram   Responses from a sociometric questionnaire indicating the number of times each student is chosen may be recorded on a tally sheet, or a *sociogram* can be constructed to provide a visual record of the social structure within the class. Figure 5.2 shows a sociogram of ten fourth-grade students who were asked to write the names of two classmates with whom they would most like to play. In this example, for the most part, girls preferred to play with girls, and boys with boys. Among the girls, Alice, Debby, and Judy seem to have a close relationship. None of these girls chose other classmates. Joan did not receive any choices, and Kim was selected as first choice only by Joan. Kim was the only girl to choose a boy. Among the boys, Bob and Steve were mutual choices, as were Ken and John. Adam received no choices, and John was the only boy to choose a girl.

The information obtained from the sociogram can help to identify isolates as well as leaders and can give the teacher a basis for congenial, effective group activities. In addition, the social preferences discovered provide insight about which social patterns should be changed and which should be encouraged. In this example, activities involving Adam and either Ken or Steve may be a positive for Adam, who in general is an isolate. Among the girls, situations should be planned to foster relationships outside of the clique. Different patterns probably will be revealed for different activities or settings. A student may be selected by several classmates as their choice for a study partner, but may receive no choices for social activities.

Information also can be provided through peer nomination techniques, in which each student

FIGURE 5.2
A sociogram

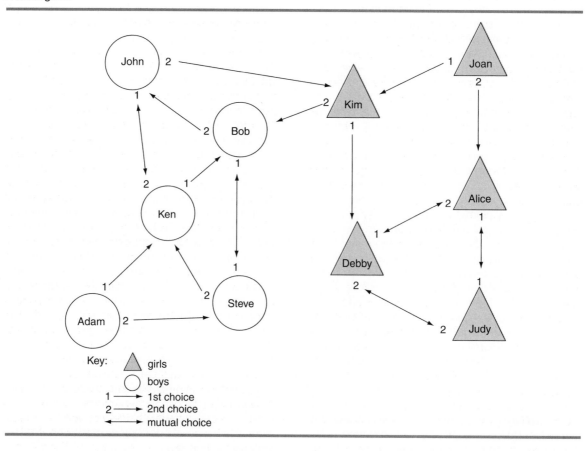

Key:
△ girls
○ boys
1 ——→ 1st choice
2 ——→ 2nd choice
←——→ mutual choice

responds to statements about attitudes or behavior by naming classmates (e.g., "Which students are very popular?" or "Which students are selfish?"). Sociograms can be scored (rather than mapped) based on combinations of positive and negative nominations, and the social status of students can be identified as popular (high number of positive nominations and low number of negative nominations), rejected (high number of negative nominations and low number of positive nominations), controversial (high numbers of positive and negative nominations), and neglected (no evaluations).

Overall, sociometric assessment can be an important component in evaluating students with learning problems. To date, Gresham and Elliott

(1989) maintain that the Coie et al. (1982) system offers the best reliability and validity.

Naturalistic Observations

Direct observation provides an in-depth study of possible problem behaviors identified by rating scales, checklists, and interviews. Moreover, defining target behaviors, observing and recording their frequency in the natural environment, and analyzing the data represent the most direct and ecologically valid assessment of students' social skills and related behaviors (Elliott, Gresham, & Heffer, 1987). Naturalistic assessment allows for a functional analysis of the antecedent events, behavioral sequence, and consequences that may influence inappropriate social behavior or decrease prosocial behaviors (Maag, 1989). This approach promotes the use of operationally defined social skills or behaviors and the development of systems for measuring and recording target behaviors. The collection of frequent data provides a sensitive index to variations in student behavior. Direct observation of social, emotional, and behavioral development includes observing the behavior, the teacher–student interaction, and the environment. The primary difficulty with naturalistic observation is that the student might not act naturally in the context in which observation occurs. If the observer suspects the student is not behaving naturally, role-play assessment may be useful.

Observation of Behavior   Direct, systematic observation of student behavior can provide information and insights about the student's social and emotional skills. Many teachers have training in personality development and work with students for several hours each day in different situations; therefore, they usually are highly qualified to observe and assess behavior. If behaviors are *described* and reported as responses seen or provided (such as "Gets out of seat," "Butts in the cafeteria line," or "Calls Bill a sissy during math seatwork") instead of as interpretations (such as "hyperactive," "disruptive," or "impulsive"), the validity of teacher observations increases. The teacher should observe the conditions under which the behavior occurs and record the frequency of occurrence. Careful observation may reveal, for example, that out-of-seat behavior occurs only during math, or that singing in class occurs when the student is sitting near Maria. The target behavior also can be measured by duration (i.e., how long the student exhibits the behavior) or by a time sampling, in which the student is observed during certain periods for specified lengths of time.

In addition to the behavior itself, the teacher also should note the events that occur immediately before and immediately after the behavior and serve to reinforce it. Information about the surrounding conditions may enable the teacher to choose management strategies. For example, a student's swearing might receive the reinforcement of attention from peers (laughter). The teacher could concentrate on eliminating peer re-inforcement and encouraging peer attention to desirable responses. Finally, daily measurement of behavior can provide feedback on the success of strategies used to resolve the behavior.

Observation of Teacher–Student Interaction   Flanders (1970) presents the *interaction analysis system* for measuring the interactions between the teacher and the students in the entire class. Flanders specifies ten behavior categories: Seven involve teacher's verbal behavior (e.g., praising or encouraging students, asking questions, and criticizing); two involve students' verbal behavior (e.g., responding to the teacher); and one is for silence or confusion. Teacher–student interactions are observed, and behaviors are recorded every 4 seconds. Data are collected for several days during short observation periods. A simplified version of the Flanders technique involves the use of a videotape or audiotape recorder instead of a trained observer. The teacher can interpret the recordings made during the day and can categorize the verbal interactions according to Flanders' ten categories. By using this assessment device, the teacher can identify verbal patterns of student–teacher interactions in the classroom.

Sprick (1985) developed a system for monitoring teacher–student interactions that focuses on the frequency of teacher responses to negative events and positive events. He suggests that a 3:1 positive-to-negative ratio is needed for effective interaction and classroom management. Other variables noted include bias toward different students (e.g., low achievers or males) and how often inappropriate behavior is reinforced.

In teacher–student interactions, a teacher occasionally may overreact to a certain behavior. Teachers must show understanding and awareness to control inappropriate reactions.

Observation of Environment   In assessing social, emotional, and behavioral development, the teacher should observe the student in different environments. The teacher then can consider the environment's influence in starting or maintaining the problem behavior. Some observation can be made outside the school setting; however, the teacher mainly should observe in-school environments (such as art class, physical education class, lunchroom, and playground). Perhaps the target behavior surfaces only in certain settings or instructional conditions. The student may become disruptive when required to remain seated for a long time during a lecture; however, when allowed to move about or participate in class discussions, his or her behavior may be acceptable. Also, a student may exhibit anxiety and withdraw when required to read orally in front of the class or to compute timed math problems, but be quite comfortable when working alone in untimed situations or in small-group activities. Thus, teacher observation of various environments can help determine the adjustments needed to improve the student's instructional program.

Role-Play Assessment This approach elicits a student's behavior in response to staged social interactions (such as receiving criticism), and the student's performance is recorded. Advances in role-play methodology (Dodge, Pettit, McClaskey, & Brown, 1986) have improved their generalizability to naturalistic observations. Moreover, role-play assessments enable the observer to determine whether the student has a social skill acquisition deficit (i.e., does not possess the skill) or a social skill performance problem (i.e., does not desire to perform the skill).

GENERAL TECHNIQUES FOR PROMOTING SOCIAL, EMOTIONAL, AND BEHAVIORAL DEVELOPMENT

The development of social, emotional, and behavioral attributes is complex because these affective domains are interdependent. Improvement in one domain frequently has a positive effect on the others. For example, positive reinforcement can help a youngster behave more appropriately, and when other students respond positively and accept the youngster, his or her self-concept improves. Fortunately, several techniques can develop positive attributes in social, emotional, and behavioral domains. The general techniques featured in this section include teach for success, focus on promoting proactivity, promote cooperation, teach self-management, model target behaviors and attributes, and focus on motivation through behavior modification. Activities for increasing on-task behavior also are provided.

Teach for Success

Many students with learning problems have low self-concepts, attention deficits, social skills deficits, or emotional problems. Because these types of affective problems can lead to aggressive, disruptive, or withdrawal behavior, students with learning problems may become difficult to manage in the classroom. Moreover, some of these students are overly negative about themselves. Sprick (1981) notes that acting out, misbehaving in a manner to get caught, and giving up or withdrawal are common manifestations of a poor self-concept. Educators agree that effective behavior management must begin with preventive techniques and that these techniques start with good teaching. Most behavioral problems of students with learning difficulties can probably be prevented with effective instruction. The development of positive social, emotional, and behavioral attributes through teaching is fundamental to a student's school success, motivation, and future learning.

Teach Effectively Effective teaching leads to academic progress, which is critical if a student with learning problems is to develop a positive self-concept regarding learning. Sprick (1981) states, "There is nothing more important for any student than believing he or she is able to learn, grow, and be successful. When in doubt about what to do to improve a child's self-concept, teach!" (Book E, p. 9). Chapters 1 through 4 of this text present frameworks for making instructional decisions, including instructional variables related to student learning. Although all the variables likely would lead to improvements in the social, emotional, and behavioral attributes of students with learning problems, those of note include ensuring high rates of student success, monitoring progress and providing feedback, and providing positive and supportive learning environments. Table 5.6 highlights some of the variables that Kameenui, Darch, and Colvin (1995) and Rieth and Evertson (1988) consider to be the most important in teaching difficult-to-teach students.

Provide Feedback The importance of feedback to success is well documented; however, the type of feedback that improves a student's social, emotional, and behavioral development needs examination. First, positive feedback or reinforcement

TABLE 5.6
Variables related to effective instruction of difficult-to-teach students

Instructional Variables	Specific Emphasis
Preinstructional Variables	
Arrangement of classroom space	Arrange classroom to facilitate smooth transitions and ease of student monitoring.
Rules and procedures	Communicate expectations and provide structure for learning.
Managing student academic work	Hold students accountable for work and keep records of progress.
Assessment	Use criterion-referenced measures to match tasks to students and monitor performance in terms of instructional objectives.
Communication of learning goals	Communicate rationales for academic tasks and clearly state learning goals.
Pacing decisions	Maintain a lively instructional pace but allow enough time for much practice. Presentation-demonstration-practice-feedback cycles appear to be most effective.
Time allocations	Plan as much time as possible for academic learning.
Instructional Delivery Variables	
Engagement time	Maintain substantive interactions with students and provide feedback. Reinforce students for being on task and for work completed.
Success rate	Maintain high rates of success because success is related to student achievement and motivation.
Academic learning time	Facilitate the amount of time students are engaged in high rates of success or appropriate goals.
Monitoring	Circulate throughout the room to check students' accuracy and progress.
Postinstructional Variables	
Testing	Regularly administer informal criterion-referenced measures (e.g., curriculum-based assessment) to assess student progress or plan instruction.
Academic feedback	Provide immediate feedback on academic work to promote learning. Praise and corrective feedback are most effective when used together.

Source: From *Students with Learning Disabilities* (p. 650), 5th ed., by C. D. Mercer, 1997, Upper Saddle River, NJ: Merrill/Prentice Hall. Copyright 1997 by Prentice-Hall Publishing Company. Reprinted by permission.

should be contingent on student performance (i.e., students should be praised for accomplishing tasks that require a reasonable amount of effort). Second, noncontingent feedback or praise can signal to students that the teacher thinks they cannot do better work; thus, students receive the message that they lack ability, which lowers their opinion of their learning capabilities. Third, students often view criticism or corrective feedback as positive when high achievers receive it (Weinstein, 1982). This feedback indicates that the teacher believes the students can do better; thus, it communicates a positive opinion about the teacher's view of a student's potential. Consequently, Bryan (1986) re-

ports that corrective feedback can help improve the self-concepts of students with learning problems. Furthermore, corrective feedback may communicate that the teacher cares about a student.

Focus on Promoting Proactivity

Many students with learning problems live a reactive existence and maintain an external locus of control. Essentially, they believe that they have little control over what happens to them. Thus, fate, bad luck, and good luck are guiding forces in their lives. This reactive existence causes individuals to believe that the conditions in their lives are out of their control, which is a terrible way to live. These students need to learn that they can control many of the events or consequences in their lives. Proactivity is based on the following belief: I can control events in my life through my own efforts (e.g., I study and I get good grades; I behave appropriately and people treat me well). A proactive or internal locus of control is much more empowering than a reactive existence. The following three techniques promote proactivity: (1) set goals, (2) give responsibility, and (3) engage in self-appreciation.

Set Goals When a student reaches goals that require considerable effort, self-worth is improved. Individuals feel good about themselves when they work hard to achieve a worthwhile goal. Goal ambitiousness is related positively to school success. In contrast, goals that are too easy often lead students to believe that the teacher thinks they are not capable of higher level achievements. Consequently, these low teacher expectations frequently lower students' beliefs about their learning potential. The teacher must stress that the students' own efforts were essential in reaching a goal. The teacher should constantly pair effort with positive or negative consequences.

Give Responsibility Students with poor affective attributes often are pleased when the teacher thinks they can accept responsibility. Giving students responsibility demonstrates a level of trust in their ability to act maturely. Some responsibilities include caring for a class pet, taking messages to the office or other classes, conducting a lunch count, tutoring other students, leading the line, making a bulletin board, using equipment, and grading papers.

Engage in Self-Appreciation Self-depreciation tends to lower a student's self-worth. Conversely, self-appreciation or positive self-talk can help improve self-worth. The teacher should reinforce students for making appropriate positive comments about themselves. Students can make lists of their positive attributes and periodically refer to them.

Promote Cooperation

To develop positive social, emotional, and behavioral attributes, students should work in a community of cooperative learners. The following three techniques promote cooperation: (1) promote positive interactions among students, (2) use peer tutoring, and (3) use cooperative learning.

Promote Positive Interactions Among Students Sprick (1981) notes that teaching students to be positive with one another benefits individual students. If the students can learn to interact positively, they will receive pleasant and friendly reactions in return. The teacher can pair students with learning problems with popular students for social group activities or on teams in instructional games so that the paired students share positive and pleasant experiences. Sprick recommends three techniques for promoting positive interactions: (1) modeling positive interactions in daily teaching, (2) practicing positive interactions through role playing specific situations, and (3) reinforcing positive interactions as they occur throughout the school day.

Use Peer Tutoring Peer tutoring typically involves pairing a competent student with one who has difficulty in a particular academic area. In addition to improving academic skills, a successful peer tutoring program can enhance self-esteem, encourage appropriate behavior, and foster positive and cooperative relationships among peers. Moreover, peer tutoring can help students with disabilities achieve in inclusive settings. For example, if assessment reveals that a student has no friends or is not accepted by peers, peer tutoring can be a strategy for enhancing positive interactions. Using information from a sociometric device, such as a sociogram, the teacher can pair a student with a preferred tutor. The student thus will be likely to model the appropriate behavior. The teacher should train the student tutor in teaching and reinforcement techniques. Tutoring sessions should have easy-to-use materials and a set routine. Self-correcting materials and instructional games provide excellent materials for peer teaching arrangements. (Chapter 2 presents guidelines for implementing several peer tutoring arrangements.)

Use Cooperative Learning Cooperative learning is an instructional arrangement in which small groups or teams of students work together to achieve team success in a manner that promotes the students' responsibility for their own learning as well as the learning of others. In cooperative learning, team goals are emphasized, and team success is achieved only if each individual learns. Regarding research findings on cooperative learning, Slavin (1991) reports that positive achievement effects are consistent across grades, subject areas, and school settings; effects are equally positive for high, average, and low achievers; and positive effects are reported in affective areas (e.g., self-esteem, intergroup relations, and ability to work cooperatively). (Chapter 2 discusses cooperative learning.)

Teach Self-Management

Many youngsters with learning difficulties cannot solve problems and make decisions effectively, which affects their performance adversely at school, home, or work. Issues related to problem solving, interpersonal relations, and generalization learning can be viewed within the context of self-management skills (Shapiro, 1989). Self-management typically is divided into three components: self-monitoring, self-evaluation, and self-reinforcement. Each component requires specific instruction.

Several researchers report success using self-management training with students who have mild disabilities (Hughes, Ruhl, & Peterson, 1988; Sander, 1991; Shapiro, 1989). Shapiro concludes that self-management instruction appears to be a promising approach for teaching students with learning problems to be more independent learners and citizens. (Chapter 4 includes guidelines for teaching self-management.)

Model Target Behaviors and Attributes

The saying "Don't do what I do, do what I say" is not appropriate for helping youngsters with learning problems develop social, emotional, and behavioral attributes. These youngsters need models to imitate and emulate regarding social skills (e.g., listening, giving encouragement, and saying "no"), emotional states (e.g., being positive and proactive), and appropriate behavior (e.g., being considerate of others and respecting property). Cognitive behavior modification is a procedure that frequently involves modeling to help youngsters internalize appropriate thinking processes related to affective behavior.

Teach Cognitive Behavior Modification

Cognitive behavior modification analyzes the thinking processes involved in performing a task. Meichenbaum (1977) discusses self-instructional training as a method to encourage appropriate responses and discourage inappropriate responses. The following sequence can be used:

1. Instruction by another person (e.g., an adult model such as the teacher performs a task while talking aloud)
2. Overt self-instruction (e.g., while performing a task, the student speaks or whispers self-instructions)
3. Covert self-instruction (e.g., the student guides performance through private speech)

Thus, inner speech is considered to be an aspect of the thinking process, and the student is encouraged to verbalize before acting. Language is thought to enhance thinking and, in turn, affect behavior. In the classroom the student can be taught to use the following self-verbalizations: questions about the task ("What does the teacher want me to do?"), answers to the question ("I'm not supposed to talk out in class"), self-instruction to guide the student through the task ("First I raise my hand and wait for the teacher to call on me"), and self-reinforcement ("I really did well that time!").

In cognitive modeling, the teacher not only should model strategies for performing a task but also should model actions and language appropriate for dealing with frustrations and failures. In addition to self-instruction, the student can be taught to use images (e.g., thinking of sitting in the classroom during recess as an image to reduce out-of-seat behavior).

Set Up Models in the Classroom   In modeling, students learn appropriate behaviors by observing and imitating others. When students observe one of their peers being rewarded for desirable behavior, they tend to follow the example of the model. Thus, they learn behaviors that have positive consequences. Likewise, unacceptable behavior can be discouraged when students watch others receive punishment for such behavior. In addition, the teacher can call attention to behavior that should be modeled: "I like the way Jimmy raised his hand instead of talking out, so I will answer his question first."

In using modeling to influence a specific behavior, the following steps are helpful: (1) select the behavior, (2) select the model, (3) give the model and the observer directions concerning their roles, (4) reinforce the model for exhibiting the behavior, and (5) reinforce the observer for imitating the behavior. The modeling process can have three effects on students: (1) new behaviors may be learned from the model, (2) previously acquired behaviors may be strengthened as the students observe similar desirable behaviors of the model being reinforced, or (3) previously acquired behaviors may be weakened as the students observe the model receiving punishment for similar unacceptable behaviors.

Focus on Motivation Through Behavior Modification

Given their failures and difficulties in acquiring information, many students with learning problems understandably lack motivation to work in school. Whereas many normally achieving students are motivated to achieve for intrinsic reasons (e.g., mastery, task completion, and enjoyment of learning new information), students with learning problems often need extrinsic reinforcers to help motivate them to work and behave. Some students with learning problems even require punishment or negative consequences to help them reduce off-task and disruptive behavior. Although some students need external reinforcers and negative consequences to work and behave, the goal of effective teachers is to help these youngsters become mature or intrinsically motivated learners. This section covers some of the behavior modification techniques that can be used to help motivate and manage students with learning problems.

The basic premise of behavior modification is that behavior is learned and is a function of that behavior's consequences. According to Wallace and Kauffman (1986), "Behavior modification refers to any systematic arrangement of environmental events to produce specific changes in observable behavior" (p. 21). Thus, it is a highly structured and systematic approach that results in strengthening, weakening, or maintaining behaviors.

After identifying and collecting baseline data on a target behavior, the teacher must observe events that happen just before the student's behavior (antecedent events) and just after the behavior (subsequent events). These events are then manipulated, and various reinforcers or rewards are used to elicit a change in the behavior. A *reinforcer* is any event that follows a behavior and results in maintaining or increasing the probability or rate of the behavior. *Positive reinforcement* means adding something pleasurable or positive to the environment (i.e., consequences that increase the probability that the behavior will occur again), whereas *negative reinforcement* means withdrawing something unpleasant or negative from the environment (i.e., avoidance of a negative consequence by performing a behavior). Reinforcement results in strengthening or increasing the target behavior.

Various social or tangible reinforcers can be used (e.g., praise, hugs, treats, and free time). The following hierarchical order of the level of reinforcers moves from extrinsic reinforcers (reinforcement from outside the performance of a task) to intrinsic reinforcers (reinforcement directly from performing a task):

Extrinsic reinforcers

1. Primary reinforcers (e.g., sleeping, eating, and drinking—necessary for survival)
2. Tangible reinforcers (e.g., food items, pencils, and certificates)
3. Token reinforcers or points with backup items or activities (e.g., chips that can be exchanged for a preferred item or activity when a certain amount is earned)
4. Social approval (e.g., gestures, touch, and verbal expressions)
5. Project or activity (e.g., running errands, being a line leader, getting free time, and playing a game)

Intrinsic reinforcers

6. Task completion
7. Feedback or result
8. Acquisition of knowledge or skill
9. Sense of mastery or accomplishment

Extrinsic reinforcers initially can be used to encourage a student to exhibit appropriate behavior or perform a task. The teacher gradually should withdraw material reinforcers and stress activities and events. As competence in a task increases, the need for extrinsic reinforcement will eventually decrease and intrinsic reinforcers will provide motivation.

Praise is a social reinforcer and is one of the most effective and convenient positive reinforcers teachers can use to manage student behavior. Paine, Radicchi, Rosellini, Deutchman, and Darch (1983) report that effective praise has several important features:

- Good praise adheres to the "if—then" rule, which states that *if* the student is behaving in the desired manner, *then* (and *only* then) the teacher praises the student.
- Good praise frequently includes students' names.
- Good praise is descriptive.
- Good praise conveys that the teacher really means what is said (i.e., it is convincing).
- Good praise is varied.
- Good praise does not disrupt the flow of individual or class activities.

In using reinforcement techniques, the teacher must remember that reinforcement immediately following the behavior is most effective. In addition, attention can act as a reinforcer for inappropriate behavior. For example, when the teacher frowns or speaks sharply, the student may interpret this as reinforcing attention. Thus, the teacher should be careful not to reinforce inappropriate behavior with attention. The teacher should shift from reinforcing everyday appropriate behavior to reinforcing academic effort as soon as possible. Behaviors such as raising a hand to talk or appropriate lining up for lunch eventually should become routine and be maintained without a great deal of teacher praise. Contingent reinforcement of academic learning promotes a higher level of functioning and improves achievement.

The *schedule of reinforcement* (i.e., the plan of conditions under which reinforcement occurs) can be either continuous or intermittent. On a *continuous schedule,* the desired behavior is reinforced every time it occurs. On an *intermittent schedule,* reinforcement is given according to either an *interval* (reinforcers given at certain times) or a *ratio* (reinforcers given after a specific number of responses).

Shaping refers to reinforcing steps toward the target behavior. The goal is broken down into an ordered sequence of steps or tasks, and reinforcement is given to those behaviors that come close to the desired behavior. The desired behavior thus is shaped by gradually increasing the requirement for reinforcement until the target behavior is obtained.

Punishment, as opposed to reinforcement, refers to presenting something negative or withdrawing something positive following the behavior. This results in decreasing the undesirable response. Kameenui et al. (1995) maintain that punishment is an important part of management, but only as a transition tool. Thus, punishment is a temporary transitional intervention that enables the teacher to deal with nonproductive behavior until the student or students return to productive behavior. Various punishment strategies are associated with different degrees of "hassle" for the teacher or class. Punishment used alone is ineffective with many students, and punishment techniques that are powerful enough to rely on as a primary management strategy are not available to teachers. Moreover, punishment can have negative side effects (e.g., low morale, revenge, and negative feelings), and the more punishment is used in the classroom the less effective it becomes (Sprick, 1981). Thus, punishment should be used as infrequently as possible, and strategies that produce the least disruption should be selected. Some mild punishment techniques include ignoring, gentle verbal reprimands, quiet time, owing time, and nonexclusionary time out. Once punishment is selected, Sprick (1981) recommends the following guidelines:

- Punishment must change the behavior in the desired direction.
- Punishment always should be used in conjunction with a reinforcement plan.
- Punishment always should be administered calmly.
- Punishment should be used discriminately.
- Once a punishable behavior is targeted, it should be punished consistently.

Paine et al. (1983) provide a step-by-step management system that combines positive reinforcement, a warning technique, and response cost (i.e., loss of a reinforcer contingent on inappropriate behavior). It includes the following steps:

1. When a student misbehaves, praise nearby students who exhibit correct behavior. Once praise is given to several students, wait a brief time (30 seconds) to see whether the misbehaving student responds. If the student responds by giving the correct behavior, praise that student.

2. If the student fails to respond positively, talk to her or him in an unemotional manner. Indicate that the student is receiving a warning and instruct her or him to begin work. The warning is more effective when it is delivered near the student and eye contact is established. The teacher should avoid getting into a conversation while giving the warning. After a short time, praise the student if she or he begins correct behavior.

3. If the student does not respond to the warning, calmly remind her or him about the warning, and then write her or his name on the chalkboard and put a mark next to it.

4. If the student fails to comply, place another mark by her or his name. This should be done without comment. Moreover, continue to praise other students for appropriate behavior.

5. At this point, if the student fails to comply, repeat step 4.

6. Use predetermined consequences for unacceptable behaviors. Unacceptable behaviors and resulting consequences should be explained at the beginning of the school year.

7. Have each mark after a student's name represent a loss of privileges. One mark could stand for 5 minutes taken from recess, two marks means 10 minutes are lost, and so on. The consequence can be similar for everyone or varied for different students. The marking system is only effective if students lose privileges that they value.

8. Finally, be sure not to give the student extra attention when she or he misses time from recess or stays after school. Consequences of the marking system should not be reinforcing in any way.

Because punishment is a transition strategy, it is best to examine and use it within the context of a management plan that focuses on stabilizing and maintaining a productive learning environment. Variables such as academic success, good teaching, motivation, and prevention of nonproductive behavior must be considered to manage a classroom effectively.

Apply Consequences with Adolescents   In managing secondary students, Kerr and Nelson (1998) report that structure and consistency are essential. The likelihood of power struggles and defiance of authority is greater with adolescents. Thus, both teacher and student must function in a structured environment in which expectations (rules), consequences, and routines have been established clearly. Effective techniques with secondary students include token economies, contingency contracting, verbal feedback, mutual goal setting, and self-control training. Moreover, the importance of involving adolescents in curriculum and management decisions is stressed throughout the literature.

Suggestions for managing consequences with adolescents include the following:

- Stress the natural consequences of behavior. For example, the natural consequence for stealing is arrest, for being tardy is detention, and so on. Thus, if a rule is broken, the stated consequence is applied. This helps reduce power struggles between the student and teacher because the student is likely to view the teacher as a person who follows rules rather than as an authority figure who maliciously applies punishment (Kerr & Nelson, 1998).

- Use conditioned reinforcers (such as points) with adolescents. They are administered easily or withheld with a minimum of teacher verbalization (Kerr & Nelson, 1998).

- Consider using peer interactions as reinforcers for adolescents.

- Develop a continuum of consequences for managing inappropriate behaviors. Public reprimands should be avoided because they increase the probability of further conflict. Use little verbal interaction and eye contact when administering a negative consequence. Response cost is a good beginning step in dealing with inappropriate behavior. Time out is another effective consequence with adolescents.

Activities for Increasing On-Task Behavior

Some social, emotional, and behavioral problems result in lowered academic performance. A student with low frustration tolerance may become overwhelmed easily when attempting to complete academic tasks requiring great effort. The problem behaviors of task avoidance and task interference also hamper the completion of academic work. The student who seldom completes timed assignments within his or her capabilities may have a problem with slowness. The following activities are suggested for increasing on-task behavior:

- Allow the student who avoids academic tasks to choose from a variety of activities within a skill area. This will allow the student to think he or she selected the work rather than having it determined by the teacher. Also, consider letting the student complete academic tasks in various ways, such as using a red pen or working in a different area of the classroom. A variety of stimuli (e.g., tape recorder, computer, and manipulative materials) can be used to maintain the student's attention to the task.

- Shortly after assigning an academic task, provide a reward for students who have started the work and completed several problems. This will encourage the student who avoids tasks to become more involved. Rewards also can be given upon task completion to encourage the student to work steadily to finish an assignment.

- To increase speed in performing academic tasks, have the student work against a timer and chart progress. For example, the number of addition problems completed correctly during a specific time can be recorded on a graph each day. As progress is made in the student's rate of work, the difficulty of the tasks can be increased.

- To discourage slowness in work, devise a contingency contract. The student and teacher can agree that if a specific part of an academic task is completed within a certain amount of time, the student will not have to complete the remainder of the assignment. The contract also should specify an accuracy criterion (such as 85 percent or more correct responses) to discourage the student from rushing incorrectly through the task. Thus, accurate work performed in a reasonable amount of time is rewarded.

- When a student shows a task interference behavior, such as looking out the window, move physically closer so that the student is aware of your presence. Also, pair the student with a productive worker and use modeling to elicit appropriate behavior.

- Prepare a series of tasks at different levels of difficulty. Allow the student with low frustration tolerance to complete the first task at his or her own pace. Gradually introduce time limits. Record the student's progress and reward steps of progress. After the student has mastered the first task at various time intervals, repeat the procedure with a more difficult task.

- Provide the student who avoids tasks with an incentive to start working: Give the student a worksheet with the first few problems already completed.

- Present academic tasks in game formats, such as start-to-finish races or card playing.

- Use self-correcting materials, which provide immediate feedback and reduce the practicing of errors. The student may avoid academic tasks to avoid failure; however, with self-correcting materials, failure is not publicly known, and the student can immediately correct responses.

- Use a spinner to provide reinforcement after the student completes an academic assignment. The spinner can be divided into several different-size pie-shaped sections, with the more preferred reinforcers on the smaller wedges and the less costly reinforcers on the larger areas. The student spins the spinner and receives the reinforcer listed on the selected spinner section. This adds reinforcement variety as well as an element of unpredictability, and thus serves as a "mystery motivator."

- Use assistance cards to help manage requests for assistance (Paine et al., 1983). Fold a 9″ × 12″ piece of construction paper into a triangular shape with two 4″ sides and a 2″ base. Tape the triangle together and write "Please Keep Working" on one side and "Please Help Me" on the other side. When help is needed, the student places the side stating "Please Help Me" toward the front of the room, thus leaving the side stating "Please Keep Working" facing the student. Provide each student with a work folder that occupies the student until the teacher is available to help. Frustration is reduced and success is increased if the work folder includes self-correcting material. The work folder should include tasks relating to the student's instructional needs (e.g., practice in a specific skill). The assistance card enables the student to request help without raising a hand or disrupting engaged academic time. The supplementary work folder enables the student to continue to work productively on another academic task in which immediate teacher assistance is not required. Also, the assistance card reminds the student to keep working.

• Use feedback charts for managing student behavior. Paine et al. (1983) note that feedback charts give the student a visible display of progress and also generate valuable data to help make educational decisions. The chart is displayed where all students can see it and is divided into four areas. For example:

Begins assigned activities promptly	Follows directions
Completes work or works entire time	Receives less than two warnings

Each student receives a blank card divided into four squares. Throughout the day, the teacher marks each square with plus marks (+) when the student performs the desired behavior. At the end of a specified time period, the student may be allowed to trade the marks for free time, playing a game, and so on. The teacher may use separate cards for different academic periods. Also, a group chart can be made and laminated so that it can be used repeatedly.

	Math		Reading		Language	
Alan	+		+		+	
			+			
Elise	+	+	+			+
	+		+			
Clayton		+	+		+	+
		+	+		+	+

• Have the student who does not complete homework earn the privilege of being allowed to do homework at home (Lieberman, 1983). Place the student on a five-day probation during which the student must stay after school and complete homework assignments within an agreed-upon time period. Then have the student alternate doing homework at home and at school every other day for five days. Finally, the student can be allowed to do all homework at home. However, if any assignments are not completed at home, the student is placed on probation for another five days. Thus, for the student the positive consequence is earning the privilege to do homework at home, as opposed to the negative consequence of staying after school for not completing homework.

☀ SOCIAL DEVELOPMENT INTERVENTIONS

Among affective domains, social competence has received extensive attention in the educational literature. Social competence is a global construct that involves the interaction of personality development variables and social interaction factors (Bender, 1995). A socially competent individual can perceive situations in which social skills can be used, can discriminate which social skill is appropriate for a given situation, and can perform the appropriate social skill in such a way that there is a high likelihood of positive consequences. Given the low social competence of many individuals with learning problems and the extensive social demands of adult living, it is apparent why social competence receives so much attention. Social skills, a component of social competence, are discrete behaviors that are learned and performed in interactive situations, and they have been the focus of many intervention studies involving students with learning problems.

Social Skills Training

Several procedures have been used to improve the social skills performance of students with learning problems (Hazel & Schumaker, 1988; Schumaker & Hazel, 1984). One technique involves the manipulation of antecedent and consequent events associated with the target social behavior. For example, environmental events can be changed in an effort to increase the probability of future occurrence of appropriate social behaviors while decreasing the probability of occurrence of inappropriate behaviors. Approaches of this technique include the use of cooperative goal structures, the delivery or the withholding of particular consequences contingent upon the occurrence of social responses, the application of group contingencies, and the use of home-based contingency management systems. Another technique that has been used to reduce the rate of inappropriate social behaviors is cognitive training aimed at teaching self-control of personal behaviors (e.g., self-recording and self-evaluation of behaviors).

Interpersonal social skills also can be increased through direct instruction. Schumaker and Hazel (1984) discuss four types of instructional interventions that have been used to facilitate the acquisition of social skills:

1. *Description* involves primarily oral techniques in which the teacher describes how to perform a skill appropriately.
2. *Modeling* involves demonstrations of the social skill either by live models or by film, audiotape, or pictorial models.
3. *Rehearsal* involves verbal repetition of required skill steps to ensure that the students have memorized the steps in sequence and can instruct themselves in what to do next, and structured practice (e.g., role-play activities) whereby the learner attempts to perform the skill.
4. *Feedback* involves verbal reinforcement following rehearsal to inform the students what steps they performed well and what behaviors need improvement.

Frequently, combinations of these procedures are included in social skills training interventions.

A social skills curriculum also can be used. Cartledge, Frew, and Zaharias (1985) and Maag (1989) note that a basic principle of social skills instruction is that behaviors chosen for instruction should be those valued by persons important in the learner's environment. In an analysis of social behaviors selected for individualized educational programs, Pray, Hall, and Markley (1992) found that academically related social skills (e.g., task-related skills such as following directions or being on task) were much more prominent than interpersonal skills (e.g., making conversation or accepting authority). In a similar vein, Mellard and Hazel (1992) maintain that nonacademic characteristics may have more effect than academics on the employment of an individual with learning problems. Thus, Pray et al. and Mellard and Hazel recommend more emphasis on interpersonal skills for these students. To foster peer interaction, attention should be given to areas such as informal conversation and play skills. The following social skills curriculum consists of four main areas:

1. *Conversation skills* include using body language, greeting others, introducing oneself, applying active listening, answering questions, interrupting correctly, asking questions, saying good-bye, and conversing.

2. *Friendship skills* include making friends, saying thank-you, giving compliments, accepting thanks, accepting compliments, joining group activities, starting activities with others, and giving help.
3. *Skills for difficult situations* include giving criticism, accepting being told "no," accepting criticism, following instructions, responding to teasing, resisting peer pressure, and apologizing.
4. *Problem-solving skills* include negotiating, giving rationales, persuading, problem solving, getting help, and asking for feedback.

Sugai and Fuller (1991) provide an excellent decision model for examining a social skills curriculum. Their model addresses background, assessment, and instruction and features insightful questions to ask in each area.

Bender and Wall (1994) note that the research indicates that social skills training has successfully helped students with learning problems; however, most of this research has focused on short-term outcomes. Research is needed to demonstrate that social skills training generalizes to the daily settings of employment, significant-other relationships, and recreation (Bender & Wall, 1994; Mellard & Hazel, 1992). In a meta-analysis of 53 studies on social skills training, Forness and Kavale (1996) found that the average amount of social skills training tended to be 30 hours or less (i.e., fewer than three hours per week for less than ten weeks) and had relatively modest effect. They suggest that longer interventions may be needed to improve long-standing social problems and result in generalization and long-term effects.

☀ SOCIAL DEVELOPMENT ACTIVITIES

The socially immature student lacks the ability to get along with peers and lacks other social skills common to his or her age group. The student may engage in antisocial behavior, failing to recognize his or her responsibilities and the rights of others. Social withdrawal may result from lack of academic success. The following activities are presented to help students who are socially immature.

• Pair a withdrawn student with a competent, socially mature peer for various activities. They must cooperate in completing an academic task together or being a team during a game. Thus, in these situations, success or failure is shared by both students.

• If one student frequently teases another, ask the teased student to ignore the one doing the teasing and reward him or her each time no response is made to the teasing. Thus, the student who is teasing receives attention neither from the teacher nor the peer for the inappropriate behavior. Also, self-recording can be used to reduce teasing. Give the student a slip of paper with lines for name and date, and spaces in which the student is to mark each time he or she teases. The marking should be monitored. Self-recording inappropriate behavior may help the student decrease teasing.

• Use the socially withdrawn or rejected student in peer teaching situations as either the tutor or tutee. A sociogram can indicate an appropriate match. Peer tutoring encourages appropriate peer contacts in a secure and structured activity.

• Use modeling techniques to teach various social skills. Praise the model for appropriate social behavior in the presence of the socially immature student.

• Encourage the withdrawn student to use a tape recorder when he or she feels like talking. Tell the student that if he or she would like to share feelings, the teacher will be glad to listen. The teacher can respond on tape if the student prefers. This is a first step in encouraging a withdrawn student to talk and discuss feelings.

• Use role playing to present a variety of possible social situations. Discuss several different mature reactions to specific problems. Thus, the student is presented with a choice of solutions to use when coping with similar social occurrences.

• When a student frequently is aggressive toward a peer, ignore the aggressive student and pay attention to the victim. Reinforce cooperative and peaceful behavior in the presence of the aggressive student and reward the student for appropriate behavior.

• Encourage the student to develop a vocabulary that expresses feelings. Glue pockets on a large piece of tagboard, and on each pocket illustrate a face showing a different expression (e.g., smiling, frowning, and serious). Write words expressing feelings (*sad, cheerful, troubled, anxious, pleased, miserable,* and *nervous*) on index cards. Instruct the student to match each word to a picture expressing that emotion. The correct face can be drawn on the back of each card so that the student can check the response. Another activity with feeling words is to provide a list of words and ask the student to write each word in a way that shows the emotion:

Afraid

Shy

Excited

Jumpy

Secondary students can increase their vocabulary to include feeling words that can be divided into the categories of *unpleasant* and *pleasant*:

Unpleasant	Pleasant
Ambivalent	Accomplished
Betrayed	Confident
Condemned	Ecstatic
Distraught	Fascinated
Dubious	Gratified
Exasperated	Infatuated

• Have each student express his or her mood or feeling at different happenings. Write events on index cards (e.g., "It's time to go to school," "I don't know what to do," "I don't have any money," "My teacher smiles at me," and "It's my birthday"). Use a piece of tagboard with pockets labeled with various moods. Each student selects a card, reads it aloud, tells how the described event makes him or her feel and why, and places the card in the pocket that corresponds to the feeling. Also, take pictures of students showing various emotions during classroom situations. These photographs can be displayed with captions telling the emotion shown and the situation in which it occurred: "Kevin is very proud. He is wearing his badge for captain of the safety patrol." By observing the pictures, students may become more sensitive to facial expressions.

• Conduct class meetings during which the students discuss any question that seems relevant to them at the time. This opportunity for personal involvement is especially appropriate for secondary students. The teacher should keep the discussion moving and see that everyone is given an opportunity to participate as much as possible.

INSTRUCTIONAL GAMES IN SOCIAL DEVELOPMENT

Many activities can be presented in a game format to stimulate interest and involvement. Games also promote positive peer relations and enable the teacher to work on specific social behaviors (e.g., cooperating, taking turns, or expressing feelings). The following games are designed to promote appropriate social behaviors.

Best and Worst Game

Materials: Paper and pencil.

Directions: The teacher describes a social situation and instructs each student to write down what would be the *best* and the *worst* thing to do in response to that event. Each student reads his or her response, and the choices presented are discussed. The student with the best response (decided by the presenter of the problem) gets to describe the next social incident and lead the discussion.

Socialization Game

Materials: Start-to-finish board; dice; set of cards containing personal questions; markers.

Directions: A game board is used to improve social skills by giving the players an opportunity to talk freely about feelings, relationships, or activities. Each player rolls the dice and moves that number of spaces on the board. The player then must take a card and respond to the question by explaining the answer to the other players. The first player to reach the finish space wins.

Sample questions: "Do you like to be alone? When?" "If you could be anyone in the world, who would you be? Why?" "What happened on the happiest day of your life?" "What would you do if you didn't go to school?"

Decision Game

Materials: Five parallel lines marked on the floor with masking tape.

Directions: The teacher explains to students that the five lines represent (from right to left) *absolutely right, somewhat right, undecided or neutral, somewhat wrong,* and *absolutely wrong.* The teacher tells a story or describes a situation and then asks students to move to the line that indicates their decision about the story or situation. Each student should explain why he or she moved to a particular line.

Sample story or situation: John saw William take two quarters from the teacher's desk and put them in his pocket. He told William to return the money but William refused to do so. John then went to the teacher and told her William had taken the money. Was the decision to tell the teacher right or wrong?

☀ COMMERCIAL SOCIAL DEVELOPMENT PROGRAMS

Various commercial programs are designed to help students get along with others. The following programs can be used to promote the social development of students with learning problems.

Getting Along with Others

Getting Along with Others: Teaching Social Effectiveness to Children (Jackson, Jackson, & Monroe, 1983) presents a direct intervention approach with systematic instructional methods. A tell–show–practice model of social skills training is used in which the students participate in role-playing activities and learn adaptive coping responses. A notebook of skill lessons and activities presents 17 core social skills (e.g., following directions, giving and receiving positive feedback, and saying "no" to stay out of trouble). The program guide provides teacher scripts and offers 32 training activities and 5 main teaching strategies as well as 9 additional techniques to enhance the learning potential in any interaction. It also includes a built-in behavior management system for reducing or eliminating problem behaviors.

Skillstreaming the Elementary School Child; Skillstreaming the Adolescent

These two manuals provide a program for teaching prosocial skills based on a structured learning method that involves modeling (demonstrating the behavioral steps that make up specific skills), student role playing (reviewing, rehearsing, and performing each of the skill steps), performance feedback (evaluating the role-play), and transfer training (developing assignments for using the skills in real-life situations). In *Skillstreaming the Elementary School Child* (McGinnis & Goldstein, 1997), 60 specific prosocial skills (such as asking for help, dealing with group pressure, and accepting consequences) are presented within the content areas of dealing with feelings, classroom survival skills, alternatives to aggression, friendship-making skills, and dealing with stress. *Skillstreaming the Adolescent* (Goldstein & McGinnis, 1997) presents 50 prosocial skills (such as starting a conversation, setting a goal, and standing up for a friend) within the content areas of beginning and advanced social skills, dealing with feelings, alternatives to aggression, dealing with stress, and planning skills. A video program is available illustrating the concepts and training procedures contained in the books.

The Walker Social Skills Curriculum

The ACCEPTS Program (Walker et al., 1983) is a social skills curriculum that teaches classroom and peer-to-peer social skills to students in kindergarten through sixth grade. The 28 classroom competencies and social skills are presented in five areas: (1) classroom skills (e.g., listening to the teacher and following classroom rules), (2) basic interaction skills (e.g., eye contact, listening, and taking turns talking), (3) getting-along skills (e.g., using polite words, sharing, and assisting others),

(4) making-friends skills (e.g., good grooming, smiling, and complimenting), and (5) coping skills (e.g., when expressing anger, when being teased, and when things don't go right). *The ACCESS Program* (Walker, Todis, Holmes, & Horton, 1988) teaches peer-to-peer skills, skills for relating to adults, and self-management skills to students at the middle- and secondary-school levels. The 30 social skills are presented in three areas: (1) relating to peers (e.g., interacting with the opposite sex, being left out, and handling group pressures), (2) relating to adults (e.g., disagreeing with adults, working independently, and developing good study habits), and (3) relating to yourself (e.g., being organized, using self-control, and feeling good about yourself). The curriculum is designed for use by both general and special education teachers and can be taught in one-to-one, small-group, or large-group instructional formats.

☀ EMOTIONAL DEVELOPMENT INTERVENTIONS

The emotional development of individuals with learning problems is being recognized as an area that warrants study and the development of related interventions. This section features selected interventions to promote emotional development and includes bibliotherapy, attribution retraining, life-space interviewing, reality therapy, techniques for improving mood states, and projective techniques.

Bibliotherapy

Bibliotherapy is a teaching technique that uses reading materials to help students better understand themselves and their problems. Characters in the books learn to cope with problems and situations similar to those faced by the students. Through identifying with the character, students release emotional tensions and achieve a better understanding of themselves and their problems. Also, characteristics, attitudes, values, and situations in reading selections can serve as models for the students.

Hoagland (1972) notes that for bibliotherapy to be effective, students must move through three phases during or immediately after reading a book: (1) *identification*—the students must become personally involved and must identify themselves or see a situation similar to some of their own situations, (2) *catharsis*—the students must release emotional tensions regarding the problems, and (3) *insight*—through empathizing with the character

or plot, students must reach a better understanding that tempers their emotional drives.

Cianciolo (1965) suggests the following steps for discussing a book with a student:

1. Retell the story and emphasize incidents, feelings, relationships, and behavior.
2. Discuss changes of feelings, relationships, and behaviors.
3. Identify similar events from the student's life or other reading selections.
4. Explore the consequences that occurred.
5. Generalize about the consequences or helpfulness of alternative behaviors.

The student should begin to realize that many other people have experienced the same problem and that there is more than one way to solve a problem.

Books chosen for a bibliotherapeutic program should focus on a particular need and should be written on the student's level. The selections also should depict realistic approaches and have lifelike characters. Suitable books can be selected from various bibliographies that are cross-indexed by theme and age level. Russell and Russell (1979) provide various activities to be used in conjunction with bibliotherapy. Although research on bibliotherapy is minimal, Lenkowsky and Lenkowsky (1978) note that the approach seems to help some students with learning problems by providing them with reading materials relevant to their own social and emotional needs.

Attribution Retraining

Attributions refer to a person's beliefs concerning the causes of events. Students have different ideas about why they succeed and fail. Those who believe in an internal locus of control explain the outcomes of their actions on the basis of their abilities or efforts. In contrast, persons with an external locus of control believe that factors outside their control, such as luck or task difficulty, determine their fates.

Students with learning disabilities are more likely than normally achieving students to believe that their successes are a function of external factors (Chapman & Boersma, 1979; Pearl, Bryan, & Donahue, 1980). Bryan (1986) notes that it would seem advantageous to induce such students to have more positive and self-serving expectations of their academic successes. As students with learning problems experience many academic failures, they are likely to lack confidence in their intellectual abilities and doubt that anything they do will help them overcome their difficulties. Thus, they may lessen their achievement efforts, especially when presented with difficult material. In other words, repeated failure can lead students to believe that they are not capable of overcoming their difficulties, and students' beliefs about their abilities can affect their achievement efforts and accomplishments.

Attribution retraining studies (Schunk, 1981; Shelton, Anastopoulos, & Linden, 1985) have found that teaching students to attribute their failures to insufficient effort can result in increased persistence and improved performance when confronted with difficulty. In these studies, students are engaged in academic tasks and are given feedback emphasizing the importance of their effort. In a review of attribution retraining research, Bryan (1986) reports that attribution retraining sessions have been shown to be somewhat successful in changing attributions and persistence behavior. Fowler and Peterson (1981) found that prompting and reinforcing students for verbalizing the appropriate effort attributions can be more effective than simply telling students when they fail that they need to try harder. In addition to stressing effort as a determinant of a student's difficulties, it also can help to teach students to attribute their failures to ineffective task strategies (Licht, 1984). Bryan notes that teachers should convey to students with learning problems that they are learning new skills and that determined application of the new skills can help them overcome their difficulties.

Ellis, Lenz, and Sabornie (1987) suggest the following instructional sequence in attribution retraining:

1. Teach students to make statements that reflect effort.
2. Teach students to attribute difficulty to ineffective strategies.
3. Arrange for students to have success with newly learned strategies.

Life-Space Interviewing

Life-space interviewing is a verbal strategy for intervention that can be used in the classroom to manage a crisis or an everyday problem. This technique attempts to structure a situation so that the student works out the problem independently. The interview is designed to be free of judgment. The teacher is simply a listener and helper as the student makes decisions about how to handle the problem.

Morse (1971) outlines the steps in life-space interviewing:

1. All students involved in the specific incident are allowed to give their own impressions of the occurrence without interruption.
2. The teacher listens and, without casting judgment, asks questions to determine the accuracy of each student's perception.
3. If the students cannot resolve the problem agreeably, the teacher may have to suggest an acceptable plan to deal with it.
4. The students and the teacher work together to develop a plan for solving similar problems in the future.

The classroom teacher may best use life-space interviewing to provide emotional first aid at times of unusual stress. Thus, the technique is used to reduce students' frustration and anxiety by giving them support during an emotional situation; change behavior and reinforce behavioral and social rules; enhance self-esteem; and assist students to solve their own everyday problems by expanding their understanding and insight into their own and others' behavior and feelings. For example, after a fight on the playground, the teacher can engage in life-space interviewing to allow students to release frustration and anger. The teacher provides support and helps students view all sides of the situation and the rights of others.

Wood and Long (1991) use the term *life-space intervention* to emphasize that a crisis always evokes verbal intervention. They note that the key to success or failure in obtaining a therapeutic outcome of a crisis is the quality of the adult's verbal intervention. The teacher's attitude and behavior as interviewer influence the effectiveness of life-space interviewing. The teacher should be polite to the student and should maintain eye contact. Asking *why* questions should be avoided, and the interviewer should try to reduce any apparent guilt feelings. In addition, the teacher should encourage the student to communicate and ask questions as they work together to develop a plan of action for present or future use. The life-space interview technique is time-consuming and requires sensitivity and emotional control from the teacher. However, it can help students see the consequences of behavior and find ways to deal with a problem.

Reality Therapy

Reality therapy, developed by Glasser (1965), is used to manage behaviors by teaching students to behave responsibly and to face reality. An interview technique similar to life-space interviewing is used in an attempt to help students make sound decisions when confronted with a problem. In reality therapy, all students are assumed to be responsible for their own behavior, and inappropriate behaviors are not excused because of unconscious motivations. During interviews the student receives emotional support, and no judgments are made of the present behavior. The teacher and the student jointly develop a plan to increase the student's responsible behavior, and the student is encouraged to make a commitment to carry out the plan. The student is expected to realize the consequences of irresponsible behavior, and no excuses are accepted. Thus, the morality of behavior is emphasized, and the student is taught socially accepted ways to handle problems.

Glasser (1965) presents a three-step format for applying reality therapy. The first step is to help the student identify the problem. This is accomplished by asking questions such as "What happened?" and "Where are you going?" The second step is to help the student develop value judgment, asking questions such as "Is the behavior helping you?" or "Is the behavior against the rules?" The third step is to involve the student in carrying out a plan to correct the inappropriate behavior (e.g., "What can you do about it?"). An application of reality therapy is featured in the following scenario:

Teacher: Michael, what just happened?
Michael: Nothing.
Teacher: I thought I saw you push Susan.
Michael: Yeah, maybe I did.
Teacher: Tell me about it.

Michael: I was running to get in line and she got in my way.
Teacher: Well, I'm sure you didn't push her on purpose, but is pushing students against the rules?
Michael: Yeah.
Teacher: What do you think should be done?
Michael: I don't know.
Teacher: Why don't you sit over there at the reading table a couple of minutes and think about what you can do to solve the problem.
Michael: Okay.
(5 minutes later)
Teacher : Got an idea?
Michael: Yeah, I think I should line up after the others for the rest of the week.
Teacher: Does that help Susan?
Michael: No.
Teacher: What can you do to help Susan?
Michael: I can tell her I'm sorry and let her line up in front of me tomorrow.
Teacher: Can you do that?
Michael: Yeah.
Teacher: Fine, I think that's an excellent plan.

Techniques for Improving Mood States

In their review of the affective research since 1984 regarding individuals with learning disabilities, Bender and Wall (1994) found no intervention studies for treating depression and suicide, anxiety, temperament, and loneliness. However, Bender (1995) offers some tentative suggestions for dealing with temperament, suicide, and general personality variables.

Temperament   Some students with learning problems have a temperament that predisposes them to be less task persistent or display less social flexibility; thus, educators should strive to develop interventions that lessen the negative effects of their temperament. Because little intervention research exists in this area, the following suggestions should be regarded as tentative:

- Reward on-task behavior, and discuss the positive consequences of completing tasks.
- Teach the student to self-monitor on-task and off-task behavior.
- Include the student in selecting some tasks to do.
- Lessen social inflexibility by helping the student make transitions among activities (e.g., periodically cue the student about a transition prior to its occurrence).
- Reward smooth transitions and discuss their positive outcomes.
- Involve the student in role-play games or situations in which students must take turns.

Suicide   The following suggestions are offered for dealing with suicide concerns:

- Take suicide-related drawings and comments (such as "I hope I die") seriously and keep records of their occurrence.
- Elicit confirmation regarding a student's suicidal signals (e.g., "Do you think about hurting yourself often?").
- Affirm a commitment to life when responding to a student's concerns (e.g., "I see how that can upset you, but isn't it nice that you have your friend to enjoy each day?").
- Have the student stay with someone if his or her thoughts or actions seem serious.
- Seek professional help in dealing with the student.

Personality Variables   The following suggested interventions focus on dealing with personality variables:

- Separate the student's problem from the person and do not criticize the student personally.
- Provide opportunities for the student to be proud (e.g., encourage sharing a special interest or talent when the content or situation is appropriate).
- Constantly point out the relationship between the student's efforts and outcomes, and encourage the student to set goals for learning. These activities may help the student develop an internal locus of control.
- Display the student's work on bulletin boards and arrange situations where outsiders (such a principal or other teachers) are able to encourage or praise the student.

Projective Techniques

The teacher can use various projective techniques to encourage students to project or express their feelings and emotions. Creative activities, such as role playing and puppetry, provide an opportunity for the student to express feelings and reduce frustrations with few constraints.

Role Playing   In role playing, students assume the role of a character and act out a brief episode that involves a problem. The role-playing process includes four steps:

1. A specific problem is identified (i.e., classroom problems or conflicts or other relevant situations).
2. After the problem is described, the roles must be established and assigned to various students. Volunteers should be sought; students should not be forced to play a role.
3. The actual role playing takes place and should be brief. The same situation can be repeated several times with different students to present many solutions to a single problem.
4. A discussion follows, focusing on the role or behavior rather than the student portraying it.

Thus, through role playing the student faces reactions of other people and learns ways to cope with similar situations.

Puppetry   Puppets can help students experience different events and express feelings and emotions. Fairy-tale characters (such as king, witch, giant, and animal) can be used to represent human emotional experiences. Students can make hand puppets and a stage. The puppet theater provides a nonthreatening atmosphere in which students can express their feelings freely as they engage in problem solving. After the puppet show, other solutions to the problems presented can be discussed.

☀ EMOTIONAL DEVELOPMENT ACTIVITIES

Activities for Improving Reactions to Authority Figures

Some students respond inappropriately to school personnel or authority figures. The student may resist coming to school and frequently may challenge the authority of the teacher and principal by arguing constantly and disobeying school rules. This negative reaction needs to be changed to promote a healthy attitude toward school and authority figures. The following activities are suggested for improving students' reactions to authority figures:

- Provide the student with positive reinforcement for attending school. For example, give the student a special treat or plan a rewarding activity each day the student arrives on time. Special privileges, snacks, and activities can be made contingent on regular school attendance.

- Pair the student who is absent frequently with a well-liked peer who has regular attendance. (Use a sociogram to determine a good match for modeling purposes.) With the teacher's guidance, the model can plan to meet the student at school for various activities and thus encourage attendance.

- Allow class members to establish some of their own rules of behavior and consequences for disobeying a rule. Discuss the need and reasons for the rules. When some rules are made by peers, students may be less inclined to challenge the teacher's authority.

- Give the student who repeatedly disobeys rules and instructions several courses of action from which to choose. When possible, avoid conflict and "showdowns" in which the student is forced to obey. Sometimes a peer can explain an assignment or rule to a student who resists adult authority and the student will comply.

- Ignore or walk away from the student whenever he or she argues with you or disobeys instructions. Isolation also can be effective in dealing with the student who argues. Reinforce obedient behavior and positive language through praise and attention.

- Invite various authority figures in the community to speak to the class and share some of their problems and experiences during their school years. Such sharing can make a positive impression on the student who shows a negative attitude.

- Use an "emotion box" in the classroom. Give the class members several forms that ask for name, date, emotion, and reasons. Ask students to complete a form and place it in the emotion box whenever they react strongly to an event in the classroom. Through this method the teacher can gain understanding about each student's reasons for undesirable and negative behaviors.

- To foster a positive attitude toward authority figures, ask the student "planned interest" questions every day (e.g., "What did you do last night?" "Did your team win its ball game?"). Also, remember the student on special days (e.g., birthday). A teacher's genuine interest in individual students encourages a positive feeling toward school attendance and authority figures.

Activities for Enhancing Self-Concept

Self-concept refers to a person's perception of his or her abilities and of how others important to the person feel about him or her. A person with a poor self-concept has feelings of inferiority and inadequacy and may express these feelings (e.g., "I can't do that"; "I'm not very smart"). Such a student may lack self-confidence and be reluctant to interact with others. The student may resist academic work due to fear of failure. The following activities are suggested to enhance self-concept:

- To make the student feel special and important, select the student to be "Student of the Week." Have the student sit in a special chair and wear a badge. Each day ask the student's classmates to write something special about her or him. They may write positive statements about the student's abilities or personal attributes. Also, the classmates can decide on other special activities they can do for the student (e.g., write a story about the student or play the student's favorite game at recess).

- To develop self-awareness, have students collect items that tell something about themselves (e.g., magazine pictures, small objects, and photographs). Encourage each student to make a collage of these items on tagboard. The center of the collage can contain a picture of the student, with the items arranged around the photograph. The students can share with others what the items represent and why they were chosen.

- Write short, personal notes to the student to provide encouragement and to let him or her know you are interested. Also, have brief conversations with the student, and provide extra encouragement when he or she is trying a new task or suffering from a disappointment.

- Use the student as a tutor in peer tutoring situations. This may boost self-esteem, and it also shows that the teacher has confidence in the student's ability to handle the task.

- Make some academic tasks look more difficult than they really are. The student will gain self-confidence when successfully completing a task perceived as very difficult. For example, a simple math worksheet to practice subtraction facts can be replaced by a worksheet that appears to contain very difficult problems but really requires the same basic skills. For example, the problem

$$394876$$
$$- 173472$$

requires the same basic skills as

3	9	4	8	7	6
-1	-7	-3	-4	-7	-2

• Provide success activities and limit failure as much as possible. For example, before requiring participation in oral reading, have the student review difficult words or listen to the story on a tape recorder. Also, using self-correcting materials keeps incorrect responses private and gives the student a chance to correct responses immediately. Provide verbal praise and correct wrong responses without hurting the student's feelings (e.g., "You're almost right," "Let's do it together," and "Nice try").

• Help the student compile a personal scrapbook. Include pictures or drawings of family, friends, and pets. If possible, take photographs in class. The scrapbook can include written accounts of trips, interests, and favorite activities.

• Set realistic goals with the student on selected tasks. Record the student's daily progress toward the goal. When the goal is achieved, point out the progress to make the student feel proud of the accomplishments.

• Emphasize the importance of student effort on academic tasks and teach the student to attribute successes and failures to amount of effort. This may result in increased persistence on difficult material and reduce doubts of intellectual ability.

☀ INSTRUCTIONAL GAMES IN EMOTIONAL DEVELOPMENT

Activities to promote emotional development can be presented in a game format. Because games often stimulate interest and motivation, they frequently engage students with emotional difficulties. The following game promotes emotional development.

Personality Game

Materials: Start-to-finish game board; cards with personality traits written on them; markers.

Directions: The cards are placed face down on the playing board (see Figure 5.3). The first player takes the top card and reads it aloud. If the player thinks the card describes him or her, the player's marker is moved forward five spaces. However, if the player believes the statement on the card does not apply, but the majority of the group thinks it does (or vice versa), the player's marker is moved back three spaces. If neither the player nor the others believes the card applies, the player's marker is not moved. The players may tell why they think a trait is or is not descriptive of their personality. After each turn the card is placed face down in the discard pile. If a blank card is picked, the player must make up a trait. Players may choose the top card from either the original card pile or the discard pile. The purpose of

the game is to help students better understand themselves. The first player to reach the finish space is the winner.

Sample cards: "I am impatient"; "I joke around a lot"; "I am kind to animals"; "I don't ever like school."

☀ COMMERCIAL EMOTIONAL DEVELOPMENT PROGRAMS

Various programs and materials are available to help students deal with emotional problems. The following programs can help students understand themselves better and develop appropriate strategies for dealing with personal problems.

Developing Understanding of Self and Others

The *DUSO* kits (Dinkmeyer & Dinkmeyer, 1982) are designed to encourage the social and emotional growth of students in kindergarten through fourth grade. *DUSO I,* for students in kindergarten through second grade, is used to develop appreciation of individual strengths and acceptance of limitations; beginning of social skills; and awareness of feelings, priorities, and choices. *DUSO II,* for third and fourth graders, helps develop a greater understanding of the purposive nature of behavior; more effective communication skills; a greater understanding of feelings and empathetic behavior; and skill in recognizing and making choices. The central character of both programs is a puppet, Duso the Dolphin. A problem situation and a story are presented, followed by role-playing and puppet activities. The kit provides hand puppets, posters, activity cards, and audiocassettes of stories and songs.

Thinking, Feeling, Behaving

Thinking, Feeling, Behaving, developed by A. Vernon (published by Research Press), is an emotional education curriculum based on the principles of Rational Emotive Therapy. The curriculum consists of one volume for youngsters in first through sixth grade and one volume for adolescents in seventh through twelfth grade. Each volume includes 90 field-tested activities arranged by grade level and organized into the categories of self-acceptance, feelings, beliefs and behavior, problem solving/decision making, and interpersonal relationships. The activities are designed for use in small-group settings and include simulation games, stories, role plays, written activities, brainstorming, and art activities. The curriculum is appropriate as a preventive or remedial program to

FIGURE 5.3
Personality game board

help students learn to use positive health concepts in overcoming irrational beliefs, negative feelings and attitudes, and the negative consequences that may result.

BEHAVIORAL DEVELOPMENT INTERVENTIONS

Discipline problems consistently rank first in order of seriousness in polls of teachers, parents, and students (Whelan, 1996). Nearly 3 million crimes occur on or around school sites each year, and in a 1994 survey, school discipline was listed as parents' top priority, along with teaching reading, math, and writing (United States General Accounting Office, 1995). Whelan maintains that broken social bonds, inordinate amounts of stress and conflict, the observation of violent behavior in relationships, and substance abuse are some of the primary reasons that youngsters face conflicts in school and are disruptive. Although many of the causes of disruptive behavior are beyond the parameters of the educational system, these conditions do not lessen the educator's responsibility to ameliorate discipline problems. Whelan maintains that one of the primary reasons that discipline problems remain a top concern is because many educators fail to use effective and efficient classroom management procedures.

If the techniques featured in this chapter in the sections on interventions (i.e., general techniques for promoting social, emotional, and behavioral development; social development interventions; and emotional development interventions) are applied, disruptive behavior should diminish to the extent that it is not a problem. In essence, when applied within a classroom community that values cooperation, feelings, and property, using the techniques listed in this chapter and in Chapter 4 should diminish or eliminate chronic disruptive behavior. The primary techniques include academic success through good teaching, the use of motivation techniques, the occasional use of mild consequences, social skills instruction, self-regulation instruction, and sensitivity to personality variables. If these techniques are unsuccessful, more intense management techniques should be used. Kameenui et al. (1995) note that three levels of intervention are needed for managing mild to severe behavioral problems. The first level of intervention is for mild behavioral problems, and 80 percent of students respond to routine instructional management at this level. At the second level of intervention, another 15 percent of students present persistent problems and require ongoing attention and a strategic intervention plan. The third level of intervention is for the remaining 5 percent of students who exhibit severe and chronic behavioral problems.

Students can be rewarded for appropriate behavior in creative ways.

A management approach grounded in teaching students appropriate behavior, responsibility, and self-regulation will succeed with almost all students. This section includes reinforcement and punishment perspectives and procedures that help with students requiring strategic management plans and vigilance.

Positive Reinforcement Plan

Knowledge and application of reinforcement principles can help manage a classroom. Many teachers apply these principles in a natural way, without taking the time to write a behavior modification plan specifying the target behavior, consequent events, schedule of reinforcement, and so forth. However, some students' behavior does not change unless a highly systematic behavior modification plan is developed and applied.

Figure 5.4 presents a record of a behavior modification plan to increase staying-in-seat behavior. The teacher used a time-sampling technique to record whether the student stayed seated during seatwork activities. Observation sessions were 30 minutes long, and the teacher used a recording sheet marked off with a row of ten squares. The teacher looked at the student every 3 minutes and recorded a "+" if the student was seated and a "–" if the student was not. As Figure 5.4 shows, the student's percentage of staying-in-seat behavior was low during $baseline_1$. However,

when the teacher began giving the student praise and attention for appropriate in-seat behavior (in sessions 11 through 20), the level of the desired behavior increased greatly. When praise and attention were withdrawn in $baseline_2$ (sessions 21 through 25), the student's staying-in-seat behavior sharply diminished. However, when praise and attention were provided again (in sessions 26 through 35), the level of the appropriate behavior quickly increased. Thus, the teacher was able to note the effects of teacher attention on modifying the student's out-of-seat behavior.

Contingency Contracting

Contracts between a student and the classroom teacher can help to motivate the student toward desirable behavior changes. A *contract* is an agreement—verbal or written—between two parties. The term *contingent* means that there is a relationship between what one does and the consequences. In behavior modification, contingency contracting is based on the Premack Principle (Premack, 1959), which states that the frequency of a less preferred activity increases when it is followed by the opportunity to engage in one that is preferred. For example, if the student would rather play outside than sit quietly in the classroom, the contingency contract might state that sitting quietly for a certain amount of time will be followed by outside play.

FIGURE 5.4

Record of a behavior modification plan to increase staying-in-seat behavior

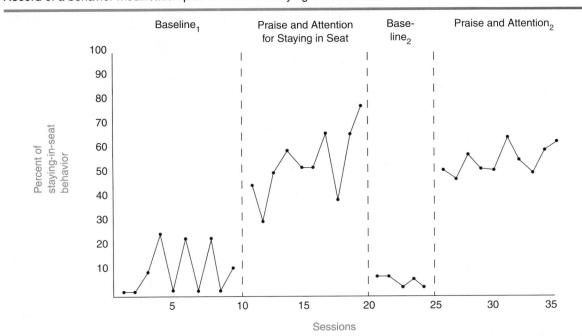

The following steps are involved in writing a contingency contract:

1. The teacher outlines the specific behavior required of the student.

2. The teacher identifies the reinforcement for which the student will work. This reinforcement should be available to the student *only* for performing the specified behavior. The required behavior or the consequent reinforcement can be determined through student–teacher discussions.

3. The teacher specifies the terms of the contract, which should include the amount or type of behavior required and the amount or type of reward.

4. The teacher watches for the specified behavior to occur and then rewards the student according to the terms of the contract.

A sample contingency contract is presented in Figure 5.5.

A contingency contract should represent agreement between the student and the teacher. The terms should be stated clearly in a positive manner and should be fair for both the student and the teacher. After both parties have signed the contract, the conditions should be monitored frequently to assess progress. In addition, all parts of the contract should be followed systematically, and the student should receive reinforcement as soon as the contract is completed.

Various types of contracts can be used. The agreement may or may not specify a time limit within which the required behavior must be performed. Intermittent reinforcers can be used in long-term contracts, and steps toward the desired behavior can be rewarded. Contracts also can include agreements between the student and other school personnel or parents. Group contracts can be used in which the entire class agrees to behave in a certain manner or perform a specified task by a designated date, and the teacher agrees to reward students who fulfill the agreement. Contingency contracting thus can promote desirable actions (social or academic) by involving students in managing their own behavior.

FIGURE 5.5
A sample contingency contract

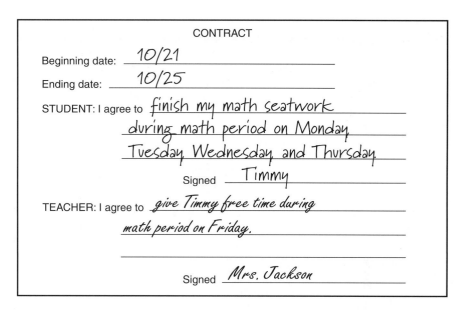

CONTRACT

Beginning date: _10/21_

Ending date: _10/25_

STUDENT: I agree to _finish my math seatwork during math period on Monday, Tuesday, Wednesday, and Thursday_

Signed _Timmy_

TEACHER: I agree to _give Timmy free time during math period on Friday._

Signed _Mrs. Jackson_

Token Systems

Token reinforcement systems are used widely in behavior modification. These systems have three basic characteristics: (1) behaviors to be reinforced are stated clearly, (2) procedures are devised for giving out a reinforcing stimulus (token) when the target behavior occurs, and (3) a set of rules is explained to govern the exchange of tokens for reinforcing objects or events.

A *token* is an item given to a student immediately after a target behavior occurs. Usually the tokens have little intrinsic value, but they acquire value when they can be exchanged for a desired object or activity. Tokens can consist of play money, trading stamps, poker chips, stars, or any other object that is easy to dispense and store. These tokens can be accumulated and then exchanged for a desired object or activity. A classroom store can be established where, at designated times, each student may purchase reinforcers by trading in earned tokens. Objects (balloons, comics, jewelry, sports trading cards, pennies, coloring books, and magazines) and activities (playing a game, listening to records, coloring, and watching a filmstrip) can be available in the store. A reward menu can be posted, listing the store items and their costs (e.g., listening to records for 10 minutes = 10 tokens; purchasing a baseball trading card = 15 tokens).

Token systems have several advantages. First, they avoid boredom because tokens can be traded for a variety of reinforcing objects or events. Second, a token system is useful with students who generally do not respond to social reinforcement. Third, tokens are administered easily, and the number can be adjusted to reflect the time and energy required to perform the target behavior. Fourth, token systems help students appreciate the relationship between desirable behavior and reinforcement. Students learn that behavior has consequences, which is likely to enhance self-control.

Blackham and Silberman (1980) stress that a token system must be developed and applied thoughtfully. They also report that problems should be expected at first, and the teacher will have to refine the system. Blackham and Silberman suggest guidelines for planning and using a token system:

- The target behaviors that earn tokens should be specified clearly. For example, individual behaviors can be posted on a student's desk. Rules governing group behavior contingencies should be reviewed frequently.
- The reinforcers that the tokens are exchanged for must be appealing and available *only* within the token system.
- The number of tokens earned must match the effort required for performing the target

behavior. If a student has great difficulty staying on task during math seatwork, the reward for staying on task must be sufficient to encourage on-task behavior.

- If possible, the teacher should keep a record of the number of tokens each student and the group earn. This type of record often provides an additional incentive to students.
- If *response cost* (token fines) is used, the conditions under which tokens are earned and lost must be specified clearly. Awarding and taking away tokens always must be related to student *behavior*. Arguments about token loss should be avoided.
- A scheduled token exchange at the end of the day usually works best.
- The system should be devised so that there is self-competition rather than competition with others.
- A well-planned token system gradually should withdraw material reinforcers and stress reinforcing activities and events. Also, praise should be combined with the tokens so that social reinforcement eventually can be used alone to maintain desirable behaviors.
- The token system should be simple, functional, and not distracting to the learning process. In school, check-mark tokens are often the easiest to use. Each student is given a card, and the teacher puts checks on it as they are earned. A special pen can be used to distinguish these checks. Other students cannot use a student's card, whereas tangible tokens might be traded or stolen.

Extrinsic Reinforcement

Many disruptive or aggressive students need extrinsic reinforcers to establish the habits of appropriate behavior. Once these habits are developed in caring environments, effort should be made to help them become intrinsically motivated. Table 5.7 provides some advantages and disadvantages of several extrinsic reinforcers.

Sprick (1981) provides the following guidelines for changing a behavior during spontaneous interventions:

- Reinforce students who are doing the behavior in an appropriate manner.
- When a misbehaving student begins to behave, reinforce the student.

- Provide fun activities for the whole class.
- Provide fun activities for a student who improves in behavior or academic performance.

Sprick recommends the following modifications when the behavior improves:

- Require more of the desired behavior for the same amount of reinforcement.
- When the behavior has reached the appropriate level of success, reinforce less frequently and less immediately.
- When delayed reinforcement has successfully maintained the desired behavior, begin to modify the reinforcement by using a less powerful reinforcer or one closer to intrinsic reinforcement.
- When the behavior has been maintained successfully with a less powerful reinforcer, switch from a continuous reinforcer to an intermittent reinforcer.

Punishment

Unfortunately, there is a tendency for some people to equate discipline with punishment. An effective classroom management plan, however, focuses on prevention or proactive strategies and minimizes the use of punishment. Sprick (1981) and Whelan (1996) maintain that an emphasis on punishment is inappropriate for several reasons:

- Punishment focuses on decreasing an inappropriate behavior rather than on teaching an appropriate behavior.
- Punishment can be self-defeating and result in such complications as poor self-image or revenge.
- Students may become anxious and learn to lie, cheat, or steal to avoid punishment. Also, anxiety interferes with learning.
- Punishment is effective only while the threat is present, and it does not eliminate the desire to engage in misbehavior.

Overall, effective classroom management does not stress punishing the misbehavior but emphasizes its correction. When misbehavior occurs, the teacher works with the student to solve it.

Although punishment is not a preferred approach, it is needed periodically as a transition stra-

TABLE 5.7

Advantages and disadvantages of extrinsic reinforcers

Type and Definition of Reinforcer	Advantages	Disadvantages
Tangible–a physical object given for appropriate behavior Examples: popcorn, crackers, stickers, pencils, books, coupons, and mazes	Are very desirable Are highly reinforcing	Must be purchased May teach incorrect associations Should be paired with praise Are temporary and should be switched to social praise as soon as possible
Token–an item, given for appropriate behavior, that can be exchanged at a later time for rewards (e.g., toys, food, or games), which may be displayed in a classroom store Examples: points, poker chips, stars, trading stamps, and play money	Are a concrete means for immediate reinforcement Provide a record of accomplishments Do not interfere with class routines	Require much organization Require planning, time, and energy to use Require an assortment of backup items May not generalize Create dependency on concrete reinforcement
Social–a social behavior provided contingent on appropriate behavior Examples: gestures (smile, wink, thumbs up, and eye contact), verbal approval (praise and encouragement), and touch (hug, shoulder pat, handshake, and high-five)	Easy to use Require little teacher effort Are always available Rarely cause criticism Are powerful reinforcers	Are sometimes not powerful enough
Activity–an action that students get to do as a reward for appropriate behavior Examples: eat lunch with teacher, run errands, have free time, lead the line, pass out books, and use the computer	Are readily available Can be combined with social reinforcers Can be built into class routines	May delay gratification May interrupt other activities

tegy for students who frequently engage in misbehavior. Kameenui et al. (1995) note that punishment serves as a transition strategy to restore a safe and productive learning environment. Some of the advantages of punishment highlight its usefulness as a transition strategy. Sprick (1981) offers the following advantages:

- Punishment can be powerful if used effectively.
- Although the behavior change may be temporary, punishment can reduce disruptive behavior rapidly.
- Punishment can provide information to the misbehaving student and other students about what is acceptable and unacceptable.

Punishment Prevention Strategies Some generic prevention strategies are discussed in the general techniques section of this chapter. Most of these strategies focus on good teaching and effective intervention skills (see Chapter 4). This section presents some low-energy strategies that help prevent the need for punishment. Punishment prevention strategies include the following:

1. ***Ensure the task is appropriate.*** The task must be within the student's ability to perform if the student tries.

2. ***Give more attention to appropriate behavior than to inappropriate behavior.*** The teacher should maintain a 3:1 attending ratio for

positive events vs. negative events in the classroom (Sprick, 1985).

3. **Reinforce students who are following the rules.** This provides examples of acceptable behavior to all students.

4. **Use gentle verbal reminders.** A gentle verbal reminder involves reminding the student of the rule that is not being followed. The reminder is delivered in an instructional manner: Eye contact is limited, body language is relaxed, voice is calm, and it happens quickly and in a matter-of-fact manner. In delivering a gentle verbal reminder, the teacher might say, "Please remember to raise your hand if you wish to speak." Giving a gentle verbal reminder provides all students with an example of unacceptable behavior.

5. **Use proximity control.** The teacher can move to stand near the student who is misbehaving or is about to misbehave. Also, students who are prone to misbehave should be seated close to the area where the teacher spends the most time.

6. **Discuss the problem with the student.** The teacher should discuss the misbehavior with the student at a neutral time. The discussion may simply involve requesting the student to stop the misbehavior. More involved discussions usually focus on a problem-solving approach in which the

pair discuss appropriate alternative behaviors or creative plans for the situation.

7. **Use a precorrection strategy for teaching appropriate behavior.** Colvin, Sugai, and Patching (1993) note that correction is reactive, focuses on consequences, stresses misbehavior, and deals with immediate events, whereas precorrection is proactive, stresses appropriate behavior, focuses on antecedents, and deals with future events. They maintain that correction often leads to more misbehavior, whereas precorrection enhances appropriate behavior. A seven-step precorrection plan is featured in Table 5.8.

8. **Ignore mild misbehavior.** The teacher should ignore behavior that is mildly disruptive (e.g., talking to others) if it does not occur frequently. Guidelines for teachers to use when ignoring misbehavior include the following:

- Ignore only what you feel comfortable ignoring.
- Ignore behavior that is displayed primarily for teacher attention.
- When ignoring, pretend the student is not present.
- Prior to ignoring, tell the class or student that you will use ignoring.
- Be aware that effective ignoring usually results in an increase in the misbehavior before the misbehavior decreases.

TABLE 5.8
Seven-step precorrection plan

Precorrection Steps	Example
1. Identify context for the predictable behavior.	Students entering the classroom immediately after luinch. (Predictable behavior: Students talking loudly, laughing, and moving around before following teacher directions.)
2. Specify expected behavior.	Students should enter the room quietly, go quickly to their desks, and begin a specified task.
3. Modify the context.	The teacher meets students at the classroom door, waits until they are quiet, and then allows them to go to their desks to begin work.
4. Conduct behavior rehearsal.	The teacher reminds students before lunch of the expected behavior following lunch. A student can be called on to explain the expected behavior.
5. Provide strong reinforcement for expected behavior.	The teacher tells the students that if they follow the teacher's requests, they will have an additional break or an extra 5 minutes at recess.
6. Prompt expected behavior.	The teacher gives a signal at the door to be quiet and points to the activity on the chalkboard. The teacher praises students who are beginning work.
7. Monitor the plan.	The teacher times how long it takes for all students to begin work and counts how many students begin the task within 10 seconds.

FIGURE 5.6

A continuum of preventive strategies and punishment strategies

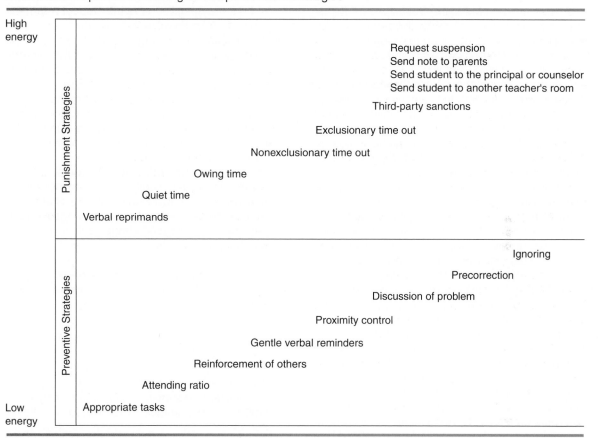

Punishment Strategies   Punishment strategies may be viewed on a continuum from least intrusive (i.e., least energy consuming) to most intrusive (i.e., most energy consuming). Kameenui et al. (1995) provide a low-energy to high-energy continuum of punishments that features the following sequence: verbal reprimands, quiet time, owing time, nonexclusionary time out, exclusionary time out, and third-party sanctions. Figure 5.6 displays a continuum of preventive strategies and punishment strategies.

Punishment strategies include the following:

1. ***Verbal reprimands.*** Reprimands conducted calmly and briefly can be effective and unobtrusive. Guidelines for implementing verbal reprimands include the following:

- During the reprimand, specify the inappropriate behavior.
- Pair the reprimand with a consequence.
- When reprimanding, stand close to the student or talk so that others do not hear.
- Follow reprimands with reinforcement.

2. ***Quiet time.*** Quiet time allows the student to think about the misbehavior and its consequences and to consider appropriate alternative behaviors. To implement quiet time, the following procedures are used:

- Instruct the student immediately to stop the inappropriate behavior.
- Instruct the student to remain quiet.
- Enforce quiet time for 1 or 2 minutes.
- Instruct the student to resume the assigned task.
- Reinforce appropriate behavior.

3. ***Owing time.*** This strategy is based on the rationale that misbehavior uses learning time and this time must be paid back. Guidelines for implementing owing time include the following:

- Specify behaviors that lead to owing time.
- Prior to implementing owing time, discuss the rationale for the strategy and how it will be conducted.
- Determine the amount of time the student owes. Requiring the student to pay back the amount of time that the misbehavior took away from learning deserves consideration.
- Specify when the student will pay back time.
- Determine what learning activity the student will engage in during payback time.

4. ***Nonexclusionary time out.*** Time out is a procedure in which access to sources of reinforcement is removed. Some examples of nonexclusionary time out are student's head on desk, lights turned off, removal of materials from student, and removal of student from group but allowing student to watch (i.e., contingent observation).

5. **Exclusionary time out.** This procedure is more obtrusive than nonexclusionary time out and involves the student moving to a new location. Examples of exclusionary time out include placing the student in another part of the room, having the student sit in a chair in the corner of the room, and having the student sit in a chair outside the classroom door. Finally, seclusion time out involves placing the student in a specially designed isolation room for a short period of time. Guidelines for implementing exclusionary time out include the following:

- Always administer time out calmly.
- Specify punishable behaviors.
- Establish time out procedures and locations for exclusionary and seclusion time outs.
- State inappropriate behavior and direct the student to take a time out.
- Lead younger children to the time-out area.
- Keep track of time for exclusionary and seclusion time outs. Recommended time is 3 minutes or less.

6. ***Third-party sanctions.*** Third-party sanctions are high cost in energy and time and involve other school personnel or parents. Third-party sanctions include the following:

- *Send student to another teacher's room.* Prior to using this strategy, the following procedures are arranged with another teacher: The student enters the new class without disruption and goes to a designated seat; students in both classrooms are instructed to ignore the student at all times, and after a specified time the student returns to the original class without disruption.
- *Send student to the principal or counselor.* This strategy results in instant removal from the room; however, it may be reinforcing and communicate that the teacher has lost control.
- *Send note to parents.* An advantage of this strategy is that it keeps parents informed; however, the note may result in severe punishment by the parents, or the student may be reinforced by the attention.
- *Request suspension.* The teacher should be aware of the school policies and procedures for suspension. Disadvantages of suspension are that it may be reinforcing, it may negatively affect the student's self-image, and it does not teach appropriate behavior.

General Guidelines for Punishment   Sprick (1981) provides the following guidelines for using punishment effectively:

- Specify acceptable and unacceptable behavior.
- Be as consistent as possible in implementing punishment.
- Always implement punishment with a concurrent plan of positive reinforcement.
- Administer punishment calmly and quickly (e.g., limit the consequence statement to 3 or fewer seconds).
- Establish punishment for as few behaviors as possible.
- Always treat students with respect.
- Monitor punishment to ensure that it is decreasing the target misbehavior.

Techniques for Managing Surface Behaviors

Long and Newman (1971) discuss 12 techniques for managing surface (observable) behaviors and helping to prevent the buildup of behavior problems:

1. *Planned ignoring.* Many behaviors will stop if they are ignored rather than given teacher attention.
2. *Signal interference.* The use of a cue (such as finger snapping) can alert the student to stop a particular behavior.

3. *Proximity control.* Some disruptive behavior can be prevented by the teacher's presence in the area of potential trouble.
4. *Interest boosting.* Some behaviors can be managed when the teacher shows a genuine interest in the student as an individual.
5. *Tension decontamination through humor.* A humorous remark by the teacher can release tension in an emotional situation.
6. *Hurdle lessons.* The teacher can lessen frustration by providing individual academic assistance.
7. *Restructuring the classroom program.* A change in the classroom program can reduce behavior problems.
8. *Support from routine.* A familiar routine can provide support to the student.
9. *Direct appeal to value areas.* The teacher needs to be aware of the student's personal values to appeal to them.
10. *Removing seductive objects.* Items that distract the student can be removed from the classroom to avoid provoking disruptive behavior.
11. *Antiseptic bouncing.* The student can be removed from the classroom without punishment (e.g., ask the student to run an errand).
12. *Physical restraint.* The teacher can restrain the student who has lost self-control and might be injured.

☀ BEHAVIORAL DEVELOPMENT ACTIVITIES

Disruptive behavior in the classroom includes actions that interfere with instruction or activities of an individual or a group. Inappropriate talking out and out-of-seat behaviors frequently disrupt the classroom. Moreover, the use of sarcasm, swear words, and temper tantrums are disturbing behaviors that need to be modified. The following activities focus on managing disruptive behavior:

• As much as possible, ignore disruptions and reward the student's complying behaviors. For example, when a student talks out during class, completely ignore the student and do not respond to what is said; however, when the student raises a hand during class, immediately recognize the student and praise the behavior. This is effective only if teacher attention is reinforcing. It may be necessary also to control peer attention to the inappropriate behavior.

• Ignore out-of-seat behaviors and give verbal praise to students who remain in their seats. Students who remain seated during work periods can be rewarded by being allowed to participate in a game involving movement (e.g., musical chairs or kickball).

• Use a timer to see how long an active student can stay seated. Time the student at various intervals during the day and reward the student for remaining seated during the interval. Record progress on a graph so that the student competes to improve the behavior. As the student progresses, gradually increase the time interval for staying seated.

• Give periodic breaks that allow the active student out-of-seat time. The student may be given errands to run, during which the student can move around or leave the room.

• Devise contingency contracts in which the student agrees to stay seated for a period of time; if the student does so, the teacher agrees to reward the student with some free out-of-seat time (such as extra recess). Likewise, a student can agree in a contract not to talk out during class for a specific amount of time in return for the reward of free talking time.

• Cut out a figure of the student that includes a large pocket and tape it to the wall. Whenever the student behaves appropriately, place a chip or token in the figure's pocket. When the student engages in an inappropriate behavior (e.g., out of seat, talking out, or use of swear words), remove a chip from the pocket. At the end of each day the chips can be traded for a reinforcing activity (e.g., free time, playing a game, or watching a filmstrip).

• To reduce swearing, suggest to the student other words that can be used (e.g., *darn, heck,* or *shoot*). Provide reinforcement every time the student refrains from swearing and uses another word.

• Use a graph to record the number of swear words or sarcastic remarks made by the student during a specific time period. This will call attention to the inappropriate remarks. Have the student compete to improve progress, and reinforce the student for improved behavior.

• When a student begins a temper tantrum, immediately remove the student to a time-out area in which the student is isolated from the teacher and peers. When the student is able to remain quiet, allow him or her to return to the classroom. In this way, the student receives little attention for inappropriate behavior. Also, be aware of the chain of behavior that leads the student to an outburst or tantrum. Apply time out or another management technique before the chain has gone too far.

• At the beginning of the day, make 15 numbered marks on the chalkboard. Explain to the class that they have an opportunity to have a 15-minute recess at the end of the day. However, for each disruptive behavior, one mark is erased from the board. At the end of the day, give the class the number of minutes of extra recess remaining on the board. Instead of recess, the minutes can be used in a special game, story time, or field trips.

☀ INSTRUCTIONAL GAMES IN BEHAVIORAL DEVELOPMENT

Game formats can be used to enable the teacher and students to focus on appropriate behaviors (e.g., staying on task, raising a hand to talk, or remaining seated). The following games are designed to promote behavioral development.

Picture Puzzle Game

Materials: A large picture of something the student is interested in or wants, cut into pieces.

Directions: Encourage appropriate behavior over a period of time by rewarding the student with a requested item or activity. The student and teacher agree on the desired behavior to be reinforced and the type of reward. Each time the student shows the desired behavior, the teacher provides a piece of the picture puzzle. Each time inappropriate behavior is observed, the teacher takes away a puzzle piece. When all the puzzle pieces to the picture are received, the student is reinforced by receiving the reward.

Work Around the Circle

Materials: Classroom chairs arranged in a circle; a timer.

Directions: Set a timer to ring at various times during intervals of from 1 to 4 minutes. When the timer rings, each student who is working may move to the next chair. Students who are caught not working must remain in their seats for that turn. Thus, students who are working appropriately rotate around the circle. When a student has completed the circle, the teacher should check the assignment and give the student free time until all students have worked their way back to their own seats.

The Principal's Game

(Paine et al., 1983)

Materials: Timer; chalkboard area for recording points.

Directions: Use this game to improve the behavior of a disruptive class of students. Begin by telling students they need to work harder and that there is a game that

can help them. In the game, teams are formed according to seating clusters or rows (i.e., one team for each row or cluster). A timer is set to ring six times during the class or day. Each time it rings, the teacher determines which teams are following classroom rules and working. If all team members are working, the whole team receives a point; however, if one or more members are not working, no points are awarded. To win, a team must receive a minimum of five points, and it is possible for all teams to win. At the end of the day or class, invite the principal to come into the room and recognize the winning teams and praise their work. In addition to the principal, other significant people (e.g., counselor, another teacher, local sports figure, or parent) can be asked to visit and recognize winning teams.

Behavior Monopoly

Materials: A game board similar to a Monopoly board that has a variety of reinforcers (including some booby prizes) written in the squares; a die; student markers.

Directions: Use the game board (see Figure 5.7) to provide the student with some type of reinforcement. Randomly identify a student displaying an appropriate behavior. Allow the student to roll the die and move the marker on the board. The student receives the reinforcer indicated on the space where the marker lands. The marker is left on that space so that it can be moved the next time the student gets to play.

Suggested Chance Cards: "Arm wrestle with teacher"; "Hop on one foot for 5 seconds"; "Send note to a friend"; "Hug the teacher"; "Pick up trash."

Speed Chase

Materials: Poster board with large speedometer dial drawn on it; cardboard arrows, each of which has a student's name on it; various small prizes.

Directions: Allow groups of students to compete to see who can complete the most classwork accurately during the day. After the teacher has checked an assignment, each student attaches an arrow to the speedometer to indicate the number of items the student performed correctly on the task. The speed on the speedometer increases according to the number of correct items on each assignment. At the end of the day, the student with the highest speed wins and picks a prize.

Modifications: Rather than competing in all subject areas for an entire day, students can record their speed in one subject area for several days. Also, the speedometer can be used to record specific behaviors during the day,

FIGURE 5.7
Behavior Monopoly game
board

Pick chance card	Trip to water fountain	Listen to record	Teacher's helper today	Read a magazine
Get two snacks	BEHAVIOR MONOPOLY			Free pick
Trip to library				10 seconds of applause
Choose prize				Throw darts at target
Go back 5 spaces	Have picture taken	Line leader		5 minutes free time

such as staying in seat or raising a hand instead of talking out. Two students who need to change the same behavior can compete. Each time the student displays the appropriate behavior, the teacher moves the student's arrow on the speedometer; the arrow is moved *back* for inappropriate behavior. The student with the highest speed at the end of the day wins the speed chase.

The Lottery

(Paine et al., 1983)

Materials: Prerecorded tape with randomly spaced "beeps"; tape recorder; space on chalkboard for recording checks by students' names.

Directions: Hold a daily lottery in which students work for the opportunity of having their names drawn at random. During the day, play a tape with six randomly distributed "beeps." Students who are following classroom rules (e.g., on task, seated, and quiet) when the beep sounds receive a check by their names on the chalkboard. Students who receive five or six checks in a day are eligible for the daily drawing. At the end of the day, two names are selected from the qualifying students. The principal or teacher phones the respective parents and tells them about their child's good behavior.

Good Behavior Game

Materials: Tally chart.

Directions: Divide the class into two teams and explain that talking out and out-of-seat behaviors are going to be recorded. Whenever a student engages in either behavior, place a mark on the tally sheet for the student's team. At the end of the day, the team with the fewest marks wins. If both teams have fewer than six marks, the whole class wins. The members of the winning team receive a previously agreed upon reward. If both teams win, reward the entire class with a 30-minute special project period.

Timer Game

Materials: Timer; point chart; prizes.

Directions: Set the timer to ring on the average of once every 20 minutes during a range of from 1 to 40 minutes. Each student who is seated when the timer rings is awarded five points. Each student's earned points are recorded on a point chart. At the end of a specified time period, the points may be traded in for prizes such as snacks or privileges.

☀ COMMERCIAL BEHAVIORAL DEVELOPMENT PROGRAMS

Various commercial materials help the teacher focus on managing the behavior of disruptive students. The following commercial programs are designed to promote behavioral development.

Getting Along

Getting Along, developed by P. Page, D. Cieloha, and M. Suid (published by American Guidance Service), is a conflict resolution program for students in kindergarten through fourth grade. The program focuses on teaching students to become more thoughtful, helpful, and respectful by challenging them to deal with the following common behavioral problems: teasing, bossiness, bullying, overcompetitiveness and poor sportsmanship, fighting, intolerance, violent play, disrespect for others' and public property, and selfishness. Music, art, reading, language, creative writing, and role-play activities are used to help students learn to identify and deal with behavioral problems. The program includes ten topic cards containing more than 100 activities, ten cartoon posters to help students identify problem behaviors, an audiocassette of ten songs, a teacher's guide, and blackline masters of activities to reinforce newly learned skills and to encourage family participation. A bilingual English and Spanish edition also is available.

The Teacher's Encyclopedia of Behavior Management; CHAMPs

The Teacher's Encyclopedia of Behavior Management (Sprick & Howard, 1995) provides practical, positive solutions to common classroom problems in kindergarten through ninth grade. More than 100 specific problem behaviors, such as absenteeism, blaming others, sloppy work, fighting, and cheating, are included. For each misbehavior, up to six detailed step-by-step plans are offered to present effective interventions that teachers can choose from or modify to fit the origin, duration, and severity of the actual situation. A companion book, *CHAMPs* (Sprick, Garrison, & Howard, 1998), assists teachers in designing a classroom management plan that overtly teaches students to behave responsibly. Eight modules (such as organization, expectations, motivation, and correction procedures) focus on varying aspects of classroom organization and behavior management. The implication steps and procedures are supported by school effectiveness research literature related to classroom and behavior management.

☀ PERSPECTIVE ON SOCIAL, EMOTIONAL, AND BEHAVIORAL DEVELOPMENT

Academic difficulties clearly cause frustration, anxiety, low self-concept, and mood swings. The degree to which these academic learning problems contribute to social, emotional, and behavioral aberrations is difficult to ascertain. An understanding of academic and social, emotional, and behavioral problems is complicated further by the position that such problems can interfere with academic learning. Certain educators continue to debate the academic deficiency/behavioral disorder relationship. Which occurred first? Which caused the other? Does the student primarily have emotional disabilities or learning problems? Moreover, some students exhibit social or emotional disabilities yet maintain excellent academic progress. These conditions and their related questions are complex, and until precise causes and valid diagnostic procedures are developed, they will continue to generate controversy. Meanwhile, perhaps the best strategy involves the direct treatment of target behaviors and the placement of youngsters in settings that provide earned success, reasonable structure, and sensitive support. This chapter offers information (i.e., assessment practices and intervention procedures) aimed at facilitating an appropriate education for students with learning problems who also have social, emotional, or behavioral problems.

The disintegration of the family and its supportive structures combines with increasing crime, violence, child abuse, and substance abuse to remind educators that perhaps at no other time in the history of civilization has it been more important for school personnel to provide safe and caring environments for students. Whelan (1996, p. 309) discusses the need for intervention and treatment to help students develop prosocial styles of relating to others:

> The schools cannot do it alone. Schools must use an interagency approach, involving all of the social service disciplines, in order to proactively respond to the problems and to provide assistance at every point in the student's life. Why should the schools be responsible for prevention and intervention programs? Because normal and dysfunctional behavior grow from

the same roots, we prevent and remedy student behavior problems by meeting developmental needs. Thus, according to Brendtro and Long (1995), the four "A's" of reclaiming school ethos are

attachment: Positive social bonds are prerequisites to prosocial behavior,

achievement: Setting high expectations means refusing to accept failure,

autonomy: True discipline lies in demanding responsibility rather than obedience, and

altruism: Through helping others, young people find proof of their own self-worth.

REFERENCES

Battle, J. (1992). *Culture-Free Self-Esteem Inventories—2.* Austin, TX: PRO-ED.

Bender, W. N. (1994). Social-emotional development: The task and the challenge. *Learning Disability Quarterly, 17,* 250–252.

Bender, W. N. (1995). *Learning disabilities: Characteristics, identification, and teaching strategies* (2nd ed.). Boston: Allyn & Bacon.

Bender, W. N., & Wall, M. E. (1994). Social-emotional development of students with learning disabilities. *Learning Disability Quarterly, 17,* 323–341.

Blackham, G. J., & Silberman, A. (1980). *Modification of child and adolescent behavior* (3rd ed.). Belmont, CA: Wadsworth.

Bracken, B. A. (1992). *Multidimensional Self Concept Scale.* Austin, TX: PRO-ED.

Brendtro, L., & Long, N. (1995). *Breaking the cycle of conflict.* Educational Foundation Leadership, *15*(5), 52–56.

Brown, L. L., & Alexander, J. (1991). *Self-Esteem Index.* Austin, TX: PRO-ED.

Brown, L. L., & Hammill, D. D. (1990). *Behavior Rating Profile—2.* Austin, TX: PRO-ED.

Bruininks, R. H., Woodcock, R. W., Weatherman, R. F., & Hill, B. K. (1996). *Scales of Independent Behavior—Revised.* Itasca, IL: Riverside.

Bryan, T. H. (1986). Self-concept and attributions of the learning disabled. *Learning Disabilities Focus, 1,* 82–89.

Cartledge, G., Frew, T., & Zaharias, J. (1985). Social skill needs of mainstreamed students: Peer and teacher perceptions. *Learning Disability Quarterly, 8,* 132–140.

Chapman, J. W., & Boersma, F. J. (1979). Learning disabilities, locus of control, and mother attitudes. *Journal of Educational Psychology, 1,* 250–258.

Cianciolo, P. J. (1965). Children's literature can affect coping behavior. *Personnel and Guidance Journal, 43*(9), 897–903.

Coie, J., Dodge, K., & Coppotelli, H. (1982). Dimensions and types of social status: A cross-age perspective. *Developmental Psychology, 18,* 557–570.

Colvin, G., Sugai, G., & Patching, B. (1993). Precorrection: An instructional approach for managing predictable problem behaviors. *Intervention in School and Clinic, 28,* 143–150.

Coopersmith, S. (1981). *Coopersmith Self-Esteem Inventories.* Palo Alto, CA: Consulting Psychologists Press.

Dinkmeyer, D., & Dinkmeyer, D., Jr. (1982). *Developing understanding of self and others* (Rev. ed.). Circle Pines, MN: American Guidance Service.

Dodge, K. A. (1983). Behavioral antecedents of peer status. *Child Development, 54,* 1400–1416.

Dodge, K. A., Pettit, G. S., McClaskey, C. L., & Brown, M. M. (1986). Social competence in children. *Monograph of the Society for Research in Child Development, 51*(2, Serial No. 213).

Elliott, S. N., Gresham, F. M., & Heffer, R. W. (1987). Social-skill interventions: Research findings and training techniques. In C. A. Maher & J. E. Zins (Eds.), *Psychoeducational interventions in the schools* (pp. 141–159). New York: Pergamon.

Ellis, E. S., Lenz, B. K., & Sabornie, E. J. (1987). Generalization and adaptation of learning strategies to natural environments: Part 2: Research into practice. *Remedial and Special Education, 8*(2), 6–23.

Fitts, W. H., & Warren, W. L. (1996). *Tennessee Self-Concept Scale: Second Edition.* Los Angeles: Western Psychological Services.

Flanders, N. (1970). *Analyzing teacher behavior.* Menlo Park, CA: Addison-Wesley.

Forness, S. R., & Kavale, K. A. (1996). Treating social skill deficits in children with learning disabilities: A meta-analysis of the research. *Learning Disability Quarterly, 19,* 2–13.

Fowler, J. W., & Peterson, P. L. (1981). Increasing reading persistence and altering attributional style of learned helpless children. *Journal of Educational Psychology, 73,* 251–260.

Glasser, W. (1965). *Reality therapy: A new approach to psychiatry.* New York: Harper & Row.

Goldstein, A. P., & McGinnis, E. (1997). *Skillstreaming the adolescent* (Rev. ed.). Champaign, IL: Research Press.

Gresham, F. M., & Elliott, S. N. (1989). Social skills assessment technology for LD students. *Learning Disability Quarterly, 12,* 141–152.

Gresham, F. M., & Elliott, S. N. (1990). *Social Skills Rating System.* Circle Pines, MN: American Guidance Service.

Gresham, F. M., Elliott, S. N., & Evans-Fernandez, S. (1992). *Student Self-Concept Scale.* Circle Pines, MN: American Guidance Service.

Gresham, F. M., & Reschly, D. J. (1988). Issues in the conceptualization, classification, and assessment of social skills in the mildly handicapped. In T. Kratochwill (Ed.), *Advances in school psychology* (pp. 203–247). Hillsdale, NJ: Erlbaum.

Hazel, J. S., & Schumaker, J. B. (1988). Social skills and learning disabilities: Current issues and recommendations for future research. In J. F. Kavanagh & T. J. Truss (Eds.), *Learning disabilities: Proceedings of the national conference* (pp. 293–344). Parkton, MD: York Press.

Hoagland, J. (1972, March). Bibliotherapy: Aiding children in personality development. *Elementary English,* 390–394.

Hughes, C. A., Ruhl, K. L., & Peterson, S. K. (1988). Teaching self-management skills. *Teaching Exceptional Children, 20*(2), 70–72.

Hutton, J. B., & Roberts, T. G. (1986). *Social-Emotional Dimension Scale.* Austin, TX: PRO-ED.

Jackson, N. F., Jackson, D. A., & Monroe, C. (1983). *Getting along with others: Teaching social effectiveness to children.* Champaign, IL: Research Press.

Kameenui, E. J., Darch, C. B., & Colvin, G. (1995, April). *Instructional classroom management.* Paper presented at the meeting of the Council for Exceptional Children, Orlando, FL.

Kaufman, M., Agard, J., & Semmel, M. (1985). *Mainstreaming: Learners and their environment.* Cambridge, MA: Brookline Books.

Kerr, M. M., & Nelson, C. M. (1998). *Strategies for managing behavior problems in the classroom* (3rd ed.). Upper Saddle River, NJ: Merrill/Prentice Hall.

Lambert, N., Nihira, K., & Leland, H. (1993). *AAMR Adaptive Behavior Scale—School* (2nd ed.). Austin, TX: PRO-ED.

Lenkowsky, B., & Lenkowsky, R. (1978). Bibliotherapy of the LD adolescent. *Academic Therapy, 14,* 179–185.

Licht, B. G. (1984). Cognitive-motivational factors that contribute to the achievement of learning-disabled children. *Annual Review of Learning Disabilities, 2,* 119–126.

Lieberman, L. M. (1983). The homework solution. *Journal of Learning Disabilities, 16,* 435.

Long, N. J., & Newman, R. G. (1971). Managing surface behavior of children in schools. In N. J. Long, W. C. Morse, & R. G. Newman (Eds.). *Conflict in the classroom: The education of emotionally disturbed children* (2nd ed.). Belmont, CA: Wadsworth.

Maag, J. W. (1989). Assessment in social skills training: Methodological and conceptual issues for research and practice. *Remedial and Special Education, 10*(4), 6–17.

McCarney, S. B., & Leigh, J. E. (1990). *Behavior Evaluation Scale—2.* Columbia, MO: Hawthorne Educational Services.

McConnell, S., & Odom, S. (1986). Sociometrics: Peer-referenced measures and the assessment of social competence. In P. Strain, M. Guralnick, & H. Walker (Eds.), *Children's social behavior: Development, assessment, and modification* (pp. 215–284). Orlando, FL: Academic Press.

McGinnis, E., & Goldstein, A. P. (1997). *Skillstreaming the elementary school child* (Rev. ed.). Champaign, IL: Research Press.

Meichenbaum, D. (1977). *Cognitive-behavior modification: An integrative approach.* New York: Plenum Press.

Mellard, D. F., & Hazel, J. S. (1992). Social competencies as a pathway to successful life transitions. *Learning Disability Quarterly, 15,* 251–271.

Morse, W. C. (1971). Worksheet on life space interviewing for teachers. In N. J. Long, W. C. Morse, & R. G. Newman (Eds.), *Conflict in the classroom: The education of emotionally disturbed children* (2nd ed.). Belmont, CA: Wadsworth.

Naglieri, J. A., LeBuffe, P. A., & Pfeiffer, S. I. (1993). *Devereux Behavior Rating Scale—School Form.* San Antonio, TX: Psychological Corporation.

Neeper, R., Lahey, B. B., & Frick, P. J. (1990). *Comprehensive Behavior Rating Scale for Children.* San Antonio, TX: Psychological Corporation.

Paine, S. C., Radicchi, J., Rosellini, L. C., Deutchman, L., & Darch, C. B. (1983). *Structuring your classroom for academic success.* Champaign, IL: Research Press.

Pearl, R., Bryan, T., & Donahue, M. (1980). Learning disabled children's attributions for success and failure. *Learning Disability Quarterly, 3*(1), 3–9.

Piers, E. V., & Harris, D. B. (1984). *The Piers-Harris Children's Self-Concept Scale: Revised manual.* Los Angeles: Western Psychological Services.

Pray, B. S., Jr., Hall, C. W., & Markley, R. P. (1992). Social skills training: An analysis of social behaviors selected for individualized education programs. *Remedial and Special Education, 13*(5), 43–49.

Premack, D. (1959). Toward empirical behavior laws: I. Positive reinforcement. *Psychological Review, 66,* 219–233.

Quay, H. C., & Peterson, D. R. (1987). *Revised Behavior Problem Checklist.* Coral Gables, FL: University of Miami.

Reynolds, C. R., & Kamphaus, R. W. (1992). *Behavior Assessment System for Children.* Circle Pines, MN: American Guidance Service.

Rieth, H., & Evertson, C. (1988). Variables related to the effective instruction of difficult-to-teach children. *Focus on Exceptional Children, 20*(5), 1–8.

Russell, A. E., & Russell, W. A. (1979). Using bibliotherapy with emotionally disturbed children. *Teaching Exceptional Children, 11,* 168–169.

Sander, N. W. (1991). Effects of a self-management strategy on task-independent behaviors of adolescents with learning disabilities. *B. C. Journal of Special Education, 15,* 64–75.

Schumaker, J. B., & Hazel, J. S. (1984). Social skills assessment and training for the learning disabled: Who's on first and what's on second? Part II. *Journal of Learning Disabilities, 17,* 492–499.

Schunk, D. H. (1981). Modeling and attributional effects on children's achievement: A self-efficacy analysis. *Journal of Educational Psychology, 73,* 93–105.

Shapiro, E. S. (1989). Teaching self-management skills to learning disabled adolescents. *Learning Disability Quarterly, 12,* 275–287.

Shelton, T. L., Anastopoulos, A. D., & Linden, J. D. (1985). An attribution training program with learning disabled children. *Journal of Learning Disabilities, 18,* 261–265.

Slavin, R. E. (1991). Synthesis of research on cooperative learning. *Educational Leadership, 48*(5), 71–82.

Sparrow, S. S., Balla, D. A., & Cicchetti, D. V. (1984). *The Vineland Adaptive Behavior Scale.* Circle Pines, MN: American Guidance Service.

Sprick, R. S. (1981). *The solution book: A guide to classroom discipline.* DeSoto, TX: SRA.

Sprick, R. S. (1985). *Discipline in the secondary classroom: A problem-by-problem survival guide.* West Nyack, NY: The Center for Applied Research in Education.

Sprick, R. S., Garrison, M., & Howard, L. M. (1998). *CHAMPs: A proactive and positive approach to classroom management.* Longmont, CO: Sopris West.

Sprick, R. S., & Howard, L. M. (1995). *The teacher's encyclopedia of behavior management: 100 problems/ 500 plans.* Longmont, CO: Sopris West.

Sugai, G., & Fuller, M. (1991). A decision model for social skills curriculum analysis. *Remedial and Special Education, 12*(4), 33–42.

United States General Accounting Office. (1995). *School safety: Promising practices for addressing school violence.* (GAO/HEHS-95-106). Washington, DC: Author.

Walker, H. M. (1983). *Walker Problem Behavior Identification Checklist.* Los Angeles: Western Psychological Services.

Walker, H. M., McConnell, S., Holmes, D., Todis, B., Walker, J., & Golden, N. (1983). *The Walker social skills curriculum: The ACCEPTS program.* Austin, TX: PRO-ED.

Walker, H. M., Todis, B., Holmes, D., & Horton, G. (1988). *The Walker social skills curriculum: The ACCESS program.* Austin, TX: PRO-ED.

Wallace, G., & Kauffman, J. M. (1986). *Teaching students with learning and behavior problems* (3rd ed.). Upper Saddle River, NJ: Merrill/Prentice Hall.

Wallace, G., Larsen, S. C., & Elksnin, L. K. (1992). *Educational assessment of learning problems: Testing for teaching* (2nd ed.). Boston: Allyn & Bacon.

Weinstein, R. S. (1982). *Expectations in the classroom: The student perspective.* Invited address, Annual Conference of the American Educational Research Association, New York.

Whelan, R. J. (1996). Classroom management. In E. L. Meyen, G. A. Vergason, & R. J. Whelan (Eds.), *Strategies for teaching exceptional children in inclusive settings* (pp. 303–310). Denver, CO: Love.

Wood, M. M., & Long, N. J. (1991). *Life space intervention: Talking with children and youth in crisis.* Austin, TX: PRO-ED.

Teaching Academic Skills

6

Assessing and Teaching Language

Oral language is a learned behavior that enables people to transmit their ideas and culture from generation to generation. The ability to communicate through language is perhaps an individual's most vital and complex characteristic. It is through speech and language that people make sense of and respond to their environment. A communication problem can be devastating because it directly affects the individual as well as others in the immediate environment as attempts are made to transmit ideas, facts, feelings, and desires. Language also is related directly to achievement and adjustment in school because it forms the basis for formulating questions, extending and clarifying information, and reducing ambiguity in new learning situations (Bashir, 1989). In addition to being part of the academic curriculum, language is a medium through which information is taught and acquired.

Language is defined as "a socially shared code or conventional system for representing concepts through the use of arbitrary symbols and rule-governed combinations of those symbols" (Owens, 1994, p. 45). In contrast, *speech* involves the actual mechanics or motor act of verbal expression. Thus, whereas speech includes spoken utterances to convey meaning, language indicates a person's knowledge of the linguistic concepts on which speech is based. Moreover, language comprises receptive skills (understanding) and expressive skills (use) and includes both written and oral forms.

A variety of terms may be used with youngsters who do not acquire language at a normal rate. Terms such as *specific language impairment, language delay,* and *language disorder* generally are used with students who are having difficulty learning language in the absence of any intellectual, sensory, or emotional problems. The American Speech-Language-Hearing Association (1992, p. 949) provides the following definition of *language disorder:*

> A language disorder is the impairment or deviant development of comprehension and/or use of a spoken, written, and/or other symbol system. The disorder may involve (1) the form of language (phonologic, morphologic, and syntactic systems), (2) the content of language (semantic system), and/or (3) the function of language in communication (pragmatic system) in any combination.

The term *language disorder* generally is used when a student exhibits difficulty learning language or is learning language in a nontypical sequence. However, the initial manifestation of a language disorder is generally a delay in language development (Mogford & Sadler, 1989). Thus, in practice, the distinction is not clear, and the terms *language disorder* and *language delay* often are used interchangeably. As Lahey (1988) states, "It is not always easy to determine whether a child's system is qualitatively different from that of any non-language-impaired child at some point in development" (p. 21).

Students with severe language impairments usually are identified at an early age and receive speech or language therapy through a prekindergarten or developmental program. A greater number of students possess a more subtle language problem and begin to show difficulties as they grow older. As curriculum demands increase in about the third or fourth grade, these students lack the language foundation required to build academic skills. Teachers often describe such students as having difficulty maintaining attention, following directions, and using the right words when speaking. Other students are identified when they begin to have difficulties in academic subjects such as reading and writing. These students need an informed classroom teacher who can identify and understand their language problems and help them receive appropriate intervention.

This chapter provides a basic understanding of language disorders in students with learning problems. Theories of language acquisition and the major components of language are discussed. Language difficulties at various stages in a student's life are included, as well as a discussion of issues involving the language skills of bilingual and culturally diverse students. Moreover, assessment techniques, service delivery models, and teaching strategies are provided. Finally, language activities, instructional games, self-correcting materials, commercial programs, and computer software programs are described.

Although certain language skills are discussed separately in this chapter, they should be understood in the context of their interactiveness and pervasive impact on a student's learning and academic success. Language is viewed as interacting with other cognitive constructs and is best assessed and remediated as a whole in social communication rather than as isolated language skills. To ensure academic success for students with language problems, the teacher and language specialist should consult each other and work cooperatively.

☀ THEORIES OF LANGUAGE ACQUISITION

Theories of language acquisition fall within three major camps: behavioristic, nativistic (or psycholinguistic), and interactionistic (or cognitive). The behavioristic position (Skinner, 1957) relies on learning principles to explain language acquisition. Braine (1971), Jenkins and Palermo (1964), and Staats (1971) are proponents of the behavioristic position. Behaviorists believe that the infant begins with no knowledge of language but possesses the ability to learn it. The child learns through reinforcement of imitation. Reinforcement of babbling (including parental attention and delight) and the shaping of vocal behavior account for the initial stages of learning. Behaviorists emphasize environmental influences and the universal laws of learning, namely operant conditioning principles. The *DISTAR Language* program (discussed in the section on commercial materials) is based on the behavioral model.

Chomsky (1965), Lenneberg (1967), and McNeil (1970) are proponents of the nativistic position. Chomsky claims that the child possesses an innate capacity for dealing with linguistic universals. The child generates a theory of grammar to help understand and produce an infinite number of sentences. Lenneberg states that the child is biologically predisposed to learn language as the brain matures. Nativistics believe that humans are "prewired" for language development and that the environment simply triggers its emergence. Language programs that teach rules for sentence transformations represent the nativistic model.

Piaget (1960), the major proponent of the interactionistic position, theorizes that the child acquires language through the interaction of perceptual-cognitive capacities and experiences. The child's environment and neurological maturation determine learning. Language and thought thus develop simultaneously as the child passes through a series of fixed developmental stages requiring more and more complex strategies of cognitive organization. Interactionists consider the capacity for language to be innate; however, unlike the nativist, the interactionist believes the child must internalize linguistic structures from the environment and must become aware of communication's social functions. Thus, language programs in the interactionistic model are based on two ideas: (1) meaning is brought to a child's language through interaction with the environment and (2) the child uses speech to control the environment. Intervention approaches based on this model emphasize natural language teaching rather than structured exercises and drills.

On the one hand, the biologists (Lenneberg, 1967) and the linguists (Chomsky, 1965) view the child as a product of the maturation process. Biologists and linguists believe that, unless physical or mental complications occur, the child's development is predetermined. This view places heavy emphasis on the child, who is considered to be biologically prepared or linguistically preprogrammed to develop language. On the other hand, behaviorists stress the influence of the environment. The child's role is passive, and development depends largely on the individuals in the child's environment who respond to his or her behavior. The interactionistic position emphasizes the child's active interactions with the environment as he or she learns to talk (Bloom, 1975).

Primarily through the work of Wiig and Semel, language intervention has focused on the linguistic model, with direct concern about language functioning through analyzing comprehension and performance according to the components of language (such as phonology) and their rules. The linguistic model has served as the basis for the creation of many language programs. These programs usually focus on a particular language skill that the student should possess. Although the content of these programs is similar (phonemes and morphemes), some are founded in behavioral theory, some in nativism, and some in interactionism.

☀ COMPONENTS OF LANGUAGE

Language refers to "a code whereby ideas about the world are expressed through a conventional system of arbitrary signals for communication"

(Lahey, 1988, p. 2). Speakers and listeners both are involved in oral language because language is heard as well as spoken. A speaker's use of this arbitrary vocal system to communicate ideas and thoughts to a listener is referred to as *expressive language,* or *production.* In this process the listener uses *receptive language,* or *comprehension.* Students with expressive language difficulties may be reluctant to participate in verbal activities, whereas students with receptive language problems may have difficulty following directions or understanding content presented orally.

To assess and plan instruction for language problems, the teacher needs to be familiar with the components of language (see Table 6.1). Bloom and Lahey (1978) classify the components of language according to form (phonology, morphology, and syntax), content (semantics), and use (pragmatics). These language components are distinct but interrelated and interactive.

Form: Phonology

Phonology is the system of rules governing sounds and sound combinations; a *phoneme* is a unit of sound that combines with other sounds to form words. A phoneme is the smallest unit of language and is distinguished from the other language components in that a phoneme alone, such as /s/ and /b/, does not convey meaning. However, when interchanged in a word, phonemes significantly alter

TABLE 6.1
Components of language

Component	Definition	Receptive Level	Expressive Level
Phonology	The sound system of a language and the linguistic rules that govern the sound combinations	Discrimination of speech sounds	Articulation of speech sounds
Morphology	The linguistic rule system that governs the structure of words and the construction of word forms from the basic elements of meaning	Understanding of grammatical structure of words	Use of grammar in words
Syntax	The linguistic rule system governing the order and combination of words to form sentences, and the relationships among the elements within a sentence	Understanding of phrases and sentences	Use of grammar in phrases and sentences
Semantics	The psycholinguistic system that patterns the content of an utterance, intent, and meanings of words and sentences	Understanding of word meanings and word relationships	Use of word meanings and word relationships
Pragmatics	The sociolinguistic system that patterns the use of language in communication, which may be expressed motorically, vocally, or verbally	Understanding of contextual language cues	Use of language in context

Source: From *Students with Learning Disabilities* (p. 422), 5th ed., by C. D. Mercer, 1997, Upper Saddle River, NJ: Merrill/Prentice Hall. Copyright 1997 by Prentice-Hall Publishing Company. Reprinted by permission.

meaning (e.g., *sat* to *bat*). The rules governing phonemes focus on how sounds can be used in different word positions and which sounds may be combined. For example, standard English does not have a sound for the combination /zt/.

The English language consists of about 40 phonemes, classified as either vowels or consonants. Vowels are categorized according to where they are produced in the mouth. The tongue may be moved up, down, forward, or backward in producing vowels. These different tongue positions are used to classify vowels as high, mid, or low (i.e., the position of the highest part of the tongue) and front, central, or back (i.e., the location of the highest position) (Owens, 1994). For example, the long /e/ sound is classified as high front because the tongue blade is high in the front of the mouth. The tip of the tongue is down for all vowels. Consonants are classified according to place and manner of articulation. For example, the phoneme /f/ can be described by place (labial) and manner (voiceless stop).

Jacobson and Halle (1956) propose three principles that influence the order of phoneme acquisition:

1. Children learn first to distinguish sounds that have the fewest features in common, such as oral-nasal (/p/, /m/), labial-dental (/p/, /t/), and stop-fricative (/p/, /f/).
2. Development of front consonants such as /p/ and /m/ precedes the development of back consonants such as /k/ and /g/.
3. Phonemes that occur infrequently among the languages of the world (such as the English short *a* in *bat*) are the last to be acquired, even though they may be frequent in the child's native language.

Owens (1994) notes that vowels are acquired by the age of 3, whereas consonant clusters and blends are not acquired until age 7 or 8. However, there are individual differences, and the age of acquisition for some sounds may vary by as much as three years.

Phonological Deficits   Problems in phonology frequently appear as articulation disorders, most commonly in the child who is developmentally delayed in consonant acquisition. The child may omit a consonant (such as saying "oo" for *you)*, substitute one consonant for another (such

as saying "wabbit" for *rabbit*), or distort a consonant. An example of a consonant distortion is the lateral emission of air in the production of /s/ in which the air escapes over the sides of the tongue (rather than the tip), resulting in a noticeably slushy quality to the sound.

In addition to problems in expression, problems in reception also can occur, such as discrimination difficulty. For example, the child may hear "Go get the nail" when the command was actually "Go get the mail." The child cannot tell the difference between /n/ and /m/, and thus does not respond correctly. Phoneme discrimination errors can occur in comprehension of consonants (/p/ for /b/ and /d/ for /t/) consonant blends (/pr/, /fr/, and /kr/ confused with /pl/, /fl/, and /kl/), and vowels (confusion of vowels produced with the tongue in a forward position such as in *pit, pet,* and *pat*) (Wiig & Semel, 1976).

Researchers recently have begun to examine the relationship between phonological disorders and academic reading performance. (Phonological awareness training, which is a prereading skill but has a strong language component, is discussed in Chapter 8.) Ackerman, Dykman, and Gardner (1990) note that students with reading disabilities tend to articulate sequences more slowly than do students without disabilities. Ackerman et al. claim that the slow-speaking student has greater difficulty sounding out and blending polysyllabic words and comprehending what is read. Moreover, Pehrsson and Denner (1988) add that many students with language disorders have organization problems, which may inhibit their ability to remember what they have read. Students with a limited phonological repertoire (i.e., unintelligible speech) who are experiencing difficulties in reading, spelling, and writing present concerns for the teacher regarding the priorities and content of appropriate intervention.

Form: Morphology

A *morpheme* is the smallest unit or segment of language that conveys meaning. Two different types of morphemes exist: roots and affixes. Root words are free morphemes that can stand alone (e.g., *car, teach,* and *tall*), whereas affixes are bound morphemes such as prefixes and suffixes that when attached to root words change the meaning of the word (e.g., *cars, teacher,* and *tallest*). *Derivational* suffixes change word class; for example, the verb *walk* becomes a noun, *walker,* with the addition of the suffix *er. Inflectional* suffixes change the meaning of a word; for example, the addition of the inflectional *s* to the word *boy* changes the meaning to "more than one boy."

A further distinction can be made between two broad classes of words in a language: content words and function words (Lahey, 1988). Similar to root words, content words convey meaning when they stand alone; they generally carry the meaning in sentences. Function words or connective words join phrases or sentences together (e.g., pronouns, articles, prepositions, and conjunctions). The meaning of connective words varies according to the context or words that they connect.

Morphological Deficits Students who are delayed in morphological development may not use appropriate inflectional endings in their speech. An elementary school student may not use the third-person *s* on verbs (e.g., "He walk"), may not use *s* on nouns or pronouns to show possession (e.g., "Mommy coat"), or may not use *er* on adjectives (e.g., "Her dog is small than mine"). Older elementary and middle school students who are delayed in morphology may lack more advanced morphemes of irregular past tense or irregular plurals (e.g., they may use such forms as *drived* for *drove* or *mans* for *men)*. Such students exhibit inconsistency regarding morphology usage (e.g., they vacillate in the use of *bringed, brang,* and *brought)*.

Students with morphological problems may not acquire and understand word formation rules at the same rate and complexity as their peers with normal language development. Disorders in form or morphology also include difficulties learning the language code and linking it to what already is known about the environment. Wiig and Semel (1984, p. 303) list the following areas in which specific morphological deficits can be found in many students with language problems:

1. The formation of noun plurals, especially the irregular forms (-s, -z, -ez, vowel changes, -ren, etc.)
2. The formation of noun possessives, both singular and plural (-'s, -s')
3. The formation of third person singular of the present tense of verbs (-s)
4. The formation of the past tense of both regular and irregular verbs (-t, -d, -ed, vowel change)
5. The formation of the comparative and superlative forms of adjectives (-er, -est)
6. The cross-categorical use of inflectional endings (-s, -'s, -s')
7. Noun derivation (-er)
8. Adverb derivation (-ly)
9. The comprehension and use of prefixes (pre-, post-, pro-, anti-, di-, de-)

Some differences in inflectional endings are observed in students who speak Black English (Baratz, 1969; Bartel, Grill, & Bryen, 1973). The teacher should be aware that some inflectional endings reflect a student's cultural difference rather than a developmental delay. Examples of inflectional differences in Black English include "John cousin" instead of "John's cousin," "fifty cent" instead of "fifty cents," and "She work here" instead of "She works here."

Form: Syntax

Syntax is a system of rules governing how words or morphemes are combined to make grammatically correct sentences. Rules of syntax specify word order, sentence organization, relationships between words and word classes or types, and other sentence constituents (Owens, 1994). Moreover, syntax specifies which word combinations are acceptable or grammatical and which word classes may appear in noun and verb phrases (e.g., adverbs modify verbs). Thus, syntax frequently is referred to as *grammar.*

Rules of grammar emerge between 18 and 24 months of age, as evidenced in a child's production of two-word sentences. The child does not change abruptly from single words to grammatical two-word sentences. There is a transition period in which a distinction can be made between two-word utterances and two words in grammatical form. Braine (1976) claims that in this transition period the child often is groping for a pattern that later is replaced by a correct grammatical form.

Wood (1976) outlines six stages in the acquisition of syntax. Stages 1 and 2 are described better with semantic rules of grammar, whereas the last four stages describe syntactic structure. Stage 3 typically begins when the child is 2 to 3 years old. At this age, the child's sentences contain a subject and a predicate. For example, in Stage 2, the child says, "No play," but in Stage 3 says, "I won't play." Stage 4 begins around 2$\frac{1}{2}$ years of age and continues to about 4 years of age. In this stage the child begins to perform operations on sentences, such as adding an element to basic sentences through the process of *conjunction.* For example, "where" can be added to the simple sentence "Daddy go" to form "Where Daddy go?" The child also can *embed* (i.e., place words within the basic sentence). For example, the sentence "No glass break" becomes "The glass didn't break." In Stage 4 the word order is changed to ask a question. For example, the question, "Man is here?" is changed to "Is the man here?" During this stage, sentences remain simple. Between 2 and 3 years of age, the child does not combine simple sentences but says them next to each other (e.g., "John bounced the ball; John hit the lamp"). Between 3 and 4 years of age the child combines simple sentences with the conjunction *and* (e.g., "John bounced the ball and hit the lamp").

Stage 5 usually begins between 3½ and 7 years of age. In this stage the child uses complete sentences that have word classes typical of adult language: nouns, pronouns, adverbs, and adjectives. The child also becomes aware of differences within the same grammatical class. This awareness is evident in the child's use of different determiners and verbs with singular and plural nouns. For example, *this* is inappropriate for use in the sentence, "This chairs are heavy." The proper determiner (singular or plural) and appropriate verb for expressing plurality must be used. This same principle applies to prepositional phrases. For example, the sentence, "We cried to the movie" is not grammatically correct because an inappropriate prepositional phrase is used. In essence, in this stage the child learns the appropriate semantic functions of words and assigns these words to the appropriate grammatical classes.

Wood's Stage 6 begins when the child is about 5 years of age and extends until 10 years of age. The child begins using complex sentence structures and learns to understand and produce sentences that imply a command ("Give me the toy"), a request ("Please pass the salt"), and a promise ("I promise to stop"). Implied commands are the easiest to acquire but often are confused with requests. The promise is difficult for children to understand, and this type of verb may not be mastered until age 10 (Wood, 1976).

Syntactic Deficits   Children who have delay in syntax use sentences that lack the length or syntactic complexity expected for their age. For example, a 6-year-old child who uses a mean sentence length of three words may say, "Where Daddy go?" instead of "Where did Daddy go?" Additional deficits in the processing of syntax include problems in comprehending sentences (such as questions or sentences that express relationship between direct and indirect objects), negation, mood (such as inferences of obligations signified by auxiliary verbs *must, have to,* and *ought*), and passive sentences (Wiig & Semel, 1976, 1984).

Students with language problems may have difficulty processing syntactic structures of increased complexity such as embedded sentences, *wh* questions, interrogatives, and negative sentences. Wiig and Semel (1984) include deficits in memory and recall, difficulties using strategies to enhance memory, and decreased selective attention as being related to deficits remembering spoken messages. Students with language problems also may tend to rely on basic sentence structures and exhibit little creativity and use of novel or interesting sentences (Simon, 1985).

Content: Semantics

Semantics refers to language meaning and is concerned with the meaning of individual words as well as the meaning produced by combinations of words. For example, the word *cup* means "a container from which to drink" and refers to an object in the child's world. An example of meaning attached to combinations of words is the phrase "Daddy's cup." These words add the meaning of possessiveness in relationship to one another (i.e., the cup belongs to Daddy). Receptive semantics refers to understanding language, whereas expressive semantics refers to producing meaningful discourse.

According to Lahey (1988), language content (semantics) has three categories. One category involves general objects (e.g., cars, ball, Mommy, and juice). The second category involves general actions (e.g., throwing, hitting, and kicking). The third category involves relations between objects (e.g., Michael and his computer, me and my puppy, and Debbie and her car) and relations between events (such as the causal relation between going swimming and getting wet). The difference between language topic and language content is reflected in the particular message called the *topic* (e.g., a Power Ranger) and the more general categorization of the message called the *content* (e.g., toys). Consequently, because youngsters from different cultures talk about different topics, they do not have the same vocabulary even though their content is often the same.

Wood (1976) outlines several stages of semantic acquisition. In Stage 1, a child develops meanings as he or she acquires first words. Wood refers to these first words as one-word sentences. The meanings of these sentences are determined by the context in which they are spoken. An 18-month-old child may use the word *doggie* quite frequently, but the context in which the child says the word may differ and imply different meanings (e.g., "There is a doggie," "That is my doggie," "Doggie is barking," or "Doggie is chasing a kitty").

At about 2 years of age, the child begins to produce two-word utterances with meanings related to concrete actions (such as "Doggie bark" or "My doggie"). In Stage 2, the child conveys more specific information verbally and continues to expand vocabulary and utterance length. However, until about the age of 7, the child defines words merely in terms of visible actions. To a 6-year-old child, a fish is "a thing that swims in a lake" and a plate is "a thing you can eat dinner on." Also, during this stage, the child typically responds to a prompt word (such as *pretty*) with a word that could follow it in a sentence (such as *flower*). Older children, around 8 years of age, frequently respond with a verbal opposite (such as *ugly*) (Brown & Berko, 1960).

In Stage 3, at 8 years of age, the child's word meanings relate directly to experiences, operations, and processes. If a child's neighbor owns a horse, the child may include this attribute in the word meaning of *horse* in addition to the attributes of "animal," "four-legged," and "a thing that can be ridden." When asked where horses live, the child may respond, "At the Kahns'." By an adult definition, this answer is not correct. The child's vocabulary is defined by the child's experiences, not those of adults. At 12 years of age, the child begins to give dictionarylike definitions for words (Wood, 1976). When asked to define *bear,* the child might respond, "a large, warm-blooded animal that hibernates in the winter." At this time the child's word definitions approach the semantic level of adults.

Semantic Deficits   Developmental delay in word meaning (semantics) is observed in youngsters who use or understand a limited number of words. The limited vocabulary may be in specific areas, such as adjectives, adverbs, prepositions, or pronouns. Students may have a longer response time when selecting vocabulary words or have difficulty retrieving or recalling a specific word (dysnomia). The student with retrieval difficulties often attempts to participate in classroom discussions but has no apparent response when called on to answer. Vocabulary difficulties may be evident in an inability to use specific words when describing objects or events (e.g., "that thing over there" or "the thing you use to write with").

Semantics delay also is evident when students assign a narrow set of attributes to each word so that each word has limited meaning. Students with semantic deficits often fail to perceive subtle changes in word meaning that follow from changes in context and may not perceive multiple meanings of frequently used words (Wiig & Secord, 1994). This leads to incomplete understanding and misinterpretations of what is heard or read. In addition, students may have figurative language problems and tend to interpret idioms, metaphors, and proverbs literally (Wiig & Semel, 1984). These problems have important classroom implications when considered with research findings by Lazar, Warr-Leeper, Nicholson, and Johnson (1989). Their study of math, reading, and language arts teachers in kindergarten through eighth grade revealed that 36 percent of all teacher utterances contained at least one multiple-meaning expression. Indirect requests (27 percent) occurred most frequently. Moreover, at least one idiom occurred in 12% of the utterances, and more idiomatic expressions were used as grade level increased. Thus, older students with language problems may become increasingly unable to follow teacher directions or understand classroom discourse. The following middle school classroom discussion exemplifies this problem. The teacher asked the students whether the expression "my father hit the roof" meant that the father literally hit the roof. One student, interpreting the nonverbal contextual cues, proudly responded, "No, it doesn't mean he literally hit the roof. It means he hit the roof with his broom or something long!"

Additional semantic difficulties experienced by students with language problems include understanding linguistic concepts (e.g., *before/after, if/then, many, some,* and *few*), perceiving logical relationships among words (e.g., comparative, possessive, spatial, and temporal), and comprehending verbal analogies (e.g., sandwich is to eat as milk is to drink) (Wiig & Semel, 1984). Moreover, students may misuse transition words (i.e., conjunctions such as *although* and *if* and phrases such as *in addition*) and avoid making complex sentences and signaling logical relationships among two arguments in sentences or sentence sequences (Wiig & Secord, 1994).

Use: Pragmatics

Bruner (1974/1975) defines *pragmatics* as the "directive function of speech through which speakers affect the behavior of others in trying to carry out their intention" (p. 283). In discussing this definition, McLean and Snyder-McLean (1978) distinguish two broad functions: controlling or influencing the listener's action ("Give me the doll") and influencing attitudes ("I think Jane would make a good class president"). These functions also are referred to as the *speaker's intent.* Bates (1976) notes that the study of meaning in language pragmatics involves how one's communicative intentions are mapped into linguistic forms. The rules then govern how language is used in social contexts to convey a variety of intentions such as requesting, asserting, and questioning. An individual's language use based on an understanding of how language works in social interactions also is referred to as *communicative competence.* Wilcox (1986) describes communicative competence as "the ability to convey effectively and efficiently an intended message to a receiver. . . . This requires not only knowledge of the conventional communicative code, but also knowledge pertaining to socially appropriate communicative behaviors" (p. 644).

One pragmatic function that occurs after 3 years of age is the indirect request or hint (Ervin-Tripp & Mitchell-Kernan, 1977; Leonard, Wilcox, Fulmer, & Davis, 1978). Prutting (1979) notes that these indirect requests frequently are used (e.g., "My mother always lets me have cookies before lunch"). Leonard et al. studied 4-, 5-, and 6-year-

old children's understanding of three types of indirect requests: affirmative construction ("Can you shut the door?"), responses with a negative element ("Can't you answer the phone?"), and affirmative construction with a negative intention ("Must you play the piano?"). The 4- and 5-year-old children understood the first two types of requests but not the third type. The 6-year-old children understood the third type of request but made mistakes. Leonard et al. interpret the mistakes to mean that understanding was not complete.

Bloom and Lahey (1978) state that the situation affects the form of the message within the pragmatics of language. The characteristics of the message that increase the likelihood that the message will be accepted as well as understood are referred to as *pragmatic presuppositions.* In adult speech these presuppositions appear as tendencies to be polite and indirect in requests. Children as young as 4 and 5 years of age show these pragmatic presuppositions when they talk politely as they make a request. Pragmatic presuppositions develop as the child matures and learns not to interrupt the speaker, talk at the wrong time, or speak too loudly for the situation.

Pragmatic Deficits Delay in pragmatics is evident when students do not use functions that are expected for their developmental age. For example, a student with a developmental age above 8 years who seriously answers "Yes" to the indirect request "Must you play the piano?" (instead of ceasing to play the piano) may be developmentally delayed in understanding indirect requests. Moreover, a student may have difficulty determining when the listener does not understand what he or she is saying and thus continue with the manner of presentation rather than adapt the speech to the listener's needs. Also, a student may enter conversations in a socially unacceptable fashion or fail to take turns when conversing. The student may either monopolize a conversation or expect the other speaker to do most of the talking with little feedback to indicate listening. Other examples of problems with language use include difficulty staying on a topic during conversation (topic maintenance), inappropriate facial expressions and body posture, immature speech, and difficulty interpreting verbal and nonverbal communication cues (Simon, 1985; Wiig & Semel,

1984). Finally, a student may have difficulty choosing the right linguistic content (i.e., gauging complexity according to the listener), using questioning strategies, and interacting well verbally in a group (Wiig & Semel, 1984). Difficulties with communicative competence are particularly frustrating because they can persist into adulthood and affect the student's academic, vocational, and social performance (Schumaker & Deshler, 1984).

☀ LANGUAGE DIFFICULTIES

Students with language problems display a wide variety of difficulties, although many of the deficits initially may be subtle. The teacher should be aware of the potential language difficulties so that students can be identified and receive appropriate services as early as possible. In spite of early intervention, many language problems are long term and require intervention that changes with the varying needs of the student. This section presents the language difficulties typically found in three age groups of students: preschool and kindergarten, elementary, and secondary. It is important to keep in mind that language is interactive and that many of these difficulties may not occur in isolation. Furthermore, because language difficulties generally do not disappear without intervention, the same deficits may span several age categories.

Preschool and Kindergarten Students

Young students with language problems are a diverse group, so it may be difficult to differentiate them from their normally developing peers. However, various researchers (Bernstein, 1993; Wiig & Semel, 1984) discuss the difficulties common to this age group. Readiness skills such as counting, naming colors, naming the days of the week, and using scissors often are delayed. The child may be unable to follow simple directions, follow the story line in a book or movie, or enjoy listening to stories. In addition, the period of normal acquisition for articulation and sound development may be delayed, so that the child exhibits immature-sounding speech. The mean length of utterances and vocabulary may be similar to that of a younger child. Word-finding difficulties and an inability to name common objects also may be noted. As a result, the child may exhibit sound substitutions such as "buzgetti" for "spaghetti." The child may produce fewer functionally appropriate and accurate responses, say phrases such as "you know" or "that thing over there," or describe rather than name objects. In addition, the child may be unable to make one-to-one correspondence between letters and sounds and have difficulty discriminating between sounds.

Furthermore, young children may have difficulty responding accurately to certain types of questions. Parnell, Amerman, and Harting (1986) note that questions regarding nonobservable persons, actions, or objects are the most difficult for young children. In an evaluation of nine *wh-* forms, *why, when,* and *what happened* were the most difficult.

Young children with language problems also may demonstrate significant deficits in symbolic, adaptive, and integrative play as compared with their linguistically matched peers. They frequently play by themselves or exhibit more nonplay and parallel play than do their peers (Roth & Clark, 1987). Behaviorally, children with language problems may have attention deficits, need additional time to understand information and formulate ideas for expression, and have a poor tolerance for frustration.

Elementary Students

A student with a language problem may exhibit a variety of difficulties in the first grade, such as a limited ability to identify sounds, difficulty analyzing and synthesizing sound sequences, and problems segmenting words into grammatical units. Temporal and spatial concepts, as well as abstract concepts such as *before-after, neither-nor, some, if/then,* and *few,* may pose particular difficulty (Snyder, 1986; Wiig & Semel, 1984). These concepts often are presented in sentences of increased length and complexity that are particularly problematic for students with subtle processing problems. The student may be seen as obstinate or noncompliant, when actually the directions are misunderstood.

In the early elementary grades, the use of manipulatives begins to decrease, and the student must gain information from the teacher's verbal presentation. As the language complexity increases with each grade advance, the student must keep up with the demands of the instructional language as well as absorb the curriculum content. By fourth grade, most of the curriculum content is presented in print, and the student with language problems may have particular difficulty making the transition from narrative to expository writing (Wallach, 1989).

Word finding (retrieval) difficulties still may exist, but the deficits may not be as evident because the student begins to use strategies involving circumlocution (i.e., talking around the word), fillers, and descriptors (Bos & Vaughn, 1998). German (1984) adds the manifestation of secondary characteristics such as tapping and saying "I know it." She claims that students with retrieval problems generally have difficulty with three indices: response time, error index or word selection process, and substitution types. Students generally do not perform similarly across the three areas, and situations often occur in which the student's speed is affected although the correct word eventually is recalled.

Problems stemming from the relationship between phonological disorders and reading achievement begin to emerge in elementary school. Students with reading problems often articulate sequences more slowly than do their peers who do not have reading difficulties. As a result, the slow-speaking student tends to have greater difficulty sounding out and blending polysyllabic words and comprehending what is read (Ackerman et al., 1990). Requirements for comprehension also change because multiple-meaning words emerge and students are required to draw conclusions and make inferences. Deficits in text comprehension lead to problems in reading independence and mastery of content material. Thus, students with language problems may have difficulties participating in group discussions, sharing ideas on a topic, and developing ideas that follow earlier learning (Bashir, 1989).

Students in elementary school also may be deficient in expressive or oral language. In a study that examined children's discourse or ability to tell a story, Merritt and Liles (1987) found that the stories told by students with language problems contained fewer story episodes and fewer main and subordinate clauses than the stories told by their peers without language problems. In addition, the students with language problems had significant difficulty integrating critical parts of a story, and these difficulties continued after maturity and intervention. Merritt and Liles conclude that stu-

dents with language problems may have difficulty forming verbal abstractions and performing the logical operations needed to interpret and understand complex concepts. The students also had difficulty formulating and expressing spoken language; such problems often are reflected in academic difficulties.

Finally, elementary students with language problems continue to exhibit difficulties in their use of language. In academic settings, this often is reflected in the student's social skills. Such students may exhibit some of the same behaviors as they did when they were younger, such as failing to adjust to their listener's needs and having difficulty joining an ongoing conversation. In addition, they may misinterpret social cues, fail to think of others' thoughts and feelings, and be unable to predict the consequences of their behavior. Also, students at this level may be able to formulate a question but have difficulty functionally using requests to obtain new information (Schwabe, Olswang, & Kriegsmann, 1986).

Secondary Students

Adolescents who have language problems exhibit a variety of difficulties that tend to become more subtle. They tend to be passive learners and often appear to lack the metacognitive strategies necessary to perform complex academic tasks. At the secondary level, the teacher is faced with the challenge of designing interventions to assist students in overcoming or compensating for their language disabilities so that they can meet the increased demands of secondary school.

Many adolescents with language problems lack the ability to use and understand higher level syntax, semantics, and pragmatics in both production and processing (Ehren & Lenz, 1989). Secondary students are expected to organize their time and complete assignments and, thus, they must follow both oral and written instruction to complete work independently. However, receptive and expressive language difficulties affect their ability to learn effectively. This creates problems in gaining information from class lectures and textbooks, completing homework, following classroom rules, demonstrating command of knowledge through test taking, expressing thoughts in writing, passing minimum competency exams, and participating in classroom discussions (Schumaker & Deshler,

1984). Some adolescents learn strategies to compensate for their language difficulties, whereas others need additional services or support. As students mature, the teacher must be aware of the changing curriculum demands. For example, intervention may change from a content-oriented approach to a functional approach in which the student is taught strategies to deal with everyday situations.

Problems in comprehension of auditory language also are persistent in adolescents and result in short-term memory problems and a decrease in the understanding of linguistic relationships (Riedlinger-Ryan & Shewan, 1984). Frequently, adolescent students with language problems have difficulty organizing information and correctly associating or categorizing it for later retrieval. Thus, they often are unable to retain and synthesize complex information because they lack the ability to organize or categorize it. Poor organization and categorization result in other problems, such as poor note-taking, test-taking, and study skills, as well as difficulty integrating information (Schumaker, Deshler, Alley, Warner, & Denton, 1984).

Difficulties also may persist in language use in the awareness of social cues, interpretation of the motives and emotions of others, and use of appropriate language. Because adolescents frequently are aware of their difficulties, behaviors such as aggression, frustration, lack of motivation, withdrawal, and inattention may arise (Hazel & Schumaker, 1988; Seidenberg, 1988; Wiig & Semel, 1984).

☀ BILINGUAL AND CULTURALLY DIVERSE STUDENTS

Bilingual students know and use more than one language. Many bilingual students speak Spanish as their first language and acquire English as a second language. A student who displays inadequate skills in understanding and speaking English has limited English proficiency. Unfortunately, some students with limited English proficiency are misdiagnosed as having learning or language impairments because of their poor academic performance or difficulty on standardized tests (Cardoza & Rueda, 1986; Mercer, 1983). As the bilingual population in the United States increases, the teacher must distinguish between students who are unfamiliar with the language and culture and

students with a true language problem. Bilingual students with language problems may need services somewhat different from those for students whose primary language is standard English. Salend and Fradd (1986) note that bilingual students have the following needs:

- Access to teachers who are proficient in English as well as in the student's native language.
- Use of nonbiased assessment and instruction to formulate appropriate individualized educational programs.
- Exposure to curriculum and alternative instructional strategies that promote the academic and social relevance of instruction.

Several factors should be considered when assessing bilingual students. To determine whether the student has limited English proficiency or a language problem, assessment should be conducted in the student's primary language to examine writing, reading, listening, and speaking skills. Language assessments should include both quantitative measures (i.e., formal tests) and qualitative measures (e.g., observations, adapted test instruction, and a language sample). It also helps to interview significant people in the student's life with the same cultural background to determine how effectively the student communicates in the primary language. Interviews can yield important information regarding the language spoken at home, attitudes toward the two languages and cultures, the parents' educational level, and a profile of the community where the student lives (Kayser, 1989).

Gersten and Woodward (1994) discuss two major instructional approaches advocated for bilingual students. In programs with a native-language emphasis, the student receives academic instruction in the primary language, whereas in sheltered English or structured immersion programs, English is used for the majority of the teaching day. Most studies indicate little or no difference in achievement between students taught with these two bilingual approaches. In both approaches, second-language instruction should be relevant rather than only a series of drills on grammar and usage. Gersten and Woodward note that many second-language programs have moved toward the increased use of natural language to promote comprehension and use of English.

Another group of culturally diverse students speaks nonstandard English by using dialects related to geographic regions or race and ethnicity. Dialectical differences may be evident in the student's pronunciation of speech sounds or in variations in morphology and syntax. For example, in Black English the use of the verb *to be* (as in "he be running") is different from standard English. As with bilingual students, language assessment of culturally diverse students should include the collection of spontaneous speech samples in naturalistic settings or interviews with other students who speak the dialect. Thus, the student's cultural background is considered and he or she is compared with others in the same language community to determine the existence of a language problem.

Students who exhibit normal production of their own primary language or dialect should not be identified as having a language problem. These students simply are producing an acceptable language variation. However, many students with limited English proficiency or dialectical differences are identified as having a language problem such as a phonological deficiency. For example, a Spanish-speaking youngster may say "cheap" for "chip," and a youngster learning Black English may say "birfday" instead of "birthday." Owens (1991) presents the major variations between standard American English and Black English, Hispanic English, and Asian English in phonology, syntax and morphology, and pragmatics and nonlinguistic features. Adler (1988) raises the following questions regarding these students: Should only standard English be taught to these students? If the dialect is rule-governed and nonstandard, rather than substandard, should the student be taught to speak "correctly" if the dialect is consistent with what is spoken in the community in which the student lives? Finally, should only English be taught to young non-standard-speaking students, or should they be allowed to retain the social dialect of their cultural peers and parents? Alder notes that the current belief appears to support teaching the use of language that is relevant to school talk (standard English) as well as everyday talk (nonstandard English). This is difficult to accomplish, however, because it requires a change in the current system and collaborative interaction between families and teachers in language arts and English. Although changes in the service delivery to bilingual and culturally diverse students are beginning to emerge, the teacher must assume the responsibility of providing quality assessment and intervention to these students to assist in the prevention of instructional problems related to a lack of English proficiency.

ASSESSMENT OF LANGUAGE SKILLS

The heterogeneity of students with language impairments and language problems makes the assessment task especially difficult, because no two students exhibit the same strengths and weaknesses. The speech and language evaluator must know not only what areas to assess but also how to interpret the findings and help make the necessary adjustments in the student's curriculum. Although most classroom teachers never conduct an in-depth assessment of a student's language skills, they should understand the implications of a language evaluation because language pervades the curriculum. In the past, speech and language assessments were viewed as separate from the curriculum and the sole responsibility of the speech and language pathologist. However, this trend is changing, with emphasis being placed on the teacher and the speech and language specialist *sharing* the responsibility for diagnosing problems and designing intervention programs to improve a student's receptive and expressive language skills (Nelson, 1989). After becoming familiar with the basic principles of language development, the teacher undoubtedly will identify numerous youngsters who exhibit language problems in the classroom and would benefit from systematic assessment and instruction in the use of spoken language.

Language assessment should be viewed not as a single isolated event but rather as an ongoing process throughout a student's education. The five major reasons for language assessment are as follows:

1. To identify students with potential language problems
2. To determine a student's language developmental level
3. To plan educational objectives and design appropriate intervention programs

4. To monitor the student's progress
5. To evaluate the language intervention program

The last three of these assessment functions are most relevant to daily instructional planning. The first of these three functions is *planning objectives.* The assessment information describes the student's language. This description is used in planning objectives that relate directly to the problem. The assessment of a morphological disorder, for example, should be specific: "The student does not use *s* on regular nouns to indicate plurality." The teacher then can plan the objective: "The student will use plural *s* on regular nouns with 90 percent accuracy when naming pictures of plural regular nouns." *Monitoring the student's progress* involves the teacher determining daily or weekly whether the student is reaching short-term instructional objectives. The sample objective of 90 percent accuracy of plural *s* when naming pictures of plural regular nouns requires an assessment procedure of counting responses. Finally, in *program evaluation,* the teacher assesses the student's progress with the materials and techniques used in the program. This information allows the teacher to determine whether she or he needs to change materials or techniques to achieve the educational objective.

Thus, language assessments of school-age youngsters should be educationally relevant and provide both diagnostic information and intervention strategies. To accomplish this goal, two levels of information should be included in the assessment: the content-oriented level and the process-oriented level. The content-oriented level examines the actual content the student has learned and identifies specific areas that require intervention (e.g., a syntactic deficit in the use of present progressive tense). The process-oriented level examines how skills are learned or acquired (e.g., the use of a strategy such as clustering digits to remember a phone number).

Language development assessment is an evaluation of the student's receptive and expressive language skills. The components assessed include phonology, morphology, syntax, semantics, and pragmatics. The teacher can assess all of these components or decide to assess only one or two specific components. An experienced examiner obtains information or observes the student before deciding what to assess. The information gathered can include various observations (e.g., the student is difficult to understand, the student has difficulty understanding what others say, the student uses short sentences, the student uses few words, or the student cannot start and maintain a discussion topic).

The student who is difficult for others to understand, but who understands what others say and uses many words and long sentences, may have problems in phonology. Thus, assessment should begin in this area. The student who uses only a few words needs to be assessed in semantics, and the student who uses short sentences needs assessment in semantic relationships and syntax.

Language assessment includes the use of formal and informal assessment procedures. Quantitative (formal) measures are used when the examiner needs to determine the student's developmental level and obtain a standardized score or classify the student. These measures include observable behaviors and result in a numerical score or an assigned classification. If the examiner wants to determine specific teaching objectives, informal measures are used. Qualitative or naturalistic measures are based on the assumption that behaviors vary across different settings, and their purpose is to determine the relevant behaviors or skills evident in the setting being examined. Assessment of both language developmental level and teaching objectives should include both types of tests. School speech and language specialists are experienced in administering and interpreting formal and informal measures of language. The teacher who is unfamiliar with these tests should consider working with the school speech and language specialist in assessing language.

Formal Language Assessment

In a formal language assessment, standardized instruments are used to compare a student's performance with pre-established criteria to determine the existence of a speech or language problem. On these instruments, a student's raw score is converted to a standardized score, language age or mental age, age equivalent, or, occasionally, a grade equivalent. Students whose scores are much lower than the scores of other students their age usually are referred for additional testing or are placed in speech and language therapy.

Some language tests provide a comprehensive measure of all language functioning. This type of test assesses receptive and expressive language in many components. For example, the *Clinical Evaluation of Language Fundamentals—3* (Semel, Wiig, & Secord, 1995) assesses morphology, syntax, and semantics. Other tests are designed to measure specific components of language. For example, the *Test of Children's Language* (Barenbaum & Newcomer, 1996) assesses receptive and expressive skills in syntax and semantics. Some tests are more specific and measure only receptive or expressive skills in one component. For example, the *Peabody Picture Vocabulary Test—Third Edition* (Dunn & Dunn, 1997) assesses receptive semantic skills.

Screening Tests   In many school districts, students are given a speech-and-language screening test when they enter preschool or kindergarten. The screening provides a general overview of a student's performance in a particular area, which can be compared with the performance of a student of the same age or grade who is developing normally. Many school districts use standardized or formal screening instruments, whereas other districts devise informal assessment instruments to identify preschool and kindergarten students who

may have potential language problems. Table 6.2 presents two formal language screening tests that assess receptive and expressive language in various components. Students who score below an acceptable level on a screening test usually are referred for a comprehensive evaluation.

One advantage of a screening is that it requires little administration time and, thus, allows a large number of students to be evaluated. When all students are screened at the beginning of their formal education, speed is an obvious concern because so many students must be evaluated. However, because of factors such as social and emotional development, participation in a preschool program, family environment, and cultural influences, only a few language skills should be expected to have been mastered by all 4- or 5-year-old children. Thus, a disadvantage to screening young children is that the screening often cannot detect subtle language problems. To illustrate, a youngster may receive high scores (80 to 90 percentiles) in both processing and production on a language screening test administered at the beginning of first grade. However, because subtle language problems were not detected at the initial screening and intervention was not made available, the student may experience academic difficulties later when faced with a more abstract and demanding fourth-grade

TABLE 6.2
Selected language screening measures

Test	Component Measured	Receptive/ Expressive	Age Norms
Adolescent Language Screening Test (Morgan & Guilford, 1984)	Phonology, morphology syntax, semantics, pragmatics	R, E	11–17 years
The dimensions of language use, content, and form are screened by seven subtests: Pragmatics, Receptive Vocabulary, Concepts, Expressive Vocabulary, Sentence Formulation, Morphology, and Phonology. Administration time is less than 15 minutes.			
Clinical Evaluation of Language Fundamentals— 3: Screening Test (Semel, Wiig, & Secord, 1996)	Phonology, morphology syntax, semantics	R, E	6–21 years
The screening test identifies the need for an in-depth diagnosis of language. The test includes parallel items from CELF—3, and the content reflects real-life situations. It screens receptive and expressive language skills in phonology, morphology, syntax, and semantics in about 10 to 15 minutes.			

curriculum. Thus, ideally, several speech and language screenings should be administered (e.g., kindergarten, third grade, sixth grade, and ninth grade); however, time constraints on public school clinicians force them to give a screening test only one time. Consequently, many students with language problems are not identified at an early age.

Diagnostic Tests   Diagnostic tests measure one or more specific language components including receptive or expressive language. As presented in Table 6.3, comprehensive tests measure a wide range of language skills, whereas other diagnostic tests assess specific speech and language components. In a comprehensive diagnostic evaluation, it generally is advisable to administer a test that provides an overall view of the student's understanding and use of language. The specific test often is determined by the student's age or level of functioning. If the examiner notices that the student has difficulty formulating words and sentences, an additional test should be administered to measure the student's ability to understand and use words (e.g., the *Test of Word Knowledge*) or apply syntactic skills (e.g., the *Carrow Elicited Language Inventory*). If the student's speech intelligibility is reduced, the examiner may administer a test of phonology to obtain additional information (e.g., the *Goldman-Fristoe Test of Articulation*). The assessment provides an overall view of the student's language skills as well as additional information concerning reported or observed areas of concern.

Although standardized language tests do not provide information regarding academic or therapeutic interventions, they do target the student's specific strengths and weaknesses. The examiner's role is to interpret the assessment information and transform it to academically relevant instructional skills and interventions.

Informal Language Assessment

Informal assessment procedures generally are combined with standardized tests to provide descriptive information regarding a student's language ability. Although standardized measures are used widely, the emphasis on including some type of informal assessment is consistent with the theoretically based descriptive approach that is critical of viewing language as a series of independent objectives. Although standardized instruments determine the need for services, they often are too narrow to assess a student's baseline performance or the communicative skills needed for academic achievement in the classroom (Hughes, 1989). Many formal tests use a small number of items to assess a particular skill, and using a small sample can lead to incorrect conclusions about the student's skill level. Thus, informal assessment often is used to affirm or refute the results of formal measures. Also, many formal measures do not give enough specific information to plan educational objectives. Therefore, informal language measures often are used to determine specific instructional objectives. Another common use of informal measures is to monitor a student's daily or weekly progress. Unlike formal measures, which are designed to assess a student over a long period of time, informal measures lend themselves to daily or weekly assessment.

The teacher may wish to interview the student's parents to obtain a case history as a form of informal assessment. This technique gives the teacher insights into the history of the student's language development. In addition, it provides information regarding the student's communicative functioning in environments other than the school setting and can result in suggestions for appropriate assessment and intervention techniques. Larson and McKinley (1995) provide general and supplemental case history forms as well as a learning style questionnaire designed for preadolescent or adolescent students.

The current emphasis in language assessment stresses the informal evaluation of a student's language within the context in which it occurs. The goal of informal language assessment is to provide insight into how the student uses communication from a functional viewpoint in a variety of settings. Specific areas to examine include the intention or purpose of language, the social communicative context, and the physical setting. Various informal techniques that include the use of spontaneous, imitative, or elicited language can be used, depending on the type of information desired.

Informal Tests of Phonology   Phonology can be assessed informally by analyzing the student's production of phonemes in single words. The examiner makes a list of all the consonant

TABLE 6.3
Selected diagnostic language measures

Test	Component Measured	Receptive/ Expressive	Age Norms
Comprehensive Measures			
Bankson Language Test—2 (Bankson, 1990)	Morphology, syntax, semantics, pragmatics	R, E	3–6 years

This instrument is organized into three general categories. Semantic knowledge includes body parts, verbs, nouns, functions, prepositions, and opposites and categories. Morphological and syntactic rules include pronouns, verb usage and tense, plurals, comparatives and superlatives, questions, and negation. Pragmatics includes controlling, ritualizing, informing, and imagining. A 20-item short form also is available to screen children for language problems.

Test	Component Measured	Receptive/ Expressive	Age Norms
Clinical Evaluation of Language Fundamentals— 3 (Semel, Wiig, & Secord, 1995)	Morphology, syntax, semantics	R, E	6–21 years

This individually administered test consists of five receptive subtests (*Sentence Structure, Concepts and Directions, Semantic Relationships, Word Classes,* and *Listening to Paragraphs*), five expressive subtests (*Word Structure, Formulated Sentences, Sentence Assembly, Recalling Sentences,* and *Word Associations*), and one optional subtest *(Rapid, Automatic Naming).* Each subtest yields standard scores and percentile ranks, and the test also yields receptive, expressive, and total language scores. Dialectical and regional variations that may be present in a student's word and sentence structure are not counted as errors if they are a natural part of the student's language system.

Test	Component Measured	Receptive/ Expressive	Age Norms
Oral and Written Language Scales: Listening Comprehension and Oral Expression (Carrow- Woolfolk, 1995)	Syntax, semantics, pragmatics	R, E	3–21 years

Neither scale on this individually administered test requires reading by the student. On the *Listening Comprehension* scale, a verbal stimulus is read aloud by the examiner, and the student responds by pointing to one of four pictures. On the *Oral Expression* scale, the student is shown a picture while a verbal stimulus is read aloud by the examiner, and the student responds orally by answering a question, completing a sentence, or generating one or more sentences. The test yields standard scores, percentile ranks, and age equivalents.

Test	Component Measured	Receptive/ Expressive	Age Norms
Test of Adolescent and Adult Language—3 (Hammill, Brown, Larsen, & Wiederholt, 1994)	Syntax, semantics	R, E	12–24 years

The test includes eight subtests designed to assess receptive and expressive aspects of spoken and written vocabulary and grammar. The composites yield scores in ten areas: listening, speaking, reading, writing, spoken language, written language, vocabulary, grammar, receptive language, and expressive language. Administration time is one to three hours, and a software scoring system is available.

Test	Component Measured	Receptive/ Expressive	Age Norms
Test of Language Development—Primary: 3 (Newcomer & Hammill, (1997)	Phonology, syntax, semantics	R, E	4–8 years

(continued on next page)

TABLE 6.3
(continued)

Test	Component Measured	Receptive/ Expressive	Age Norms
Test of Language Development—Intermediate: 3 (Hammill & Newcomer, 1997)	Syntax, semantics	R, E	8–12 years

The *TOLD–Primary: 3* has nine subtests: *Picture Vocabulary, Relational Vocabulary,* and *Oral Vocabulary* assess the understanding and meaningful use of spoken words; *Grammatic Understanding, Sentence Imitation,* and *Grammatic Completion* assess differing aspects of grammar; *Word Articulation, Phonemic Analysis,* and *Word Discrimination* measure the abilities to say words correctly and to distinguish between words that sound similar. The *TOLD–Intermediate: 3* contains six subtests: *Sentence Combining, Word Ordering,* and *Grammatic Comprehension* assess different aspects of grammar; *Picture Vocabulary, Generals,* and *Malapropisms* measure the understanding and use of word relationships, the knowledge of abstract relationships, and correcting ridiculous sentences.

Measures of Specific Components

Test	Component Measured	Receptive/ Expressive	Age Norms
Auditory Discrimination Test (Wepman, 1973)	Phonology	R	4–8 years

Forty word pairs are presented to the student for discrimination. Ten of the word pairs are identical, and the others have one differing phoneme in either the beginning, middle, or ending position. The student tells the examiner whether the word pairs sound the same or different.

Test	Component Measured	Receptive/ Expressive	Age Norms
Boehm Test of Basic Concepts— Revised (Boehm, 1986)	Semantics	R	5–7 years

Fifty pictorial items, in multiple-choice form, are arranged in approximate order of increasing difficulty and divided into two booklets. The test is read by the teacher, and students mark their answers in the test booklets. The test measures understanding of basic concepts relating to space, quantity, and time, and it can be administered individually or to small groups in about 30 minutes. A Spanish edition also is available.

Test	Component Measured	Receptive/ Expressive	Age Norms
Carrow Elicited Language Inventory (Carrow-Woolfolk, 1974)	Syntax	E	3–7 years

This norm-referenced test diagnoses expressive language deficits by having the student imitate exactly what is heard after listening to the examiner read a sentence. The stimuli range in length from two to ten words, with an average length of six words. There are 52 oral stimuli including 51 sentences and 1 phrase. Administration time is about 25 minutes.

Test	Component Measured	Receptive/ Expressive	Age Norms
Comprehensive Receptive and Expressive Vocabulary Test (Wallace & Hammill, 1994)	Semantics	R, E	4–17 years

The *Expressive Vocabulary* subtest includes 25 items that encourage and require the student to converse in detail about a particular stimulus word. The *Receptive Vocabulary* subtest consists of 61 items in which the student must point to the picture of the stimulus word said by the examiner. The subtest includes ten plates with six pictures on each plate, and the words associated with each plate relate to a particular common theme and are spaced evenly across all grade levels. Two forms are available, and the test can be individually administered in 20 to 30 minutes. Also, there is an adult level and a computerized format.

TABLE 6.3
(continued)

Test	Component Measured	Receptive/ Expressive	Age Norms
Goldman-Fristoe Test of Articulation (Goldman & Fristoe, 1986)	Phonology	E	2–16+ years

The first subtest, *Sounds in Words,* consists of 35 pictures that elicit the student's articulation of the major speech sounds in the initial, medial, and final positions. The second subtest, *Sounds in Sentences,* contains two narrative stories that are read by the examiner and illustrated by action pictures. The student is asked to retell each story. The third subtest, *Stimulability,* determines whether misarticulated phonemes are articulated correctly when the student is given maximum stimulation. The student is asked to watch and listen carefully while the sound is pronounced in a syllable, used in a word, and used in a sentence.

Test	Component Measured	Receptive/ Expressive	Age Norms
Peabody Picture Vocabulary Test—Third Edition (Dunn & Dunn, 1997)	Semantics	R	2–40 years

Stimulus pictures are presented to the student, who points to the picture (from among four choices) that best represents the corresponding stimulus word spoken by the examiner. There are two forms of 204 items each; the items are arranged in increasing order of difficulty.

Test	Component Measured	Receptive/ Expressive	Age Norms
Test for Auditory Comprehension of Language—3 (Carrow-Woolfolk, 1999)	Morphology, syntax, semantics	R	3–9 years

The test is individually administered and measures auditory comprehension of word classes and relations, grammatical morphemes, and elaborated phrase and sentence constructions. There are 142 test items in which the student looks at a set of three pictures and points to the one that best represents the meaning of the word, phrase, or sentence spoken by the examiner. No oral responses are required, and administration time is about 25 minutes. A computer program is available for scoring and data storage.

Test	Component Measured	Receptive/ Expressive	Age Norms
Test of Children's Language (Barenbaum & Newcomer, 1996)	Syntax, semantics	R, E	5–8 years

The test helps in identifying children's strengths and weaknesses in language components and in recognizing youngsters who are at risk for failure in reading and writing. Unit 1 of the test uses a storybook format to ensure children's ability in spoken language and reading. Specific skills include semantics, syntax, and listening comprehension, as well as knowledge about print, phonological awareness, and letter knowledge. Additional items assess word recognition and reading comprehension. Unit 2 includes a series of writing tasks divided into three parts: (1) copying, writing from dictation, spelling, and writing vocabulary words, (2) writing a story the student has read previously, and (3) writing an original story about the animal characters in the storybook. The test is designed for use with individuals and can be administered in about 30 to 40 minutes.

Test	Component Measured	Receptive/ Expressive	Age Norms
Test of Early Language Development—3 (Hresko, Reid, & Hammill, 1999)	Syntax, semantics	R, E	2–7 years

This individually administered test provides information directly related to the semantic (content) and syntactic (form) aspects of language. The items can be administered in about 20 minutes and assess receptive and expressive language using a variety of semantic and syntactic tasks.

(continued on next page)

TABLE 6.3
(continued)

Test	Component Measured	Receptive/ Expressive	Age Norms
Test of Pragmatic Language (Phelps-Terasaki & Phelps-Gunn, 1992)	Pragmatics	E	5–13 years

The test includes 44 items, each of which establishes a social context, to provide information within six components of pragmatic language: physical setting, audience, topic, purpose (speech acts), visual-gestural cues, and abstraction. After the examiner provides a verbal stimulus prompt and displays a picture, the student responds to the dilemma presented.

Test	Component Measured	Receptive/ Expressive	Age Norms
Test of Word Finding—2 (German, 2000)	Semantics	E	4–12 years
Test of Adolescent/Adult Word Finding (German, 1990)	Semantics	E	12–80 years

These two tests both contain naming sections in picture naming nouns, picture naming verbs, sentence completion naming, and picture naming categories. The adolescent test has an additional section in description naming. Each test also includes a comprehension section to determine whether errors are due to word-finding problems or poor word comprehension. The adolescent form also includes a brief test that provides a 10-minute assessment of word-finding abilities.

Test	Component Measured	Receptive/ Expressive	Age Norms
Test of Word Knowledge (Wiig & Secord, 1992)	Semantics	R, E	5–17 years

This test evaluates the student's ability to understand and use vocabulary words. Level 1, for students age 5 to 8, includes subtests in expressive vocabulary, word definitions, receptive vocabulary, word opposites, and synonyms (optional). Level 2, for students age 8 through 17, includes core subtests in word definitions, multiple contexts, synonyms, and figurative usage, as well as supplementary subtests in word opposites, receptive vocabulary, expressive vocabulary, and conjunctions and transition words. All stimuli are presented through visual and auditory modes to accommodate students with poor reading skills or auditory memory problems. The test yields standard scores, age equivalents, percentile ranks, and expressive and receptive language scores.

phonemes and collects pictures to depict words that contain each phoneme. There should be a picture to elicit a word with the consonant in the initial position and a picture to depict the consonant in the final position. For example, a picture of a pot will elicit initial /p/, and a picture of a map will elicit final /p/. The examiner shows the student each picture and says, "Tell me the name of each picture." A notation is made if the student says the word incorrectly, and the results are recorded on a checklist. This type of assessment requires careful, experienced listening for accurate results. Only the error sounds are recorded; for example, a /b/ sound is recorded to indicate the student said "bot" for *pot*. Also, comments

that describe the error are recorded; for example, a substitution of /b/ for /p/ is recorded as an error in voicing. The examiner lists all the phoneme errors and determines which phonemes should have been mastered at the student's developmental age. These phonemes can become targets for the student's educational objectives.

After analyzing the phoneme profile and selecting a target phoneme, the examiner should collect baseline data on the target phoneme in the student's spontaneous speech. The examiner also needs to monitor change in the student's speech after corrective instruction has begun. Informal assessment is the primary tool used to gather baseline data on the target phoneme and to monitor change in the student's speech.

Direct observation of the production of a phoneme can be used to obtain baseline data and to monitor the student's progress. The examiner engages the student in spontaneous speech with pictures or toys as stimuli to elicit speech from the student. Older students may respond to prompts such as "Tell me about your weekend." The examiner's talking should be kept to a minimum so that the student is allowed to talk. During a 3-minute sample, the examiner counts the student's correct and incorrect productions of the target phoneme. The target phoneme's frequency can be observed by charting the correct and incorrect responses (see Chapter 3 for a discussion on recording data). Accuracy is computed by dividing the number of correct target phonemes the student said by the total number of target phonemes said (correct and incorrect).

One aspect of receptive phonology that is assessed readily by informal measures is auditory discrimination. The examiner may want to verify whether the student has difficulty discriminating between two particular sounds that were confused on a formal measure. For example, the student may have confused /p/ with /b/, and the examiner may assess these sounds further with a criterion measure. The measure can consist of a list of consonant-vowel-consonant words in which only one phoneme is different (e.g., *pin—bin* or *cup—cub*). Two words are said in word pairs, and the student is asked whether the words are the same or different. The examiner records the results on a checklist and scores the responses for accuracy. Accuracy levels can be used to indicate whether the student needs help in learning to discriminate these sounds. Accuracy of 90 percent or above is a good indication that the student already can discriminate these sounds.

Informal Tests of Morphology   Informal measures of morphology can determine the mastery level of each morpheme in a hierarchy. The examiner can use Brown's (1973) rank ordering of morpheme acquisition to make sentences that assess each morpheme. Pictures are presented with the sentences to assess the use of each morpheme. If the objective is to assess use of the present progressive morpheme *ing,* the examiner may show a picture of girls playing and say, "The girls like to play. Here they are _____." The student says the missing word, "playing." When assessing the use of the morpheme *in,* the examiner may show a picture of a baby sleeping and ask, "Where is the baby? The baby is _____." The student says the missing words, "in bed."

The examiner records the results as correct or incorrect on a checklist. Analysis of the results helps the teacher determine which morphemes are mastered and which need to be taught. Also, assessing the morphemes in a hierarchical order indicates to the teacher which morpheme to teach first.

Another informal assessment of morphology is a measure of accuracy of a specific morpheme in a student's conversational speech. Mastery of a morpheme is indicated by 90 percent accuracy in a student's conversational speech (Brown, 1973). It would be time-consuming to obtain a daily or weekly conversational sample with enough occurrences of a specific morpheme to determine accuracy. An informal assessment that is less time-consuming is to have the student respond to the prompt, "Tell me about this picture." First the examiner shapes the response by showing the student a picture depicting a person jumping and asks, "What is the person doing?" If the student does not describe the action (by saying "jumping" or "jump"), the examiner can prompt the student: "Say *jumping.*" After the student gives two correct responses (description of action) to two different pictures and the question "What is the person doing?" the instruction can be changed to "Tell me about this picture." The examiner can show a series of 20 pictures, each of which elicits the present progressive *ing* form of a word. As each picture is presented, the examiner says, "Tell me about this picture." The examiner records the number of correct and incorrect responses on a checklist. The accuracy percentage is determined by dividing the correct responses by the total number of pictures. If the accuracy is 90 percent or above, the morpheme is mastered and does not need to be taught. Accuracy below 90 percent indicates that the morpheme is not mastered and may require teaching. The examiner should note whether mastery of the morpheme is expected at the student's developmental age.

An informal measure of receptive morphology is to have the student point to a picture that depicts a morpheme. The examiner says a sentence with a specific morpheme and asks the student to point to the correct picture. For example, to assess the irregular past tense of *eat,* the examiner can show a picture of a girl who has finished eating and a picture of a girl eating. The examiner says, "The girl ate." The student must point to the correct picture of the girl who has finished eating. Sequence picture cards (such as those published by SRA) can be used with this task. The examiner records the results on a checklist by marking each irregular past tense verb as correct or incorrect. The results are analyzed to determine which morphemes the student has mastered receptively. The examiner may recommend that the student master a morpheme receptively before he or she is taught to use that morpheme expressively.

Informal Tests of Syntax   Expressive syntax can be assessed informally by analyzing the student's spontaneous speech for use of grammatical forms. Spontaneous speech or language is a student's unrehearsed verbal expression that occurs naturally in real-life settings and situations. The examiner can obtain and record a spontaneous sample of the student's speech using the guidelines presented in the next section on informal tests of semantics. If the sample is used only for grammatical analysis, the guidelines can be modified so that a tape recorder is used without recording the context of each utterance. After recording, the examiner transcribes the sample and lists each utterance on a checklist, as shown in Figure 6.1. Each utterance is analyzed for the grammatical forms used, and a list is compiled of the grammatical forms that were not used. Each form is compared with norms for the student's developmental age. If the particular form is expected for the student's developmental age, a teaching objective can be planned to teach it.

An alternative informal assessment of syntax involves sentence repetition. The examiner says each sentence, and the student repeats it. In an imitation task that is long enough to tax the memory, the student frequently translates the adult sentence into the student's own language system and repeats the sentence using those rules (Salvia &

Ysseldyke, 1998). Thus, imitation tasks can elicit language forms that the student did not attempt in spontaneous speech. To increase the accuracy of the examiner's judgment, the evaluation session can be recorded on tape so that the student's responses can be checked. The examiner records the student's responses on a checklist and analyzes them for critical syntactic features. Omitted syntactic features should be included in the student's educational objectives.

Informal Tests of Semantics   Some tasks that assess semantics are complex (such as the areas of logical relationships, cause-and-effect relationships, and verbal problem solving), so informal procedures may be difficult to devise. However, for areas such as verbal opposites, categorization, and classification of words, informal testing is useful.

For the assessment of verbal opposites, SRA produces a set of cards that display pictures of 40 pairs of opposites. When paired correctly, the cards in each set illustrate two opposites (e.g., *near* and *far*). The examiner mixes the cards and asks the student to sort them into sets of opposites. The examiner observes as the student makes set combinations, and the results are recorded on a checklist. Analysis of the incorrect sets helps the teacher determine which opposites to include in teaching objectives for the student.

An informal assessment of word categorization involves having the student say words in the same category. The examiner says a word and asks the student to say as many words as possible in the same category. The words can fall into the category because of similar function or physical attribute. The examiner lists the words on a checklist as the student says them. The results are analyzed to determine whether the student can say several words in a category or whether the student says a word that is an opposite, says a rhyming word, or tends to repeat the stimulus word.

A word association task can be used to measure word classification. Young children tend to respond to a stimulus word with a word that precedes or follows the stimulus word according to the rules of syntax. This is called a *syntagmatic* response. For example, if the stimulus word is "apple," the young student may respond with "eat" or "red." Young-

FIGURE 6.1

Syntactic analysis of utterances

Utterances	present progressive *ing*	is	plural regular *s, es*	possessive *s*	I, me, mine, my you, yours	irregular past	he, him, his she, her, hers	am, are, was, were	not	can't, don't	and	but	because	reversal of copula (is it)	who, what	where
Student's Name Michael Jordan Date 3/15																
1. What this is?		X													X	
2. That all of it?																
3. This a wall.																
4. I gonna tell you.					X											
5. Yeah, but her not in today.							X		X			X				
6. Car go up and car go down.																
7. Car go sideways.																

sters shift to a response in the same grammatical category around the age of 6 to 8 years. This type of response is called *paradigmatic.* For example, if the stimulus word is "apple," the older student may respond with "orange," "banana," or another fruit. The examiner says the stimulus word, notes which kind of response the student makes, and records the response under that category (syntagmatic or paradigmatic) on a checklist. The checklist shows whether the student is categorized as a younger child with syntagmatic responses or as an older student with paradigmatic responses. The student may have responses in both categories but have most responses in one category.

Another area of semantics that can be assessed by informal measures is semantic relationships. This area can be assessed if the student's language utterances are three or fewer words. If a student uses more words, a syntactic analysis is more appropriate. Semantic relationships can be assessed informally by analyzing the student's spontaneous speech. The examiner observes the student playing or interacting with someone, codes or transcribes the conversation, and analyzes it according to error pattern. Various objects such as clay, toys, and games can be used to stimulate communication.

McLean and Snyder-McLean (1978) recommend the following steps for obtaining a speech or language sample:

1. Set up a partially structured play situation in which the student interacts with a familiar adult.

2. Use toys that the student is familiar with and that are likely to elicit a variety of responses.

3. Record the student's speech on videotape. Continue the sampling until 50 to 100 intelligible utterances are obtained. If videotape equipment is not available, record the sample on a tape recorder and have an observer record the context of each utterance.

4. Avoid talking excessively or structuring the student's verbal responses by asking questions such as "What is this?" or "What color is the doll's dress?"

5. Transcribe the tape as soon as possible.

6. List each utterance (i.e., any meaningful speech segment preceded and followed by a pause). Analyze each word in the utterance for semantic form and list each word under the appropriate category. Several two- and three-word utterances are analyzed in Figure 6.2. The two-word utterance "that ball" is listed under demonstrative

FIGURE 6.2

Format for semantic analysis of a language sample

Student's Name ___Lisa Walker___   Date Collected ___4/3___

Total Number of Utterances ___11___

Relationship Components	Demonstrative Nomination	Notice	Recurrence	Attribute Nonexistence	Descriptive	Possession	Conjunction
Two-word grammatical	That ball	Hi Mommy	More cookie	allgone cookie	Big ball pipe	Daddy	Milk cookie
Three+-word grammatical							
Nongrammatical one-word utterances							

Relationship Components	Action Agent	Action	Object	Location Agent	Action	Object	Location
Two-word grammatical							
Three+-word grammatical	Mommy	drink	milk	Daddy Mommy	sit put	car doll	here here bed
Nongrammatical one-word utterances							

because *that* plus a noun is used to point out an object or person. "More cookie" is listed under attribute because *more* modifies the noun, and "Daddy pipe" is listed under possession because it refers to Daddy's ownership of the pipe. "Milk cookie" is listed under conjunction because it refers to milk *and* cookie. The three-word utterance "Mommy drink milk" is placed in the action category (agent—Mommy; action—drink; object—milk).

7. After listing each utterance in the appropriate category, analyze the checklist to determine which semantic relationships the student did or did not use. The forms that the student did not use can be included in teaching objectives of semantic relationships. For example, if the student used three-word utterances but did not use action-object-location forms, this may be an appropriate teaching objective.

After the student's language sample is analyzed for semantic grammar, the mean length of ut-terance in morphemes is computed. Brown (1973) suggests the following sequence:

1. Transcribe the language sample.

2. Start the analysis on the second page of the transcription and count the first 100 utterances. Count only fully transcribed utterances, including utterance repetitions.

3. Count each morpheme in the 100 utter-ances. Do not count fillers ("mm" or "oh") or repe-titions, but do count "no," "yeah," and "hi." Count as single morphemes all compound words, proper names, idiomatic duplications (e.g., *night-night, choo-choo,* and *see-saw*), irregular past tenses of verbs (e.g., *got, did, went,* and *saw*), diminutives (e.g., *doggie*), and catenatives (e.g., *gonna, wanna,* and *hafta*). Count as separate morphemes all auxiliaries (*is, have, will, can, want,* and *would*) and inflections (e.g., posses-sive *s,* plural *s,* third-person singular *s,* regular past *ed,* and progressive *ing*).

4. Compute the mean length of utterance by dividing the total number of morphemes by 100.

The mean length of utterance gives the examiner a quick measure of growth over an extended time period. Many research studies report students' semantic development in terms of this measure rather than chronological age. For example, the agent-action-object semantic form may be reported as occurring in students with a mean length of utterance of three words, rather than in students of any specific chronological age.

Informal Tests of Pragmatics   Pragmatics can be assessed informally by analyzing a sample of the student's spontaneous speech to determine which pragmatic function was used. The first step is to obtain a videotaped language sample from the student. (Guidelines for obtaining a language sample are presented in the semantics section of this chapter.) If videotape equipment is not available, an observer can record what happened just before and just after each utterance. The second step is to transcribe the tape and list each utterance on a checklist, as shown in Figure 6.3. The examiner classifies the pragmatic function of an utterance by analyzing the events before and after it. For example, the student's utterance may be "Throw ball." The examiner notes that before the utterance the examiner was holding the ball and the student's arms were extended to catch the ball, and also notes that the examiner threw the ball to the student after the utterance. The utterance is classified as a request and a mark is put in the *Request* column. The examiner analyzes the checklist for each function the student did or did not use and then lists the functions that the student did not use. For example, it may be noted that the student did not use a protest function, such as "No shoes," to mean "Don't put on my shoes." The teacher can select from the pragmatic functions that were not used to determine appropriate teaching objectives.

In older students, informal assessment of pragmatics includes measures of speaking with inappropriate loudness, talking at inappropriate times, interrupting the speaker, and using indirect requests. These behaviors can be assessed by counting and recording them in several situations and on different days. A teacher may want to count and record these same behaviors in a speaker of the same age who is not delayed in pragmatics. The teacher can select a student who talks to other students and contributes during group activities, rather than a student who is quiet or has little to say. Three situations are chosen, such as group instructional time, independent work time, and lunch or playground time. The teacher counts the number of times each student interrupts other speakers, talks too loudly, and talks when the student should be listening, reading, or working. The results are recorded on charts, and the teacher compares the results of the two students. A significant difference in the two students' behaviors signifies a possible teaching objective. An appropriate objective is to decrease interruptions by increasing skills in determining when a speaker is finished talking.

Indirect requests can be assessed informally in students whose developmental age is 8 years and above by asking the student to state the implied direct requests. For example, the examiner says, "Tell me what I want you to do when I say, 'Can you close the door?'" The student says, "You want me to close the door." The examiner then says, "Tell me what I want you to do in each of the following sentences." The examiner reads indirect requests listed on a checklist and puts a check in a column to indicate whether the student's response is correct or incorrect. The results are analyzed to determine the number of errors made and the forms with which the student is having the most difficulty (i.e., the affirmative: "Can you . . . ?"; the negative: "Can't you . . . ?"; or the affirmative with negative intention: "Must you . . . ?"). These forms of indirect requests can become teaching objectives for the student.

Curriculum-Based Measurement   In curriculum-based measurement, curriculum contexts and content are used to determine appropriate language interventions by identifying activities and skills that may help the student develop more effective communicative skills. The goal is to make functional changes relevant to the student's communicative needs within the academic setting. Nelson (1989) suggests that sample language contexts and skills should include expository test comprehension, the ability to follow oral directions, narrative comprehension and production, and use of language to complete math

FIGURE 6.3

Checklist of pragmatic functions

Student's Name Julie Bates Date 2/12 Utterances	Instrumental	Protest	Request	Acquire Information	Metalinguistic	Give Information	Label	Imitate	Answer	Initiate/Terminate Social	Entertain	Other
1. Drink milk	X											
2. No milk		X										
3. Shoes on			X									
4. Car							X					
Question asked: "Where is the ball?" 5. Ball chair									X			
6. Daddy come?				X								

problems. Additional activities may include written expression, silent and oral reading, and listening comprehension of written language. Nelson (1994) discusses the philosophy and methods of curriculum-based language assessment and intervention for students with language problems.

☀ LANGUAGE SERVICE DELIVERY MODELS

Pullout Therapy Model

The most common language service delivery model is the pullout therapy model, in which the language specialist takes students from their classes and instructs those with similar difficulties in homogeneous groups. Many teachers admit that this model presents various problems and often results in ineffective and inefficient services. According to Ehren and Lenz (1989), students usually dislike this model because they do not like to be singled out as different. This becomes particularly important as peer pressure increases during adolescence. Many adolescents also do not want to continue with the same methods and activities as they had during speech instruction in elementary school, and they lack motivation to achieve because speech and language therapy is not a class they register for in their normal schedule.

The pullout method also causes students to miss course work while they are out of the classroom. This is especially devastating to students with learning problems, who can least afford to miss classroom instruction. As attempts are made to formulate a pullout schedule, the language specialist is faced with numerous scheduling concerns, such as from which subject and how often to pull the student as well as how to handle special events, tests, and absences. Scheduling problems are compounded further by the number of students who need services and the inability to provide the intensity required by certain students.

A final problem associated with the pullout model involves fragmentation of services. Because students generally are seen for therapy in a separate classroom, the services often are isolated from general classroom content and, thus, may not be consistent with classroom goals and expectations. Disagreement regarding responsibility for certain content and type of instruction increases when language goals seem irrelevant to the student's functioning or needs in the general classroom, or when the goals are derived without regard to content in the curriculum. This fragmentation of services frequently results in resentment on the part of the general classroom teacher and often hinders students who need instructional consistency to achieve academic success.

Classroom-Based Language Models

Classroom-based models involve a new delivery of traditional services, and some school systems use them in an attempt to improve the services to students with language problems and to integrate therapy goals with the student's academic needs. In spite of their differences, all classroom-based models emphasize the need for collaborative consultation between the classroom teacher and the language specialist so that resulting interventions are meaningful and relevant to natural occurrences in the classroom (Damico, 1987; Marvin, 1987). The American Speech-Language-Hearing Association (1991) Committee on Language-Learning Disorders presents a model for collaborative service delivery for students with language-learning disorders. In the collaborative service delivery model, the team members (language specialist, teacher, parents, and student) work together closely to plan and implement each student's educational program. The team devises all treatment goals, assessment methods, intervention procedures, and documentation systems to enhance the student's academic and social functioning in the school environment. The team members share responsibility for educational goals, and all services and instruction take place in the classroom. The five major types of classroom-based language models include team teaching; self-contained classroom teaching; one-to-one intervention; staff, curriculum, or program development; and consultation (Miller, 1989).

Team Teaching   In this classroom-based model, the language specialist teaches with the general or special classroom teacher. The key to this format is that the language specialist actually teaches a portion of the curriculum. The curriculum goals and objectives as well as the methods and materials to be used are established jointly by the members of the professional team. Services can be rendered in a variety of settings, including the general classroom with the general education teacher or a self-contained classroom or a resource room with a special education teacher.

Self-Contained Classroom Teaching   In this service-model format, the language specialist teaches in a self-contained language class. This format is common with younger students, and the language specialist is responsible for teaching content areas including reading, math, science, and social studies to students who need particular interventions in language processing and production. At the middle- and secondary-school levels, some language specialists offer a separate course that focuses on writing, reading, or other language areas that are difficult for students with language problems to deal with in the general curriculum.

One-to-One Intervention   The language specialist can provide one-to-one intervention to particular students in the classroom. In this approach, the language specialist must maintain close contact with the classroom teacher to provide appropriate interventions to each student regarding specific content areas, study skills, writing, and vocabulary. Classroom textbooks and materials are used to maintain relevance to ongoing classroom activities.

Staff, Curriculum, or Program Development   The language specialist can aid students indirectly by providing staff, curriculum, or program development to a school or district. For example, the specialist can plan community programs to increase student and parental awareness of the school's language objectives. The language specialist also can participate in curriculum development and evaluation or present in-service workshops to teachers or parents that focus on the effect of language on academic success. This service delivery format requires a fundamental change in the focus of the language specialist from providing direct service to students to educating those responsible for teaching the students.

Consultation   The language specialist can serve as a consultant to the various professionals who interact with students, such as general or special education teachers, psychologists, physicians, nurses, social workers, or counselors. In this model, the language specialist consults with persons who provide language interventions to the student, and an effort is made through the consultation to determine methods to improve the student's communication. An additional benefit of the consultation format is that students who do not qualify for direct services under school district guidelines benefit indirectly from the suggestions of the consultant as they affect educational and social concerns in the classroom (Damico, 1987).

Strategies-Based Model

A strategies-based service delivery model focuses on teaching specific learning strategies to students and is especially appealing to language specialists who work with middle- and secondary-school students. One of the major differences between the strategy-based model and a classroom-based model is that students are able to register for and receive a grade for the course work. The use of strategies involves increasing the student's understanding and use of metacognitive and metalinguistic skills. These skills focus on improving the student's awareness and use of strategies that enhance learning. In essence, a change is made from teaching students *what* to learn to teaching students *how* to learn.

Based on the perspective that many students with language problems show delays in metalinguistic maturation and strategic language use, Wiig (1990) discusses the need for emphasizing different reasoning strategies in language intervention. This approach to language intervention is process oriented rather than product oriented and is implemented collaboratively between language specialists and classroom teachers. Likewise, Buttrill, Niizawa, Biemer, Takahashi, and Hearn (1989) propose a strategies-based model that considers the learning characteristics of students with language problems as well as the demands of the secondary school settings to which they apply.

One of the most widely researched and developed approaches to learning strategies is the Strategies Intervention Model developed by Don Deshler and his colleagues at the University of Kansas Center for Research on Learning. Although this model is quite specific, it is based on principles applicable to strategy training in general. Deshler and Schumaker (1986) state that the ultimate goal of learning strategies is to enable students to analyze and solve novel problems in both academic and nonacademic settings. Their approach to teaching learning strategies to adolescents is based on three rationales:

1. The development and application of learning strategies or metacognitive skills are appropriate for older students who are more proficient in these skills.
2. Adolescents who learn how to learn are in a better position to learn new skills in the future.
3. Students should accept responsibility for their learning and progress.

To design relevant instruction, the language specialist must determine what curriculum demands the student is failing to meet. Student involvement and mutual goal setting also should be established to maximize motivation toward learning, and activities should be designed to promote generalization. Motivation can be enhanced by broadening the student's understanding of the skill and its application to a variety of settings. To facilitate generalization, the learning-strategies model stresses the importance of cooperative planning and consultation between the language specialist, general and special education teachers, and personnel of other support services.

☀ TEACHING LANGUAGE SKILLS

Many teachers who use direct teaching methods for remediation of reading and math problems undoubtedly select this technique for teaching language skills. With this format, the teacher directs the learning and dictates the lesson's content, pace, and sequencing. Often the student is allowed little opportunity to engage in spontaneous conversations during this highly structured skills approach. Conversely, some teachers believe that learning should be student centered, with the student dictating the lesson's content, pace, and sequencing. The teacher controls minimally and emphasizes social interaction so that communication can occur along the lines of normal conversation. To teach new concepts, the responsive interaction approach emphasizes adult expansions or modifications of the youngster's utterances, whereas elicited prompts are used in milieu teaching. Warren and Yoder (1994) suggest that it may be advantageous to use a combination of approaches based on the characteristics of the learner, the instructional context, and the skills being taught. For example, milieu teaching may be effective for teaching early vocabulary, whereas direct instruction can be used for teaching more abstract language skills.

When designing appropriate language intervention, the phonological, syntactic, semantic, and pragmatic aspects should be considered, as well as the student's cognitive skills and social environment. Wallach (1989) and Ehren and Lenz (1989) present the following general principles for meeting a student's language needs:

- The language specialist should be aware of young students with language disorders who are dismissed from language services, because academic problems may resurface later due to a breakdown in the language system and increased curriculum demands.
- Language screenings should consist of more than one test and be sensitive to subtle forms of language disorders.
- Students suspected of having learning problems should receive routine language evaluations that emphasize language and auditory processing.
- School officials should consider service delivery alternatives to the traditional pullout model, and language specialists should focus on both contextualized and decontextualized aspects of language.
- Professionals should collaborate to devise a coordinated program for students with language problems rather than implement a variety of isolated programs.
- The delivery of instruction in learning strategies should be language sensitive.
- The curriculum in language intervention should be relevant to the general curriculum, respond to setting demands, reflect areas of academic concern, integrate spoken and written language systems, and focus on generalization.
- The individual strategy preferences of students with language problems should be considered, and students should be encouraged to determine which strategies are successful in a given situation.
- Intervention should encourage student accountability and responsibility.
- Effective interventions from other disciplines should be applied.

Moreover, especially when working with young children, the following specific techniques for teaching language may be helpful:

- Teach language in a context.
- Follow the sequence of normal language development.
- Use specific and effective teaching strategies when introducing a new concept.
- Vocalize thoughts or describe actions.
- Describe what others are doing using parallel talk.
- Use modeling to provide practice on a specific language skill.
- Use expansion to show how an idea can be expressed in a more complex manner.
- Use elaboration to demonstrate how to provide more information.
- Use structured programs to provide adequate practice and feedback regarding performance.
- Use everyday activities to provide skill practice within a context.
- Recognize the relationship of comprehension and production.
- Systematically plan for and teach generalization.

Because language is interactive, the teacher should be creative when implementing teaching methods, because an activity designed to focus on a particular skill also may be useful in other areas. The remainder of this section presents strategies for increasing language comprehension, strategies for increasing language production, and imitation and modeling strategies. Parental involvement in language intervention also is discussed.

Strategies for Increasing Language Comprehension

The following strategies may improve listening skills and increase the comprehension or understanding of students with language problems:

- If the student frequently has difficulty following directions or understanding information of increased complexity, establish eye contact and maintain attention prior to presenting information.

Cue the student to listen by using silent pauses or instructions to listen to or look at the teacher. This helps to establish a mental set for listening.

• Ask the student to repeat or paraphrase directions or instructions to the teacher or a peer to ensure comprehension.

• To facilitate listening, arrange classroom seating to limit distractions from doorways and windows and to maximize the use of visual aids.

• When introducing a new concept or skill, use vocabulary that is familiar to the student and explain new vocabulary words by using familiar terms.

• Present new concepts in as many modalities as possible (e.g., auditory, visual, and kinesthetic), and use gestures to augment verbal presentations (Bos & Vaughn, 1998).

• To increase understanding of the relationship between semantic role and word order, encourage young children to act out sentences (e.g., "Mommy kiss baby") or manipulate objects and talk about their movement (Connell, 1986).

• Explain to students that listening is an active process that requires them to behave in certain ways, and teach them to identify specific behaviors associated with good listening (e.g., look, think about what is said, and repeat to yourself). Model effective listening skills by being attentive to students.

• Use introductory statements (such as "These are the main points" or "Before we begin") to provide an organizational framework and help students prepare for a task.

• Be sensitive to the students' linguistic sophistication and adjust the rate and complexity of instructional language accordingly. Use structurally simple and relatively short sentences of not more than five to ten words and limit the number of new and unfamiliar vocabulary words presented in a single lesson to five or less (Wiig & Semel, 1984).

• Teach specific memory strategies (e.g., visual imagery, clustering and grouping information, and forming associations) to help students organize, categorize, and store new information for later retrieval.

• To enhance students' recall and memorization of new vocabulary, use the keyword method, in which familiar words are associated with each new concept or word (Mastropieri, Scruggs, & Fulk, 1990).

• Engage adolescents in concrete problem-solving activities to identify those who have difficulty

thinking symbolically or using reasoning in nonsymbolic events (Moses, Klein, & Altman, 1990).

Strategies for Increasing Language Production

The following strategies focus on improving the production or expressive skills of students with language problems:

• Expect students to speak occasionally in incomplete sentences because this is normal for discourse.

• Regardless of the effectiveness of a student's communication, convey that the message is important. React first to the content of a student's message because it is most important in the communication process, and then correct the syntax error.

• When attempting to expand a young child's utterances, provide one or two additional words to the child's spontaneous utterance for the child to repeat rather than impose adult structures that are difficult to imitate. Explain that the reason for the expansion of the utterance is not to correct what the youngster is saying but to give a more complex way of expressing thought (Bos & Vaughn, 1998).

• Teach language in various natural settings (e.g., classroom, cafeteria, and playground) rather than only in isolated groups. Also, teach language skills in connection with other curriculum content (Wiig & Semel, 1984).

• Act as a good language model, and ask students to imitate what they hear. Imitation is frequently a good measure of language skills because students tend to imitate only the forms they know and not necessarily what they hear.

• Use structured language programs that provide adequate opportunities to practice a new skill as well as interactive activities for applying the skill to relevant contexts (Bos & Vaughn, 1998).

• Comment or elaborate on students' ideas to demonstrate how more information can be expressed and how concepts can be associated.

• Use activities such as role playing and charades to improve a student's use of language in different contexts and to enhance the ability to recognize the importance of nonverbal skills such as eye contact, facial expressions, and gestures. Also, model and reinforce appropriate turn-taking in conversations.

Activities involving communication toys can facilitate oral expression.

• When a student has difficulties with word retrieval, examine indices such as response time, error index (word-selection process), and substitution types (German, 1984).

• Use semantic training to improve a student's word-retrieval skills, and include strategies such as categorizing or classifying words and using associative clues (McGregor & Leonard, 1989).

• To improve a student's verbal expression, encourage storytelling activities in which the student must name all of the objects or pictures, tell what is happening, and create an ending.

• Teach generalization of language skills through three phases: an orientation phase in which the student becomes aware of the different contexts applicable, an activation phase in which practice is provided in a variety of situations, and a maintenance phase in which periodic probes are conducted to ensure proficiency is maintained (Deshler & Schumaker, 1986).

Imitation and Modeling Strategies

Two frequently used language-skills teaching strategies are imitation and modeling. In these strategies, the student gives a response that is similar to that of a model. Courtright and Courtright (1976) distinguish between modeling and imitative behavior that is mimicry. They define *imitative mimicry* as a one-to-one, literal matching response for each stimulus statement. In contrast to mimicry, *modeling* involves acquiring an abstract language

rule without giving an immediate response to the stimulus (Bandura, 1971). For example, the student observes the teacher modeling a rule several times before being required to use the rule. This strategy is apparent in the following method of teaching the use of *s* on singular verbs: The teacher models 20 different singular subject-verb sentences that describe pictures (such as "Dog runs," "Boy walks," and "Cat plays"). After the teacher models these sentences, the student is requested to describe the pictures.

Leonard (1975) recommends the use of modeling with a problem-solving set. The teacher uses a puppet as a model. Visual stimuli, such as toys or pictures of objects and people, are placed in front of the model (puppet). The teacher tells the student to listen carefully and determine which sentences earn reinforcers for the model. The model produces 10 to 20 utterances that describe the visual stimuli and deliberately gives 25 percent of the responses incorrectly. The teacher then presents the same visual stimulus to the student and encourages a response that earned a reinforcer for the model. The student and model take turns responding until the student has produced three consecutive appropriate responses that were presented previously by the model. At this point the student is presented with new visual stimuli and is required to produce unmodeled utterances.

The teacher can use imitative mimicry at one point with a student and gradually move to more spontaneous responses. When using this strategy, the teacher needs to structure the event preceding the student's response (i.e., the antecedent event). The antecedent event can have varying degrees of cueing. A teacher can use total cueing in the antecedent event ("What do you want? Tell me, 'I want an apple'") or partial cueing in the antecedent event ("Is this a ball or an orange?"). Partial cueing also can include pointing to or looking at items to help the student make a correct response. Minimal cueing can be used when the student is ready to generalize a rule. For example, the teacher can say "What's happening? What's he doing?"

The expansion model is a modeling technique frequently used by parents for language intervention. With this technique, the youngster's response is expanded by the parent or teacher. For example, the youngster says, "Car go," and the parent or teacher immediately gives the expanded model, "The car is going."

Parental Involvement

Parents of students with language problems play an important role in language intervention. Tiegerman and Siperstein (1984) note that about 60 percent of maternal utterances directed toward youngsters with language impairments are not related semantically to the child's vocal, verbal, or nonverbal behavior. However, in a study of social conversational skills of preschoolers, Girolametto (1988) found a significant increase in appropriate language when parents received training in three areas: following their child's lead in establishing joint focus on an activity, responding contingently to their child's communicative attempts, and encouraging conversation by taking turns. The training resulted in the parents being less controlling and more responsive to their children. Girolametto notes that following parental training, the children initiated more topics, were more responsive to their mother's preceding turn in conversation, allowed more verbal turns when talking, and used a more diverse vocabulary.

☀ LANGUAGE ACTIVITIES

After carefully selecting a language program, the teacher may decide to supplement to meet the specific needs of certain students. Some teachers prefer to plan a complete individualized program rather than use an available commercial program. To supplement or design an individualized program, the teacher must plan teaching activities. One advantage of planning activities is that the teacher can select and vary teaching methods and materials to fit individual students' needs.

Direct teaching activities are designed to meet specific objectives. They must, however, be supplemented with independent learning and reinforcing activities. Self-correcting materials are a good choice for independent learning of a skill, and instructional games frequently are used to reinforce newly acquired skills. Various teaching activities are presented in this section, and instructional games and self-correcting materials are described in the following sections. Activities, games, and self-correcting materials that are appropriate for use with secondary students are presented near the end of each section.

1. *To teach is + verb + ing (is jumping):* For each picture, say a model sentence that includes *is* plus verb plus *ing.* The teacher can show a picture of a girl jumping rope and say, "The girl is jumping." The teacher models ten different sentences with pictures. The student is not encouraged to respond during the modeled sentences. After the modeled sentences, the teacher shows the pictures again and asks the student to tell what is happening in each picture. After successful completion of this task, the teacher shows ten new action pictures and for each new picture says, "Tell me what's happening."

Modification: The teacher can use modeling to teach semantics, morphology, syntax, and so forth by varying the stimulus and the modeled response. For example, the morphological form of singular pronouns plus the inflectional verb ending *s* ("She walks") can be taught by using action pictures with singular subjects and changing the model to "She walks," "He runs," "He jumps," and so on. Courtright and Courtright (1976, 1979) report that generalization of a syntactic rule is significantly higher with this type of modeling than with imitative responses, in which the student repeats the model immediately after the teacher.

2. *To teach plural morpheme s on regular plural nouns:* Use modeling with problem solving to teach language rules (Leonard, 1975). Show a puppet 20 pictures that depict 20 plural nouns. The puppet names each picture and misses 25 percent of them. The teacher reinforces each correct response with a chip. After the modeling of 20 pictures, the teacher asks the student to name the pictures. After the student correctly responds to these pictures, the teacher presents 20 new pictures and asks the student to name them.

Modification: Modeling with problem solving also can be used to teach semantics, phonology, syntax, and so on. For example, to teach a syntactic rule of *they + are + verb + ing,* present pictures depicting action with a plural subject (such as children playing) and say to the puppet, "Tell me what's happening in each picture." The puppet responds using the form of *they + are + verb + ing* for each picture ("They are playing"). The puppet randomly makes 25 percent of the responses incorrect ("They play"). The teacher reinforces the correct responses with a chip. After the modeling, the teacher says, "You give the puppet a chip for each correct sentence." After successful completion of this task, the teacher says to the student, "You tell me what's happening in each picture."

3. **To teach possessive pronouns (her, his, their):** Prepare small cards with mounted pictures of a single girl, a single boy, and several children. Mount pictures of objects on separate cards. Attach the cards to rings and group all the people pictures together on one set of rings and all the object cards on another. Attach the rings and card sets to a folded cardboard stand. The student or teacher flips each card separately to form phrases (*her hat, his ball, their house,* and so forth). Coloring books are good sources of pictures.

Modification: A third set of color cards can be used in which each card is shaded a different color. The student is required to say phrases such as "Her dress is red," "His hat is yellow," or "His ball is blue."

4. **To teach classification of associated words:** Have the student sort various association pictures using the following procedure (see Figure 6.4):
- Mount individual pictures of objects commonly associated with each other on small cards. Select pictures such as ball and bat, cup and saucer, and shoe and sock from reading-readiness workbooks.
- Make a card holder with strips of tagboard stapled to a large piece of tagboard.
- Place a picture in each slot down the left side of the card holder.
- Have the student place the remaining pictures and tell how the two objects are associated.

Modification: Matching pictures and pictures that depict opposites can be used. Also, the activity can be made self-correcting by putting matching shapes on the backs of associated pictures. After sorting the pictures, the student can check the work by looking at the backs of the cards to determine whether the shapes match.

5. **To develop the use of him, her, and it:** Arrange the students in a circle, girls alternating with boys. Each student's task is to roll the ball to another student. Before doing so, however, the student must state whether the individual who receives is a "him" or a "her." After some students succeed with this task, have them hold pictures of familiar objects (such as car, ball, and house) while the other students retain their human identity. Now before rolling the ball, the student must state whether the individual receiving is an object and must say "it" before rolling the ball. If the receiver does not have a picture, the student must state "him" or "her" before rolling the ball.

Modification: All students hold pictures of objects. Before each student rolls the ball, ask the student to state whether the receiver of the ball is a "him" or a "her" and to identify the object that the receiver is holding. Then the student says the appropriate phrase (such as "her house").

6. **To teach ed on regular verbs (walked, jumped):** Have the student describe an activity as he or she is performing it. For example, the student says, "I am jumping" as he or she is jumping. Upon completion, have the student say, "I jumped very high" or "I jumped over the box." This activity can be extended by using small objects that can perform movement; for example, a doll can be made to jump, walk, or hop. Also, this activity can be used to teach irregular verb forms such as *ate, drank,* and *fell.*

7. **To teach the prepositions in, on, out of, in front of, in back of, and beside:** Use hula hoops and physical activity to teach prepositions. Tell the students to move in relation to the hoops ("Stand in the hula hoops"). At first the teacher announces and performs the activity with students; then gradually the teacher only announces the activity. Finally, the teacher has students themselves talk during the activity. For example, students say, "The hula hoop is beside me" when they move their hoops by their side.

Modification: The teacher can stand in some kind of relation to the hoop (e.g., in the hoop) and ask, "Where am I?" The students answer, "You are in the hula hoop." Each student then can have a turn standing in relation to the hula hoop and asking, "Where am I?"

8. **To teach classification of part/whole relationships:** Cut out of flannel the parts of two complete

FIGURE 6.4
Association pictures mounted
in a card holder

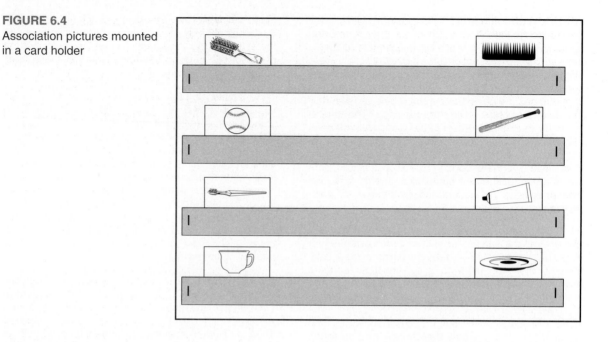

objects such as a truck. Have one truck put together on the flannelboard before beginning. Ask the student to complete the second truck by saying, "Put on the part of the truck that is the wheel," "Put on the part of the truck that is the door," and so on.

Modification: This activity also can be used to teach functional relationships. For example, ask the student to put on the part of the truck that opens to let people inside, or the part of the truck that turns to change the truck's direction.

9. ***To teach classification by function:*** Collect pictures of objects used for one function. For example, to show a bath, collect pictures of a bathtub, soap, washcloth, and towel. Have the student sort the pictures according to function. For example:
- *Sandwich:* bread, knife, peanut butter, and jelly
- *Bath:* tub or shower, washcloth, towel, and soap
- *Washing dishes:* dishes, soap, sink, sponge, drainer, and towel
- *Building:* lumber, nails, hammer, sandpaper, paint, screws, and tools

Modification: This task can be made more difficult for older students by making the functional relationships more complex (e.g., *Dressing for a party:* washing hair, fixing fingernails, brushing hair, and brushing teeth). Moreover, a picture-card deck called Functions (produced by SRA) can be used to teach classification. It includes 14 five-card sets (e.g., stamp, paper, pen, enve-

lope, and mailbox), which the student can use to match objects into sets based on function.

10. ***To classify objects that belong to the same class (animals, foods, houses, vehicles):*** Prepare a large card with four sections. In one section put a picture of a house; in the second section put a picture of an animal; in the third, a picture of a vehicle; and in the fourth, a picture of food. Collect and mount pictures of animals, foods, houses, and vehicles. Have the student sort the pictures in the four areas. An area can be made with a color or shape so that the student can sort objects or pictures according to these attributes.

11. ***To teach synonyms:*** Ask a student to call out a word for which he or she knows at least one synonym. Then ask the next student to "match" the word by

providing a synonym of it. Use a game format in which the student receives one point for each correct synonym named. If unable to think of any synonyms, the student can challenge the first player to state the synonym he or she had in mind. Any failure in this task is penalized by one point. A player fails to score a point if he or she is unable to think of a synonym, and a player is penalized one point if he or she responds with a word that is not a synonym of the word proposed by the preceding player. The object is to squeeze as many synonyms out of the original word as possible. If a player can think of only one or two synonyms, the opponent can earn points by naming some others. When the possibilities of a given word have been exhausted, a new word is used.

Modification: This activity also can be used with antonyms. For example, if *big* is the given word, an appropriate response might be *little.* Then the next player must give an antonym of *little* (e.g., *large*) without using the original word, *big.* A point is scored for each correct antonym (or synonym of the original word) given.

12. ***To teach rough and smooth as modifiers:*** Collect items that are small and rough (e.g., a piece of sandpaper, a piece of window screen, a fingernail file, a washcloth, a small rough rock, a piece of net, and a piece of bark) and collect items that are smooth (e.g., a marble, a small magnet, a small mirror, and a smooth rock). Place the rough and smooth objects in a large bag. Introduce the word *rough* by letting the students feel a rough object and talk about how it feels. Introduce the word *smooth* by letting them feel a smooth object and talk about how it feels. Now let each student reach in the bag and feel one object. Have the student decide whether the object feels rough or smooth and then take it out of the bag.

Modification: Hard and soft or heavy and light objects can be used.

13. ***To increase auditory discrimination between two phonemes:*** Draw a ladder on a piece of paper. Provide a marker and tell the student to move the marker when he or she hears two different words. Say some word pairs that consist of the same word and some that are different words. When the student consistently moves the marker only for two different words, change the task by having the student listen to words that are different by only one phoneme, such as *pair—fair.* The student moves the marker when he or she hears two different words. Some suggested pairs differing in only one phoneme are *pair—fair, purr—fur, put—foot, pork—fork,* and *pay—day.*

Modification: This activity can be modified according to how the student signals that two sounds are the same or different. The student can raise a hand, tap a pencil, move a space on a game board, or pick up a chip.

14. ***To teach negatives:*** Model a sentence without a negative and then immediately model a sentence containing a negative. For example, the teacher says, "Some for John. None for John." The student imitates the two sentences. When several sentences with negatives have been modeled correctly, the teacher only presents a sentence without a negative. The student responds by saying a sentence with a negative. A recommended sequence of negatives is as follows:

- no
- none
- nothing else
- no more
- not enough
- don't
- let's not
- we'll not
- do not
- don't do
- is no more
- does not
- is not
- did not
- nothing is
- will not
- was not

Modification: This technique can be used to teach morphology. For example, to teach plural *s* on regular nouns, the teacher can present sets of two pictures and two modeled responses, such as "one kite—two kites, one cat—two cats." After the student correctly repeats several modeled responses, the teacher presents a picture of one cat and says, "One cat." Then the teacher presents a picture of two cats, and the student says, "Two cats."

15. ***To extend the use of linguistic forms to other environments:*** Have a student act as a speaker to describe an object to a listener such that the listener can select a similar object from several objects placed in front of him or her. The speaker and listener sit back-to-back. Place three objects in front of the listener (e.g. key, comb, and ball) and one similar object (such as a comb) in front of the speaker. The speaker describes the object, and the listener is encouraged to ask questions until he or she can select the correct object.

Modification: A block-building activity can be used in which two students are seated back-to-back. The speaker and listener each have an identical set of six blocks that vary in shape, color, or size. The speaker builds a construction using all of the blocks and provides enough information so that the listener can duplicate the construction.

16. ***To use language as an effective communicator:*** Use an over-the-shoulder activity in which the speaker is the encoder and the listener is the decoder. The encoder stands behind the decoder and talks over the decoder's shoulder to tell the decoder what to do next. The encoder must give information so that the decoder understands, and the information must be revised if the decoder does not understand. For example, the

encoder may say, "Put the red triangle on top of the blue square." The decoder places the triangle above the square so that it touches the top of the square. The encoder then may say, "You have put the triangle on top of the square like a roof on a house. Instead, lay it on top of the square like a blanket." The encoder must keep revising the instructions until the decoder completely understands the message.

Modification: The encoder can draw a simple design and then talk over the decoder's shoulder to tell how to draw the same design. The decoder can stand at the chalkboard while the encoder looks at his or her own design and the one the decoder is drawing.

17. **To teach the classification of where, when, and what phrases:** Write the word *where* next to the word *place*. Tell the student that *where* refers to place. With the student, list a few phrases that refer to place. Write the word *what* next to the word *thing*. Tell the student to list some phrases that refer to things. Write the word *when* next to the word *time*. Tell the student that *when* usually refers to time. The student needs a broader concept of time than time on a clock. Time can refer to the hour, parts of a day, events of a day (such as breakfast, school, and bedtime), day of the week, and so on. Have the student list some time phrases. For practice, provide a worksheet with the three headings of *Where, What,* and *When* and have the student list the following phrases under the appropriate heading:

- on the playground
- tomorrow morning
- beside your bed
- the blue car
- on a rainy day
- her pretty dress
- my broken cup
- behind the school
- a small coat
- at my house
- before lunch
- after school

Modification: This activity also can be used to classify *who, why,* and *how* phrases. Classification of these phrases can be made self-correcting by putting the phrases on cards in a Poke Box (described in Chapter 2) with the multiple-choice words of *When, Where,* and *What* (or *Who, Why,* and *How*).

18. **To teach vocabulary likenesses:** Write the following verbs and objects on the chalkboard:

kicking	swing
pushing	house
sewing	ball
building	dress

Ask the student to tell how to pair the action words and objects. Then ask the student to tell how *kicking* the *ball* is like *pushing* a *swing*. (Help the student conclude that when you kick a ball it goes away from you, and when you push a swing it also goes away from you.) Ask the student how *sewing* a *dress* is like *building* a *house.*

(Again, help the student conclude that when you build or sew you make a complete item out of parts.) Then provide a worksheet with incomplete sentences and ask the student to select the best word to complete each sentence. For example:

- *Sweeping* is to *broom* as *hitting* is to _____. (bat, ball, catch).
- *Sleeping* is to *bed* as *sitting* is to _____. (table, chair, desk)
- *Smiling* is to *happy* as *crying* is to _____. (anger, tears, sad)
- *Eating* is to *food* as *drinking* is to _____. (thirst, water, cup)
- *Writing* is to *pencil* as *painting* is to _____. (paper, canvas, brush)

Modification: This vocabulary task of comparison of likenesses can be modified to include items based on part/whole relationships (e.g., *Fingers* are to *hands* as *toes* are to *feet).*

19. **To teach the use of relative clauses:** On the chalkboard give the student several examples of sentences that contain relative clauses. Then give the student a practice sheet with several sets of two sentences. Ask the student to combine each set of two sentences into one sentence by using a relative pronoun. For example:

- The boy broke the window. The boy ran away. (who)
- Read the book. The book is about dogs. (that)
- The boy who broke the the window ran away.
- Read the book that is about dogs.

Modification: The sentences can be combined with conjunctions such as *and, but, because,* and *so.* For example, the following sentences can be combined with *but:*

- Bob eats breakfast every day. Bob is always hungry at lunch.
- The puppy plays outside. The puppy likes to sleep in the house.
- Bob eats breakfast every day, but he is always hungry at lunch.
- The puppy plays outside, but he likes to sleep in the house.

20. **To use the conjunctions and, but, because, and so:** Use the cloze procedure with multiple-choice items. Make a list of sentences that require the use of a conjunction. Leave a blank space and give multiple choices. For example:

- I don't want ice cream _____ I would like a dessert. (or, but)
- You should take a bath _____ you are dirty. (because, but)
- You must finish your homework _____ you can play outside. (but, so)

Modification: The cloze procedure with multiple-choice items can be used to teach semantics, morphology, or other forms of syntax. For example, the following sentence requires an inflectional ending *(ed)* on a regular verb:

The boy _____ to school this morning before breakfast. (walk, walked)

21. ***To teach paraphrasing:*** Use a game format in which the students are divided into two teams. Have the first player on Team A tell the first player on Team B to do something (e.g., "Touch your nose"). The Team B player performs the action and then tells the first player on Team A to do the same thing; however, the Team A player must give the command using different words (e.g., "Put your finger on your nose"). If both players perform correctly, both teams get a point. If the player on Team B is unable to say the same command in different words, only Team A gets the point. The game continues in this manner, and the team with the most points at the end of the game wins.

Modification: The students can be required to paraphrase a short paragraph. This can be a written or oral task. For example:

> Mary woke up early because she had to arrive at school before the bell rang. She needed to go to the library before school so she could return an overdue book.

Paraphrased paragraph:

> Mary had to return an overdue book to the library before school began. Therefore, she needed to wake up earlier than usual.

22. ***To teach employment vocabulary words to secondary students:*** Cut out job ads from the newspaper and collect job application forms. Read the ads and application forms to the class and determine what words and phrases they know (such as *experience, minimum wage, waitress, waiter, good working conditions, apply in person,* and *references required*). Define the words the students do not understand. With each student, role play a job interview and use the vocabulary on the job applications.

Modification: Vocabulary words can be selected from credit applications, checkbooks, classified ads, or driver's license applications.

☀ INSTRUCTIONAL GAMES IN LANGUAGE

His, Her, or Their

Objective: To teach the use of the possessive pronouns *his, her,* and *their.*

Materials: Game board with start-to-finish format (presented in Chapter 2); one stack of picture cards depicting objects; one stack of picture cards depicting people (should include at least one picture of a boy, one picture of a girl, and one picture of several children); a spinner; markers.

Directions: The stack of object pictures and the stack of people pictures are placed face down on the game board, and each player places a marker at the start position. Each player in turn spins the spinner, notes the number on which it lands, and picks up from each stack the number of cards shown on the spinner. The player turns over the cards and makes as many pronoun and object combinations as possible (e.g., *her hat, his hat, their hat, their ball, her house,* and *his shoe*). For each combination said, the player moves the marker ahead one space and puts the used cards face down on the bottom of each stack. The players take turns, and the one who moves to the end of the game board first is the winner.

What Goes Together

Objective: To teach classification by association.

Materials: Set of 40 playing cards composed of association pictures (e.g., a card illustrating a shoe and a card illustrating a sock).

Directions: Six cards are dealt to each player (two to four players), and the remaining cards are placed face down in the center of the players. Each player combines any association sets in his or her hand and lays them face up on the table. Then each player in turn takes a card from the deck, discards one from his or her hand, and places it face up next to the deck. After the first discard, each player can select a card either from the deck or from the discard pile. The first player who displays three association sets wins. (The criteria for winning can be varied to suit the students and the situation.)

The Deck

Objective: To teach opposite words.

Materials: Deck of cards composed of pictures depicting opposite words (e.g., a card illustrating the word *up* and a card illustrating the word *down*).

Directions: An equal number of cards is dealt to each player until all cards are dealt. Each player combines any sets of opposites in his or her hand and lays them face up on the table. Then each player draws a card in turn from another player's hand. When a player has a set of opposite pictures in his or her hand, the player lays them on the table. The game continues until one player wins by pairing all the cards in his or her hand.

Whose Is It?

Objective: To teach the use of possessive personal pronoun *mine* and *'s.*

Materials: Two matching sets of 12 pictures.

Directions: The dealer lays three pictures from the first set of cards face down in front of each of the four players. The dealer then lays the entire second matching stack of cards face down on the table. The dealer turns the first card in the stack face up and asks, "Whose is it?" The first player guesses whose stack contains the matching card by saying, "Mine," "John's," or "Mary's." The player must use the possessive *'s* or possessive pronoun *mine.* Whoever the player guesses must turn over his or her cards; that is, if the player says, "John's," John must turn over his cards for everyone to see. If the card matches one in John's stack, the player who selected John gets a chip. If it does not, the card is placed face down on the bottom of the deck, and John turns his cards back face down on the table. The dealer turns the next card from the stack face up and asks the next player, "Whose is it?" The player who makes the most correct guesses receives the most chips and wins.

Say the Whole Sentence

Objective: To teach sentence construction.

Materials: Deck of cards of matching pairs with several of the pairs having only one attribute different from other pairs (e.g., three pairs of Christmas trees—one set with blue lights, one set with red lights, and one set with green lights).

Directions: Six cards are dealt to each player, and the remaining cards are placed face down in a stack on the table. Each player combines any matching sets in his or her hand and lays them face up on the table. Each player in turn asks for a card from another player by using all the attributes (e.g., "Do you have a Christmas tree with green lights?"). If the other player has that card, it is given to the first player. If the other player does not have the requested card, the first player takes a card from the deck. The first player who matches all of his or her cards wins the game.

Phonetic Bingo

Objective: To teach phoneme identification.

Materials: Cards that have five numbered columns, with each column containing five letters; discs.

Directions: Each player receives a bingo card containing letters. The caller calls out a column number and a phoneme, such as 2/p/. If that particular phoneme is in the appropriate column on the card, the player places a disc over that letter. The winner is the first player to cover five letters in a row. A list of the called-out letters can be kept to check the winning card.

1	2	3	4	5
p	d	g	t	v
g	v	p	v	t
b	t	d	g	p
t	g	b	p	b
d	p	t	d	g

Fishing for Blends

Objective: To teach /s/ blends.

Materials: Fish-shaped cards displaying /s/ blends: *st, sk, sw,* and *sl.*

Directions: The cards are placed face up in the center of the students. The caller calls out a word containing an /s/ blend, such as *skate.* The players take turns finding the correct blend from the group of fish cards. If the correct card is picked, the player gets to keep the card. When all the cards are gone from the center, the player with the most "fish" wins.

Two-Way Words

Objective: To improve use of homonyms.

Materials: Set of 20 index cards with a pair of homonyms written on each card; answer key that lists the definition of each homonym.

Directions: Two pairs of partners sit across from each other, and the dealer deals five cards to each of the four players. The first player selects one of his or her cards, makes a statement that includes either of the homonyms on the card, and then repeats the homonym (e.g., "She wore a plain dress—-plain"). The player then challenges his or her partner to make a statement that includes the other homonym on the card but gives no further clues. When the partner makes a statement (e.g., "We were in the plane"), the dealer refers to the answer key to see whether the response is correct. If the response is questionable, the dealer can ask for another statement that gives additional information concerning the meaning of the homonym (e.g., "We were flying above the clouds in the plane"). If the partner's statement is correct, the player can place the card in the middle of the table. If the partner's statement is not correct, the player must keep the card for another turn. The next player challenges his or her partner in the same way, and the partner pairs take turns. A player can challenge only his or her own partner and must use his or her own cards. The first partner pair to have all their cards in the middle of the table wins the game.

Sentence Game

Objective: To teach sentence construction.

Materials: A start-to-finish game board (presented in Chapter 2); a deck of cards displaying stimulus pictures; a spinner; markers.

Directions: Each player places a marker at the start position, and the picture cards are placed face down. The first player spins the spinner and moves the designated number of spaces. Then the player selects a card from the deck and must say a sentence using the word or words illustrated in the picture. If the sentence is complete and correct, the player remains on the square. If the word or words are not used correctly, the player moves back one square at a time and picks up another card until able to produce a correct sentence. The first player to reach the finish square wins.

Can You Answer with a Question?

Objective: To teach the use of w*ho, what,* and *where* questions.

Materials: A game board with categories and points (similar to Jeopardy game); question cards corresponding to the categories and point levels (the words range in difficulty according to their point value, and the answers are written on the back of each card).

Directions: The first player chooses a category and point value from the game board. The player is presented with a word from the chosen category and must define the word with a question. For example, the category may be *Clothes,* and the word on the card may be *shoes.* The correct answer on the back of the card is, "What do you wear on your feet?" Object categories require a *what* question. If the player selects from a place category, the answer must be in the form of a question that uses *where.* For example, if the category is *Community Places* and the word is *library,* the answer is "Where do we get books?" If the student selects from a person category, the answer must be in the form of a question that uses *who.* For example, if the category is *Community Helpers* and the words are *police officer,* the answer is "Who catches criminals?"

Suggested categories: (1) What—Clothes (hat, shoes, and dress); Animals (dog, cat, and bird); Sports Equipment (ball, bat, and glove); (2) Where—Community Places (bank, post office, and school); Fun Places (res-

taurant, zoo, and theater); Travel Depots (train station, airport, and bus station); Who—Community Helpers (firefighter, police officer, and mail carrier); Family Member (mother, father, and sister); School Personnel (principal, teacher, and librarian).

Build a Sentence

Objective: To teach combining independent clauses with conjunctions.

Materials: Thirty flannel-backed cards with independent clauses written on the front of each card; 13 flannel-backed cards with conjunctions written on the front of each card; a flannelboard.

Directions: The flannelboard is placed in the middle of the table, and the cards are dealt to the players. The first player lays down a card containing an independent clause, such as *She was late.* The second player lays down a card containing a conjunction, such as *because.* The third player must lay down a clause to complete the sentence, such as *she missed the bus.* Then the next player begins a new sentence. A player loses a turn if the player does not have an appropriate card to play. The first player who uses all of his or her cards wins the game.

Suggested clauses: She went to bed; She was tired; Mary stayed home; He made a good grade; John went to the store; He studied; She watched television; He brought some ice cream; He washed dishes; He bought a ticket; Father fussed; Mother cooked supper.

Suggested conjunctions: because; and; since.

Prefix Bingo

Objective: To teach the prefixes *in, re, un,* and *non.*

Materials: Bingo cards with various root words that can be combined with the prefixes *in, re, un,* or *non;* a spinner, with four sections, that has a prefix in each section; markers with one prefix printed on each marker (see Figure 6.5).

Directions: The first player spins the spinner, notes on which prefix it lands, and picks up a marker with that prefix on it. The player places the prefix marker on a root word with which it can be combined. The player loses a turn if the spinner lands on a prefix that cannot be combined with a root word on his or her card. The first player whose markers are in a row (vertically, horizontally, or diagonally) wins the game. The winning card is checked to make sure the prefix on each marker can be combined with the root word on which it is placed.

Modification: This game can be modified by using suffixes, such as *ful, less,* and *ly.*

FIGURE 6.5

Prefix Bingo game card and spinner

side	build	do	tire	seen
turn	tell	fill	use	sense
sent	claim	call	stick	tend
skid	happy	move	cover	born
to	tie	come	paid	fuel

Deal a Sentence

Objective: To teach sentence construction.

Materials: Fifty-five word cards containing words from the following grammatical categories: noun (9), pronoun (9), verb (15), adjective (12), article (3), conjunction (3), preposition (3), and adverb (1).

Directions: Each player receives five cards, and the remaining cards are placed face down in the center of the players. Each player organizes his or her hand to determine whether there is a sentence. Then each player selects one card from the deck and discards one card face up. The first player to make a sentence wins the hand. The number of hands played can vary according to the time available, and the player with the most points at the end of the time period wins. Another option is for the first player to earn a predetermined number of points to be the winner. Scoring can be one point for a declarative sentence, two points for using *not* in a sentence, three points for a sentence with a conjunction, and four points for a question.

Suggested words: Nouns—ball, dress, boy, girl, book, house, doll, bike, dog; Pronouns—I, you, she, he, him, they, them, it, we; Verbs—is, are, was, were, made, can, go, should, may, do, see, ride, walk, run, am; Adjectives—big, round, pretty, small, sad, happy, little, red, fast, slow, fat, funny; Articles—a, an, the; Conjunctions—and, but, or; Prepositions—to, at, with; Adverb—not.

Conjunction Square

Objective: To teach sentence construction using conjunctions.

Materials: A checkerboard with a conjunction written on each square; a stack of cards with a sentence printed on each card; checkers.

Directions: The player makes a checker move (according to the rules of the game of checkers) and takes two sentence cards. The player must combine the two sentences on the cards with the conjunction on which the checker lands. The player must make a correct sentence to keep the move. If unable to make a sentence,

the player must move the checker back to its previous position. The players continue taking turns and making sentences until one player wins the checker game.

☀ SELF-CORRECTING LANGUAGE MATERIALS

Opposites

Objective: To teach classification of word opposites.

Feedback device: Windows in the back of the Spinning Wheels show matching symbols to indicate picture or word opposites.

Materials: Spinning Wheels (described in Chapter 2); a worksheet that has one picture in the left column and two pictures on the right—-one of which illustrates the opposite of the picture on the left—-corresponding to the pictures on the Spinning Wheels; an acetate overlay (see Figure 6.6).

Directions: The student places the acetate overlay over the worksheet, selects the picture that is the opposite of the one in the left column, and marks an X on that picture. After completing the worksheet, the student checks the work with the Spinning Wheels. The student turns the wheels so that the selected picture opposites appear in the windows, and then the student turns over the wheels to see whether matching symbols appear in the back windows.

Modification: This activity can be used to teach same, different, or associated words by changing the items or pictures on the Spinning Wheels.

Time Slot

Objective: To increase skills in using verbs relating to time.

Feedback device: Symbols or line drawings on the back of the verb cards match the line drawing on the envelope with the appropriate verb form.

FIGURE 6.6
Worksheet for Opposites

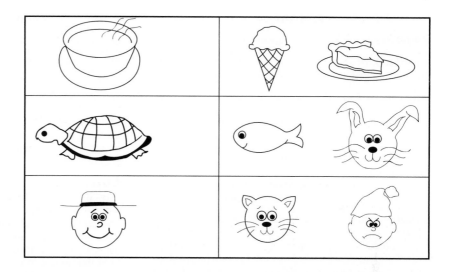

Materials: Three envelopes for present-, past-, and future-tense verbs with a different line drawing or symbol on each envelope; a set of cards with pictures depicting the time associated with various verb tenses (see Figure 6.7).

Directions: The student looks at each card to determine which verb tense the picture illustrates. The student then places each card in the envelope that denotes the answer. After sorting all the cards, the student takes the

cards out of the envelopes and checks to see whether the symbol on the back of each card matches the symbol on the front of the envelope in which it was placed.

Modifications: The activity can include several syntactic forms such as *are* + verb + *ing* or *has* + verb + *ed*. A different line drawing or symbol should be assigned to each syntactic form. Also, the activity can be modified further by using words instead of pictures and labeling the envelopes with the name of the verb tense.

FIGURE 6.7
Envelopes and cards for Time Slot

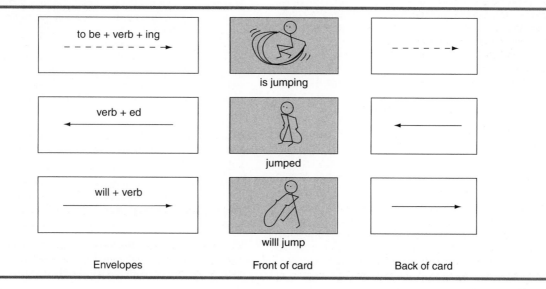

Flip-Siders

Objective: To teach classification by association.

Feedback device: Matching colors or symbols are on the back of pictures that are associated.

Materials: Flip-sider cards (presented in Chapter 2) that contain pictures of associated words (such as a sock and a shoe) and have matching colors or symbols on the back of associated pictures.

Directions: The student looks at each picture and finds the picture associated with it. The student combines the pictures and turns over the cards. The pictures that are associated have the same color or symbol on the back.

Modifications: Flip-siders can be used to teach opposites, verb tenses, and phoneme recognition. Also, the material can be modified for secondary students by combining associated pictures that illustrate cause-and-effect relationships (e.g., pictures showing a student studying and a report card with good grades, or an accident and an ambulance).

Make a Question

Objective: To teach the interrogative reversal.

Feedback device: The pieces of the puzzle strip fit together when the sentence is in question form.

Materials: A worksheet with declarative sentences; a set of puzzle pieces for each sentence that fit together when the sentence is in the form of a question.

Directions: The student rewrites each sentence on the worksheet into an interrogative reversal to ask a question. After completing the question, the student puts the corresponding puzzle pieces together to check the answer.

● The girls are at home.

● She is very tall.

When Did It Happen?

Objective: To teach the past-tense morpheme *ed*.

Feedback device: A tab pulled from a pocket in the material reveals the correct answer.

Materials: A tape recording of sentences that contain the morpheme *ed*; a card that contains the sentences and has a smiling face to circle to indicate correct use of *ed* and a frowning face to circle to indicate incorrect use of *ed*; a tab containing the answer key that fits in a pocket in the card; an acetate overlay (see Figure 6.8).

Directions: The student places the acetate overlay over the card, listens to the sentence on the tape recording, and circles the appropriate face on the answer card to indicate correct or incorrect use of *ed*. A pause on the tape is given after each sentence to allow the student time to circle the answer and pull the tab from the pocket to see whether the answer is correct. The numbers next to the faces on the tab correspond to the numbers of the sentences.

Modifications: The activity can be used to teach *is* or *ing* by making a tape with sentences that require *is* or *ing*. The activity can be modified further for older students by using written sentences, each of which the student must judge as grammatically correct or incorrect.

Word Endings with Meanings

Objective: To teach the suffixes *less* and *ful*.

Feedback device: The correct answer is revealed under a flap.

Materials: A laminated card that contains incomplete sentences that require a root word and the suffix *less* or *ful*; a laminated card illustrating a tree with roots at the bottom and the same number of branches at the top of the tree: (1) two numbered leaves on each branch are cut so that each leaf will fold back to reveal an answer underneath, (2) holes are punched in each corner of the card and a sheet of paper is attached to the back of the card with brass fasteners, (3) under each numbered leaf a suffix is written that fits the respective sentence, and (4) root words are written along the tree roots with a grease pencil (see Figure 6.9).

Directions: The student is given a laminated card that contains incomplete sentences requiring a root word and a suffix. The student circles the correct suffix with a grease pencil. After completing the sentences, the student lifts the leaves on the tree card to see the correct answers.

Modification: A sheet containing different prefixes and suffixes can be attached to the back of the tree card, and a corresponding worksheet provided.

FIGURE 6.8

Card and tab for When Did It Happen?

		Right	Wrong
1.	Yesterday the boy walked to the store.	😊	🙁
2.	At lunch the girl look at the clerk.	😊	🙁
3.	Last week the boy jump over the fence.	😊	🙁
4.	The dog chewed the ball.	😊	🙁
5.	John played all afternoon.	😊	🙁

1. 😊

Tab

Make It Say a Sentence

Objective: To teach sentence order.

Feedback device: An answer key in an envelope attached to the back of the card provides the answers.

Materials: A card containing scrambled sentences that contain conjunctions; an envelope on the back of the card; an answer key; paper.

Directions: The student looks at each scrambled sentence on the card and unscrambles the words. The student writes the unscrambled sentences on paper and checks the work by looking at the answer key in the envelope on the back of the card.

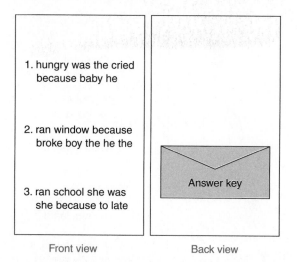

1. hungry was the cried because baby he

2. ran window because broke boy the he the

3. ran school she was she because to late

Answer key

Front view   Back view

Modifications: This self-correcting device can be used with many tasks, such as making grammatical judgments, changing declarative sentences into interrogative sentences, and using conjunctions. The cloze procedure for completing sentences with conjunctions can be adapted to this procedure by putting sentences on a card with an answer key attached. For example:

She went to the store _____ she needed to buy some groceries. (because, and)

She is going to buy milk _____ bread. (since, and)

Does It Mean the Same Thing?

Objective: To teach similarity of deep structure in two sentences.

Feedback device: An answer key on the back of the card provides the correct answers.

Materials: A card with sentence pairs, some having the same meaning (deep structure) and others having different meanings; an acetate overlay; an answer key on the back of the card (see Figure 6.10).

Directions: The student reads each set of sentences and decides whether the meaning of both sentences is the same or different. The student places the acetate overlay over the response section of the card and circles *same* or *different* to indicate the answer. After completing the task, the student turns over the card and places the acetate overlay over the answer key. The circles on the overlay should match the words circled on the answer key.

Modifications: Acetate overlays and marked answer keys can be used with sentences that use a cloze procedure with multiple choices. For example:

He heated the water _____ made coffee. (and, because)

FIGURE 6.9
Cards for Word Endings with Meanings

1. The broken car is use(ful/less) until it is fixed.
2. The basket is use(ful/less) to carry groceries.
3. I learned a lot from the meaning(ful/less) speech.
4. The poor directions were meaning(ful/less).
5. The student was vey care(ful/less) and wrote a neat letter.
6. The student was care(ful/less) and spilled paint on her dress.
7. She felt help(ful/less) when she couldn't start her car.
8. The neighbor was help(ful/less) when she loaned me her telephone.
9. The flower arrangement was pleasing and taste(ful/less).
10. The food was very bland and taste(ful/less) to me.

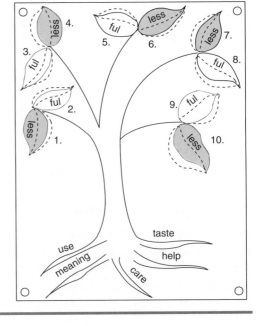

This procedure also can be used with grammatical judgments. For example:

Yesterday he walk to school.

_____ Correct   _____ Incorrect

Descriptors

Objective: To increase use of effective communication skills.

Feedback device: The correct responses are provided on the back of the stimulus card.

Materials: Cards with a small object mounted on the front of each card and a list of six descriptive categories pertaining to the object written on the back of each card; a tape recorder.

Directions: The student looks at the object on the card and records six different sentences describing the object on a tape recorder. After recording the six sentences, the student turns over the stimulus card, listens to each of the recorded sentences, and checks the appropriate descriptive category used on the back of the card.

☐ Name (pencil)

☐ Color (blue)

☐ Function (write, draw)

☐ Size (long, thin)

☐ Material of construction (wood, lead)

☐ Characteristics (point, eraser)

FIGURE 6.10
Card and acetate overlay for Does It Mean the Same Thing?

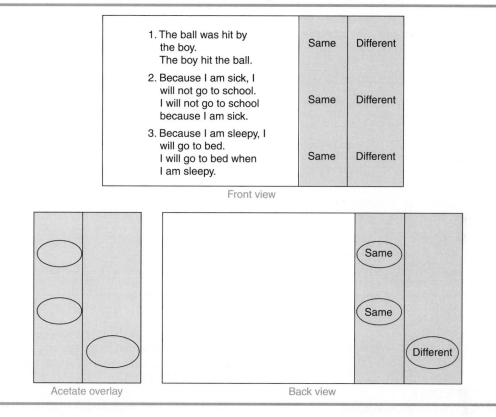

Modification: This material can be modified for younger students by using a picture of an object with two attributes (e.g., a small, red car). The student records a descriptive sentence on a tape recorder. Then the student turns over the picture card to the answer key, listens to the recording, and checks each attribute used. Answers can be coded for nonreaders—a color to indicate color category and a small object to indicate size category.

Indirect Requests

Objective: To identify indirect requests.

Feedback device: An answer key is provided on the back of the response card.

Materials: A tape recording of various indirect requests and questions; a response card with an answer key provided on the back of the card; an acetate overlay (see Figure 6.11).

Directions: The student places the acetate overlay over the response card and listens to the taped sentences. The student decides whether each sentence is a question or an indirect request and marks the answer on the overlay. After completing the task, the student turns over the response card and places the acetate overlay over the answer key to check the responses.

Taped sentences

1. What time is it?
2. Can you shut the door?
3. Won't you stop that?
4. Can't you finish your work?
5. When does the bus arrive?
6. Is the water running?
7. Must you just sit there?
8. Must you slurp your milk?
9. Can't you sit still?
10. Did the dog run away?

FIGURE 6.11

Response card for Indirect Requests

	Indirect Request	Question
1.	_____	_____
2.	_____	_____
3.	_____	_____
4.	_____	_____
5.	_____	_____
6.	_____	_____
7.	_____	_____
8.	_____	_____
9.	_____	_____
10.	_____	_____

Front of response card

	Indirect Request	Question
1.		X
2.	X	
3.	X	
4.	X	
5.		X
6.		X
7.	X	
8.	X	
9.	X	
10.		X

Back of response card

Modification: The taped sentences can be changed to questions and statements. The student identifies each sentence as a statement or question.

☀ COMMERCIAL LANGUAGE PROGRAMS

Numerous commercial language programs and materials are available to help students having difficulty with language. Selection of a program for intervention is influenced by two primary factors: the population the program serves and the theoretical model on which it is based. The theoretical model describes normal language acquisition and includes the content the student learns, the sequence in which the student learns, and how the student learns. There is a close relationship between the language program and the theoretical model of language acquisition (McLean & Snyder-McLean, 1978). Because language is interactive, no single program is appropriate for use alone, and the teacher should select programs based on the language needs of individual students. Thus, the selection of programs and materials for classroom use should reflect the developmental ages of the students for whom they are selected as well

as the purpose of the intervention. The following selected commercial language programs may be useful for teaching language skills to students with language problems.

Clinical Language Intervention Program

The *Clinical Language Intervention Program* (Semel & Wiig, 1982) focuses on teaching semantics, morphology and syntax, pragmatics, and memory to students in kindergarten through eighth grade. Within each category of language form and content, the materials and tasks are designed to elicit clearly defined intervention targets. The program includes more than 2,000 stimulus pictures, matching verbal stimuli, suggested training methods and strategies, a picture manual to promote acquisition and use of specific language skills or functions, a language activities manual of maintenance and generalization activities, and checklists for recording student progress across time.

Fast ForWord

Fast ForWord (published by Scientific Learning Corporation) is a technology-based program for students in kindergarten through twelfth grade that builds oral language comprehension skills such as phonemic awareness, auditory processing speed, phonological awareness, working memory, syntax, grammar, and sequencing. The training uses acoustically modified sound and methods of cross-training to improve receptive and expressive oral language skills within a scientifically validated optimal learning environment. The training exercises are presented in a game-like environment and include motivational rewards. Artificial speech, digitized human speech, and digital tones are used in the computerized exercises to stretch and emphasize minute speech sounds so that students are better able to distinguish among them. The methods behind *Fast ForWord* training are based on findings from research in neuroscience and neuropsychology. The *Fast ForWord* training schedule consists of 100 minutes of training per day, five days a week, under the supervision of a trained educator.

Language for Learning; Distar Language II and III

Language for Learning and *Distar Language II* and *III,* developed by S. Engelmann and J. Osborn (published by SRA), present a highly structured approach to language intervention. The program is designed for students in kindergarten through fourth grade and focuses on expressive and receptive language and cognitive development. In *Language for Learning,* students practice using complete sentences, answering questions, and following oral directions. In *Distar Language II,* students learn word and sentence skills and develop questioning and reasoning skills. The structure of spoken and written sentences is analyzed in *Distar Language III,* and students learn to follow the rules of grammar to communicate information and ideas effectively. The program uses a didactic approach, with repetition and group drills to teach language concepts. Following a script, the teacher models, elicits group and individual responses at a fast pace, and either reinforces the correct response or corrects the inappropriate response. Various language skills are taught, such as identity statements, pronouns, prepositions, and multiple attributes.

Lindamood Phoneme Sequencing Program for Reading, Spelling, and Speech

The *Lindamood Phoneme Sequencing Program for Reading, Spelling, and Speech* (Lindamood & Lindamood, 1998) presents step-by-step sensory-cognitive procedures to develop the ability to identify and sequence individual sounds and their order within words. Activities focus on the lip, tongue, and mouth actions that produce speech sounds. Phonemic awareness is brought to a conscious level, and activities progress from single phonemes through multisyllabic words. Students are taught to use sensory information from feeling, hearing, and seeing to develop a feedback system that promotes self-correction in speech, reading, and spelling. Both a classroom version and clinical version are available, and manipulatives, static-cling letters and mouth pictures, a videotape, and an audiocassette are included. A supplemental CD-ROM can be used to stimulate sensory processing and thinking regarding phonemes and their sequence in words. The program is designed for students in kindergarten through adult age.

Peabody Language Development Kits

The *Peabody Language Development Kits,* developed by L. M. Dunn, J. O. Smith, L. N. Dunn, and K. B. Horton (published by American Guidance Service), provide a multilevel program for developing oral language and cognitive skills in young children. Level P, for 4- to 5-year-old preschoolers, provides practice in labeling language, constructing sentences, and thinking logically. Level 1, for 5- to 6-year-old students, focuses on brainstorming and problem solving to prompt divergent thinking and oral expression. The kits stress overall language development rather than specific psycholinguistic processes. The activities at each level emphasize the skills of *reception* through sight, hearing, and touch; *expression* through vocal and motor behavior; and *conceptualization* through divergent, convergent, and associative thinking. Picture card decks, puppets, a sound book, story posters, and a teacher's manual are included in the kits. The teacher's manual has descriptions of daily lessons and specifies a teacher script as well as appropriate materials and activities.

Teaching Morphology Developmentally

Teaching Morphology Developmentally, developed by K. G. Shipley and C. J. Banis (published by Communication Skills Builders), is a developmental program for teaching word formation that is designed for students whose language age is between $2^1/2$ and 10 years. The 522 color stimulus cards can be used to teach more than 1,000 free morphemes and 700 bound morphemes. Specific morphemes include present progressives, plurals, possessives, past tenses, third-person singulars, and derived adjectives (comparative-superlative and irregular forms). Reproducible lists of curriculum items, pretest and posttest forms, and suggestions for developing behavioral objectives are included in the instructional guide.

COMPUTER SOFTWARE PROGRAMS IN LANGUAGE

Computer-assisted instruction can be used to improve students' speech and language skills. As well as enhancing motivation, computers appear to facilitate both social and cognitive interactions (Clements, 1987). Moreover, the use of computers tends to stimulate social use (Lipinski, Nida, Shade, & Watson, 1986), produce more positive and varied facial expressions and smiling (Hyson, 1985), and produce more spoken words per minute when compared with traditional activities such as blocks, art, or games (Muhlstein & Croft, 1986). Also, speech synthesizers such as Echo, DECtalk, and Digispeech provide speech for "talking" programs, and headphones can facilitate individual use. The following software programs focus on language skills.

Parts of Speech

Parts of Speech (produced by Optimum Resource) is designed to help students in third through twelfth grade increase grammar and vocabulary skills. Students identify nouns, pronouns, adjectives, verbs, adverbs, conjunctions, prepositions, and interjections from word lists and from within sentences and paragraphs. The 32 leveled lessons use a variety of timed and untimed activities and present more than 1,000 graded words. The teacher can customize the program by adding new words and exercises. Progress reports are available, and worksheets can be printed for later use.

Picture Gallery

Picture Gallery (produced by Psychological Corporation) is a series of CD-ROM products for use by language specialists who use visual stimuli in an educational setting. The collection features thousands of color digitized photographs that can be used to create picture sets according to each student's needs. Five CD-ROMs are available: articulation and phonology, thematic units, early concepts, advanced vocabulary, and morphology. The items can be used to facilitate the acquisition or remediation of speech or language skills.

Vocabulary Development

Vocabulary Development (produced by Optimum Resource) is a comprehensive vocabulary-building program for students in third through ninth grade that provides practice in recognizing synonyms, antonyms, homonyms, multiple meanings, prefixes, suffixes, and context clues. The program includes more than 400 words in lessons at six difficulty levels. The student automatically is advanced to the next level upon mastering the previous one. The teacher can create exercises and set difficulty levels to expand the use of the program. Practice sheets and test masters can be printed, and the program keeps records of student progress.

Words Around Me

Words Around Me (produced by Edmark) presents 275 common vocabulary words as well as 186 plurals for people, places, things, and actions. Students learn to associate spoken words with a variety of visual representations, including photographs, drawn images, and animations. Students progress through five activities (word identification, plurals, categorization, sameness, and difference), and four review games provide opportunities for reinforcement. Flash cards can be printed with or without text labels, and word collections are provided in both English and Spanish.

☀ REFERENCES

Ackerman, P. T., Dykman, R. A., & Gardner, M. Y. (1990). Counting rate, naming rate, phonological sensitivity, and memory span: Major factors in dyslexia. *Journal of Learning Disabilities, 23,* 325–327.

Adler, S. (1988). A new job description and a new task for the public school clinician: Relating effectively to the nonstandard dialect speaker. *Language, Speech, and Hearing Services in Schools, 19,* 28–33.

American Speech-Language-Hearing Association. (1991). A model for collaborative service delivery for students with language-learning disorders in the public schools. *Asha, 33*(Suppl. 5), 44–50.

American Speech-Language-Hearing Association. (1992). Definitions for communicative disorders and differences. *Asha, 24,* 949–950.

Bandura, A. (1971). Analysis of modeling processes. In A. Bandura (Ed.), *Psychological modeling: Conflicting theories.* New York: Aldine/Atherton.

Bankson, N. W. (1990). *Bankson Language Test—2.* Austin, TX: PRO-ED.

Baratz, J. C. (1969). Language and cognitive assessments of Negro children: Assumptions and research needs. *Journal of American Speech and Hearing Association, 11,* 87–91.

Barenbaum, E., & Newcomer, P. (1996). *Test of Children's Language.* Austin, TX: PRO-ED.

Bartel, N. R., Grill, J. J., & Bryen, D. N. (1973). Language characteristics of Black children: Implication for assessment. *Journal of School Psychology, 11,* 351–364.

Bashir, A. S. (1989). Language intervention and the curriculum. *Seminars in Speech and Language, 10,* 181–191.

Bates, E. (1976). Pragmatics and sociolinguistics in child language. In D. Morehead & A. Morehead (Eds.), *Normal and deficient child language* (pp. 411–463). Baltimore, MD: University Park Press.

Bernstein, D. K. (1993). Language development: The preschool years. In D. K. Bernstein & E. Tiegerman (Eds.), *Language and communication disorders in children* (3rd ed., pp. 97–122). Boston: Allyn & Bacon.

Bloom, L. (1975). Language development review. In F. D. Horowitz (Ed.), *Review of child development research* (Vol. 4). Chicago: University of Chicago Press.

Bloom, L., & Lahey, M. (1978). *Language development and language disorders.* New York: John Wiley.

Boehm, A. E. (1986). *Boehm Test of Basic Concepts— Revised.* San Antonio, TX: Psychological Corporation.

Bos, C. S., & Vaughn, S. (1998). *Strategies for teaching students with learning and behavior problems* (4th ed.). Boston: Allyn & Bacon.

Braine, M. (1971). *On two types of models of the internalization of grammar.* New York: Academic Press.

Braine, M. (1976). Children's first word combinations. *Monographs of the Society for Research in Child Development, 41* (Serial No. 164).

Brown, R. (1973). *A first language: The early stages.* Cambridge, MA: Harvard University Press.

Brown, R., & Berko, J. (1960). Word associations and acquisition of grammar. *Child Development, 31,* 1–14.

Bruner, J. S. (1974/1975). From communication to language: A psychological perspective. *Cognition, 3,* 255–287.

Buttrill, J., Niizawa, J., Biemer, C., Takahashi, C., & Hearn, S. (1989). Serving the language learning disabled adolescent: A strategies-based model. *Language, Speech, and Hearing Services in Schools, 20,* 185–201.

Cardoza, D., & Rueda, R. (1986). Educational and occupational outcomes of Hispanic learning-disabled high school students. *The Journal of Special Education, 20,* 111–126.

Carrow-Woolfolk, E. (1974). *Carrow Elicited Language Inventory.* Austin, TX: PRO-ED.

Carrow-Woolfolk, E. (1999). *Test for Auditory Comprehension of Language—3.* Austin, TX: PRO-ED.

Carrow-Woolfolk, E. (1995). *Oral and Written Language Scales: Listening Comprehension and Oral Expression.* Circle Pines, MN: American Guidance Service.

Chomsky, N. A. (1965). *Aspects of the theory of syntax.* Cambridge, MA: MIT Press.

Clements, D. H. (1987). Computers and young children: A review of research. *Young Children, 42*(1), 34–44.

Connell, P. J. (1986). Acquisition of semantic role by language-disordered children: Differences between production and comprehension. *Journal of Speech and Hearing Research, 29,* 366–374.

Courtright, J. A., & Courtright, I. C. (1976). Imitative modeling as a theoretical base for instructing language-disordered children. *Journal of Speech and Hearing Research, 19,* 655–663.

Courtright, J. A., & Courtright, I. C. (1979). Imitative modeling as a language intervention strategy: The effects of two mediating variables. *Journal of Speech and Hearing Research, 22,* 389–402.

Damico, J. S. (1987). Addressing language concerns in the schools: The SLP as a consultant. *Journal of Childhood Communication Disorders, 11,* 1–16.

Deshler, D. D., & Schumaker, J. B. (1986). Learning strategies: An instructional alternative for low achieving adolescents. *Exceptional Children, 52,* 583–590.

Dunn, L. M., & Dunn, L. M. (1997). *Peabody Picture Vocabulary Test—Third Edition.* Circle Pines, MN: American Guidance Service.

Ehren, B. J., & Lenz, B. K. (1989). Adolescents with language disorders: Special considerations in providing academically relevant language intervention. *Seminars in Speech and Language, 10,* 192–204.

Ervin-Tripp, S., & Mitchell-Kernan, C. (Eds.). (1977). *Child discourse.* New York: Academic Press.

German, D. J. (1984). Diagnosis of word-finding disorders in children with learning disabilities. *Journal of Learning Disabilities, 17,* 353–359.

German, D. J. (2000). *Test of Word Finding—3.* Austin, TX: PRO-ED.

German, D. J. (1990). *Test of Adolescent/Adult Word Finding.* Austin, TX: PRO-ED.

Gersten, R., & Woodward, J. (1994). The language-minority student and special education: Issues, trends, and paradoxes. *Exceptional Children, 60,* 310–322.

Girolametto, L. E. (1988). Improving the social-conversational skills of developmentally delayed children: An intervention study. *Journal of Speech and Hearing Disorders, 53,* 156–167.

Goldman, R., & Fristoe, M. (1986). *Goldman-Fristoe Test of Articulation.* Circle Pines, MN: American Guidance Service.

Hammill, D. D., Brown, V. L., Larsen, S. C., & Wiederholt, J. L. (1994). *Test of Adolescent and Adult Language— 3.* Austin, TX: PRO-ED.

Hammill, D. D., & Newcomer, P. L. (1997). *Test of Language Development—Intermediate: 3.* Austin, TX: PRO-ED.

Hazel, J. S., & Schumaker, J. B. (1988). Social skills and learning disabilities: Current issues and recommendations for future research. In J. F. Kavanagh & T. J. Truss (Eds.), *Learning disabilities: Proceedings of the national conference* (pp. 293–344). Parkton, MD: York Press.

Hresko, W. P., Reid, D. K., & Hammill, D. D. (1999). *Test of Early Language Development—3.* Austin, TX: PRO-ED.

Hughes, D. L. (1989). Generalization from language therapy to classroom academics. *Seminars in Speech and Language, 10,* 218–230.

Hyson, M. C. (1985). Emotions and the microcomputer. An exploratory study of young children's responses. *Computers in Human Behavior, 1,* 143–152.

Jacobson, R., & Halle, M. (1956). *Fundamentals of language.* The Hague: Mouton.

Jenkins, J. J., & Palermo, D. S. (1964). Mediation processes and the acquisition of linguistic structure. In U. Bellugi & R. Brown (Eds.), *The acquisition of language. Monographs of the Society for Research in Child Development, 29* (1, Whole No. 92).

Kayser, H. (1989). Speech and language assessment of Spanish-English speaking children. *Language, Speech, and Hearing Services in Schools, 20,* 226–241.

Lahey, M. (1988). *Language disorders and language development.* Boston: Allyn & Bacon.

Larson, V. L., & McKinley, N. (1995). *Language disorders in older students.* Eau Claire, WI: Thinking Publications.

Lazar, R. T., Warr-Leeper, G. A., Nicholson, C. B., & Johnson, S. (1989). Elementary school teachers' use of multiple meaning expressions. *Language, Speech, and Hearing Services in Schools, 20,* 420–429.

Lenneberg, E. H. (1967). *Biological foundations of language.* New York: Wiley.

Leonard, L. B. (1975). Modeling as a clinical procedure in language training. *Language, Speech, and Hearing Services in Schools, 6,* 72–85.

Leonard, L. B., Wilcox, M. J., Fulmer, K. C., & Davis, G. A. (1978). Understanding indirect requests: An investigation of children's comprehension of pragmatic meanings. *Journal of Speech and Hearing Research, 21,* 528–537.

Lindamood, P. C., & Lindamood P. D. (1998). *Lindamood phoneme sequencing program for reading, spelling, and speech* (3rd ed.). Austin, TX: PRO-ED.

Lipinski, J. M., Nida, R. E., Shade, D. D., & Watson, J. A. (1986). The effects of microcomputers on young children: An examination of free-play choices, sex differences, and social interactions. *Journal of Educational Computing Research, 2,* 147–168.

Marvin, C. A. (1987). Consultation services: Changing roles for SLPs. *Journal of Childhood Communication Disorders, 11,* 1–16.

Mastropieri, M. A., Scruggs, T. E., & Fulk, B. J. M. (1990). Teaching abstract vocabulary with the keyword method: Effects on recall and comprehension. *Journal of Learning Disabilities, 23,* 92–96, 107.

McGregor, K. K., & Leonard, L. B. (1989). Facilitating word-finding skills of language-impaired children. *Journal of Speech and Hearing Disorders, 54,* 141–147.

McLean, J. E., & Snyder-McLean, L. K. (1978). *A transactional approach to early language training.* Boston: Allyn & Bacon.

McNeil, D. (1970). The development of language. In P. H. Mussen (Ed.), *Carmichael's manual of child psychology* (Vol. 2, 3rd ed., pp. 1061–1161). New York: Wiley.

Mercer, J. R. (1983). Issues in the diagnosis of language disorders in students whose primary language is not English. *Topics in Language Disorders, 3*(3), 46–56.

Merritt, D. D., & Liles, B. Z. (1987). Story grammar ability in children with and without language disorder: Story generation, story retelling, and story comprehension. *Journal of Speech and Hearing Research, 30,* 539–552.

Miller, L. (1989). Classroom-based language intervention. *Language, Speech, and Hearing Services in Schools, 20,* 153–169.

Mogford, K., & Sadler, J. (1989). *Child language disability: Implications in an educational setting.* Philadelphia: Multilingual Matters.

Morgan, D. L., & Guilford, A. M. (1984). *Adolescent Language Screening Test.* Austin, TX: PRO-ED.

Moses, N., Klein, H. B., & Altman, E. (1990). An approach to assessing and facilitating causal language in adults with learning disabilities based on Piagetian theory. *Journal of Learning Disabilities, 23,* 220–228.

Muhlstein, E. A., & Croft, D. J. (1986). *Using the microcomputer to enhance language experiences and the development of cooperative play among preschool children.* Cupertino, CA: De Anza College. (ERIC Document Reproduction Service No. ED 269 004)

Nelson, N. W. (1989). Curriculum-based language assessment and intervention. *Language, Speech, and Hearing Services in Schools, 20,* 170–184.

Nelson, N. W. (1994). Curriculum-based assessment and intervention across the grades. In G. P. Wallach & K. G. Butler (Eds.), *Language learning disabilities in school-age children and adolescents* (pp. 104–131). Boston: Allyn & Bacon.

Newcomer, P. L., & Hammill, D. D. (1997). *Test of Language Development—Primary: 3.* Austin, TX: PRO-ED.

Owens, R. E., Jr. (1991). *Language disorders: A functional approach to assessment and intervention.* Boston: Allyn & Bacon.

Owens, R. E., Jr. (1994). Development of communication, language, and speech. In G. H. Shames, E. H. Wiig, & W. A. Secord (Eds.), *Human communication disorders: An introduction* (4th ed., pp. 36–81). Boston: Allyn & Bacon.

Parnell, M. M., Amerman, J. D., & Harting, R. D. (1986). Responses of language-disordered children to *wh*-questions. *Language, Speech, and Hearing Services in Schools, 17,* 95–106.

Pehrsson, R. S., & Denner, P. R. (1988). Semantic organizers: Implications for reading and writing. *Topics in Language Disorders, 8*(3), 24–32.

Phelps-Terasaki, D., & Phelps-Gunn, T. (1992). *Test of Pragmatic Language.* Austin, TX: PRO-ED.

Piaget, J. (1960). *The psychology of intelligence.* Patterson, NJ: Littlefield, Adams.

Prutting, C. A. (1979). Process\pra I , ses\n: The action of moving forward progressively from one point to another on the way to completion. *Journal of Speech and Hearing Disorders, 44,* 3–30.

Riedlinger-Ryan, K. J., & Shewan, C. M. (1984). Comparison of auditory comprehension skills in learning-disabled and academically achieving adolescents. *Language, Speech, and Hearing Services in Schools, 15,* 127–136.

Roth, F. P., & Clark, D. M. (1987). Symbolic play and social participation abilities of language-impaired and normally developing children. *Journal of Speech and Hearing Disorders, 52,* 17–29.

Salend, S. J., & Fradd, S. (1986). Nationwide availability of services for limited English-proficient handicapped students. *The Journal of Special Education, 20,* 127–135.

Salvia, J., & Ysseldyke, J. E. (1998). *Assessment* (7th ed.). Boston: Houghton Mifflin.

Schumaker, J. B., & Deshler, D. D. (1984). Setting demand variables: A major factor in program planning for the learning disabled adolescent. *Topics in Language Disorders, 4*(4), 22–40.

Schumaker, J. B., Deshler, D. D., Alley, G. R., Warner, M. M., & Denton, P. H. (1984). Multipass: A learning strategy for improving reading comprehension. *Learning Disabilities Quarterly, 5,* 295–304.

Schwabe, A. M., Olswang, L. B., & Kriegsmann, E. (1986). Requests for information: Linguistic, cognitive, pragmatic, and environmental variables. *Language, Speech, and Hearing Services in Schools, 17,* 38–55.

Seidenberg, P. L. (1988). Cognitive and academic instructional intervention for learning-disabled adolescents. *Topics in Language Disorders, 8*(3), 56–71.

Semel, E. M., & Wiig, E. H. (1982). *Clinical language intervention program.* San Antonio, TX: Psychological Corporation.

Semel, E. M., Wiig, E. H., & Secord, W. (1995). *Clinical Evaluation of Language Fundamentals—3.* San Antonio, TX: Psychological Corporation.

Semel, E. M., Wiig, E. H., & Secord, W. (1996). *Clinical Evaluation of Language Fundamentals—3: Screening Test.* San Antonio, TX: Psychological Corporation.

Simon, C. S. (1985). *Communication skills and classroom success.* San Diego, CA: College-Hill Press.

Skinner, B. F. (1957). *Verbal behavior.* New York: Appleton-Century-Crofts.

Snyder, L. S. (1986). Developmental language disorders: Elementary school age. In J. M. Costello & A. L. Holland (Eds.), *Handbook of speech and language disorders* (pp. 671–700). San Diego, CA: College-Hill Press.

Staats, A. (1971). Linguistic-mentalistic theory versus an explanatory S-R learning theory of language development. In D. I. Slobin (Ed.), *The ontogenesis of grammar.* New York: Academic Press.

Tiegerman, E., & Siperstein, M. (1984). Individual patterns of interaction in the mother-child dyad: Implications for the language-disordered child. *Topics in Language Disorders, 4,* 50–62.

Wallace, G., & Hammill, D. D. (1994). *Comprehensive Receptive and Expressive Vocabulary Test.* Austin, TX: PRO-ED.

Wallach, G. (1989). Current research as a map for language intervention in the school years. *Seminars in Speech and Language, 10,* 205–217.

Warren, S. F., & Yoder, P. J. (1994). Communication and language intervention: Why a constructivist approach is insufficient. *The Journal of Special Education, 28,* 248–258.

Wepman, J. (1973). *The Auditory Discrimination Test.* Palm Springs, CA: Language Research Associates.

Wiig, E. H. (1990). Linguistic transitions and learning disabilities: A strategic learning perspective. *Learning Disability Quarterly, 13,* 128–140.

Wiig, E. H., & Secord, W. (1992). *Test of Word Knowledge.* San Antonio, TX: Psychological Corporation.

Wiig, E. H., & Secord, W. A. (1994). Language disabilities in school-age children and youth. In G. H. Shames, E. H. Wiig, & W. A. Secord (Eds.), *Human communication disorders: An introduction* (4th ed., pp. 212–247). Boston: Allyn & Bacon.

Wiig, E. H., & Semel, E. M. (1976). *Language disabilities in children and adolescents.* Boston: Allyn & Bacon.

Wiig, E. H., & Semel, E. M. (1984). *Language assessment and intervention for the learning disabled* (2nd ed.). Boston: Allyn & Bacon.

Wilcox, M. J. (1986). Developmental language disorders: Preschoolers. In J. M. Costello & A. L. Holland (Eds.), *Handbook of speech and language disorders* (pp. 643–670). San Diego, CA: College-Hill Press.

Wood, B. S. (1976). *Children and communications: Verbal and nonverbal language development.* Upper Saddle River, NJ: Prentice Hall.

CHAPTER 7

Assessing Reading

About 10 to 15 percent of the general school population experience difficulty in reading (Harris & Sipay, 1990). Carnine, Silbert, and Kameenui (1997) suggest that reading difficulties are the principal cause of failure in school. Reading experiences strongly influence a student's self-image and feeling of competency; furthermore, reading failure can lead to misbehavior, anxiety, and a lack of motivation. Moreover, in American culture, learning to read is important for maintaining self-respect and for obtaining the respect of others.

Reading is a very complex task, and numerous definitions exist. In this chapter, *reading* is defined as a visual-auditory task that involves obtaining meaning from symbols (letters and words). Reading includes two basic processes: a *decoding* process and a *comprehension* process. The decoding process involves understanding the phoneme-grapheme relationships and translating printed words into a representation similar to oral language. Thus, decoding skills enable the learner to pronounce words correctly. Comprehension skills enable the learner to understand the meaning of words in isolation and in context.

☀ ORGANIZATION OF READING SKILLS

To assess or teach reading skills effectively, it is helpful to understand the general organization of reading content and related subskills. As implied in the definition, reading content is divided into word recognition skills and comprehension skills (see Figure 7.1). Reading approaches differ in the skills they stress and when to introduce them. For example, a phonics approach emphasizes the early introduction of the sound-symbol system, whereas an approach that focuses on meaning stresses learning whole words by sight at first and introduces the sound-symbol system later.

Educators commonly use seven strategies of word recognition (Ekwall & Shanker, 1989; Guszak, 1985):

1. **Configuration** is the outline or general shape of a word. Word length, uppercase letters, and letter height can provide some visual cues to the unskilled reader.

2. **Context analysis** is "the use of any surrounding information that may unlock a given word's name or meaning" (Guszak, 1985, p. 72). Semantic and syntactic (grammatical) cues help the reader predict word possibilities according to context. Likewise, pictures can provide context cues.

3. **Sight words** are words the reader recognizes without applying phonetic analysis. They include frequently used words, such as those on the Dolch list (Dolch, 1955), as well as words the reader knows instantly from repeated exposure. Many words in English that have irregular spellings are taught as sight words; that is, they are learned as whole words. In reading approaches that focus

FIGURE 7.1
An organizational framework of developmental reading skills

Source: From *Students with Learning Disabilities* (p. 518), 5th ed., by C. D. Mercer, 1997, Upper Saddle River, NJ: Merrill/Prentice Hall. Copyright 1997 by Prentice-Hall Publishing Company. Reprinted by permission.

on meaning, the whole-word method is used predominantly to introduce printed words.

4. *Phonics analysis* involves decoding words by symbol-sound associations. This involves learning phonemes and rules concerning the various sounds, such as those pertaining to single initial consonants, initial and ending consonant blends, consonant digraphs, silent consonants, short and long vowel sounds, and vowel teams and special letter combinations.

5. *Syllabication* is the process of dividing a word into its component parts. Each syllable contains a vowel sound. Some authorities place syllabication in phonics skills, whereas others include it in structural analysis (Ekwall & Shanker, 1989).

6. *Structural analysis* is the use of meaningful units such as root words, prefixes, suffixes, possessives, plurals, word families, and compound words. Comprehension of these structures permits a faster rate of reading than does analyzing individual sounds.

7. *Dictionary analysis* involves the use of a dictionary. Although seldom used for word recognition, it provides an independent means of pronouncing unknown words by using the pronunciation key symbols in a glossary or dictionary.

Five major areas are included in reading comprehension (Ekwall & Shanker, 1989; R. J. Smith & Barrett, 1979):

1. *Vocabulary development* is essential for the reader to understand the words a writer has used. A background of meaningful experience (exposure to books, people, and places) and learning words from context (through a variety of reading material) help develop vocabulary.

2. *Literal comprehension* refers to recognition and recall of explicitly stated information. Some of the skills involved in literal reading include reading for the central thought and main ideas, noting and remembering significant details, noting the order or sequence of events, and finding answers to specific questions.

3. *Inferential* (or *interpretative*) *comprehension* requires the reader to make conjectures or hypotheses based on stated information, intuition, and personal experience. Grasping cause-effect relationships, anticipating the remainder of a story, and forming opinions are inferential comprehension skills.

4. *Evaluation* or *critical reading* deals with judgments based on the reader's experiences, knowledge, or values. Evaluation focuses on qualities of accuracy, acceptability, worth, or probability of occurrence. It includes determining validity and judging the difference between reality and fantasy or fact and opinion. It also involves making value (moral) judgments and analyzing the intent of the author.

5. *Appreciation* deals with being emotionally and aesthetically sensitive to the written selection. To function at this level, the student identifies with characters and incidents and verbally can express emotional feelings about the work (e.g., excitement, fear, or boredom).

In functional reading, the student reads to obtain information. Whereas developmental reading (word recognition and comprehension) involves *learning to read,* functional reading involves *reading to learn.* Functional reading is sometimes called *study skills* because it includes locating information (using indexes, tables of contents, and encyclopedias), comprehending data (technical vocabulary, maps, and tables), outlining and summarizing, researching, and developing study patterns for specific content areas.

The scope and sequence skills list for reading presented in Appendix A is organized into word-attack skills and comprehension skills. Authorities disagree about the sequence for teaching reading skills, and research results about the sequence are inconclusive. Thus, a teacher should use a reading scope and sequence skills list in a flexible way and should tailor the sequence for assessing and teaching reading skills according to logic and experience.

DEVELOPMENT OF READING SKILLS

Chall and Stahl (1982) discuss three reading models that differ in the importance they attach to text and meaning. The *bottom-up* model emphasizes that readers proceed from text to meaning; that is, letters and words are perceived and decoded and then the text's meaning is comprehended. In contrast, the *top-down* model emphasizes that readers rely on prior knowledge and comprehension of the textual material's meaning rather than on word recognition and decoding of individual text elements. In essence, the bottom-up model focuses primarily on the reader's skill in sound-symbol association and word recognition, whereas the top-down model focuses on the reader's ability to question, hypothesize, and comprehend rather than on decoding individual text elements. The *interactive* model emphasizes both text and meaning by proposing that readers shift between attending to the text (i.e., specific letters and words) and what is in their mind (i.e., predicting or hypothesizing). For example, a reader may use a top-down approach when the material is familiar but change to a bottom-up approach when confronted with unfamiliar text.

Reading content has a structure in which the student first constructs simple relationships (such as grapheme-phoneme) and then progresses to more complex tasks (such as critical reading). Thus, the interactive model may describe the reading process most adequately, especially in the early stages of learning to read. As the reader becomes more proficient, attention to comprehension is increased and less attention is given to scrutinizing individual letters and words. Many authorities (Chall, 1983; Kirk, Kliebhan, & Lerner, 1978) believe that growth in reading skills occurs in several stages. Knowing the stages helps the teacher select assessment tasks, develop instructional goals, and choose instructional approaches. In addition, carefully monitoring student progress helps determine when the student moves from one level to the next. Chall divides reading development into six stages, from 0 to 5, covering prereading to highly skilled reading: (0) prereading, (1) initial reading or decoding, (2) confirmation, fluency, and ungluing from print, (3) reading for learning the new, (4) multiple viewpoints, and (5) construction and reconstruction.

Stage 0: Prereading

During the prereading stage, from birth to about age 6, children gradually accumulate understandings about reading. Most children learn the parts of a book (e.g., top, bottom, front, back, and page) and recognize letters, common signs, and a few words. Many children can print their own names and pretend they can read a story that has been read to them frequently. Prereading activities should include parents reading to children (especially reading that involves the child in discussions about

books, pictures, words, letters, and stories). Other appropriate activities include experiences with environmental print (e.g., food labels, menus, store names, traffic signs, and print associated with toys and play activities).

The distinction between prereading and reading activities becomes less apparent during the latter period of this stage. Harris and Sipay (1990) note that reading readiness activities (e.g., oral demonstrations of phonological awareness of words and syllables) that begin in some kindergarten classes are viewed as the teaching of specific concepts and skills that merge into reading. The question of when to begin formal reading instruction remains controversial. Early research (Gates, 1937) promoted the position that formal reading instruction should not begin until the child reaches a mental age of 6 to $6^{1}/_{2}$ years. Fortunately for the many children who need early intervention, this old research has been discredited.

In a nationwide longitudinal study of 3,959 secondary school seniors, Hanson and Farrell (1995) found that those who received a formal reading program in kindergarten outperformed comparable groups who did not participate in such a program. They conclude the following (p. 929):

> The major finding of this study, briefly stated, is: Students who learned to read in kindergarten were found to be superior in reading skills [current reading competency and reading attitude and behavior] and all other educational indicators [remediation, grades and attendance, and academic track] measured as seniors in high school. Further, this finding held up across districts and schools, as well as ethnic, gender, and social class groups. Also, there was absolutely no evidence of any negative effects from learning to read in kindergarten. Collectively, the results provide full support for the policy of teaching reading in kindergarten.

Waiting late to begin formal reading instruction has many negative implications. Research indicates that 74 percent of children who do not learn to read by third grade will be poor readers as adults (Lyon, 1995). Similarly, Juel (1988) notes that 88 percent of children who are poor readers at the end of first grade will remain poor readers at the end of fourth grade. Moreover, neurological studies suggest that deficiency in word recognition skills of some children is associated with below-normal brain activity in the left temporal region (Lyon, 1995). These children may become successful readers when they receive *early* phonological awareness training.

The critical period for teaching reading efficiently appears to differ among children. Some youngsters need early reading instruction because they are very capable of learning and handling schoolwork, and others need it because they lack certain abilities and need an early start to learn to read by third grade. Thus, what is developmentally appropriate differs from child to child. Reading instruction decisions must be based on systematic data collected on each learner. Educators now realize that difficulty of material, pace of instruction, method used, amount of individualized help, and the child's specific abilities and disabilities affect the minimum age required for efficient learning.

Stage 1: Initial Reading or Decoding

The initial reading stage (first to second grade) involves learning to use letter-sound relationships to decode printed words not recognized immediately. Children learn to recognize words and understand material in their books; however, what they can read at this stage is considerably below what they can understand in speech. Often the student reads slowly, word-by-word, trying to break a detailed, complicated code. Some students experience difficulty acquiring beginning decoding skills because they have problems with the phonological aspects of language (Perfetti, 1985). A basic phonological problem of poor readers is lack of awareness that words have parts (i.e., phonemes, syllables, and morphemes). Lyon (1995) notes that the best predictor of reading ability from kindergarten and first-grade performance is phoneme segmentation ability, which is part of phonological awareness. For many students, adequate phonics instruction involving the sequencing and blending of sounds to form words is necessary for the acquisition of basic decoding skills; however, students who have difficulty with phonics analysis may use context analysis, syllabication, or structural analysis to aid in word identification.

Much controversy exists among researchers concerning this stage in relation to the code-emphasis approach versus the meaning-emphasis approach. The code approach stresses the early introduction of the sound-symbol system and teaching phonics. The meaning approach stresses the initial learning of whole words and sentences by sight, with phonics instruction introduced later.

Stage 2: Confirmation, Fluency, and Ungluing from Print

In second and third grades, what students previously have learned is consolidated in the recognition of words and the use of decoding skills to help them comprehend easy and familiar texts. At this stage, students automatically begin to use the tools acquired previously, attain fluent reading, and are able to read grade-level material in the range of 100 to 140 words per minute with two or fewer errors. By using their decoding skills along with repetitions inherent in the language and stories read, students gain competence in using context and, consequently, improve in fluency and reading rate. Perfetti (1985) notes that when the decoding process becomes automatic (i.e., accurate and rapid), attention is freed for higher level reading comprehension skills. Most students develop rapid word recognition as a result of the familiarity that develops from extended practice; however, students with reading problems require additional practice and repetition to reach automaticity. The transition from the initial stage to the fluency stage is similar to the transition experience of a baby who at first must concentrate intensely on learning to walk and then can walk automatically without thinking about it. Students at the initial stage read automatically until an unknown word is encountered and then they try a variety of word-attack approaches. By the end of this stage, students have developed fluency and can quickly recognize familiar words, sound out words they do not recognize, and predict other words according to context. Measures of reading speed and reading accuracy should be included in reading assessment to determine which students are ready to move to the next stage of reading instruction (Perfetti, 1985).

Stage 3: Reading for Learning the New

This stage, which begins in fourth grade and continues through eighth grade, marks the beginning of reading to learn, as opposed to learning to read in earlier stages. Reading is used to gain new knowledge, experience new feelings, and learn new ideas and attitudes. Thus, students acquire a rich base of information and vocabulary concepts by reading a wide variety of materials. At this stage, silent reading is done in large units (e.g., a complete story or selection), and word study is concerned more with meanings than with recognition or decoding because the reading materials contain more unfamiliar abstract, technical, and literary words. Snider and Tarver (1987) suggest that students who read with slow and inaccurate decoding skills may fail to learn many of the concepts that are acquired typically during this stage by inference from the context and by analogical reasoning from prior knowledge. In other words, students with reading problems may be limited in learning from usual reading experiences because poor decoding skills present a barrier to the acquisition of knowledge. The resulting impoverished knowledge base may not allow students to comprehend more complex reading material. Thus, because of the cumulative effects of deficiencies at earlier stages, students with reading problems particularly need effective and efficient instruction at this stage.

Stage 4: Multiple Viewpoints

Reading at the secondary school level requires students to deal with a variety of viewpoints and to compare and evaluate information from a variety of sources. Secondary students are expected to read complex texts in advanced content areas. Through reading and studying materials that vary widely in type, content, and style, students practice acquiring difficult concepts and learning new concepts and points of view. At this level, metacognitive processes play an important role, monitoring and evaluating one's understanding of the text while reading. Instruction in comprehension monitoring should be followed by instruction in study skills and use of reference materials. The failure of a student to monitor understanding of the text may be due to an inability to decode rapidly and efficiently or to a lack of necessary information to understand the topic. To facilitate the use of textbooks with students who have difficulty reading them, Ciborowski (1995) presents a textbook teaching-learning model that focuses on activating prior knowledge, helping students become more active comprehenders and thinkers, and consolidating and extending textbook usage. Moreover, Snider and Tarver (1987) suggest that supple-

mental materials emphasizing vocabulary and background information should be developed to accompany content-area textbooks to help students with learning problems profit from reading in the content areas.

Stage 5: Construction and Reconstruction

At the college level, students read books and articles in the detail and depth that they need for their own purposes. From reading what others say, students construct knowledge for their own use. At this stage, the reader synthesizes information and forms hypotheses that usually are restricted to a specific area of study at an advanced level. Thus, reading at this stage requires extensive background knowledge in highly specialized content areas. The acquisition of highly specialized knowledge in this stage depends upon the rich base of information acquired in Stages 3 and 4, which, in turn, depends upon the accurate decoding and fluency skills developed in Stages 1 and 2.

EMERGENT LITERACY ASSESSMENT

Extensive research exists that indicates children's early experiences with print and language strongly relate to later success in learning to read. For example, letter knowledge, phoneme discrimination, and the understanding that words consist of discrete units are strong predictors of later success in learning to read (Adams, 1990; Ball, 1993; Lyon, 1995; Snow, Burns, & Griffin, 1998). During the last decade, the concept of phonological awareness has emerged to describe oral language components that develop early and are germane to later reading and spelling success. *Phonological awareness* is defined as the ability to perceive that spoken words include a series of individual sounds. In essence, phonological awareness is a conscious sensitivity to the phonological structure of language. Before assessing phonological awareness skills, a child's basic concepts about print (i.e., an understanding that the marks and squiggles on a page represent words and convey meaning) must be evaluated. Also, the child must know what a word is and be able to distinguish it from its referent (e.g., recognize that the word *lion* does not growl or roar). Emergent literacy assessment includes assessment of concepts about print and phonological awareness.

Concepts About Print

Because of different abilities and experiences with print, similar-age children can vary significantly in their knowledge of print-related concepts. An age-appropriate book for the child can be used to assess the child's knowledge of concepts about print. The child can perform the following tasks:

- Point out the front and back of the book.
- Demonstrate awareness that print contains a message.
- Indicate where to start reading on a page.
- Point to a single word and to two words.
- Indicate the direction to read words (i.e., left to right).
- Indicate that at the end of a line you sweep left to the next lower line.
- Demonstrate an understanding of the concepts of *first* and *last.*
- Indicate that you read the left page before the right page.
- Indicate that you stop at a period.
- Indicate that you pause at a comma.
- Count words in a line.
- Point to one letter.
- Point to an uppercase letter.
- Point to the top and the bottom of a page.
- Point to the top and the bottom of a picture.

Phonological Awareness

Language Components   To read, children need to know that the speech stream can be broken into phonemes and that phonemes are the units used to make words. Phonological awareness includes four hierarchical language components: word, syllable, onset and rime, and phoneme. Word awareness is the least difficult and phoneme awareness is the most difficult.

1. ***Word.*** The awareness that speech flow consists of words occurs at a very young age. When a child says a single word that has only been heard in combination with other words, the child is demonstrating the word level of phonological awareness. Counting or tapping out the number of spoken words in a sentence is an activity to assess or improve word awareness.

2. ***Syllable.*** Syllables are the easiest distinguishable units within words. Most children acquire the ability to segment words with minimal instruction. Tapping out the number of syllables in a spoken word is an activity used to develop syllable awareness.

3. ***Onset and rime.*** This component represents an intrasyllable level and is useful as an intermediate level of analysis between the syllable and the phoneme. It involves splitting syllables into onsets and rimes. An onset is the part of the syllable that precedes the vowel (e.g., *p* in *pink* and *spl* in *split*). The rime is the rest of the syllable (e.g., *up* in *cup* and *own* in *brown*). All syllables must have a rime but not all syllables have an onset (e.g., *and, off,* and *up*).

4. ***Phoneme.*** Phonemes are the smallest unit of sound. Phonemic awareness differs from phonological awareness in that it applies to the relationship between phonemes (sound) and graphemes (print) (i.e., letters have specific sounds). Phonemic awareness skills include the ability to detect, segment, and blend phonemes and to manipulate their order in words (Adams, 1990). Phonemes are impossible to segment in a pure manner because in speech flow phonemes affect the pronunciation of adjacent phonemes. Phonemic awareness is much more sophisticated and difficult than syllable or intrasyllabic analysis.

Phonological Awareness Tasks   Once an evaluator realizes that the phonological awareness language components of word, syllable, onset and rime, and phoneme develop in a hierarchical manner, the level of tasks used to assess phonological awareness must be considered. Phonological awareness assessment tasks primarily are administered to 3- to 7-year-old children. These tasks are discussed next in ascending order of difficulty.

The first four tasks are used mostly with preschoolers and beginning kindergartners and include word oddity, sentence segmentation by words, word segmentation by syllables, and sound matching by initial and final sounds of words.

1. ***Word oddity*** requires the child to recognize words as a unit of language and compare similarities and differences among three to four spoken words. For example, the child can be given three to four spoken words and must tell which one does not belong. The words may differ on initial

sounds (e.g., *pig, hill,* and *pal*), medial sounds (e.g., *pin, gun,* and *bun*), or final sounds (e.g., *doll, hop,* and *rap*). Oddity tasks usually consist of alliteration when based on initial sound and rhyme detection when based on medial and final sounds. These tasks do not require the ability to fractionate a syllable.

2. ***Sentence segmentation by words*** requires the child to listen to a sentence and count (e.g., by tapping, clapping, or marching) the number of words heard. For example, when listening to the sentence, *Jiggles jumped over the hole,* the child would tap five times, or the child would repeat the sentence while clapping once for each word. This task simply requires the child to recognize a word and count how many words are heard.

3. ***Word segmentation by syllables*** requires the child to recognize the syllables in a spoken word. The task involves counting (by tapping, clapping, or marching) the syllables in a spoken word. For example, when given the word *cat,* the child must tap once; when given the word *candy,* the child must tap twice. This task is more complex than word oddity tasks because it involves intraword analysis. About 50 percent of 4 year olds and kindergartners and 90 percent of first graders can segment words into syllables (C. R. Smith, 1995).

4. ***Sound matching*** requires the child to detect sound similarities in spoken words: The child may hear four words and be asked to match one of the last three words to the first word on the basis of beginning, middle, or ending sound. For example, in a beginning sound matching task, the teacher may say "card—farm, had, cake" and the child must match *cake* with *card.* This task also may be designed to have the child match pictures on the basis of sounds. About 50 percent of kindergartners can tell whether two words begin or end with the same sound (C. R. Smith, 1995).

The next three phonological awareness tasks are appropriate for children in kindergarten. The tasks include blending, word manipulation, and syllable splitting.

5. ***Blending*** requires the child to combine two to four spoken word segments. For example, the teacher may say "/l/. . ./a/. . ./m/. . ./p/," and the child must combine the segments and say "lamp." This task requires knowledge that strange little sounds can be smashed together to form a word (Adams, 1990). Although a child may know the individual sounds in the word, blending them requires more

abstraction than simply saying them quickly. Kindergartners are about 65 percent correct on this task (C. R. Smith, 1995).

6. ***Word manipulation*** requires the ability to delete a word segment and say what is left. This task is appropriate for kindergartners and beginning first graders when the task difficulty is controlled. The use of compound words, short words, or words with sound segments that easily are isolated is appropriate for 5- and 6-year-olds. For example, the teacher may say, "Say *football.* Now say *football* without saying *ball"* (foot) or "Say *tall.* Now say *tall* without saying /t/" (all). A task that is too difficult for most kindergartners would be "Say *driver.* Now say *driver* without saying the /v/ sound" (drier).

7. ***Syllable splitting*** requires the child to break off or isolate the first phoneme of a word or syllable and say the first phoneme or the remainder. For example, the teacher may ask for the first phoneme and say "Bear" and the child must say "/b/," or the teacher may ask for what is left and say "Feel" and the child must say "eel." This task does not require the child to think of a word as a string of phonemes; it only requires the child to attend carefully to the sounds of the syllable and break away the initial sound. Thus, the child thinks in terms of onsets and rimes rather than phonemes.

The final two tasks, phoneme segmentation and phoneme manipulation, require some formal reading instruction before most children are able to do them. Thus, children in the latter part of first grade usually are able to do these tasks. Both phoneme segmentation and phoneme manipulation are strong predictors of beginning reading acquisition (Adams, 1990).

8. ***Phoneme segmentation*** requires the child to hear a syllable and break it into its component phonemes. For example, the teacher may say "mat" and the child must tap, clap, or step (march) three times—once for each phoneme (/m/, /a/, /t/). This task is difficult because individual phonemes are not distinguishable in many words. The attributes of each phoneme spill over to adjacent sound segments. Whereas no 4-year-olds and only 17 percent of 5-year-olds succeed at this task, about 70 percent of 6-year-olds succeed (Liberman, Shankweiler, Fischer, & Carter, 1974).

9. ***Phoneme manipulation*** requires the child to add, delete, or move any designated phoneme and regenerate a word or nonword. For example,

the child must pronounce a word without the first, middle, or last phoneme (*hill* without saying /h/, *monkey* without saying /k/, or *pink* without saying /k/). Also, the child may be asked to reorder the phonemes of a syllable (e.g., say "tap" backwards—"pat").

Figure 7.2 presents a general framework for examining the progressive nature of phonological

FIGURE 7.2
General hierarchical framework of phonological awareness language components and tasks

		Language Components			
		Least Difficult ←		→ Most Difficult	
		Word	Syllable	Onset and Rime	Phoneme
Preschool/Kindergarten	Word Oddity	Select odd word			
	Sentence Segmentation by Words	Count words heard			
	Word Segmentation by Syllables		Clap or count syllables in a word		
	Sound Matching				Match initial phoneme (*card*—mat, *cat,* part) Match final phoneme (*cup*—run, *dip,* fat)
Kindergarten	Blending				Blend /d/, /o/, /g/ ("dog")
	Word Manipulation	Say "baseball" without saying "ball" ("base")	Say "winter" without saying "ter" ("win")	Say "mat" without saying /m/ ("at")	
	Syllable Splitting			Hear *pair,* say onset (/p/) Hear *pair,* say rime ("air")	
First Grade	Phoneme Segmentation				Hear *sat,* tap out phonemes (/s/, /a/, /t/)
	Phoneme Manipulation				Say "monkey" without saying /k/ ("money") Say "pal" backwards ("lap")

Tasks — Most Difficult

awareness language components (i.e., word, syllable, onset and rime, and phoneme) and the difficulty level of the respective tasks used to assess phonological awareness. The development of phonological awareness prepares the youngster to succeed in both reading and spelling. Moreover, it complements the learning of letter names and sounds, as well as phonics instruction. A good way to assess letter skills is to have the child say each letter, pronounce its sound, and give a word that begins with the letter. Chapter 8 provides activities for teaching phonological awareness.

☀ ASSESSMENT OF READING SKILLS

Once the teacher recognizes the decoding and comprehension processes of the reading task and is aware of the network of reading skills and their general developmental sequence, meaningful reading assessment can be undertaken. Because reading problems stem from many causes and the reading process is so complex, many reading difficulties can exist. Bond, Tinker, Wasson, and Wasson (1989) provide the following general classification of the more prevalent reading difficulties: faulty word identification and recognition, inappropriate directional habits, deficiencies in basic comprehension abilities, limited special comprehension abilities (such as inability to locate and retain specific facts), deficiencies in basic study skills, deficiencies in ability to adapt to reading needs of content fields, deficiencies in rate of comprehension, and poor oral reading.

In addition to indicating the student's current reading ability, assessment can point to specific strengths and weaknesses and aid in planning instructional objectives. Both commercially prepared instruments and informal measures are useful. To obtain a valid assessment of the student's reading abilities, the teacher should use a variety of assessment procedures—standardized tests, observations, and informal inventories. The information the teacher wants to obtain should help determine the type of assessment device used. For example, a group-administered reading achievement test yields information on the level of reading of the entire class, whereas more specific information about one student's certain skills can be obtained from an individually administered diagnostic reading test or

through informal assessment. The remainder of this chapter presents various formal and informal reading assessment techniques and devices.

Formal Reading Assessment

Many commercial tests have been standardized on large groups of students. Such norm-referenced tests enable the teacher to compare each student's performance with the population upon which the test was standardized. Scores from standardized reading tests are reported in several ways (such as reading grade level, reading age score, percentile, and stanine score). However, norm-referenced tests require strict administration, scoring, and interpretation procedures. In addition to norm-referenced tests, some published reading measures are criterion-referenced. These tests describe performance, rather than compare it, and can be used to determine whether the student has mastered specific instructional objectives. This section presents achievement and diagnostic tests as well as criterion-referenced tests.

Achievement and Diagnostic Tests   General achievement tests assess a student's ability in various academic areas. Achievement tests with reading subtests often are used to obtain an overall measure of reading achievement. These tests are norm-referenced and thus yield objective results that can be compared with the norms of the standardization sample. Reading survey tests measure reading skills only and, like achievement tests, are used frequently to indicate a student's general range of reading abilities. Achievement and reading survey tests are basically screening measures and can help determine which students are experiencing reading difficulties and need further assessment. Reading survey tests and achievement tests with reading subtests include the following:

- *Gates-MacGinitie Reading Tests—Fourth Edition* (MacGinitie, MacGinitie, Maria, & Dreyer, 2000). Assesses word decoding, vocabulary, and comprehension.
- *Iowa Tests of Basic Skills* (Hoover, Hieronymus, Frisbie, & Dunbar, 1996). Assesses word analysis, vocabulary, and reading comprehension.
- *Kaufman Test of Educational Achievement* (Kaufman & Kaufman, 1998). Assesses reading decoding and comprehension.

Listening to a student read provides information for planning instruction.

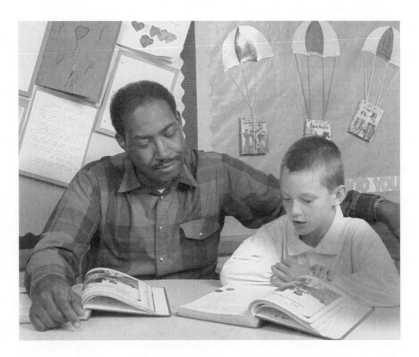

- *Metropolitan Achievement Tests—Seventh Edition* (Balow, Farr, & Hogan, 1997). Assesses word recognition, reading vocabulary, and reading comprehension.
- *Woodcock-Johnson III Tests of Achievement* (Woodcock & Mather, 2000). Assesses letter-word identification, word attack, reading fluency, reading vocabulary, and passage comprehension.

In contrast to achievement and general reading survey tests, which yield broad information, diagnostic reading tests provide a more precise, comprehensive analysis of specific reading abilities and disabilities. Diagnostic tests differ from achievement tests in that they generally have more subtests and test items related to specific reading skills. The teacher finds out *how* the student attempts to read. By identifying the student's specific strengths and weaknesses in various subskills of reading, diagnostic tests yield detailed, useful information for planning appropriate individual educational programs.

Diagnostic reading test batteries are designed to measure many reading subskills. They often include multiple subtests that sample performance in word analysis, word recognition, comprehension, and various reading-related skills. In contrast to test batteries, some diagnostic reading tests measure the student's ability in a specific skill area. Table 7.1 lists selected standardized diagnostic reading test batteries and tests of specific skills.

Criterion-Referenced Tests   Whereas norm-referenced tests compare a student's performance with the scores of others, criterion-referenced tests describe performance according to fixed criteria. The teacher discovers which skills the student has learned, which are being learned now, and which still must be taught. The teacher uses criterion-referenced reading tests to determine whether the student has mastered specific objectives, such as recognition of *ed* endings or use of the *ch* consonant digraph. Test items are presented in a hierarchy to assess a sequence of reading skills. If performance on each skill does not reach the established criterion of success (e.g., 95 percent level of proficiency), the teacher provides instruction specifically for that skill. A student who demonstrates skill mastery according to the determined criterion progresses to the next skill in the sequence. Thus, criterion-referenced tests focus on the student's ability to master

TABLE 7.1
Selected standardized diagnostic reading tests

Test	Grade Levels	Areas Assessed
Test Batteries		
Diagnostic Reading Scales (Spache, 1981)	1–7	Oral reading errors, silent reading comprehension, auditory comprehension

Three word recognition lists and 22 reading passages of increasing difficulty are included. The student's performance on the word lists, which increase in difficulty, indicates the level at which the reading passages should begin. As the student reads orally from the reading passages, the teacher notes reading errors and then checks comprehension by asking several questions following each passage. Instructional, independent, and potential reading levels are determined. Twelve supplementary phonics and word analysis tests also are included to assess areas such as consonant and vowel sounds, blending, initial consonant substitution, and auditory discrimination.

Test	Grade Levels	Areas Assessed
Durrell Analysis of Reading Difficulty (Durrell & Catterson, 1980)	1–6	Oral reading, silent reading, listening comprehension, word recognition, word analysis

Oral reading passages and accompanying comprehension questions are included, as well as paragraphs for silent reading and listening comprehension. Additional subtests are included in listening vocabulary, sounds in isolation, spelling, visual memory of words, identifying sounds in words, and prereading phonics abilities. The battery assesses a wide variety of specific skills and requires about an hour to administer. In addition to providing a profile of grade-level scores, the test includes a checklist of instructional needs on which the teacher can note particular reading difficulties. Also, the test manual contains helpful information concerning corrective instruction and program planning.

Test	Grade Levels	Areas Assessed
Stanford Diagnostic Reading Test— Fourth Edition (Karlsen & Gardner, 1995)	1–13	Phonetic analysis, vocabulary comprehension, scanning

This group-administered test is both norm-referenced and criterion-referenced. There are six levels, identified by color, and several subtests of the four skill areas are not included at all six levels; for example, phonetic analysis is included only in the first three levels, and scanning is assessed in the last three levels. Two forms are available for the last three levels. In addition to yielding percentile ranks, stanines, grade equivalents, and scaled scores, the test results can be used to identify strengths and weaknesses in specific reading skills.

Test	Grade Levels	Areas Assessed
Woodcock Reading Mastery Tests— Revised (Woodcock, 1998)	K–college and adult	Visual auditory learning, letter identification, word identification, word attack, word comprehension, passage comprehension

This battery of tests yields cluster scores (in readiness, basic skills, and comprehension) and a total reading score, as well as derived scores (age- and grade-based percentile ranks and standard scores, and age and grade equivalents). The test contains two forms (one of which omits visual-auditory learning and letter identification). A computer scoring program can be used to assist the examiner in computing scores and providing score printouts.

Test	Grade Levels	Areas Assessed
Tests of Specific Skills		
Gray Oral Reading Tests— Third Edition (Wiederholt & Bryant, 1992)	2–12	Reading miscues, reading rate, comprehension

This test includes two forms, each of which contains 13 developmentally sequenced passages with five comprehension questions. As the student reads aloud, the teacher notes reading characteristics, errors, and time elapsed in reading each paragraph. Comprehension questions are asked after each paragraph is read. A system for performing a miscue analysis of reader performance yields information in four areas: meaning similarity, function similarity, graphic/phonemic similarity,

TABLE 7.1
(continued)

Test	Grade Levels	Areas Assessed
and self-correction. Standard scores, percentile ranks, and grade equivalents are provided. The *Gray Oral Reading Tests—Diagnostic* (Bryant & Wiederholt, 1991) can be used as a supplement to the GORT–3. The student reads passages orally and responds to comprehension questions. If performance on the paragraph reading is poor, additional subtests are administered in decoding, word identification, word attack, morphemic analysis, contextual analysis, and word ordering. Thus, information is provided about graphic-phonemic, function, and meaning cues that the student uses to decipher words in print and comprehend words and ideas.		
Test of Early Reading Ability—2 (Reid, Hresko, & Hammill, 1989)	Preschool–4	Knowledge of contextual meaning, alphabet, and conventions
This test measures the actual reading ability of young children through items that focus on knowledge of contextual meaning (print in the environment, relations among vocabulary, and print in connected discourse), alphabet (letter naming, oral reading, and proofreading), and conventions of written language (book handling and other practices). Two alternative forms are available, as well as a computer software scoring system.		
Test of Phonological Awareness (Torgesen & Bryant, 1994)	K–2	Phonological awareness
This test measures young children's awareness of the individual sounds in words and can be used to identify children who may profit from instructional activities to enhance their phonological awareness in preparation for reading instruction. Both the kindergarten version and the early elementary version can be administered either individually or to groups in about 20 minutes.		
Test of Reading Comprehension—3 (Brown, Hammill, & Wiederholt, 1995)	2–12	General vocabulary, syntactic similarities, paragraph reading, sentence sequencing
This test includes eight subtests and can be administered to either groups or individuals. In addition to the four general comprehension core subtests, there are four diagnostic supplementary subtests in mathematics vocabulary, social studies vocabulary, science vocabulary, and reading the directions of schoolwork. Standard scores, grade and age equivalents, and reading comprehension quotients are provided.		
Test of Word Reading Efficiency (Torgesen, Wagner, & Rashotte, 1999)	1–college	Word reading accuracy, fluency
This test includes two subtests that can be administered quickly to monitor the growth of two word reading skills that are critical in the development of overall reading ability: the ability to accurately recognize familiar words as whole units and the ability to sound out words quickly. The Sight Word Efficiency subtest assesses the number of real printed words (sight words) that can be accurately identified within 45 seconds, and the Phonetic Decoding Efficiency subtest measures the number of pronounceable printed nonwords that can be accurately decoded within 45 seconds. Each subtest has two forms of equivalent difficulty.		

specific skills, and the assessment relates to curriculum content and instructional objectives. The student's progress is determined by comparing current performance with previous performance. Table 7.2 includes three criterion-referenced reading assessment measures.

Informal Reading Assessment

Informal assessment involves examining the student's daily work or administering teacher-constructed tests by which the teacher can assess any measurable reading skill. The teacher also can determine specific strengths and weaknesses

TABLE 7.2

Selected criterion-referenced reading tests

Test	Grade Levels	Areas Assessed
Brigance Diagnostic Comprehensive Inventory of Basic Skills—Revised (Brigance, 1999)	K–9	Word recognition, oral reading, word analysis, reading comprehension
This inventory is used primarily to establish educational objectives and monitor progress toward these objectives. Student record books show at each testing the point of competence to which the student has progressed. Also, a class record book is provided for the teacher to keep a record of each student's progress. Grade placement tests are included for selected skills.		
California Diagnostic Reading Test (1990)	K–12	Word analysis, vocabulary, comprehension, applications
This test of basic reading skills yields both criterion- and norm-referenced scores. It is divided into six levels and is not timed, with the exception of the parts of the Applications test for skimming, scanning, and reading rates. The test is designed to provide information needed to plan effective remedial programs for students who require help in acquiring basic reading skills. The Teacher's Guide suggests instructional techniques and methods to help at-risk students.		
Standardized Reading Inventory—2 (Newcomer, 1999)	K–8	Oral and silent reading, word recognition, reading comprehension
This instrument is designed like an informal reading inventory, with each of its two forms consisting of ten graded reading passages, ranging from primer to eighth-grade level. The passages include typical words found in five popular basal reading series. The student reads passages aloud while the examiner records errors in oral reading. Then the student reads the same passages silently and responds to comprehension questions. The scoring of the inventory indicates whether the student's word recognition skills and reading comprehension are at an independent, instructional, or frustration level. In addition to being criterion referenced, this instrument is also norm-referenced.		

by analyzing reading errors. Informal procedures usually offer two advantages: (1) they require less time to administer than formal tests and (2) they can be used with classroom materials during regular instruction periods (Kirk et al., 1978).

An experienced teacher can obtain diagnostic information through careful, day-to-day observations. The teacher has many opportunities to observe and informally assess the student's reading skills and can obtain information about the student's reading interests and attitudes, as well as word analysis and comprehension skills, by observing oral reading, seatwork assignments, instructional sessions, testing sessions, and recreational reading periods. Several informal observations during a period of time also can confirm or supplement the results of formal assessment tests.

When observing the student's performance on various reading tasks, the teacher should consider the following questions:

- What is the student's attitude toward reading?
- What specific reading interest does the student have?
- Is the student making progress in reading?
- What strengths and weaknesses in reading does the student exhibit?
- During oral reading, does the student read word by word or with fluency?
- What kinds of errors does the student make consistently?
- What word analysis skills does the student use?
- Does the student use context clues to recognize words?
- Does the student have a good sight vocabulary?
- Does the student appear to pay attention to the meaning of the material when reading?

Teacher observations can be recorded on a checklist of reading skills and behaviors. Figure 7.3

FIGURE 7.3

Reading diagnosis checklist

NAME _____   TEACHER _____

GRADE _____   SCHOOL _____

	28	27	26	25	24	23	22	21	20	19	18	17	16	15	14	13	12	11	10	9	8	7	6	5	4	3	2	1
1st check																												
2nd check																												
3rd check																												

28. Written Recall Limited by Spelling Ability
27. Undeveloped Dictionary Skills
26. Unable to Locate Information
25. Inability to Skim or Scan
24. High Rate of Reading at the Expense of Accuracy
23. Inability to Adjust Reading Rate
22. Low Rate of Speed
21. Comprehension Inadequate
20. Vocabulary Inadequate
19. Inadequate Ability to Use Context Clues
18. Contractions Not Known
17. Structural Analysis Difficulties
16. Phonics Difficulties: Blends, Digraphs, or Diphthongs
15. Phonics Difficulties: Vowels
14. Phonics Difficulties: Consonants
13. General Sight Vocabulary Not Up to Grade Level
12. Basic Sight Words Not Known
11. Voicing Lip Movements, Finger-Pointing, and Head Movements
10. Guesses at Words
9. Substitutions
8. Insertions
7. Inversion or Reversals
6. Repetitions
5. Omissions
4. Poor Pronunciation
3. Incorrect Phrasing
2. Word-by-Word Reading
1. Lacks Phonemic Awareness and/or Alphabet Knowledge

| Other | Study Skills | Compre-hension | Decoding | Oral Reading | Pre-reading |

The items listed above represent the most common difficulties encountered by pupils in the reading program. Following each numbered item are spaces for notation of that specific difficulty. This may be done at intervals of several months. One might use a check to indicate difficulty recognized or the letters at right to represent an even more accurate appraisal.

D—Difficulty recognized
P—Pupil progressing
N—No longer has difficulty

Source: From *Locating and Correcting Reading Difficulties* (p. xix), 7th ed., by J. L. Shanker and E. E. Ekwall, 1998, Upper Saddle River, NJ: Merrill/Prentice Hall. Copyright 1998 by Prentice-Hall Publishing Company. Reprinted by permission.

presents a reading diagnosis checklist devised by Shanker and Ekwall (1998) consisting of 28 reading or related abilities. The teacher is to check each ability three times. Specific strengths and weaknesses are noted, and progress is charted.

Teacher observation is continuous and permeates all types of informal assessment. This section presents the following informal assessment techniques: graded word lists, informal reading inventory, curriculum-based measurement, portfolio assessment, reading miscue analysis, cloze procedure, and teacher-made tests.

Graded Word Lists Graded word lists examine the student's word recognition skills. Word lists can be useful in informal diagnosis to indicate the student's sight vocabulary, to estimate the

level at which the student can read with fluency and has little difficulty with word attack, and to reveal basic weaknesses in word-attack skills as the student confronts unknown words.

The teacher can develop word lists by randomly selecting 20 to 25 words for each level from the glossaries of graded basal readers. To obtain a random sample of 25 words for each level, the teacher would divide the total number of words for each level by 25. For example, 250 total words divided by 25 would mean that every tenth word is included. The teacher should check to make sure that the words represent various phonics skills (such as consonant and vowel sounds in different positions, consonant blends, and digraphs). The words also should include prefixes, suffixes, and compound words. Sample graded word lists for

TABLE 7.3
Graded word lists

Primer	First	Second	Third	Fourth	Fifth	Sixth
not	kind	mile	beginning	worm	abandon	seventeen
funny	rocket	fair	thankful	afford	zigzag	annoy
book	behind	ago	written	player	terrific	dwindle
thank	our	need	reason	scientific	terrify	rival
good	men	fourth	bent	meek	plantation	hesitation
into	met	lazy	patient	rodeo	loaf	navigator
know	wish	field	manage	festival	hike	gorge
your	told	taken	arithmetic	hillside	relative	burglar
come	after	everything	burst	coward	available	construction
help	ready	part	bush	boom	grief	exploration
man	barn	save	gingerbread	booth	physical	technical
now	next	hide	tremble	freeze	commander	spice
show	cat	instead	planet	protest	error	spike
want	hold	bad	struggle	nervous	woodcutter	prevail
did	story	love	museum	sparrow	submarine	memorial
have	turtle	breakfast	grin	level	ignore	initiation
little	give	reach	ill	underground	disappointed	undergrowth
cake	cry	song	alarm	oxen	wrestle	ladle
home	fight	cupcake	cool	eighty	vehicle	walnut
soon	please	trunk	engine	shouldn't	international	tributary

Source: From *Analytical Reading Inventory* (pp. 78–79), 6th ed., by M. L. Woods and A. J. Moe, 1999, Upper Saddle River, NJ: Merrill/Prentice Hall. Copyright 1999 by Prentice-Hall Publishing Company. Reprinted by permission.

primer through sixth-grade level are presented in Table 7.3. The words for each grade level can be typed on separate cards for the student to read, but the teacher should have a list of all the words. Another method would be to have the student's word list on a sheet of paper and present each word through a window with the use of a tachistoscope made from oaktag or strips cut from manila folders.

Word lists can be presented in two ways. First, a timed flash exposure (1 second) can be given to assess the student's instant recognition or sight word vocabulary. Second, words the student is initially unable to recognize can be presented untimed to test ability to apply word-attack skills to unknown words. The teacher also can obtain additional information by giving prompts, such as providing an initial sound or covering part of the word.

The teacher can determine a word recognition grade-level score—indicating the student's ability to identify words—by an untimed presentation of graded word lists. In general, the level at which the student misses none or only one word is the *independent level.* At the *instructional level* the student identifies two words incorrectly; when three or more words are missed, the student has reached the *frustration level.* As well as using word lists to determine grade-level placement in word recognition, the teacher also should note specific errors in word attack. When the student mispronounces a word, the teacher should write down the mispronunciation to analyze the method of word attack and look for error patterns. For example, the student may recognize only initial consonant sounds and guess at the remainder of the word, or may not be able to blend individual sounds into whole words. The student who reads *month* as *mouth* or *long* as *large* may be responding to configuration cues, whereas a response of a completely dissimilar word, such as *after* for *field,* may indicate a lack of phonetic word-attack skills. The teacher also should note the student's skill in structural analysis (i.e., knowledge of prefixes, roots, and endings).

In addition to graded word lists devised by the teacher, published word lists are available. The widely used Dolch (1955) list includes 200 sight words that make up 50 to 65 percent of the words the student encounters in elementary school basal readers. The Dolch list was examined by D. D. Johnson (1971) in terms of current word usage. D. D. Johnson notes that 82 Dolch words are not among the 220 most frequent words in the Kucera-Francis list, which is an analysis of present-day American English. Table 7.4 presents the 220 most frequent words in the Kucera-Francis list. Using graded word lists to determine word recognition skills is often the first step in administering an informal reading inventory.

Informal Reading Inventory An informal reading inventory provides information about the student's general reading level. It uses reading passages of increasing difficulty from various graded materials, such as selections from a basal reading series with which the student is unfamiliar. In general, the passages should consist of about 50 words (at preprimer level) to 200 words (at secondary level). The student begins reading passages aloud at a level at which word-attack and comprehension tasks are handled easily. The student continues reading passages of increasing difficulty until the passages become too difficult for him or her to read. As the student reads aloud, the teacher records errors and asks three to five questions about each passage. Many kinds of questions should be used: recall of facts (who, what, and where), inference (why), and vocabulary (general or specific meanings). To assess literal comprehension, the student can be asked to state the main idea of the passage, propose a title, recall details, present a series of events or ideas, or explain the meaning of vocabulary words. Inferential comprehension can be evaluated by asking questions that force the student to go beyond the information provided in the passage. For example, the student can be asked to draw conclusions, make predictions, evaluate ideas or actions, or suggest alternative endings. The student should be allowed to reread or inspect the passage before answering comprehension questions. Otherwise, it is possible that *memory* rather than comprehension is being tested. The percentage of words read correctly for each

passage is computed by dividing the number of correctly read words by the number of words in the selection. The percentage of comprehension questions answered correctly is determined by dividing the number of correct answers by the number of questions asked.

Through this method the teacher can estimate ability at three levels: independent, instructional, and frustration (M. S. Johnson, Kress, & Pikulski, 1987). At the *independent level,* the student can read the graded passage with high accuracy, recognizing 98 to 100 percent of the words and answering the comprehension questions with 90 to 100 percent accuracy. The reading is fluent and natural, and there is no finger pointing or hesitation. At this level, the teacher can hand out supplementary materials for independent or enjoyment reading. The level at which the student needs some help is the *instructional level.* The student can recognize 95 percent of the words and comprehends about 75 percent of the material. The material is challenging but not too difficult, and the student reads in a generally relaxed manner. The teacher should provide directed reading instruction at this level. At the *frustration level,* the student reads with considerable difficulty. Word recognition is 90 percent or less, and comprehension is less than 70 percent. The student is tense and makes many errors or reversals. Reading material at this level cannot be used for instruction.

According to Carnine et al. (1997), one of the major purposes of an informal reading inventory is to help the teacher place the student at the appropriate instructional level in a basal series. Lovitt and Hansen (1976) offer guidelines for placement in a basal series: a correct reading rate of 45 to 65 words per minute with eight or fewer errors and 50 to 75 percent comprehension. Deno and Mirkin (1977) suggest that curriculum placement decisions be based on a reading rate of 50 to 99 correct words per minute with three to seven errors, whereas Starlin (1982) recommends a correct reading rate of 70 to 149 words per minute with six to ten errors.

In addition to using an inventory to record oral reading word recognition and comprehension, the teacher should note various types of reading errors such as omitting words or parts of words, inserting or substituting words, reversing a word or its letters, and repeating words. It helps to develop a system

TABLE 7.4
Kucera-Francis list of basic sight words

1. the	45. when	89. many	133. know	177. don't
2. of	46. who	90. before	134. while	178. does
3. and	47. will	91. must	135. last	179. got
4. to	48. more	92. through	136. might	180. united
5. a	49. no	93. back	137. us	181. left
6. in	50. if	94. years	138. great	182. number
7. that	51. out	95. where	139. old	183. course
8. is	52. so	96. much	140. year	184. war
9. was	53. said	97. your	141. off	185. until
10. he	54. what	98. may	142. come	186. always
11. for	55. up	99. well	143. since	187. away
12. it	56. its	100. down	144. against	188. something
13. with	57. about	101. should	145. go	189. fact
14. as	58. into	102. because	146. came	190. through
15. his	59. than	103. each	147. right	191. water
16. on	60. them	104. just	148. used	192. less
17. be	61. can	105. those	149. take	193. public
18. at	62. only	106. people	150. three	194. put
19. by	63. other	107. Mr.	151. states	195. thing
20. I	64. new	108. how	152. himself	196. almost
21. this	65. some	109. too	153. few	197. hand
22. had	66. could	110. little	154. house	198. enough
23. not	67. time	111. state	155. use	199. far
24. are	68. these	112. good	156. during	200. took
25. but	69. two	113. very	157. without	201. head
26. from	70. may	114. make	158. again	202. yet
27. or	71. then	115. would	159. place	203. government
28. have	72. do	116. still	160. American	204. system
29. an	73. first	117. own	161. around	205. better
30. they	74. any	118. see	162. however	206. set
31. which	75. my	119. men	163. home	207. told
32. one	76. now	120. work	164. small	208. nothing
33. you	77. such	121. long	165. found	209. night
34. were	78. like	122. get	166. Mrs.	210. end
35. her	79. our	123. here	167. thought	211. why
36. all	80. over	124. between	168. went	212. called
37. she	81. man	125. both	169. say	213. didn't
38. there	82. me	126. life	170. part	214. eyes
39. would	83. even	127. being	171. once	215. find
40. their	84. most	128. under	172. general	216. going
41. we	85. made	129. never	173. high	217. look
42. him	86. after	130. day	174. upon	218. asked
43. been	87. also	131. same	175. school	219. later
44. has	88. did	132. another	176. every	220. knew

Source: From *"The Dolch List Reexamined"* (pp. 455–456), by D. D. Johnson, 1971, *The Reading Teacher, 24,* 449–457. Copyright 1971 by the International Reading Association. Reprinted by permission.

for marking oral reading errors. Table 7.5 presents oral reading errors and a corresponding set of appropriate marks. Spache and Spache (1986) note that types of reading errors can have particular meanings. Omissions may indicate that the student is skipping unknown words or is reading quickly

TABLE 7.5

Oral reading errors and marking system

Type of Error	Marking System	Example
Omissions	Circle the word or parts of word omitted.	The boy went into the burning building.
Insertions	Use a caret to mark the place of insertion and write the added word or letter(s).	The children sat at the table to eat lunches.
Substitutions	Cross out the word and write the substituted word above it.	Now I recognize your name.
Reversals	For letter reversals within a word, cross out the word and write the reversal word above it.	The top is lost.
	For reversals of words, draw a curved line going over, between, and under the reversed words.	Mary looked often at the clock.
Repetitions	Draw a wavy line under the words which are repeated.	Everyone was cheering for me because I was a baseball hero.
Mispronunciations	Write the mispronounced word (indicating the student's pronunciation) over the correct word.	It was an octopus.
Hesitations	Use a slash to indicate improper hesitation.	The judge asked the jury to leave the courtroom.
Aided Words	Underline the word pronounced for the student.	The scared cat began to tremble.
Unobserved punctuation marks	Cross out the punctuation mark the student continued to read through.	Puppy saw the man. He barked and barked.
Self-corrected errors	Write **sc** over the error notation.	This month is November.

Example of a Marked Passage

The three boys were very tired from their long journey. Now they had to swim across a river. John plunged into the icy water and started to swim. He swam slowly but managed to reach the other side of the wide river.

without attention. Insertions of words that do not appear in the passage may suggest a superficial reading, a reliance on context for assistance, or a lack of interest in accuracy. Whereas omissions and insertions are more characteristic of older students, reversals are common at the primary age level or with students for whom English is a second language. Repetitions may indicate that the reader is tense and nervous or is delaying to gain time to attack the next unknown word. Mispronunciations are common among students who attempt to sound out words without knowing exceptions to phonetic rules; they also may occur in students who have low levels of listening vocabulary and are unable to use context clues. Self-corrections indicate that the reader is attempting to read more accurately and to rely upon information from the context of the sentence, whereas a dependent reader tends to make no attempt at decoding and needs the teacher to supply the unknown word.

An informal reading inventory also can be used to assess silent reading. Whereas oral reading focuses on word-attack skills, silent reading emphasizes comprehension. The student silently reads each passage and then answers comprehension questions. The percentage of correct responses indicates the student's silent reading level: independent (90 to 100 percent), instructional (75 percent), or frustration (50 percent). While the student reads silently, the teacher can note whispering, lip movements, finger pointing, facial grimaces, and fidgeting. The student also may have difficulties such as low rate, high rate at the expense of understanding, poorly organized recall, and inaccurate recall. Comprehension errors can be classified according to an analysis of skills, including recall of factual details, comprehension and summary of main ideas, understanding of sequence, making inferences, and critical reading and evaluation. The teacher can compare the student's oral and silent reading performances to determine whether there is a great difference.

In addition, the material in an informal reading inventory can be read to the student to determine listening or hearing capacity level, which is the highest level at which the student can comprehend 75 percent of the material. This provides an estimate of the student's reading potential or what the level would be if the student had no problems with the mechanics of reading.

Although it is time-consuming to use informal reading inventories because they are individually administered, they are used widely. They help the teacher to plan needed corrective instruction and to provide reading materials suited to the student's abilities. An informal reading inventory can be administered from time to time to check the student's reading progress. Several published informal reading inventories that contain graded word lists and graded passages are available. Three widely used inventories are the *Analytical Reading Inventory* (Woods & Moe, 1999), the *Informal Reading Inventory* (Burns & Roe, 1999), and the *Classroom Reading Inventory* (Silvaroli, 1997). Figure 7.4 pre-

sents a sample informal reading inventory for the second-grade level.

Curriculum-Based Measurement   Curriculum-based assessment includes any approach that uses direct observation and recording of a student's performance in the school curriculum as a basis for obtaining information to make instructional decisions. Within this model, *curriculum-based measurement (CBM)* refers to a specific set of standardized procedures in which rate samples are used to assess a student's achievement in academic skills (Deno, 1987, 1989). The assessment procedures involved in CBM are used primarily to establish district or classroom performance standards and to monitor individual student progress toward long-range goals; however, they also can be used to monitor progress toward short-range goals. Basically, in curriculum-based measurement of reading skills, basal reading passages are used to measure oral reading fluency. The student reads passages under timed conditions, the examiner counts the number of words read (correctly and incorrectly), and student performance is summarized as the rate correct.

When CBM is used to establish performance standards in reading, measures are developed from the school reading curriculum and are administered to all the students in a target group (such as all fourth graders in a school or district). The results provide data to determine standards of performance. Using CBM to establish standards involves four components: material selection, test administration, performance display and interpretation, and decision-making framework (Tindal & Marston, 1990). Selecting the appropriate material from the school curriculum begins the assessment process; an appropriate difficulty level is that which the teacher expects the student to master by the end of the semester or school year. Passages of about 200 words—excluding poetry, exercises, and excessive dialogue—from the school's reading curriculum are selected and administered to targeted students (e.g., fourth graders). A comparison of all students on the same measure provides a norm-referenced database for making instructional decisions. Four to six sample passages should be selected to provide the teacher with enough material for several administrations. All passages should reflect similar difficulty (possibly based on their readability). Once ma-

FIGURE 7.4
Sample informal reading inventory

Level 2 (118 words)

Student's Name: _____

Date: _____

Passage:
Whiz! The baseball went right by me, and I struck at the air!
"Strike one," called the man. I could feel my legs begin to shake!
Whiz! The ball went by me again, and I began to feel bad. "Strike two," screamed the man.
I held the bat back because this time I would kill the ball! I would hit it right out of the park! I was so scared that I bit down on my lip. My knees shook and my hands grew wet.
Swish! The ball came right over the plate. Crack! I hit it a good one! Then I ran like the wind. Everyone was yelling for me because I was now a baseball star!

Comprehension Questions and Possible Answers:
1. Who is the main character in this story? (the batter)
2. After strike one, how do you think the batter felt? (nervous)
   You think this because . . . (it said his legs began to shake)
3. After strike two, what did the batter plan to do? (planned to kill the ball)
4. What did it mean when the batter said, "I'll kill the ball"?
   (hit the ball real hard; try to get a home run)
5. Why was the last pitch good?
   (because it went right over the plate)
6. Do you think it was good or bad to hit the ball right out of the park? You think this because . . . (good . . . it's a home run because it will go so far the other team can't get it and the batter can run around the bases and no one can tag you; or bad because it is a run, but if you only have one ball, then it's gone)
7. How do you think the batter felt after hitting the ball? (felt good, confident)
   You think this because . . . (the story said everyone yelled because he/she was a baseball star)

Error Count:

Omissions	_____	Aided words	_____
Insertions	_____	Repetitions	_____
Substitutions	_____	Reversals	_____

Scoring Guide:

Word Recognition Errors		Comprehension Errors	
Independent	1	Independent	0
Instructional	6	Instructional	1–2
Frustration	12+	Frustration	3+

Source: Adapted from *Analytical Reading Inventory* (pp. 84–86), 6th ed., by M. L. Woods and A. J. Moe, 1999, Upper Saddle River, NJ: Merrill/Prentice Hall. Copyright 1999 by Prentice-Hall Publishing Company. Reprinted by permission.

---

terials are selected, they can be prepared by creating a student copy retyped to eliminate picture distractions and a teacher copy that has the cumulative number of words on successive lines printed along the right margin. When administering a reading passage, the teacher uses the following steps:

1. Randomly select a passage from the goal-level material.
2. Place it in front of and facing the student.
3. Keep a copy for the examiner.
4. Provide directions (see Step 3 in Figure 7.5).
5. Have the student read orally for 1 minute.

6. Score the student's performance in terms of number of words read correctly and note errors for instructional purposes.

It is helpful to administer two passages of similar readability and record the average score. When all students in the grade or class are tested and the average score for each student is computed, the teacher can develop a plot of the entire group. (Guidelines for developing a box plot of a group of students are presented in Chapter 3.) These data

FIGURE 7.5
Procedures for administering and scoring reading passages, determining long-range goals, and graphing data

---

Step 1:   Select a reading passage in which it is likely that the student will read aloud at a rate of 55 to 75 words correct per minute. This performance level represents entry level on goal-level material.

Step 2:   Have available two copies of each passage. Place the student's copy (face down) in front of and facing the student, and place the teacher's copy in front of and facing the teacher.

Step 3:   Read the directions *verbatim* for the first administration. Say to the student:
This is a story about _____ (fill in the blank with unusual adjectives and nouns found in the passage). When I say "Start," begin reading at the top of this page. If you wait on a word too long, I'll tell you the word. (Give the student 3 seconds before supplying the word.) If you come to a word you cannot read, say "Pass" and go on to the next word. Do not attempt to read as fast as you can. This is not a speed reading test. Read at a comfortable rate. At the end of 1 minute, I'll say "Stop."

Step 4:   Say "Start," and turn on the stopwatch. (Do not use the word *Go* to begin, because it implies racing, particularly when stated in the presence of the stopwatch.)

Step 5:   Follow the reading on the teacher's copy, and cross off the following incorrectly read words:

(a) Misread words such as *house* for *horse, hug* for *huge, home* for *house,* and *big* for *huge.*
(b) Words the student cannot read within about 3 seconds.
(c) Words not read (omissions); count all words in skipped lines as errors.
(d) Reversals of letters within words (such as *say* for *was*) or pairs of words (such as *the red, big dog* instead of *the big, red dog*).

The following miscues are not counted as errors: (1) proper nouns that are mispronounced more than once, (2) self-corrections, and (3) words added into the text by the student (additions or insertions).

Step 6:   At 1 minute, say "Stop," mark the last word read with a bracket (]), and quickly move to the next reading task. Place the top sheet over and to the side and tell the student you would like to continue in the same manner. Repeat this procedure until all reading tasks are completed.

Step 7:   Count the number of words read correctly and words read incorrectly by taking the cumulative count and subtracting the number of errors. For the basal reading passages, simply use the number to the right of the last full line read; add the number for words read in the next (partially read) line to obtain the total number of words read. The number of words read correctly is found by subtracting the number of words read incorrectly from the total number of words read. If the student's score falls within the range of 55 to 75 words correct per minute, test two more times at this level.

Step 8:   Test until the student reaches a level in which at least two of three scores fall in or close to the 55 to 75 words per minute (wpm) range. If the score falls above the 55 to 75 wpm range, test using a probe at a higher level. If the score falls below the 55 to 75 wpm range, test using a probe from a lower level of material. Try to find the optimal measurement level.

Step 9:   After the measurement level is identified, write the goal:
Objective: In _____ weeks the student will read _____ words correct per minute in the _____ Scott-Foresman* reader. (*Use name of reading series used with the student.)
Strategy: Use two probes per week from randomly selected passages from the reader.
Criteria: After three consecutive data points fall significantly below the aim line, changes in instruction will be made and noted on the instructional plan.

FIGURE 7.5
(continued)

Use a calendar to count the number of weeks remaining in the school year or semester. Write that number in the first blank. To calculate the number for the second blank, refer to the baseline data, the three probes scores at or near the 55 to 75 wpm range. Determine which of the three scores is the median (i.e., in rank order, the middlscore).

(a) If the student is being measured at or above the third-grade reader level, multiply the number of weeks (i.e., weeks in the instructional period) times 2 (rate of growth) and add this to the baseline score.

$$(weeks \times 2) + baseline\ median = goal$$
For example: $(30 \times 2) + 66 = 126$ wpm

(b) If the student is being measured below the third-grade reader level, multiply the number of weeks (i.e., weeks in instructional period) times 1.5 (rate of growth) and add this to the baseline median score.

$$(weeks \times 1.5) + baseline\ median = goal$$
For example: $(30 \times 1.5) + 66 = 111$ wpm

Step 10: Draw the aim line on the graph by connecting the baseline point and the goal point (see Figure 7.6).

Step 11: Write an instructional plan on the reverse side of the CBM graph.

Step 12: Implement the plan and collect CBM data twice a week. To collect CBM data, use the prepared probes from the respective reading series. Because these probes are already in a random sequence, use them in order. Try to measure the student in the same setting, at about the same time, and under the same general circumstances whenever possible. Read the directions each time so that the student consistently gets clues about the unusual words in the story. After scoring the performance, write the score in the appropriate box at the side of the graph page.

Step 13: Graph the median of the current score and the two previous scores instead of graphing every data point. This graphing system is called the *moving median* and is used to reduce the variability in the graphed data because these data are used for decision making. For example, if today's score is 66, last Thursday's was 70, and the previous Tuesday's was 59, graph the 66 because this is the median. Do not graph until three data points are collected after the baseline. Plot the moving median on the administration day even if the median score was from a previous day. In the given example, if the fourth probe (on Thursday) is 71, the last three probes would be 70, 66 and 71, and the median is 70. Thus, on the Thursday date, 70 is graphed as the median of the last three probes.

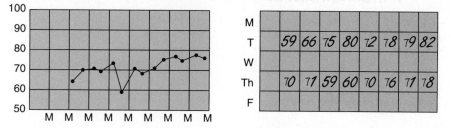

Step 14: To evaluate the effects of instruction, carefully examine the data. If the student has three consecutive scores graphed significantly below the aim line, make a change in instruction. (*Significant* is defined as ten or more points below the aim line.) Every time the student's data points fall significantly below the aim line three consecutive times, draw a vertical line on the graph after the third point (see Figure 7.6). Record the change in the reading instructional plan. If the student has six consecutive scores significantly above the aim line (six or more points above), probe with the next higher reading level book to see whether the student scores within the 55 to 75 wpm range on two of the three probes. This may mean establishing a new aim line for the student. This is done on the existing graph.

(continued on next page)

FIGURE 7.5
(continued)

Step 15: Change instruction. For ideas on what to change, consider using some of the following strategies: talk to another teacher; review suggestions in books, journals, and magazines; ask the student for ideas; or use the student's performance on the passages for error analysis.

Step 16: Use other measures for students who are word callers (i.e., can read aloud fluently but do not understand what they have read). These students can be asked to retell a story read silently, and the number of words used in the retelling can be scored and graphed. Also, these students can be asked to answer three to five comprehension questions, and the correct number of responses can be scored and graphed. The correct number of responses can be graphed between the 0 to 10 unit on the bottom of the graph chart. Examples of comprehension questions that can be asked after each assessment probe include the following: What are the main characters in the story? Where does the story take place? and What do you think will happen next?

Step 17: If the student reads more than 100 words correct per minute at or above the sixth-grade reader level on three consecutive probes, discontinue CBM. Note documentation of performance on the student's graph.

FIGURE 7.6

A curriculum-based measurement graph illustrating an aim line and intervention changes

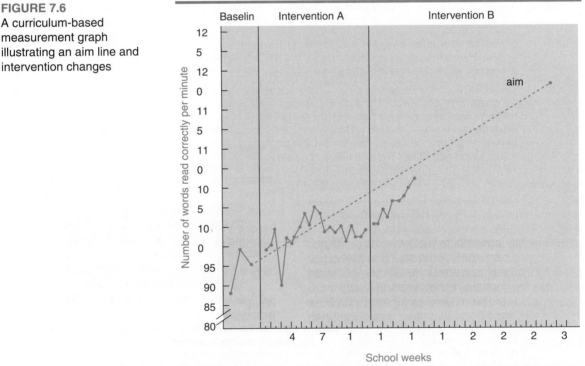

enable teachers to identify low performers who need special instruction, divide students into instructional groups, plan instructional programs, and establish long-range goals. Thus, rather than placing students into a reading material according to a percentage of correct responses, as is done with informal reading inventories, a placement validated through research can be made by placing the student in the level where her or his reading ability is most comparable to others.

A second primary use of CBM is to monitor individual student progress toward long-range goals. The teacher uses the steps in Figure 7.5, which includes the administration and scoring procedures of reading passages as well as procedures for determining long-range goals and graphing data. Figure 7.6 presents a graph of CBM data and illustrates a long-range goal or aim line and appropriate intervention changes.

When monitoring progress toward a long-range instructional goal, patterns of errors may indicate areas for remediation. These areas become the focus of short-term goals (e.g., identification of sight words, letter sounds, or facts in a story). To monitor progress on short-term goals, mastery monitoring charts that are similar to those in precision teaching are used. When the student reaches mastery on a short-term goal, a new goal is established. Monitoring continues through a series of short-term goals, and the measurement items change each time the student masters a goal. Probes or task sheets frequently are used for evaluation of student progress in timings given two or three times a week. The teacher graphs the correct responses and analyzes the data to make instructional decisions.

Potter and Wamre (1990) note that the use of oral reading rate measures in curriculum-based measurement is proving to be a viable measure of general reading skill and is consistent with developmental reading models such as Chall's (1983) stages of reading development. Moreover, research indicates that students who read more fluently also perform higher on comprehension tasks (Tindal & Marston, 1990).

Portfolio Assessment
A reading portfolio consists of a collection of materials that reflect the student's personal reading history and accomplishments as a reader. The student should participate in the selection and evaluation of the materials chosen for the portfolio. The materials can vary widely depending on the function of the portfolio assessment, which may include providing information for the teacher to use in assessing student achievement and making instructional decisions, documenting a record of student progress, and demonstrating student accomplishments to parents. Reading logs that indicate the number and variety of books read can be included, as well as checklists made from student observations and questionnaires completed by the student on reading interests and attitudes toward reading. Audiotapes of the student's best oral reading also can be collected at regular intervals. Reviews of the student's portfolio can provide information for teacher assessment as well as self-assessment by the student to evaluate reading progress and plan future activities to enhance reading achievement.

Reading Miscue Analysis
Reading miscue analysis, based on the work of K. S. Goodman (1969, 1973), is a method of analyzing the student's oral reading strategies. The selection read by the student should be a complete story or passage (i.e., have a beginning, middle, and end) that is one grade level above the material used by the student in class. It also should be unfamiliar to the student and of sufficient length and difficulty to generate a minimum of 25 miscues. Following the oral reading, the student retells the story.

Although comprehension is considered in an informal reading inventory, it is the major consideration in reading miscue analysis. The nature of the reading errors (miscues) is emphasized, rather than the number of errors made. Miscues can be classified in the following categories:

- **Semantic** miscues are similar in meaning to the text word. Some miscues indicate that the student comprehends the passage; thus, the simple substitution of a word is not important (e.g., substitution of *dad* for *father*).
- **Syntactic** miscues are the same part of speech as the text word. Some miscues show that the student fails to comprehend the meaning but at least substitutes a word that makes grammatical sense.
- **Graphic** miscues are similar to the sound-symbol relationship for the initial, medial, or final portion of the text word (such as *find* for *found*). Some miscues indicate the student's knowledge of phoneme-grapheme relationships.

It must be determined whether each miscue changed or interfered with the meaning of the information conveyed in the sentence or phrase in which it occurred. The most acceptable miscue is semantically correct, whereas syntactic and graphic errors are less acceptable. The seriousness of miscues depends on whether they consistently alter the meaning of the written passage and thus affect the student's comprehension.

Some oral mistakes reveal that the student reads with meaning (K. S. Goodman, 1969, 1973). These errors are not very serious if the purpose of reading is simply to understand. Fry (1977) suggests that distinguishing the three types of linguistic errors—semantic, syntactic, and sound-symbol—can help the classroom teacher in informal observation of any oral reading. The teacher who wants to pursue a systematic diagnosis of meaning-clue deficiencies should consult the *Reading Miscue Inventory* (Y. M. Goodman & Burke, 1972; Y. M. Goodman, Watson, & Burke, 1987). Each oral reading miscue is scored according to nine categories: dialect, intonation shift, graphic similarity, sound similarity, grammatical function, correction, grammatical acceptability, semantic acceptability, and meaning change. A short form of the *Reading Miscue Inventory* also is available (Burke, 1976).

Cloze Procedure   The cloze procedure can be used to measure reading levels and comprehen-

sion informally (Bormuth, 1968). It allows the teacher to estimate the difficulty the student will have with a specific reading material and thus helps determine whether a book is appropriate. The teacher presents an unfamiliar reading passage of about 250 words to the student. The first sentence is typed completely, but in subsequent sentences every fifth word is replaced with a blank. The blanks should be of uniform length. The remainder of the selection is typed as it appears in text. The student reads the passage and fills in the missing words or synonyms. Thus, the student must rely on context clues within the passage to make meaningful responses.

A variation of the cloze procedure is the maze procedure, in which the student is presented with a vertical array of choices for each omitted word. This changes the task from completion to multiple-choice or recognition. Another modification includes having the student select words from an answer key. The teacher also may choose to delete only every tenth word, or other appropriate words can be omitted to avoid the inadvertent

TABLE 7.6
Reading selection illustrating the cloze procedure

James Cornish lay wounded on the saloon floor! "He's been stabbed in __1__ chest!" shouted one horrified __2__. "Someone get him to __3__ hospital!" another shouted.

It __4__ a hot and humid __5__ in Chicago in 1893. __6__ arrived at the hospital __7__ a one-inch knife __8__ in his chest, dangerously __9__ his heart. Dr. Daniel __10__ Williams was called in __11__ operate.

In those days, __12__ blood transfusions and antibiotics __13__ unknown, chest surgery was __14__ attempted since it meant __15__ high risk of death. __16__ Dr. Williams began to __17__, he found that the __18__ wound had cut the __19__ and the sac around __20__ heart. Dr. Williams then __21__ history by becoming __22__ first surgeon to successfully __23__ on the human heart.

__24__ Williams did not release __25__ information for three and __26__ half years. When he __27__, the newspaper headline read, "__28__ Up His Heart," and __29__ news became known to __30__ entire world. Not only __31__ Cornish been discharged from __32__ hospital a well man, __33__ he lived fifty years __34__ his surgery. Cornish even __35__ the surgeon who had __36__ his life.

Correct Answers:

1. the	7. with	13. were	19. heart	25. this	31. had
2. bystander	8. wound	14. rarely	20. the	26. a	32. the
3. a	9. near	15. a	21. made	27. did	33. but
4. was	10. Hale	16. As	22. the	28. Sewed	34. after
5. day	11. to	17. operate	23. operate	29. the	35. outlived
6. Cornish	12. when	18. stab	24. Dr.	30. the	36. saved

Source: Adapted from *Analytical Reading Inventory* (p. 162), 5th ed., by M. L. Woods and A. J. Moe, 1995, Upper Saddle River, NJ: Merrill/Prentice Hall. Copyright 1995 by Prentice-Hall Publishing Company. Reprinted by permission.

continuous omission of articles or proper names. An example of the cloze procedure for a reading passage is presented in Table 7.6.

A reading passage using the cloze procedure can be administered either individually or in groups. Reading levels are determined by changing the number of correct responses to percentages. Bormuth (1968) suggests the following scoring of cloze passages: *independent reading level,* above 57 percent correct responses; *instructional reading level,* 44 to 57 percent correct responses; and *frustration reading level,* below 44 percent correct responses. Because identification of a correct word is easier than production of a correct word, the criterion is higher when the maze procedure is used (e.g., about 60 to 85 percent correct for instructional level). For additional information, the teacher should attempt to analyze why the student makes certain errors. Hafner (1965) notes that cloze errors can be examined according to linguistic components, cognitive types, and reasoning skills.

Teacher-Made Tests   The teacher can devise an informal test to obtain a quick estimate of a specific skill. Probe sheets can be developed to assess a particular reading objective, such as consonant sounds, vowel sounds, blends, or compound words.

A sample probe sheet to assess the student's ability to blend consonant-vowel-consonant sounds is presented in Figure 7.7. The probe is administered for 1 minute; then the correct and incorrect responses are tallied. Although the range of suggested proficiency reading rates varies in the literature, the median number of correct words per minute for saying isolated sounds is 70, and the median number of correct words per minute for saying words in a list is 80. Howell and Nolet (2000) suggest the following proficiency reading rates for saying words in text: early first grade—35 words per minute; late first grade—50 words per minute; early second grade—70 words per minute; late second grade—100 words per minute; early third grade 120 words per minute; late third grade and above—140 words per minute. Figure 7.8 presents a sample record sheet for probe assessment of various reading skills.

Teacher-made tests can be constructed by using items in standardized tests and workbook exercises as guides. A variety of items that measure a specific skill can be used (e.g., multiple-choice, true–false, completion, or matching). The teacher should be careful to include enough items to sample the skill adequately. Heilman (1985) provides an excellent informal word recognition skills test (see Figure 7.9) that the teacher can

FIGURE 7.7
Probe sheet for blending consonant-vowel-consonant sounds

luv	had	mok	hob	cuz
lit	def	cak	met	roc
nom	vig	pit	tik	fam
cum	zot	wet	bag	pod
fif	lid	hat	get	won
pik	soc	jox	vic	sut
sas	far	kah	par	gan
teg	tem	mez	zix	zec
pub	hun	nod	wol	wap
sel	top	nip	ris	dit

Name:_____

Time: _____

Number Correct:_____

Number Incorrect: _____

Comments:_____

_____

_____

FIGURE 7.8
Sample record sheet for probe assessments

Name _____ Greg _____				Grade ___ 4 ___	
Reading Areas	Session 1	Session 2	Session 3	Session 4	Suggested Rates for Proficiency	
	correct/ error	correct/ error	correct/ error	correct/ error	correct	error
Consonant Sounds (1 minute)	18/0	25/0	18/0	35/0	60–80	2 or fewer
Vowel Sounds (1 minute)	28/0	24/4	28/1	30/3	60–80	2 or fewer
Sight Words (1 minute)	28/3	35/3	41/3	44/9	70–90	2 or fewer
Grade 4 Word List (1 minute)	32/8	38/4	41/5	43/4	70–90	2 or fewer
Oral Reading (1 minute)	59/7	68/4	76/6	78/11	100–140	2 or fewer

Source: From *Students with Learning Disabilities* (p. 191), 5th ed., by C. D. Mercer, 1997, Upper Saddle River, NJ: Merrill/Prentice Hall. Copyright 1997 by Prentice-Hall Publishing Company. Reprinted by permission.

FIGURE 7.9
Informal word recognition skills test

Subtest A (pronunciation)
(Initial and final consonant sounds; short vowel sounds)

dad	self	but	ten	lift
fuss	yell	hog	sand	muff
lamp	him	jug	get	nap
puff	web	miss	pond	kill
rag	gum	pill	rob	cob
van	top	big	held	fond

Subtest B (pronunciation)
(Initial consonant blends; long and short vowel sounds)

bring	split	blue	smoke	scream
throat	clay	club	string	trip
please	twist	float	trade	glass
sky	prize	grass	flag	snail
crop	drill	blow	scene	sweet
spray	free	sled	spoon	stay

Subtest C (pronunciation)
(Consonant digraphs [*ch, sh, th, wh, qu, ng, ck*]; consonant blends)

quite	thank	check	shrink	crash
church	block	length	queen	shake
shake	quick	shove	choose	think
splash	strong	thing	truck	deck
whale	chose	which	sprung	hung
fresh	wheat	quench	tenth	quack

FIGURE 7.9
(continued)

Subtest D (pronunciation)
(Compound words; inflectional endings; contractions)

keeping	something	it's	bakery	really
pleased	can't	everybody	likes	finding
stops	quickly	lived	someone	helped
I'll	into	calls	he'll	outside
anyone	tallest	you'll	prettiest	loudest
unlock	happily	going	everything	wasn't

Subtest E (sight recognition—pronunciation)
Irregular Spellings
Consonant Irregularities

knee	rough	gnaw	is	you	limb
hour	the	who	phone	knew	whole
was	know	cough	enough	whose	knot

Vowel Irregularities

been	have	once	eye	sure	bird
give	any	do	break	chief	cough
they	to	one	love	could	dead
said	some	head	steak	none	their

Subtest F (syllabication)
(In the blank spaces, write the word in separate syllables.)

candy __can dy__	detective _____
moment _____	situation _____
locomotive _____	tiger _____
formation _____	education _____
summer _____	slippery _____
tumble _____	release _____

Subtest G (prefixes, suffixes, and syllabication)
(Pronounce each word; divide each word into syllables [see example].)

dis/con/tent/ment	prehistorical	disloyalty
recaptured	disgraceful	indebtedness
incapable	imperfection	previewing
unhappily	expandable	readjustment
exporter	independently	impassable
removable	rearrangement	submerged

Subtest H
(Sustained-reading passage)
Fred and Frank planned to go on a trip to the pond. Frank liked to swim, but Fred was not a swimmer. He chose to hunt frogs and trap crabs. With a shout, the boys were off on their hike to the lake. At first, they tried to walk in the shade. Then both took off their shirts to get a suntan.

Source: From *Phonics in Proper Perspective* (pp. 84-86), 5th ed., by A. W. Heilman, 1985, Upper Saddle River, NJ: Merrill/Prentice Hall. Copyright 1985 by Prentice-Hall Publishing Company. Reprinted by permission.

adapt for use in informal assessment. It assesses both phonics and structural analysis skills. In addition, short-form word analysis tests can be de-

vised to measure specific skills. Items also can be developed to assess specific comprehension skills, such as stating the main idea, noting de-

FIGURE 7.10
Teacher-made test items for assessing short *a* vowel sound

I. The student reads the words with short *a* in initial position.

am	ant	at
an	as	act
and	ask	add

Criterion: 7/9

II. The student reads the words with short *a* in medial position.

ham	pant	bat
can	gas	fact
hand	task	mad

Criterion: 7/9

III. The student selects the word of the pair that contains the short *a* sound.

hat—hate	plan—plane
say—sad	past—pay
ran—ray	stay—sand
tale—land	dad—pale

Criterion: 7/8

IV. The student chooses the word with the short *a* sound to complete the sentence.

The boy had a _____ on his head.
(cap, cape)

The _____ was blowing. (sail, flag)

His mother was looking at the _____.
(mail, map)

There was a _____ in the sidewalk.
(crack, nail)

The father did not _____ his son.
(blame, spank)

Criterion 4/5

---

tails, and understanding cause-and-effect relationships. Selected items for assessing the short *a* vowel sound are presented in Figure 7.10. When the student passes the informal test, the teacher can assume that he or she has mastered the objective and is ready to progress to another skill. Reading scope and sequence skills lists, such as the one included in Appendix A, can help determine the order of skill assessment and instruction. Finally, teacher-made tests often deal with reading skills the student must use daily, and they provide a measure of student progress over a specific period of time.

☀ REFERENCES

Adams, M. J. (1990). *Beginning to read: Thinking and learning about print.* Cambridge, MA: MIT Press.

Ball, E. W. (1993). Assessing phoneme awareness. *Language, Speech, and Hearing Services in Schools, 24,* 130–139.

Balow, I. H., Farr, R. C., & Hogan, T. P. (1997). *Metropolitan Achievement Tests—Seventh Edition.* San Antonio, TX: Harcourt Brace Educational Measurement.

Bond, G. L., Tinker, M. A., Wasson, B. B., & Wasson, J. B. (1989). *Reading difficulties: Their diagnosis and correction* (6th ed.). Upper Saddle River, NJ: Prentice Hall.

Bormuth, J. R. (1968). The cloze readability procedure. *Elementary English, 45,* 429–436.

Brigance, A. H. (1999). *Brigance Diagnostic Comprehensive Inventory of Basic Skills—Revised.* North Billerica, MA: Curriculum Associates.

Brown, V. L., Hammill, D. D., & Wiederholt, J. L. (1995). *Test of Reading Comprehension—3.* Austin, TX: PRO-ED.

Bryant, B. R., & Wiederholt, J. L. (1991). *Gray Oral Reading Tests—Diagnostic.* Austin, TX: PRO-ED.

Burke, C. (1976). *Reading Miscue Inventory—Short form.* Bloomfield, IN: Indiana University.

Burns, P. C., & Roe, B. D. (1999). *Informal Reading Inventory* (5th ed.). Boston: Houghton Mifflin.

California Diagnostic Reading Test. (1990). Monterey, CA: CTB/McGraw-Hill.

Carnine, D., Silbert, J., & Kameenui, E. J. (1997). *Direct instruction reading* (3rd ed.). Upper Saddle River, NJ: Merrill/Prentice Hall.

Chall, J. S. (1983). *Stages of reading development.* New York: McGraw-Hill.

Chall, J. S., & Stahl, S. A. (1982). Reading. In H. E. Mitzel (Ed.), *Encyclopedia of educational research* (5th ed., pp. 1535–1559). New York: Free Press.

Ciborowski, J. (1995). Using textbooks with students who cannot read them. *Remedial and Special Education, 16,* 90–101.

Deno, S. L. (1987). Curriculum-based measurement. *Teaching Exceptional Children, 20*(1), 41–42.

Deno, S. L. (1989). Curriculum-based measurement and special education services: A fundamental and direct relationship. In M. R. Shinn (Ed.), *Curriculum-based measurement: Assessing special children* (pp. 1–17). New York: Guilford Press.

Deno, S. L., & Mirkin, P. (1977). *Data-based program modification: A manual.* Reston, VA: Council for Exceptional Children.

Dolch, E. W. (1955). *Methods in reading.* Champaign, IL: Garrard.

Durrell, D. D., & Catterson, J. H. (1980). *Durrell analysis of reading difficulty* (3rd ed.). San Antonio, TX: Harcourt Brace Educational Measurement.

Ekwall, E. E., & Shanker, J. L. (1989). *Teaching reading in the elementary school* (3rd ed.). Upper Saddle River, NJ: Merrill/Prentice Hall.

Fry, E. (1977). *Elementary reading instruction.* New York: McGraw-Hill.

Gates, A. I. (1937). The necessary mental age for beginning reading. *Elementary School Journal, 37,* 497–508.

Goodman, K. S. (1969). Analysis of oral reading miscues: Applied psycholinguistics. *Reading Research Quarterly, 5,* 9–30.

Goodman, K. S. (1973). *Miscue analysis: Applications to reading instruction.* Urbana, IL: National Council of Teachers of English.

Goodman, Y. M., & Burke, C. L. (1972). *Reading Miscue Inventory: Manual of procedure for diagnosis and evaluation.* New York: Richard C. Owens.

Goodman, Y. M., Watson, D. J., & Burke, C. L. (1987). *Miscue Inventory: Alternative procedures.* New York: Richard C. Owens.

Guszak, F. J. (1985). *Diagnostic reading instruction in the elementary school* (3rd ed.). New York: Harper & Row.

Hafner, L. (1965). Importance of cloze. In E. T. Thurstone & L. E. Hafner (Eds.), *The philosophical and social bases for reading: 14th yearbook.* Milwaukee: National Reading Conference.

Hanson, R. A., & Farrell, D. (1995). The long-term effects on high school seniors of learning to read in kindergarten. *Reading Research Quarterly, 30,* 908–933.

Harris, A. J., & Sipay, E. R. (1990). *How to increase reading ability: A guide to developmental and remedial methods* (9th ed.). New York: Longman.

Heilman, A. W. (1985). *Phonics in proper perspective* (5th ed.). Upper Saddle River, NJ: Merrill/Prentice Hall.

Hoover, H. D., Hieronymus, A. N., Frisbie, D. A., & Dunbar, S. B. (1996). *Iowa Tests of Basic Skills.* Itasca, IL: Riverside.

Howell, K. W. & Nolet, V. (2000). *Curriculum-based evaluation: Teaching and decision making* (3rd ed.). Belmont, CA: Wadsworth/Thomson Learning.

Johnson, D. D. (1971). The Dolch list reexamined. *The Reading Teacher, 24,* 449–457.

Johnson, M. S., Kress, R. A., & Pikulski, J. J. (1987). *Informal reading inventories.* Newark, DE: International Reading Association.

Juel, C. (1988). Learning to read and write: A longitudinal study of 54 children from first through fourth grades. *Journal of Educational Psychology, 80,* 437–447.

Karlsen, B., & Gardner, E. F. (1995). *Stanford Diagnostic Reading Test—Fourth Edition.* San Antonio, TX: Harcourt Brace Educational Measurement.

Kaufman, A. S., & Kaufman, N. L. (1998). *Kaufman Test of Educational Achievement.* Circle Pines, MN: American Guidance Service.

Kirk, S. A., Kliebhan, J. M., & Lerner, J. W. (1978). *Teaching reading to slow and disabled learners.* Boston: Houghton Mifflin.

Liberman, I. Y., Shankweiler, D., Fischer, F. W., & Carter, B. (1974). Reading and the awareness of linguistic segments. *Journal of Experimental Child Psychology, 18,* 201–212.

Lovitt, T. C., & Hansen, C. L. (1976). Round one—Placing the child in the right reader. *Journal of Learning Disabilities, 9,* 347–353.

Lyon, G. R. (1995). Research initiatives in learning disabilities: Contributions from scientists supported by the National Institute of Child Health and Human Development. *Journal of Child Neurology, 10* (Suppl. 1), 120–126.

MacGinitie, W. H., MacGinitie, R. K., Maria, K., & Dreyer, L. G. (2000). *Gates-MacGinitie Reading Tests—Fourth Edition.* Itasca, IL: Riverside.

Newcomer, P. L. (1999). *Standardized Reading Inventory—2.* Austin, TX: PRO-ED.

Perfetti, C. (1985). *Reading ability.* New York: Oxford University Press.

Potter, M. L., & Wamre, H. M. (1990). Curriculum-based measurement and developmental reading models: Opportunities for cross-validation. *Exceptional Children, 57,* 16–25.

Reid, D. K., Hresko, W. P., & Hammill, D. D. (1989). *Test of Early Reading Ability—2.* Austin, TX: PRO-ED.

Shanker, J. L., & Ekwall, E. E. (1998). *Locating and correcting reading difficulties* (7th ed.). Upper Saddle River, NJ: Merrill/Prentice Hall.

Silvaroli, N. J. (1997). *Classroom Reading Inventory* (8th ed.). DeSoto, TX: McGraw-Hill.

Smith, C. R. (1995, March). *Developmental progression of phonological segmentation skills.* Paper presented at the Learning Disabilities Association International Conference, Orlando, FL.

Smith, R. J., & Barrett, T. C. (1979). *Teaching reading in the middle grades* (2nd ed.). Reading, MA: Addison-Wesley.

Snider, V. E., & Tarver, S. G. (1987). The effect of early reading failure on acquisition of knowledge among students with learning disabilities. *Journal of Learning Disabilities, 20*, 351–356, 373.

Snow, C. E., Burns, M. S., & Griffin, P. (Eds.). (1998). *Preventing reading difficulties in young children.* Washington, DC: National Academy Press.

Spache, G. D. (1981). *Diagnostic Reading Scales.* Monterey, CA: CTB McGraw-Hill.

Spache, G. D., & Spache, E. B. (1986). *Reading in the elementary school* (5th ed.). Boston: Allyn & Bacon.

Starlin, C. (1982). *On reading and writing.* Des Moines, IA: Department of Public Instruction.

Tindal, G. A., & Marston, D. B. (1990). *Classroom-based assessment: Evaluating instructional outcomes.* Upper Saddle River, NJ: Merrill/Prentice Hall.

Torgesen, J. K., & Bryant, B. R. (1994). *Test of Phonological Awareness.* Austin, TX: PRO-ED.

Torgesen, J. K., Wagner, R., & Rashotte, C. (1999). *Test of Word Reading Efficiency.* Austin, TX: PRO-ED.

Wiederholt, J. L., & Bryant, B. R. (1992). *Gray Oral Reading Tests—Third Edition.* Austin, TX: PRO-ED.

Woodcock, R. W. (1998). *Woodcock Reading Mastery Tests—Revised.* Circle Pines, MN: American Guidance Service.

Woodcock, R. W., & Mather, N. (2000). *Woodcock-Johnson III Tests of Achievement.* Itasca, IL: Riverside.

Woods, M. L., & Moe, A. J. (1999). *Analytical Reading Inventory* (6th ed.). Upper Saddle River, NJ: Merrill/Prentice Hall.

CHAPTER **8**

Teaching Reading

Through the years, reading instruction has remained the most controversial topic in education. The intense debate between educators who stress the code-emphasis reading approach and those who stress the meaning-emphasis reading approach has existed for more than a century. Consequently, teachers must choose from a plethora of materials and techniques in designing reading programs. To make instructional decisions that are best suited to the needs of diverse learners, it helps to understand the reading process.

Adams (1990) conducted a thorough review of reading research and developed a model that serves as an excellent foundation for understanding the reading process. Her model, which provides a good framework for making instructional decisions about reading, includes four interrelated processors: orthographic, phonological, meaning, and context. These processors interact to produce skilled reading.

The *orthographic processor* is the visual processor, and it receives information directly from the printed page. This visual information serves to initiate the reading process. When a reader sees a familiar word, the letters are strongly interconnected or hang together within the learner's orthographic memory. This causes the word to be recognized instantaneously. Skillful readers recognize familiar spelling patterns and break unfamiliar polysyllabic words into syllables. The ability to recognize spelling patterns quickly and break words into syllables allows students to read fluently. Poor readers tend to recognize fewer letter patterns and fail to apply syllabication strategies. This disrupts fluency and comprehension.

The *phonological processor* is the auditory processor, and it receives information from speech. The orthographic processor deals with an image or string of letters; the phonological processor interacts to determine whether the letters are pronounceable. Thus, the two processors work together to decipher sound-symbol relationships. In addition to sounding out words, phonological processing features translation of sounds into words and interpretation of those words into meaningful units. Phonological translations of words (i.e., the sounds of the word) tend to remain in memory longer than their visual images and can be recalled without visual cues. Through thinking or saying words, skillful readers renew the words' phonological activation, thus facilitating memory.

The *meaning processor* interacts with the orthographic processor (i.e., letters), the phonological processor (i.e., sounds), and the context processor to provide meaning to individual words. Because activation of the meaning processor occurs during reading, a reader's vocabulary expands substantially through reading a variety of materials.

The *context processor* constructs a fluent interpretation of the text. It works by continuously creating expectations of word meanings. Skillful readers use context to determine appropriate meanings for words. Children with limited language experiences are restricted in their ability to derive meaning from context. Once the word has been decoded, the context processor enhances the interpretations of printed information.

The four processors (i.e., knowledge of common spelling patterns, spoken forms of words, word meanings, and context) work together to produce reading. When information from one processor is weak, information from the other processors compensates. Given that the capacity or development of the four processors varies among learners and that reading approaches stress different processors, teachers must use a variety of reading approaches to meet the needs of diverse learners.

Reid Lyon, Chief of the Child Development and Behavior Branch of the National Institute of Child Health and Human Development (NICHD) of the National Institutes of Health (NIH), periodically reports on the research findings of NIH studies concerning reading development for children with and without reading difficulties. These studies have employed excellent scientific methodology for more than 30 years with large numbers of students (i.e., more than 40,000 individuals). The findings are providing much insight concerning what is known about children who have reading disabilities and how to teach them. In his 1999 report to the United States House of Representatives House Science Committee, Lyon (1999, pp. 4–5) highlights some of the NIH findings in the following passage:

Specifically, over the past 34 years a great deal of converging evidence has improved our understanding of how children learn to read, what factors impede reading development, and which instructional approaches are most beneficial at different stages of reading development. We have learned that the development of skilled reading abilities requires the integration of phonological skills, phonics skills, the development of accurate and fluent textual reading capabilities, and the development and application of reading comprehension strategies. We have learned that early language and literacy experiences from birth onward are extremely important in fostering these specific foundational skills. We have developed inexpensive screening and assessment methods to identify children in kindergarten and first grade who are at-risk for reading failure. This is a significant development given that we have also learned that children after the age of nine have an extremely difficult time improving their reading abilities. We have learned that girls are as likely as boys to have difficulties learning to read, but are frequently overlooked in the assessment process and are not likely to receive appropriate specialized instruction. We have learned that some instructional approaches, methods, and philosophies are clearly not appropriate for certain children, but continue to be employed in classrooms due to a lack of adequate teacher preparation in colleges of education. We have also learned that instructional approaches that are designed on the basis of the converging research findings work remarkably well with children who have had difficulties learning to read as long as well trained teachers provide the instruction early enough in the youngster's school tenure.

Moreover, in a 1998 report to the United States Senate Committee on Labor and Human Resources, Lyon (1998, pp. 8–9) discusses the following specific findings related to phonemic awareness, early intervention, and poor readers:

> In contrast to good readers who understand that segmented units of speech can be linked to letters and letter patterns, poor readers have substantial difficulty developing this "alphabetic principle." The culprit appears to be a deficit in phoneme awareness—the understanding that words are made up of sound segments called phonemes. Difficulties in developing phoneme awareness can have genetic and neurobiological origins or can be attributable to a lack of exposure to language patterns and usage during the preschool years. The end result is the same however. Children who lack phoneme awareness have difficulties linking speech sounds to letters—their decoding skills are labored and weak, resulting in extremely slow reading. This labored access to print renders comprehension impossible. . . . We have learned the foillowing with respect to the

role that phonemic awareness plays in the development of phonics skills and fluent and automatic word reading:

1. Phonemic awareness skills assessed in kindergarten and first grade serve as potent predictors of difficulties learning to read. We have learned how to measure phonemic awareness skills as early as the first semester in kindergarten with tasks that take only 15 minutes to administer— and over the past decade we have refined these tasks so that we can predict with approximately 80% to 90% accuracy who become good readers and who will have difficulties learning to read.
2. We have learned that the development of phonemic awareness is a necessary but not sufficient condition for learning to read. A child must integrate phonemic skills into the learning of phonics principles, must practice reading so that word recognition becomes rapid and accurate, and must learn how to actively use comprehension strategies to enhance meaning.
3. . . . We have learned that for 90% to 95% of poor readers, prevention and early intervention programs that combine instruction in phoneme awareness, phonics, fluency development, and reading comprehension strategies, provided by well trained teachers, can increase reading skills to average reading levels. However, we have also learned that if we delay intervention until nine-years-of-age (the time that most children with reading difficulties receive services), approximately 75% of the children will continue to have difficulties learning to read throughout high school.

This chapter presents a variety of reading approaches, strategies, and activities for teaching children and adolescents with learning problems. The content includes substantial information on developing comprehension, reading good literature, and the importance of student motivation to read. Moreover, because many students with learning problems need systematic experiences with decoding skills (i.e., orthographic/phonics and phonological processors/phonemic awareness) to learn to read well, this chapter also presents extensive information about code-emphasis approaches, strategies, and techniques.

DEVELOPMENTAL READING APPROACHES

Developmental reading approaches emphasize daily, sequential instruction. Most are programmed according to a normative pattern of reading growth. The basic material for instruction is usually a series of books (such as basal readers) that directs what will be taught and when. A well-developed program provides supplementary materials such as workbooks, skillpacks, wall charts, related activities, learning games, and filmstrips. To teach students with learning problems, it often is necessary to adapt developmental programs by changing the sequence, providing additional practice activities, and modifying the input-output arrangements of selected tasks. Moreover, combinations of programs often are superior to single approaches (i.e., using supplemental phonics or adding language experiences to any kind of reading). The following developmental approaches are discussed: basal, literature-based, phonics, linguistic, whole-language, language experience, and individualized reading.

Basal Reading Approach

Many teachers use a basal reading series as the core of their program. Most series include a sequential set of reading texts and supplementary materials such as workbooks, flash cards, placement and achievement tests, and filmstrips. In addition, a comprehensive teacher's manual explains the purpose of the program and provides precise instructional plans and suggestions for skill activities. The teacher's manual usually is highly structured and completely outlines each lesson, perhaps including skill objectives, new vocabulary words, motivational activities, and questions for checking comprehension on each page of the text.

The readers usually begin with preprimers and gradually increase in difficulty through the eighth grade. Some basals are changing their progression from grade-level readers to levels corresponding to stages in development. The content is based upon common student experiences and interests. Materials designed for student groups who are multiracial or disadvantaged sometimes feature settings and content to appeal to a variety of backgrounds and ethnic groups. Basals may use either a meaning-emphasis or a code-emphasis approach. Some basals feature a whole language approach and focus on whole-word recognition and comprehension through the reading of children's literature stories. Others focus on word decoding strategies such as phonics. A basal series systematically presents reading skills in word recognition, comprehension, and word attack, and controls the vocabulary from level to level. The reader, manual, and student workbook provide activities that help teach word-attack skills (including phonics), develop comprehension, and increase reading rate steadily.

Most basal readers recommend a *directed reading activity* procedure for teaching a reading lesson. The steps include the following:

1. Motivate the student to learn the material.
2. Prepare the student by presenting new concepts and vocabulary.
3. Guide the student in reading the story by asking questions that give a purpose or goal for the reading.
4. Develop or strengthen skills relating to the material through drills or workbook activities.
5. Assign work to apply the skills acquired during the lesson.
6. Evaluate the effectiveness of the lesson.

This guided reading approach can be used to increase comprehension skills. Basal readers contain stories with many details and often are divided into small parts. Thus, location exercises can be given to find the main idea or main characters as well as specific words, phrases, sentences, and paragraphs.

The basal reading approach is used in most reading programs in the United States; however, Schumm, Vaughn, Haager, and Klinger (1994) note that many widely used basal reading programs offer none or only a few teaching suggestions for planning and implementing instruction for students with reading disabilities in inclusive settings. The teacher must adjust or supplement the materials to meet the individual needs of students with reading problems. Modifications to enhance the base lesson include teacher modeling, additional examples, control of the learning set, and additional phonological awareness activities (e.g., word segmentation exercises) (Simmons, Chard, & Kameenui, 1994). Also, for supplemental reading, high interest–low vocabulary books offer a relatively easy vocabulary while maintaining an interest level appropriate for the more mature reader.

Literature-Based Reading Approach

In an effort to acquaint youngsters with good literature and motivate them to read, some teachers use a literature-based approach for beginning reading instruction. In this approach, trade books and children's literature books are leveled according to specific criteria. The leveling is organized by grade level or by reading stages (e.g., early emergent/emergent reader [kindergarten], developing reader [first grade], early independent reader [second grade], and independent reader [third grade]). Characteristics of books leveled at beginning first grade include repetition of two to three sentence patterns, simple sentence patterns, predominately oral language patterns, many familiar objects and actions, and illustrations that provide moderate to high support. Characteristics of books for students at the end of second grade include elaborated episodes and events, extended descriptions, literary language, unusual or challenging vocabulary, and low-support illustrations.

The following activities frequently are used in a literature-based reading program:

• ***Teacher reading aloud to children.*** Reading aloud to children is common in the primary grades. Some advantages of this activity are that it motivates children to read, provides an adult reading model, develops sense of story, acquaints children with books, and increases vocabulary and phonological awareness (e.g., word rhymes).

• ***Oral reading variations.*** The children first read a story or passage silently to prepare for oral reading. Variations involve choral reading in pairs, with the teacher providing help, and choral reading for the whole group, with the teacher signaling when to stop. In imitative reading, the teacher reads one or two sentences aloud and the children read the sentences back to the teacher. Choral reading helps reduce the risk of public failure for poor readers.

• ***Shared reading.*** To conduct shared reading, the teacher uses an enlarged (big book) text of familiar songs, poems, or stories. The teacher reads the text aloud to the group. Then the children are invited to join in reading the enlarged text while the teacher points to each word as it is read.

• ***Sustained silent reading.*** Everyone in the class reads silently. During this time the teacher also reads silently.

Because of the number of large- and small-group activities and choral reading, it is possible for low readers to "fake it." Thus, the teacher should listen to each child read periodically and monitor each student's progress. The success of this approach for students with learning problems depends on how much systematic instruction in letter-sound associations is provided. With whole language approaches such as this one, most letter-sound associations are taught during writing activities. To date, little research exists to support this approach with students who have learning problems.

Phonics Approach

The phonics approach teaches word recognition through learning grapheme-phoneme associations. In her comprehensive review of reading research, Adams (1990) reports that systematic phonics instruction coupled with reading meaningful connected text results in improved reading achievement for both low- and high-level reading students. She further notes that phonics instruction not only helps students decode words but also assists in spelling. After learning vowels, consonants, and blends, the student learns to sound out words by combining sounds and blending them into words. Thus, the student learns to recognize unfamiliar words by associating speech sounds with letters or groups of letters. Table 8.1 presents the sounds stressed in a phonics program. The emphasis on phonics (or decoding) in the primary grades has become almost universal in beginning reading programs (with the exception of whole language programs).

The teacher can use the synthetic method or the analytic method to teach phonics. In the *synthetic* method, the student learns that letters represent certain sounds (e.g., *b—buh*) and then finds out how to blend, or *synthesize,* the sounds to form words. This method emphasizes isolated letter sounds before the student progresses to words. The *analytic* method teaches letter sounds as integral parts of words (e.g., *b* as in *baby*). The student must learn new words based on phonics elements similar to familiar or sight words. Carnine, Silbert, and Kameenui (1997) note that synthetic phonics appears to yield better results in beginning reading than does analytic phonics. Phonics methods and materials differ on details, but the main objective is to teach the student to attack new words independently.

Phonics instruction builds on a foundation of phonemic awareness and can be integrated into a total reading program. Phonics may be added effectively to a literature-based, whole language, or

TABLE 8.1
Sounds stressed in a phonics program

Single Consonants

b	bear	*l*	lake	*t*	turtle
d	dog	*m*	money	*v*	vase
f	face	*n*	nose	*w*	wagon
h	hen	*p*	pear	*y*	yellow
j	jug	*q*	queen	*z*	zebra
k	king	*r*	rat		

The following consonants have two or more sounds:

c	cat	*g*	goat	*s*	six	*x*	xylophone
c	city	*g*	germ	*s*	is	*x*	exist
				s	sure	*x*	box

When *g* is followed by *e, i,* or *y,* it often takes the soft sound of *j,* as in *gentle* and *giant.* If it is not followed by these letters, it usually takes the hard sound, as illustrated in such words as *got* and *game.*

When *c* is followed by *e, i,* or *y,* it usually takes the soft sound heard in *cent.* If it is not followed by these letters, it usually takes the hard sound heard in *come.*

Qu usually has the sound of *kw;* however, in some words such as *bouquet,* it has the sound of *k.*

Consonant Blends

Beginning

bl	blue	*pr*	pretty	*tw*	twin
br	brown	*sc*	score	*wr*	wrench
cl	clown	*sk*	skill	*sch*	school
cr	crown	*sl*	slow	*scr*	screen
dr	dress	*sm*	small	*shr*	shrink
dw	dwell	*sn*	snail	*spl*	splash
fl	flower	*sp*	spin	*spr*	spring
fr	from	*st*	story	*squ*	squash
gl	glue	*sw*	swan	*str*	string
gr	grape	tr	tree	*thr*	throw
pl	plate				

Ending

ld	wild
mp	lamp
nd	wind
nt	went
rk	work
sk	risk

Consonant Digraphs

ch	chute	*sh*	ship
ch	choral	*th*	three
ch	church	*th*	that
gh	cough	*wh*	which
ph	graph	*wh*	who

(continued on next page)

TABLE 8.1
(continued)

Vowel Sounds

	Short Sounds		Long Sounds	
	a	bat	*a*	rake
	e	bed	*e*	jeep
	i	pig	*i*	kite
	o	lock	*o*	rope
	u	duck	*u*	mule

W is sometimes used as a vowel, as in the *aw*, *ew*, and *ow* diphthongs (see the following list). *W* is usually used as a vowel on word endings and as a consonant at the beginning of words.

Y is usually a consonant when it appears at the beginning of a word and a vowel in any other position.

Three consonants usually affect or control the sounds of some, or all, of the vowels when they follow these vowels within a syllable. They are *r, w,* and *l* (sometimes known as *R*eally *W*eird *L*etters).

r	*w*	*l*
car	law	all
her	few	bell
dirt	now	
word		
fur		

Vowel Digraphs (Most common phonemes only)

ai	pain	
ay	hay	
ea	each or weather	(Other phonemes are common for *ea*.)
ee	meet	
ei	weight or either	(Other phonemes are common for *ei*.)
ie	piece	(Other phonemes are common for *ie*.)
oa	oats	
oo	book or moon	
ou	tough (digraph) or house (diphthong)	
ow	low (digraph) or cow (diphthong)	

Of the various consonant digraphs, those that are most regular in their pronunciation are underlined here and are represented by the phrase: M*ai*ds m*ay* *ea*t *oa*k tr*ee*s. (Unfortunately, *ea* does have many exceptions!)

Diphthongs (Pronounced: dif' thongs.)

au	haul*	*oi*	soil
aw	hawk*	*ou*	trout
ew	few	*ow*	cow
ey	they*	*oy*	boy

*In a diphthong, both of the vowel letters are heard and they make a gliding sound, which is heard most easily in words like *cow* and *boy*. Some speakers may hear the examples of *au*, *aw*, and *ey* given here as digraphs (one sound) rather than diphthongs.

Source: From *Locating and Correcting Reading Difficulties* (pp. 233–235), 7th ed., by J. L. Shanker and E. E. Ekwall, 1998. Upper Saddle River, NJ: Merrill/Prentice-Hall. Copyright 1998 by Prentice-Hall Publishing Company. Reprinted by permission.

language experience approach after the student has acquired some basic sight vocabulary. Phonics is helpful with beginning readers in a developmental program or as a remedial technique for students who have a strong sight vocabulary but are unable to analyze unfamiliar words.

Guidelines for Teaching Phonics Stewart and Cegelka (1995) provide the following guidelines for teaching phonics:

1. ***Use lowercase letters for beginning instruction.*** Preschoolers' experiences with print

include much exposure to uppercase letters; however, because of environmental print (e.g., signs and names), reading primarily involves reading lowercase letters. Thus, lowercase letters are recommended for beginning phonics instruction (Adams, 1990).

2. ***Introduce most useful skills first.*** Frequently occurring letter sounds such as /m/, /s/, /t/, /a/, and /i/ are taught before less frequently occurring sounds such as /j/, /v/, /x/, and /z/. This process usually involves teaching vowel sounds early, along with sounds for the consonants *b, c, d, f, h, m, n, p, r, s,* and *t.*

3. ***Introduce easy sounds and letters first.*** Easy sounds include /m/, /s/, and /a/, whereas the sounds /l/, /x/, and /y/ are more difficult to learn. Letters that are visually similar (e.g., *b, p,* and *d; m* and *n; p* and *q;* and *v* and *w*) should be temporally spaced during instruction. Also, letters with similar sounds (/b/, /d/, and /p/; /e/ and /i/; /f/ and /v/; and /m/ and /n/) should be separated for instruction.

4. ***Introduce new letter-sound associations at a reasonable pace.*** Carnine et al. (1997) recommend introducing a new letter-sound correspondence every two or three days, with daily practice for youngsters who have limited prior experiences. Once the initial five or more sounds are mastered, a new letter-sound can be introduced even if the student experiences difficulty with one of the prior correspondences. It is important that the new correspondence be unlike the prior one that still causes difficulty (e.g., if the child experiences difficulty with a vowel, introduce a consonant).

5. ***Introduce vowels early, but teach consonants first.*** Because vowels are the most useful sounds and are essential for decoding words, they need to be presented early; however, vowels are also difficult because they frequently do not present clear letter-sound correspondences. Thus, it is helpful to present consonants first because they tend to have clear one-to-one letter-sound correspondences. Irregular consonant correspondences such as *c* in *cat* and *c* in *ice, g* in *goat* and *g* in *germ,* and *s* in *sure* and *s* in *six* should be taught later, after the alphabetic principle is established.

6. ***Emphasize the common sounds of letters first.*** With vowels, the short sound that occurs in most one-syllable words is the most common sound. The most frequently occurring sound is apparent for most consonants (e.g., /b/ in *bump,* /d/ in *dig,* /m/ in *mitt,* and /t/ in *top*), but the most frequent sounds for other consonants are less obvious (e.g., /c/ in *can,* /r/ in *rat,* /s/ in *sat,* /w/ in *wet,* and /z/ in *zoo*).

7. ***Teach continuous sounds prior to stop sounds.*** Continuous sounds can be voiced for several seconds without distortion. All vowels and some consonants (i.e., *f, l, m, n, r, s, v, w, y,* and *z*) are continuous sounds. Stop sounds primarily involve a puff of airflow and can be pronounced only momentarily. Letters with stop sounds include *b, c, d, g, h, j, k, p, q, t,* and *x.* Continuous sounds are taught first because they are easier to pronounce and hear. Carnine et al. (1997) suggest the following instructional sequence for introducing lowercase letters: *a, m, t, s, i, f, d, r, o, g, l, h, u, c, b, n, k, v, e, w, j, p, y, x, q,* and *z.*

8. ***Teach sound blending early.*** Once the student has mastered four or five sounds, instruction in sound blending is appropriate. Initial letter-sound correspondences can be used to decode consonant-vowel-consonant trigrams. When the student can blend simple consonant-vowel-consonant and vowel-consonant letter sounds into words, other word types are introduced. Carnine et al. (1997) list regular word types according to difficulty level as follows:

- Vowel-consonant and consonant-vowel-consonant words that begin with continuous sounds (e.g., *at, man*)
- Vowel-consonant-consonant words and consonant-vowel-consonant-consonant words that begin with continuous sounds (e.g., *ask, fish*)
- Consonant-vowel-consonant words that begin with stop sounds (e.g., *dot, cap*)
- Consonant-vowel-consonant-consonant words that begin with stop sounds (e.g., *desk, push*)
- Consonant-consonant-vowel-consonant words that begin with continuous sounds (e.g., *slap, frog*) and consonant-consonant-vowel-consonant words in which one of the initial sounds is a stop sound (e.g., *crib, stop*)
- Consonant-consonant-vowel-consonant-consonant words (e.g., *cramp*), consonant-consonant-consonant-vowel-consonant words (e.g., *split*), and consonant-consonant-consonant-vowel-consonant-consonant words (e.g., *scrimp*)

This order provides a framework for sequencing blending instruction.

9. ***Introduce consonant blends.*** When students have mastered the ability to blend consonant-vowel-consonant words that start with continuous sounds (e.g., *fat*) and consonant-vowel-consonant words that start with stop sounds (e.g., *dig*), words beginning with consonant blends (e.g., *spot*) are introduced. Next, words ending with consonant blends (e.g., *sick*) are taught.

10. ***Introduce consonant digraphs.*** With blends, each consonant sound is heard; however, the adjacent consonants in a digraph join to form one sound (e.g., *ship*). As with consonant blends, digraphs occur in both initial and final positions of words.

11. ***Introduce regular words prior to irregular ones.*** Beginning instruction focuses on words that are consistent with phonics rules in that they are pronounced according to their most common sounds. In addition to words that feature common letter-sound conventions, rules exist to help identify patterns for letters that have multiple sounds or combine with other letters to produce blends or digraphs (see Table 8.2). Most students require much practice with each phonics rule with words in text. Adams (1990) maintains that once youngsters achieve a critical mass of letter clusters and corresponding sounds, phonics rules and generalization are superfluous. After this critical mass is acquired, reading primarily involves adding more vocabulary. A large number of English words are irregular because they do not follow the conventions of phonics rules. Most of these words are presented after regular words in phonics instruction. Irregular words frequently are taught as sight words to be memorized. Because many sight words are high-frequency words, they need to be acquired through reading them many times. (Table 7.4 provides a list of sight words.)

12. ***Read connected text that reinforces phonics patterns.*** Adams (1990) notes that phonics is much more effective if students immediately read connected text that reinforces the letter-sound correspondences being taught. For

TABLE 8.2
Phonics rules

Consonants
1. When *c* is frequently followed by *e, i,* or *y,* it has the sound of *s,* as in *race, city, fancy.*
2. Otherwise, *c* has the sound of *k,* as in *come, attic.*
3. *G* followed by *e, i,* or *y* sounds soft like *j,* as in *gem.*
4. Otherwise *g* sounds hard, as in *gone.*
5. When *c* and *h* are next to each other, they make only one sound.
6. *Ch* is usually pronounced as it is in *kitchen,* not like *sh* (in *machine*).
7. When a word ends in *ck,* it has the same last sound, as in *look.*
8. When two of the same consonants are side by side, only one is heard, as in *butter.*
9. Sometimes *s* has the sound of *z,* as in *raisin, music.*
10. The letter *x* has the sounds of *ks* or *k* and *s,* as in *box, taxi.*

Vowels
11. When a consonant and *y* are the last letters in a one-syllable word, the *y* has the long *i* sound, as in *cry, by;* in longer words the *y* has the long *e* sound, as in *baby.*
12. The *r* gives the preceding vowel a sound that is neither long nor short, as in *car, far, fur, fir.* The letters *l* and *w* have the same effect.

Vowel Digraphs and Diphthongs
13. The first vowel is usually long and the second silent in *oa, ay, ai,* and *ee,* as in *boat, say, gain, feed.*
14. In *ea* the first letter may be long and the second silent, or it may have the short *e* sound, as in *bread.*
15. *Ou* has two sounds: one is the long sound of *o;* the other is the *ou* sound, as in *own* or *cow.* The combination *ou* has a schwa sound, as in *vigorous.*
16. These double vowels blend into a single sound: *au, aw, oi, oy,* as in *auto, awful, coin, boy.*
17. The combination *oo* has two sounds, as in *moon* and as in *wood.*

Source: From *Reading in the Elementary School* (p. 480), 5th ed., by G. D. Spache and E. B. Spache, 1986, Boston: Allyn & Bacon. Copyright 1986 by Allyn & Bacon. Reprinted by permission.

example, if a youngster is learning the short *a* sound, it helps if she or he reads stories or passages that highlight words containing that sound. Table 8.3 provides selected trade books that repeat phonics elements. Reading interesting or entertaining literature throughout phonics instruction reinforces the sound-symbol correspondences and fosters the enjoyment of reading.

Some commercial phonics programs used with students who have learning problems include *SRA/Open Court Phonics* (SRA), *Merrill Phonics Skilltext Series* (SRA), and *Phonic Remedial Reading Lessons* (Kirk, Kirk, & Minskoff, 1985).

Linguistic Approach

Bloomfield and Barnhart (1961) first introduced the linguistic approach to reading for students who were not succeeding in the basal approach. The linguistic approach emphasizes decoding print into meaningful oral language.

Many linguistic reading materials use a *whole-word* approach. Words are taught in word families and only as wholes. Beginning reading introduces words containing a short vowel and consisting of a consonant-vowel-consonant pattern. The words are selected on the basis of similar spelling patterns (such as *cab, lab, tab*), and the student must learn

TABLE 8.3
Trade books that repeat phonics elements

Short *a*	*The Cat in the Hat,* by Dr. Seuss (Random House, 1957) *The Fat Cat,* by Jack Kent (Scholastic, 1971) *The Gingerbread Man,* by Karen Schmidt (Scholastic, 1985)
Long *a*	*The Pain and the Great One,* by Judy Blume (Bradbury, 1974) *The Paper Crane,* by Molly Bang (Greenwillow, 1985) *Taste the Raindrops,* by Anna G. Hines (Greenwillow, 1983)
Short *e*	*Elephant in a Well,* by Marie Hall Ets (Viking, 1972) *Hester the Jester,* by Ben Shecter (Harper & Row, 1977) *The Little Red Hen,* by Paul Galdone (Scholastic, 1973)
Long *e*	*Brown Bear, Brown Bear, What Do You See?* by Bill Martin (Scholastic, 1983) *Little Bo-Peep,* by Paul Galdone (Clarion/Ticknor & Fields, 1986) *Never Tease a Weasel,* by Jean C. Soule (Magazine Press, 1964)
Short *i*	*Fix-It,* by David McPhail (E. P. Dutton, 1984) *My Brother, Will,* by Joan Robins (Greenwillow, 1986) *Willy the Wimp,* by Anthony Browne (Alfred A. Knopf, 1984)
Long *i*	*The Bike Lesson,* by Stan and Jan Berenstain (Random House, 1964) *If Mice Could Fly,* by John Cameron (Atheneum, 1979) *Why Can't I Fly?* by Rita Gelman (Scholastic, 1976)
Short *o*	*Fossie & the Fox,* by Patricia McKissack (Dial, 1986) *Fox in Socks,* by Dr. Seuss (Random House, 1965) *Oscar Otter,* by Nathaniel Benchley (Harper & Row, 1966)
Long *o*	*The Adventures of Mole and Troll,* by Tony Johnston (G. P. Putnam's Sons, 1977) *The Giant's Toe,* by Brock Cole (Farrar, Straus, & Giroux, 1986) *White Snow Bright, Snow,* by Alvin Tresselt (Lothrop, Lee, & Shepard, 1947)
Short *u*	*Big Gus and Little Gus,* by Lee Lorenz (Prentice Hall, 1982) *The Cut-Ups,* by James Marshall (Viking Kestrel, 1984) *Thump and Plunk,* by Janice May Udry (Harper & Row, 1981)
Long *u*	*"Excuse Me—Certainly!"* by Louis Slobodkin (Vanguard Press, 1959) *Tell Me a Trudy,* by Lore Segal (Farrar, Straus, & Giroux, 1977) *The Troll Music,* by Anita Lobel (Harper & Row, 1966)

the relationship between speech sounds and letters (i.e., between phonemes and graphemes). The student is not taught letter sounds directly, but implicitly learns them through minimal word differences (e.g., s*at*, f*at*, b*at*). Words with irregular spellings are introduced as sight words as the student progresses. After the words are learned in the spelling patterns, they are put together to form sentences.

The linguistic approach differs from the phonics approach in that linguistic readers focus on words instead of isolated sounds. Many linguistic series contain no pictures or illustrations that may provide clues and tempt the student to guess rather than decode the printed word. Although the frequent repetition of words in this approach may help students with learning problems, the use of nonsense words and phrases for pattern practice detracts from reading for comprehension.

Some commercial materials using the linguistic approach are *Basic Reading Series* (SRA), *Let's Read* (Educators Publishing Service), and *Merrill Reading Program* (SRA).

Whole Language Approach

The whole language concept (Goodman, 1986) uses students' language and experiences to increase their reading and writing abilities. Reading is taught as a holistic, meaning-oriented activity and is treated as an integrated behavior rather than being broken into a collection of separate skills. According to Altwerger, Edelsky, and Flores (1987), the main consideration regarding classroom reading and writing within the whole language framework is that there be *real* reading and writing rather than exercises in reading and writing. Thus, the emphasis is on reading for meaning rather than learning decoding skills, and the student is taught to break the code in reading within the context of meaningful content. In a classroom with a whole language orientation, the curriculum is organized around themes and units that increase language and reading skills, and reading materials consist of various relevant and functional materials such as children's literature books and resources the students need or want to read. Whole language relies heavily on literature or printed matter used for appropriate purposes (e.g., a recipe used for making a dessert rather than for finding short vowels) and on writing for varied purposes. In this approach, read-

ing is immersed in a total language arts program, and teachers develop the curriculum to offer instructional experiences relating to authentic problems and ideas. The underlying concept is that all language arts are related and should not be taught as if they were separate subjects. The premise is that students learn naturally from exposure and use.

Advocates of the whole language reading approach oppose teaching phonics in any structured, systematic way and believe that students will develop their own phonetic principles through exposure to print as they read and write. Students initially start to read meaningful, predictable whole words and then use these familiar words to begin to learn new words and phrases. To develop comprehension skills and for reading to make sense, it is believed that students must begin with a meaningful whole, and they initially are given familiar, predictable material. A constructive process is used in which students recognize familiar parts in unfamiliar written matter, and their reading is monitored to ensure it is making sense to them. While learning to read, students also are learning to write and are encouraged to write about their experiences. Goodman (1986) suggests that to implement a whole language approach in the classroom, the teacher should establish a center for reading and writing and encourage students to participate in activities such as dictating stories to an adult and then reading them, or following along while listening to audiocassettes of books. The teacher also can read to students and provide them with an opportunity to predict events within the story. In addition, the teacher can plan sustained silent reading and reading activities in which students read independently and are guided by reading conferences.

According to Chiang and Ford (1990), "Integrating the whole language strategies with other effective methods . . . can bring about a more balanced perspective with equal emphasis on fostering . . . students' positive attitudes toward reading and on facilitating a more functional and purposeful use of printed materials" (p. 34). They offer the following guidelines for implementing whole language programs with students who have learning problems:

- Read aloud to students regularly.
- Devote a few minutes each day to sustained silent reading.

- Introduce students to predictable books with patterned stories.
- Use writing activities that provide opportunities for the teacher to model writing strategies and skills.
- Include journal writing as part of the students' individualized educational programs.
- Provide meaningful printed materials in the instructional setting (e.g., simplified dictionaries and categorized lists of words).
- Establish a network to communicate with other teachers using holistic techniques in working with students with learning problems.

One accepted aspect of the whole language approach is the integration of the language arts program, especially in writing. This approach minimizes a fragmented curriculum, and students see writing as a complement of reading. However, the whole language approach to reading lacks direct instruction in specific skill strategies, and students with learning problems may need a more systematic approach to decoding and comprehension than it provides. In a review of research on the whole language approach, Stahl and Miller (1989) note that the strategy may be most effective when used early in the process of learning to read (i.e., kindergarten) and for teaching functional aspects of reading such as print concepts and expectations about reading. However, more direct approaches may better assist some students master the word recognition skills they need to understand what they are reading. Finally, research indicates that the whole language approach may have less of an effect with populations who are disadvantaged and have a lower socioeconomic status (Stahl & Miller, 1989).

Pressley and Rankin (1994) provide support for reading instruction that balances decoding instruction with authentic literary experiences and note that "reading instruction strictly consistent with whole language precepts is probably not the most effective instruction for students who are at risk for reading difficulties, including students with learning disabilities, those who are economically and socially disadvantaged, and those who are culturally and linguistically diverse" (p. 164). Thus, until whole language has been found effective at various levels with students who have learning problems, it should be used cautiously, especially

in light of the success that teachers have had in using direct instruction.

The commercial program *Learning Through Literature* (Dodds & Goodfellow, 1990/1991) is based on the use of literature for students with learning problems. Also, Norton (1992) discusses selecting material for a literature-based reading program and provides sources for children's literature.

Language Experience Approach

The language experience approach integrates the development of reading skills with the development of listening, speaking, and writing skills. The materials consist of the student's thoughts and words. According to Lee and Allen (1963), the language experience approach deals with the following thinking process: what students think about, they can talk about; what students say, they can write (or someone can write for them); and what students write (or others write for them), they can read.

The language experience approach is based upon the student's oral and written expression. The student's experiences play a major role in determining the reading material. The student dictates stories to the teacher. These stories may initially originate from the student's own drawings and artwork. The teacher writes down the stories, which become the basis of the student's initial reading experiences. Thus, the student learns to read the dictated written thoughts. In this approach, the language patterns of the reading materials are determined by the student's speech, and the content is determined by experiences. The teacher tries to broaden and enrich the base of experiences from which the student can think, speak, and read. Eventually, with help, the student can write stories. Thus, according to Hall (1981), the approach is based on the concept that "reading has the most meaning to a pupil when the materials being read are expressed in his language and are rooted in his experiences" (p. 2).

At first the teacher guides students in writing an experience chart. The story in the chart derives from students' experiences as they share information through group discussion. Experience charts may comprise several topics: narrative descriptions of experiences, reports of experiments or news events, or fictional stories the students create. The teacher writes the ideas in a first draft on the chalkboard; guides the students' suggestions and revisions; and discusses word choice, sentence structure, and the sounds of letters and words. Specific skills such as capitalization, punctuation, spelling, grammar, and correct sentence structure can be taught as needed while the chart is edited and revised. Thus, the teacher provides skill development at the appropriate time instead of following a predetermined sequence of training in reading skills. Because the students create the content, motivation and interest are usually high.

In the language experience approach, students are encouraged to proceed at their own rate. Progress is evaluated in terms of each student's ability to express ideas in oral and written form and to understand peers' writing. Progress or growth in writing mechanics, spelling, vocabulary, sentence structure, and depth of thinking is evident in the student's written work. The stories each student writes can be illustrated and bound in an attractive folder, and students can trade story notebooks.

The language experience approach is similar to whole language in that both emphasize the importance of literature, treat reading as a personal act (i.e., accept language varieties of individual students), and advocate an abundance of books written by youngsters about their own lives. However, language experience presumes that written language is a secondary system derived from oral language, whereas whole language sees oral and written language as structurally related without one being a rendition of the other (Altwerger et al., 1987). The teacher frequently may take dictation from students in the language experience approach, but dictation is less frequent in a whole language curriculum because it deprives the learners of making meaning through the act of writing. Moreover, in the language experience approach, a student's dictation often is used to teach word-attack or phonics skills, whereas whole language theory disputes that fragmented exercises can lead to comprehensive knowledge of language.

The language experience approach is mainly a way of teaching beginning reading. However, it may be just as effective at all ages for corrective instruction and motivation. When teacher organization and instruction in word-attack and comprehension skills are provided, the language experience approach can be used effectively to teach

students with learning problems. It also can be used to improve comprehension skills of older students who have developed basic decoding skills or to maintain interest and motivation. Research, however, indicates that the language experience approach may produce weaker effects with populations labeled specifically as disadvantaged (Stahl & Miller, 1989). Allen and Allen (1982) provide various language experience activities.

Individualized Reading Approach

In an individualized reading program, students select their own reading material according to interest and ability and progress at their own rate. A large collection of books (e.g., those suggested in Table 8.3 or ones used in a literature-based reading program) should be available at different reading levels, with many subjects represented at each level of difficulty. After students choose reading materials, they pace themselves and keep records of their progress. The teacher teaches word recognition and comprehension skills as each student needs them.

Each student meets once or twice a week with the teacher, at which time the teacher may ask the student to read aloud and discuss the reading material. The teacher can note reading errors and check the student's sight vocabulary, understanding of word meanings, and comprehension. Also, the teacher can guide the student regarding the next reading selection, although the choice is made by the student. From these conferences, the teacher keeps a record of the student's capabilities and progress to plan activities to develop specific skills. The teacher's role is to diagnose and prescribe, and success of the program depends on the teacher's resourcefulness and competence. Individual work can be supplemented with group activities using basal readers and workbooks to provide practice on specific reading skills.

Self-pacing and self-selection can be considered advantages of the individualized reading approach. Self-pacing builds self-confidence, and self-selection satisfies personal interests and promotes independent reading. Individualized reading also eliminates "high" and "low" reading groups and avoids competition and comparison. This approach deserves consideration for students who have ability but lack motivation. However, the value of the individualized reading approach for many students with learning problems is questionable, because it involves self-learning and lacks a systematic check of developmental skills in the reading process.

REMEDIAL READING PROGRAMS AND METHODS

Remedial programs are designed to teach reading to the student who has, or would have, difficulty learning to read in the general classroom reading program. In addition, several remedial methods are designed for students with moderate to severe reading problems (e.g., nonreaders or students who are more than one year behind in reading achievement). The remedial programs and methods discussed in this section include phonological awareness training, *Reading Mastery* and *Corrective Reading, Success for All, Reading Recovery,* multisensory reading method, neurological impress method, glass analysis, high interest–low vocabulary method, and functional reading.

Phonological Awareness Training

The ability to read and comprehend depends on rapid and automatic recognition and decoding of single words, which is dependent on the ability to segment words and syllables into phonemes. Phonological awareness is an insight that words are composed of smaller units, and deficits in phonological awareness reflect a core deficit in students with reading disabilities (Lyon, 1995). According to Torgesen, Wagner, and Rashotte (1994), "Phonological awareness is generally defined as one's sensitivity to, or explicit awareness of, the phonological structure of the words in one's language. It is measured by tasks that require children to identify, isolate, or blend the individual phonemes in words" (p. 276). Thus, phonological awareness includes the ability to perceive spoken words as a sequence of sounds as well as the ability to consciously manipulate the sounds in words (Adams, 1990). Although the relationship is reciprocal, phonological awareness precedes skilled decoding. Rather than being the ability to make letter-sound correspondences or to sound out words (as in phonics), phonological awareness refers to an awareness that comes intuitively

before such abilities. Of the components of phonological awareness, auditory blending and segmenting correlate strongly with reading acquisition (Adams, 1990) and appear to be critical dimensions in prereading instruction.

As noted in Chapter 7, some experts (Adams, 1990; Stahl, Osborn, & Lehr, 1990) indicate that the phonological awareness of children entering school may be the single most powerful determinant of reading success or failure. Individual differences in phonological awareness prior to school entry are highly related to and predictive of the ability to learn to read in the first grade (Mather, 1992). Results of a longitudinal study (Torgesen et al., 1994) indicate that inefficient development of phonological awareness in kindergarten is causally related to difficulties in acquiring alphabetic reading skills in first and second grades.

Simmons, Gunn, Smith, and Kameenui (1994) note that children who lack phonological awareness may not be able to identify sounds in words; represent the separate sounds in a word; detect and manipulate sounds within words; perceive a word as a sequence of sounds; and isolate beginning, medial, and ending sounds. Because these children are unable to infer the underlying alphabetic relationships that are essential to generalized word-reading skills, they experience difficulty in reading programs that do not provide explicit instruction in phonological decoding. Thus, there is a need for early and explicit instruction both in phonological awareness as an oral language skill and in the alphabetic principle as an aid to the development of independent word-reading skills (Adams, 1990; Liberman & Liberman, 1990). Children who are at risk for reading problems can be identified accurately even before they begin the process of learning to read (Hurford, Schauf, Bunce, Blaich, & Moore, 1994), and preventive interventions can be introduced to increase their phonological awareness.

Fortunately, phonological awareness in young children can be developed, and training in phonological awareness produces improved performance in reading. When phonemic skills do not develop naturally or children enter school with limited language backgrounds, systematic instruction may be required. Phonological awareness training prior to reading instruction may significantly reduce the incidence of reading disabilities among young children, and thus should be included in preventive or remedial programs for children who are at risk or identified with reading disabilities.

Simmons et al. (1994) present five recommendations to enhance the effectiveness of phonological awareness instruction:

1. ***Focus first on the auditory features of words.*** When asking the student to blend the sound of a word together or to identify the individual sounds in a word, instruction initially should occur without alphabetic symbols.

2. ***Move from explicit, natural segments of language to the more implicit and complex.*** Initial segmenting instruction should proceed from segmenting sentences into words, words into syllables, and syllables into phonemes.

3. ***Use phonological properties and dimensions of words to enhance performance.*** Task complexity can be controlled by initially selecting words with fewer phonemes and words in which consonant and vowel configurations can be distinguished easily (e.g., words with vowel-consonant or consonant-vowel-consonant patterns). Also, words with discrete phonemes (e.g., *rug*) are segmented more easily than those beginning and ending with consonant blends, and words that begin with continuous sounds (e.g., *sun, mat*) facilitate sound blending activities.

4. ***Scaffold blending and segmenting through explicit modeling.*** Strategies should be modeled by the teacher and practiced over time to make the blending and segmenting processes obvious and explicit.

5. ***Integrate letter-sound correspondence once learners are proficient with auditory tasks.*** Blending and segmenting skills should be applied to realistic reading, writing, and spelling situations.

Torgesen et al. (1994) note that programs designed to train phonological awareness in young children generally have been successful; however, they suggest that explicit and intense training procedures may be required to have a substantial effect on the phonological awareness of children with severe reading disabilities. Activities to develop phonological awareness and *Phonological Awareness Training for Reading* (Torgesen & Bryant, 1994) are presented later in this chapter.

Reading Mastery and *Corrective Reading*

Reading Mastery (Engelmann & Bruner, 1995) is an intensive, highly structured programmed instructional system. There are six levels for students in first through sixth grade; however, Levels I and II and Fast Cycle are designed to remediate below-average reading skills of students through third grade. Students are grouped according to their current abilities with no more than five students in a group. They sit in chairs in a quarter-circle around the teacher. Each day, one 30 minute lesson is presented. The manual specifies the sequence of presentation as well as statements and hand movements. Each student receives positive reinforcement (praise or points) for correct responses. A student who masters skills (indicated by performance on tests) changes groups.

The program uses a synthetic phonics approach and emphasizes basic decoding skills, including sound-symbol identification, left-to-right sequence, and the oral blending of sounds to make words. The program includes games to teach sequencing skills and left-to-right orientation, blending tasks to teach students to spell words by sounds ("say it slow") and to blend quickly ("say it fast"), and rhyming tasks to teach how sounds and words relate. Take-home sheets are used to practice skills. The program teaches students to concentrate on important sound combinations and word discriminations and to use a variety of word-attack skills. In Level I, students learn how to read words, sentences, and stories, both aloud and silently, and to answer literal comprehension questions about their readings. Level II expands basic reading skills, and students learn strategies for decoding difficult words and for answering interpretive comprehension questions. The program also teaches basic reasoning skills such as applying rules and completing deductions.

This direct instruction approach emphasizes learning specific skills, and the method of teaching is characterized by teacher modeling or demonstration of important skills; frequent student response; appropriate, direct feedback to students (including correction); adequate provisions for practice; and student mastery. *Reading Mastery* is fast paced, providing immediate feedback and correction procedures for various student errors.

Repetition is built into the program, and the library series reinforces skills developed in the program and provides opportunity for independent reading. Research indicates that the program has been highly effective in teaching reading to young students with learning problems (Carnine et al., 1997; Stallings, 1974).

The companion program, *Corrective Reading* (Engelmann, Hanner, & Johnson, 1999), is an advanced remedial reading program designed for students in fourth through twelfth grade who have not mastered decoding and comprehension skills. The program is divided into two strands, decoding and comprehension, each of which has four levels. Each lesson lasts 35 to 45 minutes and provides teacher-directed work, independent applications, and tests of student performance. The decoding strand follows the *Reading Mastery* format and includes word-attack basics, decoding strategies, and skill applications. The comprehension strand presents real-life situations and includes thinking basics, comprehension skills, and concept applications. The presentation book for the teacher specifies the teacher's role in each lesson. The program gives the student immediate feedback and provides a built-in reinforcement system.

Success for All

Success for All is a schoolwide restructuring program designed to provide students with early success in reading and to maintain that success through the elementary school years (Herman & Stringfield, 1995). It combines several research-supported teaching and reading approaches, including the following:

- Whole-day kindergarten
- Reading programs for 90 minutes per day
- Combination of phonics and whole language
- Homogeneous reading groups that are reassessed and regrouped every eight weeks
- One-to-one tutoring for first- through third-grade students who are experiencing difficulties in reading
- Cooperative learning
- Family support services to increase parental involvement
- A part- or full-time project facilitator to coordinate the program and provide technical assistance

The program's goal of keeping students' reading performance on grade level involves less grade retention and dependence on long-term special education services.

Longitudinal studies involving matched control schools and students indicate that *Success for All* improves achievement. Students with the lowest pretest scores made the most improvement; schools that used *Success for All* for five or more years maintained these improvements through the elementary grades (Madden, Slavin, Karweit, Dolan, & Wasik, 1993; Slavin et al., 1994; Slavin, Madden, Karweit, Dolan, & Wasik, 1992). King (1994) reports that the cost of implementing *Success for All* ranges from $261,060 to $646,500 per year.

Reading Recovery

Reading Recovery, an early intervention program developed in New Zealand for young children experiencing difficulty in beginning reading (Clay, 1985, Pinnell, DeFord, & Lyons, 1988), combines writing and reading and helps children learn phonics within meaningful written contexts. In this intervention, which combines whole language with tutoring in specific skills, low-achieving first-graders receive one-to-one tutoring for 30 minutes daily in addition to classroom reading instruction.

During the first ten days, the student reads familiar books ("roaming around the known") to establish a level of instruction. The 30-minute daily tutoring sessions follow systematic steps:

1. The student first rereads two easy books.

2. The student works on a book introduced in a previous lesson. As the student reads, the teacher conducts a diagnostic procedure (referred to as a *running record*) in which the teacher records the student's errors and reading strategies. Books are selected from a list of about 700 titles organized into 20 levels of difficulty.

3. The student manipulates plastic letters on a magnetic board to work with letters (e.g., finding little words in big words).

4. The student dictates and practices writing. The student and teacher work together on spelling difficult words before the student writes them. Spelling errors are covered with white tape and corrected. Thus, the words in the sentence are written correctly for the child to read.

5. The teacher writes the sentence on a strip of paper, cuts it up, and asks the student to recreate it. This activity also can be practiced at home.

6. The student prepares for and reads an unfamiliar book.

Students are discontinued (i.e., graduate) from the program when they are reading on grade level in their classroom and score high on *Reading Recovery* assessment instruments. Some students are removed from the program if they have participated in 60 lessons without reaching the appropriate reading performance criteria.

Teachers participate in a 30-hour workshop before school begins and a year-long course that meets for 2.5 hours weekly. Training includes observing tutoring sessions behind a one-way mirror. Teachers receive ongoing guidance from a rigorously trained "teacher leader." Training and program implementation are meant to work in conjunction.

This highly structured model emphasizes direct teaching of metacognitive strategies, learning to read by reading, teaching of phonics in the context of students' writing, and the integration of reading and writing. Although implementing a high-quality *Reading Recovery* program is difficult and time-consuming due to required training and one-to-one intervention, research indicates that it has both immediate and long-term effects in helping low-achieving students learn to read and write (Pinnell, 1990). *Reading Recovery* has successfuly taught many at-risk students to read; however, it has not been as successful with students who have moderate to severe reading problems. For example, DeFord, Pinnell, Lyons, and Young (1988) found that 2 percent of the students did not make appropriate progress in *Reading Recovery* and continued to lag behind their classmates. Also, Herman and Stringfield (1995) note that students who leave the program with fewer than 60 lessons and have not been evaluated as able to read on their grade level, such as students transferred to special education, are excluded from analysis in most studies. Thus, results of *Reading Recovery* evaluations are potentially somewhat inflated.

Multisensory Reading Method

The multisensory method is based on the premise that some students learn best when content is presented in several modalities. Frequently, kinesthetic (movement) and tactile (touch) stimulation is used along with visual and auditory modalities. The multisensory programs that feature tracing, hearing, writing, and seeing often are referred to as *VAKT* (visual-auditory-kinesthetic-tactile). To increase tactile and kinesthetic stimulation, sandpaper letters, finger paint, sand trays, raised letters, and sunken letters are used. The Fernald and the Gillingham methods, as well as word imprinting, highlight VAKT instruction. The Fernald method and word imprinting stress whole-word learning, while the Gillingham method features sound blending.

The Fernald Method   In the Fernald (1943, 1988) approach, vocabulary is selected from stories the student has dictated, and each word is taught as a whole. There is no attempt to teach phonics skills. The teacher identifies unknown words, which the student writes to develop word recognition. Each word is learned as a whole unit and is placed immediately in a context meaningful to the student. Success is stressed to help maintain a high level of motivation.

The method consists of four stages. In Stage 1, the student selects a word to learn, and the teacher writes it with a crayon in large letters. The student then traces the word with a finger, making contact with the paper (tactile-kinesthetic). While tracing, the student says each part of the word aloud (auditory). In addition, the student sees the word (visual) while tracing it and hears the word while saying it (auditory). This process is repeated until the student can write the word correctly without looking at the sample. If an error is made when tracing or writing, the student must start over so that the word always is written as a unit. If the word is correct, it is filed alphabetically in a word bank. Using the learned words, the student writes a story, which is then typed so she or he can read the words in print.

In Stage 2, the student no longer is required to trace each word but now learns each new word by looking at the teacher's written copy of the word, saying it, and writing it. The student continues to write stories and keep a word file.

In Stage 3, the student learns new words by looking at a printed word and saying it before writing it, thus learning directly from the printed word; the teacher is not required to write it. At this point the student can begin reading from books.

The teacher continually checks to ensure that the student retains learned words.

Finally, in Stage 4, the student can recognize new words by their similarity to printed words or parts of words already learned, and thus can apply reading skills and expand reading interests.

The Fernald approach uses language experience and tracing (kinesthetic) techniques. Progress is slow, and to sustain interest the student chooses the material. Success is stressed to help maintain a high level of motivation. The student is never encouraged to sound out word parts or to copy words that have been traced. Each word is learned as a whole unit and is placed immediately in a context meaningful to the student. The four stages must be mastered in sequence without modifications. This remedial approach generally is used with students with severe reading problems (Ekwall & Shanker, 1988). Moreover, the tracing technique alone can be used effectively to help students learn frequently used words with which they are having difficulty. The Fernald approach is intense, but some research (Thorpe & Borden, 1985) supports its effectiveness with students who have moderate to severe reading problems.

The Gillingham Method The Gillingham method (Gillingham & Stillman, 1970) is a highly structured, phonetically oriented approach based on the theoretical work of S. T. Orton (1937). The method requires five weekly lessons for a minimum of two years. Each letter sound is taught using a multisensory approach. Consonants and vowels with only one sound are presented on drill cards (consonants on white cards and vowels on salmon-color cards), and letters are introduced by a key word (e.g., *fun* for *f*). *Associative* processes are used, beginning with the student associating (linking) the name and sound of a letter with its printed symbol. The method involves the following procedures:

1. A drill card showing one letter is shown to the student. The teacher says the name of the letter and the student repeats it. When this has been mastered, the teacher says the sound of the letter, and the student repeats the sound. Then the card is exposed and the teacher asks, "What does this letter say?" The student is to give its sound.

2. Without presenting the drill card, the teacher makes the sound represented by the letter and says, "Tell me the name of the letter that has this sound." This strategy is essentially oral spelling.

3. The teacher carefully writes the letter and explains its form, thus instructing the student in cursive handwriting. The student traces the letter over the teacher's lines, copies it, writes it from memory, and writes it while looking away. Finally, the teacher makes the sound and says, "Write the letter that has this sound."

After mastering the first group of ten letters, (*a, b, f, h, i, j, k, m, p,* and *t*), the student is taught to blend them into words. The letters are combined to form simple consonant-vowel-consonant words (e.g., *bit, map,* and *jab*). Spelling is introduced after blending. When the teacher says a word, the student repeats it, names the letters, writes the letters while saying them (simultaneous oral spelling), and reads the written word. Sentence and story writing are introduced after the student is able to write any three-letter, phonetically pure word. Nonphonetic words are taught through drill. Consonant blends are taught after the student can read, write, and spell the words in the short stories. Syllabication, dictionary skills, and additional spelling rules also are introduced. Thus, the Gillingham method emphasizes repetition and drill; spelling and writing skills are taught in conjunction with reading skills.

Instructional materials developed for the Gillingham method include phonics drill cards or phonetic word cards, syllable concept cards, diphthong cards, and little stories. Lessons and instructions on using the materials to teach various skills are provided (Gillingham & Stillman, 1970; J. L. Orton, 1976). The procedure is highly structured and rigid, and no other reading or spelling materials may be used. Finally, several researchers (Henry & Rome, 1995; Maskel & Felton, 1995) report excellent results in word recognition and reading comprehension using the Orton-Gillingham approach in tutorial settings with students who have severe reading problems. Two adaptations of the Gillingham method include *Recipe for Reading* (Traub & Bloom, 1978) and *A Multi-Sensory Approach to Language Arts for Specific Language Disability Children* (Slingerland, 1981). The *Wilson Reading System* (produced by Wilson Language Training) also is based on Orton-Gillingham principles as well as current phonological coding research. In addition, the *Phonic Remedial Reading Lessons* (Kirk et al., 1985) (presented in the commercial materials section) use a VAKT phonics approach.

Word Imprinting   Carbo (1978) describes a multisensory procedure to help students with visual memory difficulties imprint words. It includes the following six instructional steps:

1. Look at the word and repeat it following the teacher's model.
2. Determine the meaning of the word.
3. Trace around the word to promote awareness of its configuration.
4. Trace the word itself for tactile stimulation.
5. Trace and say the word simultaneously.
6. Picture the word by looking at it, develop a visual image with eyes closed, and write the word in the air.

Polloway and Smith (1992) note that various steps of Carbo's sequence can be used to help students learn words.

Neurological Impress Method

The neurological impress method (Heckelman, 1969; Langford, Slade, & Barnett, 1974) was developed to teach reading to students with severe reading disabilities. The method consists of joint oral reading at a rapid pace by the student and the teacher. It is based on the theory that students can learn by hearing their own voice and someone else's voice jointly reading the same material. The student is seated slightly in front of the teacher, and the teacher's voice is directed into the student's ear at a close range. There is no special preparation of the material before the joint reading. The objective is simply to cover as many pages as possible in the allotted time without tiring the student. At first, the teacher should read slightly louder and faster than the student, who should be encouraged to maintain the pace and not worry about mistakes. The teacher's finger slides to the location of the words as they are being read. As the student becomes capable of leading the oral reading, the teacher can speak more softly and read slightly slower, and the student's finger can point to the reading. Thus, the student and teacher alternate between leading and following.

Instruction begins at a level slightly below that at which the student can read successfully. No attempt is made to teach any phonics skills or word

recognition, and no attention is given to comprehension of the material being read. The basic goal is for the student to attain fluent reading automatically. The neurological impress method emphasizes rapid decoding and can be most effective with students age 10 or older who spend too much time sounding out words and do not read fluently (Faas, 1980). Reading phrases rather than isolated words reveals progress, as does learning to pause for punctuation previously ignored.

Repeated Readings   A variation of the neurological impress method is the method of repeated readings (Samuels, 1979). This method requires the student to reread a short, meaningful passage several times until a satisfactory level of fluency (i.e., for students beyond third grade, 100 correct words per minute with two errors) is reached. The procedure then is repeated with a new passage. Repeated readings thus emphasize reading rate on a single passage rather than single words, and identification of words in context must be fast as well as accurate.

From her extensive review of reading interventions, Adams (1990) reports that repeated readings significantly improve students' word recognition, fluency, and comprehension. Weinstein and Cooke (1992) found that repeated readings is an effective instructional strategy to help students achieve fluency. O'Shea and O'Shea (1988) indicate that the method can be used in a variety of learning arrangements, such as small-group instruction with choral reading, peer reading with pairs of reading partners, and learning centers with the use of tape recorders. Comprehension practice can be provided through activities involving the cloze and maze procedure (i.e., reading the passage and filling in the blanks for omitted words with the words that complete phrases or sentences correctly).

Glass Analysis

Glass analysis is a procedure that uses 119 letter clusters as a decoding strategy to teach reading (Glass & Glass, 1978). Letter clusters are two or more letters in a word that represent a relatively consistent sound (e.g., in *crab* the clusters are *cr* and *ab*). Through intensive auditory and visual training, the student is guided to perceive patterns of specific letter clusters that are related to particular sounds. Teaching a word involves five steps: (1) the teacher identifies the whole word as well as the letters and sounds of the clusters, (2) the teacher pronounces the sound of the letter(s) and asks the student what letter(s) represent the sound, (3) the teacher says the letter or letters and asks the student for the sound(s), (4) the teacher takes away letters and asks the student what sound is left, and (5) the teacher asks the student to read the whole word. The student's attention to the word is essential, and the entire word is always presented. Portions of the word are never covered, nor are meaningful letter clusters broken apart. Miccinati (1981) notes that through this method, students with reading disabilities can be taught to perceive distinctive features in words. By visually and auditorily responding to redundant letter clusters, the student begins to recognize the distinctive features and synthesize the clusters to form a word. Polloway and Patton (1997) note that this approach is useful to motivate adolescents who continue to need word analysis practice.

High Interest–Low Vocabulary Method

Older students with reading problems often are frustrated because books geared to their interest level are beyond their reading ability. High interest–low vocabulary books offer a relatively easy vocabulary while maintaining an interest level appropriate for the more mature reader. As indicated in Table 8.4, several publishers produce these materials, covering a wide variety of topics (e.g., sports, mystery, science, and adventure).

The teacher can estimate the reading level of any reading material by using the Fry (1977) readability formula, presented in Figure 8.1. A computer software program, *Readability Formulas,* produced by Encyclopaedia Britannica Educational Corporation, allows the user to apply seven different readability formulas (e.g., Fry, SMOG, and Spache) to any reading selection simultaneously to determine reading level. Also, *Readability Analysis,* produced by Gamco (available from Cambridge Development Laboratory), determines the reading level of any written material according to the three readability tests (i.e., the Spache Primary Reading Formula, the Dale-Chall Readability Formula, and the Fry Readability Scale).

Functional Reading

As noted in Chapter 1, students with learning problems vary significantly in their learning characteristics. Some students achieve reading levels that enable them to pursue postsecondary education, whereas those with more severe reading problems focus on developing reading skills that enable them to function independently in a world of print. The functional approach is designed to help individuals with severe reading problems live, work, and play independently in their respective ecologies. Langone (1990) provides an ecological framework that highlights the need to anticipate the environment in which the student will need to function (e.g., shopping, employment, recreation, and home).

To help teachers select the most appropriate words for a student in a functional reading program, Polloway and Polloway (1981) offer a rank-order listing of the most essential survival vocabulary words and phrases (presented in Table 8.5).

Folk and Campbell (1978) provide a six-step program for teaching students to acquire survival and functional reading skills. The following steps focus on helping students read sight words and simple sentences and enhance their sight reading by learning some decoding skills (i.e., initial consonant and short vowel sounds):

1. Present the student with two index cards, one with the student's name and the other with another student's name. The teacher says, "This is your name. Say _____." The procedure is repeated for the second name. Then the cards are placed on the table and the student is asked to find his or her name and then to find the other student's name. A reinforcer is given for each correct response. This procedure is continued until the student can read all the students' names with 100 percent accuracy.

2. Introduce the words *boy* and *girl* by using the procedure in Step 1. A worksheet is provided that shows a line drawn from the word *boy* or *girl* to each student's name.

3. Continue the procedure with various words; as proficiency increases, use more sophisticated worksheets and activities.

4. Proceed from the presentation of nouns to adjective-noun phrases to verbs and, finally, to complete sentences. To indicate comprehension

TABLE 8.4
High interest—low vocabulary reading materials

Title	Publisher	Reading Grade Level	Interest Grade Level
American Adventure Series	Harper & Row	3–6	4–8
Basic Vocabulary Books	Garrard	2	1–6
Breakthrough Series	Allyn & Bacon	2–6	6–12
Checkered Flag Series	Field Educational Publications	2–4	7–12
Childhood of Famous Americans Series	Bobbs-Merrill	4–5	7–9
Cowboy Sam Series	Benefic Press	PP–3	1–6
Dan Frontier Series	Benefic Press	PP–4	1–7
Deep Sea Adventures	Field Educational Publications	2–5	3–11
Everyreader Series	McGraw-Hill	6–8	5–12
Fastback Books	Globe/Fearon	4–5	6–12
First Reading Books	Garrard	1	1–4
Focus on Reading	SRA	1–6	3–12
Folklore of the World Books	Garrard	2	2–8
Interesting Reading Series	Follett	2–3	7–12
Jim Forest Readers	Field Educational Publications	1–3	1–7
Junior Science Books	Garrard	4–5	6–9
Morgan Bay Mysteries	Field Educational Publications	2–4	4–11
Morrow's High Interest/Easy Reading Books	William Morrow	1–8	4–10
Mystery Adventure Series	Benefic Press	2–6	4–9
Pacemaker Classics	Globe/Fearon	2	7–12
Pacemaker True Adventure	Globe/Fearon	2	5–12
Pacemaker Story Books	Xerox Education Publications	2	7–12
Pal Paperback Kits	Xerox Education Publications	1–5	5–12
Perspectives Set	High Noon Books	3–4	6–12
Phoenix Everyreaders	Phoenix Learning Resources	4	4–12
Pleasure Reading Books	Garrard	4	3–7
Racing Wheels Series	Benefic Press	2–4	4–9
Reading For Concepts Series	McGraw-Hill	3–8	5–12
Reading Reinforcement Skilltext Series	SRA	1–5	1–8
Reading Skill Builders	Reader's Digest Services	1–4	2–5
Sailor Jack Series	Benefic Press	PP–3	1–6
Scoreboard Series	High Noon Books	2	6–11
Space Science Fiction Series	Benefic Press	2–6	4–9
Sports Mystery Stories	Benefic Press	2–4	4–9
Spotlight on Literature	SRA	3–6	6–12
Sprint Libraries	Scholastic	1–3	3–6
Super Kits	Warner Educational Services	2–5	4–12
Superstars Series	Steck-Vaughn	4–6	7–12
Teen-Age Tales	D. C. Heath	4–6	6–11
Tom & Ricky Mystery Series	High Noon Books	1	4–9
Top Picks	Reader's Digest Services	5–7	5–12
Trailblazers Series	High Noon Books	2	4–9
Turning Point	Phoenix Learning Resources	1–4	7–12
What Is It Series	Benefic Press	1–4	1–8

FIGURE 8.1

Fry's graph for estimating readability—extended

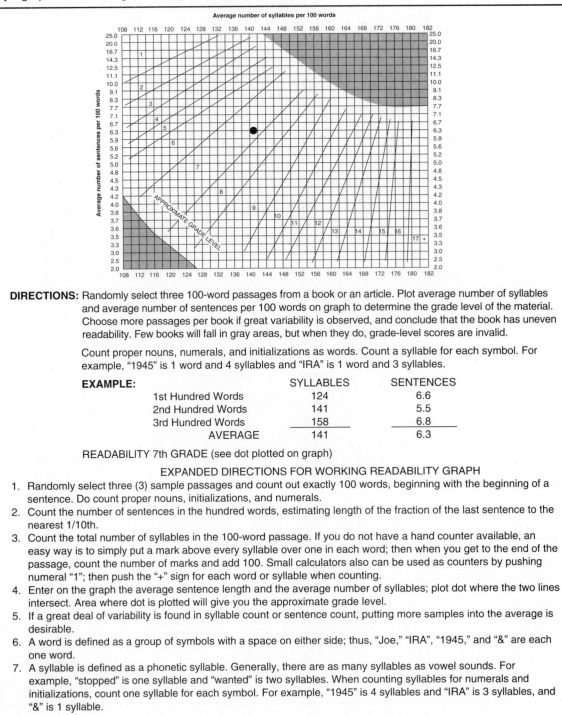

DIRECTIONS: Randomly select three 100-word passages from a book or an article. Plot average number of syllables and average number of sentences per 100 words on graph to determine the grade level of the material. Choose more passages per book if great variability is observed, and conclude that the book has uneven readability. Few books will fall in gray areas, but when they do, grade-level scores are invalid.

Count proper nouns, numerals, and initializations as words. Count a syllable for each symbol. For example, "1945" is 1 word and 4 syllables and "IRA" is 1 word and 3 syllables.

EXAMPLE:	SYLLABLES	SENTENCES
1st Hundred Words	124	6.6
2nd Hundred Words	141	5.5
3rd Hundred Words	158	6.8
AVERAGE	141	6.3

READABILITY 7th GRADE (see dot plotted on graph)

EXPANDED DIRECTIONS FOR WORKING READABILITY GRAPH

1. Randomly select three (3) sample passages and count out exactly 100 words, beginning with the beginning of a sentence. Do count proper nouns, initializations, and numerals.
2. Count the number of sentences in the hundred words, estimating length of the fraction of the last sentence to the nearest 1/10th.
3. Count the total number of syllables in the 100-word passage. If you do not have a hand counter available, an easy way is to simply put a mark above every syllable over one in each word; then when you get to the end of the passage, count the number of marks and add 100. Small calculators also can be used as counters by pushing numeral "1"; then push the "+" sign for each word or syllable when counting.
4. Enter on the graph the average sentence length and the average number of syllables; plot dot where the two lines intersect. Area where dot is plotted will give you the approximate grade level.
5. If a great deal of variability is found in syllable count or sentence count, putting more samples into the average is desirable.
6. A word is defined as a group of symbols with a space on either side; thus, "Joe," "IRA", "1945," and "&" are each one word.
7. A syllable is defined as a phonetic syllable. Generally, there are as many syllables as vowel sounds. For example, "stopped" is one syllable and "wanted" is two syllables. When counting syllables for numerals and initializations, count one syllable for each symbol. For example, "1945" is 4 syllables and "IRA" is 3 syllables, and "&" is 1 syllable.

Reprinted by permission of the authors.

TABLE 8.5

Most essential survival vocabulary words and phrases

Words		Phrases	
1. Poison	26. Ambulance	1. Don't walk	26. Wrong way
2. Danger	27. Girls	2. Fire escape	27. No fires
3. Police	28. Open	3. Fire extinguisher	28. No swimming
4. Emergency	29. Out	4. Do not enter	29. Watch your step
5. Stop	30. Combustible	5. First aid	30. Watch for children
6. Hot	31. Closed	6. Deep water	31. No diving
7. Walk	32. Condemned	7. External use only	32. Stop for pedestrians
8. Caution	33. Up	8. High voltage	33. Post office
9. Exit	34. Blasting	9. No trespassing	34. Slippery when wet
10. Men	35. Gentlemen	10. Railroad crossing	35. Help wanted
11. Women	36. Pull	11. Rest rooms	36. Slow down
12. Warning	37. Down	12. Do not touch	37. Smoking prohibited
13. Entrance	38. Detour	13. Do not use near	38. No admittance
14. Help	39. Gasoline	open flame	39. Proceed at your
15. Off	40. Inflammable	14. Do not inhale fumes	own risk
16. On	41. In	15. One way	40. Step down
17. Explosives	42. Push	16. Do not cross	41. No parking
18. Flammable	43. Nurse	17. Do not use near heat	42. Keep closed
19. Doctor	44. Information	18. Keep out	43. No turns
20. Go	45. Lifeguard	19. Keep off	44. Beware of dog
21. Telephone	46. Listen	20. Exit only	45. School zone
22. Boys	47. Private	21. No right turn	46. Dangerous curve
23. Contaminated	48. Quiet	22. Keep away	47. Hospital zone
24. Ladies	49. Look	23. Thin ice	48. Out of order
25. Dynamite	50. Wanted	24. Bus stop	49. No smoking
		25. No passing	50. Go slow

Source: Adapted from "Survival words for disabled readers" (pp. 446–447), by E. A. Polloway and C. H. Polloway, 1981, *Academic Therapy*, 16, 443–448. Copyright 1981 by Academic Therapy Publications. Reprinted by permission.

of adjective-noun phrases, the student points to the correct picture of the object; for verbs, the student produces a motor response (or correctly pronounces the verb *is*). For sentence comprehension, the student selects, from three choices, the picture that correctly depicts the sentence meaning.

5. Give words from the Dolch Reading List, give a brief definition of the word, and introduce basic word-attack skills. To indicate word comprehension, the student uses the word correctly in a phrase or sentence. Also, the student is taught each consonant sound and must master it before learning a new sound. To indicate mastery, the student gives the correct sound of the given word as well as another word that begins with the same sound. In addition, the student is shown a picture of a new word and is asked with what sound and what letter it begins. Activities involving worksheets, sorting pictures,

finding pictures that begin with specific sounds, and listening to tapes supplement this procedure.

6. Introduce vowel sounds using the procedure in Step 5.

Folk and Campbell note these steps helped students add 100 or more sight words to their vocabularies. They maintain that "the question is not whether students are competent enough to acquire basic reading skills but whether we . . . are competent enough to teach them" (p. 323).

Finally, Browder and Snell (1993) provide the following five factors to consider in determining what academic goals (if any) are appropriate for students who have moderate to severe learning problems: (1) current and future academic skill needs, (2) other skill needs, (3) chronological age, (4) the prior rate of learning in academics, and

(5) the student's and parents' preferences. Instructional decisions involve whether to use academic prosthesis to reduce the need for reading (e.g., use pictures instead of words), teach specific but limited academic skills (e.g., survival words), or teach generalized academic skills.

The *Edmark Reading Program,* presented in the section on commercial materials, is designed to allow nonreaders of all ages to master basic reading skills and become more comfortable in the reading environment.

☀ DESIGNING A READING PROGRAM

In designing a reading program, teachers are faced with the difficult task of matching a myriad of commercial programs, strategies, and techniques with a multiplicity of student learning needs. This section provides some guidelines for designing a reading program that is responsive to a diversity of learners.

Use Effective Teaching Practices

Effective teaching practices are featured in Chapter 4 and are responsive to the needs of a heterogeneous student population. In essence, they sweep with a wide instructional broom. Practices such as providing success, promoting engaged academic time, demonstrating and modeling, giving corrective feedback, and striving to motivate are germane to successful beginning reading instruction. Harris and Sipay (1990) state that teacher skill is more important than reading methodology and that teachers must know numerous instructional practices in reading to teach students with reading disabilities.

Provide Prereading Experiences

Children enter school and reading programs with different experiences concerning print. Youngsters who have not been read to and engaged in discussions about words and books with family members or adults need prereading activities to prepare them for reading instruction. Concepts about print and phonological awareness training are featured in prereading experiences. These areas are discussed in Chapter 7 and in this chapter.

Consider the Nature of Reading Development

As noted in Chapter 7, literacy and subsequent reading development tend to progress through several stages. With the expanding information about emergent literacy and beginning to read, educators are learning more about reading development. Many educators refer to literacy and beginning reading stages (e.g., early emergent/emergent reader [kindergarten], developing reader [first grade], early independent reader [second grade], and independent reader [third grade]). Extensive early prereading and reading instruction is essential for students with phonological awareness or reading problems to succeed in reading and in school. If students experience enough letter-sound associations to gain the critical mass of letter-sound correspondences needed to decode letter clusters fluently, reading success is very likely. Stewart and Cegelka (1995) state, "By second or third grade, most readers attain sufficient decoding automaticity or fluency at the visual and phonological memory levels to shift to a more holistic approach" (p. 273). At this level, reading becomes more automatic, with less effort used on word decoding and more used on comprehension. Once the student becomes fluent in word recognition, reading emphasis shifts from oral to silent reading. Thus, a student's level of reading development has implications for using explicit and implicit instruction.

Provide Explicit and Implicit Reading Instruction

The explicit-to-implicit instructional continuum is discussed in Chapter 4. This section presents how this continuum relates to reading. Primarily, the explicit position is aligned with a code-emphasis reading approach, whereas the implicit position is aligned with a meaning-emphasis reading approach.

Methods of beginning reading instruction can be divided into two major approaches: the bottom-up or code-emphasis approach, and the top-down or meaning-emphasis approach. The primary difference between the two approaches is the way decoding is taught. This is reflected in the debate over the relative importance of text versus meaning or decoding versus comprehension. In the bottom-up sequential approach, decoding skills are taught first and instruction in comprehension follows. Beginning reading programs that stress letter-sound regularity are *code-emphasis* programs. The top-down model is the basis for the spontaneous approach to reading instruction, and reading for meaning is emphasized in the first stages of instruction. Programs that stress the use of common words are *meaning-emphasis* programs.

Code-emphasis programs begin with words consisting of letters and letter combinations that have the same sound in different words. The consistency in the letter-sound relationship enables the reader to read unknown words by blending the sounds together. For example, the word *sit* is sounded out as "sss-ii-tt" and pronounced "sit." The word *ring* is sounded out as "rrr-ii-nng" and pronounced "ring." The letter *i* has the same sound in both words. Moreover, a new word is not introduced unless its component letter-sound relationships have been mastered. The phonics, linguistic, and phonological awareness training programs are classified as code-emphasis programs.

Meaning-emphasis programs begin with frequently appearing words, on the assumption that they are familiar to the reader and thus easier to learn. Students identify words by examining meaning and position in context and are encouraged to use a variety of decoding techniques, including pictures, story context, initial letters, and word configuration. Words are not controlled so that a letter has the same sound in different words. For example, the words *at, many,* and *far* may occur, though the *a* represents a different sound in each word. The whole language, language experience, and individualized reading approaches generally are classified as meaning-emphasis programs.

Code-emphasis programs are considered to be more effective in teaching students to decode (Adams, 1990; Bond & Dykstra, 1967; Chall, 1983; Dykstra, 1968). Early systematic instruction in phonics provides the skills necessary for becoming an independent reader earlier than is likely if phonics instruction is delayed and less systematic (Adams, 1990). Many researchers contend that the foundation of comprehension is accurate word recognition, which is attained over time through careful de-

coding and practice (Adams & Bruck, 1995; Beck & Juel, 1995; Chall, 1989). Thus, decoding or facility with phonics is viewed as a necessary step in the acquisition of reading comprehension and other higher level reading processes.

Supporters of the meaning-emphasis approach agree that code-emphasis programs have an advantage in teaching decoding, but they maintain that meaning-emphasis programs have an advantage in teaching comprehension. Whole language instruction, which is the current meaning-emphasis approach to beginning reading, tends to be associated with a natural, self-directed or developmental, and open view. Some whole language proponents stress that skills (including phonics) should not be taught directly but acquired from more natural reading and writing activities. Carbo (1987) stresses that most primary students are global learners who need to learn to read with reading activities such as reading books of their own choosing, engaging in choral reading, writing stories, and listening to tape recordings of interesting, well-written books.

Though the debate continues between meaning-emphasis and code-emphasis supporters, Carnine et al. (1997) strongly recommend the code-emphasis approach, especially for students with learning problems. They note that the results of almost four decades of research on beginning reading indicate that phonics programs are superior to meaning-emphasis approaches in the early grades. In a review of research on beginning instruction in reading, Adams (1990) notes that instructional approaches that include systematic phonics lead to higher achievement in both word recognition and spelling, especially in the early grades and for students who are slower or economically disadvantaged. She advocates an instructional program that includes phonics skills as well as practice reading connected text. Beginning reading instruction should stress decoding but not ignore comprehension (Carnine et al., 1997). Accurate and automatic habits in decoding lead to reading fluency, which allows attention to be directed to higher level reading comprehension. Lyon (1995) notes that slow and inaccurate decoding is the best predictor of deficits in reading comprehension. Because successful reading requires proficiency in word identification as well as

TABLE 8.6
Reading concepts and approaches organized according to explicit-to-implicit instruction

Explicit	Interactive	Implicit
Reading Concepts		
Bottom-up reading (code emphasis)	Combination	Top-down reading (meaning emphasis)
Part-to-whole learning	Combination	Whole-to-part learning
Teacher-directed instruction	Combination	Student-directed instruction
Skill emphasis	Combination	Immersion emphasis
Reading viewed as a learned behavior that requires much teacher assistance		Reading acquired naturally through exposure to text
Reading Approaches and Programs		
Literature-Based Approach with systematic phonics	*Success for All*	Literature-Based Approach with little or no phonics
Phonics Approach	*Reading Recovery*	Whole Language Approach
Phonological Awareness Training	*B.A.L.A.N.C.E.*	Language Experience Approach
Reading Mastery and *Corrective Reading*	Reciprocal Teaching	Individualized Reading Approach
Linguistic Approach	Learning Strategies	Neurological Impress Method
Multisensory Reading Method (Fernald; Gillingham; Word Imprinting)		High Interest—Low Vocabulary Method
Glass Analysis		

comprehension, competency is required in both areas. Thus, there needs to be a proper balance between systematic decoding instruction and attention to developing reading comprehension.

Mather (1992) and Gersten and Dimino (1993) suggest that because both whole language and skill-based instruction have strengths, the teacher should create a combined approach. They note that aspects of both whole language and direct instruction should be implemented to teach reading so that all students, including students at risk and with learning problems, can succeed. Chall (1987) notes that research indicates that better results are achieved when young children are taught skills systematically and directly and use them in reading. In addition, research shows that being read to and reading and writing stories and selections in which newly gained skills are applied also contribute to reading development.

An example of a model program that integrates whole language with direct instruction and precision teaching is *B.A.L.A.N.C.E.: Blending All Learning Activities Nurtures Classroom Excellence* (Hefferan & Parker, 1991), developed in Orlando, Florida (FDLRS/Action, 1600 Silver Star Road, Orlando, FL

32804). *B.A.L.A.N.C.E.* stresses direct instruction but encourages the use of writing, quality literature, and integrated subjects to enhance the application of skills. In addition, the use of precision teaching helps the teacher make decisions about students' learning and enhance their fluency.

As stated by Heilman, Blair, and Rupley (1998), "No single approach to teaching literacy [i.e., learning to read and reading to learn] works best for all students. . . . Effective reading teachers integrate features associated with different philosophies and materials to match the needs of their students" (p. 302). Moreover, Stanovich (1994, p. 259) discusses the merits of different approaches for word recognition and comprehension:

The ideas that self-discovery is the most efficacious mode of learning, that most learning can be characterized as "natural," and that cognitive components should never be isolated or fractionated during the learning process have been useful as tenets for comprehension instruction, but are markedly at variance with what is now known about the best ways to develop word recognition skill. Research has indicated that explicit instruction and teacher-directed strategy training are more efficacious and that this is especially true for at-risk children, children with learning disabilities, and . . . children with special needs.

The teacher must consider each individual case to determine which skills need corrective instruction and then select the approach most likely to be effective.

Many educators are frustrated with the ongoing war between the explicit (code) and implicit (meaning) enthusiasts and are encouraging an integration of the two ideologies. Perhaps if advocates of these two approaches joined forces, they could collaborate in an effort to combine the best of each approach and develop a synthesis of models that would serve all children. Reading research clearly indicates that phonics instruction is essential for teaching many students to read, particularly those with learning problems. Meaning-emphasis instruction just as clearly helps many youngsters learn to read for meaning and enjoyment. To teach a diversity of learners to read, both explicit and implicit reading instruction should be available at each grade. A balanced approach helps both immature and mature readers succeed. Table 8.6 presents numerous reading concepts and approaches organized according to explicit-to-implicit instruction. This information helps teachers select from a variety of explicit and implicit programs to design a balanced reading program. Finally, it is important to remember that teachers greatly influence the explicit or implicit nature of a program through their interactions with students, teaching behaviors, and resources. Few teachers use instruction that is totally explicit or implicit.

☀ TEACHING STRATEGIES IN READING

Many reading approaches and instructional techniques are available for teaching students with learning problems. Because each student with learning problems is unique, a combination of approaches and various teaching strategies are needed to meet the needs of these students. The keyword method, reciprocal teaching, and mapping strategies are effective teaching techniques.

Keyword Method

To teach new vocabulary words and the initial learning and retention of facts, Mastropieri (1988)

suggests the use of the keyword method, which is a memory-enhancing technique that relies strongly upon visual imagery. The method uses three steps: (1) *recoding*—changing a vocabulary word into a word (keyword) that sounds like part of the vocabulary word and is easy to picture (e.g., *ape* as a keyword for *apex*), (2) *relating*—integrating the keyword with its definition by imagining a picture of the keyword and its definition doing something together (e.g., an ape sitting on the highest point [apex] of a rock), and (3) *retrieving*—recalling the definition by thinking of the keyword and the picture or interactive image of the keyword.

In teaching abstract and concrete vocabulary words to students with learning problems, Mastropieri, Scruggs, and Fulk (1990) found that keyword mnemonic instruction resulted in higher levels of recall and comprehension than a rehearsal condition. Students were shown mnemonic pictures for each new vocabulary word in which the keyword was pictured interacting with its definition in a line drawing or interacting with an instance of the definition. For example, for the word *oxalis,* meaning "a cloverlike plant," an ox (keyword for oxalis) was pictured eating a cloverlike plant; for *chiton,* meaning "a loose garment," a kite (keyword for chiton) was shown in a picture of people making kites out of loose garments. In addition, when using the keyword method, the teacher can enhance fluency and application by presenting practice exercises that require students to use the new words in sentences and in oral communication.

Reciprocal Teaching

To improve reading comprehension, reciprocal teaching is an interactive teaching strategy that promotes both comprehension of text and comprehension monitoring through active participation in discussions of text (Palinscar & Brown, 1986, 1988). The teacher and students work together to comprehend text through the use of a dialogue structured by four strategies:

1. ***Predicting:*** Students are taught to make predictions about upcoming content from cues in the text or from prior knowledge of the topic. They can use text structure such as headings, subheadings, and questions embedded in the text to

hypothesize what the author will discuss. This gives students a purpose for reading (i.e., to confirm or disprove their hypotheses).

2. ***Question generating:*** Through teacher modeling and practice in generating main idea questions about the text, students learn to identify information that provides the substance for a good question. Students become more involved in the reading text when they are posing and answering questions rather than responding to teacher or text questions.

3. ***Summarizing:*** The teacher guides students in integrating the information presented in the text. For example, the students can identify or invent topic sentences, name lists with appropriate labels, and delete unimportant or repeated information. This provides students with an opportunity to monitor their understanding of the text.

4. ***Clarifying:*** The students' attention is given to reasons why the text may be difficult to understand (e.g., unfamiliar vocabulary, unclear referent words, or disorganized text). They are taught to reread or ask for help to restore meaning.

In reciprocal teaching, the teacher initially leads the dialogue and models the use of the four strategies while reading. Through guided practice, the responsibility for initiating and maintaining the dialogue is transferred to the students. Thus, there is interplay among the teacher and students, and the teacher uses explanation, instruction, and modeling with guided practice to help students independently apply the strategies and learn from text. When using the strategies or thinking skills, students are forced to focus on the reading material and, at the same time, monitor for understanding.

Englert and Mariage (1991) present a comprehension procedure that includes the reciprocal teaching format as well as semantic mapping to improve students' recall of information in expository text. In POSSE, students apply the following strategies:

P—*Predict* text ideas based on background knowledge.

O—*Organize* the predicted textual ideas and background knowledge into a semantic map based on text structure.

S—*Search* for the text structure in the expository passage by reading.

S—*Summarize* the main ideas and record the information in a semantic map.

E—*Evaluate* comprehension by comparing the semantic maps, clarify information by asking questions, and predict what information will be in the next text section.

In this procedure students take turns leading the comprehension dialogue; group interaction promotes internalization of the reading strategies. In addition, the teacher constructs a semantic map of students' ideas to visually represent the text structure and organization of ideas. Thus, text structure mapping and reciprocal teaching within the reading process are combined. In a study on the effectiveness of the intervention, Englert, Tarrant, Mariage, and Oxer (1994) report that POSSE produced powerful effects on the comprehension abilities of students with learning disabilities and was found to be a highly effective procedure for comprehension instruction regardless of students' age levels.

Mapping Strategies

Story-mapping procedures can be used to improve reading comprehension through a schema-building technique (Idol & Croll, 1987). A pictorial story map is used as an organizer for readers, and students are asked to fill in the map components as they read. The map components of a narrative story include the setting (characters, time, and place), problem, goal, action, and outcome. The teacher initially models the story-mapping procedure by pointing out information related to the story-map components and having students write the correct answer on the story-map outline. Then students independently complete the story map, with prompting from the teacher as needed. Improved comprehension results as students build a structural schema (the story-map components) that is applied to a narrative story. Story mapping brings the reader's attention to important and interrelated parts of a story and provides a framework for understanding, conceptualizing, and remembering story events.

Idol (1987) notes that a mapping strategy designed for use with expository material can improve comprehension. A critical thinking map is used that highlights the major aspects of a passage, including (1) the important events, points, or steps that lead to the main idea, (2) the main idea itself, (3) other viewpoints and opinions of the reader, (4) the reader's conclusion upon reading the passage, and (5) any relevancy the reader perceives for contemporary situations. The reader completes the map components either during or after reading a passage in the text. (Chapter 13 presents additional information on graphic organizers that enhance comprehension of content areas.)

☀ READING AND STUDY SKILLS FOR ADOLESCENTS

Reading instruction at the secondary level typically builds on the student's strengths while simultaneously working to lessen the weaknesses. Reading material should be interesting and at an instructional level. Direct and functional reading approaches primarily are used with adolescents who have learning problems. Direct instruction focuses on teaching a hierarchy of skills; in functional instruction, reading skills are not taught in isolation but within the context of real reading events. Functional instruction is the major emphasis, and it stresses the use of reading skills in real-life tasks. Moreover, the secondary teacher integrates content instruction with the teaching of reading skills that are essential for acquiring the content (Gartland, 1995).

Dixon, Carnine, and Kameenui (1992) suggest the following guidelines for teaching adolescents to read:

- Use instructional time efficiently.
- Remediate early, strategically, and often.
- Teach less but do so more thoroughly.
- Teach reading strategies explicitly.
- Use a balance of teacher-directed and student-centered activities.
- Evaluate progress frequently to determine effectiveness of instruction.

Most secondary course work requires a relatively large amount of reading, because textbooks and supplementary materials are the major sources of information. In expository materials, the vocabulary is often more difficult to decode and pronounce than that found in narrative material, and the general content is frequently beyond the reader's experiences. According to Roe, Stoodt, and Burns (1995), "Content teachers can help students comprehend content materials by teaching them the meanings of key vocabulary terms. . . . Content area teachers need to be familiar with the types of writing patterns encountered frequently in their particular disciplines, so that they can help students to better understand these patterns" (p. 9).

Secondary teachers also should be aware that older students often need to develop study skills and reading rate in addition to increasing decoding and comprehension skills. Increasing reading rate and adjusting reading rate according to purpose should help the adolescent read more efficiently in the content areas. Also, setting a purpose for reading through the use of study guides or the SQ3R method can improve comprehension. Finally, learning strategies can enhance adolescents' word identification and reading comprehension.

Reading Rate

The adolescent may need to increase reading speed to finish assignments on time and keep up with older classmates. Roe et al. (1995) note that secondary students should be made aware of poor reading habits (including forming each word as it is read, sounding out all words [familiar and unfamiliar], rereading material, and pointing to each word with the index finger) that may decrease their reading rate. Another technique for increasing rate, which often is used in a reading laboratory, is to present words and phrases with a tachistoscope and gradually reduce the presentation time, thus speeding up the student's responses. The teacher can have the student practice timed readings with stopwatches or egg timers. Progress should be reinforced and charted continuously, and timed readings should be accompanied by comprehension checks.

Rupley and Blair (1989) note that successful reading in the content areas requires the ability to adjust one's rate of reading to the type of material being read. Three types of reading are required: skimming, scanning, and studying. *Skimming* refers to covering a selection to get some of the main ideas and a general overview of the material without attending to details. In skimming, the student should read the first paragraph line by line; read bold print headings as they appear; read the first sentence of every paragraph; examine pictures, charts, and maps; and read the last paragraph. Skimming practice may involve giving the student a short amount of time to skim a content chapter and write down the main ideas or having the student skim newspaper articles and match them to headlines. *Scanning* refers to reading a selection to find a specific piece of information. When scanning, the student should use headings to locate the pages to scan for the specific information; run eyes rapidly down the page in a zigzag or winding *S* pattern; note uppercase letters if looking for a name, numbers for dates, and italicized words for vocabulary items; and read only what is needed to verify the purpose. Scanning activities may include having the student find the date of a particular event by scanning a history chapter or locate a specific person's number in a telephone directory. In *study-type reading,* the goal is total comprehension, and reading is deliberate and purposeful. Students should have these three types of reading explained to them, practice them under teacher supervision, and be given opportunities for independent practice.

Study Skills

As students learn to study various content areas, they should develop effective study skills. The SQ3R method developed by Robinson (1961) is used widely, especially for social studies and science. This method, which can provide students with learning problems with a systematic approach to better study skills, involves the following steps:

1. **Survey:** To get an overview of the reading material, the student scans the entire assignment, glancing at headings to see the major points that will be developed and reading introductory statements and summaries. The student also should inspect graphic aids such as maps, tables, graphs, and pictures. This survey provides a framework for organizing facts in the selection as the student progresses through the reading.

2. **Question:** To give a purpose for careful reading, the student devises questions that may be answered in the selection. Questions can be formed by rephrasing headings and subheadings.

3. **Read:** The student reads the material with the intent of finding the answers to the questions. The student may take notes during this careful reading.

4. **Recite:** The student looks away from the reading material and notes and briefly recites the answers to the questions. This checks on what the student has learned and helps set the information in memory.

5. **Review:** The student reviews the material and checks memory of the content by rereading portions of the selection or notes to verify answers given during the previous step. The student also can note major points under each heading. This review activity helps the student retain the material better by reinforcing the learning.

Another strategy to increase students' comprehension is for the content teacher to provide a reading guide or study organizer containing questions and statements on the content of the text material. The student should receive it beforehand and complete it while reading. A study organizer summarizes the material's main ideas and important concepts in a factual style or in a schematic form such as a flow chart, diagram, or table.

Learning Strategies

Lenz and Hughes (1990) present a word identification strategy, DISSECT, that is effective in reducing common oral reading errors such as mispronunciations, substitutions, and omissions made by adolescents with learning problems. The seven steps of the strategy include the following:

D—*Discover* the content: Skip a difficult word and read the remainder of the sentence to guess the word by using the meaning of the sentence.

I— *Isolate* the prefix: Look at the beginning of the word to see whether it is possible to box off the first several letters to create a phoneme that can be pronounced.

S—*Separate* the suffix: Look at the end of the word to see whether it is possible to box off ending letters that form a suffix.

S—*Say* the stem: If able to recognize the stem (what is left after the prefix is isolated and the suffix is separated), say the prefix, stem, and suffix together.

E—*Examine* the stem: If unable to name the stem, apply one of two rules:

1. If a stem, or any part of a stem, begins with a vowel, separate the first two letters from the stem and pronounce. If a stem, or any part of a stem, begins with a consonant, separate the

first three letters from the stem and pronounce. Apply the rule until the end of the stem is reached and then pronounce the stem by saying the dissected part. Add the prefix and suffix and reread the whole word.

2. If the first rule cannot be used, isolate the first letter of the stem and try to apply the first rule again. When vowels appear together in a word, pronounce both vowel sounds and then make one vowel sound at a time until it sounds right.

C—*Check* with someone: If unable to pronounce the word after applying the first five strategy steps, obtain assistance by checking with someone (such as a teacher, parent, or better reader) in an appropriate manner.

T—*Try* the dictionary: If personal assistance is unavailable, look up the word in the dictionary, pronounce it by using the pronunciation guide, and read the definition.

Students with learning problems also can be taught to use learning strategies designed to increase their reading comprehension. For example, the visual imagery strategy requires the student to read a passage and create representative visual images. The self-questioning strategy helps maintain interest and enhance recall by teaching the student to form questions about the content of a passage as the student reads. Learning strategies involve the student more actively in the reading process. The reader is asked to formulate questions, take notes on the content, or verbally paraphrase critical information. Thus, the student is engaged in information rehearsal and practice involving either reciting or writing down critical information.

To improve reading from content-area texts, Grant (1993) suggests a mnemonic strategy, SCROL, to help students use text headings:

S—*Survey* the headings and subheadings in the text selection to determine what information is being presented.

C—*Connect* the segments by writing key words from the headings that show how the headings relate to one another.

R—*Read* the heading segment and pay attention to words and phrases that express information about the heading.

O—*Outline* the major ideas and supporting details in the heading segment without looking at the text.

L—*Look* at the heading segment to check the outline for accuracy and correct inaccuracies.

(Chapter 13 features additional information on reading in the content areas.)

☀ READING ACTIVITIES

Many reading activities and materials help develop reading skills. Supplementary activities and materials are useful in short, concentrated drill or practice or to enhance motivation and interest by reinforcing a newly learned skill. Activities, instructional games, self-correcting materials, and computer software programs can be used to individualize instruction according to specific needs and abilities. This section presents activities in concepts about print, phonological awareness, word attack, fluency, and comprehension. Additional activities for adolescents are presented in Chapter 13.

Prereading Activities: Concepts About Print

Initial prereading activities acquaint the learner with children's literature and environmental print. These activities help develop concepts related to print.

• To help children learn concepts about print and become motivated to read, read and reread their favorite selections aloud to them. While doing this, recognize and talk about the front, bottom, top, and back of the book; the pages and how to turn them; the pictures; and the words and their left-to-right order. Reading aloud and discussing stories provide the child with an adult reading model and help the child develop a sense of book, story, word, and sounds. This activity is excellent for family members to do with a young child.

• Teach nursery rhymes to the young child and practice saying them. Also teach the alphabet song.

• To facilitate listening and thinking about readings and rereadings of stories, have the child share in the experience by retelling the story or drawing a picture related to the story. This helps the child develop a sense of story as well as the ability to predict events.

Prereading Activities: Phonological Awareness

Phonological awareness activities involve experiences with spoken language and help promote awareness of words, syllables, onsets, rimes, and phonemes as units of language. The following phonological awareness activities are, for the most part, presented in sequential order. Thus, word activities are first, followed by syllable, onset-rime, and phoneme activities.

1. Say three words and have the child select the odd word (i.e., the word that does not belong) (e.g., *tall, mall, **dog***).

2. Say a phrase or sentence and have the child tap out with a stick, make marks with chalk, or move a marker to indicate the number of words in the utterance.

3. Say two words and ask the child to indicate whether the words rhyme.

4. Say two syllables and have the child blend them into a word (e.g., /pen/ /cil/ [pencil]; /num/ /ber/ [number]).

5. Say a word and have the child tap or count out the number of syllables in the word.

6. Say a two-syllable word and have the child segment the word into syllables. Using the names of classmates is a nice variation of this task.

7. Say four words and have the child select the word that does not rhyme with the other words (e.g., *meat, beat, **head**, seat*).

8. Have the child participate in rhyming activities such as providing a word that rhymes with a dictated word or matching pictures whose names rhyme. Also, when given one word in a family, ask the child to list other words that belong to the same family and to circle like parts of the rhyming words.

9. Say the small parts of a word and have the child put the parts together (blending) to make the whole word (e.g., /d/ /og/ [dog]; /c/ /at/ [cat]). Using a puppet can be an entertaining way of presenting this activity. The puppet can tell a story but sometimes mispronounce a word by segmenting it into phonemes. The embarrassed or bashful puppet turns away from the children until they fix the word by blending it.

10. Say a target word and three other words. Have the child choose the word that rhymes with the target word (e.g., *get—race, **met**, hand*).

11. Have the child make a sound dictionary in an indexed scrapbook. On each page, paste pictures of objects or actions that illustrate words beginning with the sound. For example, pictures of a table, tent, and top can be pasted on the *T* page, and the page for words with the initial *Ch* sound can have pictures of a church, cheese, and children on it.

12. Say a target word and three other words, and have the child select the word that has the same beginning consonant sound (e.g., *tent—mat, race, **tall***), a different beginning consonant sound (e.g., *bag—**fine**, beach, ball*), the same final consonant sound (e.g., *boat—seed, read, **hat***), or a different final consonant sound (e.g., *sat—**time**, coat, mitt*).

13. Say a compound word and have the child repeat it; then have the child say the word without saying a part of the word (e.g., "Say *cupcake*. Now say *cupcake* without saying *cup*" [cake]). Say another word and have the child repeat it; then have the child say the word without saying a beginning, final, or middle sound (e.g., *mat* without /m/ [at], *card* without /d/ [car], and *tiger* without /g/ [tire]).

14. Say a word and have the child say the sound at the word's beginning (*jam—/j/*), middle (*heat—/ea/*), or end (*look—/k/*).

15. Say a word and have the child tap out the number of phonemes (e.g., *cat*—three taps [/c/ /a/ /t/]).

16. Draw a box for each phoneme in a word (e.g., for *boat*, draw three boxes). Say the word and a phoneme, and ask the child to mark an X in the box representing the position of the targeted phoneme (e.g., *boat*, /t/—last box).

17. Say a one-syllable word and ask the child to segment it into phonemes (e.g., *bun—/b/ /u/ /n/*).

18. Say a word and have the child isolate the initial sound and substitute a new sound (e.g., *man, /m/, can*). Repeat the task, focusing on final sounds and then on medial sounds. The song *I've Been Working on the Railroad* has a verse that begins with "Someone's in the kitchen with Dinah," which easily adapts to sound substitutions. "Fe-Fi-Fiddly-i-o" can become "Pe-Pi-Piddly-i-o" or "Se-Si-Siddly-i-o." The class can sing the song and be given a consonant or blend (e.g., /w/ or /th/) to substitute at the beginning of each verse.

19. Have the child segment the sound of a word by engaging in a "say it and move it" activity. Provide the child with some disks, tiles, buttons, or blocks and a laminated sheet of paper showing an arrow from left to right. Say a word or show a picture of a word, and ask the child to segment the sounds of the word and, while doing so, move an object for each sound along the arrow from left to right. The order of presentation in segmentation activities should be one sound (/e/), two-phoneme words (*up, it, or*), three-phoneme words with a continuous sound beginning letter (*map, fat*), and three-phoneme words with a stop sound beginning letter (*bet, pig*). This activity could be adapted to a start-to-finish board game, with each phoneme representing a one-space move.

20. Say a word slowly and have the child hold up one finger to represent each phoneme.

Word-Attack Activities

Accurate word recognition is attained through careful decoding and practice over time. Exposures to letter-sound associations in word-attack activities allow the student to gain the critical mass of letter-sound correspondences that is needed to decode letter clusters fluently.

• For practice in initial consonant sounds, glue pictures of simple objects on small cards and make a grid or a pocket chart in which the beginning square or pocket has consonant letters corresponding to initial sounds of the objects. To indicate the initial sound of the word, the student places each picture card next to the appropriate letter. Consonant blends, medial vowel sounds, and final consonant sounds can be practiced the same way.

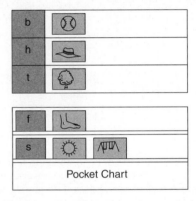

Pocket Chart

• Have the student make a picture dictionary by using a scrapbook indexed with the letters of the alphabet. The student draws pictures or cuts them out of old magazines. After learning the word shown by the picture, the student pastes the picture on the page representing the initial consonant sound. For example, a picture of a dog is pasted on the *D* page. The student-made dictionary invites interest because the student creates it and it contains only words that the student is using. If desired, completed dictionaries can be exchanged so that each student learns to read other students' dictionaries.

• Make a rotating circle device to use in practicing initial consonant sounds and word families. Cut an attractive design or object out of poster board and print the desired letters of a word family on it. Cut out a square in front of the letters. Then cut a small circle out of poster board and print the appropriate initial consonant letters on it. Attach the circle to the back of the larger poster board, positioned so that each letter will be exposed in the square opening as the circle is rotated.

• Make flash cards by pasting pictures on index cards and printing the word or phrase that tells about the picture on both the front and back of the card. Vowel cards can be made by using a picture illustrating a word that uses a specific vowel (e.g., *cat*) and writing the word and the marked vowel on the card (căt—ă). Flash cards for blends, digraphs, or diphthongs can be similarly constructed. After learning to associate the printed symbol with the picture, the student can practice reading the words on the back side of the cards.

• Make a set of word cards in which the first letter of each word is omitted and a picture illustrates the word. The student is to fill in the missing letter. The cards can be made self-correcting by writing the answer on the back or supplying a picture-coded answer key. Cards also can be made that omit letters in the medial or final position or that omit blends, digraphs, or diphthongs. The cards can be laminated and written on with a grease pencil so they can be reused.

- For general word recognition, attach labels to the doors, windows, and objects in the classroom so the student will begin to associate the printed word with the object. Also, a large picture can be made on poster board with slits next to the objects in the picture. Word cards are made for the objects in the picture, and an envelope containing paper clips is attached to the back of the picture. Instruct the student to match each word card to the appropriate object in the picture by paper-clipping it to the slit.

- To provide practice on basic sight words or sight phrases, make a ladder that will hold word or phrase cards on each rung. The student tries to climb the ladder by saying each word or phrase. When she or he reaches the top by pronouncing each word correctly, the student celebrates and begins to work on a more difficult set of cards.

- Construct a word wheel by fastening together two poster board circles, one smaller than the other, through their centers so that they rotate freely. A blend can be written on the inner circle with an opening next to it; letters to add to the blend are printed on the outer circle. The student rotates the inner wheel and reads the words as they appear in the opening. A variation of the word wheel is to print word endings and suffixes on the outer wheel and various root words on the inner wheel. The teacher gives a sentence (e.g., "The two boys are _____") and points to the root word on the inner wheel. The student rotates the wheel to find the appropriate ending and reads the word.

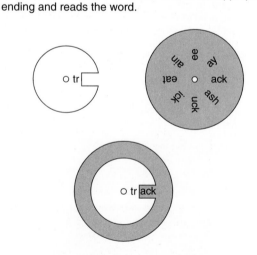

- Make a tachistoscope by cutting a window in a piece of oaktag and attaching the window card to another card of equal size to form a backing. Words or phrases are written on a strip of paper the width of the window; the student pulls the strip past the window to reveal the written words. This device can be made self-

correcting by having two windows, one of which is covered with a flap, and preparing an answer strip with picture clues. The student reads the word in the open window and lifts the flap on the other window to check the response by looking at the picture clue. Also, to develop quick recognition of sight words, a shutter can be attached to the opening so that the teacher can expose or flash each word quickly. If the word is misread, the shutter can be reopened to allow the student more time to analyze the word.

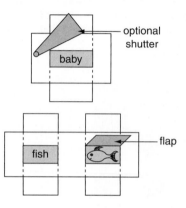

- Emphasize left-to-right orientation to help the student who frequently reverses letters in words (such as *was* for *saw* or *lap* for *pal*). Present frequently reversed words on flash cards and cover up all but the initial letter. Slowly uncover the remaining letters as the student correctly pronounces the word. Arrows drawn from left to right also may be added under the word. In addition, the student may be asked to trace troublesome words or letters with a finger and simultaneously sound out the word or letter. After tracing each word or letter, the student should attempt to write it from memory.

- To develop knowledge of contractions, give the student sentences to read in which several words are underlined that could be made into contractions. Instruct the student to change the words to the appropriate contraction while reading. For example:

- <u>There is</u> nobody <u>she will</u> go with today.
- He <u>has not</u> done the work because he <u>cannot</u> see it.
- "<u>You are</u> going to the store, <u>are not</u> you?" said Mary.

Also, the student can be asked to underline all contractions or words that could have been made into contractions in a selected reading passage. An additional activity is to have contraction races. Call out contractions and see who can give the words they stand for, or call out two words and see who can give the contraction. Shanker and Ekwall (1998) list contractions and the grade level at which they should have been mastered or taught.

- To facilitate identification of compound words, provide two lists of words and have the student draw lines to connect two words to make a compound word. Also, the student can be asked to separate compound words into two words. Activities involving compound words encourage focusing on the whole word. Such activities may help the student who has a tendency to read words by looking at the initial sound and guessing at the remainder of the word.
- To discourage a tendency to read word by word, allow the student to read familiar material or material that has a lower level vocabulary (high interest–low vocabulary stories). Have the student listen to tape recordings of familiar passages that are read fluently. The student also can read against a timer to increase speed and maintain a more appropriate pace.
- Have the student practice with phrase cards. After short, easy phrases have been mastered, longer and more difficult phrases can be introduced. The phrase cards may be arranged to tell a continuous story. Phrase reading also can be encouraged by giving the student a reading passage in which the words to be read together are underlined (e.g., <u>All the children walked quickly</u> to the car).
- On the chalkboard, write sentences that contain words with prefixes or suffixes. Ask the student to locate the root word, identify the prefix or suffix, and explain how the addition of the prefix or suffix changes the meaning of the root word.
- If the student tends to omit or repeat words when reading, tape-record his or her reading of a selected passage. Provide a copy of the passage and ask the student to follow along with a finger as the tape is played back. Have the student circle all omitted words or underline repeated words. This focuses attention on omitted or repeated words and increases the student's awareness of this tendency when reading.
- Encourage the student to use context clues instead of guessing at unknown words or substituting words. Ask the student to complete multiple-choice sentences that provide practice in context reading. For example:
  - While camping, the boys slept in a _____. (lamp, tent, trap)
  - It was raining, so she brought her _____. (umbrella, usher, clock)

In a reading passage, encourage the student to sound out the first few sounds of a troublesome word and then to read beyond it to see whether the following words give any clue concerning its meaning. Context clues as well as beginning sounds may help the student identify a difficult word.

- Provide a list of words and ask the student to arrange them in columns according to the number of syllables in each word. Improving skills in syllabication aids the older student in structural analysis and often enhances word recognition.

Fluency Activities

Once the student has had numerous exposures to highly frequent letter-sound correspondences and sounds of letter clusters, activities should focus on developing fluency. Word recognition fluency allows the reader to focus on comprehension.

- Have the student practice reading high-frequency sight words (see Table 7.4). One excellent method is to have the student repeatedly read phrases that include the sight words. This provides word-by-word readers with an experience in reading clusters of words.
- Have the student read words, phrases, or passages in 1-minute segments and try to increase the rate of words read correctly per minute. Have the student work toward rate-per-minute goals and record the results of each reading on a graph.
- Use repeated readings in which the student orally reads a passage repeatedly until a fluency rate is attained. This helps the student attain the neurological, cognitive, and affective experience of reading fluency. (Repeated readings are discussed in the section on the neurological impress method.)
- Model fluent oral reading (e.g., about 150 words per minute with two or fewer errors). Have the student read along silently in the text as fluent oral reading is modeled. Model reading can be accomplished by teacher readings, peer readings, teacher assistant readings, and taped readings.
- Have the student read aloud to other students.
- Conduct a readers' theater. Have students read their parts in a story or play.
- Review new vocabulary before reading a story or text. Multisensory techniques (e.g., Fernald or Gillingham methods) are excellent for learning new vocabulary. (Vocabulary development activities for adolescents are presented in Chapter 13.)

Comprehension Activities

The purpose of reading is to obtain meaning from words; thus, comprehension is the culminating event of the reading process. Fluency and comprehension are highly correlated (Shinn, Good, Knutson, Tilly, & Collins, 1992). Thus, the activities to build fluency listed previously also are important in developing comprehension. Additional comprehension activities (e.g., keyword method and the POSSE strategy) are presented in the teaching strategies section of this chapter, in Chapter 7 (the cloze procedure, which is easily adapted to teach comprehension), and in Chapter 13 (comprehension activities for adolescents).

• To facilitate memory of what the student has read, point out key words that reveal the text's organization and show a series of events. The student should be aware of words and phrases such as *to begin with, next, after that,* and *finally.*

• To emphasize word meaning and develop vocabulary, have the student group various words into categories. For example, the student may group words that relate to specific interests such as baseball or cooking. Words may also be grouped in categories such as "Things That Are Alive," "What Animals Do," or "Things That Eat."

• Encourage the development of a visual image by reviewing the story setting before the student reads. While reading, the student can be asked to describe images from the passage (e.g., "Do you think Ruff is a big dog?"). Also, after reading, the student can draw pictures to illustrate story settings and events.

• Model proper inflection for a particular sentence. Have the student imitate the inflection. Reading with expression increases understanding.

• Model comprehension strategies using "think alouds." Students follow along silently while the teacher reads a passage aloud and uses the following strategies:

• *Makes predictions.* Shows how to develop a hypothesis (e.g., "In the next part, I think we'll find out why the dog was barking").

• *Describes the mental picture forming from the information.* Shows how to develop images during reading (e.g., "I have a picture of a man hiding in a closet").

• *Shares an analogy.* Shows how to link prior knowledge with new information in the text (e.g., "This is like when my neighbor's house was robbed").

• *Verbalizes a confusing point.* Shows how to monitor ongoing comprehension (e.g., "This is not what I had expected").

• *Demonstrates fix-up strategies.* Shows how to correct lagging comprehension ("I'll read the next part to see whether I understand what's happening").

• Have the student read a story and then make up an appropriate title for it. The teacher can give the student several titles and ask the student to select the best one and justify the response.

• Have the student read a story in which the sentences have been numbered. Ask several detailed questions about the reading selection and require the student to give the number of the sentence in which each answer is located.

• After a selection has been read, ask the student to underline the sentences that best state or paraphrase the main idea of the selection. Then have the student list important details pertaining to the main idea. The headings "Who," "What," "Where," "When," and "Why" may be written on the paper so that details regarding each heading can be listed in the appropriate column. The student also may draw pictures to illustrate details of the selection, or answer questions requiring knowledge of the important details.

• Cut pictures out of magazines or catalogs and write descriptive statements about them. Have the student match each picture with its description.

• Cut articles out of the newspaper and cut off the headlines. Have the student read each article and then select the appropriate headline.

• To encourage attention to specific details of a reading passage, have the student read directions on how to do a given activity and then perform the activity step by step. Also, ask the student to write directions for playing a game; then another student can read the written directions to see whether they tell others how to play the game.

• Present the student with a series of paragraphs, each of which contains one word or one sentence that does not fit the meaning of the rest of the paragraph. Have the student cross out the irrelevant word or sentence and write a more appropriate one in its place.

• To enhance vocabulary development and word meaning, make a crossword puzzle in which the clues are word definitions. For young students, a modified puzzle may be made in which the puzzle supplies the first letter for each response.

• Teach vocabulary with definitions according to the following format (Carnine et al., 1997):

• State the definition and ask the student to repeat it.

• Teach and test students on positive and negative examples. Positive examples are words of the same class, and negative examples are those of a different class. For example, in teaching the meaning of the word *exit,* a positive example would be a picture of a door leading out of a movie theater, and a negative example would be a picture of a closet door. The teacher presents each example by holding up the picture, pointing to the door, and asking, "Is this an exit? How do you know?"

• Review the new word and words previously taught. Modifications include allowing the student to select words to be learned, having the student write a story using the words, or having the student use the words in an oral discussion.

• After a short story has been read, instruct the student to write a telegram telling the main events of the passage. The telegram should be limited to a specific number of words. Blank telegrams can be provided for the student's use. A variation of this activity is to provide a list of topic suggestions and have the student compose a telegram of ten or fewer words about the chosen topic.

• To facilitate distinction between the main idea and supporting details of a reading selection, have the student diagram the sentences of a paragraph. For example:

| Every day the old man and his dog took an early morning walk. |
| They always walked four blocks. |
| The dog stayed right next to the man. |
| Many people spoke to both the man and his dog. |

• To provide practice in distinguishing between cause and effect, have one student describe an event (e.g., "the dog barked"). A second student must give a reason for the event (e.g., "because a cat came into the yard"). Then a third student is asked to give a probable effect (e.g., "the cat ran home").

• To help increase speed of reading while focusing on comprehension, have the student read a short selection in a limited amount of time. Then present a series of questions based on the selection and have the student answer as many questions as possible. Also, the teacher can present questions before the student reads the selection; the student is allowed a short time to locate the answers. An additional method to increase recall of facts involves having the student read a selection orally for a specified amount of time and then write down or recite all remembered facts. The number of correct and incorrect responses can be charted to indicate progress.

• Read half of a story aloud and ask the student to predict how the story will end. Also, the student can read chapter headings of a book or look at pictures from a story, and the teacher can ask her or him to tell or write what the story probably will concern.

• Present the student with a short story in which the sentences are written in the wrong order. Ask the student to rewrite the selection, arranging the sentences in logical order so that the story makes sense. Another sequencing activity is to provide a list of events from a story the student has read and ask her or him to number the events to indicate the order in which they happened. Also, the student can arrange pictures that tell stories or show action in sequence and then write a sentence or paragraph for each picture.

• Encourage students to use metacognitive strategies such as self-questioning (e.g., What is the main topic of this passage? What do I know about it?) and making predictions and reading to test them. Also,

have students read with the intent of summarizing the passage.

• Use comprehension response frames to help students report and organize the information they learn through reading. The students (1) read the same book or story, (2) engage in discussion about the information while reading or after reading, (3) write entries into response frames, (4) work to become independent in reading and writing in the frames, and (5) share their frame entries. Figure 8.2 presents sample frame forms.

• To develop comprehension skills involving inference, ask the student several cause-and-effect questions (e.g., "What will happen if. . . ?"). Read part of a story aloud and stop at a crucial point to let the student predict what will happen next. Also, the student may be asked to judge the reading selection as being true or fantasylike.

• To develop study skills, use the daily newspaper to present comprehension activities. The student can practice locating the main idea and supporting ideas by using the editorial page and can discuss the pros and cons of the viewpoint presented. Also, the student may be asked to study the employment ads to answer various questions concerning available jobs. Grocery store ads give the student an opportunity to read for comparison shopping, and from articles in the sports section the student may be required to locate answers concerning to whom it happened, what happened, when it happened, where it happened, and why it happened. Highway maps, available at local service stations, are excellent for practice in the important skill of map reading.

• Use story maps to help students construct meanings. A story map is a graphic representation of a story's structure; it consists of the following key elements: the setting (including place, time, and major characters), the problem (most stories represent characters' attempts to solve problems), the goal (usually to alleviate the problem), the set of attempts to achieve the goal (usually the major events in the story), and the resolution (usually achieving the goal and alleviating the problem).

• Use the K-W-L procedure for increasing comprehension (Ogle, 1986). This three-step cognitive procedure helps the student recognize prior knowledge, predict new types of information to be acquired from reading, and review what is learned from reading:

K— *What I know.* The student writes down prior knowledge regarding the topic.

W—*What I want to learn.* The student anticipates or predicts what will be learned about the topic and writes it down.

L— *What I learned.* The student writes down what is learned from reading.

FIGURE 8.2
Sample frame forms

Basic Reaction Frame

I learned some interesting facts about _____ from reading this selection. First, _____

_____ .

Second, _____

_____ .

Third, _____

_____ .

However, the most interesting thing I learned was _____

_____ .

Contrast Frame

Insects differ from spiders in several ways. First, insects _____

_____ , while spiders _____ .

Second, insects _____ , while

spiders_____ .

I think the easiest way to tell an insect from a spider is_____

_____ .

- Encourage students to use comprehension monitoring when reading content-area materials. A code can be provided for reading a content selection: B = Boring, C = Clarify, D = Details, I = Interesting, and M = Main idea. While reading, students monitor their responses to the selection by writing the appropriate code letters on strips of paper attached to the pages. During post-reading discussions, the students can clarify their thinking and discuss the feelings they had while reading the selection.

☀ INSTRUCTIONAL GAMES IN READING

Bang Game

Materials: Twenty-six popsicle sticks that have a different lowercase letter written on both sides of the lower end of each stick; six popsicle sticks that have the word *BANG* written on both sides of the lower end of each stick; a small container, decorated with the word *BANG,* that holds the sticks upright with the stick ends extending beyond the upper edge.

Directions: All sticks are placed in the *BANG* container, and two to four students take turns drawing sticks and naming the letters on them. If a letter name is correct, the player keeps the stick; if a letter name is incorrect, the player returns the stick to the container. If a *BANG* stick is drawn, all sticks accumulated by the player are placed back into the container. The winner is the first person to get a predetermined number of sticks without drawing a *BANG* stick.

Modifications: The skill can be changed by writing different items on the sticks (e.g., uppercase letters [with young children saying the letter name or its sound], numbers, students' names, survival words, functional words, basic sight words, or contractions). Each set should be painted a different color to separate the sticks for each skill.

Vowel Spinner

Materials: A spinner made from a cardboard circle that is divided into five equal segments, with a vowel written in each section; two or more laminated cardboard cards containing three-, four-, or five-letter words with the vowels deleted; grease pencil.

Directions: The first student spins the spinner and must try to use the vowel the spinner stops on to complete a word on the player's card. The student uses the grease pencil to write the vowel in the selected place; the word must make sense. If unable to use the vowel, the player loses that turn. Next, the second student spins and attempts to use the indicated vowel. The players continue to take turns, and the winner is the first student to fill the card by completing every word with an appropriate vowel.

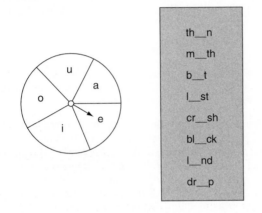

th__n

m__th

b__t

l__st

cr__sh

bl__ck

l__nd

dr__p

Blend Game

Materials: A start-to-finish game board; cards with pictures showing words containing initial blends; spinner with numbered segments; markers; answer key that gives the correct initial blend for each picture.

Directions: The first player draws the top card from the card deck, identifies the picture (e.g., flower), and tells the initial blend (*fl*). Another student can check the response by referring to the answer key. If the response is correct, the player spins the spinner and moves his or her game-board marker the number of spaces shown. The players take turns; when an incorrect response is made, the player loses that turn and does not spin the spinner. The first player to reach the finish space on the game board wins the game.

Modifications: Picture cards that illustrate words containing digraphs, diphthongs, medial vowels, or initial consonants can be used. Also, to boost interest, the game board can have various instructions on certain spaces (e.g., *Go back one space, Spin again,* and *Lose one turn*).

Word Blender

Materials: Cards of words containing initial blends, with each card cut in half to show the blend on one half and the remainder of the word on the other half.

Directions: The deck of blend cards and the deck of word cards both are shuffled and placed face down. The first player turns over the top cards from each deck. If the blend fits the letters on the word card, the player places the cards together and says the word. If the response is correct, the player keeps the cards. If the response is incorrect or the blend and letters do not form a word, the cards are placed in their respective discard piles. The players take turns trying to form words. When the decks are finished, the discard piles are shuffled and used. When all the cards have been used (or at the end of a predetermined time period), the players count their cards; the one with the most matches wins.

Modifications: The cards can present words and be cut so that the players must form words with appropriate prefixes, suffixes, or various endings.

Phonics Rummy

Materials: Phonics card sets consisting of four cards, each with a phonics element written at the top and four words listed under it containing that phonics element (a different word is underlined on each of the four cards in the set [36 cards are ample for two players; additional card sets can be added for more players]).

Directions: Eight cards are dealt face down to each player, and the remaining cards are placed face down in a stack in the middle of the players. The first player asks another player for a word using a certain phonics element to try to obtain three or four cards in a set. For example: "Mike, give me 'bat' from the *a* group" (the player pronounces the short *a* sound). If the asked player has the card, it must be given to the caller. The caller continues to ask for cards from specific players. If the person asked for a card does not have it, the caller takes the top card from the center pile. The players take turns, and when a player has three cards from a certain phonics element set, they are laid down. When the fourth card to a set that has already been laid down is drawn, it also may be put down. The winner is the player who gets rid of all the cards in his or her hand.

Modification: Instead of phonics elements, the card sets can contain four synonyms (or four antonyms) for a specific word.

Fish

Materials: A deck of word cards with three cards for each word (the word should be written in the top right-hand corner and upside down in the lower left-hand corner of the card; a picture illustrating the word can be placed in the middle).

Directions: Nine cards are dealt to each player, and the remaining cards are placed face down in the middle of the players. The first player asks another player for a match for a word in his or her hand. If the asked player has the word card, it must be given to the caller. If the asked player has two cards of that word set, both cards must be given to the caller. The caller continues to ask for cards until the person does not have the card asked for and says, "Go Fish." When told to "Go Fish," the player takes the top card from the pile. If it happens to be the word card just asked for, the player's turn continues. The players take turns, and when a player completes a set (three cards with the same word), the cards are laid down. The first player out of cards is the winner.

Word Bingo

Materials: Bingo cards (five squares across and five squares down) with a sight word written in each square; word list of the words included on all the cards; discs to use as markers.

Directions: Each student is given a bingo card and several discs. The teacher (or caller) reads a word from the word list and checks it off. The players look for the called word on their bingo cards; if it is on the card, the player covers it with a disc. The teacher continues to call out words one at a time, and the first player to cover five spaces in any direction calls out "Bingo." After calling out "Bingo," the player also must pronounce each of the covered words to win.

Modifications: Bingo cards and word lists can be derived from various categories, such as words with prefixes, words with suffixes, compound words, or words containing blends.

Word War

Materials: Word cards with several sets of identical words.

Directions: All the cards are shuffled and dealt to the players. All players simultaneously turn over one card at a time from their stacks. When two (or more) identical cards are turned up, the first player to name the word correctly takes the turned-up stacks of cards from the players who were involved in the "war." The winner is the player who gets all the cards or the most cards within a specified time period.

Dominoes

Materials: Word cards divided in half by a line, with a different word on each side of the line (the words are repeated several times on different cards).

Directions: All the cards are dealt to the players. The first player places a word card in the middle, and the next player must match words to play a card. The player must pronounce the word as the match is made. A design is formed by placing the matching card next to the word in any direction. If unable to match a word, the player loses that turn. The first player to use all of his or her cards is the winner.

Modifications: Various sets of word cards can be devised, such as words containing blends, digraphs, or diphthongs; compound words; contractions; or words with prefixes or suffixes.

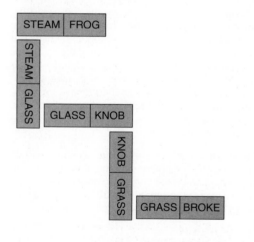

Word Game Board

Materials: Start-to-finish laminated game board with words or phrases written in the squares and some special squares containing instructions such as *Move back three squares, Take an extra turn,* or *Go back to start;* dice; markers.

Directions: The first player rolls the dice and moves a marker the indicated number of spaces. The player must pronounce correctly the word or phrase written on the square holding the marker. If the player is unable to pronounce the word or phrase correctly, the marker is moved back to where it was before the roll. When the marker lands on a special square, the player must follow the directions on that square. The players take turns, and the first player to reach the finish square is the winner.

Modifications: The board can be laminated or covered with clear plastic so that words can be written with a grease pencil and changed as needed. Also, chance dice can be used that have one number covered with a sticker. When one sticker is rolled, the player loses a turn; when two stickers are rolled (one on each die), the player goes back to the beginning square.

Word Baseball

Materials: Vocabulary words written on flash cards; answer key.

Directions: The teacher divides the class into two teams and marks first base, second base, third base, and home plate on the floor. A member of the first team goes to home plate, and the designated pitcher on the opposing team holds up a word from the player's set of flash cards. The batter must pronounce the word correctly, define it, and use it in a sentence. If the response is correct (as judged by a scorekeeper with an answer key), the batter advances to first base. Other members of the team bat, and for each "hit" (correct response) the player advances one base. Runs are scored by crossing home plate; an out occurs when a batter misses a word or its definition. Each team gets three outs, and then the opposing team comes to bat. The team with the highest score, after both teams have batted at least three times, is the winner.

Modifications: The word cards can be labeled *single, double, triple,* or *home run* to indicate the value of the hit. Also, the word cards can be divided according to words with one, two, three, or four or more syllables. The number of syllables indicates the number of bases a correct response is worth. However, in addition to reading the word, the student must state the number of syllables in that word correctly, or the batter is out. In addition, the pitcher may be allowed to select pitches (word cards) depending on who the batter is; however, once a word card has been used, it is out of the game for that team.

Chance Dice Reading Game

Materials: Two chance dice, each of which has numbers on five sides and a sticker covering the number on the sixth side; worksheets with equal items that are appropriate for each player (e.g., a list of vocabulary words to match with pictures or definitions, comprehension questions pertaining to a short reading passage, and antonyms or synonyms to be matched); an answer key for each worksheet.

Directions: Each player is given an appropriate worksheet for his or her reading level. The first player rolls both of the chance dice. If no stickers are rolled, the player answers an item on the worksheet, and the answer is checked by a student with the answer key. If the answer is correct, the item number is checked; however, if the answer is incorrect, the item number is not checked and the player must attempt that item on another turn. If one sticker is rolled on the chance dice, the player loses that turn. If two stickers are rolled (one on each die), the player is allowed to attempt to answer two items on the worksheet. This procedure is continued until one player correctly answers all the worksheet items and wins the game.

Mystery Detective Game

Materials, Directions, Modifications, and Example: This game, designed to practice reading comprehension of phrases (who, where, why, how, what, and when), uses a game-board format and is described in detail in Chapter 2. It features a self-correcting format and can be modified to offer practice in syllabication.

Comprehension Game

Materials: Start-to-finish game board with each square colored red, blue, or white; several copies of a story; a set of red cards (made from construction paper) containing comprehension questions (who, what, when, why, where, or how questions) about the story's content; a set of blue cards containing vocabulary words from the story; a set of white cards that are synonym cards and give a sentence with one word underlined; markers; spinner.

Directions: Each player reads a copy of the given story. To begin the game, the first player takes the top card from one of the card sets. If a red card is selected, the player must answer the comprehension question correctly. If a blue card is selected, the player must define the vocabulary word correctly. If a white card is selected, the player must give a synonym for the word underlined on the card. If a correct response to the card is given, the player spins the spinner and moves his or her marker the number of spaces shown. On the next turn, the player must take the top card from the card set that is the same color as the space holding his or her marker. If unable to respond to the card correctly, the player does not spin the spinner and must try another card of the same color on the next turn. The other players must decide whether each task is answered correctly; they may refer to the story to check a response. The first player to reach the finish square wins the game.

☀ SELF-CORRECTING READING MATERIALS

Flip-Siders

Feedback device: A picture clue to identify the word on the front of the card provides feedback.

Materials: Index cards with a word printed on the front and a picture illustrating that word pasted on the back.

Directions: The student looks at the word and reads it. Then the student flips over the card to check the response by looking at the picture illustrating the word.

Modifications: For phonics review, the student can look at the pictures and put all the pictures with the same beginning sound in a pile (e.g., *cat, cake, can,* and *crack*). Then the student turns over each card to see the printed word and the initial letter. Another variation is to have words written on the front of each card and the number of syllables, or the word divided into syllables, written on the back. The student reads the word, counts the number of syllables, and flips over the card to check the response. Also, for practice in vocabulary development, sets of cards can show a word on one card and its definition on another card. The backs of both cards in the set should have matching objects, numbers, or colors, or

should go together to complete a picture. When a word is paired with its definition, the student flips over the cards to see whether the reverse sides go together.

Punch-Through Cards

Feedback device: On the reverse side of the card the hole that indicates the correct answer is circled in a color.

Materials: Index cards containing pictures, with the word illustrated by each picture written underneath omitting the initial or final consonant or blend, and with three possible answers listed next to three holes (the hole next to the correct answer is circled in a color on the back); pencil (or golf tee).

Directions: The student looks at the picture and determines what letter or letters are omitted in the word. The student punches a pencil through the hole to indicate the response and then turns over the card. If the answer is correct, the pencil is in the hole circled in a color.

Modifications: Vocabulary words with three possible definitions can be presented on the cards, or the student can be required to select the appropriate synonym or antonym for a word. Also, a brief reading selection can be presented with a comprehension question and three possible answers.

Front   Back

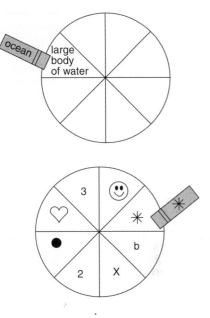

Clothespin Wheel

Feedback device: The symbol or number on the back of the clothespin matches the symbol or number on the back of the correct section of the wheel.

Materials: A 10-inch cardboard circle divided into eight sections that have definitions written in them, and a symbol or number on the back of the circle in each section; clothespins with words corresponding to the definitions written on the front and the matching symbol or number written on the back.

Directions: The student reads the definition and looks at the words on the clothespins to find the correct answer. The student clips the clothespin containing the answer to the section of the wheel with the definition and then turns the circle over. If the response is correct, the symbols or numbers on the backs of the circle section and the clothespin match.

Modifications: The student can be required to match synonyms, antonyms, or contractions with the appropriate section of the circle. Another variation is to have a word written in each section on the front with a corresponding picture in each section on the back. The student reads the word, clips a clothespin to the section, and turns over the circle to check the response by looking at the picture.

Poke Box

Feedback device: The student inserts a stylus into the hole in the Poke Box to indicate her or his response. If the answer is correct, the task card can be removed from the box because the area below the correct answer is cut out and offers no resistance to the stylus.

Materials, Directions, Modifications, and Example: The Poke Box, described in detail in Chapter 2, can be used to present various reading tasks, including synonyms, antonyms, vocabulary definitions, or comprehension questions for a selected reading passage.

Synonym Lotto

Feedback device: The correct answer is written on the back of each word card.

Materials: A large cardboard square, 6 squares across and 6 squares down, with a word written in each of the 36 squares; word cards containing synonyms for the words included on the large board and the correct responses written on the back (see Figure 8.3).

Directions: The student selects a word card and matches it with its synonym on the large board. After making the choice, the student turns over the word card to see whether the response is correct. The student continues until the entire board is covered.

FIGURE 8.3
Game board and cards for Synonym Lotto

LITTLE	ENDED	SMILED	CENT	WOMAN	TRAIL
GLAD	PRESENT	CRY	REPLY	PRETTY	SCARED
MAD	LARGE	BAG	CORRECT	DISTANT	FAST
NEARLY	GRANDMA	CHIEF	STONE	SPEAK	BEACH
HARD	BEGAN	FLAT	TRIP	SHOUT	ODD
WOODS	HURRY	WEARY	NEAR	HUNGRY	AUTO

Cards containing the following words with the appropriate synonym from the large square written on the back:

small	finished	grinned	penny	lady	path
happy	gift	weep	answer	beautiful	afraid
angry	big	pouch	right	faraway	quick
almost	Grandmother	leader	rock	talk	shore
difficult	started	level	journey	yell	strange
forest	rush	tired	close	starved	car

Modifications: The student can be required to match antonyms with words, words with pictures, contractions with contracted words, or words with definitions.

Tape Recorder Reading

Feedback device: The correct answers are provided on the tape.

Materials: A tape recording of 25 words numbered on the tape and separated by a pause between each word, and at the end of the tape a list of the correct responses; paper numbered from 1 to 25.

Directions: While listening to the tape recording, the student writes the sound heard at the beginning (or end) of each word. At the end of the 25 words, the student continues to listen to the tape to hear the correct answers and check the responses.

Modifications: The student can be instructed to write down vowel sounds, blends (in initial or final positions),

or digraphs. Another variation is to present a short reading passage on the tape. After listening to the selection, the student is instructed to turn off the recorder and write down the main ideas. Then the student can turn the recorder back on to check the work by listening to the reader's summary of the main ideas. Also, after listening to a reading selection on tape, the student can be presented with various comprehension questions, and the answers can be provided on tape. Another device that can be used to provide oral feedback is the Language Master. The student can read the word printed on the Language Master card and then run the card through the machine to hear the word read.

Comic Strips/Sentence Strips

Feedback device: The numbers to indicate correct sequence are written on the back of each section.

Materials: Laminated newspaper comic strips or sentence strips mounted on cardboard and cut into frames, with each frame numbered on the back to indicate its proper position in the sequence.

Directions: The student is given the mixed-up frames of the comic or sentence strip. The student reads the frames and then unscrambles them and arranges them in order. This develops and improves the student's ability to recognize and follow a sequence of happenings and the ability to anticipate the outcome of a situation. After arranging the frames in order, the student turns over the frames to see whether they are numbered in order, indicating the correct sequence.

Packaged Comprehension

Feedback device: The correct answers are provided on an answer key included in an envelope attached to the back of the folder.

Materials: Manila folder with a label or wrapper (such as a food can label or a candy bar wrapper) attached to the front and comprehension questions concerning the label or wrapper written inside the folder (e.g., What company makes the product? What does the product weigh?); an answer key in an envelope attached to the back of the folder.

Directions: The student reads the label or wrapper on the front of the folder and then opens the folder to read the comprehension questions. The student answers each question on a sheet of paper without rereading the label or wrapper and then checks the responses with the answers included in the answer key.

Modification: A brief reading selection or short story can be attached to the front of the folder instead of a label or wrapper. Comprehension questions concerning the reading passage are included inside the folder.

☀ COMMERCIAL READING PROGRAMS

Many commercial reading programs and materials are available for use with students who have learning problems. These materials can supplement one of the basic reading approaches to develop or improve specific skills, such as word attack or comprehension. This section presents several well-known commercial reading materials.

Edmark Reading Program

The *Edmark Reading Program* (published by PRO-ED) is designed to teach 150 sight words of varying parts of speech, plus the endings *ing, ed,* and *s,* to students with extremely limited skills. The student needs only to be able to repeat a word the teacher says and point to a response. The 227 lessons are of five formats: (1) pre-reading lessons that train the student on the match-to-sample format, (2) word recognition lessons of one to two words per lesson, (3) lessons in direction books that teach the student to follow printed directions, (4) lessons in matching pictures to phrases, and (5) lessons in a storybook in which the student orally reads 16 stories. All lessons are broken down into small, sequential steps, and reinforcement is provided. Pretests and review tests are included throughout the program, and procedures are given for charting student progress. After completing Level I of the *Edmark Reading Program,* the student may move into Level II, which introduces an additional 200 words and reinforces the 150 words previously learned. Compound words are introduced, and comprehension questions focus students' attention on the meaning within the two-page stories. Supplemental materials include spelling activities, supplemental worksheets, word bingo games, and homework activities.

Great Leaps Reading Program

Great Leaps Reading Program, developed by K. U. Campbell (published by Diarmuid), combines research-based instructional practices with powerful behavioral motivators to effectively remediate reading difficulties. Individual students work with a teacher, paraprofessional, or parent on phonics, sight phrases containing essential vocabulary, and motivating, age-appropriate stories for less than 10 minutes per day. The K–2 manual (Mercer & Campbell, 1997) also includes sound awareness and letter recognition activities. Student performance is charted on graphs. Each student makes goals, achieves success, and moves to the next step in the reading hierarchy. The program includes five levels (kindergarten through second grade, third through fifth grade, sixth through eighth grade, ninth through twelfth grade, and adult) and a collection of high-interest stories. Results of field testing with students with learning problems indicate consistent success at all age levels.

Learning Strategies Curriculum

The Learning Strategies Curriculum of the University of Kansas Center for Research on Learning (3061 Dole Center, Lawrence, KS 66045) is designed to improve a student's ability to cope with specific curriculum demands and to perform tasks independently. The learning strategies in the acquisition instructional strand enable students to gain information from written material. The *Word Identification Strategy* is aimed at quick decoding of multisyllabic words. The strategy is based on the premise that most words can be pronounced by identifying prefixes, suffixes, and stems, and by

Entertaining storybooks provide motivation to read.

following three short syllabication rules. The *Visual Imagery Strategy* improves reading comprehension by having the student form mental pictures of the events described in a passage. In the *Self-Questioning Strategy,* students form questions about key pieces of information in a passage, predict answers to those questions, and then read to find answers to the questions. Finally, the *Paraphrasing Strategy* is designed to improve comprehension by focusing attention on the important information of a passage. It directs students to read a limited section of material, ask themselves the main idea and the details of the section, and rephrase the information in their own words.

Learning Through Literature

Learning Through Literature (Dodds & Goodfellow, 1990/1991) includes 12 resource packages for teaching literature stories and poetry (kindergarten through third grade) and complete novels (third through eighth grade). Learning activities include brainstorming, exploring story grammar, word banks, process writing activities, research, and integrative curriculum activities. The four story-study packages each contain two 20-lesson thematic units in which discussion and ongoing activities develop understanding of story grammars. The eight novel-study packages each contain a single 15- to 20-lesson unit for concentrated study of one specific novel, and students participate in vocabulary exercises, discussion of background pertinent to the story, guided questioning and comprehension exercises, and story extension activities. Teacher materials include detailed lesson guides and blackline masters that provide background information, vocabulary, writing and research stimuli, and bibliographies.

Phonic Remedial Reading Lessons

Phonic Remedial Reading Lessons (Kirk et al., 1985) is a program designed to teach phonetic reading and word-attack skills to students who are reading below the third-grade level and need remedial assistance. The 77 lessons are divided into six parts and consist of words with a consistent phonic pattern. Part I introduces the most frequent sounds, including sounds of short vowels and consonants. Part II consists of two- and three-letter sequences that have a single sound. Part III includes integration of known symbols into consonant blends and common syllables. Part IV presents new configurations of sound-symbol associations. Part V provides exercises that cover exceptions to sounds previously taught. Part VI covers grammar concepts such as plurals, possessives, and past tense. The lessons emphasize learning the sounds of letters and blending letters together, and students are instructed to visualize, write, say, and hear the sounds simultaneously as each phoneme is introduced.

Phonological Awareness Training for Reading

Phonological Awareness Training for Reading (Torgesen & Bryant, 1994) is designed to increase the level of phonological awareness in youngsters and can be used with at-risk kindergartners to help prepare them for reading in first grade or with first or second graders who are having difficulty learning to read. The program takes about 12 to 14 weeks to complete if children are taught in short sessions three or four times a week. Children learn to hear the individual sounds in whole words as well as to blend individual sounds into words. All words in the program are presented on picture cards, and game boards are used to provide reinforcing activities. In the final phase of the program, children learn to generalize their acquired phonological awareness skills to reading and spelling simple words. A training manual contains instructions for all phases of the program and includes sample scripts for teaching specific concepts.

Specific Skill Series

The *Specific Skills Series* (Boning, 1998) includes exercise booklets designed to provide practice in reading comprehension skills for students reading at the prekindergarten- through eighth-grade level. The series includes nine separate skill strands: identifying inferences, getting the facts, using the context, drawing conclusions, getting the main idea, working with words, detecting the sequence, following directions, and locating the answer. The skill strands feature integrated language activities and emphasize critical reading and thinking skills. Students are allowed to work at their own pace, and the strands continue upward in sequential levels. Placement tests in each of the nine areas of reading comprehension are available.

TR Reading Comprehension Series

The *TR Reading Comprehension Series* (published by SRA) features a structured framework for teaching comprehension skills to remedial students in third through seventh grade who are reading two to three grades below level. The program consists of eight worktexts (readability level—low first grade to high fourth grade) that can be used with phonics/decoding programs and with graded readers. Each worktext contains 42 lessons that focus on the following areas of skill development: vocabulary, genres, topic and main idea, details, sequence, spatial relationships, contrast and comparison, cause and effect, critical and interpretive thinking, and study skills.

COMPUTER SOFTWARE PROGRAMS IN READING

Computer programs can be used effectively to develop basic skills in reading by providing varied drill and extra practice. Word identification skills as well as comprehension skills can be reinforced. Numerous software programs are available to reinforce sight words, expand vocabularies, provide drill in phonics, analyze words according to structural analysis, and test comprehension. Also, the teacher can use a computer to develop language experience lessons, store individual reading vocabulary tests, and produce cloze tests.

With recent technological advances, some currently available programs offer speech feedback and allow the reader to select any word on the screen for pronunciation by synthetic speech. CD-ROM equipment can play "talking books" that provide graphic images as well as digitized speech. In addition, hypermedia computer-based reading materials offer definitions and spoken pronunciation of unfamiliar words, animation and zoom-ins, full-motion graphics and video, and links to databases of related information (Boone, Higgins, Falba, & Langley, 1993). MacArthur and Haynes (1995) present a software system (Student Assistant for Learning from Text) for developing hypermedia versions of textbooks designed to help students compensate for their reading disabilities. Support features that enhance comprehension include speech synthesis, ready access to a glossary, highlighting of main ideas, questions embedded in the text at appropriate places, and summaries of important points.

Torgesen and Barker (1995) note that computer-assisted instruction and practice in reading can help students with learning problems learn to read more effectively by assisting them in acquiring accurate and fluent word identification skills. They describe computer programs that provide training in phonological awareness, specific context-free word identification, and reading of connected text. The following programs provide examples of available software that focus on reading skills.

Cloze-Plus

Cloze-Plus (produced by Milliken) develops reading comprehension skills and vocabulary through the use of structured cloze and context analysis activities. The structured cloze activities require the student to use context to complete syntax and to demonstrate comprehension. The vocabulary-in-context activities require the student to derive the meaning of a difficult or unfamiliar word by analyzing the information in the surrounding context. Both activities develop the ability to see word relationships and to derive meaning through the use of context clues. The program is designed for students in first through eighth grade, and it tracks 11 skills including same meaning/synonyms; opposite meaning/antonyms; association synthesis; categorization/classification; time/order; signal words, phrases/transitions; pronoun referents; similarities/ differences; form/function; conclusion/summary; and definition.

Let's Go Read

This series (produced by Edmark) incorporates both phonics and whole language methodologies to help students learn, practice, and apply the skills necessary to achieve reading readiness, decode hundreds of words, and comprehend imaginative stories. Level 1, *An Island Adventure,* for students in prekindergarten and kindergarten, presents more than 175 sequenced reading lessons that focus on letters and their sounds, word recognition, sounds within words, and building sentences. Students also expand their vocabulary as they learn new words in the context of pictures and sentences. Level 2, *An Ocean Adventure,* includes over 125 lessons in which students in kindergarten and first grade learn to identify and use beginning and ending blends, consonant digraphs, long vowel sounds, second sounds of letters, and the silent "e" rule. Both levels include direct participation in interactive books to build vocabulary and develop reading comprehension skills.

Reading Blaster

This series (produced by Knowledge Adventure) helps students master age-appropriate reading skills through problem-solving activities. In *Reading Blaster Ages 4–6,* a step-by-step approach is used to encourage students to read, learn sentence structures, recognize letters, use prepositions, and identify rhyming patterns. *Reading Blaster Ages 6–9* presents seven games and nine levels of difficulty to help students learn over 2,000 vocabulary words, silent letters and vowel blends, compound and rhyming words, and parts of speech. More than 75 mystery stories are included in *Reading Blaster Ages 9–12* to provide practice as students learn to read for details, find the main ideas, make inferences, draw conclusions, and build vocabulary. Finally, *Reading Blaster Vocabulary Ages 9–12* features six activities to teach students how to find the meaning and pronunciation of over 2,000 words through context clues, prefixes, suffixes, and root words.

The Reading Solution

The Reading Solution (produced by Milliken) is designed for students in fourth through twelfth grade and presents 72 reading selections (biographies, legends, short stories, and nonfiction articles) that are tailored to an individual student's grade level. Because the reading selections are vocabulary controlled by reading level, the program is appropriate for mature students reading at lower levels. The reading material is presented by line or by paragraph to improve reading rate, and the topics can be presented in a timed or untimed format. Questions specifically designed to improve comprehension are presented at the conclusion of each segment. Each level provides measurement of 25 specific comprehension skills in the areas of literal understanding, interpretation, analysis, evaluation, and appreciation. Thus, this program provides the opportunity to practice major comprehension skills and increase reading speed at the same time.

SuperSonic Phonics

SuperSonic Phonics (produced by Curriculum Associates) is an intensive phonics program designed for new readers and readers who need to strengthen their phonics skills. The program helps the student develop critical symbol-to-sound and decoding skills to enhance automatic word recognition and phonics application. The student receives clearly pronounced computer audio instructions and uses the computer mouse to complete each exercise. A repeat button allows the student to hear a sound or word as often as needed. Based on performance, the student automatically is branched to reinforcement activities (such as a reward game) or to more challenging activities. Level 1 focuses on consonants and short vowels; Level 2 includes short vowels, long vowels, silent *e,* consonant digraphs, and consonant blends; and Level 3 features short and long vowel review, vowel *r* words, vowel combination words, and two-syllable words. A management system is included that provides student performance reports.

☀ REFERENCES

Adams, M. J. (1990). *Beginning to read: Thinking and learning about print.* Cambridge, MA: MIT Press.

Adams, M. J., & Bruck, M. (1995). Resolving the "great debate." *American Educator, 19,* 7, 10–20.

Allen, R. V., & Allen, C. (1982). *Language experience activities* (2nd ed.). Boston: Houghton Mifflin.

Altwerger, B., Edelsky, C., & Flores, B. M. (1987). Whole language: What's new? *The Reading Teacher, 41,* 144–154.

Beck, I. L., & Juel, C. (1995). The role of decoding in learning to read. *American Educator, 19,* 8, 21–25, 39–42.

Bloomfield, L., & Barnhart, C. L. (1961). *Let's read—A linguistic approach.* Detroit, MI: Wayne State University Press.

Bond, G. L., & Dykstra, R. (1967). The cooperative research program in first-grade reading instruction. *Reading Research Quarterly, 2,* 5–142.

Boning, R. A. (1998). *Specific skill series* (5th ed.). DeSoto, TX: SRA.

Boone, R., Higgins, K., Falba, C., & Langley, W. (1993). Cooperative text: Reading and writing in a hypermedia environment. *LD Forum, 18*(3), 29–37.

Browder, D. M., & Snell, M. E. (1993). Functional academics. In M. E. Snell (Ed.), *Instruction of students with severe disabilities* (4th ed., pp. 442–479). Upper Saddle River, NJ: Merrill/Prentice Hall.

Carbo, M. L. (1978). A word imprinting technique for children with severe memory disorders. *Teaching Exceptional Children, 11,* 3–5.

Carbo, M. L. (1987). Matching reading styles: Correcting ineffective instruction. *Educational Leadership, 45*(2), 55–62.

Carnine, D., Silbert, J., & Kameenui, E. J. (1997). *Direct instruction reading* (3rd ed.). Upper Saddle River, NJ: Merrill/Prentice Hall.

Chall, J. S. (1983). *Learning to read: The great debate* (Updated edition). New York: McGraw-Hill.

Chall, J. S. (1987). Reading and early childhood education: The critical issues. *Principal, 66*(5), 6–9.

Chall, J. S. (1989). *Learning to Read: The Great Debate* 20 years later—A response to "Debunking the great phonics myth." *Phi Delta Kappan, 70,* 521–538.

Chiang, B., & Ford, M. (1990). Whole language alternatives for students with learning disabilities. *LD Forum, 16*(1), 31–34.

Clay, M. M. (1985). *The early detection of reading difficulties* (3rd ed.). Auckland, New Zealand: Heinemann Educational Books.

DeFord, D. E., Pinnell, G. S., Lyons, C. A., & Young, P. (1988). *Reading Recovery: Volume IX, Report of the follow-up studies.* Columbus, OH: Ohio State University.

Dixon, R., Carnine, D., & Kameenui, E. J. (1992). *Curriculum guidelines for diverse learners* (Monograph for National Center to Improve the Tools of Educators). Eugene: University of Oregon.

Dodds, T., & Goodfellow, F. (1990/1991). *Learning through literature.* DeSoto, TX: SRA.

Dykstra, R. (1968). Summary of the second-grade phase of the cooperative research program in primary reading instruction. *Reading Research Quarterly, 4,* 49–70.

Ekwall, E. E., & Shanker, J. L. (1988). *Diagnosis and remediation of the disabled reader* (3rd ed.). Boston: Allyn & Bacon.

Engelmann, S., Hanner, S., & Johnson, G. (1999). *Corrective reading.* DeSoto, TX: SRA.

Engelmann, S., & Bruner, E. C. (1995). *Reading mastery.* DeSoto, TX: SRA.

Englert, C. S., & Mariage, T. V. (1991). Making students partners in the comprehension process: Organizing the reading "POSSE." *Learning Disability Quarterly, 14,* 123–138.

Englert, C. S., Tarrant, K. L., Mariage, T. V., & Oxer, T. (1994). Lesson talk as the work of reading groups: The effectiveness of two interventions. *Journal of Learning Disabilities, 27,* 165–185.

Faas, L. A. (1980). *Children with learning problems: A handbook for teachers.* Boston: Houghton Mifflin.

Fernald, G. (1943). *Remedial techniques in basic school subjects.* New York: McGraw-Hill.

Fernald, G. (1988). *Remedial techniques in basic school subjects.* Austin, TX: PRO-ED.

Folk, M. C., & Campbell, J. (1978). Teaching functional reading to the TMR. *Education and Training of the Mentally Retarded, 13,* 322–326.

Fry, E. (1977). Fry's readability graph: Clarifications, validity, and extension to level 17. *Journal of Reading, 21,* 242–252.

Gartland, D. (1995). Reading instruction. In P. J. Schloss, M. A. Smith, & C. N. Schloss, *Instructional methods for adolescents with learning and behavior problems* (2nd ed., pp. 225–254). Boston: Allyn & Bacon.

Gersten, R., & Dimino, J. (1993). Visions and revisions: A special education perspective on the whole language controversy. *Remedial and Special Education, 14*(4), 5–13.

Gillingham, A., & Stillman, B. (1970). *Remedial training for children with specific disability in reading, spelling, and penmanship* (7th ed.). Cambridge, MA: Educators Publishing Service.

Glass, E. W., & Glass, G. G. (1978). *Glass analysis for decoding only.* New York: Easier to Learn.

Goodman, K. S. (1986). *What's whole in whole language?* Portsmouth, NH: Heinemann.

Grant, R. (1993). Strategic training for using text headings to improve students' processing of content. *Journal of Reading, 36,* 482–488.

Hall, M. (1981). *Teaching reading as a language experience* (3rd ed.). Upper Saddle River, NJ: Merrill/Prentice Hall.

Harris, A. J., & Sipay, E. R. (1990). *How to increase reading ability: A guide to developmental and remedial methods* (9th ed.). New York: Longman.

Heckelman, R. G. (1969). The neurological impress method of remedial reading instruction. *Academic Therapy, 4,* 277–282.

Hefferan, M., & Parker, S. (1991). *B.A.L.A.N.C.E.: Blending all learning activities nurtures classroom excellence.* Orlando, FL: FDLRS/Action.

Heilman, A. W., Blair, T. R., & Rupley, W. H. (1998). *Principles and practices of teaching reading* (9th ed.). Upper Saddle River, NJ: Merrill/Prentice Hall.

Henry, M. K., & Rome, S. O'C. (1995). Results of Orton-Gillingham tutoring on students with reading disabilities: A retrospective study. In C. W. McIntyre & J. S. Pickering (Eds.), *Clinical studies of multisensory structured language education for students with dyslexia and related disorders* (pp. 138–143). Salem, OR: International Multisensory Structured Language Education Council.

Herman, R., & Stringfield, S. (1995, April). *Ten promising programs for educating disadvantaged students: Evidence of impact.* Paper presented at the meeting of the American Educational Research Association, San Francisco, CA.

Hurford, D. P., Schauf, J. D., Bunce, L., Blaich, T., & Moore, K. (1994). Early identification of children at risk for reading disabilities. *Journal of Learning Disabilities, 27,* 371–382.

Idol, L. (1987). A critical thinking map to improve content area comprehension of poor readers. *Remedial and Special Education, 8*(4), 28–40.

Idol, L., & Croll, V. J. (1987). Story-mapping training as a means of improving reading comprehension. *Learning Disability Quarterly, 10,* 214–229.

King, J. A. (1994). Meeting the educational needs of at-risk students: A cost analysis of three models. *Educational Evaluation and Policy Analysis, 16*(1), 1–19.

Kirk, S. A., Kirk, W. D., & Minskoff, E. (1985). *Phonic remedial reading lessons.* Novato, CA: Academic Therapy.

Langford, K., Slade, K., & Barnett, A. (1974). An explanation of impress techniques in remedial reading. *Academic Therapy, 9,* 309–319.

Langone, J. (1990). *Teaching students with mild and moderate learning problems.* Boston: Allyn & Bacon.

Lee, D. M., & Allen, R. V. (1963). *Learning to read through experience* (2nd ed.). New York: Appleton-Century-Crofts.

Lenz, B. K., & Hughes, C. A. (1990). A word identification strategy for adolescents with learning disabilities. *Journal of Learning Disabilities, 33,* 149–158, 163.

Liberman, I. Y., & Liberman, A. M. (1990). Whole language vs. code emphasis: Underlying assumptions and their implications for reading instruction. *Annals of Dyslexia, 40,* 51–76.

Lyon, G. R. (1995). Research initiatives in learning disabilities: Contributions from scientists supported by the National Institute of Child Health and Human Development. *Journal of Child Neurology, 10*(Suppl. 1), 120–126.

Lyon, G. R. (1998). Overview of reading and literacy initiatives (Report to Committee on Labor and Human Resources, U.S. Senate). Bethesda, MD: National Institute of Child Health and Human Development, National Institutes of Health.

Lyon, G. R. (1999). Education research: Is what we don't know hurting our children? (Report to House Science Committee, Subcommittee on Basic Research, U.S. House of Representatives). Bethesda, MD: National Institute of Child Health and Human Development, National Institutes of Health.

MacArthur, C. A., & Haynes, J. B. (1995). Student assistant for learning from text (SALT): A hypermedia reading aid. *Journal of Learning Disabilities, 28,* 150–159.

Madden, N. A., Slavin, R. E., Karweit, N. L., Dolan, L. J., & Wasik, B. A. (1993). Success for All: Longitudinal effects of a restructuring program for inner-city elementary schools. *American Educational Research Journal, 30,* 123–148.

Maskel, S., & Felton, R. (1995). Analysis of achievement at the Hill Learning Development Center: 1990–1994. In C. W. McIntyre & J. S. Pickering (Eds.), *Clinical studies of multisensory structured language education for students with dyslexia and related disorders* (pp. 129–137). Salem, OR: International Multisensory Structured Language Education Council.

Mastropieri, M. A. (1988). Using the keyword method. *Teaching Exceptional Children, 20*(2), 4–8.

Mastropieri, M. A., Scruggs, T. E., & Fulk, B. J. M. (1990). Teaching abstract vocabulary with the keyword method: Effects on recall and comprehension. *Journal of Learning Disabilities, 23,* 92–96, 107.

Mather, N. (1992). Whole language reading instruction for students with learning disabilities: Caught in the cross fire. *Learning Disabilities Research & Practice, 7,* 87–95.

Mercer, C. D., & Campbell, K. U. (1997). *Great leaps reading program: Grades K–2.* Gainesville, FL: Diarmuid.

Miccinati, J. (1981). Teach reading disabled students to perceive distinctive features in words. *Journal of Learning Disabilities, 14,* 140–142.

Norton, D. E. (1992). *The impact of literature-based reading.* Upper Saddle River, NJ: Merrill/Prentice Hall.

Ogle, D. (1986). K-W-L: A teaching model that develops active reading of expository text. *The Reading Teacher, 39,* 564–570.

Orton, J. L. (1976). *A guide to teaching phonics.* Cambridge, MA: Educators Publishing Service.

Orton, S. T. (1937). *Reading, writing, and speech problems in children.* New York: W. W. Norton.

O'Shea, L. J., & O'Shea, D. J. (1988). Using repeated reading. *Teaching Exceptional Children, 20*(2), 26–29.

Palinscar, A. S., & Brown, A. L. (1986). Interactive teaching to promote independent learning from text. *The Reading Teacher, 39*(8), 771–777.

Palinscar, A. S., & Brown, A. L. (1988). Teaching and practicing thinking skills to promote comprehension in the context of group problem solving. *Remedial and Special Education, 9*(1), 53–59.

Pinnell, G. S. (1990). Success for low achievers through Reading Recovery. *Educational Leadership, 48*(1), 17–21.

Pinnell, G. S., DeFord, D. E., & Lyons, C. A. (1988). *Reading Recovery: Early intervention for at-risk first graders.* Arlington, CA: Educational Research Service.

Polloway, E. A., & Patton, J. R. (1997). *Strategies for teaching learners with special needs* (6th ed.). Upper Saddle River, NJ: Merrill/Prentice Hall.

Polloway, E. A., & Polloway, C. H. (1981). Survival words for disabled readers. *Academic Therapy, 16,* 443–448.

Polloway, E. A., & Smith, T. E. C. (1992). *Language instruction for students with disabilities* (2nd ed.). Denver, CO: Love.

Pressley, M., & Rankin, J. (1994). More about whole language methods of reading instruction for students at risk for early reading failure. *Learning Disabilities Research & Practice, 9,* 157–168.

Robinson, F. P. (1961). *Effective study.* New York: Harper & Row.

Roe, B. D., Stoodt, B. D., & Burns, P. C. (1995). *Secondary school reading instruction: The content areas* (5th ed.). Boston: Houghton Mifflin.

Rupley, W. H., & Blair, T. R. (1989). *Reading diagnosis and remediation: Classroom and clinic* (3rd ed.). Upper Saddle River, NJ: Merrill/Prentice Hall.

Samuels, S. J. (1979). The method of repeated readings. *The Reading Teacher, 32,* 403–408.

Schumm, J. S., Vaughn, S., Haager, D., & Klinger, J. K. (1994). Literacy instruction for mainstreamed students: What suggestions are provided in basal reading series? *Remedial and Special Education, 15,* 14–20.

Shanker, J. L., & Ekwall, E. E. (1998). *Locating and correcting reading difficulties* (7th ed.). Upper Saddle River, NJ: Merrill/Prentice Hall.

Shinn, M. R., Good, R. H., Knutson, N., Tilly, W. D., & Collins, V. L. (1992). Curriculum-based measurement of oral reading fluency: A confirmatory analysis of its relation to reading. *School Psychology Review, 21,* 459–479.

Simmons, D. C., Chard, D., & Kameenui, E. J. (1994). Translating research into basal reading programs: Applications of curriculum design. *LD Forum, 19*(4), 9–13.

Simmons, D. C., Gunn, B., Smith, S. B., & Kameenui, E. J. (1994). Phonological awareness: Applications of instructional design. *LD Forum, 19*(2), 7–10.

Slavin, R. E., Madden, N. A., Dolan, L. J., Wasik, B. A., Ross, S., & Smith, L. (1994). *Success for All: Longitudinal effects of systemic school-by-school reform in seven districts.* Paper presented at the meeting of the American Educational Research Association, New Orleans, LA.

Slavin, R. E., Madden, N. A., Karweit, N. L., Dolan, L. J., & Wasik, B. A. (1992). *Success for All: A relentless approach to prevention and early intervention in elementary schools.* Arlington, CA: Educational Research Service.

Slingerland, B. (1981). *A multi-sensory approach to language arts for specific language disability children: A guide for elementary teachers.* Cambridge, MA: Educators Publishing Service.

Stahl, S. A., & Miller, P. D. (1989). Whole language and language experience approaches for beginning reading: A quantitative research synthesis. *Review of Educational Research, 59,* 87–116.

Stahl, S. A., Osborn, J., & Lehr, F. (1990). *Beginning to read: Thinking and learning about print—A summary.* Urbana-Champaign, IL: University of Illinois Center for the Study of Reading.

Stallings, J. A. (1974). *Follow Through classroom observation evaluation 1972–1973* (Executive Summary SRI Project URU-7370). Menlo Park, CA: Stanford Research Institute.

Stanovich, K. E. (1994). Constructivism in reading education. *The Journal of Special Education, 28,* 259–274.

Stewart, S. R., & Cegelka, P. T. (1995). Teaching reading and spelling. In P. T. Cegelka & W. H. Berdine, *Effective instruction for students with learning difficulties* (pp. 265–301). Boston: Allyn & Bacon.

Thorpe, H. W., & Borden, K. F. (1985). The effect of multisensory instruction upon the on-task behavior and word reading accuracy of learning disabled students. *Journal of Learning Disabilities, 18,* 279–286.

Torgesen, J. K., & Barker, T. A. (1995). Computers as aids in the prevention and remediation of reading disabilities. *Learning Disability Quarterly, 18,* 76–87.

Torgesen, J. K., & Bryant, B. R. (1994). *Phonological awareness training for reading.* Austin, TX: PRO-ED.

Torgesen, J. K., Wagner, R. K., & Rashotte, C. A. (1994). Longitudinal studies of phonological processing and reading. *Journal of Learning Disabilities, 27,* 276–286.

Traub, N., & Bloom, F. (1978). *Recipe for reading.* Cambridge, MA: Educators Publishing Service.

Weinstein, G., & Cooke, N. L. (1992). The effects of two repeated reading interventions on generalization of fluency. *Learning Disability Quarterly, 15,* 21–28.

## CHAPTER 9

Assessing and Teaching Spelling

Spelling is the forming of words through the traditional arrangement of letters. Young children developmentally move through stages of invented spelling in which different types of spelling strategies are used. According to Gentry (1982), the five stages include the following characteristics:

Stage 1: *Precommunicative spelling.* The child uses scribbles, letters, and letterlike forms and shows a preference for uppercase letters. There is no understanding of phoneme-grapheme correspondence. This stage is typical of preschoolers, ages 3 through 5.

Stage 2: *Semiphonetic spelling.* The child has some awareness that letters are used to represent sounds and may use abbreviated one-, two-, or three-letter spellings to represent an entire word (e.g., *DA* for *day,* *LF* for *laugh*). Semiphonetic spellers include 5- and 6-year-olds.

Stage 3: *Phonetic spelling.* The child represents all essential sound features in spelling a word and chooses letters on the basis of sound (e.g., *PEKT* for *peeked, KOM* for *come*). Typically, 6-year-old children are phonetic spellers.

Stage 4: *Transitional spelling.* The child begins to use conventional alternatives for representing sounds and includes a vowel in every syllable (e.g., *AFTER-NEWN* for *afternoon, TRUBAL* for *trouble*). Many words are spelled correctly, but words with irregular spellings continue to be misspelled. Transitional spellers generally are around 7 or 8 years old.

Stage 5: *Correct spelling.* The child spells many words correctly and applies the basic rules of the English orthographic system. The child recognizes when words look incorrect and can consider alternative spellings. Youngsters typically reach this stage by age 8 or 9.

Formal spelling instruction, typically introduced at the beginning of the second grade, facilitates growth in Stage 5. The student extends knowledge of word structure and learns irregular spelling patterns. The ability to spell is essential because it allows one to read written words correctly. In addition, incorrect spelling often results in an unfavorable impression, and the poor speller may be considered uneducated or careless.

The English language presents inconsistent relationships between phonemes (speech sounds) and graphemes (written symbols). There are 26 letters in the alphabet; however, about 44 phonemes are used in English speech. Moreover, there are more than 500 spellings to represent the 44 phonemes (Tompkins, 1998). Thus, differences exist between the spelling of various words and the way the words are pronounced. Many students with learning problems have difficulty mastering the regular spelling system, and inconsistent spelling patterns make learning to spell even more complex.

Students who have trouble recognizing words in reading usually have poor spelling skills as well (Carpenter & Miller, 1982; Shanker & Ekwall, 1998). However, some students are able to read words but not spell them. Thus, it appears that spelling a word may be more difficult than reading a word. Reading is a *decoding* process in which the reader receives clues (such as context) for word recognition. Spelling is an *encoding* process in which the learner must respond without the benefit of a complete visual stimulus; thus, there are fewer clues. Spelling requires concentration on each letter of every word, while in reading it is not necessary to know the exact spelling of words or to attend to every letter. Some students make the same types of errors in both reading and spelling. For example, a phonetic speller may mispronounce phonetically irregular words when reading. In addition, a student who lacks phonetic word-attack skills in reading may not be able to spell because of poor phonetic skills. Whiting and Jarrico (1980) verified that normal students spell with an accuracy from 70 to 100 percent at grade level and found that the normal reader tends to make spelling errors that are readable, good phonetic equivalents of the dictated word.

To spell a word correctly, the student must apply various abilities including being able to read the word, possess knowledge and skill in certain relationships of phonics and structural analysis, apply phonics generalizations, visualize the appearance of the word, retrieve the word from memory, and use the motor capability to write the word. Spelling errors may result from confused recall of spelling rules (*takeing* for *taking*) or be related to insertion of unneeded letters (*umberella* for *umbrella*), omission of needed letters (*famly* for *family*), substitution of letters (*kome* for *come*), phonetic spelling of irregular words (*laf* for *laugh*), directional confusion (*was* for *saw*), vowels in unaccented syllables (*cottin* for *cotton*), *r*-controlled vowels (*dert* for *dirt*), letter orientation confusion (*doy* for *boy*), and reversed letter sequences (*aminals* for *animals*) (Poteet, 1980). Thus, spelling difficulties may stem from problems in visual memory, auditory memory, auditory and visual discrimination, attention deficits, or motor skills.

ASSESSMENT OF SPELLING SKILLS

A variety of techniques assess the student's spelling performance. Also, specific patterns of spelling errors may be determined. Spelling assessment can include the use of standardized and criterion-referenced tests as well as informal assessment techniques. In choosing spelling assessment techniques, the teacher should know what the test measures and its limitations, supplement the test where possible with other measures, and use informal evaluation techniques to gain specific information for planning a remedial program.

Formal Spelling Assessment

Standardized spelling tests (achievement and diagnostic) are norm-referenced, whereas other published measures of spelling are criterion-referenced. This section presents achievement tests, diagnostic tests, and criterion-referenced tests that can be used to assess spelling skills.

Achievement and Diagnostic Tests   Achievement tests that contain spelling subtests provide an estimate of the student's general spelling ability. Achievement tests assess spelling by two procedures: recall and recognition. On tests using recall, the student must write words presented orally and used in sentences. On tests using recognition, the student selects the correctly spelled word from several choices. Recall items are related to the writing stage of the writing process, whereas recognition items are essentially proofreading and are related to the editing stage

(McLoughlin & Lewis, 1994). Achievement tests yield a single score that is compared with the standardized norms and converted to a grade-equivalent score. Thus, achievement tests provide a general survey measure and may identify students who need corrective instruction and further diagnosis. Some commonly used achievement tests that include spelling subtests include the following:

- *Iowa Tests of Basic Skills* (Hoover, Hieronymus, Frisbie, & Dunbar, 1996). Assesses ability to choose the correctly spelled word from four words after hearing the word read.
- *Kaufman Test of Educational Achievement* (Kaufman & Kaufman, 1998). Assesses ability to spell 50 increasingly difficult words, each of which is said by the examiner and used in a sentence.
- *Peabody Individual Achievement Test—Revised* (Markwardt, 1998). Assesses ability to identify the correct spelling of a word after hearing the word pronounced.
- *Wide Range Achievement Test—3* (Wilkinson, 1994). Assesses skill in copying marks onto paper, writing one's name, and writing single words from dictation.

Diagnostic tests provide detailed information about the student's performance in various spelling skills. These tests are aimed at determining the student's strengths and weaknesses. Two diagnostic spelling tests are presented in Table 9.1.

Criterion-Referenced Tests   Whereas standardized norm-referenced tests (achievement and diagnostic) *compare* a student's performance with the scores of those in the norm population, criterion-referenced tests *describe* performance in terms of fixed criteria. Thus, criterion-referenced tests mainly aid in specific instructional planning, rather than determining grade-level scores or percentile ranks. The teacher can use criterion-referenced spelling tests to determine whether a student has mastered specific spelling instructional objectives (e.g., *wh* spelling, contractions, or vocational words). The teacher determines what skills the student has learned and what skills still must be taught. Also, an objective measure of progress is provided as the student moves from task to task and current performance is compared with previous performance.

TABLE 9.1

Diagnostic and criterion-referenced spelling tests

Test	Age/Grade Level
Diagnostic Tests	
Diagnostic Spelling Potential Test (Arena, 1981)	7 years–adult
The test measures traditional spelling, word recognition, visual recognition, and auditory-visual recognition. The four 90-item subtests take about 25 to 40 minutes to administer. Raw scores from each subtest can be converted to standard scores, percentiles, and grade ratings.	
Test of Written Spelling—4 (Larsen, Hammill, & Moats, 1999)	1st–12th grade
This dictated word test consists of 100 words chosen from ten basal spelling series. The test assesses the student's ability to spell words that have readily predictable spellings in sound-letter patterns as well as words whose spellings are less predictable (spelling demons). The test can be administered to individuals or small groups in about 20 minutes and yields standard scores, percentiles, spelling ages, and grade equivalents. Two equivalent forms are available.	
Criterion-Referenced Tests	
Brigance Diagnostic Comprehensive Inventory of Basic Skills—Revised (Brigance, 1999)	Kindergarten–9th grade
The test contains a section that assesses spelling skills arranged in a developmental and sequential hierarchy. Tests include spelling-dictation grade placement, initial consonants, initial clusters, suffixes, and prefixes. Also, the reference skills section contains a test on the skill of dictionary use. The instructional objectives related to each test are defined clearly. In addition to determining the student's level of achievement, the results can help the teacher develop individualized programs.	
Diagnostic Spelling Test (Kottmeyer, 1970)	2nd–6th grade
The test measures specific phonics and structural spelling elements (e.g., doubled final consonants, nonphonetic spelling, and *th* spelling). The examiner says a word and a sentence using the word, and the student is required to write the word. The two 32-item tests (one for second and third grades, and one for fourth grade and above) are designed so that each item measures a particular spelling element. A grade score is computed from the total number of correct spellings. Specific information on skills not yet mastered is obtained through an analysis of the student's errors.	

Two criterion-referenced spelling tests are presented in Table 9.1.

Informal Spelling Assessment

The teacher can obtain diagnostic information through structured observation and evaluation of the student's attitudes, written work, and oral responses. Attitudes toward spelling and willingness to use a dictionary may be noted, as well as the student's work habits and ability to handle frustration. Analysis of written work can provide information about handwriting problems that are causing errors (such as letter forms or spacing), specific types of errors, range of the student's vocabulary, and knowledge of spelling rules. In addition, the teacher should observe the student's oral responses and note problems in pronunciation, articulation, and dialect. Oral spelling responses also can indicate phonics ability and method of spelling words orally (e.g., as units, by letter, by digraphs, or by syllables).

The spelling scope and sequence skills list presented in Appendix A can be used to devise informal assessment measures and to determine appropriate instructional objectives as the student progresses in spelling. The following informal assessment techniques are discussed: dictated spelling test, informal spelling inventory, curriculum-based measurement, spelling error analysis, cloze procedure, probes, and modality testing.

Dictated Spelling Test   The dictated spelling test is a commonly used procedure for assessing various skills in spelling and determining spelling grade level. Words can be selected from any graded word list; the student's performance indicates the spelling grade level. Stephens, Hartman, and Lucas (1982) present sample assessment tasks that use dictated word lists of increasing difficulty. The instructional level is determined when the student achieves 70 to 90 percent accuracy. Dictated word lists also can assess skills in areas such as phoneme-grapheme association *(like, bike, hike)*, spelling generalizations (*stories, cries, tries*), homonyms *(pain, pane; pear, pair)*, and functional words *(menu, restaurant, cashier)*. The dictated test presented in Table 9.2 assesses selected spelling objectives for students in second and third grades. Through error analysis the teacher can readily determine areas of weakness.

The student's proficiency in spelling frequently used words and words that often are misspelled also can be determined. Shanker and Ekwall (1998) note that the 100 highest frequency words account for 60 percent of the words used in early writing. They also report that the following eight words represent 18 percent of all the words used in writing: *the, of, and, a, to, is, in,* and *you.* Moreover, Kuska, Webster, and Elford (1964) present a list of commonly misspelled words that are linguistically irregular and do not follow spelling rules (e.g., *ache, fasten, nickel, scratch,* and *double*).

Informal Spelling Inventory   An informal spelling inventory (ISI) can be used to determine the student's approximate grade level in spelling achievement. An ISI can be constructed by selecting a sample of words from spelling books in a basal spelling series (Mann, Suiter, & McClung, 1992). About 15 words should be chosen from the first-grade book and 20 words from each book for second through eighth grade. Random selection is obtained by dividing the total number of words at each level by 20. For example, 300 words at each level divided by 20 equals 15; therefore, every 15th word should be included in the ISI. For students in fourth grade and below, testing should begin with the first-level words. For students in fifth grade and above, assessment should start with words at the third level.

The test is administered in a dictated-word format. The teacher says the word, uses it in a sentence, and repeats the word. Some students prefer for only the word to be given (without a sentence), and M. R. Shinn, Tindal, and Stein (1988) suggest that a 7-second interval between words is sufficient. Testing ends when the student responds incorrectly to six consecutive words. The achievement level is the highest level at which the student responds correctly to 90 to 100 percent of the items, and the instructional level is the highest level at which the student scores 75 to 89 percent correct. Various errors made on the ISI can be analyzed to provide additional diagnostic information.

Curriculum-Based Measurement   In curriculum-based measurement of spelling skills, rate samples on words from a given spelling curriculum are used to measure the student's spelling skills. The assessment process begins with the selection of appropriate word lists. Tindal and Marston (1990) note that the word lists can reflect a phonic-regularity base (i.e., words with consistency or generalizability of the grapheme-phoneme relationships) or a frequency base (i.e., words that appear frequently in writing). Wesson (1987) suggests that the words can be from a given spelling curriculum level or from a new-words list for a particular reading series. The words can be selected randomly by printing all words in the test item pool on index cards, shuffling the cards before each measurement, and randomly picking ones to present during the measurement task.

The type of response to the spelling task can be either a selection response or a production response (Tindal & Marston, 1990). In word or sentence editing, an incorrectly spelled word is underlined or a blank space representing a specific word is presented in a phrase, and the student must select the correct word from several options to replace the underlined word or to fill in the blank. For example:

1. Her dress had a <u>stane</u> on it.
   a. staen   b. stain   c. stan   d. stene
2. The wind _____ his hat away.
   a. bled   b. blew   c. bliew   d. blued

When the teacher orally presents words from a list, the student must produce the spelling of the

TABLE 9.2
A dictated spelling test and objectives

Spelling Words	Spelling Objectives	Spelling Words Used in Sentences
1. man 2. pit 3. dug 4. web 5. dot	short vowels and selected consonants	The *man* is big. The *pit* in the fruit was hard. We *dug* a hole. She saw the spider's *web*. Don't forget to *dot* the i.
6. mask 7. drum	words beginning or ending with consonant blends	On Halloween the child wore a *mask*. He beat the *drum* in the parade.
8. line 9. cake	consonant-vowel-consonant-silent *e*	Get in *line* for lunch. We had a birthday *cake*.
10. coat 11. rain	two vowels together	Put on your winter *coat*. Take an umbrella in the *rain*.
12. ice 13. large	variant consonant sounds for *c* and *g*	*Ice* is frozen water. This is a *large* room.
14. mouth 15. town 16. boy	words containing vowel diphthongs	Open your *mouth* to brush your teeth. We went to *town* to shop. The *boy* and girl went to school.
17. bikes 18. glasses	plurals	The children got new *bikes* for their birthdays. Get some *glasses* for the drinks.
19. happy 20. monkey	short *i* sounds of *y*	John is very *happy* now. We saw a *monkey* at the zoo.
21. war 22. dirt	words with *r*-controlled vowels	Bombs were used in the *war*. The pigs were in the *dirt*.
23. foot 24. moon	two sounds of *oo*	Put the shoe on your *foot*. Three men walked on the *moon*.
25. light 26. knife	words with silent letters	Turn on the *light* so we can see. Get a fork and *knife*.
27. pill	final consonant doubled	The doctor gave me a *pill*.
28. bat 29. batter	consonant-vowel-consonant pattern in which final consonant is doubled before adding ending	The baseball player got a new *bat*. The *batter* hit a home run.
30. didn't 31. isn't	contractions	They *didn't* want to come. It *isn't* raining today.
32. take 33. taking	final *e* dropped before adding suffix	Please *take* off your coat. He is *taking* me to the show.
34. any 35. could	nonphonetic spellings	I did not have *any* lunch. Maybe you *could* go on a trip.
36. ate 37. eight 38. blue 39. blew	homonyms	Mary *ate* breakfast at home. There are *eight* children in the family. The sky is *blue*. The wind *blew* away the hat.
40. baseball	compound words	They played *baseball* outside.

word during the dictation task. The teacher dictates words for 2 minutes by saying each word twice and using homonyms in a sentence. There should be a 7-second interval between words for students in fourth through eighth grade and 10-second intervals for younger students and those with fine motor difficulties. When a production response is required, scoring can be in terms of number of words spelled correctly or number of letters in correct sequence. The latter strategy focuses on successive pairs of letters, and the blank spaces preceding the first letter and following the last letter are included in counting the pairs of letter sequences. Thus, for a word spelled correctly, the number of correct letter sequences will be one more than there are letters in the word. For example:

1. Correct spelling: l a z y (five correct letter sequences)
2. Misspelling: l a s y (three correct and two incorrect letter sequences)

Deno, Mirkin, and Wesson (1984) suggest that the instructional level is 20 to 39 correct letter sequences for students in first and second grades and 40 to 59 correct letter sequences for students in third through sixth grade. They note that the long-range goal should be 60 to 80 correct letter sequences for students in first and second grades and 80 to 140 correct letter sequences for students in third through sixth grade. An individualized error analysis can help establish appropriate instruction.

The teacher can test all students in a grade or class and develop a box plot of the entire group (see Chapter 3). Table 9.3 presents curriculum-based measurement procedures for administering and scoring spelling word lists. Poor spellers (i.e., more than one standard deviation below the mean for the group) can be identified, and instructional planning decisions can be made. A graph of a student's weekly performance in spelling can be used to evaluate instruction (see Figure 9.1).

Spelling Error Analysis   A spelling error analysis chart can be used to provide a profile of spelling strengths and weaknesses. Each time the student makes a specific error, it is recorded on the chart. Spelling errors can be analyzed in written compositions as well as on dictated tests. Taylor and Kidder (1988) examined the misspellings of first- through eighth-grade students and found that

TABLE 9.3
Curriculum-based measurement procedures for administering and scoring spelling word lists

Step 1:	Randomly select 20 words from the goal-level spelling curriculum material.
Step 2:	Present each student with lined, numbered paper.
Step 3:	Provide directions and administer the spelling test by pronouncing each word on the list in isolation, in a sentence or phrase, and again in isolation. Dictate words at a pace of one every 7 to 10 seconds, or sooner if all students finish. Do not acknowledge questions and ignore requests (such as "slow down"). Terminate testing after 2 minutes.
Step 4:	Score performance in terms of words and letter sequences correct.
Step 5:	Develop box plots of the entire group according to words spelled correctly and letters spelled correctly (see Chapter 3).
Step 6:	Analyze the individual protocols scored according to correct letter sequences. Place students in appropriate instructional groups.
Step 7:	Begin instruction based on student error patterns.
Step 8:	Introduce new words each week in accordance with the curriculum sequence. Vary the number of new words presented depending on the mastery of previous words. Graph the results of continuous assessment to evaluate instruction (see Figure 9.1). Because grouping is based on the rate of words learned, move students among groups as a function of their progress.

FIGURE 9.1

Graph of a student's weekly performance in spelling

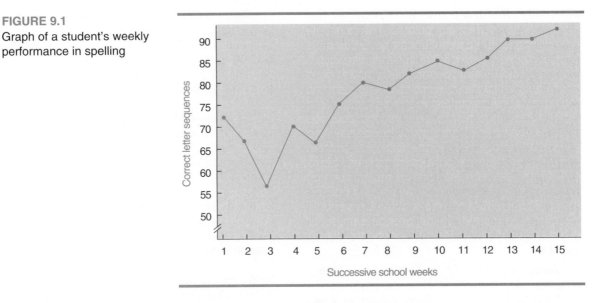

the most frequent spelling error was deleting letters in words (e.g., *hoping* for *hopping; spose* for *suppose).* Selected spelling errors may include spelling the word as it sounds (*doter* for *daughter),* omitting a letter that is pronounced (*aross* for *across),* using the wrong vowel digraph (*speach* for *speech),* reversing letters in words (*croner* for *corner),* using an incorrect vowel (*jab* for *job; anemals* for *animals),* using the wrong homonym for the meaning intended (*peace* for *piece),* inserting an unneeded letter (*ulgly* for *ugly),* doubling a consonant when not needed (*untill* for *until*), and omitting a silent letter (*bome* for *bomb*) (Hitchcock, 1989). Moreover, Edgington (1967) suggests that the following specific types of errors should be noted on a spelling error analysis chart: addition of extra letters; omission of needed letters; reversals of whole words, consonant order, or syllables; errors resulting from a student's mispronunciation or dialect; and phonetic spelling of nonphonetic words. Misspellings also can be categorized as phonetic and nonphonetic. Phonetic misspellings occur when the student attempts to use phonics rules to spell a word but applies the rule incorrectly or the word does not adhere to those rules, whereas nonphonetic spellings do not appear to be based on the application of phonics rules (McLoughlin & Lewis, 1994). Burns (1980) notes that most errors occur in vowels in midsyllables of

words; 67 percent of the errors result from substitution or omission of letters, and 20 percent result from addition, insertion, or transposition of letters. Through a careful analysis of spelling errors, the teacher can focus on consistent patterns of errors and plan appropriate instruction.

Cloze Procedure The cloze procedure is a visual means of testing spelling. The student may be required to complete a sentence by writing the correct response in the blank; for example, "The opposite of down is _____" *(up).* In addition, the student may be asked to complete a word or supply missing letters: "The clouds are in the s_____" *(sky),* or "Please give me a glass of w_t_r" *(water).* Cartwright (1969) notes that the cloze procedure is especially useful in evaluating the student's knowledge of spelling generalizations. In this case, the student is required to fill in blanks pertaining to a rule, such as doubling the final consonant before adding *ing;* for example, "The man was run__ to catch the bus" *(ning).* A multiple-choice format also may be used; for example, "Mary needed _____ to pay for her lunch" *(munny, mony, money, monie).* The cloze procedure, which is visual, can be used effectively along with the auditory dictated spelling test.

Probes Spelling skills can be assessed through the use of probe sheets. The student works on the probe sheet for 1 minute, and the teacher records the rate of correct and incorrect responses and notes any error patterns. The probe task (e.g., see picture—write word, see words—write contractions, hear word—write word, or see partial word—write missing letter) may be administered several times to give the teacher a reliable index of how well the student can perform. Starlin and Starlin (1973) suggest a proficiency rate for students in kindergarten through second grade of 30 to 50 correct letters per minute with two or fewer errors at the independent level and 15 to 29 correct letters with three to seven errors at the instructional level. For third grade through adult, the independent level is 50 to 70 correct letters per minute with two or fewer errors, and the instructional level is 25 to 49 correct letters with three to seven errors. In addition, the teacher can collect data from students who are achieving satisfactorily and use their rates for comparison when assessing a student with spelling difficulties. A sample probe sheet for spelling contractions is presented in Figure 9.2.

Modality Testing   Sensory modality preference testing, described by Westerman (1971), assesses the student's performance through combinations of five input/output channels:

1. *Auditory-vocal:* The teacher spells the word aloud, and the student orally spells the word.
2. *Auditory-motor:* The teacher spells the word aloud, and the student writes the word on paper.
3. *Visual-vocal:* The teacher shows the word on a flash card, and the student spells the word aloud.
4. *Visual-motor:* The teacher shows the word on a flash card, and the student writes the word on paper.
5. *Multisensory combination channel:* The teacher shows the word on a flash card and spells it aloud, and the student spells the word aloud and writes it on paper.

In modality testing, 40 unknown words are divided into five sets of eight words each. Two words are taught in each of the five modalities for four consecutive days, and the student is tested on a written dictation spelling test at the end of each day. On the fifth day the student is tested on all 40 words. The number of correct responses

FIGURE 9.2
Probe sheet for spelling contractions

Task: See words — Write contractions

do not	_____
I will	_____
can not	_____
have not	_____
we are	_____
I am	_____
could not	_____
is not	_____
it is	_____
you are	_____
she is	_____
are not	_____
would not	_____
I have	_____
did not	_____
they would	_____
has not	_____
was not	_____
they are	_____
he will	_____

Name: _____

Time: 1 minute

Number of correct letters written: _____

Number of incorrect letters written: _____

in each modality indicates whether the student shows a pattern of preference among modalities. This kind of assessment information is useful in planning individualized instruction. For example, students with an auditory-motor preference may learn new spelling words by using a tape recorder and writing each word after hearing it. Similarly, visual learners should be provided with many opportunities to see the word.

TEACHING SPELLING SKILLS

Stephens (1977) notes that nine spelling competencies enable the student to be an effective speller. These nine skills and corresponding subareas are presented in Table 9.4. Shanker and Ekwall (1998) note that the words most frequently misspelled by nearly all students are exceptions to phonics rules. They suggest that it may be most helpful to teach students to spell correctly those

TABLE 9.4
Spelling competencies

Competency	Subareas
Auditory discrimination	Ability to discriminate consonant sounds and vowel sounds and use correct word pronunciation
Consonants	Knowledge of consonants in initial, final, and medial positions in words and knowledge of consonant blends
Phonograms	Ability to identify phonograms in initial, medial, and final positions in words and ability to identify word phonograms
Plurals	Ability to form a plural by adding *s*, adding *es*, changing *f* to *v*, making medial changes, and knowledge of exceptions
Syllabication	Ability to divide words into syllables
Structural elements	Knowledge of root words, prefixes, and suffixes
Ending changes	Ability to change ending of words that end in final *e*, final *y*, and final consonants
Vowel digraphs and diphthongs	Ability to spell words in which a vowel digraph forms one sound *(ai, ea, ay, ei, ie)* or a diphthong forms a blend *(oe, ou, ow)*
Silent *e*	Knowledge of single-syllable words that end in silent *e*

words that appear most frequently in writing. Moreover, spelling should be emphasized in all subject matter and viewed as a skill that will enable students to be more effective writers.

Vallecorsa, Zigmond, and Henderson (1985) note that educators may need to improve their knowledge of validated methods for teaching spelling to be able to use supported techniques routinely. In a research review of spelling instruction for students with learning problems, McNaughton, Hughes, and Clark (1994) suggest that the following strategies may enhance learning of spelling skills: limiting the number of new vocabulary words introduced each day, providing opportunities for self-directed and peer-assisted instruction, directing students to name letters aloud as they are practiced, including instruction in morphemic analysis, providing immediate error imitation and correction, using motivating reinforcers, and providing periodic retesting and review. The following teaching methods and strategies provide alternatives for teaching spelling skills to students with spelling difficulties.

Rule-Based Instruction

Spelling instruction can be based on teaching rules and generalizations. After learning a general spelling rule, the student is able to use it with un-

familiar words. These rules can apply to instruction using both linguistics and phonics.

The linguistic approach to teaching spelling is based on the idea that there is regularity in phoneme-grapheme correspondence. This method stresses the systematic nature of spelling patterns. Spelling rules, generalizations, and patterns that apply to whole words are taught. Spelling words are selected according to their particular linguistic pattern (e.g., *cool, fool, pool; hitting, running, batting*).

The phonics approach to teaching spelling stresses phoneme-grapheme relationships within parts of words. The student learns to associate a sound with a particular letter or combination of letters. Thus, phonetic rules can help the student determine how sounds should be spelled. Through phonics instruction, the student can learn to spell words according to syllables. The student breaks the word into recognizable sound elements, pronounces each syllable, and then writes the letter or letters that represent each sound.

In rule-based instruction (in both linguistics and phonics), only spelling rules and generalizations that apply to a large number of words and have few exceptions should be taught. The general rule should be applicable more than 75 percent of the time. Spelling rules can be taught by guiding the student to discover rules and generalizations independently. After analyzing several words that share a common linguistic property, the student is asked to apply the rule to unfamiliar words. After the student can generalize, exceptions to the rules can be discussed. The student should be taught that rules are not steadfast and that some words do not conform to spelling rules.

Although phonetic approaches to teaching spelling are used frequently, Hanna, Hodges, and Hanna (1971) note that only about 50 percent of spellings follow regular phonetic rules. Dixon (1991) suggests that incorporating morphological analysis into spelling instruction potentially may reduce misspellings due to phonetic irregularities and, thus, facilitate students' problem-solving behavior through focusing on both phonetic and morphemic generalization.

Multisensory Approach

Spelling involves skills in the visual, auditory, and motor sensory modalities. The student must be able to exhibit visual and auditory recognition and discrimination of the letters of the alphabet and must have motor control to write the word. Hodges (1966) notes that "a child who has learned to spell a word by the use of the senses of hearing, sight, and touch is in a good position to recall the spelling of that word when he needs it in his writing because any or all the sensory modes can elicit his memory of it" (p. 39).

Fernald's (1943, 1988) multisensory approach involves four sensory modalities: visual, auditory, kinesthetic, and tactile (VAKT). In this approach, Fernald focuses on the following areas as being important in learning to spell: clear perception of word form, development of a distinct visual image of the word, and habit formation through repetition of writing until the motor pattern is automatic. The following steps are included in learning to spell a new word:

1. The teacher writes and says a word while the student watches and listens.

2. The student traces the word with a finger while simultaneously saying the word. Then the student copies or writes the word while saying it. Careful pronunciation is emphasized, with each syllable of the word dragged out slowly as it is traced or written.

3. Next, the word is written from memory. If it is incorrect, the second step is repeated. If the word is correct, it is put in a file box. Later the words in the file box are used in stories.

4. At later stages the tracing method for learning is not always needed. The student may learn the word by observing the teacher write and say it and then by writing and saying it alone. As progress is made, the student may learn the word by looking at it in print and writing it and, finally, merely by looking at it.

The Gillingham method (Gillingham & Stillman, 1970) uses an alphabetic system with repetition and drill. Letter-sound correspondences are taught using a multisensory approach—visual, auditory, and kinesthetic. Words introduced initially include only those with consistent sound-symbol correspondences. The student is given experience reading and spelling one-syllable words as well as detached regularly spelled syllables. Words of more than one syllable are learned syllable by syllable (e.g., *Sep tem ber*). Words whose spellings are not entirely consistent are sequenced carefully according to structural characteristics, and words following a pattern are grouped. The technique used in studying spelling words is called *simultaneous oral spelling.* When the teacher says a spelling word, the student repeats the word, names the letters, writes the letters while saying them aloud, and reads the written word. Letter names rather than sounds are used in this practice so that the technique can be applied to nonphonetic words. Sentence and story writing are introduced after the student is able to write any three-letter, phonetically pure word. Nonphonetic words are taught through drill. Thus, the Gillingham method differs from the Fernald (1943, 1988) approach in two major respects: words to be taught are selected carefully and sequenced or selected as needed for writing rather than being of the student's own choosing, and instruction focuses on individual letters and sounds rather than on whole words. *How to Teach Spelling* (available from Educators Publishing Service) is a comprehensive resource manual based on the Gillingham approach to reading and spelling.

Kearney and Drabman (1993) used a modified write-say spelling intervention designed to provide immediate feedback to the visual and auditory modalities of students with learning problems. The students' spelling accuracy significantly increased through the use of the following procedure:

Day 1:   Students receive the spelling word list and are asked to study on their own.

Day 2:   Following taking a test on the spelling word list and receiving verbal teacher feedback on performance, students simultaneously say aloud and write the correct spelling (letter by letter) of any incorrectly spelled word five times.

Day 3:   The procedure is repeated, except students simultaneously correctly rewrite and restate incorrectly spelled words ten consecutive times.

Day 4:   The procedure is repeated, except students simultaneously correctly rewrite and restate incorrectly spelled words 15 consecutive times.

Day 5:   To assess spelling accuracy, students write words from the list verbally presented by the teacher.

Another multisensory approach that features repetition is the cover-and-write method. The student is taught to spell words through the following steps:

1. The student looks at the word and says it.
2. The student writes the word twice while looking at it.
3. The student covers the word and writes it again.
4. The student checks the spelling by looking at it.

The steps are repeated, with the student writing the word as many as three times while looking at it, covering the word, writing it, and checking the spelling.

Test-Study-Test Technique

The test-study-test approach to teaching spelling is used frequently. The student is given a pretest at the beginning of each unit of study. The words the student misspells on the pretest become the study list. After instruction, another test determines the degree of mastery. A progress chart is kept, and words misspelled on the second test are added to the list of words for the following unit of study.

The study-test plan is similar to the test-study-test approach, except that it does not include a pretest. The student's study list consists of all of the words in the unit of study. The student is tested after completing various spelling activities. Stephens et al. (1982) note that the test-study-test method obtains better spelling results than the study-test approach. The pretest identifies words that the student already knows how to spell; the elimination of these words allows the student to focus on the unknown words.

In addition, some studies indicate that added reinforcement procedures can encourage students to study harder to obtain higher test scores. For example, Lovitt, Guppy, and Blattner (1969) noted a substantial increase in the number of perfect spelling papers when students were given the test four days a week (Tuesday through Friday) and, after receiving 100 percent on that week's word list, were excused from spelling for the rest of the week and given free time. Also, Sidman (1979) used group and individual reinforcement contingencies with middle school students. Accuracy increased when free time was provided as a reward for improved test scores. The increase was greater during group contingency conditions.

Graham and Voth (1990) recommend daily testing on new and previously introduced words from a spelling unit, as well as periodic maintenance checks to ensure mastery or to identify words that need to be reincorporated into the instructional sequence. In addition, they suggest that the tests should be corrected, with supervision, by the students themselves. Thus, the students receive immediate feedback about their efforts to learn to spell. Because some students spell the words correctly on the test but misspell them in their writing, the teacher periodically should collect samples of student writing to determine whether the students are applying in their writing what they have learned through spelling instruction. To improve accuracy and fluency, practice on misspelled words should include a variety of high-interest activities and games. In addition, peer tutoring or cooperative learning arrangements can improve spelling performance.

Study Strategies   Study techniques provide a structured format for the independent study of spelling words and help students with learning problems to organize their spelling study. Graham and Freeman (1986) found that students with learning problems who were trained to use an efficient study strategy were able to recall immedi-

Learning spelling words from topical areas enhances vocabulary and meaning.

ately the correct spelling of more words than were students who were allowed to choose their own methods for studying unknown spelling words. The study strategy included the following steps:

1. Say the word.
2. Write and say the word.
3. Check the word by comparing it with a model.
4. Trace and say the word.
5. Write the word from memory and check.
6. Repeat the first five steps.

Moreover, Foster and Torgesen (1983) found that directed study improved the long-term retention of spelling words in students with learning problems who had average short-term memory; however, students who had short-term memory deficits continued to experience difficulty in the acquisition of spelling words.

Self-correction also can have positive effects on student spelling performance. Wirtz, Gardner, Weber, and Bullara (1996) used a self-correction strategy in which students heard each spelling word presented on audiotape, wrote each spelling word, compared each word with a model on an answer key, corrected any misspellings by using proofreading marks, wrote the word correctly, and repeated the task. The effects of using this self-correction method were compared with the traditional method of having students write spelling words three times, arrange the words in alphabet-

ical order, and use the words in a sentence or in stories. In addition to improved performances on weekly spelling tests, the self-correction strategy was more effective than the traditional method in helping students maintain their ability to correctly spell previously learned words.

Visual mnemonics also can help students with learning problems remember spelling words. Greene (1994) suggests that visual mnemonic stimuli can be incorporated into the student's spelling list or put on flash cards with the mnemonic word on one side and the nonmnemonic form of the word on the other side. For example, the word *look* is presented with two eyes drawn (L👀K) and *great* has the *e* circled and slashed to indicate it is silent (g r ⊘ a t). With eyes closed, the student visualizes the word, attempts to see the mnemonic aid presented in the word, and then writes the word from memory. Moreover, the student can generate associations to facilitate recall of correct spellings (e.g., princi*pal* is your *pal*, de*ss*ert is *s*omething *s*weet).

When structural word analysis, syllable rules, and spelling patterns are taught, Wong (1986) suggests that the student use the following self-questioning strategy:

1. Do I know this word?
2. How many syllables do I hear in this word? (Write down the number of syllables.)
3. I will write the word the way I think it is spelled.

4. Do I have the right number of syllables?
5. Is there any part of the word that I am not sure how to spell? (If so, underline that part and try spelling the word again.)
6. Does the word look right to me? (If not, underline the questionable part of the word and write it again. Listen to the word to find any missing syllables.)
7. When I finish spelling, I will tell myself that I have worked hard.

Finally, individual and classwide peer tutoring can be a viable instructional alternative to provide intensive one-to-one practice with spelling words. When the tutoring sessions include structured lessons, peers can provide direct, individual instruction.

Fixed and Flow Word Lists

Spelling words frequently are presented and taught in fixed word lists. Generally, a new list of words is assigned each week. The words may be either somewhat unfamiliar or completely unknown to the students. Usually a test on each list is given on Friday. This method seldom results in spelling mastery for all students because misspelled words on the test usually are ignored or left for the students to practice independently. Another procedure using fixed word lists is to have students practice the words at their own rate until they are able to spell all of them correctly on a certain number of tests.

On a flow list of spelling words, words are dropped from each student's list when mastered (e.g., spelled correctly on two consecutive days), and then a new (unpracticed) word is added. Thus, the list is individualized, and the student does not spend time practicing known words. McGuigan (1975) developed a teaching procedure, the Add-a-Word Program, which uses flow word lists. McGuigan found that students ages 7 to 13 and adults learned words more quickly with add-a-word lists than with fixed lists, and showed similar or superior retention of learned words.

Graham and Voth (1990) emphasize that the spelling words taught to students with learning problems initially should be limited to high-frequency words and misspelled words from their writing. They recommend that weekly spelling lists be limited to 6 to 12 words (emphasizing a common structural element, if possible), and 2 or 3 words from the list should be introduced daily and practiced until the entire set of words is mastered. Likewise, Burns and Broman (1983) recommend presentation of only 5 to 10 words per week to poor spellers (20 words per week may be presented to adequate spellers). In a study of spelling performance of students with learning problems, Bryant, Drabin, and Gettinger (1981) found that a higher failure rate and greater variance in performance may occur when 3 or more new words are presented each day. They suggest that 7 to 8 new spelling words per week may be an appropriate number for these students.

MacArthur and Graham (1987) note that students with learning problems incorrectly spell 10 to 20 percent of the words they write. Thus, Graham, Harris, and Loynachan (1994) developed the Spelling for Writing list of 335 words, ordered from first- through third-grade level. The list includes words students use most often when writing, many of which are "spelling demons" and commonly misspelled words.

Imitation Methods

Stowitschek and Jobes (1977) present a method of spelling instruction that involves imitation. It is designed for students who have failed repeatedly to learn to spell through traditional procedures. The teacher provides an oral and written model of the spelling word, and the student is required to imitate the model by spelling the word aloud and writing it. The student receives immediate feedback and praise for correct responses. Incorrect responses are followed by retraining. The procedure is repeated until the student can spell and write the word without models or prompts. A spelling probe is administered after each training session to determine which words have been mastered and to check retention of learned words.

Kauffman, Hallahan, Haas, Brame, and Boren (1978) tested the effectiveness of showing the student a correct model of a spelling word as opposed to first providing a written imitation of the student's spelling error and then showing the correct model. Kauffman et al. found that including the imitation of the student's error was more effective, especially for nonphonetic words. Kauffman et al. suggest that imitation can be particularly useful in teaching words that do not follow regular phonetic rules (i.e., words for which the student must use visual memory). However, Brown (1988) conducted a series of experiments and found that exposures to incorrect spellings can interfere with subsequent spelling accuracy.

Additional Considerations

Different types of correctional procedures should be used with various kinds of spelling errors. Visual image should be emphasized with a student who omits silent letters or misspells phonologically irregular words, whereas incorrect spelling of homonyms indicates a need to stress word meanings. Also, words the student misspells in written compositions may be included in his or her spelling program. This can be motivating because the need to learn to spell those words is apparent.

Spelling also may be taught and reinforced throughout the language arts curriculum. One way to improve spelling is through word study in reading (Templeton, 1986). In oral reading the student gives close attention to the sounds of the entire word. In addition, reading gives the student the meanings of words and thus increases interest in them. The student learns the correct usage of words in sentences and can determine whether the word is written correctly. Thus, learning to spell can accompany learning to read, and a program that stresses both skills may be both effective and motivating. As discussed in Chapter 8, the language experience approach and the whole language approach incorporate reading and spelling. T. K. Shinn (1982) stresses that no student should be forced to learn to spell words that he or she cannot read and understand. Otherwise, the student really is memorizing a nonmeaningful series of letters that will not be retained. Thus, spelling lists should be produced from the student's reading vocabulary. Moreover, to facilitate maintenance and generalization, the student should be encouraged to use learned spelling words frequently in writing.

Training in dictionary usage also should be included in the spelling program. Dictionaries help the student become more independent in locating spellings and provide such information as syllabication, meaning, pronunciation, synonyms, and homonyms. Picture dictionaries can be used in the primary grades. Beginning in the fourth grade, special practice in using the dictionary often is included

in the curriculum, and the use of dictionaries may be encouraged during writing tasks. When the correct spelling of a word is not known, the student should predict possible spellings for the word by identifying root words and affixes, considering related words, and determining the sounds in the word. Then the student can check the predicted spelling by consulting a dictionary. *The Dictionary of Basic English* (available from American Guidance Service) contains more than 5,000 frequently used and essential words and provides short, clearly written definitions as well as sample phrases and sentences showing proper word usage.

In teaching spelling skills at the secondary level, the teacher should help the adolescent understand the social and practical significance of correct spelling. For example, employers place value on accurate spelling on job applications. The student's own interests and various areas of study provide new words. Vocational words also can be emphasized. At the secondary level it may be best to teach spelling in conjunction with other activities rather than to use class time solely for spelling instruction. Practice in reading and other learning activities can help the adolescent learn to spell. Success in spelling increases in importance with the finding that students' beliefs about their efficacy as spellers may affect not only their spelling performance but their writing performance as well (Rankin, Bruning, Timme, & Katkanant, 1993). Finally, strategies to compensate for poor spelling should be taught to students whose spelling problems may affect their grades in content areas. For example, the teacher can provide such students with a spelling checker, which contains frequently used words and words they often misspell. The *Speaking Homework Wiz* (produced by Franklin Electronic Publishers) provides automatic spelling correction for nearly 50,000 words and speaks 40,000 easy-to-understand definitions.

☀ SPELLING ACTIVITIES

Many activities and materials can be used to supplement a spelling program. Games and activities stimulate interest, provide practice, and add variety in teaching techniques. In addition, spelling instruction may be individualized by developing games and activities for particular individuals or small groups. The activities presented in this section and the instructional games and self-correcting materials presented in the following sections promote the development of spelling skills.

• Ask the student to complete words in sentences by filling in omitted letters. Lists of words from stories in basal readers or spelling textbooks can be used to develop reusable worksheets or dittos. For example:

The bo_ and _irl were bak___ a cak_.

• Provide a worksheet showing various words and their configurations. Ask the student to match each word with its configuration. Worksheets of specific words (e.g., reading selections or weekly spelling lists) can be made and reused for this seatwork activity.

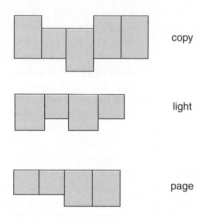

copy

light

page

• Use a hidden-word format to provide practice in letter sequence of spelling words. Provide a list of spelling words and a puzzle. Ask the student to locate the hidden spelling words and to draw a circle around them.

curve

held

ranch

young

• Have the student keep a file box of spelling words that have caused some difficulty. The words should be arranged in alphabetical order, and the cards also may contain definitions or pictures. Encourage the student to study the cards and to practice writing the words from memory. New words can be included and others deleted as the student progresses.

• In compiling the weekly spelling word list, ask class members to volunteer words, such as those they have misspelled in writing or have encountered in independent reading. The teacher may want to include on the spelling list those words the students will use frequently in their writing. Give a pretest on the words on Monday and a second test on Friday. Keep a scoreboard graph for the entire class, scaled to ten. Have each student try to move "up ten" each week on the graph by spelling more words correctly on Friday than were spelled correctly on the pretest. Thus, the student is competing against a previous score. The advanced student who gets a perfect score and the less able student who improves by ten words both receive the "up ten" mark on the graph.

• Describe a current spelling word phonetically. For example, the word *move* may be described as "a one-syllable word beginning with a consonant and ending with a vowel." Call on a student to find the word in the spelling list, then give her or him a turn to describe a word and to call on another classmate.

• Have the student work with anagram activities, in which the student is given a word and must rearrange all the letters to make a new word. For example, *smile* is an anagram for *miles,* and *sister* is an anagram for *resist.* For students having particular difficulty, Scrabble letter tiles may be used, or the student can copy the word, cut it apart, and rearrange the letters. Also, have the student work anagram puzzles, in which one letter is changed each time until the top word is changed into the bottom word. Definitions or clues may be provided. For example:

POND	small lake
_____	young horse (*pony*)
_____	nickname for Anthony (*Tony*)
_____	dial ____ (*tone*)
BONE	dog's treat

• Have a spelling bee in which the students stand in a line, and each time a student spells a word correctly the student "jumps" two persons toward the end of the line. When a student reaches the end, she or he sits down. Thus, students who need practice remain in line, and those who know the words have time for independent work.

• Begin an add-a-letter activity with a one- to two-letter word (e.g., *to*). Call on a student to make a different word by adding one letter (e.g., *top*). The letters may be rearranged, but one letter must be added each turn (e.g., *spot*). When no one can continue the process, start a new word. This can become a seatwork activity, in which each student works independently on a worksheet to add letters and make new words.

● Provide the student with a jar containing about 40 wooden cubes with letters on them (similar to alphabet blocks or Spill and Spell cubes). Spill the letters from the jar and see how many words the student can make in 5 minutes with the given letters. Link letters (letters that fit together to form words) also can be used for this activity.

● Provide spelling word cards (two cards for each word) and have the student play a concentration game. The cards are mixed up and placed face down in rows. The student turns over two cards at a time and tries to remember their location so that spelling matches can be made. When the student turns up two cards that match (i.e., the same spelling word), the cards are removed. Two students may play together by taking turns to see who can make the most matches.

● Have the student write a story or theme using the spelling list words. The theme may be on any subject and as long or as short as the student wishes to make it; however, every one of the spelling words must be included in what is written. Encourage the student to pay attention to spelling and using the words correctly.

● Encourage the student to develop memory devices to facilitate the spelling of difficult words or words that are not spelled as they sound. For example:

Station*ery* is writing pap*er*.
The princi*pal* is your *pal*.

● Present crossword puzzles that contain spelling words to give practice in writing the words and learning their meanings. Also, the student can be asked to make up a crossword puzzle that includes new and review spelling words and everyday words.

Across
1. small cat
3. not wild
6. what you hear with
7. a small clue
8. a father's boy
10. not old

Down
1. room you cook in
2. short periods of sleep
4. more than one man
5. puts in mouth and chews
9. opposite of yes

● For dictionary practice, provide a list of words (e.g., *overcoat, tongue-tied,* and *well-known*). Ask the student to locate the words in the dictionary and write *yes* or *no* to indicate whether each word is hyphenated. Also, provide sentences containing some unfamiliar words and ask the student to supply synonyms for four words in each sentence. For example:

The *clandestine* meeting was interrupted by *incorrigible bandits* who came *incognito.*

● Have a student describe a spelling word from the current week's list by giving rhyming, meaning, or descriptive clues. The other class members are given 1 minute to guess the word. The first person to say the correct word goes to the chalkboard and writes it. If the word is spelled correctly, that student gets to describe a word.

● For motivation, allow the student to practice spelling words on a typewriter or computer keyboard. The student can say the letters when typing them, thus combining sight, sound, and touch.

● Select a student to pick a word from the dictionary and write on the chalkboard the exact pronunciation for the word as found in the dictionary. It should be written letter for letter with all diacritical marks and accents. The student can ask a class member to pronounce and spell the word the correct way.

INSTRUCTIONAL GAMES IN SPELLING

Find-a-Word

Materials: Two words containing the same number of letters written on the chalkboard.

Directions: The teacher divides the class into two teams. The first student from each team goes to the chalkboard and writes any word that can be made from the letters in the given word. Then the student gives the chalk to the next student on the team and goes to the end of the line. Each student must write a new word or correct a misspelled one. The game continues until the teacher calls time. The team with the most correctly spelled words at the end of the time limit is the winner. For example:

The given words are:	*place*	*dream*
The student may write:	pace	read
	cap	mad
	leap	dear
	pal	me

Detective

Materials: Spelling words with various letters omitted written on the chalkboard.

Directions: The teacher gives the definition of each word and calls on a student to fill in the missing letters. The student goes to the chalkboard and writes in the missing letters. One point is given for each correct word or letter. The student with the most points at the end of the game is the winner. For example:

n___ghb__	person who lives next door
stor___s	short reading selections
ni___t	opposite of day

Jaws

Materials: Twenty-one index cards with one consonant printed on each card; 21 index cards with pictures corresponding to the sound of each consonant; 1 index card with "jaws" (a shark) drawn on it.

Directions: The cards are dealt to three or more players. The players check for pairs (i.e., one consonant card and a picture card that has the same beginning consonant sound) and place them on the table. The first player turns to the left and picks a card from that player. If it matches a card already held, the player places the pair on the table. The game continues until all the cards have been matched and one student is left holding "jaws."

Modification: The players can be asked to write the names of the pictures in the pairs. The player who spells the most pairs correctly wins the game.

Spell It—Keep It Card Game

Materials: Cards with spelling words printed on them placed on the chalkboard ledge with backs to the class.

Directions: The teacher divides the class into two teams. A student from the first team selects a card and reads the word. A student from the other team spells the word. If the word is spelled correctly, the student who spelled it gets to keep the card. If the word is spelled incorrectly, a student from the first team has a chance to spell it and get the card. Then a student from the second team selects a card, and the process is repeated until all cards are gone from the ledge. The winner is the team having the most cards at the end of the game.

Telegraph Spelling

Materials: Two sets of 2″ × 6″ cards with letters used in the spelling words printed on them.

Directions: The class is divided into two teams, and each student receives a letter card. The teacher pronounces a spelling word. The members of each team arrange themselves in the proper order at the front of the room. The team that correctly spells the word first wins a point. After a specified time limit, the team with the most points wins the game.

Modification: For older students, each member of the team can be assigned one or two letters of the alphabet. When the teacher gives the spelling word, the members of the team begin verbally to "transmit" (call out) the spelling of the word. There can be no more than 5 seconds between calling out letters, and other team members are not allowed to help. One point is earned for each correct response.

Spelling Bingo

Materials: Cards divided into 24 squares (four squares across and six squares down), with a different spelling word printed in each space and words in different order on each card; numerous discs or markers.

Directions: Each student receives a card and several discs. As the teacher calls out and spells a word, each student covers the given word on the card with a disc. The first student to complete a column going across, down, or diagonally calls "Bingo" and wins the game.

Modifications: The students can make their own cards by dividing their paper into 24 squares. The spelling words are written on the chalkboard, and each student writes the words in any squares on the paper. One student is selected to stand facing away from the chalkboard, and the teacher calls out words for the student to spell. For each word the student spells correctly, the other students place a disc on the corresponding square on their card. The game continues until someone calls "Bingo." The teacher keeps a list of the words and checks the winning card. Also, for young students, the bingo cards can consist of rows of selected consonants, short vowels, and long vowels. When the teacher calls a word, each student puts discs on the appropriate letters on the card.

Golf Game Board

Materials: Large game board on tagboard or laminated poster board; different-color golf tees for markers; cards with spelling words printed on them, with stars on the cards of the most difficult words (see Figure 9.3).

FIGURE 9.3
Golf game board

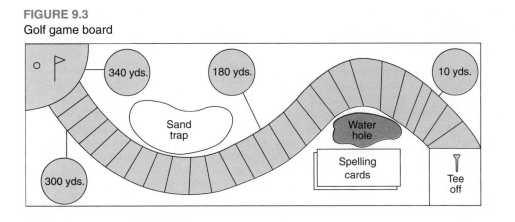

Directions: Two players each choose a golf tee and place it on the "tee off" square. The first player takes the top card and reads the word to the other player, who tries to spell the word. If the word is spelled correctly, the student moves ahead one space. If the word is spelled incorrectly, the student moves back one space. When a player correctly spells a word that has a star on the card, the student moves ahead two spaces. The first player to reach the golf hole wins the game.

Modifications

- Game boards can be made on poster board to depict various themes, such as a racetrack, rocket path, mountain path, safari, or any other start-to-finish sequence.
- The spelling cards can consist of some words spelled correctly and some words spelled incorrectly. The player draws a card and must decide whether the word is spelled correctly. If it is misspelled, the player must spell it correctly. Each player moves one space for a correct answer. A third student can use an answer key to check responses.
- Stacks of index cards containing spelling words can be color-coded or numbered according to difficulty level. Students may play with two different stacks of cards according to their ability levels. The players roll dice to determine the number of spaces they can move on the game board if they spell the word on the spelling card correctly.
- Chance dice that have one number covered with a sticker can be used. When one sticker is rolled, the player loses a turn; when two stickers are rolled (one on each die), the player goes back to the beginning square.
- For older students, the words on the spelling cards can be assigned a number of yards (in multiples of 10) according to the difficulty level of the word. Each space on the board is worth 10 yards. When a word is spelled

correctly, the player moves the number of yards indicated on the card. If a word is misspelled, the player does not advance.

Tic-Tac-Toe

Materials: A tic-tac-toe game square made of tagboard or laminated poster board; five tagboard Xs and five Os; cards with spelling words written on them.

Directions: One student chooses to mark with Xs and the other student uses Os. The first student takes the top spelling card and reads it to the opponent, who attempts to spell it. If the word is spelled correctly, the student places a marker in a square on the board. The game continues until one player has three Xs or Os in a horizontal, vertical, or diagonal row.

Modification: The class can be divided into two teams, and a paper marked X or O can be pinned on each player to indicate the X or O team. Nine chairs are placed in three rows similar to a tic-tac-toe board. A member of one team selects a card and reads the spelling word, and a member of the other team must spell it. If the word is spelled correctly, the student chooses a chair and sits in it. The game continues until one team has three members sitting in a row.

Connect the Dots

Materials: Twenty-five dots (rows of five across and five down) drawn on the chalkboard; cards with spelling words printed on them.

Directions: The students are divided into two teams. A member of the first team draws the top spelling card and reads the word to a member of the opposite team, who tries to spell it (either in writing or aloud). If the word is spelled correctly, the student draws a line connecting two dots, and that team gets another turn to try to spell a word. If a word is spelled incorrectly, the other team gets a turn. When a square is closed in by four lines, the number of the team is written in the square. The team that obtains the most squares is the winner.

Modification: Two players may play the game with a game board of dots made of tagboard covered with acetate so that marks made with a grease pencil can be erased. When a square is made, the player can write an initial in it.

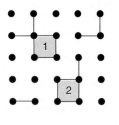

Checkers

Materials: A checker game board made of tagboard; 24 tagboard checkers (12 of one color and 12 of another), each of which has a spelling word printed on the bottom.

Directions: Two players place their checkers on the board, and they take turns moving their checkers. If one player can "jump" the opponent's checker, the opponent looks on the bottom of the checker to be jumped and reads the word aloud. If the jumping player correctly spells the word, that player is allowed to jump and pick up the opponent's checker. If the word is misspelled, the player is not allowed to make the move. The game continues until one player has obtained all of the opponent's checkers through jumping.

Modifications: Additional checkers can be made so that different spelling words are used each time the game is played. Also, regular checkers can be used when spelling word cards are provided. To make a jump, the player must spell the word on the top card correctly to the opponent.

Chance Dice Spelling Game

Materials: Two chance dice, each of which has numbers on five sides and a sticker covering the number on the sixth side; worksheets with equal items that are appropriate for each player (e.g., matching spelling words with pictures or definitions, choosing correctly spelled words from four options, dividing spelling words into syllables, and filling in omitted letters in spelling words); an answer key for each worksheet.

Directions: Each player is given an appropriate worksheet for the student's spelling word list. The first player rolls both of the chance dice. If no stickers are rolled, the player answers an item on the worksheet, and the answer is checked by a student with the answer key. If the answer is correct, the item number is checked; however, if the answer is incorrect, the item number is not checked and the player must attempt that item on another turn. If one sticker is rolled on the chance dice, the player loses a turn. If two stickers are rolled (one on each die), the player is allowed to attempt to answer two items on the worksheet. This procedure is continued until one player correctly answers all the items on the worksheet and wins the game.

TV Talent

Material: Three decorated shoe boxes; spelling words of varying difficulty printed on index cards.

Directions: The game is presented as a television show with one student acting as master of ceremonies (MC). The words are placed in the three boxes, and two players are chosen from the "audience." The first player picks a card from one of the boxes and hands it to the MC without looking at it. The MC pronounces the word, and the player writes the word on the chalkboard. If the word is spelled correctly, the player gets 5 points. The players take turns until one player earns 50 points.

Modification: The spelling words can be divided into three levels of difficulty. The easiest words are placed in the box marked 1 point; the next level, in the box marked 3 points; and the most difficult words, in the box marked 5 points. The student chooses a card from a box according to the number of points the student will attempt to earn on that turn.

Bowling

Materials: Two sets of ten numbered bowling pins; file-card box divided into ten sections, with spelling words filed according to the number of points each word is worth (1 to 10).

Directions: The bowling pins are set up or pinned to a backboard in the arrangement of a bowling game. The first player calls the number of a pin, and the opponent reads the first word from that section in the file box. If the word is spelled correctly, the pin is removed and the player gets the number of points that pin is worth. The second player takes a turn using the other set of pins. The winner is the player who earns the most points after trying to knock down all the pins.

Modification: Two pairs of players can play. The first player of the pair tries to get a strike (worth 55 points) by spelling all the words. If that player misses a word, the player's partner may try to get a spare (worth 45 points) by spelling the word the first player missed and the words for any remaining pins. If the second member of the pair misses a word, the players receive points according to the numbered pins they knocked down. The first pair of players to score a specified number of points wins the game.

Dictionary Store Hunt

Materials: One dictionary per player; a stack of cards with nouns that are unlikely to be familiar to the players (e.g., *cockatiel, metronome,* and *colander*) written on them.

Directions: Each player randomly picks five word cards. At the same starting time, each player begins to find the words in a dictionary, reads the definitions silently, and writes down the kind of store to shop in for each item. The winner is the first person to complete the hunt. Other players can check responses by looking in the dictionary as the player names the stores.

Baseball Spelling Game

Materials: Baseball diamond with three bases and home plate drawn on the chalkboard; cards with spelling words written on them.

Directions: The class is divided into two teams, and the top speller in each group can act as pitcher. The pitcher draws a card and reads the word to the first batter of the other team. If the word is spelled correctly, the first player is given a "single" and stands in front of first base on the chalkboard. If the second batter correctly spells the next word, that batter goes to first base and the player on first base moves to second base. If a word is misspelled, that player is "out"; there are three outs for each team in each inning. Before hearing a word, any batter may declare "home run"; if the word is spelled correctly, that batter clears the bases and the number of runs is added to the score. However, if the batter misspells the word, it automatically counts as the third out for the team, regardless of the actual number of outs in the inning. The team with the most runs at the end of a set number of innings wins.

Modifications: The word cards can be labeled "single," "double," "triple," and "home run" according to the difficulty level of the spelling word. After the batter spells the word correctly, the pitcher tells what the "hit" was worth according to the card. The batter moves to the appropriate base, and batters already on base advance. Also, a baseball diamond can be arranged in the room, using chairs for the bases, and the "runners" can sit in the appropriate chair when they get "hits."

Football Spelling Game

Materials: A football field, including yard lines, drawn on the chalkboard; index cards with spelling words written on them.

Directions: The class is divided into two teams, and the ball is placed (drawn) on the 50-yard line by the "referee." The referee reads a word to a member of the first team. If the player spells the word correctly, the ball is moved 10 yards toward the opponent's goal line. If the word is misspelled, the offensive team loses 10 yards. Each team gets four words in one turn; then the other team takes a turn. A team is given six points each time it crosses the opponent's goal line. The winner is the team with the most points at the end of a specified time period.

Modifications

• The football field may be made on tagboard, and two players can play using small tagboard footballs for their markers. One player draws a card and reads the word for the opponent to spell. If the word is spelled correctly, the opponent's marker is advanced 5 yards closer to the goal; if the word is misspelled, the opponent's marker is moved back 5 yards. The players take turns (one word a turn), and the first one to reach the goal line scores a touchdown and wins the game.

• The word cards can include the number of yards each spelling word is worth (1 to 10 yards), and the ball is moved accordingly.

• In addition to spelling word cards, there can be "gain" cards and "loss" cards. When the word on the spelling card is spelled correctly, the player picks a gain card; when a word is misspelled, the player draws a loss card. The gain cards denote the number of yards gained (e.g., *completed 30-yard pass; 20-yard run*). The loss cards denote the number of yards lost (e.g., *quarterback sack, lose 10 yards; tackled, 5-yard loss*). The player moves the football accordingly.

• Rather than drawing, erasing, and redrawing the ball throughout the game, a chalkboard eraser can be used as the ball. It is easy to see and move if set vertically on the chalkboard tray.

Nym Game

Materials: Two sets of three decorated coffee cans (one labeled *antonyms,* one labeled *homonyms,* and one labeled *synonyms*); cards with pairs of words written on them, which are antonyms, homonyms, or synonyms (all appropriate and acceptable antonyms, homonyms, or synonyms are given for each initial word in the word pair).

Directions: The first player draws the top card and reads and spells the first word on the card to the opponent. The opponent must spell the word that completes the word pair, use the words in sentences, and identify the word pair as antonyms, homonyms, or synonyms. If correct, the word card is placed in the appropriate can of the opponent's set. If incorrect, the card is placed in the appropriate can of the first player's set. The players take turns, and when all the cards are gone, they count their score. Each card in the homonym can is worth three points; each antonym card is worth two points; and each synonym card is worth one point. The player with the highest total score wins the game.

Spelling Dart Game

Materials: Target divided into sections for 15, 10, 5, and 1 points, drawn on heavy poster board; suction darts; a file box divided into sections labeled *15, 10, 5,* and *1* containing spelling word cards of four levels of difficulty (the most difficult words are in the 15-point section).

Directions: The target is mounted on the wall, and the first player throws a dart at it from about 10 feet away. The players determine in which section of the target the dart landed. Another player takes a card from the section of the file box corresponding to the target section. For example, if the dart landed in the 5-point section, the card would be drawn from the 5-point section in the file box. The spelling word is pronounced, and the player who threw the dart must spell the word correctly to receive that number of points. The players take turns until one player scores 50 points and wins the game.

Charades

Materials: Spelling words printed on index cards.

Directions: The class is divided into two teams. A member of the first team selects a card, reads the word silently, and then acts out the word without saying anything. There is a 2-minute time limit, after which the student picks another team member to act out the word. The first team to guess the word gets one point. If the person who guesses the word also can spell it correctly, that team gets two points. The person who guessed the word then draws a card and acts out the word. The team with the most points at the end of a specified time period wins the game.

Bottle Top Scrabble

Materials: One hundred and fifty bottle tops with letters of the alphabet written inside them with a marking pen and point values written on the outside (letters most often used should appear most; point values may be the same as those in Scrabble).

Directions: Each student selects ten tops without looking. The first player spells a word using as many of the letters as possible and adds the point values of the letters used. Then the player picks more tops to again have ten tops. The players take turns spelling words that connect with previously spelled words, as in Scrabble. After all possible bottle tops have been used, the player with the highest score is the winner.

Modification: For older students, there can be a minimum number of letters for each word (e.g., four or more). Also, the number of tops may be increased.

☀ SELF-CORRECTING SPELLING MATERIALS

Spelling Word Puzzles

Feedback device: The pieces of the puzzle fit together to indicate a correct choice.

Materials: Spelling words printed on heavy cardboard and then cut into two or more puzzle pieces.

Directions: The student looks at the puzzle pieces and fits together the pieces that correctly spell a word.

Flip-Sider Spelling Cards

Feedback device: Picture completion or the matching of objects, numbers, or colors provides feedback.

Materials: Sets of index cards with a spelling word on one card and the definition or a picture representing the word on another card; the reverse sides of the two cards that go together have the same object, number, or color, or the two cards complete a picture.

Directions: The student looks at the spelling word on a card and selects the card with the definition of that word or a picture representing it. Then the student flips over the two cards. If the student has chosen the correct definition or picture, the backs of the two cards will have the same object, number, or color, or they will complete a picture.

Modification: The front of the card can have a sentence in which the spelling word is omitted. The sentence may be a definition of the missing word, or there may be a picture illustrating the word in the blank. The spelling word that goes in the blank is written on the back of the card. The student reads the sentence, writes down the missing word, and then flips the card over to check the response.

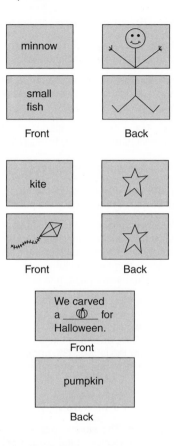

Front

Back

Front

Back

Front

Back

Spelling Spinner

Feedback device: A flap is located on the poster board. When the flap is raised, the answer is revealed.

Materials: A round disc of poster board divided into several sections, each of which has a word written at the top and a picture or definition written in the lower portion of the section; a square piece of poster board that has the round disc attached to the back with a brass fastener, with a small window cut out at the top to reveal the top portion of the disc and a larger window below it to reveal the lower portion of the disc; a flexible flap (such as vinyl wallpaper) placed over the top window.

Directions: The student turns the spinner to reveal a picture or definition in the window. The student writes the spelling word for the picture or definition and then lifts the flap to check the answer.

Modification: Discs of spelling words selected from reading selections or spelling lists may be numbered and stored so that the teacher can select a disc appropriate for an individual student.

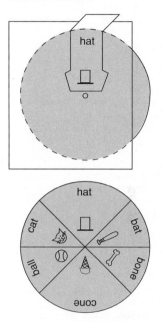

Tape Recorder Spelling

Feedback device: Following the spelling activity presented on the tape, the correct answers are given on the tape.

Materials: A tape recorder and a tape cassette that contains a spelling activity (e.g., a dictated spelling test or directions instructing the student to draw a house and label objects, such as "Add a chimney to your house and write the word *chimney*").

Directions: The student follows the instructions given on the tape recorder and writes the specified words. Following the activity, the student continues to listen to the tape to hear the correct responses and thus checks the answers.

Answer Box

Feedback device: A flap is placed over the window; when lifted, the window reveals the answer.

Materials: An Answer Box (presented in Chapter 2) and a set of index cards that present a spelling exercise.

Directions: The student writes an answer to the presented spelling problem and then lifts the flap to see the answer.

Modification: Change the two "eyes" to one long opening so that activities such as definitions or sentences with missing words can be presented.

Contraction cards to use in the Answer Box:

Definition cards to use in the modified Answer Box:

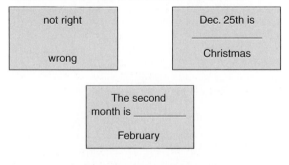

Fill in the Letters

Feedback device: When the correct letters are filled in, the message at the bottom of the page is completed. Deciphering the code thus provides feedback.

Materials: Worksheets on which the student either must cross out or add a letter so that the word is spelled correctly; blanks at the bottom of the page that give a message when the crossed-out or added letters are written in them.

Directions: The student completes the worksheet by crossing out or adding letters as indicated. Then each letter is written in the appropriate blank at the bottom of the page. If the correct letters are chosen, the student reads a message.

Color Spelling Sheet

1. rsed   5. whirte

2. bl e   6. yeljlow

3. orpange   7. br wn

4. belack   8. greben

(super job)

Spelling Crossword Puzzles

Feedback device: Only a correct response will fit in the squares and complete additional words.

Materials: A crossword puzzle in which spelling words are used (e.g., the crossword puzzle presented in the section on spelling activities).

Directions: The student completes the crossword puzzle and receives feedback by filling in the squares.

Scrambled Letters

Feedback device: The backs of the letters are numbered in the correct sequence of the spelling word.

Materials: Envelopes with pictures illustrating a word or definitions written on the front; square cards placed inside the envelopes, with each card giving a letter needed to spell the word; numbers written on the backs of the cards to represent the word's correct letter sequence.

Directions: The student reads the definition or looks at the picture on the envelope, takes the letters out of the envelope, and places them face up. The student unscrambles the letters, arranges them to spell the word, and then turns over the letters. The number order on the back of the cards indicates whether the word is spelled correctly.

Poke Box

Feedback device: The student places a stylus in the hole to indicate a response. If the correct answer is selected, the card can be pulled out of the Poke Box easily.

Materials: A Poke Box (presented in Chapter 2) and a set of index cards that present a spelling exercise (e.g., a word and three abbreviations, or a definition or picture and three words).

Directions: The student selects an answer to the presented spelling problem by inserting the stylus in the hole below the answer. The student then pulls the card, which can be removed if the answer is correct.

Abbreviation and picture cards to use in a Poke Box:

Color Magic

Feedback device: The student receives feedback by opening the folder to see the answers written in color pencil.

Materials: A color plastic folder (such as the type typically used to hold term papers), inside of which is a spelling worksheet; answers written on the worksheet in the same color as the plastic folder (i.e., if the plastic folder is red, the answers are written with a red pencil so that they will not show through the folder).

Directions: The student follows the instructions on the worksheet by reading through the color plastic folder. After writing all the answers on a sheet of paper and finishing the activity, the student opens the folder to check the responses.

☀ COMMERCIAL SPELLING PROGRAMS

The following selected basic developmental programs and corrective materials for spelling instruction may be helpful for students with spelling difficulties. Additional commercial materials include spelling calculators (e.g., Speaking Spelling and Handwriting Ace, produced by Franklin Electronic Publishers), spelling games (e.g., Scrabble, produced by Milton Bradley), and spelling reference books (e.g., Spellex Word Finder, published by Curriculum Associates).

Corrective Spelling Through Morphographs

Corrective Spelling Through Morphographs (Dixon & Engelmann, 1980) is an intensive one-year program for fourth-grade through adult students. The program includes 140 twenty-minute lessons that cover more than 12,000 words, including problem words. The student is taught basic units of meaning in written language (morphographs) that always are spelled according to specific rules. Thus, the student learns analytic techniques and generalizable rules that can be applied to words not in the program. Also available is a book of crossword puzzles, which includes puzzles correlated with the words listed in the review lessons of the program.

Instant Spelling Words for Writing

Instant Spelling Words for Writing, developed by R. G. Forest and R. A. Sitton (published by Curriculum Associates), is an eight-level series designed for writers of all ages (first grade through adult) who have difficulty spelling and proofreading. The series focuses on 1,500 high-frequency words, which cover 90 percent of all words used in writing. All spelling words are introduced as whole words in list form, and students practice writing each word at least ten times in a variety of high-interest exercises. Visual imagery is emphasized through activities involving configuration of word shapes and visual discrimination. The program teaches a multimodality word-study procedure and uses the self-corrected test-study-test method. The last exercise in every lesson is a structured writing activity. Using a total language approach, the review lessons and optional extension activities provide language arts exercises that integrate spelling with listening, speaking, reading, writing, and thinking.

Speed Spelling 1

This tutorial, phonetically based spelling program (published by PRO-ED) is designed for students of any age who have not mastered first- through sixth-grade spelling skills. *Speed Spelling 1* focuses on increasing speed and accuracy through a systematic development of sound-to-letter correspondence. The program includes 93 lessons that teach word reading, word writing, and sentence writing. Detailed branching instructions are given for students who may need additional help. One-to-one instruction is given, and each session takes about 20 minutes.

Spelling Mastery

Spelling Mastery (Dixon, Engelmann, Bauer, Steely, & Wells, 1998) is a six-level basal spelling series designed to teach spelling and strategies to students in first through sixth grade. The series begins with phonemic (sound-symbol) and whole-word strategies and then shifts to morphemic (meaning-symbol) strategies. The program emphasizes learning to spell by generalization rather than memorization, and the 20-minute daily lessons can be used with an entire class or with small groups.

Stetson Spelling Program

The *Stetson Spelling Program* (Stetson, 1988) introduces the 3,000 words most frequently used in writing, which account for 97 percent of the total words written by the average adult. The program uses effective teaching and learning strategies including pretesting, immediate feedback and self-correction, visual imagery of the whole word, spelling clusters, mnemonics, and visual memory. The 230 lessons each contain 10 to 16 words, and direct instruction is used to present a five-step spelling drill on each word. Three blackline masters books each include 1,000 words, as well as student support materials such as three-column self-corrected test forms.

Target: Spelling

This series of six consumable books (published by Steck-Vaughn) is designed to teach spelling to students with learning problems in first through seventh grade. A systematic, highly ordered format is used in which 1,260 words are presented sequentially and with constant reinforcement throughout the six books. Students are asked to learn only six to eight new words per week, and learning experiences to ensure mastery include activities such as word shapes, word search, visual discrimination, recognition in context, matching words with pictures, sound blending, rhyming, and supplying missing letters.

☼ COMPUTER SOFTWARE PROGRAMS IN SPELLING

Computer software can be used effectively to give students additional learning opportunities to improve or enrich their spelling skills. Many students with learning problems prefer to practice spelling words at a computer. Gordon, Vaughn, and Schumm (1993) report that computer-assisted instruction can develop positive attitudes toward spelling drill and practice, decrease spelling errors, promote individualized study strategies, and enhance spelling performance when used with time-delay procedures. Software programs can emphasize awareness of word structure and spelling strategies as well as use time-delay, voice simulation, and sound effects. Four techniques commonly are used in spelling software: (1) a word is flashed quickly on the screen and then erased, and the student must spell the word from memory; (2) a word is presented with the letters scrambled, and the student must unscramble the letters; (3) a word is missing within a presented sentence, and the student must use context clues to determine the word and then spell it; and (4) three or four versions of a word are shown, and the student must select the one that is spelled correctly. In addition, to aid in writing activities, some software programs offer a built-in spelling scanner that checks for mis-spelled words or typographical errors according to a predetermined file of common words. Hasselbring and Goin (1989) recommend that instructional computer programs in spelling should require the use of long-term memory, be limited in the size of the practice set of words, require practice spread over several different times, and emphasize speed as well as accuracy. The following computer programs are described to give examples of types of software that are available to reinforce spelling skills.

Spell It Deluxe

Spell It Deluxe (produced by Knowledge Adventure) is a CD-ROM spelling program that features over 4,000 words divided into 200 word lists at six levels of difficulty. Five activities are included in which students of all ages learn spelling rules, practice spelling words, work crossword puzzles, edit manuscripts, fill in missing letters, and identify correct spellings. Speech capability lets students hear each word read aloud, and spelling skills are tested with a virtual spelling bee. The word lists as well as crossword and word search puzzles can be customized.

Spelling Blaster Ages 6–9

Spelling Blaster Ages 6–9 (produced by Knowledge Adventure) includes five activities to encourage students to use phonics and context clues to master basic spelling skills while reinforcing reading skills. The program features over 1,700 words and more than 140 spelling lists of varying difficulty levels. The teacher can customize spelling lists with a word editor and monitor misspelling trends with a Spell Track feature. Printable word searches, crossword puzzles, and 25 storybooks encourage learning away from the computer.

Spelling Rules

Spelling Rules (produced by Optimum Resource) includes six progressive learning levels for students in third grade and above. This curriculum-based program covers 21 rules, including forming plurals and compound words, capitalization, and the "*i* before *e*" rule. The degree of difficulty can be set to advance automatically or to remain at the chosen level for extended study and practice. The program can be customized to include new exercises, and progress reports and exercises can be printed.

Stickybear Spellgrabber

Stickybear Spellgrabber (produced by Optimum Resource) is designed for students in first through fourth grade and includes three spelling activities that feature more than 4,000 high-frequency words. In *Picture Spell,* the student moves Stickybear through a maze and picks up letters to spell the name of an on-screen image. *Word Spell* requires the student to unscramble letters to spell and reconstruct words. In *Bear Dunk,* the student tries to guess the words letter by letter before Stickybear gets dunked in a tank of water. The program adjusts to match each student's skill level, and the teacher can create unique word lists for any specialized content.

☀ REFERENCES

Arena, J. (1981). *Diagnostic Spelling Potential Test.* Novato, CA: Academic Therapy.

Brigance, A. H. (1999). *Brigance Diagnostic Comprehensive Inventory of Basic Skills—Revised.* North Billerica, MA: Curriculum Associates.

Brown, A. S. (1988). Encountering misspellings and spelling performances: Why wrong isn't right. *Journal of Educational Psychology, 80,* 488–494.

Bryant, N. D., Drabin, I. R., & Gettinger, M. (1981). Effects of varying unit size on spelling achievement in learning disabled children. *Journal of Learning Disabilities, 14,* 200–203.

Burns, P. C. (1980). *Assessment and correction of language arts difficulties.* Upper Saddle River, NJ: Merrill/Prentice Hall.

Burns, P. C., & Broman, B. L. (1983). *The language arts in childhood education* (5th ed.). Chicago: Rand McNally.

Carpenter, D., & Miller, L. J. (1982). Spelling ability of reading disabled LD students and able readers. *Learning Disability Quarterly, 5,* 65–70.

Cartwright, G. P. (1969). Written expression and spelling. In R. M. Smith (Ed.), *Teacher diagnosis of educational difficulties* (pp. 95–117). Upper Saddle River, NJ: Merrill/Prentice Hall.

Deno, S. L., Mirkin, P. K., & Wesson, C. (1984). How to write effective data-based IEPs. *Teaching Exceptional Children, 16,* 99–104.

Dixon, R. C. (1991). The application of sameness analysis to spelling. *Journal of Learning Disabilities, 24,* 285–291, 310.

Dixon, R. C., & Engelmann, S. (1980). *Corrective spelling through morphographs.* DeSoto, TX: SRA.

Dixon, R. C., Engelmann, S., Bauer, M. M., Steely, D., & Wells, T. (1998). *Spelling mastery.* DeSoto, TX: SRA.

Edgington, R. (1967). But he spelled them right this morning. *Academic Therapy Quarterly, 3,* 58–59.

Fernald, G. (1943). *Remedial techniques in basic school subjects.* New York: McGraw-Hill.

Fernald, G. (1988). *Remedial techniques in basic school subjects.* Austin, TX: PRO-ED.

Foster, K., & Torgesen, J. K. (1983). The effects of directed study on the spelling performance of two subgroups of learning disabled students. *Learning Disability Quarterly, 6,* 252–257.

Gentry, J. R. (1982). An analysis of developmental spellings in *Gnys at wrk. The Reading Teacher, 36,* 192–200.

Gillingham, A., & Stillman, B. (1970). *Remedial training for children with specific disability in reading, spelling, and penmanship* (7th ed.). Cambridge, MA: Educators Publishing Service.

Gordon, J., Vaughn, S., & Schumm, J. S. (1993). Spelling interventions: A review of literature and implications for instruction for students with learning disabilities. *Learning Disabilities Research & Practice, 8,* 175–181.

Graham, S., & Freeman, S. (1986). Strategy training and teacher- vs. student-controlled study conditions: Effects on LD students' spelling performance. *Learning Disability Quarterly, 9,* 15–22.

Graham, S., Harris, K. R., & Loynachan, C. (1994). The Spelling for Writing list. *Journal of Learning Disabilities, 27,* 210–214.

Graham, S., & Voth, V. P. (1990). Spelling instruction: Making modifications for students with learning disabilities. *Academic Therapy, 25,* 447–457.

Greene, G. (1994). The magic of mnemonics. *LD Forum, 19*(3), 34–37.

Hanna, P. R., Hodges, R. E., & Hanna, J. S. (1971). *Spelling: Structure and strategies.* Boston: Houghton Mifflin.

Hasselbring, T. S., & Goin, L. I. (1989). Use of computers. In G. A. Robinson, J. R. Patton, E. A. Polloway, & L. R. Sargent (Eds.), *Best practices in mild mental disabilities.* Reston, VA: Division on Mental Retardation, Council for Exceptional Children.

Hitchcock, M. E. (1989). *Elementary students' invented spellings at the correct stage of spelling development.* Unpublished doctoral dissertation, University of Oklahoma, Norman.

Hodges, R. E. (1966). The psychological bases of spelling. In T. D. Horn (Ed.), *Research on handwriting and spelling.* Champaign, IL: National Council of Teachers of English.

Hoover, H. D., Hieronymus, A. N., Frisbie, D. A., & Dunbar, S. B. (1996). *Iowa Tests of Basic Skills.* Itasca, IL: Riverside.

Kauffman, J. M., Hallahan, D. P., Haas, K., Brame, T., & Boren, R. (1978). Imitating children's errors to improve their spelling performance. *Journal of Learning Disabilities, 11,* 217–222.

Kaufman, A. S., & Kaufman, N. L. (1998). *Kaufman Test of Educational Achievement.* Circle Pines, MN: American Guidance Service.

Kearney, C. A., & Drabman, R. S. (1993). The write–say method for improving spelling accuracy in children with learning disabilities. *Journal of Learning Disabilities, 26,* 52–56.

Kottmeyer, W. (1970). *Teacher's guide for remedial reading.* New York: McGraw-Hill.

Kuska, A., Webster, E. J. D., & Elford, G. (1964). *Spelling in language arts 6.* Don Mills, Ontario, Canada: Thomas Nelson & Sons.

Larsen, S. C., Hammill, D. D., & Moats, L. (1999). *Test of Written Spelling—4.* Austin, TX: PRO-ED.

Lovitt, T. C., Guppy, T. E., & Blattner, J. E. (1969). The use of free-time contingency with fourth graders to increase spelling accuracy. *Behavior Research Therapy, 7,* 151–156.

MacArthur, C., & Graham, S. (1987). Learning disabled students' composing under three methods of text production: Handwriting, word processing, and dictation. *The Journal of Special Education, 21,* 22–42.

Mann, P. H., Suiter, P. A., & McClung, R. M. (1992). *A guide to evaluating mainstreamed students* (4th ed.). Boston: Allyn & Bacon.

Markwardt, F. C., Jr. (1998). *Peabody Individual Achievement Test—Revised.* Circle Pines, MN: American Guidance Service.

McGuigan, C. A. (1975). *The effects of a flowing words list vs. fixed words lists and the implementation of procedures in the add-a-word spelling program* (Working Paper No. 52). Seattle: University of Washington, Experimental Education Unit.

McLoughlin, J. A., & Lewis, R. B. (1994). *Assessing special students* (4th ed.). Upper Saddle River, NJ: Merrill/Prentice Hall.

McNaughton, D., Hughes, C. A., & Clark, K. (1994). Spelling instruction for students with learning disabilities: Implications for research and practice. *Learning Disability Quarterly, 17,* 169–185.

Poteet, J. A. (1980). Informal assessment of written expression. *Learning Disability Quarterly, 3*(4), 88–98.

Rankin, J. L., Bruning, R. H., Timme, V. L., & Katkanant, C. (1993). Is writing affected by spelling performance and beliefs about spelling? *Applied Cognitive Psychology, 7,* 155–169.

Shanker, J. L., & Ekwall, E. E. (1998). *Locating and correcting reading difficulties* (7th ed.). Upper Saddle River, NJ: Merrill/Prentice Hall.

Shinn, M. R., Tindal, G., & Stein, S. (1988). Curriculum-based measurement and the identification of mildly handicapped students: A research review. *Professional School Psychology, 3*(1), 69–85.

Shinn, T. K. (1982). Linguistic and functional spelling strategies. In D. A. Sabatino & L. Mann (Eds.), *A handbook of diagnostic and prescriptive teaching* (pp. 263–295). Rockville, MD: Aspen Systems.

Sidman, M. T. (1979). The effects of group free time and contingency and individual free time contingency on spelling performance. *The Directive Teacher, 1,* 4–5.

Starlin, C. M., & Starlin, A. (1973). *Guides to decision making in spelling.* Bemidji, MN: Unique Curriculums Unlimited.

Stephens, T. M. (1977). *Teaching skills to children with learning and behavior disorders.* Upper Saddle River, NJ: Merrill/Prentice Hall.

Stephens, T. M., Hartman, A. C., & Lucas, V. H. (1982). *Teaching children basic skills: A curriculum handbook* (2nd ed.). Upper Saddle River, NJ: Merrill/Prentice Hall.

Stetson, E. (1988). *Stetson spelling program.* Austin, TX: PRO-ED.

Stowitschek, C. E., & Jobes, N. K. (1977). Getting the bugs out of spelling—or an alternative to the spelling bee. *Teaching Exceptional Children, 9,* 74–76.

Taylor, K. K., & Kidder, E. B. (1988). The development of spelling skills: From first grade through eighth grade. *Written Communication, 5,* 222–244.

Templeton, S. (1986). Synthesis of research on the learning and teaching of spelling. *Educational Leadership, 43*(6), 73–78.

Tindal, G. A., & Marston, D. B. (1990). *Classroom-based assessment: Evaluating instructional outcomes.* Upper Saddle River, NJ: Merrill/Prentice Hall.

Tompkins, G. E. (1998). *Language arts: Content and teaching strategies* (4th ed.). Upper Saddle River, NJ: Merrill/Prentice Hall.

Vallecorsa, A. L., Zigmond, N., & Henderson, L. M. (1985). Spelling instruction in special education classrooms: A survey of practices. *Exceptional Children, 52,* 19–24.

Wesson, C. L. (1987). Curriculum-based measurement: Increasing efficiency. *Teaching Exceptional Children, 20*(1), 46–47.

Westerman, G. S. (1971). *Spelling & writing.* San Rafael, CA: Dimensions.

Whiting, S. A., & Jarrico, S. (1980). Spelling patterns of normal readers. *Journal of Learning Disabilities, 13,* 40–42.

Wilkinson, G. S. (1994). *Wide Range Achievement Test—3.* Austin, TX: PRO-ED.

Wirtz, C. L., Gardner, R., III, Weber, K., & Bullara, D. (1996). Using self-correction to improve the spelling performance of low-achieving third graders. *Remedial and Special Education, 17,* 48–58.

Wong, B. Y. L. (1986). A cognitive approach to teaching spelling. *Exceptional Children, 53,* 169–173.

## CHAPTER 10

Assessing and Teaching Handwriting and Written Expression

Writing is a highly complex form of communication. It is both a skill and a means of self-expression. The process of writing integrates visual, motor, and conceptual abilities and is a major means through which students demonstrate their knowledge of advanced academic subjects. Moreover, Hammill and McNutt (1981) report that writing skills are among the best correlates of reading skills. Skills that correlate with reading skills include competence in writing, spelling, punctuation, capitalization, studying, making sound-letter correspondences, knowing the alphabet, and distinguishing one letter from another. Hammill and McNutt conclude that "a strong relationship exists between reading, which is theoretically a receptive form of written language, and almost all other aspects of written language" (p. 35).

Classroom instruction in handwriting usually begins in kindergarten or first grade. Readiness activities such as tracing, coloring, and copying are emphasized at first. The formation of letters, numbers, and words is stressed until about the third grade. After the third grade, more emphasis is placed on writing as a form of meaningful self-expression, and instruction focuses on using grammar and developing the quality of ideas expressed.

Handwriting and written expression tasks require sustained attention and concentration; thus, some students with learning problems have difficulty learning to write and producing written products. These students need direct, concentrated instruction to become proficient in written communication. This chapter presents the assessment and teaching of writing skills in two major problem areas: handwriting and written expression.

HANDWRITING PROBLEMS

The major objective of instruction in handwriting is legibility. To communicate thoughts effectively through writing, the student first must be taught to write legibly and fluently. Thus, instruction begins by focusing on holding the writing instrument, forming manuscript and cursive letters correctly, and maintaining proper spacing and proportion. Numerous factors contribute to handwriting difficulties: motor problems, faulty visual perception of letters and words, poor visual memory, poor instruction, and lack of motivation.

Fine motor problems also can interfere with handwriting and thus with schoolwork. For example, a student may know how to spell a word but be unable to write legibly or fast enough to keep up with the teacher; thus, the spelling may be poor. This same situation may exist in copying material from the chalkboard and working on seatwork. Unfortunately, many parents and teachers view students as academically slow when, in fact, the real problem is handwriting.

Students show a variety of handwriting problems: slowness, incorrect directionality of letters and numbers, too much or too little slant, spacing difficulty, messiness, inability to stay on a horizontal line, illegible letters, too much or too little pencil pressure, and mirror writing. Newland (1932) examined the cursive handwriting of 2,381 people and found that about 50 percent of the illegibilities involved the letters *a, e, r,* and *t.* Most commonly, people failed to close letters (such as *a* and *b*), closed top loops (such as writing *e* like *i*), looped strokes that should be nonlooped (such as writing *i* like *e*), used straight-up rather than rounded strokes (such as writing *n* like *u*), and exhibited problems with end strokes (not brought up, not brought down, or not left as horizontal). In a study of illegibilities in cursive handwriting of sixth graders, Horton (1970) reports that 12 percent of all errors were incorrect formations of the letter *r.* Thus, the majority of handwriting errors involve the incorrect writing of a few letters. Common number malformations include writing *5* like *3* ($\mathbf{5}$), *6* like *0* ($\mathbf{6}$), *7* like *9* ($\mathbf{7}$), and *9* like *4* ($\mathbf{4}$).

ASSESSMENT OF HANDWRITING SKILLS

In assessing the young student (8 or 9 years old and younger), the teacher should remember that occasional reversals, omissions, and poor spacing are normal. However, a writing problem exists if such errors continue for a long time and if the student does not improve in simple handwriting tasks. Unlike other academic skills, few standardized tests measure handwriting, and informal procedures are used widely. Minimum standards are difficult to set because activities differ in emphasis placed on speed, legibility, and character of handwriting.

Formal Handwriting Assessment

Because only a few norm-referenced measures of handwriting are available, rating scales and inventories frequently are used to assess a student's current proficiency in handwriting. Table 10.1 presents published handwriting assessment devices and includes a standardized measure as well as a rating scale. Published legibility scales provide a subjective evaluation of general handwriting competence. However, the objectivity of such scales has been questioned, and they do not highlight specific errors and illegible forms of handwriting. Thus, handwriting scales may be used best to aid the teacher in rating a writing specimen for screening purposes. To obtain information for instructional purposes, various informal assessment techniques may be helpful.

Informal Handwriting Assessment

The teacher can obtain diagnostic information informally by visually examining the student's handwriting. Writing samples can be used to determine problem areas in legibility. Mann, Suiter, and McClung (1992) suggest obtaining three samples: the student's usual, best, and fastest handwriting. The usual writing sample shows the student's work under normal, nonfatiguing conditions. For the best sample, the student is told to take time and write the sentence with best effort. Then a 3-minute timing is given to see how many times the student can write a given sentence. Sometimes a student can write legibly only when specifically asked to do so. Also, some students write well but at an extremely slow rate. By comparing the three writing samples, the teacher can determine the student's ability with regard to speed and legibility.

While observing the student during handwriting activities, the teacher should note possible problem areas by answering the following questions:

- Does the student grip the pencil correctly and in a comfortable and flexible manner?
- Is the student's paper in the proper position on the writing surface?
- Does the student sit correctly when writing, or is the head too close or too far away from the paper?
- Does the student consistently write with the same hand?
- Does the student appear extremely frustrated, nervous, or emotional when writing?
- Does the student have a negative attitude toward handwriting and appear bored and disruptive?

Additional instructional information can be obtained by analyzing the student's writing samples for error patterns in the following various aspects of handwriting:

- **Letter formation:** Letter formation involves the strokes that make up each letter. In manuscript writing, letters are composed of vertical, horizontal, and slanted lines plus circles or parts of circles, whereas cursive letters are composed of slanted lines, loops, and curved lines. To check for legibility, the teacher can use a piece of cardboard with a hole cut in the center that is slightly larger than a single letter. By exposing one letter at a time, the teacher can see more easily which letters are illegible or poorly formed.

- **Letter size, proportion, and alignment:** The size and proportion of letters are indicated by their height relationship to one another; alignment refers to the evenness of letters along the baseline, with letters of the same size being the same height. These legibility elements can be measured by using a ruler to draw lines that touch the base and tops of as many letters as possible.

- **Spacing:** Spacing should be consistent between letters within words, as well as between words and between sentences.

TABLE 10.1
Published handwriting assessment devices

Test	Age/Grade Level
Basic School Skills Inventory–Third Edition (Hammill, Leigh, Pearson, & Maddox, 1998)	4–6 years
The writing section of this inventory assesses a student's handwriting ability in various tasks: writing from left to right, grasping a pencil, writing first name, maintaining proper writing position, writing letters upon request, copying words, copying from chalkboard to paper, staying on the line, and writing last name. This norm-referenced instrument can be used to identify students who are low in handwriting readiness compared with other students their age. The rating scale also can be used as a criterion-referenced test to determine what skills need to be taught.	
Zaner-Bloser Evaluation Scales (1984)	1st–6th grade
These scales (published by Zaner-Bloser) are based on a national sampling of students' handwriting and frequently are used for assessing manuscript and cursive handwriting. There are scales for first and second grade written in manuscript style and scales for second through sixth grade written in cursive style. Five specimens of handwriting—excellent, good, average, fair, and poor—are provided for each grade level. Each scale contains a sentence or paragraph that the teacher writes on the chalkboard. The students practice writing the model and then copy the sentences in their best handwriting onto a sheet of paper. The teacher compares each paper with the five specimen sentences for the student's grade level and judges the following five elements: letter formation, vertical quality in manuscript and slant in cursive, spacing, alignment and proportion, and line quality. Each student's writing is rated according to the number of satisfactory elements. Through this method, a student's handwriting can be compared with that of students in the same grade level; however, a thorough analysis of errors is needed before planning instructional programs.	

- **Line quality:** Thickness and steadiness of the lines used to form letters should be consistent. The teacher should mark lines that waver or are too thick or too fine. Incorrect hand or body position or cramped fingers can result in inconsistent line quality.

- **Slant:** The slant of letters should be uniform. In general, manuscript letters are perpendicular to the baseline and have a straight up-and-down appearance. In cursive writing the paper is slanted, and strokes are pulled toward the body. Straight lines or lines with a uniform slant can be drawn through the letters to indicate which letters are off slant.
- **Rate:** Handwriting speed can be determined on a writing sample by asking the student to write as well and as rapidly as possible. The rate of handwriting—letters per minute (lpm)—is determined by dividing the total number of letters written by the number of writing minutes allowed. Handwriting proficiency rates include the following:

- Zaner-Bloser scales:
  Grade 1: 25 lpm
  Grade 2: 30 lpm
  Grade 3: 38 lpm
  Grade 4: 45 lpm
  Grade 5: 60 lpm
  Grade 6: 67 lpm

Table 10.2 displays a diagnostic chart for manuscript and cursive writing that highlights errors, likely causes, and remediation procedures.

TABLE 10.2
Diagnostic chart for manuscript and cursive writing

Factor	Problem	Possible Cause	Remediation
		Manuscript Writing	
Shape	Letters slanted	Paper slanted	Place paper straight and pull straight-line strokes toward center of body.
	Varies from standard	Improper mental image of letter	Have student write problem letters on chalkboard.
Size	Too large	Poor understanding of writing lines	Reteach size concept by pointing out purpose of each line on writing paper.
		Exaggerated arm movement	Reduce arm movement, especially on circle and part-circle letters.
		Improper mental image of letter	Have student write problem letters on chalkboard.
	Too small	Poor understanding of writing lines	Reteach size concept by pointing out purpose of each line on writing paper.
		Overemphasis on finger movement	Stress arm movement; check hand–pencil and arm–desk positions to be sure arm movement is possible.
		Improper mental image of letter	Have student write problem letters on chalkboard.
	Not uniform	Adjusting writing hand after each letter	Stress arm movement; move paper with nonwriting hand so writing hand can remain in proper writing position.
		Overemphasis on finger movement	Stress arm movement; check arm–desk and hand–pencil positions.
Space	Crowded letters in words	Poor understanding of space concepts	Reteach uniform spacing between letters (finger or pencil width).
	Too much space between letters	Improper lowercase letter size and shape	Review concepts of size and shape; provide appropriate corrections under size and shape.
Alignment	Letters not sitting on baseline	Improper letter formation	Evaluate work for letter shape; stress bringing straight-line strokes all the way down to baseline.
		Poor understanding of base-line concept	Review purpose of baseline on writing paper.
		Improper hand–pencil and paper–desk positions	Check positions to make sure student is able to reach baseline easily.

(continued on next page)

TABLE 10.2
(continued)

Factor	Problem	Possible Cause	Remediation
	Letters not of consistent height	Poor understanding of size concept	Review concept of letter size in relationship to lines provided on writing paper.
Line quality	Too heavy or too light	Improper writing pressure	Review hand–pencil position; place wadded paper tissue on palm of writing hand to relax writing grip; demonstrate desired line quality.
		Cursive Writing	
Shape	Letters too oval	Overemphasis of arm movement and poor image of letter	Check arm–desk position; review letter size and shape.
	Letters too narrow	Finger writing	Check positions to allow for arm movement.
		Overemphasis of straight-line stroke	Make sure straight-line stroke does not come all the way down to baseline in letters such as *l, b,* and *t.*
		Poor mental image of letter shape	Use transparent overlay for student's personal evaluation of shape.
			In all problems of letter shape, review letters in terms of the basic strokes.
Size	Letters too large	Exaggerated arm movement	Check arm–desk position for over-movement of forearm.
		Poor mental image of letter size	Review base and top line concepts in relation to $1/4$ space, $1/2$ space, and $3/4$ space; use transparent overlay for student's personal evaluation of letter size.
	Letters too small or letters not uniform	Finger movement	Check arm–desk and hand–pencil positions; stress arm movement.
		Poor mental image of letter size	Review concept of letter size ($1/4$ space, $1/2$ space, and $3/4$ space) in relation to base and top lines; use transparent overlay for student's personal evaluation of letter size.
Space	Letters in words crowded or spacing between letters uneven	Finger movement	Check arm–desk, hand–pencil positions; stress arm movement.
		Poor understanding of joining strokes	Review how letters are joined; show ending stroke of one letter joined to beginning stroke of following letter; practice writing letters in groups of five.

TABLE 10.2
(continued)

Factor	Problem	Possible Cause	Remediation
	Too much space provided between letters and words	Exaggerated arm movement	Check arm–desk position for over-movement of forearm.
		Poor understanding of joining strokes	Review joining strokes; practice writing groups of letters by rhythmic count.
	Uneven space between words	Poor understanding of between-word spacing	Review concept of spacing between words; show beginning stroke in second word starting under ending stroke of preceding word.
Alignment	Poor letter alignment along baseline	Incorrect writing position; finger movement; exaggerated arm movement	Check all writing positions; stress even, rhythmic writing movement.
		Poor understanding of baseline concept	Use repetitive exercise with emphasis on relationship of baseline to written word.
		Incorrect use of joining strokes	Review joining strokes.
	Uneven letter alignment in words relative to size	Poor understanding of size concept	Show size relationships between lower- and uppercase, and $1/4$ space, $1/2$ space, and $3/4$ space lowercase letters; use repetitive exercise with emphasis on uniform height of smaller letters.
Speed and ease	Writing becomes illegible under stress and speed (grades 4, 5, and 6)	Degree of handwriting skill is insufficient to meet speed requirements	Improve writing positions; develop more arm movement and less finger movement.
	Writing becomes illegible when writing activity is too long	Handwriting positions have not been perfected to allow handwriting ease	Improve all writing positions, especially hand–pencil position; stress arm movement.
Slant	Back slant	Left-handedness	Correct hand–pencil and paper–desk positions.
	Vertical	Poor positioning	Correct hand–pencil and paper–desk positions.
	Too far right	Overemphasis of finger movement	Make sure student pulls slant strokes toward center of body if right-handed and to left elbow if left-handed.
			Use slant line instruction sheets as aid to teaching slant.
			Use transparent overlay for student's personal evaluation.
			Review all lowercase letters that derive their shape from the slant line.
			Write lowercase alphabet on chalkboard; retrace all slant strokes in color chalk.

Probes can be used to assess a specific handwriting skill and determine instructional targets. Handwriting probe sheets can include tasks such as repeatedly writing the same letter, writing first name, writing uppercase letters, writing lowercase letters, and writing words. The student is timed for 1 minute, and daily performance on the probe sheets is charted to monitor progress. Figure 10.1 presents a probe sheet on writing uppercase manuscript letters.

FIGURE 10.1
Probe sheet for writing uppercase manuscript letters

Name: _____ Date: _____

Time: _____

Rate (letters per minute): _____ Correct

_____ Error

Comments: _____

_____

B —

G —

K —

M —

R —

S —

Y —

FIGURE 10.2
Formation of uppercase and lowercase manuscript letters and numbers

Zaner-Bloser Simplified Manuscript Font

Source: From *Zaner-Bloser Handwriting,* 1996, Columbus, OH: Zaner-Bloser. Reprinted by permission.

3. The student traces the model with a finger and may report the movements aloud while tracing.
4. The student traces the letter model with a pencil.
5. The student copies the letter on paper while looking at the model.
6. The student writes the letter from memory while saying the name of the letter.

A fading model also can be used to teach handwriting. The letter model is presented at first in heavy, dark lines, and the student traces over the model with a finger and the nonwriting end of a pencil. Portions of the model gradually are faded, and the student traces the model with a pencil. The model eventually is removed, and the student writes the letter independent of the model.

As soon as possible, activities should be provided in which words are used and the writing says something. Copying meaningless letters may result in boredom and negative attitudes toward writing. Also, in copying exercises, the letter or word model should be presented at first on the kind of paper the student uses and be placed on the student's desk. It is more difficult for some students to copy far models (e.g., letters or words written on the chalkboard) than near models because the image of a far model must be transferred through space and from different planes.

Letters that consist entirely of vertical and horizontal strokes (such as *E, F, H, I, L, T, i, l,* and *t*) are learned more easily than letters in which straight and curved lines are combined (such as *b, f, h,* and *p*). Letters with easier strokes may be taught first. The teacher should give more attention to the formation of difficult letter forms. In a study of first graders' errors in the formation of manuscript letters, Lewis and Lewis (1965) made the following observations:

- Incorrect size was the most common type of error and was seen more often in descender letters (*p, q, y, g,* and *j*).
- The most frequently reversed letters were *N, d, q,* and *y*.
- Incorrect relationship of parts occurred most frequently in the letters *k, R, M,* and *m*.
- Partial omission occurred most frequently in the letters *m, U,* and *I*.
- Additions often occurred in the letters *q, C, k, m,* and *y*.
- The most frequently misshaped letter forms were *j, G,* and *J*.

Numerous letters often are reversed, such as *b, d, p, q, s, y,* and *N.* In teaching these letters, the teacher should emphasize their correct beginning

point and direction. Students who continue to reverse letters and numbers after the age of 7 or 8 may need direct intervention techniques. As well as receiving immediate corrective feedback followed by practice saying the letter name while tracing and writing it, the student can be instructed to associate the problem letter with another letter that does not cause confusion (e.g., *c* within *d*). In addition to difficulties in formation, some students have problems spacing and aligning manuscript letters. In general, the widest space is left between straight-line letters, and the least amount of space is left between circle letters. Spacing between words equals about the size of one finger or a lowercase *o,* and twice as much space is left between sentences.

Poor formation and alignment should be pointed out to the student; however, if the student has extreme difficulty forming letters and staying on the lines of writing paper, the teacher may choose to facilitate instruction with commercial materials until the student improves. *The Talking Pen* (produced by Wayne Engineering) is an electronic pen with a small beam of infrared light in its tip. This infrared sensor picks up reflected light and triggers a buzzer. The battery-operated pen responds to any pattern of light and dark. When the tip of the pen is on a dark area, the pen is silent. If the pen is moved to a light area, it "squawks." This sound can be silenced only by placing the tip of the pen back on a dark area. Thus, by providing a dark pattern on a light background, the pen "talks" only when the pattern is traced incorrectly. Because the pen provides immediate auditory feedback, it is self-correcting and can be used without direct supervision. The pen can be used with standard headphones so that only the student knows when a mistake is made. Also, Right-Line Paper (available from PRO-ED) is produced in both wide rule and narrow rule and has a raised line superimposed on the printed line so that the writer can feel as well as see the baseline.

Transitional Writing

The transition from manuscript to cursive writing usually occurs during the second or third grade, after the student has mastered manuscript letters. However, some controversy exists concerning whether to begin with manuscript or cursive writing. Those who favor manuscript writing

(Anderson, 1966; Barbe, Milone, & Wasylyk, 1983; Herrick, 1960) claim that it requires less complex movements and reduces reading problems because most printed pages are in manuscript. In addition, manuscript writing tends to be more legible and has received acceptance in business and commercial contexts. Advocates of cursive writing (Strauss & Lehtinen, 1947) believe that it results in fewer reversals because of its rhythmic flow and that it helps the student to perceive whole words. Also, transference problems are avoided if writing begins with cursive. However, some educators (Hildreth, 1963; Templin, 1960; Western, 1977) question the need for teaching cursive writing at all and believe that manuscript writing meets the adult needs of speed and legibility. After reviewing research data concerning manuscript versus cursive writing, Graham and Miller (1980) indicate that most evidence supports manuscript instruction; however, the advantages of manuscript writing have yet to be conclusively demonstrated. Because good arguments are presented on all sides, the teacher should assess each individual situation. It may be best to teach students the form of writing used by their peers. Also, many young children want to learn cursive writing because older peers and adults use it. Regardless of the type of writing instruction, the student should be allowed to choose the mode of writing for tests and expressive writing.

Mann et al. (1992) suggest the following method for transitional writing:

1. The word is printed in manuscript.
2. The letters are connected with a dotted line in color pencil.
3. The student traces over the manuscript letter and the connecting dotted line to form the cursive writing.

The teacher may begin teaching transitional writing with the easier letters and add more difficult

letters one at a time. Certain letters must be taught specifically, such as *b, e, f, k, r, s,* and *z.* Also, when the letter *n* is in the middle or end of a word, enough space must be allowed in front of it for the additional hump needed in the cursive formation of the letter.

Hagin (1983) recommends a simplified handwriting method based on the vertical downstroke rather than the diagonal slant necessary to cursive writing. Manuscript letters are used as a bridge to a simplified writing style with connections between letters made by the natural movement to the next vertical downstroke. Thus, the simplicity of manuscript writing is combined with the speed of cursive writing. In this approach, letter forms are taught through four simple motifs (waves, pearls, wheels, and arrows) that serve as foundations for lowercase letters. After practice at the chalkboard, lessons at the desk include tracing letters on an acetate sheet placed over the printed model, trying to write the letter on the acetate without a model, matching the written letter with the model to determine whether more practice is needed, and providing a permanent record of the letters worked on in that lesson, which later can be compared with previous writing samples during self-evaluation. This approach may help students who have difficulty learning conventional cursive writing patterns.

Cursive Writing

Cursive writing instruction usually begins in the second or third grade, depending upon the skill development of the individual student. In cursive writing the strokes are connected, and fine motor coordination is required to perform many precise movements. The basic strokes in cursive writing are the slant stroke ( ), understroke ( ), downstroke ( ), and overstroke ( ) (Milone & Wasylyk, 1981). Figure 10.3 presents the letter formation of uppercase and lowercase cursive letters and numbers, with arrows and numbering to indicate stroke direction and sequence.

Many of the same techniques used to teach manuscript writing, such as the multisensory approach and fading model, also can be used in cursive writing instruction. The proper slant in cursive writing is achieved by slanting the paper and pulling strokes to the body, as described in the discussion of readiness skills.

FIGURE 10.3
Formation of uppercase and lowercase cursive letters and numbers

Zaner-Bloser Simplified Cursive Font

Source: From *Zaner-Bloser Handwriting,* 1996, Columbus, OH: Zaner-Bloser. Reprinted by permission.

Hanover (1983) suggests teaching cursive writing by grouping letters into families based on similar strokes. The letter families include the following:

- The *e* family (taught first): *e, l, h, f, b, k*
- The family with a handle to which the next letter is attached: *b, o, v, w*
- The family that emphasizes the correct formation of hump-shaped letters: *n, s, y*
- The *c* family: *c, a, d, o, q, g*
- The hump family: *n, m, v, y, x*
- The family with tails in the back: *f, q*
- The family with tails in the front: *g, p, y, z*

TABLE 10.3
Common illegibilities in handwriting

a like u	*Ce*	m like n	*n*	
a like o	*Oe*	n like u	*u*	
a like ce	*Ce*	o like a	*a*	
b like li	*li*	o like v	*v*	
be like I	*be*	p like js	*ps*	
b like k	*k*	r like n	*n*	
c like e	*e*	r like v	*v*	
c like a	*a*	r like i	*i*	
d like cl	*cl*	t like i	*i*	
e like i	*i*	t like I	*l*	
g like y	*y*	u like ee	*ee*	
g like q	*g*	u like ei	*ei*	
i like e	*e*	w like n	*n*	
h like li	*li*	w like ue	*ue*	
h like k	*k*	w like eu	*eu*	
k like ls	*ls*	x like v	*v*	
m like w	*w*	y like ij	*y*	

Newland (1932) notes that four specific letters—*a, e, r,* and *t*—contribute to a large number of errors in cursive writing. The teacher should give special attention to the proper formation of these four letters and also should focus upon the types of errors that result in common illegibilities. Table 10.3 illustrates numerous common illegibilities in forming cursive letters. After students have learned how to form cursive letters accurately, they should be taught to connect letters and to write simple words.

Typewriting and Keyboarding

The typewriter or computer may be a viable alternative for students who have severe fine motor problems or who write very slowly. Polloway and Smith (1992) note that, in addition to simplified motor movements, the advantages of typing include faster speed, the highest degree of legibility, and inherent motivation. Also, the ability to type facilitates the use of computers and word processing programs, and keyboarding is becoming a basic literacy skill because word processing is a standard method of writing. Selected computer programs available for teaching touch-typing and keyboarding include *JumpStart Typing* (Knowledge Adventure), *PAWS in Typing Town!* (SRA), *Stickybear Typing* (Optimum Resource), and *Type to Learn* (Sunburst). Moreover, AlphaSmart (produced by Intelligent Peripheral Devices) is a keyboard that weighs less than 2 pounds and is designed to let students take notes, practice keyboarding, and store reports, essays, or e-mails without having to use a computer. Later, students can transfer text into any application on a computer or directly into a printer.

☀ HANDWRITING ACTIVITIES

Numerous activities and materials enhance the development of handwriting skills. This section presents handwriting activities in three areas: readiness skills, manuscript writing, and cursive writing.

Readiness Activities

- Use body exercises to practice movements such as up and down, left and right, and forward and backward. For example, give the student the following instructions: "Raise your writing hand *up* in the air"; "Make a long straight line with your hand going from *top* to *bottom*"; Make a *circle* with your hand in front of your body"; "Make a long line from *left* to *right*."
- Have the student use scissors to cut out shapes or large letter forms. Coloring activities also can help the student develop muscle control and learn how to use a writing instrument and stay within lines. The student can be asked to color shapes or objects before cutting them out with scissors.
- In seatwork activities, have the student practice making circles by drawing balls, balloons, funny faces, coins, and apples.
- To help develop fine motor skills and strengthen hand and finger muscles, have the student participate in finger painting and clay modeling activities. Squeezing and molding clay is good exercise. Also, the student can be required to manipulate small objects such as nuts and bolts, cubes, buttons, and bottle caps.
- Have the student connect dots in dot-to-dot activities to form geometric shapes or pictures. To help

the student draw straight lines, place dots in a straight line and gradually increase the distance between them. Also, circles and squares can be completed in dot-to-dot fashion. The figures eventually can include actual letters.

• Use chalkboard activities for exercises in copying, dot-to-dot, and completing incomplete figures. The large, free movements made at the chalkboard help develop muscles of the shoulders, arms, hands, and fingers. Academic skills also can be practiced through the use of a chalkboard. A student's lack of handwriting development should not be allowed to impede the completion of academic tasks.

• Have the student practice writing movements in a tray filled with a layer of sand, salt, or cornmeal.

• Provide tracing activities by making dark-line figures (such as shapes, letters, numbers, and objects) on white paper and covering the paper with a sheet of onionskin on which the student can trace. Also, the student can trace on sheets of acetate or plastic with a felt-tip pen or a grease pencil. Clipboards can be used to hold tracing paper in its place, or the paper can be taped to the student's desk.

• Make stencils and templates of shapes, numbers, and letters from plastic, styrofoam, or cardboard. Paper clip the stencil to a piece of paper so the student can write or trace the forms. When the stencil or template is removed, the student can view the figure. Lakeshore Learning Materials produces sets of see-through alphabet templates to provide hands-on writing practice.

• To help develop visual discrimination, give the student pictures containing hidden uppercase and lowercase manuscript letters. Ask the student to locate the hidden letters. A variation of this activity is to have the student produce a picture from a letter (e.g., draw an umbrella from the letter *f*). Also, the student can be asked to think of things that different letters resemble.

Manuscript Writing Activities

• Give the student an individual copy of the alphabet and numbers 0 to 9 to use at a desk. Zaner-Bloser produces self-adhesive alphabet strips (both manuscript and cursive) that have arrows showing correct stroke directions and sequence. Encourage the student to refer to the model during writing exercises.

• Have the student form manuscript letters and numbers by drawing between the double lines of outlined letters.

• Use paper with squares to help the student maintain correct letter size and proportion.

• Have the student form manuscript letters and numbers by completing slash-to-slash and dot-to-dot activities.

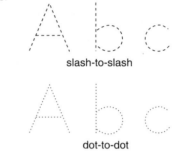

slash-to-slash

dot-to-dot

• On pieces of oaktag, print uppercase letters and their corresponding lowercase letters and cut the pair to form puzzle pieces. Have the student match the uppercase and lowercase manuscript pairs. This activity is self-correcting, because the puzzle pieces will fit together only if the letters correspond to each other. A variation of this activity would be to match manuscript letters to corresponding cursive letters.

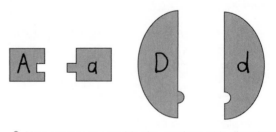

• Use arrows to provide the student with direction clues in forming specific letters.

• Use color dots to indicate the starting and stopping positions for each letter stroke.

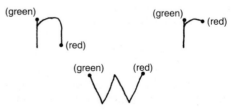

Also, letters can be color-coded to indicate their position with respect to the line on which the student is writing. Letters that stay on the line are written in green (grass letters), letters that extend above the line are written in blue (sky letters), and letters that extend below the line are written in brown (root letters). Eventually the color cueing is faded.

• Have the student who reverses letters (such as *b* and *d*) form an association to facilitate memory of the direction of the letters. For example, the student can learn to associate lowercase *b* with uppercase *B* or identify the stem of *b* with the left hand. Another method is to have the student raise the left arm in front of the body and grasp the left elbow with the right hand. When looking down, the student will see the letter *b*. For all reversal problems, encourage the student to refer to an alphabet taped to the desk before writing the letter.

• Have the student announce strokes while writing certain letters. For example:

m—"short line down; back up, around, and down; back up, around, and down"
h—"tall line down, back up halfway, around, and down"
i—"short line down, dot"

• On balsa wood, print manuscript letters and numbers and use a razor-sharp knife to groove out the wood deep enough for a pencil to follow. Have the student practice forming letters by tracing the letters and numbers with a pencil in the grooves.

• For the student who has difficulty with letter size and staying on the baseline, make a cardboard frame with a rectangular piece cut out of the frame. The student writes within the window area and thus has a barrier that stops the downward movement. Frames can be made for words with one-line, two-line, and three-line letters.

Masking tape also can be used on paper to represent baselines and margins.

• For the student who has difficulty with spacing between letters within a single word and between words themselves, make an underlay sheet. Trace over the lines on a piece of notebook paper with a felt-tip pen; then draw vertical lines on the paper one letter distance apart. This makes squares the appropriate size for letters. The student places notebook paper on top of the underlay sheet. The student can see the felt-tip pen lines and use them as cues for proper spacing. One letter is written in each square, and one square is skipped between words. An additional method for the student who has difficulty remembering to space between words involves giving the student a two-leaded pencil that has red on one end and blue on the other end. Have the student alternate colors each time a new word is written (e.g., first a blue word, then red, then blue, and so on). Changing the color serves as a cue to stop and space properly. Also, if words run together, have the student place the index finger of the nonwriting hand at the end of each word to allow space for the next word.

• Use the Practice Pad as a handwriting center to offer motivation and handwriting exercise. The student can practice any of the handwriting skills provided by the model.

Cursive Writing Activities

• To help the student see the similarity of manuscript and cursive letters, make a chart that has manuscript and corresponding cursive letters written next to each other.

• Make dot-to-dot cursive letters and have the student form the letter by connecting the dots. The dots gradually can be faded so that the student is required to complete the letter.

• Have the student trace a cursive letter several times. Gradually reduce the cues to only the first stroke and have the student finish forming the letter.

• Use arrows and color-coded dots to show direction of the stroke and beginning and ending points.

• Encourage the student to practice forming cursive letters until the written letters look like the model and show best effort; then the student can stop and proceed to another writing activity. With this method, the student practices only those letters that present difficulty.

• Have the student practice letters with similar movement patterns at the same time. Also, the student can say the strokes of the letters while writing.

• After the student has learned the correct letter formation of cursive writing, provide practice activities that involve meaningful writing. For example, on the chalkboard write an informative letter to parents and have the student copy it, giving special attention to good handwriting.

• Have the student copy a series of ten stories and draw a picture to accompany each one. When the student has completed all the stories and pictures in the series, put them together in a booklet to be displayed or taken home.

COMMERCIAL HANDWRITING PROGRAMS

Many commercial programs and materials are available to develop or improve handwriting skills. The following selected programs and materials may help students having difficulty with handwriting.

Cursive Writing Program

The *Cursive Writing Program,* developed by S. Miller and S. Engelmann (published by SRA), consists of 140 developmentally sequenced lessons designed to teach cursive writing to students who have mastered manuscript writing. The program teaches how to form letters, create words, write sentences, and improve writing speed and accuracy. The 20-minute lessons feature a simplified orthography that reduces unnecessary frills, slant arrows to assist in slanting the paper correctly, slant bars to prompt proper spacing, exercises to correct errors, and an emphasis on high-frequency word and letter combinations. Points are awarded following the successful completion of a series of exercises. The materials include a teacher presentation book and a student workbook of practice exercises.

D'Nealian Handwriting

The *D'Nealian Handwriting* program (Thurber, 1987) is designed to simplify handwriting for the readiness student through eighth grade. The forms of most lowercase manuscript letters are the basic forms of the corresponding cursive letters. Each manuscript letter is made with a continuous stroke, except the dotted letters *i* and *j* and the

crossed letters *f, t,* and *x.* The transition to cursive writing is simplified because the addition of simple joining strokes is all that is needed for all but five letters (*f, r, s, v,* and *z*). The program includes student workbooks and teacher's editions for each grade level; alphabet cards and self-sticking alphabet tapes are available.

Handwriting: A Fresh Start

Handwriting: A Fresh Start (Powers & Kaminsky, 1988) is a multisensory remedial program designed to improve cursive writing. The approach links letter forms to guided eye–hand motor skills. Verbal descriptions are paired with letter formations to combine auditory and motor feedback with visual imagery. Horizontal and vertical guidelines (power writing lines) define writing space for proper formation, sizing, and spacing letters. These cues fade gradually in later lessons. Review and reinforcement activities prompt transfer from power writing lines to regular writing lines.

Zaner-Bloser Handwriting

Zaner-Bloser Handwriting (published by Zaner-Bloser) contains a series of seven workbooks for students in kindergarten through sixth grade. For older students there are additional books that focus on common problems and corrective techniques as well as self-instruction in handwriting. Manuscript writing is introduced in kindergarten, and cursive writing is introduced in second or third grade. Letters are introduced systematically, and elements of legibility are emphasized. This revised edition features new simplified letters; for example, the cursive Q no longer looks like a 2, and the extra loops on more than half of the cursive uppercase letters are eliminated. Also, there are only four simple strokes to learn for the entire manuscript alphabet. In addition to a teacher's edition for each grade level, there are supportive materials available such as letter cards, wipe-off practice cards, evaluation guides, and home/school worksheets.

WRITTEN EXPRESSION SKILLS

Written expression, one of the highest forms of communication, reflects a person's level of comprehension, concept development, and abstraction. It is how an individual organizes ideas to convey a message. Whereas handwriting is primarily a visual-motor task that includes copying, tracing, and writing from dictation, written expression requires complex thought processes.

The skill of written expression usually is not acquired until an individual has had extensive experience with reading, spelling, and verbal expression. Problems in written expression may not be diagnosed until the upper elementary school years, when the student is required to use the various language components in written composition and emphasis is placed upon refining writing skills. Written expression is the most complex language arts skill and is based on listening, talking, handwriting, reading, and spelling. Thus, it generally is not stressed in instructional programs for learners with mild disabilities. Teachers tend instead to focus on the skills prerequisite to written expression. However, as the student acquires those prerequisite skills, instruction in written expression is warranted.

In a comparison of the written products of students with learning disabilities and their normally achieving peers in fourth, eighth, and eleventh grades, Houck and Billingsley (1989) found that students with learning disabilities write fewer words and sentences, write more words per sentence, produce fewer words with seven letters or more and fewer sentence fragments, and have a higher percentage of capitalization and spelling errors. Research indicates that the writing difficulties of students with learning disabilities result from problems with basic text production skills, scant knowledge about writing, and difficulties with planning and revising text (Graham, Harris, MacArthur, & Schwartz, 1991). Additional areas of difficulty may include idea generation, maturity of themes, organization, grammar, and theme development (Smith, 1998).

Christenson, Thurlow, Ysseldyke, and McVicar (1989) contend that written language instruction for students with mild disabilities can be improved by increasing the time allocated for instruction, teaching written language as an integrated process, and coordinating written language activities with different content areas. Students with learning problems experience a variety of writing problems, and the treatment of these difficulties in a systematic program requires that teachers at all levels allocate instructional time for writing and the review and editing of written products.

ASSESSMENT OF WRITTEN EXPRESSION SKILLS

Assessment of written expression yields information about a student's skill level and aids in instructional planning. The teacher can assess various components of written expression to determine deficiencies. A scope and sequence chart for written expression is provided in Appendix A according to the areas of capitalization and punctuation, written composition, and creative expression. It provides a skill hierarchy by grade level for assessing skills that need to be taught. Assessment techniques are presented in two broad categories: formal standardized and criterion-referenced tests and informal techniques specifically related to instructional planning.

Formal Written Expression Assessment

Many standardized survey tests of academic achievement contain some measure of written language. The most frequently assessed areas include word usage, mechanics, and grammar. However, with the shift in emphasis from the product to the process of writing, newer tests include measures of composition. Standardized achievement tests that evaluate written expression skills include the following:

- *California Achievement Tests—Fifth Edition* (1992): Assesses mechanics (punctuation and capitalization), word usage, and understanding of sentence structure and paragraph organization for students in first through twelfth grade.
- *CTB Writing Assessment System* (1993): Assesses writing samples for students in second through twelfth grade.
- *Metropolitan Achievement Tests—Seventh Edition: Writing Test* (Balow, Farr, & Hogan, 1997): Assesses ideas and development; organization, unity, and coherence; word choice; sentences; grammar and usage; and mechanics for students in first through twelfth grade.
- *Peabody Individual Achievement Test—Revised* (Markwardt, 1998): Assesses prewriting skills for students in kindergarten through first grade and written language skills for students in second through twelfth grade.
- *Woodcock Language Proficiency Battery—Revised* (Woodcock, 1991): Assesses dictation, proofing, writing samples, and writing fluency for preschoolers through adults.

Standardized diagnostic tests of written expression and criterion-referenced tests of writing skills provide additional basic information useful in planning instruction. Measures of writing skills can focus on composition skills such as organization, vocabulary, style, and originality of ideas, as well as mechanical aspects including syntax, usage, capitalization, punctuation, spelling, and handwriting. Table 10.4 describes diagnostic and criterion-referenced tests of written expression.

Informal Written Expression Assessment

The teacher begins informal assessment of written expression by obtaining representative writing samples from the student and analyzing them to determine specific weaknesses. Five major components of written expression that can be analyzed are fluency, syntax, vocabulary, structure, and content. Also, curriculum-based measurement is an informal assessment technique that uses a set of standardized procedures to assess written expression skills. Finally, portfolio assessment can give the teacher insight into student growth.

Fluency   *Fluency* is defined as quantity of verbal output and refers to the number of words written. Isaacson (1988) notes a significant correlation between fluency and other measures of writing skills. For example, a student who is able to write more words is likely to be more fluent in generating ideas as well. Fluency is related to age and includes sentence length and complexity (McCarthy, 1954; Meckel, 1963). The average sentence length in a composition is determined by counting the number of words and the number of sentences in the composition and dividing the number of words by the number of sentences. Cartwright (1968) found that the average sentence length of an 8-year-old is eight words and that this length increases one word per year through age 13. He suggests that any deviation of more than two words indicates a problem.

Syntax   *Syntax* refers to construction of sentences or the way words are put together to form phrases, clauses, and sentences. Frequent written syntax errors of students with learning disabilities include word omissions, distorted word order, incorrect verb and pronoun usage, incorrect word endings, and lack of punctuation (D. J. Johnson & Myklebust, 1967). Thomas, Englert, and Gregg (1987) found that a large proportion of the syntactic errors of older writers with learning disabilities is attributed to errors in which the student generates a phrase instead of a sentence.

One method for assessing syntactic maturity is counting the number of sentences that fall into several different categories: incomplete (fragment), simple, compound, and complex. The percentage of usage of the four sentence types in a writing sample can be computed to provide comparisons and a record of the student's progress. Cartwright (1969) suggests that the number of compound and complex sentences increases with age and that the use of incomplete and simple sentences decreases.

Another common measure of syntax is T-unit length (words per terminable unit). A T-unit is the shortest grammatically correct segment that a passage can be divided into without creating fragments (Hunt, 1965). Thus, a sentence consisting of one T-unit may have subordinate clauses, phrases, or modifiers embedded within it, whereas a compound sentence is two T-units because it can be divided into two grammatically complete units without leaving fragments. The ratio of the average T-unit length is a total count of the number of words written divided by the number of T-units present. T-unit length is positively correlated to other measures of written expression (Isaacson, 1988), and a general increase in the average T-unit length occurs throughout the school years (Morris & Crump, 1982).

Vocabulary   *Vocabulary* refers to the originality or maturity in the student's choice of words and the variety of words used in the written task. The student's vocabulary should increase with age and experience; however, Morris and Crump (1982) report that, compared with their normally achieving peers at four age levels, students with learning disabilities use fewer word types in their writing. Wiig and Secord (1994) report that some students with learning problems have adequate vocabularies for their age range but have assigned a small number of attributes to each word.

The Type Token Ratio (TTR) (W. Johnson, 1944) is a measure of vocabulary that is the ratio of different words used (types) to the total number of words used (tokens). For example, the sentence *The two boys went fishing in Noonan's Lake early yesterday morning* has a high TTR (1.0)—11 total words are used, and all 11 words are different. In contrast, the sentence *The little girl saw the little*

TABLE 10.4

Diagnostic and criterion-referenced tests of written expression

Test	Age/Grade Level

Diagnostic Tests

Oral and Written Language Scales: Written Expression   5–21 years
(Carrow-Woolfolk, 1995)

> This test measures writing skills including the use of conventions (handwriting, spelling, and punctuation), the use of syntactical forms (modifiers, phrases, and sentence structures), and the ability to communicate meaningfully (relevance, cohesiveness, and organization). The examiner presents a variety of developmentally appropriate writing prompts, either verbally, with pictures, or in print, and the student writes responses in a booklet. The scale can be administered individually or in small groups in about 15 to 25 mintues and yields standard scores, grade and age equivalents, and percentiles. Computer scoring with the ASSIST system provides a score profile, score narrative, suggested exercises, and a descriptive analysis.

Test of Early Written Language—2   3–10 years
(Hresko, Herron, & Peak, 1996)

> The test includes two forms, each with a Basic Writing and a Contextual Writing subtest. The Basic Writing subtest measures a child's ability in areas such as spelling, capitalization, punctuation, sentence construction, and metacognitive knowledge. The Contextual Writing subtest measures a child's ability to construct a story when provided with a picture prompt, and the subtest focuses on areas such as story format, cohesion, thematic maturity, ideation, and story structure. Administration time is 30 to 45 minutes; the test provides standard score quotient, percentiles, and age equivalents.

Test of Written Expression (McGhee, Bryant, Larsen, & Rivera, 1995)   6–14 years

> The test includes a series of items that assess different skills associated with writing. Also, the student reads or hears a prepared story starter and uses it as a stimulus for writing an essay. The essay is scored by evaluating performance across ideation, vocabulary, grammar, capitalization, punctuation, and spelling. The test can be administered to individuals or groups and yields standard scores and percentile ranks.

Test of Written Language—3 (Hammill & Larsen, 1996)   2nd–12th grade

> The test assesses cognitive, linguistic, and conventional components of written language by having the student look at pictures and write a complete story based on the pictures. Subtests with spontaneous formats (essay analysis) include contextual conventions—measures capitalization, punctuation, and spelling; contextual language—measures vocabulary, syntax, and grammar; and story construction—measures plot, character development, and general composition. Subtests with contrived formats include vocabulary—measures word usage; spelling—measures ability to form letters into words; style—measures punctuation and capitalization; logical sentences—measures ability to write conceptually sound sentences; and sentence combining—measures syntax. Two equivalent forms are available, and percentiles and standard scores are provided. The test can be administered to individuals or groups in about 90 minutes, and the PRO-SCORE system allows computer scoring.

Criterion-Referenced Test

Brigance Diagnostic Comprehensive Inventory of Basic Skills—Revised   K–9th grade
(Brigance, 1999)

> This criterion-referenced inventory includes a grade placement test in sentence writing. The writing section also assesses the student's strengths and weaknesses in the following areas: writing cursive lowercase and uppercase letters in sequence, quality of manuscript and cursive writing, writing personal data, capitalization, punctuation, addressing envelopes, writing a personal letter, writing a letter requesting information, and writing a customer-complaint letter. A student record book tracks assessments administered, correct and incorrect responses, progress since last testing, and instructional objectives. A class record book also is available.

boy in the little house has a fairly low TTR (.63)—11 total words are used, but only 7 of these words are different. A low TTR may indicate inadequate vocabulary for the written expression task. This technique also can be used for measuring long compositions; however, the number of different vocabulary words decreases as the total number of words in the composition increases (Carroll, 1938). When comparing several compositions produced by the same student or by different students, the same type of sample should be taken. For example, the first 50 words should be used from each composition instead of selecting the first 50 words from some compositions and the last 50 words from others.

Vocabulary variety also can be assessed by using the index of diversification (Carroll, 1938; Miller, 1951). This refers to the average number of words between each occurrence of the most frequently used word in the writing sample. Cartwright (1969) suggests dividing the total number of words in the sample by the number of *the's* or by the number of times the word used most often appears. The higher the value of the index, the more diverse the vocabulary.

Finally, vocabulary can be assessed by measuring the number of unusual words. For this assessment, a sample of the student's written expression should be compared with a list of words frequently used by other students—for example, the Dolch (1955, 1960) word list. The number of words the student uses that do not appear on the list indicates the extent of the student's vocabulary.

Structure   *Structure* includes the mechanical aspects of writing, such as punctuation, capitalization, and rules of grammar. The Grammatical-Correctness Ratio (GCR) (Stuckless & Marks, 1966) can be used to assess structure. The GCR quickly analyzes the total number of the student's grammatical errors. To obtain the GCR, a sample of the student's writing (e.g., 50 words from a composition) is scored by counting the number of grammatical errors. The error count is subtracted from 50, and this difference is divided by 50. To obtain a percentage score, this last number is multiplied by 100. Because the final result can be displayed as a percentage, GCRs can be calculated for any number of words and still yield a score that can be compared with the student's previous scores. A GCR score also can be calculated for one specific type of grammatical error or for errors in punctuation or capitalization.

Structure also can be assessed by tabulating types of errors in the writing sample. The frequency of specific errors can be recorded to target individual weaknesses. An error analysis chart (presented in Figure 10.4) provides a profile of errors in writing structure. Errors in spelling (phonetic and nonphonetic misspellings) and handwriting (problems with letter formation, spacing, consistent slant, line quality, alignment, letter size, and fluency) also can be noted.

In addition to spontaneous writing samples, teacher-made test items also can be used to analyze specific elements of writing structure. Written compositions may not include enough opportunities for various errors to occur. For example, the student may write only sentences that contain grammatical forms or punctuation the student knows how to use. Thus, to assess punctuation, the teacher can devise several short sentences in which punctuation rules are used. The sentences can be dictated for the student to write correctly or can be presented unpunctuated for the student to correct. For example:

- School starts at 8 30
- Twenty two boys are in the class
- Dr Goodman lives in Richmond Virginia
- His birthday is January 31 1943
- Blaze our Golden Retriever had four puppies

Content   *Content,* the fifth component of written expression, can be divided into accuracy, ideas, and organization (Cartwright, 1969). Similarly, Isaacson (1988) indicates that aspects of content that should be considered in assessment include idea generation, coherence of all parts of the composition to the topic or theme, organization or logical sequence, and awareness of audience. The nature of the written assignment determines how the different factors should be weighed. For example, accuracy carries more weight when the written exercise is a presentation of historical facts. Cartwright suggests rating each factor on a scale from 0 to 10. A 10 in ideas would indicate that the ideas were pertinent to the topic and represented a high degree of originality, and a 0 would indicate lack of originality or understanding of the task. Some youngsters with learning problems may have limited ideas because

FIGURE 10.4

Writing structure error analysis chart

Sample Elicitation Procedure: _____ _____ Date: _____ Students' Names	Verbs		Pro- nouns		Words					Sen- tences		Capitals			Punctuation						
	Agreement	Tense	Personal	Possessive	Additions	Substitutions	Modifiers	Negatives	Plurals	Incomplete	Run-on	Beginning sentences	Proper nouns	Inappropriate use	Period	Comma	Question mark	Apostrophe	Colon	Other	Total

of lack of experience, while others may have the ideas but not the ability to sequence them in logical order. Thomas et al. (1987) found that in expository writing (i.e., the ability to explain or provide information on a topic), students with learning disabilities frequently terminate their text prematurely, thus indicating difficulty in producing multiple factual statements about familiar topics. In addition, these students tend to repeat information and generate irrelevant items pertaining to the topic. Wallace, Larsen, and Elksnin (1992) note that evaluation of content is especially difficult because the ideas and levels of abstraction contained in the written product depend on the student's intelligence, language experiences, culture, background, and interests.

Profile of Components   By examining a student's writing sample, such as an autobiography, the teacher can determine which skills need to be introduced or remediated and which have been acquired. Poteet (1980) developed the *Checklist of Written Expression Skills,* containing four areas:

penmanship, spelling, grammar (capitalization, punctuation, and syntax), and ideation (type of writing, substance, productivity, comprehensibility, reality, and style). Likewise, Weiner (1980) devised the *Diagnostic Evaluation of Writing Skills,* consisting of the following areas: graphic (visual features), orthographic (spelling), phonologic (sound components), syntactic (grammatical), semantic (meaning), and self-monitoring.

A profile of the assessment of written expression components is presented in Figure 10.5. The profile can be used with an individual student or an entire class to record strengths and weaknesses and student progress. Although some interpretation is required, profiles standardize observations and thus yield a more reliable and valid informal assessment. Also, determining the error patterns associated with each writing component is essential for instructional planning.

Curriculum-Based Measurement   Curriculum-based measurement allows the teacher to collect data routinely and monitor instructional progress.

FIGURE 10.5

Profile of written expression components

| Students' Names | Fluency | Syntax | | Vocabulary | | | Structure | | Content | | |
	Average Sentence Length	Sentence Type Variety	T-Unit Length	Type Token Ratio	Index of Diversi-fication	Number of Unusual Words	Gram-matical Correct-ness Ratio	Type of Errors	Accuracy Rating	Ideas Rating	Organi-zational Rating

Writing skills are assessed through repeated 3-minute writing samples using stimulus story starters or topic sentences. The use of 3-minute writing samples represents a general assessment of writing skills rather than a diagnostic assessment of specific writing deficits; however, it allows the teacher to base instructional decisions on direct, repeated measurement.

Wesson (1987) notes that 30 story starters are needed for one year of measurement. When the story starters are written on note cards, the teacher can write the students' initials on the back so that the story starter is not used by the same student more than three times. The measures can be administered to a group of students rather than individually. Tindal and Marston (1990) present three evaluation strategies: (1) holistic scoring—raters review compositions within the same distribution to determine an overall impression and assign a value from a rating scale; (2) analytical scoring—writing samples are scored on specific qualities or traits (such as organization, ideas, wording, and punctuation) with operational definitions and criteria to aid the judgment process; and (3) primary-trait scoring—raters focus on the degree of consistency

in the purpose of writing according to defined traits (such as creativity and persuasion). Parker, Tindal, and Hasbrouck (1991) indicate that holistic judgments appear to be reliable in a writing process approach when there is no judgment of improvement over time; however, in a subskill mastery instructional approach, the most useful indexes for monitoring writing progress are number of correct word sequences, mean length of correct word sequences, and percent of legible words written.

To implement curriculum-based measurement of written expression, the teacher can use the steps in Table 10.5, which includes the administration and scoring procedures of written expression measures as well as procedures for determining long-range goals and graphing data. Figure 10.6 presents a graph of curriculum-based measurement data and illustrates a long-range goal or aim line. Deno, Mirkin, and Wesson (1984) provide the following mean scores for average students: first grade—14.7 words in 3 minutes, second grade—27.8 words, third grade—36.6 words, fourth grade—40.9 words, fifth grade—49.1 words, and sixth grade—53.3 words.

TABLE 10.5

Procedures for administering and scoring written expression measures, determining long-range goals, and graphing data

Step 1:	To establish a baseline, provide each student with a lined sheet of paper and the same story starter or topic sentence on any three days of a given week. Discuss writing ideas, and then have the students write for a 3-minute period. Collect the papers after 3 minutes.
Step 2:	Count the number of words or letter sequences representing words written after the given story starter or topic sentence. Ignore misspellings, content, punctuation, and organization. Continue with this procedure for two more days, giving two new story starters or topic sentences during the week. Plot the student's scores on a graph (see Figure 10.6).
Step 3:	Find the median score from the three baseline scores. This is the middle number when ranked from lowest to highest.
Step 4:	Compute the long-range goal. Count the number of weeks left in the school year or semester. Multiply the number of weeks by 2.0 (rate of growth), and add the median score obtained from the baseline week [e.g., 21 weeks $\times$ 2.0 = 42; 42 + 14 [baseline median] = 56 [goal]].
Step 5:	Plot the goal data point on the graph on the line for the last week. Draw the aim line connecting the baseline median data point to the goal data point. This represents the line that the student's performance should follow as the student progresses through the school year.
Step 6:	Beginning with the first week after the baseline, measure student performance two times each week. On two different days in a given week, provide the students with a different story starter or topic sentence. Following a brief discussion of the story starter or topic, tell the students to write for 3 minutes and say "Begin writing."
Step 7:	After the 3-minute period, say "Stop." Collect the papers and count the number of words or letter sequences representing words written after the given story starter or topic sentence.
Step 8:	Plot each score on the graph in the space corresponding with the day and week. Connect the data points.
Step 9:	Continue with this procedure throughout the year. Analyze student error patterns for information regarding writing deficits of individual students. Use this information in planning instructional lessons. Graphs also can be made to monitor progress on specific skills (e.g., capitalization, punctuation, and subject-verb agreement).

In addition to increasing student motivation to write, monitoring written expression provides the teacher with information that encourages sensitive and relevant instructional modifications. For example, for a student who has great difficulty with written expression, the following modifications are useful:

• Allow the student to copy selected words during the 3-minute timing to help get the student started. Selected words may center around a theme (e.g., marine life), word family (e.g., *cat, fat, rat, bat*), or a special interest (such as sports).

• Provide story starters that include sentences with missing words or letters. Have the student write words or letters for the blanks. Count the number of correct words that student input helped create.

• Periodically introduce specific written expression interventions (e.g., capitalization, punctuation, compound words, and contractions) and note whether student writings reflect content from instructional lessons.

• Use experiences (e.g., science project, class visitor, field trip, or movie) for story starters.

• If the student is unable to produce sentences, have the student generate words. Score the number of legible words.

Portfolio Assessment The student can compile a collection of self-produced written words to reflect efforts, progress, and achievements in written expression. Writing portfolios may include notes, diagrams, drafts, and the final version of a writing project, as well as diverse entries such as journal writings, letters, poems, or essays (Wolf, 1989). The student's self-assessment of the writings as well as the teacher's notes about the writings and the student as a writer also may be

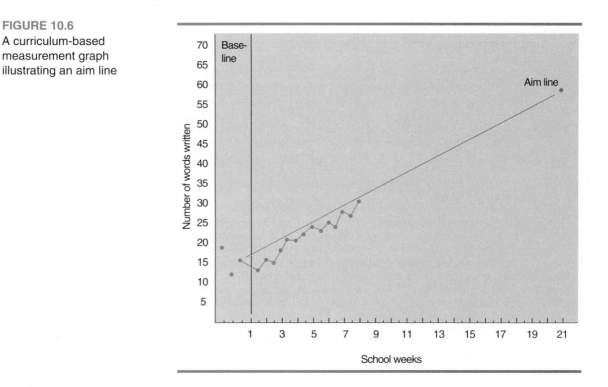

FIGURE 10.6
A curriculum-based measurement graph illustrating an aim line

included. Thus, the student is a participant in the assessment process and learns to set goals and evaluate learning in progress. For use as an assessment tool to chart student learning, performance, and growth, *Writing Portfolios* (published by Curriculum Associates) are available in two levels: primary for students in first through third grade and intermediate for students in fourth through eighth grade. These three-pocket student writing portfolios are divided into the areas of prewriting, drafting and revising, and publishing and editing, and they contain information and tips about writing as a process. The teacher's guide includes prewriting activities, writing conference forms, editing and proofreading checklists, and self-evaluations.

☀ TEACHING WRITTEN EXPRESSION SKILLS

Written expression primarily is concerned with creative writing but also includes functional writing. *Creative writing* is the personal expression of

thoughts and experiences in a unique manner, as in poetry, story writing, and personal narratives. *Functional writing* focuses on conveying information in a structured form, such as writing answers to chapter questions, social and business letters, invitations, reports and essays, or minutes of a meeting. The writing program for students with learning problems should include a range of writing experiences in both creative and functional writing. The student must learn to organize thoughts logically and follow the proper mechanics of writing (including punctuation and capitalization) to communicate clearly and accurately.

Process Approach to Writing

In teaching writing, the emphasis has shifted from the product of writing to the process involved in creating that product (Graves, 1985). The product approach focuses primarily on grammar, spelling, capitalization, punctuation, and handwriting. The process approach stresses meaning first and then skills in the context of meaning. Students work through various stages (e.g., prewriting, drafting,

TABLE 10.6

Overview of writing stages

Prewriting Stage

Select a topic for the written piece.

Consider the purpose for writing (e.g., to inform, describe, entertain, or persuade).

Identify the audience for whom the writing is intended (e.g., classmates, parents, businesspersons, or publishers).

Choose an appropriate form for the composition based on purpose and audience (e.g., story, report, poem, script, or letter).

Engage in rehearsal activities to gather and organize ideas for writing (e.g., drawing, talking, reading, interviewing, brainstorming ideas, and clustering main ideas and details).

Participate in writing a collaborative or group composition with the teacher so that the teacher can model or demonstrate the writing process and clarify questions and misconceptions.

Drafting Stage

Write a rough draft, skipping every other line and allowing adequate space for revising.

Emphasize content rather than mechanics, grammar, and spelling.

Revising Stage

Reread the rough draft and make changes by adding, substituting, deleting, and moving text.

Share the composition in writing groups in which listeners respond with compliments as well as comments and suggestions about how to improve the composition.

Make revisions based on feedback from the writing group by crossing out, drawing arrows, and writing in the space left between the writing lines.

Editing Stage

Focus on mechanics, including capitalization, punctuation, spelling, sentence structure, word usage, and formatting considerations.

Proofread the composition by reading word by word and hunting for errors (e.g., spelling, capitalization, and punctuation) rather than reading for meaning, and insert proofreading symbols to indicate needed changes.

Correct as many mechanical errors as possible and, if necessary, use a dictionary or have a conference with the teacher for instruction or a mini-lesson on a needed skill.

Publishing Stage

Publish the writing in an appropriate form (e.g., make a covered booklet or contribute to a newspaper or magazine).

Share the finished composition with classmates or appropriate audiences by reading it aloud in the class "author's chair" or displaying the writing on a bulletin board.

Source: From *Students with Learning Disabilities,* (p. 496), 5th ed., by C. D. Mercer, 1997. Upper Saddle River, NJ: Merrill/Prentice Hall. Copyright 1997 by Prentice Hall Publishing Company. Reprinted by permission.

revising, editing, and publishing) and focus their attention on one stage at a time (Tompkins, 1994). An overview of the writing stages is presented in Table 10.6.

In the process approach, the student independently selects a writing topic and rehearses (brainstorms) before writing. After drafting and redrafting for several days, the student discusses the work with the teacher or peers and then revises and edits. Revising refers to reworking the text in a way that alters its content or structure, whereas editing is the process of correcting errors in grammar, syntax, punctuation, and spelling. Finally, the product is published or shared with the audience for whom

the student has written. Thus, the teacher's role has shifted from merely assigning and assessing a product to working with the student throughout the writing process. By working through the writing process, the student develops problem-solving skills, critical thinking skills, and a positive self-image.

Isaacson (1995) discusses four characteristics of the process approach in which the teacher introduces the student to the entire process of writing, from initial idea generation to editing of the final draft:

1. *The process should be modeled.* In a prewriting discussion, the teacher should model

planning strategies by raising questions on the topic and demonstrate ways to organize information (e.g., charts or semantic maps). The teacher can model how to convert planning notes into written sentences by thinking aloud while performing the task. Finally, the teacher should model reviewing and revising strategies and show that first drafts differ greatly from the finished copy.

2. *The process can be collaborative.* Collaboration can involve either the teacher or other students in activities such as brainstorming ideas, contributing and organizing information, giving constructive feedback, and editing for mechanical errors. Writing groups can be formed to share writing and develop ideas; a peer team is also a good arrangement for editing written work.

3. *The process can be prompted.* The teacher can assist by prompting the steps of the writing process or helping with writing decisions. For example, a prompt procedure in the prewriting stage can begin with having students list isolated words related to a topic. In the editing stage the teacher can write a code in the margin for a type of error (e.g., *sp* for spelling, *v* for verb form, and *cap* for capitalization) to prompt the student to find and correct errors.

4. *The process should become self-initiated and self-monitored.* The teacher can show the student specific writing strategies and ideas for self-instructional statements, such as a sentence-writing strategy (PENS), a paragraph-writing strategy (PLEASE), an error-monitoring strategy (COPS), and an acronym for use in theme writing (TOWER), which are presented later in this chapter.

Graham and Harris (1994) note three advantages of the process approach to writing: (1) student writing is frequent and meaningful, (2) environmental conditions are created that foster self-regulated learning, and (3) the integrative nature of learning in literacy development is emphasized. However, they note that these benefits may be weakened "by an overreliance on incidental learning and by a lack of emphasis on the mechanics of writing" (p. 275). Many students with learning problems do not develop effective strategies and skills for writing without careful instruction. Thus, such students' writing may be improved by integrating the process approach to writing with skill-oriented instruction.

For students with academic learning problems, Kameenui and Simmons (1990) recommend a skills-based approach to expressive writing instruction in which basic writing skills are developed systematically for advanced exercises and applications. In this approach, the instructional emphasis focuses first on the writing and editing phases (teacher-directed) and then on the process of planning (student-initiated). Thus, the student learns to rely on writing skills when planning more complex written products.

Graham and Harris (1988) offer ten instructional recommendations for developing an effective writing program for students with written expression difficulty:

1. *Allocate time for writing instruction.* A sufficient amount of time should be allocated to writing instruction (e.g., four times per week) because students can learn and develop as writers only by writing.

2. *Expose students to a broad range of writing tasks.* Students should participate in writing activities that present highly structured problem-solving situations as well as activities that involve self-selected and expressive writing.

3. *Create a social climate conducive to writing development.* The teacher needs to be encouraging in a nonthreatening environment and should try to develop a sense of community by promoting student sharing and collaboration.

4. *Integrate writing with other academic subjects.* Writing should be integrated with other language arts activities to increase writing and develop skills.

5. *Aid students in developing the processes central to effective writing.* The composition process can be divided into a series of discrete stages (e.g., prewrite, write, and rewrite), and students can be taught appropriate task-specific and metacognitive strategies (e.g., self-instructional strategy training).

6. *Automatize skills for getting language onto paper.* The teacher should provide direct instruction in mechanical skills and sentence and paragraph production, or the mechanical requirements of composing can be removed through the use of oral dictation.

7. *Help students develop explicit knowledge about the characteristics of good writ-*

ing. Students should be given exposure to the characteristics of various literary compositions either through reading or teacher presentation of written or live models that incorporate a specific skill or style, or students should receive direct instruction in the structured elements representative of a particular literary style.

8. ***Help students develop the skills and abilities to carry out more sophisticated composing processes.*** Three methods for the development of more mature composing processes include conferences during which teachers act as collaborators, procedural facilitation in which external support is provided, and self-instructional strategy training.

9. ***Help students develop goals for improving their written products.*** Goal setting and having students evaluate their own or others' written products according to specific criteria can help students accurately monitor and evaluate progress.

10. ***Avoid instructional practices that do not improve students' writing performances.*** Skills in grammar and usage should be developed within the context of real writing tasks, and the teacher should give specific, explanatory feedback on only one or two types of frequently occurring errors at any one time.

Writing Instruction

The first step in writing instruction is to promote a positive attitude to motivate the student to write. The student must feel comfortable expressing thoughts and feelings. The teacher can promote discussion by encouraging the student to share ideas. Writing should be integrated into the entire curriculum, and the teacher should help the student understand that the purpose of writing is to communicate. Writing instruction thus begins with establishing a positive environment and then proceeds to skill development.

One of the most effective means of teaching writing skills to students with learning problems is through spontaneous written expression. Each student's writing samples can be used as a base from which to introduce instruction in various writing skills. In other words, the objective of the writing program may be for the student to express ideas and thoughts with ease. The written work then is used as the basis for skill development. Thus,

spontaneous writing samples can be used to teach written expression within the context of various instructional programs such as whole language, language experience, or direct skill instruction. The teacher can provide events (e.g., discussions, field trips, and films) that stimulate topics. At first, the student may be most comfortable writing about personal material, such as family, trips, or holidays. Some students enjoy writing each day in journals about their experiences and reactions to events. Students also enjoy writing stories about pictures or intriguing titles and completing unfinished stories (i.e., story starters or story enders). Books in which the pictures are presented in sequence without text can provide stimuli for writing activities. In general, students should choose their own writing topics. When students produce their own stories, the material is meaningful to them, and they are motivated to study it. This may be especially important for adolescents, because the stories they compose are on their level of maturity. Also, writing tasks may become more meaningful when students are allowed to work on the same writing project for an extended period of time. Students' involvement or interest in a given topic influences their ability to write about it.

To begin writing, brainstorming can generate ideas and words to be used. The student lists all words and phrases that come to mind in response to the topic. Clustering or mapping information also can help the student organize ideas for writing. The cluster or map can include main ideas, details, and examples. In these informal writing strategies and as the student begins tentatively to write ideas, content rather than mechanics is stressed.

As the student continues to be encouraged to express ideas well in writing, instruction on the more mechanical aspects of writing begins. The teacher can call attention to punctuation and capitalization errors in the student's written work, show the proper use of the skill, and point out how its use enhances meaning. Dowis and Schloss (1992) suggest using directed minilessons to teach specific skills during the writing process so that skills and content can develop concurrently. Thus, writing mechanics are explained as needed, and the student becomes aware of their importance.

The teacher should avoid excessive correction of the mechanical aspects of writing, which may discourage the student from trying to express ideas. The student may think that *how* thoughts are written is more important than *what* is written and, thus, may begin to limit vocabulary use, write only simple sentences, and avoid expressing complex and creative thoughts. Good writing models should be provided, and reinforcement should be combined with constructive criticism. The teacher should say something positive about the student's work prior to offering correction and give encouragement and praise for whatever amount the student has written. In general, more attention should be given to developing the written expression of ideas than to correcting mechanical errors. Of course, students who learn to use the right punctuation, correct grammar, and good organization are likely to become better writers. Thus, balanced instruction targets both process and mechanics. Some teachers prefer to give two grades for some writing assignments—one for ideas and one for technical skills. Also, the teacher can provide selective feedback directly to a student through oral conferences

To help improve a student's writing, the teacher should emphasize sentence and paragraph development. The student should be helped to recognize the different syntactic patterns in which ideas can be expressed. Having the student read interesting material at his or her independent reading level will expose the student to good sentences in other people's writing and may help develop a sense of English sentence constructions. Also, through orally reading or tape-recording stories, the student is likely to notice faulty sentence constructions. Learning to write unified, coherent paragraphs can be facilitated by activities in which the student categorizes or classifies ideas or organizes ideas in a logical sequence. An organizational framework can be provided through the use of content charts, semantic maps (or webbings), and pyramid diagrams that present an overview of information and visually represent how items are related (Levy & Rosenberg, 1990). Suggesting the use of transition words (such as *finally* and *in addition to*) may help the student put compositions together.

A sentence-writing strategy designed by Schumaker and Sheldon (1985) can be used to teach the basic principles of sentence construction and expression. The student learns a set of steps and formulas that facilitates the recognition and writing of different kinds of sentences. The acronym PENS helps the student remember the steps to sentence writing:

P—*Pick* a sentence type and formula.

E—*Explore* words to fit the formula.

N—*Note* the words.

S—*Search* for verbs and subjects, and check.

PENS also is used in the paragraph-writing strategy developed at the University of Kansas Center for Research on Learning to help the student write a topic sentence, detail sentences, and a clincher sentence to form a paragraph (Schumaker & Lyerla, 1991). This learning strategy teaches the student to write various types of paragraphs: sequential (narrative or step by step), descriptive, expository, and comparison and contrast. Also, *Teaching Competence in Written Language* (Phelps-Terasaki & Phelps-Gunn, 2000) contains highly structured lessons in which the student progresses effectively in a step-by-step fashion from ideas to sentences to paragraphs.

Welch (1992) presents a metacognitive strategy to teach students to write paragraphs. The use of a first-letter mnemonic cues the student how to complete the writing task independently:

P—*Pick* a topic, an audience, and the appropriate textual format (e.g., enumerative, comparison and contrast, or cause and effect).

L—*List* information about the topic to be used in sentence generation, ongoing evaluation, and organizational planning.

E—*Evaluate* whether the list is complete and plan how to organize the ideas that will be used to generate supporting sentences.

A—*Activate* the paragraph with a short and simple declarative topic sentence.

S—*Supply* supporting sentences based on items from the list.

E—*End* with a concluding sentence that rephrases the topic sentence, and *evaluate* the written work for errors in capitalization, punctuation, spelling, and appearance.

Welch notes that the intervention increases the student's metacognitive knowledge of the writing process involved in prewriting, planning, composing,

Good literature provides writing models and stimulates interest.

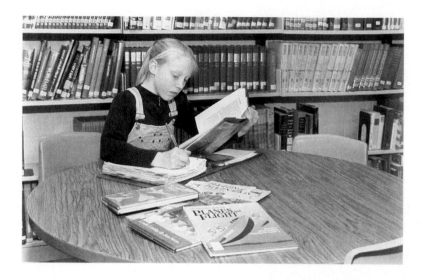

and revising, as well as improves the student's attitude toward writing and writing instruction.

As basic writing skills are acquired, the student should learn to proofread and edit. In proofreading, the student reads the written work to identify and correct errors. To edit the work, the student can be guided to look for elements in the writing such as capitalization, sentence sense, punctuation, misspelled words, margins, and paragraph indention. At first it may be helpful for the student to proofread the work several times with a different purpose in mind each time. As the student reads the work aloud, errors such as omitted words, improper punctuation, or poor organization may be noticed. Also, peer critiquing can be used as a revision strategy, and individual conferences with the teacher in a supportive atmosphere can result in constructive editing.

To cue the student to detect four kinds of common errors, the teacher can introduce COPS questions to be used as an error-monitoring strategy (Schumaker, Nolan, & Deshler, 1985). The student is instructed to ask the following questions and look for these errors:

C—Have I *capitalized* the first word and proper nouns?

O—How is the *overall* appearance? (Look at spacing, legibility, indention of paragraphs, neatness, and complete sentences.)

P—Have I put in commas, semicolons, and end *punctuation?*

S—Have I *spelled* all the words correctly?

Periodically the teacher can review COPS and encourage each student to use it daily so that it will become a habit. The teacher can require all papers to be "COPSed" before being accepted.

Because the goal of writing is to communicate ideas, students should be encouraged to share their written work. Notebooks or books of stories the students want to share may be exchanged for reading material. Also, students can be given the opportunity to read their selections voluntarily in front of other students. Through sharing stories, students receive feedback and become more motivated to improve the quality of their work. Also, the students are provided with models to help them improve their writing.

At the secondary level, greater written expression demands are placed on students. Not only are students required to take notes during class lectures and express themselves on written tests, but they also frequently must write themes and reports. Teaching theme writing through the use of the acronym TOWER provides a structured approach:

T—*Think* about content (i.e., title, major subtopics, and details).

O—*Order* topics and details.

W—*Write* the rough draft.

E—Look for *errors* (use COPS).

R—*Revise/rewrite.*

Before writing, the student can be encouraged to fill in a form with the topic at the top and ideas organized according to subtopics or paragraphs. After writing a rough draft, the student can ask COPS questions to edit the work and monitor errors.

Teachers expect written work to be reasonably neat and unconsciously may judge an assignment based on the paper's appearance. Archer and Gleason (1988) suggest a strategy using the acronym HOW to improve the appearance of written work and remind the student how the paper should look:

H— *Heading* (include name, date, subject, and page number if needed).

O— *Organized* (start on front side of paper, include a left and right margin, have at least one blank line at the top and at the bottom, and space well).

W— *Written neatly* (write words or numbers on the line, form words or numbers clearly, and neatly cross out or erase errors).

MacArthur, Schwartz, and Graham (1991) present a model for writing instruction that integrates word processing and strategy instruction into a process approach to writing. Strategy instruction in writing primarily has been used to help students learn to better internalize and regulate the cognitive activities involved in effective planning, production, and revision of text (Graham et al., 1991). To enhance the quality and quantity of writing, there should be increased focus on thinking as a critical aspect of the writing process, and writing should be practiced and applied in a variety of situations and contexts to foster generalization of these skills.

☀ WRITTEN EXPRESSION ACTIVITIES

Writing skills improve through practice. Instructional activities should be chosen for each student according to particular skill deficits. This section presents numerous activities for developing skills in fluency and syntax, vocabulary, structure, and content. Additional activities and strategies for developing written expression skills related to test taking and note taking at the secondary level are presented in Chapter 13.

Fluency and Syntax Development Activities

• Provide scrambled words from a sentence and ask the student to arrange the words to form a sentence. For example:

her quietly cat the food ate
friends yesterday Jane's left

Also, list several words and have the student write a sentence that contains all the words.

• Have the student complete partial sentences. Gradually decrease the number of words presented. For example:

Yesterday morning the dog barked at . . .
Yesterday morning the dog . . .
Yesterday morning . . .

• Provide a written paragraph that contains both incomplete and complete sentences. Ask the student to underline the subject and verb in each statement and determine which sentences are incomplete.

• Have the student practice connecting two simple sentences to make compound or complex sentences. Give a list of various words for the student to use when writing the compound or complex sentences (e.g., *but, because, or, and, after,* and *before*).

• Provide various noun and verb phrases and have the student expand each sentence by adding descriptive words. For example:

| man ate | The man in the blue shirt ate his dinner slowly. |
| dog barked | The big, black dog barked at the man with the stick. |

Also, have the student combine related sentences into one sentence. For example:

| The policeman is young. The policeman stopped the car. | The young policeman stopped the car. |
| Yesterday the boys played a football game. The game lasted two hours. | Yesterday the boys played a football game that lasted two hours. |

Vocabulary Development Activities

- Provide the student with a variety of experiences (e.g., taking structured field trips and listening to stories and poems) and include follow-up discussions of what was seen and heard. In addition, viewing films, listening to guest speakers, making a picture dictionary, and reading books, magazines, and newspapers may increase a person's vocabulary. Praise the student whenever a new vocabulary word is used appropriately.

- Discuss special interests (e.g., baseball, music, and cooking) with each student and make lists of words pertaining to the interests. New words and their definitions can be written on index cards and filed in a word box so that they can be considered for use in written compositions.

- Give the class a list of vocabulary words to learn. Write each word on a slip of paper, fold the paper slips, and place them in a decorated coffee can. The first student draws out a word and must begin a story by using the word in a sentence. Each student takes a turn drawing a word and then adds to the story by using the word. After all vocabulary words have been used, the teacher can develop an ending to the story.

- Have each student discover new words by looking and listening for them outside the classroom (e.g., on signs, on television, and in reading material). One day each week the students can share newly found words and definitions with their classmates.

- Provide a written paragraph in which various words or phrases are underlined. Have the student substitute appropriate words or expressions in each underlined area.

- Divide the class into two teams and play a game involving synonyms and antonyms. Present a word and ask each team member (alternating teams) to give a synonym. A point is awarded to each team for a correct response, and five points are taken away from the first team no longer able to give a synonym. Then the same word or a new word can be presented with the team members giving antonyms.

- Present a reading passage and ask the student to locate words or phrases according to specific questions (e.g., "Tell me the word in the second paragraph that describes Jim's car" and "Find the phrase in the last paragraph that indicates that Mary was mad at herself").

- Develop a crossword puzzle that includes words related to a single subject. Have the student complete the puzzle and then write a paragraph using all the puzzle words.

Structure Development Activities

- To help develop proper use of punctuation, cut large punctuation marks from black construction paper and pin them to students. After reviewing rules of punctuation usage, write an unpunctuated story on the chalkboard or present it on an overhead projector. As the story is read aloud, the student wearing the appropriate punctuation mark should call out its name when it is needed in the story.

- To increase awareness of the use of capital letters, have the student make a list of all capitalized words in a specific reading passage and give the reasons for their capitalization. Lists of capitalized words can be made according to various classifications, such as cities, people's names, states, and months.

- Provide a written paragraph that does not contain any capitalized words. Have the student correct the words that should be capitalized and give reasons for capitalizing them. Also, a reading selection can be dictated for the student to write, adding capitals where necessary.

- Provide written sentences that contain no capitals or punctuation and ask the student to write each sentence correctly. Also, the teacher can give a paragraph without punctuation and capitalization for the student to rewrite correctly. Tell the student the type and number of punctuation marks and capitals that must be added. To make the activity self-correcting, provide an answer key.

- Give a list of verbs or singular nouns and ask the student to write the past tense form of each verb or plural of each noun. For example:

do	*did*	child	*children*
ride	*rode*	boy	*boys*
eat	*ate*	deer	*deer*
sing	*sang*	hero	*heroes*
walk	*walked*	story	*stories*

In addition, the student can be asked to use each past tense verb or plural noun in a sentence. Sentences can be given with the verb omitted, and the student is required to choose the correct verb form from multiple-choice answers. For example:

I (*ride, rode, ridden*) the bus to school this morning.
Last Saturday we (*go, went, gone*) on a picnic.
When he (*fell, fall, fallen*), he hurt his leg.

- To work on grammatical skills, provide a paragraph with blanks that the student must complete. The blanks can require the use of different grammatical elements (e.g., plurals, verb tenses, possessive pronouns, and adverbs). A list of words for the student to use can be provided at the top of the worksheet.

- To practice editing skills, have students exchange papers and "COPS" each other's work. After the teacher reviews the material, each student can make a corrected copy of the work. The teacher also can provide a paragraph and ask the student to correct it according to the COPS questions.

Content Development Activities

- Read the beginning of an exciting story to the class and ask each student to write an ending. The students can share their work to see how others finished the story. Also, after watching a film or reading or listening to a story, the students can write a summary or abstract.

- To provide ideas for writing stories, cut three windows in a large piece of poster board. Make three circles, each of which is divided into eight sections. Write eight *Who* words on the first circle, eight *When* words on the second circle, and eight *Where* words on the third circle. Attach the circles to the back of the poster board so that the writing shows through the windows (see Figure 10.7). To find a story starter, the student spins all three wheels. Also, to give the student story ideas, the poster board can contain two windows. Two circles can be made with one containing names of circus acts (or any subject) and the other containing phrases of things they might do (see Figure 10.8). The circles are attached to the poster board, and the student spins the wheels to find the subject for the composition.

- Encourage letter writing by establishing a post office in the classroom. Make mailboxes for each student out of cardboard or milk cartons. Have students write letters, invitations, birthday cards, poems, and so forth and send them through the class postal system. Also, the teacher can use the mailboxes to return papers, give feedback, or send notes to be taken home.

- On a large piece of poster board draw four circles, each divided into six sections. On each circle write characters, descriptors, settings, or actions. In the middle of each circle attach an arrow. Have the student spin all four arrows and then write a paragraph that includes the four designated elements in the story (see Figure 10.9).

- Provide a written paragraph in which the sentences are out of sequence. Have the student rewrite the paragraph by arranging the sentences in a meaningful order. Also, the student can be given a topic sentence and a closing sentence and be asked to write three detail sentences to form a paragraph.

- To provide practice in organization skills, give the student a set of cards, each containing a different but related idea. Have the student arrange the cards in a logical sequence to form an outline and then write a composition from the outline.

- Reproduce on ditto sheets several cartoons without captions or comic strips without the words spoken by the characters. Have the student write appropriate captions or fill in the conversations. Also, provide frames from a comic strip that the student must arrange in proper sequence before writing a comic strip story. These can be shared with the class, and the funniest or best ones can be included in a book.

- Prepare a worksheet on poems. Have the student arrange the lines in the proper order or fill in blanks with appropriate words. Then give the student an opportunity to select from various titles and compose a poem. To help the student get started, suggest a first line.

- Read a tall tale to the class and ask the students to identify parts of the story that are "tall" (exaggerated). Discuss the importance of accurate or truthful statements in compositions that are not tall tales. Have each student write a tall tale, which can be shared with the class.

FIGURE 10.7
Who? When? Where? story board

FIGURE 10.8
Circus Acts story board

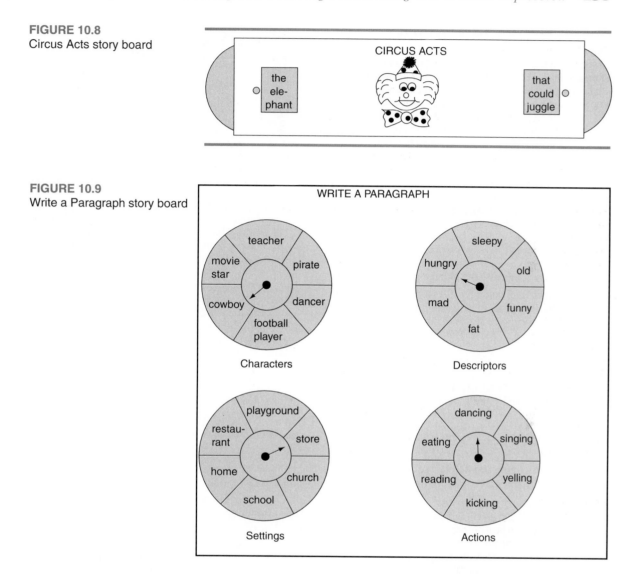

FIGURE 10.9
Write a Paragraph story board

• Have the student keep a daily diary in a spiral note-book. At the end of class each day, have the student write a diary entry that summarizes experiences, feelings, and activities of the day.

• Present letters like those that appear in a newspaper advice column such as *Dear Abby*. Have each student give advice by writing responses to the letters. The responses can be shared with classmates or compared with actual newspaper replies.

• Encourage the students to develop a monthly class newspaper to which each student can contribute some form of writing. The newspaper can contain current events articles, interviews, short stories, poems, jokes, cartoons,

comic strips, advertisements, sports articles, and want ads. Groups of students can take turns serving as editors, printers or typists, proofreaders, and distributors.

COMMERCIAL WRITTEN EXPRESSION PROGRAMS

Various published materials and programs are available for developing written expression skills. This section presents selected commercial written expression materials and programs that may be helpful to students with learning problems.

Clues for Better Writing

Clues for Better Writing (published by Curriculum Associates) is designed for students in kindergarten through fifth grade to connect reading with writing and provide strategies that promote writing success. At the kindergarten level, teacher-directed lessons feature text, artwork, and oral literature to develop early language skills. The first-grade-level book develops and reinforces skills with creative writing projects, art activities, and vocabulary exercises. In the books for second through fifth grade, students learn the five steps to successful writing: brainstorming, planning, writing, editing, and publishing. Reading samples are used for writing activities, and for each writing strand there are two structured writing lessons with open-ended writing activities. The teacher guides provide lesson objectives and directions as well as extension activities.

Everyone Write

Everyone Write (published by PRO-ED) includes a series of three books with reproducible pages for students in first through second grade, third through fourth grade, and fifth through sixth grade. The activities focus on the thinking process required of a writer, and writing skills are learned and applied congruently with reading and problem-solving skills. Instruction includes writing tasks that involve persuasive, expository, and descriptive writing; letter writing; news accounts; and personal communications. The activities relate directly to students' lives and to the curriculum areas of language arts, science, social studies, and art.

Expressive Writing 1; Expressive Writing 2

Expressive Writing 1 and *Expressive Writing 2,* developed by S. Engelmann and J. Silbert (published by SRA), present an effective writing program designed for students who read at or above the third-grade level. The program includes 50 daily 45-minute lessons that integrate sentence writing, paragraph construction, and editing skills. At the completion of the program, students are able to write, punctuate, and edit compound sentences, sentences with dependent clauses, direct quotations in dialogue form, and sentences that list items. The program, which is based on five years of field testing, includes a teacher presentation book and a student workbook, and students participate in self-evaluation activities.

Language Roundup

Language Roundup (published by SRA) includes books at five levels designed to help students learn to apply specific grammar, usage, and mechanics rules in the context of writing. Instructional modeling with examples, abundant practice exercises, and formal and informal assessment are included. Self-tests allow students to assess their own understanding and identify skills that need additional practice. The computer software program *Grammar Games* (produced by Knowledge Adventure) correlates with lessons in each book to reinforce skills.

Reasoning and Writing

Reasoning and Writing (published by SRA) is a real-life writing and thinking program that starts with templates to guide students in the process of writing and progresses to independent writing assignments. Six levels are available for students in kindergarten through eighth grade. The beginning levels develop a foundation for reading comprehension and writing and expand thinking skills. By the third level, students are fully engaged in the writing process, including drafting, revising, and editing for clarity. Knowledge of grammar and complex sentence structure is expanded, and students learn to vary word choice and sentence structure as well as to take notes, paraphrase, and evaluate evidence from various perspectives to form opinions. Editorial checklists allow the teacher to correct errors and provide precise instruction.

☀ COMPUTER SOFTWARE PROGRAMS IN WRITTEN EXPRESSION

The use of the computer as a word processor can facilitate the teaching of writing. Word processing allows the student to correct, edit, revise, and manipulate text. Because words in a word-processed document can easily be changed before the document is printed, older students may be motivated to proofread for spelling and mechanical errors as well as to make improvements in other aspects of composition writing. MacArthur (1988) notes that the visibility of writing on a word processor can facilitate interaction between the student and teacher as well as collaborative writing activities among students and sharing of work in progress. In addition, the availability of a spelling checker and the ability to produce a neat, printed copy can be especially motivating to students with spelling or handwriting difficulties. Additional features of some computer-supported writing applications include speech synthesis, pronunciation editing, visually highlighted words, spell checking, spelling assistance, spelling modifications, insertion of correctly spelled words into document, word diction-aries, word prediction, organizational assistance, and grammar correction and tutoring (Hunt-Berg, Rankin, & Beukelman, 1994).

Outhred (1989) found that the use of a word processor with students with learning problems resulted in fewer spelling errors and the produc-tion of longer stories. However, research has not confirmed the advantages of word processors for all students with learning difficulties. For exam-ple, in a study involving fifth- and sixth-grade stu-dents with learning disabilities, MacArthur and Graham (1987) found no differences on several variables (e.g., length, quality, story structure, and mechanical errors) between handwritten stories and those composed on a word processor. Isaacson (1995) notes that before a word pro-cessor can contribute effectively to the develop-ment of writing skills, the teacher must teach the necessary subskills (such as keyboarding) and self-monitoring strategies for writing that take ad-vantage of the computer's capabilities.

Write This Way (produced by Compass Learn-ing) is a voiced word processing program for stu-dents in fourth through twelfth grade that high-lights spelling and grammatical errors and guides the student to correct mistakes. Also, user-friendly desktop publishing programs such as *Print Shop* (produced by Broderbund) and *The Student Writ-ing Center* (produced by The Learning Company) make it possible to publish in a wide range of professional-looking formats. Numerous other software programs focus on specific written ex-pression skills. The following programs may facil-itate instruction of students who have difficulty with written expression skills.

Grammar Games

Grammar Games (produced by Knowledge Adventure) is designed to help students in fourth through twelfth grade master essential grammar skills. Within four ex-citing activities involving rain forest adventure stories, students learn proper punctuation, identify sentence fragments, use verbs correctly, master subject and verb agreement, identify common errors in word usage, and utilize correct forms of plurals and possessives. Each game has three levels of difficulty, and five on-screen diagnostic tests determine each student's ap-propriate starting level and assess progress. Also easily accessible is a grammar guide that provides grammar rules.

Kaplan Grammar for the Real World

In *Kaplan Grammar for the Real World* (produced by Knowledge Adventure), students in fourth through twelfth grade improve their writing, grammar, and spelling skills and learn how mastering these skills is essential to everyday life. Six activities focus on the use of punctuation and capitalization, pronouns, parts of speech, verb usage, plurals, and possessives, and a variety of creative assignments at a Hollywood studio help students improve their creative writing, proof-reading, and editing skills. Text-to-speech technology allows students to hear their scripts read back to them. The program also features automatic adjustment of dif-ficulty level, and an on-line grammar book resource is available.

Write On! Plus

Write On! Plus (produced by Humanities Software/ Sunburst) integrates process writing, word processing, skill building, and literature with writing activities. Stu-dents use their word processors to write and illustrate letters, stories, poetry, journals, and essays while prac-ticing grammar, sentence structure, and paragraph skills. The primary level for students in kindergarten to third grade includes *Beginning Writing Skills* (word fam-ilies, cloze sentences, and sentence patterns) and *Writing with Picture Books.* The elementary titles for stu-dents in third to sixth grade are *Elementary Writing Skills* (editing skills, sentence combining techniques, and punctuation rules), *Steps to Better Writing* (pre-writing, drafting, organizing, revising, and editing), and *Writing with Literature.* Students in sixth to ninth grade use *Middle School Writing Skills* (sentence develop-ment, structured paragraphs, essays, and revising), *Growing as a Writer* (writing essays, business letters, position statements, and persuasive arguments), and *Literature Studies I* and *II.* The high school level pro-grams for students in ninth through twelfth grade include *High School Writing Skills* (word choice grammar, punc-tuation, audience, sentence structure, and organiza-tion), *Essential Writing* (expository, descriptive, narra-tive, and persuasive writing; job skills; interviews; filling out forms; and follow-up), and *Responding to Great Literature.* All of the *Write On! Plus* titles can be used with the AlphaSmart keyboard and with a variety of word processors.

The Writing Trek

The Writing Trek (produced by Sunburst) features lan-guage arts projects and assignments that build writing competence and encourage creativity. Three CD-ROMs are available (fourth to sixth grade, sixth to eighth grade, and eighth to tenth grade), with each one presenting twelve structured projects based on real-life writing models. Lessons on writing concepts, such as sentence structure, punctuation, or vocabulary are incorporated into the structured projects. A personalized, interactive notebook guides students as they write and save their work, and a direct Internet link to *The Writing Trek* site lets students post and critique their written products.

The Writing Workshop

The Writing Workshop (produced by Milliken) is designed for students in third through tenth grade and covers the entire writing process from thought organization to final editing and proofreading. The complete program includes three modules. The Writing Word Processor module allows teachers and students to create their own writing activities, and the full-featured word processor includes guides to direct students to writing successful papers. The Writing Activities module features 150 writing and research paper activities that lead students through the steps of the writing process. Finally, the Writing About Literature module includes activities for 20 literature novels that are often assigned as required reading for students. Accompanying resource books are provided.

REFERENCES

Anderson, D. W. (1966). Handwriting research: Movement and quality. In T. D. Horn (Ed.), *Research on handwriting and spelling.* Champaign, IL: National Council of Teachers of English.

Archer, A. L., & Gleason, M. M. (1988). *Skills for school success.* Boston: Curriculum Associates.

Balow, I. H., Farr, R. C., & Hogan, T. P. (1992). *Metropolitan Achievement Tests—Seventh Edition: Writing Test.* San Antonio, TX: Harcourt Brace Educational Measurement.

Barbe, W., Milone, M., & Wasylyk, T. (1983). Manuscript is the "write" start. *Academic Therapy, 18,* 397–406.

California Achievement Tests—Fifth Edition. (1992). Monterey, CA: CTB/McGraw-Hill.

Carroll, J. B. (1938). Diversity of vocabulary and the harmonic series law of word-frequency distribution. *Psychological Record, 2.*

Carrow-Woolfolk, E. (1995). *Oral and Written Language Scales: Written Expression.* Circle Pines, MN: American Guidance Service.

Cartwright, G. P. (1968). Written language abilities of normal and educable mentally retarded children. *American Journal of Mental Deficiency, 72,* 499–508.

Cartwright, G. P. (1969). Written expression and spelling. In R. M. Smith (Ed.), *Teacher diagnosis of educational difficulties* (pp. 95–117). Upper Saddle River, NJ: Merrill/Prentice Hall.

Christenson, S. L., Thurlow, M. L., Ysseldyke, J. E., & McVicar, R. (1989). Written language instruction for students with mild handicaps: Is there enough quantity to ensure quality? *Learning Disability Quarterly, 12,* 219–229.

CTB Writing Assessment System. (1993). Monterey, CA: CTB/McGraw-Hill.

Deno, S. L., Mirkin, P. K., & Wesson, C. (1984). How to write effective data-based IEPs. *Teaching Exceptional Children, 16,* 99–104.

Dolch, E. W. (1955). *Methods in reading.* Champaign, IL: Garrard.

Dolch, E. W. (1960). *Better spelling.* Champaign, IL: Garrard.

Dowis, C. L., & Schloss, P. (1992). The impact of mini-lessons on writing skills. *Remedial and Special Education, 13*(5), 34–42.

Graham, S., & Harris, K. R. (1988). Instructional recommendations for teaching writing to exceptional students. *Exceptional Children, 54,* 506–512.

Graham, S., & Harris, K. R. (1994). Implications of constructivism for teaching writing to students with special needs. *The Journal of Special Education, 28,* 275–289.

Graham, S., Harris, K. R., MacArthur, C. A., & Schwartz, S. (1991). Writing and writing instruction for students with learning disabilities: Review of a research program. *Learning Disability Quarterly, 14,* 89–114.

Graham, S., & Miller, L. (1980). Handwriting research and practice: A unified approach. *Focus on Exceptional Children, 13*(2), 1–16.

Graves, D. H. (1985). All children can write. *Learning Disabilities Focus, 1*(1), 36–43.

Hagin, R. A. (1983). Write right—or left: A practical approach to handwriting. *Journal of Learning Disabilities, 16,* 266–271.

Hammill, D. D., & Larsen, S. C. (1996). *Test of Written Language—3.* Austin, TX: PRO-ED.

Hammill, D. D., Leigh, J. E., Pearson, N. A., & Maddox, T. (1998). *Basic School Skills Inventory—Third Edition.* Austin, TX: PRO-ED.

Hammill, D. D., & McNutt, G. (1981). *Correlates of reading: The consensus of thirty years of correlational research* (PRO-ED Monograph No. 1). Austin, TX: PRO-ED.

Hanover, S. (1983). Handwriting comes naturally? *Academic Therapy, 18,* 407–412.

Herrick, V. E. (1960). Handwriting and children's writing. *Elementary English, 37,* 248–258.

Hildreth, G. (1963). Simplified handwriting for today. *Journal of Educational Research, 56,* 330–333.

Hofmeister, A. M. (1981). *Handwriting resource book: Manuscript/cursive.* DeSoto, TX: SRA.

Horton, L. W. (1970). Illegibilities in the cursive handwriting of sixth graders. *Elementary School Journal, 70,* 446–450.

Houck, C. K., & Billingsley, B. S. (1989). Written expression of students with and without learning disabilities: Differences across the grades. *Journal of Learning Disabilities, 22,* 561–567, 572.

Hresko, W. P., Herron, S. R., & Peak, P. K. (1996). *Test of Early Written Language—2.* Austin, TX: PRO-ED.

Hunt, K. W. (1965). *Grammatical structures written at three grade levels* (NCTE Research Report No. 3). Champaign, IL: National Council of Teachers of English.

Hunt-Berg, M., Rankin, J. L., & Beukelman, D. R. (1994). Ponder the possibilities: Computer-supported writing for struggling writers. *Learning Disabilities Research & Practice, 9,* 169–178.

Isaacson, S. (1988). Assessing the written product: Qualitative and quantitative measures. *Exceptional Children, 54,* 528–534.

Isaacson, S. (1995). Written language. In P. J. Schloss, M. A. Smith, & C. N. Schloss, *Instructional methods for adolescents with learning and behavior problems* (2nd ed., pp. 200–224). Boston: Allyn & Bacon.

Johnson, D. J., & Myklebust, H. R. (1967). *Learning disabilities: Educational principles and practices.* New York: Grune & Stratton.

Johnson, W. (1944). Studies in language behavior. A program of research. *Psychological Monographs, 56*(2).

Kameenui, E. J., & Simmons, D. C. (1990). *Designing instructional strategies: The prevention of academic learning problems.* Upper Saddle River, NJ: Merrill/Prentice Hall.

Levy, N. R., & Rosenberg, M. S. (1990). Strategies for improving the written expression of students with learning disabilities. *LD Forum, 16,* 23–30.

Lewis, E. R., & Lewis, H. P. (1965). An analysis of errors in the formation of manuscript letters by first grade children. *American Educational Research Journal, 2,* 25–35.

MacArthur, C. A. (1988). The impact of computers on the writing process. *Exceptional Children, 54,* 536–542.

MacArthur, C., & Graham, S. (1987). Learning disabled students' composing under three methods of text production: Handwriting, word processing, and dictation. *The Journal of Special Education, 21,* 22–42.

MacArthur, C. A., Schwartz, S. S., & Graham, S. (1991). A model for writing instruction: Integrating word processing and strategy instruction into a process approach to writing. *Learning Disabilities Research & Practice, 6,* 230–236.

Mann, P. H., Suiter, P. A., & McClung, R. M. (1992). *A guide to educating mainstreamed students* (4th ed.). Boston: Allyn & Bacon.

Markham, L. R. (1976). Influences of handwriting quality on teacher evaluation of written work. *American Educational Research Journal, 13,* 277–283.

Markwardt, F. C., Jr. (1998). *Peabody Individual Achievement Test—Revised.* Circle Pines, MN: American Guidance Service.

McCarthy, D. (1954). Language development in children. In L. Carmichael (Ed.) *Manual of child psychology.* New York: Wiley.

McGhee, R., Bryant, B. R., Larsen, S. C., & Rivera, D. M. (1995). *Test of Written Expression.* Austin, TX: PRO-ED.

Meckel, H. C. (1963). Research on teaching composition and literature. In N. Gage (Ed.), *Handbook of research on teaching.* Chicago: Rand McNally.

Miller, G. A. (1951). *Language and communication.* New York: McGraw-Hill.

Milone, M. N., & Wasylyk, T. M. (1981). Handwriting in special education. *Teaching Exceptional Children, 14,* 58–61.

Morris, N. T., & Crump, D. T. (1982). Syntactic and vocabulary development in the written language of learning disabled and non-learning disabled students at four age levels. *Learning Disability Quarterly, 5,* 163–172.

Newland, T. E. (1932). An analytical study of the development of illegibilities in handwriting from the lower grades to adulthood. *Journal of Educational Research, 26,* 249–258.

Outhred, L. (1989). Word processing: Its impact on children's writing. *Journal of Learning Disabilities, 22,* 262–264.

Parker, R. I., Tindal, G., & Hasbrouck, J. (1991). Progress monitoring with objective measures of writing performance for students with mild disabilities. *Exceptional Children, 58,* 61–73.

Phelps-Terasaki, D., & Phelps-Gunn, T. (2000). *Teaching competence in written language* (2nd ed.). Austin, TX: PRO-ED.

Polloway, E. A., & Smith, T. E. C. (1992). *Language instruction for students with disabilities* (2nd ed.). Denver: Love.

Poteet, J. A. (1980). Informal assessment of written expression. *Learning Disability Quarterly, 3*(4), 88–98.

Powers, R., & Kaminsky, S. (1988). *Handwriting: A fresh start.* North Billerica, MA: Curriculum Associates.

Schumaker, J. B., & Lyerla, K. D. (1991). *The paragraph writing strategy.* Lawrence: University of Kansas Center for Research on Learning.

Schumaker, J. B., Nolan, S. M., & Deshler, D. D. (1985). *Learning strategies curriculum: The error monitoring strategy.* Lawrence: University of Kansas Center for Research on Learning.

Schumaker, J. B., & Sheldon, J. (1985). *The sentence writing strategy.* Lawrence: University of Kansas Center for Research on Learning.

Smith, C. R. (1998). *Learning disabilities: The interaction of learner, task, and setting* (4th ed.). Boston: Allyn & Bacon.

Strauss, A., & Lehtinen, L. (1947). *Psychopathology and education of the brain-injured child.* New York: Grune & Stratton.

Stuckless, E. R., & Marks, C. H. (1966). *Assessment of the written language of deaf students* (USOE Cooperative Research Project 2544). Pittsburgh, PA: University of Pittsburgh.

Templin, E. (1960). Research and comment: Handwriting, the neglected R. *Elementary English, 37,* 386–389.

Thomas, C. C., Englert, C. S., & Gregg, S. (1987). An analysis of errors and strategies in the expository writing of learning disabled students. *Remedial and Special Education, 8*(1), 21–30, 46.

Thurber, D. N. (1987). *D'Nealian handwriting* (Rev. ed.). Glenview, IL: Scott, Foresman.

Tindal, G. A., & Marston, D. B. (1990). *Classroom-based assessment: Evaluating instructional outcomes.* Upper Saddle River, NJ: Merrill/Prentice Hall.

Tompkins, G. E. (1994). *Teaching writing: Balancing process and product* (2nd ed.). Upper Saddle River, NJ: Merrill/Prentice Hall.

Tompkins, G. E. (1998). *Language arts: Content and teaching strategies* (4th ed.). Upper Saddle River, NJ: Merrill/Prentice Hall.

Wallace, G., Larsen, S. C., & Elksnin, L. K. (1992). *Educational assessment of learning problems: Testing for teaching* (2nd ed.). Boston: Allyn & Bacon.

Weiner, E. S. (1980). Diagnostic evaluation of writing skills. *Journal of Learning Disabilities, 13,* 48–53.

Welch, M. (1992). The PLEASE strategy: A metacognitive learning strategy for improving the paragraph writing of students with mild learning disabilities. *Learning Disability Quarterly, 15,* 119–128.

Wesson, C. L. (1987). Curriculum-based measurement: Increasing efficiency. *Teaching Exceptional Children, 20*(1), 46–47.

Western, R. D. (1977). Case against cursive script. *Elementary School Journal, 78,* 1–3.

Wiig, E. H., & Secord, W. A. (1994). Language disabilities in school-age children and youth. In G. H. Shames, E. H. Wiig, & W. A. Secord (Eds.), *Human communication disorders: An introduction* (4th ed., pp. 212–247). Boston: Allyn & Bacon.

Wolf, D. P. (1989). Portfolio assessment: Sampling student work. *Educational Leadership, 46*(7), 35–39.

Woodcock, R. W (1991). *Woodcock Language Proficiency Battery—Revised.* Chicago: Riverside.

Wright, C. D., & Wright, J. P. (1980). Handwriting: The effectiveness of copying from moving versus still models. *Journal of Educational Research, 74,* 95–98.

## CHAPTER 11

Assessing Math

The National Research Council (1989) claims that mathematics represents "the invisible culture of our age" that affects our daily lives. From a *practical* perspective, math knowledge influences many decisions, including the calculation of the effects of a salary increase, the comparison of interest rates on loans, and the figuring of unit prices. From a *civic* perspective, math concepts relate to public policies such as helping individuals understand taxation, debt, and statistics involving health, crime, ecology, and institutional budgets. In terms of *professional* parameters, math knowledge provides many individuals with the tools to succeed on the job. From a *recreational* perspective, math knowledge can be a source of relaxation and fun, including playing strategic games, keeping score in various card or sport games, or understanding probabilities in games. Finally, from a *cultural* viewpoint, math can be appreciated for its power to solve problems and predict outcomes.

Research indicates that the math deficiencies of students with learning problems emerge in the early years and continue throughout secondary school. Thus, math problems are common at all age levels. During the preschool and primary years, many young children cannot sort objects by size, match objects, understand the language of math, or grasp the concept of rational counting. During the elementary years, they have trouble with computational skills. In the middle and upper grades, students experience difficulty with fractions, decimals, percentages, and measurement. Secondary students may experience problems in these areas, but it is not uncommon for them to make errors similar to those of younger students (e.g., errors in place value and basic facts).

The mathematical knowledge of students with learning problems progresses about one year for each two years of school attendance (Cawley & Miller, 1989). Warner, Alley, Schumaker, Deshler, and Clark (1980) found that the math progress of students with learning disabilities reaches a plateau after seventh grade. The students in their study achieved only one more year's growth in math from seventh through twelfth grade. Both studies report that the mean math scores of students with learning disabilities in the twelfth grade are at the high-fifth grade level.

Students with learning problems in math obviously need quality instruction; however, the chal-lenge intensifies when the reforms being considered in math education are examined. The *Curriculum and Evaluation Standards for School Mathematics,* published in 1989 by the National Council of Teachers of Mathematics (NCTM), is shaping current practices and reform efforts in math education. Spurred by poor performances of American youth on national math tests, this document urges professionals to adopt the NCTM standards. Specifically, the NCTM calls for practitioners and researchers to embrace problem solving as the basis for math instruction and minimize meaningless rote drill and practice activities.

Upon initial inspection, the NCTM standards are very appealing, and their goals are widely accepted. Closer inspection, however, reveals some serious limitations regarding the education of students with learning problems. The following limitations center around the modest attention given to student diversity and the rigid adherence to select instructional paradigms:

• The standards make only modest reference to students with disabilities (Hofmeister, 1993; Hutchinson, 1993b; Rivera, 1993).

• The standards are not based on replicable, validated instructional programs. Research-supported instructional programs for students with moderate to mild disabilities are especially lacking (Hofmeister, 1993; Hutchinson, 1993b; Rivera, 1993). For example, Hutchinson states that there is "no evidence to support the claim that exposure to the proposed content and experiences will result in mathematical power for students with disabilities" (p. 20).

• The standards promote a self-discovery approach for teaching math to all students. This position ignores the wealth of teaching practices generated from the process-product research (Englert, Tarrant, & Mariage, 1992) that have proven effective with students who have moderate to mild disabilities. Moreover, strict adherence to discovery learning does not recognize the promising findings being generated from educators who promote a directed discovery approach or educators who advocate a guided discovery approach.

Reforms that produce higher standards are certain to frustrate teachers and students who are struggling with current standards and traditional curricula. For example, some states already have raised their secondary school diploma requirements to include the successful completion of Algebra I. Given that traditional mathematics instruction is failing many students (Carnine, 1991; Cawley, Miller, & School, 1987), not just those with learning problems, and that higher standards are being implemented, the reason for concern is apparent. Without better math instruction, these individuals will continue to face debilitating frustration, anxiety, and failure. Fortunately, the amount of research on teaching math has increased dramatically in the last decade, and it now is clear that appropriate curriculum and effective teaching behaviors can result in positive mathematical outcomes for students with learning problems. General and special educators must work together to ensure that students with learning problems receive adequate instruction and that the instructional reforms are sensitive to those students' unique learning and emotional needs.

☀ DEVELOPMENT OF MATH SKILLS

Mathematics has a logical structure. The student first constructs simple relationships and then progresses to more complex tasks. As the student progresses in this ordering of math tasks, the learning of skills and content transfers from each step to the next. Hierarchies or lists of math concepts and skills that are useful in planning specific interventions are provided by Heddens and Speer (1997) and Stein, Silbert, and Carnine (1997). Appendix A includes a scope and sequence skills list that shows a math hierarchy by skill area as well as a hierarchy of what commonly is stressed at each grade level. Although the hierarchy stops at sixth grade, these skills also apply to many adolescents with learning problems because their problems usually involve skills taught in the elementary grades. Basically, the hierarchy in Appendix A indicates the following skill introduction sequence: (1) addition and subtraction—first and second grades, (2) multiplication and division—third and fourth grades, (3) fractions—fourth and fifth grades, and (4) decimals and percentages—fifth and sixth grades.

Several cognitive factors are needed for a student to progress in mathematics. To begin formal math instruction, the student should be able to form and remember associations, understand basic relationships, and make simple generalizations.

More complex cognitive factors are necessary as the student progresses from lower-level math skills to higher-order skills. Moreover, lower-level math skills must be mastered before higher-order skills can be learned; thus, the concept of *learning readiness* is important in math instruction. In their *Twelve Components of Essential Mathematics,* the National Council of Supervisors of Mathematics (1988) highlights the need for students to understand basic facts and operations. Many authorities (Kirby & Becker, 1988; Underhill, Uprichard, & Heddens, 1980) claim that failure to understand basic concepts in beginning math instruction contributes heavily to later learning problems. Unfortunately, students with learning problems often fail to grasp basic math facts or to develop fluency in these initial skills.

Readiness for Number Instruction

Piaget (1965) describes several concepts basic to understanding numbers: classification, ordering and seriation, one-to-one correspondence, and conservation. Mastering these concepts is necessary for learning higher-order math skills.

Classification involves a study of relationships, such as likenesses and differences. Activities include categorizing objects according to a specific property. For example, children may group buttons according to color, then size, then shape, and so on. Most children 5 to 7 years old can judge objects as being similar or dissimilar on the basis of properties such as color, shape, size, texture, and function (Copeland, 1979).

Ordering is important for sequencing numbers. Many children do not understand order until they are 6 or 7 years of age (Copeland, 1979). They first must understand the *topological* relation of order. When counting objects, students must order them so that each object is counted only once. The teacher can display objects in a certain order and ask students to arrange identical objects in the same order. Ordering activities include sequencing blocks in a certain pattern, lining up for lunch in a specific order, and completing "pattern" games—for example, students are given a series such as X-O-X-O-X-O-X-__ and then must determine what goes in the blank.

Topological ordering involves arranging a set of items without considering a quantity relationship between each successive item. The combination of *seriation* and *ordering,* however, involves ordering items on the basis of *change* in a property, such as length, size, or color. An example of a seriation task would be arranging items of various lengths in an order from shortest to longest, with each successive item being longer than the preceding item. Children 6 to 7 years old usually master ordering and seriation (Copeland, 1979).

One-to-one correspondence is the basis for counting to determine how many, and is essential for mastering computation skills. It involves understanding that one object in a set is the same number as one object in a different set, whether or not characteristics are similar. If a teacher places small buttons in a glass one at a time and the students place the same number of large buttons in a glass one at a time, the glass containing the large buttons soon displays a higher stack. If students respond "Yes" to the question "Does each glass have the same number of buttons," they understand one-to-one correspondence. If they respond "No, because the buttons are higher in one glass," they are not applying one-to-one correspondence and instead are judging on the basis of sensory cues. Most children 5 to 7 years old master the one-to-one correspondence concept. Initial activities consist of matching identical objects, whereas later activities should involve different objects. Sample activities include giving one pencil to each child, matching each head with a hat, and matching a penny to each marble.

Piaget (1965) considers the concept of *conservation* fundamental to later numerical reasoning. Conservation means that the quantity of an object or the number of objects in a set remains constant regardless of spatial arrangement. Copeland (1979) describes two types of conservation: quantity and number. Conservation of quantity is illustrated in the familiar Piagetian experiments of pouring identical amounts of water into a tall, thin glass and a low, wide glass and rolling a piece of clay into a ball and a long roll. Students who recognize that the amount of water or clay remains constant probably understand conservation of quantity. Conservation of number involves understanding that the number of objects in a set remains constant whether the objects are close together or spread apart. The teacher can ask students to select a spoon for each of seven plates and have them check their work by putting a spoon on each plate. The teacher then can remove the spoons, put them in a stack, and ask the students whether there is still the same number of spoons and plates. If they respond "Yes," they probably understand the concept of conservation of number (Copeland, 1979). Most children master conservation between the ages of 5 and 7.

Several authorities consider an understanding of Piaget's concepts to be a prerequisite for formal math instruction. Many teachers in preschool through first grade directly teach to help students understand these concepts. Moreover, some authorities recommend that teachers in later grades should spot deficits in these concepts and provide remedial instruction.

Readiness for More Advanced Mathematics

Once formal math instruction begins, students must master operations and basic axioms to acquire skills in computation and problem solving. Operations are well-known: addition, subtraction, multiplication, and division. Basic axioms are less familiar. Some axioms that are especially important for teaching math skills to students with learning problems are commutative property of addition, commutative property of multiplication, associative property of addition and multiplication, distributive property of multiplication over addition, and inverse operations for addition and multiplication.

Commutative Property of Addition   No matter what order the same numbers are combined in, the sum remains constant:

$$a + b = b + a$$
$$3 + 4 = 4 + 3$$

Commutative Property of Multiplication Regardless of the order of the numbers being multiplied, the product remains constant:

$$a \times b = b \times a$$
$$9 \times 6 = 6 \times 9$$

Associative Property of Addition and Multiplication   Regardless of grouping arrangements, the sum or product is unchanged:

Addition

$$(a + b) + c = a + (b + c)$$
$$(4 + 3) + 2 = 4 + (3 + 2)$$

Multiplication

$$(a \times b) \times c = a \times (b \times c)$$
$$(5 \times 4) \times 3 = 5 \times (4 \times 3)$$

Distributive Property of Multiplication over Addition   This rule relates the two operations:

$$a(b + c) = (a \times b) + (a \times c)$$
$$5(4 + 3) = (5 \times 4) + (5 \times 3)$$

Inverse Operations   These axioms relate operations that are opposite in their effects. The following equations demonstrate inverse operations:

Addition and Subtraction

$$a + b = c \qquad 5 + 4 = 9$$
$$c - a = b \qquad 9 - 5 = 4$$
$$c - b = a \qquad 9 - 4 = 5$$

Multiplication and Division

$$a \times b = c \qquad 9 \times 3 = 27$$
$$c \div a = b \qquad 27 \div 9 = 3$$
$$c \div b = a \qquad 27 \div 3 = 9$$

☀ ASSESSMENT CONSIDERATIONS

The assessment of math concepts and skills follows a general-to-specific format. As presented in Figure 11.1, assessment begins with an evaluation of general math skills. At this level, a span of skills (e.g., operations, word problems, and measurement) is tested. Standardized or informal survey tests typically assess general math skills. The primary goal of assessment at this level is to identify the student's overall strengths and weaknesses. Also, standardized scores frequently are used to identify math disabilities and qualify students for special education services. Specific skill assessment usually involves standardized diagnostic tests or informal tests; however, informal tests are the preferred instruments for evaluating specific math skills. At this level, the purpose of assessment is to determine specific teaching objectives. The assessment of problem-solving skills involves examining the student's ability to solve word problems. This assessment tests the student's ability to apply mathematical concepts and operations to real-life problems and to determine problem-solving instructional objectives. Finally, diagnostic interviews and informal testing are used to evaluate the student's attitudes and feel-

ings about learning math. These affective factors frequently provide essential insights into planning math instruction. Throughout the math assessment process (general skills to attitude assessment), types of errors, level of understanding, and mastery learning must be examined.

Examining Math Errors

Although the specific error patterns of each student must be considered individually, it helps to examine some of the research regarding types of errors made by many students at different grades.

Computation   In a study of third graders, Roberts (1968) reports that careless numerical errors and poor recall of addition and multiplication facts were found with the same frequency in all levels of ability. Random responses accounted for the most errors of low-ability students, and defective algorithm techniques accounted for the most errors of students in the other three ability levels. An algorithm includes the specific steps used to compute a math problem. An algorithm is defective if it does not deliver the correct answer. For example, the student who adds 24 + 16 by adding each number without regard for place value (i.e., 2 + 4 + 1 + 6 = 13) is using a defective algorithm.

FIGURE 11.1

Math assessment progression

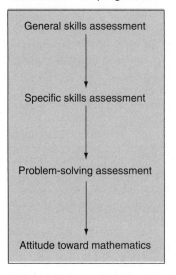

General skills assessment

↓

Specific skills assessment

↓

Problem-solving assessment

↓

Attitude toward mathematics

Cox (1975) conducted a study of error patterns across skill and ability level among students with and without learning problems. In a comparison with students without learning problems, she found that the average percentages of systematic errors in multiplication and division were much higher for the special education students. The majority of errors for all students occurred because of a failure to understand the concepts of multiplication and division. Moreover, Cox found that without intervention many of these youngsters persisted in making the same systematic errors for a long period of time.

In a study of multiplication and division errors made by 213 students with learning disabilities, Miller and Milam (1987) found that the majority were caused by a lack of prerequisite skills. Multiplication errors primarily resulted from a lack of knowledge of multiplication facts and inadequate addition skills. Division errors included many subtraction and multiplication errors. The most frequent error in division was failure to include the remainder in the quotient. According to Miller and Milam (p. 121),

> Many of the errors discovered in this study indicated a lack of student readiness for the type of task required. Students were evidently not being allowed to learn and practice the skills necessary for higher order operations. The implications are obvious: students *must* be allowed to learn in a stepwise fashion or they will not learn at all.

Kelly, Gersten, and Carnine (1990) examined the error patterns that secondary students with learning disabilities made in adding and multiplying fractions. They found that the errors of students instructed in a basal program primarily involved a confusion of the algorithms for addition and multiplication of fractions. However, an effective curriculum design decreased error patterns and resulted in better achievement. Kelly et al. conclude that a strong relationship exists between the number and types of errors and the curriculum.

The determination of a specific error is important because the type of error influences corrective intervention (e.g., whether the student receives place value instruction or specific algorithm instruction). Howell and Nolet (2000, p. 134) provide the following guidelines for conducting an error analysis:

1. Select an assessment or product that provided an opportunity for a variety of errors to occur.

2. Encourage the student to attempt everything and to show all work.
3. Try to get as many examples of meaningful errors as possible (by reviewing products on which the student was only partially correct or those that illustrate the student's best efforts).
4. Try to gain insight into the student's processes by noting patterns, or thought consistencies, in the errors.
5. Try to categorize errors or corrects by content, behavior, condition, or thought process (fact, concept, rule, strategy).
6. Note and categorize skills that were not displayed.
7. Ask yourself (or the student) "How did you arrive at this answer?"
8. Once you think you have found an error pattern, see if you can confirm it by predicting the sort of mistake a student will make and then giving a specific assessment to see if the pattern occurs.

Rivera and Bryant (1992) note the importance of conducting a *process assessment* to determine the strategies that students use to determine answers. Specifically, they suggest using passive and active process assessments. Passive process assessments involve examining a student's written work to determine error patterns and procedural strategies. Active process assessments involve a form of flexible student interviewing in which the student "thinks aloud" while solving an equation or word problem.

Ginsburg (1987) notes that student error patterns tend to fall into three categories: number facts, slips, and bugs. Number facts errors occur when the student has not mastered the basic facts. Slips consist of deficiencies in the execution of a readily available procedure (e.g., forgetting to add a regrouped number). Bugs are systematic procedural errors (e.g., always subtracting the smaller number from the larger number) that are made repeatedly during problem solving. To develop effective remedial programs, these error patterns must be identified.

The following common error patterns in addition, subtraction, multiplication, and division illustrate some of the computational difficulties of students with learning problems:

- The sums of the ones and tens are each recorded without regard for place value:

$$
\begin{array}{r} 83 \\ + 67 \\ \hline 1410 \end{array}
\qquad
\begin{array}{r} 66 \\ + 29 \\ \hline 815 \end{array}
$$

- All digits are added together (defective algorithm and no regard for place value):

$$\begin{array}{r} 67 \\ + 31 \\ \hline 1\,7 \end{array} \qquad \begin{array}{r} 58 \\ + 12 \\ \hline 16 \end{array}$$

- Digits are added from left to right. When the sum is greater than 10, the unit is carried to the next column on the right. This pattern reflects no regard for place value:

$$\begin{array}{r} \overset{21}{476} \\ + 851 \\ \hline 148 \end{array} \qquad \begin{array}{r} \overset{37}{753} \\ + 693 \\ \hline 1113 \end{array}$$

- The smaller number is subtracted from the larger number without regard for placement of the number. The upper number (minuend) is subtracted from the lower number (subtrahend), or vice versa:

$$\begin{array}{r} 627 \\ - 486 \\ \hline 261 \end{array} \qquad \begin{array}{r} 861 \\ - 489 \\ \hline 428 \end{array}$$

- Regrouping is used when it is not required:

$$\begin{array}{r} 1\overset{61}{\cancel{7}}5 \\ - 54 \\ \hline 1111 \end{array} \qquad \begin{array}{r} 1\overset{7_1}{\cancel{8}}5 \\ - 22 \\ \hline 1513 \end{array}$$

- When regrouping is required more than once, the appropriate amount is not subtracted from the column borrowed from in the second regrouping:

$$\begin{array}{r} \overset{5_{11}}{632} \\ - 147 \\ \hline 495 \end{array} \qquad \begin{array}{r} \overset{4_{11}}{523} \\ - 366 \\ \hline 167 \end{array} \qquad \begin{array}{r} \overset{4_{11}}{563} \\ - 382 \\ \hline 181 \end{array}$$

- The regrouped number is added to the multiplicand in the tens column prior to performing the multiplication operation:

$$\begin{array}{r} \overset{2}{17} \\ \times\ 4 \\ \hline 128 \end{array} \qquad \begin{array}{r} \overset{4}{46} \\ \times\ 8 \\ \hline 648 \end{array}$$

- The zero in the quotient is omitted:

Many computational errors stem from an inadequate understanding of place value. Lepore (1979) analyzed the computational errors of 79 youngsters age 12 to 14 with mild learning problems. The type of error they made most frequently involved regrouping, a procedure that requires understanding place value. Place value is introduced in the primary grades; however, students of all ages continue to make mistakes because they do not comprehend that the same digit expresses different orders of magnitude depending on its *location* in a number. Many of the error patterns presented earlier reflect an inadequate understanding of place value.

Ashlock (1998) provides a thorough listing of computational error patterns. In addition to analyzing the student's work, one of the best ways to determine error patterns is to ask the student to show how the answer was computed. The response may offer immediate insight into the error pattern and its cause. Ashlock shares a story told by Dr. Geoffrey Matthews, organizer of the Nuffield Mathematics Teaching Project in England, about a youngster who computed correctly during one school year but missed more than half of the problems the following year. In a discussion with the student, Dr. Matthews found that the child used the rule, "Begin on the side by the piano." However, the following year the piano was on the other side of the room, and the student understandably was confused.

Problem Solving   Recently, the problem-solving skills of students with learning problems have received much attention. Problem-solving skills primarily are assessed by means of word problems. Research indicates that many students with learning problems have trouble solving word problems, especially those categorized as more difficult (Russell & Ginsburg, 1984; Scheid, 1990). One way to vary the difficulty level of word problems is to vary what is unknown. For example, the following word problems increase in difficulty as a function of what is unknown.

1. Tom has 5 stickers. Pam gave him 3 more. How many stickers does Tom have now? (Result unknown)
2. Tom has 5 stickers. How many more does he need to have 7? (Change unknown)
3. Tom had some stickers. Pam gave him 3 more. Now he has 7. How many stickers did Tom have to start with? (Start unknown)

Cawley et al. (1987) found that students with math disabilities experienced difficulty with problems that include extraneous information. Montague and Bos (1990) report that students with math disabilities have difficulty predicting operations (such as multiplication or subtraction), choosing correct algorithms for multistep problems, and correctly completing problems. Also, many students with learning problems experience difficulty in transforming word problems into mathematical representations (Hutchinson, 1993b). Fortunately, several researchers (Cawley et al., 1987; Goldman, 1989; Hutchinson, 1993a; Montague, 1993) indicate that strategies exist to help such students become successful problem solvers.

Determining Level of Understanding

Students frequently memorize a fact or algorithm without understanding the concept or operation involved in the computation. This process leads to the rote memorization of information that is not comprehended. In reading, it is analogous to word calling without comprehension. An understanding of the information to be learned improves memorization and the manipulation of math concepts, operations, and axioms to solve computation and word problems. Thus, knowledge of the levels of understanding in mathematics is vital to math assessment and instruction. Underhill et al. (1980) report that there are several basic levels of learning in mathematical learning experiences. These levels are *concrete, semiconcrete,* and *abstract.*

Concrete Level The concrete level involves the manipulation of objects. This level can be used to help the student relate manipulative and computational processes. At this level the learner concentrates on both the manipulated objects and the symbolic processes (e.g., 6×3) that describe the manipulations. For example, in assessing or teaching multiplication, the teacher presents the problem

5×3 and instructs the student to display the problem using objects. The student looks at the first number, 5, and forms five groups using paper plates. The student then looks at the second number, 3, and places three objects in each plate. The student counts or adds the number of objects on the plates and says "5 groups times 3 objects equals 15 objects." This procedure illustrates that the student understands at a concrete level that 5×3 means "5 groups of 3 objects equals 15 objects." Some students demonstrate their need for concrete-level activities by counting on their fingers when requested to complete simple computational problems. Concrete experiences are important for teaching and assessing skills at all levels in the math hierarchy.

Semiconcrete Level The semiconcrete level involves working with illustrations of items in performing math tasks. Items may include dots, lines, pictures of objects, or nonsense items. Some authorities divide this level into semiconcrete and semiabstract (Underhill et al., 1980). *Semiconcrete* refers to using pictures of real objects; *semiabstract* involves the use of tallies. In this book, *semiconcrete* refers to both pictures and tallies. A worksheet that requires the learner to match sets of the same number of items is a semiconcrete-level task. One way to assess a student's understanding at this level is for the teacher to present a problem (such as 5×3) and ask the student to use drawings (i.e., lines and tallies) to solve the problem. The student looks at the first number, 5, and draws five horizontal lines. The student then looks at the second number, 3, and draws three tallies on each line. The student counts or adds the number of tallies on the lines and says "5 groups times 3 tallies equals 15 tallies." This procedure illustrates that the student knows at a semiconcrete level of understanding that 5×3 means "5 groups of 3 tallies equals 15 tallies." Many students with math learning problems need practice at this level to master a concept or fact. Often students demonstrate their reliance on this level by supplying their own graphic representations. For example, the problems $5 + 4 = \_\_$ and $3 \times 2 = \_\_$ can be approached in the following manner:

$$
\begin{array}{cc}
5\ /////\ & 3\ // \\
+4\ ////\ & \times 2\ // \\
\hline
9 & 6\ \underline{//}
\end{array}
$$

Chalkboard math activities enable students in the class to learn from teacher feedback.

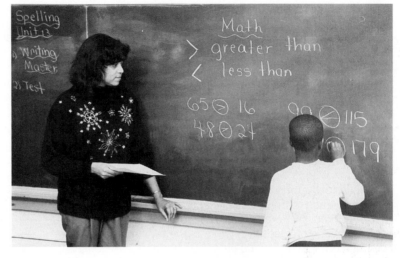

At the semiconcrete level, the emphasis is on developing associations between visual models and the numerical equations.

Abstract Level   The abstract level involves the use of numerals. For example, in computation this level involves working only with numerals to solve math problems. Students who have difficulty in math usually need experience at the concrete and semiconcrete levels before they can use numerals meaningfully. Traditionally, assessment has focused on the abstract level; however, assessment should not be limited to this level. The goal of assessment involves determining the learner's ability to relate to math computation in a meaningful way. To do this, tasks are needed at each of the levels. Sample activities for assessing levels of understanding are presented later in this chapter.

Determining Mastery Learning

Many educators use percentage scores to determine a mastery level for a skill. In many cases these scores are a valid measure of a student's mastery learning. For some students, however, percentage scores are not sufficient for assessing mastery. Many students with learning problems produce accurate answers at a slow rate and use tedious procedures (such as counting on fingers and drawing tallies for large numbers) to compute answers without understanding the math concept or operation.

Several authorities (Kirby & Becker, 1988; Lovitt, 1989) report that slow rates of computation are a primary problem of students with math disabilities. Wood, Burke, Kunzelmann, and Koenig (1978) examined the math rates of successful students, unsuccessful students, and community workers. In nearly every comparison, the rates of unsuccessful students were lower than the rates of successful students. Also, the rates of successful students were about the same as community workers.

As noted in Chapter 3, rate is an excellent measure of mastery learning. In addition to helping with retention and higher math performance, high rates of correct responses help students complete tests on time, finish homework quickly, and keep score in games. Math rate assessment involves the use of probes (i.e., a sheet of selected math problems) that are administered under timed conditions (usually 1 minute). Scores are computed by counting the number of correct and incorrect digits written per minute. A sample probe is presented later in this chapter.

☀ ASSESSMENT OF MATH SKILLS
Formal Math Assessment

Standardized math tests are norm-referenced and provide many kinds of information (e.g., math grade level, math age score, percentile, and stanine score) based on a comparison of the student's performance with the population upon which the test was standardized. Standardized tests usually are classified into two categories: achievement (or survey) and diagnostic. Other published math measures are criterion-referenced, and these tests describe performance, rather than compare it, to determine whether the student has mastered specific instructional objectives. This section presents achievement and diagnostic tests as well as criterion-referenced tests.

Achievement and Diagnostic Tests   Most achievement tests include sections covering specific academic areas, such as reading, spelling, and math. Each of these specific academic areas is divided into skill areas. For example, a math section can be divided into numerical reasoning, computation, and word problems. Achievement or survey tests cover a broad range of math skills and are designed to provide an estimate of the student's general level of achievement. They yield a single score, which is compared with standardized norms and converted into standard scores or a grade- or age-equivalent score. These tests help identify students who need further assessment. Achievement tests with math subtests include the following:

- *California Achievement Tests—Fifth Edition* (1992). Assesses computation, concepts, and applications.
- *Diagnostic Achievement Battery—2* (Newcomer, 1990). Assesses mathematics reasoning and mathematics calculation.
- *Kaufman Test of Educational Achievement* (Kaufman & Kaufman, 1998). Assesses concepts, applications, numerical reasoning, and computation.
- *Metropolitan Achievement Tests—Seventh Edition* (Balow, Farr, & Hogan, 1997). Assesses concepts and problem solving and procedures.
- *Peabody Individual Achievement Test—Revised* (Markwardt, 1998). Assesses skills ranging from matching and recognizing numbers to solving geometry and trigonometry problems.
- *Woodcock-Johnson III Tests of Achievement* (Woodcock & Mather, 2000). Assesses calculation, math fluency, and applied problems.

In contrast to achievement tests, diagnostic tests usually cover a narrower range of content and are designed to assess the student's performance in math skill areas. Diagnostic tests aim to determine the student's strengths and weaknesses. No one diagnostic test assesses all mathematical difficulties. The examiner must decide on the purpose of the assessment and select the test that is most suited to the task. Table 11.1 presents several standardized diagnostic math tests.

Criterion-Referenced Tests   Standardized tests compare one individual's score with norms, which generally does not help diagnose the student's math difficulties. However, criterion-referenced tests, which describe the student's performance in terms of criteria for specific skills, are more suited to assessing specific difficulties. Criterion-referenced survey or inventory tests usually cover several academic areas. Each of these areas is further subdivided into skill categories. Whereas survey tests locate general problem areas, diagnostic tests focus on more specific difficulties. Criterion-referenced diagnostic tests are the most suited for identifying specific math problems. Table 11.2 presents two criterion-referenced math tests.

Informal Math Assessment

Informal assessment involves examining the student's daily work samples or administering teacher-constructed tests. Informal assessment is essential for the frequent monitoring of student progress and for making relevant teaching decisions regarding individual students. Such assessment enables teachers to sample specific skills through the use of numerous test items that are related directly to the math curriculum. Because the content of standardized math tests and the content of math curriculum texts have a low degree of overlap (Tindal & Marston, 1990), the practice of assessing each student's achievement within the curriculum becomes essential. With informal techniques, the teacher also can determine the student's understanding of math concepts at the concrete, semiconcrete, and abstract levels. By asking appropriate questions and listening to students' responses, teachers can assess not only whether a student can solve a particular problem but *how* the problem is solved. Informal assessment thus is the most efficient way of determining the instructional needs of individual students.

TABLE 11.1
Selected standardized diagnostic math tests

Test	Grade Levels	Areas Assessed
Key Math Revised: A Diagnostic Inventory of Essential Skills (Connolly, 1998)	K–12	Basic concepts, operations, applications

> *Key Math Revised* is based on a comprehensive content scope and sequence and is composed of 13 subtests in three areas. Administration time is about 35 to 50 minutes. Spring and fall norms are given, and two parallel forms are available. Derived scores for the three area composites and total test include standard scores, grade and age equivalents, percentile ranks, and stanines. *Key Math-R ASSIST* software is available to provide quick derived score conversion as well as suggestions for remedial instruction.

Stanford Diagnostic Mathematics Test—Fourth Edition (Beatty, Madden, Gardner, & Karlsen, 1995)	1–13	Concepts and applications, computation

> This group-administered test is divided into six separate levels, identified by color; two forms are available for the upper three levels. Each level provides both multiple-choice and free-response formats to reveal the problem-solving process and product. In addition to yielding percentile ranks, stanines, grade equivalents, and scaled scores, the test results can be used to identify strengths and weaknesses in specific math skills.

Test of Early Mathematics Ability—2 (Ginsburg & Baroody, 1990)	Preschool–3	Concepts, counting skills, number facts, calculation

> This test of early math functioning takes about 5 to 10 minutes to administer and measures informal as well as formal (school-taught) concepts and skills. Items in informal mathematics focus on concepts of relative magnitude, counting skills, and calculation; items in formal mathematics focus on reading and writing numerals, number facts, calculational algorithms, and base-ten concepts. Results are reported as standard scores, percentiles, or age equivalents.

Test of Mathematical Abilities—2 (Brown, Cronin, & McEntire, 1994)	3–12	Story problems, computation

> In addition to information about a student's skills in two major areas (story problems and computation), the test provides related information regarding expressed attitudes toward mathematics, understanding of mathematical vocabulary used in a mathematical sense, and the application of mathematical content in real life.

Curriculum-Based Measurement   When progress is assessed within the curriculum to measure achievement, the teacher is assured that what is being assessed is what is being taught. Curriculum-based measurement (CBM) offers the teacher a standardized set of informal assessment procedures for conducting a reliable and valid assessment of a student's achievement within the math curriculum.

Curriculum-based measurement begins by assessing an entire class with a survey test of a span of appropriate skills. From the results of a survey test, a box plot (see Chapter 3) is developed for making instructional decisions. Five steps are required in developing and administering a survey test:

1. ***Identify a sequence of successive skills included in the school curriculum.*** Many

TABLE 11.2

Selected criterion-referenced math tests

Test	Grade Levels	Areas Assessed
Brigance Diagnostic Comprehensive Inventory of Basic Skills—Revised (Brigance, 1999)	K–9	Numbers, number facts, computation of whole numbers, fractions and mixed numbers, decimals, percents, time, money, measurement and geometry, metrics

This inventory provides instructional objectives and includes a recordkeeping system for monitoring progress of individual students. Also, grade placement tests in math computational skills and math problem solving are included. An option is offered that provides normed or standardized scoring.

Test	Grade Levels	Areas Assessed
California Diagnostic Math Test (1990)	1–12	Number concepts, computation, applications

This test, which includes six levels that allow testing in each student's ability range, produces both criterion- and norm-referenced scores that can be used to evaluate student progress. In addition to items focusing on number concepts, computation, and applications at all levels, there are items on life skills problems in the level for students in eighth through twelfth grade. The Teacher's Guide explains how to interpret and apply test results for classroom planning and suggests instructional techniques for methods to help at-risk students. Scoring and reporting options include handscoring as well as computer scanning.

curriculum unit tests or review tests provide a source of sequenced skills and corresponding test items. Appendix A provides a scope and sequence list of math skills developed from a review of numerous basal math programs. This review indicated that there is much agreement (90 to 95 percent) among the basal scope and sequence skills lists.

2. ***Select a span of math skills to be assessed.*** For a beginning fourth-grade class, it may be appropriate to administer a survey test of the computation skills covered in the third grade. This third-grade survey test would help identify students with math problems and provide some normative information to facilitate goal setting. Once a scope and sequence skills list across the grades has been identified, the teacher has a multitude of options for developing survey tests for different spans of skills. The options enable the teacher to identify instructional groups (such as high, average, and low achievers) or plan instruction for a new student.

3. ***Construct or select items for each skill within the range selected.*** A survey test may be used to assess computation and problem-solving skills. To maintain an adequate sample, it is a good practice to include a minimum of three items per specific skill. Table 11.3 presents a survey test of computation skills covered in a typical third-grade curriculum. This test could be used at the beginning of fourth grade to determine which students need additional teaching on third-grade skills and which are ready for fourth-grade computation skills.

4. ***Administer and score the survey test.*** The teacher instructs the students to work successive problems during the 2-minute timing. In scoring, the teacher counts all correct digits. Figure 11.2 provides detailed CBM administration directions and scoring procedures.

5. ***Display the results in a box plot, interpret the results, and plan instruction.*** To increase the accuracy of the results, it helps to develop an alternate form of the survey test and

TABLE 11.3

Survey test of third-grade computation skills

1.	$\begin{array}{r} 476 \\ +\,200 \\ \hline \end{array}$	2.	$\begin{array}{r} 807 \\ +\,407 \\ \hline \end{array}$	3.	$\begin{array}{r} 9000 \\ +\,3010 \\ \hline \end{array}$
4.	$\begin{array}{r} 3168 \\ +\,5426 \\ \hline \end{array}$	5.	$\begin{array}{r} 4727 \\ +\,2761 \\ \hline \end{array}$	6.	$\begin{array}{r} 7964 \\ +\ \ 385 \\ \hline \end{array}$
7.	$\begin{array}{r} 604 \\ -\,237 \\ \hline \end{array}$	8.	$\begin{array}{r} 704 \\ -\,369 \\ \hline \end{array}$	9.	$\begin{array}{r} 501 \\ -\,269 \\ \hline \end{array}$
10.	$\begin{array}{r} 7134 \\ -\,3487 \\ \hline \end{array}$	11.	$\begin{array}{r} 5094 \\ -\,4630 \\ \hline \end{array}$	12.	$\begin{array}{r} 8751 \\ -\,2683 \\ \hline \end{array}$
13.	$\begin{array}{r} 9 \\ \times\,8 \\ \hline \end{array}$	14.	$\begin{array}{r} 9 \\ \times\,6 \\ \hline \end{array}$	15.	$\begin{array}{r} 8 \\ \times\,7 \\ \hline \end{array}$
16.	$\begin{array}{r} 7 \\ \times\,8 \\ \hline \end{array}$	17.	$\begin{array}{r} 6 \\ \times\,9 \\ \hline \end{array}$	18.	$\begin{array}{r} 9 \\ \times\,0 \\ \hline \end{array}$
19.	$\begin{array}{r} 8 \\ \times\,0 \\ \hline \end{array}$	20.	$\begin{array}{r} 6 \\ \times\,1 \\ \hline \end{array}$	21.	$\begin{array}{r} 1 \\ \times\,8 \\ \hline \end{array}$
22.	$\begin{array}{r} 34 \\ \times\ \ 2 \\ \hline \end{array}$	23.	$\begin{array}{r} 26 \\ \times\ \ 1 \\ \hline \end{array}$	24.	$\begin{array}{r} 31 \\ \times\ \ 8 \\ \hline \end{array}$
25.	$24 \div 3 = \rule{2cm}{0.4pt}$	26.	$12 \div 2 = \rule{2cm}{0.4pt}$	27.	$4\overline{)16}$
28.	$5\overline{)16}$	29.	$4\overline{)34}$	30.	$7\overline{)58}$
31.	$\begin{array}{r} 17 \\ \times\ \ 5 \\ \hline \end{array}$	32.	$\begin{array}{r} 49 \\ \times\ \ 2 \\ \hline \end{array}$	33.	$\begin{array}{r} 16 \\ \times\ \ 4 \\ \hline \end{array}$
34.	$\begin{array}{r} 82 \\ \times\ \ 4 \\ \hline \end{array}$	35.	$\begin{array}{r} 74 \\ \times\ \ 2 \\ \hline \end{array}$	36.	$\begin{array}{r} 81 \\ \times\ \ 5 \\ \hline \end{array}$
37.	$\begin{array}{r} 342 \\ \times\ \ 2 \\ \hline \end{array}$	38.	$\begin{array}{r} 637 \\ \times\ \ 1 \\ \hline \end{array}$	39.	$\begin{array}{r} 312 \\ \times\ \ 3 \\ \hline \end{array}$
40.	$\begin{array}{r} 436 \\ \times\ \ 3 \\ \hline \end{array}$	41.	$\begin{array}{r} 578 \\ \times\ \ 6 \\ \hline \end{array}$	42.	$\begin{array}{r} 638 \\ \times\ \ 7 \\ \hline \end{array}$
43.	$3\overline{)36}$	44.	$4\overline{)44}$	45.	$2\overline{)28}$
46.	$3\overline{)51}$	47.	$4\overline{)72}$	48.	$7\overline{)84}$
49.	$\frac{1}{3}$ of 6 = $\rule{2cm}{0.4pt}$	50.	$\frac{1}{4}$ of 8 = $\rule{2cm}{0.4pt}$	51.	$\frac{1}{2}$ of 12 = $\rule{2cm}{0.4pt}$
52.	$\dfrac{1}{2} = \dfrac{\ \ }{4}$	53.	$\dfrac{2}{3} = \dfrac{\ \ }{6}$	54.	$\dfrac{2}{5} = \dfrac{\ \ }{5}$

TABLE 11.3
(continued)

Item Analysis of Survey Test	
Problems 1–3:	Addition: With zero
Problems 3–6:	Addition: Multidigit plus multidigit
Problems 7–9:	Subtraction: Regrouping more than once with zero in minuend
Problems 10–12:	Subtraction: Four-digit numbers with regrouping
Problems 13–21:	Multiplication: Facts for 6 through 9 with 0 and 1 properties and order proportions
Problems 22–24:	Multiplication: Two-digit number times one-digit number
Problems 25–27:	Division: Facts
Problems 28–30:	Division: Two-digit number divided by one-digit number, with remainder
Problems 31–33:	Multiplication: Two-digit number times one-digit number, with tens regrouping
Problems 34–36:	Multiplication: Two-digit number times one-digit number, with hundreds regrouping
Problems 37–39:	Multiplication: Three-digit number times one-digit number, without regrouping
Problems 40–42:	Multiplication: Three-digit number times one-digit number, with regrouping
Problems 43–45:	Division: Two-digit number divided by one-digit number, without regrouping
Problems 46–48:	Division: Two-digit number divided by one-digit number, with regrouping
Problems 49–51:	Fractions: Of a whole number
Problems 52–54:	Fractions: Equivalent fractions

administer both survey probes of the same skills. The results should be interpreted to help place students in instructional groups and to plan individual programs.

From an analysis of student performances on a span of skills, the teacher develops probes of specific skills for monitoring individual student progress. Specific skill monitoring usually involves a single skill until mastery is achieved. The scope and sequence skills list in Appendix A that features the sequence of skills within an operation (i.e., addition, subtraction, and so on) is useful in sequencing specific skill monitoring. Although the range of proficiency rates on math skills varies in the literature, generally a rate of 40 to 60 correct digits per minute on math computation problems is appropriate for most third-grade and above students. Starlin and Starlin (1973) suggest the following mastery rates according to specific math objectives and grade levels:

- Addition facts 0 to 9 and subtraction facts with top number 1 to 5 (grades 2 and 3): 20 to 30 correct digits per minute with two or fewer errors.
- Addition facts and subtraction facts (grades 3 and 4): 40 to 60 correct digits per minute with two or fewer errors.

- Two-column addition with regrouping (grades 4 and 5): 40 to 60 correct digits per minute with two or fewer errors.
- Two-column subtraction with regrouping (grades 4 through 6): 40 to 60 correct digits per minute with two or fewer errors.
- Multiplication facts (grades 5 and 6): 40 to 60 correct digits per minute with two or fewer errors.
- Division facts (grade 6): 40 to 60 correct digits per minute with two or fewer errors.

Likewise, Smith and Lovitt (1982) suggest that the rate of 45 to 50 correct digits per minute on addition, subtraction, multiplication, and division facts indicates mastery.

The chart in Figure 11.3 displays a student's progress on specific skills during an eight-week period. In this chart, the mastery or aim line is set at 50 correct digits per minute. The chart shows that the student has mastered two skills and has started working on a third skill.

Teacher-Constructed Tests   Teacher-constructed tests are essential for individualizing math instruction. They enable the teacher to identify problems, determine level of understanding, and monitor progress. The type of test the teacher selects depends, in part, on the purpose of the

FIGURE 11.2

Curriculum-based measurement administration directions and scoring procedures for math

---

Administration Directions

The following steps are recommended for administering 2-minute timings to individuals or groups.

1. Select the appropriate measurement (i.e., survey test or specific skill probe) and pass it face down to students.
2. Give standardized directions at the beginning of the administration. Also, use specific instructions for different parts of some tests.

   "The sheets I just passed out are math problems." If a single skill probe is used, tell the students the operation: "All problems are _____ (addition, subtraction, multiplication, or division)." If a multiple skill probe is used, say: "There are different types of problems on the sheet. There are some addition, subtraction, and multiplication problems. Look at each problem closely before you compute."

   "When I say 'Begin,' turn the sheet over and answer the problems. Start with the first problem at the beginning of the first row. Touch the problem. Work across the sheet and then go to the beginning of the next row. If you are unable to do a problem, mark an X on it and go to the next problem. If you finish one page, go to the next page. Do you have any questions?"

   "Ready, start."
3. Monitor student work to ensure that students are following the directions (i.e., working in successive rows). Watch for students who want to skip around and do the easy problems.
4. When 2 minutes have elapsed, say: "Stop. Put your pencils down."

Scoring Procedures

1. Underline each correct digit.
2. Score numerals written in reverse form (e.g., ε for 3) as correct.
3. Score a correct digit in the proper place (column) as correct.
4. Award full points (number of digits used in solving a problem) when the student has a correct answer, even if the work is not shown.
5. If the student displays work and the answer is incorrect, give credit for each digit done correctly.
6. Do not count numerals written for regrouping purposes (i.e., carried numbers).
7. Do not count remainders of zero.
8. When an X or a zero is placed correctly as a place holder, count it as one digit correct.
9. Give credit for any correct digits, even if the problem has not been completed.
10. Total the number of correct digits and record it on the paper.

Sample Scoring of Student Copy

$$\begin{array}{r} 2 \\ +4 \\ \hline 6 \end{array}$$ 1 digit correct

$$\begin{array}{r} 12 \\ +26 \\ \hline 38 \end{array}$$ 2 digits correct

$$\begin{array}{r} 38 \\ \times 9 \\ \hline 342 \end{array}$$ 3 digits correct

$$\begin{array}{r} 12R42 \\ 63\overline{)798} \\ \underline{63X} \\ 168 \\ \underline{126} \\ 42 \end{array}$$

(4 digits correct)
(3 digits correct with x)
(3 digits correct)
(3 digits correct)
(2 digits correct)

15 digits correct

$\dfrac{1}{4} + \dfrac{1}{3} =$

$\dfrac{3}{12} + \dfrac{4}{12} = \dfrac{7}{12}$

(3 digits correct) (3 digits correct) (3 digits correct)

9 digits correct

FIGURE 11.3

Chart showing a student's progress on specific skills

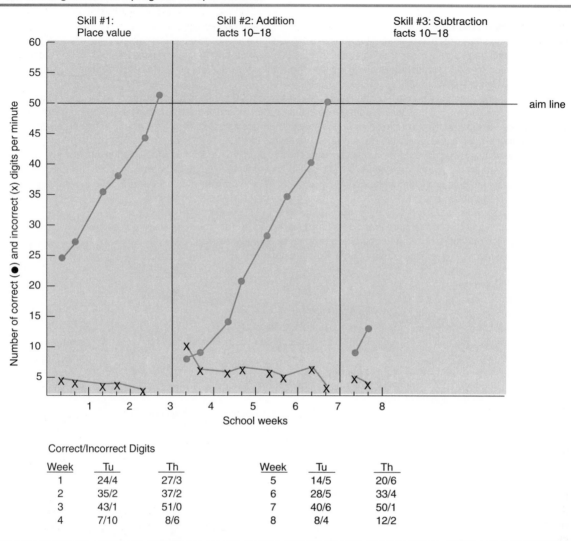

Correct/Incorrect Digits

Week	Tu	Th	Week	Tu	Th
1	24/4	27/3	5	14/5	20/6
2	35/2	37/2	6	28/5	33/4
3	43/1	51/0	7	40/6	50/1
4	7/10	8/6	8	8/4	12/2

assessment. To identify specific problem areas, the teacher may construct a survey test with items at several levels of difficulty. There are four steps to developing and using this type of test:

1. ***Select a hierarchy that includes the content area to be assessed.*** This hierarchy may come from a math program series, a curriculum guide, or a textbook. A sample math hierarchy is included in Appendix A.

2. ***Decide on the span of skills that needs to be evaluated.*** Because a hierarchy includes a wide range of skills, the teacher must select which range of skills needs to be evaluated with an individual student. This is done by examining the student's performance on published tests and by analyzing the math curriculum by grade level. In deciding on the span, the teacher should begin with items that are easy for the student and proceed to more difficult ones.

3. ***Construct items for each skill within the range selected.*** A survey test is designed to assess the student's computation (abstract) performance within a hierarchy; thus, all items are at the abstract level. If an untimed criterion approach is used, the teacher should include three items for each skill and set 67 percent or 100 percent as a passing criterion (Underhill et al., 1980). Most commercial tests do not adequately sample a specific skill. Including three items per skill helps to control the factor of carelessness and provides an adequate test sample. The use of probes can help assess specific skill mastery. To use timed probes, the teacher should construct one for each skill and establish the criterion in terms of correct and incorrect responses per minute. To obtain a valid performance, each probe should be administered at least three times. The highest rate from the three samples is used for determining the criterion. From analyzing proficiency rates, it appears that a useful criterion is a score of 40 to 60 correct digits per minute with no errors. Rate, however, can vary as a function of age, motor (handwriting) skills, and difficulty level of the task.

4. ***Score the test and interpret the student's performance.*** The teacher starts with the easiest skill items and applies the "two out of three" (67 percent) criterion or the criterion of rate correct per minute. At the point where the criterion is not achieved, the teacher analyzes the student's performance (i.e., errors, basic fact deficit, and understanding) to determine what skill to teach. The test also can be used to monitor student progress.

The division test presented in Figure 11.4 is based on the math scope and sequence skills list in Appendix A. The skills become progressively more difficult, and three items are presented for each skill. The student is sometimes less intimidated if the items in each skill area are written on index cards. The teacher scores the student's responses under each skill and determines whether the 67 percent criterion has been obtained. Failure to reach the criterion on a skill alerts the teacher to a specific area of difficulty, which can become the target of instruction and further assessment. The type of survey test presented in Figure 11.4 is commonly used to determine what to teach. However, after becoming more skillful in assessment and teaching, the teacher can construct

other diagnostic tests to determine the student's level of understanding. The scope and sequence skills list presented in Appendix A can be used to develop informal tests in other math areas.

Teacher-constructed tests can include a number of formats. The following are sample skills and related assessment items:

- Identifies before or after for numbers to 10. What numbers are missing?

$$\_ 2 \_ \_ 5 \_ 7 \_ 9$$

Fill in the spaces:

Before		After
—	9	—
—	7	—
—	3	—

- Identifies the greater or smaller number for numbers 0 to 100 and uses > and <.
Circle the greater number:

Put > or < in the ◯:

23 ◯ 32   8 ◯ 19   94 ◯ 76

13 ◯ 43   43 ◯ 29   65 ◯ 59

- Identifies place value with ones and tens. State the face value and the place value of the underlined digit:

46<u>3</u>	<u>2</u>8	48<u>4</u>3
face value ___	face value ___	face value ___
place value ___	place value ___	place value ___

Complete the following:

$$7 \text{ ones, } 3 \text{ tens} = \_\_$$
$$5 \text{ tens, } 4 \text{ ones} = \_\_$$
$$0 \text{ tens, } 3 \text{ ones} = \_\_$$

- Computes three two-digit numerals, sum of ones column greater than 20.
Add:

26	57	29
18	38	47
+ 47	+ 49	+ 36

FIGURE 11.4
Survey test: Division with whole numbers

Skill	Criterion (score in %)

1. Identify symbols for division by circling problems that require division.

$$\begin{array}{c}4\\+4\\\hline\end{array}\qquad 6\times3\qquad 6\div2\qquad 7-4\qquad \dfrac{6}{2}$$

$$4\overline{)16}\qquad 7\times4\qquad 8\div2\qquad \dfrac{9}{3}\qquad \begin{array}{c}13\\\times7\\\hline\end{array}$$

$$4\times1\qquad \begin{array}{c}6\\-2\\\hline\end{array}\qquad 8\overline{)64}\qquad 6+2\qquad 9=3$$

⬚

2. Compute basic division facts involving 1.

$1\overline{)8}\qquad\qquad 1\overline{)7}\qquad\qquad 1\overline{)1}$

⬚

3. Compute basic division facts.

$4\overline{)36}\qquad\qquad 7\overline{)42}\qquad\qquad 8\overline{)56}$

⬚

4. Compute division of a nonzero number by itself.

$7\overline{)7}\qquad\qquad 29\overline{)29}\qquad\qquad 1\overline{)1}$

⬚

5. Compute quotient of a one- or two-place dividend and a one-place divisor with a remainder.

$3\overline{)7}\qquad\qquad 4\overline{)7}\qquad\qquad 2\overline{)9}$

$8\overline{)74}\qquad\qquad 6\overline{)39}\qquad\qquad 3\overline{)17}$

⬚
⬚

6. Compute quotient with expanding dividend.

$3\overline{)9}\qquad\qquad 3\overline{)90}\qquad\qquad 3\overline{)900}$

$2\overline{)6}\qquad\qquad 2\overline{)60}\qquad\qquad 2\overline{)600}$

$4\overline{)8}\qquad\qquad 4\overline{)80}\qquad\qquad 4\overline{)800}$

⬚

7. Compute quotient of a three-place dividend with a one-place divisor.

$8\overline{)638}\qquad\qquad 6\overline{)461}\qquad\qquad 3\overline{)262}$

⬚

8. Compute quotient of a many-place dividend with a one-place divisor.

$7\overline{)47,864}\qquad 6\overline{)2783}\qquad\qquad 3\overline{)578,348}$

⬚

9. Compute quotient of a three-place dividend and a two-place divisor where divisor is a multiple of 10.

$40\overline{)681}\qquad\qquad 30\overline{)570}\qquad\qquad 10\overline{)874}$

⬚

10. Compute quotient when divisors are 100, 1000, and so on.

$100\overline{)685}\qquad 100\overline{)4360}\qquad 100\overline{)973}$

$1000\overline{)6487}\qquad 1000\overline{)99,490}\qquad 1000\overline{)7430}$

⬚
⬚

11. Compute a quotient of a three-place dividend and a two-place divisor.

$27\overline{)685}\qquad\qquad 39\overline{)871}\qquad\qquad 14\overline{)241}$

⬚

12. Compute quotient of a many-place dividend and a many-place divisor.

$649\overline{)78,741}\qquad 3641\overline{)100,877}\qquad 247\overline{)8937}$

⬚

Note: When this test is administered, the directions for items 2–12 should simply state: Solve the following division problems.

- Identifies unit faction inequalities.
  Circle the numeral that represents the smaller number of each pair:

$$\frac{1}{2} \quad \frac{1}{3} \qquad \frac{1}{6} \quad \frac{1}{2} \qquad \frac{1}{4} \quad \frac{1}{3}$$

- Writes fractions in numeral form.
  Write the fractional numerals for each of the shaded areas in numeral form:

———————   ———————

- Identifies fraction names for 1.

Fill in each ☐ :

Teacher-made probes also can be used to identify problem areas. Mixed probes are used to locate areas that need further assessment or instruction. Figure 11.5 presents a mixed probe in addition. Each of the following categories has nine items: basic addition facts of sums-to-9 (first item and then every fourth item), two-digit number plus two-digit number with no regrouping (second item and then every fourth item), two-digit number plus one-digit number with no regrouping (third item and then every fourth item), and basic addition facts of sums-to-18 (fourth item and then every fourth item). On this probe, the student can obtain a maximum score of 63 correct digits with no errors. After three timings, a high score of 40 or more correct digits per minute with no errors is a reasonable criterion for diagnostic purposes. If the student fails to reach the criterion on a mixed probe, it is important to analyze the responses and locate the items being missed. This analysis provides the teacher with information for further assessment with specific skill probes (such as 0 to 9 facts). Also, specific skill probes can be used to monitor the student's daily progress.

Assessment at the Concrete, Semiconcrete, and Abstract Levels

As discussed earlier, learning math facts and concepts progresses through three levels of understanding: concrete, semiconcrete, and abstract. Most published tests consist of abstract-level items; therefore, they do not yield information on the student's understanding at the semiconcrete and concrete levels. The student's level of understanding determines whether manipulative, pictorial, or abstract experiences are appropriate. To obtain the type of information required for effective instructional planning, the teacher can construct analytical tests that focus on both identifying difficulties and determining level of understanding. Items at the concrete level involve real objects, items at the semiconcrete level use pictures or tallies, and items at the abstract level use numerals.

Assessment at the concrete level can begin either with a written problem (such as 5 + 3 = ____), with a display of objects, or with both numerals and objects. When assessment begins with a written problem, the student is instructed to read the problem and then solve it by using objects. When assessment begins with objects, the student is instructed to look at the display of objects (e.g., ⚬⚬ + ⚬⚬ = ____) and then write the problem and solve it. When assessment begins with both numerals and objects (e.g., 5 ⚬⚬ + 3 ⚬⚬ = ____), the student uses the objects (i.e., counts, removes, or groups) to solve the problem. The preferred sequence is to (1) use both numerals and objects, (2) use only objects and have the student write the problem, and (3) use only written problems and have the student arrange objects to solve them.

Assessment at the semiconcrete or representational level can begin with a written problem, with drawings (i.e., pictures or tallies), or with both numerals and drawings (e.g., 5 ///// + 3 /// = ____). When assessment begins with a written problem, the student is instructed to solve the problem by drawing tallies. When assessment begins with pictures or tallies, the student is instructed to write the problem and solve it. When assessment begins with both numerals and drawings, the student uses the pictures or drawings to solve the problem. The preferred sequence in assessing at the semiconcrete level is to (1) use both numerals and drawings, (2) use only drawings and have the student write the problem, and (3) use only written problems and have the student generate the drawings (tallies).

Sometimes it is not feasible to present the problem through the use of objects or drawings because the operation is not implied. For

FIGURE 11.5

Mixed addition probe with no regrouping

4	22	33	9	6	36	41	6	8
+ 3	+41	+ 6	+ 7	+ 2	+62	+ 3	+ 5	+ 0
53	78	5	7	43	82	7	5	61
+44	+ 1	+ 8	+ 2	+36	+ 5	+ 4	+ 3	+37
42	8	4	33	31	9	6	24	65
+ 4	+ 7	+ 5	+52	+ 8	+ 9	+ 0	+53	+24
7	5	82	37	6	4	31	57	7
+ 6	+ 2	+13	+ 2	+ 6	+ 4	+18	+32	+ 9

Name _____   Date _____

Correct Digits: _____

Incorrect Digits: _____

Patterns: 0–9 facts _____/9

          2D + 2D _____/9

          2D + 1D _____/9

          0–18 facts _____/9

Comments: _____

_____

_____

example, in arranging the objects for subtraction, only the objects or drawings for the minuend are used in beginning the problem. The subtrahend involves taking away objects from the minuend; thus, the subtrahend is not part of the original stimulus. At the abstract level, only numerals are used in presenting and solving problems.

The examples that follow should help in developing analytical math tests in specific skill areas. Also, the instructional activities presented in Chapter 12 for each of the operations (at all three levels) can provide guidance in developing assessment items.

- Skill: Counting (1 to 5)
  Concrete level: Count the blocks.

  ☐   ☐   ☐   ☐   ☐

  Semiconcrete level: Circle five blocks.

  ☐ ☐ ☐ ☐ ☐ ☐ ☐ ☐ ☐

Abstract level: Count to five and circle the number.

1 2 3 4 5 6 7

- Skill: Addition facts (0 to 9)
  Concrete level: Write problem and sum.

  _____ + _____ = _____

Semiconcrete level: Write problem and sum.

Abstract level: Write sum.

$$\begin{array}{r} 5 \\ + 3 \\ \hline \end{array}$$

- Skill: Addition facts (0 to 18)
  Concrete level: Arrange blocks to show tens and ones, and then write sum.

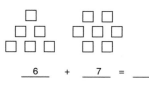

6 + 7 = ____

Student work:

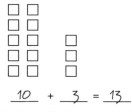

10 + 3 = 13

Semiconcrete level: Circle tens and write sum.
Student work:

10 + 3 = 13

Abstract level: Write sum.

$$\begin{array}{r} 6 \\ + 7 \\ \hline \end{array}$$

- Skill: Addition operation without regrouping
  Concrete level: Let ☐ = 1 ten and ☐ = 1 one. Write problem and sum.

Semiconcrete level: Let ◯ = 1 ten and ◦ = 1 one. Write problem and sum.

◯ ◦ ◦

+ ◯ ◦ ◦ ◦ ◦   + ___

___

Abstract level: Write sum.

$$\begin{array}{r} 12 \\ + 14 \\ \hline \end{array}$$

- Skill: Addition with regrouping ones and tens
  Concrete level: Use string to group units and write sum.
  Student work:

string for
regrouping
sets of 10

16
+ 27
43

Semiconcrete level: Circle to group units and write sum.
Student work:

16
+ 27
43

Abstract level: Write sum.

$$\begin{array}{r} 16 \\ + 27 \\ \hline \end{array}$$

- Skill: Addition with regrouping ones, tens, and hundreds
  Concrete level: Let ▭ = 1 hundred, ☐ = 1 ten, and ☐ = 1 one. Use strings to show work. Write sum.
  Student work:

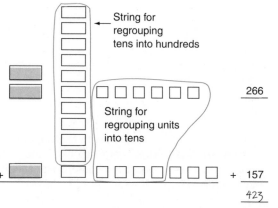

String for
regrouping
tens into hundreds

String for
regrouping
units into tens

266

+ 157
423

Semiconcrete level: Use the place value chart to show work. Write sum.

Abstract level: Write sum.

$$266$$
$$+ \ 157$$

- Skill: Basic subtraction facts
  Concrete level: Write difference or missing addend.

$$7$$
$$- \ 3$$

Student work:

$$7$$
$$- \ 3$$
$$\overline{4}$$

moved away

Semiconcrete level: Write difference or missing addend.

$$7 \quad ///////$$
$$- \ 3$$

Student work:

$$7 \quad ////XXX$$
$$- \ 3 \quad \text{cross out 3 to take away}$$
$$\overline{4}$$

Abstract level: Write difference or missing addend.

$$7$$
$$- \ 3$$

- Skill: Subtraction operation with regrouping
  Concrete level: Rearrange blocks and use strings to show work. Write difference or missing addend.

32

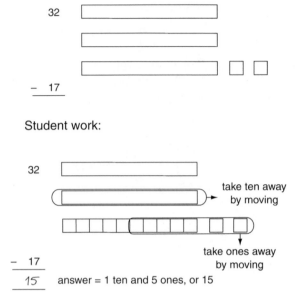

$$- \ 17$$

Student work:

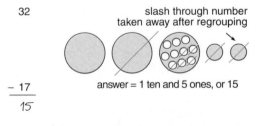

take ten away by moving

take ones away by moving

$$- \ 17$$
$$\underline{15} \quad \text{answer} = 1 \text{ ten and 5 ones, or 15}$$

Semiconcrete level: Show work with slashes. Write difference or missing addend.

Student work:

32

slash through number taken away after regrouping

$$- \ 17$$
$$\overline{15}$$

answer = 1 ten and 5 ones, or 15

Abstract level: Write difference or missing addend.

$$32$$
$$- \ 17$$

- Skill: Basic multiplication facts
  Concrete level: Write product.

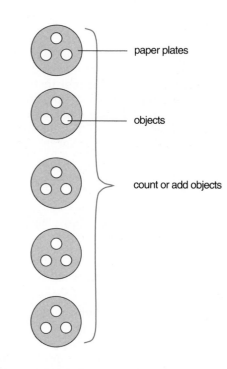

paper plates

objects

count or add objects

$$\begin{array}{r} 5 \\ \times\, 3 \\ \hline \end{array}$$

Semiconcrete level: Write product.

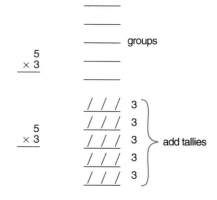

Abstract level: Write product.

$$\begin{array}{r} 5 \\ \times\, 3 \\ \hline \end{array}$$

* Skill: Basic division facts
  Concrete level: Use strings to show work. Write quotient.

○ ○ ○ ○ ○ ○ ○ ○ ○ ○ ○ ○   3⟌12

Student work:

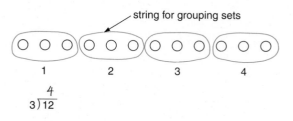

string for grouping sets

$$3\overline{)12}\;{}^{4}$$

Semiconcrete level: Connect sets to show work. Write quotient.

/ / / / / / / / / / / /   3⟌12

Student work:

/ / /   / / /   / / /   / / /
 1   2   3   4

$$3\overline{)12}\;{}^{4}$$

Abstract level: Write quotient.

$$3\overline{)12}$$

* Skill: Division with remainder
  Concrete level: Given a large matrix of blocks, figure out how many sets of 4 are in 30, or 30 ÷ 4. Use strings to show work. Write quotient.
  Student work:

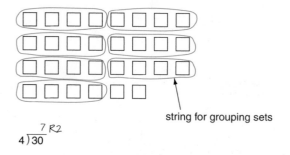

string for grouping sets

$$4\overline{)30}\;{}^{7\ R2}$$

Semiconcrete level: Circle sets to show work with tallies. Write quotient.

Student work:

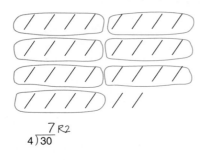

$$4\overline{\smash{\big)}30} \quad {}^{7}\,{}^{R2}$$

Abstract level: Write quotient.

$$4\overline{\smash{\big)}30}$$

- Skill: Recognize simple fractions
  Concrete level: Let ▭ = 1 or $^5/_5$ and ▢ = $^1/_5$. Stack the blocks to show $^3/_5$.
  Student work:

Semiconcrete level: Write a fraction for the shadowed part of the group.

● ● ● ○ ○ ____

Abstract level: Write the fraction for three-fifths.

- Skill: Addition of fractions with like denominators
  Concrete level: Let � = $^1/_3$. Show work with blocks. Write sum.
  Student work:

1/3	+	1/3	=	2/3

Semiconcrete level: Display the sum of $^1/_3 + ^1/_3$ by shading in the circles.

Abstract level:

$$^1/_3 + ^1/_3 = \underline{\quad}$$

- Skill: Money change for amounts up to $1.00
  Concrete level: Given real money and items with marked prices, figure out correct change if a $.39 item is purchased with a dollar.
  Semiconcrete level: Circle the coins given as change for a dollar when buying a $.39 item.

Abstract level: Answer this problem: How much change would you give when someone buys a $.39 item and gives you a dollar?

Evans, Evans, and Mercer (1986) provide a detailed discussion of periodic and continuous math assessment. Periodic assessment includes an initial testing that generates instructional objectives; periodic evaluations include checkups of general progress and in-depth evaluations of students experiencing difficulty. Continuous assessment focuses on monitoring the student's progress. It involves daily, weekly, or biweekly assessments. Stein et al. (1997, p. 11) highlight the importance of continuous assessment.

> The importance of careful monitoring cannot be overemphasized. The sooner the teacher detects a student's skill deficit, the easier it will be to remedy. For each day that a student error goes undetected, the student is, in essence, receiving practice in doing something the wrong way. To ameliorate a skill deficit, the teacher should plan to spend a couple of days reteaching for every day the student's errors go undetected. Thus, careful monitoring is a critical component of efficient instruction.

Charts can be used to locate math facts that have not been memorized. The teacher gives the student a test of selected facts (e.g., sums 0 to 9 or 10 to 18, differences 0 to 9 or 10 to 18, or products 0 to 9). Then the teacher records the student's performance on the chart: ✓ = basic fact memorized; – = basic fact not memorized. The chart for multiplication facts presented in Figure 11.6 shows that the student is experiencing difficulty with facts in-

FIGURE 11.6
Chart of a student's performance on basic multiplication facts

volving 0. The chart for subtraction facts 0 to 18 presented in Figure 11.7 suggests that the student is having difficulty with two-digit minus one-digit facts, except those involving 9 and those in which the subtrahend equals the difference.

Inspection of the sample items readily shows that the student's level of math understanding must be assessed individually. Developing and administering analytical math tests take time. Some teachers need several years to build an ample file of such tests, which then must be organized and stored in a functional system. Because of the time constraints, some teachers reserve this type of assessment for students who are not progressing with systematic math instruction and who appear to have serious math difficulties. Others include concrete experiences in their teaching and construct tests that include semiconcrete and abstract items. Instruction for students with math learning problems should include experiences at each of the three levels for teaching specific concepts and skills.

Diagnostic Math Interviews As a curriculum area, math is quite different from reading, language, or written communication. One major difference is that skill in math is not reflected in global tasks such as oral reading, language samples, or written passages. A student may know much about math but perform poorly on a math test that does not cover that specific material.

Thus, to perform a functional math assessment, the teacher needs to know what the student has been taught and is expected to know. Moreover, basals vary dramatically in their sequences and coverages of math content and grade-level scores from math tests are not comparable. Thus, placing students in math programs based on grade-level scores is strongly discouraged.

Because of growing dissatisfaction with math tests, a move toward "authentic" math assessment is evolving. This movement involves portfolio assessments typified by open-ended performance measures (California Mathematics Assessment Advisory Committee, 1990) and emphasizes that math is more than the language of numbers. Assessment procedures that ask students only to look at and write numbers are too limiting to reflect current views of math instruction. Given both the lack of consistency across programs and tests and the evolving portfolio approach, student interviews should be used when assessing math at specific levels. Interviews can provide insights into mathematical strategies, processes, products, and social-emotional reactions to math.

The diagnostic interview provides information to determine what math skills to teach the student and how to teach them. In this technique, the student expresses thought processes while solving math problems. This technique often is used in administering diagnostic math tests. Moreover, the diagnostic interview enables the teacher to identify specific problems, error patterns, or problem-solving strategies in math. A sample interview illustrates how the procedure can yield important information:

> The teacher gave Mary three multiplication problems and said, "Please do these problems and tell me how you figure out the answer." Mary solved the problems in this way:
>
> $$\begin{array}{ccc} \overset{2}{2}7 & \overset{4}{3}6 & \overset{3}{4}4 \\ \underline{\times\ 4} & \underline{\times\ 7} & \underline{\times\ 8} \\ 168 & 492 & 562 \end{array}$$

For the first problem, Mary explained, "7 times 4 equals 28. So I put my 8 here and carry the 2. 2 plus 2 equals 4, and 4 times 4 equals 16. So I put 16 here." Her explanations for the other two problems followed the same logic.

By listening to Mary and watching her solve the problems, the teacher quickly determined Mary's error pattern: She adds the number associated with

FIGURE 11.7
Chart of a student's performance on 0 to 18 subtraction facts

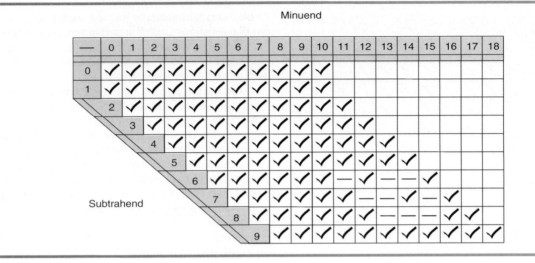

the crutch (the number carried to the tens column) *before* multiplying the tens digit. Mary explained that she had been taught to add the number being carried when regrouping in addition. After identifying Mary's error pattern and its origin, the teacher could plan instruction for teaching the correct algorithm and developing an understanding of the multiplication process. Without the interview, the teacher incorrectly may have planned instruction in the basic multiplication facts.

Clinical interviews also offer an excellent technique for identifying negative emotions and attitudes toward math. Knowledge of these feelings helps teachers adjust math instruction (e.g., using graphic cueing, prompts, reinforcement, and charts) to alter a student's feelings. Several activities can be used in an interview session to assess attitudes:

- Instruct the student to solve some math problems and observe the student's behavior (e.g., makes negative statements, becomes upset, or gives up quickly).
- Have the student respond to some oral sentence-completion tasks. The teacher starts a sentence and the student responds aloud. Sample starters include the following:
  - Math is very . . .
  - My best subject is . . .
  - During math lessons I feel . . .

- Ask the student direct questions. The following are some sample questions:
  - What is your favorite subject?
  - Do you like to do math?
  - What is your favorite thing about math?
  - What do you not like about math?
  - Do you use math outside school?
  - What would you do to make math more interesting?

The validity of the diagnostic findings depends on the quality of the exchange between teacher and student. The teacher must establish a rapport and ensure that the student feels free to respond honestly. General guidelines for conducting an interview include the following:

- Establish rapport and be alert to the student's attitudes toward math throughout the session. It often helps to start with items that are easy for the student to complete.
- Focus only on the student's problem area that is the lowest on the skill sequence. Limit each session to one area of difficulty (e.g., two-column addition with regrouping).
- Allow the student the freedom to solve the problem in his or her own way.
- Record the student's thinking processes and analyze for error patterns and problem-solving techniques.

- Once an error pattern or faulty problem-solving technique is discovered, introduce diagnostic activities for assessing the student's level of understanding. These activities should include tasks at the semiconcrete and concrete levels. (For more detailed discussions of diagnostic math interviews, see Rivera and Bryant [1992] and Stenmark [1989].)

☀ REFERENCES

Ashlock, R. B. (1998). *Error patterns in computation* (7th ed.). Upper Saddle River, NJ: Merrill/Prentice Hall.

Balow, I. H., Farr, R. C., & Hogan, T. P. (1997). *Metropolitan Achievement Tests—Seventh Edition.* San Antonio, TX: Harcourt Brace Educational Measurement.

Beatty, L. S., Madden, R., Gardner, E. F., & Karlsen, B. (1995). *Stanford Diagnostic Mathematics Test— Fourth Edition.* San Antonio, TX: Harcourt Brace Educational Measurement.

Brigance, A. H. (1999). *Brigance Diagnostic Comprehensive Inventory of Basic Skills—Revised.* North Billerica, MA: Curriculum Associates.

Brown, V. L., Cronin, M. E., & McEntire, E. (1994). *Test of Mathematical Abilities—2.* Austin, TX: PRO-ED.

California Achievement Tests—Fifth Edition. (1992). Monterey, CA: CTB/McGraw-Hill.

California Diagnostic Math Test. (1990). Monterey, CA: CTB/McGraw-Hill.

California Mathematics Assessment Advisory Committee. (1990). *Guidelines for the mathematics portfolio: Working paper.* Sacramento: California Assessment Program, California State Department of Education.

Carnine, D. (1991). Curricular interventions for teaching higher order thinking to all students: Introduction to the special series. *Journal of Learning Disabilities, 24,* 261–269.

Cawley, J. F., & Miller, J. H. (1989). Cross-sectional comparisons of the mathematical performance of children with learning disabilities: Are we on the right track toward comprehensive programming? *Journal of Learning Disabilities, 23,* 250–254, 259.

Cawley, J. F., Miller, J. H., & School, B. A. (1987). A brief inquiry of arithmetic word-problem solving among learning disabled secondary students. *Learning Disabilities Focus, 2,* 87–93.

Connolly, A. J. (1998). *Key Math—Revised: A Diagnostic Inventory of Essential Mathematics.* Circle Pines, MN: American Guidance Service.

Copeland, R. W. (1979). *Math activities for children: A diagnostic and developmental approach.* Upper Saddle River, NJ: Merrill/Prentice Hall.

Cox, L. S. (1975). Diagnosing and remediating systematic errors in addition and subtraction computations. *The Arithmetic Teacher, 22,* 151–157.

Englert, C. S., Tarrant, K. L., & Mariage, T. V. (1992). Defining and redefining instructional practice in special education: Perspectives on good teaching. *Teacher Education and Special Education, 15,* 62–86.

Evans, S. S., Evans, W. H., & Mercer, C. D. (1986). *Assessment for instruction.* Boston: Allyn & Bacon.

Ginsburg, H. P (1987). How to assess number facts, calculation, and understanding. In D. D. Hammill (Ed.), *Assessing the abilities and instructional needs of students* (pp. 483–503). Austin, TX: PRO-ED.

Ginsburg, H. P., & Baroody, A. J. (1990). *Test of Early Mathematics Ability—2.* Austin, TX: PRO-ED.

Goldman, S. R. (1989). Strategy instruction in mathematics. *Learning Disability Quarterly, 12,* 43–55.

Heddens, J. W., & Speer, W. R. (1997). *Today's mathematics. Part 2: Activities and instructional ideas* (9th ed.). Upper Saddle River, NJ: Merrill/Prentice Hall.

Hofmeister, A. M. (1993). Elitism and reform in school mathematics. *Remedial and Special Education, 14*(6), 8–13.

Howell, K. W., & Nolet, V. (2000). *Curriculum-based evaluation: Teaching and decision making* (3rd ed.). Belmont, CA: Wadsworth/Thomson Learning.

Hutchinson, N. L. (1993a). Effects of cognitive strategy instruction on algebra problem solving of adolescents with learning disabilities. *Learning Disability Quarterly, 16,* 34–63.

Hutchinson, N. L. (1993b). Second invited response: Students with disabilities and mathematics education reform—Let the dialogue begin. *Remedial and Special Education, 14*(6), 20–23.

Kaufman, A. S., & Kaufman, N. L. (1998). *Kaufman Test of Educational Achievement.* Circle Pines, MN: American Guidance Service.

Kelly, B., Gersten, R., & Carnine, D. (1990). Student error patterns as a function of curriculum design: Teaching fractions to remedial high school students and high school students with learning disabilities. *Journal of Learning Disabilities, 123,* 23–29.

Kirby, J. R., & Becker, L. D. (1988). Cognitive components of learning problems in arithmetic. *Remedial and Special Education, 9*(5), 7–15, 27.

Lepore, A. (1979). A comparison of computational errors between educable mentally handicapped and learning disability children. *Focus on Learning Problems in Mathematics, 1,* 12–33.

Lovitt, T. C. (1989). *Introduction to learning disabilities.* Boston: Allyn & Bacon.

Markwardt, F. C., Jr. (1998). *Peabody Individual Achievement Test—Revised.* Circle Pines, MN: American Guidance Service.

Miller, J. H., & Milam, C. P. (1987). Multiplication and division errors committed by learning disabled students. *Learning Disabilities Research, 2*(2), 119–122.

Montague, M. (1993). Student-centered or strategy-centered instruction: What is our purpose? *Journal of Learning Disabilities, 26,* 433–437, 481.

Montague, M., & Bos, C. S. (1990). Cognitive and metacognitive characteristics of eighth grade students' mathematical problem solving. *Learning and Individual Differences, 2,* 371–388.

National Council of Supervisors of Mathematics. (1988). *Twelve components of essential mathematics.* Minneapolis, MN: Author.

National Council of Teachers of Mathematics. (1989). *Curriculum and evaluation standards for school mathematics.* Reston, VA: Author.

National Research Council. (1989). *Everybody counts: A report to the nation on the future of mathematics education.* Washington, DC: National Academy Press.

Newcomer, P. L. (1990). *Diagnostic Achievement Battery—2.* Austin, TX: PRO-ED.

Piaget, J. (1965). *The child's conception of number.* New York: W. W. Norton.

Rivera, D. M. (1993). Examining mathematics reform and the implications for students with mathematics disabilities. *Remedial and Special Education, 14*(6), 24–27.

Rivera, D. M., & Bryant, B. R. (1992). Mathematics instruction for students with special needs. *Intervention in School and Clinic, 28*(2), 71–86.

Roberts, G. H. (1968). The failure strategies of third grade arithmetic pupils. *The Arithmetic Teacher, 15,* 442–446.

Russell, R., & Ginsburg, H. (1984). Cognitive analysis of children's mathematical difficulties. *Cognition and Instruction, 1,* 217–244.

Scheid, K. (1990). *Cognitive-based methods for teaching mathematics to students with learning problems.* Columbus, OH: LINC Resources.

Smith, D. D., & Lovitt, T. C. (1982). *The computational arithmetic program.* Austin, TX: PRO-ED.

Starlin, C. M., & Starlin, A. (1973). *Guides to decision making in computational math.* Bemidji, MN: Unique Curriculums Unlimited.

Stein, M., Silbert, J., & Carnine, D. (1997). *Designing effective mathematics instruction: A direct instruction approach* (3rd ed.). Upper Saddle River, NJ: Merrill/Prentice Hall.

Stenmark, J. K. (1989). *Assessment alternatives in mathematics.* Berkeley, CA: EQUALS, Lawrence Hall of Science, University of California.

Tindal, G. A., & Marston, D. B. (1990). *Classroom-based assessment: Evaluating instructional outcomes.* Upper Saddle River, NJ: Merrill/Prentice Hall.

Underhill, R. G., Uprichard, A. E., & Heddens, J. W. (1980). *Diagnosing mathematical difficulties.* Upper Saddle River, NJ: Merrill/Prentice Hall.

Warner, M. M., Alley, G. R., Schumaker, J. B., Deshler, D. D., & Clark, F. L. (1980). *An epidemiological study of learning disabled adolescents in secondary schools: Achievement and ability, socioeconomic status and school experiences.* (Report No. 13). Lawrence: University of Kansas Center for Research on Learning.

Wood, S., Burke, L., Kunzelmann, H., & Koenig, C. (1978). Functional criteria in basic math skill proficiency. *Journal of Special Education Technology, 2*(2), 29–36.

Woodcock, R. W., & Mather, N. (2000). *Woodcock-Johnson III Tests of Achievement.* Itasca, IL: Riverside.

CHAPTER 12

Teaching Math

The possible excitement about learning math is illustrated by the behavior of the students in the following story (Mercer, 1997, p. 568):

I recently had the opportunity to work on a math project with second-grade teachers and their students in a rural Florida school. During the last week of school I attended the end-of-the-school-year picnic. I was sitting at a table enjoying an ice cream cone when I heard a confident but quiet voice say, "I know 99 times 0." Standing beside the table was a second grader named Matt, with his hands in his pockets, waiting for my response. I decided to have some fun. I said, "How could you possibly know 99 times 0 and still be in the second grade? That must be at least a third-grade skill." Matt quickly replied, "99 times 0 is 0!" With a surprised expression, I said, "Lucky guess!" Matt looked directly at me and said, "I'll be back." Then he turned and walked away. A few minutes later, Matt approached me with several of his second-grade friends. Upon their arrival, one of Matt's friends said, "I know 1,000 times 1." I responded, "You're kidding. That problem is impossible for a second grader." The friend blurted out, "1,000!" More second graders joined our discussion. They continued to share with me their knowledge of multiplication—1,000,000 times 1, 6,000 times 0, 9 times 8, and so on. The group of 8 to 10 students consisted of normally achieving students and students with learning disabilities. They displayed their knowledge of rules, multiplication facts, and problem-solving skills. I praised them for their knowledge and smartness. I was surprised that the students continued to discuss math when they had the opportunity to be playing. That afternoon while driving home, I realized that I had learned a lesson about empowered students.

Unfortunately, this scenario of students excited about their math learning is uncommon. For many students, math problems often result in school failure and lead to much anxiety. Although deficiencies in reading are cited most often as a primary characteristic of students with learning disabilities, Mastropieri, Scruggs, and Shiah (1991) note that deficits in math are as serious a problem for many of these students.

Fleischner, Garnett, and Shepherd (1982) note that the inability to acquire and maintain math facts at fluency levels sufficient for acquiring higher-level math skills is common among students with learning problems. De Corte and Verschaffel (1981) and Russell and Ginsburg (1984) report that unfamiliarity with basic number facts plays a major role in the math difficulties of students with math learning problems. Other researchers (Garnett & Fleischner, 1983; Thornton & Toohey, 1985) report that many students with learning disabilities lack proficiency in basic number facts and are unable to retrieve answers to math facts efficiently.

As indicated in Chapter 11, reforms in math education likely will increase the overall complexity of the mathematics curriculum. General and special educators must work together to ensure that the instructional reforms are sensitive to the unique learning and emotional needs of students with learning problems. Although many students with math deficiencies exhibit characteristics (such as problems in memory, language, reading, reasoning, and metacognition) that predispose them to math disabilities, their learning difficulties often are compounded by ineffective instruction. Many authorities (Carnine, 1991; Cawley, Miller, & School, 1987; Kelly, Gersten, & Carnine, 1990; Scheid, 1990) believe that poor or traditional instruction is the primary cause of the math difficulties of many students with learning problems. Numerous studies support the position that students with math disabilities can be taught to improve their mathematical performance (Kirby & Becker, 1988; Mastropieri et al., 1991; Mercer & Miller, 1992; Rivera & Smith, 1988; Scheid, 1990).

Given the poor math progress of students with learning problems and the call for a reform in math education to increase standards, a need clearly exists to design an effective math curriculum for these students. Without better math instruction, these youngsters will continue to face much frustration and failure. Cawley and Miller (1989) report that students with learning disabilities are capable of making progress in math throughout their school years and that comprehensive programming is needed to ensure their math progress. Given the problems that students with learning problems exhibit with lower-level math skills (i.e., many students do not know the 390 basic math facts after five or more years of school) and the importance of these skills to overall math achievement, comprehensive programming to teach basic math facts is obviously needed.

This chapter is designed to help the teacher provide effective instruction to students with math problems. Included are basic terms and processes, research on effective math instruction, instructional practices for computation and problem solving (including math facts programs, concrete-semi-concrete-abstract activities, basic rules and algorithms, problem-solving interventions, functional math, estimation, and calculators), math activities, instructional games, self-correcting materials, commercial programs, and computer software programs.

☀ BASIC TERMS AND PROCESSES

Before beginning math instruction, the teacher needs to know some of the basic terms used in math. Table 12.1 presents some major terms.

The teacher also should know basic information about the organization of math content. Five areas are essential to learning addition, subtraction, multiplication, and division: understanding, basic facts, place value, structures (laws), and regrouping (Underhill, Uprichard, & Heddens, 1980). *Understanding* means comprehending the operation at the concrete, semiconcrete (representational), and abstract levels. *Basic facts* must be understood and memorized; these are the tools of computation. The basic facts are simple closed number sentences used in computation. Addition and subtraction facts involve two one-digit addends, and multiplication and division facts in-

TABLE 12.1
Math terms in basic computations

Operation	Terms
Addition	8 ← addend + 4 ←addend 12 ←sum
Subtraction (take away)	9 ←minuend −4 ←subtrahend 5 ←difference
Subtraction (add on)	9 ←sum −4 ←known addend 5 ←missing addend
Multiplication	8 ←multiplicand or factor × 5 ←multiplier or factor 40 ←product
Division	8 ←quotient or factor 6)48 ←dividend or product ↑ divisor or factor

volve two one-digit factors (Ashlock, 1998). There are 390 basic facts—100 addition, 100 subtraction, 100 multiplication, and 90 division facts. Once understanding and basic facts are mastered, the specific operation can be expanded readily by using *place value.* For example, if the student recognizes that 3×2 is 6, the place value concept can be applied to compute a series of problems such as the following:

$$
\begin{array}{ccc}
3 & 30 & 300 \\
\underline{\times 2} & \underline{\times\ 2} & \underline{\times\ 2} \\
6 & 60 & 600
\end{array}
$$

$$
\begin{array}{ccc}
3000 & 30 & 300 \\
\underline{\times\quad 2} & \underline{\times\ 20} & \underline{\times\ 20} \\
6000 & 600 & 600
\end{array}
$$

Structures are mathematical properties that help the student. A student who memorizes that 7×3 is 21 but sees 3×7 as a new problem to memorize needs to understand a basic structure (in this case, the commutative property of multiplication) to learn multiplication effectively. (Other structures are presented in Chapter 11.) The last area is *regrouping* (commonly referred to as *carrying* and *borrowing*), which must be understood to solve more complex problems in each of the four operations.

Another important factor in teaching math is knowledge of algorithms. Algorithms are the steps used in solving a math problem. Numerous algorithms are presented later in this chapter.

☀ RESEARCH ON EFFECTIVE MATH INSTRUCTION

The amount of research on teaching math has increased substantially in the last decade, and it is now clear that both curriculum design and teacher behavior directly influence the mathematics achievement of students with learning problems (Hutchinson, 1993a; Kameenui & Simmons, 1990; Kelly et al., 1990; Mastropieri et al., 1991; Mercer, Jordan, & Miller, 1994; Mercer & Miller, 1992). Although much remains to be learned about teaching math, educators need to examine existing research and literature to determine *what* should be taught in a math curriculum and the best practices for *how* to teach it. Only through the systematic examination and application of what is known about math instruction can educators ensure that the achievement levels of students with learning problems are commensurate with their potential. The components of effective math instruction are presented next.

Selecting Appropriate Mathematics Content

Mathematics educators recommend reforms in the content of the mathematics curriculum. Although computation remains a vital component, experts agree that obtaining answers through the use of written work is not sufficient. Estimating answers and cross-checking with alternative methods are stressed in the current recommendations. Moreover, the ability to think critically and the understanding of concepts, operations, and real-life applications are important goals of a mathematics curriculum. The official 1988 statement of the National Council of Supervisors of Mathematics, *Twelve Components of Essential Mathematics,* has implications for planning math instruction for students with learning problems.

1. ***Problem solving.*** Learning to solve problems by applying previously acquired information to new and different situations is one of the primary reasons for studying math. Problem solving involves solving both verbal (text) and nonverbal problems. Skills involved include using trial and error, asking relevant questions, selecting an operation, illustrating results, analyzing situations, and translating results.

2. ***Communication of mathematical ideas.*** Students must learn the language and notation of math. They should present math ideas through the use of manipulative objects, drawings, written work, and speech.

3. ***Mathematical reasoning.*** Students must learn to conduct investigations of math concepts. These skills include making tentative conclusions, recognizing patterns, and using math knowledge to support conjecture.

4. ***Application of mathematics to everyday situations.*** Students should be encouraged to translate daily experiences into mathematical representations (i.e., graphs, tables, diagrams, or math expressions) and interpret the results.

5. ***Alertness to the reasonableness of results.*** Students must be able to examine results

against viable conjecture. The use of calculators and computers makes this an essential skill.

6. ***Estimation.*** Students must be able to perform rapid mental approximations to establish the reasonableness of a math solution. In addition to approximating purchase costs, these estimations involve measurements such as length, area, volume, and weight.

7. ***Appropriate computational skills.*** Students must gain proficiency in using operations (i.e., addition, subtraction, multiplication, and division) with whole numbers and decimals. Knowledge of basic facts is essential, and mental arithmetic is important. Competence in using common fractions and decimals is necessary, and knowing when to use a calculator also is helpful.

8. ***Algebraic thinking.*** Students must learn to use letters to represent math quantities and expressions and to represent mathematical relationships and functions with graphs, tables, and equations. Students need to understand how one quantity changes as a function of another.

9. ***Measurement.*** Students must learn the basic concepts of measuring (i.e., distance, weight, time, capacity, temperature, and angles) through concrete experiences.

10. ***Geometry.*** Students must learn geometric concepts to function in a three-dimensional world. Parallelism, perpendicularity, congruence, similarity, and symmetry are important concepts. These concepts should be explored in situations that involve measurement and problem solving.

11. ***Statistics.*** Students must learn to collect and organize data to answer daily questions. Measures of central tendency and variance are important, as well as interpreting tables, maps, graphs, and charts.

12. ***Probability.*** Students must understand the basic notions of probability to predict the likelihood of future events.

Many experts recommend that math instruction focus on problem solving within an authentic context. One way to accomplish this is to introduce math concepts and operations within the context of a word problem. For example, solving division equations in algebra could be introduced with the following word problem: "Cindy plans to give 30 coupons for free pizza to 6 of her friends. How many coupons will each friend receive?" The teacher explains that this can be represented and solved through the use of simple division: 30 coupons ÷ 6 friends = __ coupons per friend. Then the teacher demonstrates how the problem can be solved through the use of algebra by giving the unknown a letter name and moving it to the left side of the equation: 30 coupons ÷ 6 friends = __ becomes 6 friends × c (coupons per friend) = 30 coupons. Furthermore, the teacher uses the students' prior knowledge about the multiplication and division relationship to solve the problem (i.e., What number multiplied by 6 equals 30?). As the lessons progress, the teacher guides and encourages the students to create their own word problems that can be solved through the use of division equations.

If mathematical content is to be authentic to learning, it must be presented in a real-world context. For example, if the instructional content fails to relate $6y + 2y + 6 = 48$ to a pragmatic word problem, then students are memorizing meaningless procedures for obtaining answers. In a study of technological math interventions with students with learning problems, Bottge and Hasselbring (1993) found that contextualized learning was a key factor.

Another consideration for determining what mathematics content to teach involves a student's prior learning. Mathematics is a logical interrelated system of concepts and operations that are hierarchically ordered. Numerous experts (Bley & Thornton, 1995; Kameenui & Simmons, 1990; Stein, Silbert, & Carnine, 1997) stress the importance of teaching students skills for which they have the necessary preskills. For example, students should know some addition facts before learning subtraction facts. Teaching students skills in which they lack the necessary preskills often leads to a limited amount of fragmented or rote learning and much frustration. A best teaching practice clearly involves teaching students the preskills that are germane to learning a new skill or beginning instruction with a skill in which students possess the essential preskills. Finally, educators must ensure that students with learning problems receive math instruction on relevant or practical math skills. For example, the teaching of Roman numerals appears to lack relevance.

Teaching the Acquisition of Math

Follow Teaching Steps A viable plan for teaching the acquisition of computation or problem-solving skills includes the following activities:

1. Assess the student's math skills and identify an appropriate instructional objective. To promote success, the objective should be relevant and one in which the student has the essential preskills.

2. Obtain a commitment from the student to learn the math skill and set goals. Discussions regarding the applications of the targeted skill help the student establish a desire to learn. Moreover, goal setting provides the student and teacher with instructional expectations and fosters motivation. Goal setting is enhanced by identifying the expected time period for reaching a mastery criterion. In their synthesis on research on good teaching, Porter and Brophy (1988) report that good teachers are clear about instructional goals and communicate expectations and why the specific expectations exist. In presenting goals, effective teachers explain what the student needs to do to achieve the goal and what the student will learn in achieving the goal (Christenson, Ysseldyke, & Thurlow, 1989). There is growing support for the premise that teachers tend to make goals too easy for students with learning problems (Anderson & Pellicer, 1990; Clifford, 1990; Fuchs, Fuchs, & Deno, 1985). Clifford reports that students need challenge rather than easy success and that tasks involving moderate risk taking provide the best level of difficulty in setting goals. She recommends that instructional environments should feature error tolerance and reward for error correction. A substantial research base (Locke & Latham, 1990; Locke, Shaw, Saari, & Latham, 1981) verifies that difficult but attainable goals lead to higher effort and achievement than do easier goals. Elementary and secondary students with learning problems have responded well to goal setting in math. Goal setting helps the students become more proactive and involved in their own learning. Moreover, students perform better when the goals are self-set rather than assigned. Miller, Strawser, and Mercer (1996) provide the following guidelines in conducting a goal-setting conference:

- Allow adequate time for the goal-setting conference (e.g., 10 to 15 minutes).
- Arrange to confer with students in a place that does not permit others to overhear.

- Encourage students to do most of the talking (i.e., the teacher should listen).
- Begin the session by guiding students through a self-evaluation of their progress.
- Listen to students' ideas without interruptions or judgmental comments.
- If necessary, lead students to revise their goals realistically by asking open-ended questions.
- Encourage students to set goals in skills at the acquisition, proficiency, maintenance, and generalization levels of learning.
- Record the results of the conference and provide copies for students. A conference form can be developed that has space to record the time frame for the goals, self-evaluation of progress in skills, the amount of time spent working on each skill, prerequisite skills that the students did not have, and the amount of time the students plan to work on each skill.

3. Use effective teaching steps to teach the math skill. These teaching steps are presented in Table 4.11, which includes a math lesson design that guides teacher–student interactions. Numerous researchers have used these steps (or variations thereof) to produce excellent math achievement in students with learning problems. Also, during the learning of new material, the student should review prior content and maintain a high success rate. Wilson, Majsterek, and Jones (1995) recommend four types of review: (1) review before beginning a math lesson, (2) review homework, (3) review within every lesson, and (4) review across lessons.

Use Teacher Modeling of Explicit Strategies

A promising feature from the recent literature entails the *substance* of teacher modeling. Instead of the traditional teacher modeling of mathematical algorithms in a meaningless context, researchers are exploring the modeling of problem-solving strategies (i.e., cognitive and metacognitive) to solve meaningful problems and develop self-regulation processes. Woodward (1991) notes that cognitive task analyses are being conducted to enable teachers to model thinking processes involved in math problem solving. Explicit teacher modeling of cognitive and metacognitive strategies in solving word problems has yielded encouraging results, and these preliminary findings (Hutchinson, 1993a; Montague, 1992, 1993) suggest that specific stra-

tegy instruction in math holds significant promise for students with learning problems. These findings support Zawaiza and Gerber's (1993) position that "successful strategy instruction . . . requires modeling of competent strategy use, sufficient and appropriate exemplar problems, ample opportunity to practice and receive correction on strategy use, and adequate opportunities for students to describe and evaluate how effectively they are employing newly learned strategies" (p. 67). Strategies that include explicit teacher modeling are presented in the section on problem-solving interventions.

Focus on Teacher–Student Interactions   A

focus on teacher–student interactions provides a timely opportunity for educators to improve the quality of instructional discourse for teaching math. Earlier research mainly stressed the role of the teacher in providing instruction to cover content, whereas recent research focuses on the dynamic nature of the dialogue between the student and the teacher to develop conceptual understandings. In this dynamic process, the teacher constantly adapts the dialogue according to student needs. Teachers are encouraged to time their interactions prescriptively so that they know when it is appropriate to provide direct instruction, give guided instruction, ask questions, challenge, offer corrective feedback, encourage, let the student work independently, reflect with the student, set instructional goals, model a cognitive or metacognitive strategy, discuss rationales for learning new declarative or procedural knowledge, or discuss transfer. When teachers prescriptively interact (i.e., base interactions on student behavior) during instruction to ensure that students develop conceptual understandings, students are treated as active agents in their own learning.

Elmore (1992) notes that teachers need extensive help to learn and apply the ideas of current research on teaching. He claims that it is unrealistic to expect teachers to accomplish this by themselves. Apparently, teacher education and commercial materials have not helped teachers to teach conceptual understandings. Most materials present information that describes how to use algorithms to solve math problems. This algorithm-driven approach provides little or no help to teachers who desire to teach the conceptual underpinnings implicit in math.

To help teachers model strategies and teach understanding of math concepts, several researchers have provided scripts or sample dialogues (Hutchinson, 1993a; Mercer & Miller, 1992; Montague, 1993). These scripts or sample dialogues provide the teacher with an initial guide on how to model metacognitive strategies explicitly and how to lead the student to conceptual understandings of math concepts (declarative knowledge) and apply declarative and procedural knowledge to solve word problems and math equations. The scripts serve as a springboard for helping teachers engage in productive teacher–student discourse. As teachers gain confidence and experience with these interactions, the sample dialogues are not needed. Sample dialogues guide the teacher through the teaching steps. The describe-and-model step features explicit teacher modeling of strategies. The guided practice step parallels scaffolding as the teacher guides the students to conceptual understandings and independent work. The independent practice step incorporates working alone and with peers to gain mastery. The feedback step is used to recognize successes and relate them to learning goals and to use errors in math for teaching and learning opportunities. The generalization-and-transfer step encourages the students to reflect on strategy uses and create their own word problems. (Table 4.11 provides a beginning format for developing sample dialogues and practice activities.)

Use the Concrete-Semiconcrete-Abstract Sequence

During the acquisition of a computational or problem-solving skill, the student must be instructed in such a way that understanding is ensured. Many authorities believe that the concrete-semiconcrete-abstract (CSA) sequence is an excellent way to teach students with learning problems to understand math concepts, operations, and applications. Lambert (1996) notes that research supports the use of manipulative objects at all grade levels to teach math concepts. Several research studies (C. A. Harris, Miller, & Mercer, 1995; Mercer & Miller, 1992) reveal that the CSA sequence is an effective way to teach math to students with learning problems. Results indicate that such students do not need large numbers of formal experiences at the concrete and semiconcrete levels to understand the basic facts. In this research, within six 30-minute lessons (three concrete and three semiconcrete), students with learning problems demonstrated an understanding of the respective operation and generalized their learning to abstract-level (numbers only) problems. Moreover, the students retained the targeted skills during follow-up testing. The CSA sequence seems to be especially useful in helping students who have deficits in *representing* or *reformulating* math from word problems to equations, equations to objects, pictures or drawings to equations, and vice versa. Because the CSA sequence requires students to represent math concepts and operations with objects and drawings, math concepts (such as addition, place value, multiplication, fractions, and equations) are understood. Examples of CSA teaching are presented later in this chapter.

Teach Concepts and Rules

The learning of concepts and rules also is germane to facilitating a student's understanding of math. A student who memorizes that 8 + 6 is 14 but sees 6 + 8 as a new problem to memorize needs to understand a basic concept (in this case, the commutative property of addition) to learn addition effectively. Likewise, the learning of subtraction is facilitated if a student understands the inverse relationship of addition and subtraction (i.e., $a + b = c$; $c - b = a$). Also, the concept of place value is difficult for many students and deserves much teacher attention. Finally, rules such as *any number times zero is zero* help students learn multiplication facts. Concrete and semiconcrete experiences are excellent ways to demonstrate concepts and rules to students.

Monitor Progress and Provide Feedback

The research is replete with the positive effects of monitoring the math progress of students with learning problems and giving feedback (Fuchs, 1986; Lloyd & Keller, 1989; Robinson, DePascale, & Roberts, 1989). Monitoring progress through the use of charts has yielded some excellent results regarding student achievement. Gersten, Carnine, and Woodward (1987) report that teachers who provide immediate corrective feedback on errors produce higher student achievement. Robinson et al. found that feedback helped students with learning disabilities complete more problems and improved accuracy from 73 percent to 94 percent.

They stress the importance of feedback (p. 28):

> Feedback is potentially even more important for learning disabled (LD) children, who may be less attentive, participate less in academic work, and make more errors than higher achieving learners. Academic environments that maximize LD students' opportunities to learn under direct teacher supervision with timely feedback are essential.

Kline, Schumaker, and Deshler (1991) developed and evaluated an elaborated feedback routine with students with learning problems. Their results indicate that this routine helps students achieve learning goals quickly and efficiently. A major factor in the routine stresses that errors represent learning opportunities for the students and teaching opportunities for the teacher. The essential features of elaborated feedback are included in the mnemonic FEEDBACK:

F—*Find* the score. Explain the grade.

E—*Enter* the score. Use a graph and goal setting and make it meaningful.

E—*Evaluate* the score in terms of the goal.

D—*Determine* errors by examining the pattern.

B—*Begin* error correction. The teacher models a similar problem.

A—*Ask* the student to apply the correction procedure.

C—*Close* out the session by giving positive feedback on correction.

K—*Kick* back and relax!

Clifford (1990) recommends that instructional environments feature error tolerance and reward for error correction. The letters *D, B, A,* and *C* in FEEDBACK stress error-correction procedures.

Maintain Flexibility   Given the heterogeneity of students with learning problems, the teacher must use some flexibility in teaching math. From the numerous learning characteristics that can affect math learning, it is apparent that a variety of teaching activities or procedures is needed. If a specific teaching activity does not result in student learning, it may help to try another. Low-stress algorithms, specific modality-oriented instruction, visual and auditory cueing, prompting, and reinforcement represent a few instructional alternatives that can be manipulated readily.

Teaching Mastery

In this discussion, *mastery learning* refers to teaching a skill to a level of automaticity. Individuals usually reach a level of automaticity when they continuously respond to math problems without hesitating to compute the answer. Most people operate at a level of automaticity when responding to questions such as What is your phone number? or What is 6 plus 2? Rate of responding is regarded as an effective measure of automaticity (Hasselbring, Goin, & Bransford, 1987; Kirby & Becker, 1988; Lovitt, 1989). Reaching mastery on a skill provides numerous benefits, including improved retention and ability to compute or solve higher-level problems. Other benefits include finishing timed tests, completing homework faster, receiving higher grades, and developing positive feelings about math.

Before mastery instruction or techniques are used, the students must possess the preskills and understand the concept related to the targeted skill. Once they understand a skill, they can be instructed at mastery level. Ashlock (1998) notes that understanding is gained through the use of concrete and semiconcrete experiences, promoting relationship insights among operations (e.g., $4 + 3 = 7$, $7 - 4 = 3$; and $8 \times 3 = 24$, $24 \div 3 = 8$, $24 \div 8 = 3$), and fostering mature ways to determine missing numbers (e.g., using algorithms such as counting up in addition, or using rules such as *any number times zero equals zero*). Students with learning problems vary considerably on the number of trials they need before achieving automaticity. Independent practice is the primary instructional format used to acquire mastery. Because practice can become boring, the teacher must try to make practice interesting or fun. Instructional games, peer teaching, computer-assisted instruction, self-correcting materials, and reinforcement are helpful in planning practice-to-mastery activities.

Several techniques are available to improve speed in math computation:

- Reinforce high rates of correct responses.
- Set a rate goal.
- Chart performances and terminate daily practice once the goal is achieved.
- Tell students to work faster.
- Challenge students to beat their last rate score.

- Teach students to use rules (e.g., any number times 2 is double that number).
- Teach efficient algorithms (such as counting up in addition).
- Drill difficult problems with flash cards.
- Play instructional math games.
- Provide rate practice in small intervals (10 to 20 seconds).
- Teach students the relationships between addition and subtraction or multiplication and division when they are learning the respective facts.

In establishing mastery rate levels for individuals, it is important to consider the learner's characteristics (such as age, academic skill, and motor ability). For example, oral responses may be more appropriate for a student who has handwriting difficulties. For most students, a rate of 40 to 60 correct digits written per minute with two or fewer errors is appropriate; however, for younger students (kindergarten through second grade), it often is necessary to lower the digits-per-minute criteria. Once a mastery level is achieved, the teacher and student are able to move to the next skill level with appropriate preskills and more confidence.

Teaching Problem Solving

Problem solving has received more attention since the National Council of Teachers of Mathematics (1980) made a statement noting that problem solving should be a top priority in math instruction. Although problem solving has received a decade of attention from educators, its exact nature remains ambiguous. The National Council of Teachers of Mathematics (1989) describes problem solving as it relates to word and computation problems. It seems reasonable that a problem-solving activity is needed for any task the student finds difficult. Thus, word and computation problems both could require problem-solving procedures. For skills in which automaticity has been achieved, problem solving is probably not a necessary procedural process.

Most authorities (Cawley et al., 1987; Fleischner, Nuzum, & Marzola, 1987; Kameenui & Simmons, 1990) interpret problem solving within the context of word problems. From an analysis of the problem-solving literature on students with learning problems, several components germane to problem solving are evident. These components include that to problem solve, the student needs to have a mathematical knowledge base, apply acquired knowledge to new and unfamiliar situations, and actively engage in thinking processes. These thinking processes involve having the student recognize a problem, plan a procedural strategy, examine the math relationships in the problem, and determine the mathematical knowledge needed to solve the problem. Then the student needs to represent the problem graphically, generate the equation, estimate the answer, sequence the computation steps, compute the answer, and check the answer for reasonableness. The student self-monitors the entire process and explores alternative ways to solve the problem. Problem solving is a complex procedure, and these descriptors are offered as a frame of reference to promote understanding and appreciation of the numerous components involved in it.

Fortunately, in spite of the complexity of the concept, the problem-solving emphasis is generating research that provides insights into how to teach students with learning difficulties to solve word problems. Paralleling the emphasis on problem solving has been a focus on strategy instruction. In strategy instruction, students learn a strategy that helps them engage in the appropriate steps needed to recognize and successfully solve a word problem. Numerous learning strategies are being developed and evaluated to teach problem-solving skills to students with learning problems. For example, mnemonics help students with memory problems acquire, remember, and apply specific math content and procedures. The following are some guidelines for problem-solving instruction:

- Link instruction to students' prior knowledge and help them connect what they know in learning new information. For example, to help students learn division facts, point out the relationship of multiplication and division (i.e., $9 \times 7 = 63$, $63 \div 9 = 7$, $63 \div 7 = 9$).
- Teach students to understand concepts and operations.
- Give students problems that pertain to daily living.
- Teach word problems simultaneously with computation skills.

• Concentrate on helping students develop a positive attitude toward math.

• Teach students learning strategies that help them become independent learners.

Cawley et al. (1987, pp. 91–92) present the following list of do's and don'ts for teachers:

Do:

1. Begin problem solving the day a child enters school.
2. Make problem solving the reason for computation.
3. Develop long-term programs of problem solving.
4. Conduct problem solving as a multimodal activity.
5. Parcel out the effects of one variable on another. If the child cannot read the problem, rewrite it. If the computation is too complex, make it simpler.
6. Have children prepare or modify problems.
7. Differentiate between process and knowledge.
8. Prepare problems in such a way that children must act upon the information. Prepare a set of problems in which all problems have the same question.
9. Present problems dealing with familiar subject matter.
10. Constantly monitor progress and modify problems to fit the child's weaknesses and progress.

Don't:

1. Use cue words to signal an operation.
2. Teach children to use computational rules to solve problems. That is, do not tell children to add when they see three different numbers.
3. Use problem-solving activities as an occasional wrap-up to computation.
4. Mark a child wrong if he or she makes a computational error in problem solving if the operation is correct.
5. Train teachers to treat problem solving as secondary to computation.
6. Assume that because the child is able to perform an arithmetic operation that he or she can automatically solve problems that use that operation.
7. Conclude that an incorrect answer automatically indicates lack of facility in problem solving.
8. Fail to realize that problem solving is the most important aspect of mathematics for daily living.
9. Fail to seize the opportunities for training in problem solving in conjunction with other subject areas.
10. Present problem solving in a haphazard manner. Order and careful planning are essential.

Specific interventions for teaching problem-solving skills are presented later in this chapter.

Teaching Generalization

As discussed in Chapter 4, *generalization* refers to the performance of the targeted behavior in different, nontraining conditions (i.e., across subjects, settings, people, behaviors, or time) without arranging the same events in the conditions that were present during training (Stokes & Baer, 1977). Students with learning problems typically have difficulty generalizing skills. A lack of instruction aimed at teaching students with learning problems to generalize math skills has contributed to their generalization problems. Ellis, Lenz, and Sabornie (1987a, 1987b) report that generalization must be taught prior to, during, and subsequent to instruction. Selected instructional practices to help students generalize math skills include the following:

1. Develop motivation to learn. It is believed that students who desire to learn a skill or strategy are most likely to generalize it. Motivation helps students feel responsible for their own learning and helps establish the independence needed to apply the new skill in settings without teacher support.

2. Throughout the instructional process, have periodic discussions with students about the rationale for learning the math skill and in which situations it is useful (e.g., homework, recreational activities, and shopping).

3. Throughout the instructional process, provide students with a variety of examples and experiences. For example, vary the manipulative objects (such as cubes, checkers, and buttons) in concrete activities, and use a variety of graphic representations (i.e., different pictures, drawings, and tallies) in semiconcrete activities. Likewise, vary the format in abstract computation or word-problem activities (e.g., present computation problems in vertical and horizontal formats). Also, vary the person doing the instruction (e.g., aide, peer, and parent).

4. Teach skills to a mastery level so that students can concentrate on using and not just remembering the skill.

5. Teach students strategies for solving multistep math problems. When students possess a strategy for solving difficult problems, they are more likely to develop independent behavior and to actively engage in the problem-solving process. Mnemonic devices frequently are used to help students retrieve appropriate strategies.

☀ INSTRUCTIONAL PRACTICES FOR COMPUTATION AND PROBLEM SOLVING

The instructional components for teaching computation presented in Figure 12.1 include teaching procedures and activities presented in the remainder of this chapter. Because many students with learning problems fail to master basic facts, two programs are discussed for teaching math facts. Following these programs, concrete-semi-concrete-abstract teaching activities, basic rules and algorithms, problem-solving interventions, functional math, estimation, and calculators are presented.

Thornton and Toohey Math Facts Program

Thornton and Toohey (1985) report substantial literature that indicates that modifying the *sequence* and *presentation* of learning tasks can improve basic fact learning among students with learning problems. They offer ten guidelines that are supported by the literature for planning and implementing basic fact instruction for students with learning problems. These guidelines form the basis for *MATHFACT,* which was developed and used successfully in Queensland, Australia (Thornton & Toohey 1982–1985). Their guidelines include the following:

1. ***Consider prerequisite learnings by looking ahead to review or reteach as necessary.*** Mathematical concepts and operations are hierarchical. Concepts that are basic to learning a new skill or concept should be taught before introducing the new material. For example, ensure that sums-to-9 facts are mastered before introducing subtraction facts.

2. ***Provide ongoing diagnosis and assessment.*** Attention to the student's rate of progress, types of errors, understanding of concepts, and learning style is basic to successful math facts instruction.

3. ***Modify the sequence in which facts are presented for learning.*** Traditional fact instruction sequences addition facts by the size of the sum. Thornton and Toohey (1985) maintain that other sequences are more effective for various

learners. For example, for immature students or those with serious deficits, they recommend beginning instruction with the 72 easiest addition facts: count-ons (+1, +2, +3) (45 facts), zeroes (19 facts), doubles (6 facts not previously encountered), and 10 sums (2 facts not previously encountered—6 + 4 and 4 + 6).

4. ***Before drill, teach students strategies for computing answers to unknown facts.*** Many students with learning problems need to be taught specific strategies to help them solve problems independently. For example:

7 + 2	6 + 3	Start BIG and count on.
6 + 0	0 + 8	Plus zero stays the same.
8 + 6	6 + 8	Order of addends does not affect sum.

Overall, the following sequence is suggested: easy addition facts, easy subtraction facts, other addition facts, and other subtraction facts.

5. ***Modify the presentation of activities to fit the learning style of each student.*** Students with learning problems are a heterogeneous population with many different learning styles and preferences. Procedures for taking advantage of various modality preferences include the following (Thornton & Toohey, 1985, pp. 52–53):

For Auditory Learners

1. Precede all actions and demonstrations with spoken instructions. Each step may have two parts: (a) oral instructions only; (b) oral instructions closely followed by a visual stimulus, concrete manipulation, or demonstration.
2. Provide a verbal summary of each step.
3. If necessary use key words to focus the child's attention (e.g., "listen").
4. Remove extraneous visual stimuli.

For Visual Learners

1. Precede all oral instructions by concrete manipulations or mimed demonstrations. Each step may have two parts: (a) presentation of the visual stimulus only; (b) visual presentation in conjunction with verbalization.
2. Have children describe mimed or demonstrated actions, pictures, or concrete manipulation.
3. Provide a visual summary of each step.

FIGURE 12.1

Instructional components for teaching computation

1. Provide concrete experiences to promote understanding.
   Example:

   4   +   3   =   _____

2. Provide semiconcrete experiences to promote understanding.
   Example: //// + ///
   $$4 + 3 = \underline{\quad}$$

3. Provide abstract activities and practice to promote mastery.
   Example: $4 + 3 = \underline{\quad}$

4. Teach rules that show patterns and relationships.
   Example: *Zero rule:* Any number plus zero equals the number.
   $$4 + 0 = 4$$
   Order rule: Addends yield the same sum regardless of their order.
   $$4 + 3 = 7 \qquad 3 + 4 = 7$$

5. Teach algorithms for solving problems.
   Example: *Fact:* $7 + 2 = \underline{\quad}$ *Algorithm:* Start BIG and count on.

6. Use mnemonics to help students remember algorithms or problem-solving procedures.
   Example: DRAW
   D–*Discover* the sign (+, −, x, ÷).
   R–*Read* the problem ("four plus three equals blank").
   A–*Answer,* or "DRAW" a conceptual representation of the problem, using lines
   and tallies, and check (4 ////   +   3 ///   =   _____).
   W–*Write* the answer (4 ////   +   3 ///   =   _7_).

7. Provide a variety of practice activities to promote mastery and generalization.
   Example: Provide vertical and horizontal problems.
   Use self-correcting materials, instructional games, peer tutoring, and computer-assisted instruction for seatwork.
   Provide activities to improve the rate of responses (e.g., 1-minute probes).

8. Teach problem solving.
   Example: Have students solve a variety of word problems.
   Have students create their own word problems.
   Provide students with strategies for solving problems.

4. Encourage children to make mental images of visual stimuli. Provide opportunity for them to reproduce these images (verbally, pictorially).
5. Use cue cards to focus children's attention.
6. Try a silent lesson.

For Kinesthetic/Tactile Learners

1. Precede all instructions by the physical manipulation of objects by the child. The teacher should guide all manipulations. Each step may have two parts: (a) physical manipulation only; (b) physical manipulation in conjunction with oral instruction.
2. Remove visual stimuli if distracting. Have children close their eyes or place objects in their hands behind their backs.
3. Provide a summary (physical manipulation of each step).
4. Use a cueing system to focus the child's attention.

5. Use textured material (pipe cleaners, sandpaper, plasticine, sandtrays, and magnetic boards).

6. ***Control the pacing.*** Knowing when to move faster or slow down is critical to good fact instruction. Continuous monitoring of fact progress can facilitate pacing.

7. ***Help students discriminate when to use a strategy, and integrate new learnings with old.*** Some students with learning problems learn a strategy and apply it to all situations. For example, a student may learn a count-on strategy and apply it to all addition facts. A student's appropriate use of a strategy should be strengthened by activities that require identifying math facts to which it applies.

8. ***Provide verbal prompts.*** Repeatedly give students verbal prompts during instruction. This helps some students independently associate the prompts with the specific facts to which they apply.

9. ***Help students develop self-monitoring skills.*** Many students with learning problems need to acquire skills that focus on *how to learn.* Such techniques as cognitive behavior modification and academic strategy training enable the student to develop self-monitoring skills that are useful across tasks and situations.

10. ***Ensure provisions for overlearning.*** Once facts are mastered, emphasis shifts to activities that help students with learning problems store them in long-term memory. This usually requires a variety of drill activities and performances on tasks at a high criterion level. Instructional games, self-correcting materials, computer-assisted instruction, peer teaching, and periodic review are a few of the activities appropriate for developing overlearning.

Mercer and Miller Math Facts Program

The *Strategic Math Series* (Mercer & Miller, 1991–1993) features seven phases to teach basic math facts:

Phase 1: Pretest
Phase 2: Teach concrete application
Phase 3: Teach representational application
Phase 4: Introduce the "DRAW" strategy
Phase 5: Teach abstract application

Phase 6: Posttest
Phase 7: Provide practice to fluency and develop problem-solving strategies

To help teach basic facts, all lessons in the *Strategic Math Series* include a sequence of procedures developed from the effective teaching research. These steps have demonstrated effectiveness with students who have learning difficulties. These instructional procedures include the following:

1. ***Give an advance organizer.*** The first component in each lesson is the advance organizer, which prepares the student for learning.

2. ***Describe and model.*** This component allows the teacher to describe and model the computation process, following two basic procedures. In Procedure 1, the teacher asks and answers questions aloud while demonstrating how to compute the answer for one or more problems on the learning sheet. In computing the problem, the teacher verbalizes thoughts so that students can better understand the thought processes involved. In Procedure 2, the teacher continues to demonstrate how to solve one or more problems, asking questions and soliciting student responses and using prompts and cues to facilitate correct responses. Thus, in Procedure 2, the teacher and the students work a problem together.

3. ***Conduct guided practice.*** Guided practice allows the teacher to instruct and support students as they move toward independently solving problems on their learning sheets. During this time, the teacher follows two basic procedures. In Procedure 1, the teacher's role is to prompt and facilitate students' thought processes. To facilitate correct responses, the teacher asks questions and solicits student responses, using prompts and cues, thereby guiding students through each problem in a way that ensures success. In Procedure 2, the teacher instructs students to solve the next few problems on the learning sheet, offering assistance to individual learners only if needed.

4. ***Conduct independent practice.*** Independent practice of facts is an integral component of the lessons. It enables the teacher to determine whether students can solve facts independently. The sample dialogues for this component consist of simple directions, including a statement that reminds students to use previously learned skills and techniques to solve problems. To enhance

generalization, students solve problems in horizontal and vertical formats; to promote mastery, the rules and relationships (structures) of each operation are covered. During this time, the teacher does not provide any assistance.

5. ***Conduct problem-solving practice.*** Like independent practice of computation facts, problem-solving practice constitutes an integral component of all lessons. To teach students the thought process involved in problem solving, the teacher uses a graduated sequence of word problems. For example, in early lessons, students solve problems involving three words; in later lessons, they write their own word problems. Along the way, students learn to extract any information that may be irrelevant to a problem. Thus, when students complete a facts program, they are able to solve word problems with and without extraneous information and to write their own word problems.

6. ***Provide feedback.*** Because proper feedback is critical to learning, a feedback component is found in all the lessons. This component follows the elaborated feedback routine developed by Kline et al. (1991), and allows the teacher to recognize and praise correct student responses, thereby preventing future errors. Feedback is facilitated through the use of a facts progress chart on which the teacher and the student plot the student's scores for the last ten problems on a learning sheet.

The *Strategic Math Series* has yielded excellent results from field testing (Mercer & Miller, 1992; Miller, Mercer, & Dillon, 1992). The field-test results indicate that 109 students with learning problems were able to acquire computational skills across facts; solve word problems with and without extraneous information; create word problems involving facts; apply a mnemonic strategy to difficult problems; increase rate of computation; and generalize math skills across examiners, settings, and tasks.

Concrete-Semiconcrete-Abstract Activities

The concrete-semiconcrete-abstract (CSA) sequence (see Chapter 11) is appropriate for teaching the understanding of math throughout the span of math concepts, skills, and word problems. The use of manipulative objects requires some specific guidelines to ensure effective results. Dunlap and Brennan (1979) offer the following guidelines:

- Before abstract experiences, instruction must proceed from concrete (manipulative) experiences to semiconcrete experiences.
- The main objective of manipulative aids is to help students understand and develop mental images of mathematical processes.
- The activity must accurately represent the actual process. For example, a direct correlation should exist between the manipulative activities and the paper-and-pencil activities.
- More than one manipulative object should be used in teaching a concept.
- The aids should be used individually by each student.
- The manipulative experience must involve the moving of objects. The learning occurs from the student's physical actions on the objects rather than from the object themselves.

Moreover, Thornton and Toohey (1986) suggest that the teacher continuously ask students questions about their actions as they manipulate objects, encourage students to verbalize their thinking, have students write out the problem being solved through the use of objects, and have students use objects to check answers.

Implicit in CSA instruction is an emphasis on enabling students to understand the concepts of math prior to memorizing facts, algorithms, and operations. According to the CSA sequence, instruction begins at the concrete level where the student uses three-dimensional objects to solve computation problems. After successfully solving problems at the concrete level, the student proceeds to the semiconcrete (or representational) level. At the semiconcrete level, students use two-dimensional drawings (i.e., pictures or lines and tallies) to solve computation problems. After successfully solving problems at this level, the student begins to work at the next level, the abstract level. At the abstract level, the student looks at the computation problem and tries to solve it without using objects or drawings. The student reads the problem, remembers the answer or thinks of a way to compute the answer, and writes the answer. No objects or drawings are used in the computation unless the student is unable to answer a problem. Because success in math requires the ability to solve problems at the abstract level, student mastery at this level is essential. The use of the CSA sequence to teach various computation skills is presented next.

Place Value To begin place value instruction at the *concrete level,* gather two plastic cups, a bundle of straws, and a set of blocks. Set the two cups on poster board; label the right one *ones* and the left one *tens.* Tell the student to count the blocks. For each block the student counts, place a straw in the ones cup. Stop when nine blocks are counted and nine straws are in the ones cup. Before picking up the tenth straw, explain that one straw in the tens cup represents ten objects. The student then takes the nine straws out of the ones cup and places one straw in the tens cup. Next, the student continues to count the blocks and place the straws. Counting proceeds in the following manner: 1 ten and 1, 1 ten and 2, . . . 3 tens and 4, 3 tens and 5, and so on. Each time a ten is reached, empty the ones cup and place a straw in the tens cup. Although the student is told that 1 ten and 1 is another name for 11, and 3 tens and 5 is another name for 35, during place value instruction encourage the student to count using the 3 tens and 5 system. The student continues with the blocks and straws until able to do the task easily.

At the *semiconcrete level,* use illustrations instead of the blocks, straws, and cups. For example:

Task: Count the items and place the correct number in each cup.

The completed task would look like this:

Gradually fade the pictures of the cups and replace them with:

tens	ones
___	___

The items may change to pictures of real objects.

At the *abstract level,* add numbers gradually in place of items. For example:

Task 1: Count the items and identify the number of tens and ones.

/ /

_____ tens   _____ ones

x x x x x x x x x x x x x

_____ tens   _____ ones

Task 2: Identify the number of tens and ones in each number.

24   _____ tens   87   _____ tens

      _____ ones   _____ ones

These activities represent only one way of providing place value instruction at the concrete, semiconcrete, and abstract levels. The teacher can expand and use different activities across the three levels.

Addition: Sums-to-9 Learning sums-to-9 underlies later math functioning. These sums are the initial facts to be mastered.

Concrete level: 6 + 3 = _____
The student looks at the first number and counts that many objects. The student looks at the second number and counts that many objects. The student counts all objects for the sum.

Example:

Semiconcrete level: 6 + 3 = _____
The student looks at the first number and draws that many tallies. The student looks at the second number and draws that many tallies. The student counts all tallies for the sum.

Example:

Abstract level: 6 + 3 = ____

The student looks at the problem and solves it without objects or drawings. The student uses an algorithm (such as start BIG and count up) or memory to solve the problem.

Example:

$$
\begin{array}{r}
6 \\
+\ 3 \\
\hline
9
\end{array}
\qquad \text{or} \qquad 6 + 3 = 9
$$

Addition: Sums-to-18   After sums-to-9 and place value to two places are learned, the student is ready for instruction in addition facts of sums-to-18.

Concrete level: 7 + 5 = ____

The student looks at the first number and counts that many objects. The student looks at the second number and counts that many objects. The student manipulates the objects to form a group of ten and a group of two. The student writes and says the answer as 1 ten and 2 ones or 12.

Example:

Semiconcrete level: 7 + 5 = ____

The student looks at the first number and draws that many tallies. The student looks at the second number and draws that many tallies. The student circles a group of ten and computes the answer as 1 ten and 2 ones.

Example:

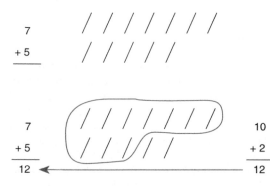

Abstract level: 7 + 5 = ____

The student answers the problem from memory or uses an algorithm.

Example:

$$
\begin{array}{r}
7 \\
+\ 5 \\
\hline
12
\end{array}
\qquad \text{or} \qquad 7 + 5 = 12
$$

Addition with Regrouping   When going from the concrete to the semiconcrete level, the teacher simply replaces real objects with pictures of objects, dots, or tallies. The step from the semiconcrete to the abstract level involves replacing pictures and tallies with numbers. The following examples are provided to assist the teacher in developing instructional tasks for addition with regrouping.

Concrete level: 26 + 17 = ____

The student looks at the first number and counts the appropriate number of objects grouped into tens and ones. The student looks at the second number and counts the appropriate number of objects grouped into tens and ones. The student looks at the total number of ones and groups them into tens. The student counts the total groups of tens and ones and writes the answer.

Example:

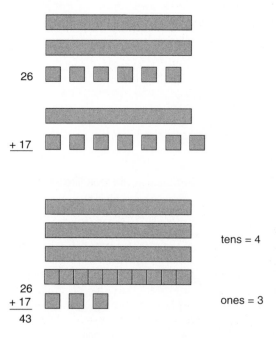

Semiconcrete level: 26 + 17 = ___
The student looks at the first number and draws tens and ones. The student looks at the second number and draws tens and ones. The student looks at the total number of ones and groups them into tens. The student counts the total groups of tens and ones and writes the answer.
Example:

26
+ 17
―――
43

= 4 tens, 3 ones

Abstract level: 26 + 17 = ___
The student uses an algorithm to solve the problem.
Example:

    27   or   27 + 17 = 43
  + 17
  ―――
    43

Subtraction Facts (1 to 9)

After the addition facts through 9 are learned, the teaching of subtraction facts (1 to 9) is simple. When the "add on" approach to subtraction is used, the student must find a missing addend instead of a difference. The missing addend approach involves the same logic used in addition; thus, the student can use knowledge of addition facts to solve subtraction problems. For example, an addition fact can be expressed as an addition *or* a subtraction equation, depending on which unknown the student is seeking to compute.

Addition: 4 + 3 = _7_ (addend + addend = sum)

Subtraction: 7 − 3 = _4_ (sum − addend = missing
                                             addend)

In the missing addend approach to subtraction, the student uses knowledge of addition facts to answer the subtraction question, "What number goes with 3 to make another name for (equal) 7?" Thus, when solving 7 − 3 = ___, the problem becomes 3 + ___ = 7. Although the missing addend approach is feasible mathematically, the "take away" approach is used more widely to teach stu-

dents with learning problems. The "take away" approach appears more relevant to the real world of subtraction when solving word problems or demonstrating the subtraction process. Subtraction tasks at each of the three levels for the facts through 9 are presented next.

Concrete level: 7 − 3 = ___
The student looks at the first number and counts the appropriate number of objects grouped into tens and ones. The student looks at the second number and takes (or moves) away the appropriate number of objects. The student counts the remaining objects for the answer.
Example:

    7
  − 3
  ―――
    4

objects taken away

Semiconcrete level: 7 − 3 = ___
The student looks at the first number and draws that many tallies. The student looks at the second number and crosses out that many tallies. The student counts the remaining tallies for the answer.
Example:

        7   ////XXX
      − 3
      ―――
        4

Abstract level: 7 − 3 = ___
The student answers the problem from memory or uses an algorithm.
Example:

      7   or   7 − 3 = 4
    − 3
    ―――
      4

Subtraction Facts (10 to 18)

When solving subtraction facts 10 to 18, the student must recognize place value (i.e., recognize that a portion of the take away number comes from the ten). It helps to teach the BBB rule: In subtraction, when the *Bottom* number in the ones column is *Bigger* than the tens number in the ones column, *Break* down the ten in the next column and trade it for 10 ones.

Concrete level: 14 − 6 = ___

The student looks at the first number, counts that many objects, and groups them as the appropriate number of tens and ones. The student looks at the second number and takes away the appropriate number of objects from the ones and from a renamed group of ten ones. The student counts the remaining objects for the answer.

Example:

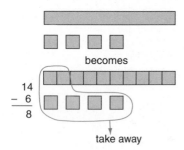

Semiconcrete level: 14 − 6 = ___

The student looks at the first number and draws a group of ten and the appropriate number of ones. The student uses the BBB rule to trade a ten for 10 ones. The student looks at the second number and crosses out the appropriate number of lines from the ones and from the 10 ones. The student counts the remaining lines for the answer.

Example:

Abstract level: 14 − 6 = ___

The student answers the problem from memory or uses an algorithm.

Example:

$$
\begin{array}{r}
14 \\
-\ 6 \\
\hline
8
\end{array}
\qquad \text{or} \qquad 14 - 6 = 8
$$

Subtraction with Regrouping   The following examples can help the teacher develop instructional tasks for subtraction with regrouping at all three levels.

Concrete level: 33 − 18 = ___

The student looks at the first number and counts that many objects and groups them as the appro-

priate number of tens and ones. The student looks at the second number, uses the BBB rule, and then takes away the appropriate number of objects from the ones and from a renamed group of 10 ones. The student counts the remaining objects for the answer.

Example:

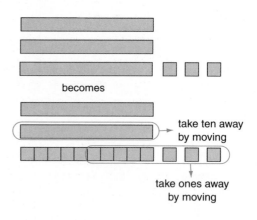

answer = 1 ten and 5 ones or 15

Semiconcrete level: 33 − 18 = ___

The student looks at the first number and draws tens and ones. The student looks at the second number, uses the BBB rule, and then crosses out the appropriate number from the ones and a renamed group of 10 ones. The student counts the remaining tens and ones for the answer.

Example:

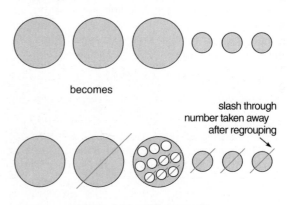

answer = 1 ten and 5 ones or 15

Abstract level: 33 − 18 = ___

The student uses an algorithm to solve the problem.

Example:

$$\begin{array}{r} 33 \\ -\ 18 \\ \hline 15 \end{array} \quad \text{or} \quad 33 - 18 = 15$$

Multiplication   The 100 multiplication facts ($\times$ 0 to $\times$ 9) are basic to more complex multiplication operations.

Concrete level: $3 \times 4 =$ _____
The student looks at the first number and selects that many containers to represent groups. The student looks at the second number and puts that many objects in each container (group). The student counts or adds objects across the groups for the answer.
  Example:

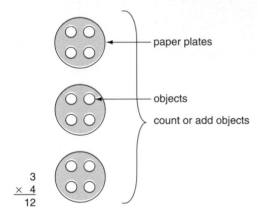

$$\begin{array}{r} 3 \\ \times\ 4 \\ \hline 12 \end{array}$$

Semiconcrete level: $3 \times 4 =$ _____
The student looks at the first number and draws that many groups using horizontal lines. The student looks at the second number and draws that many tallies in each group (i.e., horizontal line). The student counts or adds the tallies across the groups for the answer.
  Example:

$$\begin{array}{r} 3 \\ \times\ 4 \end{array} \quad \begin{array}{c} \underline{\hspace{1cm}} \\ \underline{\hspace{1cm}} \\ \underline{\hspace{1cm}} \end{array} \quad \text{groups}$$

$$\begin{array}{r} 3 \\ \times\ 4 \\ \hline 12 \end{array} \quad \begin{array}{c} \underline{/\,/\,/\,/} \\ \underline{/\,/\,/\,/} \\ \underline{/\,/\,/\,/} \end{array} \quad \begin{array}{c} 4 \\ 4 \quad \text{add tallies} \\ 4 \end{array}$$

Abstract level: $3 \times 4 =$ _____
The student answers the problem from memory or uses an algorithm.

Example:

$$\begin{array}{r} 3 \\ \times\ 4 \\ \hline 12 \end{array} \quad \text{or} \quad 3 \times 4 = 12$$

Division   Division is considered to be the most difficult of the four operations. For example, long division requires the use of division, multiplication, and subtraction in computing quotients. The following examples illustrate division problems involving solving for number of groups of objects.

Concrete level: $12 \div 4 =$ _____ or $4\overline{)12}$
The student looks at the first number, or the number within the lines, and counts that many objects. The student looks at the second number, or the number outside the lines, and groups objects according to that number. The student counts the number of groups for the answer.
  Example:

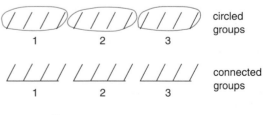

Semiconcrete level: $12 \div 4 =$ _____ or $4\overline{)12}$
The student looks at the first number, or the number within the lines, and draws that many tallies. The student looks at the second number, or the number outside the lines, and circles (or groups) that many tallies until all the tallies are within circles (groups). The student also can connect groups of tallies with lines. The student counts the number of circles (groups) for the answer.
  Example:

/ / / / / / / / / / / / tallies

becomes

(/ / / /) (/ / / /) (/ / / /) circled groups
   1   2   3

/ / / / / / / / / / / / connected groups
   1   2   3

$12 \div 4 = \underline{3}$

Abstract level: $12 \div 4 =$ ___ or $4\overline{)12}$
The student answers the problem from memory or uses an algorithm.

Example:

$$12 \div 4 = \underline{\ 3\ } \qquad \text{or} \qquad 4\overline{)12}^{\,3}$$

Division with Remainder   The following examples present division problems in which the answer contains a remainder.

Concrete level: $20 \div 3 =$ ___ or $3\overline{)20}$
The student looks at the first number, or the number within the lines, and counts that many objects. The student looks at the second number, or the number outside the lines, and groups objects (circles with string or rearranges groups) according to that number. The student counts the number of circles with string (or the rearranged groups) and the remaining number of ungrouped objects for the answer.

Example:

String around groups of 3 or remove groups of 3

} remainder

$$20 \div 3 = 6 \text{ R}2$$

Semiconcrete level: $20 \div 3 =$ ___ or $3\overline{)20}$
The student looks at the first number, or the number within the lines, and draws that many tallies. The student looks at the second number, or the number outside the lines, and circles (or groups) objects according to that number. The student counts the number of circles (groups) and the remaining number of ungrouped tallies for the answer.

Example:

$$20 \div 3 = 6 \text{ R}2$$

At this level the student also may use a grid (covered with acetate and used with an overhead pen or grease pencil) to solve division problems (e.g., determine the number of 3s in 20). In performing the task, the student counts until the 20th block is identified. Then 1s are written in the first three blocks, 2s are written in the second three blocks, and so on until no more sets of 3 are left in the first 20 blocks. For example:

1	1	1	2	2	2	3	3	3	4
4	4	5	5	5	6	6	6	X	X

student circles the 20th block
$20 \div 3 = 6$ R2

Abstract level: $20 \div 3 =$ ___ or $3\overline{)20}$
The student answers the problem from memory or uses an algorithm.

Example:

Recognition of Unit Fractions   The teacher can use the following instructional tasks to teach several skills in fractions.

Concrete level:
Let ⬜ be 1 and smaller size blocks represent fractional subregions of it. ⬜ may be a block or a container that holds fractional blocks. Use the blocks to display $1/4$, $1/3$, $1/2$, and so on.

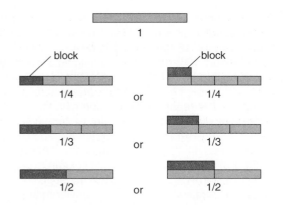

Numerous commercial materials are available for working with fractions at the concrete level (e.g., Cuisenaire rods and Unifix cubes).

Semiconcrete level:
Write the unit fraction for the designs.

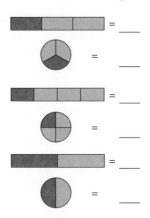

Abstract level:
Use numbers to express the unit fractions for one-fourth, one-third, and one-half.

Addition of Fractions with the Same Denominators

Concrete level: ($1/3 + 1/3$)

Semiconcrete level: ($1/4 + 2/4$)

Abstract level:

$$1/3 + 1/3 = \Box/\Box$$
$$1/4 + 2/4 = \Box/\Box$$

Addition and Subtraction of Mixed Fractions

Concrete level:
Task 1: Use real blocks ($3\,2/3 + 2\,2/3$)
Task 2: Use string ($5\,1/4 - 2\,3/4$)

Semiconcrete level:
Task 1: Use drawings ($3\,2/3 + 2\,2/3$)

+

_____

5 $4/3$

Task 2: Use lines ($5\,1/4 - 2\,3/4$)

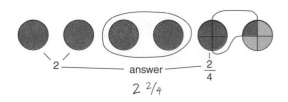

2 ———— answer ———— $\frac{2}{4}$

2 $2/4$

Abstract level:

$$\begin{array}{r} 3\frac{2}{3} \\ +\,2\frac{2}{3} \\ \hline 5\ \ ^4/_3 \end{array} = 6\,1/3$$

$$\begin{array}{r} 5\frac{1}{4} = \ \ 4\,^5/4 \\ -\,2\frac{3}{4} = \ \ 2\,^3/4 \\ \hline 2\,^2/4 = 2\,1/2 \end{array}$$

For activities on multiplying and dividing fractions at the various levels, see fraction activities presented later in this chapter.

Basic Rules and Algorithms

The teaching of basic rules and algorithms helps students compute math more efficiently. Moreover, many rules and algorithms are based on relationships that foster student understanding and computational problem solving.

Addition Rules   The following five addition rules are basic for understanding math:

1. *Order rule:* The order of addends does not affect the answer (commutative property) (6 + 3 = 9; 3 + 6 = 9).
2. *Zero rule:* Any number plus zero is the number (3 + 0 = 3; 0 + 7 = 7).
3. *One rule:* Any number plus 1 is one more than the number (i.e., count up by 1) (3 + 1 = 4; 18 + 1 = 19).
4. *Nine rule:* Any single-digit number greater than zero added to 9 results in the addend number minus 1 plus 10 (9 + 7 = 6 + 10 = 16).
5. *Tens rule:* Any single-digit number added to 10 results in the 0 in 10 being changed to the number being added to it (10 + 6 = 16).

Addition Algorithms   After the student knows addition facts through sums-to-18, an adaptation of the *tens method* (Fulkerson, 1963) may be a useful algorithm. To illustrate:

$$
\begin{array}{r}
\overset{2}{8}\,\overset{2}{6}\,7 \\
5\,\overset{5}{7}\,\overset{1}{4} \\
\overset{1}{6}\,4\,7 \\
+\,7\,8\,\overset{7}{8}\,{}^{4} \\
\hline
2874
\end{array}
$$

Beginning at the top right in the example, 7 + 4 = 11, which can be renamed as 1 ten and 1 one. A horizontal line is drawn through the 4 to represent the ten, and the ones number is written on the extension of the line. Because the line represents the ten, the student no longer needs to hold it in mind. The student uses the 1 (ones digit) that is left over to begin adding until another ten is obtained. In this example, 1 + 7 = 8; then 8 + 6 = 14. Thus, a line is drawn through the 6 to represent the ten, and the 4 ones are written on the line. Because all numbers in the ones column have been added, the 4 is recorded as the one's digit at the bottom of the column.

The two lines drawn in the ones column represent 2 tens; thus, addition in the tens column begins by carrying the 2 tens by writing *2* above the tens column. These 2 tens are added to the 6

tens, and this continues until there is a sum greater than or equal to 10 tens: 2 tens + 6 tens = 8 tens; 8 tens + 7 tens = 15 tens. A line is drawn across the 7 to represent 10 tens and the remaining 5 tens are written on the line. Then, 5 tens + 4 tens = 9 tens; 9 tens + 8 tens = 17 tens. A line is drawn across the 8, and the 7 is recorded on the line extension and as the tens digit at the bottom. In the tens column each line represents 10 tens or 1 hundred. Thus, the two lines in the tens column are carried by writing *2* at the top of the hundreds column to begin addition there. The 2 hundreds are added to 8 hundreds, and addition proceeds in a similar manner.

Another addition algorithm is referred to as *partial sums.* To illustrate:

$$
\begin{array}{r}
47 \\
+\,28 \\
\hline
15 \\
60 \\
\hline
75
\end{array}
$$

In this algorithm, when the sum of the ones column is greater than or equal to 10, it is written as a two-digit number at the bottom of the ones and tens columns. In the given example, 7 + 8 = 15, so 15 is written at the bottom of the columns. Next, the tens column is added and the sum is written below the ones column sum. In this case, 4 tens + 2 tens = 6 tens, or 60. Then the two partial sums are added.

Pearson (1986) presents a left-to-right addition algorithm that enables the student to regroup in the answer. This process offers some students a better understanding of the regrouping process. To illustrate:

$$
\begin{array}{r}
898 \\
+\,367 \\
\hline
11 \\
15 \\
15 \\
\hline
1265
\end{array}
$$

Subtraction Rules   The following six subtraction rules are basic for understanding math:

1. *Zero rule:* Any number minus zero equals the number (6 − 0 = 6; 9 − 0 = 9).
2. *One rule:* Any number minus 1 is one less (i.e., count backwards by one) (6 − 1 = 5; 19 − 1 = 18).
3. *Same number rule:* Any number minus the same number is zero (8 − 8 = 0).

4. *One less rule:* Any number minus 1 is the next smaller number ($15 - 1 = 14$).
5. *BBB rule:* In subtraction, when the *Bottom* number is *Bigger* than the top number, it is necessary to *Break* down the top number in the next column, trade it for 10 units, and then subtract.
6. *Addition/subtraction relationship rule:* In a subtraction problem, the answer (difference or missing addend) added to the number that is being subtracted (subtrahend or known addend) equals the top number (minuend or sum) ($13 - 5 = 8$; $8 + 5 = 13$). This rule enables the student to use knowledge of addition facts to solve subtraction facts. For example, to solve the problem $12 - 7$, the student asks, "What number added to 7 equals 12?"

Subtraction Algorithms   After the student has mastered subtraction facts with minuends to 18, selected algorithms are helpful. Several algorithms are based on the fact that adding or subtracting a constant number (i.e., the same number) to or from the minuend and the subtrahend does not change the answer (i.e., the difference or missing addend). To illustrate subtracting a constant to avoid regrouping:

6000	Student work:	$6000 - 1$	5999
$- 3642$		$- 3642 - 1$	$- 3641$
			2358

In the above problem, the zeros in 6000 are changed to 9s by subtracting 1. When the 1 is subtracted from both numbers, the problem is solved easily without regrouping. This algorithm is especially helpful because subtraction problems involving money frequently have zeros in the minuend (e.g., $5.00 - 2.38$; $10.00 - 6.74$).

To illustrate adding a constant to avoid regrouping:

46	Student work:	$46 + 2$	48
$- 28$		$- 28 + 2$	$- 30$
			18

In the above problem, when the bigger number is on the bottom in the ones column, a constant number that produces a zero in the ones column is added to both numbers. When the subtrahend becomes a zero, the problem is solved easily without regrouping.

Another example of adding a constant to the top and bottom numbers involves adding a ten in the top number of the ones column and a ten in the bottom number of the tens column. This helps simplify regrouping for some students. For example:

Student work: add ten to top number in ones column / add ten to bottom number in tens column

$$\begin{array}{r} 42 \\ -27 \end{array} \qquad \begin{array}{r} {}^{1}4\,2 \\ {}^{3}\!-27 \\ \hline 15 \end{array}$$

This procedure also can be used effectively to compute fractions. For example:

$$\begin{array}{r} 5\tfrac{1}{4} \\ -2\tfrac{3}{4} \end{array} \qquad \begin{array}{r} 5\tfrac{5}{4} \\ -3\tfrac{3}{4} \\ \hline 2\tfrac{2}{4} \end{array}$$

Student work: add one ($\tfrac{4}{4}$) to fraction in top number / add one (1) to whole number in bottom number

Hutchings' (1975) *low-stress method of subtraction* is an effective procedure in remedial instruction. It is based on notation for recording a minuend or sum in several ways. For example, 752 may be recorded as $6^{1}52$ or $6^{1}4^{1}2$ or $74^{1}2$. When using this notation, the regrouped sum or minuend is recorded in the middle before the recalling of subtraction facts. For example:

(a)
$$\begin{array}{r} 8472 \\ -\,6673 \end{array}$$

8	4	7	2
7	${}^{1}3$	${}^{1}6$	${}^{1}2$
$-\ 6$	6	7	3
1	7	9	9

(b)
$$\begin{array}{r} 65400062 \\ -\,21450238 \end{array}$$

6	5	4	0	0	0	6	2
6	4	${}^{1}3$	9	9	${}^{1}0$	5	${}^{1}2$
$-\ 2$	1	4	5	0	2	3	8
4	3	9	4	9	8	2	4

In this algorithm, all renaming is completed before subtraction takes place. The student is reminded that renaming is necessary each time the subtrahend (known addend) in each column is greater than the minuend (sum).

Fitzmaurice-Hayes (1984) describes a left-to-right subtraction algorithm that requires the student to regroup in the answer. This process helps students understand regrouping. To illustrate:

532	532	532	532
-246	-246	-246	-246
3	$\cancel{3}9$	$\cancel{3}\cancel{9}6$	286
	2	28	

Multiplication Rules   The following six multiplication rules are basic for understanding math:

1. *Order rule:* The order of the numbers to be multiplied does not affect the answer ($6 \times 3 = 18$; $3 \times 6 = 18$).
2. *Zero rule:* Any number times zero is zero ($8 \times 0 = 0$; $647 \times 0 = 0$).
3. *One rule:* Any number times 1 is the number ($9 \times 1 = 9$; $78 \times 1 = 78$).
4. *Two rule:* Any number times 2 is double the number ($8 \times 2 = 8 + 8$ or 16; $12 \times 2 = 12 + 12$ or 24).
5. *Five rule:* Any number times 5 involves counting by 5s the number of times indicated by the multiplier (i.e., 5×6 means counting "5, 10, 15, 20, 25, 30") ($3 \times 5 = 5 + 5 + 5$ or counting "5, 10, 15").
6. *Nine rule:* When multiplying any number by 9, the answer can be obtained by subtracting 1 from the multiplier to obtain the tens digit and then adding enough to it to make 9 to obtain the ones digit ($9 \times 4 = 36$—3 is one less than 4 and $3 + 6 = 9$).

If these rules are used, there are only 15 facts left to be memorized:

$3 \times 3 = 9$	$4 \times 8 = 32$
$3 \times 4 = 12$	$6 \times 6 = 36$
$3 \times 6 = 18$	$6 \times 7 = 42$
$3 \times 7 = 21$	$6 \times 8 = 48$
$3 \times 8 = 24$	$7 \times 7 = 49$
$4 \times 4 = 16$	$7 \times 8 = 56$
$4 \times 6 = 24$	$8 \times 8 = 64$
$4 \times 7 = 28$	

Some teachers report that these facts are learned faster by grouping the doubles ($3 \times 3 = 9$, $4 \times 4 = 16$, and so on), thus leaving only 10 facts.

Multiplication Algorithms   The *low-stress method of multiplication* (Hutchings, 1976) reduces the amount of remembering required during computation. It is based on notation for recording the products of multiplication facts in a different manner. With *drop notation,* the product of

$$\begin{array}{r} 7 \\ \times\, 8 \\ \hline \end{array}$$

may be written

$$\begin{array}{r} 7 \\ \times\, 8 \\ \hline 5 \\ 6 \end{array}$$

To illustrate:

Conventional notation:

$$\begin{array}{r} 8 \\ \times\, 7 \\ \hline 56 \end{array} \qquad \begin{array}{r} 6 \\ \times\, 6 \\ \hline 36 \end{array} \qquad \begin{array}{r} 5 \\ \times\, 1 \\ \hline 5 \end{array}$$

Drop notation:

$$\begin{array}{r} 8 \\ \times\, 7 \\ \hline 5 \\ 6 \end{array} \qquad \begin{array}{r} 6 \\ \times\, 6 \\ \hline 3 \\ 6 \end{array} \qquad \begin{array}{r} 5 \\ \times\, 1 \\ \hline 0 \\ 5 \end{array}$$

Using the drop notation, multiplication problems can be computed in the following ways:

(a)

	Step 1	Step 2	Step 3
	476	476	476
	$\times\quad 8$	$\times\quad 8$	$\times\quad 8$
	40	540	3540
	8	68	268
			3808

(b)

$$\begin{array}{r} 57764 \\ \times\qquad 7 \\ \hline 344420 \\ 59928 \\ \hline 404348 \end{array}$$

(c) using two multidigit factors:

	Step 1	Step 2	
	476	476	
	$\times\quad 38$	$\times\quad 38$	
	3540	3540	$\Big\}\times 8$
	268	268	
		1210	$\Big\}\times 3$
		218	
		18088	

This low-stress method of multiplication eliminates the regrouping requirement and allows the student to work only with multiplication facts in solving complex multiplication problems.

Another multiplication algorithm is the *partial products* algorithm. This algorithm reduces the regrouping requirement in multiplying multidigit numbers by one-digit numbers. For example:

27	
$\times\quad 6$	
42	(7×6) partial product
120	(20×6) partial product
162	

362	
$\times\quad 4$	
8	(2×4)
240	(60×4)
1200	(300×4)
1448	

Division Rules The following five division rules are basic for understanding math.

1. *Zero rule:* Zero divided by any number is zero ($9 \div 0 = 0$; $49 \div 0 = 0$).
2. *One rule:* Any number divided by 1 is the number ($8 \div 1 = 8$; $1\overline{)8}^{\,8}$; $67 \div 1 = 67$).
3. *Two rule:* Any number divided by 2 is half the number ($14 \div 2 = 7$; $2\overline{)66}^{\,33}$).
4. *Nines fact rule:* When 9 is divided into any of the 9s facts, the answer is one more than the number in the tens columns ($9\overline{)36}^{\,4}$—3 + 1 is 4; $9\overline{)45}^{\,5}$—4 + 1 is 5).
5. *Multiplication/division relationship rule:* The quotient multiplied by the divisor equals the dividend ($7 \times 5 = 35$; $35 \div 7 = 5$; $35 \div 7 = 5$). This rule enables the student to use knowledge of multiplication facts to solve division facts. For example, to solve the problem $32 \div 8$, the student asks, "What number times 8 equals 32?")

Division Algorithms Reisman (1977) notes that the following algorithms are less difficult than the traditional division algorithm. Using the algorithms is made simpler by knowing the shortcut for multiplying by multiples of 10. In the example of this algorithm, the student immediately pulls out the largest tens multiple of the divisor.

$$
\begin{array}{r|r}
28\overline{)62372} & \\
56000 & 2000 \\
\hline
6372 & \\
5600 & 200 \\
\hline
772 & \\
560 & 20 \\
\hline
212 & \\
196 & 7 \\
\hline
16 & 2227 \\
\end{array}
$$

The following algorithm helps the student identify or compute each number of the quotient when the first quotient number selected is too low.

Step 1	Step 2
	1
2	2
$23\overline{)8761}$	$23\overline{)8761}$
46	46
41	41
	23
	18

Steps 1 and 2 are repeated until no more multiplication is needed. The answer is computed by adding each column in the quotient computations.

$$
\begin{array}{r}
2 \\
78 \quad 98 \\
\text{(a)}\ 8\overline{)784} \\
56 \\
\hline
22 \\
16 \\
\hline
64 \\
64 \\
\hline
\end{array}
\qquad
\begin{array}{r}
12 \\
260 \\
\text{(b)}\ 23\overline{)8761} \\
46 \\
\hline
41 \\
23 \\
\hline
186 \\
138 \\
\hline
48 \\
46 \\
\hline
21 \\
0 \\
\hline
21 \\
\end{array}
$$

(answer is 380 R21—computed by adding each column in the quotient computations)

Fraction Algorithm Ruais (1978) describes a low-stress algorithm for teaching the addition and subtraction of fractions. The algorithm is called *ray multiplication* and consists of the following steps:

1. An overhead projection is used to drill the student on the location of geometric shapes and numbers. $\frac{\bigcirc}{\triangle}\ \frac{\square}{\diamond}$ are model items used to show the locations of bottom right, bottom left, top right, and top left.
2. The student is instructed to draw three rays (⟋): from bottom right to top left, from bottom left to top right, and from bottom left to bottom right. Thus, $\frac{\bigcirc}{\triangle}\ \frac{\square}{\diamond}$ would look like ⟋⟍ .
3. On a worksheet that has pairs of numerical fractions, the student is directed to draw the three rays and multiply along them. The student writes the answers to these multiplication tasks. After the rays are multiplied, the student writes the operation sign between the fractions in a pair. For example:

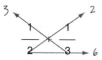

4. In this step the student writes a new fraction for each pair. The new numerator is formed by performing the correct operation on the products of the diagonal ray multiplications. The new

denominator for both fractions is the product of the horizontal ray multiplication. For example:

$$\frac{3}{6}+\frac{2}{6}$$

5. Now the student computes the sum or difference of the numerators and writes the result over the denominator. For example:

$$\frac{3}{6}+\frac{2}{6}=\frac{(3+2)}{6}=\frac{5}{6}$$

or

$$\frac{3}{6}-\frac{2}{6}=\frac{(3-2)}{6}=\frac{1}{6}$$

Ruais reports that this ray multiplication algorithm leads to reduced stress, reduced teaching time prior to mastery, and increased computation power.

Problem-Solving Interventions

In word problem solving, math problems are presented in the context of social situations, and information needed to solve each problem must be identified and then used. Some problems include extraneous information, and the number of operations may vary from one to several. Peterson, Fennema, and Carpenter (1988/1989) report that the context of simple addition and subtraction problems varies significantly and students must understand mathematical concepts and develop strategies to solve these various problems. Table 12.2 presents four basic categories of addition and subtraction word problems.

Interventions That Use Sequential Steps

RIDE is a mnemonic strategy that identifies the steps needed to solve story problems successfully:

R—*Read* the problem correctly.

I—*Identify* the relevant information.

D—*Determine* the operations and unit for expressing the answer.

E—*Enter* the correct numbers and calculate and check the answer.

Also, Watanabe (1991) presents a five-step mnemonic strategy, SIGNS, that has been used successfully to teach students with learning difficulties to solve word problems:

S—*Survey* question.

I—*Identify* key words and labels.

G—*Graphically* draw problem.

N—*Note* operation(s) needed.

S—*Solve* and check problem.

Fleischner et al. (1987) discuss a study in which they used a strategy-based intervention with a cue card to help students with learning difficulties successfully solve addition and subtraction word problems. The cue card presents the following sequence:

1. *Read:* What is the question?
2. *Reread:* What is the necessary information?
3. *Think:* Putting together? = add; Taking apart? = subtract; Do I need all the information? Is it a multistep problem?
4. *Solve:* Write the equation.
5. *Check:* Recalculate, label, and compare.

In the study, during the *Read* step, students highlighted the question and wrote the metric pounds, inches, and so on. In the *Think* step, students were instructed to circle the largest number and write it. Then they were asked to see what happened to the number (i.e., did it get smaller or larger?). Finally, students used calculators to compute the answer so that they could focus on problem solving rather than on computation.

To teach problem-solving strategies to middle school students with learning problems, Montague (1992) used explicit modeling of cognitive and metacognitive strategies. The intervention also included verbal rehearsal, corrective and positive feedback, guided practice, and mastery checks. The specific cognitive strategies included the following:

1. *Read* for understanding.
2. *Paraphrase* in your own words.
3. *Visualize* a picture or diagram.
4. *Hypothesize* a plan to solve the problem.
5. *Estimate* or predict the answer.
6. *Compute* or do the arithmetic.
7. *Check* to make sure everything is right.

Montague reports that students readily learned these strategies and applied them successfully in solving word problems. Because some students failed to maintain and generalize the strategies, she encourages the use of techniques to promote generalization. Specifically, she suggests mnemonics and verbal rehearsal as techniques to help students remember and gain access to procedural math knowledge. Finally, Montague con-

TABLE 12.2

Categories of addition and subtraction word problems

Problem Type	Sample Problems
Join (elements are added to a given set)	1. Jan had 7 cookies. Kevin gave her 4 more. How many does Jan have altogether? (result unknown) 2. Jan has 7 cookies. How many more cookies does she need to have 11 cookies altogether? (change unknown) 3. Jan had some cookies. Kevin gave her 4 more cookies. Now she has 11 cookies. How many cookies did Jan have to start with? (start unknown)
Separate (elements are removed from a given set)	1. Jan had 11 cookies. She gave 7 cookies to Kevin. How many cookies does she have left? (result unknown) 2. Jan had 11 cookies. She gave some to Kevin. Now she has 7 cookies. How many did Jan give to Kevin? (change unknown) 3. Jan had some cookies. She gave 7 to Kevin. Now she has 4 cookies left. How many cookies did Jan have to start with? (start unknown)
Part-Part-Whole (comparisons between two disjoint sets)	1. Jan has 7 oatmeal cookies and 4 chocolate cookies. How many cookies does she have? 2. Jan has 11 cookies. Seven are oatmeal and the rest are chocolate. How many chocolate cookies does Jan have?
Compare	1. Jan has 11 cookies. Kevin has 7 cookies. How many more cookies does Jan have than Kevin? 2. Kevin has 7 cookies. Jan has 4 more than Kevin. How many cookies does Jan have? 3. Jan has 11 cookies. She has 7 more cookies than Kevin. How many cookies does Kevin have?

cludes that this type of strategy instruction holds much promise for helping students with learning problems achieve in math.

Hutchinson's (1993a) intervention for teaching adolescents with learning disabilities included explicit teacher modeling of strategies for solving algebra word problems. The strategies consisted of self-questions for representing and solving algebra word problems. The intervention also featured scripts to guide instruction, teacher prompts, encouragement, corrective feedback, student think alouds, guided practice, independent practice, and the use of graphs to monitor student progress. Selected self-questions for representing algebra word problems included the following: (1) Have I read and understood the sentence? (2) Do I have the whole picture, a representation, for this problem? and (3) Have I written the representation on the worksheet? The students displayed improved performance on algebra word problems, and maintenance and transfer of the problem-solving strategy were evident.

Interventions That Use the CSA Sequence

S. C. Howell and Barnhart (1992) developed a concrete-semiconcrete-abstract instructional sequence for teaching young students to solve word problems. The concrete stage features six steps and involves the systematic manipulation of objects to represent equations. The following activity is included in the sixth step. The student reads (or has someone read aloud) the problem, "There are three blue circles and two orange circles. How many circles are there?" The student places the correct numbers and colors of circles on the display boards. The student states, "I placed three blue circles on one side and two orange circles on the other side. To find out how many circles there are, I place the groups together, so three circles plus two circles equals five circles." If this activity is done correctly, the student goes to the next stage.

In the semiconcrete stage the student is guided through six steps in which manipulative objects are replaced with pictures or drawings. In the sixth step the student represents a story problem by drawing tallies, writing the equation, and calculating the answer.

In the abstract stage a series of five questions is presented to promote a thinking strategy for solving word problems (Eicholz et al., 1985):

1. What is the question?
2. What are the numbers in the problem?
3. What do I do to the numbers?
4. What is the answer?
5. Do I need to check the answer by drawing tallies?

The final step at the abstract stage involves having the student independently write a story problem. For example, the number sequence $7 - 4 = 3$ may be written as the following story problem: "My dog had 7 puppies. There are 4 male puppies and the rest are females. How many puppies are females?"

Mercer and Miller (1991–1993) present a learning strategy approach to teach students with learning problems math facts and word problems simultaneously. The multiplication word problems as presented in Figure 12.2 feature a graduated sequence of difficulty in which students learn to solve problems with extraneous information and create their own word problems. This CSA sequence guides the student to understand and apply multiplication to real-life word problems. Field-test results indicate excellent acquisition of math facts, generalization, and problem-solving skills.

Marsh and Cooke (1996) used manipulative objects to teach word problem solving to students with math learning difficulties. Their intervention uses the following procedures:

1. The student reads a word problem aloud and receives help with unknown words.
2. The teacher rereads each line of the problem and asks the student to set up the appropriate numerical values with manipulative objects.
3. The teacher uses prompts and cues to help the student create correct concrete representations of the word problem parts.
4. The student rereads the word problem while touching and counting the respective objects.
5. The student holds up a flash card showing the correct operation to use. An incorrect response results in correction procedures.

Marsh and Cooke report that this intervention helps students generalize problem-solving strategies to solve written problems.

Functional Math

Math instruction for students with learning problems rarely equips them with skills essential for independent living. Yet, the primary goal of math instruction for these students should be to prepare them to use math in their daily adult lives. To do this, math curricula must include content that promotes this pragmatic outcome. Math in the real world involves such skills as budgeting, estimating, purchasing, hiring, playing games of chance, reading graphs and tables, and planning travel and transportation. Moreover, it involves computing costs, change, taxes, interest, measurements, and profits and losses. Table 12.3 presents the math demands of daily living within five areas: consumer, employment, homemaking, recreation, and travel.

The systematic steps discussed in Chapter 4 and in this chapter effectively teach students with moderate to severe learning problems to apply essential math skills in authentic contexts. Also, because real-life math events are oral, students need to practice mental math calculations. *Real-Life Math,* which is presented in the section on commercial programs, addresses functional math skills.

Estimation

Estimation entails the forming of an approximate answer (e.g., approximating the cost of grocery items or the dimensions of a room or yard) and the ability to check the reasonableness of calculations (e.g., the reasonableness of a calculation total on a cash register). Estimation has applications to every aspect of mathematics and is an essential part of an effective mathematics program for students with learning problems (Bezuk & Cegelka, 1995; Bley & Thornton, 1995). Ashlock (1998) notes that the ability to estimate requires a robust "number sense." Specifically, he reports that students need to be fluent in math facts, understand numeration concepts, and understand mathematical relationships and rules. For example, calculators do not tell whether an answer is reasonable. Determining reasonableness requires computational knowledge and skills. Thus, the combination of a strong number sense and instruction in estimation skills enables students with learning problems to learn and apply estimation. Also, students need to distinguish events for using estimation, mental computation, paper-and-pencil calculations, and calculators.

sand is close to it on a number line. For example, have the student locate 42 on the number line and determine whether it is closer to 40 or to 50.

- Provide cards with two-digit numbers on them (e.g., 73, 58, 13, 27, 84, 39, 42, 87, 16, and 61). Instruct the student to spread the cards on a table, mentally round each number to the nearest ten, and then combine sets of numbers that sum to 100.
- Give a group of students a set of cards in which each card includes the name of a grocery item, a picture of the item, and its price. Advertisements from newspapers or magazines can be used. After one student turns over three cards, have all members of the group estimate the amount of money needed to buy the items indicated on the cards. The students can discuss their estimates, and a record is kept of the number of times their estimates agree. If several groups are involved, they can compare the respective number of agreements. A variation of this activity involves giving the students several cards and asking them whether a specific amount of money (e.g., $20.00) is enough to buy the items. Finally, calculators can be used to compare the cost of the items with the student estimates (Bezuk & Cegelka, 1995).
- Color cue or underline the "thinking" digit (i.e., the digit to the right of the digit that changes when rounding) to help the student focus on the digit that influences the rounding process (Bley & Thornton, 1995). This activity can help the student round money amounts to make estimates (e.g., to round $7.28 to the nearest whole number, the *2* would be colored or underlined, and to round $1.76 to the nearest dime, the *6* would be colored or underlined).

Calculators

Calculators are used widely in our society, making computation accurate and easy. The National Council of Teachers of Mathematics (1980) recommends that calculators be routinely available to students in elementary school. Because effective math instruction stresses understanding, problem solving, and computation, the instructional role of calculators needs clarification. Suydam (1980) believes that calculators should be used primarily with problems that students are capable of doing by hand. Also, students should *understand* the math concept (e.g., multiplication) involved in the computation before using a calculator to solve problems. Paper and pencil may be most effective with simple computation problems, whereas calculators are better suited for complex or tedious problems (e.g., long division) (Lovitt, 1989).

Initially, students need to learn the correct procedures for using a calculator. Proper early instruction helps promote positive experiences with calculators and prepares students for successful applications of the calculator as they advance in mathematics. Some guidelines for early calculator instruction include the following:

- Encourage the student to press the *Clear* key twice prior to beginning each problem on the calculator.
- Point out the sequential number configuration on the calculator and the location of the initial function keys the student will use.
- Encourage the student to watch the display panel after each entry and check the results for reasonableness (Heddens & Speer, 1997).
- Stress that weak batteries or broken calculators can produce incorrect answers (Heddens & Speer, 1997).
- Encourage the student to operate the calculator with the hand not used for writing. This facilitates the ability to record the results with one hand and operate the calculator with the other hand (Heddens & Speer, 1997).

Hembree (1986) reviewed 79 studies on the use of calculators and reports the following findings:

- When used appropriately, calculators promote skill acquisition.
- Sustained calculator use in the fourth grade appears to interfere with skill development.
- The use of calculators when taking tests results in higher achievement scores.
- The use of calculators improves the attitudes of students toward mathematics.

Moreover, Fleischner et al. (1987) note that the use of calculators allows students to focus on problem solving rather than becoming bogged down in computations; thus, their use may be especially helpful with students who have difficulty solving problems. Heddens and Speer (1997) note that calculators can help students develop understanding of place value, reversibility, relationships among numbers, operations, and mathematical estimates. Selected activities with calculators include the following:

- Instruct the young student to place interesting or personal numbers on the display screen (e.g., age, age of best friend, today's calendar date, address number, and telephone number). Provide copies of the student's personal numbers if not known (Heddens & Speer, 1997).

- Present real-life problem situations for the student to solve on the calculator. For example, place three books on one student's desk and five books on another student's desk. State the problem situation and ask the student to use the calculator to show how many total books are on the two desks. Discuss the reasonableness of the answer.

- Instruct the student to enter *5748* into the calculator. Next, ask the student to use addition or subtraction to change *7* to *0*. Ask for the new number and discuss why *5048* is correct (i.e., subtracted 700). Repeat the task by changing *5* to *6*, *4* to *2*, and *8* to *1* (Ashlock, 1998).

- Have the student round each addend in an addition problem to the nearest hundred and estimate a sum. Then have the student use a calculator to determine the actual sum of the addends and compare the answer with the estimate. Discuss reasonableness of estimates. For example:

Student work:

329	*300*
289	*300*
474	*500*
+ 336	*300*
	1400 (estimated sum)

- Instruct the student to use the calculator to divide several numbers by 10. The student should generalize that every time the *Equals* (=) key is pressed, the decimal point of the number divided by 10 moves one space to the left (Heddens & Speer, 1997).

- Provide various math problems for the student to complete. Instruct the student to use the calculator as a self-correcting device to check answers to completed computations.

☀ MATH ACTIVITIES

Various activities can be used for teaching or practicing math skills. Activities can be used to stimulate interest, individualize instruction, extend practice, and provide variety in teaching methods. The activities presented in this section and the instructional games and self-correcting materials

presented in the following sections promote the development of math skills.

Readiness

In addition to the selected activities in this section, readiness areas and related assessment tasks are presented in Chapter 11.

Classification   Give the student a collection of circles, squares, and triangles of various colors. Have the student classify the items according to shape and then according to color. Other useful objects in classification activities are buttons, wooden blocks, dominoes, spoons, nails, and golf tees.

Ordering   Provide the student a set of different-size objects (e.g., wooden blocks, buttons, straws, nails, washers, shapes, and Cuisenaire rods). Have the student arrange them in order from the smallest to the largest or vice versa.

One-to-One Correspondence   Provide a pegboard design and instruct the student to duplicate it. Other helpful activities include putting screws on bolts, passing out papers, playing musical chairs, and adding the same part to several items (such as strings to kites, sails to boats, stems to flowers, or straws to cups).

Counting   Provide the student with Language Master cards with a number of objects to count and a taped message (such as "One, two, three— three cats").

Give the student a picture of several monkeys hanging together or a card with a number on it. Provide a barrel of toy monkeys and a hook (on the wall or on a stand) and ask the student to show the number on the picture or the card by hanging up the same number of toy monkeys.

Assign each student a secret number. Have a student knock on the door the number of times that matches his or her secret number. The class members can respond, "Come in Number Five (Seven, Fourteen, . . .)."

Have the student circle the number that corresponds to the configuration.

	4	5	6	8
	2	3	4	7
	7	6	9	8
	3	5	6	4

Attach a number line to the top of the student's desk to provide a helpful reference.

| 1 | 2 | 3 | 4 | 5 | 6 | 7 | 8 | 9 |

Greater Than, Less Than   Use a number line to help students decide which numbers are greater than and less than in completing sentences with < or > symbols (Heddens & Speer, 1997). For example:

0 1 2 3 4 5 6 7 8 9 10

Fill each blank with < or >: 7 _ 5   0 _ 4   10 _ 8

Provide a drawing of a "creature" with numbers written in the sections of the body. Instruct the student to mark an X on each body part that has a number greater than 15 and less than 39.

Place Value

Chip-Trading Games   Use chip-trading games to teach place value (Ashlock, 1998). These games stress the idea of exchanging many for one. The values of chips correspond to a numeration place value pattern. For example, white chips represent ones, blue chips represent tens, and red chips represent hundreds. The student rolls a die and receives the number of ones indicated on the die. Exchanges for higher valued chips are made according to the rules of the game (four for one if

base 4, ten for one if base 10). The first player to get a chip of a certain high value wins.

Bank Game   Use a game board and a bank to help students understand place value (Ashlock, 1998). For example:

In computing the problem

$$527$$
$$+\ 893$$

the student places 5 hundreds, 2 tens, and 7 ones blocks in the upper row. Then the student places the appropriate blocks for 893 in the second row. Starting with the ones (at green dot), the student collects 10 ones if possible and moves all remaining ones below the wide line. The student trades to the bank each 10 ones collected for the correct number of tens. The tens collected from the bank are placed at the top of the tens column. In this problem (see example), 10 ones are traded to the bank for 1 ten, and zero blocks are placed below the wide line in the ones column. Next, 10 tens are traded for a hundreds block, and 2 tens blocks are placed below the wide line in the tens column. The student trades 10 hundreds for a thousands block and then places 4 hundreds blocks below the wide line in the hundreds column. Finally, the student moves the thousands block below the wide line in the thousands column. The student counts the blocks in each column and writes the answer, 1,420.

Making Columns Present FIND as a mnemonic strategy to help the student understand and solve place value problems:

F—*Find* the columns.

I—*Insert* the ts.

N—*Name* the columns.

D—*Determine* the numbers of hundreds, tens, and ones.

For example:

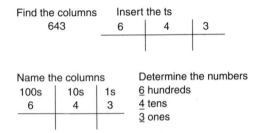

Find the columns   Insert the ts
643   6 | 4 | 3

Name the columns   Determine the numbers
100s | 10s | 1s   6 hundreds
 6 | 4 | 3   4 tens
                       3 ones

Labeling Columns Insert the initial letters for ones, tens, hundreds, and so on over their respective columns:

t th	th	h	t	o
	4	5	4	7
	1	7	5	6
+	3	3	1	1

Vertical lines can be in colors for additional cueing.

Pegboard Use a pegboard to teach borrowing and carrying. For example:

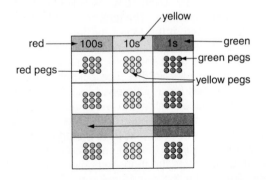

Use masking tape to divide the pegboard into three rows and three columns, with nine holes in each subdivision. An arrow is drawn from right to left on a piece of tape that separates the bottom third. This line serves as an equals sign; answers to problems always are shown by inserting pegs below this line. In addition to helping the student recall the different values for each column, color coding reminds the student to start with green (*go*). The top two rows hold the pegs representing the first two numbers in an addition or subtraction problem. To solve 5 + 6, the student starts to transfer all the pegs in the ones column to the ones section below the arrow. The student discovers that not all 11 pegs will fit in the bottom row of the ones column. Consequently, the student must exchange 10 green pegs for 1 yellow peg (10 ones for 1 ten) and carry this yellow peg into the tens column. Borrowing consists of trading 1 yellow peg for 10 green pegs and putting the green pegs in the top row of the ones column.

Dice Game Use a dice game in which three different-color dice are used. The colors correspond to color-coded lines drawn on paper to represent hundreds, tens, and ones. The student rolls the dice, writes the number in the appropriate columns, and reads it. The player with the highest number wins.

Place Value Cards Make cards with numbers on one side and tallies for the number of hundreds, tens, and so on in that number on the other side. For example:

431

Front

100s	10s	1s
////	///	/

Back

Also, strings can be attached to the cards for stringing beads to represent the number in each column.

Place Value Table Instruct the student to complete the missing spaces in the place value table (Heddens & Speer, 1997). For example:

100 Less	10 Less	1 Less		1 Greater	10 Greater	100 Greater
178			278	279		
		141	142		152	
	359		369			469
420			520			
		400	401	402		

Numerical Expanders

Use folding numerical expanders to help the student show the meaning of place value (Heddens & Speer, 1997). For example, the number 642 can be displayed in various ways:

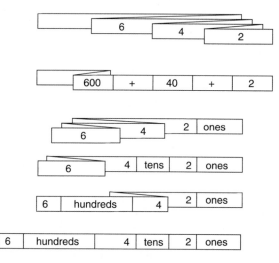

General Computation

This section presents activities that easily are adapted for any of the four operations. Many of the games and self-correcting materials presented later in this chapter also are useful with all four operations.

Small Work Samples   Present assignments in small segments. Because of attention problems or lack of interest, some students cannot complete an entire worksheet of math problems. Presenting assignments in small segments may help these students complete as many problems as their classmates. Cut a worksheet into small parts (rows), or place problems on cards that the student picks up each time a problem is completed.

Math Board   Glue library pockets on poster board and cover the outside portion of the pocket with transparent, self-adhesive paper. Use water-base felt pens to write problems on the pockets. Corresponding answers are written on cardboard strips. The student is instructed to match the correct answers to the pockets. The problems can be removed with a cloth so that new problems can be presented.

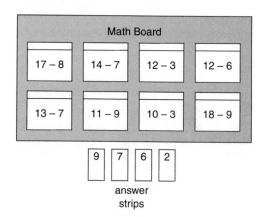

Mystery Math   Cut tagboard into 5″ × 5″ squares or draw a square on a ditto. Put a decorative drawing, decal, or picture in the middle. Space off seven or more lines on each side of the decorative square in the middle. Write numbers at random on the left side. If the concept being taught is ÷6 and the first number is 42, the first number on the right should be 7. All other lines on the right side remain blank. The process is repeated with the top and bottom lines. By looking at the top lines on the left and right sides, the student tries to figure out the mathematical function involved. The student then fills in the remaining blanks using the same function. Next the process is repeated with the top and bottom lines.

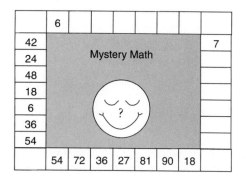

Learning Ladders   Provide the student with math problems in a vertical order on strips of paper or cardboard. Have the student start at the bottom of the "ladder" (strip) and proceed upward as problems are answered correctly. A marker is placed at the last problem answered correctly. When the student gets three markers (e.g., star, tack, or pin) on the top problem, progress is recorded and the student is allowed to take the strip home. Learning ladders also can be used to practice number identification, telling time, and coin identification.

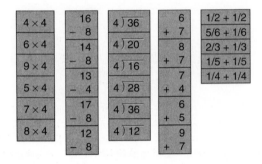

Addition

Nail Abacus   Use a nail abacus for teaching counting, place value (regrouping), and addition. Make the nail abacus by driving five finishing nails at 2-inch intervals into a wooden board 2″ by 10″ by ¹/₂″. The abacus is used by placing washers or beads on the nails. To display the number 43,062 on the abacus, two washers are placed on the ones nail, six washers are placed on the tens nail, no washers on the hundreds nail, three washers on the thousands nail, and four washers on the ten-thousands nail:

ten-thousands   thousands   hundreds   tens   ones

The student adds on the abacus by placing washers or beads on the appropriate nails and counting. For example, in solving the problem 43 + 32, the student first would place three washers on the ones nail and four washers on the tens nail. Next, 32 would be shown on the abacus by placing two washers on the ones nail and three washers on

the tens nail. Now the student computes the sums of the ones (5) and the tens (7) by counting the washers on the respective nails.

Instruct the student to follow these rules about regrouping when using the abacus:

1. Ten discs on the ones nail are exchanged for one disc on the tens nail.
2. Ten discs on the tens nail are exchanged for one disc on the hundreds nail.
3. No nail can have more than nine discs remaining.

Thus, in solving 18 + 26, several steps are used:

1. Display 18 on the abacus.
2. Leaving the 18, put 26 on the abacus.
3. Check to see whether any nails are overloaded (ten or more).
4. Because the ones nail is overloaded with 14 discs, exchange 10 ones discs for one more disc on the tens nail.
5. Record the answer in a table. For example:

Tens	Ones	
1	8	
2	6	
3	14	sum
4	4	regrouped sum

Number Line   Provide a number line to help the student compute addition facts. Number lines for use in seatwork are made easily by cutting strips from a manila folder. Besides helping the student compute, they provide models for the correct form of numerals. In computing 2 + 4, the student is taught to start at 2 and move four spaces to the right to obtain the answer (6) (see Figure 12.3). Later, the dot patterns can be eliminated and the numbers can be increased to 18.

Dot Addition   Place reference points on numerals to help students with math problems (Kramer & Krug, 1973):

FIGURE 12.3
Number line showing computation of 2 + 4

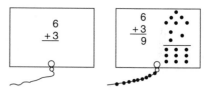

Kramer and Krug note that the system offers consistency in perception of the numbers and provides direct association between the number and its value. Actually, the dots provide a semiconcrete-level task for basic addition facts. Also, the dot cues can be faded as the student becomes proficient in learning the facts. For example:

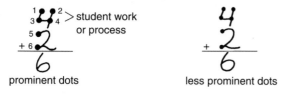

Computational Cues   Provide cues for helping the student remember to regroup or recall the steps in an algorithm. For example, the square reminds the student to carry:

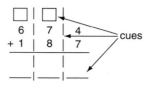

Direction Cue   For the student who adds from left to right rather than right to left, place a green dot over the ones column to serve as a reminder to begin computation there.

Bead Addition   Attach a string to cards displaying math facts so that the student can put beads on the string when solving the problem. When using the card, the student computes the addition problem by threading the right number of beads onto the shoelace or string. The student

can check the answer by looking on the back of the card.

Addition Squares   Divide a square into nine smaller squares. Instruct the student to add across and down and to fill in all missing addends or sums. If the computations are accurate, the right column addends and the bottom row addends equal the same sum.

4	7	11
6	8	14
10	15	25

— super sum

4		7
	2	
5		

231		720
		175
425		

Complete the missing squares

Addition Facts Family   Present the addition facts (sums 0 to 18) within a number family framework to help the student learn them (see Figure 12.4). By teaching that any number plus 0 equals the number, and any number plus 1 is counting by 1, only 64 facts out of 100 must be memorized. If the doubles are taught in terms of doubling the addend to compute the sum, only 56 facts remain to be memorized.

Subtraction

Nail Abacus   For solving the problem 57 − 34, have the student put 57 on the nail abacus: five

FIGURE 12.4
Addition facts family

0	1	2	3	4	5	6	7	8	9
0 | 0*	0 | 1*	0 | 2*	0 | 3*	0 | 4*	0 | 5*	0 | 6*	0 | 7*	0 | 8*	0 | 9*
	1 | 0*	2 | 0*	3 | 0*	4 | 0*	5 | 0*	6 | 0*	7 | 0*	8 | 0*	9 | 0*
		1 | 1*	1 | 2*	1 | 3*	1 | 4*	1 | 5*	1 | 6*	1 | 7*	1 | 8*
			2 | 1*	3 | 1*	4 | 1*	5 | 1*	6 | 1*	7 | 1*	8 | 1*
				2 | 2*	2 | 3	2 | 4	2 | 5	2 | 6	2 | 7
					3 | 2	4 | 2	5 | 2	6 | 2	7 | 2
						3 | 3*	3 | 4	3 | 5	3 | 6
							4 | 3	5 | 3	6 | 3
								4 | 4*	4 | 5
									5 | 4

10	11	12	13	14	15	16	17	18
1 | 9*	2 | 9	3 | 9	4 | 9	5 | 9	6 | 9	7 | 9	8 | 9	9 | 9*
9 | 1*	9 | 2	9 | 3	9 | 4	9 | 5	9 | 6	9 | 7	9 | 8	
2 | 8	3 | 8	4 | 8	5 | 8	6 | 8	7 | 8	8 | 8*		
8 | 2	8 | 3	8 | 4	8 | 5	8 | 6	8 | 7			
3 | 7	4 | 7	5 | 7	6 | 7	7 | 7*				
7 | 3	7 | 4	7 | 5	7 | 6					
4 | 6	5 | 6	6 | 6*						
6 | 4	6 | 5							
5 | 5*								

Note: Facts marked with an asterisk do not need to be memorized.

washers on the tens nail and seven washers on the ones nail. The teacher can use the "take away" or the "find the missing addend" approach. With the take away approach, the student is instructed to take away 34 (3 tens, 4 ones) from the abacus and count the remaining washers to find the difference. With the missing addend approach, the student is instructed to remove the known addend (34) from the sum (57) and count the remaining washers to determine the missing addend. For example:

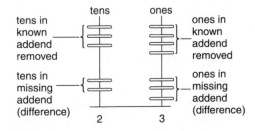

For solving 57 – 39, have the student put 57 on the abacus. Because the student cannot take 9 ones from 7 ones, 1 ten is taken off the tens nail and replaced with 10 washers on the ones nail. Now 9 washers are removed from the ones nail, and 3 washers are removed from the tens nail. The number left on the abacus is the answer.

Number Line Provide a number line to help the student compute subtraction facts. In solving the problem 14 – 8, the student is taught to start at 14 and move eight spaces to the left to obtain the answer (6) (see Figure 12.5).

Addition–Subtraction Pattern Improve understanding of the relationship between addition and subtraction by having the student compute the sum of two addends and then subtract the two addends from the sum.

FIGURE 12.5
Number line showing
computation of 14 − 8

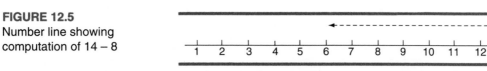

$$
\begin{array}{r}
47 \\
+ 23 \\
\hline
70
\end{array}
\qquad
\begin{array}{r}
70 \\
- 23 \\
\hline
47
\end{array}
\qquad
\begin{array}{r}
70 \\
- 47 \\
\hline
23
\end{array}
$$

Circle Cues   Use circle cues to help the student subtract with regrouping.

Let ⬤ be 100; let ◯ be 10; let • be 1.

$$
\begin{array}{r}
231 \\
-\ 64 \\
\hline
167
\end{array}
$$

1 hundred   6 tens   7 ones

The remaining circles that are not
marked through represent the answer.

Self-Monitoring Subtraction Strategy   Provide a modified worksheet format to help the student remember the strategies for regrouping in subtraction (Frank & Brown, 1992). Each problem on the worksheet has cue words above it to remind the student to follow the strategy steps:

1. Begin? In the 1s column.
2. Bigger? Which number is bigger?
3. Borrow? If the bottom number is bigger, I must borrow.
4. Basic Facts? Remember basic facts. Use drawings or touch math if needed.

For example:

		___	Begin
___	___	___	Bigger
___	___	___	Borrow
___	___	___	Basic Facts
7	6	5	
−2	8	7	

If the teacher develops a problem-solving sequence to other operations, this self-monitoring strategy can be modified for use in addition, multiplication, and division.

Multiplication

Array Multiplication   Have the student form arrays using tiles, pegboards, or other objects and determine the number of rows and columns. Ex-

plain that the number of rows and the number of columns represent the factors in a multiplication problem. Then instruct the student to write the multiplication facts represented by various arrays.

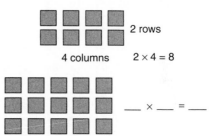

2 rows

4 columns $2 \times 4 = 8$

___ × ___ = ___

Next, present multiplication problems and have the student form the corresponding arrays.

Dot Arrays   Provide dot arrays and instruct the student to write the fact below each array.

$3 \times 4 = 12$ _____   _____

Napier's Rods   Use Napier's rods to strengthen the student's recall of multiplication facts or to check seatwork. The rods can be constructed from heavy construction paper, tongue depressors, or popsicle sticks. They consist of ten strips numbered according to the pattern presented in Figure 12.6. The numbers on top of the strips are the multiplicands, and the numbers on the index are the multipliers. The products are in the squares with the diagonal lines. By putting a strip next to the index, the student easily can determine the product of the respective factors. For example:

FIGURE 12.6
Napier's rods

Index	1	2	3	4	5	6	7	8	9
1	0/1	0/2	0/3	0/4	0/5	0/6	0/7	0/8	0/9
2	0/2	0/4	0/6	0/8	1/0	1/2	1/4	1/6	1/8
3	0/3	0/6	0/9	1/2	1/5	1/8	2/1	2/4	2/7
4	0/4	0/8	1/2	1/6	2/0	2/4	2/8	3/2	3/6
5	0/5	1/0	1/5	2/0	2/5	3/0	3/5	4/0	4/5
6	0/6	1/2	1/8	2/4	3/0	3/6	4/2	4/8	5/4
7	0/7	1/4	2/1	2/8	3/5	4/2	4/9	5/6	6/3
8	0/8	1/6	2/4	3/2	4/0	4/8	5/6	6/4	7/2
9	0/9	1/8	2/7	3/6	4/5	5/4	6/3	7/2	8/1

The rods can be used for multiplying more than one digit by a one-digit number. For example, to compute 73 × 4, the rods would be lined up accordingly:

To compute the product, the diagonal columns are added right to left.

2   9   2   } product of 73 × 4

Multiplication Chart   Provide a multiplication chart so the student can check work and do seatwork. For example:

1	2	3	4	5	6	7	8	9
2	4	6	8	10	12	14	16	18
3	6	9	12	15	18	21	24	27
4	8	12	16	20	24	28	32	36
9	18	27	36	45	54	63	72	81

Addition–Multiplication Pattern   To facilitate understanding of the relationship between addition and multiplication, have the student first add the same number several times, then multiply that number by the times it was added. For example:

$$7 + 7 + 7 + 7 + 7 = 35$$
$$7 \times 5 = 35$$

Dot Cards   Make ten sets of cards representing numerals from 1 to 9. Set 1 contains nine cards with one dot on each card; Set 2 contains nine cards with two dots on each card; Set 3 contains nine cards with three dots on each card; and so on. Instruct the student to use the cards to compute multiplication problems.

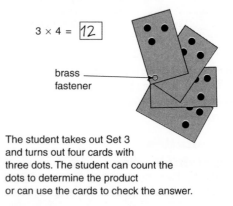

3 × 4 = 12

brass fastener

The student takes out Set 3 and turns out four cards with three dots. The student can count the dots to determine the product or can use the cards to check the answer.

Clothespin Multiplication   Instruct the student to fasten clothespins to cards to display multiplication models using groups (cards) and objects (clothespins) (Heddens & Speer, 1997). For example, the student can display 2×3 and then answer questions:

How many groups? (2)
How many pins in each group? (3)
How many total pins? (6)

Division

Number Line   To divide with the number line, have the student count backward from the dividend by the set determined by the divisor until 1 is reached. The quotient is the number of sets used in counting from the dividend to 1. In computing $18 \div 3$, for example, the student counts by threes because the divisor is 3, and then the student counts the loops for the answer. Thus, $18 \div 3 = 6$ (see Figure 12.7).

Dividing Numbers into Parts   To facilitate understanding of division, have the student divide numbers into equal parts. For example:

$$12 = \underline{}\ 3s \qquad 24 = \underline{}\ 6s$$
$$9 = \underline{}\ 3s \qquad 36 = \underline{}\ 6s$$
$$16 = \underline{}\ 4s \qquad 18 = \underline{}\ 6s$$

Dot Division   Use dots to present division problems and have the student write the numerical statement. For example:

Determining the First Digit in the Quotient   Provide several long division problems and ask the student to find the first number in the quotient.

Long Division Steps   Present a face illustrating the four steps in long division problems to remind the student to follow the steps.

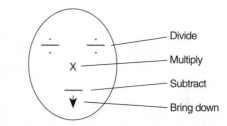

Also, the words **D**addy, **M**other, **S**ister, and **B**rother can be used to help the student remember the four steps in long division.

Fractions

Number Line   Use the fraction number line for illustrating the value of improper fractions (see Figure 12.8). Also, ask the student to indicate whether fractions are equal to one whole, greater than one whole, less than one whole, or equal to several wholes. Use the number line to illustrate simple division problems involving fractions. For example:

$$= 3 \text{ or } 1\tfrac{1}{2} \div \tfrac{1}{2} = 3$$

Fraction Chart   Use fraction charts to show the relationship of a fraction to 1 and to other fractions. Activities with the charts include determining greater-than and less-than values of fractions,

FIGURE 12.7
Number line showing
computation of $18 \div 3$

FIGURE 12.8
Fraction number line

finding the lowest common denominator, and determining equivalent fractions.

1							
1/2				1/2			
1/4		1/4		1/4		1/4	
1/8	1/8	1/8	1/8	1/8	1/8	1/8	1/8

Front

1					
1/3		1/3		1/3	
1/6	1/6	1/6	1/6	1/6	1/6
1/12	1/12	1/12	1/12	1/12	1/12	1/12	1/12	1/12	1/12	1/12	1/12

Back

Matching Graphic Form to Numerical Symbol   Have the student match fractions in word or graphic form to the numerical symbol for that fraction. To do this, provide the student with library pockets labeled $^1/_4$, $^1/_8$, and so forth and a stack of cards with graphic representations of a fraction. Have the student match the cards with the correct pocket. For example:

pocket   cards

Use discs (concrete level) or circles (semiconcrete level) to illustrate the division of fractions. For example:

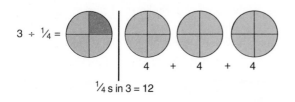

$3 \div \frac{1}{4} =$

4 + 4 + 4

$\frac{1}{4}$s in 3 = 12

Also, grids help illustrate division by fractions.

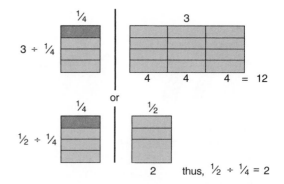

$3 \div \frac{1}{4}$

3

4   4   4   = 12

or

$\frac{1}{2} \div \frac{1}{4}$

$\frac{1}{4}$ $\frac{1}{2}$

2   thus, $\frac{1}{2} \div \frac{1}{4} = 2$

Fraction Bars   Make fraction bars out of tongue depressors, popsicle sticks, or construction paper. On each bar, the multiples of a single-digit number are written. For example:

When one bar is placed over another bar, fractions are formed. The two numbers at the extreme left indicate the fraction formed (such as $^3/_4$); the remaining fractions are a set in which each member of the set is equivalent (such as $^3/_4$, $^6/_8$, $^9/_{12}$, and so on). The fraction and its equivalents are formed by putting the 3 bar over the 5 bar. For example:

Sample activities include reading the equivalent fractions, forming fractions with other bars, and making new bars.

To compute with fraction bars, instruct the student to use the bars to add two fractions, such as $^2/_3 + ^2/_5$. The student should follow these steps:

1. Form the fraction $^2/_3$ by placing the 2 bar over the 3 bar.

2. Form the fraction $^2/_5$.

3. Look at the denominators of each fraction and locate the lowest number that is the same on each denominator bar. In this example it is 15.
4. Slide the fraction $^2/_5$ over until $^6/_{15}$ lies directly under $^{10}/_{15}$.

fractions with same denominator

5. To add, simply add the numbers on the numerator bars: $10 + 6 = 16$; thus, the sum is $^{16}/_{15}$.
6. To subtract, simply subtract one numerator from the other: $10 - 6 = 4$; thus, the difference or missing addend is $^4/_{15}$.
7. To divide $^2/_3$ by $^2/_5$, use the common denominator method:

$$^2/_3 \div ^2/_5 = ^{10}/_{15} \div ^6/_{15} =$$
$$(10 \div 6) \div (15 \div 15) =$$
$$(10 \div 6) \div 1 = 10 \div 6 = ^{10}/_6$$

Multiplying Fractions with Grids   Have the student draw a grid and represent the two fractions that are being multiplied on it. The student should follow these steps:

1. Make a rectangle and section it equally into the number of squares indicated by the product of the denominators. For example, $^2/_3 \times ^1/_4 = 12$ squares.

2. Represent $^2/_3$ on the grid by shading in the correct number of rows.

$= ^2/_3$

3. Represent $^1/_4$ by shading in the correct number of columns.

$= ^1/_4$

4. The number of squares that overlap represents the numerator of the product of $^2/_3 \times ^1/_4$; the total number of squares represents the denominator.

overlap

$= ^2/_{12}$; thus
$^2/_3 \times ^1/_4 = ^2/_{12}$

At the concrete level, the student can use tiles of different sizes.

Time

Number Line   Use a circular number line from 1 to 60 to help the student learn to tell time (Reisman, 1982), as shown in Figure 12.9. The number line can be used to help the student construct a clock face, determine the minutes "after the hour," and note the relationship between the hour-hand movement (5 increments per hour) and the minute-hand movement (60 increments per hour).

Record Schedule   Mark the correct time on clocks for each school bell. Larger clocks can be used to record major events.

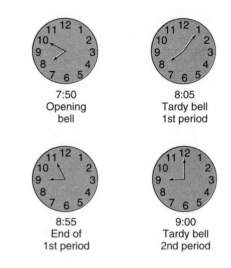

7:50
Opening
bell

8:05
Tardy bell
1st period

8:55
End of
1st period

9:00
Tardy bell
2nd period

Examining Schedules Provide the student with blank clock faces and a variety of schedules (such as those for television programs, a movie, or a bus). Have the student record schedule times on the clock faces.

Calendar Travel Provide the student with a calendar and a die. The student rolls the die and moves a marker the indicated number of spaces, beginning with the first day. Then the student records the die number and the day of the week on which the marker lands. The task is completed when the student reaches the end of the month.

FIGURE 12.9
Clock face with a circular number line

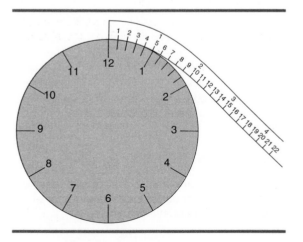

Calendar Quiz Provide the student with a calendar and a worksheet with numerous questions. Ask the student to respond to questions such as the following:

1. How many days are in a week?
2. On what day is the 27th of May?
3. List the dates of all the Wednesdays in January.
4. How many months are in a year?
5. List the months with 31 days.

Decimals/Money

Cardboard Regions Use cardboard regions for displaying decimals and fractions at the semi-concrete level. The teacher can shade in various squares and instruct the student to write the equivalent decimal. Graph paper can be glued to the cardboard regions to display specific numbers.

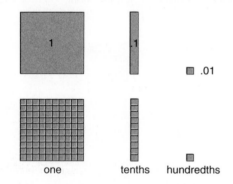

one   tenths   hundredths

Number Line Use number lines to display decimals and their fractional equivalents (see Figure 12.10). In addition to using the lines as an aid in computing decimal–fraction problems, the student can be instructed to fill in blank sections of number lines.

Completion of Missing Parts Instruct the student to fill in missing parts of various charts and figures as an activity in learning the relationship among fractions, decimals, and percentages.

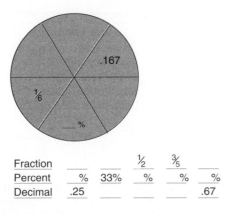

Fraction			½	⅗	
Percent	%	33%	%	%	%
Decimal	.25				.67

Expanded Place Value Chart   Use an expanded place value chart to demonstrate the relationship among column values, column names, and decimals (see Figure 12.11). An activity consists of leaving parts unlabeled and instructing the student to fill in the missing labels.

Money Cards   Use money cards to help the student determine correct change. For example, the following $10.00 change card can be used to compute correct change when a $10.00 bill is received:

$10.00 Money Card

To solve the problem of how much change to give when a $10.00 bill is received and the purchase is for $6.77, the student simply marks out the amount of the purchase on the card. The remaining money is the correct change.

Real Money   Use real money as often as possible to teach money values. For example, provide combinations of coins and ask the student to total the amounts. Money stamps from commercial publishers also can be used.

Coupon Shopping   On a manila folder, draw a chart and label the columns *Grocery Items, Price, Coupon Value,* and *Actual Cost.* In the *Coupon Value* column, write the value of the coupon or use the real coupon. Ask the student to determine the actual cost of each item. For example:

Grocery Items	Price	Coupon Value	Actual Cost
1. coffee	$3.12	10% off	_____
2. pickles	$1.14	$ .15	_____
3. cereal	$1.39	15% off	_____
4. jelly	$ .79	$ .20	_____

Taking Orders   Have the student become a waiter and write down orders from a prerecorded cassette tape. Using the menus provided, the student can look up the prices of the items ordered, compute the cost of the order, and write the total on the order pad.

Chance Shopping   Provide a block with dollar amounts on each side and a laminated shopping card with the following statements:

1. How much do you have to spend?
2. What are you buying?
3. What page is it on in the catalog?
4. How much are you spending?
5. How much do you have left?

The student tosses the block to see how much money he or she has to spend. Then the student

FIGURE 12.10
Decimal and fraction number lines

.0	.1	.2	.3	.4	.5	.6	.7	.8	.9	1.0
0/10	1/10	2/10	3/10	4/10	5/10	6/10	7/10	8/10	9/10	10/10

.00	.05	.10	.15	.20	.25	.30	.35	.40	.45	.50
0/100	5/100	10/100	15/100	20/100	25/100	30/100	35/100	40/100	45/100	50/100

0	1.4	2.8	4.2	5.6	7.0	8.4	9.8	11.2
0	1 4/10	2 8/10	4 2/10	5 6/10	7 0/10	8 4/10	9 8/10	11 2/10

FIGURE 12.11
Expanded place value chart

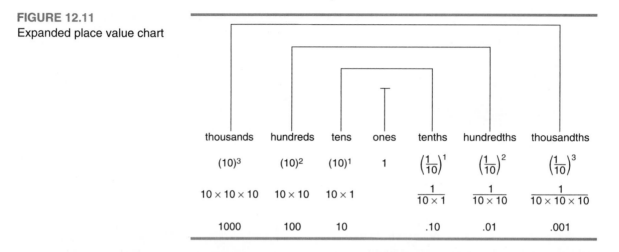

thousands	hundreds	tens	ones	tenths	hundredths	thousandths
$(10)^3$	$(10)^2$	$(10)^1$	1	$\left(\frac{1}{10}\right)^1$	$\left(\frac{1}{10}\right)^2$	$\left(\frac{1}{10}\right)^3$
$10 \times 10 \times 10$	10×10	10×1		$\frac{1}{10 \times 1}$	$\frac{1}{10 \times 10}$	$\frac{1}{10 \times 10 \times 10}$
1000	100	10		.10	.01	.001

looks through a catalog to find items that can be bought for that amount of money. Next, the student answers the questions on the card.

Store Comparison Have the student prepare a list of grocery items and find which supermarket offers the best price. The items and stores can be listed on a chart.

Check the Charge Make worksheets with instructions to check the cashier's slips and see whether they are added correctly. For example:

$1.19		$1.38
.99		2.64
.37		.26
1.03		.15
$3.38		**$4.43**

Measurement

Measure Box Provide the student with a box of objects to measure (such as popsicle stick, comb, paper clip, and straw) and a worksheet with the objects listed on it. Have the student measure the objects and record their lengths in inches and centimeters on the worksheet. This activity can be repeated for weighing objects.

Measurement and You Have the student complete the following worksheet:

Your height:
_____feet _____inches

Your weight:
_____pounds

Your speed:
Number of seconds to run 40 yards: _____seconds

Your agility:
Number of seconds to deal 52 cards:
_____seconds

Your writing speed:
Number of times you can write your first name in one minute: _____times

Number of times you can write 6s in one minute: _____times

Your reading speed:
Number of words read in one minute:
_____words

Circumference of your head: _____inches

Circumference of your waist: _____inches

Word Problems

Reality Math Use classroom activities to help an adolescent face the realities of adult life. For example, have the student locate a job in the newspaper and use the salary quoted in the paper to compute net pay. Also, have the student compute living expenses by using newspaper ads, apartment rental ads, car ads, tax guides, catalogs, and brochures with insurance rates.

Story Problems   Initially, provide the student with simple, interesting word problems. This helps the student understand that sentences may request specific math computations. For example:

1. How much are 3 marbles and 4 marbles?
2. What number represents a triple?
3. How many points is a field goal in football?
4. To get a first down in football, how many yards must you gain?
5. How many points are 10 baskets in basketball?

Have the student write a number sentence after reading a story problem. For example:

Mary has 6 comic books. She has read 2 of them. How many books does she have left to read? $6 - 2 = $ ____

Table Problems   Provide problems that include computing answers from information on a table. An interesting activity that requires computing percentages and decimals from a table is to give the student baseball standings (or football or basketball standings, depending on the season) from the newspaper with only the won/lost record beside each team. Have the student do the following:

1. Compute the percentage for each team in the American League East and the National League East.
2. Place the American and National League teams in order based on their won/lost records.
3. Determine how many teams have records over .500.
4. Determine how many percentage points the team in the American League East with the most losses is behind the team with the most wins.

☀ INSTRUCTIONAL GAMES IN MATH

Math War

Materials: Sets of index cards consisting of family patterns. (With sums-to-9, each of the numbers from 1 to 9 has a family of two one-digit addends. The entire set for sums-to-9 includes 54 cards. The family pattern for 7, for example, is $0 + 7$, $7 + 0$, $1 + 6$, $6 + 1$, $2 + 5$, $5 + 2$, $3 + 4$, $4 + 3$.)

Directions: All players shuffle their 54-card decks. With cards face down, one card at a time is turned face up. The player who turns the card showing the number fact with the largest sum wins all the turned cards. The players then turn their next card. If cards of equal sums are turned up at the same time, players with the equivalent cards declare war. They place three cards face down and turn the fourth card face up. The player whose fourth card has the highest value wins all four cards of the other players (three face-down cards and one face-up card). Whoever has the most cards after 54 cards are played wins. Another way of winning is to play until the other players only have five or ten remaining cards.

Modifications: Any set of math facts or operations can be placed on the cards (such as multiplication facts; sums-to-18; and sets of fractions, decimals, and percents). Also, students who play the game during the school day may keep the cards they win and give up the cards they lose. For homework, each player can then complete the missing cards in the deck and remove the extra cards. (Each player always comes to school with one complete deck, with no extra or missing cards.)

Pig Game

Materials: Dice, scoring pad.

Directions: Pig Game usually is played by two students with one pair of dice. The object is to be the first player to score 100 points by adding the totals on the dice after each roll. The players take turns rolling the dice; however, a player may roll as many times as desired as long as the player does not roll a 1 on one or both of the dice. If a 1 is rolled on one die, the player gives up the turn and loses all points earned during that turn. If a 1 is rolled on both dice, the player gives up the turn, loses all points, and starts again at zero.

Modifications: Wooden blocks with numerals on all sides except one can be used. A drawing of a pig is placed on the empty side. When pig dice are used, each player can be given an appropriate worksheet for his or her math level. If no pigs are rolled, the player answers an item on the worksheet, and the answer is checked by a student with the answer key. If the answer is correct, the item number is checked; however, if the answer is incorrect, the item number is not checked and the player must attempt that item on another turn. If one pig is rolled on the dice, the player loses a turn. If two pigs are rolled (one on each die), the player is allowed to attempt to answer two items on the worksheet. This procedure is continued until one player correctly answers all the items on the worksheet and wins the game. Also, to minimize erratic dice throwing, the dice can be placed in a pill container. The student shakes the container and then opens the lid to see the numbers that are upright on the dice.

Make the Numbers Count

Materials: Dice or a spinner; score sheets.

Directions: Each player is provided with a score sheet that has five columns—one each for ones, tens, hundreds, thousands, and ten thousands. The left side of the score sheet is numbered from 1 to 10. The die (showing 1 to 6) or spinner (1 to 5—can be taken from a commercial game) is rolled or spun ten times by each player. On each turn the players must enter the number shown on the die or spinner in one of the columns. For a game of ten turns, only two numbers may be put in each column. After ten turns, the columns are totaled and the player with the highest number wins.

Spinner Number	10,000s	1000s	100s	10s	1s
1. 3			3		
2. 5	5				
3. 1					1
4. 3		3			
5. 2				2	
6. 2				2	
7. 1					1
8. 4	4				
9. 5		5			
10. 5			5		
Total	9	8	8	4	2

Note: The player in this example would have had a higher score if the 4 in spin #8 had not been used in the 10,000 column. The 5 in either turn 9 or 10 could have been used there.

Rook Math

Materials: A deck of Rook cards (14 sets of four numbered cards); four dice.

Directions: The cards are shuffled, and five cards are dealt to each player. The remaining cards are placed on the table, and one card is turned up beside the deck. The player to the left of the dealer throws the four dice and attempts to match the sum on the dice with a card or cards in his or her hand. The player can lay down a single card or a combination of cards that equals the sum. The player can take the face-up card or draw from the deck. Whether the player lays down cards or not, he

or she then discards on the face-up pile. The next player then takes a turn. When one player is out of cards, the players total the cards that have been played, and the player with the highest sum wins the game.

Math Concentration

Materials: Ten stimulus cards with math problems on one side and blank on the other side; ten cards with the answers to the problems of the stimulus cards on one side and blank on the other side.

Directions: The cards are placed face down in a 5×4 array. Two or more students can play. The first player turns over a card and gives an answer. If the answer is correct, the player turns over a second card. If the second card shows the answer to the first card, the player gets to keep both cards. If an incorrect answer is given to the first card, the player does not turn over a second card. The next player then takes a turn. The winner is the player with the most cards when all cards are taken.

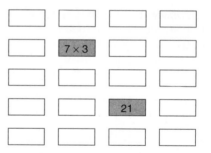

Fraction Game

Materials: One-inch cubes of wood with gummed stickers on each side marked $1/2$, $1/4$, $1/6$, $1/12$, $1/3$, and $1/12$; one-inch cardboard squares marked as follows: 24 pieces with $1/4$ label, 31 pieces with $1/6$ label, 12 pieces with $1/2$ label, 18 pieces with $1/3$ label, and 60 pieces with $1/12$ label; six game boards marked into 12 sections.

Directions: Each player is given a game board. The player attempts to collect fractional parts that will cover $12/12$ of the board without overlapping pieces. The first player throws a cube and collects the fractional piece designated by the cube. This piece is placed on the playing board. The next player then takes a turn. Play continues until a player's board is covered. If a player throws the cube and all corresponding pieces have been taken, the player receives nothing. Likewise, if the cube indicates a fraction that is larger than needed, the player collects nothing.

Toss A Bean Bag

Materials: Six one-gallon cans; bean bags; six discs with numerals written on them; masking tape; score cards.

Directions: The six cans are placed in bowling pin format and are taped together with masking tape. One disc is placed in the bottom of each can. A strip of masking tape is placed on the floor about ten feet from the cans. Each player stands behind the strip, tosses two bean bags into the cans, and adds the numbers in the bottom of the cans in which the bean bags land. If a bag does not land in a can, a 1 is used in computation. The players take turns and record their scores on their score cards. After five tosses by each player, the player with the highest score wins.

Modifications: For column addition practice, each player can toss three or four bean bags and add the numerals. Also, discs with different numbers can be used for other computations (e.g., subtraction and multiplication of whole numbers, and addition of fractions).

Multiplication and Division Facts Rummy

Materials: Forty to 52 cards containing a family of multiplication/division facts (e.g., 9×6, 6×9, $54 \div 6$, $54 \div 9$).

Directions: Seven cards are dealt to each player. The player on the dealer's left draws a card from the remaining cards. If the card matches two others in the player's hand in the same family, the player lays down the book of cards and gives the answer to each fact. If an incorrect answer is given, the cards must remain in the player's hand until the next turn. After the player lays down cards or is unable to do so, the player discards by placing a card from his or her hand face up beside the deck so that all the other discards can be seen. The next player may choose from the stack or pick up the previous discard if the player can match it with two cards in his or her hand. If there are two cards in the discard pile that match one in a player's hand, the player may pick up both cards. The player does not have to take the whole pack, provided he or she can give the correct answers of the cards between the two desired cards. Also, during a turn a player may lay down one or more cards that match another player's books. When a player is out of cards, he or she says, "Rummy," and wins the game.

Modifications: Cards can be constructed to play Place Value Rummy. One-fourth of the 52 cards display groups of tens and ones, one-fourth display standard notation, one-fourth show expanded notation, and one-fourth name the tens and ones.

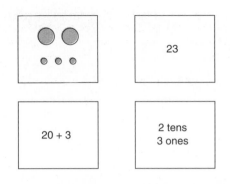

Travel Game

Materials: Large map of the United States; markers or pictures of vehicles; cards with math problems on them.

Directions: On a large map of the United States, a course across the nation is marked off into 50-mile segments. Each card presents a math problem and the number of miles it is worth (such as 50, 100, or 200 miles). Each player draws a card and responds to the problem. If correct, the player's marker is moved the number of miles indicated on the card. If incorrect, the player moves *back* the specified miles. The winner is the first player (or team) to reach the destination.

Modification: Players can be provided with cards of various difficulty levels. Each student can select cards from the desired difficulty level. The more difficult the problem, the more miles it is worth.

Basketball Math

Materials: A drawing of a basketball court on the chalkboard or on poster board; sets of cards presenting math problems labeled *lay-up, 10-foot jump shot, 15-foot jump shot,* and *3-point shot.*

Directions: The cards are divided into stacks. Each lay-up card has a problem to be answered for 2 points and two problems (slightly more difficult) that may be answered to block the lay-up. If the opposing player can answer either of the block problems, the lay-up is blocked. If the shooter answers the lay-up problem correctly and it is not blocked, the player receives 2 points. For the next most difficult stack (10-foot jump shot), there is only one block question on the card. The 15-foot jump shot has the next most difficult problems and no block questions. The 3-point-shot stack has the most difficult problems and no block questions. A time limit (e.g., 5 seconds) is set for answering the questions.

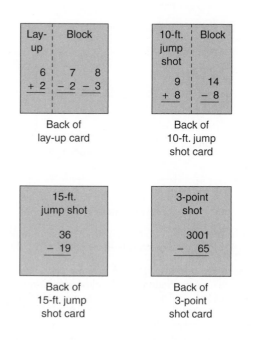

Back of
lay-up card

Back of
10-ft. jump
shot card

Back of
15-ft. jump
shot card

Back of
3-point
shot card

Counting Coins

Materials: Timer; paper and pencil.

Directions: The object of the game is to use the fewest coins to make a given sum. The leader calls out an amount (such as 65 cents). Each player must write down the coins that make the sum within a given time limit. All players who correctly sum the coins receive 1 point. The player or players who use the fewest coins receive 5 points. The first player to receive 25 points wins the game.

Rate Game

Materials: A start-to-finish game board; math worksheets and corresponding answer sheets; game markers; dice.

Directions: Each player is given an individual worksheet at the appropriate instructional level. The first player rolls one die and may elect to move his or her marker that number of spaces on the game board or to write the answers to problems on the worksheet for 10 seconds and move the marker according to the number of problems answered correctly. The opposing player uses the answer sheet to check the responses. If the choice is made to write answers on the worksheet, the player must take these results even if the number is less than the number rolled on the die. The first player to reach the finish space on the board wins the game.

Fraction Blackjack

Materials: Deck of playing cards.

Directions: All picture cards are given any value from 1 to 10. The cards are separated into two stacks: red cards (diamonds and hearts) and black cards (spades and clubs). The first player draws one card from each stack and forms a fraction using the value of the black card as the numerator and the value of the red card as the denominator. Thus, if the player draws a black 8 and a red 2, the fraction is $^8/_2$. The same player continues by drawing two more cards (one black and one red), forming the fraction, and adding the new fraction to the first fraction ($^8/_2$). This continues until the player makes a sum of 10 or as close to 10 as possible. The sum may be above or below 10, and the winner of each round is the player who gets closest to 10.

Modification: The game may be played more like traditional blackjack, in which the players take turns receiving their two cards and a player loses if the sum goes over 10.

Fraction Removal

Materials: Dice (one green and one white); paper and pencil.

Directions: Each player writes the following 22 numbers on a sheet of paper: 1.00, .50, .33, .25, .20, .26, 2.00, .66, .40, 3.00, 1.50, .75, .60, 4.00, 1.33, 1.20, 5.00, 2.50, 1.66, 1.25, .83, and 6.00. One green die and one white die are used. The green die determines the numerator, and the white die determines the denominator. Thus, a dice roll of a green 4 and a white 2 is equivalent to $^4/_2$, or 2. The decimal equivalent of this is 2.00. A roll of a green 3 and a white 5 equals or .60. Each player rolls the dice, forms the fraction, computes the decimal form, and crosses it out on his or her paper. One point is scored for each decimal crossed out, and 5 bonus points are given for each fraction rolled that is equivalent to 1.00 (e.g., $^4/_4$). The winner is the player who scores 50 points first.

Decimal Shapes
(Bright & Harvey, 1982)

Materials: A game board with sections containing numbers in decimal form; ten markers (five each of two colors); a chip marked *L* on one side and *S* on the other; an answer sheet that has the numbers on the board listed in order from smallest to largest.

Directions: Both players place their markers on the starting spaces of the board (enclosed with dark lines). The first player flips the chip. If the chip lands on the *L* side, the player must move one of his or her markers to an adjacent space having a number larger than the number the marker is on. If the chip lands on the *S* side, the player must move one of his or her markers to an adjacent space having a number smaller than the number the marker is on. If the player can move one of the markers to a space occupied by the opponent, the opponent's marker is moved back to a starting position. Only one marker may be on a space at one time. The player must move one of his or her markers, no matter what the direction, if able to do so. If unable to move, the player loses a turn. The two players take turns, and each move can be checked for correctness by using the answer sheet. The winner is the first player to get all of his or her markers to the starting spaces on the other side of the board.

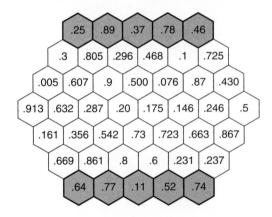

☀ SELF-CORRECTING MATH MATERIALS

Flip-Sider Math Cards

Feedback device: The correct answer is written on the back of each stimulus card.

Materials: Stimulus cards with a math problem on one side and the correct answer on the other side.

Directions: The student looks at the math problem on the card and writes the answer on a worksheet. Then the student flips over the card to check the response.

Front   Back

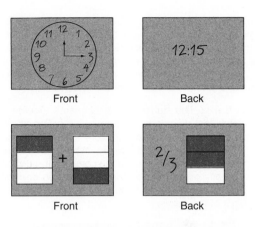

Front   Back

Front   Back

Clipping Answers

Feedback device: When the clothespin containing the correct answer is clipped to the problem on the board and the board is turned over, the symbol on the back of the clothespin matches the symbol on the back of the board.

Materials: Segmented stimulus board showing math problems on the front and symbols on the back; clothespins with answers on one side and symbols corresponding to those on the stimulus board on the other side.

Directions: The student matches the answer on the clothespin to a problem by clipping the clothespin to the problem on the board. Then the student turns over the board. If the symbol on the back of the clothespin matches the symbol on the back of the board, the answer is correct.

Modifications: For easy storage, the clothespins can be kept in a plastic bag with a zipper. Also, pizza wheels make good stimulus cards.

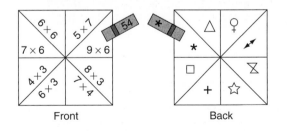

Front   Back

Math Squares

Feedback device: After completing the squares, the student can check the work by turning the squares over. If the squares are placed correctly, a message or picture appears on the back.

Materials: A set of poster board squares that include math problems and answers to problems on adjoining squares (a message or picture is written on the back of the large piece of poster board before the squares are cut); a large box with a window in the bottom, made by placing a piece of acetate over an opening.

Directions: The student fits the squares together so that each fact adjoins its correct answer. The student puts the pieces (message or picture side down) inside the box and on top of the acetate. When the puzzle is completed, the student places the cover on the box and flips the box over. If the puzzle is completed correctly, the player can read the message or view the picture on the back of the puzzle.

5x6	30 7x8	56 4x8	32
16—7	64	13—8	5
9	8x8	5	9—4
8 14—6	72 9x8	0 8x0	
42÷7	63	1/2+1/2	16
6	9x7	1	4x4
4x9	36 1/4+1/4	1/2 6—0	6

Front

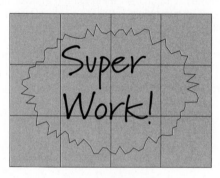

Back

Color Code Folders

Feedback device: When the worksheet is in the red folder, the problems can be seen but the answers cannot. After completing the problems on a separate sheet of paper, the student removes the worksheet from its folder to check the answers.

Materials: Red transparent folder (such as a term-paper folder); worksheet with problems written in black felt-tip pen and answers written in yellow.

Directions: The student inserts the worksheet into the red folder. Then the student numbers a separate sheet of paper and records the answer for each problem. The worksheet is removed from the folder, and the student checks the answers with those written in yellow on the worksheet.

Modification: Different colors may be used (answers can be written in the same color as the folder).

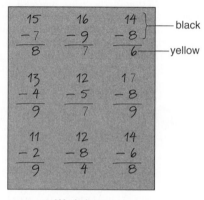

15	16	14 ← black
−7	−9	−8
8	7	6 ← yellow
13	12	17
−4	−5	−8
9	7	9
11	12	14
−2	−8	−6
9	4	8

Worksheet

yellow answers cannot be seen

Red folder
with worksheet inside

Fast Facts

Feedback device: The correct answers are written inside the open folder.

Materials: Manila folder with math problems in a column on the right side inside the folder and the answers to the problems on the left side of the same flap inside the folder (the outside flap of the folder is cut so that only the problems are exposed when the folder is closed).

Directions: The student computes the problems presented in the closed folder and then opens the folder to check the work.

6 x 8
2 x 8
4 x 8
3 x 8
7 x 8
8 x 8
1 x 8
9 x 8
0 x 8

Closed folder

48	6 x 8
16	2 x 8
32	4 x 8
24	3 x 8
56	7 x 8
64	8 x 8
8	1 x 8
72	9 x 8
0	0 x 8

Open folder

Snoopy Math

Feedback device: When the student puts a pencil in the hole of the completed problem and turns over the cutout (Snoopy), the correct answer is written next to the hole where the pencil is.

Materials: Snoopy figure cut out of poster board with (1) holes punched around the cutout, (2) a number placed near each hole, (3) an operation and a number (such as +8) written in the middle of the cutout, and (4) answers written on the other side beside the holes; pencil.

Directions: The student computes problems according to the operation and number presented in the middle of the cutout. For example, if +8 is presented, the student is to add 8 to each number near each hole. The student places a pencil in the hole beside a problem, computes the answer, and turns over Snoopy to check the response by looking at the answer where the pencil is.

Modification: Each side can be used as the problem or the answer. For example, the problems on the other side of the example +8 become –8.

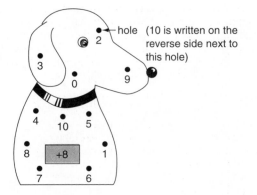

hole (10 is written on the reverse side next to this hole)

Equivalent Fractions, Decimals, and Percents

Feedback device: The correct answers are written in the bottom of each box section.

Materials: A box divided into six sections by partitions, with each section having correct answers written on the bottom of the box; a lid to the box that has six slits cut in it and a fraction, decimal, or percent written above each slit; index cards with values written on them that correspond to the slit labels.

Directions: The student places each index card in the slit named by an equivalent decimal, fraction, or percent on the card. For example, cards marked $2/6$, .33, and 33% would be placed in the slit marked $1/3$. When all the cards have been placed in a slit, the student removes the lid from the box and checks the answers by looking at the bottom of the box where the correct values for each section are listed.

☀ COMMERCIAL MATH PROGRAMS

Numerous published programs and materials are available for teaching math concepts and skills. The following selected programs and materials are useful for teaching math skills to students with learning problems.

Connecting Math Concepts

The *Connecting Math Concepts* curriculum, developed by S. E. Engelmann, D. Carnine, O. Engelmann, and B. Kelly (published by SRA), establishes relationships among math concepts and their application. The basal program includes Levels A through F for students in first through sixth grade, and skills are organized in tracks for the ongoing development of a particular topic. Suggestions are provided for problem-solving activities,

The use of manipulative objects helps students understand math operations.

games, cooperative learning activities, and the use of manipulative materials.

Corrective Mathematics

Corrective Mathematics (Engelmann & Carnine, 1982) is a remedial series in basic math for students in fourth grade through adult age who have not mastered basic skills. The basic facts are taught in addition, subtraction, multiplication, and division. The program includes the concepts of carrying and borrowing as well as translating story problems into numerical statements. Each lesson (65 in each operation area) takes 25 to 45 minutes and includes both teacher-directed instruction and independent review activities. Additional mathematics modules developed by S. E. Engelmann and D. Steely are available in basic fractions; fractions, decimals, percents; and ratios and equations.

DISTAR Arithmetic

These math kits, developed by S. E. Engelmann and D. Carnine (published by SRA), stress direct instruction within a highly systematic, intensive framework. Each kit includes a teacher's guide, teacher's presentation books, take-home workbooks for students, and group progress indicators. *DISTAR Arithmetic* is designed primarily for use with students in small groups, but suggestions are included for teaching large groups. The 160 lessons in each kit are fast-paced, and the teacher's guide specifies what the teacher should say and do. Simple skills are presented first, followed by more complex skills. Oral responses are used extensively; however, written work also is required. *DISTAR Arithmetic I* focuses on facts and fact derivation, story problems, rote counting, symbol identification, equality, addition, subtraction, and multiplication. *DISTAR Arithmetic II* broadens knowledge of basic math facts and includes strategies for problems in columns, multiplication, fraction operations, length and weight measurement, and negative numbers. The results of extensive field testing indicate that *DISTAR Arithmetic* effectively teaches math skills to economically disadvantaged children (Becker & Engelmann, 1976; Stallings & Kaskowitz, 1974).

Key Math Teach and Practice

The *Key Math Teach and Practice* program (Connolly, 1991) provides activities for the diagnosis and remediation of math difficulties. It includes essential concepts covered in kindergarten through eighth grade, and the three packages of basic concepts, operations, and applications are linked directly with the *Key Math—Revised: A Diagnostic Inventory of Essential Mathematics*. Math inventories and probes are used to determine a student's strengths and weaknesses. Instructional intervention follows a sequence of (1) foundation steps (reviewing prerequisite skills, introducing concepts and skills, and demonstrating application), (2) learning activities (moving from the use of manipulatives to pictorial to symbolic representations), and (3) drills, games, and extensions (including exercises of estimation and problem solving). A teacher's guide, a student progress record, and a scope and sequence chart also are included. In addition, *AGS Math Manipulatives* are available (such as attribute blocks, cubes, chips, tumblers, and boards) to provide hands-on learning experiences to enrich the math program.

Real-Life Math

Real-Life Math, developed by S. E. Schwartz (published by PRO-ED), stresses the development of functional math skills in teenage students with learning problems through the use of role-playing activities in which students establish their own businesses. Students complete files, handle billing forms, and conduct financial transactions with a bank. The materials include a teacher's manual, 15 spirit masters, eight stimulus posters, ten audiocassettes, five student skill books, a mail box, three desk signs, and a supply kit of checks, deposit and withdrawal slips, and saving passbooks for 20 students.

Saxon Math 54 and Math 65: Adaptations for Special Populations

The *Adaptations for Special Populations* series, designed to accompany Saxon Publishers' middle grades math textbooks, provides modifications to facilitate success of at-risk students using a general education curriculum. The two textbooks for students performing at the fourth- through sixth-grade level, feature incremental development and continual review. The Teacher's Resource Kit includes a teaching guide that explains how to adapt the textbooks for special populations as well as reproducible student materials such as a reference guide, worksheets with simple vocabulary and hints, cumulative tests, daily quizzes, and supplemental practices. Teacher support materials include placement tests, class handouts, parent letters, and recording forms. A poster set, fact cards, and an instructional video are also provided. In addition, a manipulative kit of 15 different items supplements the adaptations. Manipulatives are fully integrated into the program and help address students' various learning styles.

Strategic Math Series

The *Strategic Math Series,* developed by C. D. Mercer and S. P. Miller (published by Edge Enterprises), is designed to enable students with math difficulties to understand, acquire, remember, and apply math concepts and skills. The program is based on research in effective teaching, learning strategies, memory, mastery learning, applied behavior analysis, generalization, and student motivation. Eight instructional stages are included: pretest, concrete, representational, DRAW (mnemonic), abstract, posttest, practice to mastery, and periodic review. All lessons include scripts to guide the teacher through the instructional components of advance organizer, demonstrate/explain, guided practice, independent practice, problem solving (i.e., students learn to create their own story problems), and lesson feedback. Manuals are available for addition facts 0 to 9, subtraction facts 0 to 9, place value, addition facts 10 to 18, subtraction facts 10 to 18, multiplication facts 0 to 81, and division facts 0 to 81.

The Super Source

The Super Source (produced by Cuisenaire Dale Seymour) is an 18-volume series of teacher resource books that include classroom-tested, problem-solving activities involving the use of manipulatives. Each grade-level book (kindergarten through second grade, third through fourth grade, and fifth through sixth grade) focuses on one of six manipulatives: color tiles, Cuisenaire rods, geoboards, pattern blocks, Snap cubes, and tangrams. The three-step lesson plan and the suggested activities incorporate manipulatives into the math program and facilitate a hands-on approach to learning math. Also available are a CD-ROM and transparencies for further teaching aides. Additional math manipulatives are produced by Lakeshore Learning Materials and SRA.

COMPUTER SOFTWARE PROGRAMS IN MATH

Computer software programs in math can be used to provide motivating drill and practice activities. Some programs present game-playing situations; others effectively use animation and sound effects to maintain student interest. The computer also can provide self-correcting feedback so that the student does not practice errors. R. D. Howell, Sidorenko, and Jurica (1987) examined the effects of computer use on the learning of multiplication facts by students with learning disabilities. They found that it was necessary to combine direct teacher instruction with tutorial and drill-and-practice software for effective results. The following software programs present various math skills and can help the student understand and master these skills.

Fraction Attraction

Fraction Attraction (produced by Sunburst Communications) is designed to help students in third through eighth grade learn fundamental fraction concepts. Four animated activities strengthen students' understanding of ordering, relative size, equivalence, location of fractions on a number line, and multiple representations. Each multilevel activity features diagnostic help to assist students in correcting conceptual errors. The program is fully customizable and includes a teacher's guide with activities.

Math Blaster

The *Math Blaster* software series (produced by Knowledge Adventure) covers various math curriculum skills. *Math Blaster Ages 4–6* presents 10 activities to help students master essential early math skills such as counting to 20, learning concepts of greater than and less than, practicing addition and subtraction, and understanding number sentences. In *Math Blaster Ages 6–9,* five learning activities help students practice basic math facts; understand fractions, decimals, and percents; explore estimation and number patterns; and build problem-solving skills. Students master advanced math skills such as building equations, adding fractions, and estimating in *Math Blaster Ages 9–12. Math Blaster Pre-Algebra* presents pre-algebra concepts in a mystery setting and includes over 4,000 word problems to develop problem-solving and critical thinking skills. Finally, *Math Blaster Algebra* presents six activities to cover an entire year of algebra, while *Math Blaster Geometry* covers 52 subject areas in geometry. Each *Math Blaster* program builds on the math skills learned in the previous program and includes multiple activities in varying difficulty levels.

Math FactMaster

The *Math FactMaster* CD-ROM (produced by Curriculum Associates) offers math fact drill sessions tailored to each individual student's needs. The program remembers the facts each student has mastered from one session to the next and focuses on unmastered facts in each succeeding lesson. Facts are presented in horizontal/vertical, true/false, and open-sentence formats. Responses that are incorrect or exceed the mastery time limit set by the teacher reappear at random until the student masters them. Checkpoint activities provide word problems that use only mastered facts, and as students master facts in each session they move toward their ultimate goal of immediate recall of number facts. Individual student reports indicate mastered and unmastered facts, response times for each fact, and percentage of mastered facts in each operation.

Math Sequences

Math Sequences (produced by Milliken) provides a comprehensive, objective-based mathematics curriculum with structured drill and practice designed for students in first through eighth grade or as remediation for older students. The CD-ROM version contains 14 programs: number readiness, addition, subtraction, multiplication, division, laws of arithmetic, estimating, integers, fractions, decimals, percents, equations, measurement formulas and number theory. The program presents over 100 different problem formats, and

the range of problem levels within a sequence makes it possible to place students according to level of understanding. The work (such as carrying, borrowing, and canceling numbers) for each problem is completed on the screen. Graphic or textual reinforcements are given for a correct response. When a problem is missed more than once, the correct solution is displayed, step by step, for the student to study. The student is advanced by a level after specific achievement criteria are met or moved back a level until mastery is achieved. The management program maintains records for each student and allows the teacher to establish personalized performance levels and make individual and class assignments. In addition, a worksheet generator allows the teacher to create and print a variety of computation problems and word problems. Also, a set of 39 workbooks is integrated into the software curriculum.

WordMath

The *WordMath* programs (produced by Milliken) provide students with individualized instruction and practice in solving word problems. The lessons for students in second and third grades in *Primary WordMath* focus on addition, subtraction, and basic facts and include tutorial messages for all errors. Computation is completed on the screen and, if the student has difficulty, a step-by-step solution is given. *WordMath I* and *II* for students in fourth through eighth grade include modules in basic problems, forward/reverse order, extra numbers, hidden numbers, key words, dictionary, mixed practice, and advanced mixed practice. Graphic reinforcement supports correct answers, and tutorial error messages provide immediate assistance on the kind of error made and the particular problem worked. The program includes two levels of difficulty on each disk as well as a comprehensive management system. Supplemental workbooks are provided. The program can be used for supplemental instruction or remediation.

☀ PERSPECTIVE

Many students with learning problems experience math difficulties. However, if educational researchers can scientifically tap the potential benefits of research-driven principles and if teacher educators and publishers of commercial materials can place the products of these findings in the hands of teachers, educators have an opportunity to improve significantly the math learning of students and the math instruction of teachers. Perhaps student beliefs about learning math will change, and more math teachers will experience the satisfaction and joy of having a student approach them and say, "I know how to solve 9x − 6x + 12 = 24" . . . and the fun begins.

☀ REFERENCES

Anderson, L. W., & Pellicer, L. O. (1990). Synthesis of research on compensatory and remedial education. *Educational Leadership, 48*(1), 10–16.

Ashlock, R. B. (1998) *Error patterns in computation* (7th ed.). Upper Saddle River, NJ: Merrill/Prentice Hall.

Baroody, A. J., & Hume, J. (1991). Meaningful mathematics instruction: The case of fractions. *Remedial and Special Education, 12*(3), 54–68.

Becker, W. C., & Engelmann, S. E. (1976). *Technical report 1976–1.* Eugene: University of Oregon.

Bezuk, N. S., & Cegelka, P. T. (1995). Effective mathematics instruction for all students. In P. T. Cegelka & W. H. Berdine, *Effective instruction for students with learning difficulties* (pp. 345–383). Boston: Allyn & Bacon.

Bley, N. S., & Thornton, C. A. (1995). *Teaching mathematics to students with learning disabilities* (3rd ed.). Austin, TX: PRO-ED.

Borkowski, J. G. (1992). Metacognitive theory: A framework for teaching literacy, writing, and math skills. *Journal of Learning Disabilities, 25,* 253–257.

Bottge, B. A., & Hasselbring, T. S. (1993). A comparison of two approaches for teaching complex, authentic mathematics problems to adolescents in remedial math classes. *Exceptional Children, 59,* 556–566.

Bright, G. W., & Harvey, J. G. (1982). Using games to teach fraction concepts and skills. In L. Silvey (Ed.), *Mathematics for the middle grades (5–9): 1982 yearbook.* Reston, VA: National Council of Teachers of Mathematics.

Carnine, D. (1991). Curricular interventions for teaching higher order thinking to all students: Introduction to the special series. *Journal of Learning Disabilities, 24,* 261–269.

Carnine, D. (1992). The missing link in improving schools—Reforming educational leaders. *Direct Instruction News, 11*(3), 25–35.

Cawley, J. F., & Miller, J. H. (1989). Cross-sectional comparisons of the mathematical performance of children with learning disabilities: Are we on the right track toward comprehensive programming? *Journal of Learning Disabilities, 23,* 250–254, 259.

Cawley, J. F., Miller, J. H., & School, B. A. (1987). A brief inquiry of arithmetic word-problem solving among learning disabled secondary students. *Learning Disabilities Focus, 2,* 87–93.

Christenson, S. L., Ysseldyke, J. E., & Thurlow, M. L. (1989). Critical instructional factors for students with mild handicaps: An integrative review. *Remedial and Special Education, 10*(5), 21–31.

Clifford, M. M. (1990). Students need challenge, not easy success. *Educational Leadership, 48*(1), 22–26.

Cobb, P., Yackel, E., & Wood, T. (1992). A constructivist alternative to the representational view of mind in mathematics education. *Journal for Research in Mathematics Education, 23*(1), 2–33.

Connolly, A. J. (1991). *Key Math Teach and Practice.* Circle Pines, MN: American Guidance Service.

De Corte, E., & Verschaffel, L. (1981). Children's solution processes in elementary arithmetic problems: Analysis and improvement. *Journal of Educational Psychology, 73,* 765–779.

Dunlap, W. P., & Brennan, A. H. (1979). Developing mental images of mathematical processes. *Learning Disability Quarterly, 2*(2), 89–96.

Eicholz, R. E., O'Daffer, P. G., Fleenor, C. R., Charles, R. I., Young, S., & Barnett, C. S. (1985). *Addison-Wesley mathematics 1–3 components.* Menlo Park, CA: Addison-Wesley.

Ellis, E. S., Lenz, B. K., & Sabornie, E. J. (1987a). Generalization and adaptation of learning strategies to natural environments: Part I: Critical agents. *Remedial and Special Education, 8*(1), 6–20.

Ellis, E. S., Lenz, B. K., & Sabornie, E. J. (1987b). Generalization and adaptation of learning strategies to natural environments: Part II: Research into practice. *Remedial and Special Education, 8*(2), 6–23.

Elmore, R. F. (1992). Why restructuring alone won't improve teaching. *Educational Leadership, 49*(7), 44–48.

Engelmann, S. E., & Carnine, D. (1982). *Corrective mathematics program.* Blacklick, OH: SRA.

Englert, C. S., Tarrant, K. L., & Mariage, T. V. (1992). Defining and redefining instructional practice in special education: Perspectives on good teaching. *Teacher Education and Special Education, 15,* 62–86.

Fitzmaurice-Hayes, A. (1984). Curriculum and instructional activities: Grades 2 through 4. In J. F. Cawley (Ed.), *Developmental teaching of mathematics for the learning disabled.* Rockville, MD: Aspen Systems.

Fleischner, J. E., Garnett, K., & Shepherd, M. J. (1982). Proficiency in arithmetic basic facts computation of learning disabled and nondisabled children. *Focus on Learning Problems in Mathematics, 4,* 47–56.

Fleischner, J. E., Nuzum, M. B., & Marzola, E. S. (1987). Devising an instructional program to teach arithmetic problem-solving skills to students with learning disabilities. *Journal of Learning Disabilities, 20,* 214–217.

Frank, A. R., & Brown, D. (1992). Self-monitoring strategies in arithmetic. *Teaching Exceptional Children, 24*(2), 52–53.

Fuchs, L. S. (1986). Monitoring progress among mildly handicapped pupils: Review of current practices and research. *Remedial and Special Education, 7*(5), 5–12.

Fuchs, L. S., Fuchs, D., & Deno, S. L. (1985). The importance of goal ambitiousness and goal mastery to student achievement. *Exceptional Children, 52,* 63–71.

Fulkerson, E. (1963). Adding by tens. *The Arithmetic Teacher, 10,* 139–140.

Garnett, K., & Fleischner, J. E. (1983). Automatization and basic fact performance of normal and learning disabled children. *Learning Disability Quarterly, 6,* 223–230.

Gersten, R., Carnine, D., & Woodward, J. (1987). Direct instruction research: The third decade. *Remedial and Special Education, 8*(6), 48–56.

Harris, C. A., Miller, S. P., & Mercer, C. D. (1995). Teaching initial multiplication skills to students with disabilities in general education classrooms. *Learning Disabilities Research & Practice, 10,* 180–195.

Harris, K. R., & Pressley, M. (1991). The nature of cognitive strategy instruction: Interactive strategy construction. *Exceptional Children, 57,* 392–404.

Hasselbring, T. S., Goin, L. I., & Bransford, J. D. (1987). Developing automaticity. *Teaching Exceptional Children, 19*(3), 30–33.

Heddens, J. W., & Speer, W. R. (1997). *Today's mathematics. Part II: Activities and instructional ideas* (9th ed.). Upper Saddle River, NJ: Merrill/Prentice Hall.

Hembree, R. (1986). Research gives calculators a green light. *The Arithmetic Teacher, 34,* 18–21.

Howell, R. D., Sidorenko, E., & Jurica, J. (1987). The effects of computer use on the acquisition of multiplication facts by a student with learning disabilities. *Journal of Learning Disabilities, 20,* 336–341.

Howell, S. C., & Barnhart, R. S. (1992). Teaching word problem solving at the primary level. *Teaching Exceptional Children, 24*(2), 44–46.

Hutchings, B. (1975). Low-stress subtraction. *The Arithmetic Teacher, 22,* 226–232.

Hutchings, B. (1976). *Low-stress algorithms.* Reston, VA: National Council of Teachers of Mathematics.

Hutchinson, N. L. (1993a). Effects of cognitive strategy instruction on algebra problem solving of adolescents with learning disabilities. *Learning Disability Quarterly, 16,* 34–63.

Hutchinson, N. L. (1993b). Second invited response: Students with disabilities and mathematics education reform—Let the dialogue begin. *Remedial and Special Education, 14*(6), 20–23.

Kameenui, E. J., & Simmons, D. C. (1990). *Designing instructional strategies: The prevention of academic learning problems.* Upper Saddle River, NJ: Merrill/Prentice Hall.

Kelly, B., Gersten, R., & Carnine, D. (1990). Student error patterns as a function of curriculum design: Teaching fractions to remedial high school students and high school students with learning disabilities. *Journal of Learning Disabilities, 23,* 23–29.

Kirby, J. R., & Becker, L. D. (1988). Cognitive components of learning problems in arithmetic. *Remedial and Special Education, 9*(5), 7–15, 27.

Kline, F. M., Schumaker, J. B., & Deshler, D. D. (1991). Development and validation of feedback routines for instructing students with learning disabilities. *Learning Disability Quarterly, 14,* 191–207.

Kramer, T., & Krug, D. A. (1973). A rationale and procedure for teaching addition. *Education and Training of the Mentally Retarded, 8,* 140–144.

Lambert, M. A. (1996). Mathematics textbooks, materials, and manipulatives. *LD Forum, 21*(2), 33, 41–45.

Lenz, B. K. (1992). Cognitive approaches to teaching. In C. D. Mercer, *Students with learning disabilities* (4th ed., pp. 269–309). Upper Saddle River, NJ: Merrill/Prentice Hall.

Lloyd, J. W., & Keller, C. E. (1989). Effective mathematics instruction: Development, instruction, and programs. *Focus on Exceptional Children, 21*(7), 1–10.

Locke, E. A., & Latham, G. P. (1990). *A theory of goal setting and task performance.* Upper Saddle River, NJ: Merrill/Prentice Hall.

Locke, E. A., Shaw, K. N., Saari, L. M., & Latham, G. P. (1981). Goal setting and task performance: 1969–1980. *Psychological Bulletin, 90,* 125–152.

Lovitt, T. C. (1989). *Introduction to learning disabilities.* Boston: Allyn & Bacon.

Marsh, L. G., & Cooke, N. L. (1996). The effects of using manipulatives in teaching math problem solving to students with learning disabilities. *Learning Disabilities Research & Practice, 11,* 58–65.

Mastropieri, M. A., Scruggs, T. E., & Shiah, S. (1991). Mathematics instruction for learning disabled students: A review of research. *Learning Disabilities Research & Practice, 6,* 89–98.

Mercer, C. D. (1997). *Students with learning disabilities* (5th ed.). Upper Saddle River, NJ: Merrill/Prentice Hall.

Mercer, C. D., Enright, B., & Tharin, M. A. (1994). *Solving division equations: An algebra program for teaching students with learning problems.* Unpublished manuscript, University of Florida, Gainesville.

Mercer, C. D., Jordan, L., & Miller, S. P. (1994). Implications of constructivism for teaching math to students with mild to moderate disabilities. *The Journal of Special Education, 28,* 290–306.

Mercer, C. D., Jordan, L., & Miller, S. P. (1996). Constructivistic math instruction for diverse learners. *Learning Disabilities Research & Practice, 11,* 147–156.

Mercer, C. D., & Miller, S. P. (1991–1993). *Strategic math series* (A series of seven manuals: *Addition Facts 0 to 9; Subtraction Facts 0 to 9; Place Value: Discovering Tens and Ones; Addition Facts 10 to 18; Subtraction Facts 10 to 18; Multiplication Facts 0 to 81; Division Facts 0 to 81*). Lawrence, KS: Edge Enterprises.

Mercer, C. D., & Miller, S. P. (1992). Teaching students with learning problems in math to acquire, understand, and apply basic math facts. *Remedial and Special Education, 13*(3), 19–35, 61.

Miller, S. P., Mercer, C. D., & Dillon, A. S. (1992). CSA: Acquiring and retaining math skills. *Intervention in School and Clinic, 28,* 105–110.

Miller, S. P., Strawser, S., & Mercer, C. D. (1996). Promoting strategic math performance among students with learning disabilities. *LD Forum, 21*(2), 34–40.

Montague, M. (1992). The effects of cognitive and metacognitive strategy instruction on the mathematical problem solving of middle school students with learning disabilities. *Journal of Learning Disabilities, 25,* 230–248.

Montague, M. (1993). Student-centered or strategy-centered instruction: What is our purpose? *Journal of Learning Disabilities, 26,* 433–437, 481.

Moshman, D. (1982). Exogenous, endogenous, and dialectical constructivism. *Developmental Review, 2,* 371–384.

Mtetwa, D., & Garofalo, J. (1989). Beliefs about mathematics: An overlooked aspect of student difficulties. *Academic Therapy, 24,* 611–618.

National Council of Supervisors of Mathematics. (1988). *Twelve components of essential mathematics.* Minneapolis, MN: Author.

National Council of Teachers of Mathematics. (1980). *An agenda for action: Recommendations for school mathematics of the 1980's.* Reston, VA: Author.

National Council of Teachers of Mathematics. (1989). *Curriculum and evaluation standards for school mathematics.* Reston, VA: Author.

Paris, S. G., & Winograd, P. (1990). Promoting metacognition and motivation of exceptional children. *Remedial and Special Education, 11*(6), 7–15.

Pearson, E. S. (1986). Summing it all up: Pre-1900 algorithms. *The Arithmetic Teacher, 33,* 38–41.

Peterson, P. L., Fennema, E., & Carpenter, T. (1988/1989). Using knowledge of how students think about mathematics. *Educational Leadership, 46*(4), 42–46.

Porter, A. C., & Brophy, J. (1988). Synthesis of research on good teaching: Insights from the work of the Institute for Research on Teaching. *Educational Leadership, 45*(8), 74–85.

Pressley, M., Harris, K. R., & Marks, M. B. (1992). But good strategy instructors are constructivists! *Educational Psychology Review, 4,* 3–33.

Reid, D. K., & Stone, C. A. (1991). Why is cognitive instruction effective? Underlying learning mechanisms. *Remedial and Special Education, 12*(3), 8–19.

Reisman, F. K. (1977). *Diagnostic teaching of elementary school mathematics: Methods and content.* Chicago: Rand McNally.

Reisman, F. K. (1982). *A guide to the diagnostic teaching of arithmetic* (3rd ed.). Upper Saddle River, NJ: Merrill/Prentice Hall.

Rivera, D. M., & Smith, D. D. (1988). Using a demonstration strategy to teach midschool students with learning disabilities how to compute long division. *Journal of Learning Disabilities, 21,* 77–81.

Robinson, S. L., DePascale, C., & Roberts, F. C. (1989). Computer-delivered feedback in group-based instruction: Effects for learning disabled students in mathematics. *Learning Disabilities Focus, 5*(1), 28–35.

Rosenshine, B., & Meister, C. (1992). The use of scaffolds for teaching higher-level cognitive strategies. *Educational Leadership, 49*(7), 26–33.

Ruais, R. W. (1978). A low-stress algorithm for fractions. *Mathematics Teacher, 71,* 258–260.

Russell, R., & Ginsburg, H. (1984). Cognitive analysis of children's mathematical difficulties. *Cognition and Instruction, 1,* 217–244.

Scheid, K. (1990). *Cognitive-based methods for teaching mathematics to students with learning problems.* Columbus, OH: LINC Resources.

Stallings, J. A., & Kaskowitz, D. H. (1974). *Follow Through classroom observation evaluation.* Menlo Park, CA: Stanford Research Institute.

Stein, M., Silbert, J., & Carnine, D. (1997). *Designing effective mathematics instruction: A direct instruction approach* (3rd ed.). Upper Saddle River, NJ: Merrill/Prentice Hall.

Stokes, T. F., & Baer, D. M. (1977). An implicit technology of generalization. *Journal of Applied Behavioral Analysis, 10*(2), 349–367.

Suydam, M. N. (1980). *Using calculators in precollege education: Third annual state-of-the-art review.* Columbus, OH: Calculator Information Center.

Thornton, C. A., & Toohey, M. A. (1982–1985). *MATH-FACT: An alternative program for children with special needs* (A series of four kits: *Basic Addition Facts; Basic Subtraction Facts; Basic Multiplication Facts; Basic Division Facts*). Brisbane, Australia: Queensland Division of Special Education.

Thornton, C. A., & Toohey, M. A. (1985). Basic math facts: Guidelines for teaching and learning. *Learning Disabilities Focus, 1,* 44–57.

Thornton, C. A., & Toohey, M. A. (1986). Subtraction facts hide-and-seek cards can help. *Teaching Exceptional Children, 19,* 10–14.

Underhill, R. G., Uprichard, A. E., & Heddens, J. W. (1980). *Diagnosing mathematical difficulties.* Upper Saddle River, NJ: Merrill/Prentice Hall.

Watanabe, A. (1991). *The effects of a mathematical word problem solving strategy on problem solving performance by middle school students with mild disabilities.* Unpublished doctoral dissertation, University of Florida, Gainesville.

Wilson, R., Majsterek, D., & Jones, E. D. (1995). Mathematics instruction. In P. J. Schloss, M. A. Smith, & C. N. Schloss, *Instructional methods for adolescents with learning and behavior problems* (2nd ed., pp. 255–286). Boston: Allyn & Bacon.

Wong, B. Y. L. (1992). On cognitive process-based instruction: An introduction. *Journal of Learning Disabilities, 25,* 150–152, 172.

Woodward, J. (1991). Procedural knowledge in mathematics: The role of the curriculum. *Journal of Learning Disabilities, 24,* 242–251.

Zawaiza, T. R. W., & Gerber, M. M. (1993). Effects of explicit instruction on math word-problem solving by community college students with learning disabilities. *Learning Disability Quarterly, 16,* 64–79.

13

Teaching Learning Strategies, Content, and Study Skills

hapters 1 through 12 of this text primarily focus on helping teachers create instructional environments that assist students with academic problems to learn to listen, speak, read, write, compute, problem solve, and socialize. These foundational skills are important for early school successes and provide a basis for the expanded school demands that students face in middle school, secondary school, and postsecondary school settings. Adolescents are faced with the complex task of using these academic and social skills to acquire knowledge about science, social studies, literature, and independent living in settings that are demanding for teachers and students.

The characteristics of students with learning problems combine with the complex academic demands and difficult instructional realities to make it difficult for these adolescents to succeed in school. Figure 13.1, which contains information compiled from Bulgren and Lenz (1996) and Mercer (1997), highlights the parameters of learning characteristics, academic demands, and setting realities that operate in the middle school and secondary school arenas. Inspection of these instructional conditions make it apparent that adolescents with learning problems need intensive and explicit instruction to succeed.

Fortunately, recent efforts in the field of learning disabilities have focused on developing secondary programs. For example, the University of Kansas Institute for Research in Learning Disabilities (now the Center for Research on Learning) was established in 1978 to study the needs of adolescents

FIGURE 13.1
Instructional conditions and essential services for students with learning problems

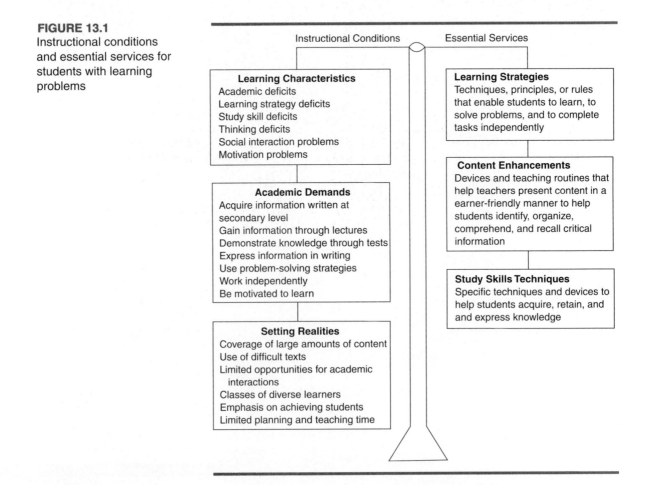

with learning disabilities and develop appropriate interventions. Under the leadership of Don Deshler, Jean Schumaker, and their colleagues, this center is having a nationwide impact. Their learning strategy materials and content enhancement routines are being used successfully to help adolescents with learning problems experience school success. Moreover, other authorities (Hoover, 1995; Meltzer et al., 1996; Wood, 1998) present study skills techniques that are effective. Figure 13.1 presents learning strategies, content enhancements, and study skills techniques as essential instructional options for students with learning problems. Following a discussion on motivation and the adolescent, this chapter presents information that assists teachers in teaching learning strategies, content, and study skills to adolescents with learning problems.

☀ MOTIVATION

Motivation to learn or participate is essential to the success of any intervention approach. The adage "You can lead a horse to water, but you can't make him drink" certainly applies to learning. For an intervention approach to be effective with a student who has learning problems, the individual must be motivated to participate. For the adolescent with learning problems, lack of motivation is often a roadblock to school success. Thus, regarding motivation, the adage may be altered to "Although you can't make a horse drink the water, you can salt the hay."

Several motivation techniques are available to help low-achieving students in secondary school. Deshler, Schumaker, and Lenz (1984) divide these approaches into two broad categories: those using extrinsic controls and those that focus on developing intrinsic motivation. From their review of motivation studies, Deshler et al. report that several extrinsic control techniques have been used successfully to improve the academic skills of adolescents with learning problems. Zigmond, Sansone, Miller, Donahoe, and Kohnke (1986) provide a list of extrinsic reinforcers that appear to be effective with adolescents. The reinforcers include the following:

- Time for listening to tapes, CDs, or records
- Tokens for progress on academics
- Charting or self-recording of academic accomplishments

- Allowances at home tied to grades
- Time to play games or enjoy a recreational activity
- Opportunity to participate in scheduling academic activities
- Tangible reinforcers such as restaurant coupons, magazines, and movie tickets
- Exemption from some homework or assignments
- Extra time for a break or lunch

The most useful techniques include token economies, contingency contracting, and verbal feedback (see Chapter 5 for descriptions of these techniques). Techniques aimed at facilitating intrinsic motivation also are receiving support.

Motivation strategies are one of the curriculum components of the Strategies Intervention Model developed at the University of Kansas Center for Research on Learning. Van Reusen and Bos (1994) note that motivation strategies within this model are defined as "techniques and procedures that involve the learner in key aspects of the learning process and are used to increase a student's commitment to learn" (p. 469). Within this context, Van Reusen and Bos examined the effectiveness of IPARS, a motivation strategy designed to foster students' active participation in IEP conferences. They found that students with learning problems who received the strategy instruction identified more goals and communicated better during the conferences than did the contrast students. Thus, motivation strategies can be used to increase students' interest in their own learning and foster their ability to gain control over their own performances.

To promote the development of active and independent learners, some motivation strategies attempt to teach self-control skills, including one or more of the following: goal setting, self-recording of progress, self-evaluation, and self-reinforcement. Seabaugh and Schumaker (1981) taught all four of these self-control subskills to adolescents with learning problems and had positive results (i.e., the number of lessons completed by the students increased from an average of one-half lesson completed per day to four lessons completed per day). Deshler et al. (1984) report that self-control training can help students with learning problems complete their assignments, and the training procedures are easy to implement and do not depend on expensive extrinsic reinforcers.

From their review of the motivation literature, Adelman and Taylor (1983) list tactics for enhancing intrinsic motivation, including the following:

1. Provide some choices in curriculum content and procedures to enhance the student's perception that learning is worthwhile, and discuss the relevance (real-life applications) of various content.

2. Through discussion, obtain a commitment to options that the student values and indicates a desire to pursue. Contractual agreements are helpful.

3. Schedule informal and formal conferences with the student to enhance her or his role in making choices and negotiating agreements.

4. Provide feedback that conveys student progress. The student must not perceive the feedback as an effort to entice and control. Self-correcting materials are useful.

Student involvement is a recurring theme in the literature on managing and motivating adolescents with learning problems. For example, in their discussion of secondary classroom management, Kerr and Nelson (1998) state, "Encourage pupils to participate in all aspects of the curriculum. This includes permitting them to make choices among tasks, curriculum, materials, and instructional sequences. In addition, they should be involved in selecting and prioritizing their own social goals, in making decisions about the classroom structure, and in setting consequences and contingencies" (p. 176). An example of procedures that teachers can use to teach students how to participate in goal setting and planning is presented by Van Reusen, Bos, Schumaker, and Deshler (1994).

Another dimension that may be included in efforts to promote student motivation relates to the beliefs that students have about themselves. Many students do not believe that they can learn or change. Ellis, Deshler, Lenz, Schumaker, and Clark (1991) present four techniques for teachers to use to help students alter their beliefs about their learning and performance:

1. Engineer instructional arrangements to promote and reinforce student independence.
2. Communicate high expectations for students through words and actions.

3. Help students identify and analyze beliefs that underlie their behavior as ineffective learners.
4. Help students discard unproductive beliefs through a variety of activities and interactions.

LEARNING STRATEGIES

A learning strategies approach helps students with learning problems cope with the complex demands of the secondary curriculum. Deshler and his colleagues at the University of Kansas Center for Research on Learning define *learning strategies* as techniques, principles, or rules that enable a student to learn, to solve problems, and to complete tasks independently. The goal of strategy development is to identify strategies that are optimally effective (i.e., help students meet the demands of both current and future tasks) and efficient (i.e., help students meet the demands of the task in appropriate, timely, resourceful, and judicious ways). The goal of strategies instruction is to teach the strategies effectively (i.e., the strategy is learned and generalized by the student) and efficiently (i.e., the strategy is learned to an optimal level with a minimum amount of effort by the teacher and the student). This approach attempts to help students learn course content (such as geography) through instruction in skills necessary to acquire, store, and express content. Basically, it focuses on teaching students how to learn and how to demonstrate command of their knowledge in performing academic tasks. For example, a reading strategy may be used by a student with fourth-grade reading skills to obtain relevant information from a textbook chapter written at the tenth-grade level. As one part of the Strategies Intervention Model, Deshler and his colleagues developed a learning strategies curriculum, whose components have been specified, developed, and validated in classrooms. Field-testing and evaluation data indicate good student progress and a high degree of consumer satisfaction (Deshler & Schumaker, 1986, 1988; Schumaker, Deshler, & Ellis, 1986). Because the strategies included in the Strategies Intervention Model have the longest history of comprehensive research and development for adolescents with learning problems, a detailed description of this approach is presented.

Learning Strategies Curriculum

The Learning Strategies Curriculum of the University of Kansas Center for Research on Learning includes intervention manuals and support materials. The manuals, available through training, advise teachers on how to provide intensive instruction to adolescents with learning problems and how to promote the acquisition, storage, and expression of information and demonstration of competence through instruction in learning strategies. The strategies included in the curriculum are listed and described in Table 13.1. (Some of these strategies are presented in other chapters of this text [Chapters 8, 10, and 12], and the study skills section of this chapter presents many skills that are organized within a strategic framework.) Each of the teacher's manuals details how to teach the strategy and how to prompt the student to transfer it across settings. Teachers are trained in the basic concepts of the strategy that previously has been validated through research, and they are encouraged to tailor strategy instruction according to their personal teaching style to meet the needs of students. Thus, while integrity in the basic features of the strategy and the instructional procedures must be retained to ensure student success, the teacher is given wide latitude to make the intervention meaningful in individual situations.

The learning strategy interventions respond to the specific needs of teachers who need instructional procedures and curricula for adolescents with learning problems. Because most special education teachers provide instruction in a support class setting rather than in the general classroom setting, the curriculum materials are used mainly to teach strategies in one setting and then prompt generalization of the strategies to additional settings (e.g., the general classroom). The student's general classroom materials are used in the process so that the student learns to associate the strategy with success in meeting naturally occurring learning demands. Changes in service delivery options permit general classroom teachers to infuse many dimensions of these strategy interventions into content-area instruction, thereby allowing the student to see the application of the strategy in natural settings. However, additional intensive instruction usually is required by the special education teacher in a support class setting because many secondary content teachers are unable to provide the explicit or intensive instruction needed to overcome the difficulties of students with learning problems.

Features of Effective Learning Strategies

Ellis and Lenz (1996) note that effective and efficient learning strategies share critical features in the parameters of content, design, and usefulness. These parameters and accompanying features are presented in Table 13.2. All strategies use a mnemonic (i.e., acronym) to organize the strategy steps and assist the student to remember the content and order of the steps. Ellis and Lenz note that content features provide guidelines for "how to think and act when planning, executing, and evaluating performance on a task and its outcomes" (p. 30). Design features focus on how the strategy is packaged. Good designs organize the content for the student's optimal learning and application. Usefulness features relate to how applicable the strategy is across settings, situations, and people.

Instructional Procedures

Several instructional procedures are used to promote the acquisition of skills by adolescents. These approaches use activities involving guided practice, modeling, peer instruction, provision of feedback, and task analysis. Since 1978, the University of Kansas Center for Research on Learning has studied how these instructional procedures are integrated and used to promote adolescent learning. The Center's research has culminated in a set of instructional procedures that integrate instructional methods into specific stages of instruction. A detailed description of instructional issues and the instructional stages is presented by Ellis and Lenz (1996) and Lenz, Ellis, and Scanlon (1996).

Table 13.3 depicts the instructional stages that are used successfully to teach adolescents with learning problems a variety of skills and strategies. These instructional stages are characterized by their intent to increase the adolescent's role in the instructional process so that the student learns to self-control learning and become empowered. Several important dimensions are built into these instructional stages. While the term *strategy* is used, the same stages are applied to promote the acquisition of many other skills as

TABLE 13.1
The Learning Strategies Curriculum of the University of Kansas Center for Research on Learning

---

Acquisition Strand

Strategic Math Series: Teaches students problem-solving procedures for acquiring and applying basic math facts. The strategies are designed to help students develop fluency in basic math facts and use strategies for solving word problems.

Word Identification Strategy: Teaches students a problem-solving procedure for quickly attacking and decoding unknown words in reading materials, allowing them to move on quickly for the purpose of comprehending the passage.

Paraphrasing Strategy: Directs students to read a limited section of material, ask themselves the main idea and the details of the section, and put that information in their own words. The strategy is designed to improve comprehension by focusing attention on the important information of a passage and by stimulating active involvement with the passage.

Self-Questioning Strategy: Aids reading comprehension by having students actively ask questions about key pieces of information in a passage and then read to find the answers for these questions.

Visual Imagery Strategy: Improves students' acquisition, storage, and recall of prose material. Students improve reading comprehension by reading short passages and visualizing the scene that is described, incorporating actors, action, and details.

Storage Strand

FIRST-Letter Mnemonic Strategy: Aids students in memorizing lists of information by teaching them to design mnemonics or memorization aids, and to find and make lists of crucial information.

Paired Associates Strategy: Aids students in memorizing pairs or small groups of information by using visual imagery, matching pertinent information with familiar objects, coding important dates, and using a first-syllable technique.

Vocabulary Strategy: Helps students learn the meaning of new vocabulary words using powerful memory-enhancement techniques. Strategy steps cue students to focus on the critical elements of the concept; to use visual imagery, associations with prior knowledge, and keyword mnemonic devices to create a study card; and to study the card to enhance comprehension and recall of the concept.

Expression and Demonstration of Competence Strand

SLANT: A Strategy for Class Participation: Helps students participate in class discussions. Students learn how to use appropriate posture, track the talker, activate their thinking, and ocntribute information.

Fundamentals in the Sentence Writing Strategy: Teaches the fundamental concepts and skills associated with writing simple sentences and how to identify subjects, verbs, prepositions, infinitives, and adjectives.

Proficiency in the Sentence Writing Strategy: Teaches students how to recognize and generate four types of sentences: simple, compound, complex, and compound-complex.

Paragraph Writing Strategy: Teaches students how to write well-organized, complete paragraphs by outlining ideas, selecting a point-of-view and tense for the paragraph, sequencing ideas, and checking their work.

Error Monitoring Strategy: Teaches students a process for detecting and correcting errors in their writing and for producing a neater written product. Students are taught to locate errors in paragraph organization, sentence structure, capitalization, overall editing and appearance, punctuation, and spelling by asking themselves a series of questions. Students correct their errors and rewrite the passage before submitting it to their teacher.

Theme Writing Strategy: Teaches students to generate ideas for themes, organize these ideas into a logical sequence, write the paragraphs, monitor errors, and rewrite the theme.

Assignment Completion Strategy: Teaches students to monitor their assignments from the time an assignment is given until it is completed and turned in to the teacher. Students write down assignments; analyze the assignments; schedule various subtasks; complete the subtasks and, ultimately, the entire task; and submit the completed assignment.

TABLE 13.1
(continued)

Test-Taking Strategy: Teaches students to allocate time during a test and read instructions and questions carefully. A question is either answered or put aside for later consideration. The obviously wrong answers are eliminated from the abandoned questions and a reasonable guess is made. The last step is to survey the entire test for unanswered questions.

InSPECT Strategy: Teaches students to detect and correct spelling errors in their documents by using a computerized spellchecker or a handheld spelling device.

well (e.g., applying for a job, accepting criticism, self-questioning, outlining, setting goals, identifying words, completing a word problem in math, and writing a paragraph).

The following instructional procedures relate to the acquisition and generalization of skills and strategies:

1. ***The student should be committed to learning the strategy and fully understand the purpose and benefits.*** The student's understanding of the potential effect of the strategy and the consequences of continued use of ineffective and inefficient strategies is the first step in the instructional process. The student must understand that the goal is to learn the content or perform a certain task successfully, rather than simply to learn a strategy. Thus, the teacher must inform the student of the strategy's goals and obtain a commitment from him or her to learn the strategy.

2. ***The physical and mental actions covered in the strategy should be fully described and explained.*** The student must be taught what to do and how to think about each step of the strategy, and the full content of the strategy should be made apparent to the student. Examples and circumstances relevant to the student's experiences should be incorporated into the presentation, and the student should play an active role in exploring and commenting on the strategy and its uses.

3. ***The student should be taught how to remember the strategy to facilitate the process of self-instruction.*** After the content of the strategy is presented to the student, the teacher should demonstrate how the strategy can be remembered easily. If a mnemonic is used, the teacher explicitly should relate the mnemonic to the intended physical and mental associations and demonstrate how

to use the mnemonic to guide the student in the self-instructional process.

4. ***The student should understand the process of learning the strategy and participate in goal-setting activities to anticipate and monitor learning.*** The student should be informed of the acquisition and generalization process, understand the goals and vocabulary associated with each step, and set goals for mastery of each step. As instruction proceeds, the student should evaluate each step as it is completed to determine whether specified learning goals have been met.

5. ***Multiple models of the strategy should be provided, and an appropriate balance between the physical and mental activities involved in the strategy should be achieved.*** The heart of strategic instruction is in the think-aloud model in which the teacher accurately and completely demonstrates the strategy's application. While a complete and thorough initial model is critical, additional modeling episodes should be inserted throughout the instructional process. In each of these models, the physical activities must be demonstrated as the associated mental activities are made apparent in an overt think-aloud depiction of the strategy.

6. ***The student should be enlisted in the model and become a full participant in guiding the strategy instructional process.*** While the modeling phase of instruction begins with the teacher, it should end with student participation in and experience with the modeling process. The teacher gradually should include the student in the model. The student eventually should be able to perform the strategy while providing many of the key mental actions associated with each step.

7. ***The strategy should be understood fully and memorized before practice in the strategy is initiated.*** Sufficient rehearsal of the strategy

TABLE 13.2
Parameters and features of effective learning strategies

Parameter	Features
Content	The strategy steps: • lead to a specific and successful outcome. • are sequenced to ensure an efficient approach for the task. • remind students to use specific cognitive and metacognitive processes. • remind students to choose and use appropriate procedures, rules, and skills. • cue the use of overt action. • are performed in a reasonable amount of time.
Design	The strategy steps: • include a remembering system. • include brief and simple working in the remembering system. • begin with an action word. • use seven or fewer steps in the remembering system.
Usefulness	The strategy: • addresses important and common problems that students encounter. • addresses demands faced over time. • is applicable across settings and situations.

steps should be provided before the student is asked to perform the strategy from memory. Before applied practice of the strategy begins, the student should know the remembering system and be able to demonstrate how to use it to guide the self-instructional process. During the forthcoming practice phase, the student must sufficiently understand the strategy and be able to concentrate on applying it rather than focus unnecessary mental effort on remembering its aspects.

8. *Practice should begin with controlled guided practice and conclude with advanced independent practice.* The goal of the initial practice stage should be mastering the strategy without having to struggle with content or situational demands. Thus, practice should occur under conditions in which the student feels comfortable or knowledgeable. As the strategy is learned, conditions that approximate actual setting and task demands should be introduced gradually until the student uses the strategy fully to meet actual learning demands.

9. *A measurement system should provide ongoing information that will demonstrate to*

the student and the teacher that the strategy is being learned and used and that the demands of the setting are being met. Knowledge of progress and performance is a critical part of the learning process. The measurement system should tell the student whether the strategy is promoting success. However, the measurement system also should provide information related to the student's mastery of the strategy.

10. *While generalization should be promoted throughout the strategy acquisition process, specific efforts to promote generalization should follow strategy acquisition.* After the strategy has been mastered, the student should attempt to generalize it. In the generalization stage, the teacher and student must work together to identify where the strategy can be used across settings and conditions, identify modifications in the strategy to make it more generalizable, and program use of the strategy across settings.

Additional information about the Strategies Intervention Model and the Learning Strategies Curriculum can be obtained by contacting the

TABLE 13.3
Stages of strategy acquisition and generalization developed by the University of Kansas Center for Research on Learning

---

Stage 1: Pretest and Make Commitments

Purpose: To motivate students to learn a new strategy and establish a baseline for instruction

Phase 1: Orientation and pretest
  Give rationales and overview
  Administer pretest
  Determine whether strategy is appropriate

Phase 2: Awareness and commitment
  Describe:
    the alternative strategy
    results others have achieved
  Ask for a commitment to learn the new strategy

Stage 2: Describe the Strategy

Purpose: To present a clear picture of the overt and covert processes and steps of the new strategy

Phase 1: Orientation and overview
  Give rationales for the strategy
  Describe situations where the strategy can be used

Phase 2: Present the strategy and the remembering system
  Describe the overall strategic processes
  Explain the remembering system and its relationship to self-instruction
  Set goals for learning the strategy

Stage 3: Model the Strategy

Purpose: To demonstrate the cognitive behaviors and physical actions involved in using the strategy

Phase 1: Orientation
  Review previous learning
  State expectations

Phase 2: Presentation
  Think aloud
  Self-instruct
  Self-monitor
  Perform task

Phase 3: Student enlistment
  Prompt involvement
  Check understanding

Stage 4: Verbal Elaboration and Rehearsal

Purpose: To ensure comprehension of the strategy and facilitate student mediation

Phase 1: Verbal elaboration
  Have students describe the intent of the strategy and the process involved
  Have students describe what each step is designed to do

Phase 2: Verbal rehearsal
  Require students to name each of the steps at an automatic level

Stage 5: Controlled Practice and Feedback

Purpose: To provide practice in controlled materials, build confidence and fluency, and gradually shift the responsibility for strategy use to students

Phase 1: Orientation and overview
  Review the strategy steps
  Prompt reports of strategy use and errors

(continued on next page)

TABLE 13.3
(continued)

Phase 2: Guided practice
  Prompt student completion of activities as teacher models
  Prompt increasing student responsibility
  Give clear instructions for peer-mediated practice

Stage 6: Advanced Practice and Feedback

Purpose: To provide practice in advanced materials (e.g., general class or work-related) and situations and gradually shift the responsibility for strategy use and feedback to students

The instructional sequence for Advanced Practice and Feedback is the same as the instructional sequence used for Controlled Practice. However, this level of practice should:
  use grade-appropriate or situation-appropriate materials
  fade prompts and cues for use and evaluation

Stage 7: Confirm Acquisition and Make Generalization Commitments

Purpose: To document mastery and to build a rationale for self-regulated generalization

Phase 1: Confirm and celebrate
  Congratulate student on meeting mastery
  Discuss achievement and attribution for success

Phase 2: Forecast and commit to generalization
  Explain goals of generalization
  Explain phases of generalization
  Prompt commitment to generalize

Stage 8: Generalization

Purpose: To ensure the use of the strategy in other settings

Phase 1: Orientation
  Prompt students to:
    discuss rationales for strategy use
    identify settings in which the strategy might be used
    discuss how to remember to use the strategy
  Evaluate appropriateness of the strategy in various settings and materials

Phase 2: Activation
  Prompt and monitor student application across settings
  Enlist assistance of other teachers
  Prompt students to:
    apply the strategy in a variety of settings, situations, materials, and assignments
    set goals for the use of the strategy
  Prompt general classroom teachers to:
    understand the strategy
    cue use of strategy
    provide feedback on strategy use

Phase 3: Adaptation
  Prompt students to:
    identify where these processes and strategies are required across settings
    identify how the strategy can be modified
    repeat application with the modified strategy

Phase 4: Maintenance
  Prompt students to:
    discuss rationales related to long-term use of the strategy
    set goals related to monitoring long-term use
    identify self-reinforcers and self-rewards

Source: From *Students with Learning Disabilities,* (pp. 388–389), 5th ed., by C. D. Mercer, 1997, Upper Saddle River, NJ: Merrill/Prentice Hall. Copyright 1997 by Prentice-Hall Publishing Company. Reprinted by permission.

Coordinator of Training, Center for Research on Learning, 3061 Robert Dole Human Development Center, The University of Kansas, Lawrence, KS 66045-2342.

☀ CONTENT INSTRUCTION

In developing programs for adolescents with learning difficulties, educators must determine how students can master the content of the secondary curriculum and, at the same time, develop important skills and strategies (Ellis & Lenz, 1990). In most educational programs, adolescents with learning problems spend the majority of their school day in general education classes.

In many cases, the general classroom teacher must individualize and modify instruction to accommodate the needs of students with learning problems. The accommodations requested from special educators may include altering either how content is delivered or evaluated or the nature or quantity of the content that the teacher expects students to master. Inclusion teachers use numerous instructional alternatives to help these students. These alternatives often are referred to as *accommodation techniques, compensatory techniques,* or *instructional adaptations.* Laurie, Buchwach, Silverman, and Zigmond (1978) recommend that special and general educators follow a problem-solving sequence in developing instructional alternatives for students with learning difficulties. Steps in a problem-solving sequence include the following:

1. Determine the requirements for "making it" in the general class.
2. Specify the course requirements that the student is not satisfying.
3. Identify factors hindering the student's performance.
4. Brainstorm possible classroom modifications.
5. Select a plan of action.
6. Implement the plan.
7. Evaluate the plan.

Determining the types of modifications needed is critical in providing program alternatives. Chapter 3 presents testing modifications as well as assessment factors for determining how a student learns, and Chapter 4 includes an extensive list of accommodations involving materials, interactive instruction, and student performance. The alternatives listed in Table 13.4 provide an overview of some modification possibilities. This section presents instructional alternatives in the following areas: content enhancements, adapting materials, assignments, tutoring, testing, and administrative considerations.

Content Enhancements

Research on learning has led to an increase in studies on how content-area teachers can present information that is sensitive to the strategies used by students. When information is presented in a manner that helps students organize, understand, and remember important information, the effect of ineffective or inefficient strategies may be minimized. To accomplish this, the content-area teacher must select enhancements that can be used during a presentation to meet specific learning goals and then must teach students how to use each enhancement successfully. For example, to help students understand something unfamiliar and abstract, the teacher may use an analogy of something that is familiar and concrete. The teacher then must present the analogy so that students see the relationship between the two concepts, and the new concept becomes meaningful. Thus, content enhancements are techniques that enable the teacher to help students identify, organize, comprehend, and retain critical content information (Lenz, Bulgren, & Hudson, 1990).

Content enhancements can be used when a lesson's content appears to require more manipulation than the teacher predicts the student can handle effectively or efficiently. According to Schumaker, Deshler, and McKnight (1991), the enhancements can be used to make abstract information more concrete, connect new knowledge with familiar knowledge, highlight relationships and organizational structures within the information to be presented, and draw the unmotivated learner's attention to the information. However, simply using a content enhancement as part of a lesson cannot be viewed as an effective practice. Research indicates that the teacher must help the student see how the enhancement is working and enlist each student's active involvement and support in using the enhancement in the learning process.

Bulgren and Lenz (1996) discuss devices and routines as two components of content enhancements

TABLE 13.4

Instructional alternatives for an inclusion teacher

Classroom Organization	Classroom Management	Methods of Presentation	Methods of Practice	Methods of Testing
Examine Grouping Arrangements	**Examine Grading System**	**Examine Content**	**Examine General Structure**	**Examine Type**
Large-group instruction	Homework	Authentic context	Amount to practice	Oral short answer
Small-group instruction	Tests	Different instructional goals	Time to practice	Oral elaborated answer
Individual instruction	Class participation	Time for learning	Group/individual practice	Written objective items
Adult with student	Goals	Amount of content	Teacher-led practice	Written essay items
Peer-mediated learning	Group projects	Difficulty of content	Independent practice	Demonstration
Computer-assisted instruction	Individual projects		Peer-mediated practice	
		Examine General Structure	Difficulty level	**Examine General Structure**
Examine Methods of Instruction	**Examine Reinforcement System**	Previews	Feedback	Group/individual
Explicit instruction	Tangibles	Organizers		Timed/untimed
Guided instruction	Points	Content enhancements	**Examine Response**	Amount tested
Implicit instruction	Praise	Assignments	Written	
	Grades	Mnemonic devices	True–false	**Examine Response**
	Special activity	Feedback	Multiple-choice	Objective— recognition
	Free time	Student involvement	Matching	Objective— recall
	Goal setting		Short answer	Essay—list
	Progress chart	**Examine Type**	Essay	Essay—short answer
	Computer time	Review	List	Essay—long answer
	Student involvement in planning	Advance organizers	Compare	
		Guided practice	Open book/ closed book	
	Examine Rules	Discussion	Create	
	Behavior expectations	Question/answer	Oral	
	Rule rationales	Videotapes	Long answer	
	Student involvement	Audiotapes	Presentation	
	Number of rules	Movies	Discussion	
		Computers		
		Transparencies	**Examine Type of Materials**	
			Texts	
			Worksheets	
			Computer	
			Audiotape	
			Videotape	

that make them effective for both general education students and students with learning problems. *Devices* are instructional tools that teachers use to promote learning. They help teachers foster explicit learning, focus on specific points, and make a concrete connection between ideas and relationships. Different types of devices are used to help students organize, understand, describe, demonstrate, and re-

call content. These devices include verbal and visual modes of presentation. Figure 13.2 presents content enhancement devices according to function (type) and mode of presentation.

Routines are strategic instructional procedures that involve students in developing, acquiring, and applying the device. Bulgren and Lenz (1996) define a teaching routine as "a set of integrated in-

FIGURE 13.2

Content enhancements

Type: used to	Mode: presentation	
	Verbal	**Visual**
Organize (arrange information in meaningful structures)	Summarization Chunking Advance organizer Post organizer Verbal cues about organization	Outline Web Hierarchical graphic organizer Table Grid Flowchart
Promote Understanding (clarify words or concepts)	Analogy Comparison Synonym Metaphor Antonym Simile Example	Symbol Concrete object Picture Model Diagram
Describe (tell a story)	Current events Past events Fictional story Hypothetical scenario Personal story	Film Filmstrip Video
Demonstrate (show through action)	Role play Dramatic portrayal	Physical gesture or movement Movable objects Demonstration
Promote Recall	Acronyms Keywords	Visual images Sketches

Source: From *Teaching Adolescents with Learning Disabilities: Strategies and Methods* (p. 446), 2nd ed., by D. D. Deshler, E. S. Ellis, and B. K. Lenz, 1996, Denver, CO: Love. Copyright 1996 by Love Publishing Company. Reprinted by permission.

structional procedures revolving around a specific teaching device designed to promote broad learning goals associated with the full spectrum of information acquisition, storage, and expression/ demonstration of content information" (p. 447). When devices are embedded in these instructional procedures, they become a routine. The University of Kansas Center for Research on Learning has developed and published the following routines:

• The *Course Organizer Routine* (Lenz, Schu- maker, Deshler, & Bulgren, 1998) includes a set of activities to help the teacher create a course around big ideas for diverse learners. It features a

mnemonic device to help the teacher reflect on course concepts and outcomes and formulate questions.

• The *Unit Organizer Routine* (Lenz, Bulgren, Schumaker, Deshler, & Boudah, 1994) includes a set of steps that the teacher uses to create a unit of instruction for diverse learners. It involves re- flecting on the content of a unit and important out- comes and the development of a graphic "road map." (This routine is presented in Chapter 4.)

• The *Lesson Organizer Routine* (Lenz, Marrs, Schumaker, & Deshler, 1993) includes a set of steps that the teacher uses to create a lesson for diverse learners. It involves reflecting on the content and important outcomes and the creation of a graphic device that serves as a "road map" for the lesson. (This routine is presented in Chapter 4.)

• The *Concept Mastery Routine* (Bulgren, Deshler, & Schumaker, 1993) features a concept diagram that allows the teacher to exhibit information related to a key concept. The teacher works with students to analyze and understand the concept.

• The *Concept Anchoring Routine* (Bulgren, Schumaker, & Deshler, 1994) features a visual device called the *anchoring table,* which allows the teacher to display information about a new concept by tying it to a familiar concept that shares critical characteristics with the target concept.

• The *Concept Comparison Routine* (Bulgren, Lenz, Deshler, & Schumaker, 1995) features a visual device called the *concept comparison table,* which enables the teacher to display information about two or more concepts or topics through analyzing the characteristics they share.

• The *Quality Assignment Routine* (Rademacher, Deshler, Schumaker, & Lenz, 1998) is a routine for planning high-quality assignments. It features a planning phase, an explanation phase, and an evaluation phase. Each interactive phase helps the teacher guide students to complete assigned tasks.

• The *Survey Routine* (Deshler, Schumaker, & McKnight, 1997) is a routine for providing an overview of a reading assignment.

• The *Clarifying Routine* (Ellis, 1997) features a set of procedures and a graphic device to enable the teacher to present information associated with new terms to students.

• The *Framing Routine* (Ellis, 1998) features several graphic devices for presenting complex sets of interrelated information to students.

• The *Recall Enhancement Routine* (Schumaker, Bulgren, Deshler, & Lenz, 1998) enables the teacher to show students how to create and use mnemonic devices.

In a review of research on the use of content enhancements (i.e., devices and routines), Hudson, Lignugaris-Kraft, and Miller (1993) found the following seven types:

1. **Advance organizers.** These enhancements help orient and prepare the student for the upcoming lesson. An advance organizer is presented before the lesson presentation and can in-

clude an array of information about the lesson. Some of the most common features include linking the lesson content to prior lessons or information, introducing the targeted content, explaining tasks to be performed by the teacher and student, providing a rationale for the lesson, and introducing materials and new vocabulary. Ellis and Friend (1991) present a simple procedure to help teachers use advance organizers. The FORM device is used to introduce content-area lessons:

F—*Focus:* What will be the focus of the lesson and the focus of students' questions?

O—*Organization:* What organizational devices will be used to make the lesson easier to learn, and what sequence of activities will be used during the lesson?

R—*Relationship:* What have you learned before that will help you now? If you master the material, how will you benefit in the future?

M—*Most important goal:* What do you need to learn if you do not learn anything else?

The teacher can adapt the advance organizer and use the aspects that help him or her deliver the content and orient students to what is being taught. In addition to the advance organizer, the teacher can use lesson organizers that reinforce the critical structure and content of the lesson. To clarify the organization and focus of the content, the teacher can use words and statements such as "first . . . , second . . . , third . . . ," and "the most important idea is . . . ." Diagrams, tables, or charts also can help students see the content structure. Organizers can be used before an instructional sequence (advance organizer), throughout an instructional sequence (lesson organizer), or at the end of an instructional sequence (post organizer). For example, to help orient students to a learning task, Schumaker et al. (1991) present a teaching routine on introducing a typical chapter. In this routine, the teacher leads students through an introductory and focused exploration of the chapter before they begin to read it. In the exploration process, the teacher guides students to discover how the chapter fits in with surrounding chapters, prompts them to discuss and rephrase the chaper title and subsections, and helps them identify the critical main ideas and vocabulary presented in the various sections of the text.

2. ***Visual displays.*** These enhancements feature several formats that graphically display the organization of the content. For example, Figure 13.3 illustrates three types of visual displays (e.g., representative, directional, and hierarchical/central). Visual displays can be combined to build powerful and sophisticated teaching routines. Concept diagramming (Bulgren et al., 1993), semantic feature analysis (Bos & Anders, 1987), and semantic webbing (Anders & Bos, 1984) are three routines that help students understand the various parts of concepts. The use of a graphic organizer is included in all of these routines. In the concept diagramming routine, the teacher helps students brainstorm information about an important concept, and these characteristics of the concept are organized into three separate lists (i.e., *always present, sometimes present,* and *never present*). Students construct a definition for the concept from the list of characteristics that are always present and then generate examples and nonexamples of the concept based on the definition. For example, Figure 13.4 presents a diagram of the mammal concept. The semantic feature analysis routine involves the use of a table in which concept examples are listed in a vertical column and important concept characteristics or features are listed in a horizontal column. By reading across the table for a given example, students can identify which concept features the example contains. Also, students can construct a table by exploring information about an example of a concept and placing a plus or minus sign in the intersection to indicate a positive or negative relationship, a zero to indicate no relationship, or a question mark if the student is unsure of the relationship. The third routine, semantic webbing, involves writing the important term, idea, or concept on the chalkboard and encouraging students to generate information. The appropriate placement of the information about the concept in relation to the original stimulus concept is discussed, and lines are drawn to indicate coordinate and subordinate relationships, examples, or features.

3. ***Study guides.*** These enhancements are used to highlight critical information. Study guides usually consist of statements or questions that stress important content, and formats include matching, short-answer questions, and framed outlines or fill in the blanks. Thus, guides can consist of outlines or lists of questions that the teacher

can use to focus student attention, point out important information, and encourage the student to inspect the material more closely. In guides involving the use of graphics, the student is directed to complete missing parts of constructed diagrams of the content. Both question- and graphic-oriented study guides are more helpful to students than self-study alone; however, the use of graphics in study guides is perceived as the most effective (Bergerud, Lovitt, & Horton, 1988).

4. ***Mnemonic devices.*** These enhancements are designed to help students remember content. They feature pictorial or verbal techniques that promote recall of unfamiliar information. Studies on how teachers can help students consolidate information into meaningful chunks of information affirm the premise that students need to understand what they must remember before reducing the memory load with the use of a mnemonic device (Nagel, Schumaker, & Deshler, 1986). Thus, the teacher and students should identify what is most important about the information presented and then label and organize it. Studies on the actual manipulations that can help students remember important information consist of a variety of tactics including creating mental images, making familiar associations, using first-letter mnemonics, or using keyword strategies. First-letter mnemonics is the primary verbal format used to help students with learning problems remember information. In this technique, students learn the first letter of a word, phrase, or sentence to cue them to remember the targeted information. For example, the word EASY is a mnemonic for remembering the following study strategy (Ellis & Lenz, 1987):

E—*Elicit wh* questions to identify important information (who, what, when, where, and why).
A—*Ask* yourself which information is least troublesome.
S—*Study* easy parts first, hardest parts last.
Y—*Yes*—do use self-reinforcement.

Popular verbal formats include keyword, mimetic, and symbolic. The keyword format pairs a picture of a familiar object that is phonetically similar to the term to be learned. The mimetic format includes pictorial representations of the targeted information; for example, to remind students of a definition of a lighthouse, a picture of a lighthouse

FIGURE 13.3
Types of visual displays

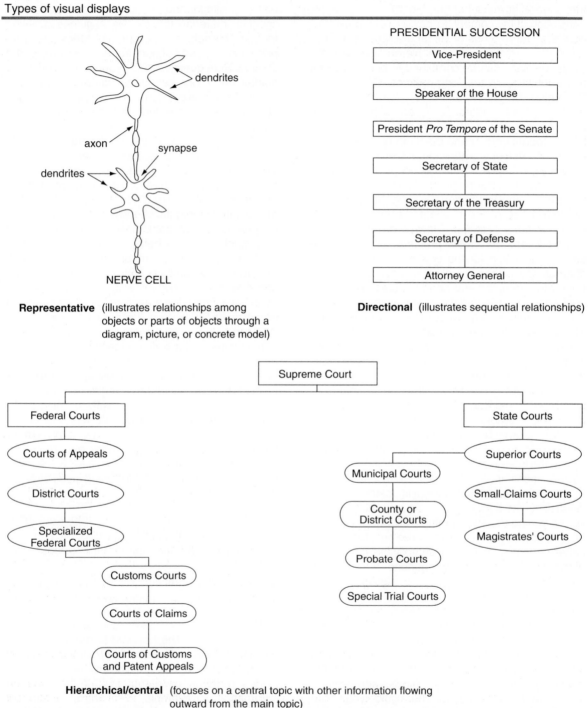

PRESIDENTIAL SUCCESSION

Vice-President
Speaker of the House
President *Pro Tempore* of the Senate
Secretary of State
Secretary of the Treasury
Secretary of Defense
Attorney General

Representative (illustrates relationships among objects or parts of objects through a diagram, picture, or concrete model)

Directional (illustrates sequential relationships)

Hierarchical/central (focuses on a central topic with other information flowing outward from the main topic)

FIGURE13.4

A concept diagram

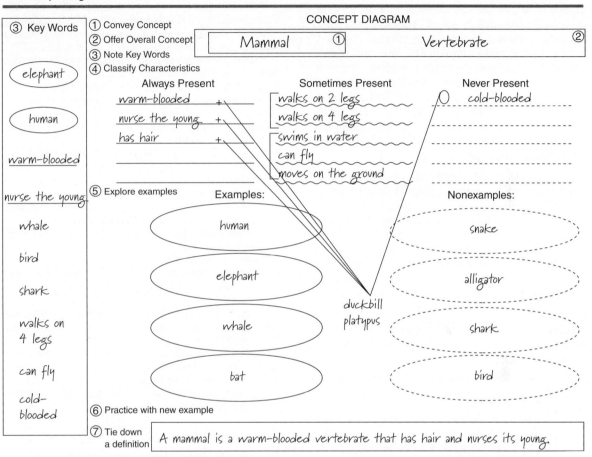

Source: From *The Content Enhancement Series: The Concept Mastery Routine* (p. 37), by J. A. Bulgren, D. D. Deshler, and J. B. Schumaker, 1993, Lawrence, KS: Edge Enterprises. Copyright 1993 by J. A. Bulgren, D. D. Deshler, and J. B. Schumaker. Reprinted by permission.

Note: The concept diagram shown in Figure 13.4 is an instructional tool developed and researched at the University of Kansas Center for Research on Learning (Bulgren, Schumaker, & Deshler, 1988). It is one of a number of teaching devices designed for teachers to use as they teach content information to classes containing diverse student populations. It is a databased teaching instrument that has been found effective when used with a planning routine as well as a teaching routine that combines cues about the instruction, specialized delivery of the content, involvement of the students in the cognitive processes, and a review of the learning process and content material (Bulgren et al., 1993). It has not been shown to be an effective tool if it is simply distributed to the students. For more information on the training workshops that accompany the use of *The Concept Mastery Routine,* contact the University of Kansas Center for Research on Learning, 3061 Dole Building, Lawrence, KS 66049, or call 913/864-4780.

is used. Symbolic mnemonics use common symbols to represent critical information; for example, doves may be used to symbolize peace.

5. ***Audio recordings.*** These enhancements include verbatim audiotapes of written materials and key information audiotapes that are used along with other materials.

6. ***Computer-assisted instruction.*** This enhancement involves delivering instruction through computers. The primary formats include

simulations and tutorials, which students usually complete independently. However, Hudson et al. (1993) note that few computer programs, to date, are designed well enough for students with learning problems to learn new content independently. In computer simulations, students review and apply facts and concepts previously learned. (Chapter 2 covers computer-assisted instruction.)

7. ***Peer-mediated instruction.*** This enhancement involves the use of classmates to teach one another. It features peer tutoring, classwide peer tutoring, and cooperative learning. (Chapter 2 presents these strategies.)

The overall results from the content enhancement research are encouraging (Bulgren & Lenz, 1996; Hudson et al., 1993). Furthermore, the research indicates that various enhancements can be used effectively at different phases in the instructional cycle. For example, mnemonic devices can be used during learning set, presentation of new material, and guided practice, whereas peer mediation can be integrated during independent practice and evaluation of student progress.

Activities for Presenting Content   The following activities may help present content to students with learning problems:

* Provide a list of simple questions before a lecture or reading assignment to serve as an effective advance organizer.
* Provide written backup to oral directions and lectures (e.g., use an outline on a handout or overhead).
* Use the following activities for presenting information to the student who has difficulty with auditory input (Towle, 1982):
  * Provide pre-presentation questions.
  * Develop vocabulary before presentation.
  * Pace presentation and give frequent examples.
  * Cluster main points.
  * Summarize.
  * Provide opportunities for student questions and discussion.
  * Repeat important points.
  * Relate content to other topics.
* For the student who has difficulty following oral presentations, provide tapes of the lectures or allow him or her to record the class presentation and discussions. In addition, good note takers can use carbon paper to make copies of their notes for problem learners, or photocopies of notes can be given to problem learners.
* Instruct the student with learning problems to sit near the front of the class. This encourages atten-

tion to teacher-directed activities and reduces distractions.
* Match a problem learner with a peer helper who can assist by explaining directions and assignments, reviewing essential information from a lecture, sharing and correcting notes, and working on joint assignments or projects.
* Use the following suggestions to help the student maintain attention and learn:
  * Combine visual and auditory presentations.
  * Establish eye contact with students during oral directions and lectures.
  * Write assignments, directions, and lecture objectives on the chalkboard.
  * Pause after questions to provide thinking time.
  * Pause after each segment while giving directions and presenting content.
  * Give examples and demonstrations.
  * Briefly review information from previous lectures, and summarize information at the end of each lecture.
  * Provide the student with time after the lecture for reviewing and improving notes.
  * Talk distinctly and at a reasonable rate.
  * Give cues concerning what is important, and refer the student to textbook pages for more clarification or information.
* Use a pause procedure during lectures to improve the recall of adolescents with learning problems (Hughes, Hendrickson, & Hudson, 1986). Pause several times during a lecture (e.g., every 6 to 12 minutes) for students to discuss the content covered. To help groups of three to four students systematically discuss the content, instruct students to use the RAP mnemonic presented in Chapter 2.

Adapting Materials

The difficulty level of texts and materials used in content-area classes may present a problem to secondary students with learning difficulties because the reading level may be several grades above the student's reading level. To assist the student in learning, it often is necessary to modify or adapt the ways in which content is presented. These modifications aim to change the format and mode of presentation while maintaining the basic content. Alternatives for adapting materials include developing parallel curriculum, simplifying texts, and taping texts.

Developing Parallel Curriculum   Parallel curriculum materials present essential content in ways that help the problem learner organize, practice, and master important information. Many school districts provide general and special educators with release time or summer employment to write curriculum guides for various courses designed for use with low achievers. Thus, a low achiever receives the standard text and a curriculum guide or booklet. For example, Project PASS (Packets Assuring Student Success) is an inclusion program for secondary students with difficulties in United States history and American government. The instructional packets are written at the third- to fifth-grade reading level and contain vocabulary, a glossary, a pretest and posttest, subject content, activities, and projects. (Information is available from Project PASS, Livonia Public School District, 15125 Farmington Road, Livonia, MI 48154.)

Moreover, some publishers offer adapted textbooks in which the content matches the grade-level textbook but is written at a lower readability level (e.g., *Wonders of Science* and *America's Story,* published by Steck-Vaughn). However, in inclusive settings, many students with learning problems prefer to use the same text that others are using; thus, it is helpful to provide the simplified materials as a supplement to help the students study the grade-level textbook.

Simplifying Texts   The simplification of textbooks assists low achievers to master essential information efficiently. The following activities and procedures can be used for simplifying texts:

- Provide the student with a highlighted text. Underlining or highlighting the main ideas, words, and concepts with a marker pen helps the student focus on relevant material. Also, deleting irrelevant or nonessential words with a dark pen identifies important content.
- Transform words into graphic aids by creating charts, graphs, drawings, or models. Also, real materials are helpful in presenting content.
- Use advance organizers to prepare the student for the reading material. These include outlines, diagrammatic overviews, study guides, questions, and directed previewing (e.g., attention to selected headings or illustrations).
- Reduce the complexity and length of work units to the extent that the low achiever receives periodic and consistent closure.
- Provide self-correcting learning materials. Self-checking answer keys at frequent intervals are helpful checkpoints to guide the student through the material.
- When simplifying texts, concentrate on content, sentence structure, and vocabulary (Beech, 1983). In simplifying content, it helps to present generalizations first and follow with supporting details, sequence events in chronological order, and cluster related material.

- For the student with limited reading skills, consider using rewritten texts. In situations where rewriting is feasible, the following guidelines are helpful:
- Keep sentences short; a five- to eight-word total is best.
- Use basic words of few syllables (e.g., use the 850 words included in Ogden's [1970] *Basic English Dictionary*).
- Use present tense and avoid passive voice.
- Use simple sentences and try to begin each sentence with a subject. Avoid appositives and parenthetical expressions. Simple sentences with the verb following the subject are easier to read than compound and complex sentences or sentences in inverted order.
- Avoid figurative or symbolic language (e.g., change "thundering herd" to "The herd galloped so hard the hoofs sounded like thunder when they hit the ground").
- Use picture clues as much as possible.
- Be certain that every pronoun has an unmistakable antecedent.
- Use new words sparingly. Repeating key words rather than using synonyms results in simpler content.
- Eliminate unnecessary words.

Taping Texts   An alternative to reading a textbook is to listen to it on tape. Taped texts can be acquired for the student in two ways. One is to qualify the student for the special recordings provided for individuals who are blind or have learning disabilities. (Applications are available from Recording for the Blind and Dyslexic, 20 Roszel Road, Princeton, NJ 08540.) In addition to making available their existing tapes, this service tape-records requested books at no charge. Another way to acquire tapes is for teachers, students, or parents to prepare them. Guidelines for taping include the following:

- Tape in a quiet place where rugs, draperies, and upholstered furniture can absorb extraneous noises.
- Place the microphone on the table about six inches from the recorder's mouth. Turn the volume control about halfway and read a portion of the material. Listen to the tape and adjust the volume and microphone location until desirable recording is obtained.
- Eliminate clicks by turning the volume on low before starting the recorder. At the end of the recording, let the tape run for a few moments and then gradually turn the volume down and off.

• Avoid recording during the first 5 seconds and take a break every 15 minutes. Use alternating voices to reduce boredom.

• Monitor the tape before giving it to the student.

• At the beginning of the tape, identify the title of the text, author, and chapters or portions to be read.

• Include the following directions in the initial text information: "Please stop the tape any time you wish to answer questions, write notes for yourself, or look at a section of the book more carefully. You will hear this sound (ring bell) at the end of each page to help you follow along in your textbook. Please turn to page ___ for the beginning of chapter ___."

• Include selected study questions at the beginning of the tape. This alerts the student to important content.

Assignments

Many special education teachers prefer to have students complete their work in the classroom so that they can observe performance and assist students who cannot complete assignments. Lenz, Ehren, and Smiley (1991) argue that students must be given the opportunity to complete work independently because assignment completion often signifies the independence of a learner in an academic setting. Lenz, Ehren, and Smiley organize assignment completion into completion knowledge and completion management. *Completion knowledge* involves the academic skills and background knowledge required to finish the assignment. *Completion management* involves the planning, integration, and organization of time, interests, and resources that facilitate the use of academic skills and knowledge. Lenz, Ehren, and Smiley also identify three basic types of assignments: study, daily work, and project. *Study assignments* require students to prepare for a test or some type of class activity, and the focus of the assignment usually is on the process rather than on a permanent product. *Daily work* consists of assignments (e.g., completion of chapter questions and worksheets) that follow up the content covered in class and are designed to promote practice and understanding of the content. *Project assignments* take more than one or two days to complete and often require stu-

dents to extend or apply content by preparing a report, theme, visual product, or presentation. Depending on the teacher's expectations, all three assignment types can be completed in the classroom setting (seatwork) or out of the classroom setting (homework) and can be performed either individually or in a group.

Research in the area of homework indicates that the more time a student spends working on homework, the higher the student's achievement (Fredrick & Walberg, 1980; Keith & Page, 1985; Walberg, 1984), even when variables such as socioeconomic status and ability are controlled (Page & Keith, 1981). Harnischfeger (1980) notes that this relationship is consistent across subject-matter areas as early as the fourth grade. Polachek, Kniesner, and Harwood (1978) also report that less-able students can compensate for their lower ability by increasing the amount of homework completed. However, to ensure the positive benefits of homework, Keith and Page note that the assignments must be appropriate for the student's ability and achievement levels.

Research findings on different types of assignments and the assignment-completion process indicate that creating better-structured and better-organized assignments may not improve the assignment-completion process if students' interest or motivation is not addressed. Thus, the teacher must attend to the basic nature and quality of the assignments. Lenz and Bulgren (1988) propose the following suggestions regarding classroom assignments to improve the achievement of adolescents with learning difficulties:

• Assignment requirements must be explicit and clear.

• Requirements should relate to important learning outcomes.

• Choices must be provided that enable students to personalize learning.

• Over time, choices should include what to learn, how to learn, and how to demonstrate what has been learned.

• Assignment completion initially should be modeled and guided in class by the teacher with student involvement.

• Students should know the dimensions of assignments and be prompted to ask questions about assignment completion.

* The process of learning about assignment completion should be considered as important as learning the content.
* Discussions regarding the quality of assignments and the outcomes associated with assignment completion should be a regular part of classroom activities.
* Students should regularly set goals related to improving the completion process and what is being learned as a result of assignment completion.
* Fewer assignments should be given, and they should emphasize the most important learning outcomes.
* Assignments should be evaluated rather than graded, and students should revise their work to improve the quality rather than the grade.
* Peers should be used frequently to promote a variety of learning models.

Meese (1994) provides the following suggestions regarding assignments for students with learning problems:

* Divide assignments into chunks and have timelines for each chunk.
* Extend time for completing assignments.
* Encourage the use of computers and calculators in assignment completion.
* Allow groups to complete some written assignments.
* Reduce the amount of copying needed throughout the assignment (i.e., having to copy assignment material from the text or the chalkboard and having to copy problems from a text).
* Require students to paraphrase an assignment's tasks.

Tutoring

At the secondary level, earning academic credits is a major instructional concern. Special education teachers often teach and assign credit for course content or provide tutoring in subject areas required for graduation (Carlson, 1981). Given the tutorial emphasis in secondary grades, Carlson (1985) suggests that guidelines or standards are needed for implementing and evaluating tutoring. He provides three principles for tutoring instruction:

1. ***Instruction should be powerful.*** To offer powerful instruction, the teacher must know the content well, provide enough time for intensive teaching, and follow the principles of effective instruction (e.g., reinforcement, engaged time, modeling, and feedback).

2. ***Instruction should result in long-range benefits to the learner.*** Effective instruction should diminish the effect that the learning difficulty may have on future learning or help the student function more adequately. In addition to immediate subject-matter content, the teacher should stress skills (e.g., study skills and test-taking skills) that increase the student's potential for later learning.

3. ***Teacher expectations for learner performance should be high.*** Success must be maintained, but expected levels of performance should not be reduced unless this is absolutely necessary.

Hammill and Bartel (1995) offer several nonacademic guidelines for tutors:

* Be dependable. Missing a few sessions can negatively affect the tutor–tutee relationship and impede the student's progress.
* Be patient during instruction. Be willing to review or go over the material until the student learns it.
* Focus on understanding the student's concerns and feelings.
* Maintain integrity by giving the student accurate feedback concerning progress.
* Respect the interpersonal relationship and handle it with sensitivity.

Information on peer tutoring is presented in Chapter 2.

Testing

Students with learning problems frequently have difficulty displaying their knowledge or skills on tests. Modifications in test formats often help them perform better. The following suggestions are provided for improving test performances:

* Give frequent, timed minitests so that testing is not such an isolated, anxiety-provoking situation. Give practice tests and have students test one another and review answers.
* Use alternative response forms when existing formats appear to hinder student expression (Towle, 1982). Variations between and within response formats (e.g., essay, multiple choice, and short answer) are possible.

- Multiple-choice alternatives include using yes-or-no questions, reducing the number of choices, providing more information from which to make a choice, and using matching items.
- Short-answer alternatives include providing a list of facts and information to use in the answer, allowing the student to list information or choose from several prepared short answers, using the cloze technique in prepared paragraphs, and scrambling information to be arranged.
- Essay alternatives include providing a partial outline for the student to complete, allowing the student to tape answers, noting important points to be included in the response, and using take-home tests.
- In addition to the written test, provide a tape of the test items. Tapes allow the student to hear instructions and items as well as read them. Also, tapes are convenient for test makeups.
- Leave ample white space between test questions, and underline key words in the directions and test items.
- Provide test-study guides that feature various answer formats (e.g., essay, multiple choice, and fill in the blank).
- Provide additional time for the student who writes slowly, or use test items that require minimal writing. Oral tests also may be given and the answers can be recorded on tape.

Administrative Considerations

Administrative support is critical to the development and maintenance of a viable program for low achievers. Principals need support from central office staff, and teachers and counselors definitely need the support of the school principal. The following supportive activities and procedures help facilitate quality programs for low-achieving students by administrative actions:

- Identify general class teachers who are the most sensitive to the needs of students with learning problems. Schedule the student with these "sensitive" teachers, and support the teachers through such activities as providing favorable scheduling—for example, an extra planning period; assigning teacher aide(s) to their classes; releasing time to develop curriculum; placing volunteers in their classes; providing in-service training tailored to their needs; offering summer employment to develop curriculum; providing opportunities to attend conferences and workshops; offering support for university coursework; providing salary supplements; recognizing the value of the program to the entire faculty; and providing a budget that allows the purchase of some useful materials.
- Support the development of a homework hotline.
- Help establish a parental involvement and training program.
- Work with guidance counselors to schedule students so that a balanced workload is maintained (e.g., a balance between demanding courses or teachers and less demanding courses or teachers).
- Encourage the development of parallel alternative curriculum for the content classes.
- Support the development of equitable diploma options for mainstreamed students.

☀ STUDY SKILLS

The ability to acquire and use study skills is a key factor in school success. Applying efficient study skills involves learning how to learn and helps individuals acquire, retain, and use new information across a variety of learning situations. Devine (1987) defines *study skills* as "those competencies associated with acquiring, recording, organizing, synthesizing, remembering, and using information and ideas found in school" (p. 5). Although study skills are viewed as important to learning, systematic instruction in study skills is not provided with the curriculum. Unfortunately, many students with learning problems lack study skills and need instruction to learn them.

Hoover (1993) provides a framework for examining and assessing study skills. These 11 study skills and their respective subskills include the following:

1. *Reading rate:* Reads at different rates for scanning, skimming, normal reading, rapid reading, and careful reading.
2. *Listening:* Attends to listening tasks, applies meaning to verbal messages, and filters out auditory distractions.
3. *Note taking/outlining:* Uses headings appropriately, takes brief and clear notes, records

important information, uses note taking and outlining for report writing, uses note taking and outlining during lectures, constructs well-organized outlines, and has organized note card format.

4. *Report writing:* Organizes thoughts, uses proper punctuation, and uses proper spelling and grammar.
5. *Oral presentation:* Participates freely, organizes presentation, uses gestures, and speaks clearly.
6. *Graphic aids:* Attends to relevant elements, understands purposes, incorporates aids in presentations, and develops own visual aids.
7. *Test taking:* Organizes answers, proofreads, reads and understands directions, identifies clue words, properly records responses, answers difficult questions last, narrows possible correct answers, and corrects previous test-taking errors.
8. *Library use:* Uses card catalog, can locate materials, understands organization of a library, understands role of media specialist.
9. *Reference/dictionary use:* Identifies components, uses guide words, understands uses of reference materials, uses reference materials for written assignments, and identifies different reference materials.
10. *Time management:* Organizes daily activities, organizes weekly and monthly schedules, understands time management, reorganizes time when necessary, and prioritizes activities.
11. *Self-management of behavior:* Monitors own behavior, changes own behavior, thinks before acting, and takes responsibility for own behavior.

Preparatory Study Skills

Preparatory study skills involve skills and factors that are relevant precursors to efficient learning. The student's attitude and motivation are critical to student effort and consequent learning. The adolescent with learning problems needs to understand the relevance of assigned tasks and exhibit an attitude that facilitates effort. Chapter 5 and the discussion on motivation presented earlier in this chapter present strategies and activities aimed at improving motivation. This section focuses on time management and self-management.

Activities for Developing Time Management Considering the many demands placed on students to complete tasks at specific times and participate in a host of competing activities (such as being with peers, joining clubs, watching television, and listening to music), time management obviously is critical to surviving in school. The adolescent with learning problems usually needs instruction in time management. Activities for teaching time management include making schedules, making time estimates, and establishing priorities:

• Give the student a five-day schedule of after-school time and ask him or her to record all activities during these time blocks. Next, have the student allocate time blocks for specific activities (see Table 13.5) and follow the schedule as much as possible. Initially it may help the student to plan a day and then gradually build to a week.
• Provide the student with a calendar to assist in scheduling daily or weekly activities. Notations can be made on the calendar to remind the student of project

TABLE 13.5
A student's after-school schedule

	Monday	Tuesday	Wednesday	Thursday	Friday
3:00–4:00	with friend eat snack	with friend eat snack	with friend eat snack	with friend eat snack	with friend eat snack
4:00–5:00	play ball	play ball	do chores	play ball	play ball
5:00–6:00	play ball	play ball	do chores	play ball	play ball
6:00–7:00	eat dinner	eat dinner	eat dinner	eat dinner	eat dinner
7:00–8:00	study	study	study	go to game	go to movie
8:00–9:00	study	watch TV	study	go to game	go to movie
9:00–10:00	play CDs	watch TV	play video games	watch TV	watch TV

due dates or test dates. The student also can keep a notebook with all academic assignments and due dates.

• Encourage the student to allow some flexibility in the daily schedule. Occasionally unexpected events will take precedence over the planned activity. Introduce new events in the daily schedule and explain how adjustments can be made (e.g., if friends invite the student to get a pizza during study time, the student can replace television time with study time). Finally, the student should show the teacher the schedule with written adjustments when applicable.

• Either provide assignments or have the student list at least four school assignments and estimate how long it will take to complete each task. Then have the student record the amount of time it actually takes to complete the assignments. These times can be written on the student's schedule. Have student practice on tasks or subject areas in which her or his estimates are consistently inaccurate (off by more than 20 percent) until the estimates become realistic.

• Have the student list and prioritize school assignments. The student can rank the activities in the order they would be completed (i.e., place a 1 beside the first activity, a 2 beside the next activity, and so on). For example:

_____ Work on social studies project due in two weeks.
_____ Write a lab report in science due in two days.
_____ Complete a math worksheet due tomorrow.
_____ Practice baseball for the game in three days.
_____ Read 20 pages in a book in preparation for an oral report due in four days.

Discuss the need to consider consequences and time factors in prioritizing lists of things to do. Review the rankings and point out the correct and incorrect rankings in terms of consequences, breaking large tasks into smaller amounts (e.g., subdividing reading material into a number of pages per day), and time factors. Also have the student practice using value steps in prioritizing activities and tasks by grouping the list into three areas: activities with high value, activities with medium value, and activities with low value.

• To enhance the efficient completion of academic tasks, encourage the student to work in an environment conducive to studying. Ideally, the study area should be relatively quiet and unstimulating. If noise (e.g., television or classmates) becomes too distracting, the student can consider using earplugs.

Activities for Developing Self-Management
Self-management helps students learn to be responsible for their own behavior. Effective self-management enables students to monitor their behavior and decrease behaviors that interfere with the completion of assigned tasks (Hoover, 1995). Self-management through self-recording, self-evaluation, and self-reinforcement is discussed in Chapter 4. Effective activities to enhance self-management include the following:

• Ensure that the student understands specific behavioral expectations regarding assignments and class routines.

• Help the student set goals and timelines regarding schoolwork.

• Focus on "if-then" discussions in which the student explores the consequences of doing or not doing school assignments. Guide the student to realize that his or her actions influence consequences in life. Stress the positive possibilities of this proactive point of view.

• Provide the student with a self-monitoring chart to monitor a target behavior. Have the student record a check mark each time the behavior is displayed.

Acquisition Study Skills

To survive in the secondary setting, students must acquire and organize information from written and spoken input. Secondary teachers use the lecture/note-taking format extensively. Students also are required to obtain and organize information from textbooks. This section presents teaching activities and strategies aimed at developing information-gathering and organization skills. The skills are organized into the following areas: listening and note taking, textbook usage, reading and study skills, reading and note-taking skills, using visual aids, and sequential study methods.

Activities for Listening and Note Taking
Note taking is defined as an individualized process for recording and organizing information into a usable format and is dependent on active student participation (Devine, 1987). According to Saski, Swicegood, and Carter (1983), researchers agree that note taking assists the student, but no one approach is considered superior. Note-taking strategies can include either an outline format that stresses the identification of a main idea and supporting subordinate ideas or a columnar format that serves as a guide for organizing and classifying information. The importance and complexity of the note-taking process suggest the need for guidelines and activities, such as the following, to facilitate its development:

• To assist with listening and note taking, teach the student to use the following strategies (Towle, 1982):
• Physically prepare for listening and note taking by sitting alertly (e.g., leaning forward) in a comfortable desk

with the essential materials (e.g., notebook, two or more pencils or pens, and textbook). Remove all extraneous materials from the desk. To encourage listening and active class participation, students can be taught to use the SLANT mnemonic presented in Chapter 4.

- Review vocabulary (e.g., from text or handouts) related to the lecture topic before the lecture begins. It helps some students to have a list of difficult vocabulary words on their desks during the lecture/note-taking session.
- Listen for organizational cues or signal words (e.g., statements referring to time spans or sequences—*first, second, phase, period, era, next,* and *finally*). H. A. Robinson (1978) provides a list of signal words to help the student. It includes words that indicate a sequence or additional ideas (e.g., *first, second, also, furthermore, again, plus, next,* and *after that*); caution words, which point to concluding ideas (e.g., *consequently, thus, therefore, in conclusion, to summarize, finally,* and *as a result*); turn words, which indicate a change in ideas (e.g., *in contrast, opposed to, however, to the contrary, on the other hand, in spite of, although, yet,* and *despite*); stop words, which signal special significance (e.g., *significantly, absolutely, whenever, without doubt,* and *without question*); and application words, which indicate concrete application of a thought (e.g., *because, for example, specifically,* and *for instance*).
- Listen for content importance by noticing such cues as change in voice, tone, pitch, pauses, and volume.
- Ask for elaboration on specific points or content when confusion exists.
- Request examples to illustrate specific concepts.
- Paraphrase certain points to check understanding.
- Ask for visual references (e.g., pages in the text).

   * Use the following guided listening and note-taking activities to provide the student with opportunities to practice a variety of skills:

- The teacher plays a 5- to 8-minute tape recording of a lecture on content appropriate to the student's needs. The teacher and student sit beside each other and simultaneously take notes.
- At the end of the tape the teacher provides corrective feedback by sharing notes with the student and explaining listening and note-taking strategies. The teacher may elect to replay the tape and point out key factors (e.g., content organization and voice cues) in listening and note taking.
- The student listens to the tape again and takes a new set of notes. At the end of the tape the student compares the new notes to the teacher's model notes and makes corrections. The student practices this procedure to criterion with several different tapes.
- Short tapes are made of selected general classroom teachers' lectures. The student practices listening

and note taking on these tapes with corrective feedback until criterion is achieved.

- As the student progresses, the lecture tapes-feedback sequence is expanded to include more teachers in various content areas.
- Eventually the student takes notes only from live lectures and uses a set of model notes (e.g., from the teacher or a classmate) to correct or complete the notes.

This activity can be used with an individual or group to assess and remediate listening and note-taking skills. Notes from proficient peers can be used as models. In addition, teacher aides can be trained to tape lectures and provide model notes.

   * To improve legibility, have student pairs read each other's notes and circle illegible words. Have each student rewrite the circled words.

   * Present directed listening activities according to the following three stages developed by Cunningham and Cunningham (1976, pp. 27–28):

1. The Readiness Stage
   a. Establish motivation for the lesson.
   b. Introduce any new or difficult concepts.
   c. Introduce any new or difficult words.
   d. Set purposes for listening.
2. The Listening-Reciting Stage
   a. Students listen to satisfy the purposes for listening set during readiness.
   b. The teacher asks several literal and inferential questions that relate to the purposes set during readiness.
   c. The students volunteer interpretive and evaluative comments about the lesson. Some class discussion may ensue.
   d. If there are errors or gaps in the students' understanding of the lesson, the teacher directs the students to relisten to certain parts of the lesson.
3. The Follow-Up Stage
   a. The teacher provides opportunities for and encourages students to engage in activities that build on and develop concepts acquired during the lesson. These may include writing, reading, small-group discussions, [and] art activities.

   * To improve listening comprehension and retention, use the following sequence of activities adapted from Manzo's (1975) guided listening procedure:

- The teacher asks the student to try to remember everything the student is about to hear.
- The teacher lectures or plays a recorded selection. If the teacher lectures, the lecture is recorded.
- The teacher reminds the student about the instructions that were given. The teacher then writes everything on

the chalkboard without making any corrections or asking specific questions.

- The teacher reads everything listed on the chalkboard and asks the student to note incorrect information and think about missing information.
- The student listens to the tape again, corrects inaccurate information, and obtains missing information.
- The information on the chalkboard is amended and expanded.
- The teacher asks which ideas on the chalkboard are the main and important ideas and which ones should be remembered for a long time. The teacher highlights these items.
- Now that the student has mastered the literal content of the selection, the teacher asks inferential questions that appear vital for understanding.
- The teacher erases the chalkboard and tests memory with items (e.g., oral multiple choice and true–false) that are not too dependent on reading or writing skills.
- The teacher tests long-term memory with a similar test several weeks later.

• Teach the student to recognize the main idea and the contributing points from which it is derived. In this way the student gains control of what to write by determining how much detail is needed in terms of expected outcome (i.e., main idea). Looking for the main and contributing ideas helps the student become a more active listener by encouraging thinking, comprehension, and questions. Also teach the student to look for the order and organization of the lecture. Stress that notes are a skeletal representation of the material.

• Teach the student to use abbreviations to reduce the writing demands of the task (e.g., *w/* for *with*, *U.S.* for *United States*).

• Encourage the use of columned note-taking formats. Saski et al. (1983) report positive feedback from secondary learning disabilities teachers regarding the use of such formats. One of their note-taking formats contains a topic sentence at the top of the page and three columns (5″, 2″, and 1″ wide) designed for recording three types of information. The first column, Basic Ideas, is for material (such as facts, figures, dates, people, and places) that will be needed for future tests. The second column, Background Information, includes pertinent related information plus ideas, facts, and topics that interest the student. This column may begin with key words or concepts from the preceding lecture. The third column, Questions, includes space for marking unclear information that needs clarification or elaboration.

Activities for Developing Skills in Textbook Usage
The textbook is a primary source of information for secondary students. Practice in correct textbook usage benefits students with learning

problems and helps them complete assignments and review pertinent information. This section features a variety of activities to help students improve their textbook usage skills.

• To assist in developing instructional objectives and measuring competence in textbook usage, administer a pre/posttest. A test format may include the following questions:

What part of the book explains how the book is organized?

The authors are listed in what part of the book?

On what page(s) would you look for information on _____?

What part of the book gives meanings of words?

How many chapters are in the book?

What part of the book provides page references for any given topic?

Define _____.

On what page would you find a chapter titled _____?

In what part of the book would you find information on a topic in the form of visual aids?

Who publishes the book?

On what pages does chapter ____ begin and end?

On what page would you find out about _____?

What is the meaning of the term _____?

What information is included in the appendix of this book?

• Instruct the student to locate specific parts of a textbook. Allow 15 seconds for each part (e.g., the index). The following format is useful:

Name of textbook _____

Give the page number of the following:

Table of contents   _____

Index   _____

Glossary   _____

Appendix   _____

• Instruct the student to use the table of contents to determine the beginning and ending page numbers of specific chapters.

• Instruct the student to use the table of contents to name the chapter in which a given topic is located. The following format is helpful:

Directions: Place the chapter title listed on the right under the correct heading listed on the left.

I. Weather	Reptiles
A.	Precipitation
B.	Nutrition—proteins and vitamins

II. Animals   Amphibians
    A.   High-pressure system
    B.   Medications
III. Health
    A.
    B.

• Discuss the purpose of a glossary and have the student look up several words in a textbook glossary.

• From a content reading assignment, instruct the student to identify key words and find their meanings in the glossary.

• Explain what an index is, how it is developed, and how it can be used. Provide a page from an index and instruct the student to locate a list of terms and write down corresponding page numbers.

• Give a question and have the student identify the key words and locate them in the index. Have the student write the page number(s) pertaining to the question topic. A suggested format is as follows:

Underline key words. Locate them in the index and write the page number on which the answer is found.

What was the population of San Francisco in 1980?
_____

What causes a tidal wave? _____

• Instruct the student to use the following cognitive strategies to help learning (Ellis & Lenz, 1987):

CAN-DO: A strategy for learning content information

C—*Create* a list of items to be learned.

A—*Ask* yourself whether the list is complete.

N—*Note* the main ideas and details using a tree diagram.

D—*Describe* each component and how it relates to others.

O—*Overlearn* main parts, then supporting details.

RIDER: A visual imagery strategy for reading comprehension

R—*Read* the sentence.

I —Make an *image* or picture in your mind.

D—*Describe* how the new image is different from the last sentence.

E—*Evaluate* the image to make sure it contains everything necessary.

R—*Repeat* the steps to RIDE as you read the next sentence.

FIST: A self-questioning strategy for reading comprehension

F—*First* sentence in the paragraph is read.

I —*Indicate* a question based on information in the first sentence.

S—*Search* for the answer to the question.

T—*Tie* the answer to the question with a paraphrase.

Activities for Developing Reading and Study Skills An extensive demand for gaining information from reading material exists at the secondary level. Students with learning problems are faced with obtaining content from a variety of reading materials. Several reading styles and rates are needed for these students to acquire essential information. Thus, students with learning problems must be taught strategies to help them acquire information quickly from a variety of printed materials.

Skimming is a systematic and efficient reading strategy that helps students in dealing with the reading and study demands of secondary classes. In this strategy, students isolate and rapidly read key sentences, phrases, and words to determine the main ideas. The steps in skimming are as follows:

1. Read the title and headings (dark print) as they appear.
2. Read the introduction (i.e., a few paragraphs at the beginning of a chapter or article).
3. Read the first sentence of each subsequent paragraph. In textbooks, the first sentence usually contains the main idea of the paragraph.
4. Read the captions of pictures and study any illustrations in the chapter.
5. Read the conclusion or chapter summary.

The following activities involving skimming are helpful in developing this reading-study skill:

• Have the student skim the major headings of a classroom text and formulate several questions for each heading. As a group activity, the teacher can require each student to generate one question for each heading.

• Discuss the terms *chronological*, *sequential*, and *causal* and provide examples of each.

Chronological—topics or events in the order of their happening. Most history books are organized chronologically.

Sequential—a step-by-step procedure. This frequently occurs in a science lab experiment or in instructions for assembling a project.

Causal—an "if—then" presentation pattern. Some texts use a causal pattern to explain a phenomenon (e.g., conditions that lead to weather happenings such as rain, lightning, and hurricanes).

• Give the student a content reading selection and a list of comprehension questions covering several main themes. Instruct the student to skim the selection and answer the questions.

• Use the following skimming activity as a pre/posttest or as practice. Provide the student with a four- to five-page passage and a list of 20 comprehension questions covering main ideas and key words. Instruct the student to use skimming techniques to read the passage quickly and gain the most important information. At the end of 5 minutes, have the student answer the comprehension questions. Set the criterion for mastery at 90 percent correct on the comprehension questions.

Scanning is another reading and study strategy that helps students with learning problems deal with the demands of acquiring information from printed material. It involves the quick reading of key sentences, phrases, and words to locate specific information. This information could be an important term, definition, or answer to a question. Scanning is a great help in reading and studying because it enables the reader to find specific items rapidly. The steps in scanning are as follows:

1. Remember the specific question to be answered.
2. Estimate in what form the answer will appear (i.e., word, name, number, graphic, or date).
3. Use the expected form of the answer as clues for locating it.
4. Look for clues by moving the eyes quickly over the page. When a section that appears to contain the answer is found, read it more carefully.
5. Find the answer, record it, and stop reading.

The following activities involve scanning:

• Give the student a list of alphabetized items. Name an item on the list and instruct the student to circle the item within 15 seconds. Once the student becomes proficient, the activity can be repeated with an unalphabetized list.

• Give the student an unalphabetized list and related questions. Read a question and instruct the student to write the number of the question next to the appropriate word. Initially, the time limit for each question is 30 seconds. As the student progresses, the time limit can be shortened to 10 seconds. A sample format is as follows:

_____ equator	_____ green	_____ sophomore
_____ mammals	_____ mare	_____ ewe
_____ sentence	_____ blue	_____ six
_____ red	_____ hog	_____ bulls

What is the name for warm-blooded animals with fur or hair?

What do you call a female sheep?

What color is grass?

What do you call a group of words that expresses a complete thought?

The American flag is red, white, and _____.

In tenth grade you are called a _____.

How many class periods are in a day?

What do you call a female horse?

What do you call male cattle?

What color is an apple?

What do you call a male pig?

What is the imaginary line that runs around the Earth?

This activity can be adapted to independent seatwork by having the student complete the task (match questions to words) within a specified time (e.g., 2 to 6 minutes).

• Give some questions from a chapter the student is studying in a class. Indicate the page number where the answer to each question is found. Have the student answer each question using the following instructions and format:

Directions: Answer each question in 60 seconds or less. Each question has four steps: (1) find the page listed, (2) read the question, (3) scan the page to find the answer, and (4) write your answer.

(page 118) How long did Nat Turner's rebellion last?

(page 72) What states were included in the Northwest Territory?

(page 164) Why did Dred Scott think he should be a free man?

(page 210) What does the term "Jim Crow" mean?

• Give some questions from a chapter the student is studying in a content area. Vary the questions so that some key words are found in the index (e.g., names, places, and events) and others are found in the chapter (e.g., section headings, italicized words, and boldface print). Instruct the student to (1) identify key words for locating information in text, (2) locate the appropriate page number, (3) read the question, (4) scan the page to locate key words, and (5) answer the question.

• Use the following activity as a pre/posttest or as a practice activity. Select ten pages from different textbooks and write ten questions on 3″ × 5″ cards (one question per card). Have two questions each to cover information contained in the heading; information contained in topic sentences; information contained in charts, graphs, or maps; information contained in the index; and information contained in key words and terms. Give the student one question along with the number of the page on which the question is answered in the text. Have the student read the question (begin timing), locate the answer, and write the answer (stop timing). Record the time. Continue in this manner until all questions are answered. Criterion is achieved when the student answers all questions correctly in a 10-minute time period (one question per minute).

Activities for Developing Reading and Note-Taking Skills

Taking notes on material read for classes facilitates memory and often makes it unnecessary to reread the material at a later time. When taking notes on reading material, the student is forced to think about the material and thus enhance recall of the content at a later date (Roe, Stoodt, & Burns, 1995). Moreover, the act of writing ideas helps the student remember content. Note taking from reading material usually follows either an outline or a paraphrasing format. This section presents activities designed to develop or improve reading and note-taking skills.

- Teach students how to use an outline format. The first step in making an outline is determining the main ideas. The next step involves locating the supportive ideas for each of the main ideas. The sequence continues by locating specific details that go with respective supportive ideas. A blank outline format helps demonstrate the proper form.

Title

I. Main concept
   A. Information supporting I
   B. Information supporting I
      1. Specific information supporting B
      2. Specific information supporting B
         a. Specific information supporting 2
         b. Specific information supporting 2
   C. Information supporting I
II. Main concept
   A. Information supporting II
   B. Information supporting II
   C. Information supporting II
      1. Specific information supporting C
      2. Specific information supporting C

- To demonstrate outlining, show the student how the headings in a textbook chapter indicate different levels of subordination. For example, in many textbooks the main headings would be Roman numerals in an outline, side headings would be uppercase letters in an outline, and italic or paragraph headings would be Arabic numerals in an outline.

- Provide partially completed outlines and instruct the student to complete them (Roe et al., 1995).

Title

I. (Given by teacher)
   A. (Given by teacher)
      1. (Completed by student)
      2. (Completed by student)
   B. (Given by teacher)
      1. (Given by teacher)
      2. (Completed by student)
II. (Completed by student)
   A. (Given by teacher)
   B. (Completed by student)

This technique can gradually increase in difficulty until the teacher provides only the structural arrangement (i.e., the Roman numerals, uppercase letters, and Arabic numerals). This task becomes more relevant if the teacher uses textbooks from the student's general content classes.

- To facilitate note taking from printed material, teach the student to use a columned format (Saski et al., 1983). For example, in the following format, the 2″ column on the left side is used to record main ideas, the 6″ column is used to record supporting details of the main ideas, and the 2″ space at the bottom is used to summarize ideas, raise questions, and note areas of concern.

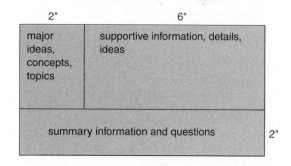

- Provide several paragraphs and several summaries. Instruct the student to select the best summary of the paragraphs. Point out the importance of locating the main idea (usually the topic sentence of a paragraph) and essential supporting details.

- Provide passages from a textbook the student is using and instruct him or her to write a summary by following these steps: (1) locate the main idea, (2) locate essential supportive details, and (3) write information as concisely as possible, leaving out illustrative material and statements that merely elaborate on main ideas.

Activities for Developing Skills in Using Visual Aids Secondary textbooks are replete with visual aids, and adolescents with learning problems need to be taught how to use and understand them. This section presents activities and techniques for developing skills in the use of various types of visual aids.

- Explain that a map represents a geographic area. Review the following map-reading steps (Roe et al., 1995): locate and comprehend the title of the map; determine map directions; interpret the map legend; apply the map's scale; discuss common map terms (e.g., latitude, longitude, equator, gulf, bay, and continent); make inferences from map material (e.g., climate, population, and industry); and understand projections (e.g., flat map or globe).
- Give the student index cards with a map legend on one side and its use or definition on the other side. Instruct the student to define or describe the legend's use and turn over the card to check the answer.
- Present road maps and instruct the student to estimate miles between locations and write directions from one place to another.
- Provide the student with a table and explain that it includes information arranged in vertical columns and horizontal rows. Review the following table-reading steps: locate and comprehend the title of the table; determine information located in columns; determine information located in rows; and locate specific information through pinpointing intersections.
- Instruct the student to make a table of respective cities and their average monthly temperatures or of the student's class periods and corresponding six-week grades.
- Use sample graphs to explain the four basic types of graphs: picture, circle, bar, and line graphs. Roe et al. (1995) recommend that teachers help students interpret graphs by reviewing the following steps:
- The purpose of the graph (usually indicated by the title but becomes more evident when the accompanying narrative is studied)
- The scale of measure on bar and line graphs
- The legend of picture graphs
- The items being compared
- The location of specific pieces of information within a graph (e.g., finding the intersection of the point of interest on the vertical axis with the point of interest on the horizontal axis)
- The trends indicated by a graph (e.g., does an amount increase or decrease over a period of time?)
- The application of graphic information to actual life situations (e.g., a graph showing the temperatures for each month in Sydney, Australia, could be used for planning what clothes to take for a particular time of the year)
- Instruct the student to make a line graph using the student's reading rate (words per minute) in textbooks for various content areas.
- Instruct the student to make a bar graph of the heights of the starting lineups for two basketball teams. A basketball program may be used to provide the data. This activity can be adapted to various sports and selected information (e.g., weights in football and batting averages in baseball).
- Have the student make a circle graph of how he or she spends time (e.g., in school, sleeping, playing, eating, and miscellaneous).
- Instruct the student to make a picture graph from the following information: Dallas scored 70 touchdowns; Washington scored 76; Miami scored 47; Pittsburgh, 64; San Francisco, 37; New York, 54; Denver, 62. Let the symbol (#) = 10 touchdowns.
- Use a model to demonstrate how diagrams are used to picture events, processes, structures, relationships, or sequences described in a textbook. Highlight the use of arrows, labeling, and various degrees of shading in diagrams.
- Instruct the student to make a diagram of a basketball play and orally present it to the teacher or class.
- For practice or for a pre/posttest format in assessing visual aids, provide the student with a map, table, graph, or diagram, and ask questions pertaining to purpose, legend, columns, and specific information from the visual aid.
- Instruct the student to use the following cognitive strategy for reading visual aids (Ellis & Lenz, 1987):

R—*Read* the written material until you are referred to a visual aid or until the material is not making sense.

V—*View* the visual aid using CLUE.

    C—*Clarify* the stated facts in the written material.

    L—*Locate* the main ideas (global) and details (specific parts).

    U—*Uncover* the signal words (look for captions or words in the visual aid).

    E—*Examine* the logic. (Does what you "read" from the picture make sense in light of what you read in the material?)

A—*Ask* yourself about the relationship between the visual aid and the written material using FUR.

    F—Ask how the visual aid and the written material *fit* together.

    U—Ask how the visual aid can help you *understand* the written material.

    R—Ask how the visual aid can help you *remember* the written material.

S—*Summarize* the most important information.

- To facilitate analysis of visual aids presented in textbook chapters or study guides, instruct the student to use the SNIPS procedure (Ellis & Friend, 1991):

S—*Start* with questions (e.g., why you are analyzing the visual aid and what is important to understand and remember about the visual aid).

N—*Note* what you can learn from the hints (such as lines, numbers, color, and title).

I —*Identify* what is important (i.e., facts).

P—*Plug* it into the chapter (i.e., note how the visual aid relates to the chapter's content).

S—*See* whether you can explain the visual aid to someone.

Sequential Study Methods   Several methods have been developed to help students obtain and organize information from textbooks. F. P. Robinson (1961) developed the SQ3R method, which remains one of the most widely known study methods. The steps in SQ3R (survey, question, read, recite, and review) are discussed in Chapter 8. Study methods clearly hold much promise for teaching secondary students with learning problems, but systematic applications are needed to determine the effectiveness of various methods with specific populations. This section presents three sequential study methods for students with learning problems.

Multipass is an adaptation of SQ3R designed to teach effective study skills to adolescents with learning problems (Schumaker, Deshler, Alley, Warner, & Denton, 1982). The Multipass steps include the following:

1. *Survey Pass* is designed for the student to determine the main ideas and organization of the chapter. In this step the student is instructed to do the following:
   a. Read the chapter title.
   b. Read the introductory paragraph.
   c. Review the chapter's relationship to adjacent chapters by examining the table of contents.
   d. Read primary subtitles of the chapter and determine the chapter organization.
   e. Note illustrations and read their captions.
   f. Read the chapter summary.
   g. Paraphrase the information gained in the preceding steps.
2. *Size-Up Pass* is designed for the student to gain specific information and facts from the chapter without reading it from beginning to end. In this step the student's instructions are as follows:

   a. Read each question at the end of the chapter and determine what information is important. If the student can answer a question, a check mark is placed next to the question.
   b. Examine the entire chapter following these guidelines: look for textual cues (e.g., italicized words, boldface print, and subtitles); transform the cue into a question (e.g., if the cue italicized word is *mitosis,* the student asks "What is mitosis?"); skim through surrounding text to locate the answer to the question; and orally paraphrase the answer without looking at the book.
   c. Paraphrase all the ideas and facts obtained from applying Step b to all contextual cues in the chapter.
3. *Sort-Out Pass* is designed to have the student self-check understanding of the chapter material. In this step the student reads and answers each question at the end of the chapter. If the student can answer a question immediately, a check mark is placed next to it. If unable to answer the question, the student follows these instructions:
   a. Think about the section that most likely contains the answer.
   b. Skim through that section for the answer and place a check mark next to the question if the answer is found.
   c. If the answer is not in that section, continue to think and skim until the answer is located and the question is marked with a check mark.

The S.O.S. strategy is an alternative version of Multipass for students with reading abilities four or more years below their grade level. It includes the same three passes over the textbook as specified in Multipass but, in addition, uses a visually marked version and an audiotaped version of the chapter. The teacher or a paraprofessional can modify the chapter (i.e., mark and tape the chapter). The marking system consists of highlighting important facts, main ideas, and key words. After the chapter is marked, it is read (not verbatim but according to markings) into a tape recorder. Thus, the tape stresses important content and reduces information that can be presented in a few sentences. Each chapter tape is limited to no more than 90 minutes. The students are taught to survey, obtain details, and test themselves (i.e., Multipass steps). During the use of the S.O.S. strategy, students complete an organizer outline. This process helps students become active learners while listening to the tape.

The PANORAMA study technique includes eight steps divided into three stages (Edwards, 1973), as follows:

Preparatory Stage:

1. *Purpose.* The learner determines why the material is being read.
2. *Adapting rate to material.* The teacher decides at what rate the material should be read. This involves maintaining flexibility of rate within sections as a function of the type of content being covered (e.g., the rate is slow on an initial reading if the main idea is being presented, whereas elaboration and expansion content may be read more rapidly).
3. *Need to pose questions.* The student uses headings or cue words to develop questions.

Intermediate Stage:

4. *Overview.* The student surveys the major parts of the chapter to determine the organization of the material.
5. *Read and relate.* The student reads the material in terms of a specified purpose, seeking specific answers to questions.
6. *Annotate.* The student makes written annotations (paraphrases and outlines) of main ideas, key words, and concepts.

Concluding Stage:

7. *Memorize.* The student uses outlines and summaries to learn the important content. Acronyms and associations are used to facilitate recall of main points.
8. *Assess.* The student assesses efforts in relation to the purpose of the reading (e.g., answers questions).

Recall Study Skills

Secondary students are expected to retain much of the information they obtain through lectures and readings. The retention of material is facilitated by rehearsal strategies. Towle (1982) states, "Rehearsal involves practicing or using information under cued conditions" (p. 92). She notes that

students need a strategy for rehearsing organized content (notes, outlines, summaries, discussions, or demonstrations).

Activities for Developing Study-Rehearsal Skills   Activities for rehearsal of material include the following:

• Have the student rehearse from various content formats (Towle, 1982). For example:
● Rehearsing notes: Rework notes, make up test questions, construct lists of important points, write summaries, and review with classmates.
● Rehearsing outlines: Verbalize the content by giving a lecture from the outline, and construct graphic aids (diagrams, charts, and graphs) from the outline.
● Rehearsing discussion: Write a summary, use supplementary materials, and give examples to support important points.
● Rehearsing demonstrations: Role play, practice segments of behavior chains, and practice with peers and critique one another.

• Encourage the student to use verbal rehearsal in reviewing content. This basic step in the learning strategies teaching sequence can be used in the initial learning of material and in reviewing it. Verbal rehearsal basically involves self-instructional training, which has received much support in facilitating learning (Meichenbaum, 1975). (Chapter 5 discusses cognitive behavior modification and the steps in verbal rehearsal.)

• Instruct the student to use questioning strategies when reviewing content. Alley and Hori (1981) increased the reading comprehension of adolescents with learning problems through a questioning treatment based on Manzo's (1969) ReQuest Procedure. The treatment consisted of the following steps:
● Appropriate reading material is selected, and the teacher and student read two or three paragraphs following these steps: both read the first sentence silently; the student asks as many questions as possible pertaining to the sentence, and the teacher answers them; the teacher asks questions pertaining to the sentence, and the student answers them.
● After several paragraphs are read using the above steps, the student is instructed to write a question or make a prediction about the outcome of the story. The student then reads and answers the question or checks the prediction.

• To help the student rehearse information for later recall, use the following activities and suggestions (Roe et al., 1995):
● Have the student review material with a specific purpose (e.g., to answer a question).

- Encourage the student to obtain an understanding of the organization of the material through outlining. This helps the student categorize information to be learned under main headings.
- Instruct the student to visualize what the text or notes are trying to present.
- Encourage the student to make notes during rehearsal. In addition to facilitating retention, writing keeps the learner actively involved.
- Have the student paraphrase the main and supporting information. Rewording the content helps improve understanding.
- Encourage the student to discuss the material with a classmate.
- Instruct the student to review notes or the text as soon as possible after initial contact with the material. Immediate review can strengthen understanding, accuracy, and associations.
- Instruct the student to rehearse to a criterion level (e.g., answer review questions at 100 percent accuracy without referring to notes or the book).
- Encourage the student to use the keyword method presented in Chapter 8.

Activities for Developing Mnemonic Devices

Nagel et al. (1986) present the mnemonic FIRST as a strategy to create mnemonics to recall information:

F—*Form* a word. For example, the student can form the word PENS to remember the parts of an atom: **p**roton, **e**lectron, **n**eutron, and **s**hell.

I—*Insert* extra letters to form a mnemonic word. For example, to remember scientific objects that have never been seen (e.g., **b**lack holes, **a**ntimatter, **c**osmic rays, and **e**arth's core), the letter *r* can be added to the first letters of the words to form BrACE.

R—*Rearrange* the first letters to form a mnemonic word. Some lists need to be memorized in order. For example, the sequence of the RAP paraphrasing strategy (*Read* the paragraph, *Ask* yourself about the main idea and two details, and *Put* it in your own words) needs to be remembered in order. With other lists, order is not important. With these lists, the first letter of each word can be manipulated to form a mnemonic word. For example, to remember the parts of the eye (i.e., **e**yelid, **i**ris, **p**upil, and **s**clera) the word PIES can be formed as a mnemonic.

S—*Shape* a sentence to form a mnemonic. For example, to remember the Roman numerals and their ascending order, the student can form the sentence **I** **v**acuumed **x**-rays last **C**hristmas **D**ay **m**orning.

T—*Try* combinations of the first four steps to create a mnemonic.

Expression Study Skills

To succeed in secondary school, students must be able to demonstrate knowledge on classroom tests, minimum competency tests, and written assignments. Moreover, the application of knowledge in real-life settings becomes important to successful independent living during and after secondary school.

Activities for Developing Test-Taking Skills

The following activities are suggested for helping students develop their test-taking skills:

- Instruct the student to determine what general information is relevant in preparing for a test. The following list can be used as a guide or reminder:

Subject content _____

Date of test _____

Chapters covered _____

Notes covered _____

Type of questions _____

Number of questions _____

Timed or untimed test _____

Information emphasized in class _____

Also, to facilitate test preparation, give the student a test that has been used previously.

- Identify vocabulary terms that are used frequently in test directions. Instruct the student to define the terms and perform the specified behavior, for example:

Compare means _____. *Contrast* means _____. Compare and contrast milk and water.

Criticize means _____. Criticize some aspect of your school schedule.

Illustrate means_____. Illustrate the difference between a triangle and a circle.

Evaluate means _____. Evaluate the importance of reading.

Other words that can be covered include *discuss, list, justify, outline, diagram, trace, match, define,* and *elaborate.*

- Present the SCORER system (Carman & Adams, 1972) as a strategy for helping students take tests. Each letter represents an important test-taking rule:

S—*Schedule* your time. The student reviews the entire test and plans time according to the number of items, point value per item, and easy and difficult items.

C—Look for *clue* words. The student searches for clue words on each item. For example, on true–false items words such as *always* and *never* usually indicate the statement is false. Words such as *usually* and *sometimes* frequently indicate the statement is true.

O—*Omit* difficult questions. Postponing hard questions until later in the testing session can improve a student's score. Specifically, Carman and Adams (p. 217) suggest that the student use the following procedure:
- Move rapidly through the test.
- When you find an easy question or one you are certain of, answer it.
- Omit the difficult ones on the first pass.
- When you skip a question, make a mark in the margin (– or √). (Do not use a red pencil or pen. Your marks could get confused with grader's marks.)
- Keep moving. Never erase. Don't dawdle. Jot brief notes in the margin for later use if you need to.
- When you have finished the easy ones, return to those with marks (– or √), and try again.
- Mark again those answers you are still not sure of. Change the – to + or √ to √√.
- In your review (that's the last R in SCORER), you will go over all the questions time permits, first the √√, then the √, then the unmarked.

R—*Read* carefully. A careful reading of test directions and each item can improve test performance. Careless reading can lead to confusion on essay items and careless errors on objective items.

E—*Estimate* your answers. On test items requiring calculations or problem solving, the student should estimate the answer. This helps correct careless errors. Moreover, if guessing is not penalized, all questions should be answered. After eliminating alternatives that are obviously incorrect, the student should take a best guess.

R—*Review* your work. The student should be encouraged to use every minute available. After all items are answered, have the student review the test. Carman and Adams (p. 222) suggest that the student use the following checklist:
- Return to the double-checked (√√) difficult questions. Reread them. Look for clue words. Look for new hints. Then go to the √ questions, and finally to the unmarked ones if there is still time.
- Don't be too eager to change answers. Change only if you have a good reason.
- Be certain you have considered all questions.
- PRINT your name on the test. If there are separate sheets, print your name on each sheet.

• Present the following activities and guidelines to help the student with answering true–false test items:
- Note the following rule to remember with true–false items: A statement must be completely true to be true. If any part of the statement is false, the whole statement is false. Instruct the student to be careful about tricky words. Some of these words include *some, many, most, everyone, no one, never,* and *always.* Demonstrate how these words cue true and false statements.
- Instruct the student to notice that directions to true–false items may vary. Sample directions include the following:

Next to each statement, print *T* for true or *F* for false.

Write the word *true* or the word *false* on the line next to each statement.

If a statement is true, do nothing to it. If a statement is false, cross out the part that makes it false. Rewrite the part you crossed out to make a true statement.

• Instruct the student to look for reworded statements in which positive or negative words have been used to change the answer.

• Present the following activities and guidelines to help the student answer multiple-choice test items:
- Explain to the student that in most multiple-choice questions several alternatives usually are easy to eliminate because they are obviously incorrect. Frequently two alternatives seem correct, but instructions require the selection of the *best* answer.
- Provide the student with sample multiple-choice items that illustrate different ways of thinking. For example, use items that include such key words as *except, not,* and *all of the above.*
- Encourage the student to use the following guidelines with multiple-choice items:

Know how many answers to select.

Be aware of the kind of answer you are seeking (e.g., for a negative question).

Remember the question.

Eliminate the obvious wrong answers.

Choose the answer that fits best.

Be careful in recording the answer.

• Present the following activities and guidelines to help the student answer essay questions:
- Instruct the student to read the directions and questions carefully and underline key words. In directions, the student should underline such parts as *answer two of the following questions.* In questions, key words include *discuss, compare, list,* and so on.
- Instruct the student to outline or organize the answer before attempting to write it. If time becomes a serious factor, the question can be finished in outline form.
- Teach the student to use the SCORER system with essay questions.

The effective use of learning strategies results in academic success for adolescents.

- Instruct the student to use the following techniques when taking all tests:
  - Review the entire test.
  - Know the time allotted for taking the test.
  - Know the value of specific questions.
  - Follow the directions carefully.
  - Notice key words in instructions and questions.
  - Reread directions and questions.
  - Go through the test and answer questions you are sure of first.
  - Place a check mark beside questions you need to return to later.
  - Return to questions that have been checked.
  - Mark an *X* at the bottom of each completed page.
  - Review all questions.
- Use a test that the student has taken previously to review ways in which performance can be improved.
- Provide the student with a machine-scorable sheet and a set of multiple-choice questions. Instruct the student to answer each test question by filling in the appropriate space. Many students with learning problems have difficulty with standardized and minimum-competency tests. Practice in using different types of answer formats helps students develop skills with these formats.
- Instruct the student to use the PIRATES test-taking strategy (Hughes, Schumaker, Deshler, & Mercer, 1993):

P—*Prepare* to succeed. Put your name and PIRATES on the test. Prioritize the test sections and allow time. Say something positive and start within 2 minutes.

I —*Inspect* the instructions. Read the instructions, underline how and where to respond, and notice special requirements.

R—*Read, Remember, Reduce.* Read the whole question, remember what you studied, and reduce the alternatives.

A—*Answer or Abandon.* Answer the question or abandon it for the moment.

T—*Turn* back. At the end of the test, go back to the abandoned items and answer them.

E—*Estimate.* Estimate unknown answers using ACE:
  A—*Avoid* absolutes.
  C—*Choose* the longest or most detailed choice.
  E—*Eliminate* similar choices.

S—*Survey.* Survey to be sure that all items are answered, and change an answer only if you are sure it is incorrect.

Activities for Developing Written Expression Skills

To survive in the secondary curriculum, students with learning problems must be able to express their knowledge in writing. Projects, papers, and essay tests require a degree of writing skills. Several methods (e.g., COPS and TOWER) and activities for teaching written expression are presented in Chapter 10. This section features some of the work from the University of Kansas Center for Research on Learning that pertains to teaching written expression strategies.

Moran, Schumaker, and Vetter (1981) conducted a study in which adolescents with learning disabilities were able to write organized paragraphs after receiving paragraph organization training. The students learned to write three paragraph styles (enumerative, sequential, and compare/contrast) by following three steps: (1) write a topic sentence, (2) write a minimum of three detail sentences, and (3) write an ending or clincher sentence.

Schumaker et al. (1981) conducted a study in which adolescents with learning disabilities were taught an error-monitoring strategy. This strategy is designed to enable a student to locate and correct errors in written material. Their results indicate that the training improved the students' ability to detect and correct errors in written work. Moreover, the error rate in the students' self-generated products was low (almost zero) after training. In addition to following the learning strategies teaching sequence, Schumaker et al. present the following steps to teach the error-monitoring strategy:

1. Provide the student with teacher-generated one-page passages, with some at the student's ability level and some at the student's grade level. Capitalization errors, appearance errors, and spelling errors are included in each passage.

2. Teach the student to detect and correct errors in the teacher-generated passages by following these procedures:

● Read each sentence separately.
● Ask the COPS questions (explained in Chapter 10).
● When an error is detected, circle it and put the correct form above the error.
● Ask for help if unsure of an item.

3. Teach the student to monitor work by following these steps:

● Use every other line as your write the rough draft.
● As you read a sentence, ask the COPS questions.
● When an error is located, write the correct form above it.
● Ask for help if unsure about a correct form.
● Copy the paragraph neatly before giving it to the teacher.
● Reread the paragraph as a final check.

Ellis and Friend (1991) present DEFENDS as a cognitive strategy for developing written expression skills when presenting a written position:

D—*Decide* on goals and theme. Decide who will read the written work and what kind of information you need to communicate.

E—*Estimate* main ideas and details. Think of at least two different main ideas that explain your theme, and note at least three details that can be used to explain each main idea.

F—*Figure* best order of main ideas and details. Decide which main idea to write about first, and note the best order for presenting the details.

E—*Express* the theme in the first sentence. State what the essay is about.

N—*Note* each main idea and supporting points. Explain the first main idea using the details, and repeat this for each of the other main ideas.

D—*Drive* home the message in the last sentence. Restate what the theme is about using different wording from the first sentence.

S—*Search* for errors and correct.

  S—*Set* editing goals.

  E—*Examine* your essay to see whether it makes sense. Read the paper aloud and make sure each sentence expresses a complete thought and makes sense.

  A—Ask yourself whether the message will be clear to others. Make sure the ideas are clear and that the order of the ideas is logical.

  R—*Reveal* picky errors. Correct all capitalization, punctuation, spelling, and grammar errors you can find, and have someone check your work.

  C—*Copy* over neatly.

  H—*Have* a last look for errors.

Activities for Developing Oral Presentation Skills   Some assignments in secondary classes require the student to present information orally. The following activities may develop the student's ability to give an oral presentation:

● Provide the student with practice in making oral presentations in one-to-one, small-group, and whole-class settings.
● Provide the student with opportunities to gain or share information orally (e.g., interviews, investigative reporting, and debates) (Hoover, 1995).
● Be flexible in structuring the conditions under which the student makes oral presentations (e.g., seated or standing, at desk, in the front of the room, member of a panel, or role play).
● Guide the student in preparing to speak by having the student (1) know the purpose of the presentation, (2) develop a presentation outline, (3) practice in a non-threatening environment, and (4) maintain a proactive attitude.

• Encourage the student to practice good body basics when presenting by using TALKS:

T—*Talk* with a pleasant voice tone.

A—*Act* confident and make eye contact with individuals.

L—*Look* at the audience.

K—*Keep* a pleasant facial expression.

S—*Stand* with a straight body posture.

COMMERCIAL LEARNING STRATEGIES AND STUDY SKILLS PROGRAMS

Commercial programs that focus on learning strategies and study skills may be helpful to adolescents with learning problems. This section presents programs that can be used to facilitate the learning of content in the secondary setting.

Advanced Skills for School Success

Advanced Skills for School Success, developed by A. Archer and M. Gleason (published by Curriculum Associates), is a teacher-directed program consisting of four modules for students in seventh through twelfth grade. Module 1, School Behaviors and Organization Skills, stresses appropriate school behaviors and organization and time management skills. The second module, Completing Daily Assignments, focuses on planning assignments, writing answers to factual and opinion questions, and proofreading. In Module 3, Effective Reading of Textbooks, students practice previewing for reading, active reading, indentation note taking, mapping a visual display of content, and writing a summary paragraph. Module 4, Learning from Verbal Presentations and Participating in Discussions, presents strategies for note taking, brainstorming, and effectively participating in class discussions. The Teacher Guides contain scripted lessons as well as review lessons and follow-up activities. Lesson books also are available for students in third through sixth grade.

The FIRST-Letter Mnemonic Strategy

The FIRST-Letter Mnemonic Strategy (Nagel et al., 1986) provides an organized way of independently approaching large bodies of information that need to be mastered. It is designed to help students identify lists of information that are important to learn, generate an appropriate title or label for each set of information, select a mnemonic device for each set of information, create a study card, and master and recall each set of information. While using this strategy, students actively manipulate information to put it into a form that is easy to remember.

The manual is part of the Learning Strategies Curriculum, and Strategies Intervention Model training is required.

The Test-Taking Strategy

The Test-Taking Strategy (Hughes et al., 1993) offers a strategy for students to use while taking classroom tests. Students learn to allocate time and priority to each section of a test, carefully read and focus on important elements in test instruction, recall information by accessing mnemonic devices, systematically and quickly progress through a test by selectively answering or abandoning questions, make well-informed guesses, check their work, and take control of the testing situation through regular use of self-talk and the application of test-wiseness principles. The strategy can be used in a variety of test-taking situations. The manual is part of the Learning Strategies Curriculum, and Strategies Intervention Model training is required.

COMPUTER SOFTWARE PROGRAMS IN LEARNING STRATEGIES AND STUDY SKILLS

Practice in preparing for and taking tests can enhance the student's ability to express knowledge in content-area classes. The following software programs focus on teaching effective study and test-taking skills.

Study to Succeed

Study to Succeed (produced by Lawrence Productions) is designed to help students make the most of their study time. The program covers listening, notetaking, study time, and reading. The SQ3R method is used.

Test-Taking Made Easy

Test-Taking Made Easy (produced by Lawrence Productions) includes five programs on preparing for tests, following test directions, and answering true–false, multiple-choice, and fill-in-the-blank test items. Graphics and a personal style of instruction present simple rules and helpful test-taking hints. This interactive program is designed for students in third through tenth grade and requires a third-grade reading level.

REFERENCES

Adelman, H. S., & Taylor, L. (1983). Enhancing motivation for overcoming learning and behavior problems. *Journal of Learning Disabilities, 16,* 384–392.

Alley, G. R., & Hori, A. K. O. (1981). *Effects of teaching a questioning strategy on reading comprehension of learning disabled adolescents* (Research Report No. 52). Lawrence: University of Kansas Center for Research on Learning.

Anders, P. L., & Bos, C. S. (1984). In the beginning: Vocabulary instruction in content classrooms. *Topics in Learning and Learning Disabilities, 3*(4), 53–65.

Beech, M. C. (1983). Simplifying text for mainstreamed students. *Journal of Learning Disabilities, 16,* 400–402.

Bergerud, D., Lovitt, T. C., & Horton, S. (1988). The effectiveness of textbook adaptations in life science for high school students with learning disabilities. *Journal of Learning Disabilities, 21,* 70–76.

Bos, C. S., & Anders, P. L. (1987). Semantic feature analysis: An interactive teaching strategy for facilitating learning from text. *Learning Disability Focus, 3*(1), 55–59.

Bulgren, J. A., Deshler, D. D., & Schumaker, J. B. (1993). *The content enhancement series: The concept mastery routine.* Lawrence, KS: Edge Enterprises.

Bulgren, J. A., & Lenz, B. K. (1996). Strategic instruction in the content areas. In D. D. Deshler, E. S. Ellis, & B. K. Lenz, *Teaching adolescents with learning disabilities: Strategies and methods* (2nd ed., pp. 409–473). Denver, CO: Love.

Bulgren, J. A., Lenz, B. K., Deshler, D. D., & Schumaker, J. B. (1995). *The content enhancement series: The concept comparison routine.* Lawrence, KS: Edge Enterprises.

Bulgren, J. A., Schumaker, J. B., & Deshler, D. D. (1988). The effectiveness of a concept teaching routine in enhancing the performance of students with learning disabilities in mainstream classes. *Learning Disability Quarterly, 11,* 3–17.

Bulgren, J. A., Schumaker, J. B., & Deshler, D. D. (1994). *The content enhancement series: The concept anchoring routine.* Lawrence, KS: Edge Enterprises.

Carlson, S. A. (1981). *Patterns and trends within exemplary special education programs in the secondary grades.* Washington, DC: National Association of State Directors of Special Education, Project FORUM.

Carlson, S. A. (1985). The ethical appropriateness of subject-matter tutoring for learning disabled adolescents. *Learning Disability Quarterly, 8,* 310–314.

Carman, R. A., & Adams, W. R. (1972). *Study skills: A student's guide for survival.* New York: Wiley.

Cunningham, P. M., & Cunningham, J. W. (1976, December). Improving listening in content area subjects. *NASSP Bulletin,* 26–31.

Deshler, D. D., & Schumaker, J. B. (1986). Learning strategies: An instructional alternative for low-achieving adolescents. *Exceptional Children, 52,* 583–590.

Deshler, D. D., & Schumaker, J. B. (1988). An instructional model for teaching students how to learn. In J. L. Graden, J. E. Zins, & M. J. Curtis (Eds.), *Alternative educational delivery systems: Enhancing instructional options for all students* (pp. 391–411). Washington, DC: National Association of School Psychologists.

Deshler, D. D., Schumaker, J. B., & Lenz, B. K. (1984). Academic and cognitive interventions for LD adolescents: Part I. *Journal of Learning Disabilities, 17,* 108–117.

Deshler, D. D., Schumaker, J. E., & McKnight, P. C. (1997). *The content enhancement series: The survey routine.* Lawrence: University of Kansas Center for Research on Learning.

Devine, T. G. (1987). *Teaching study skills: A guide for teachers.* Boston: Allyn & Bacon.

Edwards, P. (1973). Panorama: A study technique. *Journal of Reading, 17,* 132–135.

Ellis, E. S. (1997). *The content enhancement series: The clarifying routine.* Lawrence, KS: Edge Enterprises.

Ellis, E. S. (1998). *The content enhancement series: The framing routine.* Lawrence, KS: Edge Enterprises.

Ellis, E. S., Deshler, D. D., Lenz, B. K., Schumaker, J. B., & Clark, F. L. (1991). An instructional model for teaching learning strategies. *Focus on Exceptional Children, 24*(1), 1–14.

Ellis, E. S., & Friend, P. (1991). Adolescents with learning disabilities. In B. Y. L. Wong (Ed.), *Learning about learning disabilities* (pp. 505–561). San Diego, CA: Academic Press.

Ellis, E. S., & Lenz, B. K. (1987). A component analysis of effective learning strategies for LD students. *Learning Disabilities Focus, 2*(2), 94–107.

Ellis, E. S., & Lenz, B. K. (1990). Techniques for mediating content-area learning: Issues and research. *Focus on Exceptional Children, 22*(9), 1–16.

Ellis, E. S., & Lenz, B. K. (1996). Perspectives on instruction in learning strategies. In D. D. Deshler, E. S. Ellis, & B. K. Lenz, *Teaching adolescents with learning disabilities: Strategies and methods* (2nd ed., pp. 9–60). Denver, CO: Love.

Fredrick, W. C., & Walberg, H. J. (1980). Learning as a function of time. *The Journal of Educational Research, 73,* 183–204.

Hammill, D. D., & Bartel, N. R. (1995). Final thoughts. In D. D. Hammill & N. R. Bartel, *Teaching students with learning and behavior problems: Managing mild-to-moderate difficulties in resource and inclusive settings* (6th ed., pp. 451–467). Austin, TX: PRO-ED.

Harnischfeger, A. (1980). Curricular control and learning time: District policy, teacher strategy, and pupil choice. *Educational Evaluation and Policy Analysis, 2*(6), 19–30.

Hoover, J. J. (1993). *Teaching study skills to students with learning problems.* Boulder, CO: Hamilton.

Hoover, J. J. (1995). Teaching study skills to students. In D. D. Hammill & N. R. Bartel, *Teaching students with learning and behavior problems: Managing mild-to-moderate difficulties in resource and inclusive settings* (6th ed., pp. 347–389). Austin, TX: PRO-ED.

Hudson, P., Lignugaris-Kraft, B., & Miller, T. (1993). Using content enhancements to improve the performance of adolescents with learning disabilities in content classes. *Learning Disabilities Research & Practice, 8,* 106–126.

Hughes, C. A., Hendrickson, J. M., & Hudson, P. J. (1986). The pause procedure: Improving factual recall from lectures by low and high achieving middle school students. *International Journal of Instructional Media, 13*(3), 217–226.

Hughes, C. A., Schumaker, J. B., Deshler, D. D., & Mercer, C. D. (1993). *Learning strategies curriculum: The test-taking strategy* (Rev. ed.). Lawrence, KS: Edge Enterprises.

Keith, T. Z., & Page, E. B. (1985). Homework works at school: National evidence for policy changes. *School Psychology Review, 14,* 351–359.

Kerr, M. M., & Nelson, C. M. (1998). *Strategies for managing behavior problems in the classroom* (3rd ed.). Upper Saddle River, NJ: Merrill/Prentice Hall.

Laurie, T. E., Buchwach, L., Silverman, R., & Zigmond, N. (1978). Teaching secondary learning disabled students in the mainstream. *Learning Disability Quarterly, 1*(4), 62–72.

Lenz, B. K., & Bulgren, J. A. (1988). *Issues related to enhancing content acquisition for students with learning disabilities.* Lawrence: University of Kansas Center for Research on Learning.

Lenz, B. K., Bulgren, J., & Hudson, P. (1990). Content enhancement: A model for promoting the acquisition of content by individuals with learning disabilities. In T. Scruggs & B. Wong (Eds.), *Intervention research in learning disabilities* (pp. 122–165). New York: Springer-Verlag.

Lenz, B. K., Bulgren, J. A., Schumaker, J. B., Deshler, D. D., & Boudah, D. J. (1994). *The content enhancement series: The unit organizer routine.* Lawrence, KS: Edge Enterprises.

Lenz, B. K., Ehren, B. J., & Smiley, L. R. (1991). A goal attainment approach to improve completion of project-type assignments by learning disabled adolescents. *Focus on Learning Disabilities, 6,* 166–176.

Lenz, B. K., Ellis, E. S., & Scanlon, D. (1996). *Teaching learning strategies to adolescents and adults with learning disabilities.* Austin, TX: PRO-ED.

Lenz, B. K., Marrs, R. W., Schumaker, J. B., & Deshler, D. D. (1993). *The content enhancement series: The lesson organizer routine.* Lawrence, KS: Edge Enterprises.

Lenz, B. K., Schumaker, J. B., Deshler, D. D., & Bulgren, J. A. (1998). *The content enhancement series: The course organizer routine.* Lawrence, KS: Edge Enterprises.

Manzo, A. V. (1969). The ReQuest procedure. *Journal of Reading, 13,* 123–126.

Manzo, A. V. (1975). Guided reading procedure. *Journal of Reading, 18,* 287–291.

Meese, R. L. (1994). *Teaching learners with mild disabilities: Integrating research and practice.* Pacific Grove, CA: Brooks/Cole.

Meichenbaum, D. (1975). Self-instructional methods. In F. Kanter & A. Goldstein (Eds.), *Helping people change.* New York: Pergamon Press.

Meltzer, L. J., Roditi, B. N., Haynes, D. P., Biddle, K. R., Paster, M., & Taber, S. E. (1996). *Strategies for success: Classroom teaching techniques for students with learning problems.* Austin, TX: PRO-ED.

Mercer, C. D. (1997). *Students with learning disabilities* (5th ed.). Upper Saddle River, NJ: Merrill/Prentice Hall.

Moran, M. R., Schumaker, J. B., & Vetter, A. F. (1981). *Teaching a paragraph organization strategy to learning disabled adolescents* (Research Report No. 54). Lawrence: University of Kansas Center for Research on Learning.

Nagel, D. R., Schumaker, J. B., & Deshler, D. D. (1986). *The learning strategies curriculum: The FIRST-letter mnemonic strategy.* Lawrence, KS: Edge Enterprises.

Ogden, C. K. (1970). *The general basic English dictionary.* London: Evans Brothers.

Page, E. B., & Keith, T. Z. (1981). Effects of U.S. private schools: A technical analysis of two recent claims. *Educational Researcher, 10*(7), 7–17.

Polachek, S. W., Kniesner, T. J., & Harwood, H. J. (1978). Education production functions. *Journal of Educational Statistics, 3,* 209–231.

Rademacher, J. A., Deshler, D. D., Schumaker, J. B., & Lenz, B. K. (1998). *The content enhancement series: The quality assignment routine.* Lawrence, KS: Edge Enterprises.

Robinson, F. P. (1961). *Effective study.* New York: Harper and Brothers.

Robinson, H. A. (1978). *Teaching reading and study strategies: The content areas* (2nd ed.). Boston: Allyn & Bacon.

Roe, B. D., Stoodt, B. D., & Burns, P. C. (1995). *Secondary school reading instruction: The content areas* (5th ed.). Boston: Houghton Mifflin.

Saski, J., Swicegood, P., & Carter, J. (1983). Notetaking formats for learning disabled adolescents. *Learning Disability Quarterly, 6,* 265–272.

Schumaker, J. B., Bulgren, J. A., Deshler, D. D., & Lenz, B. K. (1998). *The content enhancement series: The recall enhancement routine.* Lawrence: University of Kansas Center for Research on Learning.

Schumaker, J. B., Deshler, D. D., Alley, G. R., Warner, M. M., & Denton, P. H. (1982). Multipass: A learning strategy for improving reading comprehension. *Learning Disability Quarterly, 5,* 295–304.

Schumaker, J. B., Deshler, D. D., & Ellis, E. S. (1986). Intervention issues related to the education of LD adolescents. In J. K. Torgesen & B. Y. L. Wong (Eds.), *Learning disabilities: Some new perspectives.* New York: Academic Press.

Schumaker, J. B., Deshler, D. D., & McKnight, P. C. (1991). Teaching routines for content areas at the secondary level. In G. Stover, M. R. Shinn, & H. M. Walker (Eds.), *Interventions for achievement and behavior problems* (pp. 473–494). Washington, DC: National Association of School Psychologists.

Schumaker, J. B., Deshler, D. D., Nolan, S., Clark, F. L., Alley, G. R., & Warner, M. M. (1981). *Error monitoring: A learning strategy for improving academic performance of LD adolescents* (Research Report No. 32). Lawrence: University of Kansas Center for Research on Learning.

Seabaugh, G. O., & Schumaker, J. B. (1981). *The effects of self-regulation training on the academic productivity of LD and NLD adolescents* (Research Report No. 37). Lawrence: University of Kansas Center for Research on Learning.

Towle, M. (1982). Learning how to be a student when you have a learning disability. *Journal of Learning Disabilities, 15,* 90–93.

Van Reusen, A. K., & Bos, C. S. (1994). Facilitating student participation in individualized education programs through motivation strategy instruction. *Exceptional Children, 60,* 466–475.

Van Reusen, A. K., Bos, C. S., Schumaker, J. B., & Deshler, D. D. (1994). *The self-advocacy strategy for education and transition planning.* Lawrence, KS: Edge Enterprises.

Walberg, H. J. (1984). Improving the productivity of America's schools. *Educational Leadership, 41*(8), 19–30.

Wood, J. W. (1998). *Adapting instruction to accommodate students in inclusive settings* (3rd ed.). Upper Saddle River, NJ: Merrill/Prentice Hall.

Zigmond, N., Sansone, J., Miller, S. E., Donahoe, K. A., & Kohnke, R. (1986). Teaching learning disabled students at the secondary school level: What research says to teachers. *Learning Disabilities Focus, 1*(2), 108–115.

full-time jobs, mostly at the unskilled or semi-skilled level. They receive low wages and generally work in jobs of low social status.

- *Job dissatisfaction.* Many young adults with learning disabilities report less job satisfaction than their peers without disabilities.
- *Dependent living arrangement.* About 60 to 70 percent of young adults with learning disabilities continue to live with their parents several years after leaving secondary school.
- *Social skills problems.* Many young adults with learning disabilities have problems with relationships in the work setting. These are manifested in disagreements, misunderstandings, poor communication, and inappropriate appearance.
- *Poor work habits.* Not working fast enough, difficulty coping with job pressures, possessing deficient academic skills, and having problems following directions all interfere with the job performance of many individuals with learning disabilities.
- *Job selection.* Many individuals with learning disabilities have jobs that accentuate their weaknesses. For example, they take jobs that require extensive organization when they have organizational skills deficits.

In an effort to understand what factors contribute to postschool adjustments of individuals with learning disabilities, many researchers study both individuals who have made successful adjustments and those who have not. These studies yield data on conditions or factors that appear common to most adults with learning disabilities, individuals with learning disabilities who have been successful, and individuals with learning disabilities who have been unsuccessful. Table 14.1 presents these findings summarized from the following sources: Adelman and Vogel (1993), Reiff and deFur (1992), Reiff, Ginsberg, and Gerber (1995); Sitlington et al., (1993); Spekman, Goldberg, and Herman (1993); and Spekman, Herman, and Vogel (1993).

In most of these studies, a multidimensional view is used to determine success. Some common markers of success include age-appropriate activities in relation to employment, school attendance, involvement with peers, involvement with family, participation in leisure and social activities, reported satisfaction with life, and description of endeavors in a realistic manner (i.e., perception matches reality) (Sitlington et al., 1993; Spekman et al., 1992). Likewise, a multidimensional view is used to define unsuccessful postschool adjustments and typically includes difficulty with age-appropriate activities and thoughts in work, school, family, leisure, friendships, satisfaction with life, and aspirations (Spekman et al., 1992). The findings from the research on successful adults with learning disabilities compel educators to focus on interventions that help individuals with disabilities recognize and understand their strengths and weaknesses and learn self-determination (i.e., take control of their lives to achieve positive outcomes).

In several studies, social deficits are reported as the major area of concern for adults with learning disabilities. Chelser (1982) reports the following rank ordering of areas in which 560 adults with learning disabilities felt a need for assistance:

1. Social relationships and skills
2. Career counseling
3. Developing self-esteem and confidence
4. Overcoming dependence; survival
5. Vocational training
6. Getting and holding a job
7. Reading
8. Spelling
9. Managing personal finances
10. Organizational skills

In general, problems such as social relationships of individuals with learning disabilities appear to persist in adolescents, young adults, and general adulthood; these individuals must adapt to situations that change over time and often present new challenges and problems. Studies of adults with learning disabilities who have been out of school for several years yield some encouraging findings. For example, Lewandowski and Arcangelo (1994) examined the social adjustment and self-concept of adults with and without learning disabilities who graduated from secondary school between 1982 and 1988. They found that the adults with learning disabilities were similar to the adults without learning disabilities in terms of social adjustment and self-concept. They conclude, "It appears that any negative effects of a disability classification abate once individuals leave the public school environment, and that previous forecasts of the socioemotional status of adults with learning disabilities may be unnecessarily pessimistic" (p. 598). Likewise,

TABLE 14.1

Common factors of adults with learning disabilities

All adults with learning disabilities tend to
  have learning disabilities throughout adulthood
  face more stress
  be late bloomers
  need a continuing support system
  need help in understanding their disability
  need transition planning
  need to be included in developing their own transition plan
  need assistance with problem-solving strategies

Successful adults with learning disabilities tend to
  understand and accept their learning disabilities
  maintain a proactive approach
  maintain perseverance in dealing with life events
  develop coping strategies and know how to reduce stress
  maintain emotional stability
  set appropriate goals and maintain goal-directedness
  have and use support systems (e.g., a history of tutoring and therapeutic and supportive relationships)
  maintain a sense of control in their lives (e.g., make decisions to take charge of their lives and make useful
      adaptations to move ahead)
  maintain a determination to "make it" (i.e., motivation)
  pursue careers that maximize their strengths and minimize their weaknesses
  develop creative ways to compensate and problem solve
  maintain a positive attitude toward learning
  participate in a family or community ethic that values work and independence
  graduate from secondary school
  exhibit high verbal skills

Unsuccessful adults with learning disabilities tend to
  have higher rates of unemployment if female
  not understand or accept their learning disability
  fail to take control of their lives
  maintain a sense of learned helplessness and fail to assume responsibility
  seek and promote dependent relationships
  pursue careers that accentuate their weaknesses
  have a severe math disability
  have an absence of protective factors (e.g., nurturing home environments) or factors associated with suc-
      cessful adults (e.g., support systems, proactivity, and motivation)
  drop out of secondary school

Source: From *Students with Learning Disabilities* (p. 400), 5th ed., by C. D. Mercer,1997, Upper Saddle River, NJ: Merrill/
Prentice Hall. Copyright 1997 by Prentice-Hall Publishing Company. Reprinted by permission.

Spekman et al., (1992) maintain that young adults with learning disabilities who are highly dependent on their support systems (i.e., family) tend to become more independent over time. Better jobs, improved wages, and ability to use community services facilitate independence.

Patton and Polloway (1992) report that as individuals with learning disabilities become older, their problems often become more complex. Likewise, Gerber et al., (1990) note that the complexity and interaction of variables associated with disabilities are magnified in adulthood. Cronin and Patton

(1993) note that these mediating variables need to be considered within the contexts of the following adult domains: employment and education, home and family, leisure, community involvement, emotional health, physical health, personal responsibility, and relationships. Gerber (1994) notes that consideration of the mediating variables within these contexts holds promise for more meaningful research on adults with learning disabilities.

Because many adults with disabilities do not enjoy an acceptable quality of life (U.S. Department of Education, 1994; Wehman, 1993) despite their apparent potential to do so, educators should develop and implement viable transition programs for these individuals. In an article titled "Transition: Old Wine in New Bottles," Halpern (1992) notes that educators have been trying for 30 years to prepare adolescents with disabilities to make successful transitions to adult life. The 1960s featured cooperative/work study programs, the 1970s introduced career education, and the 1980s and 1990s have focused on transition. According to Halpern, "In the area of curriculum and instruction, we are still frequently deficient in what we teach, how we teach, and where we teach. Curriculum content still tends to focus too much on remedial academics and not enough on functional skills" (p. 206).

☀ TRANSITIONS FROM SECONDARY SETTINGS

Because of the continuing failure of many students with disabilities to make positive adjustments to adult life, transition services remain a national priority (Halpern, 1992; Will, 1984). In 1990, a transition mandate was included in the Amendments to the Education of the Handicapped Act, renamed the Individuals with Disabilities Education Act (Public Law 101-476). This law (Section 602[a][19]) defines *transition* as

> a coordinated set of activities for a student, designed within an outcome-oriented process, which promotes movement from school to post-school activities, including post-secondary education, vocational training, integrated employment (including supported employment), continuing and adult education, adult services, independent living, and community participation. The coordinated set of activities shall be based upon the individual student's needs, taking into account the student's preferences and interests, and shall include: in-

struction, community experiences, the development of employment and other post-school adult living objectives, and when appropriate, acquisition.

In addition, the law (Section 602[a][20]) requires that the individualized educational program include

> a statement of the needed transition services for students beginning no later than age 16, and annually thereafter (and, when determined appropriate for the individual, beginning at age 14 or younger), including, when appropriate, a statement of the interagency responsibilities or linkages (or both) before the student leaves the school setting.

Moreover, this law mandates that all students in special education receive transition planning and that each student's need for transition services be determined during the secondary education period. These mandates ensure that the development and delivery of transition services for students with disabilities receive serious and overdue consideration (Reiff & deFur, 1992).

Transition Program Components

To be successful, transition programs need to include (1) academic programs that prepare respective students to function independently and enter work or postsecondary education, (2) career education, (3) vocational education, (4) self-advocacy training, and (5) collaboration among a multitude of professionals, parents, and employers. Rojewski (1992) reviewed nine prototype transition projects and identified seven essential components:

1. Individualized planning
2. Systematic vocational assessment, job exploration, vocational counseling, and vocational skills training
3. Academic remediation
4. Academic and vocational counseling and intervention in advocacy training, social skills, and social support
5. The identification and coordination of support systems such as vocational rehabilitation, employers, and vocational educators
6. A systematic job-seeking curriculum that features activities such as writing a resume, finding job openings, filling out applications, and interviewing for employment
7. An evaluation plan to monitor the short-term and long-term effectiveness of the program

Transition Program Participants and Transition Plans

Participants in the transition program include a variety of individuals. The primary participants and their roles include the following:

- *Special educators:* Act as transition case manager; teach job-related academic strategies, social skills, and job-finding and job-keeping program prerequisites; collaborate with the transition team to coordinate the plan; teach self-advocacy.
- *Guidance counselors:* Provide career, individual, and small-group counseling; provide career awareness and exploration information.
- *Vocational evaluator* or *school psychologist:* Conduct vocationally relevant evaluations.
- *Employers:* Provide information about job needs and requirements; provide job training sites and permanent jobs; evaluate students before and after graduation.
- *Vocational educators:* Provide vocational training both in and out of school; make instructional modifications when appropriate; obtain information regarding job needs and job requirements.
- *Parents:* Help adolescents develop realistic career goals; promote and support independence; help adolescents explore career options.
- *Students:* Acquire strategies and skills needed to be vocationally successful; work toward achieving independence; acquire strategies and skills needed for postsecondary educational settings.
- *College and university personnel:* Advise students regarding admission procedures; plan support services such as scheduling, accommodations, and advisement.
- *Vocational rehabilitation counselors:* Obtain funding for job-related services; provide vocational evaluation information; assist with job placement and provide support services; act as primary postsecondary receiving agency.

These participants are the key planners at the secondary school level; however, a school-based career development and transition program begins in elementary school and continues into adulthood. Clark and Kolstoe (1990) present a school-based career development and transition education model that covers preschool through lifelong learning opportunities. The model comprises four content elements:

1. Job-acquisition and daily living skills appropriate for current and future needs
2. Occupational information, including various occupational roles, occupational vocabulary, occupational alternatives, and basic realities about the world of work
3. Human relationships on the job, in the family, and in the community
4. Values, attitudes, and habits essential for work

Public Law 101-476 requires the development of an individualized transition plan for students with disabilities by the time they reach age 16. Because students' needs vary, the plans reflect many different types of services and providers. The *Transition Planning Inventory* (Clark & Patton, 1997) is an instrument designed to provide a systematic way to identify and plan for an individual student's transition needs (knowledge, skills, support, or services). Figure 14.1 features an individualized transition plan for a student with emotional disabilities who plans to enter full-time employment after leaving school.

☀ PROGRAM AREAS IN TRANSITION EDUCATION

Effective transition programs must prepare the student with disabilities to function successfully in many adult roles to attain an acceptable quality of life. Some of the primary curriculum areas are academic, vocational, domestic living, mobility, leisure and recreation, and accessing community services. Students planning to make the transition to postsecondary educational institutions receive their preparatory training in a curriculum that features career education and academic instruction that promotes success in higher education. The vocational aspects of the curriculum are provided through career education, vocational education, and academic programs. Domestic living, mobility, leisure and recreation, and accessing community services are covered within the independent living skills academic curriculum. Finally, an academic program that includes self-advocacy training helps the student succeed in all adult roles. This section presents the major components of a transition program: academic interventions, functional living skills instruction, career and vocational education, and self-advocacy training.

Academic Interventions

Academic interventions within transition programs consist of skill-oriented instruction or content-oriented instruction.

Skill-Oriented Instruction Skill-oriented instruction teaches students skills that relate to the academic areas they find difficult. Skills are broken down and taught to the students over time. Zigmond (1990) maintains that intensive and efficient instruction in basic academic skills is essential for helping students succeed in employment and in independent living situations. Academic interventions seem especially appropriate for ninth and tenth graders who are achieving below fourth-grade level in one of the basic skill areas. Basic skills remediation is the foundation of special education programs in the elementary school setting. The academic chapters of this text provide a wealth of information to help teachers develop academic skills with students who have learning problems.

In a review of secondary curriculum content for students with learning disabilities, Rieth and Polsgrove (1994) report several noteworthy findings. In the area of teaching reading to adolescents, they report that phonics instruction appears to be a weak intervention. In the area of spelling, they found that spelling ability appears to improve when spelling instruction is integrated with other meaning-based language arts instruction. In the area of teaching mathematics to adolescents, the use of videodisc technology has yielded impressive

FIGURE 14.1

An individualized transition plan

ITP for Student with an Emotional Disability Enrolled in a 10th Grade Diploma-Bound Program

<u>Student Profile.</u> John is a 16-year-old student. He is currently attending his neighborhood high school for four periods a day since returning to his family's home after a year-long stay in a group home for youth with emotional disabilities. John enjoys his class in auto mechanics, but has difficulty accepting responsibility for regular attendance and project completions. His academic skills are at grade level. John has signed up for a job skills class at the adult education night school to build his confidence in job interview skills. John wants to work full time after graduation.

Individualized Transition Plan

Name John Tothe Birth Date 01/31/81 Age 16 Social Security 272-95-4576

Graduation Status X Diploma Special Diploma Certificate of Completion Expects to Graduate: 1999

Describe Post-School Outcomes: Employment: Full-time independent Residential: Semi-independent

Education: No additional school Other:

Work Experience Completed: Vocational Classes: Woodshop; auto mechanics

Community-Based Instruction: 3 hrs/school day training at Sea World-Custodial

Work Experience: 8 hrs/week paid work at Sea World for 6 months

Other:

Preparation for Adulthood:

Does student have	Yes	No	When?	In Process	Adult Agency Referral:	Date to be referred	A-Active I-Inactive
Social Security Card	X				Vocational Rehabilitation	3/99	I
Driver's Education		X	12th gr		Health & Human Services	N/A	
Driver's License		X	12th gr		Community College District (Dis Stu Svcs)	N/A	
State Identification Card		X		X	Social Security (SSI)		A
Bus Identification Card		X		X	Employment Development Department	10/97	
Birth Certificate	X				County Mental Health Services	5/97	A
Resume Completed		X	11th gr	X	Department of Social Services (Dev/Dis)	N/A	
Other					Other	N/A	

(continued on next page)

FIGURE 14.1
(continued)

Prioritize Issues to be Addressed for this ITP

	Post-secondary	1	Employment/Training		Adult Agency Linkages
	Residential		Community Recreation/Leisure	2	Personal/Domestic Management
	Health and Medical		Financial and Income		Family Life and Social
3	Self-Advocacy		Mobility/Transportation		Other

Transition Domain	Transition Goals	Time-Line	Agency/Person Responsible	Evaluation
Employment/Training	John will enroll in evening job-seeking skills class.	6/97	John, Counselor	—Met —Modify —Continue
Employment/Training	John will apply for two jobs in areas of interest.	6/97	John, Teacher, Counselor	—Met —Modify —Continue
Employment/Training	John will complete application and participate in summer Hire-A-Youth program.	5/96 & 5/97	John, Counselor	—Met —Modify —Continue
Personal Management	John will attend weekly counseling meetings at County Mental Health and continue working on meeting personal goals and independent living goals.	6/97—ongoing	John, Counselor	—Met —Modify —Continue
Self-Advocacy	John will identify future lifestyle goals within each domain (i.e., employment, rec/leisure, etc.) and create a list describing his desires for each area.	9/97	John, Teacher, Parents	—Met —Modify —Continue
Self-Advocacy	John will attend and participate in his ITP meetings and be able to communicate his employment and personal goals.	9/97-6/98	John, Parents, Teachers	—Met —Modify —Continue

Prioritize Issues to be Addressed at Next ITP Meeting:

	Post-Secondary	3	Employment/Training	4	Adult Agency Linkages
1	Residential		Community Recreation/Leisure		Personal/Domestic Management
	Health and Medical	2	Financial and Income		Family Life and Social
	Self-Advocacy		Mobility/Transportation		Other

Additional Participants at Next ITP Meeting:
Name _Ms. Smith_____ Agency _County Mental Health_____

Signatures: Student_____ Parent (s)_____
Teacher_____ Adult agency_____
Transition Specialist_____ Principal_____
Counselor_____ Other_____

Source: Adapted from *Teaching Children and Adolescents with Special Needs* (pp. 386–387), 2nd ed., by J. L. Olson, and J. M. Platt, 1996, Upper Saddle River, NJ: Merrill/Prentice Hall. Copyright 1996 by Prentice-Hall Publishing Company. Reprinted by permission.

achievement gains and has been well received by teachers (Woodward & Gersten, 1992).

Several projects provide academic remediation to secondary students with learning disabilities. For example, the Pittsburgh Child Service Demonstra-tion Center developed a model that is widely used in Pittsburgh secondary schools (Buchwach, 1980). Students attend a resource room (called a *learning lab*) for no more than two periods daily. The stu-dents are removed only from English or math to receive basic skill intervention. A diagnostic systematic approach to skill development is provided, and generalization of newly learned skills is fostered by having students eventually use materials from mainstream classes in the learning lab. A second special education resource teacher functions as a liaison between the students and their mainstream teachers. In addition, this teacher works with the learning lab teacher once a week to provide a school survival skills curriculum (i.e., strands pertaining to behavior, teacher-pleasing behavior, and study skills).

Because secondary students face numerous curriculum demands and have little time to ameliorate deficits, educators are seeking ways to increase the intensity of instruction (e.g., learning labs and high-intensity learning centers). For example, *Corrective Reading* (published by SRA) can be used with adolescents with learning problems to increase the level of instructional intensity of academic remediation. Summer school programs also can provide an opportunity for high-intensity instruction without delaying graduation.

Content-Oriented Instruction   Content-oriented instruction promotes the direct acquisition of content by students. Skill or strategy instruction also is designed ultimately to lead to content-area learning, but the relationship is indirect. Content acquisition is promoted through designing content enhancements; planning courses in which the content is organized into levels of content that all students learn, most students learn, and some students learn; tutoring in the content areas; and providing equivalent-content instruction. Chapter 4 presents leveled content planning, and Chapter 13 features the use of content enhancements and equivalent-content instruction through accommodations and modifications. Moreover, Chapter 13 presents learning strategies and study skills techniques, both of which help students learn content.

In a survey of state Departments of Education, McKenzie (1991) found that content instruction by special educators is used extensively throughout the nation. In the tutorial approach, the general education teacher delivers content, but the special education teacher provides short-term assistance in mastering key aspects of the content in which the student is experiencing difficulty or failure. With the increase in inclusion, general education and special education teachers are collaborating more to deliver content in learner-friendly ways.

In a multi-state study of teachers' and supervisors' perceptions of secondary learning disabilities programs, Cline and Billingsley (1991) found that the primary program components have remained consistent over the past decade but the relative importance of these areas is changing. The four highest-rated program components of teachers and supervisors include direct teaching of content subjects, basic skills remediation, learning and study strategies, and tutorial assistance. The respondents, however, indicate that special education teachers should decrease content-area instruction and increase learning strategies instruction. Also, the results highlight a need to provide more consultation to general education teachers.

Functional Living Skills Instruction

Brolin (1995) reports that much literature supports the position that an appropriate education for students with disabilities must be implemented according to individual needs as related to the functional skills demands of adulthood. *Functional skills* are those an adult needs to perform successfully in a variety of community settings. Clark (1991) defines *functional curriculum* as instructional content that focuses on the concepts and skills needed by students in the areas of personal-social, daily living, and occupational adjustment.

A functional or essential living skills program typically is designed for secondary students whose academic skills are very low (i.e., below fourth-grade level). Functional living skills must be taught directly and systematically to some students with learning problems, or otherwise the students may never acquire these essential skills or may learn them through trial and error, which is both costly and time-consuming. Within the context of a life-centered career education curriculum, Brolin (1993) provides the following competencies and subcompetencies in daily living skills:

1. *Manages personal finance:* Counts money and makes correct change; makes responsible expenditures; keeps basic financial records; calculates and pays taxes; uses credit responsibly; uses banking services.

2. *Selects and manages a household:* Maintains home exterior and interior; uses basic appliances and tools; selects adequate housing; sets up household; maintains home grounds.

3. *Cares for personal needs:* Demonstrates knowledge of physical fitness, nutrition, and weight; exhibits proper grooming and hygiene; dresses appropriately; demonstrates knowledge of common illness prevention and treatment; practices personal safety.

4. *Raises children and meets marriage responsibilities:* Demonstrates physical care by raising children; knows psychological aspects of raising children; demonstrates marriage responsibilities.

5. *Buys, prepares, and consumes food:* Purchases food; clears food preparation areas; stores food; prepares meals; demonstrates appropriate eating habits; plans and eats balanced meals.

6. *Buys and cares for clothing:* Washes and cleans clothing; purchases clothing; irons, mends, and stores clothing.

7. *Exhibits responsible citizenship:* Demonstrates knowledge of civic rights and responsibilities; knows nature of local, state, and federal governments; demonstrates knowledge of the law and ability to follow the law; demonstrates knowledge of citizen rights and responsibilities.

8. *Utilizes recreational facilities and engages in leisure:* Demonstrates knowledge of available community resources; chooses and plans activities; demonstrates knowledge of the value of recreation; engages in group and individual activities; plans vacation time.

9. *Gets around the community:* Demonstrates knowledge of traffic rules and safety; demonstrates knowledge and use of various means of transportation; finds way around the community; drives a car.

These competencies are an excellent framework for a functional curriculum and, when combined with personal-social and occupational guidance and preparation competencies, they form the foundation of a strong career-centered education. Many of these skills can be taught within the traditional curriculum. For example, Area 1 can be included in math; Areas 3 and 5 in science; Areas 4, 7, and 9 in social studies; Areas 2 and 6 in home economics and shop; and Area 8 in music, art, and physical education.

To establish and monitor educational or prevocational objectives, the *Brigance Diagnostic Inventory of Essential Skills* (Brigance, 1981) can be used. This instrument includes measures of functional academics at the secondary level and thus assesses minimal academic and vocational competencies. The inventory includes rating scales to measure applied skills that cannot be assessed objectively, such as health practices and attitude, responsibility and self-discipline, job interview preparation, auto safety, speaking skills, and listening skills. Other practical assessments include sections on food and clothing, money and finance, travel and transportation, and oral communication and telephone skills. Also, the *Brigance Diagnostic Life Skills Inventory* (Brigance, 1994) assesses basic skills and functional life skills in the context of real-world situations. Nine skill areas are included: speaking and listening, functional writing, words on common signs and warning labels, telephone, money and finance, food, clothing, health, and travel and transportation.

Activities for Developing Functional Living Skills

Cronin (1988) presents functional curriculum tasks in the areas of consumer economics, occupational knowledge, health, community resources, and government and law. These tasks are presented across academic areas (e.g., reading and writing) at the elementary, junior high, and senior high school levels. Table 14.2 displays this information in a manner that enables the teacher to integrate these tasks and skills across academic areas and grade levels. Moreover, the following specific activities may be helpful in developing students' functional living skills:

• To focus on managing family finances, have the student keep a record of expenses for a certain period of time. The budget should include areas such as food, clothing, transportation, savings, medical expenses, and recreation. The student also may itemize his or her family's purchases during a period of time. To encourage the student to spend money wisely, provide a shopping list of products available at different stores, and require the student to compare prices or to select items based on a fixed amount of money.

• Take a field trip to a bank and a credit union facility or arrange classroom demonstrations by representatives from these establishments. A classroom bank and individual accounts can be set up to acquaint the student with checks, deposits, withdrawals, and passbooks.

TABLE 14.2
Functional curriculum tasks across academic areas

	Consumer Economics	Occupational Knowledge	Health	Community Resources	Government and Law
Elementary School					
Reading	Look for ads in the newspaper for toys.	Read books from a library on various occupations.	Read the school lunch menu.	Find a television listing in the *TV Guide*.	Read road signs and understand what they mean.
Writing	Write prices of items to be purchased.	Write the specific tasks involved in performing one of the classroom jobs.	Keep a diary of food you eat in each food group each day.	Complete an application to play on a little league team.	Write a letter to the mayor inviting him or her to visit your school.
Speaking, Listening, Viewing	Listen to a bank official talk about savings accounts.	Call a newspaper in town to inquire about delivering papers in your neighborhood.	View a film on brushing teeth.	Practice using 911 emergency number.	Discuss park playground improvements with the mayor.
Problem Solving	Decide whether you have enough coins to make a purchase from a vending machine.	Decide which job in the classroom you do best.	Role play what you should do if you have a stomach ache.	Role play the times you would use a 911 emergency number.	Find the city hall on the map. Decide whether you will walk or drive.
Interpersonal Relations	Ask for help finding items in a grocery store.	Ask a student in the class to assist you with a classroom job.	Ask the school nurse how to take care of mosquito bites.	Call the movie theater and ask the performance times of a movie.	Role play asking a policeman for help if lost.
Computation	Compute the cost of a box of cereal using a coupon.	Calculate how much you would make on a paper route at $3 per hour for 5 hours per week.	Compute the price of one tube of toothpaste if they are on sale—3 for 1.	Compute the complete cost of going to the movie (admission, food, transportation).	Compute tax on a candy bar.
Junior High School					
Reading	Read an ad for a sale locating name of store, location, phone number, and price of item.	Read a job description.	Locate poison-control numbers in phone book.	Use phone book to locate recreational program in community.	Locate and read a list of state and U.S. representatives.
Writing	Fill out a magazine order form completely.	Practice writing abbreviations for words.	Write a menu for a balanced diet.	Write a letter to a TV station about a program they just canceled.	Fill out a voter registration form.
Speaking, Listening, Viewing	Discuss saving vs. spending money.	Discuss reasons why we work.	Listen to positive and negative feedback on personal appearance.	Call a library to find out whether they have a certain book.	Discuss why we need to vote.

(continued on next page)

TABLE 14.2
(continued)

	Consumer Economics	Occupational Knowledge	Health	Community Resources	Government and Law
Problem Solving	Given $10 for the evening, choose an activity: movies, bowling, or pizza.	Decide on job environment: inside, outside, desk, travel, etc.	Role play appropriate behavior for various places (movies, church, restaurant).	Locate the skating rink on a city map and decide the best way to get there.	Decide what items have state and/or local tax.
Interpersonal Relations	Ask salesperson for help in purchasing jeans.	List questions to ask in job interview.	Discuss honesty, trust, and promise. Define each.	Call a skating rink to inquire about hours.	Call to find out what precinct you live in.
Computation	Compute the sales tax on a pair of jeans.	Compute net income.	Calculate and compare the prices of hair shampoo.	Calculate bus fare to and from the teen center.	Calculate the cost of getting a driver's license (fee, gas).

Senior High School

	Consumer Economics	Occupational Knowledge	Health	Community Resources	Government and Law
Reading	Read and compare prices of grocery store ads.	Read a job description and qualifications.	Read directions on a cough-syrup bottle.	Read a movie schedule.	Obtain and read a sales tax sheet for your county/state.
Writing	Write a check for amount of purchase.	Complete a job application.	Write a grocery list for the week, including all the food groups.	List government and community employment agencies from a phone book.	Apply for a work permit.
Speaking, Listening, Viewing	Explain the difference between charge, check, and cash purchases.	Role play calling your boss when ill.	Practice calling a doctor's office for an appointment.	Listen to a state patrolman talk about highway driving.	Describe an accident.
Problem Solving	Decide what amount you can afford to rent an apartment.	Decide what to wear to a job interview.	Decide whether you should go to a community clinic or a hospital for an injury.	Role play what you would do if your car broke down.	Decide which candidate to vote for.
Interpersonal Relations	Ask a salesperson if the store offers layaway and the costs involved.	Role play a mock interview.	Ask a pharmacist about a prescription.	Ask directions to a video store.	Call legal aid and ask what services are available.
Computation	Calculate and compare savings on items from different stores.	Calculate paycheck deductions.	Decide how many times a day to take a pill.	Compute cost of doing laundry in a laundromat vs. home.	Calculate the cost of a speeding ticket.

Source: From "Applying Curriculum for the Instruction of Life Skills" by M. E. Cronin. In *Best Practices in Mental Disabilities* (pp.44–46), Vol. 2, by G. A. Robinson, J. R. Patton, E. A. Polloway, and L. R. Sargent (Eds.), 1988, Des Moines: Iowa Department of Education, Bureau of Special Education. Copyright 1988 by Iowa Department of Education, Bureau of Special Education. Reprinted by permission.

Activities can provide extensive practice in writing checks, filling out deposit slips, and balancing a checkbook. To learn about other banking services, the student also can be required to fill out forms for obtaining a loan or opening a charge account.

• Have small-group discussions in which students examine various kinds of taxes (such as sales, gas, property, and income). Have them identify items that are taxed and determine the amount, how the tax is collected, and how it is used. The procedure for filing income tax forms can be presented by requiring each student to fill out a 1040 short form. Cut instructions from a tax guide according to numbered sections (e.g., 1—name and address, 2—Social Security number, and so on). Fasten each instruction and the corresponding section of the 1040A form to a card. Provide one sample form filled out as well as blank 1040A forms that are laminated for reuse. Instruct each student to fill out a 1040A form number by number, referring if necessary to the completed form and the individual instruction cards.

• Discuss various types of housing available in the community. Have students explore the advantages and disadvantages of each according to factors such as cost, space, utilities, and location. In discussing renting a home or apartment, include such factors as deposits, leases, and tenant rights and responsibilities. Cut out newspaper ads that list rentals and tape them to the inside of a manila folder. On index cards write questions related to the rental ads and place the cards in a pocket pasted to the folder. The student picks a card, looks for the answer in the classified ads mounted on the inside of the folder, and writes a response. An answer key can be provided by numbering the questions and assigning letters to the ads.

• Have students role play potential problems in marriage and child raising and discuss solutions. Encourage students to refer to their own life experiences when suggesting appropriate practices in raising children. Also have students identify community agencies and sources that assist in family planning and marriage problems.

• Identify emergency situations that can occur in the home (such as fire or storm damage) or with a family member (such as accident or injury). Have each student look up emergency phone numbers and make a booklet containing information on how to get help for emergencies. First-aid procedures for injury situations should be demonstrated in the classroom and listed in the student's booklet. Also, safety procedures for hazardous situations can be discussed.

• Have each student determine recreational activities in which he or she can participate, and list resources and facilities available in the community. If the student is interested in music, the teacher can tape-record five different types of music and have the student select a favorite. Then the student can explore places where that type of music is available, or the student can study favorite composers. To develop an interest in art as a leisure activity, the teacher can present prints of various types of art. The student can determine places or events in which to enjoy art during recreational time. Also, the student can participate in clubs or hobbies to explore using leisure time effectively.

Career and Vocational Education

The emphasis on career education began in the early 1970s and evolved from dissatisfaction with the educational system's ability to prepare students adequately for the future. In 1988, the U.S. Departments of Labor, Education, and Commerce surveyed 134 business representatives concerning their needs, goals, and expectations of education when hiring adolescents. One of the primary revelations involved the widening gap between the basic skills businesses need and the qualifications beginning workers possess, which costs employers a great deal in their quest to produce quality products at competitive prices.

The Council for Exceptional Children (1978, p. 1) Division on Career Development defines *career education* as

> the totality of experiences through which one learns to live a meaningful, satisfying work life. Career education provides the opportunity for children to learn, in the least restrictive environment possible, the academic, daily living, personal-social, and occupational knowledges, and highest levels of economic, personal, and social fulfillment. The individual can obtain this fulfillment through work (both paid and unpaid) and in a variety of other social roles and personal life styles including pursuits as a student, citizen, volunteer, family member, and participant in meaningful leisure time activities.

Students with learning problems often need attractive options in career training. Career-related instruction enables an individual to explore the occupational world, identify with it, and make job decisions that increase self-fulfillment. Moreover, the content places value on all work, regardless of its current social status. Cegelka and Greene (1993, pp. 142–143) state:

> By emphasizing the relationship of subject matter to various careers and occupations and by developing

needed work skills, career education sought to make education more relevant to the economic and employment realities of the day. . . . Career education has been seen as the sum of all experiences through which one learns to live a meaningful, satisfying, and productive work life.

Meers (1992) reports that career education spans kindergarten through twelfth grade and features three components: (1) instruction to help individuals live independently at home, (2) instruction to help individuals live independently in the community, and (3) vocational instruction to prepare individuals for successful employment. Thus, career education involves a comprehensive educational program, focusing on careers, that begins in early childhood and continues throughout adulthood. At the elementary level, the major objective is to introduce the student to various occupations. The primary objective at the secondary level is to shape the student's awareness of occupations into preparation for a career. Figure 14.2 presents the stages of career development.

Wiederholt and Wolffe (1990) offer a normal sequence of independent living-related developments that provide a complement to the career development stages. These independent living-related developments provide a framework of how students develop attitudes, values, interest, and information about work:

1. ***Preschool age:*** Learns to listen, cooperate, do for self, show initiative, be honest; differentiates work from other activities; understands different types of work and associated roles; develops feelings toward work.

2. ***Elementary age:*** Fantasizes different roles; understands parents' work; has continued and more complex career fantasies; is exposed to and develops understanding of a wide variety of work roles; develops understanding of good work qualities; continues to develop and implement communication skills; learns to interact appropriately with peers and authority.

3. ***Junior high school age:*** Has part-time or summer job; does chores at home; develops hobbies or special interests; begins to understand personal strengths and weaknesses; understands relative rewards, demands, and requirements of major categories of work; accepts responsibility for career decisions; begins to crystallize personal values and self-concept.

4. ***Senior high school age and older:*** Continues exploration of various career possibilities; prepares for career or initial employment; crystallizes interests; changes plans or jobs; understands and acts upon personal strengths and weaknesses; develops skills; crystallizes personal values and self-concept; handles independent living; establishes intimate relationships; refines hobbies or special interests; learns how to get jobs and holds several different jobs; learns and displays appropriate work behavior.

Career education enables an individual to explore the occupational world, to identify with it, and to make job decisions that increase self-fulfillment. Brolin (1993) recommends that career education be a major part of the curriculum for students with disabilities and that it focus on the total life plan of an individual. The total life plan facilitates growth

FIGURE 14.2
Career development stages

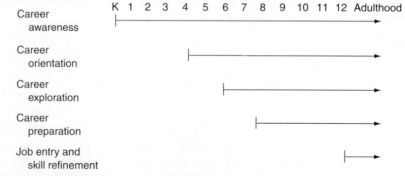

and development in all life roles and settings. In addition to the competencies in daily living skills presented earlier, Brolin includes the following competencies in personal-social skills and occupational guidance and preparation:

- ***Personal-social skills:*** Achieves self-awareness; acquires self-confidence; achieves socially responsible behavior; maintains good interpersonal skills; achieves independence; makes adequate decisions; communicates with others.
- ***Occupational guidance and preparation:*** Knows and explores occupational possibilities; selects and plans occupational choices; exhibits appropriate work habits and behavior; seeks, secures, and maintains employment; exhibits sufficient physical-manual skills; obtains specific occupational skills.

Career education has a broad emphasis and includes vocational training. Vocational education usually is provided at the secondary or postsecondary level. The American Vocational Association (1968) defines *vocational education* as education designed to develop skills, abilities, understanding, attitudes, work habits, and appreciations needed by individuals to enter and make useful and productive progress in employment. The goal of vocational education is to prepare the individual for gainful employment. Both career and vocational education are needed if students with learning problems are to make successful transitions from secondary school to adult lives. Will's (1984) support service model of transition simply identifies three levels of essential services that help students with disabilities progress from secondary school to employment. Some students with disabilities require vocational and supportive life-skills instruction as ongoing services or on a time-limited basis, whereas other students require no special support services.

Vocational training specifically focuses on developing vocational skills essential to entering the world of work. Historically, it has been difficult to obtain vocational training for students with mild disabilities. A variety of options and services are needed to provide low achievers with the programs they need. Such students can learn specialized skills in a career area in a vocational-technical school, a special vocational school, work-study off campus, and work-study on campus. Postschool alternatives include entry-level jobs, trade school, community

college, college or university, and referral to the Bureau of Vocational Rehabilitation or other appropriate community or government agencies.

A variety of measures and procedures can be used to assess students in terms of appropriate decisions on career direction. Information can be obtained informally through student–teacher interaction and a consultative process. Also, the *Brigance Diagnostic Employability Skills Inventory* (Brigance, 1995) is a criterion-referenced instrument that assesses the basic skills and employability skills needed to gain employment and succeed in the workplace. In addition, a number of standardized tests assess vocational interest or aptitude. The following instruments can be used to help secondary students choose appropriate careers based on their particular abilities and interests: *Ability Explorer* (Harrington & Harrington, 1996), *Career Decision-Making System—Revised* (Harrington & O'Shea, 1992), and *Occupational Aptitude Survey and Interest Schedule—2* (Parker, 1991). Moreover, the *Career IQ and Interest Test* (produced by PRO-ED) is an interactive CD-ROM that contains a vocational aptitude test and an interest test. Scores on the test are automatically linked to job information in the *Occupational Outlook Handbook* (published by the U.S. Department of Labor) so that individuals can obtain information concerning jobs that match their aptitudes and interests. In addition to standardized testing procedures, the work-sample method provides a means of prevocational evaluation. The work sample is a simulated task or occupational activity that is representative of tasks and activities in various employment settings. As the individual attempts different work samples, personality characteristics and skill aptitudes can be observed to indicate vocational potential.

Curriculum-based vocational assessment offers an alternative approach to commercial tests. Schloss, Smith, and Schloss (1995) note that curriculum-based vocational assessment is based on each student's learning needs and includes four primary characteristics:

1. It provides relevant information in the beginning stages of planning an individual's vocational program.
2. Assessment is an integral and ongoing part of a student's vocational program.

3. The person conducting curriculum-based vocational assessment is the same person responsible for the student's vocational instruction.

4. Informal and direct assessment measures are used to evaluate a student's progress throughout the vocational program.

When curriculum-based vocational assessment is used, information is available during all phases of the program (e.g., making placement decisions, working in vocational classes and jobs, and exiting the program). Also the assessment provides information for helping teachers collaborate with other professionals and make instructional or program modifications and for planning future job placements.

Activities for Developing Career-Related Skills   The following activities may help develop students' career-related skills:

- Invite students who have graduated recently to return to the school to discuss their jobs or problems in leaving secondary school for college, work, or military service. Selected students can be responsible for inviting alumni and for developing appropriate questions. The graduates' discussions should include positive aspects about their careers and how they handle problems encountered on the job. If possible, interested members of the class should have the opportunity to observe the individuals actually working.

- Plan field trips to visit businesses and industries and request personnel to speak with the students. A person from the business can be invited to speak to the class before or after the visit to answer questions or distribute information. During the trip, students should have enough time to observe persons performing various jobs and to record pertinent information about the job (such as job requirements, working conditions, and good and bad features of the job). Students can share their observations in class discussions after the visit.

- Divide the class into small groups and have each obtain information on one particular job per week. During group discussion, students can determine job responsibilities, identify personal and social values met through the work, and compile a list of words used on the job.

- Have each student write a want ad for what he or she considers to be the perfect job. The ad should include information such as hours, salary, qualifications, and responsibilities. Then have students check the want-ad section of the newspaper to locate ads for jobs in their interest area and compare these ads with their ideal ad. If appropriate, students can contact personnel directors of various businesses to find out the number of people recently hired, their salaries, and their qualifica-

tions. Also, visits may be arranged or volunteer or observation work can be set up with the business in which each student is most interested.

- Cut out several newspaper ads for available jobs. Have each student choose a job from the given ads and state why he or she would want that particular job and what preparation and qualifications are needed. Then have the student complete an application form for that job. The completed application can be reviewed for improvement.

- Role play interviews for various jobs. Discuss punctuality, appropriate dress, and questions to ask during the interview and acceptable responses. Role playing can build a student's self-confidence in an actual interview situation.

Self-Advocacy Training

Van Reusen, Bos, Schumaker, and Deshler (1994) provide *The Self-Advocacy Strategy for Education and Transition Planning* for teaching adolescents to identify their strengths, develop transition goals, and advocate for themselves. Specifically, students examine and plan in the following eight transition skill areas: (1) independent living skills, (2) financial and consumer skills, (3) citizenship and legal skills, (4) community involvement skills, (5) career and employment skills, (6) social and family-living skills, (7) health and wellness skills, and (8) leisure and recreation skills. Moreover, students learn communication skills to help them become self-advocates.

Finally, Durlak, Rose, and Bursuck (1994) note that several affective factors appear positively related to the successful postschool adjustments of adults with learning disabilities. Specifically, Durlak et al. identify self-determination skills as being important, and they examined the efficacy of directly teaching such skills to secondary students with learning disabilities. Their results indicate that these students were able to acquire, maintain, and generalize self-advocacy and self-awareness skills when the skills were taught using explicit instruction, opportunities to practice skills in the training setting and natural environment, and specific feedback. These findings have encouraging implications for developing secondary transition curricula for teaching affective skills.

☀ COLLEGE STUDENTS WITH SPECIAL NEEDS

Because many students with learning disabilities possess average or above intelligence and signif-

Appropriate social skills are critical to making successful transitions to colleges and careers.

icant academic strengths in select areas, a significant number make the transition from secondary school to colleges and universities. This section presents information regarding the adjustments of college students with learning disabilities.

An increasing number of students with learning disabilities are being admitted into colleges and universities. In a survey of 66 state universities and colleges, Spillane, McGuire, and Norlander (1992) found that the academic (e.g., grades, recommendations, and admission tests) and nonacademic (e.g., intelligence, motivation, and independence) criteria used to admit individuals with learning disabilities to colleges are similar to the criteria used for applicants without disabilities. Section 504 of the Rehabilitation Act of 1973 and the Americans with Disabilities Act of 1990 state that no individual should be excluded on the basis of a disability. Moreover, the Individuals with Disabilities Education Act (IDEA) states that a "qualified" college person with a disability is someone who with reasonable program modifications can meet the academic requirements. Some reasonable modifications include extended time to finish the program; course substitution, modification, or waiver of a foreign language requirement; part-time study; and extended time for tests. Scott (1994) reviews guidelines for weighing accommodation requests and presents recommendations for determining appropriate academic adjustments for college students with learning disabilities.

Section 504 also states that students must identify or refer themselves and that the university must provide full program accessibility to ensure a fair chance for success. Unfortunately, many college students with learning disabilities do not reveal their learning disability until they are in an academic crisis. Suggestions for college students with learning disabilities include the following:

- Talk to your instructors before the semester begins.
- If you think that you may have a specific learning disability, contact the disabled student services office on campus.
- Maintain realistic goals and priorities for course work.
- Keep only one calendar with all appointments and relevant dates (i.e., assignments, tests, and project due dates) clearly marked.
- Use a tape recorder during lectures and listen to the tape as soon after class as possible to reorganize your notes.
- Seek help for any questions you may have so that they can be answered before the next test.
- Sit near the front of the classroom.
- Estimate how long a given class assignment will take to complete. Build in study breaks because fatigue is a time waster.
- Obtain a course syllabus and make sure that course expectations are clear.
- Ask for reading assignments in advance if you are using books on tape.

- Use campus support services (e.g., preregistration, assistance in ordering taped books, alternative testing arrangements, specialized study aids, peer support groups, diagnostic consultation, study skills, and academic tutorial assistance).

In addition, the following selected services may help college students with learning disabilities: tutors, note takers, books on tape, proctored testing with alternative modes, tape recording, peer pairing, academic remediation, organizational skill remediation, modification in time span of program, course analysis and prescriptive scheduling, early registration, counseling (academic, vocational, and personal), lecture-pause procedure, learning strategies, social skills training, advocacy program, testing and evaluation modifications, support groups, coaching with students and faculty, and self-monitoring training.

Many recent studies focus on the status of college students with learning disabilities in terms of identification and intervention. In a review of the published work on college learning disabilities programs, Hughes and Smith (1990) note that little empirical data exist on young adults with learning disabilities in the college setting. Based on their extensive review of more than 100 studies covering a 20-year period, Hughes and Smith conclude the following:

- The intellectual functioning of college students with learning disabilities can be described as comparable to college students without learning disabilities.
- College students with learning disabilities score in the average or above-average range on intelligence tests.
- The reported reading levels vary widely with word-attack skills ranging from the second-grade level to college level. The average reading level for college students with learning disabilities is tenth grade.
- In studies using self-report measures, college students with learning disabilities most frequently report problems in reading comprehension, reading rate, and retaining information.
- Empirical evidence indicates that most college students with learning disabilities can identify their own skill problems accurately when com-

pared with measured skill levels on achievement tests.
- There is a lack of consensus on which measures should be used to evaluate the skill levels of college students with learning disabilities. This presents problems in interpreting data and findings across studies.
- Many college students with learning disabilities have problems with math computation and application, as well as with more abstract areas of math such as algebra and geometry.
- Many college students with learning disabilities have severe deficits in written expression areas such as spelling, punctuation, and sentence structure.
- Learning a foreign language presents a particularly formidable task to many college students with learning disabilities.
- Few empirical studies focus on the effectiveness of particular interventions or instructional approaches for college students with learning disabilities.

Although the development of college programs for individuals with learning disabilities is receiving much attention, few efforts have been made to validate specific interventions. In an intervention study, Ruhl, Hughes, and Gajar (1990) investigated a pause procedure for enhancing the recall of facts presented through lectures with students both with and without learning disabilities. The pause procedure consisted of providing three 2-minute periods for student discussions and note taking during a standard lecture. The procedure was effective for promoting short-term recall on objective tests for all the students. Ruhl et al. hypothesize that the pausing provides structure and time for extra processing of information presented in a class, and they note that this procedure is simple to implement in the college setting. In another study, Ruhl and Suritsky (1995) found that the pause procedure was more effective than a lecture outline for enhancing the immediate recall of lecture ideas and completeness of recorded notes of college students with learning disabilities.

It is hoped that higher education will respond to the needs of adults with learning disabilities. The Learning Disabilities Association of America (4156 Library Road, Pittsburgh, PA 15234) provides a list of colleges and universities with learning disabilities programs. Also, *The Complete Learning Disabilities Directory* (available from Grey House Publishing, Pocket Knife Square, Lakeville, CT 06039) includes entries about schools, learning centers, vocational training programs, associations and organizations, and government agencies involved in learning disabilities. The *Directory of Facilities and Services for the Learning Disabled* (published by Academic Therapy Publications) lists specialized private services as well as information about national learning disabilities support organizations.

☼ COMMERCIAL TRANSITION EDUCATION PROGRAMS

Numerous commercial programs and materials are designed to help students make successful transitions from school to work and daily living. The following commercial programs as well as the computer software programs presented in the following section may help students develop functional living skills and career-related skills.

Job Ready

Job Ready (published by Curriculum Associates) consists of two books designed to help students prepare to obtain and succeed in entry-level or semi-skilled employment. Book 1, *Understanding Work and Myself,* focuses on the identification of interests and strengths in order to choose the right job, opportunities for training, and qualities and skills employers seek. Topics in Book 2, *Finding My Job and My Success,* include job hunting, job leads, preparing for and participating in job interviews, receiving and accepting a job offer, and exiting a job. Each book contains 30 employment-related articles written at a sixth-grade reading level, plus activities for developing employment vocabulary and strengthening reading comprehension.

Steps to Self-Determination

Steps to Self-Determination, developed by S. Field and A. Hoffman (published by PRO-ED), is a 16-session curriculum designed to help secondary students learn to define and achieve important goals. The curriculum addresses five main elements of self-determination: know yourself, value yourself, plan, act and experience outcomes, and learn. Areas included are identifying strengths, weaknesses, needs and preferences; decision-making skills; rights and responsibilities; goal setting; anticipating consequences; creativity; communication skills; accessing resources and support; negotiation skills; and experiencing and learning from outcomes.

The curriculum emphasizes actively setting and working toward goals. In addition to an instructor's guide and a student activity book, the *Self-Determination Knowledge Scale* provides a pretest and posttest for the curriculum.

Tools for Transition

Tools for Transition, developed by E. Aune and J. Ness (published by American Guidance Service), is designed to prepare students with learning disabilities for postsecondary education. The program helps students identify and describe strengths and weaknesses of their learning style, apply appropriate study strategies to their learning problems, understand their legal rights and advocate for accommodations in school, select a postsecondary school and learn how to fill out applications, and explore a variety of careers by evaluating personal interests and aptitudes. Two script booklets provide role-play situations, and the student workbook reinforces lessons with exercises. A video also is provided to demonstrate and reinforce positive interpersonal behavior.

☼ COMPUTER SOFTWARE PROGRAMS IN TRANSITION EDUCATION

Computer software programs can facilitate the transition from school to employment or community life by helping students develop career-related skills and functional living skills. Computer programs also can provide helpful information on career options.

Insight: The Interactive Career Exploration Program

Insight (produced by Curriculum Associates) is an interactive career and personal exploration program designed to help students define and achieve school and employment goals. The program database includes over 750 blue- and white-collar occupations and, thus, provides a wealth of information on career options for trade-oriented and college-bound students. The program helps students determine areas of broad occupational interests; develop a profile of interests and plans, and review lists of matching or alternative occupations to link profiles with specific occupations; and identify the steps necessary to prepare and achieve their career goals. Printouts provide a record of decisions and choices as well as offer follow-up suggestions.

Job Readiness Skills Series

The *Job Readiness Skills Series* (produced by Education Associates) offers high school students and adults with interactive lessons on job readiness skills in the areas of *Career Goals, Job Applications, Good Appearance, Finding a Job, Interviews, Communication, Resumes, Positive Attitudes,* and *Written Communication.* Each CD-ROM has a unique pretest and posttest and provides branching into specific categories as well as Internet links to expand learning experiences. Student activities can be printed or completed on the screen, and the program includes management capabilities for the teacher.

Life Skills Multi-Media Series

The *Life Skills Multi-Media Series* (produced by Education Associates) is designed to help students in high school through adult age learn important consumer life skills. Nine programs are included: *Banking: Credit and Loans* (establishing credit and applying for loans), *Banking: Checking and Savings* (terms and procedures of opening accounts), *Managing Your Money* (use of paychecks and budgeting), *Skills for Buying a Car* (negotiating techniques, insurance, and responsibilities), *This Apartment's for You* (terms, leases, options, costs, and price), *On Your Own* (cleaning, cooking, and budgeting), *Life Skills for the Telephone* (using the phonebook, types of calls, and answering machines and services), *Getting Around in Today's World* (maps, directories, time management, and mass transportation), and *Consumer Shopping* (making decisions by reading labels and comparison shopping). Also included are competency requirements, a video, student activity worksheets, and assessment checklists.

☀ REFERENCES

Adelman, P. B., & Vogel, S. A. (1993). Issues in the employment of adults with learning disabilities. *Learning Disability Quarterly, 16,* 219–232.

American Vocational Association. (1968). *Definitions of terms in vocational, technical, practical arts education.* Washington, DC: Author.

Brigance, A. H. (1981). *Brigance Diagnostic Inventory of Essential Skills.* North Billerica, MA: Curriculum Associates.

Brigance, A. H. (1994). *Brigance Diagnostic Life Skills Inventory.* North Billerica, MA: Curriculum Associates.

Brigance, A. H. (1995). *Brigance Diagnostic Employability Skills Inventory.* North Billerica, MA: Curriculum Associates.

Brolin, D. E. (1993). *Life-centered career education: A competency-based approach* (4th ed.). Reston, VA: Council for Exceptional Children.

Brolin, D. E. (1995). *Career education: A functional life skills approach* (3rd ed.). Upper Saddle River, NJ: Merrill/Prentice Hall.

Buchwach, L. (1980). Child service demonstration center for secondary students with learning disabilities. In R. H. Riegel & J. P. Mathey (Eds.), *Mainstreaming at the secondary level: Seven models that work.* Plymouth, MI: Wayne County Intermediate School District.

Cegelka, P. T., & Greene, G. (1993). Transition to adulthood. In A. E. Blackhurst & W. H. Berdine (Eds.), *An introduction to special education* (3rd ed., pp. 137–175). New York: Harper Collins.

Chelser, B. (1982). ACLD vocational committee completes survey on LD adult. *ACLD Newsbriefs* (No. 146), pp. 5, 20–23.

Clark, G. M. (1991). *Functional curriculum and its place in the regular education initiative.* Paper presented at the Seventh International Conference of the Division on Career Development, Kansas City, MO.

Clark, G. M., & Kolstoe, O. P. (1990). *Career development and transition education for adolescents with disabilities.* Boston: Allyn & Bacon.

Clark, G. M., & Patton, J. R. (1997). *Transition Planning Inventory.* Austin, TX: PRO-ED.

Cline, B. V., & Billingsley, B. S. (1991). Teachers' and supervisors' perceptions of secondary learning disabilities programs: A multi-state survey. *Learning Disabilities Research & Practice, 6,* 158–165.

Council for Exceptional Children. (1978). *Position paper on career education.* Reston, VA: Author.

Cronin, M. E. (1988). Applying curriculum for the instruction of life skills. In G. A. Robinson, J. R. Patton, E. A. Polloway, & L. R. Sargent (Eds.), *Best practices in mental disabilities* (Vol. 2, pp. 41–52). Des Moines: Iowa Department of Education, Bureau of Special Education.

Cronin, M. E., & Patton, J. R. (1993). *Life skills instruction for all students with special needs: A practical guide for integrating real-life content into the curriculum.* Austin, TX: PRO-ED.

deBettencourt, L. U., Zigmond, N., & Thornton, H. (1989). Follow-up of postsecondary-age rural learning disabled graduates and dropouts. *Exceptional Children, 56,* 40–49.

Deci, E. L., & Ryan, R. M. (1985). *Intrinsic motivation and self-determination in human behavior.* New York: Plenum Press.

Durlak, C. M., Rose, E., & Bursuck, W. D. (1994). Preparing high school students with learning disabilities for the transition to postsecondary education: Teaching the skills of self-determination. *Journal of Learning Disabilities, 27,* 51–59.

Edgar, E. (1988). Employment as an outcome for mildly handicapped students: Current status and future directions. *Focus on Exceptional Children, 2*(1), 1–8.

Fourqurean, J. M., & LaCourt, T. (1990). A follow-up study of former special education students: A model for program evaluation. *Remedial and Special Education, 12*(1), 16–23.

Gerber, P. J. (1994). Researching adults with learning disabilities from an adult-development perspective. *Journal of Learning Disabilities, 27*, 6–9.

Gerber, P. J., Schneiders, C. A., Paradise, L. V., Reiff, H. B., Ginsberg, R., & Popp, P. A. (1990). Persisting problems of adults with learning disabilities: Self-reported comparisons from their school-age and adult years. *Journal of Learning Disabilities, 23*, 570–573.

Goode, D. (1990). Thinking about and discussing quality of life. In R. Schalock & M. Begab (Eds.), *Quality of life: Perspectives and issues* (pp. 41–58). Washington, DC: American Association on Mental Retardation.

Halpern, A. S. (1992). Transition: Old wine in new bottles. *Exceptional Children, 58*, 202–211.

Harrington, T. F., & Harrington, J. C. (1996). *Ability Explorer.* Chicago: Riverside.

Harrington, T. F., & O'Shea, A. J. (1992). *Career Decision-Making System—Revised.* Circle Pines, MN: American Guidance Service.

Hughes, C. A., & Smith, J. O. (1990). Cognitive and academic performance of college students with learning disabilities: A synthesis of literature. *Learning Disability Quarterly, 13*, 66–79.

Keogh, B. (1993, December). *Viewing learning disabilities through a developmental lens: The importance of time and context.* Paper presented at The Cove School and Cove Foundation meeting, Educational and Psychological Needs of Students with Learning Disabilities, Winnetka, IL.

Lewandowski, L., & Arcangelo, K. (1994). The social adjustment and self-concept of adults with learning disabilities. *Journal of Learning Disabilities, 27*, 598–605.

McKenzie, R. G. (1991). Content area instruction delivered by secondary learning disabilities teachers: A national survey. *Learning Disability Quarterly, 14*, 115–122.

Meers, G. D. (1992). Getting ready for the next century. *Teaching Exceptional Children, 24*(4), 36–39.

Parker, R. M. (1991). *Occupational Aptitude Survey and Interest Schedule—2.* Austin, TX: PRO-ED.

Patton, J. R., & Polloway, E. A. (1992). Learning disabilities: The challenges of adulthood. *Journal of Learning Disabilities, 25,* 410–416.

Polloway, E. A., Smith, J. D., & Patton, J. R. (1984). Learning disabilities: An adult development perspective. *Learning Disability Quarterly, 7,* 179–186.

Reiff, H. B., & deFur, S. (1992). Transition for youths with learning disabilities: A focus on developing independence. *Learning Disability Quarterly, 15,* 237–249.

Reiff, H. B., Ginsberg, R., & Gerber, P. J. (1995). New perspectives on teaching from successful adults with learning disabilities. *Remedial and Special Education, 16*(1), 29–37.

Rieth, H. J., & Polsgrove, L. (1994). Curriculum and instructional issues in teaching secondary students with learning disabilities. *Learning Disabilities Research & Practice, 9,* 118–126.

Rojewski, J. W. (1992). Key components of model transition services for students with learning disabilities. *Learning Disability Quarterly, 15,* 135–150.

Ruhl, K., Hughes, C., & Gajar, A. (1990). Efficacy of the pause procedure for enhancing learning disabled and nondisabled college students' long- and short-term recall of facts presented through lecture. *Learning Disability Quarterly, 13,* 55–64.

Ruhl, K. L., & Suritsky, S. (1995). The pause procedure and/or an outline: Effect on immediate free recall and lecture notes taken by college students with learning disabilities. *Learning Disability Quarterly, 18,* 2–11.

Schloss, P. J., Smith, M. A., & Schloss, C. N. (1995). *Instructional methods for adolescents with learning and behavior problems* (2nd ed.). Boston: Allyn & Bacon.

Scott, S. S. (1994). Determining reasonable academic adjustments for college students with learning disabilities. *Journal of Learning Disabilities, 27,* 403–412.

Sitlington, P. L., Frank, A. R., & Carson, R. (1993). Adult adjustment among high school graduates with mild disabilities. *Exceptional Children, 59,* 221–233.

Spekman, N. J., Goldberg, R. J., & Herman, K. L. (1992). Learning disabled children grow up: A search for factors related to success in the young adult years. *Learning Disabilities Research & Practice, 7,* 161–170.

Spekman, N. J., Goldberg, R. J., & Herman, K. L. (1993). An exploration of risk and resilience in the lives of individuals with learning disabilities. *Learning Disabilities Research & Practice, 8,* 11–18.

Spekman, N. J., Herman, K. L., & Vogel, S. A. (1993). Risk and resilience in individuals with learning disabilities: A challenge to the field. *Learning Disabilities Research & Practice, 8,* 59–65.

Spillane, S. A., McGuire, J. M., & Norlander, K. A. (1992). Undergraduate admission policies, practices, and procedures for applicants with learning disabilities. *Journal of Learning Disabilities, 25,* 665–670, 677.

U.S. Department of Education. (1994). *National transition longitudinal study: Postschool outcomes of students with disabilities* (Contract No. 300-87-0054). Washington, DC: U.S. Department of Education.

U.S. Department of Labor, Department of Education, & Department of Commerce. (1988). *Building a quality workforce.* Washington, DC: U.S. Government Printing Office.

Van Reusen, A. K., Bos, C. S., Schumaker, J. B., & Deshler, D. D. (1994). *The self-advocacy strategy for education and transition planning.* Lawrence, KS: Edge Enterprises.

Wagner, M. (1989). *The transition experience of youth with disabilities: A report from the national longitudinal transition study.* Menlo Park, CA: SRI International.

Wagner, M. (1990, April). *The school programs and school performance of secondary students classified as learning disabled: Findings from the national longitudinal transition study of special education students.* Paper presented at the meetings of Division G, American Educational Research Association, Boston.

Wehman, P. (1993). *Life beyond the classroom: Transition services for youth with disabilities.* Boston: Paul H. Brookes.

White, W. J. (1992). The postschool adjustment of persons with learning disabilities: Current status and future projections. *Journal of Learning Disabilities, 25,* 448–456.

Wiederholt, J. L., & Dunn, C. (1995). Transition from school to independent living. In D. D. Hammill & N. R. Bartel, *Teaching students with learning and behavior problems: Managing mild-to-moderate difficulties in resource and inclusive settings* (6th ed., pp. 381–417). Austin, TX: PRO-ED.

Wiederholt, J. L., & Wolffe, K. E. (1990). Preparing problem learners for independent living. In D. D. Hammill & N. R. Bartel, *Teaching students with learning and behavior problems* (5th ed., pp. 451–501). Boston: Allyn & Bacon.

Will, M. C. (1984). *OSERS programming for the transition of youth with disabilities: Bridges from school to working life.* Washington, DC: Office of Special Education and Rehabilitative Services.

Woodward, J., & Gersten, R. (1992). Innovative technology for secondary students with learning disabilities. *Exceptional Children, 58,* 407–421.

Zigmond, N. (1990). Rethinking secondary school programs for students with learning disabilities. *Focus on Exceptional Children, 23*(1), 1–24.

APPENDIX **A**

Scope and Sequence Skills Lists

KINDERGARTEN

Emergent Literacy

Participates and listens during reading situations.

Joins in to read refrains in predictable pattern books.

Develops a repertoire of favorite books, poems, rhymes, and songs.

Chooses books as a free-time activity.

Engages in talk about books and stories.

Uses book language while pretending to read.

Demonstrates awareness that print conveys meaning by trying to read.

Understands concepts about books such as knowing the front and back of a book, turning pages correctly, and using pictures as cues to meaning.

Understands concepts about print such as knowing left-to-right and top-to-bottom directionality and pointing to words one-to-one as teacher reads.

Understands difference between a letter and a word.

Knows where to begin reading.

Knows letters of own name and some letters in environment.

Recognizes own name in print.

Discusses meaning of stories.

Responds to texts in a variety of ways (orally, artistically, and dramatically).

Recounts through retelling details, events, and ideas and concepts from familiar stories, other literary materials, and informational texts.

Reads own dictated stories, pretends to read predictable pattern books, and reads some environmental print.

GRADE 1

Word Attack

Relates spoken sounds to written symbols.

Recognizes all initial and final consonant sounds (single sounds and blends up to first vowel in word).

Identifies likenesses and differences in sounds and structure of words.

Names the letter of the alphabet for single sounds heard.

Recognizes short vowels in one-syllable words and substitutes different vowels to form new words (*bad:* substitute *e = bed*).

Substitutes initial consonant to form new words.

Substitutes final consonant to form new words.

Recognizes long vowels in words ending in silent *e.*

Identifies rhyming words; decodes words with same phonogram/phonemic pattern (*at, cat, bat*).

Recognizes endings: *s, es, ed, ing.*

Identifies compound words (*football*).

Predicts and self-corrects using initial letter, final letter, and letter clusters.

Uses context clues to read words within own experience.

Comprehension

Relates printed words to objects or actions.

Follows printed directions (*Find the boy's house*).

Reads to find information.

Relates reading to personal experiences before, during, and after reading.

Draws conclusions from given facts (*What do you think happened then?*).

Recalls main ideas of what has been read aloud.

Recalls details in story.

Arranges increasing numbers of events in sequence.

Uses pictures and context clues for meaning.

Uses commas, end punctuation, and quotation marks as clues to meaning.

Identifies main characters and settings.

Makes comments and asks questions that indicate involvement with characters and story line.

Predicts events in a story.

Relates causes and effects.

Describes characters' feelings.

Discusses feelings evoked by stories.

Tells whether story is factual or fanciful (true to life or make-believe).

GRADE 2

Word Attack

Produces the consonant blends in isolation: *bl, br, cl, cr, dr, dw, fr, fl, gl, gr, mp, nd, pl, pr, qu, sc, sl, st, str, sw, scr, sm, sn, sp, spl, squ, sk, spr, tr, tw, thr, -nt, -nk, -st.*

Decodes words with consonant blends.

Substitutes initial consonant blends to form other words.

Identifies forms and sounds of consonant digraphs in initial position: *sh, ch, ph, th, wh.*

Identifies forms and sounds of consonant digraphs in final position: *sh, ch, gh, ng, ph, th, sh.*

Decodes four- and five-letter words that have regular short-vowel sounds.

Decodes words in which the vowels are long.

Decodes words with final consonant blends.

Decodes words ending in vowel-consonant plus silent *e* (*make, smoke, bone*).

Decodes consonant variants (*s—has, see; g—garden, large; c—music, ice*).

Decodes long *e* and *i* sound of *y.*

Decodes vowel diphthongs: *oi, oy, ou, ow, ew.*

Decodes words in which vowel is controlled by *r* (*far, fur, bar, more*).

Forms compound word with two known words (*baseball*).

Identifies root/base words in inflected forms of known words (*helpful, help; darkness, dark; unhappy, happy; recall, call*).

Decodes words in which final silent *e* is dropped before adding ending (*smoke, smoking*).

Identifies sounds and forms of consonant digraphs in medial position (*wishing*).

Decodes vowel digraphs/vowel teams: *oa, ai, ay, ee, ea, ie, ei.*

Identifies sounds of *a* followed by *l, w,* or *u.*

Decode suffixes (*less, ful, ness, er, est, ly*).

Decodes prefixes (*un, re, dis, pre, pro, ex, en*).

Identifies multiple sounds of long *a* (*ei, weigh; ai, straight; ay, day; ey, they*).

Decodes words with vowel digraph/vowel team irregularities (*bread, heart*).

Recognizes and knows meaning of contractions with one-letter omission.

Identifies plural endings, irregular plurals, and *'s* possessives.

Searches, predicts, monitors, and cross-checks using semantic, syntactic, pragmatic, and graphophonic cues independently.

Experiments to see what makes sense and makes a second attempt if words or phrases do not sound right or make sense.

Comprehension

Skims for information.

Reads to answer questions *who, when, where, how,* and *what.*

Makes judgments from given facts.

Draws conclusions, answering such questions as "What do you think happened next?"

Begins to use contextual clues to determine meaning of a new word.

Interprets simple figurative expressions.

Interprets feelings of characters in stories.

Recognizes the stereotyping of people in stories.
Retells characters, events, setting, problem, and solution.
Uses pragmatics to construct meaning (prior knowledge and context of situation).

GRADE 3

Word Attack

Uses phonetic clues to recognize words.
Identifies the beginning, middle, and ending sounds of each word given orally.
Recognizes silent vowels in words.
Uses consonant digraphs as an aid to word attack.
Identifies diphthongs (*ou, ow, oi, oy*) and pronounces words containing diphthongs.
Knows when to double the final consonant before adding *ing.*
Uses vowel digraphs correctly.
Reads unfamiliar words that contain *r*-controlled vowels.
Reads root words and recognizes prefixes and suffixes (*er, est, ing, ed, es, ly, un, re, less*).
Decodes silent *k* in *kn* (*know*).
Decodes silent *gh* (*through*).
Decodes words ending in *ed* (*ed, crooked; t, looked*).
Decodes *dg* (*edge*).
Divides two-syllable words.
Recognizes contractions.
Recognizes the use of the apostrophe to show ownership.
Hyphenates words using syllable rules.
Recognizes the meanings of words used in different contexts.
Selects the meaning that fits best according to the context in which the word is used.
Perseveres and problem solves when the reading task becomes difficult.
Focuses on details of print only when meaning is lost.

Comprehension

Finds main idea.
Selects facts to support main idea, lesson, theme, or moral in a variety of prose (fairy tales, tall tales, fables, legends, and myths).
Draws logical conclusions.
Reads literacy, informational, and practical materials for a variety of purposes.

Reads for a definite purpose: to enjoy, to obtain answers, and to obtain a general idea of content.
Recognizes shifts of meaning caused by using words in different contexts.
Answers specific questions about material read.
Follows written directions.
Interprets descriptive words and phrases.
Selects an appropriate title after reading an untitled selection.
Composes own questions about material read.
Makes inferences about material read.
Distinguishes between fact and opinion.
Recognizes structure of plot (summarizes sequence of events).
Recognizes that characters change as a story develops.
Identifies relationships among characters in a story.
Compares similar elements in different stories.

GRADE 4

Word Attack

Uses phonetic clues to accent unfamiliar words correctly.
Uses dictionary as an aid to attacking and pronouncing new words.
Identifies and defines prefixes and suffixes.
Reads synonyms, antonyms, and homonyms correctly at independent reading level.
Recognizes and uses words that signal relationships (*and, or, except, still, but, furthermore, especially, in this way, such as, on the other hand*).

Comprehension

Summarizes main ideas and selects facts to support main ideas.
Identifies the subtopics of a selection.
Finds factual and inferential information in answer to questions.
Compares or contrasts selections.
Compares information from different sources.
Interprets literal and figurative language.
Selects the meaning of a specific word when the meaning is implied but not stated.
Predicts possible endings based on previous events in an unfinished selection.
Recognizes theme of story.
Describes times, places, characters, and sequence of action in a story.

GRADE 5

Word Attack

Applies phonetic principles and structural analysis skills in combination with context clues to read unfamiliar words.

Uses context clues to derive meaning from unfamiliar words.

Uses phonetic clues to accent unfamiliar words correctly.

Comprehension

Investigates facts.

Identifies and recalls story facts and significant details.

Infers a character's appearance, moods, feelings, traits, and motives.

Recognizes large thought divisions within an expository work including parts, chapters, sections, acts, and scenes.

Distinguishes between good and poor summaries.

Identifies the point of view in a selection.

Analyzes a story in terms of who acted, what action was taken, and what resulted from the action.

Cites examples of one good and one bad quality of a character treated in a biography.

Recognizes structure of plot and identifies conflict or problems.

Identifies influence of setting on characters and events.

GRADE 6

Word Attack

Uses a repertoire of word-attack skills.

Uses root words, prefixes, and suffixes to derive the meaning of words.

Comprehension

Compares reading selections as to suitability for a given purpose (dramatization, reading to others, or inclusion in a bibliography).

Recognizes elements of characterization (presentation of the characters, completeness of characters, function of the characters, and relationships with other characters).

Recognizes transitional paragraphs that connect chapters, sections, and episodes.

Proves a point with factual information from the reading selections.

Interprets colloquial and figurative expressions.

Describes the rising action, climax, and falling action in a story.

Summarizes the main conflict in a story, giving the underlying causes of the conflict and the events that contributed to the conflict.

Identifies the mood of a selection and the words or phrases that establish the mood.

Identifies the basic elements of a news story *(who, what, where, when, why,* and *how).*

Analyzes and describes the point of view in an editorial.

SPELLING SCOPE AND SEQUENCE SKILLS LIST

Many spelling skills are repeated at each grade level. However, the difficulty level of the words that the spelling skill applies to increases with grade level. Boldface type denotes the initial introduction of a specific skill.

GRADE 1

Uses temporary spelling that generally can be read by others.
Spells two- and three-letter words.
Spells own first and last name correctly.

GRADE 2

Spells Consonant Sounds Correctly:

regular consonants *(bed, hat, sun, yes)*
***sh, ch, ng, wh,* and *th* (fish, much, sing, which, this, with)**
***x* spelling of *ks* (box, fox)**
***c* spelling of *k* (cold)**
***c* and *k* (cat, kept)**
***ck* (duck, black)**
***s* spelling of *s* and *z* (sun, as)**
consonant blends *(flag)*
silent consonants *(doll, hill, who, know, would)*

Spells Vowel Sounds Correctly:

short vowel in initial or medial position (*am, did***)**
long vowel spelled by a single vowel (*go, be***)**
two vowels together (*meat, rain***)**
vowel-consonant-silent *e* (*home, ride***)**

ow spelling of long *o* (*snow, grow*)
ay spelling of long *a* (*day, play*)
final *y* spelling of long *e* (*baby, very*)
final *y* spelling of long *i* (*my, why*)
oo spelling of *u* and *ü* (*good, soon*)
ow and *ou* spellings of the *ou* sound in *owl*
  and *mouse* (*down, house*)
oy spelling of the *oi* sound (*boy, toy*)
vowel sounds before *r*
the *er* spelling of *r* at the end (*over, teacher*)
er, ir, or, and *ur* spellings of *er* (*her, bird, work,*
  hurt)
the *or* and *ar* spelling of *ôr* (*for*)
the *ar* spelling of *är* (*car*)
unexpected single-vowel spellings (*from, off,*
  ***cold*)**
unexpected vowel-consonant-silent *e* (*give,*
  ***done*)**
unexpected spellings with two vowels together
  (*been, said*)
other unexpected vowel spellings (*they, are*)

Uses Morphemes to Make Structural Changes:

s plural (*cats, cows*)
s or *es* for third-person singular (*live, lives*)
s to show possession (*yours, ours*)
d or *ed* ending for past tense (*played*)
ing ending (*blowing*)
er noun agent ending (*singer, player*)
er and *est* endings (*old, older, oldest*)

Uses Devices to Aid Spelling Recall:

syllabication (*yel low, go ing*)
recognizing compounds (*today*)
recognizing rhyming words (*pet, get*)

Spells Selected Words Correctly:

simple homonyms (*to, two, too*)

GRADE 3

Spells Consonant Sounds Correctly:

regular consonants (*must, trip, ask, zoo*)
sh, ch, ng, wh, and *th* (*shoe, child, sang, while,*
  those, thank)
nk (*drunk, drank*)
x (*next*)
c spelling of *k* (*cup*)

c and *k* (*ask, cake*)
ck (*chicken, clock*)
s spelling of *s* and *z* (*gas, has*)
gh spelling of *f* (*laugh*)
consonant blends (*twin*)
silent consonants (*bell, grass, walk, catch, wrote,*
  night)

Spells Vowel Sounds Correctly:

short vowel in initial or medial position (*bad, send,*
  stop)
long vowel
  single vowel in open syllables (*paper, table*)
  two vowels together (*soap, cream, train*)
  vowel-consonant-silent *e* (*game, side, snake*)
  ow spelling of long *o* (*window*)
  ay spelling of long *a* (*always, yesterday*)
  final *y* spelling of long *e* (*city, study, sorry*)
  final *y* spelling of long *i* (*cry, try*)
oo spelling of *u* and *ü* (*cook, shoot*)
ow and *ou* spellings of the *ou* sound in *owl* and
  mouse (*flower, ground*)
vowel sounds before *r*
  the er spelling of *r* at the end (*ever, another*)
  the or spelling of *r* at the end (*color*)
  er, ir, or, and *ur* spellings of *er* (*person, third,*
    word, turning)
  the *or* and *ar* spelling of *ôr* (*horse, warm*)
  the *ar* spelling of *är* (*star, party*)
unexpected single vowels (*kind, full, cost*)
unexpected vowel-consonant-silent *e* (*whose, sure*)
unexpected spellings with two vowels together
  (*bread, great, friend*)
other unexpected vowel spellings (*aunt, says, could*)
le spelling of the *el* sound (*people, table*)

Uses Morphemes to Make Structural Changes:

***s* or *es* plural (*cups, buses, dishes*)**
changing *y* to *i* before *es* (*cry, cries*)
s or *es* for third-person singular (*jumps, races,*
  misses)
d or *ed* ending for past tense (*asked, laughed*)
ing ending (reading, thinking)
ing* ending with doubled consonant (*clapping,
  ***beginning*)**
ing* ending with dropped silent *e* (*skating,
  ***moving*)**
er noun agent ending (*painter, builder*)
er and *est* endings (*high, higher, highest*)

Uses Devices to Aid Spelling Recall:

syllabication (*bas ket, ta ble*)
recognizing compounds (*airplane, something*)
recognizing rhyming words (*hand, land*)

Spells Selected Words Correctly:

homonyms (*its—it's; eight—ate*)

Uses Dictionary Skills:

alphabetizing—sequencing of words in alphabetical order

GRADE 4

Spells Consonant Phonemes Correctly:

sh, ch, and *ng* (*ship, rich, hang*)
voiced and unvoiced *th* (*bath, those*)
***ch* spelling of *k* (*schoolhouse*)**
***wh* spelling of *hw* (*wheel*)**
***g* spelling of *g* or *j* (*frog, bridge*)**
***c* spelling of *k* or *s* (*cage, circus*)**
***ck* spelling of *k* (*luck*)**
***x* spelling of *ks* (*fix*)**
***qu* spelling of *kw* (*queen*)**
***nk* spelling of *ngk* (*monkey*)**
***ph* spelling of *f* (*elephant*)**
consonant blends (*brain*)
silent consonants (*answer*)

Spells Vowel Phonemes Correctly:

short medial vowel (*cap*)
long sound spelled with vowel-consonant-silent *e*
(*bone*)
long sound spelled with two vowels (*tie*)
long sound spelled in open syllables (*hotel*)
vowels before *r* (*fur, born*)
ou and *ow* spellings of *ou* (*count, cowboy*)
***ow* spelling of the ö sound (*unknown*)**
oo spelling of the *u* and *ü* sounds (*hook, stood*)
***oi* and *oy* spellings of *oi* (*noise, enjoy*)**
***o, al, au,* and *aw* spellings of ô (*north, tall*)**
***əl* and *l* (*castle, jungle*)**
***y* spelling of ē (*busy*)**

Uses Morphemes to Make Structural Changes:

d and *ed* ending (*recalled, untied*)

s and *es* ending (*socks, chimneys, churches*)
irregular plurals (*feet*)
doubling a final consonant before *ing* (*stepping*)
dropping final silent *e* before *ing* (*trading*)
er and *est* endings (*paler, palest*)
***ly* ending (*finally*)**
changing *y* to *i* before *es* (*bodies*)
ing ending (*interesting*)
number suffixes (*fifteen, fifty*)
**suffixes to change part of speech (*kindness,
playful, friendly*)**
**prefixes to change meaning (*unlock, ex-
change, replace, promote*)**

Uses Devices to Aid Spelling Recall:

syllable divisions (*bot tom, ho tel, cab in*)
unexpected spellings (*minute*)
compounds (*upstairs, watermelon*)

Spells Selected Words:

homonyms (*whole—hole; hymn—him*)
contractions (*aren't*)
months (*February*)

Uses Dictionary Skills:

**using guide words—recognition of words
grouped by alphabetical similarities**

GRADE 5

Spells Consonant Phonemes Correctly:

sh, ch, and *ng* (*shade, chest, among*)
voiced and unvoiced *th* (*sixth, either*)
ch spelling of *k* (*echo*)
wh spelling of *hw* (*whistle*)
g spelling of *g* or *j* (*gate, damage*)
c spelling of *k* or *s* (*cook, princess*)
ck spelling of *k* (*attack*)
x spelling of *ks* (*expect*)
qu spelling of *kw* (*quarter*)
nk spelling of *ngk* (*trunk*)
silent consonants (*ghost*)

Spells Vowel Phonemes Correctly:

short medial vowels (*bunch*)
vowel-consonant-silent *e* (*prize*)
various spellings before *r* (*term, artist*)

ou and *ow* spellings of *ou* (*outfit, shower*)
ow spelling of ō (crow)
oo spelling of the *u* and *ü* sounds (*loose, choosing*)
oi and *oy* spellings of *oi* (*join, voice*)
o, al, au, and *aw* spellings of *o* (*crawl, chalk*)
spellings of el and l (model, central)
y spelling of *ē* (*worry, crazy*)

Uses Morphemes to Make Structural Changes:

d or *ed* ending (*excited, earned*)
s or *es* ending (*beads, beaches*)
doubling final consonant before *ing* (*chopping, snapping*)
dropping final silent *e* before *ing* (*ruling, shaking*)
number suffixes (*thirteen, sixty*)

Spells Selected Words:

contractions (*they're*)

Uses Dictionary Skills:

locating words in a dictionary—ability to find words of uncertain spelling in a dictionary

GRADE 6

Spells Consonant Phonemes Correctly:

sh, ch, and *ng* consonants (*shelf, chain, gang*)
voiced and unvoiced *th* (*thread, leather*)
ch spelling of *k* (*orchestra*)
wh spelling of *hw* (*whale*)
g spelling of *g* or *j* (*cigar, pledge*)
c spelling of *k* or *s* (*cabbage, voice*)
ck spelling of *k* (*ticket*)
x spelling of *ks* (*expedition*)
qu spelling of *kw* (*acquaint*)
nk spelling of *ngk* (*plank*)
ph spelling of f (alphabet)

Spells Vowel Phonemes Correctly:

long sound with two vowels (*coach*)
long sound in open syllables (*soda*)
various spellings before *r* (*stairs, skirt*)
ou and *ow* spellings of *ou* (*growl, surround*)
ow spelling of *ō* (*narrow*)
oo spelling of *u* and *ü* (*bloom, shook*)

oi and *oy* spellings of *oi* (*spoil, voyage*)
o, al, au, and *aw* spelling of *ô* (*author, naughty*)
əl and *l* sounds (*carnival, barrel*)

Uses Morphemes to Make Structural Changes:

changing *y* to *i* before *es* (*pantries, colonies*)
forming plurals of nouns that end in o (pianos, potatoes)
ing ending (*stretching*)
er and *est* endings (*tinier, tiniest*)
ly ending (*dreadfully, especially*)
suffixes and prefixes (*harmless, attractive, dishonest, incorrect*)
d or *ed* ending (*continued, contracted*)
s or *es* ending (*insects, sandwiches*)
irregular plurals (*calves, geese*)

Uses Dictionary Skills:

locating appropriate word meaning—awareness and selection of multiple word meanings and appropriate word usage

GRADE 7 AND ABOVE

Spells Selected Words:

hyphenated words (tongue-tied)
silent letters—*b, h, m, g, p* (*pneumonia*)
letter combinations: -ient, -ian, -ium, -iasm, -iable, -ure (transient, enthusiasm)
word endings: -ance, -ence, -ense, -ogy, -cede, -ceed (biology, ignorance)

Uses Dictionary Skills:

understanding pronunciation marks—ability to interpret diacritical markings

☀ HANDWRITING SCOPE AND SEQUENCE SKILLS LIST

Many handwriting skills are emphasized at more than one grade level. Boldface type denotes a skill that has not been emphasized at a previous grade level.

KINDERGARTEN

Begins to establish a preference for either left- or right-handedness.

Voluntarily draws, paints, and scribbles.

Develops small-muscle control through the use of materials such as finger painting, clay, weaving, and puzzles.

Uses tools of writing in making letters, writing names, or attempting to write words.

Understands and applies writing readiness vocabulary given orally, such as left/right, top/bottom, beginning/end, large/small, circle, space, around, across, curve, top line, dotted line, and bottom line.

Begins to establish correct writing position of body, arms, hand, paper, and pencil.

Draws familiar objects using the basic strokes of manuscript writing.

Recognizes and legibly writes own name in manuscript letters using uppercase and lowercase letters appropriately.

Uses writing paper that is standard for manuscript writing.

GRADE 1

Establishes a preference for either left- or right-handedness.

Understands and applies writing readiness vocabulary given orally, such as left/right, top/bottom, beginning/end, large/small, circle, space, around, across, curve, top line, dotted line, and bottom line.

Draws familiar objects using the basic strokes of manuscript writing.

Begins manuscript writing using both lowercase and uppercase letters introduced to correlate with the child's reading program.

Writes at a desk with correct posture, pencil grip, and paper position; works from left to right; and forms letters in the correct direction.

Uses writing paper that is standard for manuscript writing.

Copies words neatly from near position.

Writes with firm strokes and demonstrates good spacing between letters, words, and sentences.

Writes manuscript letters independently and with firm strokes.

Writes clear, legible manuscript letters at a rate appropriate for ability.

Arranges work neatly and pleasingly on a page (i.e., uses margins and paragraph indentions and makes clean erasures).

GRADE 2

Establishes a preference for either left- or right-handedness.

Uses correct writing position of body, arm, hand, paper, and pencil.

Writes with firm strokes and demonstrates good spacing between letters, words, and sentences.

Writes clear, legible manuscript letters at a rate appropriate for ability.

Arranges work neatly and pleasingly on a page (i.e., uses margins and paragraph indentions and makes clean erasures).

Evaluates writing using a plastic overlay and identifies strengths and weaknesses.

Writes all letters of the alphabet in manuscript from memory. Recognizes the differences in using manuscript and cursive writing.

Reads simple sentences written in cursive writing on the chalkboard.

Demonstrates physical coordination to proceed to simple cursive writing.

GRADE 3

Uses correct writing position of body, arm, hand, paper, and pencil.

Uses writing paper that is standard for manuscript writing.

Evaluates writing using a plastic overlay and identifies strengths and weaknesses.

Writes with firm strokes and demonstrates good spacing between letters, words, and sentences.

Arranges work neatly and pleasingly on a page (i.e., uses margins and paragraph indentions and makes clean erasures).

Demonstrates ability to decode cursive writing by reading paragraphs of cursive writing both from the chalkboard and from paper.

Identifies cursive lowercase and uppercase letters by matching cursive letters to manuscript letters.

Begins cursive writing with lowercase letters and progresses to uppercase letters as needed.

Uses writing paper that is standard for cursive writing.

Writes all letters of the cursive alphabet using proper techniques in making each letter.

Recognizes the proper joining of letters to form words.

Writes from memory all letters of the alphabet in cursive form.

GRADE 4

Uses correct writing position of body, arm, hand, paper, and pencil.

Evaluates writing using a plastic overlay and identifies strengths and weaknesses.

Writes with firm strokes and demonstrates good spacing between letters, words, and sentences.

Arranges work neatly and pleasingly on a page (i.e., uses margins and paragraph indentions and makes clean erasures).

Uses writing paper that is standard for cursive writing.

Slants and joins the letters in a word and controls spacing between letters.

Uses cursive writing for day-to-day use.

Begins to write with a pen *if* pencil writing is smooth, fluent, and neat.

Maintains and uses manuscript writing for special needs, such as preparing charts, maps, and labels.

Writes clear, legible cursive letters at a rate appropriate for ability.

GRADE 5

Uses correct writing position of body, arm, hand, paper, and pencil.

Evaluates writing using a plastic overlay and identifies strengths and weaknesses.

Writes with firm strokes and demonstrates good spacing between letters, words, and sentences.

Arranges work neatly and pleasingly on a page (i.e., uses margins and paragraph indentions and makes clean erasures).

Uses cursive writing for day-to-day use.

Begins to write with a pen *if* pencil writing is smooth, fluent, and neat.

Writes clear, legible cursive letters at a rate appropriate for ability.

Maintains and uses manuscript writing for special needs, such as preparing charts, maps, and labels.

Reduces size of writing to "adult" proportions of letters (i.e., one-quarter space for minimum letters, one-half space for intermediate letters, and three-quarters space for tall lowercase and uppercase letters).

Takes pride in presenting neat work.

GRADE 6

Uses correct writing position of body, arm, hand, paper, and pencil.

Evaluates writing using a plastic overlay and identifies strengths and weaknesses.

Writes with firm strokes and demonstrates good spacing between letters, words, and sentences.

Arranges work neatly and pleasingly on a page (i.e., uses margins and paragraph indentions and makes clean erasures).

Uses cursive writing for day-to-day use.

Begins to write with a pen *if* pencil writing is smooth, fluent, and neat.

Maintains and uses manuscript writing for special needs, such as preparing charts, maps, and labels.

Reduces size of writing to "adult" proportions of letters (i.e., one-quarter space for minimum letters, one-half space for intermediate letters, and three-quarters space for tall lowercase and uppercase letters).

Writes clear, legible cursive letters at a rate appropriate for ability.

Customarily presents neat work.

Evaluates own progress in the basic handwriting skills pertaining to size, slant, shape, spacing, and alignment.

☀ WRITTEN EXPRESSION SCOPE AND SEQUENCE SKILLS LIST

KINDERGARTEN

Understands that writing conveys meaning.

Retells story or experience using pictures or letter strings.

Dictates experience stories.

Creates pictures for own dictated stories.

Draws a picture and then adds words (using invented spelling) about the picture.

GRADE 1

Capitalization and Punctuation

Copies sentences correctly.

Capitalizes first word of a sentence.

Capitalizes first letter of a proper name.

Uses period at the end of a sentence.

Uses question mark after a written question.

Uses period after numbers in a list.

Written Composition

Arranges scrambled words in correct sentence order.

Writes answers to simple questions.

Dictates thoughts to scribe and does copy work.

Suggests titles for dictated stories.

Forms sentences in dictating and in writing.

Writes own name and address without using a model.

Writes from both personal experience and imagination.

Writes given sentences from dictation.

Writes phrases that describe location.

Creative Expression

Uses prewriting strategies such as drawing, brainstorming, or storyboarding with support.

Dictates and begins to write captions and comments about pictures.

Writes group poems.

Writes riddles, songs, or poems.

Creates make-believe stories.

Shows increasing selectivity in choice of words to convey meanings effectively.

GRADE 2

Capitalization and Punctuation

Capitalizes titles of compositions.

Capitalizes proper names used in written compositions.

Uses comma after salutation and after closing of a friendly letter.

Uses comma between day of the month and the year.

Uses comma between names of city and state.

Written Composition

Recognizes kinds of sentences—statement and question.

Writes a paragraph of three to five sentences in accordance with specified criteria: relate to topic, capitalize first word of each sentence, use correct end punctuation, and indent first line.

Supplies titles for sentence groups.

Writes given sentences from dictation.

Copies sentences correctly.

Creative Expression

Can retell a story.

Continues and expands prewriting strategies such as drawing, brainstorming, or storyboarding.

Responds to sensory stimuli with descriptive words.

Uses a variety of descriptive words or phrases.

Writes imaginative stories in which ideas and feelings are expressed.

Draws pictures to express a theme, to inform, or to persuade.

Writes in a logical sequence including beginning, middle, and end.

GRADE 3

Capitalization and Punctuation

Capitalizes correctly the names of months, days, and holidays; first word in a line of verse; titles of books, stories, and poems; salutation and closing of letters and notes; and names of special places.

Begins to apply correct punctuation for abbreviations, initials, contractions, items in a list, quotations, questions, and exclamations.

Uses proper indention for paragraphs.

Written Composition

Gives written explanations using careful selection, relevant details, and sequential order.

Begins to proofread for accuracy and to do occasional revising.

Writes simple thank-you notes using correct form.

Builds ideas into paragraphs.

Uses a variety of sentences.
Combines short, choppy sentences into longer ones.
Avoids run-on sentences.
Keeps to one idea.
Correctly sequences ideas in sentences.
Finds and deletes sentences that do not belong in a paragraph.

Creative Expression

Demonstrates and uses prewriting strategies (drawing, brainstorming, webbing, and storyboarding).
Writes imaginative stories—imagines how others feel or how he or she might feel in another situation.
Uses a variety of words to express action, mood, sound, and feeling.
Writes original poetry.
Writes interesting dialogue.

GRADE 4

Capitalization and Punctuation

Capitalizes correctly in the following areas: proper nouns, first word of poetry line, principal words in titles, common and proper nouns, and seasons as common nouns.
Uses commas correctly in the following areas: after introductory adverbial clause, to set off interjections, to separate items in a series, to separate coordinate clauses, to set off words in direct address, and after salutation.
Uses periods correctly after declarative sentences.
Uses apostrophes correctly to show possession.

Written Composition

Makes simple outline with main ideas.
Proofreads for accuracy in writing.
Uses correct form and mechanics in writing invitations and business letters.
Compiles a list of books read, including the title and author of the books and their subjects.
Writes a paragraph defining a term, using an example.

Creative Expression

Writes descriptions of people, places, and events.
Writes narrative paragraphs in which events are presented chronologically.

Writes a story including characters, setting, and plot.
Distinguishes between imaginative and factual description.
Writes a brief story in response to a picture.

GRADE 5

Capitalization and Punctuation

Capitalizes correctly in the following areas: first word of poetry line, first word of direct quotation, seasons as common nouns, and ordinary position titles (not capitalized).
Uses commas correctly in the following areas: after introductory phrases, to set off nonrestrictive clauses, in addresses, in dates, to separate subordinate clause from main clause, to set off appositives, to set off parenthetical elements, and to separate quotations from rest of sentence.
Uses periods correctly.
Uses colons after introductory lines.
Uses apostrophes correctly in contractions and to show possession, and not in possessive pronouns.
Uses quotation marks correctly in direct quotations.
Uses hyphens in compound numbers.
Uses semicolons correctly with coordinate clauses.

Written Composition

Uses a variety of sentences—declarative, interrogative, exclamatory, and imperative.
Uses compound subjects and compound predicates.
Consistently uses transitions (e.g., *as a result of* and *in addition*).
Writes a paragraph from an outline.
Begins to organize writing by sticking to one subject and striving for a continuous thought flow.
Produces a factual report from notes and an outline.
Outlines main ideas (I, II, III) and subordinate ideas (A, B, C).
Edits writing for errors in spelling, capitalization, punctuation, and usage.
Writes a paragraph that contains a topic sentence based upon a fact and supports that fact with at least three additional facts.

Creative Expression

Records and expands sensory images, observations, memories, opinions, and individual impressions.

Writes patterned and free verse.

Develops a story plot including at least two characters, a challenge or a struggle, and a climax that results from events that prepare the reader.

Writes short scripts based on stories read by the group.

GRADE 6

Capitalization and Punctuation

Capitalizes names of outline divisions.

Writes correctly punctuated dialogue.

Correctly punctuates dictated paragraphs.

Uses underlining and quotation marks correctly for titles.

Edits own writing for correct spelling, punctuation, capitalization, and usage.

Written Composition

Develops concise statements by avoiding wordiness.

Uses complex sentences.

Checks paragraphs for accurate statements.

Uses transition words to connect ideas.

Shows improvement in complete composition—introduction, development, and conclusion.

Writes from point of view that is consistent with the intention.

Plans carefully before beginning to write and revises periodically.

Edits all writing to be read by another person and revises it in accordance with accepted mechanics of writing.

Writes a well-constructed paragraph (topic sentence, supporting details, and conclusion).

Writes a newspaper story from given facts.

Narrows topics for reports.

Writes a paragraph of comparison and contrast.

Uses correct form for business letters.

Creative Expression

Uses figurative language—similes and metaphors.

Writes descriptions and narratives.

Writes a variety of prose and verse based on personal experience.

Writes a variety of short fiction—tall tales, fables, mysteries, and adventure stories.

Describes a character by including details (the way the character looks, behaves, dresses, or speaks).

Writes original scripts to be produced by groups in the class.

☀ MATH SCOPE AND SEQUENCE SKILLS LIST[1]

By Skill Area

ADDITION HIERARCHY

Recognizes inequalities of numbers less than 10.

Understands seriation of numbers less than 10.

Recognizes the words *addend* and *sum*.

Understands the "+" sign.

Computes sums less than 10 (memorize).

Understands place value of ones and tens.

Computes sums 10 to 18, both addends less than 10 (memorize).

Computes 2D + 1D without regrouping.

Computes 2D + 2D without regrouping.

Understands place value concerning regrouping tens and ones.

Computes 2D + 1D with regrouping.

Computes 2D + 2D with regrouping.

Computes 2D + 2D + 2D with sums of ones greater than 20.

Understands place value of hundreds, tens, and ones.

Computes 3D + 3D without regrouping.

Understands place value concerning regrouping hundreds and tens.

Computes 3D + 3D with regrouping.

Estimates sums.

SUBTRACTION HIERARCHY

Finds missing addends (e.g., 4 + ___ = 9).

Understands the "−" sign.

Uses set separation as model for subtraction.

Expresses a related addition statement in subtraction form (e.g., addend + *addend* = sum ↔ sum − *addend* = addend).

---

[1]Key:

1D = one-digit number	< = less than
2D = two-digit number	> = more than
3D = three-digit number	≤ = less than or equal to

Relates the words *minuend, subtrahend,* and *difference* to *sum, given addend,* and *missing addend.*

Memorizes basic subtraction facts 0 to 9.

Understands place value of ones and tens.

Memorizes basic subtraction facts 0 to 18.

Names the difference between a two-place whole number (2D) and a one-place whole number (1D) (not a basic fact and no regrouping).

Names the difference between 2D and 2D with no regrouping.

Names the difference between 3D and 2D with no regrouping.

Names the difference between 3D and 3D with no regrouping.

Names the difference between two many-digit whole numbers with no regrouping.

Names the difference between 2D and 1D (not a basic fact) with regrouping.

Names the difference between 2D and 2D with regrouping from tens to ones.

Names the difference between 3D and 2D with regrouping from tens to ones.

Names the difference between 3D and 2D with double regrouping.

Names the difference between 3D and 3D with single regrouping.

Names the difference between 3D and 3D with double regrouping.

Names the difference between two many-place whole numbers with several regroupings.

Names the difference when a zero appears in a single place in the minuend.

Names the difference when zeros appear in the tens and ones place of the minuend.

Estimates differences.

MULTIPLICATION HIERARCHY

Recognizes sets as a model for multiplication (number of sets and number of objects in each set).

Recognizes and uses arrays as a model for multiplication; for example,

```
    2
×       ×
×       ×     3
×       ×
```

Understands the words *factor* and *product.*

Understands the "×" sign.

Understands the commutative property of multiplication; for example, $a \times (b + c) = (a \times b) + (a \times c)$ [$a \le 5, b \le 5$].

Memorizes basic multiplication facts for $a \times b$ ($a \le 5, b \le 5$).

Memorizes basic multiplication facts for $a \times b$ ($5 < a < 10, b < 10$).

Names the product if one factor is 10, 100, etc.

Expands the basic multiplication facts (e.g., 4×3 to 4×30).

Computes 2D × 1D without regrouping.

Understands place value of tens, ones, regrouping.

Computes $a \times (b + c) = (a \times b) + (a \times c)$ [$a < 10, a \times (b + c) < 100$ with regrouping] (e.g., $6 \times (10 + 3) = \underline{\quad} + \underline{\quad} = \underline{\quad}$).

Computes 2D × 1D with regrouping, product < 100.

Understands place value of hundreds, tens, ones.

Computes 2D × 1D with regrouping, product < 100.

Computes 2D × 2D with regrouping.

Computes 3D × 1D with regrouping.

Computes 3D × 2D with regrouping.

DIVISION HIERARCHY

Finds missing factor (e.g., $6 \times \underline{\quad} = 36$).

Uses symbols that indicate division ($2\overline{)6}$, $6 \div 2$, 6/2).

Expresses a related multiplication sentence as a division sentence (product ÷ factor = factor).

Computes division facts with 1 as divisor (e.g., $1\overline{)6}$).

Computes basic division facts ($a \div b$ where $a \le 81$, $b \le 9$).

Computes division of a nonzero number by itself (e.g., $12\overline{)12}$).

Computes 1D ÷ 1D with a remainder.

Estimates 2D ÷ 1D and computes 2D ÷ 1D with a remainder.

Computes quotients with expanding dividend (e.g., $3\overline{)9}$, $3\overline{)90}$, $3\overline{)900}$).

Estimates 3D ÷ 1D and computes 3D ÷ 1D (e.g., $6\overline{)747}$).

Computes quotient of many-place dividend with a one-place divisor (e.g., $4\overline{)78,743}$).

Estimates 3D ÷ 2D and computes 3D ÷ 2D where divisor is multiple of 10 (e.g., $20\overline{)684}$).

Computes quotient with divisors of 100, 1,000, etc. (e.g., $1{,}000\overline{)6{,}897}$).

Estimates 3D ÷ 2D and computes 3D ÷ 2D (e.g., $17\overline{)489}$).

Computes quotient of many-place dividend and many-place divisor (e.g., $3{,}897\overline{)487{,}876}$).

FRACTION HIERARCHY

Readiness Areas

Separates regions into subregions that are equivalent.

Expresses 1 in many different ways.

Uses the terms *fraction*, *fraction bar*, *numerator*, and *denominator*.

Models equivalent fractions on the number line.

Generates sets of equivalent fractions.

Renames fractions in simplest form.

Rewrites improper fractions as mixed numerals.

Rewrites mixed numerals as improper fractions.

Develops concept of least common denominator using the concept of least common multiple.

Compares fractional numbers.

Develops concept of least common denominator using the concept of greatest common factor.

Addition

Computes sums less than 1, same denominator.

Computes sums of mixed numerals, no regrouping, same denominator.

Computes sums between 1 and 2, same denominator, regrouping.

Computes sums of mixed numeral and nonunit fraction, regrouping, same denominator (e.g., $3^2/5 + {}^4/5$).

Computes sums of mixed numerals with regrouping, same denominator (e.g., $8^3/5 + 2^4/5$).

Computes sums less than 1, different denominators.

Computes sums of mixed numerals, no regrouping, different denominators.

Computes sums of mixed numerals, regrouping, different denominators.

Computes sums of three nonunit fractions, different denominators.

Solves word problems requiring addition of fractions.

Subtraction

Computes differences between two fractions with like denominators without regrouping, then with regrouping.

Computes differences between two fractions with unlike but related denominators without regrouping, then with regrouping.

Computes differences between two fractions with unlike and unrelated denominators without regrouping, then with regrouping.

Solves word problems requiring subtraction of fractions.

Multiplication

Computes product of whole number × unit fraction, product < 1 (e.g., $3 \times {}^1/4 = \underline{\quad}$).

Computes product of whole number × nonunit fraction, product < 1 (e.g., $2 \times {}^2/5 = \underline{\quad}$).

Gives fraction names for one (e.g., $1 = {}^?/7$).

Solves regrouping problem by writing fraction as mixed numeral, $1 < a < 2$ (e.g., $^7/5 = \underline{\quad}$).

Computes product of whole number × nonunit fraction, $1 < $ product $ < 2$ (e.g., $3 \times {}^3/5 = \underline{\quad}$).

Computes product of unit fraction × unit fraction (e.g., $^1/3 \times {}^1/4 = \underline{\quad}$).

Computes product of nonunit fraction × nonunit fraction (e.g., $^2/3 \times {}^4/5 = \underline{\quad}$).

Computes $a \times (b + c) = (a \times b) + (a \times c)$, a and b are whole numbers, c is a unit fraction, no regrouping (e.g., $3 \times (2 + {}^1/4) = \underline{\quad} + \underline{\quad}$).

Computes $a \times (b + c) = (a \times b) + (a \times c)$, a and b are whole numbers, c is a nonunit fraction, regrouping (e.g., $4 \times 3^2/5 = 4 \times (3 + {}^2/5) = \underline{\quad} + \underline{\quad} = \underline{\quad}$).

Computes product of nonunit fraction × mixed numeral using improper fractions—e.g., $^5/6 \times 2^1/3$ (change to improper fractions).

Computes product of mixed numeral × mixed numeral using improper fractions—e.g., $3^3/4 \times 1^7/8$ (use improper fractions).

Division

Computes quotient of 1 ÷ unit fraction (e.g., $1 \div {}^1/5$).

Computes quotient of whole number ÷ nonunit fraction: $1 < $ whole number $ < 10$—e.g., $2 \div {}^3/5$ (use repeated subtraction and remainder as fractional part).

Computes $^1/a \div {}^1/b$ where $a < b$ (common denominator approach) (e.g., $^1/2 \div {}^1/3$).

Computes $^a/b \div {}^c/d$ (common denominator approach) (e.g., $^3/5 \div {}^3/4$).

Computes quotient of two mixed numerals (common denominator approach) (e.g., $2^1/5 \div 1^2/3$).

DECIMAL HIERARCHY

Readiness Areas

Generates decimal place value by rewriting fractions with denominators of powers of 10.

Recognizes decimal place value to millionths place.

Reads and writes rational numbers expressed as decimals.

Rewrites fractions as decimals.

Models rational numbers expressed as decimals using the number line.

Generates equivalent decimals by appending zeroes.

Addition

Names the sum of two rational numbers expressed as decimals having the same place value.

Names the sum of two rational numbers expressed as decimals having different place values.

Names the sum of more than two rational numbers expressed as decimals having different place values.

Solves word problems requiring addition of rational numbers expressed as decimals.

Subtraction

Names the difference between two rational numbers expressed as decimals having the same place value (without regrouping and with regrouping).

Names the difference between two rational numbers expressed as decimals having different place values (without regrouping and with regrouping).

Solves word problems requiring subtraction of rational numbers expressed as decimals.

Multiplication

Names the product of two rational numbers expressed as decimals when it is necessary to append zeroes to the left of a nonzero digit as decimal holders.

Names the product of more than two rational numbers expressed as decimals.

Solves word problems requiring multiplication of rational numbers expressed as decimals.

Division

Names the quotient of rational numbers expressed as decimals when the divisor is a whole number.

Names the quotient of any two rational numbers expressed as decimals by using the division algorithm.

Solves word problems requiring division of rational numbers expressed as decimals.

Percents

Interprets the symbol for percent (%) as a fraction and as a decimal.

Rewrites percents as decimals and fractions for percents less than 100% and then for percents equal to or greater than 100%.

Rewrites fractions or decimals as percents.

Solves word problems requiring percents.

MONEY HIERARCHY

Identifies coins.

Recognizes relative value of coins.

Makes change for amounts up to $1.00. Recognizes and uses money notation.

Recognizes currency and makes change for currency.

Solves examples and word problems involving money.

TIME HIERARCHY

Relates the face of the clock with the number line through 12 for hours.

Relates the face of the clock with the number line through 60 for minutes.

Tells time by the hour.

Tells time by the minute.

Understands the difference between A.M. and P.M.

Solves examples and word problems involving time.

MEASUREMENT HIERARCHY

Linear

Uses a straightedge of arbitrary length to measure an object.

Makes a ruler of at least 12″ with 1″ markings.

Uses an inch-marked ruler to measure items.

Recognizes that 12″ measure the same length as 1 foot.

Identifies measurements of objects that are less than, greater than, or equal to 1 foot.

Introduces the symbols for inches and feet.

Makes a ruler with $1/2''$ and $1/4''$ markings to measure objects.

Uses a ruler with $1/2''$ and $1/4''$ markings to measure objects.

Estimates heights and lengths in feet and inches.

Recognizes and relates inch, foot, yard, and mile.

Solves examples involving denominate numbers related to linear measurement.

Solves word problems applying the concepts of linear measurement.

Recognizes metric units and relates them to one another.

Liquid and Dry

Recognizes relationships between and relative values of cup, pint, quart, half-gallon, and gallon.

Recognizes metric units and relates them to one another.

Solves examples involving denominate numbers related to liquid or dry measurements.

Solves word problems involving liquid measurement.

Weight

Compares relative weights of objects using a balance.

Recognizes relationships between and relative values of ounce, pound, and ton.

Weighs objects to nearest pound and ounce.

Uses the abbreviations *oz*, *lb*, and *T* in recording weights.

Recognizes metric units and relates them to one another.

Solves examples involving denominate numbers related to weight measurement.

Solves word problems involving weight measurements

Note: Portions of this skills list were adapted from *Diagnosing Mathematical Difficulties* (pp. 262–267, 278–290) by R. G. Underhill, A. E. Uprichard, and J. W. Heddens, 1980, Upper Saddle River, NJ: Merrill/Prentice Hall. Adapted by permission.

☀ MATH SCOPE AND SEQUENCE SKILLS LIST

By Grade Level

KINDERGARTEN

Position concepts: above, below, in, out, on, off, left, right, top, bottom, middle, front, back.

Classification: identity, color, size, shape, pattern.

One-to-one: as many as, using tallies to count events or objects.

Comparing: more than, less than, same.

Counting: 0 to 5.

Ordinal numbers: first, second, third.

Geometry: box, ball, square, circle, triangle, rectangle, inside, outside.

Measurement: comparing larger, smaller, taller, shorter, longer, same length.

Time: daytime, nighttime, sequence, duration, clock, calendar.

Money: value of penny, identifying nickel and dime, reading price tags, determining whether enough money.

Writing numerals: 0 to 10.

Combining sets: picture addition stories.

Sums to 5: picture addition stories.

Separating sets: picture subtraction stories.

GRADE 1

Numeration: numbers and values 1 to 10.

Matching and joining sets.

Sums to 6.

Addition properties: commutative property of addition, zero property.

Ordinal numbers: first to fifth.

Sums 7 to 10.

Families of facts: sum of 1, 2, 3, 4, 5, 6, 7, 8, 9 families (e.g., sum of 7 family is $0 + 7$, $7 + 0$, $6 + 1$, $1 + 6$, $5 + 2$, $2 + 5$, $3 + 4$, $4 + 3$).

Addition sentences: completing, writing, and choosing.

Finding missing addends (e.g., $4 + \_\_ = 7$).

Subtracting from sums or minuends to 6.

Subtracting from sums or minuends to 10.

Subtraction sentences: completing, writing, and choosing.

Money: subtracting prices, determining how much money (pennies, nickels, dimes).

Numeration/place value: counting and writing tens and ones, recognizing numbers 10 to 90, order of numbers to 100.

Counting: one more than, less than, counting by 2s, 3s, 5s, and 10s, skip-counting.

Time: calendar, hour, half hour, quarter hour.

Sums 11 to 18.

Subtracting from sums or minuends 11 to 18.

Families of facts: sum of 11 to 18 families.

Adding three addends.

Money: adding and subtracting with money.

Geometry: rectangle, square, circle, triangle.

Measurement: linear—comparing lengths, arbitrary units, metric units (centimeter, meter), customary units (inch, foot, yard); capacity—metric units (liter), customary units (cup, pint, quart); weight—kilogram; temperature—thermometer scales.

Addition of 2D + 1D without regrouping.

Addition of 2D + 2D without regrouping.

Subtraction of 2D - 1D without regrouping.

Subtraction of 2D - 2D without regrouping.

Fractions: recognizing equal parts or shapes, $^1/_2$s, $^1/_3$s, $^1/_4$s, finding $^1/_2$ of set.

Story problems: involving addition and subtraction.

GRADE 2

Numeration/place value: grouping tens and ones, order to 100, hundreds, tens, and ones.

Equations with missing numbers (e.g., 7 + __ = 14, __ + 3 = 13, 6 + 5 = __).

Three or more addends: sums to 18.

Addition of 2D numbers with regrouping.

Subtraction of 2D numbers with regrouping.

Story problems: using addition and subtraction.

Fractions: identifying and writing fractional parts, dividing shapes in half.

Time: writing times, 15-minute intervals, 5-minute intervals, telling time, calendar—earlier or later.

Geometry: solid shapes, polygons, congruent figures, symmetry.

Measurement: linear—nearest inch, perimeter in centimeters; area—square units, by counting; capacity—milliliter; volume—by counting; weight—customary units (pound, ounce); temperature—Celsius, Fahrenheit.

Multiples facts: multiples of 2, 3, 4, 5: factors 2, 3, 4, 5, 0, 1; commutative property of multiplication.

Numeration: order of numbers to 1000, 100 more than, 100 less than.

Subtraction of 3D − 2D with regrouping.

Subtraction of 3D − 3D with regrouping.

Story problems: using 3D numbers and two-step problems.

Money: half dollar, using ¢ and $, adding and subtracting money, writing amounts (e.g., $6.75).

GRADE 3

Adding zero property.

Rounding to nearest 10 or 100.

Estimating sums: to three digits.

Adding larger numbers: multidigit + multidigit.

Addition as a check for subtraction.

Subtraction with regrouping more than once and with zero in minuend.

Estimating differences: to three digits.

Subtraction of 4D numbers with regrouping.

Story problems: using addition and subtraction.

Multiplication facts: 6 to 9, zero and one properties, order property.

Multiplication of 2D × 1D without regrouping.

Division facts: 2D ÷ 1D, division equation, division and sets.

Story problems: using multiplication and division.

Division in vertical format.

Multiplication and division related: division by finding the missing factor.

Division with remainders.

Fractions of a number.

Equivalent fractions.

Measurement: linear—kilometer, mile, perimeter of polygons by adding inches; area—square centimeters by counting, square inches by counting; capacity—gallon; volume—cubic centimeters, cubic inches; mass weight—gram, kilogram; temperature—below zero.

Comparing fractions using < and >.

Geometry: areas, rectangular solid, segments, end points, sides, diagonals, symmetry, points on a grid.

Multiplication of 2D × 1D with tens regrouping.

Multiplication of 2D × 1D with hundreds regrouping.

Multiplication of 3D × 1D without regrouping.

Multiplication of 3D × 1D with regrouping.

Division of 2D numbers without regrouping (e.g., 36 ÷ 3).

Division of 2D numbers with regrouping (e.g., 51 ÷ 3).

Multiplication with addition, subtraction, and division using symbols (e.g., $8 \times 4 \div 2 - 2 =$).

GRADE 4

Rounding to nearest 100.

Numbers to millions.

Addition of numbers to six digits.

Place value of decimals.

Order and grouping properties of multiplication: $(3 \times 2) \times 4 = 24$, $3 \times (2 \times 4) = 24$.

Multiples and common multiples: 36 is a multiple of 6, 36 is a common multiple of 6 and 4.

Finding missing factor: $4 \times \underline{\quad} = 36$.

Zero as divisor.

Story problems: using addition, subtraction, multiplication, and division.

Fractions: fractions and sets, equivalent fractions, fractions of a number, numerator of 1 and more than 1.

Reducing fractions.

Adding fractions with like denominators.

Adding fractions with unlike denominators.

Subtracting fractions with like and unlike denominators.

Writing mixed numbers as fractions.

Changing fractions to mixed numbers.

Adding and subtracting mixed numbers.

Story problems: using addition and subtraction of fractions.

Measurement: linear—decimal measures, perimeter formulas, area formulas; volume—by counting, by multiplying; estimating temperature.

Multiplication of 3D × 1D with regrouping.

Multiplication of 4D × 1D with regrouping.

Estimating products.

Division of 3D number by 1D number with regrouping: including estimation.

Division of 4D number by 1D number with regrouping: including estimation.

Multiplication as a check for division.

Geometry: segments, lines, rays, angles, parallel lines.

Multiplication by 10 and multiples of 10.

Multiplication by a 2D number (e.g., 24×13).

Division by a 2D number with regrouping (e.g., $12\overline{)53}$, $15\overline{)328}$).

Decimals: writing and reading decimals to hundredths, place value of decimal numbers, adding and subtracting decimals with regrouping.

Applications: catalogs and order forms, computing averages.

GRADE 5

Values to billions.

Rounding to nearest millions and billions.

Roman numerals: I to X.

Story problems: using addition and subtraction with fractions and mixed numbers.

Least common multiples.

Multiplying by 100 and multiples of 10 and 100.

Distributive property: $(9 \times 4) \times 3 = \underline{\quad}$, $9 \times (4 \times 3) = \underline{\quad}$.

Multiplication of 3D × 2D with regrouping.

Story problems: using multiplication and division with fractions.

Factors and common factors.

Geometry: vertex, perpendicular lines, corresponding parts, naming angles, protractor, diagonals, measuring angles.

Least common denominators.

Multiplication and division of fractions.

Decimals to thousandths.

Rounding to the nearest whole number.

Measurement: linear—millimeter, decimeter, nearest $1/16$ of an inch, perimeter formulas, curved figures, circumference, area formulas by multiplying, area of triangles; capacity—fluid ounce; volume—rectangular prisms, by counting, by multiplying.

Multiplying decimals.

Dividing decimals.

Story problems: using multiplication and division with decimals.

Applications: discounts, sales tax, profits.

GRADE 6

Base two numerals.

Place value in metric system.

Multiplication: exponents.

Prime factorization.

Division with 3D numbers.

Rounding divisors.

Geometry: intersecting lines; acute, right, obtuse angles; parallelogram, rhombus, dexagon, trapezoid, kite.

Decimals: finding decimal between two numbers, decimals and money, rounding decimals, multiplying dollars, changing decimals to fractions, multiplying and dividing decimals, repeating decimals.

Measurement: linear—relation of metric units to decimal system, adding metric units, adding customary units, area formulas, parallelograms, surface areas of rectangular prisms, cylinders, circle; capacity—metric cup, kiloliter, half-gallon, comparing measures, adding measures; mass weight—milligram.

Estimating: time, volume, weight, bar graph.

Decimals and percents: converting dollars and cents, multiplying dollars

Story problems: using percent.

Applications: stocks, unit pricing, installment buying, checking account.

APPENDIX

Publishers of Books, Tests, and Materials

Academic Communication Associates, 4149 Avenida de la Plata, Oceanside, CA 92058

Academic Therapy Publications, 20 Commercial Boulevard, Novato, CA 94949

Adapt Press, 808 West Avenue North, Sioux Falls, SD 57104

Addison Wesley Longman, 2725 Sand Hill Road, Menlo Park, CA 94025

Adston Educational Enterprise, 945 East River Oaks Drive, Baton Rouge, LA 70815

Allied Education Council, P.O. Box 78, Galien, MI 49113

Allyn & Bacon, 160 Gould Street, Needham Heights, MA 02194

American Association on Mental Deficiency, 5201 Connecticut Avenue, Washington, DC 20015

American Book Company, 450 West 33rd Street, New York, NY 10001

American Guidance Service, 4201 Woodland Road, P.O. Box 99, Circle Pines, MN 55014

Appleton-Century-Crofts, 440 Park Avenue South, New York, NY 10016

Arista Corporation, 2 Park Avenue, New York, NY 10016

Aspen Publishers, 7201 McKinney Circle, P.O. Box 990, Frederick, MD 21701

Clarence L. Barnhart, Box 250, Bronxville, NY 10708

Behavioral Research Laboratories, P.O. Box 577, Palo Alto, CA 94302

Benefic Press, 10300 West Roosevelt Road, Westchester, IL 60153

Biological Sciences Curriculum Study, P.O. Box 930, Boulder, CO 80306

Bobbs-Merrill Company, 4300 West 62nd Street, Indianapolis, IN 46206

Bowmar/Noble Publishers, 4563 Colorado Boulevard, Los Angeles, CA 90039

Paul H. Brookes Publishing Company, P.O. Box 10624, Baltimore, MD 21285

Brooks/Cole Publishing Company, 511 Forest Lodge Road, Pacific Grove, CA 93950

C. C. Publications, P.O. Box 23699, Tigard, OR 97223

Childcraft Education Corporation, 20 Kilmer Road, Edison, NJ 08817

Communication Skill Builders, 3830 East Bellevue, P.O. Box 42050-CS4, Tucson, AZ 85733

Consulting Psychologists Press, 3803 East Bayshore Road, P.O. Box 11096, Palo Alto, CA 94303

Continental Press, 520 East Bainbridge Street, Elizabethtown, PA 17022

Council for Exceptional Children, 1920 Association Drive, Reston, VA 22091

CTB/McGraw-Hill, 20 Ryan Ranch Road, Monterey, CA 93940

Cuisenaire Dale Seymour Publications, 10 Bank Street, P.O. Box 5026, White Plains, NY 10602

Curriculum Associates, 153 Rangeway Road, North Billerica, MA 01862

Devereux Foundation Press, 19 South Waterloo Road, Devon, PA 19333

Diarmuid, P.O. Box 357580, Gainesville, FL 32667

Dormac, P.O. Box 752, Beaverton, OR 97075

EBSCO Publishing, 10 Estes Street, Ipswich, MA 01938

Economy Company, P.O. Box 25308, 1901 North Walnut Street, Oklahoma City, OK 73125

Edge Enterprises, 708 West 9th, Suite R4, P.O. Box 1304, Lawrence, KS 66044

Edmark Corporation, P.O. Box 3218, Redmond, WA 98073

Educational Achievement Systems, 319 Nickerson Street, Suite 112, Seattle, WA 98109

Educational Activities, 1937 Grand Avenue, Baldwin, NY 11510

Educational Performance Associates, 600 Broad Avenue, Ridgefield, NJ 07657

Educational Progress Corporation, P.O. Box 45663, Tulsa, OK 74145

Educational Service, P.O. Box 219, Stevensville, MI 49127

Educational Teaching Aids, 620 Lakeview Parkway, Vernon Hills, IL 60061

Educational Testing Service, P.O. Box 6108, Princeton, NJ 08541

Educators Publishing Service, 31 Smith Place, Cambridge, MA 02138

Enrich, Mafex Associates, 90 Cherry Street, Johnstown, PA 15907

Exceptional Education, P.O. Box 15308, Seattle, WA 98115

Field Educational Publications, 2400 Hanover Street, Palo Alto, CA 94302

Fox Reading Research Company, P.O. Box 1059, Coeur D'Alene, ID 83814

Franklin Electronic Publishers, One Franklin Plaza, Burlington, NJ 08016

Garrard Publishing Company, 1607 North Market Street, Champaign, IL 61820

General Learning Corporation, 250 James Street, Morristown, NJ 07960

Ginn and Company, 191 Spring Street, Lexington, MA 02173

Globe/Fearon Publishers, P.O. Box 2649, Columbus, OH 43216

Grune and Stratton, 111 Fifth Avenue, New York, NY 10003

Gryphon Press, 220 Montgomery Street, Highland Park, NJ 18904

Guidance Associates, 90 South Bedford Road, Mount Kisco, NY 10549

H and H Enterprises, 946 Tennessee, Lawrence, KS 66044

Harcourt Brace Educational Measurement, 555 Academic Court, San Antonio, TX 78204

Harcourt Brace Jovanovich, 6277 Sea Harbor Drive, Orlando, FL 32821

Harcourt Publishers, 301 Commerce Street, Suite 3700, Fort Worth, TX 76102

Harper and Row Publishers, 10 East 53rd Street, New York, NY 10022

Haworth Press, 10 Alice Street, Binghamton, NY 13904

Hawthorne Educational Services, 800 Gray Oak Drive, Columbia, MO 65201

Heinemann, 361 Hanover Street, Portsmouth, NH 03801

High Noon Books, 20 Commercial Boulevard, Novato, CA 94949

Houghton Mifflin, 222 Berkeley Street, Boston, MA 02116

Hubbard, P.O. Box 104, Northbrook, IL 60062

Human Development Training Institute, 1081 East Main Street, El Cajon, CA 92021

Human Sciences Press, 72 Fifth Avenue, New York, NY 10011

Ideal School Supply Company, 11000 South Lavergne Avenue, Oak Lawn, IL 60453

Incentive Publications, P.O. Box 12522, Nashville, TN 37212

Initial Teaching Alphabet Publications, 6 East 43rd Street, New York, NY 10017

Intelligent Peripheral Devices, 20400 Stevens Clark Boulevard, Suite 300, Cupertino, CA 95014

International Reading Association, 800 Barksdale Road, Newark, DE 19711

Interstate Printers and Publishers, 19 North Jackson Street, P.O. Box 50, Danville, IL 61834

Janus Books, 2501 Industrial Parkway West, Hayward, CA 94545

Jastak Associates, 1526 Gilpin Avenue, Wilmington, DE 19806

Lakeshore Learning Materials, 2695 East Dominquez Street, Carson, CA 90749

Lawrence Productions, 1800 South 35th Street, Galesburg, MI 49053

Learning Concepts, 2501 North Lamar Boulevard, Austin, TX 78705

Learning Skills, 17951-G Sky Park Circle, Irvine, CA 92707

LinguiSystems, 3100 4th Avenue, East Moline, IL 61244

Lippincott Williams and Wilkins, 530 Walnut Street, Philadelphia, PA 19106

Little, Brown and Company, 34 Beacon Street, Boston, MA 02108

Love Publishing Company, 1777 South Bellaire Street, Denver, CO 80222

Lyons and Carnahan, 407 East 25th Street, Chicago, IL 60616

Mafex Associates, 90 Cherry Street, Box 519, Johnstown, PA 15907

Mayfield Publishing Company, 1240 Villa Street, Mountain View, CA 94041

McGraw-Hill Book Company, 1221 Avenue of the Americas, New York, NY 10020

Media Materials, 111 Kane Street, Baltimore, MD 21224

Melton Book Company, 111 Leslie Street, Dallas, TX 75207

Melton Peninsula, 1949 Stemmons Freeway, Dallas, TX 75207

Milton Bradley Company, 74 Park Street, Springfield, MA 01101

Modern Curriculum Press, 4350 Equity Drive, P.O. Box 2649, Columbus, OH 43216

Modern Education Corporation, P.O. Box 721, Tulsa, OK 74101

William C. Morrow, 105 Madison Avenue, New York, NY 10016

C. V. Mosby Company, 11830 Westline Industrial Drive, Saint Louis, MO 63141

New Readers Press, 1320 Jamesville Avenue, Box 131, Syracuse, NY 13210

Newby Visualanguage, Box 121-E, Eagleville, PA 19408

Noble and Noble Publishers, 1 Dag Hammarskjold Plaza, New York, NY 10017

Numark Publications, 104-20 Queens Boulevard, Forest Hills, NY 11375

Open Court Publishing Company, 332 South Michigan, Suite 200, Chicago, IL 60604

Opportunities for Learning, 20417 Nordhoff Street, Chatsworth, CA 91311

Parker Brothers, P.O. Box 900, Salem, MA 01970

Phoenix Learning Resources, 2349 Chaffee Drive, St. Louis, MO 63146

Phonovisual Products, 12216 Parklawn Drive, Rockville, MD 20852

Prentice Hall, One Lake Street, Upper Saddle River, NJ 07458

PRO-ED, 8700 Shoal Creek Boulevard, Austin, TX 78757

Psychological Corporation, Harcourt Brace Jovanovich, 555 Academic Court, San Antonio, TX 78204

Rand McNally, 8255 North Central Park, Skokie, IL 60076

Random House/Singer School Division, 201 East 50th Street, New York, NY 10022

Reader's Digest Services, Educational Division, Pleasantville, NJ 10570

Reading Joy, P.O. Box 404, Naperville, IL 60540

Research Press, Box 9177, Champaign, IL 61826

Riverside Publishing Company, 425 Spring Lake Drive, Itasca, IL 60143

Saxon Publishers, 2450 John Saxon Boulevard, Norman, OK 73071

Scholastic, 555 Broadway, New York, NY 10012

Scientific Learning Corporation, 1995 University Avenue, Suite 400, Berkeley, CA 94704

Scott, Foresman and Company, 1900 East Lake Avenue, Glenview, IL 60025

Selchow and Righter, 505 East Union Street, Bay Shore, NY 11706

Select-Ed, 117 North Chester, Olathe, KS 66061

L. W. Singer, A Division of Random House, 210 East 50th Street, New York, NY 10022

Slosson Educational Publications, 140 Pine Street, East Aurora, NY 14052

Society for Visual Education, 1345 Diversey Parkway, Chicago, IL 60614

Sopris West, 4093 Specialty Place, Longmont, CO 80504

South-Western Publishing Company, 5101 Madison Road, Cincinnati, OH 45227

Special Child Publications, 4635 Union Bay Place Northeast, Seattle, WA 98105

Special Learning Corporation, 42 Boston Post Road, Guilford, CT 06437

SRA, 220 East Danieldale Road, DeSoto, TX 75115

Steck-Vaughn Publishing Company, P.O. Box 690789, Orlando, FL 32819

Stoelting Company, 620 Wheat Lane, Wood Dale, IL 60191

Syracuse University Press, 1011 East Water Street, Syracuse, NY 13210

Teachers College Press, P.O. Box 20, Williston, VT 05495

Teaching Strategies, P.O. Box 5205, Eugene, OR 97405

Texas Instruments, 2305 University Avenue, Lubbock, TX 79415

Thinking Publications, 424 Galloway Street, P.O. Box 163, Eau Claire, WI 54702

Charles C Thomas Publisher, 2600 South First Street, Springfield, IL 62794

Trend Enterprises, P.O. Box 43073, Saint Paul, MN 55164

Troll Associates, 100 Corporate Drive, Mahwah, NJ 07430

University of Illinois Press, 1325 South Oak Street, Champaign, IL 61820

University Park Press, 233 East Redwood Street, Baltimore, MD 21202

VORT Corporation, P.O. Box 60132, Palo Alto, CA 95306

Wadsworth/Thomson Learning, 10 Davis Drive, Belmont, CA 94002

George Wahr Publishing Company, 316 State Street, Ann Arbor, MI 41808

Walker Educational Book Corporation, 720 Fifth Avenue, New York, NY 10019

Warner Educational Services, 75 Rockefeller Plaza, New York, NY 10019

Wayne Engineering, 1825 Willow Road, Northfield, IL 60093

West Publishing Company, 50 West Kellogg Boulevard, P.O. Box 64526, Saint Paul, MN 55164

Western Psychological Services, 12031 Wilshire Boulevard, Los Angeles, CA 90225

Wilcox & Follett Book Company, 1000 West Washington Boulevard, Chicago, IL 60607

John Wiley and Sons, 605 Third Avenue, New York, NY 10158

Wilson Language Training, 175 West Main Street, Millbury, MA 01527

B. L. Winch and Associates, 45 Hitching Post Drive, Building 29, Rolling Hills Estates, CA 90274

Xerox Education Publications, 245 Long Hill Road, Middletown, CT 06457

Zaner-Bloser, 2200 West Fifth Avenue, P.O. Box 16764, Columbus, OH 43216

Richard L. Zweig Associates, 20800 Beach Boulevard, Huntington Beach, CA 92648

Producers and Distributors of Educational Computer Software

Academic Communication Associates, 4149 Avenida de la Plata, Oceanside, CA 92058

Academic Software, c/o Software City, 22 East Quackenbush Avenue, Dumont, NJ 07628

American Educational Computer, 525 University Avenue, Palo Alto, CA 94301

American Micro Media, P.O. Box 306, Red Hook, NY 12571

Avant-Garde Creations, P.O. Box 30160, Eugene, OR 97403

BMI Educational Services, Hay Press Road, Dayton, NJ 08810

Borg-Warner Educational System, 600 West University Drive, Arlington, IL 60004

Broderbund, 500 Redwood Boulevard, Novato, CA 94947

Cambridge Development Laboratory, 86 West Street, Waltham, MA 02451

CCV Software, P.O. Box 6724, Charleston, WV 25362

Charles Clark Company, 168 Express Drive South, Brentwood, NY 11717

Classroom Consorta Media, 28 Bay Street, Staten Island, NY 10301

Compass Learning, 9920 Pacific Heights Boulevard, San Diego, CA 92122

COMPU-TATIONS, P.O. Box 502, Troy, MI 48099

Computer Courseware Services, 300 York Avenue, Saint Paul, MN 55101

Computer Curriculum Corporation, P.O. Box 3711, Sunnydale, CA 94088

Computer-Ed, 1 Everett Road, Carmel, NY 10512

Cross Educational Software, 1802 North Trenton, Box 1536, Ruston, LA 71270

Dilithium Software, P.O. Box 606, Beaverton, OR 97075

Dorsett Educational Systems, P.O. Box 1226, Norman, OK 73070

Edmark, P.O. Box 97021, Redmond, WA 98073

Education Associates, 340 Crab Orchard Road, P.O. Box 4290, Frankfort, KY 40604

Educational Activities, P.O. Box 392, Freeport, NY 11520

Educational Computing Systems, 106 Fairbanks, Oak Ridge, TN 37830

Educational Micro Systems, P.O. Box 471, Chester, NJ 07930

Educational Software Consultants, P.O. Box 30846, Orlando, FL 32862

Educational Systems Software, 23720 El Toro Road, P.O. Box E, El Toro, CA 92630

Educational Teaching Aids, 159 West Kinzie Street, Chicago, IL 60610

Edu-Ware Services, 28035 Dorothy Drive, Agoura, CA 91301

Encyclopaedia Britannica Educational Corporation, 425 North Michigan Avenue, Chicago, IL 60611

Follett Software Company, 1391 Corporate Drive, McHenry, IL 60050

Gamco Industries, Box 1911, Big Spring, TX 79720

J. L. Hammett Company, Box 545, Braintree, MA 02184

Harcourt Brace Jovanovich, 6277 Sea Harbor Drive, Orlando, FL 32821

Houghton Mifflin, 222 Berkeley Street, Boston, MA 02116

Humanities Software, P.O. Box 950, 408 Columbia Street, Hood River, OR 97031

Huntington Computing, P.O. Box 1297, Corcoran, CA 93212

K-12 Micromedia Publishing, 16 McKee Drive, Mahwah, NJ 07430

Knowledge Adventure, 4100 West 190th Street, Torrance, CA 90504

Krell Software, 1320 Stony Brook Road, Stony Brook, NY 11790

The Learning Company, One Athenaeum Street, Cambridge, MA 02142

Learning Lab Software, 21000 Nordhoff Street, Chatsworth, CA 91311

Learning Systems, P.O. Box 9046, Fort Collins, CO 80525

Little Bee Educational Programs, P.O. Box 262, Massillon, OH 44648

Love Publishing Company, 1777 South Bellaire Street, Denver, CO 80222

Magic Lantern Computers, 406 South Park Street, Madison, WI 53715

MARCK, 280 Linden Avenue, Branford, CT 06405

MECC, 6160 Summit Drive North, Minneapolis, MN 55430

Media Materials, 1821 Portal Street, Baltimore, MD 21224

Mercer Systems, 87 Scooter Lane, Nicksville, NY 11801

Merry Bee Communications, 815 Crest Drive, Omaha, NE 68046

The Micro Center, P.O. Box 6, Pleasantville, NY 10570

Microcomputer Workshops, 103 Puritan Drive, Port Chester, NY 10573

Micrograms Software, 9934 North Alpine Road, Suite 108, Machesney Park, IL 61115

Midwest Visual Equipment Company, 6500 North Hamlin, Chicago, IL 60645

Milliken Publishing Company, 1100 Research Boulevard, P.O. Box 21579, Saint Louis, MO 63132

Milton Bradley Educational Division, 443 Shaker Road, East Longmeadow, MA 01028

Mindplay, 160 West Fort Lowell Road, Tucson, AZ 85705

New Media Schoolhouse, P.O. Box 505, Pound Ridge, NY 10576

Opportunities for Learning, 20417 Nordhoff Street, Department 9, Chatsworth, CA 91311

Optimum Resource, 18 Hunter Road, Hilton Head, SC 29926

Orange Cherry New Media Schoolhouse, P.O. Box 390, 69 Westchester Avenue, Pound Ridge, NY 10576

Queue, 338 Commerce Drive, Fairfield, CT 06432

Quicksoft, 537 Willamette, Eugene, OR 97401

Random House School Division, 201 East 50th Street, New York, NY 10022

Reader's Digest Services, Educational Division, Pleasantville, NY 10570

Right On Programs, Division of Computeam, P.O. Box 977, Huntington, NY 11743

Scholastic Software, 2931 East McCarty Street, Jefferson City, MO 65102

Scott, Foresman and Company, 1900 East Lake Avenue, Glenview, IL 60025

Society for Visual Education, 1345 Diversey Parkway, Department CC-1, Chicago, IL 60614

Southwest EdPsych Services, P.O. Box 1870, Phoenix, AZ 85001

South-Western Publishing Company, 5101 Madison Road, Cincinnati, OH 45227

Spinnaker Software, 201 Broadway, Cambridge, MA 02139

SRA, 220 East Danieldale Road, DeSoto, TX 75115

Sunburst Communications, 101 Castleton Street, P.O. Box 1 00, Pleasantville, NY 10570

Teacher Support Software, 1035 Northwest 57th Street, Gainesville, FL 32605

Texas Instruments, P.O. Box 10508, Mail Station 5849, Lubbock, TX 79408

AUTHOR INDEX

SUBJECT INDEX

Contents

Acknowledgments

I have been working in networking and security for over 15 years. When my editor and agent asked me to write a book on networking and security, I thought, Sure! How difficult could it be?

You never know the limits of your own knowledge until you write a book. In researching and writing this book, I learned more about the fine details within specific protocols than I ever imagined. This has been a truly rewarding experience.

I would like to thank the people who allowed this book to become as encompassing and accurate as possible by providing expertise, feedback, and the occasional heated discussion: Erik Lillestolen, Ragavan Srinivasan, Ellen Mitchell, Willis Marti, Rachael Lininger, Mark Rasch, Howard Krawetz, Paul Ferguson, Valdis Kletnieks, and Tim McGuffin. I am indebted to Michelle Mach and Bill Hayes for their incredible guidance, support, and red ink. Any errors are strictly my own, but without the help from these people, there would have been many more errors. I must also thank Neil Salkind for twisting my arm and convincing me to write a book, as well as Clay Andres, Jim Walsh, Jenifer Niles, Jennifer Blaney, and all the people at StudioB, Charles River Media, and Thomson Delmar Learning for making this possible.

I am grateful to the University of California at Santa Cruz and Texas A&M University for formalizing my knowledge and allowing me to experience many different aspects of computer science. In particular, I thank the late Dr. David Huffman, my mentor who showed me that thinking outside the box could lead to amazing results. I also must express my sincerest gratitude to my high school history teacher, Gil "Essay" Solis. Even if I never need to remember that the Battle of New Orleans happened in 1814, I continue to use my essay writing skills. And of course, I thank my family for being there.

Finally, I would like to thank Vint Cerf, Robert Kahn, the late Jon Postel, and the other members of the Internet Architecture Board for designing an amazing system: the Internet.

Part I

Overview

Network security is the identification and mitigation of undesirable information flow. Understanding the impacts, ramifications, and options requires a basic background in general computer security processes, network theory, and for some protocols, a basic understanding of cryptography. This knowledge can be used both offensively and defensively. Ethics determine whether the knowledge is used to increase social value.

In Part I we will cover:

- Security
- Ethics
- Network Theory
- Basic Cryptography

1 ∷ Security

In This Chapter

- Importance
- Threat Models
- Concepts
- Common Mitigation Methods
- Certifications
- People and Staff

1.1 IMPORTANCE

Security is an assessment of risk. Secure environments do not just appear; they are designed and developed through an intentional effort. Secure solutions must be thorough; one weakness can compromise an otherwise secure system.

In today's online and connected world, where computers outsell TVs [CNET1996] and e-commerce surpasses brick-and-mortar sales by a significant margin [Oswald2005], secure network environments are an ever-growing need. Weaknesses within the network have lead to the rapid growth of identity theft and daily computer virus outbreaks. Software developers and network administrators are being held accountable for compromises within their systems, while attackers remain anonymous. This book provides a basis for designing, developing, implementing, analyzing, and maintaining networks and network protocols. The book covers how these systems currently operate, what works, and the limitations that lead to security weaknesses.

This book is divided onto nine parts. Part I discusses the fundamentals needed to understand network security. These include the definition of security terms (Chapter 1, "Security"), security ethics (Chapter 2, "Ethics"), the OSI network model (Chapter 3, "Network Theory"), and an overview of cryptography (Chapter 4, "Basic Cryptography"). Parts II through VIII discuss each of the seven layers in the OSI network model. Each part begins with a chapter describing the overall layer, its security role, common vulnerabilities, and mitigation techniques. Each overview is followed by explicit examples of common protocols within the layer and their respective security issues. The final section, Part IX, summarizes the common risks for secure network design and development. This includes the impact of modularity on security (Chapter 24, "Modularity and Security") and a summary of the general security issues (Chapter 25, "Issues Summary"). The companion CD-ROM includes sample source code and many of the references mentioned in this book.

ON THE CD

Network protocols number in the thousands. This book is not intended to be all encompassing, so only the most common protocols are mentioned and evaluated in depth. Although the adoption of protocols and standards such as gigabit Ethernet, Dynamic Host Configuration Protocol (DHCP), Secure Multipurpose Internet Mail Extensions (S/MIME), and Wireless Application Protocol (WAP) is growing, they are not as common as other protocols found in the same network layers. The general risks and options covered at each layer are applicable to both common and uncommon protocols. Detailed risks for any specific protocol usually have counterparts in other protocols; just because DHCP is not dissected does not imply that it is secure. In addition, many of the fine details within network standards and protocols are not discussed; the primary focus of this book is network security, not general networking.

1.1.1 Terminology

Within the security community, some words have specific meanings, whereas other words commonly associated with computer security have virtually no meaning. Common security vocabulary [Schneider1999] includes the following:

Vulnerability: A defect or weakness in the feasibility, design, implementation, operation, or maintenance of a system.

Threat: An adversary who is capable and motivated to exploit a vulnerability.

Attack: The use or exploitation of a vulnerability. This term is neither malicious nor benevolent. A bad guy may attack a system, and a good guy may attack a problem.

Attacker: The person or process that initiates an attack. This can be synonymous with *threat*.

Exploit: The instantiation of a vulnerability; something that can be used for an attack. A single vulnerability may lead to multiple exploits, but not every vulnerability may have an exploit (e.g., theoretical vulnerabilities).

Target: The person, company, or system that is directly vulnerable and impacted by the exploit. Some exploits have multiple impacts, with both primary (main) targets and secondary (incidental) targets.

Attack vector: The path from an attacker to a target. This includes tools and techniques.

Defender: The person or process that mitigates or prevents an attack.

Compromise: The successful exploitation of a target by an attacker.

Risk: A qualitative assessment describing the likelihood of an attacker/threat using an exploit to successfully bypass a defender, attack a vulnerability, and compromise a system.

Not all vulnerabilities are programming errors; some are due to design oversight. For example, the email protocol SMTP was never designed for security, so the protocol does not have security defects. But SMTP does have vulnerabilities due to the lack of security in the design.

The term *hacker* is closely associated with computer security. But in contrast to the common terminology, hacker has conflicting definitions. This term originally referred to people with highly technical skills. Later it became associated with technical malcontents and online anarchists. Today, people with virtually no technical skills are called hackers if they use a computer. To avoid the ongoing definition debate, this book does not use the term hacker to describe an individual. Instead, the terms *attacker* and *defender* are used. When the particular side of an exploit is clearly benevolent or malicious, the terms *good guy* and *bad guy* are used, but a good guy may be an attacker or a defender, and may be a person or a process.

1.1.2 Types of Security Issues

Conventional wisdom says that security is used to keep out undesirable elements and keep honest people honest. In actuality, security does not just mean saving the system from bad guys and malicious software. Security means preserving data integrity, providing authorized access, and maintaining privacy. Thus, preventing a user from accidentally deleting or corrupting an important file is just as essential to security as stopping a malicious user. The vast majority of security issues are aimed at data protection and privacy issues, ensuring that users do not do something they should not do.

There are many ways to examine network security issues. In general, a threat can either come from an account on the system (*local access*), or from a system across a network (*remote access*). But someone with *physical access* to a system may also pose a threat.

1.1.3 What Is Secure?

Security does not mean "invulnerable." Even the most secured computer system will probably lose data if it is near a strong electromagnetic pulse (i.e., nuclear blast). Security means that, in a general-use environment, the system will not be openly vulnerable to attacks, data loss, or privacy issues. Attackers may still be able to access a secured system, but it will be much more difficult for them, and attacks may be more easily detected.

In computer networking, *security* is the mitigation of undesirable information flow. This includes both reactive and preventative measures. *Risk management* refers to the processes for mitigating security issues. For example, the risk from an unwanted network access can be managed by using a firewall. Although the firewall may not prevent 100 percent of the threat, it reduces the risk to the point of being considered secure. Security is a relative term to the environment, based on a measurement of acceptable risk. A solution may be secure enough for a home user but considered insecure for corporate or government environments.

Many people confuse security with the similar term "robustness." In general, a *robust system* may not be secure—a robust system may not lose data, but attackers may still compromise the system. In contrast, a *secure system* implies robustness because data is protected from attackers, processes, and innocent mistakes.

1.1.4 Compromise Response

Network security includes three critical elements: prevention, detection, and response. The combination of these elements determines the overall effectiveness of a system's security.

1.1.4.1 Prevention

Prevention addresses the steps taken to deter an attacker or mitigate a system compromise. These measures range from the physical network architecture, firewall elements, and antivirus systems, to system hardening and user education. An environment that relies solely on preventative measures may be difficult to compromise, but the impact from a compromise may be extreme. A common example is a home computer that strictly relies on an antivirus system for protection. Most antivirus systems use signatures to identify known viruses, but these signatures

1.2.1.1 Internal Attacker Motivation

Hostile insiders are usually disgruntled employees or corporate spies. Although occasionally a competitor or organized gang plants an employee into a company, more often the employee is already present and becomes motivated to attack the company from the inside. Although the motivational factors are incident specific, they usually include one of the following:

Personal issues: Personal problems may provide motivation. A disagreement with a boss or coworker, or general frustration, may trigger an attack.

Unfair disadvantage: The employee may feel mistreated by the company and view his insider access as a way to fight back.

Greed: An employee may see value in selling insider access to an interested external party. For example, in 2004, an insider at America Online (AOL) sold 92 million customer e-mail addresses to spammers [Krim2004].

Curiosity: Although not necessarily malicious, the employee's curiosity and exploration of the company's internals may create problems.

Ignorance: The employee may not be aware that specific information should be confidential.

Each of these motivating factors may cause significant damage. Although corporate policies set the groundwork for legal reactions and employee education, they are generally not a deterrent to insiders. For example, an employee that feels mistreated is probably not concerned about being fired. And user education is unlikely to prevent an intern from placing sensitive information in their résumé.

The "No Touch" Audit

In 2005, a large corporation hired an external auditor to scan for networking weaknesses. This style of auditing begins with identifying and mapping the corporate network. Unfortunately, the hiring department was not the same as the computer support division. This developed into an internal department war within the company. The result was an audit restriction: conduct the network survey without touching any system owned by the corporation. This restriction even forbade the auditors from accessing the company's public Web site.

Fortunately for the auditors, the company's employees and business partners leaked a significant amount of public information. Through the use of press releases, public white papers released by the corporation's technology partners, employee online résumés, and postings in public newsgroups, the auditors created a very detailed map of the company's network. The map included the network architecture, router specifications, type and quantity of servers, operating system versions, and specific applications used by the company. Even network policies such as scheduled backups and downtimes were identified. The audit demonstrated the severity of innocent information leaks from insiders: the corporate network was vulnerable.

1.2.1.2 Internal Attacker Damage

The damage caused by insiders can range from theft to vandalism and from information leakage to destruction. Theft and vandalism are generally associated with the corporate catch phrases "we trust people here" and "people get fired for that." But, there is a deeper level of importance. By the time the problem is caught, the damage is done: expensive hardware is missing or destroyed, data and privacy is lost, and time must be spent identifying and recreating damaged information. In the case of industrial espionage, risk assessments must occur, and project goals usually require significant adjustments.

The simplest way to protect against theft and vandalism is to take basic precautions: monitor the systems for abnormal downtime, lock down expensive equipment, place main servers behind locked doors, and use video cameras. Even with these precautions, a determined thief will find a way to access data and hardware. Store valuable data in redundant locations, lock away backup tapes and CD-ROMs, and maintain redundant or compatible equipment as short-term emergency replacements.

Keeping all of this in mind, there are few things that can stop a determined insider with a screwdriver. Detection is as important as prevention, if not more important.

Information leakage and destruction are more difficult to control. Backup and usage policies may limit any long-term impact, but they do not provide short-term solutions. Preventative measures such as access restrictions and internal IDSs limit the overall potential impact. Access restrictions reduce the likelihood of an attack, whereas an internal IDS provides rapid notification of a problem.

The security of the corporation begins with the security of the network. Although not a complete solution, securing the corporate network can mitigate many of the risks posed by insiders. Security options include designing secure solutions, hardening systems and networks, and monitoring for potential risks.

1.2.1.3 External Attacker Motivation

External attackers generally have many more motivating factors than internal attackers. Although external attacks share many of the same motivations as internal attackers, there may be other driving forces:

Political: The attack may be used to make a statement.

Status: An attacker may use the attack as bragging rights or to demonstrate his skills.

Power: An attacker may use the attack to show his technical superiority.

Any list of motivating factors for external attackers is only partial; anything may be a driving factor. In some cases, the attacker may want "a system"—the selection may be arbitrary based on general criteria such as features or accessibility. In other cases, the attack may be specific; the attacker doesn't want *a* system, he wants *your* system.

The primary mitigation options for external attackers revolve around network security. By preventing unauthorized access to network systems, a company can reduce the likelihood of a successful attack. Networks with adequate redundancy and fail-over detection can withstand even large-scale network attacks.

More Power!

The need for computing resources can be a significant driving factor. An attacker may have heard of a new exploit but lack the resources to test the exploit. Without access to the necessary resources, the attacker turns to someone else that has the resources. This type of "show me" attack generally happens shortly after a new exploit is made public.

The infamous distributed denial-of-service (DDoS), where many computers attack a single computer on the network, was likely developed by rival users in online chat rooms (IRC—Internet relay chat). The motivation is direct: more computers yield more resources for the attack. In February 2001, a 15-year-old Canadian called "Mafiaboy" conducted DDoS attacks against online powerhouses including Yahoo!, eBay, Amazon, CNN, ZDNet, and e*trade.

Although exploits and network attacks are generally malicious, resources may also serve nonmalicious purposes. For example, in 1998, William Aaron Blosser used spare computer cycles at US West to compute prime numbers [Blosser1998]. Although not malicious, this did result in an abuse of network resources.

1.2.1.4 Bridging Internal and External Attackers

In some cases, external attackers solicit information or access from internal sources. When this partnership happens, the result can be disastrous. In May 2005, insiders at Bank of America and Sumimoto Bank assisted external attackers in compromising bank accounts and stealing money. Bank of America identified 670,000 compromised bank accounts [Reconnex2005], and the thieves stole £220 million from Sumitomo Bank [Scott2005].

The combined problem of internal and external attackers can only be mitigated through a combined defense against internal and external attackers. In this situation, the network is one of the few common venues.

1.2.2 Intentional versus Accidental

Although intentional attacks receive significant attention, accidental attacks are very common. Router misconfigurations, system oversights, incompatibility, and human error all add to accidental attacks. Although accidental application problems, such as deleting a critical file (or an entire database) are significant, accidents concerning the network generally impact a wider group. For example, a backhoe may knock out networking access for a neighborhood, or a misconfigured router may create a routing loop, congesting a network used by an entire company.

> **An Attack, or an Interesting Event?**
> Most users dread system attacks, whereas most system administrators generally overlook "interesting events." So how can someone distinguish an attack from an innocent event or user error? A good rule of thumb is "if it happens once, it's a fluke; if it happens twice, it's a coincidence; if it happens three times, it's an attack." This means, for example, a problematic application that generates one error, one time is not an attack. But, if this same application causes the same problem many times, then it is a threat to the system's security.

1.3 CONCEPTS

Five basic concepts form the foundation of risk management: confidentiality, authentication, authorization, integrity, and repudiation. A system can be strong in one area and weak in another, which leads to a potential vulnerability. For example, bank ATM systems use PIN numbers to identify customers and grant access. Although the PIN supplies authorization, it may not supply integrity (the PIN may be stolen) or confidentiality (anyone can see you at the ATM).

1.3.1 Confidentiality and Privacy

Confidentiality is the ability to operate in private. Systems that provide confidentiality mitigate the risks from an eavesdropper or attacker. The level of required confidentiality varies with needs of an environment. For example, email is transmitted in plain text. Any person that can intercept the email may read it, including mail relay systems. An encrypted email ensures that the content cannot be read, but the sender and recipient may still be disclosed; at minimum, an attacker can see that an email was sent. By embedding a hidden message within an email (steganography) or generating many fake emails (chaffing), a sender may lower the likelihood of an attacker identifying the communication and ensure a higher degree of privacy.

1.3.2 Authentication

Authentication permits one system to determine the origin of another system. This becomes essential in an online community, where two systems are usually not directly connected. Anyone can attempt to impersonate anyone else. Authentication systems provide a means to identify a system or data as authentic.

1.3.3 Authorization and Access Control

Not everyone (nor everything) is equal. Based on authentication, systems, processes, and users are offered different levels of access. *Authorization* is the level of access control that is permitted. For example, anyone may dial a phone number to an office building—there is no access control restricting who may dial. But not everyone may enter the building—access is restricted to authorized staff, and the authorization is based on an ID, badge, or key authentication.

1.3.4 Integrity

When transmitting information, a recipient should be able to validate that the information was not modified in transit. Information tampering or modification changes the *integrity* of the information. A system with a high degree of integrity should be difficult to tamper.

1.3.5 Nonrepudiation

Authentication ensures that the sender is who he says he is. Integrity ensures that a message is not tampered with. But what links the message to the originator? The ability to *repute*, or deny, originating a message is key to security. If an attacker falsifies a document, the forged originator should be able to repute the document. *Nonrepudiation* ensures that an originator cannot falsely repute information. A system that includes authentication, integrity, and nonrepudiation should be able to detect tampered information and prevent valid information from being falsely rejected.

1.4 COMMON MITIGATION METHODS

Regardless of the environment—hardware, software, network, and physical—there are a few basic approaches for mitigating security risks. These general approaches work by proactively limiting the impact from a security breach.

1.4.1 Compartmentalize

Despite our best efforts, systems have bugs. Although these unplanned limitations can impact functionality, large multifunctional systems are more prone to problems. In particular, a flaw in a multifunctional system likely impacts the entire system. For example, a stereo with a built-in CD player may not work if either the stereo or CD player breaks. Similarly, an all-in-one network device that includes a firewall, virus scanner, and IDS may perform none of these tasks if one of these functions is misconfigured or vulnerable to an exploit.

The simplest way to mitigate the risk from a multifunction system failure is to separate out the functionality. Tasks and functions are divided into units containing limited functionality. These units can then be integrated into a larger system. Although the failure of one component may reduce the functionality of the larger system, the failure should not negate the functionality from other units; the scope of a failure is limited to the defective unit.

Compartmentalized functionality has an additional benefit: mix and match. Independent units can be integrated with many other units. With multifunction systems, components are tightly integrated—it becomes difficult to use one function independently. A multifunction network device is unlikely to permit using one function (e.g., an integrated virus scanner) with a different product (e.g., an external IDS from a different vendor). Compartmentalized units lead to additional security: a failure by one vendor does not imply insecurity within every unit.

Independent units do have a few limitations. Each independent unit requires its own configuration; there may not be a system for configuring all units at once. Tightly integrated multifunctional systems can be very desirable with respect to maintenance.

1.4.2 Secure Fail

Unexpected events happen, from an intentional attacker to a lightning strike. When a failure occurs, the impacted units should securely fail and not increase the threat level. For example, a firewall that fails should block all access. The alternative, a firewall that fails and permits all traffic, may not be immediately noticed and may allow an attacker inside the network.

1.4.3 Defense-in-Depth

A single security precaution prevents a single attack. Other attack methods may not be prevented and may bypass the security option altogether. More security options and more varieties of security options yield a system that is more difficult to exploit. For example, a castle in Europe may employ a high wall to deter attacks. But they also use other security options: a moat, drawbridge, and portcullis. If attackers still manage to storm the castle, narrow hallways and twisting stairwells provide advantages to defenders.

This same concept, with layers of security providing *defense-in-depth*, works well for computer networks. A single firewall is good; multiple firewalls are better. Antivirus scanners on computers are good, but also using an antivirus scanner on network traffic and on the email server may prevent widespread outbreaks.

Using tools and services from multiple vendors generally yields more security. For example, a company that only uses Cisco firewalls faces a risk from a Cisco-specific compromise. In contrast, a home user that employs both SMC and Linksys firewalls is unlikely to be breached by a vendor-specific attack. A few companies take variety to an extreme. For example, backups may be stored in triplicate, using three different backup systems on three different computer platforms with three different operating systems. The benefit is critical: a single failure from any one system is not likely to impact the other two systems.

The primary limitations from a defense-in-depth approach are complexity and compatibility. A network with three virus scanners may prevent 99 percent of computer viruses, but the maintenance cost is three times greater. Moreover, the different scanners may be incompatible on the same system.

1.4.4 Security-by-Obscurity

A provably secure solution means that an attacker, knowing all the implementation details, will be unable to realistically bypass a security precaution. Many cryptographic systems fall into this category; an attacker who has the encrypted data and algorithm cannot decrypt the data within a meaningful timeframe. (Given 200 years and 1,000 computers, anything is possible.) In contrast, many security precautions become weaker when implementation details are provided. For example, protecting a wireless network by not telling anyone that it exists is a viable security option as long as nobody discovers the network signal. *Security-by-obscurity* denotes any mechanism that is only secure due to a lack of knowledge.

Security-by-obscurity is a viable addition to defense-in-depth, but it should not be the only line of defense. Examples of commonly practiced security-by-obscurity solutions include password management (don't tell anyone your password) and server details. It is hard enough to compromise a server, but it becomes nearly impossible to compromise a specific system when (1) the type of host is unknown, (2) the location of the host is unknown, and (3) the defenses protecting the host are unknown.

Passwords

Login passwords are an example of security-by-obscurity. Passwords are only effective as long as they remain secret. An ongoing debate concerns the use of passwords. Should passwords be long or short, complicated or simple, static or changed regularly?

Many companies and institutions have strict password policies. These policies include length (e.g., at least eight characters) as well as selection (letters, numbers, no repetition, must include at least one symbol, etc.). Although these passwords are less vulnerable to brute-force guessing and dictionary attacks, they are more likely to be written down or forgotten. The alternative are weak passwords that can be easily remembered but are vulnerable to brute-force guessing.

Whereas many secure organizations require complicated passwords, the banking industry has taken a different tact. Bank account PIN codes are a type of password. PINs rarely change, use a small character set (10 digits: 0 - 9), and usually consist of only 4 characters—a total of 10,000 different combinations. The type and length of a PIN were chosen to reduce the need to write down the combination. Multiple login failures block the account and prevent brute-force attacks, and the main security comes from the bank's closed network—preventing access to the password file.

1.4.5 Security and Usability

There is a common misconception within the software development community of a tradeoff between security and usability: the more secure the system, the less usable it becomes. Actually, this is only true in extreme cases. For example, most software exploits today rely on buffer overflows and unvalidated parameters. Correcting an overflow condition and validating parameters does not impact the usability, but does improve the system's security. In the case of network security, a home user that does not run any external network servers will not be impacted by a firewall that blocks remote users from accessing the system. A corporate server is no less usable if the system is hardened, with all unnecessary services and applications disabled.

In extreme cases, there are usability tradeoffs. For example, systems that require multiple authentication tokens (besides a username and password) may be difficult to use. And a firewall that constantly prompts for user confirmation is likely a bigger annoyance than a security measure. In general, these issues are due to implementation and design faults, rather than security theory.

Usability does not strictly refer to restrictive functionality. Usability includes cost and performance. A secure solution that costs more than the data it protects is likely restrictive—most home users will not pay $10,000 for a firewall that protects a $1,000 computer. Similarly, a mitigation option that severely impacts performance may not be a viable option. Encrypted tunnel technologies may provide a secure network connection, but the overhead of the encryption may make some protocols, such as H.323 video conferencing, sluggish to the point of being unusable.

1.5 PEOPLE AND STAFF

People respond to security threats. The quality, reliability, and experience of the people defending the network directly reflect the security of the network. The primary concern becomes determining whom to trust. Between access and potential damage, insiders always pose the biggest risk. Selecting system administrators, network administrators, audit managers, and response personnel is much more important than the type of networking hardware. The main criteria for selecting dependable personnel are education, experience, and track record.

1.5.1 Education

U.S. News and World Report publishes annual rankings of schools, segmented by majors. In 1999, only 4 of the top 10 schools offered courses in computer security (Table 1.1). The remaining schools included aspects of security in specific nonsecurity courses. For example, a course in database may have a section on database security.

Before 2001, few schools offered courses specifically on computer security. People with degrees in computer science are unlikely to have security-specific degrees. In contrast, today there are formal college degrees such as Masters in Information Assurance and Masters in Information Security. Although many companies provide short seminars on security, these are not a replacement for a comprehensive education. Moreover, smaller companies may not have the resources to provide short security seminars or classes.

Due to the newness of these courses and degrees, experienced security personnel are unlikely to have these credentials. Most security experts have strong backgrounds in software development, networking, quality assurance, and system administration. Their security expertise comes through experience.

TABLE 1.1   Computer Security Courses Taught in Top U.S. Computer Science Programs

University	Total Computer Courses	Computer Security Courses	Security Course Level	"Security" Mentioned in Other Course Descriptions
Massachusetts Institute of Technology	176**	1	U	2
Stanford University	168	2	U	0
University of Illinois, Urbana-Champaign	99	0	--	4
University of Washington	89	0	--	2
Carnegie Mellon University	81	0	--	3
University of California, Berkeley	73	1	G	2
Cornell University	66	0	--	2
University of Texas, Austin	60	0	--	1
Princeton University	58	1	U	2
University of Michigan, Ann Arbor	56	0	--	2

Programs ranked by *U.S. News and World Report*, (1999); class information as listed on university Web sites, course catalogs, and syllabuses. ** Includes computer science and electrical engineering courses. U=undergraduate G=graduate

1.5.2 Experience

Although education provides the theoretical tools needed to understand and address security needs, experience shows the ability to apply the knowledge. A computer security major with a degree but no experience is unlikely to be as effective as a mathematics major with more than a decade of experience.

Successful attackers rarely work alone. They operate in groups, communicating ideas and solving problems as a team. When problems arise, attackers readily consult other people for insight. Similarly, defenders should not work alone. Security personnel should have a strong track record of working within a group, both as a follower and as a team leader.

1.5.3 Track Record

Trust between team members is essential. People with a history of loyalty and professionalism make better security staff members than people with a history of outbursts or unethical behavior.

A common topic of debate within the security community centers around *reformed hackers*—people convicted of computer crimes who have changed their ways and want to assist in protecting systems. The main issue is risk: a convicted felon with a continuous history of deceitful practices is less likely to be loyal and trustworthy than someone who has never shown unethical behavior. A convicted attacker may have detailed knowledge of attack methods, but the conviction shows a grievous lapse in ethical judgment. Moreover, the ability to attack a system does not imply knowledge regarding the defense of a system. Attacking a system requires a different skill set from system defense. Education, experience, and track record are independent factors that lead to the overall security aptitude of a staff member.

A simple check for a criminal history, strong credit rating, and strong references can provide insight into trustworthiness. Even without a criminal record, people who are regularly criticized for improper behavior are usually less desirable.

1.6 CERTIFICATIONS

Detailed background checks are not always a viable option; education, experience, and track records are not always easy to verify. Certification programs provide a general skill set baseline and a superficial assessment of a candidate's knowledge level. Ongoing maintenance of a certification shows a commitment level.

Although there are literally hundreds of security certifications, the majority is vendor- or product-specific. For example, the MSCE—Microsoft Certified Engineer—provides a minimum level of familiarity with Microsoft platforms. But MSCE knowledge may not translate into general, operating system independent knowledge, nor does certification imply experience. Apple, IBM, Microsoft, Cisco, Avaya, and most other major technology companies provide vendor-specific certifications. These certifications primarily focus on vendor-specific solutions and do not imply general security knowledge. Vendor-specific certifications are desirable when seeking a vendor-specific solution.

Vendor-neutral certifications are designed to measure general concepts, rather than vendor-specific products. A person with a vendor-neutral security certification may understand basic security principles but not how to apply them in a Cisco, Apple, or other vendor-specific environment. In general, vendor-neutral certifications are more desirable because few principles change under specific vendor platforms.

Computer security certifications are relatively new. More than 30 different vendor-neutral certification programs are available. As these programs evolve, some are expected to become obsolete, others will fill niches, and a few will rise to dominate the certification landscape. Out of the 30 vendor-neutral certification programs, 6 commercial programs appear to be more desirable than all others: CISSP, SSCP, GIAC, CISA, CISM, and Security+ certifications (Table 1.2) [VanAuken2005]. Each of these programs requires some type of examination and registration fee. Whereas a few require projects or a demonstration of knowledge application, most only use multiple-choice questions. Many of these programs require experience prior to the examination and an agreement to abide by a specific code of ethics (Table 1.3). Just as each certification has different requirements and covers different aspects of computer security, renewal requirements vary dramatically (Table 1.4). Certifications may require annual or bi-annual renewal fees, exams, or security-related continuing education.

TABLE 1.2   Common Types of Security Certifications

Certification:	CISSP	SSCP	GIAC	CISA	CISM	Security+
Name:	Certified Information Systems Security Professional	Systems Security Certified Professional	Global Information Assurance Certification	Certified Information Security Auditor	Certified Information Security Manager	Security+I
Organization:	International Information Systems Security Certification Consortiium (ISC)²	International Information Systems Security Certification Consortiium (ISC)²	SANS Institute	Information Systems Audit and Control Association (ISACA)	Information Systems Audit and Control Association (ISACA)	Computing Technology Industry Association (CompTIA)
Certifies:	Knowledge of international standards for information security. Covers 10 areas of knowledge.	Knowledge of information security policies, standards, and procedures.	Knowledge of information security policies, standards, and procedures.	Information systems auditing, control and security knowledge.	Architect, manage and assess information security projects.	Security-related skills.

1.6.1 CISSP AND SSCP

The International Information Systems Security Certification Consortium, Inc., or (ISC)², offers two certifications: the Certified Information Systems Security Professional (CISSP), and the Systems Security Certified Professional (SSCP). The CISSP covers the widest scope, testing knowledge across 10 different areas of computer security:

- Access control systems and methodology
- Applications and systems development

TABLE 1.3   Security Certification Examination Requirements

Requirements:	CISSP	SSCP	GIAC	CISA	CISM	Security+
Code of Ethics:	Yes	Yes	No	Yes	Yes	No
Exam Type:	1 exam, 250 multiple choice	1 exam, 125 multiple choice	1 practical, 2 online	1 exam, 200 multiple choice	1 exam, 200 multiple choice	1 exam, 100 questions
Required Relevant Experience:	4 years	1 year	None	5 years	5 years including 3 years in at least 3 areas of security management	None
Other:	College degree can substitute for experience	None	Courses offered to supplement exams	College credit can subsistute for experience	College credit can substitute for experience	Network+ certification and 2 years experience recommended

TABLE 1.4   Security Certification Renewal Requirements

Renewal:	CISSP	SSCP	GIAC	CISA	CISM	Security+
Fee:	Annual	Annual	Every 2 years	Annual	Annual	None
Renewal Exam:	Exam every 3 years	Exam every 3 years	Every 2 years	Annual	Annual	None
Renewal Exam Type:	1 exam, 250 multiple choice	None	Refresher exam required	None	None	None
Continuing Education:	20 Continuing Professional Education credits	60 Continuing Professional Education credits	None	20 hours per year; 120 hours in 3 years	20 hours per year; 120 hours in 3 years	None
Other:	Must be in good standing	None	Renewal includes revised coursework	Certifications periodically audited by ISACA	Certifications periodically audited by ISACA	None

- Business continuity planning
- Cryptography
- Law, investigation, and ethics
- Operations security
- Physical security
- Security architecture and models
- Security management practices
- Telecommunications and networking

To achieve CISSP certification, an applicant must agree to a code of ethics, have a minimum of 4 years of computer security experience, and pass a 250-question multiple-choice exam. College degrees are acceptable in lieu of some experience.

The CISSP also includes three focused certifications, the Information Systems Security Engineering Professional (ISSEP), Information Systems Security Architecture Professional (ISSAP), and Information Systems Security Management Professional (ISSMP). Someone with a CISSP may also test for these certifications.

The CISSP requires an annual renewal and, every three years, a renewal exam. In addition to the renewal fees and exams, the CISSP requires continuing education credits. These credits indicate continuous exposure and education in the computer security field.

The SSCP is a lighter offering of the CISSP, covering only seven areas:

- Access control
- Administration
- Audit and monitoring
- Cryptography
- Data communications
- Malicious code and malware
- Risk, response, and recovery

In addition, the SSCP only requires 125 questions and 1 year of experience. As with the CISSP, the SSCP requires a renewal exam every 3 years and continuing education.

1.6.2 GIAC

The SANS Institute offers a suite of Global Information Assurance Certification (GIAC) programs. Each GIAC program covers one area of computer security. For example, there is a GIAC Certified Firewall Analyst, GIAC Certified Intrusion Analyst, and GIAC Web Application Security. Some GIAC programs are vendor-specific, such as the GIAC Securing Oracle and GIAC .Net, but most are intended to be vendor-neutral.

Unlike the CISSP and SSCP, the GIAC does not require a code of ethics or previous experience—although passing the exams without experience may prove difficult—and no continuing education experience is required to renew. But the GIAC does include some unique offerings. To become GIAC certified, an applicant must pass a practical exam, where the knowledge is applied. In addition, the GIAC requires a renewal exam every two years.

1.6.3 CISA and CISM

The Information Systems Audit and Control Association (ISACA) offers two certifications: the Certified Information Security Auditor (CISA) and Certified Information Security Manager (CISM). The former covers system auditing, control, and security knowledge, whereas the latter addresses architecture, management, and security project assessment. Unlike the CISSP and SSCP, the CISA and CISM are not directly related. The CISA is intended for auditors and administrators, and the CISM is directed toward managers.

Both the CISA and CISM have similar requirements. Both include a code of ethics, 200 multiple-choice questions, and 5 years of experience. College credits are an acceptable substitute for some of the experience requirement. Although neither requires a renewal exam, both require a minimum of 20 continuing education or application hours per year, with no less than 120 hours in any 3-year period. ISACA enforces this requirement with random audits of certified members.

1.6.4 Security+

Of the rising security certifications, the Computing Technology Industry Association (CompTIA)'s Security+ certification appears weakest. The Security+ exam covers a wide range of topics, including communication security, infrastructure security, cryptography, access control, authentication, external attacks, and operational security. Although no experience is required, CompTIA strongly recommends 2 years experience and the CompTIA Network+ certification.

The weakest aspect of the Security+ certification is the lack of a renewal requirement. No retesting of knowledge and no continuing education is required (but no renewal fee either).

1.6.5 Certification Weaknesses

Certifications provide a baseline for expected knowledge level and experience, but certifications do not necessarily guarantee the minimal qualifications. Issues such as substituting college credits for experience, purchasing continuing education credits, and conflicting codes of ethics lead to an uneven quality among certified individuals.

1.6.5.1 College Experience

Many certification programs permit the exchange of college credits or degrees in lieu of experience. But not all colleges are accredited, and not all degrees are the same; some degrees have more value. For example, most junior colleges do not offer the same educational scope as an Ivy League degree. Similarly, transfer students know that college credits from one institution may not be transferable to another institution. Yet, for certifications, nearly all credits are treated as equal. With few exceptions, all college credits or degrees in the computer security field are acceptable. Ironically, although educational degrees are acceptable in lieu of experience, most certifications do not accept other certifications as substitutes for experience.

1.6.5.2 Cost of Certifications

Certification programs, such as the CISSP, SSCP, CISA, and CISM, require continuing education credits. The continuing professional education (CPE) credits, or continuing educational units (CEU), roughly translate into hours of service. Many lectures and seminars can be counted as credits. Although these events expose an individual to new knowledge, few actually require interaction or test the knowledge. Furthermore, most of these seminars are not free, with costs ranging from $5 to more than $2,000. An unscrupulous individual can simply buy continuing education hours.

Many professional organizations support certifications and assist their members in acquiring CPE credits. For example, the International Information Systems Forensics Association (IISFA, *http://www.infoforensics.org/*) and Information Systems Security Association (ISSA, *http://issa.org/*) offer CPE credit toward CISSP and SSCP certifications. Members may acquire credits by attending chapter meetings and presentations or by holding board positions. Most of the monthly ISSA chapter meetings are free for members, under $25 for nonmembers, and provide up to three CPE units per meeting (one unit per meeting is common). A person that joins two organizations and attends meetings can cover most of their CPE needs.

1.6.5.3 Uneven Continuing Education

The quality of security-oriented presentations varies. Many small seminars are by vendors, providing credit hours toward certification renewal with vendor-specific solutions. Yet cutting-edge and informative presentations at well-respected conferences do not necessarily count toward continuing education. Although hands-on workshops at these professional conferences offer credit hours, conference presentations do not usually count toward certification renewal.

As an example, the Black Hat Briefings (*http://www.blackhat.com/*) is a well-respected security conference, offering both seminars and workshops on cutting-edge security topics. Defcon, promoted as an "underground hacker conference," is traditionally held immediately after Black Hat. Many of the same speakers present at both conferences. Even though both conferences offer many of the same presentations, in 2005, only Black Hat counted toward CPE credits. This implies that CPE credits relate to the forum and not the content.

1.6.5.4 Breach of Ethics

(ISC)^2, ISACA, and other organizations require adherence to a code of ethics. Although the code of ethics suggests a level of professional responsibility, certifying organizations find it difficult to enforce or validate compliance. Breaching the code of ethics will not trouble an unethical individual, and an ethical individual probably does not need the code anyway.

Required code of ethics may lead to conflicts with corporate policies. For example, the CISSP must agree to "Protect society, the commonwealth, and the infrastructure" [CISSP2005]. Releasing information concerning a critical exploit may aid society, the commonwealth, and the infrastructure, but if it goes against a corporate decision, it may have legal ramifications. Employees with CISSP certifications may face a choice between their jobs and their certifications.

Some codes of ethics also include demands for preferential treatment. For example, the (ISC)^2 code of ethics says, "All other things equal, prefer those who are certified and who adhere to these canons" [CISSP2005]. This implies that, given two equally qualified candidates, a CISSP or SSCP must be chosen over a noncertified, CISA, GIAC, or other-certified person. This appears to contradict with another (ISC)^2 ethical requirement, "Treat all constituents fairly."

1.6.5.5 Validating Certification

Anyone can claim to hold a certification. As such, an employer needs a means to validate the certification. Few organizations provide easy access to certification validation, and many certification lookup services only provide a name and city. If an applicant resides in a large city and has a common name, such as "John Smith," then validating the credential may be difficult.

Although it is important to verify certifications, it is critical to know that a certification has been revoked. An individual whose certification has been revoked is not only uncertified but explicitly unqualified for certification. Revocation may occur due to breaching a required code of ethics, cheating on tests, or falsifying CPE units. Unfortunately, most organizations only provide methods to validate a claimed certification and not a method to identify revoked certifications. In addition, "expired" and "revoked" may be indistinguishable.

1.6.5.6 Comparing Certifications

Colleges and universities strive to maintain accreditation in their educational programs. All degrees from accredited schools and programs are comparable because they all provide the same baseline requirements. In contrast, no two certifications are equivalent; a CISSP is not the same as a CISA. Different certifications cover different core elements. Due to the uneven nature, certifications should be desirable, but not required. When comparing candidates, employers should only consider certifications when all experience and education are equivalent.

SUMMARY

Network security is the application of security concepts toward the networking infrastructure. This includes understanding the applicable threat models, mitigation methods, and concepts. In physical security, an attacker requires physical access; application security is generally limited to the application or operating system. In contrast, network security focuses on intersystem dependencies and communications, and a network attacker is usually located remotely.

The ability to identify potential threats, apply practical mitigation options, and react to attacks depends on the detailed knowledge of networking risks and solutions. This book describes basic networking concepts from a security orientation.

Security administrators and related personnel must identify, analyze, and mitigate network security risks. The quality of these people directly leads toward the ability to address these needs. Education, experience, and a positive track record are core attributes for qualified staff. Computer security certification programs provide a baseline for identifying qualified personnel.

REVIEW QUESTIONS

1. Name three critical elements for mitigating security risks.
2. Which is a more costly threat, internal or external attackers?
3. What are the five foundation concepts for security?
4. What is defense-in-depth?
5. What are some criteria for selecting dependable security personnel?

DISCUSSION TOPICS

1. Define security, network security, and risk management.
2. Describe a recent vulnerability. Identify the threat, exploit, primary target(s), and any secondary targets.
3. Describe a recent network compromise. Speculate on the attacker(s) and possible motivations.
4. Compare benefits and limitations of applying security-by-obscurity.
5. Choose a certification program not described in this chapter. Compare and contrast the offerings with the CISSP, CISA, CISM, and GIAC.

ADDITIONAL RESOURCES

Many resources are available for both general security guidelines as well as specific security implementations. The Open Web Application Security Project (*http://www.owasp.org/*) provides many white papers on effective security guidelines. Similar resources are available from the Internet Storm Center (*http://isc.sans.org/*) and Computer Emergency Response Team (CERT) (*http://www.cert.org/*). Many countries operate their own CERT branches, such as the United States (*http://www.us-cert.gov/*) and Australia (*http://www.auscert.org.au/*). The Black Hat Briefings (*http://www.blackhat.com/*) and Defcon conference (*http://www.defcon.org/*) make past presentations publicly available.

Security bulletins are available from CERT, as well as cutting-edge forums such as Security Focus' Bugtraq (*http://www.securityfocus.com/*) and the Full Disclosure mailing list (*http://lists.grok.org.uk/full-disclosure-charter.html*). Bugtraq and Full Disclosure discuss some of the most recent developments in computer security.

With the hundreds of certifications available, it can be difficult to tell one from another. A few online sites provide lists of vendor-specific and vendor-neutral certifications. One example is CertCities (*http://certcities.com/certs/other/default.asp*). They provide a list of more than 100 certifications as well as program details.

Besides the certifications from organizations such as SANS Institute, (ISC)^2, and ISACA, there are also security certifications for the government sector. For example, the Committee on National Security Systems (CNSS) at the U.S. National Security Agency offers a set of information assurance training courses and certifications. CNSSI 4013 is designed for system administrators, whereas CNSSI 4014 is for information systems security officers.

2 Ethics

In This Chapter

- Ethical Training
- Ethical, Social, and Legal Considerations
- Intellectual Property
- Computer Crimes

Every field has a sense of right and wrong—behaviors that are considered acceptable and unacceptable by peers and associates. Long-established fields, such as the legal and medical professions, have extensive written guidelines for appropriate behavior, which newer fields such as computer science lack.

Discussions concerning computer ethics are a relatively new development within computer science. Although it may be technically possible to crack an encryption, hijack a network, or disable a host, it may not be ethical, moral, or legal. Teaching computer security is a complicated task. Even though it is desirable to educate the good guys, there is concern that bad guys may learn a new attack method, or worse, a good guy may become a bad guy. Understanding acceptable behavior requires knowledge of ethical, social, and legal values as well as the consequences of inappropriate actions.

2.1 ETHICAL TRAINING

Morals are a sense of right and wrong. The application of moral guidance is situation dependent and develops over time. Without proper guidance, a person may develop a set of morals that significantly differs from those accepted by society.

Conveying a sense of right and wrong is just as important as transferring technical knowledge. Computer security teaches how to both attack and defend a network. Without the correct moral guidance and training, someone with the technical knowledge may develop questionable morals.

In 1985, the Association for Computing Machinery held a panel on hacking [Harvey1985] and discussed moral implications. They compared computer security training to a martial art. Brian Harvey addressed the core concern as a question of training: "Skill in Karate is a deadly weapon; to give that weapon to a young person is an affirmation of trust rather than suspicion. Why do Karate classes for kids work? Why don't they lead to an epidemic of juvenile murders?" The rationale is based on moral direction, set by a combination of discipline, access to power, apprenticeship, and experimentation.

2.1.1 Discipline

Within karate, both the beginner and expert adhere to rules of etiquette and ethics. The same rules are applied to both people, regardless of skill level. As a result, beginners do not feel unfairly restricted by a set of arbitrary rules. The master conveys ethical behavior by direct teaching and by example.

In contrast, computer knowledge is commonly learned through independent study. Individuals frequently learn skills in isolation or through brief interactions. Few computer professionals begin their knowledge with long-term assistance from a master. Instead, ethical behavior is amended to existing knowledge through advanced education programs and long-term associations with experts who display acceptable behavior.

The risk of a computer security expert with questionable morals can be mitigated through support from society, academics, and corporate leadership. Security professionals should be encouraged to develop long-term associations with respected experts. Similarly, experts should reach out as mentors for beginners.

Ph34r My Fu!

In 1985, Brian Harvey wrote a paper for the ACM suggesting that computer security should be taught similar to a martial art [Harvey1985]. In martial arts, the master educates the student by example without placing the student in a harmful situation or allowing the student to harm himself (or anyone else).

Harvey's analogy used Karate as an example, but the example changed over time. By 1987, analogies began to use Karate, Judo, Tae Kwon Do, and other martial arts. Internet users eventually adopted Kung Fu as the preferred analogy. It was later shortened to "Fu" and used to imply skill with computers.

Although some accounts of this etymology refer to David Carradine's TV series, "Kung Fu" (1972-1975), the popular "elite hacker" phrases such as "fear my fu" (ph34r my fu) and "my fu is stronger" did not surface until the early 1990s, after Harvey's paper. Ironically, many people who use "fu" to describe technical competence lack formal training and discipline.

2.1.2 Access and Power

Reading is not the same as doing. A person who reads about airplanes is not qualified to fly an airplane. Similarly, someone who only hears about computer security is not a trained security professional. Skill requires experience, and experience requires direct access to powerful tools. Computer security tools are neither good nor evil—they are tools. Just as a hammer can be used to build a home or cause bodily harm, a packet sniffer can be used to diagnose a network problem or compromise network connections. Ethical usage of the tool depends on the person and situation.

That Depends

Lawyers rarely give direct answers. Anyone who has asked for legal advice has likely heard the phrase "that depends." Legality and ethics depend on the situation, interpretation, and established history, which is also true in network security.

For example, a *packet sniffer* is a common security tool for capturing network traffic for analysis. The traffic may include passwords, private email messages, and other personal information. Most packet sniffers require little skill to operate. In essence, anyone can run a packet sniffer. But whether running a packet filter is illegal, socially unacceptable, or unethical depends on the situation. For example, if the sniffer is used "just for fun," then the behavior may be questionable—how will the collected information be used? In contrast, if a manager asks an employee to run the sniffer, then it may be socially or legally acceptable, but it can still be unethical. What if the data is used to determine whether someone should be fired? This is a different situation than determining whether a network is vulnerable to weak passwords or has been infected with a virus.

2.1.3 Apprenticeship and Experimentation

Mentors allow an individual to learn computer security and ethical behavior. A person who only learns security gains the skills without the moral values. Independent learning may also not grant exposure to uncommon or difficult problems—untrained security personnel may be unprepared for real-world situations.

Learning computer security means defending and exploiting technology, but hands-on learning should be performed in a safe environment. As an analogy, most major cities offer skateboard parks as a safe environment for skateboarders. They may perform extreme stunts without breaking laws or injuring others. Similarly, network security training requires an isolated network where exploits can be tested without causing damage outside the test bed. Without a safe environment, students may hone their skills on unsuspecting victims. An ideal environment includes a variety of network devices, operating systems, and configurations that are intended to provide a range of attack vectors and defense options.

2.1.4 Professions

Professions such as medical doctors, attorneys, accountants, and librarians have many similarities. Each of these fields includes formal associations, specific areas of influence, and professional training requirements. Yet, these occupations have clear distinctions from the field of computer science.

2.1.4.1 Formal Associations

Trained professional occupations are usually associated with well-defined associations. For example, lawyers report to specific state bar associations or national groups such as the American Bar Association or the Italian Ordine degli Avvocati e Procuaratori di Milano.

Professional organizations define standards of conduct for members and provide a central point for reporting breaches of ethics. A lawyer who is not a member of the bar is deemed a questionable lawyer, and some states require bar membership in order to practice law.

In contrast, there is no centrally required association for computer science. Although the Association for Computer Machinery (ACM) and Institute of Electrical and Electronic Engineering (IEEE) are available, people operating in the profession do not need to be members; lacking a membership is rarely a deterrent to employment. As mentioned in Chapter 1, formal certification programs for computer security are just developing and lack consistency, membership enforcement, and an established level of respect. There are also no clearly defined niche organizations. The specialty field of "computer security" is covered by hundreds of known (and lesser-known) associations.

2.1.4.2 Area of Influence

Most professional occupations focus on one area of study. For example, the American Medical Association (AMA) covers "medical" for physicians. Although the AMA may provide legal advice to members, it does not provide membership to lawyers, accountants, or auto mechanics. More specialized organizations focus on members with associated specialties—a geriatric cardiologist is unlikely to be a member of the American Academy of Pediatrics.

Computer science and security organizations lack focus. The CISSP certification (Chapter 1) is awarded to anyone who passes the exam, regardless of profession. A physician who also manages his clinic's network is as qualified as a software quality assurance specialist. Without a clearly defined focus, the field becomes contaminated by outside influences. A single guiding standard of conduct becomes impractical.

2.1.4.3 Professional Training

Most professional occupations require formal training. Physicians, attorneys, and accountants undergo years of formal schooling before being awarded certifications. Few of these professionals learned their skills in isolation. Along with learning necessary skills, these professionals also learn ethics. People who clearly display unacceptable behavior do not complete the training.

Computer science, including networking and security, is unlike other professions. The skills needed for these occupations are commonly self-taught. Computer professionals regularly boast about how young they were when they started or reminisce about their first computers. Whereas surgeons rarely boast about carving poultry when they were 12, computer programmers who were programming at an early age wear it as a badge of honor. Unfortunately, self-training teaches skills but not ethics.

Formal college education, regardless of the field of study, provides an ethical basis. Plagiarism, fraud, and illegal activities are unacceptable by all majors. As a result, people with advanced educations display positive social values and are incarcerated less often [Karpowitz2004]. In the computer field, people lacking college degrees have committed the most notorious exploits; Kevin Mitnick, Kevin Poulsen, Adrian Lamo, Jonathan James, MafiaBoy (real name withheld due to age), and Mark Abene are notable examples [Wikipedia2006a]. A formal education is not required to use a computer, develop software, or exploit vulnerabilities. This makes the field prone to a wide range of skills and moral values.

2.2 ETHICAL, SOCIAL, AND LEGAL CONSIDERATIONS

Moral values combine three decision attributes: ethical, social, and legal. Each of these attributes is distinct but interdependent.

The term *ethics* refers to a sense of honesty and dishonesty. These are individual values; actions that are ethical to one person may be unethical to another. Ethical actions are situation dependent. Scanning a network or capturing packets may be considered ethical in one situation but undesirable in another.

Groups of people with similar ethics develop a moral code. Peer groups and organizations may have *social values* that determine appropriate behavior. Acceptable social values may vary between groups, regions, and cultures. For example, colleges may teach students how to write computer viruses and analyze malware. Although writing viruses is an acceptable behavior within this forum, there is no consensus among the wider group of Internet users, and some security experts consider it to be an unacceptable practice [Hulme2003].

Legal restrictions are developed for one of three purposes. If there is no consensus for social values, then laws can be created to provide interpretation. Laws can also be used to specify consequences for unacceptable behavior. For example, digital trespassing is a felony in the United States with a punishment ranging from a fine to incarceration. Finally, laws can be used to impose a minority opinion or competitive edge.

Although they are closely related, there is a distinction between ethical, social, and legal values. Not every unethical action is illegal, and not every legal action is socially acceptable. Each is dependent on the situation. By understanding the ethical, social, and legal implications, decisions can be made that mitigate conflict or undesirable consequences.

Hat Trick

In computer security, people commonly refer to hat colors. As with the old Western movies, good guys wear *white hats*, and bad guys wear *black hats*. The distinction between white and black refers more to ethics than skill. People identified as white hats strive to show strong ethical behavior. Their actions are (usually) socially acceptable and legal. In contrast, black hats may ignore ethical, social, or legal values. They may hold different social values, feeling that laws are unjust or that their actions are ethical. The difference between a white hat and a black hat is the morality-based label placed by society.

On occasion, some people are called *gray hats*. These people may perform socially unacceptable or illegal actions while claiming ethical behavior. For example, compromising a bad guy's home computer to disable an attack has the right intent, even if the action is illegal.

2.2.1 Moral Example: Home Computing

In most countries, there is no limitation on what a user can place on his home computer. Just because the software exists, however, does not mean that it should be used.

As an example, Web filters are commonly used to restrict network access. Parents may use them to prevent a child from accessing adult-content Web sites. But filters can also track network access. Using a filter to spy on a spouse's network activities can be an invasion of privacy. Even though it is the same technology, it can be used in acceptable and unacceptable ways.

To elaborate on this example, China has a long history of filtering network access. Although this is the same type of technology used to block a child's access to pornographic Web sites, it is applied to a much larger scale. Many countries outside of China have called this censorship an unacceptable practice; this is a difference in social values. An action considered socially unacceptable to some members of the international community appears acceptable to the Chinese government.

2.2.2 Moral Example: Michael Lynn versus Cisco

When security vulnerabilities are discovered, it is considered socially acceptable to inform the appropriate vendors before any public disclosure. This gives the vendor a chance to respond to risks and develop mitigation options before informing bad guys who would exploit new weaknesses. One debate topic concerns how long to wait before the public disclosure. Some vendors may view a risk as a low priority, have limited resources, or may choose not to address the issue. As a result, going public too soon may pressure the vendor into releasing an incomplete solution, and not going public soon enough may give the bad guys an edge.

In 2005, Michael Lynn was selected as a speaker at the Black Hat Briefings security conference. His topic, "The Holy Grail: Cisco ISO Shellcode and Exploitation Techniques," became a heated controversy. The talk discussed vulnerabilities in Cisco routers that had been reported to the company months earlier. Cisco did not want the information made public, and took steps to prevent the presentation including (1) removing the talk from the printed conference proceedings, and (2) threatening Lynn with legal action.

From an ethical perspective, Michael Lynn appears to have felt that making the exploit public was the right thing to do. Cisco had been nonresponsive toward correcting the problem and was not disclosing the risks to its customers.

Socially, Michael Lynn's actions were met with a favorable reaction from the security community. Although some people disagreed with Lynn's choice of disclosure, Cisco was widely criticized for initiating legal action and failing to respond to security vulnerabilities.

Legally, Lynn walked into a minefield. Cisco and Lynn's employer, Internet Security Systems (ISS), served him with an injunction, preventing further disclosure

[Cisco2005]. To give the presentation, Lynn had to quit his job at ISS. And the Black Hat conference was forbidden from disseminating the presentation materials and associated video.

The line between right and wrong, acceptable and unacceptable is not always clear. And doing what seems like the right thing may still have undesirable results.

2.2.3 Moral Framework

A *moral framework* forms the basis of ethical decision making. By understanding the ethical, social, and legal implications, decisions can be made that reflect positive moral values. Steps can be taken to develop a moral framework [Markkula2006]:

Recognize ethical issues: Problems cannot be addressed until they are first identified. Being able to identify situations with potential ethical, social, and legal implications is critical to making moral decisions.

Gather information: What facts are necessary to create an informed decision? A single decision may impact many different people. Who is likely to be impacted by a decision and how will they be affected? Are there known ramifications or responses to particular actions? Not all information may be present. What information is known to be unavailable?

Test hypothetical decisions: Determine a good solution for the problem and evaluate it for ethical, social, and legal implications. Consider reviewing the decision with peers or trusted colleagues—other people usually offer different opinions and valuable insights. Also consider a wider impact: if the decision were made public, how would the public react?

Implement and reflect: Act on the decision and evaluate the reaction. Did it turn out as expected, or did unidentified issues develop? Given the same circumstances, would the same decisions be made or would the situation be handled differently? Reflection on past decisions is an ongoing process. Some actions may take years for all of the repercussions to be identified.

Knowing how to react to a moral decision, before needing to make a decision, is a critical skill that takes effort and practice. Without this skill, unethical behavior is likely to be repeated.

2.3 INTELLECTUAL PROPERTY

Actions that are right and wrong are not always obvious. Laws can turn an otherwise reasonable decision into an undesirable choice. Intellectual property laws are subtle and can impact network security. The Internet contains a significant amount of information that is readily available. In many situations, it becomes easier to copy and "leverage" existing works rather than re-create technology. This can lead to issues due to copyright, trademark, licensing, and fair use.

2.3.1 Copyright

Most countries support some form of copyright protection. *Copyright* means that the works cannot be used without permission or attribution. In some countries, the works must be labeled with an owners name, copyright symbol (©), date, and a formal notice such as "All rights reserved." In the United States, all created works are automatically copyrighted by the author—even if the works are not explicitly denoted by a copyright notation.

2.3.1.1 Copyright Limitations

Not everything can be copyrighted. Literary works, music, and source code can be protected, but intangible items such as ideas or unrecorded improvisation cannot be copyrighted. Items that are not under copyright protection (or under trademark or license restrictions) are in the *public domain*, and are freely available to anyone.

Copyrights are usually not indefinite. In the United States, works created before 1978 remain under copyright for 50 years after the author's death. (After 1978, copyrights could be renewed for up to 75 years.) [Rosenbaum1994]

2.3.1.2 Open Source and Licensing

There is a large amount of information sharing within the computer community. Open source projects allow other developers to see how specific code functions. Even though code is readily accessible, it may not be public domain.

Software licenses attempt to clarify open source usage and copyright terms. For example, the GNU General Public License (GPL) permits source code to be used as long as all associated source code is publicly accessible. In contrast, the MIT public license does not restrict usage. Software without a declared license cannot be arbitrarily associated with GPL, MIT, or other public license, and unlicensed software still falls under copyright law. In addition, open source software under one license should not be re-licensed without permission. Software marked with as GPL is not supposed to be reclassified under the Mozilla Public License (MPL) without permission from the author.

Open source is not the same as GPL. GPL is a specific open source license, but other licenses exist. Code can be declared as open source without being licensed as GPL.

2.3.2 Fair Use

Whereas copyrights and licensing restrict usage, *fair use* laws (or *fair dealing*) permit use of protected information without infringement. Fair use laws vary between regions and countries, but, in general, they allow copyrighted items to be mentioned in passing; used for nonprofit, educational purposes; or included for parody. For example, a paragraph may be included without permission in another work, but a larger selection may be considered copyright infringement.

Hear No Evil

Simply put, stealing is wrong. Yet people still do it even though they know they should not. Online file sharing is one example of a behavior that breaches copyrights but seems socially acceptable. In 2004, over 85% of teenagers in the United States were aware that books, movies, music, software, and games were protected by some form of copyright. Even so, more than 50% of these same teenagers admitted to downloading these items, and 43% felt that uploading (distributing) copyright materials was okay [Jackson2005].

Illegal file sharing is an example that is legally wrong, yet socially acceptable. Although people know it is wrong, they do it anyway. Socially, illegal file sharing is widely practiced and not affiliated with any stigma. Openly discussing copyright material downloads is acceptable.

Legality is a different issue. Legally, copyright items must be distributed according to their licensing agreements. The Motion Picture Association of America (MPAA) and Recording Industry Association of America (RIAA) have filed lawsuits against more than 17,000 people for illegal file swapping [Borland2005].

Although companies have the right to protect their intellectual property, they do not always do it correctly. Section 512 of the Digital Millennium Copyright Act (DMCA) protects service providers from secondary copyright infringement due to customer actions. If a user puts a music file on a Web site or shares through a peer-to-peer network, the hosting company cannot be held liable for distributing copyright information. Yet between 2002 and 2005, 30% of takedown notices were arguably covered by fair use, and Section 512 protected an additional 50% of copyright violation notifications. Adding to misuse of the DMCA, competitors to copyright holders initiated 57% of takedown notices sent to search engines, such as Google [Urban2005]. This was likely more for stifling competition than protecting copyrights.

2.3.3 Trademark

Trademarks are used to protect product identities. "Microsoft" is a trademarked name. Trademarks deter other companies from impersonating the Microsoft name, logo, or symbol. Having a trademark does not imply uniqueness—other "Microsoft" companies can exist, as long as they do not compete with the existing trademark or cause market confusion.

In the United States, trademarks do not need to be registered, and they are valid as long as they are used. If a trademarked name, logo, or slogan is abandoned, then other people may adopt the name, logo, or slogan. For example, in 2002 NBC used the TV slogan "if you haven't seen it, it's new to you." Because the slogan has not been used for more than two years, it may be considered abandoned. This same logic applies to network technologies. For example, domain names (Chapter 17) may represent trademarks. If a domain name expires, other companies can acquire the domain.

2.3.4 Patents

Patents are used to protect intellectual property such as methods, systems, or processes. They are intended to protect items that are not universal or obvious. Although they do not cover business practices or natural events, they do protect specific solutions. For example, a specific network adaptor may be patented, the name of the adaptor can be trademarked, and the firmware may be copyrighted.

Just as copyrights and trademarks are country specific, patents may need to be registered nationally and internationally. Patents usually last a fixed number of years before the technology enters into the public domain.

Patent pending is a term commonly used to indicate that a patent application has been filed, but it does not provide any protection. The protection only comes when a patent is awarded.

2.3.5 Impact on Network Security

Copyrights, trademarks, and patents can directly impact moral behavior within the fields of networking and security. Most proprietary protocols are protected though copyright and patent laws. Attempts to reverse engineer these technologies for the development of competing products can lead to copyright or patent infringement. Even developing packet sniffers for viewing proprietary protocols can be illegal depending on the development method, labeling, and motivation.

Networking terms can also be trademarked, preventing compatible systems from being given compatible names. For example, "NetMeeting" is a registered trademark of Microsoft, Inc. Other compatible videoconferencing solutions may say that they are "NetMeeting compatible" as long as they identify Microsoft's trademark, but other uses of the term may be prohibited.

Trademarked terms can lead to confusing definitions. For example, SPAM (uppercase) is a registered trademark of Hormel Foods Corporation, but "spam" (lowercase) refers to undesirable email. Whereas spam is widely used to imply something that is undesirable, such as unsolicited email or telemarketing text messages, the exact definition of *undesirable* varies. Simply using a trademarked term incorrectly in a public forum can lead to undesirable consequences.

Licensing restrictions can also impact network security. For example, computer viruses spread rapidly and can impact millions of computers. Antivirus systems can detect and prevent virus infections. Unfortunately, most antivirus solutions are not freely available. Patents, copyrights, and licensing restrictions prevent open distribution of these technologies, allowing computer viruses to spread to unprotected systems.

2.4 COMPUTER CRIMES

Computer security frequently faces ethical, social, and legal challenges. Whereas unethical or socially unacceptable behavior can leave a stigma, legal repercussions can result in stiff penalties.

2.4.1 Motive and Intent

A literal interpretation of the law (the *letter of the law*) is significant for evaluating legality, however, the primary factors in any legal interpretation are motive and intent. Accidentally capturing personal information while debugging a network problem may be argued as acceptable, but threatening to use the information for profit could be interpreted as extortion, digital trespassing, or an invasion of privacy. To defend against potential litigation, intention and motivation should be clearly documented before performing an action. If appropriate authorization cannot be acquired, then the action should not be performed. (Of course, this depends on ethical and social measures of acceptance.)

Besides motive and intent, damages are a significant consideration. Many illegal actions are not prosecuted because damage cannot be quantified or is insubstantial. In addition, court costs may surpass some damages. Just because an action was not prosecuted does not mean it was legally permitted.

2.4.2 Libel and Defamation

It is easy to feel anonymous on the Internet. This can lead to a suspension of ethics, where people do things online that they would normally not do. For example, up to 15% of IT managers view online pornography at work [Websense2004]. This behavior is usually socially unacceptable, so it is done in private and with a sense of anonymity. Similarly, online chat rooms can be very risqué if the members feel anonymous. If the anonymity were removed, the behaviors would likely change.

Online anonymity can also lead to libel. Spreading false information and performing defamation of character attacks is easy when there is little threat of being caught. Because the risk of discovery is low, people appear willing to forgo ethical, social, and legally acceptable behavior. For example, in 2005, the online encyclopedia, Wikipedia, was found to contain a false biography [Seigenthaler2005]. The biography of John Seigenthaler, Sr. included false information that was added as a "gag." Yet Brian Chase, the author of the gag, did not come forward until an online sleuth tracked him down [Page2005]. Chase would probably not have edited the Wikipedia entry if he were not anonymous.

Moral Responsibility

In 2005, Brian Chase modified the online encyclopedia, Wikipedia, to contain false information for the biography of John Seigenthaler, Sr. [Wikipedia2006]. Newspapers and TV quickly picked up this inaccuracy. One paper, *The Register*, wrote a scathing review of Wikipedia titled, "There's no Wikipedia entry for 'moral responsibility'" [Orlowski2005]. Being a dynamic online resource, the open source community quickly added an entry for "moral responsibility" to the Wikipedia. Ironically, the content for "moral responsibility" was copy from copyrighted information. It only took a few hours for the Wikipedia operators to identify the plagiarism, block the entry (Figure 2.1), and replace the text with a viable alternate definition.

2.4.3 Forgery and Impersonation

Along with anonymity comes impersonation. Many network protocols, including SMTP, NNTP, chat rooms (IRC, instant messaging), and Web forums (e.g., blogs), assume that people are honest about their identities. Yet, in many cases, it is easy to select an alternate name, age, or even gender. Not only can fictitious identities be developed, but real identities can also be impersonated. Although the technology may permit false and impersonated information, this behavior is generally considered unacceptable.

FIGURE 2.1 The Wikipedia definition for "moral responsibility" declaring copyright infringement [Wikipedia2005]. This figure is Copyright (c) 2005, Wikipedia and included under the terms of the GNU Free Documentation License. Details and licensing information are included on the CD-ROM.

2.4.4 Handling Evidence

The technologies that permit anonymity also impact legal prosecution. Just as individuals may use anonymity for providing privacy, forgery and impersonation can also provide vectors for misuse during criminal investigations. With physical crimes, there are established procedures for handling evidence. Each item is carefully handled and catalogued to avoid contamination and tampering. Logs identify each handler (*chain of custody*). In contrast, computer technology has unique evidence-handling requirements.

Power: Should a device be left on or turned off? Turning off a computer can lose the contents of volatile memory (e.g., RAM), and most cell phones require a password to be turned back on. In contrast, leaving a system on may result in additional logs—if critical logs are rotated or expired, then evidence may be lost.

Original: Computer files can be copied without modifying the source. This effectively creates multiple originals. With physical evidence, there is only one gun, but in the digital world, there can be many original copies. Maintaining a chain of custody can be difficult when copies are distributed. Similarly, claiming damage from digital theft can be difficult if the original was never lost.

Tampering: In the online world, bits can be changed. It becomes very possible to tamper with evidence. Bits and data values can be modified in subtle and undetectable ways.

Handling network evidence is even more difficult because it is temporal. The bits only exist as they pass along the network connection. Storage may denote aspects of the communication instance, but not the actual communication. Adding to the complexity, some interception and collection methods may modify the original traffic or not store all of the temporal information. For example, packet sniffers may record the data within a packet and timestamp for the start of a packet, but may not record the time for the end of the packet, gap between packets, or voltage used for transferring the data along the wire.

2.4.5 Expectation of Privacy

Privacy is the expectation that confidential or personal information disclosed in a private manner will not become public. Many countries have laws that protect this expectation. Personal information such as Social Security numbers, bank account numbers, and even shopping habits can be shared with an understanding that the information should not become public.

Some technologies are designed to enforce privacy. Cryptography (Chapter 4) is commonly used to ensure that private information is transferred and stored in a way that supports the expectation. But privacy-oriented technologies are not required. Email and chat room content may be unencrypted while relaying through public systems, but the senders can still have an expectation of privacy. A reasonable expectation of privacy does not apply when information is knowingly exposed to the public. Unfortunately, networks are complex. Was the sender of an email aware that the contents were sent over a public network without any technologies for enforcing privacy? Is communication in a private chat room still private if it was not encrypted? Even though networking tools can intercept unprotected information, the collected information may still be classified as private.

2.4.6 Preparing for the Future

Security professionals are constantly faced with decisions that include ethical, social, and legal repercussions. By addressing hypothetical situations, professionals can prepare for how they will react in real situations. These situations are used to develop a clear understanding of ethical, social, and legal issues as well as ramifications for inappropriate behavior. Ideally, good guys will not even act questionably when there is no chance of getting caught. Some sample situations that periodically arise include the following:

- Is it acceptable to scan a host?
- When is packet collection allowed, and when is it taboo?
- Can information captured from the network be released publicly?
- Is it appropriate to crack cryptography used for privacy in a public forum?
- Should software, data files, or sensitive information be shared with other people?
- Should accessing compromised systems be permitted?
- Can good guys use techniques developed by bad guys? What if the usage is directed against bad guys?
- How can bad guys employ techniques developed by good guys?
- Should exploits be researched or verified using unauthorized systems?
- When is it appropriate to publicly disclose a new vulnerability?
- When evaluating exploits, do the ends justify the means?

Each of these questions can be applied to scenarios where they become ethically right or wrong, socially acceptable or unacceptable, and legal or illegal. There is no single correct answer. Knowing how to recognize and apply moral behavior is the sign of a trained professional. In some situations, this can be more important than knowing system exploits and defense options.

SUMMARY

In computer security, ethical, social, and legal behavior separates the good guys from the bad guys. Although both sides have access to the same technology and resources, only the good guys strive for moral behavior. Morals and ethics are more than a lofty, disembodied concept; there can be real consequences for inappropriate behavior. Morality is a balancing act between personal ethics, social values, and legally acceptable actions.

Teaching acceptable behavior along with computer security skills is a difficult task. Students should be given access to powerful tools in an environment where the tools can be safely used. Ethical, social, and legal behavior related to security, intellectual property, and computer crime should be clearly explained and constantly reinforced. And most importantly, moral frameworks must be developed and applied.

REVIEW QUESTIONS

1. Is a packet sniffer an example of a tool used for moral or immoral purposes?
2. What three components form the basis of a moral judgment?
3. What are three ways to protect intellectual property?
4. List three difficulties for handling computer evidence.

DISCUSSION TOPICS

1. Unauthorized software relicensing can be a significant deterrent for companies wanting to adopt open source technologies. For example, open source software may have originally been licensed as proprietary but relicensed as GPL without permission. What are some options for resolving potential open source licensing conflicts?
2. Open source software is based on a desire to share among the software community. When is it inappropriate to use open source software? Describe some situations where releasing software as open source is undesirable. What are the ethical, social, and legal considerations for each of these situations?
3. Select any question found in Section 2.4.6. Describe a situation that is ethically right but socially unacceptable and illegal. Describe alternate situations that are only socially acceptable or only legal. Under what circumstances would someone with strong moral judgment choose a solution that appears dishonest, unacceptable, or illegal?
4. News reports constantly include arrests for technical crimes and criticisms of corporate reactions to network security risks and breaches. Select a current news report on this topic. Identify and evaluate the decisions within a moral framework. Was the situation handled in an acceptable manner? What alternate decisions could have been made? For alternate decisions, what are possible outcomes? Was the applied action the best solution to the problem?

ADDITIONAL RESOURCES

Telling people what is right and wrong passes social values, but it does not necessarily convey ethical behavior. In addition, it may not prepare the listener for unforeseen situations. The following are two resources that address ethical behavior (although not necessarily computer-specific):

■ Bear, L. A., Moldonado-Bear, R., *Free Markets, Finance, Ethics, and Law*, Prentice Hall, 1994. ISBN 0-134-57896-1.

■ Furnell, S., *Cybercrime: Vandalizing the Information Society*, Pearson Education Limited, 2002. ISBN 0-201-72159-7.

Although many laws impact computers and security, some of the more notable U.S. laws include the following:

■ California Senate Bill *SB 1386* requires notifying individuals when personal information may have been compromised.

■ The *Gramm-Leach-Bliley Act* (GLBA) influences policies and procedures for computer security at financial institutions.

■ The *Sarbanes-Oxley Act* (SOX) requires accountability for publicly traded companies.

■ The *Health Insurance Portability and Accountability Act* (HIPAA) mandates protection for patient records among the health and medical fields.

Outside of the United States, there are regulations such as the *Data Protection Act* (DPA) in the United Kingdom, *95/46/EC* for the European Union, and the *Personal Information Protection and Electronic Documents Act* (PIPEDA) in Canada. Each are aimed at protecting privacy and security.

Intellectual property is widely documented. The U.S. Patent and Trademark Office *http://www.uspto.gov/* offers many sources for information on patents, trademarks, and copyrights. The Wikipedia site *http://www.wikipedia.org/* is another excellent resource for defining these terms as well as showing some differences between countries.

3 Network Theory

In This Chapter

- Standards Bodies
- Network Stacks
- Layers and Protocols
- Common Tools

The early digital computers, from the Mark I and ENIAC to the early personal computers such as the Commodore PET and Apple][+, were designed primarily for solitary usage. Sharing information between computers was primarily accomplished using portable media: punch cards, cassette tapes, or floppy disks. Transporting data between computers was time consuming and inefficient. Computer networks were developed as a means to transfer information rapidly between distant locations. Over the past 30 years, computer networks have exploded in importance—from a convenience to a necessity. Today, the network has become more important than the computer. A critical computer that is offline can cost companies thousands of dollars; a critical network that is offline can cost companies millions.

Two options surfaced for developing the initial network implementation. Either each application requiring network access could provide network support independently, or all applications could use the same implementation. Although the former may be optimal for a specific application, it lacks interoperability and maintainability. Changes to a protocol, for example, require changes to every application. In contrast, the latter provides a single well-defined communication system that is centralized, interoperable, and maintainable. Both types of networks are in use today, but the use of an open standard for interoperability is much more common. The Internet is an example of a large, diverse network that uses open standards for interoperability, but many multiplayer gaming systems use proprietary protocols to communicate between players. Some government networks use confidential protocols that are not compatible with the Internet.

Interoperable network systems are designed using a set of layers called a *stack*. In theory, a stack contains all the elements necessary for accessing a network. Specific applications and implementations may not use all available elements, but the elements combine to ensure network compatibility. All stacks that share a common layer can intercommunicate through the common layer.

This chapter covers the basic networking concepts that are required for understanding network security. This chapter is not intended as an in-depth discussion of networking theory, design, or development.

3.1 STANDARDS BODIES

Standards allow compatibility between systems created by different manufacturers. Whereas some standards are accepted though common usage (de facto standards include many RFC documents), others are approved by governing bodies. The field of computer networking contains a wide variety of groups providing official standards. Although some of these organizations cover unique niches, others overlap in jurisdiction. Table 3.1 lists the most common organizations. Government organizations, corporations, niche associations, and informal groups may also specify standards.

TABLE 3.1   Common Standards Organizations for Networking

Abbreviation	Standards Body/Purpose
ANSI	American National Standards Institute
	Communication standards
IEEE-SA	Institute of Electrical and Electronics Engineers, Standards Association
	Low-layer network standards $\rightarrow$

Abbreviation	Standards Body/Purpose
ISO	International Standards Organization
	Information technology standards
IEC	International Electrotechnical Commission
	Electrical, electronic, and related technical standards
IETF	Internet Engineering Task Force
	Governing body over the Request For Comments (RFC) proposals for standards; network protocol standards

By adhering to standards, separate systems can be ensured to interact in a compatible fashion. Although new approaches may be faster, more efficient, or less expensive, they may not be compatible with existing systems. In general, "standard" is better than "better."

3.1.1 Standards

Network standards come from a variety of sources. The most common include the following:

Request For Comments (RFC): RFCs provide de facto standard information. They provide a forum for detailing network functionality and compatibility information. Some RFCs are provided for informational insight, whereas others define actual network standards.

Best Current Practices (BCP): BCPs are a subset of RFCs endorsed by the IETF.

For Your Information (FYI): As with BCP, the FYI documents are a subset of RFCs; however, BCP documents are technical, and FYI documents are informational.

Standards (STD): STD is a subset of RFCs that deals with networking standards.

Internet Experiment Note (IEN): The Internet Working Group developed the IEN as a set of technical documents, similar to RFCs. This group of documents merged with the RFC in 1982.

Many of the RFC documents are cross-referenced with BCP, FYI, STD, and IEN numeric identifiers.

3.1.2 RFC

In 1969, a series of documents called *Request For Comments* (RFC) were created. The RFCs were intended to record the unofficial development notes of the ARPANET (which later became the Internet). These documents quickly became the de facto standards used for developing network protocols. Today, RFC documents are treated much more as a standard than true "request for comments"; few RFCs are debated after becoming accepted.

The submission process for RFCs has evolved over the years, but the basics have not changed [RFC1000, RFC2026]. First, a standard is proposed. Anyone can propose a standard. If the proposal has merit, then the submitter creates a draft of the standard. The draft is opened to the community for review and comment, and may undergo many revisions. Eventually, the draft is either dropped as unacceptable or becomes accepted and assigned an RFC numeric identifier.

There are four main risks to the RFC process. First, many RFCs are informational and not proposed standards. Even though they do not define standards, many RFCs are still implemented as standards (see Chapter 22). This means that some RFCs, which have not been scrutinized for implementation issues, may be widely adopted and implemented.

The second risk from RFCs comes from a lack of security. Very few RFCs discuss potential security issues, and some RFCs mention security concerns but offer no mitigation options. Moreover, the few RFCs that discuss security issues are not necessarily vetted by security personnel and do not detail known security risks. For example, RFC2786 discusses the Diffie-Hellman cryptographic key exchange. But this RFC does not detail the risks associated with the algorithm nor mention any experts that evaluated the protocol. Without these details, a noncryptographer could implement the protocol and introduce significant vulnerabilities.

Special interests pose one of the largest risks to the RFC process. Many companies propose parts of standards, but keep other parts proprietary. For example, Microsoft proposed RFC2361, which defines the video/vnd.avi and audio/vnd.wave meta-tags but does not discuss the proprietary AVI format. Similarly, Macromedia's Real Time Streaming Protocol (RTSP—RFC2326) discusses the download mechanism but not the proprietary media formats used in the examples. Both of these are in sharp contrast to Kerberos, PPP, and other RFCs, where all related details are also defined as open standards.

The final risk to the RFC process comes from missing standards. Many peer-to-peer (P2P) and Instant Messaging (IM) formats are widely used but not defined by RFC standards. Similarly, Voice-over-IP (VoIP) and Internet telephony encase open standards within proprietary formats. A VoIP client from one vendor will not work with VoIP servers from other vendors. This is very different from the Web standards defined by RFCs; a browser from one company will work with a Web server from any other company.

> **Get the Message?**
>
> Instant Messaging is partially defined by a few RFCs. RFC2778 and RFC2779 are informational, whereas RFC3859 through RFC3862 are destined to become standards. Each of these describes session management but not details concerning implementation.
>
> Although each of the IM RFCs discusses high-level interactions, they do not describe any consistent packet format. This is a sharp contrast with other protocols defined by RFCs. Telnet, FTP, SMTP, HTTP, DNS, and others protocol standards include high-level descriptions as well as implementation-specific details. RFCs are intended to assist the implementation of interoperable network devices. Without detailed information, there is no compatibility. As such, IM solutions from different vendors are not compatible.

3.2 NETWORK STACKS

Each system on the Internet uses a network *stack* to manage network data. The stack is divided into *layers* and each layer includes network protocols for specific functionality. Network layers are conceptual, not physical or a byproduct of implementation. Different stacks can still be compatible across networks.

There are many ways to represent network stacks. The two most common are the ISO OSI and TCP/IP stacks. Both define specific layers for functionality. Within each layer are protocols, standards, and conventions for communicating information.

In addition to the OSI and TCP/IP stacks, multiple stacks may be used sequentially or nested, where a single layer in a stack expands to reveal an entire stack. This provides additional functionality when a single stack is not sufficient.

3.2.1 Network Stack Design

Network stacks are designed to be modular and flexible, allowing information to flow between diverse environments. The modular design allows new hardware, software, network configurations, and network protocols to communicate without redesigning the entire network. These design goals permit layers to operate independently and provide the opportunity for reliable data transfers.

3.2.1.1 Layer Independence

The different layers within a stack simplify the implementation requirements by segmenting functionality. In theory, a single layer may be replaced without impacting the entire stack. Changing a protocol used by one layer does not require changing the protocols used in any other layer.

For example, two computers may use different hardware, different operating systems, and different software. But as long as the network layers implement compatible protocols, the two computers can communicate across a network. This independence allows a cell phone with a Web browser to access a distant supercomputer. The two network stacks need to be compatible, but they do not need to be identical. Functionality found in one stack, layer, or protocol may not be required on a different system.

Although the conceptual design calls for independence between layers, actual implementations are often dependent. Commonly, a protocol is implemented at one layer with a specific protocol requirement at another layer. But even dependent protocols usually provide some degree of flexibility and are not hardware- and operating system-specific; entire stacks are usually flexible even when specific protocols are not.

3.2.1.2 Network Reliability

Most network layers provide a degree of reliability. Depending on the protocol, transmission errors may be detected or corrected. The simplest standards use checksums to validate data transfers. More complex protocols rely on cryptographic algorithms. By dividing the network stack into layers, the architecture provides many opportunities for identifying and addressing transmission errors.

Many protocols in a network stack provide error detection. Although this can appear redundant, the duplication provides additional reliability and modularity. Whereas *error-free reliability* identifies complex errors, *error-free modularity* ensures that protocols are robust:

Error-Free Reliability: Different protocols in different layers detect different types of errors. For example, a simple checksum may identify one wrong bit, but two wrong bits are undetectable. Whereas a simple checksum may be acceptable for one protocol, a different protocol may be impacted by more complex errors. Because layers operate independently, each layer must validate its own information.

Error-Free Modularity: Each layer is intended to operate independently. This means that one layer cannot assume that other layers performed any error checking. If the data transfer must be reliable, then protocols cannot assume that another layer validated the information.

3.2.1.3 Types of Errors

In general, there are three types of transmission errors: spurious, burst, and intentional. A *spurious* error occurs when a single bit (or byte) changes value. This may occur due to a short amount of transmission interference. For example, if the transmitted data is 01010101 then a spurious error could appear as 01011101.

A *burst* error appears as a sequential segment of incorrect data. Most commonly, this appears as a sequence of identical bits (e.g., 00000 or 11111). The repeated bits could be due to a defective logic gate or a sustained level of interference. A long burst of variable interference may generate "random" data. Although it is possible for spurious or burst errors to pass an error-detection algorithm, most detection algorithms are chosen to limit the number of undetected errors.

The final error category is intentional. *Intentional* errors occur when data is systematically modified. Although these may appear as spurious or burst errors, intentional errors are frequently designed to bypass error detection. When critical network data becomes intentionally corrupted, the result is a denial of service. In contrast, undetected data modifications can lead to a system compromise.

The network stack provides multiple opportunities for error detection. This means an attacker faces a significant challenge when transmitting intentionally modified data that can bypass all error-detection systems. Even when every layer's protocol uses a simple error-detection algorithm, such as a checksum, the requirement to bypass multiple checksums increases the difficulty.

> *Simple checksums, even from multiple layers, are usually not a significant deterrent against intentionally modified data that is intended to appear error-free. In contrast, a single cryptographic error-detection system can be a very successful deterrent. But because layers operate independently, a network application has no guarantee that a sufficiently complex detection algorithm is employed within the stack.*

3.2.2 ISO OSI

In 1983, the International Standards Organization (ISO) released specifications for the Open Systems Interconnection (OSI) network model [ISO7498]. The OSI model defines a seven-layer stack, with each layer providing a specific network function (Table 3.2).

3.2.2.1 Lower OSI Layers

The lower four layers form the network services and communicate data across the network. The first layer, the *physical layer*, focuses on transporting data across a medium to another networked system. This layer ensures that data transmitted

TABLE 3.2   ISO OSI Network Model

Layer	Name	Purpose	Book Section
7	Application	End-user applications	Part VIII
6	Presentation	Data conversion	Part VII
5	Session	Extended duration connection management	Part VI
4	Transport	Data collection and aggregation	Part V
3	Network	Remote network routing and addressing	Part IV
2	Data Link	Local network routing and addressing	Part III
1	Physical	Data transport media	Part II

matches the data received, but it does not protect from data collisions—where two nodes transmit at the same time—or prevent external noise from appearing as transmitted data. The physical layer defines the medium and medium specifications. Examples of layer 1 standards include 10Base-2, 100Base-T, ISDN, and modem protocols such as V.33 and V.42bis. Part II discusses the physical layer, including a detailed look at common wired protocols, common wireless protocols, and the security risks involved in different network configurations.

The physical layer does not address noise or transmission collisions. Instead, the second layer manages this type of error detection. The *data link layer* ensures that data received from the physical layer is intended for the host and is complete, that is, not a fractional data transfer. This layer provides transmission management and simple error detection from collisions and external interference. Additionally, the data link layer manages node addressing on a network with more than two hosts. The most common example of a data link protocol is the IEEE 802 standard, including CSMA/CD and LLC (Chapter 10). Other sample data link protocols include PPP and SLIP (Chapter 9). Part III details the security impacts from simplified data link protocols in point-to-point networks and complex multinode network MAC addressing, including the threats from ARP attacks such as poisoning and flooding.

The third layer, the *network layer*, routes data between adjacent networks and permits connectivity between vastly different data link and physical specifications. Examples of network layer protocols include IP, BGP, IGRP, IPX, and X.25. Part IV covers the general security risks and options that relate to the network layer. The Internet Protocol (IP) is examined in detail, including many different types of IP attacks (Chapter 12). The network layer permits connections between distant networks, which leads to fundamental concerns regarding anonymity (Chapter 13).

The *transport layer* defines ports, permitting different network services to be enabled at the same time. The network and data link layers may transmit data along a variety of paths; the recipient may receive data out-of-sequence. The transport layer addresses data sequencing by placing blocks of data in the correct order. Example transport layer protocols include TCP, UDP, NetBIOS-DG, and many AppleTalk protocols such as ATP, ADSP, and AEP. Part V examples the transport layer, TCP (in particular), and related security implications.

3.2.2.2 Upper OSI Layers

The upper three layers form the end-user layers and assist application management. The fifth layer, the *session layer*, provides support for connections that may exist even when the lower network infrastructure changes. For example, a user may log in to a remote server. The lower OSI layers can drop, reset, or change the network connection, but the user remains logged in. This is commonly used for database and naming services such as DNS and LDAP. The session layer also provides support for remote services such as RPC and RTP. Part VI covers the risks associated with the session layer with a particular focus on one of the most crucial, yet insecure, protocols on the Internet: DNS.

The sixth layer, the *presentation layer*, was originally designed to handle data conversion, such as from ASCII to EBCDIC, but today is commonly used to provide transparent compression and encryption support. Few stacks implement protocols in the presentation layer—this layer is usually transparent. A few examples of presentation layer protocols include LPP, SSH, and SSL. Part VII looks at the presentation layer, with SSL and SSH as examples.

At the top of the stack is the *application layer*. This seventh layer provides application-specific support, and acts as the final interface between network and non-network components of an application. Most user applications implement application layer protocols. There is a handful of presentation layer protocols, but there are thousands of application layer protocols. More common examples include Telnet, FTP, HTTP (Web), SMTP (email), SNMP, X-Windows, NTP, BootP, DHCP, NFS, and SMB. Although each of these protocols have specific security concerns, most share general risks and have common mitigation options. Part VIII looks at general application layer issues and solutions and offers SMTP and HTTP as specific examples.

Almost Consistent

The seven layers of the OSI model are distinct, but their purposes are sometimes interpreted inconsistently. For example, the transport layer is sometimes associated with the upper layers rather than the lower layers. Whereas the lower layers provide network addressing and routing, the upper layers supply service and support. The transport layer provides high-level control for service addressing and low-level control for application management. Thus, the transport layer can belong either or both categories.

The original layer definitions predate the use of cryptography or security methodologies. As such, any layer may implement any cryptographic or security-oriented protocol.

Although the OSI stack contains seven layers, it is sometimes described as having an eighth layer. Layer 0, or the physical medium, is sometimes separated from layer 1, the physical layer. This is commonly done for clarification when the same physical medium can be used with differing signal protocols. Similarly, an imaginary layer 8 is sometimes associated with anything beyond the standard stack. Jokingly called "OSI layer 8," the human layer (or user layer) is one common example.

3.2.3 DoD TCP/IP Stack

Before the ISO OSI network model, there was TCP/IP. In 1969, the U.S. Department of Defense (DoD) created the TCP/IP stack. This four-layer stack defines the functionality needed for connection-oriented communication. Although the distinct layers in the OSI model are beneficial as teaching aids, the TCP/IP stack is most commonly implemented. Both of these network models are compatible; the functionality in one can be mapped into the functionality of the other (Figure 3.1).

The lowest layer of the TCP/IP stack is the *network interface*. This single layer is a combination of the OSI's physical and data link layers. The network interface layer defines the communication medium, flow control, error detection, and local network addressing. In contrast to the OSI physical layer, the TCP/IP model's network interface layer does not define the physical medium—it only defines the communication across the medium.

The TCP/IP model's Internet layer performs the same duties as the OSI network layer. This layer manages internetwork addressing and routing.

The TCP/IP transport layer is almost identical to the OSI transport layer. The minor exception concerns terminology. In the OSI model, network connections may be defined as connection-oriented or connection-less, indicating whether transmission confirmation is required or not. In the TCP/IP model, there is no distinction within the terminology, although both types of traffic are supported.

FIGURE 3.1 The ISO OSI and DoD TCP/IP stacks.

The final TCP/IP layer is equivalent to all of the upper layers in the OSI model. The TCP/IP application layer provides session, presentation, and application-specific support. Unlike the OSI model, the TCP/IP model does not distinguish session and presentation from application.

Was That Four Layers or Five?
The TCP/IP network stack is sometimes described as having five layers. The fifth layer, hardware, separates the physical medium definition from the local network addressing and flow control. In the five-layer TCP/IP model, the hardware layer is equivalent to the OSI physical layer.

3.2.4 OSI versus TCP/TP

Although any networking protocol can be placed in the OSI or TCP/IP models, each model has a distinct purpose. The TCP/IP model requires each application to manage the end-to-end communications. Only the basic networking functions are defined. In contrast, the OSI model uses a strict layered hierarchy that contains both networking and networking-related functionality.

Although the TCP/IP model is more simplistic than the OSI model, it is also much older and the de facto standard. The Internet is built on TCP/IP. The OSI model, with its well-defined segmented layers, is preferable as a teaching tool, but not every layer may fit cleanly in the OSI model. (See Sections 3.4.2 and 3.4.3.)

3.2.5 Other Stacks

Although the OSI and TCP/IP models are the most common stacks, other stacks exist. For example, the Data Over Cable Service Interface Specification (DOCSIS) stack is commonly used with cable and DSL modems (Figure 3.2). DOCSIS defines a multilayer stack, but the layers do not correspond with the ISO OSI layers. The OSI physical layer corresponds with the lowest DOCSIS layer. The first layer, the DOCSIS physical layer, is split into three components: the actual medium, the modulation layer that manages the radio or optical signals, and the transmission layer that handles the actual data transfer and receipt. The layer is also divided between uplink and downlink directions. The DOCSIS data link layer is similar to the OSI data link layer except that it includes MPEG encoding and compression. The upper layers of the DOCSIS stack mirror the OSI stack, with one addition: DOCSIS includes control messages along with the upper layers.

FIGURE 3.2   Aligning the DOCSIS and OSI network stacks.

Other stacks are not as common as OSI or TCP/IP, but there is generally a mapping between different models.

3.2.6 User Layers

The network stacks only cover network-oriented protocols and standards. For example, the application layer provides network support to user-level applications. Programs (or functions) that do not use the network are not in the application layer and not part of the network stack. Outside the network stack are the user, system, and kernel spaces. Commonly called the *user layers*, these spaces host nonnetwork-oriented applications such as games, word processors, and databases.

3.3 MULTIPLE STACKS

In both the OSI and TCP/IP models, each network stack is intended as a linear transaction: transmissions flow down the stack, and received data flows up. There are no loops or jumps within a stack. Although some layers may perform no function, these layers still exist as empty layers. When looping functionality is required, a second stack is introduced. For example, an initial connection may use one network stack to perform authentication and a second stack to manage the authenticated data. An *authentication stack* is an example of two stacks in sequence. Similarly, a virtual network may use an established network connection (one stack) as a virtual medium for another stack. These stacks within stacks permit the creation of virtual private networks (VPNs). Finally, adjacent stacks permit the conversion from one protocol to another.

3.3.1 Sequential Stacks

Stacks may be placed in sequence, so that the application layer of one stack connects to the physical layer of the next (Figure 3.3). Sequential stacks are commonly used for authentication. As an authentication stack, the first stack blocks the initial network connection. The application associated with the stack manages the transfer and authentication of credentials. When the credentials are validated, the next stack handles the connection.

3.3.2 Stacks Within Stacks

Each layer of a stack may modify the data. The only condition is that a modification during sending must be reversible during receipt. Modifications may include encapsulation (adding headers and trailers around the data) or encoding, where the data is transformed into another representation. Encoding examples include SLIP's simple character replacements (Chapter 9) and the encryption and compression provided by Secure Shell (Chapter 20).

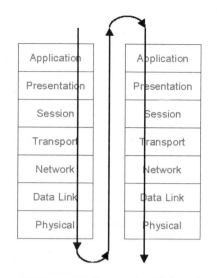

FIGURE 3.3 Two sequential stacks.

Because any data that passes down a sending stack appears the same after it passes back up the receiving stack, stacks can be nested. In a nested stack, a protocol in a specific layer may contain all the elements, from application to physical layer, of another stack. Nesting is commonly used when a network-based application fills the role of a single network protocol. A Sockets proxy (Socks) is an example of a stack within a stack (Figure 3.4). Socks is used to proxy connections through a remote system. Socks manages this by intercepting and modifying the IP headers of a data transmission. Rather than modifying all IP applications to use Socks, most Socks implementations intercept the network stack. After the data passes through the network layer, the Socks protocol redirects the data to a new stack rather than the remaining data link and physical layers. The new stack modifies the data for use with the Socks protocol, and then passes the data through the Socks data link and physical layers—the lower layer for the Socks stack may differ from the original lower layers.

Upon receipt by the Socks server, the external stack is pealed away, the IP layer is replaced, and the data is transmitted using the proxy's data link and physical layers.

3.3.3 VPN

A virtual private network (VPN) is a common example of nested stacks. In a VPN, the physical layer of one stack is actually an application for the next stack. Secure Shell (SSH) and stunnel are examples of protocols that can tunnel other protocols. The basic concept redirects the physical medium to an application that contains an

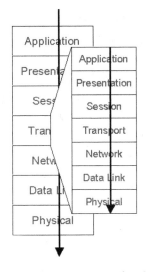

FIGURE 3.4 Example of a
stack within a stack.

established connection. (This is discussed in detail in Chapters 9, 19, and 20.) The
data for the virtual connection is tunneled through the application.

Tunneling is only part of a VPN. The second part requires network routing to
be directed through the tunnel. This redirection can make two remote networks appear adjacent. VPNs are commonly used to connect two private networks over a
public connection. The connection is done in three steps:

1. **Establish the public connection**. A dual-homed host, existing on both a
   private network and a public network, is used to connect to another dual-
   homed host. The connection is across a public network.
2. **Create the tunnel**. An application, such as `ssh` or `stunnel`, is used to tunnel a connection between the two hosts.
3. **Create the network**. A networking protocol, such as PPP, is initiated
   through the tunnel. This allows network traffic to flow between the private
   networks.

After establishing the VPN connection, network traffic is routed across the virtual network. Nodes using the virtual network may experience a latency related to
the tunneling, but the two networks will appear adjacent.

3.4 LAYERS AND PROTOCOLS

Each layer in a stack may contain one or more protocols. A protocol implements a specific functionality associated with the layer. Although there are only two widely used stacks, and only a few layers to define each stack, there are literally thousands of standardized protocols, and even more that are considered nonstandard. Whereas stacks and layers are conceptual, protocols are specific definitions for the layer concepts. Two nodes on a network may use very different software to implement a particular protocol, but two implementations of a protocol should be compatible.

Because protocols apply the layer concepts, they may not fit perfectly into a single layer. Misaligned mappings and additional functionality can lead to an imperfect association between a protocol and a particular layer or stack.

3.4.1 Mapping Protocols to Layers

In general, the convention is to design and implement protocols so that they map directly into one layer. A single protocol should not perform tasks found in multiple layers. Unfortunately, due to poor design, ambiguous layer functionality, and technical constraints, many protocols are tightly associated with multiple layers. Moreover, a protocol may be designed for one stack, such as the TCP/IP stack, and therefore not have a perfect mapping into another stack like the ISO OSI model. For example, the IEEE 802 standard is designed for the TCP/IP stack and defines the network interface layer. Subelements of the standard, such as IEEE 802.3 are closely associated with the OSI data link layer, whereas IEEE 802.3z describes the OSI physical layer for Gigabit Ethernet. The set of IEEE 802 standards fit well into the TCP/IP model but not into the OSI model.

In addition to matching multiple layers, some standards and protocols define portions of layers. The IEEE 802.2 standard defines a subsection of the OSI data link layer, and resides above the IEEE 802.3 definition (see Chapters 5 and 7).

3.4.2 Misaligned Mappings

Protocols are often tightly associated between layers. Although this usually happens within a single layer, such as the association between SLIP and CSLIP—a compressed version of SLIP—the association can occur between layers. For example, IP resides in the network layer. But IP uses the Internet Control Message Protocol (ICMP) for routing and traffic management. Some of the ICMP functionality clearly resides in the network layer, as a sublayer above IP. But other ICMP functions appear to cover functionality found in the transport layer. For example, ICMP manages the IP flow control, which is network layer functionality. But ICMP can also define data to be transported, such as the content of an ICMP Echo (ping) packet. The capability to define data for the network layer occurs in the transport layer. Thus, ICMP contains both network and transport layer attributes.

Because protocols represent a specific implementation and not an abstract concept, and because protocols may be designed for an alternate stack, many protocols do not map properly into a specific stack model. Although there may not be a perfect mapping, there remains a general alignment.

3.4.3 Different Layers, Different Views

The implementation of a specific protocol or standard may incorporate the functionality from multiple layers. As such, different people may associate protocols with different layers. A very common example is the Secure Shell (SSH) executable, ssh. This executable is primarily used to implement an encrypted tunnel. Encryption is a modification of the data and usually associated with the OSI presentation layer; however, ssh implements a few other functions:

Login Functionality: SSH provides user authentication. The authentication covers the entire protocol's connection and permits an extended connection. Extended connection support is usually associated with the OSI session layer.

Remote Procedures: The SSH daemon, sshd, can provide specific services, or functions. This is reminiscent of remote procedure calls (RPC), a function usually associated with the OSI session layer.

Command Prompt: When ssh is used by itself, it may run a remote program or start a login shell. Both remote program execution and providing a login shell are OSI application layer functions.

SSH fits well within the application layer of the DoD TCP/IP stack, but it does not fit well within the ISO OSI model. Although SSH is best described as an OSI presentation layer protocol, it is commonly included in the session or application layers.

Another example of an ill-fitted protocol is SAMBA, the open source implementation of Microsoft's Server Message Block (SMB) protocol. SMB is used to share resources, such as disk drives or printers, between computers. SMB is an application layer protocol that is dependent on the NetBIOS protocol. NetBIOS is sometimes classified within the transport layer, but also provides named pipe support—session layer functionality. The implementation of the SAMBA client includes SMB, NetBIOS, named pipes, and even an FTP-style interface—an application layer function that interfaces with the SMB application layer. The SAMBA client includes OSI transport, session, and application layer functionality.

3.5 COMMON TOOLS

Network maintenance and security requires tools for querying, collecting, assessing, and analyzing network traffic and connected nodes. Although there are a large variety of tools and many are open source, only a few regularly exist on most operating systems. Some of the more popular tools may need to be downloaded and installed. The common tools perform general functions, and the specific tools test explicit functions.

3.5.1 Querying Tools

Querying tools permit an administrator to test network connectivity and the functionality of specific protocols. These tools test connectivity to a particular network protocol. A successful query indicates network connectivity from the local host to the queried protocol on the remote host, but does not indicate full connectivity within the stack. Common query tools include the following:

Arp: A tool that lists the local ARP table (data link layer, see Chapter 10), modifies the ARP table, and more importantly, generates an ARP network request. If the arp command cannot identify a host on the local network, then the host is not on the local network (or not online).

Ping: A simple tool that generates an ICMP echo request. A successful ping indicates connectivity along the physical, data link, and network layers.

Netstat: The netstat command is available on nearly all networked operating systems, although the parameters and output format may vary. This tool provides a variety of network related status reports, including current network connections, routing tables, and number of bytes transmitted and received. Metrics can be displayed by network interface or protocol.

Telnet: Although originally designed for establishing a remote shell connection, telnet is commonly used to test connections to remote TCP services. Telneting to a specific port on a remote host can test the connectivity of the entire remote network stack. The netcat application (nc) is a common alternative to telnet.

Nmap: Nmap is an extremely powerful tool for identifying remote hosts. Nmap is capable of identifying active hosts (e.g., an ICMP ping scan) and transport layer ports (TCP and UDP). In addition, it contains fingerprinting capabilities. Nmap not only identifies available TCP network services on a remote host, but it can attempt to identify the type of services (Web, email, etc.) and identify remote operating systems.

p0f: Similar to nmap's operating system fingerprinting service, p0f estimates the type of remote operating system based on packet sequencing and related attributes.

3.5.2 Collection Tools

Collection tools are used to gather network traffic for analysis:

TCPdump: TCPdump interfaces with the data link layer and collects all packets received by the local host. Although the application's name is *TCP*dump, it can collect all network traffic that reaches the data link layer, including ARP, IP, TCP, UDP, and higher protocols. TCPdump is the de facto standard for network data collection; collected data is usually stored in the tcpdump format.

Snort: Snort is a very sophisticated alternative to tcpdump. Snort permits complex packet filtering and alerts based on specific matches. This application is the basis of many open source IDSs.

3.5.3 Assessment Tools

Vulnerability assessment tools analyze network interfaces for known and potential risks. Any segment of the network stack may be analyzed, although most tools primarily focus on the OSI session, presentation, and application layers.

Three common assessment tools are Nessus, SATAN, and Saint. These tools analyze services on remote hosts for known risks. Analysis methods include port scans that identify potential network services, packet-based host profiling, and specific service assessment. After identifying the remote network service's port, the service is queried. Frequently, the tools can identify not only the type of service but also the exact version and patch level of the service. The identified service is then compared to a list of known service exploits.

Although these tools offer very powerful ways for administrators to quickly check their own networks for known risks, attackers can use these same tools to scan for vulnerable hosts. An attacker may use Saint to scan a subnet for particular vulnerabilities and later return with appropriate exploits.

Not all of the scans performed by these tools are harmless. For example, many of the scan options in Nessus are explicitly hostile. These scans test for overflow and write-enabled vulnerabilities. In addition, many services do not handle network scans well. Nessus scans that are not denoted as hostile may still hang, reboot, or otherwise impair the target system.

3.5.4 Analysis Tools

Analysis tools are used to view and interpret collected packets, and to generate explicit test cases. Ethereal is an example of a powerful analysis tool that can reconstruct network connections and decode hundreds of different network protocols.

Ethereal has one specific limitation: it can only passively collect and analyze data. Ethereal has no way to inject packets. Without this functionality, it cannot generate specific test cases. A separate analysis tool, `hping`, offers a simple command-line interface for generating custom ICMP, UDP, and TCP packets (as well as other protocols).

SUMMARY

The Internet is designed for interoperability between networked systems. To assist the development of compatible architectures, stack models are used. Each stack contains multiple layers with distinct functionality. Protocols and standards apply the concepts from each stack.

Although there are many different stack definitions, most are compatible. Functionality in one stack can be mapped to functionality in another stack, but the functionality may not be a one-to-one layer mapping. The inaccuracies from converting between different stacks can lead to ambiguity when placing a specific protocol within a specific layer.

Although there are only a few common stacks, there are a large variety of protocols and standards across the layers. Just as there are many different protocols, there are even more applications that implement protocols. Although security risks from a specific application can be easily addressed, the errors, omissions, and oversights in standards, protocols, layers, and stack definitions lead to fundamental flaws that impact all applications.

REVIEW QUESTIONS

1. What is the IETF and what does it do?
2. Name two network stacks.
3. What is a VPN?
4. Are "layers" concepts or implementations?
5. What is a collection tool?

DISCUSSION TOPICS

1. Define *stack*, *layer*, and *protocol*. Where are security concepts such as authentication, validity, and nonrepudiation specified? Where are they implemented?
2. Can a stack implement the OSI network layers in a different order and still be compatible with the DoD TCP/IP and ISO OSI models? When would it be desirable to change the order?
3. Some layers define multiple functions. For example, the transport layer provides both ports and sequencing. Describe some reasons why these functions are not split into their own layers.

ADDITIONAL RESOURCES

W. Richard Stevens has many of excellent books on networking. These books are considered by many to be the de facto standard for network development.

- Stevens, W. Richard, et al., *Unix Network Programming, Vol. 1 & 2*. Addison-Wesley Professional, 2003.
- Stevens, W. Richard, et al., *TCP/IP Illustrated, Vol. 1, 2, & 3*. Addison-Wesley Professional, 1993.

In addition, Herbert Thomas offers an exceptional book on the Linux network architecture.

- Herbert, Thomas, *The Linux TCP/IP Stack: Networking for Embedded Systems*. Charles River Media, 2004.

Besides these general networking sources, there are books on nearly every specific protocol and standard, from 10Base-T and IP, to email and Web. Many of these books provide implementation, configuration, and security considerations for applications that implement specific protocols. Other books focus on the protocols themselves.

Understanding the shear number of protocols, and the relationship between them, can be daunting. Agilent's Test and Measurement Systems offers a poster that lists many of the common protocols and their relationships within the ISO OSI model. This poster, titled *Network Communication Protocols*, is freely available from the Agilent Web site (*http://www.agilent.com/*) as part number 5968-3611E. (Finding the poster on Agilent's Web site can be difficult, but most Web search engines can quickly find it by the part number.)

4 Basic Cryptography

In This Chapter

- Securing Information
- Necessary Elements
- Authentication and Keys
- Cryptography and Randomness
- Hashes
- Ciphers
- Encryption
- Steganography

Network stacks, such as the ISO OSI model and DoD TCP/IP stack, address data flow functionality, but do not define methods for securing information. Instead, information security is left to the individual protocol implementations. Although cryptography, steganography, and various authentication methods are used by many different protocols, they are not explicitly defined for any single stack layer. Encryption may occur within the network layer, presentation layer, or any other layer of the network stack. Moreover, different protocols at different layers may use different algorithms and approaches for securing information.

Although cryptography is not standard in the OSI model and not widely implemented (most protocols do not support cryptography), a few key protocols do implement cryptographic solutions. This chapter covers the basics of cryptography and related elements for securing information.

4.1 SECURING INFORMATION

There are three basic approaches to securing information: prevention, restriction, and cryptography. Access to information can be prevented. If an attacker cannot access information, then the information is safe from the attacker. For network security, isolated networks and restrictive architectures are generally sufficient deterrents. For example, many government offices have two computers that are not networked to each other. One computer accesses the public Internet, and the other only operates on a classified network. Without a connection between the two computers, it becomes difficult for an attacker on the unclassified network to attack the classified network. A classified network security breach indicates a conscious effort and not an accidental configuration error.

When networks cannot be isolated, access can still be restricted. Most remote login systems require a username and password. Different types of authentication exist for different security needs. Although authentication restricts access, it generally does not hinder eavesdropping-related attacks.

Cryptography is the most common approach for securing networks. Cryptography encodes data so that only the intended recipients can decode the message. Cryptographic systems include random number generators, hashes, ciphers, and encryption algorithms. *Steganography* (hiding information) is commonly associated with cryptographic algorithms.

4.2 NECESSARY ELEMENTS

Every cryptographic process has five main elements: the algorithm, environment, key, plaintext, and ciphertext. Encryption cannot work without each of these components. However, an attacker may know one or more of these required elements and use them to determine other elements.

4.2.1 Plaintext and Ciphertext

Cryptography is used to protect data from unintended recipients. The decoded data is called *plaintext*, but the data may not necessarily be text. Images and binary files may also be encrypted. Encrypted plaintext is called *ciphertext*. Ciphertext provides confidentiality by preventing unauthorized recipients from viewing the plaintext.

4.2.2 Algorithm

An *encryption algorithm* is used to convert plaintext (P) into ciphertext (C) and vice versa. This requires encryption (E) and decryption (D) functions, such that

$$E(P) = C \tag{4.1}$$

$$D(C) = P \tag{4.2}$$

Encryption algorithms are idempotent (see upcoming Note). Each encryption creates ciphertext that can be decrypted into plaintext. Repeated encryptions may generate different ciphertext, but the original plaintext can always be recovered.

In an idempotent *function, the same input always generates the same output. With encryption algorithms, random numbers can be used to generate differing ciphertext that decodes to the same plaintext. Random values may be used to pad the plaintext or modify ciphertext in noncritical ways. The only requirement is the combination of the encoding and decoding functions: D(E(P))=P.*

In contrast to encryption algorithms, cryptographic *hash algorithms* are not reversible and may not be unique. Hash functions perform a many-to-one mapping from the plaintext to a hash value. For example, a 4-MB file may be summarized by a 32-bit hash value. Many different plaintexts can generate the same hash value. These *hash collisions* are generally rare for strong algorithms and are not predictable for cryptographic hash algorithms.

4.2.3 Environment

Cryptographic environments specify implementation-specific options. Encryption algorithms (e.g., DES, Blowfish, and AES), hash functions (e.g., RC4, MD5), and key exchanges (e.g., DH and ADH) are well defined but vary between platforms. For example, the Diffie-Hellman key exchange (DH) can use very large integers. One implementation may use 64-bit integers, whereas another uses 256-bit integers. Although different bit sizes do not impact the mathematics behind the algorithm, it does impact platform compatibility. If the environment is unknown, then it can be as effective at deterring an attacker as using a novel encryption system.

Common environment factors include the following:

Endian: The byte order of integers can result in unexpected complexities. Motorola processors historically use *big endian*, where the highest-order byte is listed first. Intel processors generally use *little endian*, storing the lowest-order byte first. Network protocols generally use big endian.

Data size: The size of data structures can vary between protocols and platforms. For example, in ANSI-C, the size of an integer, `sizeof(int)`, varies by processor, compiler, and operating system. On most Intel platforms (e.g., ia64 and i386), an int is 4 bytes. But on an SGI Onyx2 running IRIX, integers can be 32 bytes.

Data wrapping: Many protocols encode, pack, or wrap data with additional information. If the wrapping method is unknown, then it can obscure the data.

Variable values: Many algorithms have modifiable variables. For example, the DES encryption algorithm uses an iterative loop. Nearly all DES implementations loop 16 times. Changing the number of loops creates an incompatible encryption system but does not invalidate DES.

As long as the encryption and decryption algorithms use the same environment, they will be compatible. But changing the environment can increase the difficulty for an attacker. Given a large number of environment variables, an attacker faces an exponentially difficult barrier for identifying the specific environment.

4.2.4 Key

Cryptographic algorithms convert plaintext to ciphertext in a nonpredictable way. The resulting ciphertext cannot be predetermined from the plaintext. Most cryptographic systems incorporate random number algorithms. The random number generator (R) is seeded with a specific value. The *seed* and plaintext generates the ciphertext. A *key* (K) may be used as the seed value or combined with a hash function to generate the initial seed value.

$$E(K,P) = C \tag{4.3}$$

$$D(K,C) = P \tag{4.4}$$

Without a key, the algorithm performs an *encoding*, not an encryption. The same plaintext will always generate the same ciphertext. Any attacker knowing the algorithm can readily decode the ciphertext. Encryption algorithms use keys to vary the ciphertext; plaintext encrypted with different keys generates different ciphertexts. Without knowing the correct key, an attacker cannot decode the ciphertext.

4.2.5 Cracking Cryptographic Systems

When attackers target a cryptographic system, they attempt to defeat the algorithms through *cryptanalysis*. This is usually done by intercepting the ciphertext, determining the algorithms and environment, and using them to derive the plaintext. In general, the more elements an attacker has, the easier the system is to defeat. For example, when attacking the encryption from the Secure Shell (SSH) protocol (Chapter 20), the environment and ciphertext are known. The algorithm used by SSH is limited to DES, 3DES, or Blowfish. Because the attacker does not know the plaintext or key, these define the attack vectors.

Determining plaintext is not always an attacker's goal. Attackers frequently attempt to identify algorithms or keys. Sometimes determining the exact content of the plaintext is not realistic, but even determining how a defender uses encryption can assist an attacker. Chapter 20 details a timing attack against the SSH environment that can be used to determine the plaintext contents of some encrypted packets—and this does not require knowing the algorithm or keys.

4.3 AUTHENTICATION AND KEYS

When a user remotely connects to a computer, he is identified with the system. If the user is authenticated, then access is provided. Unidentified users are blocked. The many types of authentication mechanisms generally fall into one of three classifications:

- **Something you know:** Passwords and PIN numbers are types of information used to access systems. The authentication assumes that knowledge of these secrets is sufficient to authenticate the user.
- **Something you have:** Room keys and badges are physical items that provide authentication. Physical keys and badges can be copied, however, digital badges and keys can deter counterfeiting efforts.
- **Something you are:** Biometrics, such as fingerprints, iris and retina patterns, and even handwriting patterns, are distinctive. Unlike the other two classifications, these do not require memorization and cannot be easily passed to other people.

Simple authentication systems may use only one type of authentication, such as a password. Single authentication methods are called *one-part authentication*. Authentication systems that require many elements from one category are also called one-part authentication. In general, a system that requires two types of memorized information is just as secure as a system that requires one larger piece of memorized information. Needing two digital keys to enter a system is no safer than needing one digital key.

More complex systems use *two-part* or *three-part authentication*, indicating elements from two or three authentication classes. For example, requiring a password and fingerprint is much stronger than requiring either alone.

In cryptography, keys are used to access data. The keys may come from a variety of elements, including passwords, random numbers, and *hashes* (digital summaries) of provided information.

Something You Are... Missing

Each of the three authentication classifications has distinct weaknesses. The most common type of authentication relies on passwords. Users are expected to memorize these bits of information, but they often forget them. Up to 80 percent of system administration help calls concern forgotten passwords [Hayday2003]. In addition, attackers can steal passwords—they only needs to observe the password to compromise it. Users that access many systems are left with a dilemma: they can use many passwords but risk forgetting them, or they can use one password and potentially compromise all of their systems. In addition, users commonly write down passwords, allowing another vector for password theft.

Physical keys, such as digital tokens, badges, and USB dongles (devices that plug into USB sockets) can be misplaced or stolen. Damage is also common—most digital keys are pocket size and do not survive washing machine rinse cycles.

Biometric authentication systems are often touted as secure because the information cannot be duplicated, stolen, or misplaced. But these solutions have their own limitations. For example, biometric devices that require fingerprint identification block access to people who are missing fingers or hands. Similarly, a variety of eye diseases can impact iris and retina identification. Even voice identification can be deterred by the common cold. Although biometrics are very accurate, they are also very restrictive and influenced by temporary and permanent physical changes.

4.3.1 Key Management Risks

Regardless of the key type, key data must be stored on the computer system for use in a cryptographic system. Passwords, physical key identifiers, and biometric information are stored in files and databases. An attacker who can compromise a database of fingerprints can generate authoritative fingerprint information—without having access to the physical finger. There are three main approaches for protecting password information. The first approach simply restricts direct access to the key database. Although the database must be accessible, this does not necessarily mean direct access. Restrictive filters and programming interfaces can mitigate the need for direct access.

The second approach encrypts the key information within the repository. The *Pretty Good Privacy* system (PGP), for example, uses a cryptographic key to encode and decode data. A PGP key must be stored on the local system. To protect the key from theft, it is encrypted using a password. Only a user that provides the correct password can decrypt and use the key. This effectively wraps one-part authentication (something you have, the PGP key) with one-part authentication (something you know, the PGP key password); however, this aspect of PGP does not offer two-part authentication.

Instead of storing the actual key, the third approach stores a hash, or *digest*, of the key. Any key that generates the same hash value is considered to be acceptable. Many password systems use this approach, including Unix /etc/passwd entries and LDAP SHA1 passwords. To reverse, or *crack*, these password systems, an attacker must identify a password combination that generates the same hash. Tools such as John The Ripper (*http://www.openwall.com/john/*) and Rainbow Crack (*http://www.antsight.com/zsl/rainbowcrack/*) are used to guess passwords and identify hash matches.

That's a Password?

The Unix /etc/passwd file stores username and account information. Traditionally, it also stores a hash of the user's password. If the password were stored in plaintext, any user on the system could see all other passwords. Instead, the password is encoded. Older Unix systems used an algorithm called *crypt*. Crypt uses a modified version of the DES encryption algorithm—modified to be a hash instead of an algorithm that supports decryption. Later versions of Unix switched to MD5. (OpenBSD uses a variant of the Blowfish encryption algorithm.)

People commonly use the same password on multiple systems. By using a hash function, these systems ensure that the password cannot be recovered. Even if an administrator's account becomes compromised, the passwords remain safe.

In addition to using strong hash functions, most Unix systems have moved the passwords out of the /etc/passwd file. The /etc/shadow file stores passwords, whereas /etc/passwd stores user information. The shadow file is only accessible by an administrator. Regular users on the system cannot view the hashed passwords. This prevents dictionary attacks against the known hash values. Finally, /etc/shadow is not exported from the system. Remote attackers see access denial, local attackers see access restriction, and compromised administration accounts are faced with information that cannot be decoded.

4.3.2 Keys and Automated Systems

When an automated system uses encryption, the key must be made available to the system. This means that any attacker with access to the system will have access to the key. Although many complicated systems attempt to encrypt, encode, or hide keys that are used by automated systems, these are all instances of security-by-obscurity. Automated systems generally do not wait for information from manual sources; the data must be available when the system needs it. If the key is available to automated systems, then the key is potentially available to all users, friend and foe.

4.3.3 Symmetrical versus Asymmetrical Keys

The two primary types of keys are symmetrical and asymmetrical. *Symmetrical keys* means the same key is used for encryption and decryption. When using a network-based encryption system, both ends of the network require the same key. Risks are associated with the initial transfer of the key (it can be intercepted), but after the transfer, it can be used to safely encrypt data. DES, Blowfish, and AES are examples of encryption algorithms that use symmetrical keys.

Asymmetrical algorithms, such as PGP, use one key to encrypt and a different key to decrypt. The key pairs, called the *public* and *private keys*, allow key exchanges without risk. Both systems exchange public keys, but do not reveal their private keys. The public key is used for encryption and generates ciphertext—any user can encrypt the data—but only the private key can decrypt the ciphertext. In this scenario, an interceptor that sees the asymmetrical key exchange cannot crack the algorithm.

The public key is not always used for encryption. The private key can also create ciphertext. In this situation, anyone with the public key can decode the ciphertext. The benefit of this approach comes from nonrepudiation; the sender cannot claim that he did not encode a message, and all recipients know that the message is authentic. This is commonly referred to as a *cryptographic signature*. A sender may use private and public keys for encoding a message; the recipient's public key ensures message privacy, and the sender's private key signs the encryption, which ensures nonrepudiation.

In general, symmetrical algorithms are faster than asymmetrical. Many systems initiate the communication flow with asymmetrical keys. Then a symmetrical key is transmitted using the asymmetrical encoding. When both ends have the symmetrical key, they switch over to the faster symmetrical algorithm. This type of handshake ensures the safe transfer of the symmetrical key between two authenticated parties and provides the speed benefits of a symmetrical algorithm.

4.3.4 Key Exchange

Symmetrical and asymmetrical keys require the keys to be shared before use. In 1976, Whitfield Diffie and Martin Hellman developed an algorithm to exchange a secret key in a public forum without compromising the key [Diffie1976]. Called the *Diffie-Hellman key exchange* (DH), this algorithm is based on a mathematical property: factorization is more difficult than multiplication. DH is commonly used in network protocols because keys are not always preshared. IPsec, IPv6, SCTP, SSH, and SSL all support the DH key exchange.

The file dh.c *on the companion CD-ROM contains sample code that performs a Diffie-Hellman key exchange.*

ON THE CD

In the basic DH algorithm, two parties share a predetermined prime number and primitive root. A *primitive root* (r) is any number where the modulus of its exponents covers every value (v) up to the prime number (p).

For each $v=1...p$; there exists some k: $r^k \bmod p = v$ (4.5)

For example, if the prime number is 7,919, then 3 is a primitive root, but 107 is not. The primitive root is used to generate shared secret values. By covering all possible values (v) up to the prime, the primitive root ensures that an attacker must scan up to 7,919 values to identify the key.

This simple example used 7,919, which is too small to be a secure prime value. Most implementations use much longer prime numbers, where the time needed to compute each r^k becomes prohibitive. Good prime numbers can be 300 digits or longer.

The prime number and root can be publicly known and traded. Disclosing this information does not impact the security of the algorithm. Each party also selects a private key. The private keys a and b are combined with the primitive root and prime numbers to generate public keys, A and B:

$$A = r^a \bmod p \qquad (4.6)$$

$$B = r^b \bmod p \qquad (4.7)$$

The public keys are exchanged and used to determine the shared secret (s):

$$s = r^A \bmod p = r^B \bmod p \qquad (4.8)$$

The shared secret (s) is known to both parties but was never transmitted over the network. An attacker who observes the key exchange knows the public keys (A and B), prime number (p), and primitive root (r), however, to derive the shared secret, the attacker must also determine both private keys. If the prime number has 300 digits (requiring 1024 bits, or 128 bytes, of storage), then it can take a very long time (decades or centuries) to identify the shared secret. Alternatively, the attacker could simply try all of the possible shared secret values—an equally daunting task.

4.3.5 Certificates and Certificate Authorities

The Diffie-Hellman key exchange provides the means to generate a shared secret value, but it does not authenticate either party. Although a man-in-the-middle (MitM) attack cannot compromise an observed key exchange, the MitM can impersonate either end of the key exchange. If an attacker wants to compromise the key exchange between a client and server, he can intercept the initial key exchange. This allows the attacker to exchange keys with the client and server independently and then relay data between them.

Certificates and certificate authorities provide the means to authenticate the ends of a key exchange. A *certificate* is a unique data sequence associated with a host. A *certificate authority* (CA) is a trusted third party that can validate a certificate. When the client and server exchange public keys, they each query the CA with the public certificates. Only authenticated certificates are accepted.

One of the most widely used certificate systems is the Secure Sockets Layer (SSL) protocol. SSL is a presentation layer protocol commonly used to provide security to Web connections—HTTPS is HTTP with SSL. Although certificates do provide authentication, they are not always used in a secure manner. The main risks concern automation, bidirectional trust, and the trustworthiness of the CA server—each of these are detailed in Chapter 21.

4.3.6 Kerberos

The *Kerberos* session layer protocol is an example of a strong certificate-based system. Kerberos uses a *key distribution center* (KDC) for initially granting a certificate. The client must authenticate with the KDC. The authentication requires two parts: a password or digital token, and a client-side certificate. The Kerberos *Authentication Server* (AS) validates the certificate. The result from the KDC and AS exchange is an authenticated client, with the client holding an authentication key.

The KDC and AS allows the client to communicate with a *Ticket-Granting Service* (TGS). Each network service requires a ticket, or service-specific certification, for granting access. The authenticated client requests the service and duration, and is provided a *Ticket-Granting Ticket* (TGT). The client may use the service as long as the TGT is valid.

For example, if a user wants to access a Web server using Kerberos, then:

1. The user logs in to the system, validating himself with the KDC and AS.
2. The user's Web browser uses the key to request a TGT from the TGS for accessing the Web server.
3. The browser then provides the TGT to the Web server, granting access to the server.

With Kerberos, all keys have durations. The TGT may expire, requiring a new TGT to be requested from the TGS. Session may also expire or require renewal.

In addition to authenticating connections and users, Kerberos provides a foundation for encryption. Each key and certificate encrypts traffic. As a result, an attacker cannot view information transfers, replay packets, or hijack sessions. If an attacker does manage to crack a session, it will happen long after the session has expired. An attacker is better off targeting an end user or server system than attacking the network traffic.

Kerberos is an example of a secure network protocol. It properly employs authentication and privacy through the use of encryption and key management. In addition, Kerberos is an open standard (RFC4120), with source code available from MIT (*http://web.mit.edu/kerberos/*). Systems that use Kerberos include IBM's Distributed Computing Environment (DCE), Sun RPC, Microsoft Windows 2000 and XP, and some versions of X-Windows.

Unfortunately, Kerberos does have limitations. The overhead and management of Kerberos limits its practical usage. In addition, variations of the implementation are not compatible. For example, the MIT Kerberos is not compatible with the Kerberos security in Windows 2000. Finally, applications must be modified to use Kerberos—the protocol is not transparently supported.

4.4 CRYPTOGRAPHY AND RANDOMNESS

An ideal cryptographic system is not predictable. A particular plaintext value generates a specific ciphertext value, but the ciphertext is unknown without applying the algorithm. This prevents an attacker from readily determining the plaintext from the ciphertext. Three common methods are used to obscure, or randomize, the plaintext-ciphertext relationship: random number generators, confusion, and diffusion. These methods combine to form cryptographic *substitution boxes* (S-box). An S-box is used to obscure the relationship between the plaintext and ciphertext.

4.4.1 Random Numbers

Most cryptographic algorithms are based on a controlled random number genera-tor. Given an input, the generator creates an output. But one input and output pair cannot be used to determine a different input and output pair. For example, a sim-ple linear congruence pseudo-random number generator [RFC1750] bases the out-put on the previous value:

$$v_{i+1} = (v_i \cdot a + b) \bmod c \qquad (4.9)$$

Given the same inputs (v_i, a, b, and c), it generates the same output (v_{i+1}); how-ever, the output value is not immediately predictable without applying the algo-rithm. Most random systems store the previous value. For example, in ANSI-C, the srand() function initializes (*seeds*) the first value (v_0). All subsequent calls to the rand() function update the previous value.

In cryptography, the random algorithm is seeded using the key. The random values are combined with the plaintext to create ciphertext. In decryption, the ran-dom sequence is re-seeded, and the random elements are removed, leaving the plaintext.

More complicated random number generators use a variety of mathematical operators, including addition, multiplication, bit shifting, and logical AND, OR, and XOR. In addition, some use external data sources for generating *entropy* (in-formation) to mix into the random algorithm. In general, external entropy is not desirable for cryptographic systems because the random sequence cannot be re-generated to decode the ciphertext.

Encryption with external entropy creates a different ciphertext each time. But the dif-ference may not always impact the decoding. As long as the external entropy can be added and not change the decoded plaintext, it can be used to deter cryptanalysis.

4.4.2 Confusion and Diffusion

In 1948, Claude Shannon described two properties for obscuring plaintext con-tents: confusion and diffusion [Shannon1949]. *Confusion* refers to data substitu-tion. For example, a Caesar cipher performs letter-by-letter substitutions (e.g., replace all occurrences of "*a*" with "*w*"). Similarly, Rot13 rotates each letter by 13 characters ("*a*" becomes "*n*", "*b*" becomes "*o*", etc.). More complex systems may perform substitutions across bit patterns or blocks of data.

Ciphers that strictly rely on confusion use the replacement character sequence as the cryptographic key. With Rot13, the key is known, but other ciphers may require statistical analysis or brute-force guessing to determine the key.

Even though confusion impairs readability, it remains vulnerable to crypt-analysis. In English, the letter "*e*" is the most common letter. Caesar and Rot13 ciphers do not remove this property—the most common letter from an encoded English paragraph is likely "*e.*" Complex substitutions may require additional analysis, but they are still vulnerable to frequency and pattern recognition.

Diffusion spreads data. This can be a simple bitwise rotation or a more complex *weaving*. For example, the bits 110011 may be woven by rotation (100111 or 111001) or by interlacing (e.g., patterns such as odd and then even positions: 101101). When diffusion is used across a large block of data, individual byte frequencies can be obscured.

4.4.3 S-Box

S-boxes combine elements from random generators, confusion, and diffusion. For example, the *Data Encryption Standard* (DES) uses 8 different S-boxes to mix blocks of 64 bits. Sixty-four bits of plaintext are fed into the S-boxes to generate 64 bits of ciphertext. This first pass through all 8 S-boxes is called a *round*. DES then feeds the output into the S-boxes again. In total, DES uses 16 rounds to generate the final ciphertext.

The basic concept of combining S-boxes and rounds exists with most cryptographic systems. The *Advanced Encryption Standard* (AES) uses more complicated S-boxes than DES but fewer rounds. The MD5 cryptographic checksum uses 4 small S-boxes, 16 times each per round, through 4 rounds.

CRC

4.5 HASHES

Secure systems validate data integrity, checking for intentional information tampering as well as accidental corruption. The degree of validation varies based on the needs of the environment. For example, SLIP (Chapter 9) operates over a point-to-point serial cable. SLIP offers no validation or integrity checking because a direct serial connection is generally black and white with regards to operation: it is either functional or it is not. In contrast, the SSH (Chapter 20) network protocol has packets that traverse many networks, and the SSH contents are intended to be private. SSH uses a very sophisticated integrity detection system.

Most integrity validation systems use hash functions. A hash function maps a large set of input into a few bits of data that describe the input. Although it is likely that many different inputs generate the same hash value, identifying the cases where the input does not match the hash value can validate integrity. Data tampering and corruption usually results in mismatched hash values.

Five main types of hash functions are used with network protocols: parity, checksum, CRC, cryptographic, and signed cryptographic. Although most network protocols use simple parity, checksum, or CRC hashes, a few protocols use more secure cryptographic hashes.

4.5.1 Parity

The simplest type of hash function is a parity check. A *parity check* sets a single bit to 0 or 1, depending on the number of 1 bits in the input sequence. For example, if the input is 00110101, then the 1-bit parity is 0. An even number of bits is assigned 1, and an odd number is assigned 0. A reverse parity check swaps the value assignment (0 indicates odd). A 1-bit parity check can detect single bit errors, but multiple-bit errors that change an even number of bits retain the same parity value. Although parity checks are common for physical and data link layer protocols [RFC935], weak error detection makes parity checks undesirable for higher-layer network protocols.

4.5.2 Checksum

A *checksum* extends the parity concept by adding bits. For example, an 8-bit checksum will segment the input into 8-bit sections and add each of the sections (ignoring any bit overflows). The resulting 8-bit number is the checksum. An 8-bit checksum can detect multiple bit errors, as long as the total difference is not a multiple of 256. Similarly, a 16-bit checksum adds each set of 16 bits. The resulting checksum can detect that error totals do not differ by 65,536.

Checksums are commonly used by protocols such as IP, TCP, and UDP. The Internet Checksum, defined in RFC1071, uses a *one's complement*. In effect, the checksum is reversed and represented as a 16-bit value.

4.5.3 CRC

A *cyclic redundancy check* (CRC) uses a polynomial function as an extension to a checksum. The polynomial function acts as an S-box, generating pseudo-uniqueness. Each piece of data is modified using the S-box and then combined in a similar fashion as a checksum. There are many different CRC functions—each with different polynomials and combination methods (Table 4.1). Although any polynomial can work as a CRC, choosing one that lowers the degree of repetition can be difficult.

TABLE 4.1 Different CRC Polynomial Functions

Name	CRC (bits)	Polynomial	Equation
ATM HEC	8	0x107	$x^8 + x^2 + x + 1$
CRC-10	10	0x633	$x^{10} + x^9 + x^5 + x^4 + x + 1$
CRC-12	12	0x180F	$x^{12} + x^{11} + x^3 + x^2 + x + 1$
CRC-CCITT	16	0x1021	$x^{16} + x^{12} + x^5 + 1$
CRC-DNP	16	0x3D65	$x^{16} + x^{13} + x^{12} + x^{11} + x^{10} + x^8 + x^6 + x^5 + x^2 + 1$
CRC-16	16	0x8005	$x^{16} + x^{15} + x^2 + 1$
CRC-32	32	0x4C11DB7	$x^{32} + x^{26} + x^{23} + x^{22} + x^{16} + x^{12} + x^{11} + x^{10} + x^8 + x^7 + x^5 + x^4 + x^2 + x + 1$
CRC-64-ISO	64	0x1B	$x^{64} + x^4 + x^3 + x + 1$

Rather than computing each CRC value every time, precomputed tables are used. The tables are commonly based on a particular factor of the polynomial. In addition, many polynomials match bit patterns—computing the actual polynomial is not necessary. For example, CRC-CCITT matches the bit-wise polynomial 0001 0000 0010 0001 ($2^{12}+2^5+2^0$ or 0x1021)—the 2^{16} term is not needed because it is a 16-bit checksum. Listing 4.1 is a function that precomputes the CRC-CCITT table, and Listing 4.2 shows the full table.

LISTING 4.1 CRC-CCITT Initialization

```
/***********************************************
 CRC_CCITT_Init(): Initialize the CRC-CCITT table.
 This is a 16-bit CRC.
 ***********************************************/
u_int *    CRC_CCITT_Init  ()
{
  static u_int CRC_table[256];
  u_int i;
  u_int Bits;
  u_int CRC;

  for(i=0; i<256; i++)
    {
    CRC = (i << 8);
    for(Bits=0; Bits<8; Bits++)
      {
      CRC = CRC * 2;
      if (CRC & 0x10000) . CRC = CRC ^ 0x1021;
```

```
        }
      CRC_table[i] = (CRC & 0xffff);
      }

    return(CRC_table);
} /* CRC_CCITT_Init() */
```

LISTING 4.2   The CRC-CCITT Precomputed Table

00 - 07:	0000 1021 2042 3063 4084 50a5 60c6 70e7
08 - 0F:	8108 9129 a14a b16b c18c d1ad e1ce f1ef
10 - 17:	1231 0210 3273 2252 52b5 4294 72f7 62d6
18 - 1F:	9339 8318 b37b a35a d3bd c39c f3ff e3de
20 - 27:	2462 3443 0420 1401 64e6 74c7 44a4 5485
28 - 2F:	a56a b54b 8528 9509 e5ee f5cf c5ac d58d
30 - 37:	3653 2672 1611 0630 76d7 66f6 5695 46b4
38 - 3F:	b75b a77a 9719 8738 f7df e7fe d79d c7bc
40 - 47:	48c4 58e5 6886 78a7 0840 1861 2802 3823
48 - 4F:	c9cc d9ed e98e f9af 8948 9969 a90a b92b
50 - 57:	5af5 4ad4 7ab7 6a96 1a71 0a50 3a33 2a12
58 - 5F:	dbfd cbdc fbbf eb9e 9b79 8b58 bb3b ab1a
60 - 67:	6ca6 7c87 4ce4 5cc5 2c22 3c03 0c60 1c41
68 - 6F:	edae fd8f cdec ddcd ad2a bd0b 8d68 9d49
70 - 77:	7e97 6eb6 5ed5 4ef4 3e13 2e32 1e51 0e70
78 - 7F:	ff9f efbe dfdd cffc bf1b af3a 9f59 8f78
80 - 87:	9188 81a9 b1ca a1eb d10c c12d f14e e16f
88 - 8F:	1080 00a1 30c2 20e3 5004 4025 7046 6067
90 - 97:	83b9 9398 a3fb b3da c33d d31c e37f f35e
98 - 9F:	02b1 1290 22f3 32d2 4235 5214 6277 7256
A0 - A7:	b5ea a5cb 95a8 8589 f56e e54f d52c c50d
A8 - AF:	34e2 24c3 14a0 0481 7466 6447 5424 4405
B0 - B7:	a7db b7fa 8799 97b8 e75f f77e c71d d73c
B8 - BF:	26d3 36f2 0691 16b0 6657 7676 4615 5634
C0 - C7:	d94c c96d f90e e92f 99c8 89e9 b98a a9ab
C8 - CF:	5844 4865 7806 6827 18c0 08e1 3882 28a3
D0 - D7:	cb7d db5c eb3f fb1e 8bf9 9bd8 abbb bb9a
D8 - DF:	4a75 5a54 6a37 7a16 0af1 1ad0 2ab3 3a92
E0 - E7:	fd2e ed0f dd6c cd4d bdaa ad8b 9de8 8dc9
E8 - EF:	7c26 6c07 5c64 4c45 3ca2 2c83 1ce0 0cc1
F0 - F7:	ef1f ff3e cf5d df7c af9b bfba 8fd9 9ff8
F8 - FF:	6e17 7e36 4e55 5e74 2e93 3eb2 0ed1 1ef0

For the CRC-CCITT algorithm, each byte is combined with the previous CRC value and the index table:

```
CRC[i+1] = ((CRC[i]<<8)^Table[(((CRC[i]>>8)^Byte)&0xff)]) & 0xffff
```

The resulting CRC value indicates the hash value for use with the integrity check. Different CRC functions are used with different protocols. For example, CRC-CCITT is used with the X.25 network protocol, and CRC-16 is used by LHA compression. CRC-32 is used by the Zip compression system as well as Ethernet and FDDI data link protocols.

4.5.4 Cryptographic Hash Functions

Parity, checksum, and CRC do provide integrity checking, but they also have a high probability for generating hash collisions. *Cryptographic hash functions* use much larger bit spaces. Rather than relying on complex polynomials, these functions rely on S-boxes to encode the data. Cryptographic hash functions generate a *digest*, or fingerprint, from the data. Although collisions are possible, different data generally have different hash values. Unlike the simpler integrity functions, the impact from a single bit change is not identifiable without running the cryptographic hash.

MD5 and SHA1 are examples of cryptographic hash functions. The *Message Digest algorithm #5* (MD5) generates a 128-bit digest [RFC1321]. The US Secure Hash Algorithm #1 (SHA1) generates a 160-bit digest and was intended to replace MD5 [RFC3174]. MD5 and SHA1 are very common for security-oriented systems. Other hash functions, such as MD2, MD4, Tiger, SNEFRU, HAVAL, and RIPEMD-160 are less common.

Hash and Crash Collisions

Cryptographic hash functions are intended to be nonpredictive. Although two sets of data can generate the same digest, finding two sets of data is supposed to be nondeterministic. An attacker should not be able to easily modify data and create a specific hash value. For this reason, many protocols rely on MD5 and SHA1 to validate information. If the information does not match the digest, then the data cannot be validated.

In August 2004, Xiaoyun Wang, Dengguo Feng, Xuejia Lai, and Hongbo Yu published a paper that discussed how to compute collisions for many cryptographic hash functions, including MD5 [Wang2004]. The attack reduces the number of permutations needed to create a specific hash value. In theory, an attacker can compromise a data set and modify the data in such a way that the MD5 digest does not change. This type of modification would not be detected. In December 2004, Dan Kaminsky released a proof-of-concept program that did just that: it modified a file, creating two distinct files that generate the same MD5 digest [Kaminsky2004].

4.5.5 Sparse Hash Mappings

The largest risk to cryptographic hash functions comes from sparse hash mappings. Algorithms such as MD5 and SHA1 work very well for large data sets but offer little protection for small data sets. For example, if the data set is known to consist of five lowercase letters, then there are only 11,881,376 combinations (a relatively small number). Given the hash value, the data can be determined by testing all the data combinations. In any situation where the data set is smaller than the size of the digest, the hash mapping becomes *sparse*—few of the possible hash values are ever used. Because SHA1 generates a 160-bit digest (20 bytes), caution should be used when using SHA1 to validate less than 20 bytes of data. Similarly, if the data set is limited (e.g., only containing letters or numbers), then it simplifies the search process for an attacker.

Ultimately Weak

Internet Relay Chat (IRC) is an application layer protocol that allows real-time text communication. (IRC was the predecessor to Instant Messaging.) Using IRC, individuals and groups can talk to each other in real time, but, they can also see each other's network address. Many denial-of-service attacks were originally developed as a way to disable or inconvenience other people on IRC channels.

There are many different IRC servers. Some offer cloaking capabilities, where the user's network address is hidden from plain sight. UltimateIRCd 3.0.1 (*http://freshmeat.net/projects/ultimateircd/*) is one such IRC server. Rather than seeing the IP address 10.1.5.6, users see the cloaked value fbb8a3c.16b4fba6.11de379d.20846cb9. A regular user is unable to identify the IP address from the cloaked value; the cloak protects users from being targeted by denial-of-service attacks.

UltimateIRCd uses MD5 to perform the cloaking. The IP address a.b.c.d becomes MD5(d).MD5(c).MD5(b).MD5(a). Normally, MD5 is a strong cryptographic hash function. In this case, however, it is used to protect sparse data. IP addresses only use 256 digits. An attacker can precompute all 256 possible MD5 hash values and then look up any address.

NOTE
ON THE CD

On the CD-ROM is a copy of UnUltimate.c—an uncloaking program that reverses the UltimateIRCd 3.0.1 server's MD5 cloak. The server code is also provided.

4.5.6 Signed Cryptographic Hashes and HMAC

Cryptographic hash functions such as MD5 and SHA1 are well defined. Any recipient of the data can validate the contents. A *message authentication code* (MAC) is any cryptographic hash function that uses a key to generate a permutation. When using a MAC, only recipients with the key can validate the data with the digest.

There are many ways to implement a MAC. The simplest method encrypts the hash with a key. Only key holders can decrypt the data and validate the hash. Using this approach, a parity, checksum, or CRC that is encrypted can be good enough to validate the data.

An alternate approach uses a *hashed message authentication code* (HMAC) [RFC2104]. This approach mixes the key with two cryptographic hash calls:

```
Hash(Key XOR outerpad, Hash(Key XOR innerpad, Data))
```

The inner pads and outer pads (innerpad and outerpad) ensure that two different key values are used. Also, passing one digest into a second hash function increases the variability. Listing 4.3 provides an example using MD5 as the hash function.

LISTING 4.3   HMAC Using MD5

```
void Hmac_MD5 (char Key[64], char Digest[64],
               char *Data, int DataLen)
{
  MD5_CTX context;
  char innerpad[64], outterpad[64];

  /* XOR key with innerpad and outerpad values */
  for(i=0; i<64; i++)
    {
    innerpad[i] = Key[i] ^ 0x36;
    outterpad[i] = Key[i] ^ 0x5c;
    }

  MD5Init(&context); /* initialize the inner context */
  MD5Update(&context,innerpad,64)   /* MD5 the inner key */
  MD5Update(&context,Data,DataLen); /* MD5 the data */
  MD5Final(Digest, &context);       /* Compute digest */

  MD5Init(&context); /* initalize the outer context */
  MD5Update(&context,outterpad,64); /* MD5 outer key */
  MD5Update(&context,digest, 16);   /* MD5 with previous digest */
  MD5Final(digest, &context);       /* Compute new digest */
} /* Hmac_MD5 */
```

For most network protocols, the integrity check is passed along with the packet. Protocols that depend on parity, checksum, CRC, and basic cryptographic hash algorithms are vulnerable to modification. Because the algorithms are well known, an attacker can modify the data and send a valid hash value along with the data. By using an HMAC, tampered data will not be validated; the attacker cannot create a valid HMAC without also having the key. HMAC is used by some of the most secure network protocols, including IPsec, IPv6, Secure Shell (SSH), SSL, and Kerberos.

4.6 CIPHERS

In cryptography, there is a clear distinction between encryption and encoding. *Encoding* is a translation from one format to another. Although encodings may not be immediately readable, they offer no protection with regards to information tampering or authentication. Common encoding systems include XOR, Rot13, Mime (or Base64), and UUencoding. More complicated systems include monoalphabetic and polyalphabetic ciphers, such as the Caesar cipher.

In contrast to encoding, *encryption* provides options for privacy and authentication. An encryption algorithm, such as DES or AES, is used to encode data in such a way that the contents are protected from unintended recipients.

Encoding and encryption algorithms are *ciphers*. A cipher refers to any system that transforms data. Ciphers contain encoding and decoding components. Encryption and decryption functions provide the encoding and decoding functionality. In contrast, hashes are not ciphers because there is no decoding component.

4.6.1 Simple Ciphers

The simplest ciphers use a fixed algorithm for encoding and decoding data. For example, the *logical exclusive-or operator* (XOR) can perform a simple encoding. Each letter is encoding by performing a bit-wise XOR with a key. If the key is ABC, then the string YES becomes the ASCII characters 0+8. If the string is larger than the key, then the key is repeated to cover the string.

Mime, or *Base64*, encoding is commonly used in email attachments. Email is not designed for transferring binary files. To prevent data corruption, binary files are Base64 encoded [RFC1421]. The Base64 algorithm converts every 3 binary bytes into 4 printable characters that can be safely transferred via email. The encoding algorithm converts three 8-bit blocks into four 6-bit blocks (Figure 4.1). Because 6 bits can hold 64 different combinations, they are mapped to letters (26 lowercase + 26 uppercase), numbers, and two symbols (+ and /). If the plaintext does not end on a 3-byte boundary, then equal signs are used at the end of the encoding. The decoding algorithm reverses this process.

XOR and Base64 are not secure ciphers. Each transforms data but can be readily reversed and provides neither privacy nor data validation. But, on occasion, they are found in places where security is desirable. For example, Web pages that use Basic Authentication for login access transmit a Base64-encoded username and password. Any eavesdropper can readily decipher the login credentials.

FIGURE 4.1   Base64 encoding.

4.6.2 Monoalphabetic and Polyalphabetic Ciphers

More complex ciphers perform character substitutions. Rot13 substitutes each letter with the letter offset by 13 characters. This makes Rot13 a shift substitution cipher—it shifts letters by 13 characters. The Caesar cipher, used by Julius Caesar to communicate with his generals, is another example of a shift substitution cipher. In a Caesar cipher, the number of characters shifted may vary between encodings.

The Vigenere cipher, proposed by Blaise de Vigenere in the sixteenth century, replaces letters with other letters but not by shifting the alphabet. For example, "A" may map to "G," and "B" maps to "W." The letter mappings are consistent but not sequential.

Rot13, Caesar, and Vigenere ciphers are examples of *monoalphabetic* ciphers. Each replaces one *alphabet* (set of characters) with a different alphabet. A *polyalphabetic* cipher replaces one alphabet with multiple alphabets. For example, a polyalphabetic shift substitution cipher may use two alphabets. The original letters are alternately replaced using the different alphabets.

4.6.3 One-Time Pads

Monoalphabetic and polyalphabetic ciphers are vulnerable to character frequency attacks [FM34-40-2]. For example, the letter "e" is the most common English letter. A ciphertext encoding of English text will contain a character that repeats with the same frequency. One-time pads address this issue.

A *one-time pad* is a sequence of random characters that does not repeat. Each random character is combined with each plaintext character, resulting in a keyed ciphertext. Only a recipient with the same one-time pad can generate the same sequence of random characters and decode the message.

In the physical world, a one-time pad is literally a pad of paper with random characters and each sheet is used once. Only the intended recipients have identical paper pads.

In the digital world, a secret key can be used to seed a random number generator. Each character generated is combined using XOR (or a similar function) to encode and decode the ciphertext. Although XOR is normally insecure, the lack of key repetition makes a one-time pad more secure than other strong-encryption algorithms. The only weaknesses are the key size used to seed the random number generator and the "randomness" of the generated sequence. If the generator only takes a 16-bit seed, then there are only 65,536 different combinations. Similarly, if the generator does not create very random data, then the sequence may be vulnerable to a frequency analysis.

4.6.4 Book Ciphers

Book ciphers extend the one-time pad concept to a lookup table (*book*). The book represents the key and environment for encoding the data. For example, the ciphertext "18 32 32" cannot be decoded without using the proper book. In this case, the cipher indicates word offsets from the first paragraph of this chapter (decoding as "do not use"). Book ciphers cannot be decoded unless the recipient has a copy of the correct book.

Many compression algorithms operate like book ciphers, replacing a short ciphertext value with a longer plaintext value. In most cases, compressed files include the lookup table or information needed to recreate the table. But some systems use predetermined books that are not known to external attackers.

The simplest book ciphers use predetermined code lists. The lists determine the type of information that can be encoded. Any system that uses many abbreviations or numeric shortcuts is effectively a book ciphers to outsiders.

4.7 ENCRYPTION

Encryption ciphers use keys to create permutations in the ciphertext. Encrypting a plaintext message with two different keys generates two different ciphertexts. Unlike cryptographic hash functions, encryption algorithms are intentionally reversible. Given a ciphertext and the correct key, the original plaintext can be derived.

The many different encryption algorithms are primarily divided into streaming and block ciphers, with block ciphers being more common. Block ciphers have a few limitations that are mitigated by different block cipher modes. Together, ciphers and modes provide a wide range of algorithms for selection. When comparing algorithms, key size and speed are the primary factors.

4.7.1 Streaming and Block Ciphers

Encryption algorithms fall under two categories: streaming and block. *Streaming ciphers* encode plaintext on a byte-by-byte basis—they operate on data streams. A one-time pad is an example of a streaming cipher. Another example is Rivest Cipher #4 (RC4). RC4 is a symmetrical key streaming cipher commonly used by wireless networks for WEP encryption (Chapter 7) and by SSL (Chapter 21). In each of these cases, the amount of data to encrypt varies, so a stream cipher's byte-by-byte encryption adds little to the transmitted packet size.

Block ciphers operate on data segments. For example, DES applies a 56-bit key to a 64-bit data block. If the plaintext size is smaller than 64 bits, then it is padded. But the algorithm itself only operates on 64-bit blocks. Table 4.2 lists common ciphers with their respective block and key sizes.

TABLE 4.2   Common Block Ciphers

Name	Key Size (bits)	Block Size (bits)
DES	56	64
IDEA	128	64
CAST-128	variable, up to 128	64
RC2	variable, up to 128	64
3DES (Triple-DES)	168	64
Blowfish	variable, 32 to 448	64
SEED	128	128
Serpent	128, 192, or 256	128
Twofish	128, 192, or 256	128
AES (Rijndael)	128, 192, or 256	128, 192, or 256

4.7.2 Block Cipher Modes

Block ciphers have a fundamental weakness: each block is encrypted independently. If a 64-bit sequence appears twice in the plaintext, then a 64-bit block cipher will generate two identical 64-bit ciphertexts. To mitigate this issue, *modes* are used to add variability between blocks.

A variety of modes can be used to seed one block with the results of the previous block. This chaining allows a block cipher to emulate a streaming cipher and reduces the likelihood of a redundant ciphertext block. Common modes include the following:

Electronic Codebook Mode (ECB): ECB splits the plaintext into blocks, and encrypts blocks separately. There is no linking between blocks; each ECB ciphertext block is vulnerable to attack.

Triple ECB Mode: To strengthen weak keys, multiple keys can be used. In 3ECB, the plaintext is encrypted with the first key, decrypted with the second, and re-encrypted with the third.

Cipher Block Chaining Mode (CBC): The ciphertext from the previous block is XORed with the next plaintext block. This deters block-based attacks, but one error in a ciphertext block will corrupt the remainder of the message.

Cipher Feedback Mode (CFB): For the first block, an *initialization vector* (IV) is XORed with the plaintext before encryption. The IV is simply a large binary sequence (number, string, or array) that changes between each ciphertext encoding. In CFB mode, subsequent blocks use the previous ciphertext block in place of the IV. New IVs can be periodically selected to prevent data corruption from impacting an entire message. CFB is effective when the IV does not repeat with the plaintext. But, if the IV repeats with a duplicate initial plaintext block, then the ciphertext also duplicates.

Output Feedback Mode (OFB): For the first block, OFB encrypts the IV with the key. This is used to generate a sequence that is XORed with the first plaintext block (similar to a one-time pad). Subsequent blocks use the previous ciphertext block in place of the IV.

The variety of ciphers, key sizes, block sizes, and block modes allow encryption algorithms to be selected based on a best-fit model. Algorithms can be weighed based on speed, complexity, key sizes, corruption recovery, and other aspects.

Is Bigger Always Better?

Cryptographic attacks attempt to reduce the effective key strength. If some bits are used in relation to other bits, then finding one set of bits can be used to determine the related set. For example, *Triple-DES* (3DES) uses 3ECB to increase the key strength. Because the Data Encryption Standard (DES) uses one 56-bit key, 3DES uses three keys for a total of 168 bits. But 3ECB does not always increase the key strength linearly. Although 3DES uses three keys, the effective key strength is only 112 bits. The attack method requires 7,000 TB (terabytes)—or 2^{56} bytes—of memory. Because this attack is currently not practical for most attackers, 3DES is applicable with 168-bit key strength and theoretically at 112bits.

The American Encryption Standard (AES) was introduced in 2000 as a replacement for DES. AES supports large keys and block sizes, and uses many S-boxes with few rounds. Although AES is large, it is relatively fast, requiring a low processing overhead. In contrast, 3DES uses a smaller key and block size with fewer S-boxes but takes much more processing time to encrypt and decrypt messages.

Similar to 3DES, AES was found to be vulnerable to a potential attack. In 2002, an attack was found that reduced the effective key size from 2^{256} to around 2^{100} [Courtois2002, Schneier2002]. Although AES does not appear to be as strong as originally expected, these theoretical attacks make AES about as effective as 3DES while retaining the performance improvements. (This was a huge finding in the cryptanalysis community, but it has little impact on practical usage.)

4.8 STEGANOGRAPHY

Although encryption is designed to provide authentication and privacy, it does not prevent attackers from observing traffic. An attacker may not know the contents of a data transfer but can see that a data transfer occurred. *Steganography* addresses the visibility-related risks from a data transfer. Encryption protects data by preventing readability—the data can be observed but not understood. Steganography prevents data from being seen. In steganographic encoding environments, the heuristics encode ciphertext, obscuring detection efforts.

Steganography applies camouflage to information. Although forum-specific information is expected, subtle modifications can be used to convey an entirely different message. For example, data may be hidden in images so that the image does not appear noticeably different. Image steganography may encode data within a few pixels. A casual observer will not notice any difference to the image. More complicated algorithms store data in unused bits within the file, or modify image compression rates, index tables, and internal data structures.

Beyond images, steganography can be used to store data in any format, including text. Text-based steganography may alter character spacing, punctuation, line breaks, and even word choice. Strong steganographic systems are undetectable by casual observers. For example, the first paragraph of this section (Section 4.8) ends with a steganographic text message. In the last sentence of that first paragraph, the first letter of each word spells out a hidden message.

It is difficult to identify steganographic messages, but they can be found. Covert channels that use steganography have been observed and validated in forums such as newsgroups (NNTP), email and spam (SMTP), Web pages, and IRC. Secret messages have been seen hidden in images, text, HTML, and even in packet headers for IP, TCP, and UDP. Steganography may use any part of the environment for camouflage. For example, the message may not be in the network packets but rather in the timing between packets. Steganography can even use keys to create permutations within the selection of hiding places. When steganography is combined with cryptography, the resulting ciphertext becomes very difficult to observe, and even if it is seen, it remains undecipherable.

The largest limitation to steganography is the camouflage size. If a 10 KB image is modified to store a few bytes of data, then few people will notice. But if the same image is modified to store 500 KB of information, then the change will likely be noticed. This is similar to the encryption problem when the key is significantly smaller than the data. Without taking special precautions, an encryption algorithm may fall victim to a pattern repetition attack. Similarly, too little camouflage allows detection of the steganographic message.

SUMMARY

The ISO OSI network stack focuses on functionality definitions, but not information security. Data authentication and protection is left to each independent protocol. Information validity is primarily implemented using checksum functions. Obviously tampered or corrupt information can be readily identified, but privacy, authentication, and nonrepudiation are rarely addressed.

Protocols that support cryptography are primarily used for privacy and authentication. Encryption protocols and signed cryptographic hash functions ensure that only authorized recipients can view and validate the information. Encryption addresses privacy, whereas steganography addresses detection. If an attacker does not see the data, then the data cannot be attacked.

REVIEW QUESTIONS

1. What are three methods for protecting information?
2. List five elements common to every cipher.
3. What are symmetrical and asymmetrical cryptographic algorithms?
4. Is Base64 encoding an example of confusion or diffusion?

5. How does an HMAC provide authentication support?
6. Is a hash function a type of cipher?
7. Why are block cipher modes necessary?
8. Can steganography hide images in text?

DISCUSSION TOPICS

1. Section 4.1 mentions three methods for securing information: prevention, restriction, and encryption. An alternate implementation splits data into separate pieces so that no single person holds all the pieces. For example, a safe may need three keys held by three different people. Is splitting information a form of prevention or restriction? Or is it a fourth option? If it is a fourth option, are there other options (a fifth or sixth)?

2. Cryptographic hash functions are commonly used for storing passwords. Examples include /etc/passwd (using crypt or MD5) and LDAP (using SHA1). Why are encryption algorithms such as DES or AES not used for storing passwords?

3. Which poses a greater risk, a sparse hash mapping or a high collision rate? When is one preferable over the other?

4. What is the difference between an encoding, encryption, and hash?

5. Which is stronger, a one-time pad with a 128-bit random number generator, or a 128-bit encryption algorithm such as IDEA, RC2, SEED, or Twofish?

6. Compare and contrast the security-by-obscurity in steganography with the security-by-obscurity in cryptographic algorithms. Which is harder for an attacker to defeat?

ADDITIONAL RESOURCES

The book *Applied Cryptography: Protocols, Algorithms, and Source Code in C* by Bruce Schneier (John Wiley & Sons, Inc., 1996; ISBN 0-471-12845-7) is considered to be the de facto source for introductory cryptography and cryptanalysis. Online, the Wikipedia site offers additional introductory information on cryptography and ciphers (*http://en.wikipedia.org/wiki/Cryptography* and *http://en.wikipedia.org/wiki/cipher*). In addition, the *U.S. Department of the Army's Field Manual* 34-40-2 provides an excellent introduction into cryptanalysis for monoalphabetic and polyalphabetic ciphers.

For steganography, Peter Wayner's *Disappearing Cryptography: Information Hiding: Steganography & Watermarking* (Elsevier Science [USA], 2002; ISBN 1-

55860-769-2) and Eric Cole's *Hiding in Plain Sight: Steganography and the Art of Covert Communications* (Wiley, 2003; ISBN 0-4714-4449-9) offer excellent insight. Unfortunately, most texts on this topic only discuss image-based steganography. Other types of steganography are equally common on the Internet but rarely discussed in detail.

Part

II

OSI Layer 1

In This Part

- Physical Layer
- Physical LAN
- Wireless Networking

L ayer 1 of the ISO OSI model is the *physical layer*. This layer is concerned with the transport of data between nodes on the network. The security issues center around access to the physical layer. Two examples of this layer are physical/wired networks and wireless networks.

5 Physical Layer

In This Chapter

- Types of Physical Mediums
- Physical Network Components
- Physical Network Risks
- Topologies
- Physical Layer Security
- Tracking Attacks

The OSI model begins with the physical layer. This incorporates the physical network mediums, network interface cards (NIC), and operating system drivers for controlling the NIC. What sets this layer apart from all other OSI layers is a physical representation; all other layers are virtual. The type of physical medium and network layout (topology) determines the physical security of the network.

The physical medium does not need to be corporeal. Wireless connections are an example of an intangible physical medium.

The OSI physical layer has one purpose: to directly communicate with the physical medium over a physical link. This communication includes establishing the physical link, transmitting data over the link, and receiving data from the link.

Depending on the type of medium, the physical link may also require activation and deactivation. The transmission and reception of data on the physical layer follows a five-step cycle:

1. A program generates data and sends it to the physical device driver.
2. The physical device driver uses the NIC to transmit the data over the physical link.
3. The NIC on the recipient system receives the data.
4. The data is passed to the recipient's physical device driver.
5. The physical device driver passes the data to higher OSI layers for processing.

The physical layer operates independent of the data sent or received—it only ensures that data is transmitted and received properly, not that the data itself is proper. For example, the program calling the physical device driver could be a Web request or just sending random bits. The physical layer ensures that the transmitted data is not corrupted, but it does not validate the content of the transmitted information

5.1 TYPES OF PHYSICAL MEDIUMS

A *physical medium* is anything that can transmit and receive data. Data signal transmissions include modulating electric voltage, radio frequencies (RF), and light. The type of medium and modulation define the OSI layer 1 protocol. Sample protocols that are commonly used include wired protocols, fiber optics, high-volume trunk lines, dynamic connections (e.g., dialup), and wireless networks. The physical layer protocols include standards that describe the physical medium and the mechanisms for transmitting and receiving data across the medium.

5.1.1 Wired Network Protocols

Wired networks comprise some of the most common physical layer protocols. These wired networks connect end-user computers to servers and branching subnetworks from high-bandwidth trunk lines in buildings and small offices. The largest risks to wired networks come from broken cables, disconnected connectors, and eavesdropping due to direct physical access.

Coax cable was commonly used for wired networks. The 10Base-2 standard, also known as thinnet or Ethernet, used a 50-ohm coaxial cable (RG58) to transmit amplitude modulated RF signals. The designation "10Base-2" denotes a maximum throughput of 10 million bits per second—10 megabits or 10 Mbps—over two wires (coaxial cable). The maximum cable length was 185 meters. A similar standard—10Base-5 (thicknet)—also used RG58 but had a maximum cable length of 500 meters. Thicknet was uncommon outside of most corporate infrastructures.

10Base-T and 100Base-T use twisted-pair wire such as category 3 (Cat3), Cat5, or Cat5e cable with an RJ45 connector. These standards use a low-voltage alternating current to transmit data at 10 Mbps and 100 Mbps, respectively. Faster networks, such as 1000Base-T, can provide Gigabit Ethernet over Cat5e or Cat6 cable. The maximum cable length depends on the category of cable used and the speeds being transmitted.

Cable modems are common for residential service. These use a variety of standards that manage an amplitude modulation RF signal over a coaxial cable (RG57). The data signals operate using different protocols for downstream (64-QAM, 256-QAM) and upstream (QPSK, 16-QAM). Higher layer protocols such as DOCSIS and NTSC manage the modem authentication and data transfer.

5.1.2 Fiber-Optic Networks

Fiber-optic cables carry pulses of light. This medium is commonly used with the Fiber Distributed Data Interface (FDDI) protocol. FDDI is an OSI layer 2 protocol and operates as a high-speed token ring, achieving 100 Mbps and faster. High-speed networks, such as 10-Gb Ethernet, also commonly use fiber-optic cables.

Fiber-optic networks are generally more expensive than wired networks but provide much higher bandwidths. Unlike wired networks, fiber optics are not electrically conductive. If a power surge strikes one node on a wired network, there is a potential for blowing out every node on the network. In contrast, a surge to a node on a fiber network only impacts that node. Fiber networks are commonly found in high-bandwidth and mission-critical environments.

Surge protectors and uninterruptible power supplies (UPS) are commonly used to mitigate the impact from power spikes and brownouts. But some surge protectors do not provide protection from lightning strikes. Be sure the read the owner's manual, terms, and conditions carefully.

5.1.3 Trunk Lines

Trunk lines connect major network hubs with other hubs, providing very large bandwidths. Some trunk lines use copper wire, and others use fiber-optic cable. As an example, T-1, T-3, and FT-1 are trunk phone line connections, and the number indicates the type. A *T-1* is a "trunk level 1" link. It contains 24 channels, with each channel supporting a data rate of 64 Kbps. A *T-3* is a "trunk level 3" link, consisting of three T-1 links, or 672 separate channels. A *fractional T-1* (FT-1) consists of a subset of channels from a T-1 connection and is usually used for leased lines. The physical medium for a T-1 line may be copper wire or fiber-optic cable, and may vary by region. The standards for trunk links also vary by country: a European E-3 consists of 480 channels and is similar to a Japanese J-3 (also 480 channels but a slightly lower throughput).

Other types of trunk lines include OC-1, OC-3, OC-12, and OC-48. These optical cable networks are commonly used by phone companies and can achieve over 2.4 Gbps (OC-48).

5.1.4 Dynamic Networks

Not every network medium is static and always connected. *Dynamic networks* provide a large portion of home and small office network connections and are used when static networks are not required. Dynamic networks generally consist of a *modem* (MOdulator and DEModulator) for connecting to an Internet service provider (ISP). A standard modem sends a data signal over a voice phone line. Dozens of subprotocols for modems include speed (V.34, V.90, K56Flex), error correction (V.42, MNP 2-4), and compression (V.42bis, V.44, MNP 5). A *digital subscriber line* (DSL) is a high-speed digital phone connection over a Plain Old Telephone System (POTS) link. For higher bandwidths, there is ISDN; the *Integrated Services Digital Network* is a type of FT-1 link that includes two 64 Kbps lines (B channels) and one 16 Kbps control channel (D channel).

Dynamic networks are generally less expensive for end consumers, but they do not provide the same high bandwidth as wired, fiber-optic, or trunk network connections. But these networks have one significant security benefit: they are not always connected. When the modem disconnects from the ISP, the network is no longer vulnerable to remote network attacks.

5.1.5 Wireless

Wireless networks are frequently used in places where traditional wired, fiber-optic, and trunk lines are unavailable, too costly, or too difficult to install. Rather than wiring an entire home for using a network, wireless networks permit the computer to be anywhere as long as it can access the wireless hub's radio signal.

IEEE 802.11, also called *wireless fidelity* (WiFi), defines a suite of protocols commonly used for wireless networking. These protocols usually include a suffix that defines the frequency and throughput. For example, 802.11a uses the 5 GHz spectrum and can potentially achieve 54 Mbps. Both 802.11b and 802.11g use the 2.4 GHz spectrum, and may reach 11 Mbps and 54 Mbps, respectively.

Wireless networks can be very inexpensive to deploy because they require only a network *access point* (AP, or "hotspot") and a wireless network interface (SP, or *subscriber point*). Wireless networks do not require any physical medium installation such as cables. But this lack of physical infrastructure means that the network signal is not contained. A remote attacker who can receive the AP radio signal can attack the physical network. In addition, *radio frequency interference* (RFI) may diminish the effective range and throughput of a wireless AP. For example, using a 2.4 GHz cordless phone near an 802.11g hub may dramatically impede the network's range and speed.

5.2 PHYSICAL NETWORK COMPONENTS

The physical layer consists of network components that transmit and receive data over a physical medium.

A network *node* is any device that connects to and uses the network. Nodes usually consist of computers, bridges, routers, gateways, and switches. Nodes may also include load balancers, fail-over relays, and IDSs. NICs connect nodes to the physical medium.

Connectors physically links two distinct physical mediums. For example, a building that uses 100Base-T as a network may use connectors to link two network segments. The two network segments are usually the same medium, so connectors can translate between compatible mediums. For example, a connector may link a network using RG58 (thinnet) cable to a network using RG57 (usually used by cable TV). But a connector cannot link between vastly different mediums. For example, an RG58 network uses RF modulation to carry a signal, whereas Cat5 uses voltage modulation. A connector cannot directly link RG58 to Cat5. Instead, a bridge (OSI layer 2) connects incompatible network mediums.

Connectors usually appear as taps or hubs. A *tap* is a connector used to attach a node to the network link, whereas a *hub* acts as a set of connectors. A single hub may link multiple network segments and include many taps (ports).

Physical mediums lose data coherence over distance. *Amplifiers* are used to boost a signal's strength, lengthening the maximum distance between two nodes. *Repeaters* are similar to amplifiers in that they replay the signal. But unlike amplifiers, repeaters actively receive and retransmit signals. The retransmission may be over a different frequency or medium.

Each physical medium has a limitation to the amount of data that can be transmitted. *Multiplexers* split data among parallel physical mediums to improve data transmission rates. For example, transmitting 4000 bits of data over a single radio frequency is not as fast as splitting the bits and transmitting 1000 bits each over four different radio frequencies in parallel. In this example, using a multiplexer can result in a 400 percent speed increase. *Concentrators* receive the multiple signals and recombine them into the original data stream.

5.3 PHYSICAL NETWORK RISKS

Physical network attacks focus on the physical network components. The attacks include eavesdropping, replay, insertion, and denial-of-service (DoS). Fortunately, these attacks are limited to attackers with physical access; restricting physical access limits the attack viability.

5.3.1 Eavesdropping

Physical connectors permit direct access to the network medium. This direct access results in an attacker's ability to eavesdrop on the data as it passes through the physical medium. Networks are vulnerable to *eavesdropping* when they have open taps, accessible taps, or physical access to the medium. For example, an attacker can use a network hub with an open port to directly interface with the network and record all network traffic. Disabling or restricting access to open ports can mitigate this risk.

When an open tap is unavailable, an existing network tap may pose a risk. The network tap can be disconnected from an existing node and plugged into a hostile node. Alternatively, an existing network tap can be connected to a simple bridge or splitter (e.g., an RG58 T-connector) creating an open tap for the hostile system. Open network taps are slightly more vulnerable than tap hijacking because there is no system to disconnect. When disconnecting a node for a physical insertion attack, network users could notice a node being temporarily disabled.

For physical cabling, the network link can be cut and a connector spliced in-line, permitting a network tap. In most cases, NICs cannot recognize the network topology. An attacker can unplug a NIC from a network and insert a hub in front of the NIC. This is usually faster than splicing and just as effective for acquiring a network tap. Both splicing and insertion attacks can be detected as an interruption in the physical link connectivity. Unfortunately, networks that are prone to interference and occasional disconnects may obscure a splicing or insertion attack. This type of physical layer attack may not be noticed.

More devious than splicing and insertion are vampire clips. Named for their capability to suck the life out of a victim, a vampire clip is a network connector that attaches to a cable. This sensitive connector detects RF variations in a cable and transfers them to a secondary cable. Although most commonly used for audio and video, these detectors work equally well on RG58 and Cat5 cabling.

Using a similar concept to vampire clips, a TEMPEST attack uses a highly sensitive receiver to intercept the RF radiation that is emitted from monitors, computer chips, or network cabling. Although shielded cabling, such as RG58, is unlikely to be vulnerable to this style of attack, network adaptors and unshielded connectors remain vulnerable. In theory, an attacker could be located across the street and accurately eavesdrop on a network.

Wireless networks are vulnerable to broadcast interception and RFI disruptions, which are detailed in Chapter 7.

> **Can You Hear Me Now?**
> New technologies are being developed for addressing risks from eavesdropping. One example is quantum networking [Aoun2004]. Quantum networks rely on the properties of polarized quantum particles. In theory, an eavesdropper would change the signal's polarization, resulting in a detectable variation.

5.3.2 Replay

Eavesdropping is a relatively passive attack and can be frequently done without detection. Because most network connectors permit transmission as well as reception, an attacker can actively transmit data into the network. *Replay attacks* rely on recording signals received over the network and echoing them back onto the network. This type of attack does not require knowing the meaning of the data that is replayed—whatever is recorded is played back.

5.3.3 Insertion

Similar to a replay attack, an *insertion* attack transmits data. But rather than replaying data recorded from the medium, the insertion attack transmits new data. These attacks are usually used to access higher OSI layers on a target system. For example, if a network limits access based on physical layer authentication, an attacker may eavesdrop on the network and insert data after the authentication is completed.

5.3.4 Denial of Service (DoS)

Physical networks are most vulnerable to *DoS* attacks, both accidental and intentional. Simple physical actions, such as accidentally kicking out a hub's power supply from the wall outlet, or bumping and dislodging a network connector, are common forms of an accidental DoS. Intentional DoS attacks include physically cutting a cable or plugging a low-voltage cable into a high-voltage source (and blowing out every device on the network in the process). For RF cables and wireless networks, RFI can effectively disrupt a network. Common sources of unintentional RFI include vacuum cleaners and microwave ovens. Simply vacuuming too close to a Cat5 cable can disrupt the network connection.

Although RFI is usually unintentional, intentional RFI can wreak havoc with equipment—damaging electronics and destroying data. Simple RF "noise" generators can interfere with signal reception, and directional high-energy RF devices

(HERF guns) are inexpensive and can knock out electronics from more than 100 feet away. A *HERF gun* is essentially a highly focused, directional radio transmitter that sends an RF burst. In many cases, simply power cycling an electronic device can reverse the impact from a HERF attack, but, in other cases, the electronics may actually be damaged.

When Animals Attack...

Intentional physical network attacks, such as wiretapping and war driving (Chapters 6 and 7), are relatively uncommon and seldom impact more than one physical network. Network attacks are usually unintentional.

The largest network outages have involved accidental service interruptions at the physical network level. On August 14, 2003, a cascading power failure affected 50 million people in the Northeastern United States and Canada. The power failure began just after 4:00 P.M. and was not fully restored for over 48 hours. During that time, more than 3,500 companies lost network connectivity. Although the majority of the network outages were directly due to the power failure, subsequent systems became unavailable as routers automatically directed traffic around the impacted areas, using weaker network segments. A few of these segments, unable to manage the sudden traffic increase, collapsed under the network load [Cowie2004]. A series of similar power outages impacted California, Oregon, Washington, and adjacent states in 2001, but did not last as long.

Network outages are commonly due to weather, construction, animals, equipment failure, and human error. These service interruptions account for the majority of physical layer attacks. On a local scale, most outages are weather related, stemming from rain, wind, snow, or ice. Tree limbs frequently damage residential power and phone lines. Even though backhoes cutting underground cables are frequently cited for causing outages, they are rare compared to animal attacks. Rodents chewing through cables can account for as much as 25 percent of phone and power disruptions [Sipler2004]. Insects and birds have caused many outages as well. In regions with underwater cables, boat anchors pose a hazard as they snag on submerged lines. Control circuitry and human error cause occasional service interruptions, such as a nine-hour telephone outage in 1990 [Dryburgh2004], but such misconfigurations are less common than animals or weather.

5.4 TOPOLOGIES

The physical link mediums and components combine to form the physical network. The ways they combine determine the network topology (layout). The four commonly used network topologies (Figure 5.1) are bus, star, ring, and broadcast.

Each of the topologies offers a tradeoff between usability and security. Small networks may use single topology architectures, but large networks generally appear as a hybrid where connectors join different topologies.

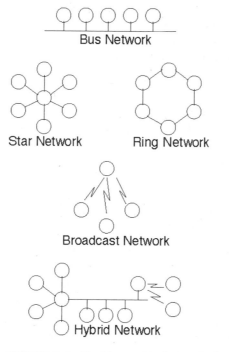

FIGURE 5.1 The five network topologies: bus, star, ring, broadcast, and hybrid.

5.4.1 Bus Networks

A *bus network* consists of a single link that includes all nodes. In a bus architecture, any transmission on the network is received by every node on the network. The primary benefit from a bus network is simplicity: nodes can be readily added and removed without significantly impacting the network. This benefit impacts security, however, in that any node on the network can readily eavesdrop on traffic from every node on the network, and a single physical DoS attack (from cutting the network to RFI) affects all nodes on the network. In addition, bus networks can suffer from performance degradation if too many nodes attempt to transmit at once. Network collisions, when two nodes transmit data at the same time, are common and can lower overall network performance. For example, two nodes (one transmitting and the other receiving) on a 10 Mbps link may benchmark their throughput at nearly 10 Mbps. But four nodes using only a single 10 Mbps bus network may benchmark their throughput at less than 5 Mbps due to network collisions.

5.4.2 Star Networks

A *star network* topology relies on a central hub for communicating with nodes. Unlike bus networks, nodes are not connected to the same physical branch and cannot necessarily observe all data from all nodes. The physical network topology of star networks does not necessarily correspond with the network traffic topology. For example, in a twisted-pair network every RJ45 connector links a node (computer) to a central hub—this is physically a star network.

Hubs usually cannot distinguish where the transmitted data needs to go, so they act as simple connectors/repeaters. They allow all branches of the star architecture see all traffic and the data flow looks like a bus network. But if the hub acts as a bridge or switch (OSI layer 2), then it can interpret the network data and direct it to the correct branches of the star network. In this configuration, the nodes may not see all traffic. If the nodes do not see all network traffic, then the threat from eavesdropping, insertion, and replay attacks is reduced.

Star networks differ from bus networks is several significant ways. Based on cost and extendibility, star networks are usually not as effective as bus networks because nodes cannot be extended off other nodes, as in a bus extension. Moreover, hubs have a limited number of ports. When all ports are used, the hub introduces an added cost for expansion. Star networks, however, can be more efficient than bus networks. Most hubs act as amplifiers, ensuring that a node can be physically far away from other nodes on the network. In contrast, a bus network's maximum distance is physically as long as the distance between the furthest nodes.

From a security viewpoint, star networks can be more resilient to DoS. RFI or network problems with one branch of the network may not propagate past the central hub. Star networks that use star topologies for data flow are more secure than bus networks because a single node cannot readily eavesdrop on neighboring nodes.

Hubs can provide a centralized point for authenticating new network nodes. In a bus network, any node can attach to the bus; authentication happens between nodes, not along the bus. In contrast, star networks may use the hub for authenticating new nodes before accessing a network. For example, modem pools operate as a star network hub, with each phone line acting as one branch. Modem pools may validate new nodes though Caller-ID, username/password authentication, or smart tokens (cards that generate random code sequences). The person dialing in is not granted access to the network until the hub authenticates the caller. The hub includes the option to authenticate new nodes prior to accessing any network layer. This authentication may occur within any of the higher OSI layers, but generally does not occur within the physical network layer.

Unfortunately, star networks have one significant limitation: the hub acts as a central point of failure. If the hub becomes inaccessible for any reason, then the network collapses.

5.4.3 Ring Networks

The *ring network* topology moves the hub from the center of the network to each node. Each node in a ring network contains two connections that lead to two neighboring nodes. Data is passed through the neighboring nodes until it reaches the destination. Ring networks typically maintain two paths between each node: clockwise and counter-clockwise around the ring. As with a bus network, new nodes can be easily added without disturbing the data flow. (In contrast, star networks can result in downtime if the hub runs out of ports and must be expanded.) The result is a robust network: any single network outage will not disrupt the entire ring architecture.

From a security perspective, ring networks are midway between a bus and star network. A single node on the ring can only eavesdrop on the traffic that it receives. Because half of the traffic likely takes a route that does not include the node, the node cannot eavesdrop on all the traffic. In addition, the impact from DoS is limited to the response by the adjacent nodes; if the neighbors do not propagate the DoS, then the DoS has little impact.

As with star networks, ring networks can either be implemented in a physical topology or data link topology. An example of a data link topology is a Token Ring network. In this configuration, all nodes connect to a media access unit (MAU). The physical layout appears similar to a star network, with the MAU acting as a central hub. Every node receives all data on the token ring, The data flow resembles a bus network, but the MAU uses a media access flag (token at OSI layer 2) to indicate when a node may transmit data. A Token Ring network is a tight integration between OSI layer 1 and layer 2.

Ring networks are not necessarily limited to two NICs per node. Although rare, these networks can be expanded to form nets, meshes, and fully connected networks. A two-dimensional grid network consists of four NICs per node, arranged in a grid fashion. Grid routing procedures, such as NW-first (send data North then West before trying South or East), can be very complex. Beyond the installation costs and expansion impact, these networks introduce an extreme level of robustness by providing multiple paths between nodes. They also can improve network speed by splitting data across different routes, and they can improve security by reducing the impact from eavesdropping and DoS.

NOTE *Some Token Ring network cards include multiple channels in one physical device. For example, a single IBM Token Ring card supplies two channels, reducing the number of necessary network cards.*

Expensive Rings

Ring networks can be very robust, but robustness has a cost: implementation expense and speed. Physical layer ring networks require two NICs per node, and many types of ring networks require specialized hardware. This additional cost can become prohibitive for large networks.

Ring networks are usually not as fast as bus networks or star networks. In a bus network, data is transmitted on the bus and received by the destination system (and every other system). The result is that data transmits very quickly. For a star network, the data traverses one relay system: the hub. The result is a small delay between the data arriving at the hub and being relayed out. Ring networks require the data to be relayed multiple times as it passes through adjacent nodes. This results in a slower data transmission rate—usually by a few microseconds. For example, a few nodes on a 10 Mbps bus network transfers data faster than a 10 Mbps ring network. Token Ring network delays are equivalent to relaying data through a series of network bridges.

5.4.4 Broadcast Networks

Broadcast networks are used when data is transmitted over radio frequencies rather than over a point-to-point wire. These networks are very desirable due to their low cost and simple setup—a network only needs a hub (access point, or AP) and a network card containing a transmitter (subscriber point, or SP); they do not require cables linking every node. The only requirement is for the radio signal to be strong enough between the AP and SP.

Broadcast and wireless networks extend on the limitations from the bus network. For example, in a bus network, every node can receive all transmitted data. In a wireless network, anyone with a radio receiver can receive all transmitted data. Similarly, bus networks have limited throughput due to network collisions, but network collisions can be detected. In a wireless network, two distant nodes may not able to hear each other transmitting. In this situation, the AP either becomes unable to distinguish one signal from another, resulting in a network collision, or the AP only receives the stronger signal; the weaker signal is effectively shut out.

Bus networks are very vulnerable to DoS from network interference; interference along the network impacts every node. Broadcast networks become even more susceptible because RFI is no longer limited to noise inserted on a local network bus. Something as innocuous as a neighbor's refrigerator may interfere with your local wireless network.

In addition to the similar limitations to bus networks, broadcast networks include many unique security risks. These are detailed in Chapter 7 and include sniffing, impersonation, and antenna placement.

5.4.5 Hybrid Networks

A *hybrid network* connects multiple network architectures to permit a combination of benefits. For example, a company may use a star architecture for connecting departments but a bus architecture within each department. The benefits for this example include cost, speed, and security.

A hybrid network can be more cost effective than a star network because a single hub is less expensive than supplying a hub for everyone in a department. Using star topology between divisions and a bus within a department limits the cost.

Hybrid topologies can distribute network loads, resulting in faster networks. An active node within a department may impact the bus speed for that department, but the impact will not be felt among other departments.

Hybrid topologies reduce security risks from homogenous networks. A risk impacting one department is compartmentalized to that department. For example, an eavesdropper in the human resources department cannot spy on data from the finance department. Similarly, a hub that becomes disabled may not impact an entire corporation.

Hybrid networks are commonly used to mitigate risks. In Part IV, we will cover how OSI layer 3 uses network segmentation and hybrid architectures to limit system compromises.

5.5 PHYSICAL LAYER SECURITY

The physical layer is strictly concerned with providing access to the physical link, and encoding and decoding data transmitted across the physical media. None of the common physical layer protocols directly provide security. Instead, authentication, authorization, and validation are managed at higher OSI layers, usually by the data link, network, or session layers.

Many physical layer protocols are tightly associated with higher layers for authentication. Examples include dialup lines and wireless networking. Dialup networking frequently relies on PPP or SLIP (layer 2 protocols) to authenticate the user. Similarly, wireless networking uses the Wired Equivalent Privacy (WEP) protocol and MAC address filtering to authenticate clients. These are discussed more in Chapters 6 and 7.

In many cases, the physical layer is implemented as part of an authentication stack (Figure 5.2). The *authentication stack* is an OSI stack that sits in front of the network client's OSI stack, and manages the authentication for the network. When data arrives at a node, the authentication stack processes the data and validates the information. Authenticated information is then passed to the node's OSI stack.

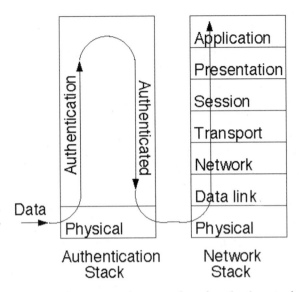

FIGURE 5.2 A sample network authentication stack.

5.6 TRACKING ATTACKS

The capability to identify the source of a physical layer attack depends on the network medium and configuration. In a bus network, each node generates a signal that is received by all other nodes on the bus. Identifying the source of a network problem can be very difficult in this configuration. In contrast, a star network can quickly narrow down the search for an offending node to a specific port on a hub; if there is only one node using the port, then the port can be readily identified.

Breaks in wires and RFI can be much more difficult to locate than an unknown node on a large network. Tools such as time delay reflectivity (TDR) link testers and TDX meters (for measuring RFI and crosstalk along a cable) simplify the search process but may not be readily available. In general, problems at the physical layer cannot be easily diagnosed without special tools.

The size of the network also leads to the ability to diagnose problems. Small networks can identify network problems by removing each node until the problem vanishes. This quickly identifies an offending node or network connection, but this solution is not practical for large networks and does not identify impedance problems. For example, a network may have two incompatible nodes on the same network, such as 10Base-2 and 10Base-5, which both use RG58. Using the same RG58 cable for both networks can result in a network incompatibility that may not be identified by individual node removal.

Needles and Haystacks

A major IT vendor used a star network with a bus data flow for its internal network. Every one of the more than 2,000 nodes could see every other node. During a network audit, one node was identified as having no owner. Unfortunately, the physical location of the node was also unknown, and the bus topology did not lend itself to readily identifying the computer's owner. To resolve this issue, the IT staff creatively modified a network card by disabling the DCD (data carrier detect) signal. This modification permitted the network card to transmit at any time and would likely cause a network data collision. They then watched for packets that used the MAC address (data link layer) of the unknown host. Each time they saw packets from the host, they intentionally transmitted to corrupt the packet. Although they could not identify the node, they could prevent it from successfully using the network. Within minutes, the IT office's phone rang as the node's owner called in to report that his network was down.

SUMMARY

All computers in a network must be connected, either directly or indirectly, through the physical layer. This layer provides connectivity between networked elements. Multiple local networks may be linked using connectors or network devices, but the physical layer is only concerned with providing connectivity—other networking aspects, such as data flows and routing, are managed by higher-layer protocols.

Although few explicit mechanisms exist in the physical layer protocols for providing security, different network configurations and topologies provide implicit security options.

REVIEW QUESTIONS

1. List two types of network mediums that use RF to transmit signals.
2. What are connectors?
3. Name four types of physical network risks.
4. Which network topology has a single point of failure?
5. What is an authentication stack?
6. What types of network attacks are difficult to diagnose without special equipment?

DISCUSSION TOPICS

1. Explain how the security concepts of authentication, authorization, integrity, nonrepudiation, and confidentiality are managed by the different network topologies: bus, star, ring, and broadcast.
2. Diagram the physical layer of a network (e.g., the building where you work). Is the topology a bus, star, ring, broadcast, or hybrid? Does the physical layer data flow use the same topology? Describe some of the security risks and mitigation options.
3. Create a program to detect disconnects in the physical layer connection. Which types of disconnect can be detected? Which cannot be detected?
4. A star network physical topology may operate as a bus network data flow topology. Describe a physical bus network that operates as a star network data flow. What are the impacts to the security of this network?

ADDITIONAL RESOURCES

IEEE is the primary standards organization for physical media protocols. The main protocols are denoted by an index number. Protocol variants, such as faster speeds or subtly different media, are denoted by an alphabetic extension. For example, IEEE 802.3 defines the common twisted-pair protocol 10Base-T. IEEE 802.3a is coaxial 10Base-2. IEEE 802.3u defines 100Base-T, gigabit 1000Base-T is IEEE 802.3z, and 10gigabit is 802.3ae. Similarly, IEEE 802.11 defines wireless networks. Besides the standards organizations, there are many reference works for understanding the details within specific protocols.

- IEEE, CSMA/CD Access Method and Physical Layer Specifications. IEEE Std 802.3-2002.
- IEEE, Amendment: Media Access Control (MAC) Parameters, Physical Layers, and Management Parameters for 10 Gbps Operation. IEEE Std 802.3ae-2002.
- IEEE, Wireless LAN Medium Access Control (MAC) and Physical Layer (PHY) specifications: High-speed Physical Layer in the 5 GHz Band. IEEE Std 802.11a-1999.
- IEEE, Wireless LAN Medium Access Control (MAC) and Physical Layer (PHY) specifications: Higher-Speed Physical Layer Extension in the 2.4 GHz Band. IEEE Std 802.11b-1999.
- Spurgeon, Charles, *Ethernet : The Definitive Guide*. O'Reilly, 2000.
- Gast, Matthew, *802.11 Wireless Networks: The Definitive Guide*. O'Reilly, 2002.

6 Physical LAN

In This Chapter

- Physical LAN Regions
- Types of Attacks
- Firewalls
- Privileged Zones
- LAN Connections

The ISO OSI physical layer can be implemented using a wired or wireless medium. This chapter discusses the common physical layer configurations and security issues with wired networks.

6.1 PHYSICAL LAN REGIONS

Networks are divided into segments based on a combination of the four lower OSI layers. Different segments may represent regions such as a LAN, WAN, DMZ, and MAN. The configuration of these network regions defines the impact from a physical network attack (Figure 6.1). Physical networks may also contain dynamic connections, such as dialup networks. The capability to connect to a physical network directly relates to the security of the physical network.

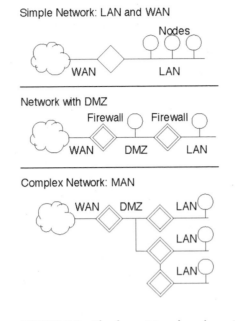

FIGURE 6.1 The four network regions: LAN, MAN, DMZ, and WAN.

6.1.1 LAN

A *local area network* (LAN) consists of local physical and data link layers. A group of LANs may be combined using network devices that operate at the data link, network, or higher layers. The definition of a LAN is not explicit—a LAN in a home may consist of one physical network, whereas a LAN for a company may incorporate hundreds of independent physical networks, forming an *intranet*. A LAN is local to the people who control it, and LAN traffic is usually considered trustworthy.

6.1.2 WAN

Networks connect to other networks. Anything that is not considered local (LAN) is part of the *wide area network* (WAN) or *extranet*. The WAN consists of all networks that are connected to the LAN either directly or indirectly but are not local. Unlike the LAN, network traffic on the WAN is potentially hostile and usually untrusted.

6.1.3 DMZ

The *demilitarized zone* (DMZ) defines an explicit network segmentation between the LAN and WAN. Network traffic on a LAN is generally considered authorized and friendly. A user on a LAN usually has easier and direct access to internal network resources. In contrast, network traffic on the WAN is usually unauthorized for accessing internal LAN resources. The DMZ separates the LAN and WAN traffic by providing a location for higher OSI layers to filter network traffic.

6.1.4 MAN

Many large organizations consist of multiple, independent LANs. Sometimes called an "internal-LAN" or "corporate-LAN," a *metropolitan area network* (MAN) consists of closely linked LAN clusters. A large company may contain a different LAN for each division, a MAN for the overall company internal network, and a DMZ between the MAN and WAN.

6.2 TYPE OF ATTACKS

The main threats to wired networks consist of disruption, interference, sniffing, replay, and insertion attacks. Mitigating the risk from unintentional attacks (DoS by disruption or interference) is different from reducing risk from intentional attacks.

6.2.1 Disruption

Any break to the physical network connectivity prevents the network from functioning. Common disruptions within a network segment include power outages and disconnected network cabling. Mitigation options usually include backup power supplies and restricted access to core networking devices.

A Simple Disruption

Unfortunately, network disruptions can come from anywhere. A science department at a Midwest university had a problem: the department's primary network printer was powered off each evening by an unknown event. After a few days of investigation, the cause was identified. Each evening the custodial staff would enter the building. They would plug the vacuum cleaner into the same power strip as the printer, causing a power spike that reached the surge protector in front of the printer. The surge protector cut power to the printer while the vacuum cleaner was in use. After the custodial staff left, power was restored but the printer remained off. This network attack was due to an unintentional power disruption. The solution for this problem was simple: the custodial staff was asked to use a different outlet.

6.2.2 Interference

Physical networks require physical connectivity. The medium used to convey network traffic can also transport other signals. If an unauthorized signal (interference) enters the medium, then network devices may be unable to distinguish data from noise. Fortunately, most physical layer protocols specify mediums with explicit shielding requirements that prevent ambient noise from entering a network. Data-encoding techniques can also mitigate the impact from interference. Most specifications define a degree of tolerance for interference—a high amount of radio frequency interference (RFI) near a network cable can still render the cable useless for transporting data.

6.2.3 Intentional Attacks

Threats from sniffing, replay, and insertion attacks are usually intentional. Fortunately, they can all be mitigated through network configuration. Common options include firewalls and network configurations that employ a DMZ, onion, or garlic orientation.

6.3 FIREWALLS

The separation between network segments is only as effective as the device that connects them. Systems that are directly connected to the Internet have no protection. *Firewalls* are a type of system that filters network traffic as it passes between network segments and can protect specific network protocols. For example, a filtering Web proxy (OSI layer 7) is effectively a Web firewall. Firewalls are primarily associated with the lower OSI layers: physical, data link, network, and transport. Any mitigation option that relies on filtering network traffic can be implemented in a firewall.

Firewalls span at least two network segments. One segment is for the trusted LAN, and one is for the untrusted WAN, although the firewall implementation may have any number of network ports. Firewalls may be provided as software or hardware. Both types of firewalls are capable of providing both inbound and outbound protection.

Soft or Hard, Where?

There are two types of firewall solutions: hardware and software. Both are implemented in software (or firmware), both are configurable, and both run on computers (or microcomputers). The difference between a *software firewall* and a *hardware firewall* is the network integration.

A *hardware firewall* exists as a stand-alone system. It can see network traffic but not running applications. In contrast, a *software firewall* is integrated into an end-user workstation. This allows the software firewall to associate network traffic with running applications, but it only sees traffic that passes through the workstation. A PC that acts as a workstation, filters packets, *and* relays traffic can be both a hardware and software firewall at the same time; it is a hardware firewall for relayed network traffic but a software firewall to the local system.

6.3.1 Software Firewalls

A *software firewall* places the network filtering directly on a computer that runs network applications. In this configuration, the network adapter appears as the firewall's WAN, and there is essentially no physical medium between the firewall, LAN, and node. The firewall only protects the computer running the firewall.

A software firewall is not the same as installing firewall software on an isolated computer. A software firewall means the protection is integrated into an end-user system.

Software firewalls can be very desirable under some circumstances:

Cost: Software solutions are generally less expensive than hardware solutions.

Complexity: For nontechnical people, installing software is generally easier than installing hardware because there are no wires or additional hardware to plug in.

Flexibility: Frequent changes to a firewall's configuration can usually be handled easier through software than hardware.

Personalization: A firewall on the local computer can observe current applications and automatically adjust the network filter's configuration.

Outbound filtering: As with personalization, outbound (*egress*) filtering is best performed close to the system creating the traffic. A software firewall places the egress filtering as close to the system as possible: it resides *on* the system.

Although software firewalls can address risks from higher-layer protocols, the physical network is not protected: any inbound traffic must reach the computer, and all outbound traffic is visible to the firewall's WAN.

Software firewalls require a host operating system. Specific driver implementations under the operating systems pose risks to the firewall. All network traffic from the WAN must reach the computer before it can be filtered by the software firewall. This means that the signal is (1) received by the computer, (2) processed by the physical layer driver on the computer, and (3) may pass multiple OSI layers before reaching the software firewall. Any vulnerable driver implementation below the software firewall can lead to a system compromise.

Although not necessarily ideal for filtering inbound packets, software firewalls are very effective for filtering outbound packets. A software firewall can match data attempting to leave a LAN with processes on the system. Unauthorized data can be identified and immediately restricted. In contrast, a hardware firewall only sees the network request after the data has left the computer. There is no method for a hardware firewall to determine whether or not the data is intentional and authorized.

An attack, such as a DoS, can significantly impact a computer using a software firewall because the firewall must defend against the DoS. This can appear as a sudden resource drain (slow response time) for anyone using the computer.

A software firewall only protects the computer running the software. The protection does not extend to other systems on the network that also connect to the WAN. But the firewall does protect systems that relay through the firewall host.

6.3.2 Hardware Firewalls

A *hardware firewall* creates a clear, physical distinction between the computer on the LAN and the WAN. The hardware firewall is placed between the LAN computers and the WAN. For home users, the firewall is positioned between the computer and the cable, DSL, or telephone modem. The hardware firewall provides additional protections not available from a software firewall.

For egress filtering, any network traffic that exits the computer stays on the LAN. Only traffic intended to leave the LAN passes through the firewall. But unlike software firewalls, a hardware firewall is distinct from the computers on the LAN; the firewall cannot identify the application generating the network traffic and therefore cannot customize the outbound filtering process.

Although a hardware firewall is still a network device and may contain risks from specific driver implementations, an attacker must first compromise the firewall before attempting to compromise a system on the LAN. Because the firewall is a dedicated hardware device, it is generally more difficult to compromise, and attacks, such as a DoS, are stopped at the firewall. Computers inside the LAN may notice a slow response time for accessing systems on the WAN, but there is no impact between systems in the LAN. For networks with a single computer in the LAN, such as a residential computer, the computer will still be responsive, but the network may appear sluggish.

Regardless of whether the firewall is hardware or software, the benefits from a residential firewall are not limited to cable, DSL, or telephone modems. Customers with satellite, ISDN, and other connections face the same security threats.

6.3.3 Home Users and Firewalls

Malicious network attackers commonly target home users because over 65 percent of homes do not use any type of firewall [Roberts2004]. According to the Internet Storm Center, an unprotected computer on the network will likely be compromised in less than 30 minutes [ISC2005]. Because most ISPs offer little or no protection from malicious network traffic, most people using DSL, cable, or telephone modems are vulnerable. The reasons home users do not use firewalls vary, but they commonly include the following:

Perceived cost: A home firewall solution is an additional cost. Most home users do not factor in any return on investment from the network protection. In addition, many software firewalls are free for personal use or bundled with the operating system. For example, Windows XP includes a personal firewall, and most versions of Linux and BSD include `iptables`, `tcpwrappers`, and other filtering options.

Complexity: Any type of firewall is more complex than no firewall.

Nontechnical: Most home users do not realize that they are vulnerable. In addition, many service providers run ad campaigns touting security but not specifying details. Few home users realize that security is relative, so these campaigns spread a misconception of protection.

Oversight: Many home users do not know what protections their ISPs provide (if any). Many also do not realize that network connectivity is bidirectional.

Confusion: Security protection at the OSI application layer, such as a spam filter or antivirus system, does not provide protection for the lower OSI layers. People commonly believe that one type of protection covers all risks.

Total value: Many home users believe that they have nothing of value on their systems. They forget that simply having a system on the network is valuable to an attacker.

On the Campaign Trail

Most home users are not technical. When they are told that a system is "secure," they do not question *how* or *from what.* Advertisers frequently tout security without providing necessary details, which leads to a false sense of security for most home users. For example, Comcast says it provides security for cable modem users: "Comcast Security Channel features McAfee virus protection, firewall and parental controls to help ensure a safe online environment for your family" [Comcast2006]. Although Comcast offers security options, they do not mention that a user must install anything. In 2001, America Online modified its ad campaign in response to complaints about security misrepresentation from the Council of Better Business Bureaus [Saunders2001]. When an advertiser says it offers security, customers must remember to ask *how* and *from what.*

6.4 PRIVILEGED ZONES

A single firewall essentially creates a barrier between the less trusted WAN and the more trusted LAN. A single firewall defines two *privileged zones*. Within an organization, there are frequently many different degrees of trust. These can be explicitly defined at the physical layer by using *segmented topology*: a series of zones that segment each level of trust. The most common topologies are DMZ, onion, and garlic, named after their layered structures (Figure 6.2).

The terms LAN and WAN are relative to the levels of trust. A corporate data center located deep within a company may view the LAN as the critical servers and the WAN as "everything else"—a data center's WAN usually includes other intranet network segments.

6.4.1 DMZ

The *DMZ* is an isolated network segment between the LAN and WAN. Although physical connectivity exists between the DMZ and LAN, the connection relies on a network device, such as a router or gateway, at a higher OSI layer to complete the connectivity. This provides three key benefits for network security by limiting data flow, limiting physical connectivity, and providing a monitoring access point.

Network devices (firewalls) that link a LAN to a DMZ ensure that data within a LAN only flows to the DMZ when it is explicitly intended to pass to the DMZ or WAN. Similarly, data from the WAN cannot pass from the DMZ to the LAN

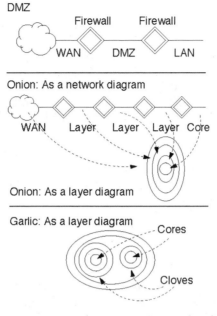

FIGURE 6.2 The DMZ, onion, and garlic network configurations.

unless the firewall permits the data flow. This limitation prevents an attacker from arbitrarily entering a LAN from the WAN.

Any network device in the DMZ cannot sniff traffic on the LAN. The DMZ only receives traffic flowing between the LAN and WAN. Because the capability to sniff network traffic is essential to a replay or insertion attack, the DMZ prevents all three intentional attack methods. In addition, a DoS from the WAN or external interference is blocked at the DMZ and does not disrupt the LAN.

Firewalls are designed to restrict unauthorized access. Other systems, such as an intrusion detection system (IDS) and intrusion prevention system (IPS) can leverage a DMZ. Because all traffic entering or leaving the LAN must pass through the DMZ, IDS and IPS systems can monitor the DMZ for suspicious network traffic and rapidly identify a potential compromise.

The DMZ defines a physical separation between the LAN and WAN, but the firewall determines the effectiveness of the DMZ. Higher OSI layer protocols may pass through a firewall and impact the LAN's security, but the DMZ still prevents sniffing LAN traffic outside of the LAN. Networks that are not vulnerable to sniffing are also not vulnerable to replay and insertion attacks.

Home Sweet Home

Many homes are connected to the Internet using a cable modem. The cable modem acts as a bridge, converting RG57 network cable signals into 10Base-T (or 100Base-T or USB) Ethernet signals. But the cable modem does not filter any network traffic. People with cable modems frequently see the network activity light blink when their computers are not using the network. This activity comes from the WAN. Unfortunately, this also means that any hostile entity on the WAN can directly access any computer plugged directly into the cable modem. If the computer is vulnerable to any network attacks, then the system can be readily compromised. To mitigate this risk, home users should use a software or hardware firewall to separate their computer (and LAN) from the WAN.

6.4.2 Onion

An *onion network* appears as sequential layers of LANs divided by firewalls. Each layer is called a ring and acts as an independent network segment between the adjacent rings. The center layer of the onion is called a core; each onion only contains one core. The firewalls between the layers restrict access to each layer, with the core being the most restrictive. For example, a bank may implement a DMZ between the Internet and its network, with only an external Web server in the DMZ. A second fortified layer (ring) is placed between the DMZ and application servers—the firewall only permits specific requests from the DMZ to the application servers. A third ring separates the database systems containing customer information—this firewall only permits specific requests from the application servers to access the databases. A series of sequential isolated regions is called an onion network or *onion topology*, after the many layers of skin within an onion.

Onion topologies usually number each ring starting with the inside. The core is ring zero. Lower numbers imply more trust.

Beyond the security aspect, an onion topology also improves network traffic performance. In a bus network, all traffic reaches every node. For an onion network, traffic not intended for an internal ring does not enter the internal ring. This results in more bandwidth being available for internal rings.

6.4.3 Garlic

A cluster of layered networks forms a *garlic network*, also called a bubble or cell network. Each of the onion networks is called a clove, and each clove contains a core.

Different cloves may be at different depths and may include subnetworks containing additional cloves. The primary security feature of a garlic network is organization: a node in one layer (or core) cannot communicate with a different layer unless the traffic traverses one path in the network.

Garlic topologies are optimal for large organizations with distinct divisions, and each division includes multiple layers of trust. For example, IBM is a large company with a multinational presence. The MAN consists of all the different primary office locations. Internal zones separate the offices—as much for limiting unnecessary network traffic as for network security. Each office may include multiple divisions (human resources, finance, research & development, etc.) that do not need to be on the same physical LAN, and mission-critical servers (such as databases or backup systems) are frequently kept in internal zones. The result is a garlic network, with each clove containing a division with mission-critical systems.

Garlic networks provide many benefits to large corporations:

Lower bandwidth: LANs within the MAN do not receive excess network traffic from other networks.

Intentional attack mitigation: Attackers cannot sniff traffic beyond the immediate LAN.

Service protection: Layered firewalls provide protection from intentional and accidental DoS attacks.

Service segmentation: If any particular LAN loses connectivity, it does not impact exterior rings or other cloves. LANs outside of the impacted region maintain their network connectivity.

6.5 LAN CONNECTIONS

To exploit a security risk at the physical layer, the attacker must connect to the LAN. LANs are generally dynamic, with systems periodically appearing and disappearing, but the type of physical network connection is either static or dynamic.

6.5.1 Static Connections

A *static connection* is a physical link between the node and network. The link is always present even when the node is offline. Static connections usually appear as a physical wire connecting nodes to the network. An attacker has many choices for exploiting a static connection because it is a direct link to the physical network, including risks from open taps, tap hijacking, splicing, and vampire clips.

6.5.2 Dynamic Connections

Dynamic network links may vary the physical linkage between or during the network connection. A good example of a dynamic network link is a dialup modem pool. The physical path between the modem server and modem client varies with each phone call; sequential calls may come from different computers and take different routes through the telephone system. Because the path is dynamic, tapping into the modem connection becomes very difficult unless the attacker taps into the client or server's phone link; identifying the network route and tapping into the phone link at some arbitrary point between the client and server is difficult (unless you are the phone company).

Dynamic networks are sometimes called *transient networks* because connections may not be long term. For telephone modems, connections may last a few hours, but days or weeks are unlikely. In contrast, cable modems may use a long-term dynamic connection—remaining online for months or longer without a static network address.

6.5.2.1 Modem Risks

Telephone modem connections have some similar risks and functions with cable modem networks. For example, both convert network traffic to a different medium, both permit bidirectional network connectivity, and both have similar benefits from firewalls. But there are a couple of significant differences between these mediums: speed and access.

Telephone modems have a significantly lower transfer rate than cable modems. This results in slower network connections and a higher vulnerability from DoS attacks. For example, a single attacker generating 20 ICMP "ping" packets per second against a cable modem is unlikely to cause any noticeable network latency. In contrast, the same "ping" attack against a 56 Kbps telephone modem can result in a significant DoS.

Cable modems rarely connect to a corporate LAN. Instead, users connect to the Internet and access services over the WAN. Telephone modem connections usually connect directly to a modem pool. Some pools, such as most dialup ISPs, are isolated and provide similar access as a cable modem. But many companies operate internal modem pools that provide direct LAN access. If an attacker knows a phone number for a modem pool, they can directly attack the corporate LAN using a telephone modem.

Fortunately, telephone modems offer authentication options to restrict physical layer access from the dynamic modem connection. Each modem server includes a network stack that is processed before passing data to the LAN. This stack operates as a firewall, separating the modems from the LAN, and provides a point for authentication prior to granting access.

6.5.2.2 Modem Authentication Credentials

Many modem pools require login credentials such as a username and password for authentication. OSI layer 2 protocols such as PPP and SLIP can request and authenticate login credentials. The network connection is linked to the LAN until the login credentials are authenticated.

Usernames and passwords can be compromised in many ways, from simple brute-force guessing to complicated password cracking or dialup wiretapping. An alternate form of authentication uses smart tokens. These cryptographic systems generate dynamic values to ensure a different authentication certificate each time. As with passwords, smart tokens can authenticate connections at any of the higher OSI layers.

With most credential-based systems, including passwords and smart tokens, the authentication occurs at the initiation of the connection. There is usually no authentication after the link is established. A modem user that connects to a modem pool and successfully authenticates is still vulnerable to physical layer eavesdropping and hijacking.

6.5.2.3 Caller-ID

Caller-ID systems (OSI layer 2) can authenticate a caller based on the calling phone number. When the phone call is placed, the local telephone exchange transmits an automatic number identification (ANI) code. The answering phone receives the code as Caller-ID authentication.

Unfortunately, Caller-ID is not always accurate. The Caller-ID code can be faked (spoofed) using an ISDN, PBX, or VoIP system. Operator-assisted calling, where the operator enters the caller's phone number manually—operator number identification (ONI)—can be used to deliberately provide an alternate Caller-ID value.

6.5.2.4 Automated Callback

Many secure systems perform a callback, where the modem pool calls the client rather than answering the phone call. To initiate a phone call, the caller dials (signals) a predetermined phone number. The receiving system may answer the call (or just record that the phone rang), and may authenticate the caller using Caller-ID or other credentials. Then the modem pools calls the client back. The callback may be to the Caller-ID number or a static number. The client answers the callback and completes any remaining authentication steps.

The result from this complicated handshake is an outbound call—from the modem pool to the caller—that cannot be intercepted through Caller-ID spoofing. But, automated callbacks can be intercepted and redirected through simple systems such as call forwarding.

6.5.2.5 Creating Secure Dynamic Connections

A very secure dialup system will use two or more authentication mechanisms. The combined elements may include passwords, smart cards, Caller-ID, automated callback, and validation based on other credentials. This defense-in-depth limits the impact from a single compromise.

SUMMARY

The physical layer usually does not include direct security precautions. Nothing in the common wired protocols (IEEE 802.3) provides or enforces network security; however, the physical network configuration, placement of firewalls, and authentication stack locations directly leads to stronger physical network security. The security within the wired physical layer depends on the following elements:

Network medium: RG58, Cat5e, fiber, and so on.

Physical access to the medium: Cutting, splicing, or open ports.

Network topology: Bus, star, ring, broadcast, or hybrid.

Network zones: DMZ, onion, or garlic.

Node connectivity: Static or dynamic.

Authentication stack: Placement and types of credentials.

REVIEW QUESTIONS

1. Name four network regions.
2. List five types of threats to the LAN.
3. What is egress filtering?
4. What is a segmented network topology?
5. What are three methods for authenticating dynamic LAN connections?

DISCUSSION TOPICS

1. Many home users employ both software and hardware firewalls. Describe the benefits from using both types of firewalls. How do the benefits differ for computers located in large companies?

2. Install and configure a firewall that filters outbound network traffic. Are there any unexpected network communications that are intercepted by the firewall?

3. Rogue modem servers pose a large risk for corporations. These appear as unauthorized modems within a corporate network and are usually installed by employees that desire easy access to the corporate LAN from an off-site location. Describe some of the risks from rogue modem servers and mitigation options.

4. The security within the physical layer depends on a combination of the network medium, network configuration, and network zones. Describe some of the security trade offs between using a bus or star topology within the different network zones.

5. What are the security impacts to allowing dynamic node connections (for example, a modem pool) within the different rings and cloves of a garlic network? Is it better to have a modem pool in the DMZ or deep within the core of a clove? Does the same hold true for an onion network?

6. Hybrid networks may include shortcuts between layers within a garlic network. Figure 6.3 illustrates one such hybrid network. Explain the security ramifications of allowing direct access beyond the strict garlic model.

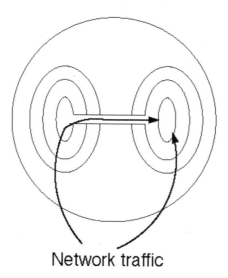

Network traffic

FIGURE 6.3   A hybrid network based on a garlic model.

ADDITIONAL RESOURCES

Many resources exist for configuring firewalls and DMZs. Some are available on the Web, but they are not necessarily detailed or complete. Other resources include reference material. The information in these resources can be readily applied to DMZ, onion, and garlic configurations.

- Schmied, Will, et al., *Building DMZs for Enterprise Networks*. Syngress Publishing, Inc., 2003.
- Zwicky, Elizabeth, et al., *Building Internet Firewalls*. O'Reilly & Associates, Inc., 2000.
- Allen, Julia, *The CERT Guide to System and Network Security Practices*. Addison-Wesley, 2001.

Caller-ID is commonly treated as a secure authentication approach. For example, credit card companies use Caller-ID to activate new credit cards, and many secure corporate environments rely on Caller-ID for authenticating dialup network connections. But many sources exist that explain how Caller-ID works and how to spoof other telephone numbers. For example, the Alt.Phreaking Frequently Asked Questions (FAQ) describes Caller-ID and different methods to modify the Caller-ID value: *http://phreaks.freeshell.org/texts/apfaq/FAQ.html*. A similar document exist at RootSecure: *http://www.rootsecure.net/?p=reports/callerid_spoofing*.

7 Wireless Networking

In This Chapter

- Wireless Spectrum
- Wireless Protocols
- Wireless Risks
- Risk Mitigation Options

Wireless networks are widely found within residential and small office areas. Compared to wired networks, wireless networks are easier to install and less expensive than running wires through walls; however, wireless networks are not ideal in all situations. This chapter discusses basic wireless LAN infrastructures, security implications, and some mitigation options.

7.1 WIRELESS SPECTRUM

Most wireless networks are based on the IEEE 802.11 set of standards. Different versions of the standards define different physical layer requirements. Currently, the most common are 802.11a, 802.11b, and 802.11g.

802.11a: Specifies the 5 GHz radio frequency with a maximum link rate of 54 Mbps per channel.

802.11b: Specifies the 2.4 GHz radio frequency with a maximum link rate of 11 Mbps per channel.

802.11g: Specifies the same spectrum as 802.11b but permits a link rate of 54 Mbps.

The 2.4 GHz and 5 GHz frequency bands were selected based guidelines from the Federal Communication Commission (FCC). The FCC defined these frequencies as ISM and U-NII and designated them for general use.

ISM: The frequency range 2.4 GHz to 2.485 GHz was originally defined for use by *industry, scientific, and medical* (ISM) purposes. Today, the ISM band operates as a general-purpose, unlicensed frequency range. Besides hosting 802.11b and 802.11g, the 2.4 GHz band also hosts cordless phones, garage door openers, pagers, and other wireless devices.

U-NII: The frequency ranges 5.15 to 5.35 GHz and 5.725 to 5.825 GHz are designated as the *Unlicensed National Information Infrastructure* (UNII) band. The use of U-NII is similar to ISB: cordless phones, pages, and wireless devices, including 802.11a, use this frequency range.

Both ISM and U-NII are license-free, general-purpose frequencies. This means any wireless device can use these frequencies without registering with the FCC or acquiring a specific broadcast license. These are relatively crowded spectrums, with interference from other devices being an occasional but significant problem. Overcrowding usually appears as a weak wireless signal or a signal with occasional disconnects. Besides defining the frequency band, 802.11b and 802.11g define 11 channels within the band. The channels are intended to relieve band congestion—whereas one channel may be overly crowded or yield a weak signal, another channel may offer better performance.

Besides being license-free, these radio bands have physical properties that are useful for wireless networks. 2.4 GHz and 5 GHz are microwave frequencies, which means they are not significantly impacted by reflection or refraction as they pass through physical objects. Similarly, they are not impacted by natural events such as temperature inversions or solar flares, and the signals can easily pass though most building materials such as wood and drywall. A home user is unlikely to have problems with the signal itself.

The primary preference for 802.11b/g over 802.11a stems from the line-of-sight range. The U-NII band is a little more susceptible to line-of-sight interference, including walls, metals, water, and people (people being 70 percent water).

Stop That Signal!

Wireless radio signals travel in a straight line, allowing line-of-sight connections. (If the antenna is visible, then it can access the signal.) The main factors for limiting wireless radio wave propagation are transmitted power, material density, and moisture. As radio waves get farther from the transmission source, the signal becomes weaker. Wireless network signals have well-defined power and frequency requirements, and, in most cases, cannot be received beyond 1,000 feet (with normal antennas). This means a home user is unlikely to worry about his network being accessible across town, but the next-door neighbor is fair game.

Microwaves cannot pass though dense materials such as granite, marble, or metal—particularly when the metal is grounded. Solid barriers such as steel doors, elevator shafts, and even filing cabinets may block wireless network access. Similarly, water absorbs microwaves, so placing the wireless access point next to a fish tank may not be a good idea.

7.2 WIRELESS PROTOCOLS

The 802.11 specification is part of the IEEE 802 suite of standards that define both medium (wireless frequencies or physical wires) and device identification. Because many wireless devices may share the same frequency, 802.11 defines how a wireless network *subscriber point* (SP) identifies the correct wireless network *access point* (AP). These include a service set identifier (SSID) and wired equivalent privacy (WEP).

7.2.1 SSID

The *service set identifier* (SSID) is a 32-character text string used to identify an AP and distinguish it from other APs. For example, 802.11b defines a frequency range (2.4 GHz) and 11 channels within that range. An AP may be placed on any single channel, but many APs may share the same channel. The SSID is used to distinguish APs that share a channel.

7.2.2 WEP

IEEE 802.11 defines the *wired equivalent privacy* (WEP) protocol, providing a degree of security to wireless networks. In a wired network, privacy is limited to physical access—if an attacker cannot gain physical access to the network, then the physical network is likely secure. In contrast, wireless networks broadcast a radio signal. Anyone who can receive the signal immediately gains physical access to the medium. WEP defines a cryptographic authentication system that deters unauthenticated SP access. The WEP cryptography includes keys and encryption. But, the cryptographic algorithm specified by WEP is weak and easily compromised.

7.2.2.1 WEP Keys

WEP supports two types of encryption: 64 bit and 128 bit. These correspond with 40-bit and 104-bit length secret keys, respectively. These *keys* are used to authenticate network access.

There are two ways to create the secret key. The first method simply allows the user to enter in the 8- or 16-character hexadecimal number that represents the key; however, this is not a convenient method for most people. As an alternative, many AP configurations permit the use of a text-based password for generating the secret keys. A text password is hashed into a 40-bit (or 104-bit) encryption key. To maintain device compatibility, nearly every wireless vendor implements the same hash functions. The same text password should generate the same key independent of the vendor.

Regardless of the generation method, the AP and SP must have the same key. Although this key is never transmitted, it is used for encrypting the wireless data stream.

7.2.2.2 WEP 40-Bit Password Hash

ON THE CD The algorithm used to convert a text string into a secret key differs based the encryption strength. The CD-ROM contains source code for WEP-password—a program that generates WEP keys based on text strings.

For the 40-bit encryption, a simple pseudo-random number generator is seeded based on the password (Listing 7.1). The generator creates four variants from the single password, any of which may be used as the WEP key.

LISTING 7.1 Source Code to Generate a 40-Bit WEP Key from a Text String

```
/************************************************
Create40bit(): Given a string, generate a 40-bit
(64bit WEP) public key.  Display the key in hex.
4 keys are created for every 1 password.
************************************************/
void    Create40bit    (char *Text)
{
  int i,j;
  int Seed[4] = {0,0,0,0};
  int TextLen;
```

```
unsigned int Rand=0;
unsigned int Value;

/* Create the seed based on the string */
TextLen = strlen(Text);
for (i=0; i<TextLen; i++)     Seed[i%4] ^= Text[i];

/* Create the initial random number */
Rand = Seed[0] | (Seed[1]<<8) | (Seed[2]<<16) | (Seed[3]<<24);

/* Create the keys */
for (i=0; i<4; i++) /* create 4 keys */
  {
  printf("  Key #%d: ",i);
  for (j=0; j<5; j++) /* 5 bytes x 8 bits = 40 bits */
    {
    Rand = Rand * 0x343fd + 0x269ec3;
    Value = (Rand >> 16) & 0xff;
    printf("%02x",Value);
    }
  printf("\n");
  }
} /* Create40bit() */
```

7.2.2.3 WEP 104-Bit Password Hash

Unlike the 40-bit hash function, the 104-bit key generation uses the MD5 cryptographic hash algorithm. The text password must consist of 64 characters. When the user specifies a shorter password, the phrase is repeated until 64 characters are present. For example, the password "Simplistic" becomes "SimplisticSimplisticSimplisticSimplisticSimplisticSimplisticSimp." Longer passwords are truncated at 64 characters. The 64-character password is then hashed using MD5, creating a 128-bit hash. Finally, the first 104 bits of the hash become the secret key (Listing 7.2).

LISTING 7.2   Source Code to Generate a 104-Bit WEP Key from a Text String

```
/***********************************************
 Create104bit(): Given a string, generate a 104-bit
 (128bit WEP) public key.  Display the key in hex.
 1 keys is created for every string.
 Unlike 40bit WEP, this uses MD5 as a hash function.
 ***********************************************/
void    Create104bit    (char *Text)
{
  char PasswordBuffer[65];
  int i;
  int TextLen;
  MD5_CTX Context;        /* the MD5 state machine (context) */
```

```
        unsigned char Result[16];

        /* Initialize the password by concatenating the same string
           until we reach 64 bytes */
        TextLen = strlen(Text);
        for(i=0; i<64; i++)   PasswordBuffer[i] = Text[i%TextLen];

        /* Initialize the MD5 context */
        MD5_Init(&Context);

        /* Create the 128-bit signature */
        MD5_Update(&Context,PasswordBuffer,64);
        MD5_Final(Result,&Context);

        /* Display only the first 104 bits (13 bytes) */
        printf("  Key: ");
        for(i=0; i<13; i++)   printf("%02x",Result[i]);
        printf("\n");
    } /* Create104bit() */
```

7.2.2.4 WEP Encryption

WEP encryption uses the RC4 stream cipher encryption algorithm. For each packet being transmitted, an *initial vector* (IV) is generated. For 64-bit WEP, the IV is 14 bits long; the IV for 128-bit encryption is 24 bits long. The IV is combined with the secret key to seed the RC4 encryption. RC4 then encrypts the data. The transmitted packet includes the unencoded IV, the encoded data stream, and a CRC checksum. In most cases, the IV is changed between every packet to prevent data repetition.

When the AP or SP receives data, the encryption process is reversed. The RC4 algorithm combines the secret key with the unencoded IV that was transmitted with the packet. This combination is used to decode the encrypted data. The final CRC is checked to validate the decoded data.

7.2.3 WEP Cracking

Although the concept behind WEP encryption is solid, the implementation uses weak security elements. In particular, there are relatively few IV values. For attackers to crack the WEP encryption, they only need to determine the secret key. There are two main approaches for cracking WEP: brute-force password guessing and data analysis.

Although RC4 is not considered an extremely strong encryption algorithm by today's standards, the weaknesses in WEP are not primarily centered on RC4. The WEP weaknesses are due to weak key and IV selections.

7.2.3.1 Brute-Force WEP Cracking

The WEP password is usually based on a hash from a dictionary or common word. Simply guessing passwords and encoding them as a WEP key may quickly crack a WEP system. A *dictionary attack* cycles through a word list, trying every word as a possible key.

WEP and 802.11 define no method for deterring dictionary attacks—an attacker can try thousands of keys without ever being denied access and without ever having the AP generate a log entry concerning a possible attack. From the AP's viewpoint, there is no distinction between a corrupt packet due to a CRC error (e.g., poor radio signal) and a corrupt packet due to a decryption problem (brute-force key attack).

Many APs are configured using weak passwords. These may include people's names, addresses, or manufacturer brands. Amazingly, one security professional reported that a significant number of WEP keys are the same as the SSID. If the SSID says "ABC Corporation" then the WEP key may be the text string "ABC Corporation."

7.2.3.2 Data Analysis WEP Cracking

WEP encryption makes one weak assumption: if an attacker does not see the same IV, then he cannot crack the data stream. In reality, IV values repeat. For 64-bit encryption, there are only 4,096 (2^{12}) different IV values. If the IV does not change between packets, then a duplicate is immediately available. But if the IV changes between each packet, then a duplicate IV will be observed after no more than 4097 packets. When an attacker captures two packets with a duplicate IV, it is just a matter of trying different key sequences to find the ones that result in an RC4 decryption with the correct CRC checksum. By assuming weak passwords for creating the secret key, the search process can be sped up.

Given two packets with the same IV, the entire 64-bit WEP analysis can take a few minutes. 128-bit encryption may take a few hours, depending on the computer's speed. The primary limiting factor is packet volume: if there is very little network traffic, then an attacker must wait a long time before seeing a duplicate IV. But a patient attacker will eventually see a duplicate IV. And given a duplicate IV, it is only a matter of time before an attacker determines the secret key.

7.3 WIRELESS RISKS

Wireless networks face a number of risks that do not appear in wired infrastructures. These include packet sniffing, SSID information, impersonations, parasites, and direct security breaches.

7.3.1 Packet Sniffing

Packet sniffing is the simplest form of network attack. The data flow on a wireless network is essentially a bus topology. Whereas individual SPs may not necessarily hear each other, every SP receives all data transmitted by the AP. This means that anyone connected to the AP can observe at least half of a client's network traffic (and usually all the traffic). This can directly lead to session hijacking or attacks against other OSI layers.

But That's Illegal!

As identity theft becomes more prevalent on the Internet, wireless packet sniffing is becoming a serious threat. In November 2003, three men in Michigan were charged with conspiracy, computer fraud, wire fraud, and possession of unauthorized access devices [Poulsen2003]. The trio had discovered an unprotected wireless network at a home improvement store and allegedly accessed credit card information. The exploitation was made possible due to the open network, allowing direct access into the store's LAN. In other packet-sniffing cases, attackers have passively received wireless packets from hotels and coffee houses, intercepting user's credentials as the victims check their email or log in to work.

On a more entertaining focus, tools such as Etherpeg (*http://www.etherpeg.org/*) and Driftnet (*http://freshmeat.net/projects/driftnet/*) permit capturing images that are transmitted over wireless networks. The resulting collogue represents Web sites people access. Although not generally considered hostile, this still represents an exploitation of the physical layer.

In all of these situations, direct access to the medium directly leads to physical network attacks. Even if the networks used WEP, the ability to sniff the wireless packets would permit WEP cracking and only temporarily deter an attacker.

7.3.2 SSID Information

Many residential and corporate wireless networks provide an attractive nuisance. SSIDs are commonly set to a company's name, family name, or street address. This suggests to potential attackers the type of data they may be able to compromise. For example, an SSID that broadcasts "Bank of Colorado" is much more attractive to attackers than one that broadcasts "Default" or "GL27." The value in the SSID may attract attackers as well as assist users.

War Driving

In the late 1970s, network attackers used *war dialers* to find vulnerable systems. Glamorized in the 1983 movie *War Games*, a war dialer consisted of a computer with a modem. The computer would dial hundreds of phone numbers, looking for one that answered with a modem. This brute-force search permitted an attacker to identify potential LAN APs (and in the movie's case, start a nuclear war).

As technology advanced and wireless networks became popular, war drivers developed. Similar to war dialing, *war driving* consists of a computer with a wireless network card. War drivers roam neighborhoods and streets logging the SSID of every AP they encounter. Many war drivers also use global positioning systems (GPS) to pinpoint the AP's location in the log files.

7.3.3 Impersonation

AP *impersonation* may be intentional or accidental. Anyone can enable an AP, and the SSID can say anything. Attackers may establish a new AP near an existing AP and assign it the same SSID. This creates an impersonation problem for SPs, called an Evil Twin attack. If users want to connect to a known AP, such as their company or a local coffee shop, which AP should they connect to? For sites that provide multiple APs, such as hotels, libraries, or schools, how can a SP distinguish the real APs from an impostor? From the SP's viewpoint, all APs with the same SSID look identical.

WEP may be useful as a distinguishing factor for separating imposter APs from true sites. Unfortunately, with WEP cracking, an attacker can determine the WEP secret key and assign it to the imposter's AP.

An imposter has many options after catching an unaware victim:

DoS: The attacker may choose to prevent network access, causing a DoS against the victim.

Man-in-the-middle (MitM): The imposter may tunnel traffic through a collection system, intercepting or modifying data intended for use by the victim. The victim may identify a MitM attack if a LAN resource is unavailable.

Tunneling: Using an SP as well as an AP, an attacker can create a tunnel between the imposter AP and the true AP. The victim cannot readily identify this sophisticated MitM attack because all desired LAN access is available.

Unintentionally, two sites, such as residential neighbors, may enable APs using the same (usually default) settings. In this situation, they may not be aware or even care that they are using someone else's network.

7.3.4 Parasites

In wireless networking terms, a *parasite* (or leech) is an unwelcome person that simply wants to access the Internet through an open AP. If a wireless network is open (no WEP), a parasite may connect to surf the Web or check email. Parasites are usually uninterested in LAN services and do not obey (or care about) network usage costs, LAN policies such as "no porn," or bandwidth limitations—they just want to access the Internet. These people frequently appear in hotels, coffee shops, bookstores, and other places where laptops are common but Internet access may not be available or free. Fortunately, most parasites are sufficiently deterred by WEP.

7.3.5 Direct Security Breaches

Although rare, some attackers are not interested in "a" network—they want "your" network. In this situation, wireless networks permit direct access to the physical network layer. As mentioned earlier, WEP is not a deterrent against a determined attacker.

7.4 RISK MITIGATION OPTIONS

As with wired networks, wireless mediums provide no inherent security mechanisms. Any attacker who can intercept the wireless signal gains immediate access to the physical network. To mitigate this situation, there are three types of solutions. The first set of options lessens the attractiveness of the wireless network. This is technically security-by-obscurity, but labeling the SSID, disabling SSID broadcasting, and selective antenna placement are active ingredients toward defense-in-depth. The second set of options limit an attacker's ability to connect and use the wireless router. MAC filtering, WEP, and other cryptographic systems define different stages for an authentication stack. Finally, the type of network architecture can limit the impact from a successful attacker.

7.4.1 SSID Labeling

The value set in the SSID may provide information to an attacker. All things being equal, an attacker is more likely to attack a known target. For example, the SSID string "Baby Care," "Sandwiches," or "Corporate Office" may advertise to an attacker the type of company that owns the wireless router. Other SSIDs may advertise a router's owner or location, such as "The Walters" or "203 Sunnybrook." In contrast, default SSID values, such as "Default" or "Linksys," may suggest a weakened target for an attacker—if the administrator did not configure this default value, then other systems accessible by the wireless network are also likely set to default values.

In a best case, the SSID should be informative to the owner but obscure to an attacker. For example, "CSL3-5" may indicate the Computer Security Lab #3 router in building 5. Other creative settings may include warnings, such as "DO NOT ENTER" or "Go away."

7.4.2 Broadcasting SSID

The default setting for most wireless routers includes SSID broadcasting. The router broadcasts the SSID every few seconds so other users looking for the AP will be able to find it. The constant broadcast can be disabled, requiring users to know the SSID's name prior to connecting. Although this does not disable all of the different SSID broadcast mechanisms, it does significantly reduce the risk of discovery by war drivers and parasites.

7.4.3 Antenna Placement

Where the wireless antenna is placed directly impacts who can access the signal. APs placed on the second floor of a home, near a front window are very likely to be received by people across the street. In contrast, an antenna placed in the corner of a basement has the range limited by the surrounding materials; rebar in basement walls act as a grounding plane and the moisture in the soil significantly reduces signal range. Many companies resort to grounded metal hoods over the antennas to restrict signal propagation to a specific direction.

Although careful antenna placement may limit a signal's strength in a particular direction, it is unlikely to prevent a determined attacker. Directional antennas can boost a SPs capability to connect to an AP by accessing signals that are very distant and very weak.

Can You Hear Me Now?

Most wireless APs have effective ranges between 300 and 1,000 feet. SPs beyond that distance are unlikely to access the AP due to a weak signal. But a Pringles™ potato chip canister can be turned into a directional antenna with a range of over a mile.

In 2003, the Defcon computer security conference in Las Vegas held a Wi-Fi Shootout contest (*http://www.wifi-shootout.com/*). The contest's goal was to determine the maximum range for a Wi-Fi network connection, without using any external amplifiers. A group called the Adversarial Science Lab connected to a wireless AP more than 35 miles away. Their antenna consisted of metal poles, window screening, cardboard, duct tape, and aluminum foil. The total cost of the antenna was under $100, with parts purchased at a home improvement store. In 2004, team P.A.D. achieved a record 55.1 miles. P.A.D. established a solid connection with an 802.11b AP. And, in 2005, a group called iFiber Redwire smashed the previous record by establishing an 11 Mbps connection over a record distance of 125 miles without the use of an external amplifier (but with very large antennas).

7.4.4 MAC Filtering

Although careful SSID management and antenna placement may lower the risk from casual attackers, they provide no mitigation option for a determined attacker. Instead, an authentication stack can restrict access from an attacker who can receive the wireless signal. The additional stack adds another layer of protection by requiring specific credentials to connect. The simplest type of authentication is based on the OSI layer 2 media access control (MAC). As covered in Part III, the MAC address is a pseudo-unique identifier assigned to every network card. Many APs permit an administrator to explicitly list the MAC addresses that may connect to the router. This prevents attackers from connecting with an unknown MAC addresses.

Unfortunately, most network cards permit the user to specify alternate MAC addresses. Because the MAC is transmitted in every packet, an attacker only needs to receive a packet to identify a valid MAC address.

7.4.5 WEP: Better Than Nothing

Although WEP is not a significant deterrent for a technical attacker, it is certainly a better alternative to providing an open network. Any security is better than no security, even if it is weak. A skilled attacker can trivially bypass SSID settings, antenna placement, and MAC filtering. These mitigation options limit discovery but do not prevent wireless connections. In contrast, WEP actively prevents connections, even if only for a few minutes.

From a legal viewpoint, WEP has a significant purpose: WEP defines intent. An attacker who enters an unprotected network (no WEP) may claim that the wireless network posed an attractive nuisance, or that he was not aware that the network was private. This makes successful prosecution (assuming the attacker can be identified) based strictly on wireless access difficult. In contrast, an attacker who decrypts and accesses a WEP-enabled network clearly demonstrates intent.

7.4.6 Other Cryptographic Systems

WEP is one example of a cryptographic system used in a wireless network authentication stack, but it is not the only cryptographic system available. For example, IEEE 802.11i defines a method for supporting authentication protocols called the

Wi-Fi Protected Access (WPA). Authentication systems, such as the 802.11i-based Temporal Key Integrity Protocol (TKIP), address the issues surrounding static WEP keys. Other systems include the Extensible Authentication Protocol (EAP), which is designed to deter MitM attacks.

The suite of authentication protocols is not limited to open standards. In 2000, Cisco introduced a proprietary variant of EAP called LEAP. This protocol has since been cracked by software such as ASLEAP (*http://asleap.sourceforge.net/*).

Although many of these alternatives to WEP provide sufficient security for limiting unauthorized connections, they have two primary drawbacks: compatibility and observability.

7.4.6.1 Alternate Authentication Compatibility

WEP is essentially universally available and accepted. Nearly all wireless network routers support WEP, and WEP from any vendor's network card will work with WEP from any other vendor's wireless router. This universal acceptance leads to a higher likelihood of adoption.

There are many other authentication systems, such as TTLS, TLS, EAP, LEAP, PEAP, and MD5. Although different vendors support some of these protocols, few vendors support all of them. Currently, none of these authentication alternatives are universally supported. This leads to an incompatibility between vendor hardware and drivers. The authentication stack offered by one vendor may not be supported or compatible with other vendors. Users are left with the option of either (1) using a strong authentication stack but being locked to a specific vendor and risking incompatibility with other wireless sites, or (2) using the known-weak WEP authentication but retaining compatibility. As seen with Cisco's LEAP (and cracking tool ASLEAP), being locked to one vendor may not enhance the security of your network: authentication systems that are secure today may not be secure tomorrow.

7.4.6.2 Alternate Authentication Observability

A wireless network authentication stack ensures that only authorized SPs connect to the AP. And combining the stack with encryption deters an attacker from monitoring network data. But these security measures do not prevent an attacker from gaining insight. Even if attackers cannot access a network, they can still count packets. By monitoring network traffic volume, an attacker can gain insight into how the network is being used.

No packets: A wireless network that generates no measurable volume is inactive. An attacker can determine when a network is in use.

Packet directions: In many cases, the attacker can determine whether the data is flowing from the AP to SP, or vice versa. Even if the data is encrypted at a low

OSI layer (preventing the packet from disclosing direction), a directional antenna system can determine which transmitter is in use.

High directional volume: A significant and constant data flow likely represents an upload or download. The duration of the volume can be used to estimate the transfer size.

High bidirectional volume: A significant and constant bidirectional data flow may indicate a network application such as X-Windows or an online game.

Low volume: Low volume packets with irregular pauses are likely a human typing over the network. The attacker may not know what is being typed, but he can determine "typing."

Depending on the volume, duration, and pause patterns, an attacker may be able to determine the type of network usage. An attacker may not know the details of what a network is transporting, but the attacker can make an educated guess as to the type of traffic based on volume analysis.

7.4.7 Network Architecture

Wireless networks permit anyone within receiving range to access the physical medium. Whereas authentication stacks may deter attackers from connecting, a properly designed network architecture can limit the impact from an attacker who successfully connects to the wireless router. Architectural decisions, such as a DMZ or VPN, can restrict the activities from a connected attacker.

7.4.7.1 Wireless and DMZ

The DMZ separates a potentially hostile network from the internal LAN. When used with a wireless network, the DMZ isolates the wireless systems from the remainder of the LAN. In this configuration, any SP that connects to the AP is only able to access the DMZ. Further access requires the ability to authenticate or bypass the DMZ's firewalls.

Although most residential wireless routers act as a firewall, separating the WAN from the LAN, more residential wireless routers do not separate the wireless hosts from the wired hosts—both reside on the same LAN. A simple solution (Figure 7.1) uses two home firewalls. The first contains the AP and connects to the WAN. The second, internal router does not support wireless and separates the internal LAN from the wireless network. Although all users on the wireless network can connect to the WAN, the LAN remains protected. The primary limitation with this approach is usability—a home user may not be able to file-share with a wireless system. But this limitation may be countered by the security consideration: do you really want to share files with anyone who connects to the AP, even if it is an uninvited guest?

FIGURE 7.1   A simple home DMZ
for isolating the wireless network
from the LAN.

7.4.7.2 Wireless and VPN

In addition to a DMZ or firewall to separate the wireless network from the LAN, the network may be configured to require a *virtual private network* (VPN). Just as the authentication stack is a network stack in series with the host's network stack, a VPN resides in series. The VPN tunnels network traffic between hosts or subnets, ensuring privacy along a public path. Solutions such as Secure Shell (SSH), Open-VPN (a solution based on secure socket layer—SSL—technology), CIPE, PPTP, Virtual Tunnel (VTun), Tinc, and many others are widely available and supported. Different VPN solutions have different tradeoffs, such as the capability to tunnel TCP or UDP, and impact to speed, but a firewall that requires an established VPN is much less vulnerable to attack.

In an ideal architecture that uses an onion or garlic configuration, the AP is placed in a core, and the core firewall only permits access beyond the core through an established VPN. Hosts on the VPN are granted access to the LAN and WAN. In this scenario, an attacker can connect to the AP but cannot access the LAN or WAN due to the firewall. In contrast, authorized users can access the LAN and perform tasks, such as checking email, sharing files, or administrating the network, in a secure manner.

SUMMARY

The 2.4 GHz and 5 GHz bands are not the only type of wireless mediums. Microwave networks, Bluetooth-enabled devices, and infrared systems all have similar limitations. The primary differences among these mediums are range, power requirements, and bandwidth. The limitations found in Wi-Fi networks can be directly applied to other wireless mediums.

Although wireless networks face the same risks as wired networks—anyone with access to the medium can attack the network—the problem is expanded due to the broadcast nature of the network. In a wired network, only people with physical access to the wire can access the network medium. There is relatively little fear from attackers that lack physical access. In a wireless network, anyone who receives the signal, regardless of distance or location, can attack the network. The risks from wireless networks can be mitigated through the combination of authentication stacks, firewalls, and VPNs, creating a secure network topology.

REVIEW QUESTIONS

1. Why are ISM frequencies more desirable than U-NII?
2. Is WEP an example of strong security? Why or why not?
3. What are five types of wireless risks?
4. What are two common limitations to deploying strong wireless security solutions?

DISCUSSION TOPICS

1. Using a laptop, wireless network card, and wireless network sniffing software (for example, AirSnort, WiStumbler, or WiFiScanner), travel around parts of your local town. Describe some of the expectations and how they vary from any findings.

   - How many APs are detectable?
   - What percentage have WEP enabled?
   - How many use default SSIDs, or SSIDs that describe the AP location?
   - Does walking or driving find more APs?
   - Is there a significant difference between business districts and residential neighborhoods?
   - Are there more APs in newer or older residential areas?

2. Create an RF shield to limit an AP's normal range to a room or building. Describe some of the complications.

3. Explain the benefits and limitations to using WEP along with other authentication or VPN protocols.

4. The technical limitations with WEP include the use of a static key and short IV. Are there other limitations? Describe an ideal replacement for WEP. For example, if there is a constantly changing key, how is it negotiated between the SP and AP? Are strong cryptographic algorithms, such as AES, required?

5. Wireless networks are desirable when the facility is not prewired for Cat5 or thinnet. The capability to broadcast the network through walls simplifies the networking infrastructure, but wireless networks are not always ideal. Historic buildings commonly have thick, stonewalls that prevent wireless signal propagation. For this situation, describe some alternatives to running cables or drilling holes (or otherwise damaging the building). Consider the impact to building aesthetics and safety. For example, increasing the signal strength to 1000 Watts on both the AP and SP may enable the network, but the microwaves will likely cook anything living nearby.

ADDITIONAL RESOURCES

The FCC defines the use of the ISM and U-NII in 47 C.F.R. Section 15 defines the U-NII bands (47 CFR 15.407) and the ISM bands (47 CFR 15.247).

Part III

OSI Layer 2

In This Part

■ Data Link Layer
■ SLIP and PPP
■ MAC and ARP

L ayer 2 of the ISO OSI model is the data link layer. This layer frames information, manages data synchronization, determines data recipients, and controls the physical layer. The security issues primarily concern data framing and recipient addressing. Two examples of this layer are the point-to-point network protocols (SLIP and PPP) and the multinode addressing protocols (MAC and ARP).

8 Data Link Layer

In This Chapter

- Data Flow
- Common Uses
- Layered Data Link Protocols
- Uncommon Uses
- Common Mitigation Options

The OSI layer 2, data link layer, provides reliable transmission of data over the physical layer. The data link layer accomplishes this by segmenting data into message frames for transmission. As data is received from the physical layer, each frame is identified and validated. The message frames may include additional data such as routing information, address information, and flow control.

Although the layers in the ISO OSI stack are intended to operate independently of other layers, this is not always the case. Data link protocols frequently have tight associations with physical layer protocols. Different physical mediums and standards specify different data link protocols.

8.1 DATA FLOW

The general flow through the data link layer appears as a four-step process for transmitting and receiving data. The data link layer receives information from Layer 3 (or higher), encodes the information into message frames, includes any error detection/correction information, and submits each frame to the physical layer. The receiving flow reverses this process.

8.1.1 Transmitting Data

The data link layer receives data from the network layer (OSI layer 3) for transmission across the network. Because the node may generate data faster than the network transfer speed, the data link layer may cache data for transmission. But, if the transmission cache fills, then the data link layer informs the network layer that the data was not transmitted. For example, the send(), sendto(), and write() functions found in C programs return the number of transmitted bytes. The number of transmitted bytes may be less than the number of bytes passed to these functions.

The C functions send(), sendto(), *and* write(), *and their reading counterparts may access the data link, network, or transport layers. Which layer is accessed depends on how the network socket was established. A* RAW *network socket accesses the data link layer. Other types of sockets include* INET *(network layer),* STREAM *(transport layer, TCP), and* DGRAM *(transport layer UDP).*

Although the physical layer is assumed to correctly transmit and receive the data link information, nothing prevents the data from interacting with different data link protocols using the same physical medium. For example, a wireless network that supports both 802.11b and 802.11g could, in theory, confuse traffic from the different protocols. To mitigate this issue, many wireless routers downgrade all traffic to the slower 802.11b protocol even if only one wireless client (on a network with many wireless nodes) is using 802.11b.

In addition, complex errors within the physical layer could allow corrupted data to reach the data link layer. If the data link layer uses a simple checksum to validate a packet's contents, then a few erroneous bits could appear as a packet with a valid checksum. For example, if the checksum is a simple parity bit, then 10110011 has the parity 1. If any two bits in the sequence change, then the parity remains the same. More complex checksums may require more bits changed, but the underlying problem remains.

To address potential data corruption, many data link protocols use an error detection scheme (e.g., checksum) and/or error correction system (e.g., Hamming code) for the data. These protocols encode the data and error mitigation information within the message frame. The frame may also include addressing or routing information.

Finally, the data is passed from the data link layer to the physical layer for transmission across the physical network. If the network is temporarily unavailable due to network traffic or transmission delays, then the data link protocol will hold the data until the physical layer is ready to transmit.

Many protocols include a transmission timeout value. If the data cannot be transmitted in a reasonable amount of time, then the system may silently drop the packet or send an error code up the stack.

8.1.2 Receiving Data

Receipt of data from the physical layer follows a four-step process that is similar to data transmission. First, the data is received from the physical layer. The physical layer generates a stream of data, so the session layer identifies the start of data by identifying the message frame. Bits of data outside of the message frame are considered to be noise.

Each message frame is validated using the error detection (or correction) code. Although it is possibly to have a significant number of errors that generate a valid checksum, the general case is a single bit error (or a few incorrect bits) will result in an invalid frame. Invalid frames may generate a signal for a retransmission, or may prevent the transmission of a data link acknowledgement.

If the frame contains address information, then the address is checked against the local node. Only information intended for the node is processed.

NOTE

Some systems check address information before validating the checksum. The only requirement is to perform both address and checksum validation sometime before accepting the data. But the order of the checks may vary between systems and protocols.

Accepted messages (those with valid frames and appropriate addressing) have the frame removed. The data is placed into a receiving buffer for network layer. C programming functions such as read(), recv(), and recvfrom() are used to retrieve data from the buffer. If the receiving buffer fills, then a flow control message is sent to the physical layer, or the receiving packet is lost. This situation may happen if the receiving node is not reading network data fast enough.

8.2 COMMON USES

The data link layer provides reliable data transfers between adjacent nodes on the network. This layer does not attempt to connect separate network or span different physical network mediums. The most common uses for data link protocols include the following:

- Navigating data between point-to-point networks
- Multihost networks
- High-speed frame relay networks
- Switched networks
- Bridging separate network segments
- Access restrictions

8.2.1 Point-to-Point Networks

Different physical network configurations permit different numbers of nodes to exist on a network segment. The simplest configuration use *point-to-point networks*, where modems, microwave networks, or direct cable connections link two nodes directly. The data link message frame is used for error checking. For simplex physical mediums, only one node may transmit at a time, so the message frames ensure that one node does not dominate the network bandwidth. Duplex physical mediums permit both nodes to transmit at the same time. In this case, the message frame provides flow control, ensuring that a slow node does not drop packets when the receiving buffer fills.

Examples of point-to-point data link protocols include the Point-to-Point Protocol (PPP) and Serial Link Internet Protocol (SLIP). These protocols are detailed in Chapter 9.

8.2.2 Multihost Networks

As described in Chapter 4, a single physical layer medium may include multiple hosts. Any node connected to the physical layer may transmit data, and every node receives the transmitted data. In this environment, the message frame may include addressing formation. The addressing may indicate a single node recipient (*unicast*), multiple node recipients (*multicast*), or all nodes as recipients (*broadcast*). Most addressing schemes include the source (sender) and destination (recipients) in the message frame.

The most common multihost data link protocol is the *media access control* (MAC), defined by the IEEE 8023 standard. The MAC provides a network-unique address (hardware address) used to identify a specific node on the physical network. To identify a node's hardware address, the data link layer includes an Address Resolution Protocol (ARP), as well as Reverse ARP (RARP), which is detailed in Chapter 10. Ethernet, Token Ring, and FDDI networks use variations of MAC addressing.

Other data link addressing schemes include the AppleTalk Address Resolution Protocol (AARP), the multilink protocol (MP) for X.25 networks, and the Cisco Data Exchange Interface (DXI) for Asynchronous Transfer Mode (ATM) networks.

8.2.3 Frame Relay

Frame relays are very high-speed networks, usually intended for ISDN, F-T1, or faster networks. With most data link protocols, the message frames are uniform in length. This simplifies the receiving and processing of each frame. For high-speed networks, uniform length frames can result in a significant amount of padded network traffic. Frame relays resolve this issue by using variable-length frames. In addition, most frame relays multiplex transmissions to increase bandwidth. When multiplexing frames, it becomes essential to receive the bits in the correct order, so frame relays may use a variety of approaches to enumerate the multiple data streams. The message frame's control codes become essential for negotiating the multiplexed streams.

8.2.4 Switches

When two networks use the same physical medium, they can be connecting using a physical layer connector, such as a hub. Although *hubs* connect separate physical layers, they do not distinguish higher layer protocols. Traffic received on one hub port is transmitted to all of the hub ports. Hubs are acceptable for small networks, but the network bandwidth consumption of large networks makes hubs undesirable. At the other extreme, frame relays provide very high bandwidth but are relatively expensive. Switches provide the tradeoff between high bandwidth and low cost.

Switches are essentially intelligent hubs that monitor data link layer addressing. When a node transmits, the switch analyzes the message frame for address information. If the address is unknown, then the switch acts as a hub and relays the data to every port. If the frame contains address information (such as an ARP packet for MAC addressing), then the address is stored and associated with a particular port on the switch. This way, other frames going to the same address do not need to be sent to all ports; they are just sent to the port associated with the address.

The level of sophistication within a switch varies. Simple switches can only route traffic between two ports (or broadcast to all ports) at one time. More complicated switches permit unrelated traffic to flow between unrelated ports. Common options include parallel traffic and multiple address support:

Parallel traffic: Some switches can manage multiple conversations at a time, such as Node *A* talking to Node *B* with a simultaneous conversation between two other nodes: *C* and *D*. These switches improve network throughput by only forwarding network traffic to the ports that need it.

Multiple addresses: The simplest switches can only associate one address per port, but more advanced switches can associate many addresses per port. The latter has the benefit of supporting very complicated network topologies without sending traffic to every port.

Most switches implement some level of traffic control. This prevents one conversation from locking out traffic from a second conversation. For example, if Node *A* is sending a high volume of traffic to Node *B*, this will not prevent Node *C* from also contacting Node *B*. The simplest traffic control systems use a round-robin approach, where each port on the switch has a turn to communicate. Very sophisticated switches can assign priority levels to different ports, so traffic from one port is delivered at a higher priority than traffic from another port.

8.2.5 Bridges

Hubs and switches are closely tied to the physical layer; they cannot span different types of physical media (Figure 8.1). *Bridges* are OSI layer 2 devices that can span different physical media. For example, a bridge can link a 10Base-2 network with a 100Base-T network. The bridge receives the data from one physical layer and sends it to a different physical layer. In the process, the bridge may need to temporarily buffer the message frame.

There are many different implementations of MAC addressing. 10Base-2 and 100Base-T commonly use 802.3 Ethernet MAC addressing. MAC addressing for Token Ring and FDDI networks use different variations of the MAC protocol.

Bridges can be used as long as the data link layer's protocol is consistent between the networks. For example, a bridge can span a 10Base-2 and 100Base-T network because both use MAC addressing. But a bridge cannot change the data link (or higher layer) protocol; a bridge cannot convert traffic from OSI layer 2 MAC addressing to X.25 addressing, and a bridge cannot span the connection from an Ethernet MAC to a Token Ring MAC. Although both use MAC addressing, each implements it slightly differently.

To link networks that use different data link protocols, a network layer (OSI layer 3) *router* is required (see Chapter 11). Similarly, *gateways* span OSI layer 4 protocols and permit conversions between network-layer protocols.

8.2.6 Access Restriction

For multihost networks, network or hardware addressing is used to direct unicast/multicast network traffic. Within a node, the address is used to filter out undesirable message frames. Some network devices also use the sender's address as an authentication token. Senders without the correct network address are denied access to the node. This type of filtering is commonly found in bridges, routers, and gateways. For example, most wireless routers permit restricting AP connections based on the SP's hardware address. An SP that does not provide a permitted hardware address is blocked from connecting to the AP.

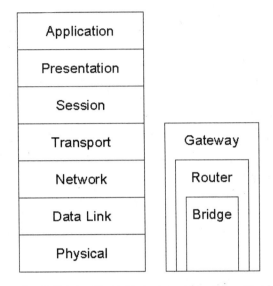

FIGURE 8.1 The OSI stack and location of bridges, routers, and gateways.

8.3 LAYERED DATA LINK PROTOCOLS

For point-to-point networks, a single data link layer protocol, such as SLIP, can perform all of the required functionality; however, few data link layer protocols span the entire layer. Instead, the data link layer usually contains multiple protocols that, together, provide the full data link functionality. The lower protocols manage the physical layer communications. The middle layer protocols manage routing and addressing, and upper layer protocols control network discovery.

8.3.1 Low-Level Protocols

The lower level data link protocols are directly associated with the physical layer. Examples include the following:

FDDI: This layer 2 protocol acts as a high-speed Token Ring over fiber-optic networks.

LAPF: The standard ITU Q.921 defines the Link Access Protocol for Frame Mode Services. This frame relay protocol is commonly used on ISDN, F-T1, and faster networks.

PPP: The Point-to-Point Protocol commonly connects dynamic connections, such as modem or ISDN.

Carrier Sense Multiple Access/Collision Detection: One of the most common protocols, CSMA/CD is part of the IEEE 802.3 standard and is used for most end-user Ethernet traffic. This protocol determines when data may be transmitted and detects when collisions occur. The physical layer is commonly twisted pair (10Base-T or 100Base-T), or coax such as 10Base-2 or 10Base-5.

8.3.2 Middle-Level Protocols

The middle protocols within the data link layer manage addressing. These are closely associated with specific lower-level layer 2 protocols. For example, IEEE 802.2 defines two data link sublayers: MAC and LLC. The MAC defines a unique address on a particular network. The various 802 standards (802.3, 802.4, 802.5, etc.) define the management of the MAC address. In particular, different types of networks may use different types of MAC addressing. The logical link control (LLC) is the higher portion that provides a consistent interface regardless of the MAC format.

8.3.3 High-Level Protocols

The high-level data link layer protocols manage address discovery. For example, when using MAC addressing, the ARP is used to identify the MAC address of a particular host. Because bridges may identify adjacent bridges, the IEEE 802.1 spanning tree protocol ensures that network loops do not lead to network feedback (where the same bits go round and round).

Other higher-level protocols include the AppleTalk Address Resolution Protocol (AARP) and the multilink protocol (MP) for X.25 networks.

8.4 UNCOMMON USES

The data link layer commonly provides an interface to the physical layer, ensuring that data is transmitted safely between two nodes on a network; however, these are not the only uses for the data link layer. Uncommon usage can indicate a network under attack. These include attacks based on promiscuous network monitoring, network load, addressing, out-of-frame data, and covert channels.

Although there are many types of uncommon uses (and abuses), each of these requires direct physical access to the network. The scope for these attacks is limited to the range of the data link layer. Because the data link layer does not extend beyond bridges, networks that are connected by routers or gateways are protected from these abuses.

8.4.1 Promiscuous Mode

Under normal usage, network-addressing schemes (e.g., MAC) prevent upper stack layers from receiving data that is not intended for the node. Many network interfaces support the disabling of the address filter. Nodes operating in *promiscuous mode* receive all message frames, not just those intended for the node. Promiscuous mode allows an attacker to receive all data from the network.

8.4.1.1 Promiscuous Mode Attacks

Promiscuous mode is commonly used as a network analysis and debugging tool. By switching the network adapter into promiscuous mode, a network administrator (or developer) can view all local network traffic. Malformed packets and routing issues can quickly be identified. Unfortunately, attackers can also use this tool. Common attack vectors include the following:

Plaintext: Any data transmitted in plaintext (not encrypted) is readily viewable by an attacker. The data may include login credentials (e.g., username and password), email contents, Web pages, or other information.

Reconnaissance: An attacker may observe the quantity and types of systems on a network, types of traffic, and times when the network is active.

Hijacking: By knowing the type of data on a network, an attacker may attempt to take over an established connection.

Detection: By monitoring network traffic, attackers can gain an early warning that their presence has been detected. Similarly, defenders may use a node in promiscuous mode to identify possible network compromises.

8.4.1.2 Common Tools

Many tools that switch the network interface into promiscuous mode and capture network packets are intended for network administrators. Common tools for analyzing networks in promiscuous mode include:

Tcpdump (*http://www.tcpdump.org/*): A simple tool to capture network packets in promiscuous mode.

Snort (*http://www.snort.org/*): A powerful packet-capturing tool that includes extensions for IDS, IPS, and other applications.

Ngrep (*http://ngrep.sourceforge.net/*): The *network grep* tool permits scanning network traffic for specific byte sequences.

Ethereal (*http://www.ethereal.com/*): One of the most powerful packet analysis tools available. This application captures packets, reconstructs communications, and deciphers most protocols from OSI layers 2 and up.

The ability to analyze network traffic can benefit administrators and attackers. Many companies have workplace policies concerning network analyzers. In some Fortune 500 companies, using unauthorized analyzers can be grounds for termination. More effective policies limit the intended usage and not the tools. Companies that forbid these tools limit the abilities of network administrators and developers. Debugging network issues may take much more time if the problem cannot be directly analyzed. In contrast, permitting these tools can aid attackers.

8.4.1.3 Detecting Promiscuous Mode

Promiscuous mode works by disabling OSI layer 1 and layer 2 filtering. All data received by the host is passed to OSI network layer (and above) for processing. Promiscuous mode permits attackers, defenders, and network administrators to receive and analyze all network traffic. Promiscuous mode does have one significant limitation in that many higher layer protocols assume that the lower layers have vetted the network data. If the data within a packet requires a reply, higher layer protocols may reply. Three examples include ARP (high layer 2), ICMP (layer 3), and DNS (called via layer 7).

8.4.1.4 Detection Using ARP

ARP packets are used to associate IP addresses (OSI layer 3) with hardware addresses (OSI layer 2). Each ARP packet contains a hardware address and IP address. Under normal usage, the receiving node first checks the hardware address. If the address indicates that it is intended for the node, then the ARP's IP address query is processed.

If the hardware address does not match the host, then the data link layer normally rejects the packet. In promiscuous mode, however, the packet is accepted and an ARP response is generated. Promiscuous mode can be remotely detected by transmitting ARP packets with invalid hardware addresses but valid IP addresses—one packet, containing one IP address, is sent to each node.

Promiscuous mode processing relies on a combination of compatible hardware, drivers, and operating systems. Different systems may require different ARP packets for detecting promiscuous mode (Table 8.1). In particular, the ARP requests may require the use of unicast or multicast data link addressing [Sanai2001], and different hardware (and hardware drivers) may generate different results.

TABLE 8.1 ARP Responses to Different MAC Destination Addresses

MAC Destination	Win9x/ME	Win2000/NT	Linux 2.4/2.6	Mac OS X 10.3
FF:FF:FF:FF:FF:FF	Always	Always	Always	Always
FF:FF:00:00:00:00	Promiscuous	Promiscuous	Always	Promiscuous
FF:00:00:00:00:00	Promiscuous	Never	Always	Promiscuous
01:00:5E:00:00:00	Never	Never	Promiscuous	Promiscuous
01:00:5E:00:00:01	Always	Always	Always	Always

The ARP test also works for other protocols. For example, sending a TCP connect request with an invalid MAC address (unicast) and valid IP address will receive a reply from many older systems when they are operating in promiscuous mode. Newer operating systems require multicast packets to bypass kernel-level packet inspections during promiscuous mode.

The arp_pd.c *program on the CD-ROM performs promiscuous mode detection using ARP packets.*

8.4.1.5 Detection Using ICMP

The ICMP Echo packet (also known as a *ping* packet) normally generates an ICMP reply from an active host. Multiple ICMP packets should generate multiple replies with similar latencies. Under promiscuous mode, the node receives more packets to process and therefore has a larger latency. This is particularly true when the network is under a significantly high load.

8.4.1.6 Detection Using DNS

Many packet-capturing tools perform hostname lookups for IP addresses that are captured. Monitoring DNS requests can determine which hosts are performing many hostname lookups. This may indicate a host that is capturing packets.

8.4.2 Load Attacks

Although closely linked to firmware, the data link layer is essentially a software layer. This means that it needs a processor to handle every packet. Whereas most data link address filters require very low overhead, the upper OSI layers frequently require significant CPU resources. A *data link load attack* appears as packets designed to increase a node's CPU load.

In a multihost network, every host receives every broadcast frame. These frames must be passed through the data link layer, where they are either managed by the upper data link layer protocols, or by higher OSI layers. The simple process of receiving and processing (or discarding) a single broadcast message frame does not consume many resources. But multiplying that same process by thousands of broadcast packets results in a significant overhead for the node. This attack is unlikely to be significant for regular workstations or bridges, however, it can be very serious for real-time or mission critical servers.

8.4.3 Address Attacks

Most addressing schemes permit a node to change the effective network address. If two nodes are configured for the same address, both will likely respond to network traffic. The result usually causes both nodes to reject network connections.

Systems that use network addresses as access tokens can be quickly defeated. An attacker just needs to change the addresses to any of the permitted values. By observing the network in promiscuous mode, an attacker can identify the acceptable addresses. Address filtering is a viable security-by-obscurity solution, but it should not be the only security option.

8.4.4 Out-of-Frame Data

In general, data that is not enclosed in a message frame is discarded. Information can be transmitted across the physical layer and not be included in a message frame. This *out-of-frame data* can consume network bandwidth or convey information in a nonstandard (covert) fashion.

Network interfaces operating in promiscuous mode may receive the out-of-frame data, but this ability depends on the interface between the physical and data link layers. For example, a 100Base-T Ethernet card may capture framed and unframed data, but wireless network cards usually discard any unframed data as noise.

8.4.5 Covert Channels

The data link layer can serve alternate purposes besides framing and transmitting data. Many higher OSI layer functions can be implemented to appear as part of the data link layer. Attackers can create backdoors and remote control protocols that appear as data link layer protocols. Examples include the following:

Out-of-Frame Data: Information can be hidden outside of standard message frames. Most nodes will likely ignore this data.

Addressing Information: Nodes ignore frames when the destination address is not the node. Invalid address information is usually not detected.

Invalid Frames: Invalid frames are normally discarded. A covert channel may intentionally create frames with invalid checksums.

Frame Size: For networks that support variable frame sizes, the size or padding within a frame may be used to pass subtle information that is difficult to detect.

Protocol Specific: Many standard protocols can be used in nonstandard ways to hide and transport information. For example, ARP packets for ATM networks can easily work on an Ethernet (or other non-ATM) network. Similarly, using ARP on an AppleTalk (AARP) network is permitted. These packets are valid and can pass through bridges, but are generally undetectable.

The range of a data link covert channel is usually limited. Bridges, being unable to recognize the nonstandard protocol, usually discard the packets. As a result, data link covert channels are usually restricted to the local network.

8.4.6 Physical Layer Risks

In theory, the data link layer operates independent from the physical layer. (In reality, many data link protocols are closely associated with physical mediums.) Usually the physical layer can be replaced without impacting the data link layer. For example, changing from 10Base-T to 100Base-T does not require a change to the data link layer. Because of this independence, the data link layer remains vulnerable to all physical layer risks:

- A physical layer attacker has direct access to the data link message frames.
- A physical layer attacker can eavesdrop on all data link traffic.
- A physical layer attacker can record and replay data link traffic. The replayed data will be acceptable to the data link layer.
- A physical layer attacker can use an insertion attack to generate a load attack with valid data link message frames.

8.5 COMMON MITIGATION OPTIONS

There are few options for combating the risks from the data link layer. The options that do exist include hard-coding hardware addresses, data link and higher-layer authentication schemes, and a few analyzers and tools.

8.5.1 Hard-Coding

Although the risk of interception in a point-to-point network is low, multinode networks are vulnerable to attacks against the data link addressing system. Attackers can hijack, intercept, and redirect hardware addresses. To mitigate this issue, address tables can be statically populated. Although not necessarily viable for large and dynamic networks, static address tables do provide a level of protection from an attacker who attempts to attack dynamically populated address tables.

Static address tables protect against changes to established systems, and they also deter unauthorized connections. For example, a dialup server may store a list of acceptable Caller-ID values. Callers providing a different Caller-ID value are rejected. Similarly, many wireless networks restrict client access by using a table of permitted wireless MAC addresses.

8.5.2 Data Link Authentication

Few data link layer protocols implement cryptography; the processing overhead for cryptographic data link protocols can be very expensive and inadvertently result in a load attack for busy networks. Instead, the two main cryptographic solutions are CHAP and PAP, both defined in RFC1334. These solutions are primarily used for point-to-point connections.

8.5.2.1 CHAP

The *Challenge-Handshake Authentication Protocol* (CHAP) uses a shared key to authenticate the initial network connection:

1. The client connects to the server.
2. The server issues a challenge. This is a value based on a one-way hash using the secret key.
3. The client validates the challenge by comparing it with the expected hash value.
4. The client sends its own hash to the server.
5. The server validates the response.

Only fully validated connections are permitted. CHAP provides a means to authenticate two nodes, but it does not perform any validation or encryption after the connection is established.

8.5.2.2 PAP

The *Password Authentication Protocol* (PAP) is a much simpler protocol than CHAP. The login credentials (id and password) are transmitted in plaintext from the client to the server. If the server accepts the credentials, then the connection is permitted. There is no encryption and no protection from interception or replay attacks.

8.5.3 Higher-Layer Authentication

The most popular solution for protecting the data link layer depends on higher-layer protocols. The assumption is that any authentication, validation, or cryptographic system will operate higher up the stack and provide protection against interception, reply, and other network attacks. Unfortunately, this assumption is usually incorrect. Higher layer protocols may offer no security mechanisms, offer weak security options, or direct their solutions to a different set of problems. Few higher-layer protocols attempt to authenticate the data link layer.

8.5.4 Analyzers and Tools

Network applications, such as IDS and IPS, rely on the capability to monitor the network in promiscuous mode. Tools such as tcpdump, snort, and ethereal can readily collect, identify, and analyze unexpected network traffic.

SUMMARY

The OSI data link layer provides reliable data transfers over the physical layer by segmenting data into message frames. For multinode networks, the data link layer also provides address routing, directing message frames to the required nodes and informing all other nodes to ignore the specified frames.

The data link layer, by itself, offers few security precautions. Node addresses can be hijacked, false data can be inserted into the network, and promiscuous nodes can receive and analyze network traffic. The few mitigation options are not complete—promiscuous mode detection can be complex and inaccurate, and hard-coded hardware addresses do not prevent hijacking or eavesdropping. Fortunately, attacks against the data link layer require direct access to the physical layer; remote attackers cannot directly attack the data link layer.

REVIEW QUESTIONS

1. What is a message frame?
2. How many nodes can be in a point-to-point network?
3. What is an example of a data link layer protocol that does not segment the layer?

4. What is promiscuous mode?
5. List three mitigation options for the data link layer.

DISCUSSION TOPICS

1. Describe why message frames are used to segment data. What other methods could be used to provide the data link layer functionality? Are these methods dependent on the physical layer?
2. Morse code and Radio Teletype (RTTY, such as BAUDOT, AMTOR, and ASCII) are data link communication protocols that do not use message frames. Describe some of the complications associated with these protocols.
3. Why is hardware addressing not required on point-to-point networks?

ADDITIONAL RESOURCES

The IEEE 802 standard forms the basis for most data link layer protocols. This standard includes many subsections such as

IEEE 802.1: This provides the standards for network management.

IEEE 802.2: This divides the data link layer into two main sublayers: the MAC and LLC. Although the MAC may vary based on the physical network, the LCC provides a constant interface.

IEEE 802.3: This defines the MAC layer for (Ethernet) bus networks that use CSMA/CD.

IEEE 802.4: This defines the MAC layer for bus networks that use token passing for flow control.

IEEE 802.5: This defines the MAC layer for Token Ring networks.

IEEE 802.6: This defines network management for MANs.

Promiscuous mode can be a significant risk to some networks. Early detection of hosts operating in promiscuous mode can mitigate risks. There are many different methods for detecting promiscuous mode beyond the methods listed in this chapter. Robert Graham's document "Sniffing (network wiretap, sniffer)" provides an extended list of detection methods. This document is available online at *http://cerberus.sourcefire.com/~jeff/papers/Robert_Graham/sniffing-faq.html.*

9 SLIP and PPP

In This Chapter

- Simplified Data Link Services
- Point-to-Point Protocols
- Common Risks
- Similar Threats

The OSI data link layer is intended to frame data from higher layers for transmission across the physical layer. The message frames are used to mitigate data errors received from the physical layer. For multinode networks, the data link layer provides node-addressing support, so nodes do not spend time processing message frames that are intended for some other node. The data link layer also manages the transmission and flow control for the physical layer, ensuring that two nodes do not collide at the physical layer. Even though this layer provides all three of these functions, the implementation can be significantly simplified on a point-to-point network.

A *point-to-point network* implies that there are only two nodes on the network. All data transmitted by the first node is intended for the second node, and vice versa. As such, the data link layer can be simplified. Two common protocols that provide data link services over point-to-point networks are the Serial Line Internet Protocol (SLIP) and Point-to-Point Protocol (PPP).

9.1 SIMPLIFIED DATA LINK SERVICES

In a point-to-point network, many of the complexities from a multinode network vanish, and core functionality can be simplified. This includes simpler framing methods, flow control, and address support.

9.1.1 Simplified Flow Control

The physical layer ensures that the data received matches the data transmitted, but it does not address transmission collisions. When two nodes transmit at the same time, data becomes overwritten and corrupted. The data link layer determines when it appears safe to transmit, detects collisions, and retries when there are data errors. This is required functionality on a multinode network because any node may transmit at any time.

In a ring network, such as Token Ring or FDDI, the data link layer arbitrates when data is safe to transmit. Without this arbitration, any node could transmit at any time.

In a point-to-point network, there are only two nodes, so arbitration and flow management can be dramatically simplified. The most common types of point-to-point networks use simplex, half-duplex, or full-duplex connections.

9.1.1.1 Simplex

A *simplex* channel means that all data flows in one direction; there is never a reply from a simplex channel. For networking, there are two simplex channels, with one in each direction. Because there is never another node transmitting on the same channel, the flow control is simplified: there is no data link layer flow control because it is always safe to transmit. Examples of simplex networks include ATM, FDDI, satellite networks, and cable modems.

9.1.1.2 Half-Duplex

Half-duplex channels are bidirectional, but only one node may transmit at a time. In this situation, either a node is transmitting, or it is listening. It is very plausible for one node to dominate the channel, essentially locking out the other node. In half-duplex networks, each node must periodically check to see if the other node wants to transmit. Examples of half-duplex networks include some dialup, serial cable, and wireless network configurations.

9.1.1.3 Full-Duplex

In a *full-duplex* network, one channel is bidirectional, but both nodes can transmit at the same time. Examples include many fiber-optic systems, where the transmitted light pulses do not interfere with the received light pulses. Some FDDI, optical cable networks, and telephone modem protocols use full-duplex channels. When using a full-duplex channel in a point-to-point network, the data link flow control system is unnecessary because it is always clear to transmit.

9.1.2 Simplified Message Framing

Message framing ensures that the transmitted data is received in its entirety. Although the physical layer ensures that the data received matches the data transmitted, simultaneous transmissions can corrupt the data. The message frame identifies possible collisions, but the flow control from point-to-point networks limits the likelihood of a collision. In point-to-point networks, the message frame only needs to indicate when it is clear for the other side to transmit.

9.1.3 Simplified Address Support

In a multinode network, the message frame must be addressed to the appropriate node. In a point-to-point network, however, all transmitted data are only intended for the other node on the network. As such, hardware addresses are not required. For backward compatibility, the LLC may report the hardware address as being all zeros or a set value based on the current connection's session. For example, a user with a dialup modem may have the data link layer assign a random MAC address to the connection. After the connection terminates, the next connection may have a different MAC address. In many implementations, the data link layer's MAC address may appear to be the system's assigned IP address; an assigned dialup IP address of 1.2.3.4 may generate the MAC address 00:00:01:02:03:04. The next time the user dials into the service provider, the system may be assigned a new IP address and generate a new MAC address.

9.2 POINT-TO-POINT PROTOCOLS

Two common point-to-point protocols are SLIP and PPP. These are commonly used over direct-wired connections, such as serial cables, telephone lines, or high-speed dialup such as DSL. Besides direct-wired connections, they can also be used for VPN tunneling over a network.

9.2.1 SLIP

The *Serial Line Internet Protocol* (SLIP) is defined by RFC1055. This simple protocol was originally designed for serial connection. SLIP provides no initial headers and only offers a few defined bytes:

END: The byte 0xC0 denotes the end of a frame.

ESC: The byte 0xDB denotes an escape character.

Encoded END: If the data stream contains the END byte (0xC0), then SLIP re-encodes the character as 0xDB 0xDC.

Encoded ESC: If the data stream contains the ESC byte (0xDB), then SLIP re-encodes the character as 0xDB 0xDD.

When the OSI network layer has data to transmit, SLIP immediately begins transmitting the data. At the end of the transmission, an END byte is sent. The only modifications to the data are the encoded escape sequences, which are used to prevent the interpretation of a premature END.

Although SLIP is one of the simplest data link protocols, it leaves the network open to a variety of risks, including error detection, data size issues, network service support, and configuration options.

9.2.1.1 Error Detection

SLIP contains no mechanism for error detection, such as a framing checksum. SLIP assumes that higher layer protocols will detect any possible transmission corruption. This can lead to serious problems when the physical layer is prone to errors (e.g., noisy phone line) or when the network layer uses a simple checksum system.

9.2.1.2 Maximum Transmission Units

The *maximum transmission unit* (MTU) defines the largest size message frame that is permitted. Larger message frames are usually rejected in lieu of causing a buffer overflow in the data link driver. The SLIP message frame has MTU restrictions. The receiving system must be able to handle arbitrarily large SLIP message frames.

As a convention, most SLIP drivers restrict frames to 1006 bytes (not including the END character). This size is based on the Berkeley Unix SLIP drivers, a de facto standard. But nothing in the protocol specifies an actual maximum size.

SLIP also permits transmitting an END END sequence, resulting in a zero-length datagram transmission. Higher layer protocols must be able to handle (and properly reject) zero-length data.

9.2.1.3 No Network Service

Many multinode data link protocols include support for multiple network layer protocols. When data is received, the information is passed to the appropriate network layer driver. SLIP contains no header information and no network service identifier. As such, SLIP is generally used with TCP/IP only.

9.2.1.4 Parameter Negotiations

A SLIP connection requires a number of parameters. Because it relies on a TCP/IP network layer, both nodes need IP addresses. The MTU should be consistent between both ends of the network, and the network should authenticate users to prevent unauthorized connections.

Unfortunately, SLIP provides no mechanism for negotiating protocol options or authenticating traffic. The user must configure the SLIP driver with an appropriate network layer IP address and MTU. Flow control, such as simplex or half-duplex, is determined by the physical layer.

Authentication for SLIP connections generally occurs at the physical layer. As users connect to the service provider, they are prompted for login credentials. After authentication, the SLIP connection is initiated. After authenticating, the service provider may supply the appropriate MTU and IP addresses before switching to the SLIP connection.

SLIP does not support other options, such as encryption and compression.

9.2.2 PPP

In contrast to SLIP, the *Point-to-Point Protocol* (PPP) provides all data link functionality. Many RFCs cover different aspects of PPP: RFC 1332, 1333, 1334, 1377, 1378, 1549, 1551, 1638, 1762, 1763, and 1764. The main standard for PPP is defined in RFC1661.

The PPP message frame includes a header that specifies the size of data within the frame and type of network service that should receive the frame. PPP also includes a data link control protocol for negotiating IP addresses, MTU, and basic authentication. In addition, PPP provides link quality support, such as an echo control frame for determining if the other side is still connected. Unfortunately, PPP does not provide a means to protect authentication credentials, detect transmission errors, or deter replay attacks.

9.2.2.1 Authentication

For authentication, PPP supports both PAP and CHAP, but only one should be used. The PPP driver should first attempt the stronger of the two (usually CHAP) and then regress to the other option if the authentication method is unavailable. Although CHAP and PAP both provide a means to transmit authentication credentials, neither provides encryption; the authentication is vulnerable to eavesdropping and replay attacks at the physical layer.

Neither PAP nor CHAP natively supports password encoding. Some extensions to these protocols, such as DH-CHAP (Diffie-Hellman negotiation for hash algorithms), MS-CHAP and MS-CHAPv2 (Microsoft NT hashing), and EAP-MS-CHAPv2 (includes the use of the Extensible Authentication Protocol), extend the authentication system to use one-way encryption rather than a plaintext transfer.

Although PPP is vulnerable to physical layer attacks, these attacks are rare. The larger risk comes from the storage of login credentials on the server. For PAP and CHAP, the login credentials must be stored on the PPP server. If they are stored in plaintext, then anyone with access to the server may compromise the PAP/CHAP authentication. Even if the file is stored encrypted, the method for decrypting the file must be located on the PPP server.

9.2.2.2 Transmission Error Detection

Although PPP includes a frame header and tail, it does not include a checksum for frame validation. The recipient will not detect frames modified in transit. Noisy phone lines, bad network connections, and intentional insertion attacks are not detected. As with SLIP, PPP assumes that error detection will occur at a higher OSI layer.

9.2.2.3 Replay Attack Transmission

PPP's message frame header contains packet and protocol information but not sequence identification. Because PPP was designed for a point-to-point network, it assumes that packets cannot be received out of order. Nonsequential, missing, and duplicate packets are not identified by PPP. As with SLIP, PPP assumes that a higher OSI layer will detect these issues.

Although these are not significant issues with serial and dialup connections, PPP can be used with most physical layer options. If the physical layer permits nonsequential transmissions, then PPP may generate transmission problems. Examples include using PPP with asynchronous transfer mode (ATM) or grid networks. In these examples, data may take any number of paths, may not be received sequentially, and in some situations may generate duplicate transmissions. Similarly, PPP may be used as a tunnel protocol. Tunneling PPP over UDP (another asynchronous protocol) can lead to dropped or nonsequential PPP message frames. Ideally, PPP should be used with physical layer protocols that only provide a single route between nodes.

An attacker with physical access to the network may insert or duplicate PPP traffic without difficulty. This opens the network to insertion and replay attacks.

9.2.2.4 Other Attacks

As with SLIP, PPP provides no encryption. An attacker on the network can readily observe, corrupt, modify, or insert PPP message frames transmissions. Because the network is point-to-point, both ends of the network can be attacked simultaneously.

9.2.3 Tunneling

VPNs are commonly supported using PPP (and less common with SLIP). In a VPN, the physical layer, data link layer, and possibly higher OSI layers operate as a virtual physical medium. A true network connection is established between two nodes, and then PPP is initiated over the connection, establishing the virtual point-to-point network. Common tunneling systems include PPP over SSH and PPP over Ethernet (PPPoE). When tunneling with PPP or SLIP, the tunneled packet header can degrade throughput performance. CPPP and CSLIP address this issue.

9.2.3.1 PPP over SSH

Secure Shell (SSH—described in Chapter 20) is an OSI layer 6 port forwarding protocol that employs strong authentication and encryption. SSH creates a single network connection that is authenticated, validated, and encrypted. Any TCP (OSI layer 4) connection can be tunneled over the SSH connection, but SSH only tunnels TCP ports. Under normal usage, the remote server's network is not directly accessible by the SSH client. By using an SSH tunneled port as a virtual physical medium, PPP can establish a point-to-point network connection. The result is an encrypted, authenticated, and validated PPP tunnel between hosts. This tunnel can forward packets from one network to the other—even over the Internet—with little threat from eavesdropping, replay, or insertion attacks.

An example PPP over SSH connection can be established using a single PPP command (Listing 9.1). This command establishes a SSH connection between the local system and remote host, and then initiates a PPP connection. The PPP connection is created with the local IP address 10.100.100.100 and remote address 10.200.200.200. No PPP authentication (noauth) is provided because the SSH connection already authenticates the user.

LISTING 9.1 Example PPP over SSH Connection

```
% sudo pppd nodetach noauth passive pty \
   "ssh root@remotehost pppd nodetach notty noauth" \
   ipparam vpn 10.100.100.100:10.200.200.200
Using interface ppp0
Connect: ppp0 <--> /dev/pts/5
Deflate (15) compression enabled
local  IP address 10.100.100.100
remote IP address 10.200.200.200
```

For the sample in Listing 9.1, the remote user must be able to run pppd noauth. *This usually requires root access. When using this command without SSH certificates, there are two password prompts. The first is for the local* sudo *command, and the second is for the remote* ssh login. *Because* pppd *is executing the* ssh *command, no other user-level prompting is permitted.*

After establishing the PPP over SSH connection, one or both sides of the network may add a network routing entry such as route add -net 10.200.200.200 netmask 255.0.0.0 or route add default gw 10.200.200.200. The former specifies routing all 10.*x*.*x*.*x* subnet traffic over the VPN tunnel. The latter sets the VPN as the default gateway; this is a desirable option for tunneling all network traffic.

9.2.3.2 PPPoE

PPP may be tunneled over another data link layer. *PPP over Ethernet* (PPPoE), defined in RFC2516, extends PPP to tunnel over IEEE 802.3 networks. Many cable and DSL connections use PPPoE because PPP provides a mechanism for negotiating authentication, IP address, connection options, and connection management. The PPPoE server is called the *access concentrator* (AC) because it provides access for all PPPoE clients.

PPPoE does have a few specified limitations:

MTU: The largest MTU value can be no greater than 1,492 octets. The MTU for Ethernet is defined as 1,500 octets, but PPPoE uses 6 octets and PPP uses 2.

Broadcast: PPPoE uses a broadcast address to identify the PPPoE server. Normally the PPPoE server responds, but a hostile node may also reply.

AC DoS: The AC can undergo a DoS if there are too many requests for connection allocations. To mitigate this risk, the AC may use a cookie to tag requests. Multiple requests from the same hardware address should receive the same client address.

9.2.3.3 CSLIP and CPPP

When tunneling PPP or SLIP over another protocol, the overhead from repeated packet headers can significantly impact performance. For example, TCP surrounds data with at least 20 bytes of header. IP adds another 20 bytes. So IP(TCP(data)) increases the transmitted size by at least 40 bytes more than the data size. When tunneling PPP over a SSH connection, the resulting stack MAC(IP(TCP(SSH(PPP(IP (TCP(data))))))) contains at least 80 bytes of TCP/IP header plus the PPP and SSH headers. The resulting overhead leads to significant speed impacts:

Transmit Size: When tunneling, there are 80 additional bytes of data per packet. More headers mean more data to transmit and slower throughput.

Message Frames: Many data link protocols have well-defined MTUs. Ethernet, for example, has an MTU of 1,500 bytes. Without tunneling, TCP/IP and MAC headers are at least 54 bytes, or about 4 percent of the MTU. With tunneling, the TCP/IP and PPP headers add an additional 3 percent plus the overhead from SSH.

Stack Processing: When transmitting and receiving, twice as many layers must process each byte of data. This leads to computational overhead.

Although the increase in transmitted data and message frames can be negligible over a high-speed network, these can lead to significant performance impacts over low-bandwidth connections, such as dialup lines. For modem connections, a 3 percent speed loss is noticeable. The stack-processing overhead may not be visible on a fast home computer or workstation, but the overhead can be prohibitive for hardware systems, mission-critical systems, or real-time systems.

Generally hardware-based network devices can process packets faster than software, but they use slower processors and do not analyze all data within the packet. Tunneling through a hardware device is relatively quick; however, tunneling to a hardware device requires processing the entire packet. The limited processing capabilities can significantly impact the capabilities to handle tunneled connections.

To address the increased data size, RFC1144 defines a method to compress TCP/IP headers. The technique includes removing unnecessary fields and applying Lempel-Ziv compression. For example, every TCP and IP header includes a checksum. Because the inner data is not being transmitted immediately, however, there is no need to include the inner checksums. This results in a 4-byte reduction. Together with Lempel-Ziv compression, the initial 40-byte header can be reduced to approximately 16 bytes.

Using this compression system with PPP and SLIP yields the *CPPP* and *CSLIP* protocols. Although there is still a size increase from the tunnel, the overhead is not as dramatic with CPPP/CSLIP as it is with PPP and SLIP.

Although CPPP and CSLIP compress the tunneled TCP/IP headers, they do not attempt to compress internal data. Some intermediate protocols support data compression. For example, SSH supports compressing data. Although this may not be desirable for high-speed connections, the SSH compression can be enabled for slower networks or tunneled connections.

Unfortunately, there are few options for resolving the stack processing issue. Tunneling implies a duplication of OSI layer processing. To resolve this, a non-tunneling system should be used. For example, IPsec provides VPN support without stack repetition.

9.3 COMMON RISKS

The largest risks from PPP and SLIP concern authentication, bidirectional communication, and user education. Although eavesdropping, replay, and insertion attacks are possible, these attacks require access to the physical layer. Because a point-to-point network only contains two nodes on the network, physical layer threats against the data link layer are usually not a significant consideration.

9.3.1 Authentication

SLIP provides no authentication mechanism. Instead, an authentication stack is usually used prior to enabling SLIP. In contrast, PPP supports both PAP and CHAP for authentication [RFC1334]. PAP uses a simple credential system containing a username and password; the username and password are sent to the server unencrypted and then validated against the known credentials.

In contrast to PAP, CHAP uses a more complicated system based on a key exchange and a shared secret key (Figure 9.1). Rather than transmitting the credentials directly, CHAP transmits a username from the client (*peer*) to the server (*authenticator*). The server replies with an 8-bit ID and a variable-length random number. The ID is used to match challenges with responses—it maintains the CHAP session. The client returns an MD5 hash of the ID, shared secret (account password), and random number. The server computes its own hash and compares it with the client's hash. A match indicates the same shared secret.

Unlike PAP, CHAP authentication is relatively secure and can be used across a network that may be vulnerable to eavesdropping; however, CHAP has two limitations. First, it only authenticates the initial connection. After authentication, PPP provides no additional security—someone with eavesdropping capabilities can hijack the connection after the authentication. Second, if an eavesdropper captures two CHAP negotiations with small-length random numbers, then the hash may be vulnerable to a brute-force cracking attack.

In both PAP and CHAP, the server must contain a file with all credential information. SLIP and PPP do not support stronger authentication methods, such as those based on hardware tokens or biometrics. And, neither SLIP nor PPP encrypts the data transmission, so an eavesdropper can observe login credentials.

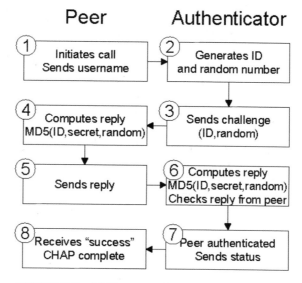

FIGURE 9.1 CHAP processing.

9.3.2 Bidirectional Communication

PPP and SLIP provide full-data link support in that the node may communicate with a remote network, and the remote network may communicate with the node. PPP and SLIP provide full bidirectional communication support. As such, any network service operating on the remote client is accessible by the entire network. Most dialup users do not use home firewalls, so any open network service may leave the system vulnerable.

Software firewalls, or home dialup firewalls such as some models of the SMC Barricade, offer approaches to mitigate the risk from open network services.

9.3.3 User Education

More important than bidirectional communication is user education. Most dialup, DSL, and cable modem users may not be consciously aware that their connections are bidirectional. Moreover, home firewalls can interfere with some online games and conferencing software such as Microsoft NetMeeting. As such, these preventative measures may be disabled and leave systems at risk.

You Can't Do That!

Most universities provide dialup support for students and faculty. One faculty member was positive that his dialup connection was not bidirectional. He challenged members of the computer department's support staff to prove him wrong. The proof took three minutes.

First, a login monitor was enabled to identify when the faculty member was online. Then his IP address was identified. This allowed the attackers to know which of the dialup connections to attack. After being alerted to the victim's presence, the attackers simply used Telnet to connect to the address and were greeted with a login prompt. The login was guessed: root, with no password. Then the attacker saw the command prompt, showing a successful login. (The faculty member had never bothered to set the root password on his home computer.) A friendly telephone call and recital of some of his directories changed his viewpoint on dialup security.

Ironically, this faculty member worked for a computer science department. If he was not aware of the threat, how many home users are aware?

9.4 SIMILAR THREATS

The risks from point-to-point networks, such as PPP and SLIP, extend to other point-to-point systems. High-speed dialup connections such as DSL and ATM use point-to-point physical connections—DSL uses PPPoE [RFC2516], and ATM uses PPPoA [RFC2364]. For these configurations, the data link layer provides a virtually transparent connection. An attacker with physical layer access is not impeded by any data link security.

SUMMARY

The data link layer performs three main tasks: segment data into message frames, address message frames, and control the physical layer flow. In a point-to-point network, these tasks are greatly simplified because there are assumed to be only two nodes on the network. Because of this assumption, physical layer attacks remain the greatest risk to the data link layer; the assumption is that there is no third node capable of accessing the network.

The SLIP and PPP protocols take advantage of the simplified network architecture. SLIP reduces the data link layer to a minimal frame requirement, whereas PPP provides minimal support for network layer protocols, authentication, and link control. Unfortunately, PPP provides no additional security beyond the initial authentication.

Both SLIP and PPP can be used as tunneling protocols, creating a virtual point-to-point network over a more secure network connection. Although useful for establishing a VPN, the primary impact is performance.

As with any data link protocol, SLIP and PPP are bidirectional. When connecting to the Internet, both enable external attackers to access the local computer system.

REVIEW QUESTIONS

1. List three data link functions that are simplified by point-to-point networks.
2. Which is a simpler point-to-point data link protocol, SLIP or PPP?
3. Why is user education a concern for point-to-point protocols?

DISCUSSION TOPICS

1. Explain the differences between general data link layer protocols and point-to-point protocols. Describe how these lead to the simplification of the data link layer requirements.
2. There is only one significant RFC covering SLIP, but there are dozens that cover PPP. Explain some of the reasons why PPP is more preferable than SLIP.
3. Describe what would be needed to use PPP as a VPN without tunneling through a higher-layer protocol such as SSH.

ADDITIONAL RESOURCES

SLIP is defined in RFC1055, *A Nonstandard for Transmission of IP Datagrams Over Serial Lines: SLIP*.

PPP is primarily defined in RFC1661, *The Point-to-Point Protocol (PPP)*. Other related documents include RFC1332, *The PPP Internet Protocol Control Protocol (IPCP)*, RFC1333, *PPP Link Quality Monitoring*, and RFC1334, *PPP Authentication Protocols*. The CHAP authentication method was updated in RFC1994, *PPP Challenge Handshake Authentication Protocol (CHAP)*.

PPP has been extended to support many types of point-to-point networks. Each of these extensions includes modifications for maximum performance or additional data link support options. As new data link layers and configurations are introduced, these documents are revised and new ones are added.

- RFC1376, *The PPP DECnet Phase IV Control Protocol (DNCP)*
- RFC1377, *The PPP OSI Network Layer Control Protocol (OSINLCP)*
- RFC1378, *The PPP AppleTalk Control Protocol (ATCP)*
- RFC1551, *Novell IPX Over Various WAN Media (IPXWAN)*
- RFC1638, *PPP Bridging Control Protocol (BCP)*
- RFC1662, *PPP in HDLC-like Framing*
- RFC1762, *The PPP DECnet Phase IV Control Protocol (DNCP)*
- RFC1763, *The PPP Banyan Vines Control Protocol (BVCP)*
- RFC1764, *The PPP XNS IDP Control Protocol (XNSCP)*
- RFC2153, *PPP Vendor Extensions*
- RFC2364, *PPP Over AAL5 (PPPoA)*
- RFC2516, *A Method for Transmitting PPP Over Ethernet (PPPoE)*

Both SLIP and PPP can benefit from compression algorithms. RFC1144, *Compressing TCP/IP Headers for Low-Speed Serial Links*, provides a general method for compressing TCP/IP headers and leads to CSLIP and CPPP. RFC1962, *The PPP Compression Control Protocol (CCP)*, and RFC1974, *PPP Stac LZS Compression Protocol*, provide a PPP-specific compression options.

10 MAC and ARP

On multiple node networks, systems use network addressing to direct data. This addressing happens in the data link layer (OSI layer 2). Any of three addressing methods may be supplied:

Unicast: Each data link message frame is intended for a specific node. All other nodes (nonrecipients) should ignore the message frame.

Multicast: The message frame is intended for a specific set of nodes but not every node.

Broadcast: The message frame is intended for all nodes on the physical network.

One of the most common addressing methods is defined by the IEEE 802 standard. The MAC defines a unique network address to each node on the network and methods for interfacing with the data link layer.

10.1 DATA LINK SUBLAYERS

IEEE 802 splits the OSI data link layer into two sublayers: LLC and MAC. The LLC comprises the upper half of the data link layer, and the MAC is the lower half.

10.1.1 LLC

The *logical link control* (LLC) is defined by the IEEE 802.2 standard and resides in the upper portion of the data link layer. It provides four functions: link management, SAP management, connection management, and sequence management. The LLC provides a consistent interface with the upper OSI layers regardless of the physical layer.

10.1.1.1 Link Management

The LLC provides the control mechanisms for protocols that require flow control. This is commonly seen in Token Ring networks but not common for Ethernet (10Base-2, 100Base-T, etc.). Many quality-of-service protocols, such as those used by ATM and wireless, use LLC link management to compute the quality.

In addition to quality of service, data link standards such as *Spanning Tree* (IEEE 802.1) use the LLC. Spanning Tree is used by bridges and ensures that routing loops do not form. Each bridge sends out a Spanning Tree message frame with an identifier. If a message frame is received with the same identifier, then the route is assumed to have a loop. Spanning Tree breaks loops by not sending message frames to hardware address that form loops. Although Spanning Tree breaks bridging loops, it also opens the network to a simple DoS attack. Any attacker on the network can reply to the Spanning Tree packet causing the bridge to assume that every path is a loop. This results in a bridge that will not bridge traffic.

10.1.1.2 SAP Management

Service Access Points (SAPs) are ports to network layer (OSI layer 3) protocols. Each network layer protocol uses a different 16-bit identifier to identify the network protocol. For example, IP is 0x0800, IPv6 is 0x86DD, and AppleTalk is 0x809B. The two SAP bytes are divided into a destination (DSAP) and source (SSAP), 1 byte each.

The *Sub Network Access Protocol* (SNAP) was added to IEEE 802.2 to extend the number of DSAP/SSAP values. Using SNAP, the LLC is not limited to 1 byte for each DSAP and SSAP. Instead, the SNAP defines a 3-byte Organizationally Unique ID (OUI) and a 2-byte protocol type.

10.1.1.3 Connection Management

The LLC determines whether the data link layer should use a connection-oriented or connection-less communication flow. The type of connection is independent of higher layer protocols. For example, UDP is an OSI layer 4 connection-less protocol, and TCP is an OSI layer 4 connection-oriented protocol. However, both TCP and UDP may use connection-less (or connection-oriented) data link protocols.

10.1.1.4 Sequence Management

For connection-oriented data link traffic and connection-less traffic that requires a confirmation, the LLC includes a sequence number and uses a sliding window system. The sequence numbers ensure that each message frame is received in the correct order. The sliding window reduces communication overhead by only requiring occasional acknowledgements rather than an acknowledgement after every transmission.

10.1.2 MAC

The *media access control* (MAC) sublayer provides two key functions: transmission control and network addressing.

10.1.2.1 Transmission Control

Many of the different IEEE 802.*x* standards define the medium access control. For example, IEEE 802.3 defines the *Carrier Sense Multiple Access with Collision Detection* (CSMA/CD) for Ethernet. CSMA/CD determines when it is safe to transmit. When a node has data to transmit, CSMA specifies that the node first listen to the network. If nobody else is transmitting, then the data is transmitted; however, CSMA provides no means to prevent two nodes from both hearing an empty network and transmitting at the same time. This results in a collision. Collision Detection (CD) monitors the network for additional voltage—above and beyond a single transmitting host. Additional voltage indicates a collision. Upon detecting a collision, the node immediately stops transmitting, waits a few microseconds, and then repeats the process. If the node cannot transmit the data within a specified timeframe or fails to transmit after a few retries, then a network error is passed to the higher OSI layers. Nodes with defective carrier-detection systems may fail to properly detect network traffic and repeatedly corrupt network data.

> **Big MAC Attack**
>
> The term "MAC" may be used many different ways. Although they have the same acronym, *media* access control is not the same as *medium* access control. The medium access control refers to transmission and collision detection, such as CSMA/CD. In contrast, the media access control is commonly associated with the entire OSI layer 2 protocol (LLC + medium access control). Additionally, MAC may refer to the hardware address: MAC address. This ambiguity can result in communication problems between people discussing the network. Is a "MAC attack" related to the hardware address, collision detection, or overall data link layer?

10.1.2.2 Network Addressing

Every node on the network requires a unique address. This hardware address allows unicast and multicast packets to be processed by the recipient node. As each packet is received, the destination hardware address is compared against the local hardware address. If the addresses match, then the packet is processed. Mismatches indicate a packet that is not intended for the node, so the node quietly drops the packet.

Ethernet network cards use a preset 6-byte code to specify the MAC address. These are usually written in a colon-delimitated format: 00:11:22:33:44:55. The first three octets are the *Organizationally Unique Identifier* (OUI). These usually determine the manufacturer. For example, 00:C0:4F:*xx:xx:xx* is a Dell Computer network card, and 00:08:83:*xx:xx:xx* denotes a Hewlett-Packard network card. In addition, the IEEE registration authority supplies an OUI subset called the *Individual Address Block* (IAB). The IAB defines the first 24 bits, only allowing 12 bits for unique identification. For example, Microsoft is allocated the MAC addresses range 00:30:00:00:30:00 to 00:30:00:00:3F:FF.

The first three octets define the OUI. The remaining three octets are vendor specific—they may indicate the particular make and model of the network card or a third-party vendor. Some portion of the last three octets is pseudo-unique; two identical network cards purchased at the same time will likely have different 6-octet sequences. However, there are a limited number of unique octets. For example, a manufacturer may use two octets as a unique identifier (65,536 combinations) but mass-produce 200,000 network cards. To resolve potential address duplications, most network cards permit the network driver to override the preset MAC address. As such, any user can change the MAC address to any value.

Because an attacker can change his MAC address, authentication based on MAC addresses is weak at best. An attacker can readily assume any other MAC address. Similarly, an attacker may change his MAC address for the duration of an attack, which makes it difficult to track down the actual node.

Attackers may target the MAC address through hardware profiling reconnaissance, impersonation, and load attacks.

10.1.2.3 Acquiring Hardware Addresses

The LLC ensures that multinode and point-to-point network interfaces use the same interface. Each physical layer interface is associated with a unique identifier (name) and MAC address. Additional information, such as a network layer IP address, may also be associated with an interface. Although hardware addresses are only needed for multinode networks, point-to-point networks are also assigned hardware addresses by the LLC. For example, the hardware address for the loopback interface (lo, localhost, etc.) is usually assigned the hardware address 00:00:00:00:00:00.

The getmac.c program on the CD-ROM displays all network interfaces, hardware addresses, and associated IP addresses. The main component uses the ioctl() function to list information associated with each interface (Listing 10.1). An example output from getmac (Listing 10.2) shows both multinode and point-to-point network interfaces.

LISTING 10.1 The ListInterface Function from the getmac.c Program

```
/********************************************************
 ListInterface(): A computer may have multiple network cards.
 List each interface, hardware address, and IP address.
 ********************************************************/
void    ListInterface   ()
{
  struct ifreq Interface;
  struct ifreq *InterfacePointer; /* pointer to an interface */
  struct ifconf InterfaceConfig;
  char Buffer[0x8000];  /* configuration data (make it big) */
  int i;
  int Socket;

  /* Prepare a socket */
  /*** Any socket will work, don't require root ***/
  Socket = socket(AF_INET,SOCK_STREAM,0);
  if (Socket < 0)
    {
    printf("ERROR: Failed to open socket.\n");
    exit(-1);
    }

  /** SIOCGIFCONF returns list of interfaces **/
  InterfaceConfig.ifc_len = sizeof(Buffer);
  InterfaceConfig.ifc_buf = Buffer;
```

```
      if (ioctl(Socket,SIOCGIFCONF,&InterfaceConfig) < 0)
        {
        printf("Error obtaining %s IP address\n",Interface.ifr_name);
        exit(-1);
        }
    /** list every interface **/
    for(i=0; i*sizeof(struct ifreq) < InterfaceConfig.ifc_len; i++)
        {
        InterfacePointer=&(InterfaceConfig.ifc_req[i]);

        /* Load the interface mac address */
        strcpy(Interface.ifr_name,InterfacePointer->ifr_name);

        ioctl(Socket,SIOCGIFHWADDR,&Interface);

        /* Display the results */
        /** The "unsigned int" and "0xff" are just so negative
            characters appear as positive values between
            0 and 255. **/
        printf("Interface: %-6s  ",InterfacePointer->ifr_name);
        printf("MAC: %02x:%02x:%02x:%02x:%02x:%02x  ",
            (unsigned)(Interface.ifr_hwaddr.sa_data[0])&0xff,
            (unsigned)(Interface.ifr_hwaddr.sa_data[1])&0xff,
            (unsigned)(Interface.ifr_hwaddr.sa_data[2])&0xff,
            (unsigned)(Interface.ifr_hwaddr.sa_data[3])&0xff,
            (unsigned)(Interface.ifr_hwaddr.sa_data[4])&0xff,
            (unsigned)(Interface.ifr_hwaddr.sa_data[5])&0xff
            );
        printf("IP: %u.%u.%u.%u\n",
            (unsigned)(InterfacePointer->ifr_addr.sa_data[2])&0xff,
            (unsigned)(InterfacePointer->ifr_addr.sa_data[3])&0xff,
            (unsigned)(InterfacePointer->ifr_addr.sa_data[4])&0xff,
            (unsigned)(InterfacePointer->ifr_addr.sa_data[5])&0xff
            );
        }
    close(Socket);
} /* ListInterface() */
```

LISTING 10.2 Sample Output from `getmac.c`

```
Interface: lo      MAC: 00:00:00:00:00:00  IP: 127.0.0.1
Interface: eth0    MAC: 00:60:08:ca:2e:2c  IP: 10.1.1.247
Interface: eth1    MAC: 00:01:03:69:4d:77  IP: 10.2.21.38
```

10.1.3 MAC Vulnerabilities

Although the MAC provides the means to communicate information between hosts on a network, it also introduces potential attack vectors. Attackers may use

MAC information for reconnaissance, impersonation, or for directed load-based attacks.

10.1.3.1 Hardware Profiling Attacks

The first step in attacking a system is reconnaissance. An attacker blindly attempting to attack an unknown system will rarely be successful. The OUI provides hardware and operating system information to an attacker. For example, if an attacker sees a source MAC address with the OUI 00:0D:93, then the attacker knows the manufacturer is Apple Computers. The operating system associated with the MAC address is likely a version of MacOS and not Windows, Solaris, or other operating system. Similarly, 00:20:F2 indicates Sun Microsystems—the host is likely running a version of SunOS or Solaris.

Attacks against the data link layer are rare and require direct physical layer access. Although hardware profiling is a viable information reconnaissance technique, the attacker is likely to already know the type of system. In environments where it is desirable to obscure the hardware profile, most network drivers permit changing the MAC address. The method to change the MAC address differs by operating system and may not be supported by some drivers:

> **Windows 2000:** The advanced configuration for most network adapters permits setting the hardware address (Figure 10.1).
>
> **RedHat Linux:** The root user can use the ifconfig command to change the adapter's hardware address. This is a three-step process. First, the interface must be taken down, ifconfig eth0 down. Then the hardware address is changed, ifconfig eth0 hw ether 00:11:22:33:44:55. Finally, the interface is brought back up: ifconfig eth0 up.
>
> **Mac OS X:** The Macintosh OS X operating system uses a variation of the ifconfig command: ifconfig en0 ether 00:11:22:33:44:55. Unlike Linux, the interface does not need to be down to change the address.

Some network adaptors, such as some Macintosh Powerbook's wireless network cards, do not support changes to the MAC address. In some situations, this is a limitation of the hardware; in other cases, this is a driver limitation.

10.1.3.2 Impersonation Attacks

Users with administration privileges can change their MAC address. An attacker may intentionally change the address to duplicate another node on the network. If both systems are active on the network, it is likely that both systems will interfere with each other. The attack effectively becomes a DoS.

FIGURE 10.1   Changing the hardware address under Windows 2000.

In some situations, two nodes can coexist on the same network with the same hardware address. If both systems use different network layer (OSI layer 3) services or different data link SAPs, then they may operate without interference. This type of impersonation may bypass some IDSs, particularly when specific nodes are filtered based on hardware address.

Finally, the impersonation attack may be used to bypass MAC filtering. Systems that validate access based on MAC addresses can be bypassed by impersonating an appropriate hardware address.

10.1.3.3 Load Attacks

As well as being part of the OUI, the first octet contains addressing flags. The least significant bit of the first octet indicates a multicast packet. Every odd value for the first octet is a multicast. The value FF indicates a broadcast packet. Attackers can quickly initiate a load attack because they can change their MAC address to be a broadcast or multicast address. Although this will have no impact on the attacker's system, all other nodes on the network will attempt to process every packet intended for the attacker's node.

An example of this style of a load attack assigns the hardware address FF:FF:00:00:00:00 to the attacker's node. All other nodes on the network will view packets directed to the attacker's node as a broadcast packet.

Although most versions of Linux, BSD, MacOS, and Windows support setting a broadcast address as the MAC address, this is operating system- and driver-specific. Under Windows XP, one test system did not support changing the MAC address, and another disabled the network card when a broadcast address was entered, removing it from the list of available network devices. The card could only be re-enabled through the hardware device manager.

10.2 ARP AND RARP

The *Address Resolution Protocol* (ARP) is an example of a service access protocol. ARP, defined in RFC826, assists the network layer (OSI layer 3) by converting IP addresses to hardware addresses. The *Reverse Address Resolution Protocol* (RARP) converts a hardware address to an IP address.

ARP packets include a function code such as ARP request, ARP reply, RARP request, and RARP reply. ARP and RARP requests are broadcast packets that include the query information. For example, an ARP request contains an IP address. The expectation is that all nodes will receive the broadcast, but only one node will claim the IP address. The node that identifies the IP address will transmit an ARP reply (unicast) back to the querying host. The query results are stored in an ARP table, which is viewable with the arp command (Listing 10.3). The ARP table lists all nodes on the local network that have responded to ARP requests.

LISTING 10.3 Sample Output from the arp Command

```
$ /sbin/arp
Address      HWtype  HWaddress          Flags Mask    Iface
10.1.3.1     ether   00:50:18:03:C0:20  C             eth0
10.1.3.2     ether   00:C0:F0:40:42:2F  C             eth0
10.1.3.3     ether   00:11:D8:AB:22:F4  C             eth0
```

ARP traffic is not passed beyond the local network. Bridges, routers, and gateways do not relay ARP packets. Nodes that are not on the local network will never be listed in the local ARP table.

10.2.1 ARP Poisoning

Mapping IP addresses to hardware addresses (and vice versa) can add a delay to network connections. *ARP tables* contain a temporary cache of recently seen MAC addresses. Therefore, ARP packets are only required when a new IP address (or MAC address) lookup needs to be performed. Unfortunately, these cached entries open the system to ARP poisoning, where an invalid or intentionally inaccurate entry is used to populate the table.

ON THE CD

ARP replies are not authenticated, but ARP reply values are placed into the ARP table. Moreover, if a later ARP reply is received, it can overwrite existing ARP table entries. The arp_stuff.c program on the CR-ROM and in Listing 10.4 is one example of a tool for poisoning ARP tables. This program generates an ARP reply and sends a fake MAC address and IP address pair to a target system. As the target processes the packet, it adds the ARP reply's information to the system's ARP table. In this attack, no ARP request is required.

LISTING 10.4 Code Fraction from arp_stuff.c for Poisoning an ARP Table

```
void LoadInterface (int Socket, char *InterfaceName,
    struct sockaddr_ll *SocketData)
{
  struct ifreq Interface;
  memset(SocketData,0,sizeof(struct sockaddr_ll));
  SocketData->sll_protocol = htons(ETHERTYPE_ARP);
  SocketData->sll_halen    = ETH_ALEN;
  strcpy(Interface.ifr_name,InterfaceName);
  ioctl(Socket,SIOCGIFINDEX,&Interface);
  SocketData->sll_ifindex  = Interface.ifr_ifindex;
  ioctl(Socket,SIOCGIFHWADDR,&Interface);
  memcpy(SocketData->sll_addr,Interface.ifr_hwaddr.sa_data,
         ETH_ALEN);
} /* LoadInterface() */

/***********************************************************/
int    main    (int argc, char *argv[])
{
  packet Packet;
  struct sockaddr_ll SocketData;
  in_addr_t IPaddress;
  int Socket;
  int rc;

  /* load Ethernet header */
  memset(&Packet,0,sizeof(packet));
  Text2Bin(argv[3],Packet.ether_header.ether_shost,ETH_ALEN);
  Text2Bin(argv[5],Packet.ether_header.ether_dhost,ETH_ALEN);
  Packet.ether_header.ether_type = htons(ETHERTYPE_ARP);

  /* load ARP header */
  Packet.arp_header.ar_hrd = htons(ARPHRD_ETHER);
  Packet.arp_header.ar_pro = htons(ETH_P_IP);
```

```
Packet.arp_header.ar_hln = ETH_ALEN;
Packet.arp_header.ar_pln = 4;
Packet.arp_header.ar_op  = htons(ARPOP_REPLY);

/* Load ARP data */
/** store the fake source ARP and IP address **/
Hex2Bin(argv[3],Packet.arp_sha,6);
IPaddress = ntohl(inet_addr(argv[2]));
Packet.arp_sip[0] = (IPaddress & 0xff000000) >> 24;
Packet.arp_sip[1] = (IPaddress & 0x00ff0000) >> 16;
Packet.arp_sip[2] = (IPaddress & 0x0000ff00) >> 8;
Packet.arp_sip[3] = (IPaddress & 0x000000ff) >> 0;
/** set the real target ARP and IP address **/
Hex2Bin(argv[5],Packet.arp_tha,6);
IPaddress = ntohl(inet_addr(argv[4]));
Packet.arp_tip[0] = (IPaddress & 0xff000000) >> 24;
Packet.arp_tip[1] = (IPaddress & 0x00ff0000) >> 16;
Packet.arp_tip[2] = (IPaddress & 0x0000ff00) >> 8;
Packet.arp_tip[3] = (IPaddress & 0x000000ff) >> 0;

Socket = socket(PF_PACKET,SOCK_RAW,htons(ETHERTYPE_ARP));
LoadInterface(Socket,argv[1],&SocketData);

/* Send data.  sendto() does not require a connection */
rc = sendto(Socket,&Packet,sizeof(Packet),0,
            (struct sockaddr *)(&SocketData),sizeof(SocketData));
close(Socket);
return(0);
} /* main() */
```

10.2.2 ARP Poisoning Impact

The result from an ARP poisoning can range from a resource attack to a DoS or MitM attack.

10.2.2.1 Resource Attack

Some systems have a limited number of ARP entries that can be cached. By sending a large number of false ARP entries, the ARP table can fill up. When the table fills, there are only two options: ignore additional ARP entries or throw out the oldest entries. If the system ignores additional entries, then no new nodes on the local network can be contacted. If the node throws out the oldest ARP entry, then the result is a much slower network performance due to constant ARP queries for each packet that the system wants to transmit.

10.2.2.2 Denial of Service (DoS)

Newer ARP replies overwrite older ARP replies in the ARP table. If an entry in the ARP table is overwritten with a bad MAC address, then future connections to the overwritten node's IP address will fail. For example, if the ARP table entry `00:11:22:33:44:55` = `10.1.2.3` is overwritten by the poisoned ARP reply `00:11:11:11:11:11` = `10.1.2.3`, then all subsequent traffic to `10.1.2.3` will fail because it will be sent to the wrong MAC address.

10.2.2.3 Man-in-the-Middle (MitM)

The MitM attack routes all traffic through a hostile node. Similar to the DoS attack, the ARP table entry is overwritten with a different machine's MAC address. In this situation, the new node will receive all traffic intended for the old node. By poisoning both nodes (Figure 10.2), the hostile node can establish a successful MitM.

FIGURE 10.2 ARP poisoning as a MitM attack.

10.2.3 Mitigating ARP Poisoning

Although very problematic, the scope of an ARP poisoning attack is limited to the local network; ARP packets do not travel beyond bridges, routers, or gateways. Although the range of the attack is limited, it can still impact network security. The few options for limiting the impact of ARP attacks include hard-coding ARP tables, expiring ARP entries, filtering ARP replies, and locking ARP tables.

10.2.3.1 Hard-Coding ARP Tables

Normally ARP tables are populated dynamically, as each ARP reply is received; however, ARP tables can be populated statically using the operating system's arp command. This command statically sets a MAC address and IP address pair into the ARP table and prevents future modification.

10.2.3.2 Expiring ARP Entries

Cached entries in an ARP table may timeout. Expired entries, where the same MAC and IP address combination are not observed, can be removed from the ARP table. This mitigation option limits the impact from resource attacks.

10.2.3.3 Filtering ARP Replies

Not every ARP reply must be inserted into the ARP table. Linux and BSD limit cache entries to ARP requests that were sent by the local host. This prevents unsolicited ARP replies from entering the ARP table. In contrast, most Windows operating systems accept unsolicited ARP replies and insert them into the ARP table. Although ARP reply filtering does prevent unsolicited entries, it does not prevent new replies from overwriting existing entries.

10.2.3.4 Locking ARP Tables

ARP tables can be temporarily locked. In this situation, an established connection (such as an IP connection) locks the ARP table entry for a short duration. During this time, new ARP replies cannot overwrite the locked table entry—ensuring that an established connection cannot be changed while it is established and mitigating MitM attacks. A MitM attack can only be initiated during the short duration between the system's ARP request and initiating network connection. Systems that support ARP table locking are uncommon.

10.3 NETWORK ROUTING

Network devices such as switches and bridges commonly use ARP packets. In particular, these devices focus on ARP replies. Unfortunately, these systems are susceptible to ARP attacks such as switch poisoning and switch flooding.

10.3.1 Switches

Network hubs and switches link two or more network segments that use the same physical medium. Data transmitted on one network segment is retransmitted through the hub to all other network segments. *Hubs* are considered "dumb" network devices because they simply receive and retransmit data.

In contrast to hubs, *switches* are "smart" network devices. Switches maintain their own internal ARP table and associate each ARP reply with a physical port on the switch. As each packet is received, the switch identifies the destination MAC address and routes the packet to the specific port rather than sending it to every port. Switches only retransmit the packet to every port when the destination MAC address is unknown.

A switch can identify MAC addresses in three ways:

ARP Requests: Many switches know how to generate ARP requests. When an unknown destination is encountered, the switch generates an ARP request across every port and waits for a reply.

ARP Replies: Any ARP reply, even one not generated by the switch, is used to populate and update the switch's ARP table.

Frame Headers: Each message frame contains a source MAC address. The switch can use this to associate the source MAC address with a specific port.

10.3.2 Bridges

Bridges link two networks that use the same data link protocol. For example, a bridge may span networks that use coaxial 10Base-2 and twisted pair 100Base-T. Both of these physical layer media use the same LLC, MAC, and CSMA/CD protocols. As with switches, bridges may associate MAC addresses with specific interfaces. Any message frame, where the source and destination addresses are on the same network (and same bridge interface), are not retransmitted through the bridge. Similarly, bridges with multiple interfaces may route message fames based on an internal ARP table.

10.3.3 Switch Attacks

As with any network node, switches and bridges are vulnerable to poisoning and flooding attacks.

10.3.3.1 Switch Poisoning Attacks

Switches maintain an ARP table to route traffic through the switch to specific physical network ports. An ARP poisoning attack can corrupt the ARP table. The poisoning ARP reply can associate another node's MAC address with a different port. This effectively cuts off the victim node from the network and sends all traffic intended for the victim through the attacker's port. Because switch poisoning redirects network traffic, this attack allows connection hijacking.

10.3.3.2 Switch Flooding Attacks

Nodes operating in promiscuous mode cannot receive any network traffic beyond the immediate local network. Switches and bridges normally ensure that nodes only receive traffic intended for the local physical network. An attacker, using ARP poisoning, can flood a switch's ARP table. Because switches cannot afford to drop packets, most switches regress to a hub state when the switch's ARP table fills. In this state, all nodes receive all traffic; a node operating in promiscuous mode can begin receiving all network traffic that passes through the switch.

Most bridges and high-end switches support static ARP entries. Using static ARP tables in these network devices can mitigate the impact from switch flooding and poisoning.

Although flooding attacks can enable network monitoring by a promiscuous node, segmenting the network with multiple switches and bridges still mitigates the impact from this attack. For example, an onion network topology can have any single bridge/switch overwhelmed by a flooding attack, but not everyone will be compromised. As each device regresses to a hub state, the overall network volume increases. Eventually the network will become unusable due to too much network traffic; the onion topology will limit the DoS to a few rings. In addition, IDS and IPS monitors will likely detect a sudden increase in network traffic (and ARP replies), indicating a network attack.

10.4 PHYSICAL LAYER RISKS

Although the IEEE 802 data link layer is closely associated with the physical layer, it does operate independently. As such, all risks associated with the physical layer also impact the data link layer. For example, nothing within this data link layer can identify a splicing or insertion attack against the physical layer. Because the MAC frame information does not contain timestamps or cryptography, physical layer replay and insertion attacks are successful. The assumption is that higher-layer protocols will detect and prevent these types of attacks.

SUMMARY

The IEEE 802.x standards for the data link layer are among the most common data link standards. IEEE 802.x is commonly used on thinnet, thicknet, twisted pair, fiber optic, and Token Ring networks. The largest threats come from MAC address information leakage, MAC address hijacking, and poisoned ARP packets. But the scope of the risk is limited to the local network. Network devices such as bridges and switches can limit the scope of an attack. Similarly, careful ARP table management can limit the impact from poisoned ARP replies.

REVIEW QUESTIONS

1. Which IEEE 802 sublayer manages hardware addressing?
2. What is ARP poisoning?
3. How can switches be forced into a hub-like mode?

DISCUSSION TOPICS

1. Describe a method for detecting ARP poisoning. Explain the benefits and limitations for the approach, and options to mitigate the limitations.
2. Create a tool to generate false RARP replies. Can RARP be used for attacks, similar to ARP poisoning? Do the fake RARP packets affect switches?
3. Explain the difference between the LLC and MAC sublayers.
4. Explain why the data link layer is tightly coupled with the physical layer. Describe a physical layer medium that cannot be adequately managed by the IEEE 802.3 MAC.
5. In a lab environment, configure a network with a switch and three hosts: A, B, and C. Set host A to continually send ICMP echo (ping) requests to host B. Using host C, generate many different forged ARP packets.

   - Does the switch regress to hub mode? Describe a method for detecting the regression.
   - Determine the size of the switch's internal ARP table. Estimate the ARP table's timeout value.
   - Why is the sequence of pings between hosts A and B required? Does the A to B traffic need to be ICMP?

ADDITIONAL RESOURCES

IEEE maintains a list of OUI octets. Although not complete, the list includes many of the common MAC address octet-triplets that form the OUI. This list is available online at *http://standards.ieee.org/regauth/oui/oui.txt*. In addition, the AIB list is available at *http://standards.ieee.org/regauth/oui/iab.txt*.

ON THE CD

The CD-ROM contains `getmac.c` and `arp_stuff.c`, tools (with source code) for listing MAC addresses and generating poisoned ARP packets. Other tools for listing MAC addresses include the Unix `ifconfig` and Windows `ipconfig` commands. For generating poisoned ARP packets, programs such as Seringe and Snarp are publicly available. Arpd from the Honeynet Project permits impersonating multiple MAC addresses on a single host, and Arpwatch by the LBL Network Research Group can detect ARP poisoning attacks.

Part IV

OSI Layer 3

In This Part

- Network Layer
- Internet Protocol (IP)
- Anonymity

Layer 3 of the ISO OSI model is the network layer. This layer addresses packets and routes them through distinct networks. The network layer also provides quality-of-service and data fragmentation support above the data link layer. The Internet Protocol (IP) is a widely used example of a network layer protocol. General network layer security issues concern recipient addressing, control channel manipulations, and anonymity.

11   Network Layer

In This Chapter

- Routing
- Routing Risks
- Addressing
- Risks to Address Schemes
- Fragmentation
- Fragmentation Risks
- Quality of Service
- Quality-of-Service Attacks
- Security

The *network layer* extends the data link layer functionality to internetwork connections. The data link layer provides three functions: addressing, data fragmentation, and quality of service. For the data link layer, these functions are only provided to the local network. The network layer extends these functions between networks. Whereas the data link layer is focused on the physical connections, the network layer focuses on the network topology.

11.1 ROUTING

Network *routing* permits two distinct data link layers to communicate. Without network routing, the data link layer would require all nodes to communicate directly with all other nodes on the network. Large networks would become bottlenecked due to the cross-communication. The network layer permits individual networks to communicate on an as-needed basis.

Routers are network devices that perform network routing. The appropriate route for delivery depends on a set of routing tables. Routing metrics determine optimal routing paths.

11.1.1 Routers

Routers are network nodes that span two distinct data link networks. Any node that spans two distinct data link networks may act as a router. A router that connects two networks is *dual-homed*; a *multihomed* router connects many different networks.

Routers span networks that support the same addressing schemes. Two networks may use different physical layer mediums and data link protocols, but a router can span them if the address convention is consistent. For example, a multihomed router may support IP over WiFi, 10Base-T, 100Base-T, and a cable modem connection. *Multiprotocol routers* may offer support for different network layer protocols, such as IP, IPX, and DECnet, but cannot convert traffic between the protocols. To convert between network protocols, *gateways*—OSI layer 4 devices—are required.

11.1.2 Routing Tables

Routers maintain an internal table that associates adjacent networks with network interfaces. The *routing table* is consulted whenever a packet is received. As the router's data link layer receives each packet, the network address in the packet is identified and compared against the routing table. Based on the match in the routing table, the data is repackaged in a new data link message frame and sent out the appropriate network interface.

The `netstat` command is found on most operating systems. The command `netstat -r` displays the local routing table (Listing 11.1). Each destination network is associated with a network interface and router address on the network. Most computers use at least two network interfaces. The first is the *loopback*, also called *localhost*. Unix systems may denote this host by the interface name `lo` or `lo0`. The loopback route is used for self-connections, where a network process on the host connects to a service on the same host.

The remaining Unix network interfaces denote the types and number of network adapters. For example, `en0` (or `eth0`) is the first Ethernet adaptor; `en1` is the second Ethernet adaptor. On Windows systems, a numeric identifier represents each network interface (Listing 11.2).

LISTING 11.1 Sample Netstat Usage from Unix

```
% netstat -rn
Routing tables
Internet:
Destination      Gateway        Flags    Refs     Use   Netif Expire
default          10.1.3.254     UGSc       0        0    en0
10.1.3/24        link#4         UCS        2        0    en0
10.1.3.180       127.0.0.1      UHS        0        0    lo0
10.1.3.254       link#4         UHLW       1        0    en0
127              127.0.0.1      UCS        0        0    lo0
127.0.0.1        127.0.0.1      UH       146   150535    lo0
169.254          link#4         UCS        0        0    en0
192.168.1        link#5         UCS        1        0    en1
192.168.1.150    127.0.0.1      UHS        0        0    lo0
```

LISTING 11.2 Sample Netstat Usage from Windows 2000

```
C:\>netstat -r
Route Table
===========================================================================
Interface List
0x1 ........................... MS TCP Loopback interface
0x1000003 ...00 c0 f0 41 31 a7 .... Intel DC21140 Ethernet Adapter
===========================================================================
===========================================================================
Active Routes:
Network Destination        Netmask          Gateway    Interface  Metric
        0.0.0.0          0.0.0.0      10.1.3.254     10.1.3.1       1
       10.0.0.0        255.0.0.0       10.1.3.1     10.1.3.1       1
       10.1.3.1  255.255.255.255      127.0.0.1    127.0.0.1       1
 10.255.255.255  255.255.255.255       10.1.3.1     10.1.3.1       1
      127.0.0.0        255.0.0.0      127.0.0.1    127.0.0.1       1
      224.0.0.0        224.0.0.0       10.1.3.1     10.1.3.1       1
255.255.255.255  255.255.255.255       10.1.3.1     10.1.3.1       1
Default Gateway:       10.1.3.254
===========================================================================
```

Routing tables not only indicate immediately adjacent networks but also paths to remote networks and network metrics.

11.1.3 Routing Metrics

In a point-to-point network, there is only one path between nodes, so metrics concerning the cost of the route are not important. Where there is only one path between nodes, either the traffic takes the path or the nodes do not communicate.

In multinode networks with routers, there can be multiple paths to the same destination. A host's routing table may list many routers, and a multihomed router may have a variety of choices for directing traffic to a specific network. *Routing metrics* provide a basis for selecting an optimal route when there are multiple choices.

Different networks may use different routing metrics and may weigh the metrics based on specific network needs. For example, one route may be shorter, relaying through fewer routers but slower than another route. In general, metrics are based on a combination of criteria:

Bandwidth: The available network capacity may drive the routing metric. For example, a router with a choice between T-3 and DSL links may weigh the T-3 as more desirable due to the higher bandwidth.

Delay: A higher bandwidth network is not always more desirable. Many satellite links offer high bandwidth but also have significant delays between the transmission at one end and receipt at the other end.

Load: A particular network connection may require more computer resources. VPN and encrypted tunnels, for example, can generate a significant load. An SSH tunnel may offer privacy, but the overhead from the tunnel is computationally expensive. The load may be on an end node or intermediate router.

Path Length: The route connecting two networks may traverse many intermediate networks. Some paths are shorter than other paths.

Service Quality: A high-speed network that periodically goes down or corrupts data may be less desirable than a slower, but more reliable, network connection.

Communication Cost: Many network providers apply a service costs per packet or duration. Although the network itself may be very fast, short, and reliable, the cost may be less than desirable.

Network routing metrics are analogous to using the post office, UPS, or FedEx to deliver a package. The post office may be more convenient and less expensive, but UPS or FedEx may offer faster or more reliable services. Similar choices exist when making a phone call. A cell phone may be convenient but have a per-minute limitation or quality issues. Standard telephones generally offer better quality and a per-minute or per-call charge.

Routing table metrics are configured to best represent the optimal path. The metrics do not need to be static—they may change over time as routes become more or less desirable. For example, a cell phone may have unlimited long distance during evenings, making the cell phone's desirability change at different times of the day.

The routing table metric is usually summarized to a single numerical value. Low values are usually more desirable, but not always—this is specific to each router's configuration. Although dynamic metrics may change the summary value, there is no method for the router to determine why a metric of 10 is less desirable than a metric of 8. The router only needs to know that the 8 is more desirable. Similarly, two paths with metrics of 10 may be equally undesirable for completely different reasons.

11.1.4 Applying Routes

A dual-homed router requires two network stacks—one for each interface. Data addressed to one interface's data link address is received, and the destination's network layer address is identified. The network address is compared with the routing table. If there is only one path, then the packet is forwarded through the appropriate network interface. If there are multiple paths, then the most desirable path is used. In the event that a path is unavailable, a different path is selected.

Occasionally, there may be multiple "best" paths. A router's configuration determines how to resolve multiple choices:

Default Route: One path is arbitrarily designated as the default path.

Round Robin: The router alternates between equally weighed paths.

Load Balanced: Traffic is alternated between paths based on usage.

Alphabetical: All things being equal, one interface may be chosen over another based on a sorted order.

11.2 ROUTING RISKS

In the OSI model, network routers are the only option for communicating with distant networks. Direct attacks against the router will, at minimum, interfere with the capability to communicate with other networks. Even when the physical and data link layers remain intact, the network layer can be disabled, which prevents network routing.

Router-based attacks appear in many forms: direct attacks, table poisoning, table flooding, metric attacks, and router looping attacks.

11.2.1 Direct Router Attacks

A *direct router attack* takes the form of a DoS or system compromise. A DoS prevents the router from performing the basic routing function, which effectively disables network connectivity. Historically, these attacks have been load based: if the network volume on a particular interface is too high, then the router will be unable to manage the traffic, including traffic from other network interfaces.

Although most PCs have very fast processors, most hardware routers use slower CPUs. A 2 GHz PC running Linux may make a dependable router, but a Cisco PIX is a commonly used commercial router that uses a 60 MHz processor. Hardware solutions are typically faster than software solutions, but slower processors can be overwhelmed with less effort.

Although rare, router compromises can be devastating. The router can be reconfigured to forward traffic to a different host, block traffic from specific hosts, or arbitrarily allocate new, covert subnets. Because routers span multiple subnets, a compromise router impacts the integrity and privacy of every network connected to it.

11.2.2 Router Table Poisoning

As with the data link layer's ARP table, the network layer's routing table is vulnerable to poisoning attacks. Few network protocols authenticate the network's traffic. Forged or compromised network traffic can overwrite, insert, or remove routing table entries. The result is not very different from a compromised router: the poisoned table can be reconfigured to forward traffic to a different host, block traffic from specific hosts, or arbitrarily allocate new, covert subnets.

Network layer protocols support dynamic routing tables, where the table is automatically generated and updated based on the observed network traffic. These protocols are more vulnerable because (1) a new node may generate poisoning data, and (2) few dynamic nodes are verifiable. Critical routers should use static routing tables to deter poisoning.

11.2.3 Router Table Flooding

Routers generally do not have large hard drives or RAM for storing routing tables. The routing table size is usually limited. Devices that do not use static routes must manage route expiration and table filling. An attacker can generate fake data that the router will use to populate the routing table. When routing tables fill, the router has three options: ignore, discard oldest, or discard worst routes:

Ignore New Routes: Routers may choose to ignore new routes. An attacker will be unable to dislodge established table entries but can prevent new, valid entries from being inserted into the table.

Discard Oldest Routes: As with ARP tables, routing tables may discard routes that are not used. A large flooding attack can dislodge established table entries.

Discard Worst Routes: The router may consider routing table metrics. Less desirable paths can be replaced with more desirable routes. Although default or highly desirable routes are unlikely to be replaced, new routes that appear desirable may dislodge table entries for alternate paths.

For a router table flooding attack to be successful, the attacker must know how the router responds to a full routing table. For example, an attack that generates many fake paths that appear optimal is effective if the router discards the worst routes, but the attack will have little impact if the router ignores all new paths.

Most dynamic routing tables also support static entries. Critical routes should be configured as static entries.

11.2.4 Routing Metric Attacks

A *routing metric attack* poisons the dynamic metrics within a routing table. This attack can make a preferred path appear less desirable. For example, most data link and network layer protocols support quality-of-service packets. These are used for flow control as well as determining connectivity quality. An attacker who forges quality-of-service packets can modify dynamic metrics. The result may be slower throughput, longer paths, or more expensive networking costs. In the worst case, the router may disable a desirable path.

Just as static paths mitigate flooding attacks, metric attacks are defeated by static metrics. Fixed paths should use static metrics. In networks where dynamic metrics are critical, refresh rates should be adjusted so the router rechecks desirable routes often.

11.2.5 Router Looping Attacks

Many network protocols attempt to detect and prevent network *loops*, where data forwarded though one interface is routed to a different interface on the same router. Network loops cause excessive bandwidth consumption and can result in feedback that consumes all available network bandwidth. Whereas some network layer protocols provide means to expire undelivered packets, many protocols exist to assist in the detection of network loops. Protocols such as the data link layer's Spanning Tree (IEEE 802.1), and the network layer's Border Gateway Protocol (BGP) [RFC1772] and Routing Information Protocol (RIP) [RFC2453] provide the means to detect network loops.

When a network router identifies a network loop, the path is removed from the routing table. A looping attack generates a false reply to a loop check, making the router falsely identify a network loop. The result is a desirable network path that is disabled. Although static values can prevent table and metric attacks, looping attacks can still disable paths.

Fortunately, looping attacks are difficult to perform. An attacker must control two systems—one on each router interface being attacked. As the loop-check query is observed by one system, a message is sent to the second system with the reply information. The second system creates the false loop reply and sends it to the router.

As stated in RFC2453, "The basic RIP protocol is not a secure protocol." Security can be added through the use of cryptography. For example, RFC2082 adds an MD5 checksum to the RIP packet, and each router contains a shared secret, preventing an attacker from blindingly sending valid RIP replies. More complicated schemes may use asymmetrical keys or encrypted RIP packets.

Many network protocols assign a *time-to-live* (TTL) value to packets. The TTL is decremented by each network relay. If the TTL reaches zero, then the packet is assumed to be undeliverable. TTLs break network loops by preventing the packet from indefinitely relaying through a loop.

11.3 ADDRESSING

The data link layer provides address support for multinode networks. Each address simply needs to be a unique sequence. The data link layer does not use addressing for any other purpose besides identifying a unique node on the network. Data link layer addressing is analogous to referencing people by their first names. As long as there is only one person named Bart in a room, there is no confusion when someone mentions Bart's name.

Network layer addressing not only provides a unique address but also provides a method to route information to that address. Even though there are many people named Bart, there is only one at 742 Evergreen Terrace in Springfield. The address provides routing information for Bart's messages.

Network addresses are independent of network cards or nodes. The same address may be assigned to many different nodes. This is common for fail-over server clusters, where a duplicate node compensates for any adjacent node failures. Different NICs on the same node may also have the same address. This is common for fail-over network interfaces and dual-homed systems that contain two network interfaces on two different subnets. Similarly, a single NIC may be assigned multiple network addresses (*multihosting*). Although a one-to-one association of addresses to NICs is common, it is not a requirement.

The two approaches for providing address information are numeric and name routing.

11.3.1 Numeric Addressing

Numeric addressing uses a sequence of numbers to identify a particular node on a specific network. This is analogous to contacting someone with a telephone number. The phone number routes the call to a particular location. Telephone numbers contain country codes, regional exchanges, and unique identifiers to route calls. For networking, the numeric address includes a subnet identifier and unique identifier. Different network layer protocols use different numerical routing systems. Examples of numerical routing protocols include IP, IPv6, VINES, IPX, and X.25.

Different numeric addressing schemes permit different node depths. If all end nodes are at the same depth from the uppermost router, then the network has a *uniform depth*. X.25 and IPX are examples of uniform depth protocols. In contrast, IP and IPv6 provide *variable depth* networks, where different nodes may be much further away from central routers. In contrast, VINES provides an *ad hoc* network, where there is no central routing system.

11.3.1.1 X.25

The X.25 network layer protocol applies the concept of telephone network address routing to data connections. The X.25 standard defines functions found in the OSI physical, data link, and network layers. Each of these subfunctions are defined by subset protocols of X.25. For example, the X.25 physical layer is managed by the X.21bis modem protocol—similar to V.24 and V.28. The X.25 data link layer is implemented using the Link Access Procedure, Balanced (LAPB) protocol, and the network addressing functionality is defined by X.121 [Cisco2001].

Each X.121 network address consists of three main components. The first component is a three-digit country code, similar to a telephone country code. The second component is a one-digit regional exchange identifier for identifying a particular *packet switched network* (PSN). The final component is a *national terminal number* (NTN) that may consist of up to 10 digits. The country and PSN identifiers identify a particular subnet, and the NTN identifies the unique node of the network. An X.121 address can be up to 14 digits long.

Two additional fields preface the X.121 address header. The first specifies the source address length, and the second is the length for the destination address. Although these are critical to interpreting the headers, they are not essential for understanding the addressing scheme.

X.121 is an example of a *uniform-depth addressing* scheme. All end nodes connect to a PSN, and all PSNs connect to a set of country routers. Each country router must know how to connect to other country routers and to the local PSNs. In contrast, the PSN only needs to route data between the country router and the end nodes.

11.3.1.2 IPX

IPX is a network protocol commonly associated with Novell NetWare. IPX uses a simplified addressing scheme. Each node is assigned a 12-byte address. The first 4 bytes identify the network number, and the next 6 bytes provide the unique node ID. The remaining 2 bytes define a service identifier.

To route data between nodes, the data is forwarded to the network's router and the 10-byte network address is analyzed. Each router maintains a table that associates network numbers to network interfaces. The routing table is used to direct traffic to the appropriate network. A single router may connect to multiple networks or other routers, which permits large networks; however, each router requires a table for navigating the network.

In addition to the address information, each IPX address header includes 2 bytes that are unique to IPX: they define a service. IPX services are used in lieu of a control protocol and tell the IPX driver how to interpret the packet. For example, the service 0x451 defines a NetWare Core Protocol (NCP) packet, and 0x456 is a diagnostic packet.

11.3.1.3 VINES

Banyan *Virtual Integrated Network Service* (VINES) provides network addressing and is part of Xerox Corporation's Xerox Network Systems (XNS) protocol suite. VINES uses an addressing scheme similar to IPX but does not use a centralized router. This defines an *ad hoc* network.

Each node on a VINES network is referenced by a 48-bit numeric address. The first 32 bits identify the server associated with the network. The remaining 16 bits identify each unique node.

Whereas X.25 and IPX use predefined network addresses, VINES strictly uses dynamic addresses. Each client initially requests a network address from the network server. The server provides the node with the server's number and unique node address. Although there may be many servers on the same physical network, the node only associates with one server.

In a VINES network, any host may contain multiple network interfaces, with each interface on a different network. All dual-homed nodes may act as routers. VINES routing tables are dynamically passed between nodes. As a routing table is received, the metrics are updated and merged with other received tables. The resulting merged table determines the accessible paths.

11.3.1.4 IP

The *Internet Protocol* (IP) is one of them most widely used network layer protocols (see Chapter 12). This protocol, described in RFC791, uses four bytes to provide address information. The bytes are usually written in a dotted-decimal format:

A.B.C.D, for example, 10.1.3.100. Subnet identification is based on bit-masked subsets. The network mask 255.255.0.0 combines with the IP address 10.1.3.100 to define the 10.1.*x*.*x* subnet. Any IP address that begins with 10.1 is a valid member of this subnet.

Unlike IPX or X.25 networks, an IP network may be very deep—the number of routers that must be traversed to reach a node varies with each network path.

11.3.1.5 IP Network Routing

When a packet is received by a router, the router examines the subnet for the packet's destination. The destination address is compared with a routing table containing a list of known networks and netmasks. The packet is then forwarded through the appropriate network interface. If there is no known path to the destination, then the packet is forwarded to a default router.

As an example (Figure 11.1), consider a machine on the 192.168.15.*x* subnet that wants to route a packet to a host at 10.50.45.111. Because the destination is not on the local subnet, it is passed to a default router. The default router handles all traffic intended for other networks. In this example, the 10.*x*.*x*.*x* subnet is not in the local network, so the data is passed to a different router that (hopefully) knows how to route to the destination's subnet. The 10.*x*.*x*.*x* router knows the different fractional subnets and passes the data to the appropriate subnet (10.50.*x*.*x*). The final router directs the traffic to the specific destination node.

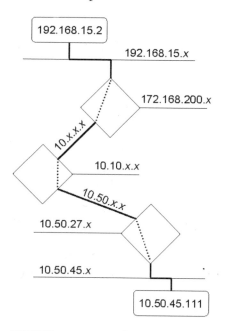

FIGURE 11.1 Sample IP network routing.

11.3.1.6 IP Multiple Routes

IP networks permit multiple routes to a particular destination. Each routing table entry is associated with a metric that indicates the cost of the network connection. The cost may indicate the number of bridges between networks, the network speed, or other factors such as service provider usage charges. If one network path is unavailable, the router simply chooses an alternate route. When no alternate routes are available, the packet's destination is considered unreachable.

The Cold War

The U.S. Department of Defense established the Advanced Research Projects Agency (ARPA) in 1958 after the Soviet Union launched the Sputnik spy satellite. ARPA was responsible for developing new military technologies. In 1972, ARPA became DARPA (*D* for Defense).

One of the ARPA projects was a network for linking computers. The ARPANET, as it was called, linked computers from military, university, and strategic corporations. ARPANET was designed as a decentralized network— a single nuclear strike would not be able to disable the entire network, and traffic would route around any disabled network segment. By the mid-1980s, the ARPANET had transformed into the Internet, connecting millions of computers worldwide. The TCP/IP network stack, as well as IP network addressing, evolved from ARPANET.

Today's Internet contains many different routes between major network segments. When a single segment becomes unavailable due to a power outage, backhoe, or network attack, the remainder of the Internet simply routes around the impacted segment.

11.3.1.7 Dynamic IP Allocation

IP addresses can be assigned statically or dynamically. *Static* addresses require an administrator to assign a specific IP address, subnet mask, and default gateway to each node.

Although IP does not natively support dynamic allocations, protocols such as OSI layer 7's Dynamic Host Configuration Protocol (DHCP) [RFC2131] and Bootstrap Protocol (BootP) [RFC1534] provide dynamic address support. For *dynamic addresses*, a server exists on the network to respond to broadcast queries for an IP address. The address server associates an IP address with the node's hardware address, ensuring that the same address is not provided to two different nodes.

11.3.1.8 IPv6

The IP has undergone many revisions. The commonly used IP is also referred to as IPv4—the fourth revision. IPv4 was refined in 1981 by RFC791. Today, the largest limitation to IPv4 is address space; there are only 4,210,752 predefined subnets. To extend subnet allocation, IPv6 was introduced in 1995 [RFC1883]. IPv6 extends IP addresses from 32 bits to 128 bits. IPv6 is often called IPng, or *IP Next Generation.*

Most IPv4 subnets are allocated to companies in the United States. IPv6 is widely adopted outside of the United States, where IPv4 subnets are more difficult to acquire.

IPv6 address notation can be daunting. Addresses are usually written as 32 hex digits: `0011:2233:4455:6677:8899:AABB:CCDD:EEFF`. Leading zeros between colons can be omitted, as can repeating "`::`" sequences. Thus, `1080:0000:0000:0000:0000:0007:1205:7A1E` can be written as `1080:0:0:0:0:7:1205:7A1E` or `1080::7:1205:7A1E`.

For compatibility, IPv6 supports the inclusion of IPv4 addresses. The IPv4 address `10.5.193.40` is the same as the IPv6 address `0:0:0:0:0:FFFF:10.5.193.40` or simply `:FFFF:10.5.193.40`.

Network routing is similar to IPv4, where addresses and netmasks are associated with router interfaces. Unlike IPv4, IPv6 multicasting is a defined, routable address range [RFC2375].

11.3.2 Name-Based Addressing

Numeric addressing requires advanced knowledge of the overall topology. Numeric routing requires the router to know the location of each numeric network. For example, each router on an IP and IPv6 network must know its own subnets as well as a path that leads to other subnets. A poorly organized network may allocate too many addresses for one network segment and not enough for a different segment.

IPv6 was created because IPv4 allocated too many subnets to large corporations and not enough to smaller providers. IPv6 is more common outside of the United States because IPv4 allocations are unevenly distributed. (Because the ARPA developed the Internet, the United States took most of the addresses.) Relatively few IPv4 subnets are available outside of the United States.

Although numeric addressing is very common, name-based network addressing provides more flexibility. Rather than allocating networks and subnets based on numerical addresses, *name-based addressing* uses text strings to identify each node. Longer strings permit more complicated networks. Two examples of name-based protocols for addressing include AX.25 and NBRP.

11.3.2.1 AX.25

AX.25 modifies X.25 networking to support name-based routing. Amateur radio packet networks commonly use this protocol. AX.25 is the amateur radio version of X.25 and is an example of an ad hoc addressing scheme.

Standard X.25 uses numeric routing, with each address containing routing elements [RFC981]. In AX.25, each routing element is a string containing a unique identifier (usually an amateur radio call sign). As the packet is relayed, the address of the router is appended to the source address (Figure 11.2). Routing tables are constructed dynamically based on the headers each router observes.

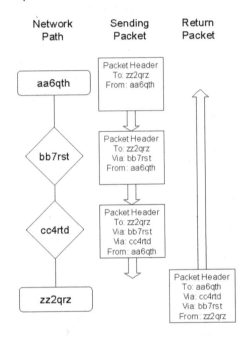

FIGURE 11.2   AX.25 address routing.

11.3.2.2 NBRP

The *Name-Based Routing Protocol* (NBRP) is an addressing scheme used by Translating Relaying Internet Architecture integrating Active Directories (TRIAD— *http://www.dsg.stanford.edu/triad/*). Although not widely used, NBRP is an example of an organized naming scheme.

Each NRBP node is defined by a segmented name, where each segment determines a particular routing path. For example, happy.go.lucky.lan defines the node happy that is located off the go subnet. The go subnet is reachable from the lucky subnet, and lucky is branched from the top-level lan subnet. Although NBRP uses an addressing scheme similar to DNS (OSI layer 5), DNS does not use NBRP.

NBRP is far more flexible than IP or IPv6 because any number of nodes and subnets can be derived from a parent subnet. NBRP does not have address space limitations beyond the maximum length of a node's address.

11.4 RISKS TO ADDRESS SCHEMES

The OSI network layer does not define any facilities for address authentication or validation. Numeric and name-based addressing schemes are vulnerable to address impersonation and hijacking. Although static addressing schemes limit the risk from rogue network devices, ad hoc networks face risks from consumption, false release, and false allocation attacks.

11.4.1 Address Impersonation

In the OSI data link layer, conflicts can arise when two nodes have the same hardware address. The same is true for network layer addresses. Routers, for example, will not know which hardware address to associate with the network address. The router may resolve this based on the last observed packet, first observed packet, or first ARP table entry containing the network address, or the router may simply alternate between available options.

Two nodes with the same network address are desirable in high-availability failover clusters. When one node becomes unavailable, another node accepts the network traffic without data loss. Unplanned impersonations can prevent a node from receiving packets, however, and this leads to intermittent or interrupted network connectivity.

11.4.2 Address Hijacking

When two nodes exist on the same subnet with the same network address, the node that responds fastest can maintain a network connection. If one node is consistently slower at responding, then it becomes effectively locked out from all network traffic. An attacker with a faster node may observe network traffic in promiscuous mode, assume the network identity of another node, and hijack an established network connection. In this situation, the attacker must be able to observe network traffic and respond faster. But, the attacker may not need any authentication credentials. For example, a Telnet session (OSI layer 7) may be hijacked after the user login. The hijacker can control the remote terminal without needing to provide credentials because Telnet only authenticates initial connections.

Unintentional hijacking attacks can occur when a user simply configures a computer with an already-in-use network address. In the worst-case scenario, the user may allocate the router's local network address to a fast workstation, effectively preventing all nodes on the network from communicating with the router.

11.4.3 Dynamic Allocation Consumption

Network protocols that support dynamic network address allocation include VINES, and IP or IPv6 with DHCP. Each server that provides network addresses only has a limited number of addresses. When all addresses have been allocated, new nodes cannot be added to the network. An *allocation consumption attack* requests all available addresses to be marked as allocated. One host can generate a significant number of false requests for address allocation to ensure that other nodes are blocked from network access.

11.4.4 False Release Attacks

Most dynamic address allocation schemes provide some method for deallocating an address. When a node no longer requires a network address, it can inform the allocation server to release the address to make it available to other nodes joining the network. A *false release attack* occurs when an attacker impersonates an allocated address and specifies the release of the address. The result is that the victim node begins to operate with an unallocated network address, making it vulnerable to impersonation attacks from future address allocations.

Although some DHCP servers validate the hardware address before accepting release requests, this is not a foolproof solution for mitigating this risk. An attacker capable of generating a false release can also impersonate the hardware address. For mission-critical environments, DHCP and other dynamic allocation systems should not be used. Critical systems should use static addresses.

11.4.5 False Dynamic Allocation

For a node to request a new network address, it must first contact the allocation server. Unfortunately, the server may not be known. VINES and DHCP servers resolve this issue by responding to broadcast requests for allocation. Attackers may configure their own allocation servers and respond to the broadcast request faster than the official servers.

Allocation responses usually include a set of configuration information. For example, DHCP usually supplies an IP address, netmask, default gateway, and DNS server list. An attacker can effectively provide false information to a new node and establish a MitM attack based on network routing.

11.5 FRAGMENTATION

Each network protocol has limitations concerning maximum packet size, and these may vary based on the physical network infrastructure. For example, most IP implementations use a default *maximum transmission unit* (MTU) of 1,500 bytes. However, IP over SMIDS [RFC1209] uses 9,180 bytes, and IP over ATM AAL5 [RFC1626] specifies an MTU of at least 8,300 bytes. When data from a higher OSI layer is larger than the MTU, the network protocol can *fragment* the data into blocks matching the MTU size. When receiving data, the network protocol reassembles the fragments into the original (larger) data block.

For optimal performance, the network and data link fragments should be the same size (including room for headers), although this may not be feasible when changing data link protocols. A router that spans networks with differing MTUs may collect fragments, reassemble packets, and then refragment the data for better network performance.

The network layer is responsible for fragmenting data from higher OSI layers into network packets and then reassembling the fragments upon receipt. Fragments may be managed using a sequence number or offset value.

11.5.1 Fragments and Sequence Numbers

The data link layer may not preserve the order of transmission, and alternate routes may shuffle the order that the packets are received. One method to ensure proper reassembly is to label each fragment with a sequence number. As each fragment is received, they are reassembled in order.

A flag is required to determine when the last fragment is received. This may be included in the first fragment as an identifier stating the total number of fragments. Alternately, each packet may contain the total number of fragments (e.g., "this is number seven of nine"), or the last fragment may contain an end-of-fragment marker. When all fragments are received, the reassembled data block is passed up the network stack.

IPX is an example of a network protocol that uses sequence numbers for fragmentation tracking. IPX's Sequenced Packet Exchange (SPX) protocol includes the fragment sequence number as well as the total number of fragments.

11.5.2 Fragments and Offsets

When using fragments with offsets, each packet contains an identification field, length, and memory offset value. The identification field identifies fragments from the same data block. Instead of including a sequence number, an offset is provided that identifies which part of the original sequence appears in the packet. Finally, the length of the fragment packet is known. Each packet in the sequence contains a flag that identifies it as being part of a fragment; the last packet uses a flag identifying the end of the series (Listing 11.3). IP and IPv6 are examples of network protocols that use offsets for managing fragments.

LISTING 11.3   Sample Packet Fragmentation

```
Original data size: 3000 bytes.
Fragmented IP packets using offsets and an MTU of 1200 bytes:
  Packet #1: length 1200, flag=fragment, offset=0
  Packet #2: length 1200, flag=fragment, offset=1200
  Packet #3: length 600, flag=last_fragment, offset=2400
Fragmented IPX packets using sequences and an MTU of 1200 bytes:
  Packet #1: length 1200, sequence = 1 of 3
  Packet #2: length 1200, sequence = 2 of 3
  Packet #3: length 600, sequence = 3 of 3
```

Fragment management with offsets has one significant gain over sequence numbering: fragments can be fragmented. When using sequence numbers, fragmented data cannot be further fragmented (such as going to a network with a smaller MTU) without first reassembling the entire packet. For example, packet #2 cannot be split because packets #1 and #3 already exist. In contrast, fragments with offsets can always be split. The two packets contain smaller total lengths and different offset values.

11.6 FRAGMENTATION RISKS

All fragmentation schemes face two main risks: missing fragments and assembled data size. In addition, the type of fragmentation management can lead to missing data segments.

11.6.1 Missing Fragment Attacks

A large packet cannot be processed until all fragments are received. Each of the fragments must be held in memory allocated to the stack. The amount of memory is generally fixed. When the memory fills, no more fragmented packets can be received until more memory is allocated, or some of the memory is freed.

A *missing fragment attack* occurs when a large packet is fragmented, and one fragment is never delivered. This attack consumes resources allocated to the network protocol. To prevent a fragment from being held indefinitely, most stacks associate a fragment timeout value with the network layer protocol. For example, the Linux command sysctl net.ipv4.ipfrag_time displays the number of seconds an IPv4 fragment will be held before being discarded. On most Linux systems, the default value is 30 seconds. This means, a fragmentation attack must be repeated at least every 30 seconds to be effective at consuming system resources. Although the timeout value differs between operating systems, the basic concept remains: due to packet timeouts, the attack is only viable for a limited duration.

In addition, most systems allocate maximum memory sizes for fragment reassembly. The Linux command `sysctl net.ipv4.ipfrag_high_thresh` shows the number of bytes allocated to the Linux IPv4 driver. If the total size of the fragmented data is greater than the maximum allocated memory, then fragments will be ignored until the existing fragments time out. This can lead to a temporary DoS for processing fragments—lasting the timeout duration. In addition, some operating systems allow the specification of the number of fragmented packets. The BSD command `sysctl net.inet6.ip6.maxfragpackets` displays the maximum number of IPv6 fragments at any time.

For systems that are potentially vulnerable to missing fragment attacks, the timeout and memory allocation values can be modified to reflect optimal values.

Specifying very short fragment timeout values can prevent data from being received. For example, a timeout value of three seconds can block most 14.4 modems from transmitting fragments from a 60 KB packet. By the time all fragments are transmitted, the first fragments have already timed out.

11.6.2 Maximum Unfragmented Size

Few fragment management schemes transmit the total packet size. Instead, an end-of-fragment packet is used to identify the final fragment. Because the total size is unknown, the network protocol should be able to receive the maximum reassembled packet size. For example, the IP header specifies 13 bits for the fragment offset. That means the maximum offset value is 16,383 bytes. Together with the maximum IP data size of 65,471 bytes (65,535 for the packet minus 64 bytes of header), the IP fragmentation scheme yields a maximum data size of 81,854 bytes before fragmentation. IP cannot transmit a single data block that is greater than 80 KB.

In contrast to IP's offset scheme, IPX specifies a 2-byte fragmentation counter, permitting 65,536 fragments of 65,535 bytes each; IPX is capable of transmitting a single data block of 4,294,901,760 bytes. Although IPX can transmit very large data blocks, the recipient computer is unlikely to have allocated 4 GB to the IPX driver. Furthermore, the network is unlikely to transmit all of the parts before the fragmentation timeout period begins expiring packet fragments.

The maximum reassembled data size is likely prohibited due to implementation specifications such as fragment timeout values, available memory, and maximum allowed fragment packets. Fortunately, this is not a significant problem because the most common OSI layer 4 protocols (TCP, UDP, NetBIOS, etc.) specify data sizes smaller than these maximum values. This limitation is primarily a concern for nonstandard (or transparent) OSI transport layer protocols.

11.6.3 Fragment Reassembly

Fragments need identifiers to specify the fragment order. Each protocol implementation must be able to handle odd cases that could lead to potential attacks.

> **Fragment Duplication:** What if the same fragment ID is seen twice? More importantly, what if the duplicate fragment contains different data? The implementation may choose to ignore the second fragment, overwrite the first fragment, or discard all of the fragments as corrupt.

> **Fragment Overlap:** For protocols such as IP and IPv6, the protocol specifies fragment offsets. What if the offsets overlap? Similar to fragment duplication, what if the overlapping fragments contain different data?

The resolutions for these situations are implementation specific. Although each network protocol specifies how to fragment and reassemble data, most do not cover duplication and overlap.

RFC791 specifies that IP packets containing "the same data either identically or through a partial overlap" will overwrite the reassembly buffer; however, there is no specification for when the data differs. In most IP implementations, fragments with different data also overwrite the buffer, but this is not always the case.

11.7 QUALITY OF SERVICE

The network layer provides six quality-of-service functions for use by the transport layer. These services assist in ensuring optimal data flow.

> **Connection Management:** The network layer provides the means to establish and release network connections. This acts as a point-to-point tunnel for transferring between two nodes. The network layer also ensures that multiple connections can be established between the same nodes without creating communication interference. Connection management can include delivery confirmation for connection-oriented services.

> **Flow Control:** The network layer provides a means for internetwork nodes to modify transfer rates. A node that is slower, either due to local resources (CPU,

RAM, etc.) or due to differing transfer rates (e.g., fast download but slow upload) can negotiate an optimal transmission rate for a connection.

Flow Management: Network layer protocols may provide the means for redirecting connections to other nodes, networks, or transport-layer services to best provide network support.

Error Status: If a packet cannot be delivered, the network protocol provides a means to report the failure back to the originating node. Tools such as `traceroute` commonly use the error status to determine the path between nodes. The `traceroute` command sends echo requests with different TTL values and then watches for the resulting error status.

Node Status: The network protocol provides a means to determine whether a node is accessible. This is commonly called an *echo* request because a packet is transmitted and the node waits for the reply.

Reset: The network protocol may transmit a reset signal that informs the remote node to drop all fragments, discard pending data, and reinitialize the connection.

11.8 QUALITY-OF-SERVICE ATTACKS

Each quality-of-service function opens attack vectors. Because network traffic relays through unknown hosts, a network node has no means to distinguish a real quality-of-service packet from a forged packet. Attackers may exploit quality-of-service functions to hinder or intercept network traffic.

Connection Management: The network layer provides the means to establish and release network connections. This acts as a point-to-point tunnel for transferring between two nodes. The network layer also ensures that multiple connections can be established between the same nodes without creating communication interference. Connection management can include delivery confirmation for connection-oriented services.

Flow Control: False packets may request a node to "slow down" or "send smaller packets" leading to impaired communication performance.

Flow Management: An attacker may redirect an established network connection to a different remote host. This may lead to a MitM or hijacking attack. In the best case, it can result in a DoS.

Error Status: False error reports can result in premature disconnects (DoS). Alternately, tools such as `paratrace` (*http://www.doxpara.com/paketto/*) extend the `traceroute` functionality for tracing hosts inside firewalls. The `paratrace` tool works by duplicating packets in an established connections and varying the TTL. The result is that errors generated from expired TTLs—even from within a firewall—are returned to the caller. This permits an attacker to conduct reconnaissance on a remote network that is otherwise protected by a firewall.

Node Status: The node status can be used for simple reconnaissance by determining whether a target is reachable and can lead to more damaging attacks. The simplest type of distributed denial of service (DDoS) is a Smurf attack (see Chapter 12). In this attack, one host generates many echo requests to many hosts across the network. Each echo request specifies a forged sender—the target of the DDoS. The result is a bombardment of echo replies sent to the target node. A large enough attack can cripple large networks due to the high volume of echo replies.

Reset: Any attacker who forges a reset packet can effectively disrupt a network connection.

The effectiveness of each of these attacks depends on the network protocol. For example, IPv6 uses cryptography to encrypt network connections. As such, it becomes very difficult for an attacker to successfully forge a redirection or reset packet. Less secure protocols, such as IP and IPX, are protected by a level of obscurity: an attacker must know the connection exists, and in many cases, know additional information provided by the transport layer.

An attacker along the path between networks can view all traffic between the networks. This position provides information that can assist in successfully exploiting quality-of-service functionality. But an arbitrary remote attacker—not on the path between hosts—will find it difficult to successfully exploit most of these attack vectors.

11.9 SECURITY

The network layer offers many services for ensuring successful internetwork data transfers, but it does not describe methods for securing the network transfer. Moreover, most network layer protocols do not implement features for authenticating, validating, or otherwise protecting network data. The general risks that face the network layer include eavesdropping, impersonation, and insertion attacks.

Risks from lower layers, such as data link interception and replay attacks, are not mitigated by most network protocols. Instead, the assumption is that security precautions will be implemented by higher-layer protocols. Although there are few cryptographic solutions, a well-chosen network architecture and filtering applications can mitigate many security risks.

Adding to the complexity, many OSI protocols are dependent on adjacent OSI layers. Network incompatibility can prevent some secure solutions from being viable options.

11.9.1 Secure Protocols

The network layer does not define security precautions. Instead, security features are left to specific network layer protocols. The most common protocols, such as IP, IPX, and VINES, do not provide any security precautions beyond simple checksums. Although checksums can detect data errors, they are trivial for an attacker to compute. For example, RFC1071 describes the checksum used within IP packets, including source code written in C and assembly language.

Few network layer protocols explicitly include security options. IPv6 and IPsec are the two best-known examples. IPsec is a combination of security-oriented additions to IP. For example, RFC2401, 2402, 2406, and 2409 describe authentication headers, data encapsulation, and key exchange methods applied to IP.

Whereas IPsec provides extensions to the existing IP protocol, IPv6 was a complete redesign. Besides extending the IP address space, IPv6 also includes supports authentication and data encapsulation via encryption. Both of these additional features are optional, however, and require both the client and server to enable this functionality.

11.9.2 Network Incompatibility

The OSI stack is designed as a framework for combining independent protocols. In theory, one network protocol can replace another without modifying the higher OSI layer protocols. For example, the transport layer protocol UDP is network-protocol independent. UDP can use IPv6, IPX, VINES, or any other network layer protocol for internetwork support. Unfortunately, this is only true in theory.

Most network applications include code for managing the transport and/or network layer protocols. Switching from IP to IPX can break the network implementation for Web browsers, email clients, and other network-oriented tools. Similarly, many transport protocols are closely tied to specific network layer protocols. Whereas UDP (layer 4) can be used over IPX (layer 3), SPX (layer 4) is closely associated with IPX (layer 3) functionality and cannot be easily used with other network protocols.

Similarly, although IPv6 supports data encryption for confidentiality, many higher-layer protocols and applications may not support IPv6. The network layer may provide security features that higher-layer protocols cannot access.

11.9.3 Architecture

As mentioned in Part II, the physical network topology provides some implicit security features. Reducing access to the physical layer lessens the risk from eavesdropping, intercept, and replay attacks. Without being able to observe the network traffic, an attacker is limited to blind attacks and guesswork for attacking a network.

Although data link layer is secured with an authenticated or encrypted tunnel, such as CHAP or a VPN, this only protects the data link connection. Hostile network layer traffic that can enter the data link tunnel is just as allowed and protected as regular network layer traffic.

11.9.4 Server Filtering

Filters operating on IP addresses can mitigate some authentication issues. For example, network servers (OSI layer 7) that rely on applications such as `iptables` or `tcpwrapper` can restrict access based on the client's IP address. Similar filtering is provided by the `inetd.sec` file (for the `inetd network` daemon) and by `xinetd` for limiting access to spawned servers. Although this acts as a level of security-by-obscurity, an attacker must know the acceptable network addresses to access the servers.

11.9.5 Firewalls and Egress Filtering

Routers normally pass traffic from one network interface to another. Firewalls can be implemented within routers and restrict access based on IP address. Rather than routing all traffic, only traffic from specific network interfaces can be given access. Although remote attackers may impersonate different IP addresses, they cannot receive the reply unless they are on the route between the target host and the impersonated network.

Filtering inbound traffic can reduce the success of an impersonation attack, but it does not prevent the network from originating an impersonation. *Outbound (egress) filtering* restricts packet relaying based on network addressing. For example, if a router links the $10.1.x.x$ subnet to the $192.168.x.x$ subnet, then it should not expect to see IP addresses beginning with 192.168 to come from the $10.1.x.x$ interface. The egress filter blocks obviously incorrect packets (due to misconfiguration or forgery) from being routed between networks.

SUMMARY

The network layer is one of the most complicated OSI layers. It provides address, fragmentation, and quality-of-service functionality with a large variety of choices and implementation options. Each of the implementation options provides functional tradeoffs and risks. Some mitigation options exist, but they are primarily based on restricting dynamic functionality. A few security-oriented network layer options exist, but they are rare compared to the common network protocols.

REVIEW QUESTIONS

1. How do routers know which should receive the routed data?
2. What are three possible consequences from router table flooding?
3. What type of addressing does AX.25 use?
4. Does the OSI network layer define facilities for address authentication or validation?
5. What are two schemes to manage packet fragments?
6. What happens if the fragment reassembly timeout value is set too low?
7. List six quality-of-service functions provided by the network layer.
8. What is the primary difference between IPsec and IPng?

DISCUSSION TOPICS

1. Compare and contrast numeric addressing and name-based network addressing. What are the functionality and security tradeoffs? Why is numeric addressing more common?
2. Describe some reasons why key exchanges are uncommon for network protocols. What are impacts to speed, trust, and the security from first-time network connections? Do key exchanges work for connection-less services?
3. Create a tool that generates four packet fragments. The first fragment has data containing all ones (0x01 0x01, etc.). The second fragment contains all twos (0x02 0x02, etc.). The third fragment reuses the second packet's fragment identifier, but contains all threes. The final fragment, containing all fours, marks the end of the fragment. Transmit the four packets to a system on the network. What is received? The system may receive 111222444, 111333444, or no data depending on the fragmentation management system. Retry the experiment with different receiving operating systems.

ADDITIONAL RESOURCES

Nearly all network resources cover IPv4 to some degree. Publications vary from software development to architecture, and from general protocols to specific operating system details. In contrast, resources covering IPsec and IPv6 are not as common and primarily focus on the security benefits. The security implications from IPv4, IPsec, and IPv6 are covered in Chapter 12.

For software development, the resources listed in Chapter 3 provide detailed information on IPv4 and network layer protocols in general. Detailed information on X.25 and AX.25 is available from the AX.25 archive at *ftp://ftp.funet.fi/pub/ham/ unix/Linux/packet/ax25/*.

12 Internet Protocol (IP)

In This Chapter

- IP Addressing
- ICMP
- General Risks
- Security Options

The *Internet Protocol* (IP) is the single most common network layer protocol. Whereas other network protocols are only found in limited environments, IP has permeated most industries, business sectors, and residential services. In 2004, there were an estimated 900 million people worldwide with online access [Zooknic2004, ClickZ2005], and nearly all support IP for network addressing.

The Defense Advanced Research Projects Agency (DARPA) initially developed IP in response to the Soviet Cold War threat. Although the network has evolved from primarily government, military, and academic members (ARPANET) to commercial and personal use (Internet), the fundamental technology behind this communication protocol has not changed in more than three decades. Transmission speeds have increased from kilobits per second to gigabits per second, and computer-processing power has jumped from kilohertz to gigahertz, but IP remains the same. Two vastly different computers can still communicate over the same Internet.

IP was designed for routing information between networks. Its fault-tolerant design enables data to move around disabled or unavailable network segments. The failure of a single node or subnet should not impact the entire network. Although network robustness was a consideration, general security issues were not significant design concerns. Many of IP's security risks stem from fundamental oversights made 30 years ago, whereas other exploits stem from common implementation flaws and similar coding traits.

12.1 IP ADDRESSING

As discussed in Section 11.3.1.4, IP uses a numeric routing system to identify subnets and specific addresses. Each IP address contains 4 bytes, usually written in a dotted-decimal format (*A.B.C.D*) that denotes the subnet and unique identifier.

Although IP addresses are commonly represented in the dotted format, they may also be written in hex or decimal. For example, the IP address 10.1.3.100 can also be written as 0x0A010364 or 167,838,564 ((10x256x256x256)+(1x256x256)+ (3x256)+100). Although the dotted format is most common, many Web browsers (and other applications) also support hostnames written as integers.

The integer representation is frequently used to obscure some hostnames from being immediately identifiable. For example, people who distribute junk email may use integers for hostnames to bypass some spam filters and to obscure the address from regular users. Fortunately, it is relatively straightforward to convert hex and integers to IP addresses (Listing 12.1).

LISTING 12.1 Sample Code to Convert a Decimal IP Address to Hex and Dotted Format

```
/* Convert a decimal number to an IP address */
/* Displays IP address in decimal, hex, and dotted format. */
#include <stdlib.h>
#include <stdio.h>

int main (int argc, char *argv[])
{
  long Num;

  if (argc != 2)
    {
    printf("Usage: %s 12345678\n",argv[0]);
    exit(-1);
    }

  Num=atol(argv[1]);
  printf("%ld = %08lx = %d.%d.%d.%d\n", Num, Num,
```

```
            (Num >> 24)&0xff, (Num >> 16)&0xff,
            (Num >> 8)&0xff, (Num)&0xff);
    } /* main() */
```

12.1.1 Subnet Classes

The three main categories of subnets (Table 12.1) are class-A, class-B, and class-C. A *class-A* subnet contains 1 bit to designate a class-A style address, 7 bits for the network, and the remaining 3 bytes as unique identifiers (*B.C.D*). There are only 64 different class-A subnets defined by the 7 bits of network addressing, but there are16,777,216 unique identifiers per subnet. Class-A subnets are commonly referenced by their 1-byte subnet identifiers. For example, the host 10.27.65.2 resides in "Net10."

The *class-B* subnet is defined by having the first 2 bits "10." The next 14 bits identify the subnet, and the remaining 2 bytes define the unique identifier. There are 16,384 unique class-B subnets. Class-B subnets are commonly described by the subnet bytes *A.B*, with the unique host denoted by *C.D*.

Class-C subnets begin with the 3 bits "110" and use the next 22 bits for the unique subnet. Although there are 4,194,304 unique class-C subnets, each only contains 256 unique addresses. Class-C subnets are commonly described by the first 3 bytes. For example, the host 192.168.15.2 is in the 192.168.15 subnet.

TABLE 12.1 IP Subnet Classes

Class	High-Order Bits	Subnet Range	Unique Nodes per Subnet
A	0	0.*x.x.x* – 127.*x.x.x*	16,777,216
B	10	128.*n.x.x* – 191.*n.x.x*	65,536
C	110	192.*n.n.x* – 223.*n.n.x*	256
D	1110	224.*n.n.n* – 239.*n.n.n*	special; multicast packets [RFC3171]
E	11110	240.*n.n.n* – 247.*n.n.n*	reserved [RFC3330]
F	111110	248.*n.n.n* – 251.*n.n.n*	special; extended addressing [RFC1365]
others	111111	252.*n.n.n* – 255.*n.n.n*	reserved

n identifies part of the subnet. *x* identifies a byte for the unique identifier.

The remaining IP network addresses begin with the bit sequence "111" and define a set of extended addresses. These denote special-purpose network addresses, and few are defined [RFC3330]. One example is Net224. The subnet 224.*x*.*x*.*x* is used for multicast IP addresses.

12.1.2 Network Masks

A subnet can be identified based on a combination of the network address and a *network mask*. A network mask, or *netmask*, is a set of 4 bytes that are combined using a bitwise-AND to define the subnet (Table 12.2). If two addresses, when combined with a netmask, yield the same value, then both addresses are on the same subnet.

TABLE 12.2   Sample Subnet Combination

	IP Address	Binary Format
Address:	10.1.5.100	00001010.00000001.00000101.01100100
Netmask:	255.0.0.0	11111111.00000000.00000000.00000000
Combine Address with Netmask Using a Bitwise-AND Subnet:	10.0.0.0	00001010.00000000.00000000.00000000

The type of network class can be used to determine a netmask. For example, the address 10.5.193.40 can also be written in hex as 0A05C128, or in binary, 00001010 00000101 11000001 00101000. Because the first bit is zero, this is a class-A address. The first 8 bits identify the subnet: Net10. A class-A subnet only has an 8-bit netmask, so the netmask is 255.0.0.0. The netmask may also be written in hex as FF000000 or by the shorthand "/8". The shorthand notation specifies the number of sequential bits that form the netmask.

Network address space may be subdivided beyond the standard classes. For example, the class-A subnet 12.*x*.*x*.*x* (Net12) may be subdivided based on bit ordering. Net12 may contain any combination of 256 class-B subnets; 65,535 class-C subnets; or fractional subnets. A *fractional subnet* does not use a network mask that ends on a byte boundary. Whereas a class-A subnet uses an 8-bit mask, a fractional subnet may contain any number of bits in the mask. The subnet 12.15.128.0/21 defines the address range 12.15.128.0 to 12.15.135.255 within Net12.

Although netmasks are usually denoted by a series of sequential bits, this is not required. A nonsequential network, such as the netmask 255.255.**170**.0 *(11111111 11111111 **10101010** 00000000) is just as usable as a sequential netmask.*

NOTE

12.1.3 Broadcast Addresses

The IP network protocol supports broadcast addressing. Packets with a destination address of 255.255.255.255 are treated as local broadcast packets [RFC1812]. This broadcast address is not routable; it is strictly used for local IP broadcasts.

12.1.3.1 Routable Broadcast Addresses

Along with the 255.255.255.255 broadcast address, each subnet contains a local broadcast address. The last IP address in a subnet is typically used as a broadcast address. For example, the subnet 192.168.0.0/16 has the broadcast address 192.168.255.255. This permits a remote host to transmit a broadcast packet to a remote network. For the example subnet, the Linux command to ping the entire 192.168.0.0/16 subnet is

```
ping -b 192.168.255.255
```

This command displays all nodes that respond to the ping request. Unlike the Linux command, the Windows ping command only shows that *a* system responded. It does not indicate which system responded.

The last IP address is typically a broadcast address, but it is not required. Any IP address can be configured as a subnet's broadcast address. And some network devices support disabling the subnet broadcast address entirely.

12.1.3.2 Determine Subnet Size

Although subnets may appear as class-A, class-B, or class-C, the actual size of the subnet may vary. An attacker can use broadcast pings to determine the size of a remote subnet. By increasing the netmask by 1 bit and determining the relative broadcast address, a ping scan can determine the likely size of the subnet.

To prevent this type of scan from revealing all systems on a network, most routers respond to the echo request but do not forward the packet to the entire subnet. This scan detects the router, not all hosts on the subnet. Other options to deter this type of scan include blocking ICMP echo requests, disabling broadcast addresses, or moving the broadcast address to a different IP address. Although it is possible to configure a router to respond to all ICMP echo requests, this is generally undesirable because an attacker may attempt to perform a detailed attack against all IP addresses that reply.

12.1.4 Routing

Each system in an IP network maintains a routing table that associates a network address and netmask with a network interface. When a packet is being transmitted, the destination IP address is compared with the subnet associated with each interface. When a match is found, the data is transmitted through the associated interface.

Routing tables may also associate a *gateway*, or external router, with a particular route. The gateway is a router that will relay packets to the desired subnet. Gateways are used when a remote network is not directly reachable from the transmitting host.

Each routing table contains a *default gateway*. This is a gateway that should receive all traffic that does not match any other known routers. Most PCs and single-homed workstations only contain a default gateway in the routing table.

12.1.5 Metrics

Routing tables do not require uniqueness. Two different table entries may route to the same subnet. This overlap permits fail-over redundancy—when one route is unavailable, the next one is attempted. To distinguish between alternate paths, routing tables include a numerical metric. Routes with lower metrics identify more desirable paths. A metric of "0" indicates an adjacent network.

When a packet is ready for transmission, the route with the lowest metric is attempted first. If there is a transmission failure, then the next path is attempted. When two paths have identical metrics, the decision may be resolved through round robin, load balancing, first listed, or default route selection.

Although systems are supposed to use fallback routes, this is not always the case. For example, if a PC has two network cards on the same network, it may conclude that neither route is available if one card fails. Similarly, if the default route is unavailable, some operating systems will not select an alternate default route. Finally, if the data link layer does not report any errors, then the network layer may not detect transmission problems and may not select alternate routes. Each of these conditions appears as a network connectivity problem, even though the routing table and network adaptors may seem to be configured correctly.

Decisions, Decisions

An employee called into a corporate helpdesk to report that his laptop could not connect to the Internet from a conference room. The laptop worked fine from his desk and from his home, but not from the conference room. At first glance, the routing table appeared correct; both the wireless and wired network interfaces were configured properly.

The helpdesk engineer began asking questions about the employee's usage. When at his desk, the laptop used a wired connection. At home, the laptop used a wireless access point. In the conference room, the employee used a wired connection; however, a wireless AP was available. (This caused a subtle problem).

When the laptop was in the conference room, it had two default routes: one over the wired network and one that was wireless. Although the wired network could connect to the Internet, the default route for the wireless network was being selected first. For security reasons, the wireless AP could only access a limited network, not the corporate intranet or external systems. All packets leaving his laptop were using the wireless connection instead of the wired. By disabling the wireless network, the problem was resolved. Alternately, the employee could have removed the default route for the wireless network or assigned the wireless route a higher metric.

12.1.6 TTL

IP networks may contain very long routes between two subnets. IP networks may also contain loops. Long routes may be desirable, but loops can quickly consume all network bandwidth. To avoid packets being indefinitely forwarded through loops, IP uses a *time-to-live* (TTL) counter. The TTL is decremented each time the packet passes through a router. If the TTL reaches zero, then the destination is considered to be unreachable and the packet is discarded. For IP, the TTL is 1 byte, with a maximum value of 255. Subnets connected by more than 254 routers are unreachable.

Many operating systems do not begin with a TTL of 255. For example, many Linux and BSD distributions use a default TTL value of 64 [RFC1340]. Windows 2000 uses a default TTL of 128. The default setting is operating system specific and may be changed by a system administrator. Under Linux, BSD, and most other Unix platforms, the command `sysctl -a | grep ttl` displays the default TTL setting. Different TTL settings may limit bidirectional communication. A packet from a sender to a recipient may be deliverable, but the return packet may decrement to a TTL of zero before being delivered.

12.1.7 Nonroutable Addresses

Some network addresses are not intended to be publicly available. RFC1918 defines three sets of reserved network addresses: `10.0.0.0/8`, `172.16.0.0/12`, and `192.168.0.0/16`. These addresses are intended for private networks. Other nonroutable addresses include extended addresses, such as `250.0.0.0/8`, and loopback addresses (Net127), such as `127.0.0.1`.

12.2 ICMP

One of the network layer's core functions is to provide quality-of-service support. IP does this through the Internet Control Message Protocol (ICMP). ICMP provides support for testing, flow control, and error handling (Table 12.2). Whereas many of the ICMP types are strictly responses, other types define bidirectional query/reply services.

NOTE

ON THE CD

The CD-ROM contains `icmpgen.c`, *a program for generating test ICMP packets.*

TABLE 12.2   Common ICMP Functions

Type	Name	Service	Purpose
8/0	Echo Request/Reply	Testing	Determine connectivity
11	Time Exceeded	Testing/Error	Determine if the TTL expired
3	Destination Unreachable	Error	Identify failed delivery
4	Source Quench	Service	Basic flow control
5	Redirect	Service	Indicate more desirable route
17/18	Mask Solicitation	Service	Identify subnets
9/10	Router Advertisement	Service	Identify viable routers

12.2.1 ICMP Support

Each ICMP packet contains three parts. The first part indicates the type of ICMP packet (e.g., `ICMP_UNREACH`, 0x03), numeric code for the packet type, and checksum for the ICMP header. The second part contains code type specific data. The final part contains packet data.

Although ICMP is a specified requirement for IP, not every system implements all functionality. For example, a host may support echo requests but not support router advertisement. Other examples include the following:

ICMP Checksums: RFC791 defines the ICMP checksum (Listing 12.2), but does not specify the behavior if the checksum is invalid. For example, some versions of Linux appear to ignore ICMP checksums, whereas Windows, OS/2, and BSD drop invalid packets. Many routers ignore checking the ICMP checksum in lieu of faster processing time.

LISTING 12.2   Sample Code to Compute ICMP Checksum

```
/*****************************************************
   IcmpCksum(): Compute ICMP checksum.
   Packet includes the ICMP header and data.
   Returns the checksum in network-byte order.
   *****************************************************/
int IcmpCksum        (unsigned char *Packet, int PacketSize)
{
  int i;
  long Sum=0;        /* at least 32 bits */
  int FinalCksum;    /* at least 16 bits */

  /* Algorithm: Add all 16-bit words */
  for(i=0; i<PacketSize-1; i+=2)
    {
    if (i==2) continue; /* skip the stored checksum value */
    /* add to the checksum */
    Sum = Sum + ((Packet[i]*256) + Packet[i+1]);
    }
  /* Take care of any odd numbered packets */
  if (PacketSize % 2) { Sum += (Packet[i]*256); }

  Sum = (Sum >> 16)+(Sum & 0xffff); /* add upper word to lower */
  Sum += (Sum >> 16); /* add carry */
  FinalCksum = ((~Sum) & 0xffff);  /* one's compliment */
  return(htons(FinalCksum)); /* return in network-byte order */
} /* IcmpCksum() */
```

Undefined Codes: Each type of ICMP packet may include codes for defining subtypes. For example, type 3 indicates an unreachable destination. The various codes for type 3 describe the actual failure. Yet nearly every operating system responds to an ICMP echo request when an undefined code is provide.

Broadcast Addresses: Some hosts handle broadcast addresses differently. An echo request sent to the 255.255.255.255 broadcast address may receive a different set of replies than a request sent to a specific subnet (e.g., 10.255.255.255 in the 10.0.0.0/8 subnet).

12.2.2 Echo Request and Reply

The ICMP echo service provides a basic test to determine whether a host is accessible. A host will transmit an echo request (*ping*) to a remote system. The remote system receives the request and generates an echo reply (*pong*) back to the calling system. If the transmitting system does not receive a pong, then the remote system may be offline or unavailable. Similarly, the delay between the ping and pong can be used to measure network latency. The `ping` command is available on most operating systems. This command generates an ICMP echo request and waits for a reply.

Unfortunately, attackers may use the ICMP echo server for attacks and reconnaissance. Common attacks include ping scans, the Ping of Death, and Smurf attacks.

12.2.2.1 Ping Scans

The first step in attacking a system is simply identifying that the target exists. *Ping scans*, or *ping sweeps*, can be used to search subnets for systems that are online. A ping sweep generates many ICMP echo requests that are directed toward each IP address on a subnet. Each echo reply indicates a potential target for an attacker. Tools such as `nmap` and `spray` can perform ping scans.

A ping scan can be very tough on a network, generating thousands of packets in a few seconds. Repeated scans can be effective DoS attacks by consuming bandwidth, particularly when many hosts reply.

An alternate form of a ping sweep uses an ICMP echo request sent to a broadcast network address for the destination. Rather than scanning an entire subnet, a single ICMP echo request is broadcasted to the network, and every host on the network replies.

A direct method to prevent detection from ping sweeps is to disable ICMP echo support. Under Linux, this can be accomplished with the commands:

```
sysctl -w net.ipv4.icmp_echo_ignore_all=1
sysctl -w net.ipv4.icmp_echo_ignore_broadcasts=1
```

Many firewalls contain the option to discard ping requests. However, inexpensive home firewalls may not support disabling ICMP echo requests, or they may only support discarding pings from the WAN.

12.2.2.2 Ping of Death

The echo request includes a payload for testing network capacity and MTU. This permits a network administrator to identify whether network issues are related to packet size. For example, small packets may be delivered, but large packets may fail.

Unfortunately, not all systems handle the MTU properly. In 1996, a vulnerability was discovered where an ICMP payload could be larger than the expected MTU. Dubbed the *Ping of Death*, the oversized packet would cause systems to overflow network stack space, which resulted in a system crash or hang [CERT1996].

The problem stems from an assumption concerning packet sizes. Most transport layer protocols specify MTU size that is smaller than the network layer's maximum transfer size. For example, TCP specifies an MTU no greater than 65,536 bytes, whereas IP can transport 81,854 bytes (size before fragmentation). As such, most operating systems only allocate 64 Kb of address space for packets. But, IP can transmit much larger packets. An echo request can contain more data than the available buffer size, which causes an overflow at the recipient.

In November 1996, nearly all operating systems were vulnerable to the Ping of Death (although there were a few exceptions). Today, most networked hosts are not vulnerable to this attack. But, new network products are constantly released and occasionally vulnerable [Bugtraq2000, Trifinite2004].

12.2.2.3 Smurf Attack

An ICMP packet contains a source and a destination, but no authentication is associated with either address. Hosts that receive an echo request send an echo reply to the request's source address. A *Smurf attack* specifies a victim's IP address as the destination and then sprays thousands of systems with ICMP echo requests. Each system that receives the echo request sends an echo reply to the victim. Even though a single echo reply is a small packet, thousands can easily overwhelm a network. Because the true source of the attack is not associated with the packet, the victim is overwhelmed by a DoS from an anonymous attacker.

Although Smurf attacks have been known since 1998 [CERT1998], there are few local solutions to deter this style of attack. In general, hosts should be configured to ignore ICMP echo requests, and external routers should not forward ICMP echo requests or replies. Egress filtering can be used to impede a host from initiating a Smurf attack by blocking packets with forged source addresses.

> **Smurf-A-Riffic!**
>
> The Smurf attack gained its name from some little blue cartoon characters. Pierre Culliford originally created the Smurfs in 1958. In the early 1980s, Hanna and Barbara animated the Smurfs for NBC. The theme throughout each cartoon was the power of teamwork. Although a single Smurf was weak, a group of Smurfs could conquer any problem.
>
> With regards to the network-based Smurf attack: A single echo reply is harmless, but a million can shut down a network.

12.2.3 Time Exceeded

ICMP provides error-handling support for IP. One such error concerns undeliverable packets. If the TTL of a packet reaches zero before delivery, the router is supposed to drop the packet and transmit an ICMP error message to the source. There are two types of TTL expiration messages: *TTL count exceeded* and *TTL reassembly expired*. A TTL count exceeded indicates that the TTL counter decremented to zero before being delivered. The TTL reassembly expiration error indicates that fragments began to expire before all parts were received.

The TTL can be used for an uncommon attack, allowing the identification of hosts that reside behind firewalls. The parasitic scanning tool (parascan) from the Paketto Keiretsu tool suite (*http://www.doxpara.com/*) varies the TTL field to identify the path to a remote host. This tool operates by performing a replay attack against an already established connection; however, the replay packets are modified with different TTL values. Normally firewalls block route detection; tools such as traceroute cannot scan inside a firewall. By replaying traffic from an existing connection, parascan can pass through firewalls; because existing bidirectional traffic is already established, the modified packets are allowed through. As each TTL value is attempted, different routers—even those inside a private network—generate ICMP TTL exceeded messages. This allows the scanning host to identify the full path to a protected host.

12.2.4 Destination Unreachable

There are a variety of reasons that the network layer cannot deliver a packet. All of these are reported to the network layer through an ICMP destination unreachable packet. Each unreachable packet includes a code describing the reason for the error. Table 12.3 lists the defined return codes.

TABLE 12.3   ICMP Destination Unreachable Codes

Code	Purpose
UNREACH_NET	Network unreachable
UNREACH_HOST	Host unreachable; implies network is reachable
UNREACH_PROTOCOL	OSI transport layer protocol unavailable
UNREACH_PORT	OSI transport layer port unavailable
UNREACH_NEEDFRAG	Fragmentation required, but the "don't fragment" flag was set
UNREACH_SRCFAIL	Source routing failed
UNREACH_NET_UNKNOWN	Network is unknown
UNREACH_HOST_UNKNOWN	Host is unknown
UNREACH_ISOLATED	Network or host is isolated
UNREACH_NET_PROHIB	Access to the network is prohibited
UNREACH_HOST_PROHIB	Access to the host is prohibited →

Code	Purpose
UNREACH_TOSNET	Type of service (TOS) is unavailable for the network
UNREACH_TOSHOST	TOS is unavailable for the host
UNREACH_FILTER_PROHIB	Prohibited filtering
UNREACH_HOST_PRECEDENCE	Unreachable due to host precedence; indicates low priority host
UNREACH_PRECEDENCE_CUTOFF	Unreachable due to precedence cut-off; indicates low priority traffic

12.2.4.1 Unreachable Packet Format

Each ICMP packet contains three parts. The first part indicates the type of ICMP packet (e.g., ICMP_UNREACH, 0x03), the numeric code for the packet type, and the checksum for the ICMP header. The second part contains code type specific data. For unreachable packets, this is an unused field. The final part contains information that relates to the packet. For unreachable packets, this is the header from the failed packet. The OSI transport layer uses the header to identify the failed connection.

12.2.4.2 Unreachable Attacks

Attackers that monitor IP traffic can create ICMP unreachable packets and transmit them to the packet source. Any router along the path is expected to return ICMP packets for errors, and the routers along the path are unknown to the sender, so the attacker's packet will not appear abnormal. As a result, an attacker can use ICMP to terminate arbitrary network connections. This becomes an effective DoS attack.

12.2.4.1 Unknown Unreachable

ICMP destination unreachable packets are intended to inform a host when a packet cannot be delivered. Yet, there are several situations where a destination unreachable packet may not be generated or received:

TTL Exceeded: Different hosts use different default TTL values. The TTL on the ICMP packet may expire before being delivered. For example, the sender may use a TTL of 128, whereas the router that detected the error uses a TTL of 64. If the sender and router are more than 64 hops away, the ICMP error will never reach the sender.

Firewalls: Many firewalls and routers do not forward ICMP traffic. The error reply may become filtered.

Undetected Failure: The packet may become lost in transit due to a transmission error or routing failure.

12.2.5 Source Quench

ICMP provides a very basic form of flow control. If the transmitting system is sending packets too quickly, the receiving system may send a *source quench* request. This request informs the sender to "send slower." Source quench has a number of limitations:

No Specified Rate: The source quench request does not specify a transmission rate. Different senders will slow by different amounts. A host being overwhelmed by network traffic may need to send many source quench requests.

No Specified Duration: The source quench does not include a duration for the request. The quench request takes effect immediately and lasts for the remainder of the network connection. To remove a source quench request, a new connection must replace the old connection.

No Send Faster: Although source quench is used to request a slower transmission rate, there is no support for increasing the transmission rate. Established connections may get slower and slower, but they can never speed up.

No Authentication: An attacker can flood an established connection with forged source quench requests. The result is an extremely slow network connection.

According to RFC1812, "Research seems to suggest that Source Quench consumes network bandwidth but is an ineffective (and unfair) antidote to congestion." Routers and nodes may choose to ignore source quench requests altogether.

12.2.6 Redirect

When a network contains multiple routers, one route may be more desirable than another. Routers have the option of providing ICMP redirect messages to a host. These packets inform the node to use an alternate route. Using this approach, a single node may have a very small routing table (just a default gateway) and learn of alternate routes dynamically and as needed.

The four types of supported redirection are for a network, host, type of service (TOS) for a network, and TOS for a host. These allow redirections based on the destination's subnet, specific address, or OSI transport layer service.

The most damaging attacks can come from redirect requests. An attacker can forge a redirect request that informs a host to send data to a nonexistent gateway

(DoS) or to a hostile node, which lead to a MitM attack. For these reasons, secure nodes should ignore redirect requests and use preconfigured routing tables.

To disable redirect support under Linux, use a command similar to

```
sysctl -w net.ipv6.conf.eth0.accept_redirects=0
```

The network adapter (e.g., eth0) may differ between hosts. Windows 2000 can disable ICMP redirects by changing the registry value for `EnableICMPRedirect` in the `HKEY_LOCAL_MACHINE\SYSTEM\CurrentControlSet\Services\Tcpip\Parameters` registry key.

12.2.7 Mask Solicitation

ICMP provides a service for one host to request the network mask from another host. Defined in RFC950, a new host on the network may transmit an ICMP mask solicitation. The responding hosts supply enough information for the new host to identify the subnet. The subnet is identified by the responder's IP address and the mask provided in the ICMP data.

Although originally designed for automated network configuration, few systems use ICMP mask solicitation. Instead, other protocols such as BootP and DHCP (both OSI layer 7) are used for configuring hosts on a network. Although most systems do not support this ICMP service, the ones that do may supply a remote attacker with information concerning the network configuration.

12.2.8 Router Advertisement

Router discovery provides a way for nodes to discover neighboring routers. Described in RFC1256, each ICMP router advertisement lists the networks reachable from the sender. Hosts may passively receive router advertisements or may actively send an address request. An address request asks all routers to reply.

The information in the router advertisement does not specify the quality of the router. Poor route selections, such as a slow or long path, is intended to be corrected through ICMP redirects.

12.3 GENERAL RISKS

Although widely available, IP contains a number of fundamental flaws that lead to general security risks. These risks include address conflicts, hijacking, replay attacks, packet storms, and covert channels. Implementation oversights can add to other common risks such as fragmentation attacks.

12.3.1 Addressing Conflicts

In the data link layer, two nodes cannot have the same hardware address if they reside on the same network. Duplicate addresses lead to ambiguous routing. Similarly, two nodes on the entire Internet cannot share the same network address. If a node is assigned an IP address but exists on the wrong subnet, then it becomes nonroutable. And, if two nodes are on the same subnet and have the same network address, then routing becomes ambiguous.

In this situation, the machine that responds fastest usually locks out the slower system. This happens because IP only tracks the first packet received. But, if a switch is used on the subnet, then the slower system may lock out the faster system. This happens because the packet sent by the slower host poisons the switch's ARP table, which redirects all traffic to the slower node. (See Chapter 10 for more information on ARP poisoning.)

12.3.2 IP Hijacking

IP hijacking occurs when one node assumes the IP address of another node. An ideal hijacking occurs without creating a detectable address conflict. There are three basic ways to perform IP hijacking:

Unused Address Hijacking: If a system, such as a laptop, is temporarily offline, then the attacker can use the IP address without generating a conflict. More forceful attacks may conduct a DoS attack against an active node to essentially force the system offline.

Redirect Hijacking: Through the use ICMP redirect messages, an attacker can redirect network connections to alternate hosts.

Promiscuous Hijacking: A node along the network path can intercept and respond to IP packets. This method works as long as the attacker is somewhere along the path between the source and destination.

Many systems rely on IP addresses as an authentication mechanism. Examples from Unix include tcpwrappers (files /etc/hosts.allow and /etc/hosts.deny), .rhosts, and /etc/inetd.sec. Even common applications such as mail servers and X-Windows (xhost) restrict access by IP addresses and subnets. The ability to hijack an IP address severely limits the effectiveness of these access control systems.

12.3.3 Replay Attacks

IP is a stateless protocol. Even though IP traffic may be connection-oriented, the state is only maintained for individual packets (or groups of fragmented packets) and not between different packet transmissions. This means an attacker may record and replay packets at any time. Although higher-layer protocols may recognize and reject the IP contents, the IP data is still valid.

12.3.4 Packet Storms

Packet storms are a general class of attack, where a network becomes overwhelmed by traffic. One type of packet storm is an *amplification attack*, where a single packet request generates a flurry of replies. ICMP requests, when sent to a broadcast address, can generate a large number of replies. This leads to a packet storm based on an amplification attack.

Other packet storms can occur when a network device improperly handles ICMP errors. RFC1812 describes many situations where ICMP errors should not be generated:

- Do not generate an ICMP error in reply to an ICMP error.
- Do not generate an ICMP error if the ICMP header is invalid.
- Do not send an ICMP error to a broadcast or multicast address.
- Do not generate ICMP errors for individual packet fragments; only generate errors for the first packet.

Systems that do not abide by these guidelines may generate many ICMP errors and flood a network. Moreover, if two such devices exist on a network, then they may amplify errors off of each other, which leads to a crippling packet storm that consumes all available bandwidth.

12.3.5 Fragmentation Attacks

IP supports the ability to fragment large data transmissions and reassemble them upon receipt. Although this concept is straightforward, many implementations are error prone. Two examples of fragmentation attacks are Teardrop and Nestea. These address implementation bugs rather than protocol issues, but these vulnerabilities occasionally resurface in new network devices.

12.3.5.1 Teardrop

The *Teardrop attack* was first reported to the Bugtraq mailing list in November 1997 [GPR1997]. When operating systems, such as Linux or Windows, reassemble packets, they perform a loop to copy all the data to a new memory allocation. Although they do check to ensure that they do not copy fragments that are too large, they overlooked the situation where fragments overlap. For example, the first fragment may contain 1,000 bytes. The second fragment starts at an offset inside the first fragment, such as 6 bytes into the first fragment, and contains a length that does not cover the entire overlap—the second fragment is completely contained in the first fragment. In this situation, the end of the fragment becomes much shorter than the end of the reassembled packet. Because the reassembly loop copies from the fragment's offset to the end of the reassembled packet, the result is that too much data is copied.

There are many variations of the fragmentation overlap, or *Teardrop*, attack. These variations use an assortment of overlap patterns, packet types, and traffic volume. Some are combined with other network attacks to increase the likelihood of a successful DoS.

In 1997, every version of Linux and Windows was vulnerable to the Teardrop attack [CERT1997]. These systems would crash or hang. Although patches have been issued for the many variations of Teardrop, new network devices are occasionally vulnerable.

12.3.5.2 Nestea

Teardrop led to an explosion in variations of the fragment-offset attack method. *Nestea* was released in 1998 and is one of the most common variations. This attack exploited an off-by-one assembly bug in many network stacks. Whereas Teardrop impacted most operating systems, Nestea only impacted a few devices—crashing Linux systems and some routers.

Today, few systems are vulnerable to Nestea, and those systems are also likely vulnerable to Teardrop attacks.

12.3.5.3 Targa

The *Targa* attack method originally developed as a rapid method to conduct many different IP-based DoS attacks. Targa included Teardrop, Nestea, LAND (Chapter 15), and many other attacks. *Targa3* was the third major revision to Targa. This system generated random IP packets with invalid fragmentation, services, checksums, and data lengths. Receiving hosts with vulnerable network stacks would crash. Today, administrators and developers may use Targa3 for evaluating a system's capability to handle corrupt packets.

12.3.6 Covert Channels

ICMP is an expected control protocol. Many firewalls and IDS systems perform a basic check of the ICMP header before relaying the traffic, but the contents of the ICMP packet are not always scrutinized. This means ICMP can pass though some firewalls and IDS systems without detection. This capability makes ICMP an ideal tool for transporting covert information.

Loki2 (*http://www.phrack.org/show.php?p=51&a=6*) is one example of ICMP used as a covert channel. This system tunnels remote access within ICMP. The data being transported, shell requests and replies, are hidden within echo request and reply packets. A system watching for suspicious activity will only see a rise in ping traffic. Besides tunneling data, Loki2 offers options for strong cryptography, UDP or ICMP tunneling (UDP is useful if the firewall filters ICMP packets), and configurable parameters for controlling tuning the remote session parameters.

12.4 SECURITY OPTIONS

IP is the most common network layer protocol. Any system on the Internet must support IP. Although IP has a significant number of fundamental flaws and implementation-specific vulnerabilities, there are a few steps that can mitigate risk exposure. These include disabling unnecessary features, using nonroutable IP addresses, filtering IP traffic, and employing security-oriented protocols when possible.

12.4.1 Disable ICMP

Although RFC791 describes ICMP as providing testing, flow control, and error handling, none of the functions provided by ICMP are essential for network routing. Testing is not always needed, and the physical, data link, and higher layers can better manage flow control. Although the error-handling functions are desirable, they are not always reliable. Combined with the security risks associated with ICMP, it becomes safer and more efficient to completely disable ICMP support.

Unfortunately, most operating systems do not provide the means to completely disable ICMP (aside from recompiling a kernel). As such, ICMP should be bidirectionally filtered at the firewall.

12.4.2 Nonroutable Addresses

Hosts that do not need to be directly connected to the Internet can use nonroutable network addresses. RFC1597 defines a set of subnets that are not routable. The subnets are designated for use on private networks (Table 12.4).

TABLE 12.4   Nonroutable Subnets

Address Range	Scope
10.0.0.0 - 10.255.255.255	Class-A
172.16.0.0- 172.31.255.255	16 Class-B
192.168.0.0 - 192.168.255.255	256 Class-C

By using nonroutable network addresses, an attacker on the network cannot directly query the protected host. Moreover, security is no longer based strictly on firewalls and filtering. If a firewall is temporarily misconfigured or disabled, the hosts become isolated from the network rather than directly vulnerable.

Internet access to the private LAN can be provided through dual-homed proxies or network address translation (NAT).

12.4.3 Network Address Translation (NAT)

Network address translation (NAT) is an OSI layer 4 (transport layer) service that relays packets from an isolated network through a common gateway [RFC1631, RFC2663]. The NAT gateway is a dual-homed system bridging the Internet (outside) with a private network (inside).

For each outbound packet, the NAT server stores a mapping in an internal relay table. The table contains (1) the source's IP address and transport layer port, (2) the destination's IP address and transport layer port, and (3) a port number for the NAT server's external interface. The packet is then relayed to the outside network using the NAT server's external IP address and port number. The external destination views the packet as coming from the NAT server and not from the internal system.

When the NAT server receives a packet on the outside network interface, it compares the packet's destination with the internal relay table. The packet is then forwarded to the internal source.

Using a NAT server, many private hosts can relay through the same external IP address. NAT servers provide two security-oriented side effects: anonymity and privacy.

> **Limited Anonymity:** All packets relaying through a NAT server appear to come from the NAT server. Although the external destination of the packet is known, the internal source is anonymous. An attacker may be able to identify the ISP and specific IP address of the NAT server, but the attacker does not know which system behind the NAT server is responsible for the connection.

> **Nonroutable Privacy:** An attacker cannot initiate the connection to an internal host. Any packet that reaches the NAT server's external interface but does not have an internal relay table entry is dropped. The drop occurs because NAT server does not know how to route the packet—there is no internal destination. This side effect turns a NAT server into a very effective firewall, blocking uninvited external traffic.

Most small-office/home-office (SOHO) firewalls, such as those provided by SMC, Linksys, Netgear, and D-Link, use NAT for the primary firewall functionality. This has the benefit of supporting multiple systems on a single DSL or cable modem connection while providing nonroutable privacy.

IP Reallocations

In the mid-1990s, it became apparent that the allocations of IP addresses were uneven. Some network providers were allocated very large subnets, whereas other providers had very few. Due to the uneven allocation, some networks (and countries!) were running out of IP addresses. Although many solutions were developed, NAT was one of the most successful.

Using NAT, a single service provider could share one routable IP address among thousands of nonroutable addresses. In theory, one external NAT address could support an entire company. In truth, load balancing and port limitations limit the number of hosts that can reside behind a NAT server. Usually NAT servers are configured to provide proxy support for 100 to 1,000 hosts. Special-purpose proxies, such as Web proxies, can alleviate much of the NAT server's network load.

An alternative to using NAT is IPv6. IPv6 provides more network addresses. But IPv6 could face the same allocation issues as IPv4 if the subnets are not carefully distributed.

When addresses first appeared misallocated, a common cry was to reallocate the Internet. Many class-A networks were initially allocated to companies that were believed to be long-term technology leaders. For example, Net3 was allocated to General Electric and Net9 was provided to IBM [IANA2005, RFC1166]. In 2002, Hewlett-Packard (HP) acquired Compaq computers. HP had been allocated Net15. Compaq, having previously acquired DEC, gave HP a second class-A network: Net16. The two class-A networks provide HP with enough address space for over 33 million systems; HP has more address space than all of Taiwan (15,546,372) and Brazil (15,097,741) combined.

While reallocating IPv4 subnets could ease the issues around limited address space, it comes with a hefty cost. Forcing every company in the world to reassign network addresses can cost billions and disrupt Internet operations. Most systems within companies such as Hewlett-Packard, IBM, and General Electric do not need routable network addresses; corporate firewalls prevent Internet traffic from routing directly to hosts. These companies could use private networks with NAT for external access, but the corporate cost currently outweighs the network need.

12.4.4 Reverse-NAT (RNAT)

The largest drawback with NAT is the inability to host a network server. Because all network traffic must initiate from within the private network, a server cannot reside within the private subnet. Normally NAT cannot be used when a network hosts Web, email, or other network services.

Reverse-NAT (RNAT) is an OSI layer 4 protocol that provides a static mapping from an external port on the NAT server to an internal port and IP address on the private network. Using RNAT, an external connection to port 80 (HTTP) on the NAT server can be routed to a Web server on the private subnet.

Many home firewalls provide both NAT and RNAT services. NAT provides the firewall functionality, whereas RNAT permits service-oriented applications. Most of these firewalls also provide support for a catchall server on the private subnet. Sometimes called a *DMZ Host*, the catchall server receives all external connections that are not covered by other RNAT mappings. But unlike a true DMZ, the DMZ host resides in the private network. If the DMZ host is compromised, it can directly attack other private systems.

12.4.5 IP Filtering

Most true (non-NAT) firewalls support packet filtering based on the IP packet header. Filter rules can restrict packets based on specific hosts, subnets, or type of service (e.g., TCP, UDP, or ICMP). This filtering can apply to the source or destination address to provide maximum control over IP support.

As mentioned in Section 12.4.1, ICMP traffic should be disabled. An IP filtering firewall can easily be configured to drop all ICMP packets. This effectively filters out the undesirable traffic.

Whereas an OSI layer 3 firewall only views the IP packet header, a layer 4 firewall can also filter based on specific ports and services. This can be used to restrict access to Web or email servers; only Web requests can reach the Web server, and only email can reach the email server.

12.4.6 Egress Filtering

Most firewalls are configured to be very restrictive for incoming (outside to inside) traffic while being unrestricted for outbound traffic. This configuration provides the maximum amount of safety from an external attacker while offering the maximum convenience to internal users. But, this configuration allows an attacker within the internal network to stage an attack against an external source. Attacks, such as those that use forged sender IP addresses, can originate from within the internal network.

Egress filtering applies firewall rules to outbound traffic. The simplest egress filters operate at the network layer by preventing packets with forged (or misconfigured) sources addresses from exiting the network. More complicated egress filtering can be performed at higher OSI layers (Table 12.5).

Although IP addresses can be forged, egress filtering prevents forged addresses from exiting a network.

TABLE 12.5 Sample Egress Filtering by OSI Layer

Layer	Type of Filtering
7 (Application)	Web URL restrictions (e.g., anti-porn filters); email/spam filtering; virus scanning
6 (Presentation)	VPN and SSL authentication
5 (Session)	Restrictive DNS and LDAP access
4 (Transport)	Port access restrictions (e.g., forbid IRC or chatroom software)
3 (Network)	Host and subnet restrictions based on network address; inbound and egress filtering
2 (Data Link)	Host based on source hardware address
1 (Physical)	None

12.4.7 IPsec

The main security issues around IP concern authentication, validation, and privacy:

No Authentication: Any host can transmit an IP packet and make the packet appear to come from another host; there is no authentication.

No Validation: IP packets use a simple checksum to validate the content's integrity. If corruption occurs at the network, data link, or physical layers, the checksum will likely identify the error. But the checksum does not provide protection against an intentional modification. An attacker can intercept a packet, modify the contents, and apply a valid checksum.

No Privacy: All IP data is transmitted without any encoding. Unless a higher OSI layer provides some method of encryption, the data is effectively transmitted unencoded (plaintext). An attacker can observe the contents of every packet.

A suite of RFCs was developed to address these limitations. For example, RFC2402 describes an authentication header for IP packets. RFC2409 defines a key exchange system. *IPsec* is a collection of security standards for the network layer. By designing IPsec as a collection of standards, new security options can be added, and less-secure solutions can be removed.

Using IPsec, two hosts can communicate using an authenticated and encrypted network protocol. Authentication may be performed based on the network layer host, subnet, type of service, transport layer port, or application layer user. Unlike regular IP, higher-layer protocols do not need to provide their own encryption and do not need to be modified to use IPsec. This makes IPsec ideal for secure connections and VPN solutions.

12.4.8 IPv6

IPv6 provides a network layer that replaces the older IPv4 (IP) protocol. IPv4 was used as a basis, whereas IPv6 contains a different (and optimized) header format as well as some significant improvements.

Address Space: IPv6 increases the address space from 32 bits to 128 bits. This mitigates the impact from poor IPv4 subnet allocations. Although IPv6 does provide more address space, the protocol has not been widely adopted yet; it is too soon to tell if the addresses are properly allocated. IPv6 could face the same allocation shortage as IPv4, although it is less likely to happen.

Broadcast Routing: For IPv4, multicast packets and remote network broadcasting were afterthoughts. As such, most IPv4 routers do not support relaying IPv4 multicast packets. In contrast, IPv6 natively supports routing multicast and broadcast packets.

Integrated Security: IPv6 includes functionality for authenticating and encrypting connections at the network layer. Higher-layer protocols do not need to be modified for use over the encrypted channel.

Integrated VPN: IPv6 natively supports encapsulation, which allows network tunneling. Together with encryption and authentication, IPv6 provides a full VPN solution.

From a security aspect, IPv6 and IPsec are essentially equivalent. Both provide strong authentication, encryption, and VPN support. IPv6 includes integrated security features with the option to extend the protocol, and IPsec incorporates a variety of independent security solutions. Many of the features found in IPsec and IPv6 are based on the same RFC specifications.

The main distinction between IPsec and IPv6 is support. IPsec is an optional extension to IPv4. An application may request IPsec, only to find that it is not available. In contrast, the security in IPv6 is mandatory. All stacks that support IPv6 must support the integrated security settings, even if the calling application does not require it to be activated.

NOTE

From a usability aspect, the effort to switch from IPv4 to IPv6 is nontrivial. Routers and network devices must all be upgraded to support the IPv6 protocol. Many newer systems either support IPv6 immediately or have IPv6 drivers available, but other devices, such as older routers, will need to be replaced. In contrast, any router that supports IPv4 can readily support IPsec. IPsec only needs to be supported by the source and destination, not by the intermediate systems.

By providing a larger address space, IPv6 forces the use of a larger network header. The IPv4 header adds a minimum of 20 bytes to each packet. In contrast, IPv6 adds a minimum of 40 bytes to each packet. Although the IPv6 header is optimized compared to IPv4, longer network addresses lead to longer headers. The overall result is that IPv6 normally consumes more bandwidth than IPv4.

Both IPsec and IPv6 perform bidirectional exchanges before establishing authenticated and encrypted connections. This generates more traffic than the "insecure" IPv4. Similarly, IPsec and IPv6 both include header options for encrypting data. This increases the header sizes for both secure protocols. Taking all of this into account, IPv6 still generates larger headers than IPsec because IPsec uses the smaller IPv4 header for addressing.

SUMMARY

IP is fundamental to modern network communications. It provides the means to address and route packets between very distinct and distant networks. Unfortunately this protocol, which predates the Internet, was never designed for security.

OSI network layer protocols are intended to provide node addressing, network routing, data fragmentation, and quality-of-service functionality. Although IP provides strong support for address and routing, there is no support for authentication, authorization, or privacy. IP's data fragmentation support is a solid concept but provides many opportunities for implementation errors and vulnerabilities. Each of the quality-of-service functions provided by ICMP opens hosts and networks to exploitation.

The security options for IP range from architectural design (NAT and RNAT) to address selection and filtering. Although IPsec and IPv6 provide alternative support for authentication and privacy, they do not address the fundamental limitations of IP: a finite address space and an inability to authenticate new hosts that have not previously been encountered.

REVIEW QUESTIONS

1. What type of network address is 192.168.144.4?
2. What is the purpose of ICMP?
3. List five fundamental problems for all IP implementations.

4. What is the primary tradeoff when disabling ICMP support?

DISCUSSION TOPICS

1. Consider a host that has two or more network interfaces. If this host transmits a broadcast echo request using `ping -b 255.255.255.255`, which network interface is used during the transmission? Is the broadcast sent through all interfaces, or just one? And if only one, which one?
2. When sending an echo request to a broadcast packet on a remote network, only one host usually responds. Which host responds and why?
3. Some systems do not validate the ICMP checksum. Describe some ways an attacker may use this oversight.
4. Consider a tool that generates packets with forged IP addresses. Discuss the difficulties encountered when attacking a remote host. Why are hosts on the local subnet more vulnerable? Does having direct access to the same data link and physical layer assist a network layer attacker?
5. Given that IPsec and IPv6 include equivalent security features such as key exchanges, encapsulation, tunneling, and encryption, discuss the tradeoff between IPsec and IPv6.

ADDITIONAL RESOURCES

Many RFCs form the basis of IPsec and IPv6. For IPsec, the primary RFCs include the following:

- *RFC2104: HMAC: Keyed-Hashing for Message Authentication*
- *RFC2401: Security Architecture for the Internet Protocol*
- *RFC2402: IP Authentication Header*
- *RFC2403: The Use of HMAC-MD5-96 within ESP and AH*
- *RFC2404: The Use of HMAC-SHA-1-96 within ESP and AH*
- *RFC2405: The ESP DES-CBC Cipher Algorithm with Explicit IV*
- *RFC2406: IP Encapsulating Security Payload (ESP)*
- *RFC2407: The Internet IP Security Domain of Interpretation for ISAKMP*
- *RFC2408: Internet Security Association and Key Management Protocol (ISAKMP)*
- *RFC2409: The Internet Key Exchange (IKE)*
- *RFC2410: The NULL Encryption Algorithm and Its Use with IPsec*
- *RFC2411: IP Security Document Roadmap*
- *RFC2412: The OAKLEY Key Determination Protocol*

IPv6 is an older protocol than IPsec and has undergone revisions since the release of IPsec. The original RFCs that define IPsec include the following:

- *RFC1825: Security Architecture for the Internet Protocol*—replaced by RFC2401
- *RFC1826: IP Authentication Header*—replaced by RFC2402
- *RFC1827: IP Encapsulating Security Payload (ESP)*—replaced by RFC2406
- *RFC1883: Internet Protocol, Version 6 (IPv6) Specification*—replaced by RFC2460
- *RFC1884: IP Version 6 Addressing Architecture*—replaced by RFC2373
- *RFC1885: Internet Control Message Protocol (ICMPv6) for the Internet Protocol Version 6 (IPv6) Specification*—replaced by RFC2463
- *RFC2374: An IPv6 Aggregatable Global Unicast Address Format*
- *RFC2375: IPv6 Multicast Address Assignments*

13 Anonymity

In This Chapter

- Why Be Anonymous?
- Privacy versus Anonymity
- Network Anonymity
- Common Limitations

The OSI network layer allows two nodes, located on different subnets, to communicate. The data passed between networks provides the means to identify the sender and recipient. For example, each IP packet contains a source and destination IP address. All nodes along the path, from the source to the destination, can observe the communication and identify the nodes involved. Anonymous networks are not natively supported by most network protocols but are viable through a variety of routing and hiding techniques.

13.1 WHY BE ANONYMOUS?

The network layer is designed for direct communication between a client and a server. Although this directness is apropos for automated systems and regular network connections, it lacks privacy and can lead to identity exposure. It is not always desirable to have all network traffic traceable to specific individuals.

13.1.1 Anonymity Motivations

Although everyone seems to have their own reasons for wanting to be anonymous online, there are a few general categories:

Doing Something Wrong: The Internet provides many opportunities to learn and explore, but it also includes items that are ethically, culturally, or politically undesirable. Whether it is viewing online pornography, compromising a remote server, or just maintaining a blog about your favorite company to hate, anonymity deters identification. Without a concern for being identified, activities can be performed without fear of being ostracized or arrested. For example, in article R.645-1 of the French penal code, it is illegal to purchase Nazi memorabilia. This ruling was upheld in November 2000, after Yahoo!, Inc. permitted the sale of Nazi articles to French citizens (*http://www.gigalaw.com/library/france-yahoo-2000-11-20.html*). A World War II historian in France may want to consider using an anonymity system when purchasing items online.

Detection Avoidance: When tracking online anarchists, pedophiles, and other people involved in illegal activities, good guys may use anonymity systems to prevent tipping off the bad guys. For example, if carders (people who illegally trade stolen identities and credit cards) notice Web logs entries from `fbi.gov`, they might become concerned and move their operations. Through the use of anonymity systems, law enforcement can closely monitor the bad guys without losing their edge.

Marketing Avoidance: With the amount of information available from online visitors, entire markets have grown around the collection and sale of personal information. Anonymity systems can be used to avoid tracking systems and mitigate the impact from online marketing sites.

Embarrassment: Accessing Web sites for medical information, secret hobbies, or family photos can lead to embarrassing situations when publicly discovered. Anonymity can reduce the likelihood of exposure.

Retaliation: Open and honest feedback is not always accepted. Feedback to teachers, management, and other people in positions of power is more likely to be honest if there is no fear of identification or retaliation.

Helpful Feedback

A department in a Fortune-100 computer company was having difficulty keeping projects on schedule. The managers opened a Web forum where employees could provide feedback, suggestions, and criticism—anything that could possible lead to an improvement. Unfortunately, none of the employees used the new system.

Although the feedback system did not display employee names or personal information, everyone in the department knew two things: (1) the Web server logged IP addresses and (2) some of the managers did not take criticism well. The fear of potential retaliation kept people from using the system.

After two months, an anonymous employee left a note on the department manager's desk. The note asked for a system that prevented the logging of IP addresses. The anonymity system was used for both reading and posting messages—someone viewing logs or network traffic would be unable to identify individuals. Within a week of deployment, the anonymous forum was widely used and produced useful feedback.

13.1.2 Identity Exposure

An observer that identifies a single IP address can frequently identify physical attributes concerning the source node. These include physical location based on hostname and WHOIS information, path and timing determination, and raw data. An observer watching an entire network transaction can identify additional attributes and details.

13.1.2.1 Hostname

Network addresses are frequently long and difficult for humans to remember. DNS (see Chapter 17) provides a means to map a text-string hostname to a network address. For example, it is easier to remember the hostname www.hackerfactor.com than to recall the IPv6 address fe80::211:d8ff:fea9:224e. Administrators of small networks frequently choose colorful system names and may follow themes such as Roman Gods (e.g., the server is "zeus", the backup system is "apollo") or ice cream flavors. But themed naming does not scale well for large class-A or class-B networks. Larger networks commonly use descriptive attributes. For example:

- A company may name hosts after their purpose. The hostname www is commonly used for Web servers, and smtp, mail, or email (e.g., mail.google.com) may be used for a mail server.

- A small company or department may name hosts after users. For example, `js7022` may be the hostname for John Smith at telephone extension 7022. Large ISPs may simply include the unique identifier from the network address in place of a person's name.

- Domain names commonly represent physical attributes. Large service providers may encode the network type and physical location into the hostname. For example, the IP address `67.174.125.100` maps to the hostname `c-67-174-125-100.hsd1.co.comcast.net`. The first segment identifies the customer's IP address. The second segment identifies the type of service: `HSD1` is high-speed data circuit #1. The third part represents the state (`co` is Colorado), and the final part identifies the service provider. This IP address identifies a high-speed data (cable modem) user in Colorado. Similarly, `geogpc1.leeds.ac.uk` is likely a PC in the geography lab at the University of Leeds (`ac` is academic), United Kingdom.

Encoded locations are frequently abbreviated. The Sarangworld Traceroute Project (*http://www.sarangworld.com/TRACEROUTE/*) provides a listing of common domain name translations.

13.1.2.2 Subnet to Country

Even if the hostname does not provide location information, network addresses may be mapped to regions. For example, each country has been allocated specific subnets. The company MaxMind (*http://www.maxmind.com/*) provides a detailed mapping of subnets to countries. For example, knowing that the IP address matches the `222.123/16` subnet places the system in Hong Kong. Although hosts may be located anywhere in the world, and subnets may span continents, subnet identification is generally accurate.

NOTE

ON THE CD

The companion CD-ROM contains a copy of the MaxMind GeoIPCountryWhois.csv *file as well as the Perl script* ip2country *for accessing the file.*

13.1.2.3 Path and Timing

When a target hostname is not informative, the hostnames found along the path can provide information about the host. The `traceroute` tool, for example, not only identifies the path to a host but also lists each of the intermediate hosts. For example, the path from a host in Colorado to `www.2600.com` (Listing 13.1) traverses Denver, Colorado (`dvmco`), New York (`n54ny`), and New Jersey (`nwrnj`). The final resolved host comes from Net Access Corporation (`nac.com`) in New Jersey. Although the IP address `207.99.30.226` could be hosted anywhere, it is likely in New Jersey.

LISTING 13.1   Sample Traceroute to www.2600.com (207.99.30.226)

```
 1  chunky (10.1.3.254)  1.214 ms  1.125 ms  1.120 ms
 2  * * *
 3  12.244.71.81 (12.244.71.81)  11.944 ms  10.626 ms  11.086 ms
 4  12.244.71.109 (12.244.71.109)  34.843 ms  32.849 ms  11.604 ms
 5  12.124.157.53 (12.124.157.53)  11.754 ms  11.924 ms  31.173 ms
 6  gbr1-p40.dvmco.ip.att.net (12.123.36.146)  190.253 ms  65.018
    ms  232.452 ms
 7  12.122.1.37 (12.122.1.37)  49.812 ms  49.838 ms  50.181 ms
 8  12.122.10.117 (12.122.10.117)  52.512 ms  51.788 ms  50.214 ms
 9  tbr1-cl1.n54ny.ip.att.net (12.122.10.1)  51.888 ms  51.170 ms
    53.143 ms
10  gar1-p3100.nwrnj.ip.att.net (12.123.214.181)  50.073 ms
    49.130 ms  49.690 ms
11  * * *
12  2.ge-0-0-0.gbr1.nwr.nac.net (209.123.11.213)  50.906 ms
    55.347 ms  51.985 ms
13  0.so-7-3-0.gbr2.oct.nac.net (209.123.11.58)  53.554 ms  51.895
    ms  50.962 ms
14  207.99.30.226 (207.99.30.226)  55.004 ms  54.572 ms  53.974 ms
```

When the final host in a traceroute listing is unknown, there is a possibility for the host to be distant from the last known host. Network timing can identify relative distances. Network connections can span states or continents, so longer paths generally take more time. In Listing 13.1, hosts 3, 4, and 5 are relatively close. Similarly, hosts 7, 8, and 9 have similar timings and are likely close to each other. Many routers treat ICMP echo requests as low-priority packets, so the timing variation for hosts 4, 5, and 6 are likely due to slow request processing. However, hosts 7 and 8 are distinctly slower than hosts 3 and 4. Thus, the first six hosts are likely in or near Denver, while hosts 9 and 10 are likely in or near New York. Because the target host (#14) has similar times to the New York and New Jersey hosts, it is unlikely to be located in Japan, Australia, or even San Francisco; it is likely located in or near New Jersey (including New York). As long as the timings are relatively similar, the location can be assumed to be relatively similar.

13.1.2.4 WHOIS

DNS maps IP addresses to hostnames but does not provide registration or contact information. The WHOIS service (OSI layer 7) does provide registration and contact information [RFC954]. This service permits administrators to identify and contact domain managers. It can also be used to identify the physical location if the query corresponds with a single entity.

WHOIS information frequently differs from physical machine locations. Instead, WHOIS returns the registrar's information. This information may not be accurate nor represent the physical location of the systems.

When a Stranger Calls...

A coworker reported that a boy was harassing his daughter. The boy had reportedly met his daughter online. Unfortunately, the boy has begun calling their home telephone asking to speak to her. Surprisingly, the daughter had never given out the home phone number. So how did he find her?

The boy knew the girl's last name from her login ID. Although her surname was not common, it could have been in any city across the nation. Her IP address's hostname narrowed the search to one area of one city. Using an online phone book, the boy had looked up the surname and city, and narrowed the results by street address. He quickly discovered the girl's home telephone number.

The daughter had thought she was anonymous because she did not give out her name. Unfortunately, the act of connecting to the forum revealed more than enough information.

13.1.2.5 Data Content Exposure

Even if the network address is hidden, an individual can be identified as long as the data content is not protected. Few network protocols provide encryption support; most network traffic uses plaintext. An observer on the network can readily intercept and read messages. Thus, logins to bank accounts, email services, and specific remote systems can provide identity information.

13.1.2.6 Transaction Monitoring

An attacker who can monitor an entire transaction gains more than the ability to identify the source, destination, and raw data. Even if the raw data is encoded, an observer can identify items such as time of day, number and duration of connections, and connection volume. The identification of habitual patterns can lead to user and activity identification.

For example, a VPN provides a point-to-point (or network edge-to-edge) connection. An attacker monitoring the VPN cannot view the raw data but can identify (1) the source and destination of the VPN tunnel, (2) the times when the tunnel is in use, and (3) the volume within the tunnel. This information can aid an attacker. For example, a DoS may be timed for the maximum impact, or an attempt to compromise the VPN may be performed when detection is least likely to occur.

13.1.3 Data Retention

Network connections are transient; they only exist while the connection is established. When the connection ends, there is no trace of the existing connection. However, network logs may be archived or retained for months or years. These records usually show when a connection occurred and the network addresses involved in the connection.

Similar to logs, many network applications cache data for faster access. Although caches may be more volatile than logs, they still record transaction histories. Caches may include network addresses as well as query and response data.

13.2 PRIVACY VERSUS ANONYMITY

Although they are similar concepts, *privacy* is not the same as *anonymity*. *Network privacy* prevents an observer from viewing information transmitted over the network. Examples of network privacy include encoding systems, cryptography, and steganography (see Chapter 3). *Network anonymity* prevents the identification of connection participants. SSH, SSL, and IPsec are examples of network privacy, but they do not provide anonymity. Similarly, many network anonymity systems, such as proxies and blind drops, do not provide privacy.

There are three distinct attributes for network anonymity: source, destination, and link identity protections.

13.2.1 Source Anonymity

When a packet is transmitted across a network, it is sent from a specific source host and delivered to a destination across the network. *Source anonymity* prevents an observer from identifying the source of the transmission. Even the destination host may not be able to identify the source. The ability to obscure the source address impacts bidirectional communication and permits impersonation.

13.2.1.1 Bidirectional Communication

Network connections may be connection-less or connection-oriented. In a connection-less environment, the sender expects to transmit data but does not expect a confirmation or reply. Connection-less network services are ideal for source anonymity because the receiver does not need to know the source. ICMP is an example of a connection-less network protocol. Similarly, UDP (OSI layer 4) is also connection-less and suitable for source anonymity.

Connection-oriented network services expect bidirectional communication. If the source address is anonymous, then the sender will never see an expected reply. Sender anonymity must be provided through a means other than providing a false sender address. Most commonly, anonymity is provided through relaying systems (see Section 13.3).

13.2.1.2 Impersonation

If the sender can set the packet's network address to any value, then it can be set to impersonate another system. This is the basis behind many DoS attacks, including the Smurf attack. For example, data link switch attacks (Chapter 10) use a combination of MAC and IP addresses to poison a local network device. Similar attacks can occur when impersonated IP addresses are used to attack transport layer protocols such as TCP and UDP (Chapter 15).

Impersonations not only permit a sender to remain anonymous, but they also allow attackers to intentionally misdirect any search for them. Tracking based on false sender addresses can be more difficult than tracking invalid addresses because invalid addresses are readily recognizable as invalid.

Egress filter is one example of a preventative measure against attacks that use impersonation. But, egress filtering is most effective close to the sender. A sender using a false address may pass all egress filters beyond the nearest routers. For example, if a sender on Net100 sends a packet that claims to be from Net200 to someone on Net300, only the Net100 router will be able to identify the packet as having a false sender. All other routers will see the packet coming from the correct ports.

13.2.2 Destination Anonymity

Although hiding the sender address still allows a packet to be delivered, hiding the destination address is a much more difficult problem. Without specifying the destination within the network header, the packet cannot be routed and delivered. There are three main approaches for hiding a destination address: broadcasting, intercepting, and higher layer relaying.

13.2.2.1 Broadcast Protection

Broadcast and multicast packets permit a large number of network devices to receive the same message. Although the intended recipient can be narrowed down to the list of hosts that receive the transmission, the specific destination is unknown.

13.2.2.2 Interception

The sender may transmit a packet along a path with the intention of having the packet intercepted by the destination. For example, a sender at 10.1.3.1 may send a packet to 192.168.100.1, knowing that it will pass through specific subnets. The destination host, operating in promiscuous mode along the path, receives the packet as it passes through the subnet.

While it is very difficult to identify this type of anonymous destination, it is also difficult to configure and not necessarily reliable. Few subnets contain multiple routers as well as hosts. Instead, a subnet with hosts usually contains only one router. A single router may link multiple subnets, but usually does not pass data along a bus network for another router. This means few hosts can intercept data as it passes through the Internet. Most hosts operating in promiscuous mode will be unable to intercept the packet.

Similarly difficult, the Internet is intended as a dynamic environment. Generally there is no guarantee that packets will take a specific route. Network outages and dynamic load balancing may prevent the packet from being sent past an intercepting destination.

13.2.2.3 Higher-Layer Relaying

One of the most common approaches for hiding destinations uses higher OSI layers to relay data. In this approach, each relay changes the source and destination network address. The true destination address is encoded along with the data, and not exposed until the last relay receives the message. Examples of higher layer relaying include proxy servers and onion routers (Section 13.3).

13.2.3 Link Anonymity

Even if the sender and recipient are unknown, they may be traceable due to access correlations. For example, routers relay traffic between networks. By monitoring a router, an attacker can narrow down the source and destination subnets. Although this may not identify the actual sender's host, it does permit tracking the path used by the anonymous packet. Tracking multiple routers can permit identifying specific hosts. Although this approach can be used to trace long-term anonymous transmissions, it can usually be defeated through the use of short duration transactions and constantly changing networks.

Attackers in the middle can observe connects, disconnects, and volume. These can be used to correlate habitual patterns and channel use. For example, a series of anonymous packets that occurs daily for an eight-hour period may be used to identify a time zone—people usually work during daylight hours. High traffic volume may indicate an automated process or a graphically intensive application, whereas low and sporadic traffic may indicate manual input.

13.3 NETWORK ANONYMITY

There are many approaches for applying network anonymity. The simplest approaches use moving addresses or blind drops, but these are not necessarily convenient or fast. Proxies and specialized routing networks can provide higher-layer re-laying, and chaffing is commonly used to provide camouflage.

13.3.1 Moving Addresses

One of the simplest forms of sender anonymity uses mobile addressing. The sending system is temporarily configured with a different network address on the same sub-net. The temporary configuration is used for the anonymous connection. When the connection completes, the original network address is restored. Listing 13.2 provides an example of a moving address. In this example, the host at 10.0.2.15 is temporar-ily moved to the unused address 10.0.2.17. The temporary address is valid because (1) it is on the same subnet, and (2) it is unused so there is no address collision.

LISTING 13.2 Example Moving Addresses

```
# ifconfig   # show the current configuration
lo0: flags=8049<UP,LOOPBACK,RUNNING,MULTICAST> mtu 33224
    inet 127.0.0.1 netmask 0xff000000
ne3: flags=8863<UP,BROADCAST,NOTRAILERS,RUNNING,SIMPLEX,MULTICAST>
    mtu 1500
    address: 52:54:00:12:34:56 media: Ethernet autoselect
    inet 10.0.2.15 netmask 0xff000000 broadcast 10.255.255.255

# ping -c 3 10.0.2.2  # send data from 10.0.2.15 to 10.0.2.2
PING 10.0.2.2 (10.0.2.2): 56 data bytes
64 bytes from 10.0.2.2: icmp_seq=0 ttl=255 time=3.662 ms
64 bytes from 10.0.2.2: icmp_seq=1 ttl=255 time=3.338 ms
64 bytes from 10.0.2.2: icmp_seq=2 ttl=255 time=0.953 ms
--- 10.0.2.2 ping statistics ---
3 packets transmitted, 3 packets received, 0.0% packet loss
round-trip min/avg/max/std-dev = 0.953/2.651/3.662/1.207 ms

# ifconfig ne3 down
# ifconfig ne3 10.0.2.17  # change the IP address
# ifconfig ne3 up
# ifconfig ne3  # check the configuration
ne3: flags=8863<UP,BROADCAST,NOTRAILERS,RUNNING,SIMPLEX,MULTICAST>
    mtu 1500
    address: 52:54:00:12:34:56 media: Ethernet autoselect
    inet 10.0.2.17 netmask 0xff000000 broadcast 10.255.255.255

# ping -c 3 10.0.2.2  # send packets from 10.0.2.17 to 10.0.2.2
PING 10.0.2.2 (10.0.2.2): 56 data bytes
64 bytes from 10.0.2.2: icmp_seq=0 ttl=255 time=2.175 ms
64 bytes from 10.0.2.2: icmp_seq=1 ttl=255 time=0.976 ms
64 bytes from 10.0.2.2: icmp_seq=2 ttl=255 time=1.006 ms
--- 10.0.2.2 ping statistics ---
```

```
3 packets transmitted, 3 packets received, 0.0% packet loss
round-trip min/avg/max/std-dev = 0.976/1.385/2.175/0.559 ms

# ifconfig ne3 down
# ifconfig ne3 10.0.2.15    # put the system back so nobody knows
# ifconfig ne3 up
# ifconfig ne3  # check the configuration
ne3: flags=8863<UP,BROADCAST,NOTRAILERS,RUNNING,SIMPLEX,MULTICAST>
    mtu 1500
    address: 52:54:00:12:34:56 media: Ethernet autoselect
    inet 10.0.2.15 netmask 0xff000000 broadcast 10.255.255.255
```

Although network logs may record this new server, only logs from the local network or switch will be able to identify that a system changed addresses rather than a new system appeared on the subnet.

For a more complete moving address, the MAC address should also be changed. This prevents correlating the same hardware address with two different IP addresses.

In addition, the anonymous user may consider changing subnets. Open network jacks provide an easy method to connect to a new subnet. Free, public, or open wireless networks also provide easy access to different IP addresses and subnets. Tracking a roving system is significantly more difficult that tracking a stationary system because both the IP address and subnet changes.

13.3.2 Blind Drops

A *blind drop* is an intermediate system that is accessible by both the source and destination. When transmitting data, the anonymous sender stores the message at a blind drop. Later, the destination connects to the blind drop and retrieves the message. This type of system grants anonymity to both sender and recipient.

Government agents and online criminals frequently use blind drops. For example, an agent may place a file on a blind-drop Web site. Later, the agency will anonymously receive the file. The blind drop protects both the agent and agency from identification. Similarly, many *phishers*, online criminals that capture credit card information, use free email accounts as blind drops. When account information is compromised, it is sent to the email account. The phisher can anonymously harvest the collection information from the drop point. This indirection prevents phishers from being readily identified.

Blind drops have two significant drawbacks: speed and identification.

Speed: Unless both sender and recipient are carefully synchronized, the system may experience long delays before the drop off and the pick up. Blind drops are best used when communication is not time critical.

Drop Identification: An observer will likely be able to identify the blind drop and may determine pick up and drop off patterns. The use of cryptography can prevent an observer or interceptor from viewing the content at the drop site.

Blind drops are not ideal for rapid communication. Similarly, they may be intercepted and disabled, preventing message delivery. But a blind drop is easy to implement and offers bidirectional anonymity between the sender and recipient.

13.3.3 Proxies

Proxies act as protocol relays, forwarding messages from the sender to the recipient. A sender can connect to a proxy and only expose the proxy's network address to the destination. The proxy anonymizes the sender. An observer between the proxy and the destination will see the connection but not be able to identify the sender. In contrast, an observer located between the sender and the proxy generally does not know the connection's destination.

Many proxies are protocol specific. *Socksified servers* (SOCKS) provide the capability to relay network traffic. The two most common SOCKS protocols are SOCKSv4 (version 4) and SOCKSv5 (version 5) [RFC1928]. SOCKSv4 only supports connection-oriented communications such as TCP (OSI layer 4). SOCKSv5 extends SOCKSv4 to support connection-less protocols such as UDP (OSI layer 4). The SOCKS proxies support relaying any higher OSI layer protocol (layers 5 and above). Other common proxy methods focus on protocols such as HTTP [RFC2616], FTP [RFC959], and telnet [RFC854].

Besides providing anonymity, proxies are commonly used as egress filters within corporations. By providing a single egress router to the Internet, corporate proxies create a single point for intrusion monitoring. Additionally, proxies can perform connection filtering based on subnets and network addresses. Someone inside the company can connect out to the Internet, but an attacker on the Internet cannot connect to the proxy and relay into the company.

Proxies are fast enough to provide real-time connectivity, but they have other limitations:

Logs: Many proxy servers, including corporate proxies, maintain connection logs. Although an observer between the proxy and the destination cannot identify the sender, the owner of the proxy can identify the sender, recipient, and any unencrypted content.

Inside Observers: Most proxy protocols do not provide encryption. An observer between the sender and the proxy will likely be able to identify the destination as well as the content. Even if the content is encrypted between the sender and destination, the proxy must still be able to identify the destination's network address.

To address these issues, senders may relay between multiple proxies. This *chaining* prevents intermediate proxies from logging the sender's network address. Many compromised systems include proxy support without logging. Malware such as Berbew, Sobig, and Sasser install proxy servers as anonymous relays. A defender tracing an attacker's IP address will likely discover a compromised host (and no logs) instead of the attacker's location.

Botnets

Viruses are very common on the Internet. According to some surveys, one in five systems is infected [Roberts2004]. Other surveys are much more dire; China may have infection rates as high as 80 percent [CNN2002]. Most infected systems are not independent. Instead, a small group (or an individual) controls a network of infected systems. These *zombie networks*, or *botnets*, can be remotely controlled to perform DoS attacks, transmit unwanted email (spam), capture individual keystrokes and other sensitive information, and provide proxy networks.

Small botnets may consist of a few hundred computers. This is more than enough to cause a successful DoS attack against a host or a subnet. Large botnets can be in excess of 50,000 infected hosts [Honeynet2005].

When used as a proxy, botnets can supply a variety of proxy services. The Sobig virus, for example, supported SOCKS, Web, FTP, POP3, and email proxies [Lurhq2003]. To ensure anonymity, virus proxy services do not log connections. An attacker may configure a few hosts in a botnet to provide proxy relays and connect to chat rooms or compromised systems indirectly. To further obscure the trail, one or more compromised hosts in the chain may be *nuked*, or destroyed, to protect the sender's identity.

13.3.4 Mesh and Grid Routing

SOCKS and similar proxies only provide one level of indirection to separate the source from the destination. Although proxy servers can be chained, the chain is relatively static and causes significant speed impacts. Each packet must relay through a proxy server that may not be along the optimal route. Connections that may take a few microseconds to travel directly can take a few seconds when going through a series of chained proxies. Moreover, an attacker at any of the proxies may be able to identify the source and destination, either through observing data content or connection sequences.

Mesh and grid networks provide an alternative to chained proxies. Originally designed for high-availability networking, mesh and grid networks consist of a series of relays arranged in a predetermined pattern. A *grid network* places each node in a geometric grid pattern. Although typically portrayed as a two-dimensional grid with each node containing four links to other nodes, grids can be three-dimensional (or *n*-dimensional), and nodes can be arranged in triangular, square, or even octagonal patterns. In contrast to the highly organized patterns that form grid networks, different nodes in a *mesh network* may contain different numbers of links, but each node is connected to at least two other nodes.

Regardless of the organization, redundancy is the driving concept behind grid and mesh networks. If any single node becomes unavailable or overworked, traffic can easily follow a different path. There are always multiple paths through these decentralized configurations.

From an anonymity viewpoint, grids and meshes that operate at the network layer are ideal for obscuring sender, recipient, and connection content. Each packet from the sender will take an unknown, likely changing route to the destination. An attacker at any one of the relays may never see the traffic, or will only see a portion of the communication.

Although a packet traversing a grid or mesh network must contain source and destination information, these relate to the grid/mesh and not the sender and recipient. For example, a secure grid network may assign private keys to each node. The sender encodes the packet with the grid's destination node's public key. The grid routes the data to the destination where it is decoded. After decoding, the packet is forwarded out of the grid-proxy to the destination. An attacker within the grid cannot observe the transaction without compromising the destination. And in a decentralized network, the destination may change between packets.

One example of a mesh anonymity system is JAP: Java Anon Proxy (*http://anon.inf.tu-dresden.de/index_en.html*). JAP provides anonymity for Web requests through the use of a mix network. A *mix* is essentially a mesh network with random paths.

13.3.5 Onion Routing

In a mesh or grid network, the network determines the route. If a node is unavailable, then data is routed through a different path. *Onion routing* leaves the path selection to the sender. The basic onion routing approach is as follows:

1. The sender acquires a list of available nodes in the onion network. The list includes public keys for each node.

2. The sender selects a few nodes that will form the path through the network.
3. The sender encodes the data and path using each node's public key. The resulting encoded data must be decoded by the correct node in the correct order. In particular, no node can see further than one hop through the path.
4. The data is sent to the first node, where it is decoded and the next node in the path is identified.
5. The data is decoded and forwarded until the unencrypted data is identified.
6. The final node in the path connects to the destination and delivers the data.

An example of an onion routing system is Tor: **T**he Second-Generation **O**nion **R**outer (available at *http://tor.eff.org*, *http://onion-router.nrl.navy.mil/*, and *http://tor.freehaven.net/*). Originally started by the Office of Naval Research in the mid-1990s, it quickly became a supported DARPA project. Tor is designed to provide anonymity from network analysis while providing bidirectional connectivity. This is achieved by supporting only connection-oriented network protocols, such as TCP (OSI layer 4). Each TCP connection establishes a path through the proxy network and the path is maintained until the TCP connection is closed.

Tor provides sender, destination, and link anonymity:

Sender Anonymity: The sender cannot be identified by arbitrary nodes within the network nor by the destination; the destination only sees the final Tor node's network address.

Destination Anonymity: The destination is unknown by any Tor node except for the final node. And only the final node can view the content of the packet.

Link Anonymity: Because the source randomly chooses the path for each TCP connection, a Tor node can only observe the volume from a single TCP transaction. There is not enough information to identify long-term patterns.

Tor provides general anonymity, but it does have a few limitations:

Source Identification: Although the data is encrypted, the first node can identify the source's network address. This is simply done by comparing the connection's address with the list of known Tor nodes. If the connection is not from a known Tor node, then it is a source.

Tor Monitoring: An attacker who can monitor a large number of Tor nodes can statistically model traffic and potentially identify source, destinations, and links.

Tor Nodes: By default, Tor version 2.0 usually uses 3 or 4 nodes per path. This is chosen as a tradeoff between anonymity and performance. Assuming true random selection and a Tor network of 300 nodes, a single node can expect to be used as both a source and a destination approximately once out of every 900 connections. For a system that generates a high number of Tor connections, a single node may be able to correlate the observed source with the observed destination.

Path Reuse: Tor is not fast when it comes to establishing a new path through the set of Tor nodes. The path, called a *circuit*, may be reused for multiple TCP connections rather than establishing a new circuit each time. This increases the likelihood of a volume analysis.

DNS Leakage: Whereas many applications may tunnel data through Tor, many others may resolve hostnames directly. An attacker (preferably at the destination) monitoring DNS queries may be able to correlate clients performing DNS lookups with Tor connections. The DNS lookup can leak the sender's identity.

The ideal Tor client will use Tor for DNS lookups and periodically change the circuit through the network.

13.3.6 Chaffing

In 1997, AT&T researchers developed an anonymity system called Crowds. Their slogan, *Anonymity loves company*, succinctly defines a critical element to identity disclosure. Even with the most sophisticated anonymity system, a user can still be tracked and identified if nobody else uses the system. The only user of a system, or someone using a system in a unique way, can easily be traced. The best anonymity systems are the ones that are used by many people. A packet with an undisclosed source and destination cannot be linked to other packets if there is a crowd of equally anonymous packets from many users.

Unfortunately, a large volume of users may not always be available. *Chaffing* is a method to generate artificial traffic, allowing a solitary connection to be hidden by noise. The four types of chaffing are directional, volume, size, and sequential. In each of these approaches, less chaffing is required as more users employ a particular anonymity system.

Winnowing Wheat from Chaff

Science fiction author Theodore Sturgeon once said, "Sure, ninety percent of science fiction is crud. That's because ninety percent of everything is crud." This has been adapted as Sturgeon's Law: 90 percent of everything is crap. In networking terms, the issue focuses on separating signal from noise. This is commonly referred to as winnowing, or separating, wheat from chaff.

In a networking environment, connections are usually direct. Noise can be readily filtered out and connections can be immediately identified. For anonymity, the desire is to increase the amount of noise. The additional noise (chaff) increases the difficulty for an observer to identify the true signal (wheat).

13.3.6.1 Directional Chaffing

When observing network traffic, all packets flow from a source to a destination. Even if proxies or relays obscure the source and destination, the packet still follows a point-to-point direction. If very little traffic traverses a particular path or flows to a specific destination, then all traffic is likely related. This permits analysis of the link.

Directional chaffing addresses the point-to-point issue by generating many fake packets that traverse many different paths. An observer will be unable to separate the true data from the noise.

13.3.6.2 Volume Chaffing

When observing an anonymous network connection, the volume of traffic can reveal information about the content, even if the content is encrypted. Some examples are shown in Table 13.1.

TABLE 13.1 Correlating Data Flow Volume with Activity

Transmit	Reply	Possibly Purpose
Low, Irregular	High, Bursts	Transmitting keystrokes, receiving application replies
Low, Bursts	High, Bursts	Downloading small files (e.g., Web, FTP)
Low, Bursts	High, Sustained	Downloading large files (e.g., Web, music)
High, Sustained	Low, Bursts	Uploading large files
High, Bursts	Low, Bursts	Uploading small files (e.g., email, FTP)
High, Sustained	High Sustained	Graphic/audio intensive (games, VoIP, real-time forums)

To avoid volume analysis, *volume chaffing* can be used to generate arbitrary data. The additional traffic is used to normalize the overall volume. For example, all observed data could appear as a high, sustained volume even if the true content consists of low volume with irregular bursts. Similarly, chaffing can be used to slow down high-volume traffic so that it appears to be low volume.

Volume chaffing should be used before establishing and after terminating a connection. This prevents the identification of a connection. Otherwise, if the chaffing only appears when a connection is present, then an observer can identify the presence and duration of a connection.

13.3.6.3 Size Chaffing

The network and data link layers fragment data to fit into transmission blocks. For maximum throughput, each block is filled to the maximum data size. The last fragment is commonly smaller than previous fragments. An observer can use this information to determine the size of the data being transmitted. For example, if the MTU is 1,500 bytes and the third packet contains 100 bytes, then the total data size is likely 3,100 bytes (two 1,500-byte packets plus a 100-byte fragment). An observer may not know what the data contains but does know the data size.

Size chaffing varies the size of the transmitted blocks. This may take either of two forms: normal or random transmit sizes. When using the *normal transmission sizes*, all packets appear to be the same size. Larger packets are cut to a smaller size, and smaller packets are padded to appear larger. Normalizing the packet size prevents size identification. In contrast, *random transmit sizes* constantly change the transmitted data size. Large packets may be split, and small packets may be padded, but few sequential packets will appear to be the same size. Without the ability to observe data content, both of these approaches can defeat data size detection.

13.3.6.4 Sequential Chaffing

Normally packets are transmitted in a sequential order. An attacker collecting packets can be fairly certain that the packets are in order. If the data is encrypted, then knowing the transmission sequence can aid in cracking the encryption.

Sequential chaffing reorders packets before transmission. Although two packets captured minutes apart may be in order, packets captured a few seconds apart are likely out of order. For attackers to crack any encryption, they must first identify the packet order. If there are 8 packets in an unknown order, the chaffing yields 40,320 combinations (8 factorial). This dramatically increases the difficulty.

13.4 COMMON LIMITATIONS

Most anonymity systems are directed at protecting identification based on the network layer; however, factors beyond the network layer can lead to identification:

Higher-Level Information Leakage: Many higher-layer OSI protocols explicitly include identification information. Web sites use tracking cookies, email discloses addresses, and someone may post personal information to a forum. Even if the anonymity system uses encryption, the data must be decrypted before is can be used. Information leakage from higher protocols can compromise an otherwise anonymous connection.

Timing Attacks: Automated systems frequently operate on specific schedules, and people may have particular hours when they are online. Analyzing occurrence rates and durations can separate a person from an automated process, isolate connection functionality, and identify probably geographic regions. An attacker can optimize his attack to take advantage of known timings, and people desiring anonymity can be tracked.

Habitual and Sequential Patterns: Similar to timing attacks, habitual behavior and sequential accesses can identify an individual. For example, visitors to the Whitehouse Web site (*http://www.whitehouse.gov*) may normally load all images then they click on one of the top stories. When using Tor, each Web connection may go through a different node. By tracking all connection from Tor nodes, Web administrators can identify (1) where the anonymous individual visited, (2) how long they stayed on each Web page, and (3) the estimated speed of the anonymous sender's network connection. If the anonymous person repeats the pattern daily, then his activities can be tracked over time. Similar patterns can be formed by correlation the order links are accessed, average timings between accesses, and amount of data transmitted and received.

Speed: Anonymity is not fast. Chaffing consumes network bandwidth, and relays add noticeable connectivity delays. Cryptography, for data privacy, adds additional delays.

In addition to the common limitations, there are a few methods to directly attack and breach anonymity. These can be implemented as a conscious effort.

Cookies: Many Web sites use cookies to track visitors. Even if the Web browser uses an anonymous network connection, cookies can permit tracking the user online.

Web Bugs: Besides Web browsers, many applications process URLs. Email clients and Instant Messaging (IM) systems, for example, can load images from remote Web sites simply by opening an email or receiving a link. By intentionally sending an anonymous target a Web bug, an attacker can force a breach of anonymity. If the bug is acquired directly, then the actual network address is disclosed. If the bug is accessed using the anonymity system, then timing analysis and information disclosure can attack the anonymity.

DNS Leaks: Many applications do not tunnel all data through the anonymous channel. DNS lookups are commonly performed directly. If an attacker sends a unique hostname to an anonymous target, then watching the DNS resolution can identify the target's network address.

Trojans and Callback Bombs: An anonymous download may transfer hostile code to the anonymous sender or anonymous recipient. These systems can establish direct connections to a remote server that permits identification of an otherwise anonymous node. Alternately, the malware can use the anonymous connection and transmit information that reveals an identity.

SUMMARY

The OSI network layer permits communication between two nodes across the network through the use of network-wide addressing. Network addresses disclose more than routing information, however. In particular, an attacker can identify a specific individual's location and identity.

To remain anonymous online, defenders have a selection of tools. Moving network addresses and subnets can make location identification difficult. Blind drops, proxies, relays, and onion networks can obscure both the source and destination. Chaffing can also deter network transfer analysis.

Network anonymity is feasible, but it is vulnerable to disclosure from higher-layer protocols and usage. Attackers may identify individuals based on habitual patterns, transmitted content, and time-based analysis.

REVIEW QUESTIONS

1. Why would an online detective desire anonymity?
2. List three types of anonymity.
3. What type(s) of anonymity does Tor provide?
4. When discussing anonymity, what is high-level information leakage?

DISCUSSION TOPICS

1. Describe some scenarios where traceroute may report a large time difference between two hosts. What is required for a traceroute listing to contain two adjacent hosts with very similar time delays but vastly different physical locations?
2. Time-based analysis compares network traffic with the time the traffic is observed. For example, connections that occur Monday through Friday

for eight hours likely indicates work hours. This can be used to estimate the time zone of the sender. Describe a chaffing approach that can defeat a time-based analysis. Identify the usability and long-term impact from such a system.

3. An online user employs an email-based blind drop to remain anonymous. Describe some approaches to ferret out the user's identity.

4. Use a large, public onion routing system, such as Tor, to anonymize Web requests. Connect to the URL *http://www.google.com/*. Flush the browser's cache and repeat the experiment. (Because Tor caches functional onion routes, it will need to be restarted to flush the stored path.) What Web page is returned? How does the server know which page to return?

ADDITIONAL RESOURCES

IEEE has devoted a number of resources to privacy, security, and anonymity. Information about the IEEE's Technical Committee on Security and Privacy is available at *http://www.ieee-security.org/*, and the IEEE journal on Security and Privacy is at *http://www.computer.org/security/*.

Many books describe the types of information disclosed online and how to track people who would otherwise be anonymous. Some examples include the following:

- McKeown, Kevin and Dave Stern. *Your Secrets Are My Business: Security Expert Reveals How Your Trash, License Plate, Credit Cards, Computer, and Even Your Email Make You an Easy Target for Today's Information Thieves.* Plume, 2000. ISBN 0-452-28204-7.
- Wang, Wallace. *Steal This Computer Book 3: What They Won't Tell You About the Internet.* No Starch Press, 2003. ISBN 1-593-27000-3.
- Foster, Donald. *Author Unknown: On the Trail of Anonymous.* Henry Holt & Company, 2000. ISBN 0-805-06357-9.

Although these books do not focus entirely on online or network-layer identification (e.g., *Author Unknown* does not track people online), the methods and approaches discussed directly apply to online identity exposure.

Part

V

OSI Layer 4

In This Part

- Transport Layer
- TCP

Layer 4 of the ISO OSI model is the *transport layer*. This layer provides an interface between the upper application layers and lower networking layers. The transport layer provides packet ordering and service identification. The two most common transport layer protocols are TCP and UDP, which represent connection-oriented and connection-less protocols.

14 Transport Layer

In This Chapter

- Common Protocols
- Core Transport Layer Functions
- Gateways
- General Risks

The lower layers of the OSI network model, the networking layers, define the functionality for communicating between nodes on a network. The physical layer provides connectivity, the data link layer identifies unique nodes, and the network layer provides inter-network routing. In contrast, the upper layers provide application support. For example, the session layer manages long-term connections, the presentation layer formats data, and the application layer provides service-specific functionality.

The *transport layer* defines an interface between the lower networking layers and upper application-oriented layers. In many networking stacks, the top interface to the transport layer is an *application programming interface* (API). For example, *sockets* is a popular interface to both TCP and UDP on Unix systems. WinSocks provides similar API functionality for Windows systems. The transport and lower OSI layers are usually implemented within the operating system, whereas higher layer functionality may be implemented by separate applications that interface with the stack through the API.

14.1 COMMON PROTOCOLS

Although there are hundreds of application layer protocols (FTP, HTTP, SMTP, SNMP, and DHCP are only the beginning of a long list), dozens of common physical layer standards (Ethernet, 802.11, etc.), and many choices for network layer protocols (IP, IPv6, IPX, X.25, etc.), there are relatively few transport layer protocols. Unlike the physical, data link, and network layers, transport protocols are usually independent of the lower layers.

The two most common transport protocols are *Transmission Control Protocol* (TCP) and *User Datagram Protocol* (UDP). These are supported by nearly all network layer protocols. Other transport protocols are less common and include SCTP, NetBIOS-DG, and a variety of AppleTalk protocols.

14.1.1 TCP and UDP

TCP and UDP are almost universally supported. The main distinction comes from their connection management: TCP is a connection-oriented protocol, whereas UDP is for connection-less communications. Both of these protocols are detailed in Chapter 15.

TCP is commonly used for established bidirectional communication [RFC793]. Application layer protocols such as Web (HTTP), email (SMTP), and Secure Shell (SSH) use TCP. TCP acknowledges all transmitted data, which provides a degree of security through transmission validation.

TCP validates the amount of data transmitted but not the data itself.

In contrast to TCP, UDP is connection-less [RFC768]. UDP transmits data but does not validate that the data was received. Because UDP does not wait for acknowledgements, it generally transmits data much faster than TCP; however, UDP does not detect lost packets. UDP is commonly used by higher-layer protocols where the loss of a single packet does not affect the data transfer. For example, streaming audio across the network uses a large number of packets, but each packet contains a very small amount of audio data. The loss of a single packet may result in small audio distortions but does not usually degrade the reception significantly. Streaming video uses even more bandwidth. The loss of a packet may make an image temporarily appear blocky but does not corrupt the entire image. For these reasons, UDP is preferred by many application layer protocols that provide audio and video, such as VoIP and Microsoft NetMeeting. Although these protocols could use TCP, the delays from connection-oriented packet acknowledgements can noticeably impact quality.

Not every high-layer protocol that uses UDP supports packet loss. For example, the application layer's *network file system* protocol (NFS) uses UDP for fast file transfers, even though a lost packet will result in file corruption or extended delays due to retries.

Transport Overhead

UDP has a very simple packet format. Each UDP packet (called a *datagram*) contains 4 bytes for source and destination ports (2 bytes each—ports are discussed in Section 14.2.1), the length of the datagram (2 bytes), and a 16-bit checksum. The remainder of the datagram contains the data to be transmitted. The entire UDP header contains 8 bytes.

In contrast to UDP, TCP is connection-oriented; it must provide additional information for sequencing and control information. Like UDP, the TCP header includes source and destination ports (2 bytes each), but TCP also include a 4-byte sequence number. TCP is much more sophisticated than UDP and provides options for flow control and data size [RFC793, RFC1122, RFC2001]. Whereas UDP headers always contain 8 bytes, TCP headers can vary in size. The smallest TCP header requires 20 bytes.

When transferring a large file, UDP requires significantly less overhead. For example, when transmitting a 1 MB file (1,048,576 bytes), both TCP and UDP divide the data into packets (or datagrams). Although the amount of data per packet can vary, systems generally try to restrict one transport-layer packet to the data link MTU size. For Ethernet, the MTU is 1,500 bytes, and an IP header consumes 20 bytes. The minimum TCP header is 20 bytes, which results in 1,460 bytes of data per packet, 719 packets to transfer 1 MB, and a total of 14,380 bytes from the header. In contrast, UDP only requires 8 bytes for the header, resulting in 1,472 bytes of data per packet and 713 packets for a total overhead of 5,704 bytes. TCP requires more than a 250 percent increase in overhead compared to UDP—and this does not include the initial TCP protocol negotiation, packet acknowledgements, or connection management (none of which exist in UDP).

14.1.2 SCTP

Although TCP and UDP are widely used, there were not designed for security—both have limited facilities for authenticating data and no method for supporting privacy. In addition, TCP's continual acknowledgements can hinder large data stream transmissions. Designed as a replacement to TCP, the *Stream Control*

Transmission Protocol (SCTP) addresses these shortcomings [RFC2960, RFC3286, RFC3309]. For example, SCTP uses a sliding window for packet acknowledgements. Rather than periodically stopping transmission and waiting for an acknowledgement, an acknowledgement window is provided. Large data streams can continue transmitting while receiving periodic acknowledgements. This provides connection-oriented functionality with a lower overhead than TCP.

SCTP includes support for packet authentication and encryption. RFC2960 defines the option to include a Message Authentication Code in SCTP and to encrypt user data. The cryptographic functions used by SCTP are the same security precautions used by IPsec and IPv6 [RFC1750]. As with IPsec and IPv6, SCTP can only provide security when connecting to a known host and using preshared keys.

RFC2960 is one of the few RFCs that discusses all the security ramifications, including authentication, privacy, and nonrepudiation.

Although SCTP provides better security and performance than TCP, it has not been widely adopted. SCTP drivers are available for Linux and BSD, but these drivers do not currently ship with most operating system distributions. In addition, SCTP is not supported by most firewalls and NAT systems and lacks compatibility with TCP. All of this impedes widespread adoption.

14.1.3 NetBIOS-DG

File-sharing protocols, such as NFS, use UDP for data transfers. The lower overhead from UDP makes it more desirable than TCP. For Windows, the protocol of choice is NetBIOS. The *NetBIOS Datagram Service* (NetBIOS-DG) provides similar functionality to UDP. NetBIOS-DG is used for transporting data between Windows systems.

The NetBIOS API provides functionality at the OSI session and transport layers. NetBIOS-DG is a transport layer function, whereas NetBIOS-NS (name server) and NetBIOS-SSN (session service network) are examples of session layer functionality.

NetBIOS-DG is an open protocol defined by RFC1001 and RFC1002, however, it is commonly associated with the proprietary Microsoft *Server Message Block* (SMB) protocol. Although the open source community has attempted to reverse engineer SMB for Linux and Unix systems, these ports are constantly under development. The open source SAMBA project (*http://www.samba.org/*) offers a very usable implementation of NetBIOS for supporting SMB. But, the SAMBA implementation does not provide 100 percent of the functionality found on Windows systems.

The NetBIOS protocol is strongly associated with Windows operating systems. Microsoft's Network Neighborhood and Shares (drive and device sharing) use NetBIOS to communicate. This protocol was designed for local networks but regularly appears across large networks and the Internet. Unfortunately, NetBIOS is generally considered an external risk because the common implementations provide direct access to services and files on the system. Between November 2004 and 2005, the Internet Storm Center recorded in excess of 500,000 scans per day for the NetBIOS ports 137/udp and 139/udp, and 50,000 for port 138/udp. Most of these scans were conducted by malware and computer viruses. Together, these ports denote some of the most widely scanned and exploited services on the Internet. To limit virus outbreaks, many ISPs automatically filter these NetBIOS ports.

Although the NetBIOS ports 137, 138, and 139 (TCP and UDP) are heavily scanned, they are not as targeted as the SMB-over-TCP port 445/tcp. Between November 2004 and 2005, the Internet Storm Center recorded in excess of 5,000,000 packets scans per day. Although many service providers filter the NetBIOS ports, 445/tcp is not regularly filtered.

14.1.4 AppleTalk

Similar to NetBIOS for Windows, Apple's operating systems incorporate the AppleTalk protocol. AppleTalk includes a variety of transport protocols that are optimized for specific tasks. For example, the AppleTalk Data Stream Protocol (ADSP) is optimized for streaming data, whereas the Name Binding Protocol (NBP) is used for hostname resolution. Other AppleTalk transport protocols include the AppleTalk Transaction Protocol (ATP) and Echo Protocol (AEP).

Most Apple products have strong support for AppleTalk, TCP, and UDP.

Although AppleTalk is a proprietary protocol, the open source Netatalk project (*http://netatalk.sourceforge.net/*) provides full AppleTalk support to Linux, BSD, and Unix systems.

14.2 CORE TRANSPORT LAYER FUNCTIONS

The transport layer abstracts the networking functionality from the upper application layers. This includes connection management, packet assembly, and service identification. The two core elements that make these functions possible are transport layer ports and sequencing.

14.2.1 Ports and Sockets

The transport layer uses the network layer to establish a connection to another node. The network layer's route provides a *socket* across the network [RFC793]. Sockets may either be active or passive. An *active socket* indicates an established network connection, either on a client or server. In contrast, a *passive socket* is one that is not in use. Servers use passive sockets while awaiting and listening for network connections.

The transport layer creates *ports*. Each port contains a unique identifier for a specific higher-layer service. A single socket may host many ports, but a port requires a socket. Ports may be associated with specific higher-layer protocols or dynamically allocated. For example, the Web (HTTP) uses a service on port 80 of the TCP protocol—denoted as 80/tcp. Email uses 25/tcp, and DNS uses both 53/udp and 53/tcp. By assigning services to known ports, every client knows how to find each service. If the service is not on a standard port, then someone (or something) must specify where the port is located. For example, the remote procedure call (RPC) protocol uses a well-known port for communicating the dynamic port numbers for specific services.

Although servers are usually assigned specific ports, clients may use any port. The server learns the client's port number when the client connects to the server. Each transport layer header specifies the source and destination port numbers.

Most remote network attacks target specific services on specific ports. But, many denial-of-service attacks may target ports or sockets. This places the transport layer in a unique position: transport attack vectors include ports, sockets, and specific protocol implementations.

Socket to Me

The term *sockets* has two meanings that are context specific. First, it can refer to a general programming interface. Unix *sockets programming* uses the sockets API for accessing transport layer protocols. Within the transport layer, however, sockets have a different meaning. A socket is a network connection, defined by four values: source network address, source port, destination network address, and destination port [RFC793]. A half-opened socket indicates a socket with source values but no destination.

14.2.2 Sequencing

The transport layer receives a block of data from the upper layers and separates the data into *packets*. Each packet is assigned a unique *sequence identifier* that is used to track the packet. The transport layer maintains a list of sequence numbers that have been used on a port—new sequence numbers are not used until the entire sequence is used. This prevents a packet with a duplicate sequence number from being confused with a previously seen packet. Packets that are clearly out of sequence are either held until the full sequence is received or simply rejected.

Because sequence numbers are used to maintain the transport layer's ordering, they form a common attack vector. Sequencing can be used for transport layer hijacking.

For some connection-less protocols, packet ordering and sequencing are not required. UDP, for example, does not provide sequencing.

14.2.3 Sequence Hijacking

An attacker who observes a transport layer packet must identify the sequence to insert or hijack the connection. If the attacker sends forged packets that are out of sequence, then they will likely be ignored by the target system; however, forged packets with valid sequence numbers can appear authentic and acceptable to the target system. For this reason, sequence numbers may not be generated incrementally. If the observed packet sequence is #1, #2, #3, then the attacker may assume the next packet is #4. If the observed sequence is #1, #352, #80, then an attacker may not be able to predict the next sequence number. In addition, if all sequence identifiers are used before the sequence repeats, then an attacker can simply observe all identifiers until there is only one left.

14.2.3.1 Random Sequence Numbers

Random initial sequence numbers are commonly used at the start of a transport connection. This deters an attacker from guessing the first packet; however, random sequence numbers within an established connected-oriented transport connection are uncommon. Instead, transport layer protocol such as TCP and SCTP use the packet header to indicate the current sequence number as well as the next number. An attacker who observes this type of header knows the next sequence number to imitate. In addition, the attacker can specify the next forged packet sequence number, effectively locking out half of an established connection. If the transport connection provides an established login, then the attacker immediately gains access to the login.

Because a socket connection includes both source and destination, a hijacker must assume the identity of either the source or the destination. This can be done through redirection or impersonation. For example, ICMP allows the redirection of connections to other hosts or ports. In addition, the victim may undergo some form of DoS attack to remove any competition with an impersonator.

14.2.3.2 Blind Sequence Attacks

Although common transport protocols are vulnerable to attackers that can observe the packets, they are not necessarily vulnerable to attackers that cannot intercept the data stream (*blind attackers*). Sequence numbers are commonly started with an initial random value but increment throughout the course of the session. An observer can easily identify the sequence pattern and hijack the session, but a blind attacker cannot identify the initial sequence number. As such, a blind attacker cannot determine the sequence number and compromise a transport layer connection.

14.2.3.3 Sequence Reconnaissance Attacks

Unfortunately, many transport layer protocol implementations use a pseudo-random number generator that becomes predictable. The complexity of the random number generator directly leads to the predictability of the packet sequence. An attacker can establish many transport connections and determine the pattern for initial sequence numbers. This weakness allows a blind attacker to potentially compromise transport layer connections. Older operating systems, such as TCP for OS/2 and Windows 95, use very predictable packet sequences. Newer network devices may use random positive increments (e.g., Linux and Windows 2000) or very random values (e.g., OpenBSD and related BSD systems). Tools such as Nmap (`nmap -O -v`) evaluate the quality of the sequence generating system.

Although most modern operating systems use very random algorithms for generating transport layer sequence numbers, network gateways and other devices do not. Many gateways, firewalls, and mobile devices use trivial, pseudo-random number generators.

14.2.3.4 Hijacking Mitigation Options

There are few solutions to transport layer hijacking. Most services that require security rely on higher OSI layer protocols to authenticate connections. For example, SSH connections can be hijacked through TCP, but the hijacker is unlikely to be able to authenticate or respond correctly to SSH packets. This type of hijacking appears as an established SSH connection that suddenly disconnects. This results in a secure failure, where the service stops the attack but does nothing to prevent an ongoing DoS attack. Secure transport layer protocols, such as SCTP, are seldom deployed but do provide options for transport authenticating connections between known hosts.

14.2.4 Connection Management

Much of the transport layer functionality operates similarly to the lower networking layers. For example, transport layer protocols may be connection-oriented or connection-less. In a *connection-oriented* protocol, the recipient acknowledges each data transfer; *connection-less* protocols do not. This is the same concept used by the OSI network, data link, and physical layers—each supports connection-oriented and connection-less protocols. There is no connectivity dependency between the OSI layers, however. A stack may be implemented with a connection-less physical layer (e.g., 10Base-2), a connection-oriented data link layer (IEEE 802.5 Token Ring), a connection-less network layer (IP), and a connection-oriented transport layer (TCP). Even if the transport protocol is connection-oriented, the lower protocols are not required to be connection-oriented.

Although it is possible to have connection-oriented protocols at each of the OSI layers, the resulting communication overhead can be overwhelming. Using connection-oriented protocols at the data link, network, and transport layers can more than quadruple the amount of physical layer traffic.

The ability to mix-and-match connection methods allows improved performance and reliability. For example, many computers only have one network adapter that supports a twisted pair physical layer protocol (commonly 10Base-T or 100-Base-T). These are connection-less protocols. The data link layer, IEEE 802.2 and 802.3, can support connection-oriented connections but nearly always operates in a connection-less mode. The network layer, IPv4 or IPv6, is connection-less (unless security is enabled through IPsec or IPv6 security). This means that the data transfer is likely connection-less. The transport layer can apply connection-oriented functionality even when the lower layers are connection-less. Because only one layer is providing a connection-oriented service, data does not need to be validated at every step. A single acknowledgement can be received at a higher OSI layer and validate the data transfer.

In the worst-case performance scenario, each layer uses a connection-oriented protocol. This means that each transport layer packet needs a transport layer acknowledgement. A single transport layer packet may be split into multiple network layer packets, resulting in multiple network-layer acknowledgements for each transport layer packet. Similarly, the data link and physical layers may subdivide the data and require transfer acknowledgements. Although this type of worst-case scenario is rarely, if ever, observed in common network environments, the scenario does appear to a lesser degree with VPNs. For example, both IPv6 and SSH provide VPN support, and both provide connection-oriented services. Tunneling a protocol that depends on TCP over SSH through an IPv6 connection introduces three layers of connection-oriented services and therefore leads to more packets being generated.

In contrast to the performance loss, connection-oriented layers do improve reliability by validating the transfer at each stage. The four types of connection-oriented confirmations are per packet, per set, sliding window, and implicit. Each of these approaches balances tradeoffs between performance and reliability.

Proxies and Tunnels

Both proxies and tunnels relay packets. Both also typically use connection-oriented services, although connection-less protocols do exist. The big difference between proxies and tunnels is in *how* they relay packets.

When using a *tunnel*, such as a VPN, an entire network stack is relayed. If an application protocol that uses the TCP connection-oriented transport protocol (e.g., HTTP or SMTP) is tunneled, then all TCP acknowledgements must also traverse the tunnel. Because all traffic is tunneled, the result is a secure connection, but the number of packets needed for sending the data increases.

In contrast, *proxies* only relay higher-layer protocols. A transport layer proxy, such as a SOCKS server (Chapter 13), only relays session, presentation, and application layer protocols. Transport layer acknowledgements are not relayed through a transport layer proxy. Similarly, NAT (Chapter 12) functions as a network layer proxy. When using NAT, transport layer acknowledgements are relayed, but network layer acknowledgements are not. In general, tunneling generates more packets, which leads to more network overhead and lower performance but also more security options. In contrast, because proxies do not relay acknowledgements, they usually generate less traffic and offer higher performance but only add security through indirection.

Tunneling protocols that use cryptography and authentication are less vulnerable to eavesdropping, hijacking, and MitM attacks than proxies with cryptographic support. This is because a transport layer proxy must decode the transport layer before relaying the data.

14.2.4.1 Per-Packet Confirmation

The simplest type of connection-oriented service uses *per-packet confirmation*. Each transmitted packet receives an acknowledgement. This increases the bandwidth at the physical layer, regardless of the layer performing the per-packet confirmation. To reduce bandwidth consumption, most protocols generate very small acknowledgement packets; the acknowledgement is generally smaller than the data.

14.2.4.2 Per-Set Confirmation

In *per-set confirmation*, a group of packets may be transmitted with one acknowledgement accounting for the entire group. The NFS application layer protocol uses per-set confirmation for file transfers. The confirmation reports the packets received, as well as the ones that were missed.

Many applications that use UDP can also use TCP. For example, NFS may use TCP or UDP but uses UDP by default.

14.2.4.3 Sliding Window Confirmation

The *sliding window confirmation* approach extends the concept of per-set confirmation. Rather than transmitting a block of data and then waiting for a reply, the sliding window continually transmits data. Acknowledgements are sent periodically and confirm a set of transmitted packets. Some acknowledgements may identify a few packets, whereas others can identify many. Sliding windows result in faster transmission rates because the sender does not stop unless no acknowledgements are received. Sliding window confirmation is used by protocols such as TCP and SCTP.

Unfortunately, sliding windows also offer attackers a window of opportunity. In per-packet confirmation and per-set confirmation, the attacker must respond faster than the destination's acknowledgement. With sliding windows, there is a longer period for the attacker to attempt to hijack or poison a connection. Chapter 15 discusses blind TCP attacks that exploit weaknesses in the sliding window approach.

14.2.4.4 Implicit Confirmation

Not every connection-oriented protocol is explicitly connection-oriented. Some protocols, such as those that use cryptography, may be designated as connectionless but actually provide connection-oriented acknowledgements. For example, when the presentation layer protocol SSL (Chapter 19) uses encryption, transport layer packets are chained together through the SSL encryption. Even if the transport layer is connection-less (e.g., UDP), the overall transport operates in a connection-oriented fashion; if a packet is not confirmed, then the encryption fails.

Encryption within the transport or higher layers can lead to implicit connection-oriented communications. Examples include the Kerberos session layer protocol and the presentation layer protocols SSH and SSL.

Few transport protocols support authentication or encryption, but none also support connection-less cryptography. SCTP, for example, supports authentication and encryption but is a connection-oriented protocol. Connection-less transport protocols, such as UDP and NetBIOS-DG, do not provide cryptographic support.

14.2.5 Packet Ordering

The transport layer may divide data into multiple packets, combine small data blocks into larger packets, and multiplex packets through multiple connections. Moreover, the network layer routes the packets to remote systems but does not guarantee the order of the packet's arrival. Different routes may result in different packet ordering. To ensure that the upper OSI layers receive data as it was sent, the transport layer uses the packet sequence numbers to ensure data ordering.

The Nagel Algorithm

Packet headers generate a large amount of overhead. For example, a TCP packet sent over IP on a 100Base-T network contains a minimum of 54 bytes of packet header: 14 for MAC addressing, 20 for IP, and 20 for TCP. When transmitting a series of short bytes, such as keyboard entries in a terminal window, the header size comprises a majority of the data being sent. If there are enough small packets, then network congestion due to acknowledgement delays may occur.

In 1984, John Nagel proposed a solution to this type of network congestion. Detailed in RFC896, the approach delays transmissions at the transport layer. Rather than sending every keystroke, systems may wait for a fraction of a second (usually 200 ms to 500 ms—the time between keystrokes) in case more small data blocks need to be transmitted. When the transfer buffer fills, or a timeout occurs, the data is placed in a packet and sent through the socket, reducing the number of headers needed to perform the transfer. This method of waiting for a packet to fill a transport buffer is commonly referred to as the *Nagel Algorithm*.

The Nagel Algorithm does improve network performance, but it can negatively impact software that requires real-time input. Applications may disable the Nagel algorithm by using the socket option TCP_NODELAY (Listing 14.1) to force real-time data transmissions. But, disabling the Nagel algorithm can lead to time-based attacks, such as the SSH timing attack discussed in Chapter 20.

LISTING 14.1 Code Sample for Disabling the Nagel Algorithm for TCP Connections

```
int On=1;
tcp_socket = socket(PF_INET, SOCK_STREAM, 0);
setsockopt(tcp_socket, IPPROTO_TCP, TCP_NODELAY, &On, sizeof(On));
```

14.2.6 Keep-Alive

Network and lower OSI layers may connect and reconnect as needed, without impacting the transport layer. Network devices such as NAT routers (Chapter 12), however, may decide a transport layer connection is terminated when no traffic is seen after a few minutes. NAT devices and firewalls normally store a table of addresses, ports, and protocols that are permitted to enter the network. After a timeout from lack of use, table entries are dropped. The result is that a low-volume transport layer connections may become disconnected due to network timeouts.

The connection timeout duration varies among firewalls. Some SOHO NAT firewalls timeout after 10 minutes. Heavy-duty commercial firewalls may timeout after hours.

To prevent network timeouts, many transport layer protocols support keep-alive packets. A *keep-alive packet* creates network traffic without transferring application data. These are intended to prevent timeouts from low activity.

Low-end network devices simply look for traffic from a known remote network address that uses a specified protocol (e.g., TCP or UDP) and port. An attacker can use this information to keep a path through a firewall or NAT router open long after the actual connection has terminated. By sending forged packets that specify the source address, destination address, protocol, and port, the attacker can keep the path through the firewall open indefinitely. In the worst case, the network service inside the firewall may be susceptible to attacks from forged packets. At best, the firewall (or NAT device) is vulnerable to a DoS as the attacker keeps all ports open—filling the table of allowed connections and preventing new connections.

Higher-end firewalls and NAT devices support *stateful packet inspection* (SPI). SPI monitors transport layer packets to identify sequence numbers and connect/disconnect requests. Using SPI, an attacker cannot trivially bypass a firewall; however, SPI can only analyze transport protocols that it knows—usually TCP and UDP. Other transport protocols, such as NetBIOS-DG or SCTP are usually not be monitored by SPI systems.

14.3 GATEWAYS

Bridges, routers, and gateways refer to network devices that convert between protocols. *Bridges* (Chapter 8) operate at the data link layer and span networks that may use different physical layer standards. *Routers* (Chapter 11) operate at the network layer and can pass traffic between separate data link layers. Similarly, *gateways* are transport layer devices that can pass data between different network layer protocols. For example, a gateway may link traffic from an IPv6 network to an X.25 network.

Gateways operate at the transport layer and can filter connections based on data link, network, or transport protocols. For example, a gateway may only pass authenticated IPv6 traffic a private IP network or allow all TCP data to pass from a specific hardware address to a specific subnet. Because of its filtering capabilities, the term "gateway" is frequently synonymous with "firewall."

What's in a Name?

The term *gateway* may be used with network or transport layer devices, but with different meanings. At the network layer, a gateway is any device that links two networks. This term is usually seen as a *default gateway* or default routing device.

At the transport layer, *gateway* has a very different meaning. *Bridge*, *router*, and *gateway* define specific terms that correspond with OSI stack functionality (layers 2, 3, and 4, respectively). Not all devices with these names operate at these layers, however. For example, many home firewall routers support transport-layer analysis. The capability to perform stateful packet inspections (SPI) requires transport layer support—a router at the network layer cannot perform SPI. The NetGear *WGR614 Wireless Router* is technically a gateway because it supports SPI. Similarly, the SMC *Barricade Router* (e.g., the 7004ABR) provides RNAT based on port and protocol (this requires gateway functionality). To add to the terminology confusion, Belkin offers a product called a *Wireless DSL/Cable Gateway Router*.

Product names do not necessarily reflect their functionality or technical definitions. A device labeled as a *router* may actually be a gateway, and a *gateway* may actually be a router. Similarly, many devices marketed as *hubs* may actually be switches, bridges, routers, or gateways. When evaluating network devices for security implications, be aware that the product's name may not match the functionality.

14.4 GENERAL RISKS

The main risks for all transport protocols center around sequence numbers and ports. To hijack a transport connection, the attacker must compromise the packet sequencing. Transport layer ports directly lead to network services. By targeting a port, a remote attacker can target a specific high-layer service. The transport layer can also lead to reconnaissance attacks, including port scans and information leakage.

14.4.1 Transport Layer Hijacking

Hijacking attacks can occur at any of the OSI layers. Physical layer hijacking intercepts the physical medium. Data link and network layer hijacking are based on impersonating addresses. A transport layer hijacking requires two elements:

■ The attacker must perform some type of network layer compromise. The attacker may intercept the network traffic by using a node in promiscuous mode, simple address impersonation, or a MitM attack.
■ The attacker must identify the transport sequencing.

From an attacker's viewpoint, the packet's sequence numbers lead to transport layer hijacking and assist in reconstructing observed data transfers. Without the ability to intercept and continue the transport sequencing, packets will not be acknowledged and new packets will not be accepted. Most protocols, such as TCP and SCTP, include the packet sequence number, next sequence number, and acknowledgement for a previous sequence number. Some protocols, such as TCP, permit combining these in one packet header. An attacker who observes a TCP packet can identify the next packet in the sequence as well as any packets needing acknowledgements. In general, the ability to hijack a transport layer connection depends on the sequence number's quality.

To complete a hijacking, the attacker must impersonate the network layer traffic. The forged packet must contain the correct source address, destination address, source port, and destination port.

As described in Section 14.2.3, randomized sequence numbers can reduce the risk of a transport layer hijacking. Systems with less-random sequences are more vulnerable. Protocols that do not use sequence numbers, such as UDP, are extremely vulnerable.

14.4.2 One Port versus Multiple Ports

Some services only require one port to function, whereas others require many ports. By reducing the number of ports on a node, the number of attack vectors can be reduced. A server with 100 active services usually has 100 ports that can be attacked. *Hardened servers* reduce the number of open ports to only essential services. A public Web server may only have HTTP (80/tcp) and a remote console such as SSH (22/tcp) open.

In general, having fewer open ports leads to safer systems. But, some services support multiplexing ports or opening new ports based on service requests. (This leads to the essential question: which is safer, a hundred small ports or one really big port?) For example, a proxy may only have one port open (e.g., 1080/tcp for SOCKS), but that one port can lead to connections on many other systems and many other ports.

Similarly, SSH supports port forwarding. Even though SSH only uses one port, a remote client may forward traffic from many ports into the SSH secure tunnel. Even though the SSH tunnel itself may be secure, the tunnel's end points may not be.

14.4.3 Static versus Dynamic Port Assignments

For a remote client to connect to a server it needs two items. First, it needs the network address of the server. Host resolution systems, such as /etc/hosts and DNS, provide this information. Second, the remote client must know the transport protocol and port. If a Web server is running on 80/tcp, then connecting to a different location, such as 1435/udp, will not reach the Web server. For TCP and UDP, port numbers below 1024 are considered privileged and reserved. This port range is usually restricted to network services operated by an administrator, and many of these ports are assigned to well-known services. In contrast, ports above 1024 are usable by any application on a node.

When a client initially connects to a server, the connection is made to a well-known port on the server. In contrast, the client usually uses an *ephemeral port*, selected from a range of dynamic ports. For the server to reply to the client, the client includes its network address and port number in the packet.

Firewalls use port information to provide network access. For example, a firewall in front of an email server will allow external requests to route to 25/tcp on a specific internal host. Firewalls with egress filtering and routers with NAT support dynamically track packet sessions. A remote host on one port can talk to a local host on another port.

Some higher-layer protocols do not use a fixed port number. Examples include RPC, FTP (data connection), and NetMeeting. Rather than using a single port for all communication, a control service is operated on a well-known port, and dynamic ports are opened for data transfers. The initial connection to the control service generates a message that identifies the dynamic port number.

Dynamic ports are useful when the application spawns off processes for managing network activity. (Having different applications use the same port number can create processing issues.) Dynamic ports create a security risk because a large port range must be accessible to the network. For example, FTP creates a second port for transferring data. This dynamic port may appear on any unused port number. Without opening a firewall for all ports, FTP's data connection will be blocked. There are three viable options for FTP to function through a firewall:

- The firewall can be opened to permit all higher (>1023) ports. This creates a huge vulnerability because the firewall effectively permits most network traffic. Any application that uses a higher port number would become susceptible to a remote network attack.

■ The firewall may understand FTP. These firewalls can identify dynamic ports and permit traffic on an as-needed basis. Although this is a viable solution for well-known protocols such as FTP, less common (or more complex) protocols such a RPC and NetMeeting may not be supported.

■ The protocol can be rewritten to not require a dynamic port. Newer versions of FTP support passive transfers [RFC1579]. In normal FTP mode, the client initiates a control port connection to the server, and the server initiates a data port connection to the client. In passive FTP mode, the client initiates both control and data connections.

■ FTP can be replaced with more secure options. Application layer protocols such as rsync, scp, and sftp provide similar functionality without the need for dynamic ports.

14.4.4 Port Scans

To attack a service, the service's port must be identified. *Port scans* work by attempting to connect to each port on a host. If the port responds, then an active service is likely listening on the port. If the service is on a well-known port, then it increases the likelihood of service identification. Fortunately, there are many methods for defending against port scans, including nonstandard port usage, no reply, always reply, knock-knock protocols, proactive detection, and intentional delays.

14.4.4.1 Types of Scans

Scans can be performed in one of two ways. *Targeted port scans* test for specific ports. For example, each time a new network vulnerability is identified, attackers begin scanning subnets for systems with vulnerable ports. Scanning a class-C network for a single port can be done with 256 packets (one per host). Scans across class-B subnets can be performed in minutes, whereas class-A subnets may take hours.

The alternative to a targeted port scan is a *port sweep*. Sweeps test all potential ports on one or more hosts. For example, both TCP and UDP allow 65,536 possible ports. That means there are up to 65,536 potential services per protocol. Port sweeps usually take minutes to complete; scanning all TCP ports on a single host takes just as long as scanning a class-B subnet for one specific port. The result is a list of ports on the host that appear to contain services. Nmap (*http://www.inse-cure.org/nmap/*), Nessus (*http://www.nessus.org/*), and Paketto Keiretsu's scanrand (*http://www.doxpara.com/*) are three examples of tools that perform port sweeps.

Most IDS and IPS products can detect rapid port scans and sweeps. Long delays can prevent the scan's detection, but it also increases the scanning duration. Rather than taking seconds to scan a class-C network, it may take hours. For example, Nmap's "paranoid mode" waits 5 minutes between each individual port scan. Scanning 256 ports takes more than 21 hours (but it is very unlikely to be detected by an IDS or IPS).

14.4.4.2 Nonstandard Ports

Many services run on well-known ports. If an attacker sees that a well-known port exists, then the type of available service can be assumed. However, well-known services can be hosted on nonstandard ports to obscure the type of service. For example, SSH usually operates on 22/tcp. Moving SSH to 7766/tcp creates a level of obscurity; only users who know it runs on port 7766/tcp can connect to the server. An attacker may see that there is a service on port 7766/tcp, but the service will likely be ignored because it is nonstandard. In particular, many automated attack systems only target known services.

Nmap and Nessus take port scanning to the next step. Both of these tools make no assumptions concerning the type of running service. Instead, they identify ports and test for known service attributes (*fingerprints*). Both of these tools would find the open port on 7766/tcp and then detect the SSH server.

When moving a service to an alternate port number, steps should be taken to ensure that the port is not allocated to another service. Many of the high-level port numbers (>1023) are assigned to specific services. IANA provides the official list of TCP and UDP port assignments at *http://www.iana.org/assignments/port-numbers*. In addition, the Internet Storm Center *http://isc.sans.org/* allows visitors to see how often a port number is scanned. A good alternate port should not be assigned to any services nor heavily scanned.

14.4.4.3 No Reply Defense

Because port scans look for packet replies, some systems alter replies. For example, BSD systems do not respond to packet requests against inactive ports. An attacker scanning a BSD system cannot tell if the scan's packet failed to reach the target or was ignored by the target. In general, this causes the scanning system to wait for a timeout before assuming the scan failed. By forcing timeout delays, scans may take hours (depending on the scanning tool).

14.4.4.4 Always Reply Defense

When systems such as BSD fail to respond to closed ports, the appearance of open ports becomes clear: these are active services. The alternative to not responding is to always respond. In this configuration, the scanning tool cannot distinguish a closed port from an open port. Tools that attempt to fingerprint services can waste hours polling ports that contain no services.

14.4.4.5 Knock-Knock Protocols

One of the cleverest defenses against port detection is *port knocking*, also known as a *knock-knock protocol*. Normally services are always running in case a client connects. This leaves the port open and vulnerable to scanning detection. A knock-knock server does not keep the port open. Instead, it monitors other ports or network protocols for an expected packet sequence. When the sequence is observed, the service is started. For example, a SSH server may not bind to a port until the host first sees an ICMP packet with an abnormal data size of 700 bytes. An attacker scanning for SSH servers will not generate the required ICMP packet and will not see SSH running on the server.

Knock-knock protocols can be very simple—requiring a single packet as the key—or very complex, involving many packets and many protocols in a predetermined configuration. One server may require a single TCP packet, whereas another may require a sequence of TCP and UDP packets before activating the service. More complicated sequences can be difficult for an observer to identify or duplicate but introduce usability issues by being inconvenient to the user.

> **Who's There?**
>
> During prohibition (1920-1933), the consumption of alcohol was prohibited in the United States. *Speakeasies* appeared in cities as underground clubs for drinking. To enter a speakeasy, one needed to know the time, location, and a secret. The secret was frequently a special knock on the door (rat-a-tat ... tat) along with a codeword whispered by the door. If the codes were correct then the door would open. This allowed desirable patrons in, and kept out law enforcement and suspicious people.
>
> This same speakeasy concept applies to port knocking. Rather than tapping a door, the special sequence is played to a networked host. By performing the correct knock, desirable clients can connect to the server.

14.4.4.6 Active Scan Detection

Although the common options for defending against port scans are technically security-by-obscurity, they are effective at slowing down attackers. In contrast, proactive security options are available. An IDS can observe a series of connections from a scanning host and block access from the host. In addition, *honeypot ports* can be used to temporarily shutdown a server. If scanning is unusual, then a connection to one or more honeypot ports can denote an undesirable scan.

14.4.4.7 Intentional Delays

Tarpitting is a technique used to impede hostile systems. The goal of the tarpit is to delay the attacker as much as possible. For example, LaBrea (*http://labrea.source-forge.net/*) monitors the network for queries to nonexisting hosts and generates replies to the queries. The result is a scan that contains many false replies. An automated scanning and attacking system would become bogged down as it targets nonexisting hosts.

Other tarpitting attacks can intentionally slow established connections. A tarpitting honeypot may use long delays between packets or restrict data transfer sizes to a few bytes at a time.

A tarpitting system may exist at any OSI layer. Email servers (Chapter 22) sometimes use this technique to slow down spam senders. Although email is accepted, delays can be added between each message. A spammer may send one or two messages quickly, but a hundred could take a very long time.

Although this approach does not stop scans or block connections, it does impede attackers. An automated attack system can be caught by the delays, preventing attacks against vulnerable hosts.

14.4.5 Information Leakage

With few exceptions, transport layer protocols do not encrypt the data being transmitted. When combined with common physical, data link, and network protocols, the first four OSI layers leave information protection to individual protocols; there is nothing inherent in the layers that offer security. An observer on the network that can monitor packet traffic can view the contents within the transport protocol. In general, the session, presentation, or application layers are expected to provide authentication and encryption.

SUMMARY

The OSI transport layer provides the essential link between low-level network routing and high-level services. The transport layer manages network connections, assigns ports to services, and ensures that packets are received from the network in the correct order.

The primary threats to transport protocols include sequence identification, hijacking, and port detection. Although these threats, along with information leakage, are a significant concern, the transport layer itself defines no authentication or encryption mechanisms. As a result, most transport protocols provide limited security options.

REVIEW QUESTIONS

1. What is an example of a transport protocol that supports authentication?
2. List four types of connection-oriented packet confirmations.
3. Can a gateway convert TCP traffic to UDP?
4. If a new exploit is known to impact Apache Web servers, what type of port scan should an administrator use to identify potentially vulnerable servers on his network?

DISCUSSION TOPICS

1. Using a transport layer sequence prediction tool such as Nmap, evaluate a variety of network devices. In addition to operating systems such as Windows, Linux, and BSD, evaluate network routers, firewalls, VoIP, and hand-held devices. Which devices have the most random sequence generators? Is there a reason why some classes of devices are more predictable?
2. Why are there no connection-less transport protocols that support authentication or encryption? Assuming there were such a protocol, how would it perform authentication validation or a cryptographic key exchange? If the cryptographic requirements were preshared, how could it prevent replay attacks?
3. In general, which is more secure, a connection-less or connection-oriented transport protocol? Does the type of threat make a difference? For example, what if the attacker is not along the network path between the client and server, and what if he is?
4. How can port knocking benefit anonymity? Can port knocking identify a user without disclosing his identity to the world? Is it practical for port scanners to test for unknown knock-knock protocols?

ADDITIONAL RESOURCES

The NetBIOS protocol is used by the Windows operating systems for identifying other Windows computers on the network and sharing files. Although documentation is not fully available, RFC1001 and RFC1002 provide some insight into this protocol.

The suite of AppleTalk protocols is proprietary but much better documented than NetBIOS. The manual for Netatalk (*http://netatalk.sourceforge.net/*) provides an excellent starting point for understanding the various AppleTalk protocols, their purposes, and functionality.

Although TCP and UDP are widely supported, experimental transport protocols are constantly being created and evaluated. In April 2005, the Data Transport Research Group developed a paper titled *A Survey of Transport Protocols Other than Standard TCP* (*http://www.welzl.at/research/publications/Survey of Transport Protocols Other than Standard TCP.pdf*). This document compares many TCP variants and alternatives.

Martin Krzywinski manages the *Port Knocking* Web site at *http://www.port-knocking.org/*. This site includes detailed descriptions of how knock-knock protocols work as well as links to many port-knocking implementations.

15 TCP

In This Chapter

- Connection-Oriented Protocol
- TCP Connections
- TCP Reconnaissance
- TCP Hijacking
- TCP DoS
- Mitigation Options
- UDP

The *Transmission Control Protocol* (TCP) is the single most widely used transport layer protocol. TCP is used by the majority of the common application layer protocols, including FTP, email (SMTP), Web (HTTP), Telnet, and Secure Shell (SSH). Nearly every application layer protocol that requires a connection-oriented service uses TCP. Even though physical, data link, and network layer protocols may vary, TCP is effectively available universally.

Although TCP is a common basis for connection-oriented transport services, the *User Datagram Protocol* (UDP) provides connection-less support. DNS, real-time collaboration (e.g., VoIP and NetMeeting), and file-sharing protocols such as NFS and SMB, commonly use UDP. Together, TCP and UDP account for more than 98 percent of all packets traversing the Internet [Estan2004].

TCP's functionality provides reliable and ordered end-to-end communication. When viewed independently, each of the functions, from connection to data exchange and from state flags to sequence numbering, pose no direct security risk. Instead, the risks come from combining the various functions. These combinations can be used for reconnaissance, hijacking, or effective DoS attacks. Due to their high availability, exploits that impact TCP and UDP are likely to threaten virtually every service on the network.

TCP and TCP/IP

TCP was designed for the transport layer in the DoD TCP/IP stack (see Chapter 3). Because of this close association, the transport layer for the TCP/IP stack is sometimes called "TCP" instead of "Transport." Adding confusion, TCP is sometimes mistakenly called "TCP/IP"—using the stack name instead of the protocol's name. Similarly, UDP is sometimes mistakenly referred to as "UDP/IP." For clarification, TCP and UDP are protocols, and TCP/IP is the DoD network stack. (And, UDP/IP does not exist.)

15.1 CONNECTION-ORIENTED PROTOCOL

TCP is a connection-oriented protocol and offers two guarantees for higher layer protocols: reliable data delivery and sequential data ordering. As a transport layer protocol, TCP also provides facilities for flow control and multiple connections [RFC793].

TCP uses a byte-stream data flow model. In this model, the byte ordering is important, but the TCP packets are not. TCP packets may be combined or split as long as the data's byte ordering is maintained. This is different from other protocols such as IEEE 802.1, PPP, and IP, where the message blocks delimitate data flow.

TCP uses a segmented header to enclose transmission data (Figure 15.1). Besides the basic 20-byte header, TCP also may include optional header information. The smallest TCP packet (containing no data and no options) is 20 bytes, whereas the largest can exceed 64 KB. Usually a TCP packet with data is only a few kilobytes in size, which ensures that one TCP packet can fit within one data link layer frame.

NOTE

The data being transmitted by the TCP packet is often called application data or user data. Although the data may come from the application layer or user layer (outside the OSI stack), the session or presentation layers can also generate transport data.

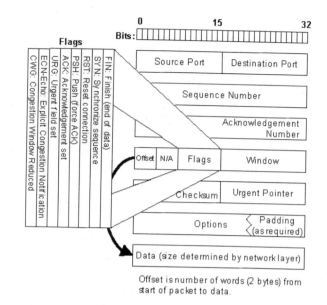

FIGURE 15.1 A basic TCP header.

15.1.1 Reliable Acknowledgements

TCP guarantees reliable data delivery. Each byte sent by a TCP packet is confirmed with an acknowledgement. If no acknowledgement is received, then it assumes that the data transfer failed. To reduce the number of acknowledgements, TCP uses a windowing system. This system acknowledges the amount of data received.

15.1.1.1 Checksums

TCP encases the application data within a TCP header. The TCP header includes a simple checksum value to detect transmission corruptions. The checksum function is a 16-bit CRC function, similar to the checksum used by IP, and covers the entire TCP header and application data. Corrupted packets with invalid checksums (that somehow manage to pass lower layer checks) are discarded and not acknowledged.

Although RFC791 and RFC793 state that TCP packets with invalid checksums should be discarded, some TCP implementations do not validate checksums. By skipping the validation, portable devices, gateways, and packet filters can reduce per-packet processing time and improve speed performance.

15.1.1.2 Retries

To ensure data is properly delivered, TCP resends unacknowledged data. The retry time interval varies based on the network speed, but is usually less than 2 minutes. Data transfers may be retried many times before the connection is assumed to be inactive and closed. This long duration can hang applications that wait for TCP to deliver data. For example, if an application blocks on writing to the network socket, then the application may appear temporarily hung while TCP waits for transfer confirmation. If there are 7 retries, 1 minute apart, then an application may hang for 7 minutes before detecting the failed connection. Under most Linux systems, TCP defaults to 15 retries (see the Linux command, `sysctl net.ipv4.tcp_retries2`); delays under Linux can be as long as 30 minutes. Most Windows systems retry 5 times, resulting in shorter delays.

Retransmission timeout (RTO) durations are based on the *round trip time* (RTT) of each TCP packet. This is a measurement based on the time it takes to receive an acknowledgement for a given packet transmission [RFC793]. In general, faster networks have smaller RTT values, leading to a shorter retry duration. In the best case, a fast network will result in rapid detection of unacknowledged packets. In the worse case, TCP may hang for minutes as it times out and retries.

15.1.2 Sequence Numbers

TCP guarantees the order of application data delivery. Although lower layer protocols may transmit and receive packets out of order, TCP will reconstruct the ordering before passing the data up the stack to an application. The reconstruction is based on sequence numbers. Each TCP packet is assigned a sequence number, and subsequent packets increase the sequence number by the amount of data transported. For example, if the sequence number is 12345 and 100 bytes of application data are transmitted, then the next sequence number will be 12445.

TCP provides full-duplex communication; both sides may transmit data at the same time. To minimize the number of packets, each TCP packet may data transfer *and* acknowledge a previous transmission. The packet header stores the current sequence number for the data being transmitted, as well as an acknowledgement for previous data received.

TCP does not acknowledge data receipt directly. A direct confirmation would acknowledge each transmitted packet. Instead, the TCP *acknowledgement packet* (ACK) confirms the data but not the packet itself. Each ACK includes the next expected sequence number. If all data has been received, then the next expected sequence number would match the next transmission's sequence number. Using this approach, a gateway or proxy can collect packets, combine (or split) TCP data, and reformat the data into new packets. The reply identifies the amount of data received and not individual packets.

15.1.3 Flow Control

TCP manages data flow using control flags and windows. These two methods combine to provide transport state, acknowledgements, priority, and optimized buffering.

15.1.3.1 Control Flags

Each TCP packet header contains 12 bits for use as control flags. One flag denotes an acknowledgement, another identifies a reset request, and a third defines urgent data. In total, there are six primary control flags (Table 15.1). The flags do not need to be used symmetrically. For example, the client may send a reset to the server to tell the server to resend all unacknowledged data; however, this does not reset the data from the client to the server—it only resets the state from the server to the client.

TABLE 15.1 TCP Control Flags [RFC793, RFC3168]

Name	Bit	Purpose
FIN	0x001	Finish; denotes the end of a connection
SYN	0x002	Synchronize; denotes the start of a connection
RST	0x004	Reset; requests a connection reset
PSH	0x008	Push; require recipient to passed all data up the stack and send an acknowledgement
ACK	0x010	Acknowledge; sender acknowledges receipt of data
URG	0x020	Urgent; data in this packet takes precedence over regular data transfers and handling
ECE	0x040	Explicit Congestion Notification – Echo; allows notification when packets are dropped
CWR	0x080	Congestion Window Reduced; notifies recipient when less window space is available
Remainder	0xF00	Reserved

15.1.3.2 Window Size

In a basic connection-oriented system, each transmission is acknowledged. The acknowledgement confirms data delivery, but creates significant overhead and delays. For example, if the transport layer needs to pass 100 KB of data, it may segment the data into 100 packets containing 1 KB each. Each of the 100 packets would require a confirmation—another 100 packets. To reduce the amount of bidirectional communication, TCP allows each packet header to define the amount of data that can be transferred before requiring an ACK. If the client specifies a window size of 8,192 bytes, then the server can send up to 8,192 bytes of data before requiring an ACK.

For large transfers, larger window sizes can be used; however, the TCP header only supports 16 bits for the window size—a maximum of 65,535 bytes. RFC1323 defines an optional extension to the TCP header for window scaling. The scale indicates the number of bits to right-shift the window size. As an example, a window value of 0x05B4 indicates a 1460-byte window. But when combined with a right-shift of 3 (multiply by 2^3, or shift the bits 3 positions), the value denotes 11,680 bytes.

A window size of 1460 bytes is very common. It is based on an Ethernet packet data size of 1,500 bytes (MTU 1500), minus the 20 bytes for the IP header and the 20-byte minimum for the TCP header. A shift of "3" indicates that the recipient can buffer up to eight (2^3) packets before forcing an acknowledgement.

NOTE

Even when using large transfer sizes, it can be desirable to force an acknowledgement before the recipient's buffer fills. The sender's *push flag* (PSH) is usually sent with the last packet in a large block. This flag informs the recipient to acknowledge the entire data transfer before the next transfer begins.

15.1.4 Multiple Connections and Ports

The source and destination port numbers are combined with the source and destination network addresses to define each TCP connection. Data from one set of ports and addresses (one connection) is not intermixed with data from another set of ports and addresses. This allows the host system to manage many connections at once.

A TCP server binds to a specific port. For a client to connect to the server, it must first acquire its own local port number. Then it connects to a server and establishes a unique transport session defined by the network client and server addresses as well as the transport client and server ports. This unique combination of source and destination ports and network addresses allows a single Web server to operate on 80/tcp while transferring data to a variety of clients. As long as the clients have different network addresses—or the same network address but different client ports—the connection remains unique.

15.2 TCP CONNECTIONS

TCP maintains three basic states: initialization, data exchange, and disconnect.

15.2.1 TCP Connection Initialization

Initialization uses a *three-way handshake*: SYN, SYN-ACK, and ACK (Figure 15.2). The client initially sends a TCP packet containing the SYN flag to a specific port on the server. The packet contains the initial sequence number that will be used by the client. The server replies with both SYN and ACK flags set (SYN-ACK). The server sets its initial sequence number and acknowledges the client's sequence number. Finally, the client transmits an ACK and confirms the server's sequence number. Using this approach, both sides confirm the established connection. If the ACK from either side fails to transfer, then data cannot be transmitted and the failure can be detected.

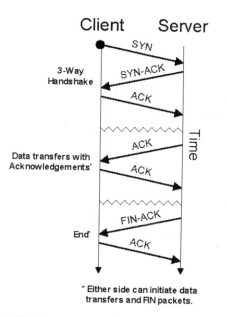

FIGURE 15.2 TCP three-way initialization handshake, data transfer, and connection termination.

Besides exchanging initial sequence numbers, the TCP header may also include information concerning the window size and other TCP options; however, the initial handshake does not transfer any application data.

The SYN flag is only used during the initial connection. Any SYN flags sent after establishing the connection are either ignored or generate a reset packet. Because the SYN packet may be retransmitted due to an initial connection timeout or duplicated by lower network protocols, it is possible for duplicate SYN packets to be received. After the SYN-ACK is transmitted, the client's sequence number is incremented by one. This makes duplicate SYN packets appear with invalid sequence numbers, forcing the packet to be ignored. In contrast, a SYN with a valid sequence number indicates a network problem (or an attack) and forces a connection reset.

15.2.2 TCP Data Exchange

After establishing a TCP connection with the three-way handshake, data packets may be transmitted. Each data packet includes an ACK flag and the data. When the client sends data to the server, the server increments the client's sequence number (a counter) and acknowledges the data with an ACK packet. The server may include response data along with the data acknowledgement.

To reduce the network congestion from acknowledging every packet, the window size identifies the amount of data that may be transmitted before requiring an acknowledgement. If the receiver's window size is 3,000 bytes, then the sender may send up to 3,000 bytes before requiring an ACK. But there is a risk: the receiver assumes that the sender is tracking the amount of data transmitted. However, there is nothing to stop the sender from transmitting more data. The receiver must ignore or drop data received after its buffer fills and before the ACK is transmitted. For this reason, both sides in a TCP connection must track acknowledgements to ensure that no data is lost. The sender knows information was lost when no ACK is received.

When neither side transmits data, the idle connection takes no network bandwidth. Network proxies and NATs may view inactivity as a terminated connection. There is an extension to TCP for generating keep-alive packets [RFC1122], but it must be listed as a supported TCP option during the initial three-way handshake; support is not mandatory nor guaranteed. A keep-alive packet may break a connection or generate a reset if the recipient does not support it. In general, higher-layer protocols that anticipate long periods of inactivity are expected to generate their own keep-alive packets.

15.2.3 TCP Disconnect

TCP identifies the end of a connection when one side transmits a packet containing a *finish flag* (FIN). The closure is completed when the recipient transmits an ACK for the FIN. As with the SYN packets, the FIN packets are not expected to transmit data. If any data is transmitted after the FIN, then the recipient responds with a reset (RST).

Using a FIN packet generates a graceful shutdown of the connection, but aborts can also terminate connections. An abort is signaled by an immediate RST (without a FIN) and can happen at any time.

15.3 TCP RECONNAISSANCE

The network services that bind to TCP ports provide direct access to the host system. If the service provides access to the hard drive, then any remote user has the potential to access the hard drive. Whereas network protocols such as IP and IPv6 provide the means to reach a remote host, TCP provides a port into the system. By identifying the type of system and type of service, an attacker can select appropriate attack vectors.

15.3.1 Operating System Profiling

Most TCP implementations allow parameter customization for optimizing connections. Systems may specify larger window sizes, define more retries, or include specific TCP options such as timestamps [RFC793]. The default selections of these values are operating system specific. Windows does not use the same default settings as Linux or Cisco. Moreover, some settings are very specific; in some cases, these can identify specific operating system versions and patch levels.

15.3.1.1 Initial Window Size

Different operating systems use different initial window sizes. Although the initial value can be modified, most systems use the default value. When the server (or client) receives the initial window size, it can use this information to identify the type of operating system that transmitted the data. For example, Windows 2000 uses an initial window size of 16,384 bytes, Windows XP specifies 64,240 bytes, and Debian Linux defaults to 5,840 bytes (1,460 bytes with a scale value of 2^2). If the initial window size from a TCP connection specifies 16,384 bytes, then the sending system is potentially running Windows 2000 and not Debian or Windows XP.

As TCP conversations continue, the window size usually increases. This results in improved performance from established connections. Active connections may have very large window sizes. Larger windows yield lower overhead from individual acknowledgements. As with the initial window size, the amount that the window increases is also operating system specific. Either end of the conversation, or an observer along the network path, can use the initial window size and increment information to fingerprint the operating systems involved.

15.3.1.2 TCP Options

Each TCP packet can contain optional TCP header values, including window scaling, maximum segment size, SACK support, and timestamp information. Different operating systems support different option selections, values, and ordering. A default RedHat Linux 7.1 system (2.4 kernel) includes five options: a maximum segment size of 1,460 bytes, SACK support, timestamp information, a no-operation

(NOP), and a window scale of zero. Debian Linux 3.1 (2.6 kernel) includes the same options but with a window scale of two. In contrast, Windows XP includes nine options: maximum segment of 1,460 bytes, NOP, window scale of zero, NOP, NOP, timestamp, NOP, NOP, and SACK support. An SMC 7004 Barricade router only includes one option: specifying the maximum segment.

By observing the initial TCP options, values, and ordering, specific operating systems can be identified. In some cases, the TCP options can be unique enough to identify the operating system as well as the patch level. Knowing the patch level of a system greatly assists an attacker because it identifies unpatched vulnerabilities.

15.3.1.3 Sequence Numbering

Although all systems that implement TCP increment sequence numbers the same way, the initial sequence number is operating system specific. The initial SYN and SYN-ACK packets exchange the starting sequence numbers for the connection. Although a single TCP connection cannot disclose identifiable information, a series of rapid connections can disclose the pattern used to establish the initial connection.

Older operating systems, such as Windows 95, Windows 98, and OS/2, and embedded systems (e.g., VxWorks) linearly increment each new sequence number. A series of SYN requests will be met with a series of SYN-ACK replies that contain sequential set of numbers. For example, each SYN-ACK reply from OS/2 version 3.0 increases the initial sequence number by 64,000. The D-Link DI-604 home router increases the sequence based on the current time. Linux systems use positive incrementing sequence numbers, but the amount of each increment is not linear. In contrast, most BSD systems use very random initial increment values. As with the initial window size and TCP options, sequence numbering can be used to identify operating system, version, and patch-level version information.

15.3.1.4 Client Port Numbering

Although servers are bound to a fixed TCP port number, clients choose any available port number for use with the connection. The server's port number must be fixed so the client knows where to connect. But, the server can determine the client's dynamic port number from the TCP header. Repeated connections from the client to one or more servers will show different port numbers for each connection. Different operating systems use different dynamic, or *ephemeral*, port ranges for selection by the client.

Ports 0 to 1023 are usually reserved for well-known services. Even if a server is not using one of these port numbers, clients will not normally use them for outbound connections. Similarly, TCP ports 49,152 to 65,535 are usually reserved for private ports. Different operating systems use different subsets of the remaining range for ephemeral ports. For example, RedHat Linux 7.1 defaults to the range

1024 to 4999. Ubuntu Linux 5.04 uses the range 32,768 to 61,000. The Linux command `sysctl net.ipv4.ip_local_port_range` displays the ephemeral port range. Under FreeBSD and Mac OS X, the command is `sysctl –a | grep portrange`. By observing the ephemeral port range used by a client, the type of operating system can be narrowed down, and in some cases, uniquely identified.

15.3.1.5 Retries

When a TCP packet does not receive an acknowledgement, the packet is resent. The number of retries and duration between retries is operating system specific. Fingerprinting based on retries can be done in several ways:

SYN retries: Without responding, count the number of SYN packets and the duration between packets. Most Windows systems transmit three SYN packets, 3 seconds apart before giving up. Linux defaults to five, but the duration progressively expands—the first two are 3 seconds apart, then 6 seconds, 12 seconds, and so on.

SYN-ACK retries: A client can connect to a server (generating a SYN) and observe the number of SYN-ACK replies.

ACK retries: After establishing the connection, the system can fail to provide an ACK. The number of observed retries from an established connection is generally more than from SYN or SYN-ACK retries.

15.3.2 Profiling Tools

There are a few popular tools for profiling systems, including Snacktime, p0f, and Nmap:

ON THE CD

Snacktime: This open source tool fingerprints hosts based on TCP window sizes, options, and retry durations. It only needs to query one open TCP port to fingerprint a system. This tool is included on the CD-ROM.

p0f and Nmap: These tools query two ports to detect subtle changes in the server's TCP configuration. In this technique, one port must be open and another port must be closed. Besides determining the operating system type, these tools can also identify how long the system has been running.

To better study the people who perform system profiling, the Honeynet Project offers a tool called *honeyd* (*http://www.honeyd.org/*). This tool creates virtual online systems for use as *honeypots*—systems used to monitor malicious activity. Honeyd can impersonate most operating systems. Tools such as Nmap and p0f cannot distinguish a real Windows NT 4 SP3 system from a virtual one.

Honeyd does have a few limitations. Although it does impersonate the internal stack, it does not impersonate the default ephemeral port ranges, TCP option ordering, or retry durations. Although Nmap may identify a Linux honeyd system as "Windows NT 4 SP3," Snacktime may detect discrepancies in the results.

15.3.3 Anti-Profiling Options

Profiling is a useful diagnostic technique, but it can also be used for reconnaissance prior to an attack. An attacker can use network profiling to identify underlying operating systems and patch levels. For example, an attacker who identifies a FreeBSD operating system will likely decide against trying a Windows-specific exploit and select a FreeBSD exploit. By changing the default window size, retry timeouts, TCP options, and ephemeral port range, a system can alter its appearance. A Windows XP system that looks like a Debian Linux system may face fewer Windows-specific attacks. Because changing a system's default TCP settings is uncommon, attackers are likely to trust misinformation derived from reconnaissance.

Most network viruses blindly attempt exploits against all network addresses. Changing the system's profile will not mitigate these attacks. Directed attacks based on system profiling can be misled, however, resulting in fewer profile-specific attacks.

TCP ports provide an entrance into the system. Many network viruses scan for well-known server ports. If an open port is found on a host, then an exploit is attempted. To scan large networks, most viruses limit the number of TCP SYN retries—sending one or two before moving on. Although uncommon, TCP servers may use a simple knock-knock protocol (see Chapter 14) to limit the impact from virus scans. Rather than acknowledging the first SYN packet, the server may wait for the third. Although this increases the time for an initial TCP connection, skipping the first two SYN packets decreases the chances of detection by automated reconnaissance.

15.3.4 Port Scans

TCP *port scans* are used to identify running services. A port scan attempts to connect to ports and records the results. In general, there are four types of replies to any connection attempts:

SYN-ACK: If a service is running on the port, then a SYN-ACK will be returned to the client. This is a positive identification. To prevent detection, some firewalls always return a SYN-ACK, even if no service is available. As a result of this countermeasure, a scanner cannot identify open ports.

RST: If no service is running, many systems return an RST packet. This provides a quick confirmation that there is no service on the port.

ICMP Unreachable: If the host is unreachable, then an ICMP packet may be returned indicating a failure. This leaves the port state unknown because it could not be reached for testing. Firewalls, such as *lokkit* and *iptables* used by RedHat Linux, return an ICMP Unreachable instead of a TCP RST packet to confuse scanners.

Nothing: If the packet fails to reach the host, there may be no reply at all. SYN requests will timeout without a SYN-ACK. Although this usually means that the host is unreachable or offline, some firewalls and operating systems intentionally ignore packets sent to closed ports. For example, OpenBSD and Hewlett-Packard's Virtual Vault do not reply to connections against closed ports. This prevents a remote client from distinguishing a closed port from an unreachable host.

Port scans can either be full or partial. A *full port scan* completes the entire three-way handshake. In contrast, a *partial port scan* only waits for the SYN-ACK. Although a full port scan can identify the type of service on an open port, a partial scan identifies only that a service exists.

15.3.5 Logging

Logging is important for detecting system scans and network attacks. Many network services log connections, including timestamps, client network addresses, and related connection information. Few systems log raw TCP traffic. Instead, higher OSI layers usually perform logging. Higher layers do not log TCP connections until the handshake completes. This is important because, with TCP, the connection is not complete until the full three-way handshake is performed. As a result, partial port scans—where the full handshake is not completed—are usually not logged.

Network monitoring tools, such as IDS and IPS, commonly monitor and log SYN requests as well as any traffic not included as part of an established connection. Just as SYN packets are recorded, unsolicited ACK and RST packets are also logged. Based on the frequency, type, and order of these packets, network scans from tools such as Nmap and p0f can be identified. In the case of an IPS, reactive steps can be taken before the scan completes to prevent too much information leakage and to limit service detection. If an attacker cannot identify the type of system, then his ability to compromise the system greatly diminishes.

15.4 TCP HIJACKING

TCP hijacking refers to any attack that interferes with a TCP connection. These attacks usually appear as a DoS, where the connection prematurely terminates. *Full session hijacking*, although rare, occurs when an attacker not only disconnects one end of the TCP connection but continues the other side of the connection. For example, an attacker may wait for a user to log in to a remote server and then hijack the connection. The user (TCP client) receives a disconnect (or TCP timeout). Meanwhile, the server does not notice that the attacker has replaced the client—without logging in.

15.4.1 Full Session Hijacking

Full session hijacking usually requires an attacker to have direct data link layer access. Operating in promiscuous mode, the attacker observes the network addresses, ports, and sequence numbers used within the connection. Using this information, the attacker attempts to respond faster than one end of the TCP connection. This becomes a *race condition*, where a difference of microseconds indicates a success or failure. A successful hijacking provides the attacker with a connected session to a network service, and a failed hijacking attempt usually results in a DoS or is simply ignored.

An attacker can gain an advantage in the race condition in many ways. For example, the attacker can flood the client with packets, reducing the victim's ability to send ACK packets. Because the victim no longer has a valid TCP session, his system

> **May I Cut In?**
> Early TCP hijacking attempts evolved around telnet and FTP. These protocols allowed an attacker to gain a remote login without needing login credentials. Although telnet and FTP use plaintext passwords (no encryption), an attacker who misses the initial login can still hijack the session. Because of these risks, most system administrators have switched to using SSH for remote access (see Chapter 20). SSH provides encryption and authentication; hijack attempts result in a DoS but not a system compromise.
>
> Although SSH is not vulnerable to a full session hijacking, other protocols remain at risk. During Defcon 12 (July 2004), a few attendees demonstrated TCP hijacking over wireless networks. Using a tool called *airpwn* (*http://sourceforge.net/projects/airpwn*), they monitored Web requests and changed the replies for downloaded images and files. Rather than seeing regular Web pages and pictures, victims saw pages and images sent by the hijackers.

generates RST packets in reply to the packets from the server. A second attack may also be used to prevent server ACKs from generating RST packets from the victim. For this reason, an IDS that detects a DoS may actually indicate a more severe problem: a TCP hijacking.

15.4.2 ICMP and TCP Hijacking

ICMP packets are used to communicate between IP and TCP (see Chapter 12). ICMP can be used to report unsuccessful connections or to redirect network services. When used maliciously, ICMP can redirect TCP connections to different ports or different hosts. Although an attacker must still know the TCP sequence numbers, an ICMP attack does not require using a DoS to disable either end of the original connection.

15.5 TCP DOS

A DoS attack can serve two purposes for an attacker. First, it can disable a victim. Someone attempting to check email will be unable to check email, and attempts to remotely administer a host can be blocked.

The second use for a DoS is more surreptitious. DoS attacks are very noticeable and quickly gain the attention of administrators. An attacker may perform a DoS against one system while subtly exploiting a different system. While administrator ·focuses on the DoS, they may not notice the second attack.

TCP is very vulnerable to DoS attacks. Any interference with the port numbers or sequencing will result in a disconnection. Although hijacking can cause a DoS, it is not the only type of attack. TCP DoS attacks may come from SYN, RST, or ICMP packets, and the attacker does not need direct network access (promiscuous mode) to perform the attacks.

15.5.1 SYN Attacks

Each TCP implementation allocates memory for managing connections. Each connection must include the network addresses, ports, window size information, sequence numbers, as well as buffer space for incoming and outgoing packets. Each server allocates memory when a SYN is received. A *SYN attack* transmits a large number of SYN packets in order to consume all available memory. If the TCP implementation can only manage 250 concurrent connections, then it only takes 250 SYN packets to block additional connections.

SYN packets are tracked on per-service and per-system levels. A Web server may be limited to 100 simultaneous connections, even if the host system supports 250 simultaneous connections across all services. In this example, 100 SYN packets to the Web server will block Web access, and 250 SYN packets to a variety of services on the same host will block all network access (including Web).

Each time a SYN packet is sent to an open service, it generates a SYN-ACK response. If the handshake is not completed, then the connection times out. The result is an effective DoS: an attacker sends a flood of SYN requests, and the server becomes blocked until the pending connections timeout.

There are a few options to mitigate the risk from a SYN attack:

Increase SYN Queue: The number of pending SYN connections can be increased. Under Linux, this is done with the `sysctl tcp_max_syn_backlog` command. By increasing the number of connections, an attacker must generate more packets.

Decrease SYN Timeout: The timeout for unacknowledged SYN-ACK packets can be reduced. In theory, if the SYN queue cannot be filled before timeouts occurs, then the system will not be impacted by the attack. In actuality, this simply lowers the impact from the attack, but a large enough attack will still be successful. When the attack stops, the decreased timeout value assists in a rapid recovery.

Enable SYN Cookies: Most Linux and BSD systems support SYN cookies. *SYN cookies* use the initial SYN-ACK serial number to specify connection information. Instead of basing the sequence number on a random value, it is populated with state information. Rather than allocating memory when a SYN is received, SYN cookie support allocates memory when the first ACK is received with a valid cookie as the acknowledgement serial number. Because SYN attacks do not complete the handshake, there is no memory consumption from these attacks.

Different operating systems permit different SYN attack mitigation options. Linux and BSD systems are the most configurable; they support all of the mitigation options. Mac OS X (a BSD variant) does not include SYN cookie support but can modify SYN queue sizes and timeout durations. Windows is the least flexible, only permitting modification of the queue sizes. This is done by editing the Windows Registry entry for `My Computer\HKEY_LOCAL_MACHINES\SYSTEM\CurrentControlSet\Services\Tcpip\Parameters`. DWORD fields such as `SynAttackProtect`, `TcpMaxHalfOpen`, and `TcpMaxHalfOpenRetries` can be added to control the SYN queue. Additional tips for protecting Windows systems are available from the *Registry Guide for Windows* (*http://www.winguides.com/registry/display.php/1236/*).

15.5.2 RST and FIN Attacks

In a *RST attack*, RST (or FIN) packets are sent to abnormally terminate an established connection. If an attacker can view the network traffic, then he can inject an RST packet and terminate the victim's established connection. The only requirement is for the RST packet to appear as part of the established connection.

Blind TCP reset attacks occur when the attacker cannot intercept or observe the network connection. In this attack, forged RST packets are sent with a variety of sequence and port values. Eventually one will become valid and terminate the connection.

A sequence number contains 4 bytes, so there are 4,294,967,296 potential sequence numbers for generating a reset. An attacker does not need to send 4 billion packets, however, because the TCP window supports ACKs for *any* of the bytes transmitted. If the window for acknowledgement is 1,000 bytes, then 4 million packets are needed. A window of 32,768 bytes is common, which reduces the number of packets to a realistic range of 131,072. If the initial window size is larger, then fewer packets are needed. For example, Windows XP uses an initial window size of 64,240 bytes. This reduces the number of packets needed to 66,858.

For example, TCP over IP and Ethernet yield a minimum packet size of 72 bytes. Assuming a 10 Mbps connection, 131,072 packets can be transmitted in approximately 10 seconds (Table 15.2). Similarly, 66,858 packets can be transmitted in about half the time.

TABLE 15.2   Best-Case Transmission Speeds for TCP Blind Reset Attacks

	10 Mbps Ethernet	100 Mbps Ethernet
Packet Size (bytes)	72	72
Packet Size (bits)	576	576
Ethernet Speed (bits/second)	10,000,000	100,000,000
Per Packet Transmission (seconds)	0.0000576	0.00000576
Packets in the Attack	131,072	131,072
Total Packet Transmission Time (seconds)	7.5497472	0.75497472
Ethernet uses a framed transmit window, with gaps between transmissions.		
Inter-packet Gap (seconds)	0.0000096	0.00000096
Gaps Between Packets	131,071	131,071
Total Gap Transmission Time (seconds)	1.2582816	0.12582816
Total Transmission Time (seconds)	8.8080288	0.88080288

Transmission times vary. The attacking system may not be able to generate traffic as fast as the network can transport information. Each bridge, router, and gateway adds delay. Noise at the physical layer may impact speeds, and other traffic on the same network can consume bandwidth. All of this impacts the transfer rate.

In a truly blind attack, the attacker does not know the client's ephemeral port number. Although this could be any of 65,536 values, most operating systems only use a few thousand possible ports. If 131,072 packets can be sent in 10 seconds, then 521,011,200 packets (for each of the 3,975 ephemeral ports on a RedHat Linux 7.1 system) can take 11 hours. By knowing the client's operating system, an attacker can deduce the ephemeral range and probable window size, which dramatically reduces the effort for a blind TCP reset attack.

The duration of a blind TCP reset attack usually matches the network speed. As the attack packets are generated, the actual TCP connection remains in use and the sequence range continues to increase. The range of sequence values for a successful attack is a moving target. The longer it takes to generate the attack packets, the more the target range will move.

15.5.3 ICMP Attacks

Similar to TCP reset attacks, ICMP packets can be used to specify a terminated connection. Blind ICMP attacks can also disable TCP connections. Unlike TCP reset attacks—where valid port and address combinations are always allowed to pass through—disabling ICMP at a firewall can block ICMP attacks.

15.5.4 LAND Attack

In 1997, a novel TCP attack was discovered: a single TCP packet could cripple or crash a system. In this attack, a SYN packet is sent to an open service on a known port. The reply address and port are forged to point back to the same system. For example, the SYN packet will be sent to 10.1.3.5 on port 515/tcp and appear to be from 10.1.3.5 on port 515/tcp. This results in the server sending packets to itself, which creates a feedback loop.

Called the *LAND attack*, these feedback loops impacted most LAN daemons (LAN-D). Windows 95 would quickly crash. Other systems would consume 100 percent of the available CPU or hang. In addition, some systems would only need one LAND packet, although other systems needed a few. (A large list of impacted operating systems is available at *http://www.insecure.org/sploits/land.ip.DOS.html*.)

Variations of the LAND attack were soon developed. For example, La Tierra (Spanish for "the land") sends LAND packets to multiple ports—crashing Windows NT. Other variations ranged from sending RST packets to bouncing packets between two ports on the same system. Although most of today's major operating systems are not vulnerable to LAND attacks, smaller hand-held devices and dedicated network systems are occasionally found to be susceptible.

15.6 MITIGATION OPTIONS

Although TCP is almost universally available, few vendors use the same implementation. TCP under Linux is different from TCP under BSD, HP-UX, AIX, IRIX, and Windows. Even different versions and patches can lead to implementation differences. Although a heterogeneous network in unlikely to be impacted by a single TCP attack, each server on the network likely has its own quirks. The main implementation risks come from these unique implementations and interactions with lower layer protocols. Mitigation options revolve around alternating system profiles and detecting attacks.

15.6.1 Alter System Profile

TCP and network service attacks fall under two categories: blind and directed. *Blind attacks* make no assumptions concerning the target system. A TCP port is tested for an exploit, and positive results are recorded. Most computer viruses use this approach.

Directed attacks target specific operating system platforms and network services. These come in two phases. First, reconnaissance identifies potential targets. The second phase attacks viable candidates. By changing the system profile, identification by potential attackers is mitigated. Profile options that can be changed to produce a different profile include SYN timeouts, retry counts, retry durations, initial window sizes, available TCP options, and initial sequence values.

Many TCP ports are standardized; specific ports are bound to specific services. For example, port 22/tcp is used by SSH and HTTP uses 80/tcp. An attacker who sees an open port on 80/tcp can expect to access a Web server. Although these port numbers are standard, they are not required. Running a SSH server on port 27272/tcp instead of port 22/tcp can reduce the likelihood of an attack against the SSH server.

Although moving servers to nonstandard ports can reduce the threat from a blind attack, directed attacks may use tools such as Nessus and Nmap to identify the type of service bound to an open port. In addition, moving well-known services, such as SMTP, to a nonstandard port can block communications—other mail servers will not be able to find the nonstandard mail port.

15.6.2 Block Attack Vectors

Firewalls are used to restrict network access. If a home or small office does not provide any external network services, then a firewall can block all external SYN packets. Similarly, if a DMZ only hosts a Web server, then only the Web ports (usually 80/tcp for HTTP and 445/tcp for HTTPS) should be allowed through the firewall.

As mentioned in Chapter 12, ICMP was designed to communicate network layer control messages, but it is not essential for network functionality. Blocking ICMP traffic can eliminate risks to TCP from remote ICMP flooding, hijacking, and reset attacks.

15.6.3 Identify Network Devices

Identifying network devices and known vulnerabilities can assist the development of preventative measures. If a host is known to be vulnerable to LAND attacks, then a firewall can be placed in front of the host to block LAND attacks.

Simple network devices, such as inexpensive home firewalls, hand-held phones, PDAs, and other portable devices with network support, may not implement all of TCP. Invalid usage of TCP, such as wrong checksums or an unexpected SYN flag, may be ignored or handled incorrectly.

15.6.4 Stateful Packet Inspection (SPI)

Many firewalls support *stateful packet inspection* (SPI). SPI tracks the state of TCP connections and rejects packets that do not match the known state. For example, a RST sent to a closed port can be silently dropped rather than delivered to the host. Similarly, out-of-sequence packets can be discarded before reaching the receiving host. SPI can reduce the impact from unsuccessful hijacking attempts, reset attacks, and remote system profiling.

15.6.5 Intrusion Detection System (IDS)

IDSs monitor the network for nonstandard or unexpected packets. An IDS can quickly identify remote system profiling, TCP port scans, hijack attempts, and DoS attacks. Snort (*http://www.snort.org/*) is one example of an open source IDS; many commercial IDS products are also available.

Although IDSs can detect an attack, these systems are also known to generate a large number of false-positive results. The output can overwhelm most administrators, and tuning is usually nontrivial. In addition, administrators who solely rely on IDS reports may miss network attacks. An attacker may intentionally trigger an avalanche of IDS alerts to draw an administrator's attention away from a subtle network attack. Even if the true attack is identified by the IDS, the report will be buried by more obvious simultaneous attacks.

15.6.6 Intrusion Prevention System (IPS)

IPSs extend the IDS approach from logging to action. Whereas IDSs record attacks, IPSs actively disable attack vectors and take corrective action. If an IPS identifies a port scan, it readily blocks the remainder of the scan and limits the scan's effectiveness.

15.6.7 Higher-Layer Protocols

TCP provides no authentication for information from lower-layer protocols. ARP and network-based attacks can significantly impact TCP. Although sequence numbers and ephemeral port selection can reduce the impact from replay attacks, the TCP headers can be modified before insertion. In general, it is assumed that higher-layer protocols will authenticate traffic and detect potential attacks.

15.7 UDP

TCP provides a connection-oriented service that guarantees packet delivery and order of delivery; however, the overhead from guaranteed delivery is not always essential. Some higher-layer protocols, such as H.323 (used by VoIP and NetMeeting; *http://www.openh323.org/*), manage message ordering and retries. In other cases, network connectivity is direct and reliable, so dropped packets and resequencing are not significant risks. And some protocols, such as DNS, use short information transfers, so elaborate connection validation ends up generating more network traffic than the actual application's request and reply. As a result, full connectivity at the transport layer is not always essential. The *User Datagram Protocol* (UDP) is a simplified transport protocol commonly used for connection-less services [RFC768].

Because many of the TCP functions are not needed (e.g., sequence numbers and flow control), UDP packets have a simplified header. The header only includes a source port, destination port, data length, and checksum. Whereas a TCP header adds a minimum of 20 bytes to each packet, UDP only adds 8 bytes. In addition, UDP transmissions do not generate acknowledgements.

Although UDP requires significantly less network bandwidth than TCP, it is more prone to attack. UDP attacks are usually based on unvalidated packets and impersonation.

15.7.1 Unvalidated Inbound Sources

In TCP, each client is authenticated with the server through the use of a three-way handshake. Completion of the handshake implies a valid network host. In contrast, UDP servers perform no initial handshake. Any host can connect to a UDP server, and the connection is not authenticated.

With TCP, the server faces flooding from SYN packets but usually not from ACK or RST packets. In contrast, any type of UDP packet can potentially flood a server. Servers buffer a finite number of UDP packets. Under Linux, the command `sysctl net.unix.max_dgram_qlen` shows the default number of queued UDP packets (usually set to 10). If more UDP packets are received, then the additional packets are dropped until the buffer is emptied. UDP packets can quickly overwhelm slow UDP services. For example, a slow computer receiving streaming audio may drop UDP packets, resulting in clipped audio.

15.7.2 UDP Hijacking

UDP servers receive packets from any hosts without authentication. As a result, any client can send a packet to any UDP server. Management of any session or connection must be handled by higher-layer protocols. Unfortunately, this means that UDP is very vulnerable to hijacking. An attacker can easily forge the correct network addresses and UDP ports to insert data into the recipient. A blind UDP attack only needs to guess the ephemeral port number—no more than 65,536 guesses and usually only takes a few seconds. In contrast, a blind TCP attack can require hundreds of thousands of packets and takes minutes to guess the port and sequence numbers.

15.7.3 UDP Keep-Alive Attack

TCP has clear designations for opening and closing a session. A SYN initiates a connection, whereas a FIN closes the connection. Firewalls and proxies can dynamically open and close connections as needed.

In contrast to TCP, UDP has no clear indicators for open or closed connections. As a result, most firewalls open UDP ports when the first outbound connection is seen but do not close the port until after a period of inactivity. Attackers can use this weakness to hold open UDP ports. Even if the client is no longer listening to the packets, an attacker can send UDP packets into the firewall to keep the firewall's port open. If enough ports are kept open, then no new ports can be opened. This effectively disables UDP through the firewall.

15.7.4 UDP Smurf Attack

ICMP Smurf attackers are detailed in Chapter 12. This attack uses forged return addresses to flood a remote network (or host) with packets. UDP is also prone to this attack. In a UDP Smurf Attack, a forged packet is sent to a UDP server. The attacker forges the victim's network address as the packer sender. The server responds by sending one or more UDP packets to the victim. Although a few UDP packets will not significantly impact a network, thousands per second can cripple a network.

15.7.5 UDP Reconnaissance

Unlike TCP, UDP offers few options for system profiling and reconnaissance. Because UDP has no window size, sequence number, or header options, these cannot be used to profile the system.

UDP port scans rely on ICMP and packet replies. If no UDP service exists on a scanned port, then an ICMP "Destination unreachable" packet is returned. In contrast, some UDP services return replies to failed connection. Any UDP reply indicates an existing service. No reply indicates a service that received the packet and did not reply. The only way to defeat this type of port scan is to not return any ICMP packets. This makes no reply indistinguishable from no service.

SUMMARY

TCP is the single most widely used transport protocol. Nearly all network-enabled devices and systems support it. Together with UDP, these protocols account for more than 98 percent of all Internet traffic. Yet, neither protocol provides options for authentication or privacy. Both protocols can be used to profile systems, although TCP profiling is usually more informative. Hijacking and insertion attacks pose direct risks from attackers that reside along the path between systems, and blind attacks are realistic threats. In addition, both protocols offer many vectors for DoS attacks.

The primary mitigation options depend on altering system profiles, filtering undesirable traffic, and using IDS or IPS tools to detect and deter attacks.

REVIEW QUESTIONS

1. What is the difference between TCP and TCP/IP?
2. How does TCP increment sequence numbers?
3. What is the TCP three-way handshake?
4. List the types of TCP information that can be used to profile an operating system.
5. If a client's connection to a server is hijacked, what happens to the client's connection?
6. Can a successful LAND attack hijack a connection?
7. List five ways to mitigate threats from TCP attacks.
8. What is one technique that can reduce attack vectors from IP, TCP, and UDP?

DISCUSSION TOPICS

1. Collect a set of network devices, such as home firewalls, network-enabled phones, PDAs, palmtops, and music players. Use nmap to scan for open network services, and ethereal (or similar analysis tool) to evaluate TCP packets. Do the devices have unique TCP profiles? How do the devices respond to invalid TCP checksums or LAND attacks?
2. Why are there few alternatives to TCP and UDP, and none that are widely adopted?
3. Besides changing TCP configuration parameters on a host, what are some ways to obscure a system profile? Can a router that supports NAT (Chapter 12) hide the system profile?

ADDITIONAL RESOURCES

TCP is defined by many different RFCs. Some describe usage, and others discuss risks and mitigation options:

- *RFC793: Transmission Control Protocol*
- *RFC1122: Requirements for Internet Hosts—Communication Layers*
- *RFC1323: TCP Extensions for High Performance*
- *RFC1337: TIME-WAIT Assassination Hazards in TCP*
- *RFC1644: T/TCP—TCP Extensions for Transactions Functional Specification*
- *RFC1750: Randomness Recommendations for Security*
- *RFC2018: TCP Selective Acknowledgment Options*
- *RFC2581: TCP Congestion Control*
- *RFC3168: The Addition of Explicit Congestion Notification (ECN) to IP*

Many documents discuss risks and exploits that impact TCP. Some excellent sources include the following:

- Andrews, Jeremy, "Understanding TCP Reset Attacks." May 10, 2004. Available online at *http://kerneltrap.org/node/3072*.
- Watson, Paul, "Slipping in the Window: TCP Reset attacks." December 2003. Available online at *http://www.osvdb.org/reference/SlippingInTheWindow_v1.0.doc*.
- Gont, F., "ICMP A ttacks against TCP. RFC Internet-Draft," The Internet Society, September 2004. Available online at *http://www.gont.com.ar/drafts/icmp-attacks-against-tcp.html*.

■ Gont, F., "TCP's Reaction to Soft Errors. RFC Internet-Draft," The Internet Society, October 2004. Available online at *http://www.gont.com.ar/drafts/tcp-soft-errors.html*.

Part VI

OSI Layer 5

Layer 5 of the ISO OSI model is the *session layer*. This layer manages long-term dialogs between two networked systems. The session layer manages the lower networking layers, ensuring that higher-layer protocols have network resources available as needed. Few network applications employ all of the session layer features. Instead, specific session-layer functions are used by the few session-layer protocols. The Domain Name System (DNS) is the most widely used session layer protocol and historically the most insecure.

16 | Session Layer

In This Chapter

- Session Example: WAP
- Session State Machine
- Sessions and Stacks
- Common Risks

The *session layer* is designed to manage long-term dialogs, called *sessions*, between a session user and a session provider. These high-level connections may last much longer than any of the lower-layer transport, network, or data link connections. The session layer ensures that OSI lower-layer resources are available when higher-layer protocols (OSI presentation and application layers) require them. This requires maintaining the state for the network connection and the capability to recover from any failed state.

Using the session layer, a user may log in to a remote system, disconnect the network, change ISPs, gain a new IP address, *and* then continue the login session—as though nothing ever happened. Behind the scenes, the session layer reconnects to the remote host using the new transport, network, data link, and physical layers; (in theory) the reconnection does not disrupt the session's connection. This type of complex activity is viable as long as the session does not terminate or expire. The session layer provides the foundation for mobile computing.

16.1 SESSION EXAMPLE: WAP

Cell phones support roaming. A person can make a telephone call and travel miles without dropping the call. The technology behind this is a form of the session layer. The cell phone and cell sites ensure that *a* connection is available. The details concerning *which* connection is in use remains hidden from the caller. A session layer manages the phone call's session.

Similarly protocols, such as the Wireless Application Protocol (WAP), support mobile computing. Developed in 1997, WAP is slowly becoming adopted for wireless computers. WAP allows wireless computers to change wireless access points (AP) without dropping connections.

Contrary to the naming, the "Application" in Wireless *Application* Protocol does not refer to the OSI application layer. Instead, WAP consists of a suite of protocols based on the OSI model (Table 16.1). The lowest WAP layer is the transport layer. This corresponds with the Wireless Datagram Protocol (WDP)—similar to the UDP protocol.

Unlike the OSI model, the WAP stack splits the session layers into specific functions. The WAP security layer uses the Wireless Transport Layer Security protocol (WTLS) to provide end-to-end authentication and encryption. The transaction layer's Wireless Transaction Protocol (WTP) provides different types of data transactions (lossy connection-less, loss-less connection-less, and connection-oriented) and manages any message duplication. Finally, the Wireless Session Protocol (WSP) offers support for session-oriented mobility.

The final WAP layer is the application layer that corresponds with the OSI application layer. The Wireless Application Environment (WAE) is primarily aimed toward Web-enabled services on wireless devices. It provides privacy and internationalized language support for data connections.

TABLE 16.1 OSI and WAP Layers and Protocols

OSI Layer	WAP Layer	Protocol
Application	Application	Wireless Application Environment (WAE)
Session	Session	Wireless Session Protocol (WSP)
Session	Transaction	Wireless Transaction Protocol (WTP)
Session	Security	Wireless Transaction Security Protocol (WTSP)
Transport	Transport	Wireless Datagram Protocol (WDP)

The full specification for WAP, and all of the associated protocols, is available from the Open Mobile Alliance (OMA) at *http://www.openmobilealliance.org/*.

16.2 SESSION STATE MACHINE

The OSI session layer is primarily defined by two standards: ISO 8326 (ITU X.215) and ISO 8327 (ITU X.225). These standards define a complex finite state machine for managing connections, communications, control, quality of service, and other session attributes.

Each state within the session layer corresponds with a functional primitive. These well-defined *primitives* determine the available functionality. Adding to the complexity of the finite state machine, primitives are commonly referenced by cryptic abbreviations defined in ISO 8326 and 8327. For example, "SUABind" is a Session User ABort indicator, and "SRELcnf+" is a Service RELease positive confirmation. Table 16.2 lists the state names for providers (services), and Table 16.3 lists the states for users (clients). The specifications for the session layer not only include the state names and functionality, but they also detail the acceptable transformations between states.

Although all OSI layers define specific functionality, the session layer provides detailed requirements for implementation. These details are much more defined for the session layer than any other layer. This makes the session layer's implementation much stricter than other OSI layers.

TABLE 16.2   Provider States

State	Name	State	Name
SACTDind	Activity-discard indication	SACTDcnf	Activity-discard confirm
SACTEind	Activity-end indication	SACTEcnf	Activity-end confirm
SACTIind	Activity-interrupt indication	SACTIcnf	Activity-interrupt confirm
SACTRind	Activity-resume indication	SACTSind	Activity-start indication
SCDind	Capability-data indication	SCDcnf	Capability-data confirm
SCGind	Control-give indication	SCONind	Connect indication
SCONcnf+	Connect/accept confirm	SCONcnf-	Connect/reject confirm
SDTind	Data indication	SEXind	Expedited-data indication
SGTind	Token-give indication	SPABind	Provider abort indication
SPERind	Provider exception-report indication	SPTind	Token-please indication
SRELind	Release indication	SRELcnf+	Release/accept confirm
SRELcnf-	Release/reject confirm	SRSYNind	Resynchronize indication

$\rightarrow$

State	Name	State	Name
SRSYNcnf	Resynchronize confirm	SSYNMind	Sync-major indication
SSYNMcnf	Sync-major confirm	SSYNmind	Sync-minor indication
SSYNmdind	Sync-minor indication	SSYNmcnf	Sync-minor confirm
STDind	Typed-data indication	SUABind	User abort indication
SUERind	User exception-report indication	STA 01	Idle state
STA 02A	Wait for connect confirm	STA 03	Wait for release confirm
STA 04A	Wait for sync-major confirm	STA 04B	Wait for activity-end confirm
STA 05A	Wait for resynchronize confirm	STA 05B	Wait for activity-interrupt confirm
STA 05C	Wait for activity-discard confirm	STA 08	Wait for connect confirm response
STA 09	Wait for release response	STA 10A	Wait for sync-major response
STA 10B	Wait for activity-end response	STA 11A	Wait for resynchronize response
STA 11B	Wait for activity-interrupt response	STA 11C	Wait for activity-discard response
STA 19	Wait for a recovery indication	STA 20	Wait for a recovery request
STA 21	Wait for capability-data confirm	STA 22	Wait for capability data response
STA 713	Data transfer state		

TABLE 16.3 User States

State	Name	State	Name
SACTDreq	Activity-discard request	SACTDrsp	Activity-discard response
SACTEreq	Activity-end request	SACTErsp	Activity-end response
SACTIreq	Activity-interrupt request	SACTIrsp	Activity-interrupt response
SACTRreq	Activity-resume request	SACTSreq	Activity-start request
SCDreq	Capability-data request	SCDrsp	Capability-data response

$\rightarrow$

State	Name	State	Name
SCGreq	Control-give request	SCONreq	Connect request
SCONrsp+	Connect/accept response	SCONrsp-	Connect/reject response
SDTreq	Data request	SEXreq	Expedited-data request
SGTreq	Token-give request	SPTreq	Token-please request
SRELreq	Release request	SRELrsp+	Release/accept response
SRELrsp-	Release/reject response	SRSYNreq(a)	Resynchronize/abandon request
SRSYNreq(r)	Resynchronize/restart request	SRSYNreq(s)	Resynchronize/set request
SRSYNrsp	Resynchronize response	SSYNMreq	Sync-major request
SSYNMrsp	Sync-major response	SSYNmreq	Sync-minor request
SSYNmdreq	Sync-minor request	SSYNmrsp	Sync-minor response
STDreq	Typed-data request	SUABreq	User abort request
SUERreq	User exception-report request		

Not every session layer protocol implements every state associated with the session layer. Rather, only states used by a protocol are required. For example, DNS (Chapter 17) uses very short-duration sessions, so major and minor synchronization requests are not needed.

16.2.1 Connection States

The OSI session layer defines three basic connection states: connect, release, and abort.

Connect: A new session layer connection is established. A single session layer may control multiple session.

Release: This terminates an established session.

Abort: At any time, the finite state machine may enter an invalid state. An abort message abruptly terminates an established session.

Each established session is assigned a unique identifier. When the session layer receives data from the transport layer, it checks the current state associated with the identifier against the received state transformation. If the transformation is permitted, then the session's state changes and an action is performed. If the transformation is forbidden, either by the state machine or due to invalid parameters, then the session is aborted.

16.2.2 Session Network Usage

A single session layer connection may span multiple transport layer (and lower layer) connections. Sessions may change transport protocols, network addresses, or routes without interfering with the session.

Sequential Network Connections: Each session may choose to end (*drop*) a transport layer connection at any time. As long as a new connection is established within the timeframe required by the session layer, lower layers may dynamically connect and disconnect as needed. Dropping network connections can be desirable when maintaining connections for idle sessions consumes network resources. For example, a telephone modem-based physical layer may be dropped when the network is not in use. This reduces calling charges. In addition, different routes may become desirable at different times of the day. Dropping and re-establishing connections may permit lower layers to optimize routing performance.

Parallel Network Connections: Depending on the lower-layer protocols, parallel connections may provide faster performance than a single network connection. The session layer definition permits a single session to be multiplexed across many network connections.

Although a single session may use sequential or parallel network connections, the session layer definition explicitly forbids a single network connection from multiplexing multiple sessions. Each transport layer connection must be associated with a single session. This restriction simplifies session management by specifying one session identifier per network connection.

Ironically, the "single session per network connection" restriction becomes moot when using a VPN. The tunnel through other protocols may use a single transport layer to transfer data from multiple sessions.

16.2.3 Communication States

After establishing a session between two hosts, data may be transferred and states may be modified. Any data transfer or state change can be accepted or rejected. To prevent a total transaction loss, the session layer provides two levels of synchronization: major and minor (Figure 16.1).

Session Data

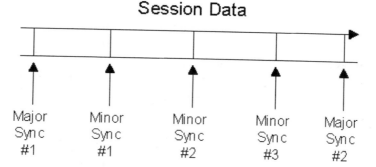

FIGURE 16.1   Major and minor synchronization points within an established session dialog.

Major Synchronization: Major synchronization permits confirmation of large session transactions within a single dialog. All transactions within the major synchronization are independent of transactions before and after the synchronization point. Each major point must be explicitly confirmed.

Minor Synchronization: Minor synchronization permits confirmation of action subsets within a major synchronization block. The scope of each major synchronization point may contain many minor points. Minor points do not need to be explicitly confirmed; confirming the major synchronization confirms all minor points within the larger scope.

Resynchronization: The session layer may issue a resynchronization request. This causes the state to roll back to the previous major or minor synchronization point. Resynchronization permits a session to abandon or restart a dialog segment. But, resynchronizations cannot be used to undo already confirmed synchronization points.

16.2.4 Flow Control Functionality

The session layer provides two different methods for controlling data flow. The first method focuses on data transfers and processing rates. The second approach manages bidirectional communications.

The session layer defines two types of data transfer: normal and expedited. An expedited data transfer permits user data or state management to bypass normal routing. Expedited data sent after normal data may be processed first. For example, consider a dialog that is confirmed through a major synchronization point. Normally there is no means to undo the confirmation after it is requested. However, an expedited transfer can be used to send a resynchronize before the confirmation. Similarly, a confirmation can be expedited to bypass a resynchronization request.

In both of these situations, the ability to bypass a normal request becomes a race condition against processing time and network speed.

Each of the lower layers of the network stack provides full-duplex and half-duplex support. A data link layer may be half-duplex although the network layer may use full-duplex. Similarly, the session layer may operate as full- or half-duplex. In full-duplex mode, both state machines may communicate at the same time. The user state may change independently of the service state.

In half-duplex mode, the user and service states operate together in lock step. One side (e.g., user) may transmit, and the other side (e.g., service) listens. The communication management is provided through a token system; only the side with the token can transmit. Normally the token is passed through a "give token" request (SGTind). To prevent one side from dominating the connection, the session layer provides support for bidirectional control requests. The listening side may transmit a "please token" request (SPTind), indicating the desire to transmit.

16.2.5 Quality-of-Service Functionality

The session layer includes many functional primitives for providing a desirable quality-of-service level. These include timing delays, flow control, and message priority.

Timing Delays: The session layer predefines a variety of delay options including permitted connection, reconnection, transit, and release settings. As long as these delays are longer than the inherent delays from the lower OSI protocols, the session layer cloaks all potential timeouts from the higher OSI protocols.

Throughput: The session layer provides a facility for flow control by regulating network throughput. Although the transport and lower OSI protocols may regulate their own throughput, the settings are not maintained between connections. For example, two different TCP connections—even to the same IP address—initially begin with the same throughput. Both connections must regulate throughput independently. In contrast, the session layer can ensure that all connections associated with an established session are regulated similarly.

Priority: Different transport layer connections may be assigned different priority levels. This can lead to optimal data transfers.

Timer: In addition to issuing synchronization and resynchronization requests for controlling state acknowledgements, ISO 8327 also defines a timer. The timer can be set to ensure that a confirmation occurs within a specified timeframe. If the timer expires, then it can generate an exception or disconnect, depending on the state.

16.2.6 Session Layer Functionality

The lower OSI layers provide basic functionality for establishing a reliable network connection. The session layer extends these concepts across multiple network connections. It is capable of providing flow control and full-duplex/half-duplex support regardless of the lower-layer capabilities. In addition, the session layer can recover from a terminated connection before needing to report the disconnection to the user-level application.

Unfortunately, this high degree of flexibility does not come easily. With all the required functionality and complexity, few session layer protocols implement the entire specified standard. The session layer's role is frequently trivialized as a system for managing sessions and flow control. In addition, most session layer protocols perform similar niche operations: hostname lookups, database transactions, or remote procedure calls.

16.3 SESSIONS AND STACKS

The session layer is uniquely associated with the ISO OSI network stack. This complex functionality was explicitly assigned to a single layer because many protocols could leverage this functionality.

16.3.1 Sessions and TCP/IP

The DoD TCP/IP stack predates the OSI model and does not separate out session-oriented functionality. Every network application based on the TCP/IP stack must manage sessions independently, and few applications manage sessions the same way. For example, Web sites use a variety of methods for maintaining sessions, including the following:

Cookies: Cookies are strings generates by a Web server and passed to a browser. The browser then returns the cookie with each subsequent Web request. If the server sees the same cookie, then it knows it is the same session.

Basic Authentication: Web pages can employ simple authentication schemes, such as Basic Authentication, where a username and password is transmitted with each request.

Cookies and Basic Authentication are two different session-management approaches. Users may restart their computers or change IP addresses and still reconnect to a Web server using the same session (not needing to log in again). Other session-management systems include Digest Authentication, Microsoft's Integrated Windows Authentication, and certificate mapping. Each of these session-management systems is only used by Web-based applications. Other applications do not rely on the same cookies or session-management systems and do not reuse session information.

It can be argued that Microsoft's Integrated Windows Authentication supports session reuse. This system uses Windows domain information for providing authentication credentials. Logging into the domain permits reusing login information for Web connections. But, authenticating a Web login first may not authenticate other applications for using the same session, and changing IP addresses invalidates the session.

Different Web-based session-management systems exist because most Web browsers (and servers) were developed using the TCP/IP stack. This stack does not define session-oriented functionality, so each system needed to define it independently. In other cases, the complexity of the session layer was not worth the effort to implement it completely. In either case, independent implementations result in critical issues:

Complexity: Each application must define and manage its own session information. This increases the complexity of the applications and results in more opportunities for exploitation.

Vulnerability: If there is an implementational vulnerability in a lower-level protocol, such as IP or UDP, then a single patch fixes the problem. All applications that use the impacted protocol inherit the repair. In contrast, few applications share session layer implementations. A flaw within the session layer impacts each application independently. Fixes cannot be applied through a common library. For example, Netscape, Mozilla, and Firefox are all Web browsers that stem from the same source code base. If a flaw is discovered in cookie management, each browser must be patched independently because they all operate separately. In contrast, if they used a common session-management library, then one patch would cure all.

A vulnerability due to independence can be a strength instead of a weakness. The threat may not exist in an unrelated implementation. This reduces the profile of the vulnerability, which leads to security through diversity.

16.3.2 Sessions and OSI

In contrast to the TCP/IP stack, the OSI model's session layer permits consistency and reuse between different network services. Examples of shared session-layer protocols include name services, remote procedure calls, remote file systems, and authentications systems.

Layer Ordering

The TCP/IP stack permits sessions to be managed anywhere within the application layer. Periodically, the question arises as to the ordering of the OSI layers that correspond with the TCP/IP application layer. In particular, why is the session layer located below the presentation layer? The answer is due to core functionality.

The session layer is content independent. A higher layer creates the data and the session layer wraps the data within a session. In contrast, the OSI application layer generates data and the presentation layer transforms the data. All OSI layers below the presentation layer do not focus on data content.

Additionally, the session layer manages multiple network connections. All network activities below the session layer may occur many times during a single session. Because the presentation layer may negotiate functionality (e.g., compression, encryption, or transformation), this high-level negotiation would need to be repeated each time the session layer initiates a new network connection.

16.3.2.1 Name Services

Few people memorize IP addresses. Instead, text-based hostnames are associated with network addresses. This allows hosts to be easily remembered. Because IP uses IP addresses and not hostnames, a system must exist to map hostnames to IP addresses (and vice versa). The simplest approach uses a flat file, such as `/etc/hosts`. This file contains a list IP addresses and their hostname aliases.

Host files are simple to maintain but are not easily distributed across a network. Changes to one host file must be pushed to all systems on the network. Complexities arise when a system is offline during the push, or a new host is brought online. Instead, network-based naming services are used for large networks. Common naming services include the Domain Name System (DNS—detailed in Chapter 17), Lightweight Directory Access Protocol (LDAP), and NetBIOS-NS. Each of these systems provides facilities to convert between hostnames and network addresses.

Common library functions, such as `gethostbyname()` and `gethostbyaddr()`, permit many applications to use the same session layer protocol for name lookups. Any vulnerability in a DNS or LDAP function can be patched at a single location and immediately mitigates the threat to any program that shares the protocol library.

16.3.2.2 Remote Procedure Calls

A *remote procedure call* (RPC) is a way to use a networked host as an extension of the local system. Procedures and functions are executed on remote hosts rather than locally. For example, programs that perform protein modeling are very resource intensive. Programs such as NAMD (*http://www.ks.uiuc.edu/Research/namd*) are computationally expensive and require large amounts of RAM. To improve processing time, RPCs are used to distribute the workload across many computers. Computations that may take hundreds of days on a single computer are completed in a fraction of that time using a distributed network. RPCs permits an application to offload work to a remote host, and then receive the results later.

Many different RPC implementations exist. Examples include Sun RPC [RFC1050], Secure RPC [RFC1057], Open Network Computing (ONC) RPC [RFC1831], the Open Software Foundation's Distributed Computing Environment (OSF DCE RPC), and Kerberos RPC. Each of these protocols permits applications to define and use remote functionality. The RPC protocols define the means to connect to the remote function and transfer function parameters (including complex data structures). In addition, many printing protocols, such as LPR [RFC1179] and Microsoft's SMB printing service, are also considered types of RPCs.

16.3.2.3 Remote File Systems

Although RPC permits using remote functions, other protocols permit using remote disk space. A remote server can *share* a file, directory, or partition to hosts on the network. This establishes an accessible remote file system. The remote file system can then be *mounted* by a networked host and accessed. Beyond any detectable network delays, the session layer ensures that the remote file system appears transparent to the local user. Remote file systems have many uses:

Limited Disk Space: Remote file systems permit storing data when the local system has limited disk space.

Collaboration Space: In work environments, data is commonly shared between groups or departments. Remote file systems permit many users to share access to common data.

Random Access: Not everyone (nor every application) needs all data in a common directory. Rather than attempting to identify the needed files, remote file systems permit listing files and transferring their contents on an as-needed basis.

Session layer protocols that provide support for remote file systems include the Network File System (NFS) [RFC3010], Cryptographic File System (CFS) [Blaze1995], and Server Message Block (SMB)—also known as Microsoft's Network Neighborhood.

16.3.2.4 Authentication Systems

The session layer is ideal for user authentication. Each established session indicates authenticated communication. The session layer can also be used to encrypt data and provide session-based privacy.

For example, Remote Authentication Dial In User Service (RADIUS) authenticates dynamic physical layer connections (e.g., dialup modem). As each modem connects, the RADIUS server authenticates the connection. Credentials such as username and password, CHAP, and one-time passwords (OTP) are commonly supported authentication methods. The authentication establishes a session. Lower OSI layer attackers must identify the session and state to successfully compromise the security. With the addition of an encrypted session, the threat of eavesdropping, hijacking, or insertion attacks from the lower layers is effectively mitigated.

Other session layer authentication systems include Kerberos (detailed in Chapter 4) and DCE. Both of these systems use cryptographic-based services to provide authentication tickets for service access. Each *ticket* corresponds to an authenticated session. Each session layer service is associated with a different type of ticket; a remote host cannot access a session service without providing an appropriate ticket. An initial session is used to determine the access to ticket generation. For example, can a user generate any kind of ticket or only specific services? One authenticated user may be permitted access to a remote printer, whereas another user may access a remote file system or RPC service.

Who Let the Dogs Out?

Most network protocols and applications are named after their functionality or purpose. The Transport Control Protocol (TCP) provides transport layer support, nmap performs *network map*ping, and DNS provides a domain naming service. Kerberos is one of the few systems that does not follow this convention.

Kerberos is named after a beast from Greek mythology. Cerberus (alternately spelled Serberus or Kerberos) guards the entrance to Hades, the Underworld. Depicted as a three-headed dog with a dragon's tail, Cerberus allows only the dead to enter Hades and forbids them from leaving.

Cerberus represents an ideal security system: desirable elements can enter, undesirable are filtered. But like most security systems, nothing is perfect. A few mortals did manage to pass Cerberus and enter Hades. Orpheus played music that put the guardian to sleep, Hercules wrestled Cerberus and carried him to the surface, and Psyche pacified Cerberus by feeding him cake (bread covered with honey). Many ancient Greeks were buried with gold and cake to assist them on their passage through Hades. The expression "a sop to Cerberus" refers to anything given to pacify or bribe a troublemaker.

Fortunately, Kerberos has not lived up to its namesake. Cracking the security in Kerberos is not a "piece of cake."

16.4 COMMON RISKS

Between functionality that is not explicitly mentioned in the TCP/IP model and its complex OSI definition, session layer protocols are relatively rare and usually insecure. The most notable exceptions are DNS and Kerberos. DNS is nearly universal in its support, but it is historically insecure. In contrast, Kerberos is very secure but relatively uncommon. The most common risks that face session layer protocols include authentication and authorization, hijacking, MitM attacks, and information leakage.

16.4.1 Authentication and Authorization

Session layer protocols maintain state through a session identifier. Ideally, the identifier should be provided after authenticating the user. Unfortunately, few protocols use strong authentication methods:

DNS: In general, there is no authentication. Any host may query data from a DNS server. A few DNS implementations rely on network addresses for authentication; however, as shown in Part IV, network addresses can be forged or hijacked. Although authentication based on network address is better than no authentication, it is not strong authentication.

NFS: NFS uses an export file (/etc/exports) to specify the remotely accessible directories. This file also lists the remote hosts that may access the exported directories. As with DNS, authentication is based on network addressing; however, NFS also supports restrictions based on hostnames.

SMB: The Microsoft Network Neighborhood permits drives, directories, and system services to be remotely accessible. Early versions of SMB, such as the implementation found under Windows 95, Windows 98, and SAMBA, use plaintext passwords for authentication. This opened the system to risks from network sniffing. Later versions of Windows, such as Windows 2000 and XP, support encrypted passwords. Although encryption is more secure, the system remains vulnerable to brute-force guessing and guest accounts that require no passwords.

16.4.2 Session Hijacking

Session layer protocols maintain state through a session identifier, and the identifiers are usually valid for an extended period. If the session identifier is not encoded, then an attacker may acquire the session identifier and hijack the session. This is a common style of network attack.

Web cookies readily lend themselves to session hijacking. Many computer viruses, such as Sasser and Berbew, harvest Web cookies from infected hosts. These cookies store active session information, allowing an attacker to effectively hijack a session. For example, some variants of Agobot looked for Web cookies associated with Bank of America and sent them to a remote system managed by the attacker. Using the stolen cookie, the attacker could access the Bank of America account without needing login credentials.

To mitigate attacks from stolen sessions, cookies should be disabled or removed when the browser closes. Cookies may also be cryptographically linked to a specific network address. Because network addresses are difficult to forge outside of the local network, hijacking becomes much more difficult. In addition, Web servers configure Web cookies with specific lifetimes; after expiration, the cookie is no longer valid. These servers can protect their customers by assigning cookies with short lifetimes. Unless the cookie is stolen and used immediately, the expired session has little value to an attacker.

Kerberos uses many of these mitigation steps. Each ticket has a limited duration. Before the ticket expires, the client "renews" the ticket by requesting a new session identifier. Kerberos tickets are associated with client-specific information (client certificate, session key, etc.) and are cryptographically protected. Assuming an attacker can get past the encryption and impersonate the client, the limited session duration restricts the window of opportunity for a viable exploit.

16.4.3 Blind Session Attacks

The length of the session identifier is protocol specific. For example, DNS and SMB use 16-bit identifiers. If the session uses a connection-less transport service, then it is vulnerable to a blind session attack.

In a *blind session attack*, the attacker cannot actually see the established session traffic. Instead, the attacker sends a series of session requests—each with a different identifier. For short session identifiers that are used over long durations, an attacker can try every possible combination in a few seconds. The simplest attacks send a session reset, effectively disconnecting an established connection.

As an example, the 16-bit identifier used by SMB yields 65,536 combinations and may be used over long durations. SMB supports both UDP (connection-less) and TCP (connection-oriented) transport layer protocols. When using TCP, a blind attacker must guess the TCP sequence number (that changes rapidly) and the session identifier. This becomes a very difficult attack. For connection-less transport services, however, the attacker only needs to guess session identifier.

In contrast to SMB, DNS is not as vulnerable to blind session attacks. This is because DNS does not maintain long-duration sessions over connection-less transport protocols.

16.4.4 Man-in-the-Middle (MitM)

Session layer protocols are potentially vulnerable to MitM attacks. The attacks may come from the session layer or lower. For session layer MitM attacks, the attacker must intercept the network request prior authenticating with the server. The MitM then independently authenticates with both the client and true server, and relays requests between the client and server.

Lower OSI layer MitM attacks are more difficult to identify and prevent. All of the exploits from protocols such as IP, TCP, and IEEE 802 can be used to intercept network traffic and observe session layer information.

The most direct method to defeat MitM attacks requires preshared keys between the client and server. The authentication at any layer will block a MitM at that layer or lower. For example, if IPsec is used, then a network layer MitM is blocked and a data link layer MitM only sees encrypted data. Unfortunately, preshared keys are not always available, and an attacker may intercept requests to a trusted third party, such as a certificate authority. In cases where the session is established between two unauthenticated hosts, a MitM is always possible.

In general, session-based services should be filtered at the firewall. This prevents unauthenticated traffic from being established at the session layer. Protocols such as RPC, NFS, SMB, LDAP, and LPR should not be externally available.

16.4.5 Information Leakage and Privacy

Although the session layer standards define session and state maintenance, they do not specify authentication or privacy support. In most cases, session layer protocols use weak authentication and no encryption. Any attacker along the route from the client to the server can sniff network traffic and view the entire session. For example, DNS, NFS, and (older) SMB perform no data encryption. An attacker who sniffs network traffic can readily observe the entire session.

Privacy is generally expected to come from higher OSI layers (presentation or application). For the session layer, some protocols do provide encryption support. Secure NFS is an extension of NFS that uses DES encryption, and later versions of SMB encrypt session content. Many RPC implementations use some variation of Kerberos for strong authentication and encryption. The most common session layer protocol, DNS, offers no widely accepted cryptographic solution.

SUMMARY

The sheer complexity of the session layer suggests ample opportunity for exploitation. Attackers may target session identifiers, content, or authentication. Although there are some secure session protocols, these are not widely used. Instead, individual session layer implementations that offer weak (or no) security options are the norm.

REVIEW QUESTIONS

1. What is WAP?
2. Define major and minor synchronization points.
3. Which of the following is not a session layer protocol: LDAP, Kerberos, FTP, or NFS?
4. List four common session layer risks.

DISCUSSION TOPICS

1. The session layer is defined by a complex system for managing states. What are the minimum states required for session management? What are the tradeoffs with regards to functionality and security?
2. The TCP/IP stack does not separate out the session layer from the application layer. Describe the tradeoffs and impacts from developing with the TCP/IP stack instead of the OSI stack.
3. Assume a network uses a secure session layer protocol that provides strong authentication and encryption. What are the security impacts from lower layer vulnerabilities?
4. Chapter 13 discusses anonymity and the OSI network layer. How does the session layer impact network anonymity? Can there be an anonymous session?

ADDITIONAL RESOURCES

The specifications for the session layer, ISO 8326 (ITU X.215) and ISO 8327 (ITU X.225), are not the easiest documents to understand. Fausto Caneschi published a summary of the protocols for the ACM:

Caneschi, F., "Hints for the Interpretation of the ISO Session Layer." *ACM SIGCOMM Computer Communication Review*, Vol. 14, Issue 4 July/Aug 1986, pp. 34-72.

RADIUS is a common authentication protocol for the session layer. It is defined by a series of RFCs, including RFC2548, 2809, 2865 2866, 2867, 2868, 2869, 2882, and 3162.

17 DNS

In This Chapter

- Common Uses
- DNS Protocol
- Distributed Architecture
- Direct Risks
- Technical Risks
- Social Risks
- Reconnaissance and Exploitation
- Mitigation Options

In the early days of the Internet, hosts were referenced by IP addresses. Although this was functional, it was inconvenient—few people could memorize many different IP addresses. The simple resolution was to use meaningful strings (hostnames) instead of IP addresses [RFC226]. By 1983, lists of hosts and their IP addresses were available for download [RFC881, RFC921, RFC952]. These lists mapped hostnames to IP addresses and vice versa.

During this time, another need developed. Email [RFC524] was becoming a core requirement of the network, but not every host operated an email server. The host lists were extended to include mail servers. Email sent to a particular host could be delivered to a different mail server.

Host lists provided necessary information but were not dynamic. New hosts added to the network needed to wait for the updated list to be propagated across the network. In addition, as more hosts became network enabled, the distribution of host lists became a network bottleneck. Out of this evolving environment, DNS was formed. The *Domain Name System* (DNS) is an extendible, distributed data management system [RFC1034]. It provides support for dynamic updates, hostname and network address mapping, and additional information about hosts and domains.

DNS was designed for massively large networks. The current DNS system easily distributes the workload and supports the millions of computers on the Internet. DNS provides individuals and companies the ability to change their DNS content as needed. In addition, DNS is an extendible information system that allows any type of host-related information to be accessed by remote systems. DNS was never designed for security, however. This oversight in architecture has opened DNS to a variety of implementation-independent attacks. The attack vectors include direct DNS vulnerabilities, technical attacks that exploit configuration weaknesses, information reconnaissance, and social attacks that target the human interfaces to DNS.

Top of the Bottom

DNS has earned the dubious honor of being "the Internet's highest security risk." Each year, the SANS Institute releases two Top 10 lists of Internet risks, called the "SANS Top 20 Internet Security Vulnerabilities" (*http://www.sans. org/top20/*). The first list addresses risks specific to Windows. The second list covers Unix systems and the Internet in general. DNS has been in the Top 10 of the Unix/general list since the lists were started (Table 17.1).

TABLE 17.1 DNS in the SANS Top 10 Internet Security Vulnerabilities

DNS Ranking	Year	Comments
#1	2000	Six critical vulnerabilities in BIND
#3	2001	RPC (#1) and Sendmail (#2) displace DNS for top honor
#9	2002	RPC (#1) and LPD (#7) join DNS as session layer protocols in the Top 10
#1	2003	DNS and RPC (#2) lead the list due to configuration vulnerabilities
#1	2004	Risks from misconfigured and unpatched BIND systems

Many of the risks with DNS come from a specific implementation—the Berkeley Internet Name Daemon (BIND). BIND is the most common DNS server and is used on the vast majority of name servers. Because BIND is designed for Unix, DNS and BIND are placed in the Unix Top 10 list. However, BIND has been ported to many non-Unix operating systems, including Windows.

BIND is not the only DNS server. Alternatives to BIND include the Name Server Daemon (NSD) (*http://www.nlnetlabs.nl/nsd/*), PowerDNS, djbDNS, and DNS Server for Windows. Although BIND does have occasional implementation errors, the maintainers usually have patches available shortly after risks are identified. However, patches and different implementations do not address the vulnerabilities inherent to the DNS protocol.

17.1 COMMON USES

Just as IP is the most common network layer protocol, DNS is the most common session layer protocol. Although IP provides address support between networks, DNS provides memorable hostnames and meta-information for other network services. Nearly every network-enabled application supports hostname lookups through DNS servers. The most common uses for DNS are hostname-to-address mapping and mail server identification. DNS can also provide additional information about hosts and domains.

17.1.1 Hostname-to-Address Mapping

Converting between hostnames and IP addresses is the most common use for DNS. DNS can perform forward lookups or reverse lookups. A *forward lookup* converts a hostname to an IP address. A *reverse lookup* identifies the hostnames associated with an IP address.

17.1.1.1 Software Development

When programming, there are four main functions used to perform DNS resolutions. These are provided by the resolver library and perform the actual hostname lookups. The resolver library may access a local hosts file, such as `C:\Windows\System32\Drivers\Etc\Hosts` or `/etc/hosts`, DNS, LDAP, NIS, or other name resolution system. The calling program has no option to specify the name resolution method.

`sethostent:` This function initializes the DNS library. In some implementations, this function takes a Boolean parameter to indicate whether TCP or UDP should be used for the connection. This is the case for Linux and BSD. Other operating systems do not require `sethostent` or simply ignore any passed parameters. In general, `sethostent` should be called before performing any hostname lookups.

gethostbyname: This function performs a forward lookup. Given a hostname, it returns the network address(es) associated with the hostname.

gethostbyaddr: This function performs a reverse lookup. Given a network address, it returns the hostname (and aliases) associated with the address.

endhostent: After performing a hostname lookup, this closes the library call. If `sethostent` specifies a TCP connection, then this function closes the connection. Also, if a host's file was used for the hostname lookup, then this call closes the file.

DNS (and other name resolution systems) provides a many-to-many mapping between hostnames and addresses. A single IP address may match a variety of hostnames, and a single hostname may map to a set of network addresses. The data structure returned by `gethostbyname` and `gethostbyaddr` provides a list of matches. In addition, hostname mapping may not be symmetrical. For example, the hostname `chutney` may resolve to `10.1.3.5`, but a reverse lookup of `10.1.3.5` may not return `chutney`. This is common for servers that host many domain names.

17.1.1.2 Common Lookup Tools

There are many command-line tools for looking up hostnames. The more common tools include the following:

host: The `host` command performs a simple hostname (or address) lookup. It returns all address information. For example, `host www.google.com` returns a list of IP addresses and hostname aliases used by Google. Different versions of the `host` command use different parameters. Some versions allow specifying a DNS server or returning other types of information beyond network addressing. (See `dig`.) In general, the `host` command performs the lookup but does not disclose where it performed the lookup—the user cannot distinguish a host file from a DNS access.

nslookup: The name server lookup tool provides an interactive interface for performing DNS queries. Unlike the `host` command, `nslookup` explicitly states the source of the resolution information. Users may also specify the DNS server for performing the lookup. Although useful, some operating systems consider `nslookup` to be obsolete and replace it with `dig`.

dig: The domain information groper (`dig`) is a powerful tool for performing hostname lookups. Unlike `host` or `nslookup`, `dig` displays all information from the entire DNS request. Although very informative, the cryptic output from dig is not intended for nontechnical users (Listing 17.1).

LISTING 17.1 Outputs from Different Hostname Lookup Systems

```
$ host www.google.com
www.google.com is an alias for www.l.google.com.
www.l.google.com has address 64.233.161.99
www.l.google.com has address 64.233.161.104
www.l.google.com has address 64.233.161.147
www.google.com is an alias for www.l.google.com.
www.google.com is an alias for www.l.google.com.

$ nslookup www.google.com
Server:   10.1.3.250
Address:  10.1.3.250#53

Non-authoritative answer:
www.google.com     canonical name = www.l.google.com.
Name:   www.l.google.com
Address: 64.233.161.147
Name:   www.l.google.com
Address: 64.233.161.99
Name:   www.l.google.com
Address: 64.233.161.104

$ dig www.google.com
; <<>> DiG 9.3.0rc4 <<>> www.google.com
;; global options:  printcmd
;; Got answer:
;; ->>HEADER<<- opcode: QUERY, status: NOERROR, id: 1580
;; flags: qr rd ra
;; QUERY: 1, ANSWER: 4, AUTHORITY: 5, ADDITIONAL: 5

;; QUESTION SECTION:
;www.google.com.                      IN      A

;; ANSWER SECTION:
www.google.com.           492   IN    CNAME   www.l.google.com.
www.l.google.com.    41   IN    A     64.233.161.104
www.l.google.com.    41   IN    A     64.233.161.147
www.l.google.com.    41   IN    A     64.233.161.99

;; AUTHORITY SECTION:
l.google.com.             21153   IN      NS      a.l.google.com.
l.google.com.             21153   IN      NS      b.l.google.com.
l.google.com.             21153   IN      NS      c.l.google.com.
l.google.com.             21153   IN      NS      e.l.google.com.
```

```
l.google.com.            21153   IN    NS    f.l.google.com.

;; ADDITIONAL SECTION:
a.l.google.com.          14492   IN    A     216.239.53.9
b.l.google.com.          13988   IN    A     64.233.179.9
c.l.google.com.          15747   IN    A     64.233.161.9
e.l.google.com.          18886   IN    A     66.102.11.9
f.l.google.com.          20183   IN    A     72.14.207.9

;; Query time: 4 msec
;; SERVER: 10.1.3.250#53(10.1.3.250)
;; WHEN: Thu Sep 22 18:08:18 2005
;; MSG SIZE  rcvd: 260
```

17.1.2 Naming Confusion Attack Vectors

Many lookup systems use simple algorithms to determine when to use `gethostby-name` and `gethostbyaddr`. Simple algorithms lead to simple exploits.

17.1.2.1 Numerical Names

One common algorithm for determining a forward or reverse lookup checks the hostname for letters. If the hostname contains a single letter, then the system uses `gethostbyname`. Otherwise, `gethostbyaddr` is used.

Simple algorithms only check the first character. Most hostname strings do not begin with a number.

Assigning a numerical name to a host can easily defeat this system. For example, the following hostnames can be placed in a DNS server configuration file:

```
491 IN A 10.1.3.49   ; hostname is "491"
49.1 IN A 10.1.3.49    ; hostname is "49.1"
49.1.2 IN A 10.1.3.49
49.1.2.3 IN A 10.1.3.49
49 in ptr 49.1.2.3.   ; reverse of 10.1.3.49 is the name "49.1.2.3"
```

The first hostname, 491 is assigned the IP address 10.1.3.49. The hostname is not a valid octal for an IP address, so it should not lead to any hostname confusion. The `host` and `nslookup` commands (from BIND 9.3) correctly find the IP address from the hostname; however, `dig` (from BIND 9.3) calls `gethostbyaddr` instead of `gethostbyname`. Hostnames without letters trigger the wrong lookup from `dig`. When using a hostname with numbers and dots, such as 49.1, 49.1.2, or 49.1.2.3, all three lookup programs use the incorrect `gethostbyaddr` call.

Similarly, reverse lookups can cause problems. The example IP address 10.1.3.49 resolves to the hostname 49.1.2.3. Although host and nslookup correctly perform the reverse lookup, dig does not.

17.1.2.2 Dotted Names

Hostnames may contain letters, numbers, or a few symbols. The dot character is normally used to separate hostname segments (hostname, domain, subdomain, etc.). For example, the hostname www.google.com contains the segments www, google, and com. If the hostname cannot be resolved, then the local domain is appended and the lookup is retried.

Anyone wanting to obscure a hostname can specify a name with a dot. For example, the domain test.lan may have the hostname www.google.com. A lookup of the hostname without the domain reveals the information for the host www in the google.com domain. However, a lookup with the domain, www.google.com.test.lan, resolves to a different system.

17.1.2.3 Name Formatting

Hostname sizes and character sets can also cause problems. Originally, hostnames were defined as 64 characters consisting of letters, numbers, and a few symbols. Some registration systems have attempted to extend or redefine the hostname format:

- Although fully qualified hostnames, with domain names, could be up to 64 characters, many operating systems in the 1980s and 1990s required hostname elements to be no longer than 8 characters. This included SunOS and HP-UX. Although recent versions of these operating systems do not have this limitation, hostnames are still recommended to be no longer than eight characters for backwards compatibility.
- Some international providers have opted to extend the character set to include nonprintable ASCII or multibyte characters.
- Many developers have chosen to support hostname sizes that are either smaller than 64 characters or much larger.

Applications that expect fixed hostname lengths or specific character sets may be vulnerable to memory overflows or parsing issues. For example, in April 2005, the security vendor iDefense announced a vulnerability in the Internet Explorer (IE) Web browser. IE would generate a buffer overflow if the URL's hostname was longer than 256 characters.

17.1.2.4 Exploited Anonymity

Inconsistencies based on numerical naming, dotted names, and variable formats cause problems for hostname lookup systems. A defender, wanting to keep systems hidden, may consider using hostnames that cannot be resolved by common network analysis tools. Only tools that can handle these naming conflicts can resolve the defender's hostnames and perform lookups.

17.1.2.5 Missing Lookups

Not all hostnames contain network address mappings. Similarly, not all hostnames with network addresses contain reverse lookup information. For example, a domain name may be associated with mail exchange (MX) and text (TXT) records but not be associated with a network address. A Web server that hosts many domains may only have a reverse lookup for the primary name and not for all of its aliases.

17.1.3 Mail Servers

The computer that people use for daily work is usually not the same system used for receiving email. Instead, domains usually provide centralized mail servers. Email is sent to a central mail server and then retrieved by individual users. If email is sent to `user@workstation.domain` then it could be directed to `user@mail.domain` instead.

Network addresses and hostnames do not provide the necessary routing information for identifying the correct mail server. Instead, DNS is used to provide mail server information. Just as DNS associates hostnames with network addresses, it also associates mail exchange server with network addresses, subnets, hostnames, and domains. This is done through the use of DNS *mail exchange* (MX) records. Each MX record specifies the hostname (or network address) of a mail server. Each mail server either knows how to deliver the email, or it knows how to forward the email. (See Chapter 22 for details on email.)

Multiple MX records can be associated with a host. This provides redundancy for delivery in case one route is unavailable. To prioritize mailer routes, each MX record includes a priority. The MX priority is similar to the metric used in routing tables: lower-priority values should be tried first, and two MX records with the same priority are considered equivalent routes. MX information can be retrieved using `host`, `nslookup`, or `dig`. For example, `host -t MX gmail.com` retrieves the list of MX records for Google's Gmail service.

Using DNS for hosting MX records leads to many risks. A misconfigured (or intentionally compromised) DNS server can redirect email to alternate mail servers.

17.1.4 Additional Data

DNS is a viable option for associating any type of meta-information with host-names or IP addresses. Besides MX records, DNS information may contain:

HINFO: The HINFO record provides text-based host information. Some domains use this to include company descriptions, computer make and models, or contact information.

NS: This field specifies the authoritative name server for hostname resolutions. Different hosts may have different NS records.

TXT: This is a generic text field associated with a particular host. The contents are arbitrary but usually limited to printable ASCII characters.

Although the DNS header supports 65,536 different types of associated information, only a few dozen are defined (Listing 17.2). Some DNS proposals have opted to overload existing types rather than define new types. Examples include SPF, DK, and OzymanDNS.

LISTING 17.2 Types of DNS Associated Data from RFC883

```
enum TYPE
  {
  TYPE_A=1,    /* host address */
  TYPE_NS,     /* authoritative name server */
  TYPE_MD,     /* mail destination (Obsolete - use MX) */
  TYPE_MF,     /* mail forwarder (Obsolete - use MX) */
  TYPE_CNAME,  /* canonical name for an alias */
  TYPE_SOA,    /* start of a zone of authority */
  TYPE_MB,     /* mailbox domain name (EXPERIMENTAL) */
  TYPE_MG,     /* mail group member (EXPERIMENTAL) */
  TYPE_MR,     /* mail rename domain name (EXPERIMENTAL) */
  TYPE_NULL,   /* a NULL RR (EXPERIMENTAL) */
  TYPE_WKS,    /* well known service description */
  TYPE_PTR,    /* domain name pointer */
  TYPE_HINFO,  /* host information */
  TYPE_MINFO,  /* mailbox or mail list information */
  TYPE_MX,     /* mail exchange */
  TYPE_TXT,    /* text strings */
  TYPE_AAAA=0x1c, /* IPv6 address request — RFC1886 */
  /** QTYPE are a superset of TYPE **/
  QTYPE_AXFR=252,    /* request for a transfer of an entire zone */
  QTYPE_MAILB=253,   /* request for mailbox records (MB/MG/MR) */
  QTYPE_MAILA=254,   /* request for mail agents (Obsolete by MX) */
  QTYPE_ALL=255      /* request for all records (symbol "*") */
  };
typedef enum TYPE TYPE;
```

17.1.4.1 Sender Policy Framework Overloading

Sender Policy Framework (SPF) is an example of a protocol that overloads existing DNS data types. SPF is an attempt to authenticate email and reduce undesirable email (spam). This protocol works by storing sender information in the TXT field. For example:

```
$ host -t txt pobox.com
pobox.com descriptive text "v=spf1 mx mx:fallback-relay.%{d}
a:webmail.%{d} a:smtp.%{d} a:outgoing.smtp.%{d}
a:discard-reports.%{d} a:discards.%{d} mx:stor" "e.discard.%{d}
a:emerald.%{d} redirect=%{l1r+}._at_.%{o}._spf.%{d}"
```

The TXT field contains the SPF information. It specifies the authorized sources for email from the pobox.com domain.

17.1.4.2 Domain Keys Overloading

SPF is not the only protocol to overload existing DNS fields. Another anti-spam solution, Yahoo! Domain Keys (DK), uses two levels of overloading. First, DK defines a reserved hostname: _domainkey. For example, Yahoo! uses _domainkey.yahoo.com. The TXT field associated with this reserved hostname includes information related to DK authentication.

```
$ host -t txt _domainkey.yahoo.com
_domainkey.yahoo.com descriptive text "t=y\; o=~\;
n=http://antispam.yahoo.com/domainkeys"
```

17.1.4.3 OzymanDNS Overloading

At the 2004 Black Hat Briefings security conference, Dan Kaminsky demonstrated a set of tools called OzymanDNS. The Aska and Geta tools in OzymanDNS overload A, TXT, and CNAME fields with data. Using these tools, entire files can be distributed and stored on DNS servers. Kaminsky's presentation at Black Hat included playing an audio file that he had distributed across a few thousand DNS servers. Each server held a few bytes of data.

17.1.4.4 Custom DNS

The functionality in BIND (and other common DNS servers) is well defined. The same DNS query will return the same DNS results; however, the implementation is independent of the protocol. Custom DNS servers do not need to return the same information each time; a custom DNS server could return different information based on the request source or time of day. For example, an administrator could configure a custom server to return real-time network and host status in the TXT fields. A covert channel could easily hide information within a DNS response.

17.2 DNS PROTOCOL

The DNS protocol uses a simple request/reply system [RFC1035]. Both request and reply packets use the same format. The first 12 bytes of the packet form the DNS header (Listing 17.3). The header identifies the type of request and number of parameters. After the header, there are four blocks of optional information. These are the queries, answers, name servers, and addition records.

LISTING 17.3 DNS Header Format and Flags

```
/*** DNS packet header format ***/
struct DNS_RR /* request/reply */
  {
  u_int16_t ID;            /* session serial number */
  u_int8_t Flags;          /* see FLAGs */
  u_int8_t Rcode;          /* see RCODE */
  u_int16_t Qcount;        /* # entries in the question section */
  u_int16_t Acount;        /* # entries in the answer section */
  u_int16_t NScount;       /* # name server records
                              in authority section */
  u_int16_t ARcount;       /* # resource records
                              in additional records section */
  /* NOTE: MTU for UDP is 512 bytes.
     512 bytes - header = 500 data bytes */
  unsigned char Data[500];    /* data */
  };
typedef struct DNS_RR DNS_RR;

/*** Flags for DNS header.  OR these together. ***/
#define FLAG_REPLY 0x80      /* is this a query or reply?
                                0=query, 1=reply */
#define FLAG_OPCODE_MASK 0x30        /* query mask */
#define FLAG_OPCODE_QUERY 0x00       /* standard query */
#define FLAG_OPCODE_IQUERY 0x10      /* inverse query */
#define FLAG_OPCODE_STATUS 0x20      /* server status request */
/* other opcode values bits reserved */
#define FLAG_AA 0x04         /* authoritative answer */
#define FLAG_TC 0x02         /* message truncated */
#define FLAG_RD 0x01         /* recursion denied */

/* Flags added to the rcode byte */
#define FLAG_RA 0x80         /* recursion available */
#define FLAG_AAA 0x20        /* answer authenticated */
#define RCODE_MASK 0x0f
enum RCODE
  {
  RCODE_NO_ERROR=0,        /* no error condition */
```

```
        RCODE_FORMAT_ERROR,    /* format error */
        RCODE_SERVER_ERROR,    /* server error */
        RCODE_NAME_ERROR,      /* name error */
        RCODE_NA,              /* not implemented (not available) */
        RCODE_REFUSED,         /* refused */
     };
  typedef enum RCODE RCODE;
```

17.2.1 Packet Information

Each DNS packet begins with a session identifier. The query, as well as any responses, uses the same session identifier.

After the identifier, the packet header contains 2 bytes for flags and return codes. The flags specify the type of packet (query or reply), type of query (forward/standard, reverse/inverse, or status), and whether the information is authoritative. The return code specifies if the query succeeded or failed.

The amount of information in the four data segments varies. A simple query usually has one set of information in the query section and no data in the other three sections. In contrast, a simple reply may repeat the query but will contain information in the answer section. Additional information, such as pointers to authoritative name servers, is included in the remaining two sections.

17.2.2 Simple DNS Server

By default, DNS is connection-less and runs on port 53/UDP. An optional DNS service on port 53/TCP can be used for connection-oriented requests. A basic DNS server receives requests and provides replies. Listing 17.4 shows a very simple DNS server that receives DNS requests and always provides the same reply: a single IP address and TXT comment. The full source code is available on the CD-ROM as dnsd.c.

ON THE CD

Queries to this simple DNS daemon from host, nslookup, and dig return the same reply. Each request receives the IP address and TXT information specified when starting the server (Listing 17.5). More complex DNS servers, such as BIND and NSD, relay requests to other DNS servers, use internal databases for storing hostnames, and cache responses from relayed requests.

LISTING 17.4 Simple DNS Daemon

```
int main    (int argc, char *argv[])
{
  int UDPsocket;    /* server socket */
  DNS_RR Request,Reply;
  int RequestLen,ReplyLen;
```

```
struct sockaddr_in Server;
struct sockaddr Client;
int ClientLen;
int Len;
int Ipaddr;

if (argc != 4)
  {
  printf("Simple DNS server that always returns ");
  printf("the same reply.\n");
  printf("Usage: %s ipaddress hostname text\n",argv[0]);
  printf("  ipaddress: IP address to reply (1.2.3.4)\n");
  printf("  hostname:  hostname to reply (cow.farm.lan)\n");
  printf("  text:      text comment to reply ");
  printf("(\"Text in quotes\")\n");
  exit(-1);
  }

UDPsocket = socket(AF_INET,SOCK_DGRAM,0);
if (UDPsocket < 0)
  {
  fprintf(stderr,"ERROR: Unable to open socket.\n");
  exit(-1);
  }

Server.sin_family = AF_INET;
Server.sin_addr.s_addr = INADDR_ANY;
/* DNS normally runs on port 53/UDP */
Server.sin_port = htons(53);
if (bind(UDPsocket,(struct sockaddr *)(&Server),sizeof(Server)))
  {
  fprintf(stderr,"ERROR: Failed to bind to port 53/UDP.\n");
  exit(-1);
  }

/* Now listen for requests and reply */
while(1)
  {
  ClientLen=sizeof(Client);
  RequestLen = recvfrom(UDPsocket,&Request,sizeof(Request),0,
                     &Client,&ClientLen);
  if (RequestLen >= 12)    /* 12 bytes is minimum */
    {
    /* Process packet request */
    memset(&Reply,0,sizeof(Reply));
    Reply.ID = Request.ID;
    /* set authoritative reply */
    Reply.Flags = FLAG_REPLY | FLAG_AA;
    Reply.Rcode = RCODE_SERVER_ERROR; /* assume error */
```

```
ReplyLen = 12;

/* check if it is a request we can handle */
if ((Request.Flags & FLAG_REPLY) == 0)
  {
  Reply.Rcode = RCODE_NO_ERROR;
  Reply.Acount = htons(2); /* 2 replies: hostname and TXT */
  Len=0;

  /* Reply #1: hostname and IP address */
  /* store hostname */
  Reply.Data[Len++]=strlen(argv[2]);
  memcpy(Reply.Data+Len,argv[2],strlen(argv[2]));
  Len+=strlen(argv[2]);
  Reply.Data[Len++] = 0; /* end of string */
  /* set upper byte of TYPE */
  Reply.Data[Len++] = (TYPE_A/256)&0xff;
  /* set lower byte of TYPE */
  Reply.Data[Len++] = (TYPE_A)&0xff;
  /* set CLASS */
  Reply.Data[Len++] = (CLASS_IN/256)&0xff;
  Reply.Data[Len++] = (CLASS_IN)&0xff;
  /* set TTL */
  Reply.Data[Len++] = 0; /* TTL = 4 bytes */
  Reply.Data[Len++] = 0; /* TTL */
  Reply.Data[Len++] = 0; /* TTL */
  /* lowest part of TTL = 10 seconds */
  Reply.Data[Len++] = 10;
  /* set data length: octets */
  Reply.Data[Len++] = 0;
  Reply.Data[Len++] = 4;
  Ipaddr = ntohl(inet_addr(argv[1]));
  Reply.Data[Len++] = (Ipaddr >> 24) & 0xff;
  Reply.Data[Len++] = (Ipaddr >> 16) & 0xff;
  Reply.Data[Len++] = (Ipaddr >> 8) & 0xff;
  Reply.Data[Len++] = (Ipaddr) & 0xff;

  /* Reply #2: hostname and TXT string */
  Reply.Data[Len++]=0xc0; /* make this a pointer */
  Reply.Data[Len++]=0x0c; /* point to name (start of data) */
  /* set TYPE */
  Reply.Data[Len++] = (TYPE_TXT/256)&0xff;
  Reply.Data[Len++] = (TYPE_TXT)&0xff;
  /* set CLASS */
  Reply.Data[Len++] = (CLASS_IN/256)&0xff;
  Reply.Data[Len++] = (CLASS_IN)&0xff;
  /* set TTL to 10 seconds */
  Reply.Data[Len++] = 0; /* TTL = 4 bytes */
```

```
            Reply.Data[Len++] = 0; /* TTL */
            Reply.Data[Len++] = 0; /* TTL */
            Reply.Data[Len++] = 10; /* lowest part of TTL */
            Reply.Data[Len++] = 0; /* upper part of data length */
            Reply.Data[Len++] = strlen(argv[3])+1; /* data length */
            Reply.Data[Len++] = strlen(argv[3]); /* string length */
            memcpy(Reply.Data+Len,argv[3],strlen(argv[3]));
            Len += strlen(argv[3]);

            ReplyLen += Len; /* total size of packet */
        } /* if request */

        sendto(UDPsocket,&Reply,ReplyLen,0,&Client,ClientLen);
        } /* if at least 12 bytes */
    } /* while(1) */

    /* Should never get here! */
    return(0);
} /* main() */
```

LISTING 17.5   Sample Queries and Replies from Simple DNS Daemon

```
As root, start the DNSD server on the local host (127.0.0.1)
$ sudo ./dnsd 1.2.3.4 myhostname.mydomain "My TXT field" &
Query the DNSD server located on 127.0.0.1
$ host www.google.com 127.0.0.1
myhostname\.mydomain has address 1.2.3.4
myhostname\.mydomain descriptive text "My TXT field"
$ nslookup www.google.com 127.0.0.1
Server:         127.0.0.1
Address:        127.0.0.1#53

Name:           myhostname\.mydomain
Address: 1.2.3.4
myhostname\.mydomain           text = "My TXT field"

$ dig @127.0.0.1 www.google.com
; <<>> DiG 9.3.0rc4 <<>> @127.0.0.1 www.google.com
;; global options:  printcmd
;; Got answer:
;; ->>HEADER<<- opcode: QUERY, status: NOERROR, id: 15518
;; flags: qr aa; QUERY: 0, ANSWER: 2, AUTHORITY: 0, ADDITIONAL: 0

;; ANSWER SECTION:
myhostname\.mydomain.        10      IN      A       1.2.3.4
myhostname\.mydomain.        10      IN      TXT     "My TXT field"

;; Query time: 13 msec
```

```
;; SERVER: 127.0.0.1#53(127.0.0.1)
;; WHEN: Sat Sep 24 15:04:56 2005
;; MSG SIZE  rcvd: 72
```

17.3 DISTRIBUTED ARCHITECTURE

No single server or network can handle all of the DNS queries generated by the Internet. Instead, DNS uses a distributed architecture. Domains and network providers divide the hostname management workload. By dividing the workload between different layers of DNS servers (Figure 17.1), no single system becomes overwhelmed. There are five main types of DNS servers: root, TLD, primary, secondary, and caching. Each type plays a critical role in dividing the workload and managing hostnames.

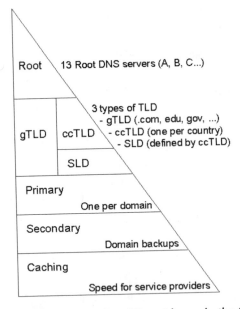

FIGURE 17.1 The different layers in the DNS architecture.

17.3.1 Root Servers

The root level DNS servers are the primary source for performing name resolution. The root servers do not store hostnames. Instead, these systems contain pointers to other name servers. For example, if a user wants to look up the hostname `hen.chicken.coop` then the root server will redirect the query to the top level domain (TLD)servers that manage the coop domain. For reverse lookups, the root servers maintain lists of subnets and servers that manage the subnets.

TABLE 17.2   Root DNS Servers

Name	IPv4/IPv6 Address	Operator
A	198.41.0.4	VeriSign Naming and Directory Services
B	192.228.79.201/2001:478:65::53	Information Sciences Institute
C	192.33.4.12	Cogent Communications
D	128.8.10.90	University of Maryland
E	192.203.230.10	NASA Ames Research Center
F	192.5.5.241/2001:500::1035	Internet Systems Consortium, Inc.
G	192.112.36.4	U.S. DOD Network Information Center
H	128.63.2.53/2001:500:1::803f:235	U.S. Army Research Lab
I	192.36.148.17	Autonomica/NORDUnet
J	192.58.128.30	VeriSign Naming and Directory Services
K	193.0.14.129/2001:7fd::1	Reseaux IP Europeans - Network Coordination Centre
L	198.32.64.12	Internet Corporation for Assigned Names and Numbers
M	202.12.27.33/2001:dc3::35	WIDE Project

The number of root-level DNS servers has expanded over time. In September 2005, there were 13 root servers (Table 17.2). The official list of servers is maintained at *http://www.root-servers.org/*. Each of the root servers represents a cluster of systems and not a single host. For example, F.root-servers.org has servers operating in 30 different locations around the world. The distribution and redundancy permits load balancing and mitigates the impact from a DoS attack.

17.3.2 Top Level Domain Servers

Hostnames are presented in a hierarchical format. Each dot in a hostname indicates another level in the hierarchy. For example, www.ucsc.edu is the host www in the domain ucsc within the *top level domain* (TLD) edu. The final extension on any *fully qualified hostname*—the individual host with full domain—indicates the TLD. On the Internet, all fully qualified hostnames contain a TLD from a limited selection. The type of TLD usually determines to type of domain.

As with the root-level servers, TLD servers do not store individual hostnames. Instead, these servers maintain pointers to the official primary name servers for a domain. The *primary name servers* are the authoritative source for specific host-name resolution. The root and TLD servers provide the means for an arbitrary host on the Internet to identify a specific primary name server. RFC2240 defines three types of TLD servers: gTLD, ccTLD, and SLD.

17.3.2.1 Generic Top Level Domain (gTLD)

The generic top level domains (gTLD) specify types of services. The most widely used gTLD is .com, which generally designates a commercial-oriented entity. Other common gTLDs include .net and .edu for network and educational services, respectively. Originally there were only six gTLDs [RFC1032], but more have since been added. Table 17.3 lists the gTLD allocations (as of September 2005) and their purposes. In addition, other domains are being considered including .cat, .jobs, .kid, .mobi, .post, .tel, .travel, and .xxx.

TABLE 17.3 gTLD Allocations

Year Established	gTLD	Purpose
1985	COM	General commerce or commercial
1985	EDU	Educational
1985	GOV	U.S. Government
1985	NET	Network services
1985	ORG	Nonprofit organization
1985	MIL	U.S. Military
1985	ARPA	Reserved for reverse lookups
1988	INT	Organizations established by international treaties
2000	AERO	Air-transport industry
2000	BIZ	Businesses
2000	COOP	Cooperative associations
2000	INFO	Informational services
2000	MUSEUM	Reserved for museums
2000	NAME	Reserved for individuals (noncommercial)
2000	PRO	Credentialed professionals and related organizations

A few gTLDs are treated as reserved for testing, but they are not officially reserved domains. These include .example, .invalid, .localhost, .localdomain, and .test. The .lan gTLD is commonly used for private, internal networks. Any gTLD that is not known by the root servers operates privately.

As with the root servers, there are many gTLD servers. These have letters for hostnames and exist in the gtld or gtld-servers domain of their respective gTLDs, and not every gTLD is recognized by all root servers. For example, the .pro gTLD is managed by a.gtld.pro, b.gtld.pro, and c.gtld.pro. Only the A, G, and J root servers identify this gTLD. A simple script (Listing 17.6) can be used to identify the list of gTLD servers.

LISTING 17.6   Shell Script to List gTLD Servers

```
#!/bin/sh
# for each root server
for root in a b c d e f g h i j k l m ; do
  echo "$root.root-servers.net"
  # for each gTLD
  for gtld in com edu gov net org mil arpa \
    int aero biz coop info museum name pro ; do
    # List the gTLDs know by the root server
    host -t ns $gtld $root.root-servers.net | \
      grep -v ":" | grep server
  done
done
```

17.3.2.2 Country Code Top Level Domain (ccTLD)

The country code top level domains (ccTLD) allocate domain space to each country. Each domain suffix is a two-letter country code defined by ISO 3166. For example, .uk is the United Kingdom, .jp is Japan, and .us is the United States of America.

17.3.2.3 Secondary Level Domain (SLD)

Within each ccTLD are *secondary level domains* (SLD) that serve the same descriptive purpose as the gTLDs. For example, www.leeds.ac.uk is the host www in the leeds domain. The SLD is ac indicating an *academic* institution, and the gTLD .uk indicates the United Kingdom. The University of Leeds (in the United Kingdom) manages this hostname.

Different ccTLDs define different SLDs, but common secondary domains include the following:

Academic: Universities, colleges, and elementary schools may use ac, acad, ed, or edu.

Commercial: Commercial entities may appear as co or com.

Organization: Noncommercial organizations may use or or org.

Government: Governments may appear as gov or a localized variation. For example, the government of France uses gouv.fr., and Canada uses gc.ca (gc is the Government of Canada).

Military: Military services may appear as mil, mi, or may represent the type of military organization such as navy.us.

17.3.3 Primary and Secondary Servers

The *primary* DNS servers are owned and managed by specific domains. These servers provide authoritative replies for hostname resolution within the domain. For example, the domain ibm.com is managed by a set of IBM-owned name servers such as ns.watson.ibm.com and ns.austin.ibm.com. These name servers can resolve all hostnames within their domain.

Secondary name servers provide authoritative responses but may not be directly owned or managed by the domain. Secondary servers receive periodic updates from primary servers. These updates, or *zone transfers*, are accomplished through a TCP connection. All authoritative information from the primary is transferred to the secondary.

17.3.4 Caching Servers

Hostnames are rarely accessed once. For example, if one person visits a Web site, then that person is likely to visit the same site again later. Similarly, if one site is popular, then many people are likely to request the same hostname lookup. *Caching DNS servers* receive and relay new requests and cache replies for faster access. Although these servers provide unauthenticated results, the results are generated much faster than if the host needed to query a root, ccTLD, SLD, and primary DNS server.

The duration for data to be held within a caching DNS server varies based on the data. Each DNS reply includes a cache timeout duration. The data should be held until the information expires. Usually the duration is between a day and a week. If the timeout value is too low, then the primary and secondary DNS servers must field more requests. In contrast, a timeout value set too large can lead to slow updates; a change to a DNS entry may take days to propagate across the Internet.

Most large companies and Internet providers operate caching DNS servers for their customers. This provides hostname resolution results faster than individual queries to the official hosting sites. In addition, caching servers remove network load by limiting the need to send requests to all of the different root, gTLD, ccTLD, SLD, and primary servers.

17.3.5 DNS Management

The distributive nature of DNS makes it difficult for a single entity to control. Instead, different organizations are responsible for different levels of servers. Each of the root servers operates under the guidance of the Internet Corporation for Assigned Names and Numbers (ICANN) (*http://www.icann.org/*). ICANN accredits the root servers to ensure that they maintain compatibility. ICANN also defines the gTLD and ccTLD suffixes and authorizes domain registration providers. Each of the domain registrants can allocate new domain names and insert primary name server information into the TLDs. The InterNIC Web site (*http://www.internic.net/*) includes a list of more than 500 accredited registrars.

Domain names are closely associated with network addresses. The Internet Assigned Numbers Authority (IANA) is responsible for allocating blocks of network addresses to organizations. One person, Jonathan (Jon) Postel, effectively operated IANA until his untimely death in 1998. Pastel was one of the most important pioneers for the Internet (and the author of many RFCs that define the Internet). Since his passing, the duties of IANA have been distributed among a set of Regional Internet Registry (RIR) providers.

Each RIR provides network address allocations, domain registration (DNS and WHOIS), and reverse DNS for a global region. For example, the American Registry for Internet Numbers (ARIN) provides support for the United States and Canada. Other RIRs include AfriNIC (Africa), APNIC (Asia and Pacific), LACNIC (Mexico and Latin America), and RIPE (Europe, the Middle East, and parts of Asia).

Individuals, companies, and other online entities submit domain names to local DNS registrars. The local registrars update the RIR, and the RIR informs the TLD providers. However, the individuals, companies, and online entities are responsible for their own primary DNS servers. In many cases, the primary and secondary DNS hosting is outsourced to third-party providers. Determining the group responsible for managing DNS depends on the level within the DNS hierarchy.

17.4 DIRECT RISKS

DNS has the reputation of being the most insecure protocol on the Internet. The fundamental security flaw in DNS revolves around the assumed trust between DNS servers: DNS systems assume that servers do not intentionally provide misinformation. Moreover, the DNS protocol provides no means for authenticating clients with servers, and vice versa. The lack of authentication permits attackers to target the trust relationship.

DNS is vulnerable to a variety of trust-based attacks. These attacks include unauthenticated responses, cache poisoning, and blind ID attacks. In addition, some DNS implementations are vulnerable to corrupt DNS packets.

Pharming

Online fraud takes many forms. *Phishing* refers to online fraud through impersonation. Usually phishing uses email or Web sites that impersonate well-respected companies, such as banks or network service providers. The nature of phishing has changed over time, from simple forged emails and fake Web sites to complex cons and computer viruses that capture confidential information.

Some types of phishing have exploited DNS weaknesses. The term *pharming* describes DNS risks applied to phishing or online fraud. Most (if not all) of the DNS risks listed in this chapter have been used for fraud against legitimate companies.

17.4.1 Unauthenticated Responses

DNS uses a session identifier to match requests with replies, but the session identifier provides no authentication (Figure 17.2). An attacker that observes a DNS request can forge a DNS reply. The false reply includes the observed session identifier. The result is an unauthenticated response that appears authentic. The attacker may even set the authoritative flag in the packet, removing any doubt as to the data's accuracy. The requester receives the reply and accepts the unauthenticated response. The result is an attacker that can control the hostname lookups and consequently redirect victim connections.

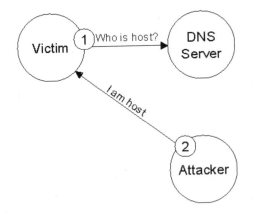

FIGURE 17.2 Unauthenticated DNS response attack.

17.4.1.1 DNS Performance versus Security

Slow DNS lookups can result in slow application performance. To enhance the response time, DNS uses two approaches: parallel requests and connectionless-packets. When a DNS system generates a request, it sends the query to a group of servers. The requests are sent in parallel and the requester can accept an answer from any of the servers. Because different servers respond at different rates, the fastest response is used for name resolution. Unfortunately, this also provides attackers with a window of opportunity. Because any server may respond to a request, an attacker may also respond.

The DNS protocol may operate over TCP or UDP. Being a connection-oriented service, TCP is generally slower than UDP because it must negotiate each connection. Because UDP has no negotiation, most DNS queries use UDP. Unfortunately, this also simplifies attacks—an attacker only needs to generate a UDP packet and not hijack a TCP connection.

17.4.1.2 DNS Poisoning

DNS trust-based attacks use a similar technique to ARP poisoning (Chapter 10) and IP hijacking through ICMP redirection (Chapter 12). In each of these cases, an attacker provides false information. Whereas ARP poisoning is limited to the local network, DNS poisoning can occur anywhere along the network. Although IP hijacking can be prevented through ICMP filtering, DNS replies cannot be filtered. Even restricting DNS replies based on the server's network address does not provide any additional security. Because DNS uses UDP, an attacker can forge the sender's network address just as easily as forging the DNS session identifier.

17.4.2 DNS Cache Poisoning

Whereas unauthenticated responses target a requester, DNS cache poisoning targets any type of caching DNS server. An attacker observes a DNS request and generates a forged DNS reply. The reply appears authoritative and contains a long cache timeout value. A poisoned DNS server will provide the false data to any data request. For example, a caching DNS server can be poisoned so that the hostname www.happydomain.lan is mapped to the localhost address (127.0.0.1). Any DNS host requesting a lookup for www.happydomain.lan receives the localhost address rather than the true address. This makes the domain unreachable. Moreover, the incorrect information will be provides as long as the poisoned information is in the cache.

There are few viable options for mitigating DNS cache poisoning. DNS servers may be configured with an upper limit for cached data storage. For example, if the server is configured for a maximum cache period of 24 hours, then a poisoned reply containing a 7-day cache timeout will expire after 24 hours. However, the attack is still viable for the 24-hour window.

Although an attacker can generate a fake DNS reply, they cannot easily prevent a valid DNS server from replying. Caching servers may discard cache entries when multiple replies are received with differing values. This prevents the propagation of tainted information (but impacts the cache performance).

17.4.3 Blind ID Attack

Unauthenticated responses and cache poisoning usually require an attacker to observe the DNS request and session identifier. But observing a request is not always essential. An attacker may choose a common domain name and begin an attack when the hostname appears to timeout. This attack method generates a flood of DNS replies, each containing a different session identifier (Figure 17.3).

FIGURE 17.3 Blind ID attack.

For example, consider a caching server with data that expires in a few seconds (Listing 17.7). In this example, the hostname entry expires in 158 seconds, and the IP addresses expire in 127 seconds. When they expire, the caching server (dnscache) relays the next request to other DNS servers. The replies from these servers repopulate the cache.

Because the attacker knows when the cache expires, the attack can be precisely timed. The only thing needed is for the caching server to generate a request after the cache expires. The attacker can initiate this process by sending a request to the server when the cache is known to expire.

During this window of opportunity, the attacker can generate 65,536 false DNS packets—one for each session identifier. If the correct session identifier is generated before a real server can provide the true reply, then the caching server becomes poisoned. If the attack fails, then the attacker must wait for the cache to expire before trying again. This type of attack is a *race condition*; the attack does not always succeed. If tried enough times, however, it will eventually succeed.

LISTING 17.7   Example Listing of a DNS Cache Expiration

```
$ dig @dnscache www.google.com
; <<>> DiG 9.3.0rc4 <<>> @dnscache www.google.com
;; Got answer:
;; ->>HEADER<<- opcode: QUERY, status: NOERROR, id: 14183
;; flags: qr rd ra
;; QUERY: 1, ANSWER: 4, AUTHORITY: 5, ADDITIONAL: 5

;; QUESTION SECTION:
;www.google.com.                         IN      A

;; ANSWER SECTION:
www.google.com.         158     IN      CNAME   www.l.google.com.
www.l.google.com.       127     IN      A       64.233.161.99
www.l.google.com.       127     IN      A       64.233.161.104
www.l.google.com.       127     IN      A       64.233.161.147
```

In theory, a blind attacker must also guess the UDP port number, however, most DNS servers reuse the same port number for subsequent queries. By reusing the same port, the DNS software does not need to manage a suite of UDP network connections and does not spend time binding to new UDP ports. Unfortunately, this also means that the attacker can determine the port to attack before initiating the attack. Although rare, DNS servers can rotate their UDP ports when making queries. This lessens the risk from a blind attack but increases the software complexity because multiple ports must be managed.

17.4.4 Corrupt DNS Packets

The DNS protocol specifies data sizes for queries and replies. Some DNS implementations do not properly check data boundaries. A packet may claim to have more data than it actually contains or may not contain enough data. These can result in buffer overflows and underflows.

Similarly, the DNS data fields can contain codes for jumping within the packet. This shorthand permits repeat domain names to be reused rather than duplicated in the packet. A misconfigured jump can result in an overflow or infinite processing loop (when the jump leads to itself).

Although most of today's DNS hosts are not vulnerable to these exploits, new network devices are released often. Many new devices rely on DNS for name lookups but implement their own version of the protocol rather than porting a vetted DNS library. These unique implementations are commonly vulnerable to malformed DNS packets.

17.5 TECHNICAL RISKS

Although the direct DNS risks impact fundamental issues with the protocol, technical risks are based on configuration issues. The ability to impact or modify a DNS server's data directly leads to DNS compromises. Technical risks include DNS domain hijacking, server hijacking, update durations, and DDNS.

17.5.1 DNS Domain Hijacking

Any owner of a DNS server can configure the server to act as a primary source for any domain. DNS does not contain the concept of domain ownership. If a company wants to configure its internal DNS server to be a primary source for the `mi-crosoft.com` domain, there is nothing to stop it. The DNS hierarchy prevents this type of configuration from flooding the Internet with invalid information. If the DNS server is high enough up the chain of servers (e.g., a SLD, ccTLD, or large service provider caching server), however, then it can be used to hijack entire domains.

DNS domain hijacking has viable uses. Many computer worms, viruses, spyware, and assorted malware report information to remote hosts on the Internet. Besides "do not become infected," the most common approach for mitigating these risks is to disable the malware collection hosts. If the host is unreachable, then it cannot collect information. When the malware sites are specified by IP addresses, egress filtering at the firewall can prevent user access. When the malware accesses a remote host by name, however, DNS becomes the best filtering option. The local DNS server can be configured to reject hostname lookups for malware sites. If the hostname cannot be resolved to an IP address, then the host becomes unreachable.

Using the DNS server to block undesirable hostname lookups can block access to undesirable sites that host services related to porn, fraud, and malware. Many sites take the filtering beyond online risks. Some providers have been reported to filter liberal and conservative viewpoints or to serve political agendas. Web sites such as *2600 The Hacker Quarterly*, abortion and sex education sites, and even political candidates have been victims of domain hijacking. China has been repeatedly criticized for hijacking domain names—preventing access to certain Web sites and countries [Zittrain2003, DIT2004].

The Name Game

Not all domain hijacking is intentional. In 1999, a Fortune-500 company fell victim to an accidental domain hijacking. Many large companies have branches worldwide. This company had a large branch in Japan. A major ISP in Japan saw that emails from the company were using a network route through the ISP, and the route was not optimal. By changing the ISP's DNS server (modifying the MX records), the email would be directed to an optimal route.

Unfortunately, the ISP implemented it wrong. Rather than setting the ISP as a less-desirable route, they were set to be *more* desirable. And the information was loaded into a very high-level DNS server. The Fortune-500 company saw their email volume drop dramatically as all emails were routed through the ISP. The ISP saw their volume increase to such as level that they fell under an unintentional DoS attack. Although the problem was identified and corrected within a few hours, it took nearly five days for the changes to propagate to all the caching DNS servers.

Although uncommon, this type of unintentional DNS hijacking occurs more often than expected. Most large corporations experience similar misconfigurations every few years.

17.5.2 DNS Server Hijacking

DNS servers can be hijacked. The hijacked server can be configured to provide different host information or include new hostnames. DNS hijacking generally takes one of two forms: system compromises and IP hijacking.

17.5.2.1 DNS System Compromise

A DNS server runs as an application on a computer system. If an attacker can gain access to the computer system, then the attacker can gain access to the DNS server. This means that the server is vulnerable to any potential compromise to the hosting system. For example, if the host is running an old print server that is vulnerable to a remote exploit, then the DNS server is vulnerable due to the remote exploit.

To mitigate the risk of a system compromise, critical DNS servers should run on hardened systems. A *hardened system* has all unnecessary network services disabled. In the case of DNS, the DNS server should be the only accessible network service. In reality, most large companies provide SSH for remote administration, but all other services are disabled.

17.5.2.2 DNS IP Hijacking

DNS is an OSI layer 5 protocol. This means that it is vulnerable to all lower-layer risks. Because most DNS servers operate using UDP or TCP over IP, they are vulnerable to IP (and ARP) hijacking. If an attacker can intercept the IP (or ARP) packets, then the attacker can impersonate the DNS server. Although very rare, this style of DNS hijacking can be very damaging.

17.5.3 Update Durations

Caching DNS servers associate a timeout with each DNS item. The timeouts prevent data from becoming invalid as host configurations change. Unfortunately, if the timeout value is too high, then changes cannot be performed immediately. For example, if the Web server www.local.lan resides at 10.1.2.3, then it cannot be immediately moved to 10.1.2.4. If the administrators immediately relocate the host, then caching servers will point to the wrong address. Instead, both IP addresses should be functional during the transition period.

17.5.4 Dynamic DNS

The Dynamic Host Configuration Protocol (DHCP) [RFC2131] is commonly used to assign network information to hosts on local networks. DHCP provides new hosts with network addresses, default gateways, and DNS server information. These hosts are only accessible by their network addresses, however, so a user wanting to connect to a DHCP-assigned host cannot access the host by a hostname.

Dynamic DNS (DDNS) [RFC2136] addresses the hostname issue for DHCP. Using DDNS, a DHCP client can place a hostname in the local DNS system. Although the DHCP client may be assigned a new network address each time it connects to the network, DDNS ensures that the hostname always points to the host's new network address.

Clients can readily configure DDNS hostnames. For example, under Debian Linux's DHCP3 package, the file /etc/dhcp3/dhclient.conf offers a send hostname field for specifying the DDNS hostname.

Unfortunately, DDNS permits name hijacking. Any hostname that is not associated with an active DHCP address can be requested. If a host is offline or unavailable, then another host can readily hijack the hostname. As long as the hijacked name is associated with a valid DHCP host, the true host cannot request the name.

17.6 SOCIAL RISKS

DNS plays a critical role for the Internet. The ability to compromise or hijack a hostname directly leads to DoS, MitM, and other system attacks. DNS servers have direct risks and technical attacks, but there are other methods for compromising a host or domain. These risks target the human factor. Social risks for DNS include similar hostnames, automatic name completion, social engineering, and domain renewals.

TABLE 17.4   Similar Hostnames Registered Between December 28 and December 31, 2003

babnkofamerica.com	bajkofamerica.com	baniofamerica.com
banjofamerica.com	bankofameeica.com	bankofameryca.com
bankofsmerica.com	vbankofamerica.com	bahkofamerica.com
bankkfamerica.com	banklfamerica.com	bankofajerica.com
bankofakerica.com	bankofamdrica.com	bankofamedica.com
bankofamefica.com	bankofamericq.com	bankofamericz.com
bankofamerixa.com	bankofamerjca.com	bankofamerkca.com
bankofameruca.com	bankofamrrica.com	bankofamsrica.com
bankofamwrica.com	bankofqmerica.com	bankofzmerica.com
banuofamerica.com	bqnkofamerica.com	bznkofamerica.com
wwwwbankofamerica.com		

17.6.1 Similar Hostnames

When using a keyboard, typographical errors are common. It is not uncommon for a user to enter in a wrong hostname. Attackers can use this knowledge to hijack connections. For example, if a user wants to connect to Bank of America (bankofamerica.com), they may accidentally enter bonkofamerica.com. If an attacker owns the similar hostname, then they can impersonate the actual site and attack the user's connection. In December 2003, over 30 variations of bankofamerica.com were registered over a 4-day period (Table 17.4). Each variation represents a common typographical error. Some of these domains, such as bankofajerica.com, were used for fraud and shut down. (bankofajerica.com was re-registered 1 year later.)

17.6.2 Automatic Name Completion

Many Web browsers support automatic name completion. Rather than typing in the TLD (e.g., .com), users can just enter the middle of the hostname. Automatic name completion appends a series of TLD suffixes until the hostname is found. Usually .com is tried first. If a Web site does not end with a .com, then an attacker can effectively hijack the domain by registering the .com name.

One of the most widely known examples of name completion hijacking is whitehouse.com. In 1997, Dan Parisi registered the domain and set up a pornographic Web site [Pelline1997]. The President of the United States uses the hostname whitehouse.gov. Users that entered whitehouse in their Web browsers had auto-completion take them to a porn site rather than the President's Web site. Although this Web site is no longer hosting pornography [Rosen2004], it clearly demonstrated the power of hijacking through automatic name completion.

A Rose By Any Other Name...

In 2004, a teenager in Germany hijacked the eBay domain [Fiutak2004]. He had read about domain name ownership transfers and submitted a few of them. He submitted transfers for several German Web sites including google.de, amazon.de, and ebay.de. Although most of the transfer requests were denied, the ebay.de site was successfully transferred.

Similarly, in January 2005, Panix—the oldest commercial ISP in New York—had its domain hijacked. This caused a service disruption that lasted days [Varghese2005].

To prevent domain hijacking, some domain registrars support domain locking. A locked domain cannot be transferred unless it is first unlocked.

17.6.3 Social Engineering

Social engineering is a term used to describe sociological persuasion. Rather than using computers and scripts to compromise a system, a social engineer uses guise and conman techniques. They may use emails or telephones to convey authority and acquire the information that they desire.

Domain names are registered through a limited number of name registrars. If the registrar can be convinced that a user is an authoritative owner of a domain, the domain's information can be modified or transferred.

17.6.4 Domain Renewals

Domain name registrars do not assign domains indefinitely. Instead, domains have expiration dates. Expiration allows abandoned domains to be released. Usually domains are registered for one, two, or five years. If a domain owner does not pay attention to the expiration date, then they may forget to renew their domain. When a name expires, anyone can register the same name. This allows an attacker to intentionally grab a domain and impersonate a known company.

17.6.5 Other Social Attacks

There are many other types of social attacks against domain names. Wildcard DNS services permit any unknown hostname to resolve to a single address. For example, if `hostiledomain.net` supports wildcard matching, then `anything.hostiledomain.net` will resolve to an address. This includes names such as `www.bankofamerica.com.hostiledomain.net`, where the user may not notice that the hostname is not Bank of America.

Search engine ranking can also be used for domain hijacking. If the owner of `hostiledomain.net` designs his Web site carefully, then it may be listed first by search engines. A user searching for "Bank of America" may see the result for `hostiledomain.net` listed first and assume that it is the correct site.

Social attacks against DNS are limited only by the degree of imagination. As long as hostnames are independent of network addressing, social attacks will be effective against DNS.

17.7 RECONNAISSANCE AND EXPLOITATION

DNS allows an attacker to gain insight about potential targets. Reconnaissance about a domain may come from hostnames, zone transfers, host listings, and DNS fields. Knowing information about a host can directly lead to exploitable risks and additional reconnaissance. Along with exploitation and information gathering, DNS can also be used to hide information.

17.7.1 Hostnames

Hostnames can provide valuable information to an attacker. Small companies, departments, or domains may use themed hostnames. Knowing the theme can provide information about the administrator. For example, if the hostnames `eminiar`, `gothos`, `thasus`, and `vendikar` appear in the hostname listing, then the administrator is likely a Star Trek fan (these are the names of Star Trek planets). This information is valuable to social engineers. A social engineer that contacts the administrator may create a friendship bond over a common trait. The bond can be exploited to gain trust and can be used as a conduit for collecting information leaks that can aid attacks. Similarly, passwords are frequently chosen based on themes. Knowing the computer theme may assist password discovery.

Whereas small companies use colorful themes, larger companies usually use employee names, phone numbers, or IDs along with department abbreviations. This information discloses employee information, department sizes, and contact points for social engineering.

Hostnames may also disclose the type of network service available. For example, most hosts named www (any domain) likely run Web servers. The host ftp runs an FTP server. Variations of ns, dns, and bind (e.g., ns1 or adns02) are likely primary or secondary name servers. If an attacker knows a vulnerability for mail servers, then the focus may be placed on hosts named mail or smtp (SMTP/email services) rather than hosts named ns or www.

17.7.2 Zone Transfers

The DNS protocol provides a facility to transfer all domain information between servers. These *zone transfers* provide an approach for rapidly updating secondary and caching servers. Whereas DNS uses UDP for individual lookups, zone transfers rely on TCP. The recipient of a zone transfer receives all domain information, including hostnames, network addresses, mail exchangers, and other DNS information.

Zone transfers are designed to streamline DNS distribution. A secondary DNS server may request a zone transfer from a primary server, or the primary may push a zone transfer to a secondary. Although the secondary likely caches some DNS information that it will not use, it will not repeatedly query the primary for individual host information. The simplest zone transfer can be performed with the Unix host command (from the BIND distribution). The command host -l domain ns.domain performs a zone transfer for the domain from the primary name server ns.domain.

Attackers can use zone transfers for reconnaissance. Because a zone transfer lists all hostnames in the domain, the attacker immediately gains a list of potential targets. If a particular network address in a subnet does not exist in a domain transfer, then there is no need to scan or attempt to compromise the missing host.

The most direct method to mitigate risks from zone transfers is to disable this functionality. Although many companies disable zone transfers, a surprisingly large number of DNS servers provide this functionality. If zone transfers are required for populating secondary or caching servers, then it should be configured as a push from the primary DNS server rather than a pull request initiated by a secondary.

Other technologies, such as DNSSEC [RFC4033, 4034, 4035], define methods for cryptographically authenticating zone information. DNSSEC can also authenticate secondary and caching servers that are permitted to conduct zone transfers.

17.7.3 Host Listing

When DNS zone transfers are not available, hosts may still be discovered using a brute-force domain scan (Listing 17.8). The technique simply iterates through all network addresses in a subnet. Each address that has a hostname (reverse lookup) can be readily discovered. A second search of the discovered hostnames can identify name aliases and additional DNS information.

NOTE

The full ListHosts.c *program is included on the CD-ROM.*

ON THE CD

Some DNS servers mitigate this attack by restricting the number of lookups that can be requested by any particular network address. For example, the host 10.1.2.3 may only be allowed to query a DNS server 100 times per hour. Attackers that use proxies or relay requests through a variety of DNS caches can overcome this type of restriction.

LISTING 17.8 Code to List Hosts in a Domain

```
/*****************************************************
ListRange(): Scan a range of IP addresses.
List any that resolve.
*****************************************************/
void        ListRange        (uint32_t Start, uint32_t Stop)
{
  int i;
  char *S, AddrIP[100];
  struct hostent *Hent;
  struct in_addr AddrIn;
  int Counter=0;

  /* process each IP address */
  for( ; Start <= Stop ; Start++)
    {
    memset(AddrIP,0,sizeof(AddrIP));
    AddrIn.s_addr = htonl(Start);
    strcpy(AddrIP,inet_ntoa(AddrIn));
    sethostent(1);
    /* check for a hostname */
    Hent = gethostbyaddr((char *)&AddrIn,sizeof(AddrIn),AF_INET);
    if (Hent)        S = Hent->h_name;
    else    S = NULL;
    if (S)
      {
      printf("%s %s\n",AddrIP,S);
      /* check every alias */
      for(i=0; Hent->h_aliases[i]; i++)
```

```
        {
        S = Hent->h_aliases[i];
        printf("          %s\n",S);
        fflush(stdout);
        }
      }
    } /* for() */
  endhostent();
} /* ListRange() */
```

17.7.4 DNS Fields

Different DNS fields can disclose information to attackers. For example, any host listed in the MX field runs a mail server on port 25/TCP. Similarly, hosts listed in the NS field run DNS servers. Although less common today, the HINFO field is intended to store host information. This may include operating system, architecture, or contact information. Finally, the TXT field is used for generic comments. This information may provide additional insight for an attacker.

17.7.5 Information Hiding

Each piece of DNS information is associated with a 2-byte type field. NS, MX, and TXT are three of the 65,536 possible values (they are 2, 15, and 16, respectively) [RFC1035]. Because new types may be defined in the future, many DNS servers permit caching unknown field types. These undefined fields can be used to store covert information—only clients that know to ask for the information will receive it.

17.8 MITIGATION OPTIONS

DNS was designed to manage meta-information for network addresses. It was designed for speed, flexibility, and scalability but not security; it offers no authentication mechanisms and assumes all queries are trustworthy. As such, there are few options to mitigate DNS risks. The main approaches for securing DNS rely on server-specific configurations, defined trust, and alternate resolution methods.

Most DNS mitigation options rely on security-by-obscurity and patching. Basic preventative measures include direct, technical, reconnaissance, and social threat mitigation.

17.8.1 Direct Threat Mitigation

Basic maintenance and network segmentation can limit the impact from direct threats:

Patch: Exploits and enhancements for DNS servers are released regularly. DNS servers and their host platforms should be regularly patched and maintained.

Separate Internal and External Domains: DNS servers should be separated. Large networks should consider dividing servers between internal network segments. This limits the impact from any single corrupt server and divides the DNS workload.

Restricted Zone Transfers: Zone transfers can be restricted to specific hosts and identified by network address or hardware address. This approach is vulnerable to MAC and IP impersonation attacks but does provide protection against arbitrary hosts requesting zone transfers.

Authenticated Zone Transfers: Using digitally signed and authenticated zone transfers can reduce the risk from zone transfer interception and poisoning.

Limit Cache Durations: Reducing cache durations below the values specified in the DNS replies shortens the vulnerability window from cache poisoning.

Reject Mismatched Replies: If a caching DNS server receives multiple replies with different values, the entire cache should be flushed. Although this negatively impacts cache performance, it eliminates the risk from long-term cache poisoning.

17.8.2 Technical Threat Mitigation

Technical risks require preventative measures for the network, host, and local environment:

Harden Servers: Restricting the number of remotely accessible processes limits the number of potential attack vectors. Hardened servers have a lower threat profile from technical attacks.

Firewall: Placing a hardware firewall in front of a DNS server limits the number of remote attack vectors.

17.8.3 Reconnaissance Threat Mitigation

The threat from an attacker performing reconnaissance can be limited by the information provided. Although DNS cannot be completely disabled, the type and amount of information available can be restricted:

Limit Zone Transfers: Zone transfers should be restricted to authenticated hosts only. Although this does not prevent brute-force host lookups, it does hinder reconnaissance.

Set Request Limits: Limit the number of DNS requests that can be performed by any single network address. Although not preventing brute-force domain listings, this does introduce an obstacle.

Remove Reverse Lookups: If reverse lookups are not essential, then remove them. This limits the impact from brute-force domain listings.

Separate Internal and External Domains: DNS servers should be separated, ensuring that LAN information remains in the LAN. In particular, internal-only hostnames should not be externally viewable.

Remove Excess Information: TXT, CNAME, and HINFO information that is not directly applicable to external users should be removed. If an external visitor does not need to see the HINFO data for a host, then the data should not be accessible.

Hide Version: For DNS servers that permit local login or remote status reports, the version of DNS may be disclosed. Because different versions correspond with different explicit exploits, the version should be modified to report false information, or removed altogether.

17.8.4 Social Threat Mitigation

Although "user education" is desirable for preventing risks from similar hostnames and automatic name completion, it is not the only option:

Monitor Similar Domains: Constantly search for domain name variations. When similar hostnames are identified, DNS providers can be asked to shut them down. Although this is a complicated and time-consuming task, there are services that specialize in monitoring for similar domain names.

Lock Domains: Use domain registrars that support domain locking. This requires additional information such as account information or passwords to transfer domain names.

Use Valid Contacts: Providing one or more valid contact values in the domain registration permits users and registrars to contact the domain owner. But, this does not require specifying people's names or personal information—a social engineer could use this information to attack the domain owner.

24/7 Support: Select a domain registrar that provides round-the-clock support. Be sure the registrar can be contacted at any time in case there is a domain issue.

Self-Hosting: Large companies may choose to become their own registrar for their domain.

If a domain is hijacked, immediately contact the domain registrar. If the registrar is unavailable or unable to resolve the issue, contact the TLD. For example, VeriSign is the contact for .com and .net domains. In addition, ICANN can be contacted by emailing *transfers@icann.org*.

17.8.5 Optimal DNS Configurations

BIND is the most common DNS server implementation. There are many documents that specify how to tighten the configuration of BIND servers. Some of these documents include "Securing BIND: How to Prevent Your DNS Server from Being Hacked" (*http://www.giac.org/certified_professionals/practicals/gsec/0756.php*) and "Defense in Depth of DNS" (*http://www.sans.org/rr/whitepapers/dns/867.php*). In addition, the Internet Security Consortium offers many resources for configuring and securing BIND (*http://www.isc.org/index.pl?/sw/bind/*).

The availability of security-oriented server documentation varies between vendors. Although BIND has many supporting documents, other servers offer few resources (or none at all).

17.8.6 Defining Trusted Replies

DNS servers normally provide no notion of trust. A DNS client cannot determine whether a reply is valid. The *DNS Security Extensions* (DNSSEC—*http://www.dnssec.net/*) provide signatures for authenticating information and digitally signs every response. However, DNSSEC requires authentication keys to be distributed prior to use. If the keys are not shared prior to the lookup, then the client has no means to validate the authentication. In addition, DNSSEC does not prevent domain hijacking—a server that supports DNSSEC can sign results for a domain that it is impersonating. DNSSEC only authenticates the server, not the content.

More common than DNSSEC, companies usually mange two DNS servers: one in the LAN and one in the WAN. The LAN server provides DNS support to all internal hosts. This prevents an external hijacker from compromising DNS queries that stay within the local network. The WAN DNS server provides information to external hosts and remains vulnerable.

17.8.7 Alternate Resolution Methods

There are other domain name resolution methods besides DNS. These include static files (e.g., /etc/hosts), LDAP, and NIS. Although alternate solutions work well within local networks, only DNS is widely supported between external networks.

For critical systems, DNS should not be used as a trusted information source. Instead, network addresses should be stored in local host files or resolved through trusted naming services. When authentication is required, other network protocols should perform security checks. For example, DNS may resolve a hostname to a network address, but IPv6, IPsec, SSH, SSL, or Kerberos should authenticate the resolved host.

NOTE

Many secure protocols perform authentication through a third-party host. In this situation, the authentication authority should not be identified through DNS. If the authenticating authority is identified using DNS, then an attacker can change the DNS entry for the authenticator. This can make it possible for the attacker to authenticate his own server.

SUMMARY

DNS provides an essential function for the Internet: it provides meta-information across the entire Internet. DNS provides hostname to network address mapping, domain information, and mail service reference support, and is extendable to providing other types of information. DNS is highly distributed and very scalable—working well for both small LANs and global networks. However, DNS was never designed for security.

DNS lacks basic authentication services and effectively trusts all data within the DNS protocol. Regardless of the implementation, all DNS clients are vulnerable to domain hijacking and forged replies. Beyond the fundamental security oversights and configuration issues, this protocol is vulnerable to social engineering exploits; a DNS server can be compromised without ever using the DNS protocol. Unlike other network protocols, there are few options for security DNS information.

REVIEW QUESTIONS

1. List three types of information DNS associates with hosts.
2. Can a DNS packet contain both query and answer information?
3. What are the different types of TLD servers?
4. What are "direct risks" to DNS?
5. How is domain hijacking different from server hijacking?
6. What type of DNS attack does not require a computer?
7. What is a zone transfer?

DISCUSSION TOPICS

1. Consider domain names from various technical and financial companies. What information is (or can be) stored at each of the different types of DNS servers?

2. Which type of DNS risk (direct, technical, social, or reconnaissance) is likely most damaging when used by a remote network attacker? When used for pharming?

3. DNSSEC associates a domain server with an authenticating key. Describe some of the issues concerning key distribution. Why is DNSSEC not widely deployed?

4. DNS exposes other network protocols to risks due to untrustworthy host-name information. Are there large-scale alternatives to DNS?

ADDITIONAL RESOURCES

The issues associated with DNS are well understood and widely documented. Ross Rader's white paper, titled "One History of DNS," provides an excellent discussion of the history, evolution, and political influences that have lead to today's DNS. This document is available online at *http://www.byte.org/one-history-of-dns.pdf* and on the companion CD-ROM. The SANS Institute provides many white papers on specific DNS issues including the following:

ON THE CD

- Irving, Christopher, "The Achilles Heal of DNS." SANS Institute, 2003. Available online at *http://www.sans.org/rr/whitepapers/dns/565.php*.
- Martin, Derek, "Securing BIND: How to Prevent Your DNS Server from Being Hacked." SANS GIAC Security Essentials Certification, SANS Institute, 2002. Available online at *http://www.giac.org/certified_professionals/practicals/gsec/0756.php*.
- Teoh, Cheng, "Defense in Depth for DNS. GSEC Version 1.4b." SANS Institute, 2003. Available online at *http://www.sans.org/rr/whitepapers/dns/867.php*.

The issues concerning DNSSEC are not as well documented as DNS. NLnet Labs hosts a short history of DNSSEC at *http://www.nlnetlabs.nl/dnssec/history.html* that lists the troubles deploying a secure DNS replacement. A larger list of DNSSEC documents, including weaknesses and analysis, can be found at the DNSSEC Web site (*http://www.dnssec.net/*).

Part

VII

OSI Layer 6

In This Part

- Presentation Layer
- SSL
- SSH

Layer 6 of the ISO OSI model is the presentation layer. This layer establishes session requests and transforms data into machine-independent formats. Although originally defined for data manipulation, this layer is commonly used by security-oriented protocols. Two common presentation layer protocols are SSL and SSH.

18 Presentation Layer

In This Chapter

- Common Usage
- Session Management
- VPN Technologies

In the early days of computers, there were few standards; every computer vendor created a unique, stand-alone product. Differences between systems ranged from byte ordering (little or big endian) and byte/word size to line representation and character sets such as ASCII and EBCDIC. Many of these differences still exist today. Traditionally, Motorola processors use big endian byte order, where the highest byte is stored first, whereas Intel uses little endian, where the lowest byte is stored first. Microsoft and DOS-based operating systems use a carriage return and line feed to separate lines in text files (represented as CRLF, 0x0d 0x0a, or \r\n), whereas Unix and Linux only use line feeds (LF, 0x0a, \n).

For networked computers to communicate, application data needs to be transformed into a machine-independent representation. The OSI *presentation layer* defines the functionality for this conversion. This layer manages syntax negotiation and data transformation. The presentation layer also manages the session layer, creating and terminating session requests.

18.1 COMMON USAGE

Although originally defined to convert data between character sets, much of the presentation layer's functionality is obsolete. For example, ASCII has become a standard for character representation, whereas EBCDIC remains a mere footnote in history. In addition, most network applications now use system-independent data formats and do not require presentation layer transformations. Because the translation requirement is no longer present, this layer frequently appears transparent within the OSI network stack.

As technology has evolved, many new functional requirements have emerged that were not specified in the original ISO OSI network model. Most notably, encoding, compression, and encryption are absent from the OSI stack's definition. Although each layer can provide protocols that support these functions, is it not necessarily best to employ these functions at every layer. For example, encryption is computationally expensive. A system that applies encryption at every layer of the network stack will process data slower than a system that only performs encryption once. In addition, compressed files cannot usually be compressed a second time. Providing compression at every layer may actually generate more data than a one-pass compression stack. Encoding, compression, and encryption are forms of data transformation, so the presentation layer has grown into the role of providing these functions.

Lost in Translation

File formats and presentation layer protocols are often confused. The *Hyper-Text Markup Language* (HTML) is one such example. Many people refer to HTML as a presentation layer protocol because it (1) is machine independent, (2) defines Web page presentation layouts, and (3) is closely associated with networking through Web servers. However, HTML is not a presentation layer protocol. When HTML is passed from a Web server to a browser, there is no data translation, and the layout presentation is based on the browser's interpretation of the data—an activity that occurs outside of the network stack.

Other file formats could benefit from the presentation layer, but they do not use it. JPEG, for example, is a graphical file format. The JPEG header defines the byte order within the file: "MM" for Motorola's big endian or "II" for Intel's little endian. Rather than requiring every JPEG picture viewer to support both MM and II formats, the presentation layer could transparently translate between formats. Ideally, the presentation layer should, during transfer, translate the picture to the most efficient format: MM for big endian systems and II for little endian. Instead, the presentation layer is not used, and viewers must support both endian formats.

Few applications still perform the originally defined translation functionality. One example is FTP. The *file transfer protocol* traces back to RFC114 (April 1971). The original FTP supported translations between ASCII, EBCDIC, and other character sets. Although the protocol has undergone many revisions (and most systems no longer support EBCDIC), today's FTP still converts between DOS CRLF and Unix LF text files.

18.1.1 Encoding

When information is passed between systems, data may be encoded to prevent misinterpretation. For example, if an application only supports 7-bit ASCII data (e.g., email), then binary data may be base64-encoded (see Chapter 4) to prevent the data transfer from corrupting the data.

Encoding may also define the amount of data and protocol. Although the hypertext transport protocol (HTTP) was designed for the DoD TCP/IP stack, it contains OSI presentation layer functionality. Each HTTP request negotiates the data transfer protocol. Choices include HTTP/1.0 or HTTP/1.1, compressed or "raw" data transfers, whether to allow many replies per network connection (or just one request per TCP connection), and even data chunking—segmenting the transferred information into blocks.

Other, less common, presentation layer protocols that perform encoding and negotiation include the lightweight presentation protocol (LPP), the ISO presentation protocol (ISO PP), and the AppleTalk Filing Protocol (AFP).

There are many standards for converting information for network translations. One of the most common is the *Abstract Syntax Notation* (ASN.1). ASN.1 describes a standard for converting between machine-specific data types and network data streams. Using ASN.1, an application can convert an internal data structure into a machine-independent format. Besides ASN.1, other translation formats include BNF notation, the CCITT X.409 standard, CORBA, and extensible markup language (XML) formats such as SOAP and DOM.

There is a distinction between using ASN.1, BNF, XML, and other encoding methods as machine-independent file formats and presentation layer protocols. This distinction is based on when the encoding is generated and interpreted. If the network stack generates it, then it is a protocol. However, if it is used by an application outside of the network, then it is a file format. Databases may use an XML protocol to share information over a network, or may export records to an XML file. Transferring an XML file over a network does not make it a presentation layer protocol.

18.1.2 Compression

Data compression transforms data from a *low entropy state*, where information may be redundant or unnecessary, to a *high entropy state*, where every bit has a unique purpose. In a *loss-less compression* algorithm, the data can be decompressed back to the original state. Loss-less compression algorithms include the Huffman minimum redundancy encoding [Huffman1952] and Lempel-Ziv coding [Lempel1977]. In contrast, *lossy compression* algorithms, such as those used by JPEG and MP3 files, can reconstruct similar (but not identical) patterns to the original. For network communications, most protocols use loss-less compression algorithms. Lossy compression may be used by multimedia applications that transmit audio or video but is not ideal for transferring exact bit sequences.

Compressed data cannot be compressed a second time. Compressing an already compressed file usually makes a larger file because it was already in a maximum entropy state. By compressing data at the presentation layer, all lower layers receive less information to transport. Lower layer protocols that do support compression, such as CPPP and IPv6, only compress the packet header and not the user's data. This is because a higher OSI layer may already compress the user's data. Other network systems, such as the DOCSIS stack, selectively compress certain types of data, such as voice, text, and HTML, but not binary files or images. This way, DOCSIS will not attempt to compress already compressed data.

18.1.3 Encryption

Data encryption is one of the most promising uses of the presentation layer. By applying cryptography at the presentation layer, information transmissions can be authenticated and encoded for privacy without modification to lower-layer protocols. SSL and SSH (Chapters 19 and 20) are presentation layer protocols that provide cryptographic functionality.

Many cryptographic algorithms require negotiated parameters. For example, Diffie-Hellman key exchanges and X.509 certificate validation require exchanging public information. Because the presentation layer allows negotiation of syntax methods, it is ideal for negotiating cryptographic parameters.

From a security viewpoint, applying cryptography at the presentation layer minimizes risk from an attacker. If any of the lower layers are hijacked or compromised, an attacker can only create a DoS. Encryption protects the transported data. Insertion and replay attacks are generally ineffective due to cryptographic authentication. To intercept intelligible data or hijack a network connection, an attacker must target the presentation layer, application layer, or hosting system; lower-layer attacks becomes ineffective.

18.2 SESSION MANAGEMENT

To negotiation data formats and syntax, the presentation layer must establish a session layer connection. The negotiated information only needs to be negotiated at the beginning of the session; settings can remain throughout the session. Some presentation layer protocols, such as SSH, permit periodic renegotiations within a session, but each session requires an initial negotiation.

The presentation layer manages session creation, termination, and error management. If the session layer fails for any reason, the presentation layer manages the failure. This may include reestablishing the session (and renegotiating the presentation options) or informing the application layer of the error.

18.3 VPN TECHNOLOGIES

A VPN may be implemented at any of the OSI layers. IPv6 provides VPN functionality for the network layer, and SCTP allows VPNs at the transport layer. SSL and SSH can provide VPN support at the presentation layer. *Where* the VPN is implemented leads to tradeoffs. Lower-layer protocols can implement entire virtual networks; IPv6 can tunnel entire subnetworks and provide broadcast and multicast support. Any network application can use the tunnel transparently. In contrast, higher-layer VPNs may not be transparent but do not need special routers for tunneling the protocol. For example, IPv6 requires routers that support IPv6 packets, whereas SSH can create a VPN over any supported network protocol.

18.3.1 VPN and Transparency

Presentation layer VPNs are usually point-to-point and not necessarily transparent. The application layer must know about the VPN at the presentation layer to use it. Although SSH does support tunneling transport layer ports, it does not natively tunnel network layer traffic. Instead, PPP (or other low-layer protocols) are used to establish a network path within an SSH connection.

18.3.2 VPN and Security

VPN technologies are usually associated with secure data encapsulation. SSH, IPsec, and IPv6 all use some form of cryptography along with the VPN. These systems provide endpoint authentication as well as data validation and privacy; however, security is not essential to VPN technologies. The *Generic Routing Encapsulation* (GRE) [RFC1701, RFC2784] is one such example. GRE allows a network layer protocol to tunnel another network layer protocol. The *Point-to-Point*

Transport Protocol (PPTP) uses GRE to create a transport layer VPN [RFC2637]. In effect, PPTP uses GRE to tunnel PPP traffic. As stated in RFC2637:

> The GRE packets forming the tunnel itself are not cryptographically protected. Because the PPP negotiations are carried out over the tunnel, it may be possible for an attacker to eavesdrop on and modify those negotiations.

Even though VPN stands for Virtual *Private* Network, the privacy part of the name is related to routing. A private network operates independently of the Internet. A VPN may be dependent on the Internet but managed and routed differently. The privacy in a VPN is not achieved through cryptography. Instead, cryptography offers a different form of privacy—protection from undesirable observers.

SUMMARY

The presentation layer is used to transform user data between machine-specific formats. Originally, this included translations between character sets and byte ordering. The presentation layer manages the session layer and any required presentation syntax negotiation. This functionality has allowed this rarely used layer to provide data encoding, compression, and encryption.

REVIEW QUESTIONS

1. Name a protocol that provides information translation for text files.
2. Give two reasons the presentation layer is ideal for encrypting user data.
3. What are three session-management functions provided by the presentation layer?

DISCUSSION TOPICS

1. Why is the presentation layer located above the session layer? Given its limited functionality for information translation, would it be better located above the application layer or below the session layer?
2. The DoD TCP/IP stack does not separate the OSI session, presentation, and application layer functionality. Does the lack of separation lead to less-secure protocols? Do the three OSI layers split functionality that would be better combined?

3. When is a VPN at the presentation layer more desirable than one at the network layer? When it is less desirable? Is there a benefit to using a VPN at both the presentation and network layers (a VPN in a VPN)? What are the limitations?

ADDITIONAL RESOURCES

ISO 8822 and 8823 define the presentation layer and functionality. The related documents, ISO 8824 and 8825, define ASN.1.

The World Wide Web Consortium (W3C) (*http://www.w3c.org/*) provides the XML standard. W3C also provides standards for many XML derivative works, including HTML, SOAP, and DOM.

The Object Management Group (OMG) provides CORBA and other presentation standards. They can be found at *http://www.omg.org/* and *http://www.corba. org/*.

19 SSL

In This Chapter

- Common SSL Usage
- SSL Functionality
- Certificates
- Risks
- HTTPS

The *Secure Socket Layer* (SSL) protocol provides a framework for passing information through an authenticated and encrypted tunnel. Each SSL connection defines a point-to-point tunnel between a client and a server. The SSL protocol operates within the presentation layer and allows the client and server to negotiate authentication, encryption, and checksum algorithms.

SSL, by itself, is a system for negotiating protocols. SSL does not provide security nor natively include cryptography; there is no security from SSL by itself. The security in SSL comes from the negotiated protocols. For example, the client may support DES, 3DES, and AES encryption, whereas the server supports 3DES and RC2. Using SSL, both systems can negotiate communication using their common 3DES encryption algorithm. A variety of authentication, encryption, and checksum functions may be incorporated into SSL.

19.1 COMMON SSL USAGE

SSL is used to tunnel plaintext data through an encrypted tunnel. Application-layer protocols that normally transmit unencrypted data gain encryption, authentication, validation, and nonrepudiation by using SSL. For example, the Web uses HTTP for transmitting and receiving HTML data normally via plaintext transfers. HTTP over SSL is called *HTTPS*. It uses SSL to encrypt the Web requests and replies. HTTPS is the most common use of SSL. Other uses include `stelnet` and `sftp`—telnet and FTP over SSL.

Because SSL is a presentation-layer protocol, any application-layer protocol may use SSL. Although most SSL-enabled applications explicitly link to an SSL library, stand-alone SSL applications can proxy application data through an SSL connection. Example generic proxies include `s_client` and `s_server` from OpenSSL, and the stand-alone Stunnel application (*http://www.stunnel.org/*).

19.2 SSL FUNCTIONALITY

Netscape initially developed SSL for securing Web-based connections. Without some type of encoding, HTTP would send Web traffic—including passwords and logins—in plaintext across the network.

In any protocol, cryptography leads to two critical issues. First, different countries have different laws regarding cryptography. Thirty-nine countries, including the United States, Russia, and Japan, have signed the Wassenaar Arrangement. This agreement regulates cryptographic software as munitions and tools of war. Non-Wassenaar countries have differing levels of cryptographic controls. For example, China and Israel have stricter regulations concerning the import, export, and usage of cryptographic systems. In contrast, South Africa, Chile, and Lebanon have virtually no restrictions. [RSA2000] Because different countries have different restrictions, any protocol that uses cryptography would fall under differing regulations, which hinders worldwide adoption.

Second, new and stronger algorithms are constantly being developed. If a protocol is tightly coupled to a specific algorithm, then it could quickly become outdated. Similarly, if a cryptographic algorithm were later shown to be weak, then a tightly coupled protocol would become a weak or insecure protocol.

SSL arose from these two requirements. SSL is not closely tied to any particular cryptographic algorithm. It allows a selection from different algorithms and permits new algorithms to be added. Because different systems support different algorithms, SSL provides the means to negotiate algorithms. SSL operates in three distinct phases: negotiation, key exchange, and data transfer.

19.2.1 SSL Connection

The first phase of the SSL protocol establishes network connectivity. Because SSL operates at the presentation layer, a network socket must be established through the lower layers. In particular, SSL operates independently of the transport layer, network addressing, and lower OSI layers. In addition, SSL operates above the session layer. Because the session layer manages disconnects and reconnects at the transport and network layers, these do not necessarily reset SSL connections.

To track the connection state, SSL maintains a *context*. The context is an abstract data structure that stores session, negotiation, and data transfer information. Initially the context is empty (set to default values). The SSL initialization handshake is used to populate the context with state and connection information.

19.2.2 SSL Negotiation

During the connection handshake, the SSL client and server negotiate cryptographic algorithms. The client transfers a list of supported cipher combinations. The list is transmitted in priority order—the first cipher is more desirable than the second cipher, the second is more desirable than the third, and so on. The server evaluates the cipher list and selects the first combination that is supported by the server. If no combination is viable, then there can be no SSL connection.

The cipher combinations specify four cryptographic elements: SSL version, key exchange, encryption cipher, and validation algorithm. The different available combinations form the list of available cipher sets. Table 19.1 shows a set of cipher combinations used by SSL. Other combinations, besides those in Table 19.1, are also possible.

Although SSL only provides a framework for negotiating and managing cryptographic systems, it is commonly described as an encryption system. This is because different versions of SSL are closely affiliated with specific cipher combinations called cipher suites.

TABLE 19.1 SSL Cipher Suites from OpenSSL 0.9.7e

SSL 2

SSL2-DES-CBC-MD5	SSL2-DES-CBC3-MD5	SSL2-EXP-RC2-CBC-MD5
SSL2-EXP-RC4-MD5	SSL2-RC2-CBC-MD5	SSL2-RC4-64-MD5
SSL2-RC4-MD5		→

SSL 3

SSL3-ADH-AES128-SHA	SSL3-ADH-AES256-SHA
SSL3-ADH-DES-CBC-SHA	SSL3-ADH-DES-CBC3-SHA
SSL3-ADH-RC4-MD5	SSL3-AES128-SHA
SSL3-AES256-SHA	SSL3-DES-CBC-SHA
SSL3-DES-CBC3-SHA	SSL3-DHE-DSS-AES128-SHA
SSL3-DHE-DSS-AES256-SHA	SSL3-DHE-DSS-RC4-SHA
SSL3-DHE-RSA-AES128-SHA	SSL3-DHE-RSA-AES256-SHA
SSL3-EDH-DSS-DES-CBC-SHA	SSL3-EDH-DSS-DES-CBC3-SHA
SSL3-EDH-RSA-DES-CBC-SHA	SSL3-EDH-RSA-DES-CBC3-SHA
SSL3-EXP-ADH-DES-CBC-SHA	SSL3-EXP-ADH-RC4-MD5
SSL3-EXP-DES-CBC-SHA	SSL3-EXP-EDH-DSS-DES-CBC-SHA
SSL3-EXP-EDH-RSA-DES-CBC-SHA	
SSL3-EXP-RC2-CBC-MD5	SSL3-EXP-RC4-MD5
SSL3-EXP1024-DES-CBC-SHA	SSL3-EXP1024-DHE-DSS-DES-CBC-SHA
SSL3-EXP1024-DHE-DSS-RC4-SHA	SSL3-EXP1024-RC2-CBC-MD5
SSL3-EXP1024-RC4-MD5	SSL3-EXP1024-RC4-SHA
SSL3-NULL-MD5	SSL3-NULL-SHA
SSL3-RC4-MD5	SSL3-RC4-SHA

19.2.2.1 SSL Version

There are many versions of the SSL protocol. Although SSLv1 (version 1) is seldom used, SSLv2 and SSLv3 are common. In addition, the *Transport Layer Security* (TLS) protocol may be used [RFC2246]. TLSv1 was designed as an open replacement for the patented SSL.

19.2.2.2 SSL Key Exchange and Authentication Algorithm

After establishing the connection and negotiating the cipher set, a key exchange is performed using the negotiated method. Many key exchange algorithms are supported by SSL. The most common are the following:

- Diffie-Hellman key exchange (DH)
- RSA (named after its authors: Rivest, Shamir, and Adleman)
- Digital Signature Algorithm (DSA) from the Digital Signature Standard (DSS)

A fourth system, called Fortezza, uses a digital token-based system for key exchanges, authentication, and encryption. Although it is supported by the SSL protocol, many SSL implementations ignore this option.

There are many variations for each of these key exchange systems. For example, the DH key exchange includes ephemeral Diffie-Hellman (abbreviated EDH or DHE) and anonymous Diffie-Hellman (ADH). DHE provides *forward secrecy*—every connection uses a new set of DH keys so a compromised connection cannot be used to crack previous connections. In contrast, ADH may not change keys between each connection. Both ADH and DHE are commonly used with digital signature algorithms such as RSA and DSS. ADH does not use a signature-based authentication system, which leaves it open to MitM attacks.

The DH key exchange is used for generating a shared secret value (see Chapter 4). In contrast, the RSA and DSS algorithms sign a digital challenge. Both parties can validate the challenge signature to validate the remote host. SSL systems may negotiate different DH variations as well as digital challenges. A client may propose key exchange algorithms such as "DHE with RSA," "ADH with DSA," or a la cart ciphers such as "ADH" or "RSA."

19.2.2.3 Encryption Cipher

In addition to the key exchange and authentication algorithm, the negotiated cipher set specifies an encryption cipher. The selection includes the cipher (DES, 3DES, RC2, RC4, and AES) and a choice of bit sizes and block chaining algorithms. For example, the client may specify "AES256" for 256-bit AES encryption or "DES-CBC" for DES with CBC chaining (see Chapter 4 for chaining methods and encryption algorithms).

19.2.2.4 Null Cipher

SSL provides a method for negotiating ciphers, but it does not specify that ciphers need to be strong or secure. Insecure algorithms, such as ADH, are usually included in the cipher suite but may be disabled by default. A client requesting SSL3-ADH-DES-CBC-SHA will be unable to use this combination to connect to a server if ADH is not enabled.

The *null cipher* is another example of an insecure option. This cipher performs no authentication and no encryption—data is transmitted unencoded. The null cipher is usually used for testing and debugging; it is not intended for secure communication. Network programmers may enable and use the null cipher along with a packet sniffer (such as Ethereal, `snort`, or `tcpdump`) to diagnose network communication problems. Without the null cipher, packet sniffers would be unable to identify network corruption because encryption prevents viewing application data.

Although the null cipher is not secure, it is available for use by most SSL implementations. OpenSSL (*http://www.openssl.org/*), the GNU Transport Layer Security Library (*http://www.gnu.org/software/gnutls/*), and Microsoft's SSL all include the null cipher option. Fortunately, the null cipher is usually disabled by default. It takes a conscious effort to enable the null cipher for use with SSL, and it must be enabled on both ends of the SSL connection. Unfortunately, developers occasionally forget to disable the null cipher after testing. Potentially, a client and server could negotiate and use the null cipher for transferring sensitive information.

19.2.2.5 Validation Cipher

Although key exchanges provide authentication, and encryption offers privacy, neither explicitly performs integrity checking. Although it is unlikely that a corrupt packet would pass decryption and authentication, data validation is not explicitly provided. For explicit validation of data integrity, SSL supports MD5 and SHA1 digests.

Although in theory every combination of key exchange, encryption algorithm, and validation cipher is possible, some variations are never implemented. For example, the DSS algorithm explicitly specifies use of the SHA1 digest. Although DSS could be used with MD5, the specification of DSS explicitly restricts the validation algorithm.

19.2.3 SSL Key Exchange

During the initialization handshake, the client transmits a list of desirable ciphers and a *digital challenge*. The challenge is used to initialize the selected key exchange. The server signs the challenge and the client validates the signature.

SSL may also transfer certificates. The X.509 certificate contains information that can be validated by a third party (section 19.3 discusses certificates). The RSA and DSS algorithms can validate certificates.

The *key exchange* permits authentication between the client and server. This mitigates the threat from a MitM attack. When using certificates or preshared keys, the exchange also validates the identity of the client and server. Although the key exchanges are performed using asymmetrical algorithms, the authenticated connection can be used to transfer a seed for use with a symmetrical (and faster) encryption algorithm. For example, SSL3-DHE-DSS-AES256-SHA specifies using SSLv3 to communicate. DHE is used to initially exchange a shared secret key, and DSS validates the client and server. After validation, both ends begin using the symmetrical 256-bit AES algorithm for encrypting data transfers. Throughout this entire process, SHA1 is used for validating packet contents.

19.2.4 SSL Data Transfer

Following the algorithm negotiation and key exchange, both ends may transfer application data. Information from the OSI application layer is encrypted using the negotiated algorithm (e.g., DES or AES) and passed down the OSI stack. On the receiving end, the SSL protocol receives the encrypted data from the OSI session layer, decrypts the data, and passes the information up to the application layer.

19.2.5 SSL Communication Flow

The different negotiations used by SSL, including cryptographic algorithms, key exchanges, and certificates, are performed concurrently (Figure 19.1).

Step 1: The client sends a `hello` record that includes the version of SSL being used (usually TLS 1.0), a list of viable cipher specifications (see Table 19.1), and a random challenge.

Step 2: The server responds with the selected cipher set and either a server certificate (*server-side certificate*) or part of a key exchange. The server may also request a certificate from the client (*client-side certificate*). The server generates a response to the random challenge that can be validated by the client. This allows the client to identify the server—preventing potential MitM attacks between the client and the server. This does not validate the server; it only prevents a MitM from hijacking the established connection.

Step 3: If the server provides a certificate, then the client contacts a certificate authority (CA) and validates the certificate. Although it is considered secure for the client to validate the certificate, there is nothing in SSL requiring certificate validation. Contacting a CA can add time to the initial connection. If speed is an issue, then the client may choose to not validate the server's certificate. In addition, some cipher sets, such as SSL3-NULL-MD5 and SSL3-RC4-MD5, do not require a server certificate.

Step 4: The client responds to the server, initiating a key exchange. If a client-side certificate is available, then the client may provide it. (If the server requests a client-side certificate, then one must be provided.) If the server provides a certificate, then the client also provides a message encrypted with the certificate. Similar to Step 2, this allows the server to identify but not validate the client.

Step 5: If the client provides a certificate to the server, then the server may contact a CA to authenticate the client. As with Step 3, the server is not required to validate the client, but servers usually validate client-side certificates.

Step 6: The server sends an encrypted handshake to complete the validation process. At this point, the negotiations and exchanges are complete; the client and server are both authenticated and validated. An attacker cannot act as a MitM or impersonate the client and server. All further communication uses the agreed upon symmetrical encryption algorithm, which is seeded with the negotiated key exchange values.

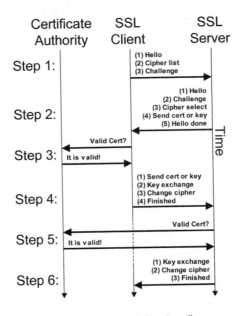

FIGURE 19.1 SSL initialization flow between client and server.

SSL includes a few out-of-band signals for managing the encrypted tunnel. These include the `hello` record for initiating the handshake, a `cipher change` signal to begin using symmetrical encryption, and a `finished` signal to denote the end of an SSL connection. RFC2246 includes a few other signals for managing retransmissions, failures, and renegotiations.

19.3 CERTIFICATES

Although many systems employ key exchange technologies to mitigate MitM hijacking, SSL's strength comes from endpoint validation. Through the use of digital certificates, the client can authenticate the server and vice versa. SSL supports two types of certificates. Server-side certificates are stored on the server, and client-side certificates are stored on client. Although there is support for different certificate formats, SSLv1 and TLS currently use the X.509 certificate format.

Certificates are sometimes called certs as a shorthand notation. A cert is a certificate.

19.3.1 X.509 Certificates

Each *X.509 certificate* follows a well-defined format and provides information for identification and validation [RFC2459]. Each X.509 certificate defines three components: identification, public key, and private key.

19.3.1.1 X.509 Identification

The X.509 identification contains field-value pairs that provide information about the certificate. The data is stored in the ASN.1 format. Some of the certificate fields form a *distinguished name* (DN) that identifies the certificate. Some of the common DN attributes are listed in Table 19.2. For example, the DN for HTTPS on Amazon.com is

```
/C=US/ST=Washington/L=Seattle/O=Amazon.com Inc./CN=www.amazon.com
```

The identification also includes the issuer's information. For Amazon.com, this is

```
/C=US/O=RSA Data Security, Inc./OU=Secure Server Certification
Authority
```

TABLE 19.2   Common Distinguished Name Attributes

Field Name	Purpose
CN	Common name (usually a person or server)
O	Organization (e.g., company name)
OU	Organization unit (e.g., department in a company)
C	Two-digit country code
ST	State or province
L	Locality (e.g., city or address)
Email	Email address for contact

Not every attribute in the distinguished name is required. In addition, attributes can be repeated. For example, a certificate may include multiple organization unit (OU) fields.

When the certificate is passed from the server to the client, the client can use the DN to validate the server's certificate with a CA. Together with the public key, the CA can validate that the key belongs with the DN.

Some clients may also use the DN to validate the server. For example, if the common name (CN) is www.amazon.com, but the certificate comes from www.badguy.com, then the certificate may be forged or stolen. In general, certificates should only come from the correct domain.

19.3.1.2 X.509 Public and Private Keys

SSL uses the X.509 certificate as a container for transferring keys in a *Public Key Infrastructure* (PKI). The PKI defines a set of public and private keys. The public X.509 certificate is used to transport the identification and public key across the network, whereas the private key is not shared. During the key exchange, a message is encoded with the private key and decoded with the public key to authenticate each party.

If the system only uses server-side certificates, then only one side can be validated. A basic key exchange prevents hijacking established SSL connections but does not authenticate the client.

The two main certificate validation algorithms are RSA and DSS. In RSA, the key exchange encodes a message with the private key and decodes it with the public key to authenticate each party. DSS transmits a digest of the public key rather than the key itself. When compared with RSA, DSS further impairs an attacker by preventing a direct attack against the public key.

19.3.2 Server Certificates

Server-side certificates are used to validate the server to the client. The server sends a public key (or in the case of DSS, a public key digest) to the client. It is up to the client to validate the certificate. Validation is usually done in one of two automated ways. The client may already have a copy of the server's key. This copy can be used to validate the server. More often, the client consults a trusted third-party that can validate the certificate. A trusted *certificate authority* (CA) is usually not the same host as the system being validated, so it can validate the certification.

Some domains operate their own CA servers for validating their certificates. This is problematic because it allows attackers to validate their own certificates. For example, VeriSign runs its own CA servers. If an attacker compromises the verisign.com DNS entry, then there is no way for a client to validate that VeriSign's certificate is authentic.

A third option is commonly used by interactive systems, such as Web browsers using HTTPS. If the certificate cannot be verified automatically, then the user is prompted to validate the certificate. Unfortunately, most users do not manually verify certificates—users usually just select "yes" or "ok" to continue. The desire to access the Web site is usually stronger than the perceived threat of an attack. As a result, interactive prompting for certificates usually leads to risks and high potentials for exploitation.

19.3.3 Client Certificates

Client-side certificates are used to authenticate the client to the server. Very secure systems use these to ensure that only authorized clients access the OSI application layer. Failure to provide a required, valid client-side certificate blocks the SSL connection. In addition, if both client and server use certificates, then it alleviates the threat of a MitM attack.

Without client-side certificates, the client is effectively anonymous to the server. In lieu of certificates, client-side identification may be passed to the application layer in the form of a username and password. For example, most online banks only use server-side certificates that authenticate the bank to the client. For client-side authentication, banks rely on the application layer, which is usually in the form of a username and password that is transmitted over the established SSL connection.

In many cases, client-side certificates are not necessary. Using only a server-side certificate, the client can be sure that the server is not an imposter, and an established SSL connection is not vulnerable to session hijacking.

Although a trusted third party usually validates server-side certificates, the server usually authenticates client-side certificates. Each client-side certificate is generated by the server and distributed before the first client connection. By authenticating certificates locally, the server gains a speed improvement over querying a remote system for authentication. In this situation, the server acts as its own CA.

19.3.4 Certificate Authority (CA)

A CA is a system that can validate a certificate. Although the CA server may be hosted by the certificate's domain (or on the same server as the certificate), they are usually hosted on separate systems or in remote domains. The system using the CA server for validation trusts the results from the CA server. For example, a client that sends a server-side certificate to the CA server trusts that the CA server will properly validate the certificate.

To prevent a hijacker from impersonating a CA server, most servers preshare their own public keys. A client validating a server-side certificate will encode the certificate with the CA server's public key. A domain-name hijacker will be unable to decode the request and cannot reply to the client.

A trusted CA server may perform any of three actions:

Accept: The certificate is found to be valid. The CA server responds with an acceptance.

Reject: The certificate is invalid, and the submitter is asked to reject the certificate. This usually happens for expired certificates, but invalid certificates can also lead to rejections.

Revoke: In the event that a certificate is compromised, the CA server can be ordered to revoke a certificate. Checking for revocation is very important because it is the only way to distinguish a valid and active certificate from a compromised certificate.

Certificates contain start and end dates that specify when they are valid. Although a client can check these dates, a client without a sense of time (or with an unset clock) may pass expired certificates to a CA server. Expired certificates generate revocation replies.

19.3.5 Certificate Generation

To validate a certificate, the CA server must know about the private certificate that contains the private key. This is a multistep process. First, the server generates a public and private key pair. For example, this can be done with OpenSSL using

```
openssl genrsa —des3 2048 -out key
```

OpenSSL will prompt for a pass phrase for protecting the private key. This deters attackers that manage to compromise the system and copy key files.

After generating system keys, a *certificate-signing request* (CSR) is generated and passed to the CA server:

```
openssl req -new -key key -out key.csr
```

The CSR (`key.csr`) contains a public key and is sent to the CA server. The CA server uses the CSR to encode an identity certificate. This identity certificate is used by the SSL certificate exchange to authenticate the server. Although this process is indirect—requiring a key pair, CSR, and identity certificate—it prevents an attacker from hijacking the initial key generation and distribution.

19.4 RISKS

The concepts behind SSL are secure. When properly implemented, SSL authenticates the server, optionally authenticates the client, and prevents established connections from being intercepted. Many SSL-based solutions do not fully implement secured environments, however. The most common risks to SSL come from four areas: certificate distribution, authentication, failure handling, and risks from lower-layer protocols.

19.4.1 Certificate Distribution

SSL relies on preshared certificates. If certificates are not exchanged in a secure way, they can be intercepted and compromised. For example, many companies use email to send client-side certificates to users. An attacker who accesses the email can use the client-side certificate.

Usually the CA server generates the certificates for use on the SSL server, but many SSL servers generate public and private certificates for use with clients. This generation may not use a CSR nor allow users to host their own private keys. As a result, the initial client-side certificate may not be protected (or only protected by a password).

Mailboxes, Etc.

Because of its convenience, email is commonly used to distribute certificates. For example, VeriSign is one of the largest CA servers. According to VeriSign, 93 percent of Fortune 500 companies use Versign's SSL services [Versign2005]. VeriSign uses email to distribute certificates for use on SSL servers. Although the emails should not be saved, a compromised email is unlikely to compromise the SSL server; an attacker would need the emailed certificate from VeriSign as well as the private key stored on the SSL server.

In contrast, client-side certificates pose a very large risk when emailed. The certificate itself is minimally protected—usually by nothing more than a password selected by the user. In addition, users may not delete emails containing their certificates, and deleted email may actually be stored in a "deleted mail" folder (for easy recovery). When combined with automated backup systems, it becomes very likely that the email containing the client-side certificate is stored where many users (and potential attackers) can access it.

19.4.2 Self-Certification

X.509 certificates specify the CA server. An attacker running an SSL server can generate certificates that point to a CA server operated by the attacker. In this situation, the certificate is valid, but the CA server should not be trusted.

To mitigate this risk, many applications (including Web browsers) maintain a list of trusted CA servers. Any CA server not in the list requires special consideration before extending trust.

19.4.3 Absent Client Certificate

As mentioned in Section 19.3.3, client-side certificates are not always used. If the server stores sensitive information required by the client, then the server should be *authenticated*. If the SSL client holds information used by the SSL server, then the client should also be *certified*.

Unfortunately, most SSL environments do not implement client-side certificates. Instead, the OSI application layer authenticates clients. SSL's security does not extend to higher OSI layers; SSL (without client-side certificates) protects the transport of application-layer data but does not protect the server against application layer attacks. For example, an attacker can anonymously connect using SSL and attack a Web server over HTTPS. When combines with anonymous relays and proxy systems, an attacker has little risk of being identified. Although client-side certificates do not prevent application-layer attacks against the server, they do allow the attacker to be identified.

To mitigate this risk, secure SSL environments should use both client and server certificates. This prevents unauthenticated clients from accessing the server's application layer. In addition, the application layer should require client authentication (e.g., username and password). Together this results in two-part authentication: something you have (the SSL certificate) and something you know (username and password).

19.4.4 Automated Systems

SSL is commonly used for communication between automated systems. This includes automated Web tools, backup and restore systems, and secure logging facilities. Although SSL does provide secure communications when it works, many automated systems fail to account for situations when SSL fails. For example, if an SSL certificate is invalid, an automated program may use it anyway (potential compromise) or cease to function (DoS). Many automated SSL systems do not check for certificate expiration or for SSL server and certificate matching (potential certificate theft).

More important than managing invalid certificates, few automated systems can recover from a revoked SSL certificate. Because automated systems cannot prompt for passwords, certificates are stored in a format that can be immediately stolen and used; the security of the certificate relies on the security of the entire host. Stolen certificates are a real possibility.

Regardless of how a certificate fails, an automated system that fails securely would not use the unauthenticated SSL connection. Unfortunately, many automated systems cannot be manually corrected when SSL fails. For example, a remote monitoring system with SSL-protected remote administration becomes a *rogue* (not under the control of the administrator) when SSL fails. To prevent rogue systems, automated systems sometimes contain backdoor options for downloading new SSL certificates. An attacker can use this type of backdoor for installing his own certificates on the remote device.

To mitigate risks from SSL, automated systems should rely on other authentication systems beyond SSL. When SSL in unavailable, alternate secure communication methods should be accessible. Although SSL does prevent established session hijacking, certificate authentication has minimal value to most remote administration systems.

19.4.5 Human Error

Human error, whether from insecure certificate storage or manually authorizing unknown certificates, is the leading cause of SSL insecurity. Although user education can reduce this risk, educating everyone is impractical. The fact that many SSL-enabled applications prompt users to resolve unauthenticated certificates shows a significant flaw in the implementation. When other secure protocols are unable to authenticate, they do not prompt the user for a resolution. For example, IPsec, IPv6, SCTP, and Kerberos do not use connections when authentication fails.

Very secure SSL implementations allow users to validate authenticated SSL connections but do not prompt users to resolve unauthenticated connections. Unfortunately, very secure SSL implementations are virtually nonexistent.

19.4.6 Lower-Layer Protocols

SSL is not a stack unto itself; it is a layer within a stack. As a result, risks from lower layers can impact SSL's effectiveness. For example, Chapter 17 discusses a large number of ways to hijack and modify DNS. An attacker can use this approach to successfully attack SSL:

1. The attacker creates a proxy that relays requests to a known host, such as a bank.

2. The attacker poisons DNS so requests for the bank resolve to the attacker. This forces clients to use the attacker's proxy to access the bank.
3. When a client (victim) requests an SSL connection to the bank, such as an HTTPS Web page, the attacker returns his own SSL certificate.
4. The client contacts the CA server to validate the certificate. The CA server's IP address is found using DNS.
5. Using the authenticated certificate, the client continues to use the attacker's system. The attacker, having established a MitM attack, can access and modify all of the SSL traffic.

This style of attack may generate a warning to the user, such as an unauthenticated CA server or invalid certificate. For an attacker, these issues can be addressed many ways:

■ Because the CA server is found using DNS, the attacker may also impersonate the CA server.
■ The attacker may contact the CA, impersonating the target company. A successful social engineer can acquire new certificates for use on hostile servers. This attack method was successfully used against Microsoft in January 2001 by acquiring certificates from VeriSign [MS01-017].
■ The attacker may register a known domain name through a different CA server. For example, PayPal uses VeriSign. If the attacker registers a certificate for pay-pal.com through an alternate CA, such as Equifax, then the certificate is valid but owned by the attacker. This will not generate any warnings for the client.

There are few mitigation options for these attack vectors. These attacks rely on automated validation systems to not check for alternate and conflicting certificates.

19.5 HTTPS

Secure Web pages usually use HTTPS—HTTP over SSL. Web browsers generally indicate SSL connections by displaying a small lock in the browser. Unfortunately, these little locks tend to have little meaning, and when combined with human error, offer little security.

19.5.1 Little Locks

Web browsers display a small lock to indicate SSL connections. The lock usually appears in the lower-right corner (or upper-right corner) of the browser, but different browsers may display it in different locations (and may use a lock or a key

icon). Although the lock is intended to indicate a secure Web page, the meaning of
the lock is misleading. Consider a Web page that accesses two different Web sites
(Listing 19.1). This page works by loading a frame with two parts—each part goes
to a different Web site, and only one uses SSL.

LISTING 19.1 SSL Key Text

```
<HTML>
<head><title>SSL Key Test</title></head>
<frameset rows="50%,*">
  <frame src="http://www.microsoft.com/">
  <frame src="https://licensing.microsoft.com/">
</frameset>
</HTML>
```

The state of the little lock depends on the connection for the outermost text
page, not the internal links. Even though the second Microsoft link uses HTTPS,
most browsers do not display a lock if the frame page is loaded using HTTP (Figure 19.2). Similarly, if the frame page is loaded using HTTPS, then the lock is present even though the first Microsoft link does not use HTTPS.

FIGURE 19.2 Example of the SSL Key Test using HTTP. (Microsoft
product screen shots reprinted with permission from Microsoft Corporation.)

On browsers such as Mozilla, Netscape, Firefox, Internet Explorer, Safari, and
Opera, the user may click on the lock to view SSL connection information. Even in
this situation, however, only the SSL connection for the frame is displayed. As of

December 2005, current browsers do not permit viewing information from more than one SSL connection. If the frame test is loaded using HTTPS, then the SSL information for the frame is accessible, but the SSL information for the internal frames is inaccessible. As another example, in 2006, PayPal loaded images from many different servers (Figure 19.3) using different SSL connections and different certificates. Information about each of these dependent SSL connections is not accessible for viewing—even though they are all different.

Address	Type	
https://www.paypalobjects.com/en_US/i/btn/btn_SignUpNow.gif	Image	
https://www.paypalobjects.com/en_US/i/scr/pixel.gif	Image	
https://www.paypalobjects.com/en_US/i/header/spot_globe.gif	Image	
https://www.paypalobjects.com/en_US/i/scr/pixel.gif	Image	
https://www.paypalobjects.com/en_US/i/header/hpPrivacy_shopwoutsharing_563x115.jpg	Image	
https://www.paypalobjects.com/en_US/i/header/spot_buyerTab_178x29.gif	Image	
https://www.paypalobjects.com/en_US/i/scr/pixel.gif	Image	
https://www.paypalobjects.com/en_US/i/header/spot_sellMerchTab_374x29.gif	Image	
https://securepics.ebaystatic.com/paypal/site/us/dc_whatispaypal_183x90.gif	Image	
https://securepics.ebaystatic.com/paypal/site/us/dchb_eMarketing2_183x90.gif.gif	Image	
https://www.paypalobjects.com/en_US/i/bnr/bnr_fpo3_183x50.gif	Image	
https://securepics.ebaystatic.com/paypal/site/whatsnewcorners/scr_tLftCnr_10x10.jpg	Image	
https://securepics.ebaystatic.com/pics/paypal/site/whatsnewcorners/pixel.gif	Image	
https://securepics.ebaystatic.com/paypal/site/whatsnewcorners/scr_tRgtCnr_10x10.jpg	Image	
https://securepics.ebaystatic.com/paypal/site/whatsnewcorners/pixel.gif	Image	
https://securepics.ebaystatic.com/paypal/site/whatsnewcorners/pixel.gif	Image	
https://securepics.ebaystatic.com/paypal/site/whatsnewcorners/pixel.gif	Image	
https://securepics.ebaystatic.com/paypal/site/whatsnewcorners/pixel.gif	Image	
https://securepics.ebaystatic.com/paypal/site/whatsnewcorners/pixel.gif	Image	
https://securepics.ebaystatic.com/paypal/site/whatsnewcorners/scr_bLftCnr_10x10.jpg	Image	
https://securepics.ebaystatic.com/paypal/site/whatsnewcorners/pixel.gif	Image	
https://securepics.ebaystatic.com/paypal/site/whatsnewcorners/scr_bRgtCnr_10x10.jpg	Image	
https://securepics.ebaystatic.com/paypal/site/whatsnewcorners/pixel.gif	Image	
https://www.paypalobjects.com/en_US/i/logo/verisign.gif	Image	
https://www.paypalobjects.com/en_US/i/logo/trustmark.gif	Image	
https://www.paypalobjects.com/en_US/i/logo/bbbmark.gif	Image	

FIGURE 19.3 Hyperlinks found at *https://www.paypal.com/*.

Microsoft, PayPal, Amazon.com, and most other companies implement SSL correctly. The problems with the little lock icon are due to the client's Web browser and not the HTTPS server.

The little lock on most Web browsers only indicates that there is an SSL connection but not which connection. In addition, if the main URL does not use HTTPS, then there may not be a little lock at all, even if SSL is used within the Web page.

Framed!

HTML frames can be used to make one Web page appear to be affiliated with a different Web site. Fortunately, there are ways to prevent a Web page from being wrapped in an unauthorized frame. The `target` option for `<BASE>`, `<FORM>`, and `<a HREF>` HTML tags specifies which frame should contain the information. Specifying `target="_top"` loads the linked page as the top layer, outside of any frames; however, this does not place the current page outside of frames. To unframe the current page, JavaScript is needed (Listing 19.2).

LISTING 19.2 JavaScript for Removing Unauthorized Frames

```
<script type="text/javascript">
<!-
function BecomeTop()
  {
  // Reload current page as top (outside of frames)
  if (self != top) window.open(location.href,"_top","");
  }
// -->
</script>
<BODY onLoad="BecomeTop()">
```

The Web Design Group maintains an HTML FAQ that describes other ways to remove frames. The FAQ is available online at (*http://www.html-help.com/faq/html/ frames.html*).

19.5.2 HTTPS and Human Error

Beyond the problems with the little lock icon, users usually accept unauthenticated certificates. Browser errors from expired certificates, unknown or not trusted CA servers, hosts that do not match certificates, and validation errors usually give users the option to continue with the unauthenticated connection. Most Web browsers display SSL Web pages even if the certificate is clearly corrupted, expired, or revoked. Users are given the option to "reject" an invalid certificate, accept it "just for this session," or "always accept." In most cases, users typically accept for the session or always accept; users rarely reject invalid certificates. For these reasons, SSL provides a minimal amount of security for users. Although an established connection cannot be hijacked or observed, neither party may be authenticated.

Due to risks from lower-layer protocols and automated validation systems, a valid certificate is not necessarily a sign of trustworthiness. An attacker can still control an authenticated host and perform MitM attacks. An invalid certificate—for any reason—is clearly a sign of a problem. Users and applications should not accept certificates or use SSL connections that fail authentication.

There are few mitigation options for this problem beyond educating users. Although Web browsers should not permit the use of unauthenticated SSL connections, this is not always the case. The few browsers that do support rejecting unauthenticated connections still default to prompting the user.

SUMMARY

The SSL protocol provides a framework for key exchanges, authentication, and encryption. It is flexible and extendible, allowing new algorithms to be added without replacing session- and application-layer implementations. SSL is commonly used to tunnel insecure protocols over a secured network connection. Unfortunately, limitations surrounding certificate management and distribution can limit SSL's effectiveness. Issues surround authentication management and error handling for both manual and automated systems. In addition, SSL remains vulnerable to some forms of server impersonation.

REVIEW QUESTIONS

1. What three items are negotiated by SSL before user data can be transferred?
2. What are HTTPS and stelnet?
3. What are four tasks performed by CA servers?
4. What are the four main types of risks for SSL?
5. What does it mean when a Web browser displays a little lock?

DISCUSSION TOPICS

1. Viruses such as Berbew and Agobot compromise SSL connections by intercepting Web browser function calls. Before data is passed from the browser to the SSL tunnel, the virus intercepts it. Is this risk a limitation of SSL? Describe some methods for detecting this type of system compromise.
2. Use a Web browser to visit sites such as PayPal, eBay, and online banks. Using HTTPS for the connection, which certificate is associated with the little lock in the browser? View HTML source code from these sites—how many certificates are actually used? By connecting to each image that uses

HTTPS, does the certificate displayed by the little lock change? What are some options to resolve this problem?

3. Configure a Web server and browser to use the Null cipher. Do Web pages still use the little lock? What does the little lock indicate?

4. Web browsers such as Netscape and Firefox have options for warning users when weak encryption functions are selected. What are the likely results from this type of warning? What would be a better option for dealing with weak ciphers? Which pose bigger risks: weak ciphers, poor certificate management, or misleading SSL indicators (little locks)?

ADDITIONAL RESOURCES

SSL is assigned patent number 5,657,390 from the U.S. Patent and Trademark Office (*http://www.uspto.gov/*). Filed on August 25, 1995 and awarded two years later to Netscape Communications Corporation, this patent describes the *SSL application program apparatus and method*. The patent discusses SSL communication from the initial handshake and negotiation to transport and out-of-band signals. The successor to SSL, TLS, is described in RFC2246. Both SSL and TLS are well documented by the OpenSSL project (*http://www.openssl.org/*).

Attacks against SSL are not limited to certificate management and user education. Sophisticated attacks against key exchanges and encryption methods are also threats. For example, David Brumley and Dan Boneh published a paper in March 2003 titled "Remote Timing Attacks Are Practical" (*http://www.zone-h.org/download/file=3021/*).

20 ▪ SSH

Few network protocols are designed with security as a primary consideration. Although the *Secure Socket Layer* (SSL) protocol (Chapter 19) has security in its name, it was actually designed as a framework and not as a secure protocol. In contrast, protocols such as SCTP, Kerberos, and *Secure Shell* (SSH) were designed with security as a primary goal.

SSH is a point-to-point tunneling protocol that is designed to pass encrypted traffic between two specific hosts. Along with tunneling traffic at the presentation layer, SSH also can provide application layer functionality, including a login shell similar to telnet (over the encrypted tunnel), and FTP-type services. The `sftp` system is an implementation of an FTP-like protocol over SSH.

20.1 SSH AND SECURITY

The SSH protocol addresses each of the basic security concepts (see Chapter 1):

Confidentiality: Each SSH connection is encrypted, preventing an eavesdropper from viewing information. For added security, SSH periodically re-exchanges keys to ensure that a compromise of one set of keys does not compromise the entire session. In contrast, CTCP, IPsec, and IPv6 only exchange keys at the beginning of the connection.

Authentication: Before establishing a connection, the client must authenticate the server *and* the server must authenticate the client. Client authentication can be any combination of certificates (keys), passwords, or digital tokens. Although SSH is usually used with one-part authentication (a password or a key), it can support two- and three-part authentication systems. The server only uses a certificate to authenticate with the client.

There are three types of keys with SSH. Cryptographic keys *are used to seed cryptographic algorithms,* host keys *are used to authenticate SSH servers, and* client keys *are asymmetrical keys used as digital certificates for authentication.*

Authorization: SSH limits the traffic that can enter the tunnel and can restrict how data exits the tunnel. For remote login access, SSH restricts authorization to the user's login privileges.

Integrity: SSH uses encryption and cryptographic checksums to validate each packet. Any packet that fails an integrity check is viewed as an attack, which terminates the connection.

Nonrepudiation: Each packet is cryptographically signed using an HMAC, ensuring that the data actually came from the sender.

SSH has three primary uses: establish a secure network tunnel, provide a VPN with port-forwarding characteristics, and supply application-layer login functionality.

20.2 THE SSH PROTOCOL

The SSH protocol operates in five phases: algorithm negotiation, key exchange, server authentication, client authentication, and data transfer.

20.2.1 Phase 1: Algorithm Negotiation

As with SSL, SSH supports a variety of cryptographic algorithms. Upon the initial connection, the systems negotiate the cryptographic algorithms that will be used. Different SSH versions and platforms support different algorithms. For encryption, 3DES is required for default compatibility between SSH clients and servers. Other algorithms, such as DES, IDEA, CAST, AES, and Blowfish, are optional. SSH authentication may use RSA or DSA keys. The integrity algorithm depends on the version of SSH. The older version, SSHv1 (SSH version 1), uses MD5 for performing integrity checks. SSHv2 uses SHA1.

The SSH algorithm negotiation is very similar to SSL. The client offers a list of supported cipher combinations, and the server responds with its selection. There are some significant differences between the negotiations for SSL and SSH:

Combinations: Unlike SSL, where cipher sets are predefined, SSH keeps them separate. Any combination of cryptographic key exchange, host-key (certificate) exchange, encryption, MAC, and compression algorithms are supported. Although SSL only supports DSS certificates with MD5 checksums (as defined by the DSS specification), SSH can support DSS with MD5 or SHA1.

Weak Ciphers: Some SSL cipher sets include weak ciphers that are generally undesirable. They are included because they are part of predefined, standard cipher sets. SSL clients, such as Web browsers, may warn the user when weak ciphers are selected. In contrast, SSH simply does not support weak algorithms. If an algorithm is considered weak, then it is not offered as an option.

Bidirectional Negotiation: With SSL and SSH, the client offers a list of ciphers, and the server makes a selection; however, SSH follows this with a list of ciphers from the server, and the client makes a selection. It becomes very possible for the negotiation to result in two different sets of algorithms. The client may use 128-bit AES when transmitting to the server, and the server may select 3DES when responding to the client. A cryptanalysis attack against the traffic may require cracking two completely different algorithms.

20.2.2 Phase 2: Key Negotiation

The algorithm negotiation is immediately followed with a key exchange using the Diffie-Hellman (DH) algorithm. SSH performs key exchanges periodically—usually every hour. This way, if an attacker does manage to identify the keys, only a one-hour window of the conversation is compromised. Considering that SSH uses a large key size (512 bits or larger), an attacker is unlikely to crack any session within a usable timeframe.

20.2.3 Phase 3: Server Authentication

After completing the key exchange, all information is transmitted using encryption. The first data transmitted is the SSH server's public key. If the server has never been seen before, then the client prompts the user to validate the key. After validation, the server's key is added to the client's list of known servers. However, if the server *has* been seen before, then the client compares the key with the cached version. If the cache does not match, then the client usually aborts—unlike HTTPS (Chapter 19), the SSH user is not prompted to continue when the server fails to validate.

Most SSH clients associate server keys with network addresses. Unfortunately, servers are occasionally reinstalled or assigned new addresses. The result is a mismatch between the server's key and the client's cache. The user must resolve the issue, and the resolution varies with different SSH clients:

OpenSSH: The OpenSSH client (*http://www.openssh.org/*) is used on most Unix systems. For OpenSSH, users must manually edit their host-key cache files to remove the mismatched server entry. The file is stored in the user's home directory: `$HOME/.ssh/known_hosts`. For users who connect to many SSH servers, this can be a very large file. To resolve mismatched cache entries, users must edit the file and delete the line for the offending server. This is significantly different from HTTPS, where most browsers prompt users to continue.

PuTTY: For Windows SSH clients, PuTTY (*http://www.putty.nl/*) is common. PuTTY stores the host-key cache in the Registry under `HKEY_CURRENT_USER\Software\SimonTatham\PuTTY`. But rather than editing the Registry, PuTTY prompts the user when the host key does not match. The user has the option to accept the new host key and overwrite the old one.

Mocha Telnet: For PocketPC, WindowsCE, PalmOS, mobile phones, and most other platforms, Mocha Telnet (*http://www.mochasoft.dk/*) is available for supporting SSH. Unlike OpenSSH and PuTTY, Mocha Telnet does not cache server keys. As a result, all servers are always accepted.

Other SSH clients, such as F-Secure SSH, ZOC, and Pragma SSH all use different caching methods. Resolving mismatched keys requires knowing the specific type of SSH client.

20.2.4 Phase 4: Client Authentication

After authenticating the server, the client is authenticated. The client may transmit any combination of a password, a challenge signed by the client key, or a digital identifier for authentication. If the authentication works, then the client successfully connects. If the authentication fails, however, the client is disconnected. SSH servers may permit multiple password retries, but repeated failures result in a dis-connection.

20.2.5 Phase 5: Data Transfer

After negotiating the algorithms, exchanging keys, and authenticating both the client and server, an encrypted VPN tunnel is established. The SSH VPN permits multiple channels—similar to the transport layer's ports. Through concurrent channels, SSH supports many simultaneous connections. For example, a login shell may be on channel #0, an X11 graphical traffic on channel #1, and a VPN proxy on channel #2. All of this data transfers across an encrypted tunnel that changes keys every few minutes.

20.3 COMMON SSH USES

SSH was originally designed as a replacement for less-secure Unix commands. Telnet, FTP, rlogin, rcp, and rsh provide login access, file transfer functionality, and remote command execution, but they transmit passwords in plaintext. The systems are also vulnerable to TCP hijacking (and UDP hijacking, in the case of FTP). SSH provides all of these functionalities over an encrypted channel. For example, the OpenSSH client, ssh, supports command-line options for performing these operations. SSH also provides support for arbitrary port forwarding and automated system usage.

20.3.1 Remote Login

Using OpenSSH's ssh without any command options provides a login prompt. The basic usage is ssh *hostname* or ssh *user@hostname*. These commands establish an SSH tunnel to the server, *hostname*, using the account name *user*. When creating a command-line shell, the SSH client provides both application layer and presentation layer functionality.

20.3.2 Remote Command Execution

The OpenSSH client permits operating similar to the BSD remote-shell command, rsh. After specifying the user and hostname, any other options are treated as a command. The command is executed immediately after logging in. For example, the command ssh user@hostname ls will remotely log in to hostname as user and execute the command ls. The file streams STDIN, STDOUT, and STDERR (standard input, output, and error) are passed across the SSH tunnels, so the output from ls is transmitted back to the client. Specifying no command is the same as specifying the user's login shell. For example, if the user uses /bin/sh, then ssh user@hostname is the same as ssh user@hostname /bin/sh.

As mentioned in Chapter 9 (Section 9.2.3.1), SSH can support very complex remote command execution. SSH can tunnel anything that uses STDIN, STDOUT, and STDERR to communicate—including VPN software.

20.3.3 File Transfers

There are two methods for performing SSH file transfers. The first method uses remote command execution. In effect, the tunnel is used to pass the file. Sample transfer commands include the following:

```
ssh user@hostname "cat remotefile" > localfile
cat localfile | ssh user@hostname "cat > remotefile"
ssh user@hostname "tar —cf — directory" | tar —xvf —
tar —cf — directory | ssh user@hostname "tar —xvf —"
```

The first two examples download and upload a single file. The second two examples transfer entire directories. In both cases, the data is converted to a single character stream and transmitted over STDOUT and STDIN (respectively).

The second method uses SSH subsystems. The SSH server permits the execution of well-defined applications. This is similar to the Unix inetd system, where different network ports are used to run different applications. Using the -s option, different subsystems can be selected. The default subsystem is a login shell, but SSH's FTP is a common, default subsystem. By specifying -s sftp, the sftp-server service is accessed. As with regular FTP servers, FTP clients are specifically designed to interact with the server. As such, the SSH command sftp presents the user with an FTP-like interface for transferring files.

Just as sftp resembles FTP, scp resembles the remote-copy command, rcp. Using scp, files can be transferred between systems through the SSH tunnel.

20.3.4 Port Forwarding

Although SSH forwards streams such as STDIN, STDOUT, and STDERR, it can also forward TCP ports. Using the OpenSSH options -R and -L, a port on the local system can be passed to the remote end, and vice versa. As an example, the X11 graphical protocol uses 6000/tcp. SSH can relay data to this port and allow X11 traffic to pass over the encrypted tunnel.

Users do not need to remember the —R and —L options for forwarding X11. The -X option enables X11 forwarding.

Do Not Disturb

When using wireless networks at hotels, anyone with a wireless packet sniffer can intercept Web traffic. Surfing the Web from a hotel (or coffee shop or airport) is neither safe nor private. Even using SSL does not guarantee security; however, SSH can add security for traveling computer users.

Most Web browsers support the use of Web proxies. The proxies may either be HTTP or SOCKS. This functionality can be combined with SSH to secure Web connections. Before going on the trip:

- Install an SSH server on a trusted host. Allow users across the Internet to access the SSH server. All other network services should be blocked by a firewall.

- Configure a SOCKS server on the trusted host's port 1080/tcp. The SOCKS server should not be accessible by anyone except users already logged in to the host.

Then, when traveling, use SSH to encrypt the Web traffic:

- Use the command ssh user@hostname –L 8888:localhost:1080 to establish a secure tunnel from 8888/tcp on the local system to the remote SOCKS server.

- Configure the Web browser to use a SOCKS proxy on port 8888/tcp on the local system.

Using this configuration, all Web connections—HTTP and HTTPS—will pass through the SSH tunnel and relay out to the trusted proxy. Although the connection is only as secure as HTTP (or HTTPS) from the trusted server, the connection between the hotel and the proxy is very secure. An attacker at the hotel will not be able to intercept Web traffic.

20.3.5 Automated Systems

SSL is commonly used by automated systems for establishing secure connections. However, as mentioned in Chapter 19, SSL has many limitations when used by automated systems. For example, SSL clients are vulnerable to MitM attacks, DNS poisoning, and risks from handling invalid certificates. In contrast, SSH addresses many of SSL's limitations:

Authentication: Using preshared client keys, SSH connections authenticate both the client and the server. Unlike SSL, SSH does not require a third-party for validation. This means that SSH will not inherit risks when using DNS.

Configuring SSH with preshared client keys is no more difficult than using SSL's client-side certificates.

MitM Protection: With SSL, client-side authentication is optional, allowing potential MitM attacks. With SSH, client authentication is mandatory. As a result, SSH is unlikely to be compromised by a MitM attack.

Extendibility: With SSL, each application must be designed to use SSL. Wrapper applications, such as stunnel, can be used for adding SSL support to pre-defined executables. In contrast, SSH permits any command-line application to be executed remotely and can be quickly integrated with applications through scripts.

Failure Options: When SSL connections fail to authenticate, the cause may be unknown. Did the server fail? Was it the client? Is there a problem with the CA? This leads to development options where failures may be ignored. In contrast, a failure to authenticate with SSH indicates a clear problem and is fatal to the connection.

20.4 SSH LIMITATIONS

Security is the primary design for SSH. As a result, there are limitations for other usability issues, including anonymous logins, speed, and UDP support.

20.4.1 Anonymous Logins

One of the largest benefits of using the Internet is flexibility. Any client can connect to any server and communicate (assuming they use the same protocol). For example, FTP and HTTP are common application-layer protocols that permit any process to transfer files between systems. The client may be new and unfamiliar to the server, but the service is available. With these protocols, the client can be anonymous and unknown, but there is a limitation: the network streams are insecure and vulnerable to MitM and hijacking attacks.

In contrast to FTP and HTTP, SSH is the opposite extreme: connections are not vulnerable to attack, but anonymous and unknown connections are not permitted. For example, although the sftp client can establish a secure connection and transfer files like FTP, it does not permit anonymous logins. Anonymous FTP sites cannot be converted to use SSH without requiring a valid login. Similarly, HTTP over SSH requires a valid login—an arbitrary user with an SSH client cannot connect. Although offering security, SSH breaks the use model for flexibility by forbidding anonymous and unknown connections.

FTP and HTTP allow any clients to connect but offer no security. SSH offers security but does not allow arbitrary clients to connect. SSL tries to fill the middle ground, offering arbitrary connections and protection from network attacks. Unfortunately, without preshared certificates, trusted CAs, and proper authentication failure handling, SSL is vulnerable to MitM attacks.

20.4.2 Speed

SSH requires a significant amount of overhead. The initial connection and negotiation generates around 17 packets before encryption can be used. This includes 3 packets for the initial TCP handshake, 4 packets for SSH version identification, (2 transmits and 2 TCP ACKs), and 10 or more packets for negotiating algorithms and keys. The initial host-key validation and login banner may add another 17 packets—and this does not even include the client-side authentication (usually another 4 packets). This initial negotiation generates significantly more overhead than 12 packets used by SSL.

After the initial connection, SSH encrypts, computes checksums, and cryptographically signs every packet, which results in a huge performance overhead. Each of these operations is computationally expensive. Usually the network is the slowest link between two computers. A 75 MHz Pentium (1990 technology) can easily handle 100 Mbps connections. But with SSH and a sustained high traffic volume, the computational processing time can become a bottleneck—even on systems with gigahertz CPUs. This overhead becomes noticeable when using VoIP, online games, or X-Windows over SSH. As a result, SSH is not ideal for systems that generate many connections in a short period or have high-speed performance requirements.

20.4.3 SSH and UDP

SSH is ideal for tunneling any point-to-point data stream. STDIN, STDOUT, STDERR, and TCP are all point-to-point implementations. Protocols that are not point-to-point, such as UDP, cannot be tunneled, however, because without an established point-to-point connection, the SSH system does not know where to relay packets. This is the same problem found with NAT systems (Chapter 12).

When a UDP service is required over an SSH connection, the solution is usually PPP over SSH. As discussed in Chapter 9 (Section 9.2.3.1), PPP can be combined with SSH, creating an encrypted VPN connection. Although PPP generates a low overhead, it also creates a lot of traffic. In the best case, the transmitted data is small—much less than the MTU for TCP—creating a one-to-one relationship between PPP-over-SSH traffic and actual network traffic; the only significant overhead becomes the SSH processing speed. Unfortunately, small packets are uncommon when transferring large files or running network-intensive applications. As a result, SSH's poor performance is very apparent. Although the VPN is secure and supports both TCP and UDP, it is slow.

20.5 RISKS

From an attacker's viewpoint, SSH lives up to its name. Few attackers will attempt to compromise an established SSH connection, and full SSH hijacking is unheard of. Hijacking attempts simply result in a disconnection. Although there are few options to mitigate SSH risks, few are needed. The biggest risks to SSH come from default settings, MitM attacks, and client-key transport. To a lesser extent, volume analysis is also a risk.

20.5.1 Default Settings

Although a default installation of the SSH client and server are very secure, leaving default settings can lead to security risks. The most common attack against SSH is a brute-force login. Accounts such as "root" and "admin" are checked against a password list (or for no password at all). Although this is not a limitation with SSH, SSH does provide a method to connect into a system with user privileges. Weak accounts on the system can be brute-forced through SSH.

Fortunately, SSH provides many options for mitigating brute-force login attacks. For example, root logins can be denied, the number of password retries can be limited, and the number of reconnections can be throttled. On more secure systems, the SSH server can require client keys—immediately stopping all brute-force password attempts. In addition, SSH can be combined with firewalls such as iptables to restrict connections to specific remote hosts.

On rare occasions, remote overflows are discovered with certain SSH versions. As a result, attackers continually scan for SSH on its default port: 22/tcp. SSH can be easily moved to other ports. In addition, the SSH server can be recompiled to display an alternate version string. This ensures that the detection of an SSH server does not disclose the true version information.

20.5.2 MitM

A MitM attack against SSH is very difficult. It primarily happens when a client connects to the server for the first time. (Few users actually check the server string. Usually it is just accepted.) To succeed at this type of attack, the attacker must:

1. Know the client has not connected to the server before.
2. Know that there is no client key (or know the public key for the client key).
3. Know when the client will be connecting.

4. Intercept the TCP connection.

Although the latter two requirements are plausible on a compromised network, the first two requirements are usually guessed. If the attacker guesses right, then the hijacker's SSH server key is accepted and the MitM is completed. But if the client-key is unknown, then the client-side authentication will fail. If the client has seen the server before, then a warning is usually displayed. Unlike SSL, warnings are rarely displayed with SSH, so the victim notices when a warning is displayed.

20.5.3 Transferring Client Keys

As with PGP and SSL, SSH is most vulnerable when transferring keys across the network. An SSH key has two components: a private key and a public key. Both keys are stored as files. Transporting the keys between systems opens them to interception. Similar to PGP, the SSH keys may be password protected. Most users only maintain one private key. If this key becomes compromised, then it effectively compromises all systems that only require the client key for authentication.

SSH client keys can be password protected, but no password is an option. Most automated systems that use SSH do not password protect the keys. If the keys were password protected, then the password would still need to be stored on the system for use by the automated application.

Fortunately, users rarely email or transfer private SSH client keys. Although the public ones may be openly transported, private ones are kept private. In addition, many users use SSH (with password-only authentication) to transfer keys between systems. This ensures a secure transport.

20.5.4 Volume Analysis

As discussed in Chapter 4, cryptographic systems include five elements: the plaintext, ciphertext, algorithm, key, and environment. For SSH, the plaintext is only accessible outside of the encrypted tunnel, leaving the ciphertext accessible to attackers. SSH uses strong algorithms and long keys to reduce the risk from cryptanalysis. However, the environment used by SSH can reveal the type of data passing through the encrypted tunnel. An attacker can identify how the tunnel is being used and determine the contents of some encrypted packets without ever cracking the cryptography.

A network *volume analysis* evaluates the overall number of packets to identify content. In the most general sense, a large number of packets being transmitted indicates activity, whereas little or no volume indicates little or no activity. Network traffic schemes, such as the Nagel algorithm (see Chapter 14) and chaffing (Chapter 13) can obscure data, which impairs volume analysis. Fortunately for the attacker, SSH does not use chaffing and disables the Nagel algorithm. As a result, every set of data passed to SSH is immediately transmitted, and an acknowledgement is returned. This can be used to identify keyboard usage, carriage returns, and sometimes applications.

20.5.4.1 SSH Initialization

Packet-capturing tools can observe the SSH initialization but cannot identify the encrypted packet contents. Because authentication is encrypted, the type of authentication used is generally unknown. However, by viewing the timing and delays between the packets, as well as the encrypted packet sizes, the authentication system can be identified (Figure 20.1). For example:

- A noticeable delay within the initialization implies that the user entered a password. No delay with a transfer indicates a client key.
- A small delay at the beginning of the connection indicates a client key. The SSHv2 initialization takes approximately 44 TCP packets. The delay will be around the ninth packet (server key exchange initialization—704 bytes) and thirteenth packet (DH key exchange reply—346 bytes). The delay is due to certificate-related computations. When only using a password, the extra computation time is not needed.
- A small delay at the beginning followed by a long delay suggests a certificate and a human-entered password.

20.5.4.2 Identifying Keystrokes

In September 2001, three researchers at the University of California, Berkeley disclosed a timing attack against SSH that could identify keystrokes [Song2001]. For most typists, the average delay between key presses is less than 200 milliseconds; this is why TCP's Nagel algorithm delays packet transmission by 200 ms. However, SSH disables the Nagel algorithm. When SSH connects to a login shell, every keystroke generates a short packet. As a result, a series of encrypted SSH packet that are small and separated by around 200 ms indicates human typing. In addition, each keystroke is echoed back by the terminal. The result is an observed three packets for every keystroke: the key being transmitted from the client to the server, the terminal echo with ACK, and the client's final TCP ACK (Figure 20.2). On a 10 Mbps network, these three packets usually appear with less than a thousandth of a second separation, although keystrokes are much further apart—on the order of hundredths of a second apart.

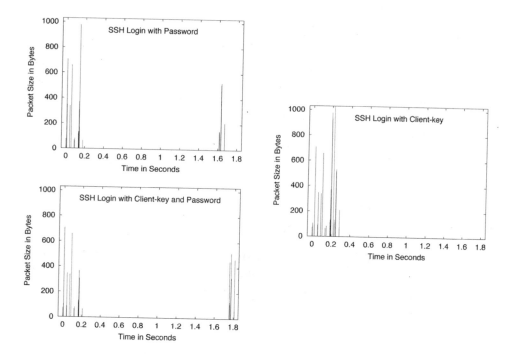

FIGURE 20.1   SSH initialization packet sizes over time.

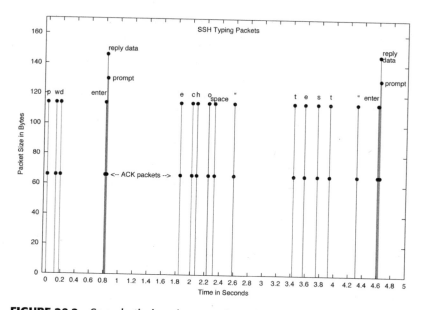

FIGURE 20.2   Sample timings in seconds and packet sizes in bytes for keystrokes sent over SSH.

20.5.4.3 Identifying Packet Contents

In a command shell, keystrokes are used to enter commands, and the Enter key executes the command. This appears in the packet capture as a set of identified keystrokes, followed by a short data burst from the server. The size of the data burst indicates the amount of data generated. In addition, each burst will be followed by a command prompt—the prompt will likely be a packet that is the same size at the end of each burst. Using this information, each press of the Enter key can be identified.

Human factors, combined with packet analysis, can hint at packet contents. For example:

- Three keys pressed quickly and followed by an Enter key are likely a Unix command, such as pwd, cwd, or who. The size of the reply packet can help narrow down the likely command. (Most other three-letter Unix commands are followed by parameters.) Although the exact command may be unknown, the number of characters is definite.
- Repetitive backspaces are usually pressed at a fixed interval, although different people have different intervals.
- Spaces are usually followed by a short pause, so the number of words on each line can be estimated.

In addition, side-traffic sniffing can also identify likely commands. If DNS lookups are generated, or other TCP or UDP connections are established, then the command may be guessed. For example, if an attacker observes four characters, a space, and six more characters followed by an Enter key, then a two-word command was likely typed. If this is immediately followed by a DNS query for the system chunky, then the typed command was likely host chunky.

20.5.4.4 Identifying Applications

Keyboard entry is not the only identifiable type of SSH packet. Different applications generate different packet sequences. For example, the traffic generated by starting the Firefox Web browser over X-Windows tunneled through SSH is consistent and unique. Firefox differs from xterm, xclock, Mozilla, and other X-Windows applications. Even editors such as vi and emacs generate distinct volume patterns.

20.5.4.5 Mitigating Volume Analysis

An attacker can use packet volume analysis to gain insight into how the encrypted channel is being used, even if the exact keys are unknown. In some cases, the exact contents of the channel can be determined without ever attempting to crack the cryptographic protection.

SSH has nothing native to mitigate the risks from volume analysis, but steps can be taken to lessen the likelihood of identification. For example, the observer cannot distinguish different SSH channels. A chaffing program can be used to generate constant noise over a second channel (such as a forwarded TCP port) to deter volume analysis.

SUMMARY

SSH is one of the most secure protocols on the Internet. It uses strong encryption, reliable authentication, and good default settings. SSH addresses many of the limitations found in common remote login applications, as well as security-oriented protocols such as SSL. The limitations for SSH primarily center around authentication, transporting client keys and accepting new host keys, as well as speed. More importantly, its biggest weakness is minor: a rare attack based on packet-volume analysis.

REVIEW QUESTIONS

1. What are some common uses for SSH?
2. What types of authentication does SSH support?
3. Does SSH forward UDP packets?
4. Does SSH's sftp support anonymous logins?
5. Is DNS poisoning a risk for SSH connections?

DISCUSSION TOPICS

1. Using two Unix workstations and an X-Windows Web browser, time how long it takes to start the browser over the SSH connection. Repeat the experiment with a non-SSH connection (try using set DISPLAY=remote-host:0). Is one method noticeably slower? What SSH options can be used to improve performance? For example, is one encryption algorithm faster than another?
2. Use a packet sniffer to monitor SSH connections. Can keystrokes or specific applications be identified? Does sniffing non-SSH packets assist in determining typed keys or activity?
3. SSL, IPsec, and IPv6 support encryption without chaffing. Are these systems vulnerable to the same volume analysis attack used against SSH?

4. Is there a benefit to using SSH over an established VPN such as IPv6 or IPsec? Is there a benefit to using HTTPS over SSH?

ADDITIONAL RESOURCES

SSH is widely supported and well documented. The OpenSSH project (*http://www.openssh.org/*) offers detailed and technical information, as well as help files and source code. *SSH, The Secure Shell: The Definitive Guide* by Daniel Barrett, Richard Silverman, and Robert Byrnes (O'Reilly Media, May 2005, ISBN 0-596-00895-3) is an excellent resource that offers real-world usage, examples, and advice for configuring and using SSH. In addition, the online Unix manuals for OpenSSH, including ssh(1), sshd(8), ssh_config(5), and sshd_config(5), are very descriptive and informative.

Part
VIII
OSI Layer 7

In This Part

- Application Layer
- SMTP
- HTTP

L ayer 7 of the ISO OSI model is the application layer. This layer provides application-specific network support. There are thousands of application layer protocols; some fill specific niches whereas others provide generalized functions. Two of the most widely used application layer protocols are SMTP (email) and HTTP (Web).

21 Application Layer

In This Chapter

- Common Formats
- General Risks

The OSI application layer provides application-specific network support and interfaces with the user-level software. The application layer is the most flexible of the OSI layers and allows a variety of application-specific protocols. Unlike other layers, this layer does not define specific functionality requirements. As a result, there are thousands of application layer protocols—ranging from very specific to very general. These protocols can support any type of required functionality. Some common application layer protocols include the following:

Network Diagnostics: SNMP, RSTAT, RWHO

File Access and Data Transfer: NFS, SMB, FTP, TFTP, HTTP, LPD

System Configuration: NTP, DHCP, BOOTP

Remote Command Execution: RLOGIN, REXEC, RSH, Telnet, SSH

Remote Desktop Access: VNC, RDP

Graphics and Audio: X-Windows, RTP, RTSP, VoIP

Authentication: TACACS

The set of possible functions are not limited to this list, and many protocols fit more than one category. HTTP for example, was designed for generic data transfer. Not only can it be used for file access, but it can also provide streaming data or configuration information.

In general, application layer protocols interface between the user's application and the presentation and lower OSI layers. The network communication provides identification, configuration, and other application layer parameters, as well as application data. For example, the Line Printer Daemon protocol (LPD) submits information to a network printer [RFC1179]. The user-level applications `lpr`, `lp`, and `enscript` accept data from the user (or another nonnetwork application) and encode the data using the LPD protocol. This specifies the print server, print queue, cover page information, and page configuration, as well as the data to print. The LPD-encoded data is passed to the presentation layer and down the network stack, transporting the data to the server for printing. LPD can also be used to query the printer's status, cancel a print job, or clear a print queue. In this process, there is a clear distinction between the application, data, and protocol.

TACACS

The Terminal Access Controller Access Control System (TACACS) is an example of an application layer protocol that provides authentication, authorization, and accounting functionality. Created for accessing terminal servers and network devices, the TACACS client sends a username and password to a server, and is granted access based on the authorization associated with the credentials [RFC1492]. After authenticating, the client may access the terminal server or request a SLIP connection (see Chapter 9). The security and usage of TACACS is very similar to protocols such as telnet and FTP; the main distinction is TACACS' focus on connections to terminal servers and routers.

TACACS has undergone many revisions. XTACACS (extended TACACS) separated the authentication and authorization components in TACACS to create a more modular protocol. XTACACS also switched to a signature authentication scheme, similar to Kerberos, where the password is never transmitted. Cisco elaborated on XTACACS, creating a variant called TACACS+ that includes encryption between the client and server.

Although TACACS+ does provide authentication, authorization, and privacy (via encryption), it does contain a few limitations. For example, the protocol is vulnerable to replay attacks, and the cryptographic session identifier is vulnerable to collision attacks—similar to the encryption weaknesses with

WEP (Chapter 7). The encryption is also stream based, so the length of the encrypted password may be identifiable even if the actual letters are unknown. The Openwall Project detailed a number of vulnerabilities in TACACS+ in its OW-001-tac_plus advisory (*http://www.openwall.com/advisories/OW-001-tac_plus/*).

21.1 COMMON FORMATS

Although the data formats for application layer protocols vary greatly, there are some common elements. Most application layer protocols use a binary command structure, text-based command-reply, meta headers, or XML for communication. In addition, these protocols can be based on push or pull technologies.

21.1.1 Push versus Pull

Push technologies allow one system to initiate a data transfer to another system without a request from the recipient. For example, TV and radio are common mass-media push technologies. Application layer push-oriented protocols include email (SMTP) and VoIP.

In contrast to push systems, *pull technologies* require the recipient to issue a request for information retrieval. Example protocols include the Web (HTTP), newsgroups (NNTP), and remote login protocols such as SSH and Telnet.

Most network protocols are pull technologies, although some may have push elements. For example, DNS (OSI layer 5) allows users to pull data, but servers can push data to other servers. Similarly, the simple network management protocol (SNMP) allows clients to push configuration changes to servers or pull values from servers. (As discussed in Chapter 23, HTTP also has push functionality but is primarily used as a pull technology.)

21.1.2 Binary Commands

A *binary command structure* uses a predefined command set. For example, the integer "1" may indicate "GET" and "2" might specify "REPLY." These fixed control sets limit a protocol's flexibility—actions outside of the predefined command set are unavailable. Fixed control sets are useful when the protocol does not require a wide range of functionality. For example, LPD (RFC1179) only defines 35 different commands. LPD does not require remote command execution or audio controls, so these functions are not part of the fixed control set.

Binary command sets are not necessarily static. SNMP uses a binary command set for basic functions (e.g., Get, Get Next, and Set) but uses a variable-length numeric parameter to specify management items. Called the *management information base* (MIB—RFC1156), the numeric parameters identify paths within a virtual tree. For example, the identifier 1.3.6.1.2.1.1.1.1.0 denotes the first branch, followed by the third branch, sixth branch, and so on. This particular *object identifier* (OID) denotes the system description. Different network devices use different MIBs that define different binary command structures. However, support for any particular OID is specific to the SNMP implementation and installed MIBs.

21.1.3 Command-Reply

Command-reply controls are used for bidirectional communication. For these systems, a command is sent, and a reply is received. The commands are usually text based to allow new commands to be easily added.

Example command-reply protocols include HTTP, FTP, SMTP, and POP3. For example, the Post Office Protocol version 3 (POP3—RFC1939) uses commands such as STAT for status, LIST to retrieve the list of emails, RETR to retrieve a specific message, and DELE to delete an email from the server. FTP has commands such as GET, PUT, and DEL.

What Is Telnet?

Telnet was one of the first official network protocols, and it supplies remote login access. A user can use the telnet application to connect to a remote host and access a login shell. Although telnet is primarily defined in RFC137, its history spans over 100 RFCs. (Telnet.org offers a very complete list of RFCs at *http://www.telnet.org/htm/dev.htm*).

The telnet protocol is sometimes used as an example of a command-reply protocol. The user types a command, and the remote server replies. But telnet actually uses a binary command structure for communicating between the client and server. Each command contains 3 bytes: 0xFF identifies an *interpret as command* (IAC) character, and 2 bytes define the specific command and options. All other bytes are simply user data. The specific telnet commands are listed in Table 21.1. The full list of commands and options are described in the telnet(1) online manual. Most of the IAC commands are not visible to the telnet user. Instead, when a user types a command and sees a reply, the visible command reply occurs at the user layer. The telnet protocol simply passes the user data between the client and the server, although IAC commands are occasionally generated. For example, pressing the backspace key triggers an IAC EC sequence, which causes a character to be erased.

TABLE 21.1   Telnet IAC Values

Abbreviation	Code	Purpose
SE	0xF0	Subnegotiation parameter end.
NOP	0xF1	No operation.
DM	0xF2	Data mark, used for data synchronization.
BRK	0xF3	Break.
IP	0xF4	Interrupt process.
AO	0xF4	Abort output.
AYT	0xF6	Are you there? (A primitive ping-like request.)
EC	0xF7	Erase character.
EL	0xF8	Erase line.
GA	0xF9	Go ahead.
SB	0xFA	Subnegotiation parameter begin.
WILL	0xFB	Indicates supported parameters.
WONT	0xFC	Indicates unsupported parameters.
DO	0xFD	Requests remote connection to support parameters.
DONT	0xFE	Requests remote connection to not support parameters.
IAC	0xFF	Interpret as command.

21.1.3.1 Command-Reply Flexibility

Although command-reply methods are well defined, they are not always enabled or accessible. For example, SMTP (RC2821) defines the VRFY command for verifying email addresses on the mail server. Due to information leakage (disclosure of valid email addresses), VRFY is usually disabled in modern mail systems. SMTP is detailed in Chapter 22.

Just as commands can be disabled, new commands can be added. For example, the HTTP (RFC1945) only defines three commands: GET, HEAD, and POST. Additional commands, such as CONNECT, OPTIONS, DELETE, and TRACE were added later [RFC2616]. In a command-reply system, unknown commands simply return an error code. In contrast, a binary command system usually has no method for defining new commands. HTTP is detailed in Chapter 23.

21.1.3.2 Command-Reply Limitations

Most command-reply controls resemble natural languages, which lead to readability and easier software development. Besides the command, parameters supply additional options.

Although a command-reply structure provides flexibility, there are a few limitations. For example, most protocols use English words for specifying commands. This can create problems for non-English speakers. In addition, most commands use a single word that may not directly indicate functionality, and sometimes the word is significantly abbreviated. To a non-English speaker, "VRFY" may be no more informative than four random letters. Similarly, would someone in Germany recognize that "HEAD" is the HTTP command for retrieving a file's status? The HEAD command comes from returning the head of the data stream—the meta header. Commands in other languages would be equally confusing. (Would the Spanish command "ALTO" mean "HIGH," "TOP," or "STOP"?)

A second limitation concerns internationalization. Although protocols are extendible, allowing new commands to be added, the character sets are usually not internationalized. Chinese, Korean, and other multibyte character sets are usually not supported.

HTTP is commonly used to transfer HTML documents. Although HTML supports international, multibyte languages, HTTP only supports English commands. All Web servers in China use an English command set.

Regardless of the language, command words usually take many bytes. Sending the command DELETE uses 6 bytes, whereas the binary command 3 uses 1 byte. Most command-reply implementations result in low entropy and high bandwidth consumption.

21.1.4 Meta Headers

Binary commands have a limited range of functions. It can be difficult (or impossible) to specify a complicated action using a binary command set. In contrast, command-reply systems can permit long, descriptive controls. However, each control is limited to the specific command. *Meta headers* associate dynamic configuration data with specific data blocks. Defined in RFC822, meta headers were originally defined to assist SMTP for email routing but have since been incorporated into many protocols. Besides SMTP, meta headers are used by HTTP, the Network News Transport Protocol (NNTP—RFC1036), and Multipurpose Internet Mail Extensions (MIME—RFC1521).

Meta headers consist of `field: value` pairs. Each `field` specifies a setting, and each `value` is the data for the setting. Different protocols may support different field types, and there are few rules for meta headers:

- A field name cannot contain a colon (:). The colon separates the field name from the value. In most implementations, a space is required after the colon.
- Field names are case-insensitive. `Color:`, `color:`, and `CoLoR:` are all treated equally, although values may be case-sensitive. Protocols manage the semantic interpretation of values.
- There is one field-value pair per line. The line ends at the newline character.
- Long values can be split between lines. If the next line begins with a space, then it indicates a continuation rather than a new field.
- A blank line separates the meta header from the data.
- A backslash can be used to quote a character. For example, `\"` denotes the double quote character and should not be interpreted as the beginning or end of a string. To use a backslash in a string, the backslash should be quoted with a backslash: `\\`.

Using a meta header, additional configuration options can be associated with a data set. The values may define character sets for the data, specify file locations, or contain processing instructions. Unlike command-reply controls, unknown meta headers can usually be ignored. If the meta header "Character-Set: Big5" is unknown, the data will likely remain valid, even if the recipient does not understand Chinese.

21.1.5 XML

Although meta headers associate additional information with a data block, they do not provide the means to associate additional information with any specific piece of data inside the data block. Each meta header covers the entire associated data block. The *eXtensible Markup Language* (XML) resolves this deficiency.

XML uses tags to indicate the beginning and end of a subblock of data. Each tag is enclosed in brackets: `<tagname>`. A slash before the tag's name indicates the end of the tag's scope. For example: `<quote>Quoted user-data</quote>`. Tags may also include attributes, in the format `field=value`. These are similar to the meta header `field: value` pairs, but the scope is restricted to the data within the tag rather than the entire data block. Finally, tags can be nested. For example, `<underline><bold size=2>Big text</bold></underline>` could be used by a word processor to denote underlined and bold text.

Because XML uses less-than (<) and greater-than (>) signs for brackets around tags, user data cannot contain these characters. Instead, XML defines a sequence that begins with an ampersand (&) and ends with a semicolon (;) as a tokenized character. For example, < becomes a < and > becomes a >. Other defined sequences include © (copyright symbol), " (double quote character), and & (ampersand). In addition, ASCII characters can be specified by their decimal values. For example, & is ASCII character 38—an ampersand.

21.1.5.1 XML Variations

XML was derived from the *Standard Generalized Markup Language* (SGML). SGML defined a method for association meta-information with data. XML's variation of SGML uses a fairly strict rule set. For example, each beginning tag must have an end, and only proper nesting is permitted. Standalone tags such as `<leftopen>` and mixed nesting such as `<1><2></1></2>` are forbidden. But different SGML implementations have different requirements. The most notable is the HTML used on Web pages.

Although HTML looks similar to XML, HTML uses a subset of the SGML rules. Under HTML, some tags do not have or need closed tags. (Although `<li>` specifies line items, `</li>` is not required by HTML.) In addition, most Web browsers permit mixed nesting. Under XML, all user data must be within the scope of some tag, but HTML permits text to appear outside of the scope. Finally, most Web browsers are lenient with regards to bad formatting. Missing less-than signs, use of `<` and `&` instead of `&lt;` and `&amp;`, and missing quotes are all tolerated. Other SGML-like variations may bend or enforce other rules, but the basic concept—using tags with additional information to define scopes—remains the same.

XML specifies the tag format but not the tag names. There are no predefined formatting tags in XML. Instead, tag definitions are implementation specific. HTML defines specific tags and tag attributes for functionality. For example, `<u>text</u>` underlines text and `<ol>...</ol>` provides an ordered list. HTML version 2 defined new tags that did not exist in HTML version 1. As another example, xmlCIM describes the XML for the Common Information Model (CIM). The XML tags and attributes defined by xmlCIM are not the same as HTML.

The current version of HTML is 4.01, which was last updated in 1997. The Extended HTML (XHTML) format is intended to replace HTML 4.01.

21.1.5.2 XML as a Network Protocol

Most systems that use XML strictly treat it as a file format. Examples include HTML, Real Simple Syndication (RSS), and the Extensible Messaging and Presence Protocol (XMPP) [RFC3920 – 3923] used by the Jabber instant messaging system.

Although XML is transmitted across the network, it is transmitted as user data. The XML performs no action or configuration with regards to the network itself.

Generally, XML is used as a file format, but a few network protocols actually use XML for the application layer. In these protocols, XML defines connectivity parameters, data handling, and session information. Examples include the following:

Blocks Extensible Exchange Protocol: The BEEP protocol (originally called BXXP) uses XML for controlling bidirectional communication [RFC3080, RFC3081].

XML-RPC: This protocol combines HTTP and XML for handling remote procedure calls.

Simple Object Access Protocol: SOAP is a successor to XML-RPC and uses XML to encode objects and function calls within the application layer.

Microsoft .NET: The Microsoft .NET infrastructure is designed to use SOAP for extra-system and inter-system communication.

21.2 GENERAL RISKS

Along with sharing similar communication methods, most application layer protocols share similar risks and attack vectors. The most common types of application layer risks are due to inherited risks from lower-layer protocols, authentication issues, and direct system access.

21.2.1 Inherited Vulnerabilities

With few exceptions, the most common protocols do not offer strong security options. As a result, risks from lower OSI layers impact higher-layer protocols. Most network application developers assume that lower-layer protocols manage security risks and open attack vectors from further down the network stack. For example, few application layer protocols encrypt data. As a result, most applications pass plaintext through the presentation, session, transport, network, and data link layers without encryption. An attacker on the network can use a packet sniffer to intercept unencrypted data. The *plaintext attack vector* is common for most application layer protocols.

Similar to plaintext, few application layer protocols authenticate both client and server. This leads to an inherited *MitM attack vector*. An attacker with network access can intercept and hijack communications from most application layer protocols.

There are a few options to mitigate the risks from lower-layer protocols:

Secure Lower Layer Protocols: The network application can specify the use of more secure lower-layer protocols. For example, IPsec or IPv6 with encryption can be selected, and SSL (or TLS) can be used to tunnel information more securely. Just as lower-layer risks are inherited, safer lower-layer protocols supply defense-in-depth and prevent plaintext and low-level hijacking attacks.

Application Encryption: Rather than relying on lower layers for security, the application layer can perform data encryption and validation.

Nonstandard Application: Using nonstandard applications can provide security-by-obscurity. Attackers generally target known protocols. An unknown protocol takes time to analyze and can discourage many would-be attackers. Unfortunately, nonstandard applications can lead to compatibility issues—compatibility becomes a tradeoff for security.

21.2.2 Authentication Issues

Although plaintext and MitM attack vectors are very real threats, few application-layer protocols require any type of authentication. HTTP and SMTP both permit unauthenticated clients to connect to unauthenticated servers. Even telnet, with its plaintext username and password, leaves authentication to the user layer; the telnet protocol itself performs no authentication.

When using telnet to log in to a system, the login prompt appears because of the remote shell (user layer). If the shell does not prompt for a password, then there is no authentication. Telnet, by itself, offers no authentication mechanism.

Application layer protocols that perform authentication may still be vulnerable to attacks from plaintext data transfers (e.g., HTTP's Basic Authentication). Even in the best cases, authentication is usually performed once, at the beginning of the connection. Hijacking attacks can be used to access established sessions after the initial authentication. For example, FTP servers require a username and password to login. FTP insecurely transfers authentication credentials in plaintext and only authenticates during the initial connection. An attacker sniffing packets will see the credentials, and a TCP hijacker will not be prompted for subsequent authentication information.

The simplest solution to this issue is to require encryption during authentication and periodically re-authenticate. For connections without logins, key exchange systems such as anonymous Diffie-Hellman (ADH) can be used (see Chapter 4). Although ADH does not protect against initial MitM attacks, it does help prevent established connection hijacking by supporting encryption and signed data transfers.

21.2.3 Direct System Access

Application layer protocols directly interface with applications on the operating system. Many applications have disk, file, and command execution permission, and these functions are accessible through the network. As a result, connections to the application layer frequently lead to exploitation. If a network server has any type of overflow or unchecked usage, then it is a viable attack vector. Even if authentication is used, a lack of continual authentication can permit a hijacker to acquire an established session.

Robust programming is the only mitigation option to direct system risks. In *robust programming*, all assumptions are tested. When software is not robust, it becomes vulnerable to software defects, and defects lead to exploitation. For example, buffer overflows and other input validation errors account for as much as 50 percent of all remote exploits (Table 21.2). To resolve this, parameters that are expected to be a specific length should have their lengths checked before use, and parameter data types should be validated.

Other risks to nonrobust applications come from parameter data types. If a parameter is expected to be an integer, then it should be checked before use. A string or other value should not be assumed to be valid. Many remote application exploits target input assumptions. For example, the remote input may specify a file, path, or command for execution. An attacker who specifies an alternate file, path, or command may exploit an unchecked parameter. In general, information received from unauthenticated and unvalidated connections should not contain directly executable commands. When remote commands are required, a lookup table on the server should translate the command string to an executable operation. Unknown command strings are blocked from exploitation.

TABLE 21.2 Percent of Remote Exploits from Buffer Overflows [NIST2006]

Year	Number of Remote Exploits	Percent of Buffer Overflows
1997	56	22%
1998	73	30%
1999	194	21%
2000	278	27%
2001	643	38%
2002	795	41%
2003	512	41%
2004	1209	52%

Risks from buffer overflows and unchecked parameters are usually implementation specific. Although one instant messaging client may have a remote overflow, clients by other vendors may not have the same risk. Risks due to the application layer are not the same as risks due to user-layer interpretation. Crashing a network file system (NFS) server due to a corrupt packet is an application layer risk. In contrast, using NFS to delete files on the server is not an application layer issue; NFS deletion is a user-level function.

Threats from the client to the server are most common, but they are not the only risks. Hostile servers can use an established network connection to attack a remote client. This is commonly seen with Web viruses, where accessing an infected Web server spreads the malware.

Feed a Cold, Starve a Fever

Most viruses spread through user-level functionality. The network transports the hostile code, but the user's application permits the execution. Computer viruses such as Sobig, Blaster, and Sasser were spread by the network but required user-level functionality to initiate the infection.

In contrast, most network worms exploit the application layer. The various Zotob worms, for example, scanned the network for vulnerable hosts. When one was found, a remote network connection was established to transfer the worm. A remote overflow in the server's application layer permitted execution. These worms self-propagated by exploiting vulnerable application layer implementations.

SUMMARY

The flexibility of the application layer permits a wide range of network services. Although services may have very different functions, most follow one of four communication forms: binary command sets, command-reply sequences, meta headers, or XML. In addition, many application layer protocols and implementations have issues with regards to inherited risks from lower OSI layers, authentication, and direct system access.

REVIEW QUESTIONS

1. What are four common methods for application layer communication?
2. Which communication method does telnet use?
3. What are the three general risks that impact application layer protocols?

4. Name two types of vulnerabilities that are inherited by the application layer.

DISCUSSION TOPICS

1. Use a packet sniffer to collect communication samples from a wide range of application protocols. For example, collect samples from HTTP, FTP, klogin (Kerberos login), telnet, VoIP, and LPD. Continue collecting protocol samples until there are representatives from each of the command method categories. Which command method is most common? Which is less common? Why is one more common than another?

2. Which command method is most secure? List some protocols that use this method. Why do other protocols not use it? Does the type of command set imply a level of security?

3. Separating application layer exploits from user-level risks can be difficult. Identify the three most common computer worms or viruses today. How do they spread? Do they exploit the application layer or user layer (or both)? Give specific examples.

ADDITIONAL RESOURCES

The OSI application layer is formally defined by two documents. ISO 8649 defines the Association Control Service Element (ACSE) services. It describes the functionality available to the application layer. ISO 8650 defines the ACSE protocol and details the available communication states.

XML is quickly growing in popularity as a method to embed meta information into data streams. Although it is heavily used as a file format, it is also making inroads as a network communication format. Many Web sites and books discuss implementation details for supporting XML, but the World Wide Web Consortium (W3C) has taken the role as the official standards organization for XML. The W3C's definition for XML is available at *http://www.w3.org/XML/*. The W3C is also responsible for standardizing HTML, SOAP, and other instantiations of XML.

22 SMTP

In This Chapter

- A Brief History of Email
- Email Goals
- Common Servers
- Risks
- Email Ethics

More people use email than cell phones, Web, or instant messaging (IM) systems [Radicati2005]. Corporations have become so dependent on email that a single day without it can result in millions of dollars in losses. The *Simple Mail Transfer Protocol* (SMTP), one of the most widely used Internet protocols, is responsible for transferring and routing email.

Many email transfer protocols exist. Microsoft Exchange servers use the Message Application Programming Interface (MAPI). The Instant Message Access Protocol (IMAP, RFC3501) and version 3 of the Post Office Protocol (POP3, RFC1939) are also common. Although these alternatives are common in corporate environments, they usually do not extend to email access outside of the company. SMTP and ESMTP (extended SMTP) are the de facto standards for general email transfers.

22.1 A BRIEF HISTORY OF EMAIL

SMTP has a long history with many significant protocol changes. The earliest form of SMTP was created as an extension to FTP. In February 1973, RFC458 was released. This document described a basic mail delivery system that used FTP (RFC114). Because of this lineage, modern SMTP servers have network interfaces that closely resemble FTP interfaces.

By May 1973, email addressing was defined [RFC510]. Addresses used a `username@location` format to allow the FTP client to deposit mail into a remote server for a specific recipient. Although the Internet was relatively small, FTP mail was a relatively hot topic. In June 1973, the first independent proposal for a stand-alone email protocol was released. This document, RFC524, set the basis for the modern email system. Over the next 30 years, many RFCs were released that added and extended SMTP functionality. RFC821 (August 1982) and RFC2821 (April 2001) attempted to consolidate all of the prior modifications into one standard, but even these have been extended.

RFC524 provided the framework for today's SMTP but was not intended to be a standard. Titled, "A Proposed Mail Protocol," Jim White wrote:

Although one can (I think) and might, implement software on the basis of this document, this REALLY IS a Request for Comments. Comments, questions, position papers are solicited. There are, I'm sure, bugs in the protocol specified here, and I hope that readers will point them out via RFC as they discover them.

Unfortunately, the protocol defined by RFC524 did not include authentication or validation. (And nobody pointed out the oversight.) These shortcomings have lead to problems from unsolicited and forged emails.

22.2 EMAIL GOALS

SMTP was designed for the timely, but not immediate, delivery of text messages. This is different and distinct from other communication protocols. For example, IRC and Jabber provide real-time communication. All intended recipients see each message immediately. In contrast, email may take a few seconds, minutes, or even hours to be delivered. SMTP was also not designed for transferring binary data—attachments and binary file support were added later.

The initial Internet was designed for robustness. Nearing the end of the Cold War, the network was initially designed for redundancy so that a single nuclear strike would not disable the entire network. SMTP followed this same design: a single network failure would not prevent email delivery. Instead, email messages are passed host-to-host until it reaches the destination. As long as a path exists, email will be delivered.

Besides timely and robust delivery, SMTP was designed to be extendable. This flexible protocol can be easily extended to support most data formats, encryption systems, and some authentication.

22.2.1 SMTP Data Format

SMTP uses a simple file transfer protocol to deliver email. Each email message is a file, and each file contains three components: meta header, blank line, and content. The meta header consists of `field: value` pairs. These are used to identify recipients, subject, and routing information. These header entries are used for tracing emails and identifying delivery information. A single blank line is used to separate the header from the content.

Email content is defined as printable ASCII characters. Other types of content, such as binary files and non-English languages, must be encoded in printable ASCII. Formats, such as Base64 or MIME encoding [RFC2045—RFC2049] are commonly used. Similarly, content originally contained one text block. MIME formatting permits subdivisions of the content to allow a single email to contain multiple attachments.

22.2.2 SMTP Command Structure

SMTP defines a command and response environment for communicating between a *mail user agent* (MUA—mail client) and *message transport agent* (MTA—mail server). The MUA connects to the MTA and issues a set of commands based on the information in the data's email headers. Each of these commands (Table 22.1) is well defined and must be supported by an SMTP-compatible system.

TABLE 22.1   SMTP Commands

Command	Example	Purpose
HELO *domain*	**HELO roach.lan**	Tells the MTA the domain for sender's information
EHLO *domain*	**EHLO roach.lan**	Similar to HELO but specifies ESMTP support
MAIL FROM: *address*	**MAIL FROM: santa@npole.org**	Specifies the email sender address
RCPT TO: *address*	**RCPT TO: grinch@xmas.mil**	Specifies one recipient for the email $\rightarrow$

Command	Example	Purpose
DATA	DATA	Specifies the start of the email content
QUIT	QUIT	Ends the SMTP/ESMTP connection

Some commands are intended to be used in a specific order. For example, HELO (or EHLO) must be the first command. And there can be only one MAIL FROM per email. Other commands may be used repeatedly; RCPT TO may be repeatedly provided for delivery to many users.

The DATA command is the only multiline command. After issuing a DATA command, all subsequent bytes form the SMTP meta header and content. A period (.) on a line by itself indicates the end of the data.

22.2.2.1 MTA Return Codes

Each MUA sends a command to the server, and the server responds with an acknowledgement. The return codes follow a format originally defined for FTP (RFC114). Each code has a three-digit identifier. The first digit tells the class of code. The second identifies the response category (Table 22.2), and the remaining digit tells the exact code type. A text string that describes the code in a human-readable form follows each code. For example, after the MUA sends a HELO, the MTA may respond with 250 hostname Hello host [192.168.1.5], pleased to meet you. The code 250 indicates a positive completion and no syntax issues.

TABLE 22.2 MTA Return Codes Classes

Code	Purpose
1xx	Positive Preliminary reply
2xx	Positive Completion reply
3xx	Positive Intermediate reply
4xx	Transient Negative Completion reply
5xx	Permanent Negative Completion reply
x0x	Syntax issues
x1x	Informational response
x2x	Connection-oriented reply

$\rightarrow$

Code	Purpose
x3x	Unused
x4x	Unused
x5x	Mail system

22.2.2.2 Sending Email

To send email, the MUA must connect to the MTA and transmit a series of commands. After each command, the MTA provides a status reply. Figure 22.1 shows a sample SMTP command and response session. In this example, Telnet is used as the MUA. Figure 22.2 shows the email generated by this example.

```
% telnet rudolf 25
Trying...
Connected to rudolf.npole.org.
Escape character is '^]'.
220 rudolf.npole.org ESMTP Sendmail 8.8.6 (PHNE_17135)/8.7.3 SMKit7.1.1
hp hp; Thu, 25 Apr 2002 09:17:17 -0600 (MDT)
helo ranch.npole.org
250 rudolf.npole.org Hello ranch.npole.org [10.2.241.27], pleased to
meet you
mail from: santa@npole.org
250 santa@npole.org... Sender ok
rcpt to: grinch@xmas.mil
250 grinch@xmas.mil... Recipient ok
data
354 Enter mail, end with "." on a line by itself
Subject: Ho ho ho

I know you've been a bad boy.
.
250 JAA19237 Message accepted for delivery
quit
221 rudolf.npole.org closing connection
Connection closed by foreign host.
```

FIGURE 22.1   Sample SMTP session with MUA information (in bold).

Many of the SMTP headers are specified by default. If the MUA does not provide the headers in the DATA, then the values are filled in by the MTA. These include the Date and Message-ID headers. However, the MUA may specify these values. Just

```
Received: from exchange2.npole.org ([10.8.16.2]) by exchange.npole.org
with
     SMTP (Microsoft Exchange Internet Mail Service Version 5.5.2653.13)
     id J2DYC3G1; Thu, 25 Apr 2002 08:19:32 -0700
Received: from rudolf.npole.org (rudolf.npole.org [10.2.23.20])
     by exchange2.npole.org (Postfix) with ESMTP id 97BB3C0093F
     for <grinch@xmas.mil>; Thu, 25 Apr 2002 08:19:32 -0700 (PDT)
Received: from ranch.npole.org (IDENT:santa@npole.org [10.2.241.27])
     by rudolf.npole.org with SMTP (8.8.6 (PHNE_17135)/8.7.3 SMKit7.1.1
     hp hp) id JAA19237 for grinch@xmas.mil;
     Thu, 25 Apr 2002 09:17:31 -0600 (MDT)
Date: Thu, 25 Apr 2002 09:17:31 -0600 (MDT)
From: santa@npole.org
Subject: Ho ho ho
Message-Id: <200204251517.JAA19237@rudolf.npole.org>
To: grinch@xmas.mil

I know you've been a bad boy.
```

FIGURE 22.2   Sample email from SMTP session.

as the MUA specifies the Subject, other fields such as the Date and Message-ID may also be provided.

22.2.2.3 Command Exploitation

Many of the MTA commands can leak information, and attackers can use this information to identify potential weaknesses. For example, upon connecting to the MTA, an initial return code is displayed. Many MTAs include the exact version number and patch level of the email server. An attacker can view this information and readily identify possible vulnerabilities.

Some commands are required, and others are optional. For example, MAIL FROM, RCPT TO, and DATA are required for sending email, but the HELP command is optional. HELP is commonly used to display the list of available commands. Just as the initial connection lists version information, the HELP command may also include the MTA version and patch level. Even when the version information is not available, the list of available commands may sometimes identify the type of server (Figure 22.3).

Other optional commands, such as VRFY and EXPN, are used to verify and expand email addresses. Attackers can use these to scan the host for a list of email addresses. Between 1995 and 2003, many unsolicited mailing lists were generated by repeatedly calling VRFY and EXPN with common account names. The replies were used to generate lists of valid email addresses.

```
$ telnet localhost 25
Trying 127.0.0.1...
Connected to localhost.
Escape character is '^]'.
220 rudolf.npole.org ESMTP Sendmail 8.11.6/8.11.6; Sun, 15 Jan 2006
09:51:22 -0700
HELP
214-2.0.0 This is sendmail version 8.11.6
214-2.0.0 Topics:
214-2.0.0     HELO     EHLO    MAIL    RCPT    DATA
214-2.0.0     RSET     NOOP    QUIT    HELP    VRFY
214-2.0.0     EXPN     VERB    ETRN    DSN     AUTH
214-2.0.0     STARTTLS
214-2.0.0 For more info use "HELP <topic>".
214-2.0.0 To report bugs in the implementation send email to
214-2.0.0     sendmail-bugs@sendmail.org.
214-2.0.0 For local information send email to Postmaster at your site.
214 2.0.0 End of HELP info
```

FIGURE 22.3   MTA version information in the initial connection and HELP menu.

Secure mail systems are usually modified to not list version information at the initial connections or in the HELP reply. Most production MTAs do not provide any of the optional commands.

Some MTAs are intentionally configured to list incorrect mailer versions. This usually requires modification of the MTA configuration files. The belief is that false information is more damaging than no information. An attacker who observes false information is likely to believe it is real.

22.3 COMMON SERVERS

There are hundreds of MTA providers and implementations. Some handle general mail delivery, whereas others specialize in mailing lists, network types, or additional features (e.g., calendars and shared workgroup space). Although there are many MTA options, most mail servers on the Internet either use Sendmail, Microsoft Exchange, Qmail, or Postfix [Timme2004, Credentia2003]. Each of these mailer options has tradeoffs with regards to performance, features, and security.

22.3.1 Sendmail

The Sendmail MTA (*http://www.sendmail.org/*) is the single most common mail transport agent. It is open source and provided as the default MTA distribution for most Unix systems. Sendmail is a master email daemon; it receives, processes, forwards, and delivers email.

Sendmail is also one of the oldest MTA implementations—it dates back to 1979 as the program `delivermail`. Being old and widely used is a strong benefit for any application. It implies durability, extendibility, supportability, and overall usefulness. However, Sendmail does have significant limitations. For example, Sendmail consistently benchmarks as one of the slowest MTAs. The configuration file is very complex, and Sendmail is historically known as the second most insecure network applications in the Internet. (Sendmail is second only to DNS, and Sendmail uses DNS.) Between 1993 and 2003, there were 65 software releases, averaging one release every 2 months. Many of these releases address security issues.

Sendmail is readily identifiable by the SMTP welcome message, HELP file identifier, and version information placed in the email header. Attackers can readily identify Sendmail, including the version and patch level. This allows an attacker to identify all unpatched risks. For mitigation, administrators should consider changing or removing the Sendmail identification strings and regularly check for updates and patches.

22.3.2 Microsoft Exchange

Similar to Sendmail, the Microsoft Exchange server is a monolithic server designed as an alternative to SMTP. Within the MTA, the system uses the proprietary *Exchange* data format, but it also supports communicating with standard SMTP MTAs.

From a security viewpoint, Exchange is not as vulnerable as Sendmail. The total number of exploits for Exchange is significantly less than Sendmail, but risks to Sendmail are patched rapidly—usually in days. In contrast, Exchange is patched much less frequently and Microsoft sometimes downplays risks. Some vulnerabilities with Exchange have been unpatched for months (or longer), and most patches are released several months after the vulnerability's initial discovery.

22.3.3 Qmail

Qmail (*http://www.qmail.org/*) is intended as a replacement for Sendmail. It was designed for performance, reliability, simplicity, and modularity. As a result, Qmail is very fast and relatively easy to configure and maintain. Because of its impressive performance, it is widely used by systems that manage large mailing lists and high volume traffic.

Security was a primary design goal for Qmail. The MTA defines a clear separation between files and programs, limits code that runs as root (Unix administrative privileges), and implements defense-in-depth. As a result, there have only been two known exploits for Qmail since 1997, and both were patched shortly after identification.

22.3.4 Postfix

Postfix (*http://www.postfix.org/*) began as an alternative to Sendmail. In 1998, Web-based application servers were modularly designed to handle high loads and limit the impact from security exploits. Wietse Venema adapted these Web-based techniques to email delivery. The result is Postfix: a fast, efficient, flexible, modular, and secure MTA.

Although fewer systems use Postfix than Sendmail or Microsoft Exchange, Postfix is the fastest growing MTA. In 2003, less than 3 percent of MTAs were using Postfix. By 2005, Postfix had grown to over 20 percent. Postfix is currently included by default on some Linux and BSD distributions.

Postfix employs dozens of special-purpose applications but maintains the same command-line options as Sendmail. This makes it a viable drop-in replacement for the more common Sendmail system. Postfix does not have the same security issues as Sendmail. Instead, it implements many security-oriented concepts:

Least privileged: Each module runs with the minimum permissions necessary.

Insulation: Each module performs one task independently from other modules.

Controlled environment: No modules operate as other users.

No SUID: No Postfix module runs with "set user id" access. In Unix, SUID is used to change access privileges.

Trust: The concept of trust between modules is well defined and constantly validated.

Large Inputs: Application memory is properly handled to mitigate risks from overflows.

From a security perspective, Postfix is secure upon installation. It does not disclose version information and consciously implements concepts for secure applications. As a result, Postfix has only had one reported exploit in eight years, and it was a DoS attack.

22.4 RISKS

SMTP was designed for reliable and timely message delivery, but it was not designed for security. When the protocol was first designed, robustness was a more serious concern than security. This oversight has led to a series of security risks that are independent of the MUA and MTA implementation.

22.4.1 Forged Headers and Spam

As shown earlier in Figures 22.1 and 22.2, the MUA can specify email headers. Each email relay is expected to append a Received header to the beginning of the email. These headers form a simple paper trail for tracing the message. The bottom Received header was added first, and the top header was added last.

Forged email headers occur when the sender intentionally inserts false header information. Well-behaved MUA and MTA systems only add valid headers, but malicious systems may add false information, remove valid headers, or modify existing headers. Distinguishing valid headers from invalid can become very difficult.

All attributes of the email header can be forged, with the exception of the final valid Received headers. The subject, date, recipients, content, and even the initial received headers can be trivially forged with the SMTP DATA command. But when the email is sent to a true MTA, a valid Received header is added to the beginning of the message. This will contain a valid timestamp and originator IP address. Additional mail relays may contain similar headers and remain valid.

22.4.1.1 Forged Emails

Forged email can lead to very serious problems. Consider a message that appears to come from a manager, firing an employee. Because email can be trivially forged, is the employee really fired? Email is commonly used for communication between companies; a single forged email could break a company. The problems with forgeries are not limited to false senders. Nonrepudiation plays a critical role with email—how can senders show that they did not send an email?

22.4.1.2 Spam

Undesirable email (*spam*) is an example of abuse due to forged emails (Figure 22.4). Although the email may appear to come from one person (e.g., "Jerrod"—with an email address in Chile), it likely came from someone else. The example spam in Figure 22.4 originated from 216.133.219.154 but contains many forged headers. These headers obscure the ability to identify the sender. (The WHOIS listing and nmap scan identified a system in the United States running Windows; however, this system was likely compromised and simply relaying spam.)

```
Received: from 25EECCE8 (unknown[216.133.219.154](misconfigured
sender))
        by rwcrmxc21.comcast.net (rwcrmxc21) with SMTP
        id <20060115230410r2100f5ccie>; Sun, 15 Jan 2006 23:05:04 +0000
Received: from 61.166.141.14 (unknown [61.166.141.14])
        by 204.127.202.26 with SMTP id allocate67074;
        Sun, 15 Jan 2006 15:00:55 -0800
Message-Id: <24916.704613beryl6943@eon.net.au>
MIME-Version: 1.0
Date: Sun, 15 Jan 2006 15:00:55 -0800
From: "Jerrod Basil " <Gilbertk_Whitfeld6@collahuasi.cl>
To: homeuser145@comcast.net
Subject: The findings support an earlier review by the U.S.
```

Have you ever stopped to wonder how much an average man pays for his
medicines? Painkillers, drugs to improve the quality of life, weight
reducing tablets, and many more. What's worse, the same medicine costs
a lot more if it is branded.

We have over 172 Meds ready to order and be shipped

So why should you pay more especially when you can get the same drugs
at a much cheaper cost? At Health Suite, we bring you the same drugs,
the generic version - the same quality, the same formula at a very
reasonable price.

Viagra low as 67.28
Cialis low as 93.73

http://Beaverq<AC6>Qx.isearcofa.com

Thank you
Harry

FIGURE 22.4 Sample undesirable email message using forged headers (in bold).

In 2005, spam was estimated to account for 80 percent of all email [Postini2006].
Spam is made possible due to a lack of authentication and the low skill level required
for generating forged headers. Anti-spam solutions primarily focus on filtering and
intercept an average of 90 percent of all spam [FTC2005]. Unfortunately, the techniques used by spammers continually change—static anti-spam systems become ineffective over time. Filters do not only target spam, they also occasionally misclassify
nonspam messages. In addition, current anti-spam solutions do not prevent the initial generation, network traversal, or relaying of forged emails. Until these issues are
addressed, there will be no long-term solution for combating spam.

22.4.1.3 Identifying Forged Emails

Separating valid emails from forgeries can be very difficult. In general, a single forged header indicates that all information below it is forged. Fortunately, some fields are well defined:

Received: The Received header should contain a "from" and "by" address. The "by" address on one header should match the "from" address on the next header. Most forged Received headers do not properly chain the "from" and "by" addresses. Received headers should also contain a timestamp and a tracking number. If these do not exist, or the time shows a significant delay, then the header is likely forged.

Not every MTA generates one Received header. For example, Qmail usually generates three Received headers and separates the "from" and "by" addresses.

NOTE

Date: The Date header should be RFC822 compliant, for example, Sun, 15 Jan 2006 16:45:27 -0700. Dates that are in nonstandard formats are likely forged.

From, To, CC: Although multiple sender and recipients are permitted by the SMTP standard, most applications only generate one of each header. Multiple carbon-copy (CC) or From lines indicate a forged header.

Message-ID: The Message-ID is intended to be a unique header assigned to the email. Different MUAs create different Message-ID formats. A very nonstandard (or missing) Message-ID can suggest a forged email.

The most obvious attributes come from the sender and the contents. If the sender is unknown and the contents are undesirable, then the email is likely unsolicited, and the headers are probably forged.

22.4.1.4 Mail Logs

Most email servers maintain transaction logs. The unique identifier added to the Received header should match log entries created by the MTA. When tracing an email, mail logs can help determine the true origination. Logs usually include sender, recipient, timestamps, IP addresses, and even process identifiers. When forging email, servers listed in false headers will not have log entries, and systems that originated the forged email may contain account information for the true sender.

Although mail logs can be used to trace emails to the true originator, they are not always accessible. Logs from different servers (or countries) are usually inaccessible. In addition, anonymity techniques, such as relaying through open proxies, can prevent determination of the true origination source.

22.4.2 Relaying and Interception

SMTP does not always send email directly from the sender to the recipient. Mail relays are commonly used to route information. As a result, any host can be a relay. Mail relays are determined by the MX records in DNS (see Chapter 17).

SMTP administrators need no special permission to operate a relay, and email is transmitted in plaintext. As a result, relay owners can read emails, and each email relay has the opportunity to intercept and modify message contents.

To mitigate interception risks, sensitive emails can use encrypted contents. PGP is one example of a common encryption method used with email [RFC2440]. But encryption technology has its own limitations when used with email:

Compatibility: Not every email encryption implementation adheres to a standard. For example, email that is PGP encrypted with mutt (a Unix mail client) may not be readily viewable by someone using Microsoft Outlook (with PGP support). More complicated cryptographic systems lead to more security but less compatibility with other email users.

General Correspondence: A significant strength of email is the ability to send a message to anyone—even a complete stranger. Current cryptographic systems require the sender to have made a prior acquaintance with the recipient. This usually includes the exchanging of cryptographic keys.

Besides cryptography, many other solutions have been proposed for validating email. Unfortunately, each of these solutions fails to address the issues of trust and authentication when connecting to an MTA. For example, the proposed Sender Policy Framework standard (SPF—*http://spf.pobox.com/*) restricts how a user can send email but does not authenticate the user. Computational challenges, such as Microsoft's Penny Black (*http://research.microsoft.com/research/sv/PennyBlack/*), penalize mass mailers but offer no authentication options.

22.4.3 SMTP and DNS

The most significant risk to SMTP comes from a dependency on DNS. As discussed in Chapter 17, DNS is used to identify mail relays; however, DNS is extremely vulnerable to many forms of attack. As a result, email can be compromised through DNS. Email can be routed to a hostile relay or simply blocked from delivery.

22.4.4 Lower-Layer Protocols

Just as SMTP is impacted by exploits to DNS, SMTP can also be impacted by lower network layer protocols. MAC, IP, and TCP hijacking can each compromise email being transported. Because SMTP provides no means to encrypt data content, any attacker along the network path can view all passing emails.

In general, if security is a significant concern, then email should not be used. In particular, plaintext email should not be used to transfer passwords, credit card information, or confidential information.

SMTP offers no more privacy than talking on a cell phone in a crowded restaurant. Any stranger within earshot can listen to the conversation.

22.5 EMAIL ETHICS

The problems with email are not limited to technical authentication, interception, and header forgery. Email contents are actual documents passed between a sender and a recipient. Ethical and legal issues arise due to ownership and distribution. For example, under U.S. copyright law, the author of a document holds the copyright—regardless of whether the document explicitly says "Copyright."

The transmission of a document through email usually does not indicate a transfer of ownership, but it also does not indicate privacy. For example, in the court case of *Bonita P. Bourke, et al. versus Nissan Motor Corporation* (California Court of Appeals, Second Appellate District, Case No. B068705, July 26, 1993), it was found that companies can review employee emails, even if the contents are personal in nature. A similar finding came out of *Bill McLaren, Jr. versus Microsoft Corp.* (Case No. 05-97-00824, 1999 Tex. App. Lexis 4103, Tex. Crt. of App., May 28,1999). In addition, *Re: Collins* (86 Cal.App.4th 1176, 104 Cal. Rptr. 2d 108, 2001) found that blocking email from delivery is acceptable (for maximum security prisoners).

22.5.1 Email Handling and Usage

Questions concerning the handling of email contents are not clear-cut, and neither are acceptable uses. There is no technical reason why a recipient cannot forward email to other people. Even if the email is marked as confidential or classified, it can still be distributed.

Many companies have policies on email management that detail how and when email may be forwarded and who owns the rights to the contents. However, policies do not prevent propagation any more than a ONE WAY sign stops cars from driving the wrong way down a one-way street. Although policies can direct proper behavior, they do not prevent policy breaches.

22.5.2 Email Impersonation

It takes very little effort to send email as if it were from someone else. The easiest impersonations simply require configuring a mail client (MUA) with someone else's email address. More complicated impersonations may use automated tools to relay through proxies, communicate with MTAs, and provide elaborate, forged headers.

Impersonation is not always a bad thing. Many systems, such as mailing list re-mailers (listserv), commonly repeat a sender's information—the email may not be directly from the person, but it is usually sent on someone's behalf. The method used for remailing as someone else is the same approach used to impersonate someone else: an alternate sender name is specified for the SMTP MAIL FROM. Although email technology permits impersonation, intentional misrepresentation is generally considered ethically unacceptable and is illegal in countries such as the United States, Australia, and the entire European Union.

SMTP offers no options to mitigate risks from unauthorized senders; however, SMTP extensions, such as cryptographic solutions, can be used to authenticate and validate the sender.

Even if an email is encrypted, digitally signed, and validated, there is no mechanism to restrict distribution.

22.5.3 Receiving Notification

Email offers a single communication path, from the sender to the recipient. Although lower OSI protocols, such as TCP, may validate data transmission, SMTP does not validate email delivery. If a recipient claims to not have received an email, there is no easy way to validate the delivery. As a result, SMTP was extended to include delivery notification. Two methods are defined: return receipts and disposition notifications.

Return Receipts: Return receipts (RFC2076) are intended to deliver an email back to the sender upon delivery. The email should be generated by the final MTA. The Return-Receipt-To header includes the email address for the receipt. But, because spam senders can use this to validate mailing lists, few MTAs enable Return-Receipt support.

Disposition Notifications: The Disposition-Notification-To header (RFC2289) operates similarly to return receipts, but the reply is generated when the email is displayed. Although return receipts are generated by the MTA, the email viewer generates disposition notifications. Most email clients prompt the user before replying to disposition notification requests—the user may choose not to confirm receipt.

Although return receipts and disposition notifications can be used to confirm delivery, there is still no verification of receipt. For example, email may be delivered to an intermediary such as the CEO's secretary for screening. Even if a return receipt or disposition notification is received, there is no guarantee that the intended recipient received the message. In a truly hostile environment, a malicious user may generate a confirmation of delivery and then delete the email—without the intended recipient ever knowing.

Without some type of receipt or notification, email recipients have a wide range of options for claiming to have never received an email. Although email relays rarely lose messages, a misconfiguration can result in a temporary loss. More commonly, spam filters intercept nonspam email messages. Even if the recipient actually does receive the message, he can still falsely blame a spam filter—this is believable. When mailboxes fill, most MTAs return a message denoting a failure to deliver mail—but some MTAs silently fail. A recipient can falsely claim to have lost mail due to a full mailbox. Or they can simply blame an unknown computer problem for deleting messages. Although SMTP usually provides timely message deliveries, there is no consistent method to validate that an email had reached the intended recipient.

Be Careful What You Wish For

Email chain letters have circulated around the Internet for decades. In 1989, eight-year-old Craig Shergold had a brain tumor and a dream—he dreamed of being in the *Guinness Book of World Records* for receiving the most greeting cards. And he successfully accomplished this dream in 1990, after receiving over 16 million cards. In 1991, Craig's tumor was successfully removed and he fully recovered.

Unfortunately, the story does not end there. Some unknown person converted the dream to an email chain letter. The letter has undergone many revisions, including a claim to be on behalf of the Make-A-Wish Foundation. In each of the revisions, the letter requested the recipient to forward it to other people. According to the Make-A-Wish Foundation, "His wish was fulfilled by another wish-granting organization not associated with the Make-A-Wish Foundation." [Wish2006] This email chain letter has propagated for years, generating millions of emails.

Any email can be created, modified, and passed to other recipients. The sender and people listed in the contents have no control over how an email is propagated, where it is sent, or whether it should be passed to other recipients. Only the recipient can control email propagation.

SUMMARY

SMTP is a ubiquitous technology, used by more people than cell phones, chat rooms, or the Web. It offers the timely delivery of messages and is flexible enough to support future needs such as attachments and encryption. But SMTP has a few significant limitations: email generation is unauthenticated and not validated. Forged email can be trivially forwarded, and real email can be propagated indefinitely, which leads to problems with trust, spam, and nonrepudiation.

REVIEW QUESTIONS

1. What protocol was used as a basis for SMTP?
2. List three goals for SMTP.
3. Which of these servers are most secure: Sendmail, Microsoft Exchange, Qmail, or Postfix? Which are least secure?
4. What are four direct risks to SMTP communications?
5. Who owns email? The sender or the recipient?

DISCUSSION TOPICS

1. Which is more desirable, an MTA with plenty of support but frequent vulnerabilities, or one with few known vulnerabilities but relatively little support?
2. Configure an isolated test network with three accounts: sender1, sender2, and recipient. In the test network, send two emails to the recipient. The first email should not be forged and be sent from sender1. The second email should be forged, appearing to come from sender2. Can the recipient identify the forged email? What aspects of the email make it appear forged? Repeat the experiment with different mail servers. Do different MTAs impact the ability to create a forged email? What if the email must relay through multiple MTAs? Can a forged email be generated that cannot be detected as being forged?
3. Given that email is trivial to forge and offers no security, is it acceptable to use email for corresponding with financial institutions or online vendors? Should military commands be transmitted using email?
4. During the Microsoft Anti-Trust trials (*http://www.usdoj.gov/atr/cases/ms_index.htm*—2001-2005), email evidence played a major role. In his testimony, Bill Gates claimed to not have received some emails and could not recall sending other emails. Regardless of personal viewpoints related to the

trial, is it possible for email to have been sent as Bill Gates without his knowledge? Could email have been sent to Mr. Gates without him receiving it? Describe some technologies, methods, and skill sets necessary for supporting Mr. Gates' testimony. How could claims of forgery and interception be debunked? In general, can email ever be a "smoking gun"?

ADDITIONAL RESOURCES

Sendmail is the de facto standard for mail transport agents. The book, *Sendmail*, by Bryan Costales and Eric Allman (O'Reilly Media, Inc., ISBN 1-565-92839-3) is the definitive guide to configuring and using Sendmail.

Spam is a long and complex problem. Documents such as "Anti-Spam Solutions and Security" (*http://www.securityfocus.com/infocus/1763*) briefly discuss some of the issues surrounding spam-filtering systems. Specific types of spam are monitored by different organizations. For example, the Federal Trade Commission (*http://www.ftc.gov/*) provides links to many anti-spam resources. The Anti-Phishing Working Group (*http://www.antiphishing.org/*) monitors phishing fraud, and the SpamHaus Project (*http://www.spamhaus.org/*) tracks spam groups.

23 HTTP

In This Chapter

- HTTP Goals
- URL
- URL Exploitation
- General HTTP Risks

The *HyperText Transport Protocol* (HTTP) is one of the most widely used application layer protocols, which forms the basis of the *World Wide Web* (Web) and Web-related protocols. Although more people use email than any other protocol, HTTP generates a majority of network volume [Radicati2005, Mellia2002]. Most email messages are a few kilobytes in size—with few emails containing large attachments. In contrast, it is not uncommon for Web pages to contain many megabytes of images and content.

23.1 HTTP GOALS

HTTP was designed as a flexible, real-time data transfer protocol. The original specification for HTTP version 1.0 was defined in RFC1945. This specification was later revised in RFC2616 to HTTP 1.1 as an elaboration to the HTTP standard.

Although HTTP is commonly used to transfer HTML (an XML-based content and formatting specification), the protocol is independent of the content being transferred. HTTP can easily transfer text or binary files and documents or images.

23.1.1 HTTP Command-Reply

RFC1945 details a command-reply protocol that uses meta information to augment requests and responses. In HTTP 1.0, each TCP connection contained up to four elements:

Command: A keyword command, such as GET or POST, followed by a resource identifier and the HTTP version. For example: GET /index.html HTTP/1.0.

Meta Information: A series of field: value pairs for augmenting the request information. This information may specify language, acceptable response formats, authentication credentials, and other request attributes.

Blank Line: A single blank line indicates the end of the HTTP meta header. If no meta header is present, then the request is simply the command and a blank line.

Optional Data: When using the request to upload files, data is provided after the blank line. The meta header Content-Length: indicates the amount of data being uploaded.

The server's reply follows the client's request. The reply is similar to the request, containing four elements:

Status: The overall status of the reply is returned. This includes a numeric code and text description. (Similar to the FTP and SMTP status replies.)

Meta Information: A series of field: value pairs for augmenting the reply. These may include information about language, file format, modification times, and server-specific information.

Blank Line: A single blank line indicates the end of the HTTP meta header.

Optional Data: Most HTTP replies contain data provided after the blank line. Under HTTP/1.0, the Content-Length: header is not required (and may not be accurate). The data transfer is completed when the TCP connection is closed.

Figure 23.1 shows a sample HTTP request to HackerFactor.com and the subsequent reply. In this example, the client sends three lines: a command (GET), a single meta header, and a blank line. The reply includes the status, five meta headers, and the HTML content.

```
GET / HTTP/1.0
Host: www.hackerfactor.com

HTTP/1.1 200 OK
Date: Sat, 21 Jan 2006 16:49:12 GMT
Server: Apache/1.3.34 (Unix) mod_pointer/0.8 PHP/4.4.1
X-Powered-By: PHP/4.4.1
Connection: close
Content-Type: text/html

<html>
<head><title>Hacker Factor Solutions</title></head>
...
</html>
```

FIGURE 23.1 An HTTP request (in bold) to *www.hackerfactor.com* and reply.

23.1.2 HTTP Command Structure

HTTP defines many different commands for managing the resource identifier and meta information. The most common commands are used with the Web: GET, HEAD, and POST.

GET: The GET command indicates data retrieval from the server. The request specifies the information to retrieve, and the reply contains the information.

HEAD: The HEAD command is similar to GET, but it only returns the associated meta header, not the actual data. This command is commonly used when checking the existence or status of data on the Web server without requiring data retrieval.

POST: Whereas GET is used to download information, POST provides upload functionality. The request contains meta information that describes the data being uploaded, as well as the data itself. The reply to a POST may not only contain status information but also response data.

Besides the three commands used by the Web, RFC1945 defines other general-purpose commands. These commands may not be supported by Web servers, but can be supported by other types of HTTP servers.

PUT: An alternative to POST, this command specifies that the data be placed in the location specified by the resource identifier. This is different from a POST, where the resource identifier is used for processing the uploaded information.

DELETE: This command requests the removal of the resource identifier from the server.

LINK: This command is used to create a relationship between a resource identifier and some other source. Meta information is intended to identify the linked source.

UNLINK: The UNLINK command removes a relationship established by the LINK command.

23.1.3 Return Codes

After processing a response, an HTTP server replies with a status code. The status code follows a three-digit structure, similar to SMTP. The first digit identifies the type of reply, and the remaining two digits denote the specific reply (Table 23.1). Common codes from HTTP servers include 200 (OK), 301 (moved permanently), 302 (moved temporarily), 404 (file not found), and 500 (internal server error).

TABLE 23.1 HTTP Return Codes Classes

Code	Purpose
1xx	*Informational.* (Generally unused; not supported by HTTP 1.0.)
2xx	*Successful.* The request was received without processing errors.
3xx	*Redirection.* The reply indicates relocation information.
4xx	*Client Error.* The request could not be processed due to an error in the request.
5xx	*Server Error.* The request could not be processed due to a server problem.

For some HTTP attacks, the returned status code can be used for reconnaissance. For example, not every Web server returns the same text string with the return code. Differences in the text string can be used to fingerprint a server. In addition, many resource identifiers are not linked through standard queries. An attacker may use HEAD or GET requests to scan for hidden resources. Return code changes between 200 and 404 can be used to determine the existence of the scanned resource. In addition, different 4*xx* and 5*xx* status codes can be used to identify different resource handling methods on the server.

23.1.4 HTTP Extensions

As with most popular protocols, HTTP is constantly evolving. HTTP 1.0 was released in 1996. In 1999, HTTP 1.1 was solidified as RFC2616. During this time, additional meta headers and commands were added to the protocol.

23.1.4.1 Maintaining State

Normally, each HTTP request operates independently; there is no relationship between subsequent HTTP requests. Although independence simplifies functional requirements, it does not lead to an ability to maintain state.

RFC2109 introduced cookies as a state management mechanism. *Cookies* are strings set by an HTTP server that define a known state. Cookies are set by the server using a `Set-Cookie:` meta header. The client is expected to return the cookie (in a `Cookie:` header) at each subsequent request to the server's domain. For example:

```
Set-Cookie: v1us=43D327891078A3DE; path=/; expires=Wed, 19 Feb
2020 14:28:00 GMT; domain=.usatoday.com
```

In this example, the client would return `Cookie: v1us=43D297898078A1DE`. Multiple cookies can be included in a response by using a semicolon as a delimiter (`Cookie: v1us=43D297898078A1DE; v2gb=5E7F8238`).

Cookies raise encoding, privacy, and misuse issues. For example:

Encoding Risk: Different servers encode cookies differently. Poorly designed servers may store user information in a plaintext (or easy to decipher) format. As a result, an attacker can change cookie values and gain access to other sessions. To reduce this risk, many servers use cryptography to encode cookies or simply assign long random strings as session designators. Both options reduce the risk of an attacker guessing a different session identifier.

Cookie Theft: In many cases, cookies are used for tracking authorized users. An attacker who gains access to an authentication cookie gains authentication. Viruses, such as Agobot and Gaobot, captured cookies from bank logins. These cookies allowed attackers to access bank accounts without providing login credentials. To mitigate this risk, some systems link cookies to other attributes, such as network addresses. In addition, critical cookies can be set to expire quickly to reduce the window of opportunity for theft.

Privacy: Cookies allow sites to track usage patterns. This data can be used to build user profiles and assist in direct marketing efforts. To mitigate this risk and protect privacy, many Web browsers allow the disabling of cookies or clearing of stored cookies between uses.

Cross-Site Cookies: Any HTTP server can assign any cookie for any domain. Hostile sites can use this capability to assign cookies for other domains. To mitigate this risk, most browsers have an option to only allow cookies for the server's domain. For example, the HTTP server `tv.images.usatoday.com` can authoritatively assign a cookie for the host `tv.images.usatoday.com`, and for the domains `images.usatoday.com` and `usatoday.com`.

Although cookies are commonly used for maintaining state, they are not the only option. Web servers also can place state information in the resource identifier. Different HTML hyperlinks are used to indicate state.

23.1.4.2 HTTP 1.1 Extensions

HTTP 1.1 introduced many extensions to HTTP 1.0. For example, rather than using one command reply per TCP connection, HTTP 1.1 permits multiple commands to be sent over a connection. Using the HTTP header `Connection: open`, a client can indicate that the server should not close the connection after returning data. Instead, a server response can be followed by another client request.

To support `Connection: open`, the server must return the size of the data. Under HTTP 1.0, the `Content-Length:` header from the server was optional (and not always accurate). Under HTTP 1.1, the length is a required element and must match the amount of returned data.

HTTP 1.1 also provided data chunking [RFC2616]. If the server takes too long to respond to a request, it raises the risk of having the client timeout. Data chunking allows the server to return parts of the reply without having the client expire the connection. Each data chunk is prefaced by the size of the chunk. A zero-size chunk indicates the end of the data.

Beyond GET, HEAD, and POST, HTTP 1.1 introduced commands for connection management.

CONNECT: This command permits a client to control and redirect HTTP proxy connections. However, the CONNECT option can also lead to exploitation. Some proxies support redirections to localhost or other servers that allow attackers to CONNECT to restricted systems [FrSIRT/ADV-2005-1537].

TRACE: This debugging command allows a client to view how a command is forwarded. Unfortunately, like the CONNECT command, TRACE can be used to exploit server vulnerabilities [FrSIRT/ADV-2005-2226].

OPTIONS: This command provides a list of Web-based communication options and services available on the HTTP server. This information can be directly used as reconnaissance. For example, OPTIONS can be used to identify Web-DAV (RFC2518) support. WebDAV has a long history of exploitable functionality [Microsoft2003].

In general, HTTP commands that are not necessary for server use should be disabled.

23.1.4.3 Basic Authentication

HTTP 1.0 does define a minor amount of authentication. Called *Basic Authentication*, the server provides a *realm* (string) to the client. The client must return a username and password combination for access to the realm. To prevent communication issues, the username and password are Base64 (MIME) encoded. For example, username:password becomes the request header Authorization: Basic dXNlcm5hbWU6cGFzc3dvcmQ. Because a colon (:) delimitates the username from the password, a username cannot contain a colon.

Basic Authentication is viable for authenticating users but offers no privacy. An attacker who observes the HTTP request can immediately intercept the valid login credentials.

Other authentication methods, such as Digest Authentication [RFC2617], use shared secret information and a cryptographic hash function (usually MD5) to authenticate. Although this does not prevent replay attacks from accessing information, it does deter theft of login credentials.

23.1.4.4 SSL Security

By itself, HTTP is a simple transfer system. Although the data being transmitted may be ASCII text or binary, there is no encryption of the data. An attacker who intercepts HTTP network traffic can readily view all of the transmitted requests, replies, and data.

To provide security, HTTP is commonly tunneled through an SSL connection (see Chapter 19). *HTTPS* is HTTP over SSL. Although SSL is not a fool-proof encryption system, it does offer a layer of encryption between the client and the server. An attacker cannot easily compromise an SSL connection.

HTTPS is usually implemented with server-side certificates but not client-side certificates. As a result, the server may appear authenticated, but the client is unknown. Other authentication methods, such as Basic Authentication or cookies, are usually used in conjunction with HTTPS. Although HTTPS does mitigate risks from external attackers, without client-side certificates, it offers no protection to the server from hostile clients.

23.1.4.5 Related Protocols

Although HTTP is commonly associated with the Web, it has also been extended to other protocols. For example, *Real Simple Syndication* (RSS) uses HTTP for transferring XML files, *Real Time Streaming Protocol* (RTSP—RFC2326) adapts HTTP for multimedia streaming, and Jabber uses HTTP to transfer XMPP instant messaging information. These extensions show that HTTP is extendible beyond Web usage.

Although the Web uses HTTP, HTTP is not the same as the Web. The Web describes the content transferred using HTTP, but other protocols also use HTTP. Referring to HTTP as the Web is like calling every vehicle on the road a "car"—cars, trucks, motorcycles, and other vehicles all share the road.

23.2 URL

HTTP uses a *uniform resource locator* (URL) as a shorthand notation for specifying the type of query [RFC1738]. This notation not only allows the identification of remote services and files but also leads to exploitable attack vectors.

> **My Name Is URL**
>
> The acronym URL is sometimes defined as a *Universal* Resource Locator, *Uniform* Resource Locator, or *Unique* Resource Locator. This ambiguity comes from the close relationship between a URL and URI: a URL contains a URI, and the definition for a URI is ambiguous. The URI may be called a *Universal*, *Uniform*, or *Unique Resource Indicator*. RFC1630 uses the term "universal" to define a URI, but RFC2396 redefines URI as "uniform." Although RFCs do not use the term "unique," many RFC draft documents do use this definition. Similarly, URL is normally associated with "uniform" but is sometimes called "unique" or "universal" as a carry-over from the URI definition.
>
> Fortunately, these variations do not interfere with the implementation. Because the abbreviations are more common than the definitions, everyone who discusses a "URL" (or "URI") talks about the same concept.

23.2.1 URL Format

Each URL defines a protocol, account information, server information, and a *uniform resource indicator* (URI) that specifies the exact instruction, for example, `http://www.hackerfactor.com/` or `ftp://anonymous:guest@ftp.wustl.edu/`. The actual format of a URL is `service://username:password@server:port/URI?options#anchor`, but many of these fields are optional.

Service: This specifies the application layer protocol. Common examples are HTTP, HTTPS, and FTP, but other protocols such as the Trivial File Transfer Protocol (TFTP) and telnet are acceptable. Although the service must be specified, many Web browsers assume the default service is HTTP. Each service is followed by a colon (`:`).

Server Information: Two slashes (`//`) indicate the start of optional server information. Some protocols may not require this information, but protocols such as HTTP and HTTPS do require it.

Username:Password@: An optional username may be specified for services that require login information. This is common for FTP and telnet services. In addition, an optional password may be specified. However, because a colon (`:`) is used to separate the username from the password, the username cannot contain a colon. Similarly, because slashes (`/`) are used to separate fields within the URL, neither the username nor password may contain a slash. An `@` symbol before the server information denotes login information. (For this reason, the `@` is also an invalid character in a username or password.)

Server: The server's address is specified for protocols such as HTTP and FTP. This name may be included in many different formats. For example, a DNS name or network address may be provided. Raw network address, such as IPv4 `10.1.2.3` or IPv6 `4E65:616C:::2BAD:E911` can be enclosed in square backets: `http://[10.1.2.3]/` or `https://[4E65:616C:::2BAD:E911]/`. In addition, most Web browsers accept integer network representations (e.g., `10.1.2.3` is `167838211`).

Port: The port for the network service can be optionally specified by using a colon (`:`) after the server address. Most protocols have default port numbers. For example, HTTP is 80/tcp, HTTPS is 443/tcp, and FTP is 21/tcp. Alternate ports can be specified as well.

URI: A slash separates the server information from the query information. The URL contains a specific directive for the service on the specified host. For HTTP, this usually appears as a directory path (`/directory1/directory2/directory3/filename`), although the path does not need to actually exist on the server. Instead, this is actually a service directive and may refer to a file, application, or database query.

Query: The URI may end with an optional query, denoted by a question mark (`?`). Queries act as optional parameters for the URI. Although the format is implementation specific, many Web servers use an ampersand

(&) to separate parameters. For example, Amazon.com may show a URI such as `/gp/product/1584504641?_encoding=UTF8&node=172282`. The query includes two parameters: `_encoding` and `node`.

Anchor: Under HTTP, the hash character (`#`) denotes an anchor within an HTML document. This character and subsequent string are never transmitted to the server. Instead, when the HTML document is returned, the browser can quickly jump down to the designated anchor point.

23.2.2 Dynamic Submission Methods

There are three common approaches for submitting information to a server. The first approach uses the URL query field to pass variables and parameter information to the HTTP server's CGI application. This is one of the most common approaches.

A second approach uses the URI's path to indicate parameters to a CGI application. For example, the URL `http://www.securityfocus.com/archive/1/422489/30/0/threaded` contains a path that defines a query. The URI is a virtual path, with each numerical element describing a query term.

The third approach places query information in the submitted data. For example,

```
http://server/cgi-bin/env.cgi?test=7&name=Neal
```

will generate the request

```
GET /cgi-bin/env.cgi?test=7&name=Neal HTTP/1.0
```

and may be treated the same as

```
POST /cgi-bin/env.cgi HTTP/1.0
Content-Length: 17

test=7&name=Neal
```

Although submitted data is usually associated with POST requests, a GET command can also include submitted data.

Each of these three methods may be used independently or combined. In addition, they may be combined with less common methods, such as cookie modification and virtual hostname:

Cookie Modification: Client-side scripting tools such as Javascript can set and modify cookie content. The cookie may be used to pass query information.

Virtual Hostname: Many Web servers can be configured to support different virtual domains on the same server. The server's hostname can be used as a query parameter. For example, the hostnames `add.server.lan` and `delete.server.lan` may be used for database modification.

23.3 URL EXPLOITATION

URLs provide the means for a user to easily identify a network resource. The URL identifies the service, server, and resource parameters. An attacker who can plant a hostile URL may be able to direct a victim to an alternate location, which leads to a viable compromise. There are many methods for attacking a URL; some of the more common approaches include hostname resolution attacks, hostname cloaking, URI cloaking, cutting and splicing, and query abuse.

23.3.1 Hostname Resolution Attacks

URLs commonly use hostnames to reference servers. This allows users to easily remember distinct text strings (e.g., `www.yahoo.com`) rather than unremarkable network addresses (e.g., `68.142.226.40`). If an attacker can redirect the hostname resolution system, then the query can be sent to an alternate server. This redirection can form a MitM, impersonation, or DoS attack.

Chapter 17 discusses many methods for compromising DNS and name-resolution systems. For URLs, social risks, such as similar hostnames and automatic completion, are more common than direct DNS compromises. Although less common than social risks, some viruses actively modify local hosts file (e.g., `/etc/hosts` or `C:\Windows\System32\Drivers\Etc\Hosts`). This allows local hostname lookups to skip DNS altogether and send victims to alternate servers.

23.3.2 Host Cloaking

There are options for camouflaging a hostname without modifying the hostname-resolution system. For example, a network address can be expressed as an integer instead of a network address. Uncommon tools, such as `int2ip` (Chapter 12, Listing 12.1), can convert an integer to a network address, but few regular Web users would use these overly technical tools—a significant percentage of computer users cannot even identify a *URL* [Pierce2001], let alone the hostname within a URL. For this reason, integer cloaking of network addresses is very successful.

An alternate cloaking method uses the username field in the URL. Most Web servers do not require URL-based authentication, so the username (and password) fields are ignored. An attacker can insert a hostname in place of the username and assume that the user will not notice that `http://www.wellsfargo.com@hostile-`

host.ru/ is a server in Russia (.ru) with the username www.wellsfargo.com, and not Wells Fargo Bank. Phishing and other impersonation attacks commonly use this form of cloaking.

In December 2003, a browser-specific vulnerability was identified that assisted host cloaking [CERT2003]. If a %01 or 0x01 was placed in the username field of a URL, then Internet Explorer would not display the entire hostname. For example, http://www.wellsfargo.com%01@hostilehost.ru/index.html would display as http://www.wellsfargo.com in the browser's address bar. Variations of this vulnerability, such as using %00 instead of %01, impacted Unix-based browsers as well as Windows.

23.3.3 URI Cloaking

The URI is intended to specify resources and parameters, but not all characters are valid. For example, because HTTP queries use spaces to separate the command, URI, and version information, the URI cannot contain a space. To allow a larger character set, URI characters can be encoded with a percent sign and the ASCII hex value of the character. For example, http://host/~neal/ is the same as http://host/%7Eneal/ (hex byte 0x7E is the ASCII character "~"). Spaces are represented as %20, and a percent is %25. HTTP systems convert all URI-encoded characters prior to processing to mitigate equivalency issues.

Spaces are very common in URLs. A shorthand for including a space is to use a plus (+) sign.

Attackers can use URI-encoding to camouflage hostnames and URI information. For example, http://bank.com%2Ehostilehost.ru/ is the hostname bank.com.hostilehost.ru and not bank.com. Similarly, characters within the URI can be cloaked, preventing most users from understanding the URL contents.

23.3.4 Cutting and Splicing

A URL defines a logical path to a remote resource. This path can be easily modified. The two most common modification methods are cutting and splicing.

Cutting, or URL shortening, simply requires the removal of URI elements. If the URL is http://www.amw.com/fugitives/search.cfm then a simple cutting would be http://www.amw.com/fugitives/. Although a secure server will return content or a 404 error, many servers return open directories that can be browsed. Private Web pages—that would otherwise be hidden—can be observed. This form of reconnaissance can be a predecessor to an attack.

Although document directories are commonly protected from cutting, image directories can still remain open. Images that are not linked to normal Web pages may remain viewable.

In contrast to cutting, *splicing* adds information to a URL. For example, most Apache Web servers have "images" and "icons" directories. The URL `http://www.securityfocus.com/` can be sliced to become `http://www.securityfocus.com/icons/`. Even if the directory is not open, the type of return code can denote the directory's presence. For example, `/icons/` may return an access permission error, whereas `/icons2/` returns a file-not-found error. Different error messages can confirm a resource's existence even if the resource cannot be accessed. Table 23.2 lists come common spliced terms.

TABLE 23.2 Common Spliced URL Terms

Term	Purpose
`/icons/`	Directory containing default server icons. Timestamps can determine installation date and version information.
`/images/`	Directory containing system images.
`/docs/` and `/manual/`	Default server files.
`/usage/`	Default server usage files.
`/cgi-bin/` or `/cgibin/`	Directory containing executables on the server.
`/_vti_cnf/`	Directory created by FrontPage.
`/tmp/` or `/temp/`	Directory containing temporary files.
`/private/`	Directory containing private information (in a publicly accessible location).
`/Thumbs.db`	Image cache from Windows systems.

Cutting and splicing can be used independently or combined. Although the results are strictly reconnaissance, the information revealed can identify system information and uncover private information left in a publicly accessible environment. To mitigate exposure from cutting and splicing, HTTP servers should be hardened:

■ Default directories should be removed if they are not needed. This lessens the risk of system-, version-, and patch-level identification.

- Open directory browsing should be disabled. This prevents unlinked files from being readily identified.
- The default reply for an access permission error should be the same as a file-not-found error. An attacker should be unable to identify private resources on the server.
- Private and temporary files should not be placed on public servers.
- Directories and files that are not part of visible content should be removed from public servers. For example, most `Thumbs.db` files are a residue from bulk file uploads rather than essential Web content.

23.3.5 Query Abuse

Whereas cutting and splicing modify a URI's path, options stored within a URI can also be modified. Most URL's that include options are CGI applications. *CGI* is the common gateway interface standard, used for interfacing applications with HTTP servers. This allows the server to deliver dynamic content rather than static Web pages. URI options are usually used to control CGI functionality.

Most URI options are in a `field=value` format. For example, `http://server/cgi-bin/index.cgi?offset=30&limit=30&c=11` passes three parameters to the `index.cgi` application. Changing parameter values, such as from `c=11` to `c=10`, can lead to changes in the application's functionality. This type of parameter modification can lead to reconnaissance or exploitation. For example, an attacker can identify value ranges and different response codes leading to a more detailed understanding of the system. In some cases, the parameter values may be other URLs or file paths, which can potentially grant access to information outside of the HTTP server's general use. When parameters are used to store state information, attackers can modify the values and potentially access information intended for another user.

To mitigate the risks from option modification, CGI applications should validate all parameters:

- If the parameters must be in a specific range, the range should be checked.
- If the parameter indicates a login state, it should be validated.
- If a parameter denotes that an event occurred (e.g., an error or file creation), then the code should validate that the event was present.
- Long and complex state information can lower the chances of an attacker successfully guessing another user's authentication information.
- Filenames and paths should not be passed to CGI applications. Instead, a lookup table can map parameter values to allowed files or paths. This way, an alternate file (or path) cannot lead to unauthorized remote access.

■ All parameters should be treated as strings to CGI applications. Executable function names and parameters should never be passed in a URL. Common exploits include using "`..`" to traverse directory hierarchies, pipe characters (|) to execute code, and single and double quotes to interfere with quoting.

23.3.6 SQL Injections

One common type of query abuse modifies *Structured Query Language* (SQL) commands. SQL is commonly used for accessing database information. In an *SQL injection* attack, the parameters and options submitted to a URL are directly sent to a database query. Through the use of unchecked inputs, an attacker can modify a query request. For example, the SQL query may say:

```
SELECT login, password, name
FROM accounts
WHERE login = '$LOGIN';
```

A sample URL may access this using `http://server/cgi-bin/account?login=bob`. This would set `$LOGIN` to have the value `bob`. But a hostile user may submit a URI such as

```
/cgi-bin/account?login=bob';+INSERT+INTO+accounts+('evil','pass',
'Evil User');commit;1='x
```

This URI expands in the SQL query as

```
SELECT login, password, name
FROM accounts
WHERE login = 'bob';
INSERT INTO accounts ('evil','pass','Evil User');
commit;
1='x';
```

The single quote in the URI allows completion of the SQL query, and the additional values become active SQL statements. This example inserts a new account with the login `evil` and password `pass`. Using this form of an attack, an attacker can SELECT alternate data, INSERT new data, DELETE existing data, CREATE new tables, or DROP existing tables. Any function available by the SQL server is accessible to the attacker.

There are a few steps for mitigating SQL injection attacks:

Quote Variables: All parameters sent by the HTTP client should be quoted so that they do not expand into executable statements.

Validate Parameters: All input parameters should be validated before use. Unsafe characters, such as single quotes, double quotes, and pattern-matching characters should be quoted, removed, or outright rejected. If an input should be a number, then nonnumber characters should be rejected by the CGI application. Other data formats, such as email addresses or usernames, should be validated against an acceptable character set.

Use Lookup Tables: Rather than using table information supplied by the client, lookup tables should be used. For example, instead of having the parameter `table=account`, the client can specify `table=1`. A lookup table in the CGI application will convert `1` to `account`. This prevents attackers from specifying arbitrary database tables.

Restrict Error Codes: Database error messages should not be passed to the end user. Instead, all errors should be caught by the CGI application and converted to a useful user-level message. Providing database errors to the user only aids attackers and can lead to further SQL injection attacks.

23.3.7 Cross-Site Scripting

Cross-Site Scripting (XSS) attacks occur when data submitted to the server by one user is sent to another user. For example, many online forums and blogs allow users to post content and hyperlinks. The postings become immediately accessible to other users. If an attacker posts hostile JavaScript, Java, or an executable (e.g., a virus), then all other users can be potentially impacted though the XSS attack vector.

Although posting active code, such as JavaScript or a virus, can lead to a direct attack, inactive attacks may contain links to hostile sites or false information. For example, a fake news article posted to the *USA Today* blog may be interpreted as being real.

To mitigate the risks from XSS attacks, information posted by users should be screened. HTML and active elements should be audited or filtered. Many Web-based forums either do not allow the inclusion of HTML content in postings or significantly restrict the permitted HTML elements. When possible, a moderator should evaluate all postings before making information publicly available.

Google Bombing

The purpose of the XSS attack may not always be obvious. Although the placement of a virus on a Web page is likely for distributing the virus, the placement of a URL may be less obvious. Is the URL intended for human visitors or automated systems? Some XSS attacks target Web log reading systems (operated by administrators) rather than regular users.

One less-obvious example concerns the ordering of Google results. When a search term is entered into the Google search engine, the results are sorted based on a rating value. If a company or Web site wants a higher position in the returned set, then it needs a higher rating.

The Google PageRank (PR) system uses a patented weight-based technology (U.S. Patent 6,285,999). In this system, the links on a Web page carry little or no weight. Instead, rank is based on the number of Web pages that refer to the URL. To increase the PageRank value for a Web page, other pages can be created with links pointing to it. Some Web sites, to improve their position in the Google results, intentionally place links on open blogs and Web forums. This results in a significant number of references to one Web site. In turn, this moves a site higher in the returned list. When done correctly, an undesirable or less relevant Web site can be forced to the top of the Google results list.

PageRank associates words in hypertext links with specific URLs. This can lead to *Google Bombing*—where specific words or phrases are associated with specific Web pages. For example, in 2005 and 2006, a Google search for the phrase "miserable failure" returned the *Biography of President George W. Bush (http://www.whitehouse.gov/president/gwbbio.html)* as the first link, even though the phrase does not appear anywhere on the page. This high ranking is due to the intentional placement in open forums of hyperlinks containing the phrase with a link to the biography.

The technique used for Google Bombing (as well as the term) is credited to Adam Mathes. Mr. Mathes first discussed this approach in April 2001 [Ott2004].

23.4 GENERAL HTTP RISKS

HTTP was designed for flexibility and real-time file transfers, but security was not part of the definition. Instead, applications that use HTTP are expected to provide authentication, validation, and privacy. This leads to risks based on unauthenticated HTTP systems. In addition, HTTP server configurations and CGI applications can expose the system to remote exploitation.

23.4.1 Unauthenticated Client

HTTP does not provide many options for authenticating the HTTP client to the server. Basic Authentication, although widely available, offers no privacy for transferring credentials. Because of plaintext data transfers, Basic Authentication is as insecure as telnet and FTP. Although SSH can be used as a replacement for telnet and FTP, the slow connection rate for SSH makes it undesirable for replacing HTTP.

Other HTTP authentication systems, such as Digest Authentication, are less supported. Pre-1999 Web browsers, such as Internet Explorer 4.0 and Netscape 5.0, do not support Digest Authentication. In addition, the digest is transferred in plaintext, making it vulnerable to dictionary attacks.

HTTPS with client-side SSL certificates does provide client authentication, but few systems use client-side certificates. In addition, SSL has its own set of risks based on authentication (see Chapter 19). However, using Basic Authentication or Digest Authentication over HTTPS is usually sufficient for providing authentication and privacy. In general, few HTTP systems authenticate the client.

23.4.2 Unauthenticated Server

Just as the client is unauthenticated, the server is usually unauthenticated too. Clients rely on hostnames or network addresses for server identification. Hostname identification is vulnerable to DNS attacks (Chapter 17), and network addresses are vulnerable to network hijacking (Chapters 12 and 15). Although SSL does provide some amount of validation, browser usability issues (Chapter 19) frequently hinder users from properly validating systems. Without client and server certificates, SSL provides privacy but offers only limited authentication support.

23.4.3 Client Privacy

In general, HTTP operates in an idempotent environment; each HTTP request is independent. Cookies and authentication schemes can track users, but the tracking is limited to specific servers. Although each of these methods have generated significant backlash from privacy advocates, the scopes are limited to a single server (or domain). However, one HTTP header does provide cross-server tracking. The "Referer" header is provided by Web browsers and indicates where the linked URL came from. For example, if a user visits a Web page at `http://server1/example.html` and clicks on a link to `http://server2/different.html`, then the second HTTP request will resemble Listing 25.1.

LISTING 25.1   Sample Request with Referer Header

```
GET  /different.html HTTP/1.0
Host: server2
Referer: http://server1/example.html
```

Is it a typographical error? This HTTP header is spelled "Referer," not "Referrer." Of all the people who reviewed RFC1945, nobody caught the spelling error. It is now widely adopted and part of the standard.

The Referer header is used by Web sites to collect visitor statistics. By tracking this information, a site can identify which other sites link to them. But the Referer header contains an entire URL. If the referencing URL contains query options, such as a link from the Google or Alta Vista search engine, then the destination server can identify the terms being queried. If the referring URL contains login credentials, then the destination receives these credentials. Only URLs that are entered into the browser's address bar have no Referer value.

23.4.4 Information Leakage

Most HTTP clients and servers leak a significant amount of information. The HTTP request header usually discloses the type of Web browser, including version and operating system. Similarly, the HTTP reply header frequently includes the type of server, version, and supported plug-ins. Although servers can be hardened to conceal this information, CGI applications frequently modify replies based on the type of browser (user agent). A hardened browser that sends no identifying information may be blocked from accessing a server.

NOTE

Just as nmap (http://www.insecure.org/nmap/) allows the fingerprinting of network systems, httprint (http://net-square.com/httprint/) allows the fingerprinting of Web servers. Even if the server is modified to return a different server description, the meta header values, ordering, and error codes may still lead to server identification. The httprint tool determines server types based on a database of distinctive Web server signatures.

The meta information from HTTP replies includes a timestamp. Usually used for caching systems, it can also reveal server information. Timestamps are usually the last modified time for a file, whereas CGI applications usually return the current time. By viewing the timestamp, an attacker can identify whether data is static (from a file) or dynamic (from an application). In addition, static timestamps can reveal the last updated time. File that are old imply a directory that is rarely monitored, whereas files that are updated daily or weekly can indicate when either administrators or automated scripts access the system. An attacker can use these timestamps to plan attacks. For example, if the files indicate an administrator who works between 02:00 and 09:00 GMT, then an attack around 15:00 GMT will likely occur when the administrator is not present.

23.4.5 Server Location Profiling

Although IP addresses can be used to narrow a server to a particular region, country, or city, many large corporations have subnets that span countries. HTTP servers leak information that can be used to geographically locate the server. For example, the HTTP "Date:" meta header is intended to return the current time in GMT (+0000). But open directories usually list the time in the server's local time zone. By subtracting the local time from the reported GMT time, the time zone hosting the server can be identified. Servers are also configured using the local language. HTML error messages can be used to approximate nationality of the server.

For example, if GMT says Feb 5 2006, 16:53:05 and the local time is Feb 5 2006, 17:53:05, then the server is likely in GMT-0100—Europe. If the server generates HTML error messages in German, then the system is likely in Germany, Switzerland, or Austria; not France, Croatia, or Bulgaria. Daylight savings time (DST) can also be used to identify the country because many countries begin and end DST at different times.

Knowing the server's nationality and location can benefit an attacker's timing. An attacker can estimate when the administrators are asleep, when shift changes for large installations occur, and when natural disasters or unexpected events likely impact the hosting site. All of this can be used to time an attack for when it will be less likely noticed and when response will be slowest.

To mitigate the risk from location profiling, disclosure of time, location, and system-language information should be minimal. Many Web applications can report time relative to a Web user's profile rather than the local time. Highly sensitive systems should either not disclose time zone and native-language information, or should be configured with an alternate time zone and default language setting. Configuring systems to use GMT can also deter location profiling.

23.4.6 Access to Operating System

The OSI application layer directly interfaces with the host operating system. HTTP servers provide direct access by accessing files or applications (via CGI programs) to process HTTP commands. Through modifying URL paths and options, direct operating system vulnerabilities can be remotely accessed. For example, the Code Red worm exploited a buffer overflow on Windows IIS servers in 2001 [CERT2002]. The HTTP request looked similar to:

```
GET /default.ida?NNNNNNNNNNNNNNNNNNNNNNNNNNNNNNNNNNNNNNNNNNNNNNNNNNN
NNNNNNNNNNNNNNNNNNNNNNNNNNNNNNNNNNNNNNNNNNNNNNNNNNNNNNNNNNNNNNNNNNNNN
NNNNNNNNNNNNNNNNNNNNNNNNNNNNNNNNNNNNNNNNNNNNNNNNNNNNNNNNNNNNNNNNNNNNN
NNNNNNNNNNNNNNNNNNNNNNNNNNNNNNNNNNNNNNNNNNNNNNN%u9090%u6858%ucbd3%u780
1%u9090%u6858%ucbd3%u7801%u9090%u6858%ucbd3%u7801%u9090%u9090%u819
0%u00c3%u0003%u8b00%u531b%u53ff%u0078%u0000%u00=a HTTP/1.0
```

This overflow exploitation permitted direct access to the underlying operating system through a vulnerable application. HTTP servers require direct system access regardless of the application. The only exposure issue is the degree of freedom for accessing the system. Even open directories or file timestamps can be used for reconnaissance before an attack.

23.4.7 Insecure Applications

Although privacy issues, XSS, open directories, and information leakage can lead to attack vectors, insecure CGI applications pose the greatest risk. Applications may use compiled executables, interpretive languages such as Perl or Bourne Shell, or embedded languages supported by the HTTP server. PHP, ASP, and application servers such as TomCat, WebLogic, JBoss, and WebSphere pose just as much risk as stand-alone applications.

Most mitigation options for application risks come through robust programming. *Robust programming* (also called *idiot proofing* or *bomb-proof programming*) tests and manages software assumptions [Bishop2003]. Rather than assuming data will be a specific length, type, or format, the application validates the assumption before using the data. Similarly, return codes from function calls are checked to ensure proper execution. In general, if an application has any form of programming flaw, then the flaw can lead to security vulnerabilities.

Web servers themselves can also be hardened. The Open Web Application Security Project (OWASP) provides a detailed list of security precautions for Web servers [OWASP2005]. These options include authentication, authorization, session, and privacy management.

NOTE

ON THE CD

The OWASP white paper, "A Guide to Building Secure Web Applications and Web Services," and Matt Bishop's paper on "Robust Programming" are included on the CD-ROM.

23.4.8 Lower-Layer Protocols

HTTP remains vulnerable to risks from lower-layer protocols. DNS attacks, TCP hijacking, and lower-layer attacks can interfere with HTTP, intercept information, or hijack connections. Even with SSL and Digest Authentication, HTTP is still vulnerable to end-point attacks, where a client with authorization attacks a server (or vice versa). For example, an attacker may establish an SSL connection and authenticate using valid credentials and then attempt to exploit CGI applications. Although the attacker may be identifiable, this does not prevent the attack.

SUMMARY

HTTP is a flexible, real-time data transfer protocol. It provides a command-reply structure with meta data support and has been extended to many network services including, Web, RSS, and RTSP.

Although designed for extensibility, HTTP natively offers few security options. HTTP includes authentication but uses plaintext transfers that compromise privacy. It offers flexibility but provides vectors for remotely attacking the host operating system. When combined with SSL, HTTP gains stronger privacy and authentication support, but also inherits SSL's weaknesses.

REVIEW QUESTIONS

1. What do cookies do for HTTP?
2. Which parts of the HTTP request can be used to transfer user data?
3. Does robust programming mitigate query abuse?
4. Is Basic Authentication a viable option for security-focused Web sites?

DISCUSSION TOPICS

1. In public discussions, the Web and HTTP are frequently used interchangeably. Explain why this is or is not accurate.
2. SMTP (Chapter 22) provides timely, but not immediate, message delivery. Is HTTP a viable alternative to SMTP? SMTP is a push technology, whereas HTTP is a pull technology. What would need to change for HTTP to be used as a push technology?
3. Identify alternatives to SSL for providing privacy and authentication to HTTP. (One example could be a Diffie-Hellman key exchange with data encryption.) What limitations would impact the security, performance, or HTTP use models? Is HTTP's Basic Authentication over IPv6 a viable alternative?

ADDITIONAL RESOURCES

The World Wide Web Consortium (*http://www.w3c.org/*) and RFCs from the IETF provide the official resources for HTTP. Most changes, additions, and modifications to the protocol are well documented by these organizations.

Web search engines, such as Google, Yahoo!, and Alta Vista, inventory every Web page they can find. This information can also be used to identify vulnerabilities. Johnny Long's Web site on *Google Hacking* (*http://johnny.ihackstuff.com/*) shows many forms of information leakage and server weaknesses that can be exploited by cutting and splicing.

Part

IX

General Issues

In This Part

- Modularity and Security
- Issues Summary

Network security allows the identification and mitigation of undesirable information flow. Under the ISO OSI model, security is implemented in compartmentalized layers. Security within and between layers has its own tradeoffs with regards to trust, flexibility, and performance.

24

Modularity and Security

In This Chapter

- Software Methodologies
- Software Engineering Principles
- Impact on Security
- The Hacker Mentality
- New Protocols

The ISO OSI and DoD TCP/IP network stacks are based on sound software engineering principles. Each stack is divided into independent layers based on functionality and requirements. Each protocol within each layer is interfaced through an abstract interface; protocols within a layer use the communication interface provided by the layer. Independent layers tradeoff security for flexibility, extendibility, and interoperability.

24.1 SOFTWARE METHODOLOGIES

There are three common methodologies for developing software projects: procedural, functional, and object-oriented. Each of these methodologies has its own strengths and limitations; no one method is better than another, although one may be better suited for a particular task. Each network stack, layer, and individual protocol implements one or more of these methodologies, and the selection is independent of other protocols. For example, a stack may be functional, a specific layer may be object-oriented, and a protocol within the layer may be procedural. The chosen methodology impacts the fundamental security aspects of the network stack.

24.1.1 Procedural Methodology

The *procedural methodology* divides functionality into sets of subroutines. Each subroutine may perform one or more complicated tasks and may modify global state elements. The inputs to a subroutine may come from passed parameters, global elements, or external systems. This makes parameter validation difficult. A subroutine may also return a value, set global elements, or activate external systems. The inputs and outputs of a subroutine may be nondeterministic, which makes completeness (accounting for all situations) and testing difficult. Applications developed with a procedural methodology usually have many tightly integrated subroutines and can be rapidly developed. In addition, customized software interfaces and global elements can lead to faster performance.

Usually small programs are created using a procedural methodology. Large, procedural applications end up being monolithic, unstructured, and difficult to extend. Because network stacks are designed for flexibility, they are usually not procedural in nature. But when generic protocol interfaces are mostly unused, functionality can be simplified and combined into tight subroutines. Minimal network stack implementations, such as those found in some handheld devices, cell phones, and single-purpose networked devices (e.g., a networked power supply), may use procedural stacks to reduce overhead.

24.1.2 Functional Methodology

The *functional methodology* segments all actions into distinct and isolated units called *functions*. Each function performs a single task with little or no modifications to global elements. Functions are accessed through well-defined interfaces; one function can be replaced with an equivalent function as long as the interface definition does not change. The functional methodology also lends itself to *recursion*, where a function may call itself directly or indirectly without interfering with the results.

The functional methodology is very desirable for network stack development. Each layer is accessed through a well-defined interface and provides specific functionality. Both of these factors simplify parameter checking and software testing. Functional recursion is used when protocols are tunneled though other protocols, such as VPN technologies. Similarly, each protocol within a layer may be enabled as a function to allow protocols to be used interchangeably.

24.1.3 Object-Oriented Methodology

The third major methodology is *object-oriented* (OO). This methodology is a combination of functional and procedural. Each object defines a specific functionality and uses well-defined interfaces, similar to the functional methodology. But objects may perform multiple tasks—each object defines a set of related functions. In addition, each object may contain internal state variables that appear relatively global to the object, and functions within the object may be tightly integrated. The result is a combination of functional and procedural methodologies: sets of objects use a functional methodology to communicate, but within an object, the elements may be procedural.

Whereas network stacks are designed using a functional methodology, most individual protocols use an OO methodology. For example, TCP is a transport layer protocol. It uses a standard interface and can be readily replaced with UDP or SCTP. This gives TCP functional properties; however, TCP uses buffers for maintaining connections and reassembling data. This buffer space is shared among all applications that use TCP; if one application fails to manage its TCP connections properly, it can negatively impact all TCP connections, which is a procedural-based failure. Because TCP has both functional and procedural properties, it is an OO design. If TCP were implemented using a functional methodology, then every TCP instance would have its own independent buffer space.

The implementation of TCP is operating system specific. Whereas Linux and Windows use an OO methodology for the protocol, other systems may use functional or procedural implementations.

24.1.4 Converging Methodologies

Not all stacks are clearly part of one methodology. For example, the DOCSIS stack's control messages (Chapter 3) are more procedural than functional, but they are not clearly one or the other.

Although general stack layers are functional, many protocols permit higher layer applications to directly influence internal protocol states. For example, the C functions ioctl() and fcntl() permit direct access to low-level drivers, including specific protocol state spaces. Although Linux and Windows provide IP and TCP as OO protocols, these implementations permit external manipulation of internal state elements. Similarly, the Unix command sysctl() (and the Windows Registry) can modify active and future connection states and protocol options.

Although the three methodologies define interactions, they are independent of the implementation method. For example, a stack may be developed using a functional methodology but implemented using a procedural programming language. An OO programming language, such as C++ or Java, supports many OO features but can still be used to develop procedural or functional applications. The type of programming language is independent of the software methodology.

From a network security viewpoint, knowing the type of methodology and programming language can assist in identifying potential attack vectors. For example, if a protocol is implemented using a procedural methodology, then it may not be easily tunneled or used as a VPN. Protocols that are strictly functional limit the scope of a security breach, but they may not support higher-level debugging, diagnostics, or real-time configuration changes.

24.2 SOFTWARE ENGINEERING PRINCIPLES

The overall OSI network stack is designed using sound software engineering principles. For example, there are well-defined APIs between layers that allow integration through standardization. Any system can use TCP through the sockets API—the interface does not need to vary between TCP implementations. The OSI stack's architecture applies many design principles:

Modularity and Compartmentalization: Each layer and protocol performs one set of tasks. Network issues are isolated and distinct functions (e.g., session management versus network addressing) are kept independent.

Abstraction: The internals of each protocol and layer are hidden from higher and lower layers. A Web browser may connect to a server without ever knowing how the data is routed or even whether it is using IPv4 or IPv6.

Simplicity: Each protocol performs one set of functions. Different layers and different protocols perform distinct functions. As a result, new protocols can be used to replace other protocols, usually with no impact to other layers.

Flexibility and Extensibility: New protocols can be added to provide new functionality. Because each protocol performs a limited set of tasks, the type of data being received or transmitted is not a consideration to the protocol. For example, data passed to IP may be from a Web browser, SSL client, or VPN—IP treats all data the same way, independent of the type of data.

Reusability: Similar to flexibility, each protocol may be used and reused without interfering with existing connections.

Scalability: Each network layer and protocol is designed to be scalable. A single TCP implementation in a network stack may manage thousands of concurrent connections. The primary limitation for scalability comes from the hosting system's resources. A slow CPU may become overwhelmed by many concurrent requests, but this limitation is independent of the protocol's implementation.

Each of these software principles is independent of the methodologies. For example, a procedural method may use modular subroutines and support reusability. Conversely, a functional method may use very complex and dependent functions. An ideal system will use a methodology that best fits the problem and apply the software engineering principles.

By combining these principles, software can be quickly developed, maintained, debugged, or expanded with less effort than modifying a monolithic application. The OSI stack applies these principles. New protocols can be added to the OSI stack, existing protocols can be upgraded, and weak protocols can be enhanced.

24.3 IMPACT ON SECURITY

Each network protocol is designed using a standard interface and provides functionality independent of other protocols. For example, IEEE 802.3 routes data between systems on the same network but does not address intersystem routing. IP manages intersystem routing but not hostname resolution. The principles that lead to independent protocol development allow the network stack to be flexible, reusable, and extendible. However, this independence comes at a tradeoff: security at one layer is independent of security at other layers.

24.3.1 Transitive Authentication

Many protocols provide authentication, validation, privacy, and nonrepudiation (Table 24.1); however, each of these protocols only offers security for themselves. For example, a client that authenticates using WEP does not authenticate with the application. Each layer of authentication is independent of other layers. Passing the security precautions at any single layer does not imply security at any other—lower or higher—layer.

TABLE 24.1 Security-Oriented Protocols and Options

OSI Layer	Protocols and Options
Physical	WEP, Caller-ID, Callback
Data Link	MAC authentication, CHAP, PAP
Network	IP filtering, IPsec, IPv6
Transport	TCP/UDP filtering, SPI, SCTP, NAT, RNAT
Session	RADIUS, Kerberos
Presentation	SSL/TLS, SSH
Application	TACACS, HTTP authentication

The result of protocol independence is a weakness for defense-in-depth. An attacker may need to overcome many security precautions, but each precaution is independent. For example, an attacker can crack a WEP password, impersonate a MAC and IP address, and hijack an established TCP connection to bypass security precautions in the first four OSI layers. Authentication, validation, and privacy at any one layer are not transitive—one secure layer does not imply security at other layers.

24.3.2 Defining Network Trust

Most network protocols only operate within one layer and are independent of other layers. As a result, the security found in one layer is not passed to other layers. Most network stacks assume that some layer will perform authentication, validation, and other security checks. This assumption establishes a false level of trust between protocols. Applications may assume that the information has not been intercepted or altered, but no steps are taken to validate this assumption. Most network connections operate with little or no explicit security precautions.

A few network protocols do explicitly enable security options and trust the results found in other layers. For example, HTTPS uses HTTP over SSL. The authenticated credentials from SSL can be passed to HTTP to create an authenticated HTTP connection that spans two OSI layers. Similarly, most presentation and application protocols that use Kerberos can inherit the authenticated credentials and validated network information.

24.4 THE HACKER MENTALITY

Although the term "hacker" has undergone a variety of definitions over the past 30 years, the definition of the *hacker mentality*, or *hacker factor*, has remained consistent. The hacker mentality is the ability to see alternatives to existing situations. Sometimes called "thinking outside the box," the hacker factor applies software, systems, and architectures to methods other than the original design. This important aspect of computer security identifies risks, limitations, and options beyond the original specifications.

One example of the hacker mentality is the use of NAT as a firewall (see Chapter 12). NAT was not designed for firewalls. It was designed as a solution to the IP address-assignment problem. NAT allows multiple hosts to share a common external address. The side effect—that inbound traffic cannot be routed when there is no outbound path—is as effective as an inbound filter on a firewall but is not a firewall by design. "NAT as a firewall" is a benevolent example of the hacker mentality.

As an example of deception, Sergey Lyubka (also known as "devnull") developed a VPN solution that tunnels TCP over SMTP. The `mproxy` system (*http://www.silversoft.net/projects.html*) uses email to extend a private network. Although this VPN is slow, SMTP is ubiquitous, and this system can bypass most corporate firewalls. Attackers and administrators may create a backdoor path into a private network. An attacker would use it as an alternate (and likely undetectable) path into the network, and an administrator may use it as an obscure method around an otherwise-hardened perimeter.

Although some examples of the hacker mentality are benevolent, attackers can also use this approach to identify and attack network weaknesses. To identify potential attack vectors, detect exploits, and deter attacks, the security professional must understand that all network protocols can be used differently from the original design or be misused altogether.

24.4.1 Alternate Protocols Uses

Many protocols can be used outside of their defined specifications. This is usually done to bypass existing systems, such as firewalls, or to prevent detection by IDS and IPS applications. Many examples of protocols being used differently are covered in earlier chapters.

> **Telnet Over ICMP:** One of the early backdoor systems modified the telnet application to use ICMP rather than TCP. At the time, ICMP was usually permitted through firewalls, so this approach could bypass existing perimeter security precautions. Today, NAT and corporate proxies are widely used, so inbound ICMP cannot bypass most firewall configurations.

> **Knock-Knock Protocols:** As discussed in Chapter 14, port knocking uses connection attempts and packet options to signal clandestine services. Although a TCP SYN packet is usually used to initiate a connection, it can be used as a messaging system instead.

> **Covert Messages:** Nearly all protocols offer some degree of flexibility in timing, data ordering, and information management (splitting, padding, unused bytes, etc.). These options and unused elements can be leveraged for passing alternative information. For example, DNS can be used as a generic distributed data system (Chapter 17). DNS is not limited to storing hostname information.

> **Reconnaissance:** Most protocols include system-specific information that can be used to profile hosts and identify possible attack vectors. SMTP leaks version and patch information (Chapter 22), TCP SYN Scan (Chapter 14) and OS profiling (Chapter 15) can identify vulnerable services and systems, and HTTP timestamps can expose server location and nationality (Chapter 23).

Alternate protocol uses are difficult to detect. A few high-end IDS and IPS applications learn expected network behavior. Unexpected network traffic is flagged as suspicious behavior, but poorly trained IDS/IPS applications generate many false reports. An attacker can generate suspicious activity as chaffing for an actual attack.

24.4.2 Misused Protocols

Some protocols can be misused to prevent communication rather than perform alternate communication functions. The DoS attack is a common example. Whether it is ICMP or SYN flooding, TCP disconnect attacks, or intentional SSH packet corruptions, a DoS disables communications. Nearly all protocols are vulnerable to DoS attacks either directly or through a dependency on lower layer protocols.

Not every protocol misuse is a form of DoS. Some manufacturers intentionally provide incompatible protocols to restrict usage. Most IM and VoIP implementations use nonstandard protocols to communicate. An IM client for Yahoo! cannot access the Microsoft MSN system unless it supports two different IM protocols. Similarly, VoIP from Skype uses a different protocol than Vonage, even though they use the same audio communication standard. Adding to the complexity, some competing companies use the same server port number for different protocols or custom protocol extensions that conflict with competitors—both force incompatibilities.

24.5 NEW PROTOCOLS

New network protocols are constantly being added. The IANA provides official TCP and UDP assigned ports at *http://www.iana.org/assignments/port-numbers*. IANA also provides official lists for MAC address values, IP version numbers, and IP service types (all found at *http://www.iana.org/numbers.html*). The official protocol-value lists are only to resolve discrepancies between conflicting applications; technically, anyone can assign any protocol to any number. The only limitation is compatibility. For example, TCP is normally IP protocol type 6; however, TCP will work equally well as IP protocol 122. As long as all systems needing to use the same protocol use the same configurations, they will be compatible.

24.5.1 Flexibility Limitations

Although in theory, any protocol can use any configuration (and not just the assigned configurations), there are some limitations due to applications processing (Table 24.2). Using standards in nonstandard ways can prevent network routing or trigger alerts on IDS and IPS systems.

Fortunately, the impact from nonstandard usage is less severe for the upper layers (session, presentation, and application) because these protocols do not manage

TABLE 24.2   Lower Layer Impact from Nonstandard Configurations

Layer	Impact
Physical	Hardware modifications needed for senders and recipients.
Data Link	Compatible device drivers needed on all nodes. Bridges must be customized.
Network	Routers that do not understand the protocol will be unable to route traffic.
Transport	Gateways, firewalls, and NAT systems may fail to route unknown protocols or route them incorrectly.

routing across the network. Although a nonstandard DNS server may be incompatible with standard servers and trigger IDS alerts, the data will properly route across the Internet. In contrast, changes to lower-layer protocols may prevent packets from passing between networks. For example, many firewalls are configured to pass TCP or UDP transport packets but will drop all other packets. A custom protocol may fail to pass the firewall. If the custom protocol reuses the IP service type 17 (UDP), then it may be dropped as a corrupt UDP packet.

24.5.2 Protocol Conflicts

Reusing standard protocol assignments or using nonstandard configurations can lead to protocol conflicts. For example, if two different protocols both use IPv6 packet type 17 (standard UDP), then they can result in conflicts at the transport layer. The unknown protocol could be dropped as invalid, generate a resend request (to resolve corruption), or be misinterpreted by the recipient as a valid packet. Similarly, running a Web server on 22/tcp (the standard port for SSH) may result in many SSH connections to the Web server. The Web server must be able to handle invalid and malformed requests, and the SSH client must handle HTTP replies without crashing.

NOTE

Although distinct protocols, such as SSH and HTTP, are unlikely to cause data corruption, similar protocols can lead to higher-layer incompatibility. For example, HTTP, RSS, and RTSP are all similar. An HTTP request to an RTSP server will likely work, but it will generate an undesirable result.

Standard application layer protocols, such as HTTP, SMTP, and SSH, are usually found on standard transport layer ports. When relocated, they are usually moved to unassigned port numbers; however, unassigned port numbers have their own set of issues:

Multiple Applications: Many applications may use the same nonstandard port number. The most common examples come from computer viruses, worms, and trojans. The port 31337/tcp is used by many trojan systems, including BackOrifice, ADMworm, and LinuxRootkit IV [ISC2006]. These applications are not compatible, and only one can use port 31337/tcp at the same time.

Server Discovery: A client must know how to contact a server. If the protocol operates on a nonstandard port, then general network clients may be unable to find the server. Requiring users to download custom applications for accessing nonstandard servers is usually undesirable; malware cannot be distinguished from desirable applications without some type of analysis.

24.5.3 Desirable Incompatibility

Sometimes protocol incompatibility is desirable. For example, if a private network reassigns IPv6 from Ethernet protocol 0x0800 to 0x0900, then most precompiled viruses will fail to spread across the network. Similarly, precompiled network scanners will fail to work if the OSI data link protocol reassigns the interface configuration for enabling promiscuous mode (or disables promiscuous mode altogether). Although each of these options provide security-by-obscurity, they are likely to stop many common attacker vectors.

Many proprietary protocols use the same nonstandard configuration values as competing protocols. This allows a vendor to specify that not only will its software be used, but the competition's software will not be used. Incompatible, proprietary protocols can lead to a business advantage in the marketplace.

Finally, protocol incompatibility can be desirable for bypassing existing restrictions. For example, if an ISP does not permit running a Web server on port 80/tcp, then the server can be moved to a different port number.

SUMMARY

The OSI stack uses a careful selection of effective software methodologies and engineering principles. These allow the adding and upgrading or protocols with little impact to other protocols. Although compartmentalization offers flexibility and modularity, it leads to a tradeoff with security. Passing the security features at any one layer does not imply security at any other layer.

REVIEW QUESTIONS

1. List the three common software methodologies.
2. Which engineering principle is emphasized by the functional methodology?
3. What is a protocol that uses transitive authentication between layers?
4. What are two general classes of exploitation by the hacker mentality?
5. Describe three situations where protocol incompatibility is desirable.

DISCUSSION TOPICS

1. Which engineering principles are explicitly used by the DNS protocol? Which principles does wireless networking (802.11g) use? Are the different principles used evenly, or are some use more than others (e.g., is modularity used more than abstraction)? Does the use of more engineering principles lead to better protocol security? Do certain principles lead to better security?
2. HTTPS uses SSL to provide authentication. This authentication can be transferred to HTTP for an authenticated connection. Is this transfer always performed? Are there some situations where the credentials cannot be easily passed to the application layer? Describe a situation where they are not transferred. What are the ramifications of HTTP ignoring SSL credentials?
3. What would need to change within the network stack to support transitive authentication? How would this impact flexibility, scalability, and overall development effort?

ADDITIONAL RESOURCES

Many resources cover software engineering methodologies and principles, or security, but few resources cover both topics. The Software Engineering Institute (SEI) at Carnegie Mellon University (*http://www.sei.cmu.edu/*) offers a wide variety of resources and papers for effective software engineering. Some of the papers and books address software development, whereas others cover software security. Similar to SEI, SIGSOFT (*http://www.sigsoft.org/*) is an ACM special interest group that focuses on software development.

25 Issues Summary

In This Chapter

- The OSI Model
- Eight Common Security Oversights
- Eight Common Mitigation Options
- Applying Security Example: Agobot

Network security is a complicated issue, spanning standards, architectures, implementations, and privileges. Secure environments are designed and developed through a conscious effort. Although most of the common network protocols have significant limitations, security is a measurement of risk. If all users on a private network are trusted, then very insecure protocols can be used without fear of exploitation or attack. Even across the Internet, the likelihood of an SSL-based impersonation or SSH hijacking is extremely low; these protocols are usually safe enough.

Each OSI layer shares common risks among protocols within the layer. General layer-specific mitigation options can be applied to most protocols. By understanding these risks and options, the amount of risk can be identified, evaluated, and managed.

25.1 THE OSI MODEL

The ISO OSI network model describes a seven-layer architecture for developing protocols. Other stacks, such as the DoD TCP/IP and DOCSIS stacks, define their own layers and functionality. Protocols written for one stack can be functionally mapped onto other stacks. The main risks from the OSI model come from forcing specifications, confusing terminology, and varying standards.

25.1.1 Forcing Specifications

Not all protocols easily fit into a network stack. Secure Shell (Chapter 20) is one such example. As implemented, SSH primarily provides OSI presentation-layer functionality, but session and application functionality are also provided. HTTP (Chapter 23) primarily provides application-layer support but offers session-layer services through cookies, authentication schemes, and referral URLs. HTTP also has presentation-layer functionality through data chunking. Even lower-layer protocols, such as IEEE 802.3 and ICMP, do not quite fit into a single OSI layer.

The issues around stacks and protocol mapping are widely known. Linus Torvalds, the creator of Linux, described it in a blunt, but succinct, way [Torvalds2005]:

> We still talk about the seven layers model, because it's a convenient model for discussion, but that has absolutely zero to do with any real-life software engineering. In other words, it's a way to talk about things, not to implement them.

The OSI specifications describe "what to build" and not "how to build it." Whether defining a stack or a specific protocol, the specifications are designed to assist compatibility. Individual implementation details are left to the developers. As a result, developers may blur the lines between different layers, and independent protocols may use very dependent functionality.

More complicated specifications are less likely to be adopted. For example, the OSI session layer is extremely complicated; there are few session layer protocols. In contrast, the application layer is extremely relaxed and includes thousands of protocols. Because many security precautions are complex, many developers choose not to implement them or take shortcuts during implementation.

25.1.2 Confusing Terminology

Although specifications are intended to allow compatibility between different implementations, confusing terminology can impede support. Terms such as MAC, router, gateway, and even TCP (compared with TCP/IP) have multiple meanings.

Problem diagnosis can be delayed due to confusing terminology. For example, delays from reviewing a gateway's configuration (instead of some other device also called a *router*) can be the difference between a major and a minor security breach.

25.1.3 Open Standards versus Proprietary

An ongoing debate in network security concerns the use of open source and proprietary protocols. *Open standards*, such as IP, TCP, DNS, SSH, and HTTP, have no hidden specifications. RFC documents, IEEE standards, and other public records cover these open definitions in detail. As a result, any developer can create a compatible protocol.

Protocols based on open standards have a few limitations. Whereas any developer can view them, any attacker can analyze them for potential attack vectors. Although many qualified people can review the specifications, having "more eyes" viewing the documents is no guarantee that all problems will be identified. Whether the issue is a spelling error (HTTP's "Referer" header from RFC1923) or more serious issues concerning security oversights (e.g., SMTP, Chapter 22), being an open standard is no guarantee of quality or security.

In contrast, *proprietary protocols* are usually not publicly available or have limited public documentation. Although there are a few exceptions (e.g., AppleTalk), most proprietary protocols offer few public details. For example, the Microsoft SMB protocol and most VoIP implementations are proprietary—few technical details are widely and publicly available. The largest benefit from proprietary protocols comes from a marketing edge. Direct competition cannot easily interface with an undocumented system. Although few people know all of the details behind proprietary protocols, "few eyes" does not imply security. SMB has numerous exploits, and VoIP security risks are being identified.

Many protocols are endorsed by standards organizations such as the IEEE, W3C, and IETF; however, even endorsements do not imply security. SSL (Chapter 19) is widely endorsed for Web security, yet it contains many limitations. In contrast, SSH (Chapter 20) is extremely secure but was not endorsed until years after it was available.

The security of a protocol does not depend on the number of reviewers or endorsements. Network security is a result of conscious efforts during the specification's design and the protocol's implementation. As evident from email's spam problem, an insecure design cannot be resolved by a strong implementation. Overflows and application layer exploits have shown that very secure designs may not be implemented in a robust fashion, whereas SSL demonstrated that a secure solution may not be applied in a secure way.

25.2 EIGHT COMMON SECURITY OVERSIGHTS

Although there are many potential vectors for attacking a network system, network security risks can be generalized into eight common categories:

1. Assuming Security Managed by Other Layers
2. Assuming Transitive Authentication
3. Assuming Continuous Authentication
4. Assuming Implementation Completeness
5. Failing to Program Robustly
6. Failing to Handle Error Conditions
7. Disregarding DoS
8. Failing to Learn from Mistakes

25.2.1 Assuming Security Managed by Other Layers

Protocols at every layer of the OSI model assume security will be handled by some other layer. Lower-level protocols, such as MAC, SLIP, PPP, IP, UDP, and TCP, either provide no data validation or a minimal checksum validation. These protocols assume that authentication, authorization, privacy, and nonrepudiation are managed by some higher layer. Higher-layer protocols such as DNS, SMTP, and HTTP also make assumptions. These protocols assume lower-layer protocols will provide any required information protection.

25.2.2 Assuming Transitive Authentication

A few protocols explicitly offer information protection. IPsec, IPv6 (with security features enabled), SCTP, SSL, and SSH are just a few examples of security-conscious protocols. Yet, even these protocols lead to inherent risks. The use of a single secure protocol at one layer does not imply security at any other layer. A stack that uses IPsec will authenticate the network routing and protect information through encryption, but an attacker can still conduct a DoS attack. SSL may authenticate clients and servers, but it does not prevent a hostile client from attacking the server over the authenticated connection.

25.2.3 Assuming Continuous Authentication

Most network protocols only authenticate during the initial connection. After the connection, protocols assume that each side does not change. Protocols such as MAC, IP, TCP, FTP, and telnet, all make this assumption. As a result, these protocols are vulnerable to connection hijacking. Other protocols, such as IPsec, IPv6, SCTP, and SSL, do support reauthentication, but the request for subsequent authentications are connection specific; the request may need initiation from a higher layer. Only a few protocols, such as Kerberos and SSH, actively and continuously reauthenticate connections.

25.2.4 Assuming Implementation Completeness

Specifications and standards are guidelines for implementation. They detail *what* to build but not *how* to build it. Many network applications do not need all of the required functionality, so not every feature is implemented. Processing resources may also limit implementation options. For example, the session layer (Chapter 16) describes over 100 different states, but DNS (Chapter 17) only implements a few of them; the other states are not required by DNS. As another example, OpenSSH (Chapter 20) authenticates servers based on a cache of known server keys; it is designed for systems with ample resources. In contrast, Mocha Telnet is a SSH client designed for handheld devices and low-resource systems. It reduces system requirements by always assuming the server is valid. Similarly, many bridges, routers, and gateways do not validate lower-layer protocol checksums (e.g., IP and TCP) as a tradeoff for faster processing performance. Even if a protocol is designed for very secure environments, the implementation may lack many desired features.

A few network protocols do attempt to force implementation completeness. The most notable are IPv6, Kerberos, and SSH. Although IPsec is an optional addition to IPv4, the same security features are required under IPv6. Although an application may not require the security found in IPv6, the option to enable it is always present. Kerberos and SSH both specify a required reauthentication stage. Although the duration between authentication requests may vary, the functionality is required. Unfortunately, forcing completeness can also lead to risks. SSL supports many weak cryptographic algorithms due to completeness. Cipher sets containing weak options are usually supported even though they may hinder security.

25.2.5 Failing to Program Robustly

Buffer overflows, unchecked variables, and assumed values continually pose risks to protocols. Even if a protocol has a provably secure design and is fully implemented, unchecked assumptions can lead to exploitation. Although this is a significant issue for HTTP CGI applications (Chapter 23), it can also impact lower-layer protocols. Corrupt DNS packets (Chapter 17) and the ICMP Ping of Death (Chapter 12) are two examples where implementations fail to check parameter assumptions.

25.2.6 Failing to Handle Error Conditions

Although specifications design how software should work, they frequently omit error-condition handling. For example, RFC791 does not define the handling of invalid ICMP checksums (Chapter 12). Invalid packets may be accepted or dropped, depending on the implementation. As another example, a TCP SYN packet should not contain any application data. But what if it does? The result may be dropped data, an invalid SYN request, or a double meaning for the SYN-ACK response (acknowledging the SYN request and the data).

New protocol extensions can lead to unknown parameters sent to older systems. These can also lead to rejections, errors, or other problems. For example, the HTTP 1.1 `Connection: open` header indicates that the connection will not be closed after the reply. This can cause problems when an older HTTP 1.0 client connects to a minimal HTTP 1.1 server that does not implement the full RFC2616 standard. The result is a connection that does not terminate until it times out.

In most cases, error conditions can be handled by default deny policies and connection resets. A *default deny* policy forbids anything that is not explicitly permitted. This blocks questionable or undesirable information but can also prevent adoption of new protocols. Gateways that only pass TCP and UDP may default deny all other protocols, which blocks the use of SCTP, NetBIOS-DG, and other alternate transport protocols.

25.2.7 Disregarding DoS

DoS attacks are commonly disregarded when designing network architectures. A DoS does not hijack a connection or lead to unauthorized privilege escalation, it only blocks access. The misunderstanding stems from fatalistic perceptions:

Everything is vulnerable: All protocols are vulnerable to some form of DoS attack, and there are no perfect mitigation options.

Solutions are not transitive: Regardless of the mitigation options taken to deter a DoS at the transport layer, one pair of wire cutters can provide an effective DoS. There are few options to deter a disgruntled employee with a screwdriver.

Pessimistic software developers frequently view DoS attacks as inevitable with no viable solution [Tina2004]. Although there is no universal solution for every DoS attack, each type of attack is different. By identifying each attack vector, steps can be taken to mitigate the impact from a DoS. For example, most network service providers contract with multiple backbone providers. This redundancy prevents a single break in a connection from disabling all communications. Low TCP timeout values and SYN cookies can lessen the impact from TCP SYN floods. Server farming, where many servers are used to divide workload, can reduce the risk of an HTTP-based DoS. Simply filtering ICMP traffic can prevent many ICMP attacks from reaching vulnerable servers.

As an extreme example, a distributed DoS attack (DDoS), such as a Smurf attack (Chapter 12), is one of the most difficult to defend against due to many attacking systems and a single victim location. Yet even a DDoS attack can be rendered harmless. In 2001, the CodeRed worm infected systems and directed a DDoS against the White House Web site (*http://www.whitehouse.gov/*) [Leyden2001]. Before the attack could begin, the site was moved to a distributed hosting service. The result was an unfocused DDoS; the attack was rendered harmless.

25.2.8 Failing to Learn from Mistakes

Many widely discussed and used exploit techniques continue to resurface. For example, the Ping of Death (Chapter 12) impacted many operating systems. Yet even with the knowledge of this attack method, new network devices continue to appear years later with the same vulnerability. ICMP-based Smurf, redirection, and disconnect attacks can be blocked by widespread adoption of ICMP filtering; however, most home consumer firewall systems do not support ICMP filtering. Even SSL (Chapter 19) falls into this category—the limitations of DNS and third-party dependencies were well known long before SSL was ever invented.

Old exploits frequently find new victims. As long as developers and vendors do not consider old exploit methods before releasing new network devices, services, and protocols, new victims will inevitably fall to preventable attacks. DNS and SMTP are excellent examples of insecure protocols that are still used as templates for newer protocols. Developers must learn from these mistakes rather than copy them.

25.3 EIGHT COMMON MITIGATION OPTIONS

Just as there are common security oversights, there are also common mitigation options that, in general, can lessen the impact from many exploits.

1. Cryptography
2. Multipart Authentication
3. Defense-in-Depth
4. Hardening Servers
5. Stay Informed
6. Patch! Patch! Patch!
7. Policies and Procedures
8. Preparing for Attacks

25.3.1 Cryptography

Encoding, encryption, and cryptographic hash systems, such as those discussed in Chapter 4, are widely trusted for providing privacy and authentication validation. Even the weakest cryptographic algorithms, such as crypt and DES, are significantly more secure than no encryption at all. Although encryption cannot be used to protect arbitrary connections from initial hijacking attacks, it can prevent an established connection from being hijacked and reduce the risk from eavesdropping, replay, and insertion attacks.

A wide selection of algorithms are available for supporting different key strength, block size, and processor requirements. Algorithms with specific export and proprietary (or open standard) needs are also available. Whether the requirement is for symmetrical or asymmetrical keys, and block or streaming data, nearly all protocols can incorporate some form of cryptography. Not every protocol requires a cryptographic solution, but for a secure connection, some layer should employ some form of cryptography.

25.3.2 Multipart Authentication

Most systems rely on one-part authentication—usually a username and password. Although this does deter simple attacks, it is also vulnerable to identity theft. Any attacker who compromises this single credential can be authenticated by the system. Multiple authentication options deter identity theft. When combined with continuous or periodic reauthentication, this solution mitigates risks from initial connection impersonation and established connection hijacking.

25.3.3 Defense-in-Depth

No single security measure protects against all risks. A home firewall may stop a computer virus from spreading into the network, but it does not stop users from downloading the same virus from a compromised Web site. Similarly, IPv6 can provide a secure and authenticated network connection, but it does not stop hostile DNS packets from traversing the VPN tunnel. Different attack vectors and different risks require different solutions. The more layers of security that are employed lead to a lower likelihood that a single attacker will successfully compromise hosts on the network. Table 25.1 lists some security-oriented protocols that can be used to create defense-in-depth. Even without employing different protocols, there are options to increase the security of a network. Table 25.2 shows some viable options for hardening networks.

Not every security-oriented protocol always has security features enabled. Although IPsec and IPv6 explicitly support encryption and authentication, only IPsec always has it enabled. IPv6 can be used without the security enabled. For IPv6, security is an option.

25.3.4 Hardening Servers

Networks are used to communicate information between systems. The communication is brief and transient—after the transmission is completed, the data is gone. Only nodes on a network provide temporal support. For this reason, a remote attacker usually targets nodes on the network rather than the network itself. By hardening servers, it becomes more difficult for a remote attacker to gain access to nodes on a network. There are a few basic steps for hardening a network node: disabling services, filtering protocols, and monitoring for unexpected activity.

TABLE 25.1   Sampling of Security-Oriented Protocols

OSI Layer	Protocol
Layer 1	WEP, Quantum Networks
Layer 2	CHAP, PAP, Caller-ID, Callback
Layer 3	NAT and RNAT, IPsec, IPv6
Layer 4	SCTP
Layer 5	WAP, RADIUS, Kerberos
Layer 6	SSL, SSH
Layer 7	TACACS, HTTP Digest Authentication, SSH for `sftp` and `scp`, SSL for `stelnet`

TABLE 25.2   Sampling of Viable Security Precautions and Choices

OSI Layer	Options
Layer 1	Architecture selection, Communication medium
Layer 2	MAC authentication, Static ARP tables, Promiscuous mode detection
Layer 3	Address filtering, Static routing tables, ICMP filtering, IDS, IPS
Layer 4	TCP and UDP filtering, Egress filtering, TCP timeout tuning, UDP buffer space, Profile modification, Knock-knock protocols, SPI, IDS, IPS
Layer 5	Hardened DNS servers
Layer 6	Adjust reauthentication interval, Disable weak and null ciphers
Layer 7	Robust programming

25.3.4.1 Disable Services and Protocols

Unnecessary services and unused protocols can be disabled. If UDP is not part of the network stack, then UDP-based attacks cannot impact the system. If the system is not a mail server, then SMTP can be safely removed. Determining what to disable can be a complicated process. Tools such as Bastille (*http://www.bastille-linux.org/*) automate system hardening.

Hardening Windows systems is much more complicated than running a tool. Books, such as *Hardening Windows* by Jonathan Hassell (Apress, 2004), *Hardening Windows Systems* by Roberta Bragg (McGraw-Hill, 2004), and *Hacking Exposed Windows 2000* by Joel Scambray and Stuart McClure (McGraw-Hill, 2003) are just a few examples of the available resources.

25.3.4.2 Filtering Accessible Protocols

Tools, such as tcpwrappers and software firewalls, can block unauthorized communications. In addition, external firewalls and IPS devices can restrict unauthorized traffic.

25.3.4.3 Monitor Hardened Servers

Systems can be monitored for suspicious activity. Antivirus software can continually scan PCs for infection. Unix software such as tripwire (*http://sourceforge. net/projects/tripwire*) and tiger (*http://www.net.tamu.edu/network/tools/tiger.html*) can detect unauthorized file system changes. Although intrusions are not expected on hardened nodes, an administrator who does not monitor nodes will never know if the system has been compromised.

25.3.5 Stay Informed

New security risks and vulnerabilities are announced daily. By monitoring security forums, administrators can learn about potential risks before they become problems. The information from security forums can be staggering—the most active can generate hundreds of emails per day that include exploits, advisories, and open discussions. Knowing what forum to monitor is just as important as knowing which risks apply to a specific network. There are three basic types of forums: high volume, low volume, and occasional.

25.3.5.1 High-Volume Forums

High-volume forums are usually email-based, although discussions may also be available on Web sites. The two most widely used high-volume forums are BugTraq and Full Disclosure. BugTraq (*http://www.securityfocus.com/archive/1*) is a moderated forum. The moderator tries to remove unrelated discussions, spam, and personal attacks (*flame wars*) from the distribution. In contrast, Full Disclosure (*http://lists. grok.org.uk/pipermail/full-disclosure/*) is an unmoderated and self-regulating forum. Both of these forums are commonly used to disclose new risks, discuss exploits, provide proof-of-concept tools, and communicate mitigation options.

Wide ranges of participants use high-volume forums. Both seasoned professionals and rank amateurs may post messages. Many postings in BugTraq and Full Disclosure are open questions—the quality of the replies varies greatly. Some of the postings also contain commentary that may or may not be based on fact. Winnowing the wheat from the chaff can be daunting at times.

25.3.5.2 Low-Volume Forums

The amount of information generated by BugTraq and Full Disclosure can be overwhelming. BugTraq offers a digest form, where the moderator selects specific topics and sends out a specific messages rather than entire discussions. Instead of receiving hundreds of emails per day, the digest may only generate one or two a day that represents key topics.

Many organizations provide their own daily summaries of important issues. The Internet Storm Center (*http://isc.sans.org/*), Department of Homeland Security (*http://www.dhs.gov/*), and the Institute for Information Infrastructure Protection (*http://www.thei3p.org/news/*) all provide daily (or on weekdays) summaries. These services summarize important technical, legal, and political changes that impact computer and network security.

25.3.5.3 Occasional Forums

Many companies offer their own list of advisories. Although these are only updated occasionally, they are usually authoritative sources for new vulnerabilities and mitigation options. For example, Microsoft's TechNet (*http://technet.microsoft.com/*) offers security bulletins for Windows systems. iDefense (*http://www.idefense.com/*) and CERT (*http://www.cert.org/*) offer advisories for many operating systems but neither update regularly.

25.3.6 Patch! Patch! Patch!

Vulnerabilities do not just vanish after patches are released. Instead, attackers continually scan for systems that can be exploited. Computer viruses such as Code Red, Nimba, Blaster, and Gaobot all made history due to the speed that they infected new systems. Yet all of these viruses exploited vulnerabilities for which patches were available. Even though CodeRed was first announced in July 2001, it is still observed on infected systems more than four years later.

Security is not static. A system that is secure today may not be secure tomorrow. A conscious effort must be taken to monitor for potential exploits and take preventative measures before an attacker strikes. Although online forums allow an administrator to stay informed, steps must be taken to block known vulnerabilities.

When to Patch

The decision to patch or wait is not always black and white. Patches are frequently released shortly after vulnerability disclosures. These patches have undergone a rapid development life cycle and minimal amount of testing. Occasionally patches are recalled because they cause more problems than they fix. For example, in 2001, Microsoft released a patch for a very high risk. The patch, which addressed an overflow condition in the Remote Data Protocol (RDP) of the network stack, ended up making the operating system unstable [Fisher2001]. The faster patches are released, the more likely they are to have problems.

Not all patches are provided by software vendors. Frequently, workarounds for code created by other developers are quickly circulated when vendors cannot or do not respond fast enough to a threat. These temporary solutions may not be as rigorously tested as vendor patches and may simply disable desirable functionality.

Waiting for a patch can place a network at risk, however, applying a new patch can be just as risky. Adding to the complexity, applying nonvendor solutions can impact support agreements. This leads to a risky tradeoff: patch now and risk damages from an unstable or nonvendor solution or wait until the patch is tested by other people and considered stable.

25.3.7 Policies and Procedures

Although policies and procedures do not stop network attacks, they do provide guidelines for managing and evaluating security risks. Most policies define acceptable use of the network, privacy levels, and software deployment options. Contact points for specific types of risks are identified, and escalation processes are defined. When an attacker targets a network, the first question should not be "what should I do?"

The SANS Security Policy Project (*http://www.sans.org/resources/policies/*) offers many documents for defining policies and procedures. For some businesses, there are legal ramifications for maintaining clearly defined operating procedures. The United States has many regulations for specific industries. A few examples include the following:

- *Health Insurance Portability and Accountability Act of 1996* (HIPAA) defines requirements for the health field.
- *Gramm-Leach-Bliley Act of 1999* (GLB) provides specifications for financial institutions.

- *Sarbanes-Oxley Act of 2002* (SOX) requires accountability for publicly traded companies.
- Educational facilities must abide by the *Family Educational Rights and Privacy Act* (FERPA).

Outside of the United States, frameworks such as the *International Convergence of Capital Measurement and Capital Standards* (also called Basel II) applies to international banks, and the *European Union Data Protection Directive* defines the management of personal information. Creating security policies is not just a good idea; in many cases, security policies are legally required.

25.3.8 Preparing for Attacks

Although risks can be weighed and mitigated, inactivity can lead to complacency. Watching logs and forums can provide information about potential attacks, but they do not always help prepare for attacks. To properly evaluate risk, networks should be regularly tested:

Design for Yourself: Prepare networks and nodes so that the designers and developers cannot breach the security. If the local administrators know how to breach the system, then there are active vectors that can be targeted by remote attackers.

Hold Drills: Divide the administration team into a set of attackers and defenders. Can people with inside knowledge find ways past the existing security? Do the policies and procedures work?

External Auditors: Many companies specialize in security evaluations. Because these people are not familiar with the network, they are likely to attack the system differently than the architects and developers. Even if hiring outside consultants is not an option, most organizations have people who were not part of the system development or day-to-day management. These attackers can provide a unique view into the existing network security.

Auditors who are familiar with a system will use their familiarity. Unbiased assessments from new auditors can lead to novel discoveries.

25.3.8.1 Reevaluating Systems

Regardless of the approach taken, systems should be periodically tested. Critical systems may be tested quarterly or semi-annually by different sets of auditors. Less important systems may only require evaluations annually.

25.3.8.2 Evaluating Risks

Security is a measurement of risk, and not all risks are equal. One model for comparing risks measures five elements, each on a scale from 1 to 3—with low risks being assigned a "1" and "3" going to high risks.

Exploitation (E): How easily can the vulnerability be exploited? Does it require technical or insider knowledge, or can nontechnical attackers be threats? Automated attack systems are usually assigned a high risk (3), although very technical attacks are usually assigned a "1."

Scope (S): Assuming that the vulnerability is exploited, what is impacted? A single, isolated system may be a low risk. All systems running specific software is usually a moderate risk, but an exploit that impacts an entire network is a high risk.

Impact (I): What is the impact from an exploit? Reconnaissance usually does not impact a system, so it would be a low risk, as would a DoS against a non-critical system. But a remote access compromise of a critical system would be a high risk.

Future Impact (F): Not all vulnerabilities can be exploited due to external factors. For example, an insecure host may be protected by an external firewall; however, a change to the firewall's configuration may expose the host. Although threats from this area do not currently pose an exploitable risk, they should not be ignored during future development or deployment.

Mitigation Options (M): What steps are currently taken to mitigate the threat? Data encryption with multipart authentication may be a "3," although no direct preventative steps are assigned a 0.

These items combine to determine the risk metric (R):

$$E + S + I + F - M = R \tag{25.1}$$

More urgent issues have higher risk values. Manpower, funding, and time are finite, and most companies cannot realistically address every risk. But knowing how to weigh and compare very different threats can make better use of the existing resources. For example, in 2001, a series of overflow conditions were found to exist in the Macromedia Flash player [CERT2001]. The vulnerabilities only needed a few bytes to crash a Web browser ($E=3$). The result was a DoS ($I=2$) that could crash computers. At the time, Macromedia claimed to have their software on 90 percent of Internet-enabled systems ($S=3$). The exposure of multiple exploits lead to risks from other, potentially unknown exploits ($F=2$), and the mitigation option was to disable Flash support ($M=0$). The overall risk (R) became 10 out of 12, making it a high risk.

25.4 APPLYING SECURITY EXAMPLE: AGOBOT

The Agobot virus (also known as Phatbot and Gaobot) provides an excellent example for network security and risk mitigation technology. The LURHQ Threat Intelligence Group provides a summary of this virus's capabilities at *http://www. lurhq.com/phatbot.html*. In addition, the source code for different variations of Agobot has also been publicly released. Using this information, the virus's functionality can be directly compared against known mitigation options.

 Agobot is sometimes called a trojan, worm, or spyware due to its different methods for distribution and supported functionality. Alternately, it may be called by the generic term, malware.

25.4.1 Agobot Functionality

Agobot was described as "the Swiss army knife of Trojan horses" [Phatbot2004]. This virus could spread through email, infected Web pages, or across Microsoft Shares (shared network drives over SMB). The virus was relatively large and contained many different functions:

- Remote Control
- Benchmarking
- Remote Service Support
- Spam Support
- Vulnerability Scanning
- Packet Sniffing
- Packet Redirection
- Network Attacks

Most systems infected with Agobot became *botnet* members—armies of remotely controlled hosts that are available for generating spam, scanning networks, and conducting DoS attacks.

Beyond these networking capabilities, Agobot could manage the infected system. A remote attacker could log off system users, reboot the system, enable and disable Windows services, and execute remote commands on the infected host. Agobot provided full remote administration capabilities.

Although the primary author of Agobot was arrested in 2004 [Sophos2004], the source code was publicly released. As a result, other virus writers quickly developed thousands of variants. Each variant contains minor changes to existing functionality, and many variants contain additional features. Although up-to-date antivirus software can identify Agobot before an infection, these systems usually use signature-based detection. New variants do not match known virus signatures and therefore are allowed to infect systems. In contrast, security-oriented network decisions can dramatically reduce the impact from viruses such as Agobot, without knowing the specific variant.

25.4.2 Agobot Remote Control

Agobot supported a remote control channel. This allowed a remote attacker to control the infected host and mange very large botnets of infected hosts (see Chapter 13). Because many infected hosts were located behind firewalls, an outside attacker could not initiate a connection to the infected system. Instead, the virus would initiate the connection to an IRC or peer-to-peer (P2P) service, and wait for instructions.

Egress filtering of IRC and P2P connections could prevent access to the control channel. Many P2P and IRC servers run on nonstandard port numbers to bypass egress filtering. IDS and IPS systems can be configured to analyze application-layer data within each packet and alert when IRC or P2P traffic is identified.

25.4.3 Agobot Benchmarking

After infecting a host, Agobot could be commanded to benchmark the victim's network speed by connecting to specific servers and transferring data. A remote attacker can use the benchmark information to determine the value of the compromised system. Slow hosts may not be valuable for staging network attacks but could be used for relaying spam.

Networks that used authenticated proxy systems, such as SOCKSv5 with passwords enabled, could prevent these connections. Similarly, host-specific egress filtering would stop the connection from completing.

Although finely tuned IDS and IPS configurations could potentially identify the unexpected benchmarking; most likely, these systems would not identify the activity. The Agobot speed tests appear as HTTP connections.

Tuning IDS and IPS applications is not trivial. Although a very finely tuned system could detect nearly all of Agobot's activities, this is an unlikely situation. More realistically, these detection tools would only notice network scans and attacks.

25.4.4 Agobot Remote Service Support

Agobot included many network services that could be remotely activated. The services include an FTP server for distribution and propagation, and SOCKS, HTTP, and HTTPS proxies. Agobot also included an IDENT service for IRC communications.

Periodic use of nmap and scanrand could detect unauthorized services on nodes, mitigating the risk. Firewalls could prevent remote hosts from accessing the unauthorized services. Some software firewalls support egress filtering and would prevent the infected host from accessing the network. In addition, IDS and IPS applications could identify abnormal communication to these network services.

25.4.5 Agobot Spam Support

Agobot supported the uploading of email mailing lists and spam templates. These could be used to send millions of unsolicited emails. Most versions of Agobot specifically targeted AOL services, but variants could send email to non-AOL SMTP and Microsoft Exchange servers.

There are many options for blocking this type of activity. Private networks can require all email to pass through a central server. Along with egress filtering, this prevents direct outbound email connections and provides a central location for detecting outbound spam. An SMTP egress filter can ensure that outbound mail does not contain spam or invalid sender information. IDS services can trigger alerts when a large volume of email is generated. On the recipient end, inbound spam filters can reduce the likelihood of undesirable email delivery.

25.4.6 Agobot Vulnerability Scanning

Agobot can scan for well-known vulnerabilities and potential exploits. The list of known vulnerabilities varies between different Agobot releases but usually included remote attacks against Windows services such as NetBIOS, DCOM, LSASS, and WebDAV. Agobot could also scan for backdoor systems provided by DameWare (remote control software) and competing viruses such as MyDoom, Bagle, and Anubis. None of the scans searched for new or novel weaknesses—some scans checked for exploits that were several years old—and all weaknesses had patches available.

Besides using IDS and IPS devices to detect network scanning, systems with patches for these known exploits were not at risk. Honeypot hosts could also detect scans, and tarpitting hosts could slow scan rates (see Chapter 14). Egress filters on firewalls could prevent the infection from spreading outside the network, even if internal systems were infected.

25.4.7 Agobot Packet Sniffing

The Agobot virus could enable promiscuous mode on the infected host. It could sniff for these specific types of packets:

IRC: Agobot watched for IRC authentication credentials and operator (administrator) status.

FTP: Login credentials were captured.

HTTP: All packets containing `Set-Cookie:` values were captured. It also targeted packets from PayPal.

Vulnerable Services: The initial data transfer from every TCP connection was monitored. Because many connections announced the type and version of service, Agobot watched for services with known vulnerabilities. Strings such as `OpenSSL/0.9.6`, `Serv-U FTP Server`, and `OpenSSH_2` indicated potentially vulnerable servers.

Network switches (Chapter 8) and a star network configuration (Chapter 5) limit the amount of traffic that can be intercepted by a promiscuous host. In addition, promiscuous mode can be detected with a variety of techniques, as detailed in Chapter 8. In the event that Agobot intercepted data, encrypted protocols such as IPsec, IPv6, SSH, and SSL can ensure data privacy. Patching services would remove risks from known vulnerable servers.

25.4.8 Agobot Packet Redirection

The Agobot virus was capable of intercepting TCP and GRE packets (Chapters 15 and 18, respectively). It could redirect requests initiated by an infected host and retransmit data outside of the network.

As with Agobot's packet sniffing, systems and architectures for addressing risks from promiscuous mode could mitigate this threat. In addition, SSH and SSL could encrypt data so that compromised packets could not be decoded.

25.4.9 Agobot Network Attacks

As with many viruses, Agobot was designed to assist with DoS attacks. It included support for ICMP Smurf (Chapter 12), SYN flooding (Chapter 15), UDP flooding (Chapter 15), spoofed UDP flooding (UDP packets with false source addresses), Targa3 (Chapter 12), and other DoS attacks.

Protocol parameter turning and egress filtering can mitigate each type of DoS attack. Although IDS and IPS detection of other Agobot functions depends on the type of defense configuration, each of these DoS attacks are detectable by all IDS and IPS implementations.

SUMMARY

Secure environments do not just appear; they are designed and developed through an intentional effort. Although the ISO OSI stack provides an architecture for communicating over the network, it does not define how the stack should be implemented. Individual protocols provided detailed specifications but are also implementation independent. As a result, the impact to network security is often overlooked during the design of new protocols. The eight common security oversights and mitigation options provide guidance for identifying potential risks, evaluating threats, and defining viable solutions.

REVIEW QUESTIONS

1. Does the OSI model define general development guidelines or specific implementation requirements?
2. If a layer uses a secure protocol, can higher layers assume that all lower layers are secure?
3. What is BugTraq?
4. Which of Agobot's features are unlikely to be detected by an IDS?

DISCUSSION TOPICS

1. Should security features be defined in the OSI model? Should they be listed in specific protocol definitions? What are the tradeoffs for defining (or not defining) security within the stack?
2. Consider the eight common security oversights. Which is the biggest risk? What types of risks are less important? Does the amount of risk depend on the environment? If so, what is the greatest risk for a home user on the Internet? Does the greatest risk change for a corporate DMZ, LAN, MAN, or WAN?
3. Some form of cryptography should be employed to add privacy to network connections. Is it better to add the cryptography at a lower layer (e.g., IPsec) or at a higher layer (e.g., SSH)? In what situations is a lower-layer encryption more desirable? Are there situations where a higher layer is optimal for managing encryption?
4. Select any of the current virus, trojan, spyware, or worm threats. Similar to the Agobot analysis in Section 25.4, evaluate the functionality of the malware and identify network security steps that could be taken to mitigate the risks. Do the steps vary with specific types of malware?

Appendix

A About the CD-ROM

The companion CD-ROM contains all the sources discussed in this book, the referenced RFCs, and additional files.

LICENSING

All sources on the CD-ROM are provided as open source. These files are not licensed under GPL, MIT, MPL, or other common open source licenses unless explicitly specified.

Document and Figure Licensing

RFC documents: All included RFC documents are managed by the IETF and included with their permission. If you are using Windows, these files should be opened under Word or Internet Explorer in order to view them.

"A Guide to Building Secure Web Applications and Web Services": This white paper by the Open Web Application Security Project is provided under the distribution terms specified within the document.

Figure 2.1: This figure is provided by the Wikipedia under the GNU Free Documentation License (GFDL). Copies of this figure and license are provided.

"One History of DNS": This white paper is by Ross Wm. Rader and included with his permission.

"Robust Programming": This paper by Matt Bishop is provided under the distribution terms specified within the document.

Source Code Licensing

Unless specified, Neal Krawetz and Hacker Factor Solutions created all source code included on the CD-ROM. The source code is included with permission. This code

525

is provided as is, without any warranty of its effectiveness, usability, or accuracy. Usage is granted for noncommercial and commercial applications as long as all developers that use the code purchase a copy of *Introduction to Network Security* by Dr. Neal Krawetz.

Neal Krawetz and Hacker Factor Solutions did not develop the following files. These are included on the CD-ROM under the terms of their individual licenses:

GeoIP Free Country Database: The GeoIP Free Country Database is Copyright (c) 2003 MaxMind LLC and included with their permission.

MD5: Solar Designer wrote the source code for the MD5 algorithm in 2001. It is part of the Openwall GNU/*/Linux (OWL) Project, Post Office Protocol (POP3) server. The source code provided is licensed as "relaxed BSD and (L)GPL-compatible."

Snacktime: `snacktime.tgz` is distributed under the terms of the GNU General Public License version 2.

Ultimate IRC Server: `Ultimate3.0.1.tar.gz` is distributed under the terms of the GNU General Public License version 2.

FOLDERS

The RFC directory contains all RFC documents referenced in this book.

The CD-ROM contains a directory for each chapter in the book. Within each of these directories are sub-directories containing each RFC document referenced by the chapter as well as source code, figures, and supplemental information.

SYSTEM REQUIREMENTS

Unless specified, source code has been tested under Red Hat Linux 7.2, Ubuntu Linux 5.04, OpenBSD 3.4, Mac OS X 10.3, and Windows with the Cygwin compiler. The files `arp_pd.c` and `arp_stuff.c` have only been tested under Linux.

PC and Windows

- CD-ROM drive
- Network interface
- 64 MB RAM
- 60 MB of disk space
- Recent version of Windows, such as Windows 2000 or XP or later

- The Cygwin compiler, freely available from http://cygwin.com/ (recommended)

Linux, BSD, and Mac OS X

- x86 or PowerPC architecture
- Red Hat 7.0 or later; Ubuntu 5.04 or later; OpenBSD 3.4 or later; Mac OS X 10.0 or later; or compatible operating systems
- CD-ROM drive

BUILDING SOURCES

Each source code directory contains a `Makefile` for compiling the executables.

B
Answers to Review Questions

CHAPTER 1

1. **Name three critical elements for mitigating security risks.**
   Prevention, detection, and response.
2. **Which is a more costly threat, internal or external attackers?**
   Internal—these attackers know the system's inner workings.
3. **What are the five foundation concepts for security?**
   Confidentiality, authentication, authorization, integrity, and nonrepudiation.
4. **What is defense-in-depth?**
   A security plan that uses many layers with different security precautions.
5. **What are some criteria for selecting dependable security personnel?**
   Education, experience, track record, and certifications.

CHAPTER 2

1. **Is a packet sniffer an example of a tool used for moral or immoral purposes?**
   Tools are neither good nor evil. Morality is based on the situation.
2. **What three components form the basis of a moral judgment?**
   Ethical, social, and legal considerations.
3. **What are three ways to protect intellectual property?**
   Copyrights, trademarks, and patents.
4. **List three difficulties for handling computer evidence.**
   Determining whether a device should be powered off, tracking "original" sources, and detecting evidence tampering.

CHAPTER 3

1. **Who is the IETF and what does it do?**
   Internet Engineering Task Force—an organization that manages the Request for Comments (RFC) guidelines and de facto standards.
2. **Name two network stacks.**
   ISO OSI and DoD TCP/IP.
3. **What is a VPN?**
   A virtual private network (VPN) is an example of a nested stack used for tunneling protocols within other protocols.
4. **Are "layers" concepts or implementations?**
   Layers are concepts. Protocols and standards are implementations.
5. **What is a collection tool?**
   Any tool that gathers data for analysis.

CHAPTER 4

1. **What are three methods for protecting information?**
   Prevent direct access, restrict direct access, and encode information that can be directly accessed.
2. **List five elements common to every cipher.**
   Algorithm, environment, key, plaintext, and ciphertext.
3. **What are symmetrical and asymmetrical cryptographic algorithms?**
   Symmetrical algorithms use the same key for encryption and decryption. Asymmetrical algorithms use one key to encrypt and a different key to decrypt.
4. **Is Base64 encoding an example of confusion or diffusion?**
   Confusion. Base64 replaces three 8-bit character sequences with four 6-bit character sequences.
5. **How does an HMAC provide authentication support?**
   The cryptographic hash value is signed using a key. Only recipients with the key can validate the hash. Having access to the key provides authentication.
6. **Is a hash function a type of cipher?**
   No. Hash functions do not contain a decryption function.
7. **Why are block cipher modes necessary?**
   When encrypting large plaintext messages, block ciphers may repeat ciphertext blocks. Each duplicate plaintext block generates a duplicate ciphertext block. Block cipher modes remove the redundancy.

8. **Can steganography hide images in text?**
   Steganography can store any type of data in any type of camouflage. The only limitations are the size of the camouflage and the ability to hide information without detection.

CHAPTER 5

1. **List two types of network mediums that use RF to transmit signals.**
   Wired and wireless networks.
2. **What are connectors?**
   Connectors are network components that physically link two distinct mediums.
3. **Name four types of physical network risks.**
   Eavesdropping, replay, insertion, and DoS.
4. **Which network topology has a single point of failure?**
   Star networks.
5. **What is an authentication stack?**
   An authentication stack is a parallel stack that validates network access.
6. **What types of network attacks are difficult to diagnose without special equipment?**
   Breaks in wires and radio frequency interference (RFI).

CHAPTER 6

1. **Name four network regions.**
   LAN, WAN, MAN, and DNZ.
2. **List five types of threats to the LAN.**
   Disruption, interference, sniffing, replay, and insertion attacks.
3. **What is egress filtering?**
   Filtering outbound network traffic.
4. **What is a segmented network topology?**
   A series of zones, separated by firewalls, that segments the network into distinct levels of trust.
5. **What are three methods for authenticating dynamic LAN connections?**
   Authentication credentials, such as username and passwords, Caller-ID, and callback systems.

CHAPTER 7

1. **Why are ISM frequencies more desirable than U-NII?**
   ISM is less susceptible to line-of-sight interference.
2. **Is WEP an example of strong security? Why or why not?**
   No. WEP's cryptographic limitations make it weak security, but a viable option for defense-in-depth.
3. **What are five types of wireless risks?**
   Packet sniffing, SSID information leakage, impersonations, parasites, and direct security breaches.
4. **What are two common limitations to deploying strong wireless security solutions?**
   Strong systems are not widely compatible and are vulnerable to observability.

CHAPTER 8

1. **What is a message frame?**
   A message frame is an encoding of packet data for transmitting over the physical layer. The frame allows the receiver to determine when a packet is received properly.
2. **How many nodes can be in a point-to-point network?**
   Two.
3. **What is an example of a data link layer protocol that does not segment the layer?**
   SLIP—this point-to-point data link protocol does not segment the data link layer.
4. **What is promiscuous mode?**
   Promiscuous mode bypasses data link layer address filtering.
5. **List three mitigation options for the data link layer.**
   Hard-coding hardware addresses, strong authentication options, and data link monitoring tools for advanced notification of potential attacks.

CHAPTER 9

1. **List three data link functions that are simplified by point-to-point networks.**
   Framing methods, flow control, and address support.

2. **Which is a simpler point-to-point data link protocol, SLIP or PPP?**
   SLIP.

3. **Why is user education a concern for point-to-point protocols?**
   Users forget that these protocols permit inbound connections, and firewalls may not exist or be disabled.

CHAPTER 10

1. **Which IEEE 802 sublayer manages hardware addressing?**
   MAC.

2. **What is ARP poisoning?**
   ARP tables contain cached information. ARP poisoning places false information into ARP tables.

3. **How can switches be forced into a hub-like mode?**
   Use ARP poisoning to fill the switch's ARP cache.

CHAPTER 11

1. **How do routers know which should receive the routed data?**
   Routers use router tables to associate networks with network interfaces.

2. **What are three possible consequences from router table flooding?**
   New routes may be ignored, older routes may be discarded, or less desirable routes may be discarded.

3. **What type of addressing does AX.25 use?**
   Name-based routing.

4. **Does the OSI network layer define facilities for address authentication or validation?**
   No, these are protocol specific.

5. **What are two schemes to manage packet fragments?**
   Fragment sequence number and fragment offset value.

6. **What happens if the fragment reassembly timeout value is set too low?**
   Packet fragments from slow networks may timeout before all fragments are received.

7. **List six quality-of-service functions provided by the network layer.**
   Connection management, flow control, flow management, error status, node status, and network reset.

8. **What is the primary difference between IPsec and IPng?**
   IPsec uses 32 bits for address space. IPng (or IPv6) uses 128 bits for addressing. Both offer options for authentication and encryption.

CHAPTER 12

1. **What type of network address is 192.168.144.4?**
   A class-C network address that is also a nonroutable network address [RFC1918].
2. **What is the purpose of ICMP?**
   ICMP provides quality-of-service support for IP.
3. **List five fundamental problems for all IP protocol implementations.**
   Address conflicts, hijacking, replay attacks, packet storms, and covert channels.
4. **What is the primary tradeoff when disabling ICMP support?**
   IP loses quality-of-service support but significantly reduces its vulnerability profile.

CHAPTER 13

1. **Why would an online detective desire anonymity?**
   Anonymity prevents the people being investigated from readily identifying the detective.
2. **List three types of anonymity.**
   Source, destination, and link identity.
3. **What type(s) of anonymity does Tor provide?**
   Tor uses onion routing proxies to provide source, destination, and link anonymity.
4. **When discussing anonymity, what is high-level information leakage?**
   Information transmitted through an anonymizing system that exposes identity information.

CHAPTER 14

1. **What is an example of a transport protocol that supports authentication?**
   The Stream Control Transmission Protocol (SCTP) defines support for authentication and encryption.
2. **List four types of connection-oriented packet confirmations.**
   Per packet confirmation, per set of packets, sliding window, and implicit confirmation.
3. **Can a gateway convert TCP traffic to UDP?**
   No.

4. **If a new exploit is known to impact Apache Web servers, what type of port scan should an administrator use to identify potentially vulnerable servers on his network?**

A targeted port scan can quickly identify Web servers on standard ports.

CHAPTER 15

1. **What is the difference between TCP and TCP/IP?**

TCP is a DoD and OSI transport layer protocol. TCP/IP is the DoD network stack that includes the transport layer.

2. **How does TCP increment sequence numbers?**

The sequence number is incremented based on the number of data bytes transmitted. If 100 bytes are transmitted, then the sequence number increases by 100.

3. **What is the TCP three-way handshake?**

The client sends a SYN to the server. The server replies with a SYN-ACK. Finally, the client confirms with an ACK.

4. **List the types of TCP information that can be used to profile an operating system.**

Initial window size, TCP option values, TCP option ordering, initial sequence numbering, ephemeral port range, retry count, and retry timeout duration.

5. **If a client's connection to a server is hijacked, what happens to the client's connection?**

The client sees the connection disconnect.

6. **Can a successful LAND attack hijack a connection?**

No. A LAND attack can only disable a network stack (or the system hosting the stack).

7. **List five ways to mitigate threats from TCP attacks.**

Modify the system profile, block potential attack vectors, identify and protect vulnerable network devices, employ detection and prevention tools (e.g., SPI, IDS, or IPS), and rely on higher-layer protocols for validating the connection.

8. **What is one technique that can reduce attack vectors from IP, TCP, and UDP?**

Filter ICMP packets at the firewall.

CHAPTER 16

1. **What is WAP?**
   Wireless Application Protocol—a set of protocols that supports roaming.
2. **Define major and minor synchronization points.**
   Major synchronization points permit confirmation of large session transactions within a single dialog. Minor synchronization points permit confirmation of action subsets within a major synchronization block
3. **Which of the following is not a session layer protocol: LDAP, Kerberos, FTP, or NFS?**
   FTP is an OSI application layer protocol.
4. **List four common session layer risks.**
   Authentication (and authorization), hijacking, MitM attacks, and information leakage.

CHAPTER 17

1. **List three type of information DNS associates with hosts.**
   Hostname to address mapping, mail server identification, and additional meta information such as text comments and contact information.
2. **Can a DNS packet contain both query and answer information?**
   Yes.
3. **What are the different types of TLD servers?**
   gTLD, ccTLD, and SLD.
4. **What are "direct risks" to DNS?**
   Direct risks are fundamental limitations to the DNS protocol.
5. **How is domain hijacking different from server hijacking?**
   Domain hijacking redirects a domain's management. Server hijacking compromises the system hosting the DNS server.
6. **What type of DNS attack does not require a computer?**
   Social engineering.
7. **What is a zone transfer?**
   A zone transfer is the bulk downloading of an entire set of domain information.

CHAPTER 18

1. **Name a protocol that provides information translation for text files.**
   FTP supports translating between CRLF and LF text file formats.

2. **Give two reasons why the presentation layer is ideal for encrypting user data.**

The presentation layer supports protocol negotiations, including cryptographic parameters. In addition, by encrypting data high up the OSI stack, lower layers do not need to provide cryptographic support to protect the data.

3. **What are three session-management functions provided by the presentation layer?**

Session creation, termination, and error handling.

CHAPTER 19

1. **What three items are negotiated by SSL before user-data can be transferred?**

The cipher set, key exchanges, and authentication.

2. **What are HTTPS and stelnet?**

HTTPS is HTTP over SSL; stelnet is telnet over SSL.

3. **What are four tasks performed by CA servers?**

Accept, reject, revoke, and generate certificates.

4. **What are the four main types of risks for SSL?**

Certificate distribution, authentication, failure handling, and risks from lower-layer protocols.

5. **What does it mean when a Web browser displays a little lock?**

It indicates that an SSL connection to a Web server has successfully authenticated but it does not necessarily indicate which connections are authenticated.

CHAPTER 20

1. **What are some common uses for SSH?**

There are many common uses, including the following:
- Establish a secure network tunnel.
- Provide a VPN with port-forwarding characteristics.
- Supply application-layer login functionality.
- Provide remote command execution functionality.
- Provide secure file transfer support.

2. **What types of authentication does SSH support?**

Server-side using host keys, and client-side using client keys, passwords, or both keys and passwords.

3. **Does SSH forward UDP packets?**
   Not by default because UDP packets are not part of a predefined point-to-point network. SSH can be combined with PPP to provide UDP support.
4. **Does SSH's sftp support anonymous logins?**
   No. All SSH clients must be associated with an account on the server system.
5. **Is DNS poisoning a risk for SSH connections?**
   Usually, no. Host keys can detect a hijacking based on DNS poisoning, but some SSH clients (e.g., Mocha Telnet) do not cache known host keys. In addition, the first connection to an SSH server could be hijacked without detection.

CHAPTER 21

1. **What are four common methods for application layer communication?**
   Binary command sets, command-reply sequences, meta headers, and XML.
2. **Which communication method does telnet use?**
   Telnet uses a binary command set.
3. **What are the three general risks that impact application layer protocols?**
   Inherited vulnerabilities from lower-layer protocols, authentication issues, and direct system access.
4. **Name two types of vulnerabilities that are inherited by the application layer.**
   Plaintext and MitM attacks.

CHAPTER 22

1. **What protocol was used as a basis for SMTP?**
   SMTP was based on FTP.
2. **List three goals for SMTP.**
   Timely delivery, robust mail routing, and an extendible message format.
3. **Which of these servers are most secure: Sendmail, Microsoft Exchange, Qmail, or Postfix? Which are least secure?**
   Generally, Qmail and Postfix are most secure (Postfix is arguably slightly safer than Qmail). Sendmail and Microsoft Exchange are the least secure. Historically, Sendmail has more vulnerabilities than Microsoft Exchange, but Sendmail's vulnerabilities are patched faster.

4. **What are four direct risks to SMTP communications?**
   Forged headers, interception, DNS, and risks from lower-layer protocols.
5. **Who owns email? The sender or the recipient?**
   This is an open topic for debate, with no clear answer.

CHAPTER 23

1. **What do cookies do for HTTP?**
   Cookies allow an HTTP server to sustain a session across multiple HTTP client requests. Without cookies, each HTTP request would be stateless.
2. **Which parts of the HTTP request can be used to transfer user data?**
   Data may be transferred in the URI, URL options, meta header fields, or HTTP data segment.
3. **Does robust programming mitigate query abuse?**
   Yes. By testing and validating parameters, query abuse can be identified and managed.
4. **Is Basic Authentication a viable option for security-focused Web sites?**
   No. Basic Authentication uses encoding but not encryption. Without a privacy-enabling technology such as SSL, Basic Authentication is an insecure authentication method.

CHAPTER 24

1. **List the three common software methodologies.**
   Procedural, functional, and object-oriented.
2. **Which engineering principle is emphasized by the functional methodology?**
   Compartmentalization, where each module performs a single task, matches the functional methodology.
3. **What is a protocol that uses transitive authentication between layers?**
   Any protocol that spans layers, such as HTTPS. HTTPS spans the presentation layer (SSL) and the application layer (HTTP); however, the transitive authentication does not span to lower layers.
4. **What are two general classes of exploitation by the hacker mentality?**
   Protocols can be used for alternate functionality, and protocols can be misused to block functionality.
5. **Describe three situations where protocol incompatibility is desirable.**
   Privacy: Incompatibility keeps out undesirable elements.
   Competition: Proprietary protocols provide a marketplace advantage.

Bypassing: Incompatible protocols can bypass some existing security defenses.

CHAPTER 25

1. **Does the OSI model define general development guidelines or specific implementation requirements?**
   General guidelines.
2. **If a layer uses a secure protocol, can higher layers assume that all lower layers are secure?**
   No. Security is not transitive between layers.
3. **What is BugTraq?**
   BugTraq is a high-volume security forum where new risks are publicly disclosed and evaluated.
4. **Which of Agobot's features are unlikely to be detected by an IDS?**
   Benchmarking and packet sniffing are unlikely to be readily identified by an IDS. In addition, the remote control, remote service support, and packet redirection may not be identified.

Appendix

C RFC References

The following is a list of RFC references used in this book. They are available online at *http://www.ietf.org/rfc/* and *http://www.faqs.org/rfcs/*, and are also provided on the companion CD-ROM.

ON THE CD

114: A File Transfer Protocol

137: TELNET Protocol

226: Standardization of Host Mneumonics [sic]

458: Mail Retrieval via FTP

510: Request for Network Mailbox Addresses

524: A Proposed Mail Protocol

768: User Datagram Protocol

791: Internet Protocol

793: Transmission Control Protocol

821: Simple Mail Transfer Protocol

822: Standard for the Format of ARPA Internet Text Messages

826: An Ethernet Address Resolution Protocol – or – Converting Network Protocol Addresses to 48-bit Ethernet Address for Transmission on Ethernet Hardware

854: Telnet Protocol Specification

881: The Domain Names Plan and Schedule

883: Domain Names – Implementation and Specification

896: Congestion Control in IP/TCP Internetworks

921: Domain Name System Implementation Schedule – Revised

935: Reliable Link Layer Protocols

950: Internet Standard Subnetting Procedure

952: DoD Internet Host Table Specification

954: NICNAME/WHOIS

959: File Transfer Protocol (FTP)

981: An Experimental Multiple-Path Routing Algorithm

1000: The Request for Comments Reference Guide

1001: Protocol Standard for a NetBIOS Service on a TCP/UDP Transport: Concepts and Methods

1002: Protocol Standard for a NetBIOS Services on a TCP/UDP Transport: Detailed Specifications

1032: Domain Administrators Guide

1034: Domain Names – Concepts and Facilities

1035: Domain Names – Implementation and Specification

1036: Standard for Interchange of USENET Messages

1050: RPC: Remote Procedure Call Protocol Specification

1055: A Nonstandard for Transmission of IP Datagrams Over Serial Lines: SLIP

1057: RPC: Remote Procedure Call Protocol Specification Version 2

1071: Computing the Internet Checksum

1122: Requirements for Internet Hosts – Communication Layers

1144: Compressing TCP/IP Headers for Low-Speed Serial Links

1156: Management Information Base for Network Management of TCP/IP-based Internets

1166: Internet Numbers

1179: Line Printer Daemon Protocol

1209: The Transmission of IP Datagrams over the SMDS Service

1256: ICMP Router Discovery Messages

1321: The MD5 Message-Digest Algorithm

1323: TCP Extensions for High Performance

1332: The PPP Internet Protocol Control Protocol (IPCP)

1333: PPP Link Quality Monitoring

1334: PPP Authentication Protocols

1337: TIME-WAIT Assassination Hazards in TCP

1340: Assigned Numbers

1365: An IP Address Extension Proposal

1376: The PPP DECnet Phase IV Control Protocol (DNCP)

1377: The PPP OSI Network Layer Control Protocol (OSINLCP)

1378: The PPP AppleTalk Control Protocol (ATCP)

1421: Privacy Enhancement for Internet Electronic Mail: Part I: Message Encryption and Authentication Procedures

1492: An Access Control Protocol, Sometimes Called TACACS

1521: MIME (Multipurpose Internet Mail Extensions) Part One: Mechanisms for Specifying and Describing the Format of Internet Message Bodies

1534: Interoperation Between DHCP and BOOTP

1549: PPP in HDLC Framing

1551: Novell IPX Over Various WAN Media (IPXWAN)

1579: Firewall-Friendly FTP

1597: Address Allocation for Private Internets

1626: Default IP MTU for use over ATM AAL5

1630: Universal Resource Identifiers in WWW: A Unifying Syntax for the Expression of Names and Addresses of Objects on the Network as Used in the World Wide Web

1631: The IP Network Address Translator (NAT)

1638: PPP Bridging Control Protocol (BCP)

1644: T/TCP – TCP Extensions for Transactions Functional Specification

1661: The Point-to-Point Protocol (PPP)

1662: PPP in HDLC-like Framing

1701: Generic Routing Encapsulation (GRE)

1738: Uniform Resource Locators (URL)

1750: Randomness Recommendations for Security

1762: The PPP DECnet Phase IV Control Protocol (DNCP)

1763: The PPP Banyan Vines Control Protocol (BVCP)

1764: The PPP XNS IDP Control Protocol (XNSCP)

1772: Application of the Border Gateway Protocol in the Internet

1812: Requirements for IP Version 4 Routers

1825: Security Architecture for the Internet Protocol

1826: IP Authentication Header

1827: IP Encapsulating Security Payload (ESP)

1831: RPC: Remote Procedure Call Protocol Specification Version 2

1883: Internet Protocol, Version 6 (IPv6) Specification

1884: IP Version 6 Addressing Architecture

1885: Internet Control Message Protocol (ICMPv6) for the Internet Protocol Version 6 (IPv6) Specification

1886: DNS Extensions to Support IP version 6

1918: Address Allocation for Private Internets

1923: RIPv1 Applicability Statement for Historic Status

1928: SOCKS Protocol Version 5

1939: Post Office Protocol – Version 3

1945: Hypertext Transfer Protocol – HTTP/1.0

1962: The PPP Compression Control Protocol (CCP)

1974: PPP Stac LZS Compression Protocol

1994: PPP Challenge Handshake Authentication Protocol (CHAP)

2001: TCP Slow Start, Congestion Avoidance, Fast Retransmit, and Fast Recovery Algorithms

2018: TCP Selective Acknowledgment Options

2026: The Internet Standards Process – Revision 3

2045: Multipurpose Internet Mail Extensions (MIME) Part One: Format of Internet Message Bodies

2046: Multipurpose Internet Mail Extensions (MIME) Part Two: Media Types

2047: MIME (Multipurpose Internet Mail Extensions) Part Three: Message Header Extensions for Non-ASCII Text

2048: Multipurpose Internet Mail Extensions (MIME) Part Four: Registration Procedures

2049: Multipurpose Internet Mail Extensions (MIME) Part Five: Conformance Criteria and Examples

2076: Common Internet Message Headers

2082: RIP-2 MD5 Authentication

2104: HMAC: Keyed-Hashing for Message Authentication

2109: HTTP State Management Mechanism

2131: Dynamic Host Configuration Protocol

2136: Dynamic Updates in the Domain Name System (DNS UPDATE)

2153: PPP Vendor Extensions

2240: A Legal Basis for Domain Name Allocation

2246: The TLS Protocol Version 1.0

2289: A One-Time Password System

2326: Real Time Streaming Protocol (RTSP)

2350: Expectations for Computer Security Incident Response

2361: WAVE and AVI Codec Registries

2364: PPP Over AAL5

2373: IP Version 6 Addressing Architecture

2374: An IPv6 Aggregatable Global Unicast Address Format

2375: IPv6 Multicast Address Assignments

2396: Uniform Resource Identifiers (URI): Generic Syntax

2401: Security Architecture for the Internet Protocol

2402: IP Authentication Header

2403: The Use of HMAC-MD5-96 within ESP and AH

2404: The Use of HMAC-SHA-1-96 within ESP and AH

2405: The ESP DES-CBC Cipher Algorithm With Explicit IV

2406: IP Encapsulating Security Payload (ESP)

2407: The Internet IP Security Domain of Interpretation for ISAKMP

2408: Internet Security Association and Key Management Protocol (ISAKMP)

2409: The Internet Key Exchange (IKE)

2410: The NULL Encryption Algorithm and Its Use With IPsec

2411: IP Security Document Roadmap

2412: The OAKLEY Key Determination Protocol

2440: OpenPGP Message Format

2453: RIP Version 2

2459: Internet X.509 Public Key Infrastructure Certificate and CRL Profile

2460: Internet Protocol, Version 6 (IPv6) Specification

2463: Internet Control Message Protocol (ICMPv6) for the Internet Protocol Version 6 (IPv6) Specification

2516: A Method for Transmitting PPP Over Ethernet (PPPoE)

2518: HTTP Extensions for Distributed Authoring – WEBDAV

2548: Microsoft Vendor-specific RADIUS Attributes

2581: TCP Congestion Control

2616: Hypertext Transfer Protocol – HTTP/1.1

2617: HTTP Authentication: Basic and Digest Access Authentication

2637: Point-to-Point Tunneling Protocol (PPTP)

2663: IP Network Address Translator (NAT) Terminology and Considerations

2778: A Model for Presence and Instant Messaging

2779: Instant Messaging / Presence Protocol Requirements

2784: Generic Routing Encapsulation (GRE)

2786: Diffie-Helman USM Key Management Information Base and Textual Convention

2809: Implementation of L2TP Compulsory Tunneling via RADIUS

2821: Simple Mail Transfer Protocol

2865: Remote Authentication Dial In User Service (RADIUS)

2866: RADIUS Accounting

2867: RADIUS Accounting Modifications for Tunnel Protocol Support

2868: RADIUS Attributes for Tunnel Protocol Support

2869: RADIUS Extensions

2882: Network Access Servers Requirements: Extended RADIUS Practices

2960: Stream Control Transmission Protocol

3010: NFS Version 4 Protocol

3080: The Blocks Extensible Exchange Protocol Core

3081: Mapping the BEEP Core onto TCP

3162: RADIUS and IPv6

3168: The Addition of Explicit Congestion Notification (ECN) to IP

3171: IANA Guidelines for IPv4 Multicast Address Assignments

3174: US Secure Hash Algorithm 1 (SHA1)

3286: An Introduction to the Stream Control Transmission Protocol (SCTP)

3309: Stream Control Transmission Protocol (SCTP) Checksum Change

3330: Special-Use IPv4 Addresses

3501: Internet Message Access Protocol – Version 4rev1

3859: Common Profile for Presence (CPP)

3860: Common Profile for Instant Messaging (CPIM)

3861: Address Resolution for Instant Messaging and Presence

3862: Common Presence and Instant Messaging (CPIM): Message Format

3921: Extensible Messaging and Presence Protocol (XMPP): Instant Messaging and Presence

3922: Mapping the Extensible Messaging and Presence Protocol (XMPP) to Common Presence and Instant Messaging (CPIM)

3923: End-to-End Signing and Object Encryption for the Extensible Messaging and Presence Protocol (XMPP)

3920: Extensible Messaging and Presence Protocol (XMPP): Core

4033: DNS Security Introduction and Requirements

4034: Resource Records for the DNS Security Extensions

4035: Protocol Modifications for the DNS Security Extensions

4120: The Kerberos Network Authentication Service (V5)

Appendix

D References

[Allen2001] Allen, Julia, *The CERT Guide to System and Network Security Practices.* Addison-Wesley, 2001.

[Aoun2004] Aoun, Bassam, "Quantum Networking." Available online at *http://arxiv.org/abs/quant-ph/0401076,* 2004.

[Bishop2003] Bishop, Matt, "Robust Programming." Available online at *http://nob.cs.ucdavis.edu/bishop/secprog/robust.html,* University of California at Davis, August 5, 2003.

[Blaze1995] Blaze, Matt, and Steve Bellovin, "Session-layer Encryption." Available online at *ftp://research.att.com/dist/mab/sesscrypt.ps,* Proc. 1995 USENIX Security Workshop, Salt Lake City, June, 1995.

[Blosser1998] Blosser, William, *Search Warrant Case Number 98-S191M.* U.S. District Court, State and District of Colorado, 1998.

[Borland2005] Borland, John, "RIAA sues 751 file-swappers." Available online at *http://news.com/RIAA+Sues+751+file-swappers/2110-1025_35996959.html,* CNET News.com, December 15, 2005.

[Bugtraq2000] BugTraq, "Cayman 3220H DSL Router 'ping of death' Vulnerability." Available online at *http://www.securityfocus.com/bid/1240/info,* Security Focus, Bugtraq ID 1240, May, 2000.

[CERT1996] CERT, "Advisory CA-1996-26 Denial-of-Service Attack via ping." Available online at *http://www.cert.org/advisories/CA-1996-26.html,* December, 1996.

[CERT1997] CERT, "Advisory CA-1997-28 IP Denial-of-Service Attacks." Available online at *http://www.cert.org/advisories/CA-1997-28.html,* December, 1997.

[CERT1998] CERT, "Advisory CA-1998-01 SMURF IP Denial-of-Service Attacks." Availaable online at *http://www.cert.org/advisories/CA-1998-01.html.*

[CERT2001] CERT, "Vulnerability Note VU#475645 Macromedia Flash Plug-in Contains Buffer Overflow." Available online at *http://www.kb.cert.org/vuls/id/475645,* June, 2001.

[CERT2002] CERT, "Advisory CA-2001-19 'Code Red' Worm Exploiting Buffer Overflow in IIS Indexing Service DLL." Available online at *http://www.cert.org/advisories/CA-2001-19.html*, January, 2002.

[CERT2003] CERT, "Vulnerability Note VU#652278: Microsoft Internet Explorer Does Not Properly Display URLs." Available online at *http://www.kb.cert.org/vuls/id/652278*, December, 2003.

[Cisco2001] Cisco Systems, *Internetwork Troubleshooting Handbook,* 2nd Ed. Cisco Press, 2001.

[Cisco2005] *Cisco Systems, Inc. and Internet Security Systems, Inc. versus Michael Lynn and Blackhat, Inc.* U.S. District Court, Northern District of California, San Francisco Division. Case number 05-CV-0343, Judge Hon. Jeffrey White. July 28, 2005.

[CISSP2005] CISSP, *Code of Ethics.* International Information Systems Security Certification Consortium, 2005.

[ClickZ2005] ClickZ Stats Staff, "Population Explosion." Available online at *http://www.clickz.com/stats/sectors/geographics/article.php/5911_151151*, Incisive Interactive Marketing LLC, July 7, 2005.

[CNET1996] CNET News.com Staff, "PC Sales Push TV Out of the Picture." Available online at *http://news.com.com/2100-1033-210768.html*, April 30, 1996.

[CNN2002] CNN, *China Computers Face Virus Epidemic.* Available online at *http://archives.cnn.com/2002/WORLD/asiapcf/east/10/10/china.virus/*, October 10, 2002.

[Comcast2006] Comcast Corporation, "Features Designed for Real Life." Available online at *http://www.comcast.com/Benefits/CHSIDetails/Slot5PageOne.asp* (accessed on March 5, 2006).

[Courtois2002] Courtois, Nicolas, and Josef Pieprzyk, "Cryptanalysis of Block Ciphers with Overdefined Systems of Equations." Available online at *http://eprint.iacr.org/*, Cryptology ePrint Archive, Report 2002/044, November, 2002.

[Cowie2004] Cowie, James, et al., *Impact of the 2003 Blackouts on Internet Communications: Preliminary Report.* Renesys Corporation, 2004.

[Credentia2003] Credentia, "E-Mail Server Survey Results for April 2003." Available online at *http://www.credentia.cc/research/surveys/smtp/200304/*, 2003.

[Diffie1976] Diffie, W., and M. Hellman, "New Directions in Cryptography," *IEEE Transactions on Information Theory*, 22:6, (November 1976): pp. 644–654.

[DIT2004] Dynamic Internet Technology, Inc., "Verisign's Proposed Deployment of Root DNS Server Will Expand China's Nationwide DNS Hijacking

Capability." Available online at *http://www.dit-inc.us/report/verisign.htm*, February 27, 2004.

[Dryburgh2004] Dryburgh, Lee, et al., *Signaling System No. 7: The Role of SS7*. Cisco Press, 2004.

[Estan2004] Estan, Cristian, et al., *Building a Better NetFlow*. CAIDA, August 4, 2004.

[Fisher2001] Fisher, Dennis, "Microsoft Issues Patch with Problems." Available online at *http://www.eweek.com/article2/0,1895,40735,00.asp*, *eWeek.com*, October 29, 2001.

[Fiutak2004] Fiutak, Martin, "Teenager Admits eBay Domain Hijack." Available online at *http://news.com.com/Teenager+admits+eBay+domain+hijack/2100-1029_3-5355785.html*, CNET News.com, September 8, 2004.

[FM34-40-2] Department of the Army, "Basic Cryptanalysis." *Field Manual No. 34-40-2*. Washington, DC, September 13, 1990.

[FrSIRT/ADV-2005-1537] *Astaro Security Linux HTTP CONNECT Security Bypass Vulnerability*. FrSIRT advisory ADV-2005-1537, August 26, 2005.

[FrSIRT/ADV-2005-2226] *Solaris Management Console HTTP TRACE Cross Site Scripting Issue*. FrSIRT advisory ADV-2005-2226, October 27, 2005.

[FTC2005] FTC, "Email Address Harvesting and the Effectiveness of Anti-Spam Filters." Available online at *http://www.ftc.gov/opa/2005/11/spamharvest.pdf*, November, 2005.

[GPR1997] GPR, "Linux IP Fragment Overlap Bug." Email correspondence to Bugtraq mailing list, November 13, 1997.

[Harvey1985] Harvey, B., "Computer Hacking and Ethics," in *Positive Alternatives to Computer Misuse: A Report of the Proceedings of an ACM Panel on Hacking*, J. A. N. Lee et al., ACM Headquarters, New York, 1985.

[Hayday2003] Hayday, Graham, "Counting the Cost of Forgotten Passwords." Available online at *http://news.zdnet.co.uk/business/employment/0,39020648,2128691,00.htm*, ZDNet News, January 14, 2003.

[Honeynet2005] Honeynet Project and Research Alliance, "Know Your Enemy: Tracking Botnets." Available online at *http://www.honeynet.org/papers/bots/*, March 13, 2005.

[Huffman1952] Huffman, D. A., "A Method for the Construction of Minimum Redundancy Codes," *Proceedings of the IRE*, Vol. 40, (1952): pp. 1098–1101.

[Hulme2003] Hulme, George, "Virus-Writing Class Creates Stir." Available online at *http://www.informationweek.com/story/showArticle.jhtml?articleID=10100296*, InformationWeek, May 27, 2003.

[IANA2005] IANA, "Internet Protocol V4 Address Space." Available online at *http://www.iana.org/assignments/ipv4-address-space*, June 30, 2005.

[ISC2005] Internet Storm Center, operated by the SANS Institute, provides a Survival Time History at *http://isc.sans.org/survivalhistory.php*. The range typically varies from 9 minutes to 30 minutes.

[ISC2006] Internet Storm Center, operated by the SANS Institute, provides a port-scan history, including the list of known malware that uses the port.

[ISO7498] ISO, *Information Processing Systems—Open Systems Interconnection —Basic Reference Model*, ISO 7489, International Standards Organization, 1984.

[Jackson2005] Jackson, S., and D. Mayster, *Fact Sheet: The Cyber Frontier and Children*, Business Software Alliance, July 8, 2005.

[Kaminsky2004] Kaminsky, Dan, "MD5 to Be Considered Harmful Someday." Available online at *http://eprint.iacr.org/*, Cryptology ePrint Archive, Report 2004/357, December, 2004.

[Karpowitz2004] Karpowitz, D., and Kenner, M., *Education as Crime Prevention: The Case for Reinstalling Pell Grant Eligibility for the Incarcerated*. Bard Prison Initiative, Bard College, 2004.

[Krim2004] Krim, Jonathan, "Insider Case at AOL Shows Vulnerability." *Washington Post*, (June 26, 2004): pp. E01. Available online at *http://www.washingtonpost.com/wp-dyn/articles/A6703-2004Jun25.html*.

[Lempel1977] Lempel, A., and J. Ziv, "A Universal Algorithm for Sequential Data Compression." *IEEE Transactions on Information Theory*, Vol. 23, (1977): pp. 337–342.

[Leyden2001] Leyden, John, "White House Web Site Moves to Linux." *The Register*, (July 24, 2001). Available online at *http://www.theregister.co.uk/ 2001/ 07/24/white_house_web_site_moves/*.

[Lurhq2003] Lurhq Threat Intelligence Group, "Sobig.a and the Spam You Received Today." Available online at *http://www.lurhq.com/sobig.html*, April 21, 2003.

[Markkula2006] Markkula Center for Applied Ethics, "A Framework for Thinking Ethically." Available online at *http://www.scu.edu/ethics/practicing/ decision/framework.html*, (accessed on March 3, 2006).

[Mellia2002] Mellia, M., A. Carpani, and R. Lo Cigno, *Measuring IP and TCP Behavior on Edge Nodes*. IEEE Globecom, Taipei, TW, November 17-21, 2002.

[Microsoft2003] *Microsoft Security Bulletin MS03-007*. Available online at *http://www.microsoft.com/technet/security/bulletin/MS03-007.mspx*, May 30, 2003.

[MS01-017] "Erroneous VeriSign-Issued Digital Certificates Post Spoofing Hazard." *Microsoft Security Bulletin MS01-017*, Microsoft TechNet, (March 22, 2001).

[NIST2006] National Vulnerability Database, query for percent of remote exploits due to input validation error between 1997 and 2004. National Institute of Standards and Technology. Available online at *http://nvd.nist.gov/statistics.cfm,* (accessed on January 4, 2006).

[Orlowski2005] Orlowski, Andrew, "There's No Wikipedia entry for 'moral responsiblity'." Available online at *http://www.theregister.co.uk/2005/12/12/wikipedia_no_responsibility/, The Register,* December 12, 2005.

[Oswald2005] Oswald, Ed, "iTunes Outsells Brick and Mortar Stores." Available online at *http://www.betanews.com/article/iTunes_Outsells_Brick_and_Mortar_Stores/1132675229, BetaNews,* November 22, 2005.

[Ott2004] Ott, Stephan, "Google Bombing." Available online at *http://www.linksandlaw.com/technicalbackground-google-bombing.htm,* 2004, (accessed January 24, 2006).

[OWASP2005] *A Guide to Building Secure Web Applications and Web Services,* The Open Web Application Security Project, 2.0.1 Black Hat Edition. Available online at *http://www.owasp.org/index.jsp,* July 27, 2005.

[Page2005] Page, Susan, "Author Apologizes for Fake Wikipedia Biography." Available online at *http://www.usatoday.com/tech/news/2005-12-11-wikipedia-apology_x.htm, USA Today,* December 11, 2005.

[Pelline1997] Pelline, Jeff, *Whitehouse.com Goes to Porn.* Available online at *http://news.com.com/2100-1023-202985.html?legacy=cnet,* CNET News.com, September 5, 1997.

[Phatbot2004] Phatbot source code, `phatbot_current`. Files are dated between March 21, 2004 and March 23, 2004.

[Pierce2001] Pierce, Elizabeth, Karl Lloyd, and James Solak, "Lessons Learned from Piloting a Computer Literacy Test for Placement and Remedial Decisions." *Journal of Information Systems Education,* Vol. 12, Num. 2 (2001): pp. 81–92.

[Postini2006] "Postini 2006 Message Management & Threat Report." Postini, Inc., January 2006.

[Poulsen2003] Poulsen, Kevin, *Wireless Hacking Bust in Michigan.* Available online at *http://www.securityfocus.com/news/7438,* SecurityFocus, November 12, 2003.

[Radicati2005] The Radicati Group, Inc., "Active Policy Management—Third Generation Compliance for Today's Corporate Environment." White paper, February, 2005.

[Reconnex2005] Reconnex News, "Reconnex Alert: Multiple Banks Involved in What Officials Say May Be Largest Case of Identity Fraud in Banking Industry to Date." Available online at *http://www.reconnex.net/news/news_articles/pr_05.25.05.asp,* 2005.

[Roberts2004] Roberts, Paul, *Your PC May Be Less Secure Than You Think.* Available online at *http://www.pcworld.com/news/article/0,aid,118311, 00.asp, PC World*, IDG News Service, October 24, 2004.

[Rosen2004] Rosencrance, Linda, "WhiteHouse.com Domain Name Up for Sale." Available online at *http://www.whois.sc/news/2004-02/white-house.html*, Whois Source, Name Intelligence, Inc., February 10, 2004.

[Rosenbaum1994] Rosenbaum, David, *Patents, Trademarks, and Copyrights: Practical Strategies for Protecting Your Ideas,* 2nd ed. Career Press, Inc., 1994.

[RSA2000] RSA Laboratories, "6.5.1 What Are the Cryptographic Policies of Some Countries?" *RSA Laboratories' Frequently Asked Questions About Today's Cryptography, Version 4.1.* RSA Security Inc., 2000.

[Sanai2001] Sanai, Daiji, *Detection of Promiscuous Mode Using ARP Packets.* Security Friday, 2001.

[Saunders2001] Saunders, Christopher, "AOL Tweaks Ads on Watchdog Recommendation." Available online at *http://www.clickz.com/news/article.php/ 742441*, ClickZ News, April 13, 2001.

[Schneider1999] Schneider, Fred, *Trust in Cyberspace.* National Academy Press, Washington D.C., 1999.

[Schneier2002] Schneier, Bruce, "AES News." Available online at *http://www. schneier.com/crypto-gram-0209.html, Crypto-Gram Newsletter*, Counterpane Internet Security, Inc., September 15, 2002.

[Scott2005] Scott-Joynt, Jeremy, "The Enemy Within." Available online at *http://news.bbc.co.uk/1/hi/business/4510561.stm*, BBC News, UK Edition, 2005.

[Seigenthaler2005] Seigenthaler, John, "A False Wikipedia 'Biography'." Available online at *http://www.usatoday.com/news/opinion/editorials/2005-11-29-wikipedia-edit_x.htm, USA Today*, November 29, 2005.

[Shannon1949] Shannon, C. E., "Communication Theory of Secrecy Systems." *Bell Systems Technical Journal,* Vol. 28, (October, 1949): pp. 656–715.

[Sipler2004] Sipler, Bob, *Five-year Electric Service Reliability Study: 1999-2003.* Oregon investor-owned utilities, 2004.

[Song2001] Song, Dawn Xiaodong, David Wagner, and Xuqing Tian, "Timing Analysis of Keystrokes and Timing Attacks on SSH." Available online at *http://packetstormsecurity.nl/papers/cryptography/ssh-timing.pdf*, September 3, 2001.

[Sophos2004] "Suspected Agobot Trojan Author Arrested in Germany, Sophos Comments." Available online at *http://www.sophos.com/pressoffice/news/ articles/2004/05/va_agobotarrest.html*, Sophos Plc., May 12, 2004.

[Timme2004] Timme, Falko, *Mail Server Survey March 2004.* Available online at *http://www.falkotimme.com/projects/survey_smtp_032004.php, 2004.*

[Tina2004] Tina, "Re: Dos Attack." *http://www.onlinemarketingtoday.com/ news/archives/website-development/website-development-p-2191.htm,* Online Marketing Today, discussion forum posting, March 15, 2004. Similar view on the impact of DoS attacks have been voiced by Marcel Ljung on The InteropNet Labs forum, November 13, 2003 (*http://www.ilabs.interop.net/ 1068716533/index_html*).

[Torvalds2005] Torvalds, Linus, "Re: I Request Inclusion of SAS Transport Layer and AIC-94xx into the Kernel." Available online at *http://lkml. org/lkml/2005/9/29/233,* Linux Kernel Mailing List, email posting, September 29, 2005.

[Trifinite2004] *BlueSmack*. Available online at *http://trifinite.org/trifinite_stuff_ bluesmack.html,* Trifinite, 2004.

[Urban2005] Urban, J., and L. Quilter, "Efficient Process of 'Chilling Effects'? Takedown Notices Under Section 512 of the Digital Millennium Copyright Act, Summary Report." University of Southern California, November 21, 2005.

[VanAuken2005] VanAuken, Joanne, "Infosec Certifications: Beyond Basic Training." *Secure Enterprise,* Vol. 2, Issue 7, (July, 2005): pp. 28–31.

[Varghese2005] Varghese, Sam, *New York ISP's domain hijacked.* Available online at *http://www.smh.com.au/news/Breaking/New-York-ISPs-domain-hijacked/2005/01/17/1105810810053.html, The Sydney Morning Herald,* January 17, 2005.

[Verisign2005] "Free SSL Trial Certificate." Available online at *https://www. verisign.com/cgi-bin/clearsales_cgi/leadgen.htm?form_id=5191,* December 17, 2005.

[Wang2004] Wang, Xiaoyun, et al., *Collisions for Hash Functions MD4, MD5, HAVAL-128 and RIPEMD.* Available online at *http://eprint.iacr.org/,* Cryptology ePrint Archive, Report 2004/199, August, 2004.

[Websense2004] *Web@Work: Survey Results.* Websense, Inc., 2004.

[West2003] West-Brown, Moira, et al., *Handbook for Computer Security Incident Response Teams (CSIRTs).* Carnegie Mellon Software Engineering Institute; CMU/SEI-2003-HB-002.

[Wikipedia2005] Wikipedia contributors, "Moral Responsibility." *Wikipedia, The Free Encyclopedia, http://en.wikipedia.org/w/index.php?title=Moral_ responsibility&oldid=31066916* (accessed December 12, 2005).

[Wikipedia2006] Wikipedia contributors, "Moral Responsibility." *Wikipedia, The Free Encyclopedia, http://en.wikipedia.org/w/index.php?title= Talk:Moral_responsibility&oldid=40714617* (accessed February 27, 2006).

[Wikipedia2006a] Wikipedia contributors, "Black Hat." *Wikipedia, The Free Encyclopedia, http://en.wikipedia.org/w/index.php?title=Black_hat&oldid= 40624135* (accessed March 3, 2006).

[Wish2006] *Chainletters*, Make-A-Wish Foundation. Available online at *http://www.wish.org/home/chainletters.htm* (viewed on January 16, 2006).

[Zittrain2003] Zittrain, Jonathan, and Benjamin Edelman, *Internet Filtering in China*. IEEE Internet Computing, (March/April 2003): pp. 70–77. A variation is online as *Empirical Analysis of Internet Filtering in China* at *http://cyber.law.harvard.edu/filtering/china/*

[Zooknic2004] *Geography of Internet Users*. Available online at *http://www.zooknic.com/*, Zooknic Internet Intelligence, September 2004.

Glossary of Network Security Terms

AES: The Advanced Encryption Standard. A widely used cryptographic algorithm intended to replace DES.

amplification attack: A type of packet storm where an intermediate host generates more data than it receives.

anonymity: The ability to operate without being identified.

ANSI: American National Standards Institute; provides communication standards.

AP: A wireless access point or hub.

application layer: The seventh ISO OSI layer; manages end-user applications.

ARP: Address Resolution Protocol; used by Media Access Control for requesting MAC addresses. ARP matches network addresses to hardware addresses. See *RARP*.

ARP poisoning: An attack vector that corrupts an ARP table.

ARP table: A local cache on a node that lists known network and hardware address mappings.

ARPA: Advanced Research Projects Agency. See *DARPA*.

ARPANET: The first large-scale distributed network. Later became the Internet.

Asymmetrical Encryption Algorithm: The key used to encrypt a message is different from the decryption key.

attack: The use or exploitation of a vulnerability.

attack vector: The path from an attacker to a target, including tools and techniques.

attacker: The person or process that initiates an attack.

authenticate: The ability to determine the origin of another system.

authentication: The identification of an authorized entity.

authorize: The ability to specify the level of permitted access control.

blind drop: An intermediate system that temporarily stores information for an anonymous source and destination.

botnet: A set of (usually compromised) hosts that can be remotely controlled.

bridge: An OSI layer 2 device that can span different physical media.

broadcast networks: A network topology that sends data radio frequencies instead of wires.

bubble network: See *garlic network*.

bus network: A network topology that consists of a single link. All nodes on the network connect to the link.

CA: See *certificate authority*.

caching DNS server: Any DNS server that temporarily stores DNS information.

carders: People that illegally trade stolen identities and credit cards.

ccTLD: Country Code Top Level Domain DNS server; a set of servers that manage country code domain extensions.

cell network: See *garlic network*.

CERT: Computer Emergency Response Team.

certificate authority: A trusted host that can validate a certificate.

chaff: Data used to camouflage or obscure true network traffic.

chain of custody: A record of information possession.

ciphertext: Encoded information. See *cryptography* and *plaintext*.

CISA: Certified Information Security Auditor.

CISM: Certified Information Security Manager.

CISSP: Certified Information Systems Security Professional.

compartmentalize: A security technique for dividing systems based on functional attributes to reduce the scope of any single flaw.

compromise: The successful exploitation of a target by an attacker.

CompTIA: Computing Technology Industry Association.

confidentiality: The ability to operate in private.

confusion: A form of data substitution for cryptographic algorithms.

connection-less protocol: Any protocol that does not confirm information transfers.

connection-oriented protocol: Any protocol that confirms information transfers.

cookie: Information used to track state across a stateless protocol.

copyright: A form of intellectual property protection that restricts usage.

covert channel: The use of a known communication method as camouflage for a private information transmission.

CPPP: Compressed PPP.

cross-site scripting: Any HTTP attack where hostile information supplied to the server by one client becomes accessible to other clients.

cryptanalysis: Any attempt to decode an encrypted message through statistical or logical analysis.

cryptographic hash function: A hash algorithm based on a cryptographic system.

cryptography: Encoding and decoding data so that only the intended recipients can access the information.

CSLIP: Compressed SLIP.

cutting: A term used to describe URL modification by removing elements from the URI.

DARPA: Defense Advanced Research Projects Agency; the government organization responsible for developing the ARPANET and Internet.

data link layer: The second ISO OSI layer; manages local network routing and addressing.

datagram: A UDP packet.

DDNS: Dynamic DNS; a method for associating hostnames with DHCP addresses.

DDoS: See *distributed denial-of-service.*

decryption algorithm: See *encryption algorithm.*

defender: The person or process that mitigates or prevents an attack.

defense-in-depth: A security concept that involves layering different security methods.

denial-of-service (DoS): An attack where network functionality is disrupted by preventing use of the service.

DES: The Data Encryption Standard; a widely used cryptographic algorithm.

destination anonymity: Prevents an observer from identifying the transmission's destination.

DHCP: Dynamic Host Configuration Protocol; a method for dynamically assigning network addresses, routing information, and DNS settings to nodes.

Diffie-Hellman key exchange: An algorithm used to exchange a symmetrical key in a public forum without compromising the key.

diffusion: A form of information mixing for cryptographic algorithms.

digest: See *hash algorithm.*

directional chaffing: False data designed to obscure the true route.

disruption: An attack that prevents network functionality.

distributed denial-of-service (DDoS): A DoS that uses many systems to attack a target.

DMZ: Demilitarized Zone; a separate network region that provides a buffer zone between the WAN and LAN.

DNS server hijacking: Any exploit that compromises the control or management of a DNS server.

DNS: Domain Name Service; a session-layer protocol that associates hostnames and meta information with network addresses and domains.

DoD TCP/IP: The Department of Defense's four-layer network stack.

DoD: U.S. Department of Defense.

domain hijacking: Any exploit that compromises the control or management of a DNS domain.

domain locking: A service provided by DNS registrars that prevents domain transfers until the domain is unlocked.

DoS: See *denial-of-service.*

dual-homed: A node that concurrently resides on two distinct networks.

dynamic network: A network link that may vary between or during the network connection.

eavesdropping: An attack vector where information is intercepted without detection.

egress filtering: Packet filtering for outbound traffic.

encryption algorithm: A function that converts plaintext to ciphertext. The function is reversible using a decryption algorithm.

entropy: A unit of useful information compared against the total information. It can be characterized as the opposite of redundancy. High entropy implies that most (or all) of the total information is useful.

exploit: The instantiation of a vulnerability; something that can be used for an attack.

fail dealing: See *fair use.*

fair use: Legal rights to use copyright information for limited purposes.

firewall: A node that filters network traffic as it passes between network segments.

forward secrecy: A cryptographic concept where the loss of one key does not compromise earlier encrypted information.

full-duplex channel: A bidirectional communication channel and multiple nodes may transmit without causing interference.

functional methodology: A programming approach that uses local elements and functions.

garlic network: A network topology that separates network regions so they can be nested or at the same level.

gateway: An OSI layer 4 device that supports conversions between different network protocols. Alternately used as a general term for a bridge or router.

GIAC: Global Information Assurance Certification provided by the SANS Institute.

Google bombing: A form of XSS attack used to associate specific content with a Google keyword search.

gTLD: Generic Top Level Domain DNS server; a set of servers that manages the generic domains such as .com and .net.

hacker factor: See *hacker mentality.*

hacker mentality: An ability to see alternatives to existing situations or apply technology in unexpected ways; thinking outside the box.

half-duplex channel: A bidirectional communication channel where only one node may transmit at a time.

hardened system: A system with all unnecessary services disabled.

hardware firewall: A firewall that operates independently of other computer systems.

hash algorithm: An encoding function that is not reversible. Also called a *digest*.

hash collision: Given two different input sequences, a hash algorithm generates the same output value.

HMAC: Hashed message authentication code. An algorithm to sign and authenticate data.

hotspot: See *AP*.

HTML: HyperText Markup Language; a data format derived from SGML.

HTTP: HyperText Transport Protocol; an application layer protocol.

HTTPS: HTTP over SSL.

hub: A device that connects separate physical layers.

hybrid network: A network topology that combines one or more bus, star, ring, or broadcast networks.

ICMP: Internet Control Message Protocol; a quality-of-service protocol for IP.

idempotent: A mathematic term indicating a stateless function that, given the same input parameters, generates the same results each time.

IDS: Intrusion detection system; a system that monitors for potential threats or exploits.

IEEE: Institute of Electrical and Electronics Engineers.

IEEE-SA: Institute of Electrical and Electronics Engineers, Standards Association; an organization that provides low-level network standards.

IETF: Internet Engineering Task Force; an organization that governs over the RFC standards.

impersonation: An attack vector where identification credentials are duplicated.

insertion: An attack vector that places new information into a transmission.

integrity: The ability to detect information tampering or modification.

interference: An attack that uses an unauthorized transmission to disrupt network functionality.

Internet: The large-scale distributed network that evolved from ARPANET.

IP: Internet Protocol.

IPng: Internet Protocol Next Generation. See *IPv6*.

IPS: Intrusion prevention system; an IDS that can also deter attacks and mitigate exposure.

IPsec: A set of extensions to IP for authentication and encryption support.

IPv4: See *IP*.

IPv6: Internet Protocol version 6, which is a replacement for IP that uses a larger address space and support for authentication and encryption.

ISACA: Information Systems Audit and Control Association; the organization that provides CISA and CISM certifications.

(ISC)²: International Information Systems Security Certification Consortium, Inc.; the organization that provides CISSP and SSCP certifications.

ISO: International Standards Organization; an organization that provides information technology standards.

ISO OSI: International Standards Organization's Open Systems Interconnection; a seven-layer network stack.

Kerberos: An OSI session layer protocol that enforces authentication, validation, and encryption.

Knock-Knock protocol: See *port knocking*.

LAN: Local area network; a network region that is locally controlled.

LAND attack: A TCP network attack where packets appear to come from the originating system.

layer: A conceptual definition for specific protocol functionality.

letter of the law: A literal interpretation of laws.

link anonymity: Prevents an observer from correlating network traffic with a source or destination.

load attack: An attack vector that attempts to increase the workload of a node or network.

MAC: The definition is context sensitive. In networking, MAC refers to the MAC address or an OSI layer 2 protocol (media access control). In cryptography, it is a message authentication code used as cryptographic function.

MAC address: A data link layer hardware address.

MAN: Metropolitan area network; a network region that is locally controlled but contains many LANs.

man-in-the-middle: An attack vector where data is relayed through an attacker's node.

media access control (MAC): A data link layer protocol that provides access control and addressing.

medium access control: A data link layer function for transmission and collision detection.

medium: See *physical medium*.

MitM: See *man-in-the-middle*.

moral framework: A basis of ethical decision making.

morals: A sense of right and wrong.

multihomed: A node that concurrently resides on multiple distinct networks.

multihost network: A network consisting of many nodes.

multipart authentication: An authentication approach that uses more than one form of information for determining credentials. See *one-part authentication*.

multiprotocol router: A router that supports different network-layer protocols.

Nagel algorithm: The delaying of TCP packets by a few microseconds to optimize data transfers. Named after John Nagel.

name-based addressing: A network-addressing scheme that uses text strings for node identification and routing.

NAT: Network Address Translation; a system that multiplexes many internal network addresses into one external network address.

Nestea attack: network attack that exploits a fragmentation reconstruction vulnerability based on an off-by-one overlap.

network anonymity: Prevents the identification of connection participants.

network layer: The third ISO OSI layer, which manages remote network routing and addressing.

network privacy: Prevents an observer from viewing information transmitted over the network.

node: A host or system on a network.

nonrepudiation: Ensuring that an originator cannot falsely repute information.

null cipher: A cipher that performs no encryption; usually used for debugging network traffic.

numeric addressing: A network-addressing scheme that uses numeric identifiers for identifying nodes and routing traffic.

object-oriented methodology: A programming approach that combines functional and procedural methodologies.

one-part authentication: The use of a single authentication mechanism (something you know, something you have, or something you are).

onion network: A network topology that nests different network regions.

onion routing: An anonymizing routing system where information is relayed through a dynamic set of proxies.

open standards: Specifications that are publicly available.

OSI: Open Systems Interconnection network stack. See *ISO OSI*.

packet sniffing: A form of eavesdropping where packets are intercepted.

packet storm: An attack vector where a network becomes overwhelmed by traffic.

patents: A form of intellectual property protection for systems, methods, or processes.

pharming: Any DNS risks applied to phishing or fraud.

phishing: A term that denotes online fraud through impersonation.

physical layer: The first ISO OSI layer, which manages data transport media.

physical medium: Anything that can transmit and receive data.

Ping of Death: An attack vector based on an oversized ICMP echo request packet.

ping: An ICMP echo request packet.

plaintext: Unencrypted or decoded information. See *cryptography* and *ciphertext*.

point-to-point network: A network consisting of two nodes that are directly connected.

port knocking: A system that uses connection attempts and packet options to enable clandestine services.

PPP: Point-to-Point protocol.

presentation layer: The sixth ISO OSI layer, which manages system-independent data conversion.

Pretty Good Privacy (PGP): An asymmetrical encryption system.

primary DNS server: A DNS server that manages a specific domain.

private key: One of two keys in an asymmetrical encryption algorithm; this key is not shared. See *public key*.

procedural methodology: A programming approach that uses global elements and subroutines.

promiscuous mode: A network mode where all traffic is received by a node.

protocol: The implementation of a specific functionality associated with a layer.

proxy: Any network device that relays a protocol.

public key: One of two keys in an asymmetrical encryption algorithm; this key can be widely shared. See *private key*.

pull technology: Any technology where the client initiates the transmission of data from a server.

push technology: Any technology where the server initiates the transmission of data to a client.

RARP: Reverse Address Resolution Protocol; matches hardware addresses to network addresses. See *ARP*.

replay: An attack vector that resends data previously intercepted.

RF: Radio Frequency.

RFC: Request For Comments; a set of networking-related specification.

RFI: Radio Frequency Interference.

ring network: A network topology that uses each node to relay messages.

RIR: Regional Internet Registry; a set of organizations that manages network address allocation.

risk: A qualitative assessment describing the likelihood of an attacker/threat using an exploit to successfully bypass a defender, attack a vulnerability, and compromise a system.

RNAT: Reverse NAT; a system that redirects specific network ports to internal hosts.

robust programming: A software development method that tests parameters and assumptions.

root server: A top-level DNS server.

route: The network path used by transmitted information.

router: An OSI layer 3 device that supports conversions between different data link protocols.

router table flooding: An attack vector that fills a dynamic routing table.

router table poisoning: An attack vector that modifies a routing table.

routing metric: A value that provides a basis for selecting an optimal route when there are multiple choices. See *routing table*.

routing table: A local network table that associates subnets with network interfaces on a node.

RPC: Remote Procedure Call.

secondary DNS server: An official backup of a primary DNS server.

secure fail: When a failure occurs, the impacted does not increase the threat level.

security-by-obscurity: A security concept for protecting systems by not disclosing information.

sequence hijacking: By observing a sequence of transport layer packets, an attacker can intercept and control an established connection.

sequential chaffing: Reordering of network traffic to obscure packet order.

session: Long-term dialogs.

session hijacking: An attack vector that compromises an established session.

session layer: The fifth ISO OSI layer; manages extended duration connections.

SGML: The Standard Generalized Markup Language.

simplex channel: A channel where all data flows in one direction.

size chaffing: False data designed to obscure the true size of network traffic.

SLD: Secondary Level Domain DNS server; a set of servers that manage generic extensions for ccTLD servers.

SLIP: Serial Line Internet Protocol; a simple point-to-point protocol.

SMTP: Simple Mail Transfer Protocol; an application layer protocol for delivering email.

Smurf attack: A DDoS attack that uses forged ICMP or UDP packets.

social engineering: A compromise through sociological persuasion.

SOCKS: Socksified Server; a proxy for the TCP and UDP transport layer protocols.

SOCKSv4: Socks Server version 4; a proxy that relays TCP packets. See *SOCKS*.

SOCKSv5: Socks Server version 5; a proxy that relays TCP and UDP packets. See *SOCKS*.

software firewall: A firewall that resides on a computer system.

source anonymity: Prevents an observer from identifying the source of the transmission.

SP: A wireless subscriber point or wireless client.

SPI: Stateful packet inspection; used by firewalls to validate TCP packet states.

splicing: URL modification by adding elements to the URL.

SQL injection attack: An attack that modifies URL contents to exploit server-side database vulnerabilities.

SSCP: Systems Security Certified Professional.

SSH: Secure Shell protocol; a tunneling protocol with OSI session, presentation, and application layer functionality.

SSID: A wireless Service Set Identifier; used to identify specific APs.

SSL: Secure Socket Layer protocol; an OSI presentation layer protocol.

stack: A conceptual set of well-defined functional layers for protocol implementation.

star network: A network topology that relies on a central hub for communicating with nodes.

static network: A consistent link between a node and a network.

steganography: Hiding information within other information so that only the intended recipient will observe the hidden message.

Substitution Box (S-box): A system that performs data manipulations for encryption and decryption algorithms. See *confusion* and *diffusion*.

switch: A device that connects separate physical layers and routes information based on node addresses.

Symmetrical Encryption Algorithm: The same key is used to encrypt and decrypt a message.

TACACS: Terminal Access Controller Access Control System; an OSI application layer protocol that provides authentication, authorization, and accounting functionality.

target: The person, company, or system that is directly vulnerable and impacted by the exploit.

tarpitting: Any defense method designed to delay an attacking system.

TCP: Transport Control Protocol; an OSI transport layer protocol.

TCP/IP: See *DoD TCP/IP*.

teardrop attack: A network attack that exploits a fragmentation reconstruction vulnerability based on overlapping fragments.

threat: An adversary who is capable and motivated to exploit a vulnerability.

three-part authentication: The use of three different authentication mechanisms. See *one-part authentication*.

TLD: Top Level Domain DNS server, a set of servers that manage domain name suffixes.

TLS: Transport Layer Security; a replacement for SSL.

Tor: The Onion Router; an onion routing network for anonymous network connections.

trademark: A form of intellectual property protection for names, logos, and symbols.

transport layer: The forth ISO OSI layer; manages data collection and aggregation.

tunnel: A network stack used to transfer information from another network stack.

two-part authentication: The use of two different authentication mechanisms. See *one-part authentication*.

UDP: User Datagram Protocol; an OSI transport layer protocol.

URI: Uniform Resource Indicator; alternately Universal or Unique Resource Indicator.

URL: Universal Resource Locator.

volume analysis: A forensic method that determines data content based on network traffic patterns.

volume chaffing: False data designed to obscure the true information volume.

VPN: Virtual Private Network; a network created by tunneling data through a second protocol stack.

vulnerability: A defect or weakness in the feasibility, design, implementation, operation, or maintenance of a system.

WAN: wide area network; the network region outside of local control and ownership.

WAP: Wireless Application Protocol; a session-based roaming wireless protocol.

war driving: A reconnaissance vector that detects APs and SSIDs.

WEP: Wired Equivalent Privacy; a form of wireless network security.

X.509: A format for transferring certificate information.

XML: The eXtensible Markup Language; a data format based on SGML.

XSS: See *cross-site scripting*.

zone transfer: A method for bulk transferring a domain's DNS table to another host.

Index